Accounting Standards

1995/96

Extant at 30 April 1995

Accounting Standards

1995/96

Extant at 30 April 1995

General Editor

Richard M Wilkins

Consultant to the Accounting Standards Board

9 ian 1997

Accountancy
BOOKS

The Institute of Chartered Accountants
in England and Wales
Gloucester House
399 Silbury Boulevard
Central Milton Keynes
MK9 2HL
Tel: 01908 248000

ISBN 1 85355 582 7

Financial Reporting Standards and UITF Abstracts are issued by the Accounting Standards Board in respect of their application in the United Kingdom and by the Institute of Chartered Accountants in Ireland in respect of their application in the Republic of Ireland.

Typeset by Create Publishing Services, Bath, Avon
Printed by The Bath Press, Avon

Contents

Preface

This book presents in one convenient bound volume all UK accounting standards and UITF abstracts extant at 30 April 1995; in this edition, as indicated below, they have been updated for amendments made since the documents were originally issued. It also reprints those UK Exposure Drafts and Discussion Documents issued by the Accounting Standards Board (ASB) that have not been superseded by later documents, together with the two outstanding Exposure Drafts issued by the Accounting Standards Committee (ASC).

This book also contains a summary of the history of the ASC, the report of the Review Committee on the Making of Accounting Standards and the present standard-setting regime. In addition, the ASB's Statement of Aims, the texts of relevant Technical Releases issued by the ASC and the ICAEW and some ICAEW Statements on accounting recommendations are included. There is also a section on Statements of Recommended Practice.

This edition includes all the major documents issued by the ASB in the year to April 1995. This includes the following:

- two accounting standards – FRS 6 on 'Acquisitions and mergers' (superseding SSAP 23 and FRED 6) and FRS 7 on 'Fair values in acquisition accounting' (superseding FRED 7). In view of the lengthy transition to FRS 6 (which is only mandatory for accounting periods commencing on or after 23 December 1994) SSAP 23 is also reproduced in this volume. Similarly various paragraphs of SSAP 22 that are superseded by FRSs 6 and 7 are also reproduced (with footnotes indicating the paragraphs concerned);
- three UITF Abstracts – 10 on 'Disclosure of directors' share options, 11 on 'Capital instruments: issuer call options' and 12 on 'Lessee accounting for reverse premiums and similar incentives';
- the Discussion draft of Chapter 7 of the Statement of Principles on 'The reporting entity';
- two Discussion Papers – 'Associates and joint ventures' and 'Accounting for taxes'.

In addition two Technical Releases issued by the ICAEW during the year have been included. These were 'The application of FRS 5 to general insurance transactions' and a Discussion Paper on 'Materiality in financial reporting'.

Following the policy initiated in last year's edition amendments to accounging standards have been incorporated into the text of the relevant documents, so that the book presents the text current at 30 April 1995. Amendments were made to SSAP 19 in July 1994 and to FRS 5 in December 1994. Also as last year where references in documents reproduced to companies legislation in Great Britain, International Accounting Standards, etc., have become outdated, footnotes have been added to refer to the current legal or other references. However, it should be noted that no attempt has been made to update any Irish legal references (for either Northern Ireland or the

Republic). There are three exceptions to this general policy regarding footnotes, in each case noted at the beginning of the document concerned. Two of these are in Part Ten, the ICAEW Accounting Recommendations, the first being the 1982 statement on realised profits (where in the interests of clarity the text itself has been updated to refer to current companies legislation) and the second being the 1986 statement on trust accounts (where the many references to tax law have not been updated). The third exception is the charities SORP, which is expected to be replaced in summer 1995 by a revised SORP.

The ASC was replaced by the ASB on 1 August 1990 and the ASB adopted the 22 SSAPs extant at that date. Adoption by the ASB gives the SSAPs the status of 'accounting standards' within the terms of Part VII of the Companies Act 1985. Under Part VII, directors of companies, other than most small or medium-sized companies, are under a statutory duty to disclose in all accounts for financial periods commencing on or after 23 December 1989 whether the accounts have been prepared in accordance with applicable accounting standards, particulars of any material departure from those standards and the reason for the departure. Under section 245B of the Act, where the accounts of a company do not comply with the requirements of the Act, the court may order the preparation of revised accounts, and that all or part of the costs be borne by such of the directors as were party to the approval of the defective accounts.

Part One

Introduction

Introduction

HISTORY OF THE ACCOUNTING STANDARDS COMMITTEE

The Accounting Standards Committee ('ASC'), originally known as the Accounting Standards Steering Committee, was set up in January 1970 by the Council of The Institute of Chartered Accountants in England and Wales with the object of developing definitive standards for financial reporting.

The Institute of Chartered Accountants of Scotland and the Institute of Chartered Accountants in Ireland became members of the Committee in 1970, the Chartered Association of Certified Accountants and the Chartered Institute of Management Accountants joined in 1971 and the Chartered Institute of Public Finance and Accountancy in 1976.

From 1 February 1976 the ASC was reconstituted as a joint committee of the six member bodies who then acted collectively through the Consultative Committee of Accountancy Bodies ('CCAB'). On 1 January 1986, the CCAB was incorporated and the ASC became a Committee of CCAB Limited.

The Councils of the six major accountancy bodies in the United Kingdom and Ireland approved and issued accounting standards following proposals developed by the ASC.

On 1 August 1990 the ASC was replaced by the Accounting Standards Board ('ASB').

During its existence the ASC issued 55 EDs, 2 SORPs, 28 discussion papers and other documents and 65 technical releases. It also franked 14 industry SORPs. Thirty-four SSAPs or revised SSAPs were recommended to and approved by the Councils of the six member-bodies of CCAB.

The CCAB agreed that 'all statements (Exposure Drafts, Discussion Papers, Technical Releases and similar documents) issued by ASC and extant at 1 August 1990 will remain documents of record under the aegis of the CCAB. SORPs issued or franked by ASC will continue in force under the aegis of CCAB until formally withdrawn or superseded'.

REPORT OF THE REVIEW COMMITTEE ON THE MAKING OF ACCOUNTING STANDARDS

The Review Committee, under the Chairmanship of Sir Ron Dearing, was appointed in November 1987 by the CCAB to review and make recommendations on the standard-setting process.

In September 1988 the Review Committee presented its report to the CCAB. The Report's recommendations included:

- Accounting standards should remain, as far as possible, the responsibility of auditors, preparers and users of accounts and there should not be a general move towards incorporating them into law.

- A Financial Reporting Council should be created covering at high level a wide constituency of interests, whose Chairman would be appointed jointly by the Secretary of State for Trade and Industry and the Governor of the Bank of England, to guide the standard-setting body on work programmes and issues of public concern; to see that the work on accounting standards is properly financed; and to act as a powerful proactive public influence for securing good accounting practice.
- The task of devising accounting standards should be discharged by a newly constituted, expert Accounting Standards Board, with a full-time Chairman and Technical Director. Its total membership would not exceed nine. The Board would issue standards on its own authority. In the interests of clearly drawn standards avoiding compromise decisions, a majority of two thirds of the Board would suffice for approval of a standard. Government would have observer status.
- The Accounting Standards Board should establish a capability of high standing to publish authoritative, though non-mandatory, guidance on emerging issues.
- A Review Panel should be established to examine contentious departures from accounting standards by large companies.

THE PRESENT STANDARD-SETTING REGIME

General

In 1990 the Government announced the establishment of the Financial Reporting Council under the Chairmanship of Sir Ron Dearing. Sir Sydney Lipworth was appointed Chairman with effect from 1 January 1994. The present arrangements for setting accounting standards and enforcing compliance follow closely the recommendations of the Review Committee. The organisation is as shown in the diagram on page 5.

The ASB replaced the ASC on 1 August 1990. The funding for the present organisation is drawn from three broad sectors: the accountancy profession; the financial community; and the Government.

Accounting Standards

The Companies Act 1989 introduced into the Companies Act 1985 a definition of 'accounting standards' along with the requirement for directors of companies, other than most small or medium sized companies, to disclose whether the accounts have been prepared in accordance with applicable accounting standards, particulars of any material departure from those standards and the reasons for the departure. Under section 245B of the Companies Act 1985, where the accounts of a company do not comply with the requirements of the Act, the court may order the preparation of revised accounts, and that all or part of the costs be borne by such of the directors as were party to the approval of the defective accounts.

At its first meeting the ASB unanimously agreed to adopt the 22 extant SSAPs issued by the ASC. Adoption by the ASB gives the SSAPs the status of accounting standards within the meaning of the Companies Act 1985. In adopting the SSAPs the ASB noted that with the passage of time certain legal references in the SSAPs have become outdated, and the ASB drew attention in particular to TR805 dated July 1990 issued by

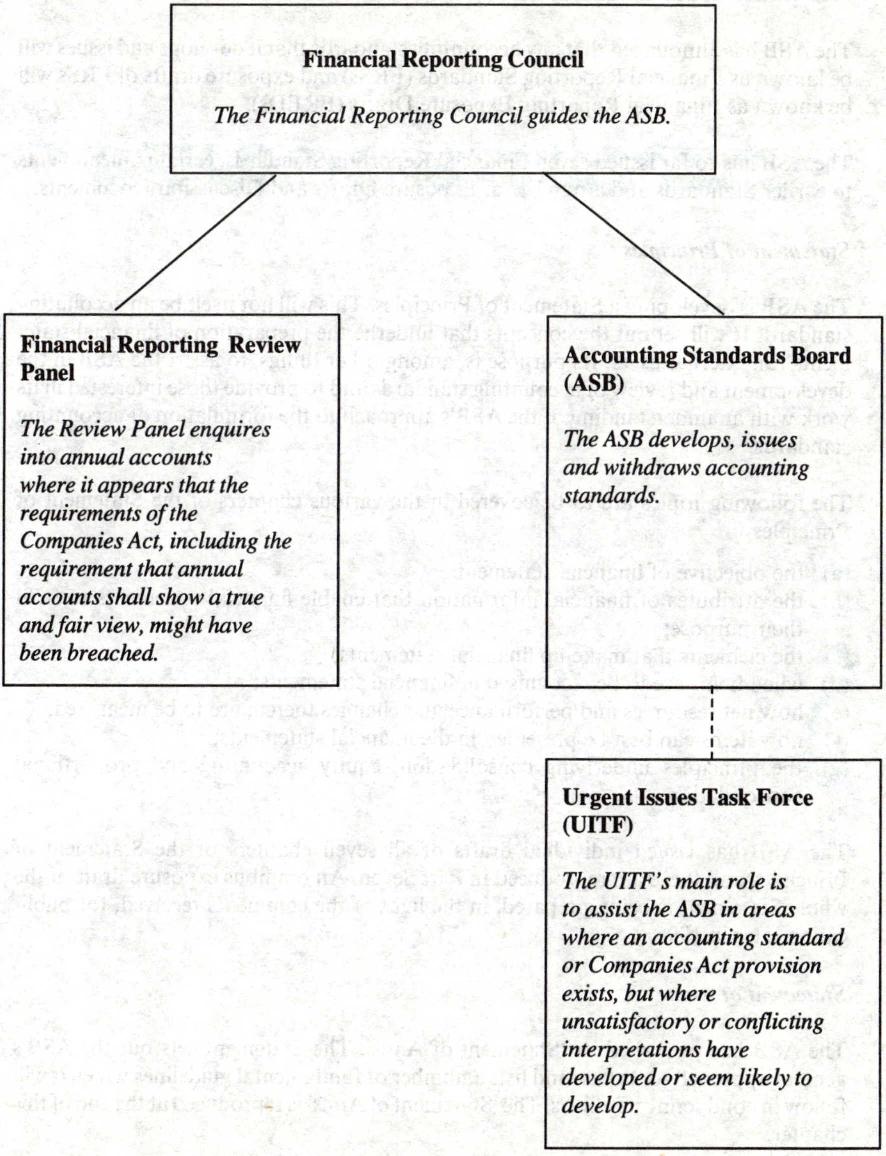
Financial Reporting Council
The Financial Reporting Council guides the ASB.
Financial Reporting Review Panel
The Review Panel enquires into annual accounts where it appears that the requirements of the Companies Act, including the requirement that annual accounts shall show a true and fair view, might have been breached.
Accounting Standards Board (ASB)
The ASB develops, issues and withdraws accounting standards.
Urgent Issues Task Force (UITF)
The UITF's main role is to assist the ASB in areas where an accounting standard or Companies Act provision exists, but where unsatisfactory or conflicting interpretations have developed or seem likely to develop.

the ASC. The TR updates references in the SSAPs that are no longer correct. The matters dealt with in the TR do not represent changes of practice or substantive changes to the standards, nor have they been formally approved by the Councils of the CCAB bodies, and are listed as a matter of record only. The TR does not deal with changes subsequent to 1990. The preface to this volume explains the updating that has been carried out to the documents that have been included herein.

The ASB has announced that any accounting standards that it develops and issues will be known as Financial Reporting Standards (FRSs) and exposure drafts of FRSs will be known as Financial Reporting Exposure Drafts (FREDs).

The ASB has so far issued seven Financial Reporting Standards, certain amendments to earlier Standards and a number of Exposure Drafts and Discussion Documents.

Statement of Principles

The ASB is developing a Statement of Principles. This will not itself be an accounting standard. It will set out the concepts that underlie the preparation of financial statements for external users. Its purpose is, among other things, to assist the ASB in the development and review of accounting standards and to provide those interested in its work with an understanding of the ASB's approach to the formulation of accounting standards.

The following topics are to be covered in the various chapters of the Statement of Principles:

(a) the objective of financial statements;
(b) the attributes of financial information that enable financial statements to fulfil their purpose;
(c) the elements that make up financial statements;
(d) when items are to be recognised in financial statements;
(e) how net resources and performance and changes therein are to be measured;
(f) how items can best be presented in the financial statements;
(g) the principles underlying consolidation, equity accounting and proportional consolidation.

The ASB has issued individual drafts of all seven chapters of the Statement of Principles and these are reproduced in Part Seven. An omnibus exposure draft of the whole Statement is being prepared, in the light of the comments received, for publication later in 1995.

Statement of Aims

The ASB has published its 'Statement of Aims'. The Statement sets out the ASB's general approach to its task and lists a number of fundamental guidelines which it will follow in conducting its affairs. The 'Statement of Aims' is reproduced at the end of this chapter.

Consultation

The ASB has stated that it is anxious to operate the maximum possible consultation and be as open as possible in its dealings. In addition to issuing exposure drafts of FRSs and of chapters from its Statement of Principles the ASB has announced that it will also publish working drafts for discussion ('Discussion drafts') on individual topics as they reach appropriate stages of development.

Urgent Issues Task Force abstracts

The UITF's main role is to assist the ASB in areas where an accounting standard or a Companies Act provision exists, but where unsatisfactory or conflicting interpretations have developed or seem likely to develop. In such circumstances it operates by seeking a consensus as to the accounting treatment that should be adopted. Such a consensus is reached against the background of the ASB's declared aim of relying on principles rather than detailed prescription.

The ASB makes the UITF abstracts publicly available for the guidance of users, preparers and auditors of financial information.

Extant abstracts should be considered to be part of the corpus of practices forming the basis for determining what constitutes a true and fair view. Such abstracts consequently may be taken into consideration by the Financial Reporting Review Panel in deciding whether financial statements call for review.

The ASB's Foreword to UITF abstracts is reproduced in Part Four. This explains the authority, scope and application of the UITF abstracts issued by the ASB. These abstracts set out the consensus reached by its Urgent Issues Task Force on particular issues.

Statements of Recommended Practice

The ASC developed and issued two SORPs together with an Explanatory foreword to SORPs. In addition the ASC 'franked' SORPs developed by bodies representative of the industry/sector to which the SORP would apply. The ASB has announced that it will not issue its own SORPs. However, SORPs will be developed by bodies recognised by the ASB to provide guidance on the application of accounting standards to specific industries. The ASB will not 'frank' such SORPs. Instead, where it is satisfied about certain particulars it will require to be appended to the SORP a 'negative assurance statement'. Further details are contained in Part Six.

Statement of aims

AIMS

The aims of the Accounting Standards Board (the Board) are to establish and improve standards of financial accounting and reporting, for the benefit of users, preparers, and auditors of financial information.

ACHIEVING THE AIMS

The Board intends to achieve its aims by:

1 Developing principles to guide it in establishing standards and to provide a framework within which others can exercise judgement in resolving accounting issues.

2 Issuing new accounting standards, or amending existing ones, in response to evolving business practices, new economic developments and deficiencies being identified in current practice.

Addressing urgent issues promptly.

FUNDAMENTAL GUIDELINES

The Board follows certain guidelines in conducting its affairs:

1 To be objective and to ensure that the information resulting from the application of accounting standards faithfully represents the underlying commercial activity. Such information should be neutral in the sense that it is free from any form of bias intended to influence users in a particular direction and should not be designed to favour any group of users or preparers.

2 To ensure that accounting standards are clearly expressed and supported by a reasoned analysis of the issues.

3 To determine what should be incorporated in accounting standards based on research, public consultation and careful deliberation about the usefulness of the resulting information.

4 To ensure that through a process of regular communication, accounting standards are produced with due regard to international developments.

5 To ensure that there is consistency both from one accounting standard to another and between accounting standards and company law.

6 To issue accounting standards only when the expected benefits exceed the perceived costs. The Board recognises that reliable cost/benefit calculations are seldom possible. However, it will always assess the need for standards in terms of the significance and extent of the problem being addressed and will choose the standard which appears to be most effective in cost/benefit terms.

7 To take account of the desire of the financial community for evolutionary rather than revolutionary change in the reporting process where this is consistent with the objectives outlined above.

WITHDRAWN STANDARDS

Accounting Standards			
		Date issued	*Date withdrawn*
SSAP 6	Extraordinary items and prior year adjustments (revised August 1986) Superseded by FRS 3	April 1974	October 1992
SSAP 7	Accounting for changes in the purchasing power of money (Provisional)	May 1974	January 1978
SSAP 10	Statements of source and application of funds Superseded by FRS 1	July 1975	September 1991
SSAP 11	Accounting for deferred tax Superseded by SSAP 15	August 1975	October 1978
SSAP 14	Group accounts Superseded by FRS 2	September 1978	July 1992
SSAP 16	Current cost accounting*	March 1980	July 1988
SSAP 23	Accounting for acquisitions and mergers Superseded by FRS 6	April 1985	September 1994†
UITF Abstracts			
UITF 1	Convertible bonds-supplemental interest/premium Superseded by FRS 4	July 1991	December 1993
UITF 2	Restructuring costs Superseded by FRS 3	October 1991	October 1992
UITF 8	Repurchase of own debt Superseded by FRS 4	March 1993	December 1993

* *See statement by the ASC on the withdrawal of SSAP 16 (TR 707) reproduced in Part Nine. SSAP 16 was suspended in June 1985.*

† *As FRS 6 is not mandatory until accounting periods commencing on or after 23 December 1994 SSAP 23 is still reproduced in this volume.*

Part Two

Accounting Standards

Foreword to accounting standards

(Issued June 1993)

Contents

Foreword to accounting standards

INTRODUCTION

This foreword explains the authority, scope and application of accounting standards issued or adopted by the Accounting Standards Board (the Board)*. The foreword also considers the procedure by which the Board issues accounting standards and their relationship to International Accounting Standards, issued by the International Accounting Standards Committee. 1

The Board at its meeting on 24 August 1990 agreed to adopt the 22 extant Statements of Standard Accounting Practice (SSAPs) issued by the Councils of the six major accountancy bodies following proposals developed by the Accounting Standards Committee (ASC)†. Adoption by the Board gave these SSAPs the status of accounting standards within Part VII of the Companies Act 1985,‡ (the Act) and within Part VIII of the Companies (Northern Ireland) Order 1986§ (the Order). This status will apply until each SSAP is amended, rescinded or replaced by new accounting standards. 2

Accounting standards developed by the Board are designated Financial Reporting Standards (FRSs). Accounting standards developed by the ASC and adopted by the Board continue to be known as SSAPs. 3

FRSs are based on the Statement of Principles for Financial Reporting currently in issue, which addresses the concepts underlying the information presented in financial statements. The objective of this Statement of Principles is to provide a framework for the consistent and logical formulation of individual accounting standards. The 4

******The Accounting Standards Board is a committee of The Accounting Standards Board Limited. The Accounting Standards Board Limited is prescribed as a standard setting body for the purposes of Section 256(1) of the Companies Act 1985 with effect from 20 August 1990 by The Accounting Standards (Prescribed Body) Regulations 1990 (S.I. 1990 No. 1667). The Accounting Standards Board Limited is prescribed as a standard setting body for Northern Ireland for the purposes of Article 264(1) of the Companies (Northern Ireland) Order 1986 with effect from 15 October 1990, by the Accounting Standards (Prescribed Body) Regulations (Northern Ireland) 1990 (S.R. 1990 No. 338).*

†Prior to 1 August 1990 accounting standards in the United Kingdom and Republic of Ireland were issued by the Councils of the six major accountancy bodies following proposals developed by the ASC. Since 1 August 1990 the Board has taken over the role of issuing accounting standards applicable in the United Kingdom. The Institute of Chartered Accountants in Ireland issues accounting standards applicable in the Republic of Ireland.

‡References to the Companies Act 1985 are to that Act as amended by, inter alia, the Companies Act 1989 and the Companies Act 1985 (Bank Accounts) Regulations 1991 (S.I. 1991 No. 2705)

§References to the Companies (Northern Ireland) Order 1986 (S.I. 1986 No. 1032 (N.I. 6)) are to that Order as amended by, inter alia, the Companies (Northern Ireland) Order 1990 (S.I. 1990 No. 593 (N.I. 5)), the Companies (No. 2) (Northern Ireland) Order 1990 (S.I. 1990 No. 1504 (N.I. 10)) and the Companies (1986 Order) (Bank Accounts) Regulations (Northern Ireland) Order (S.R. 1992 No. 258).

framework also provides a basis on which others can exercise judgement in resolving accounting issues.

5 The Board may issue pronouncements other than FRSs, including the Urgent Issues Task Force 'Abstracts'. The Board will indicate the authority, scope and application of pronouncements other than FRSs as they are issued. UITF Abstracts are the subject of a separate foreword.

AIMS OF THE ACCOUNTING STANDARDS BOARD

6 The aims of the Board are set out in the document 'The Accounting Standards Board – Statement of Aims'.

AUTHORITY OF ACCOUNTING STANDARDS

7 FRSs issued and SSAPs adopted by the Board are 'accounting standards' for the purposes of the Act, which requires accounts, other than those prepared by small or medium-sized companies (as defined by the Act), to state whether they have been prepared in accordance with applicable accounting standards and to give particulars of any material departure from those standards and the reasons for it. References to accounting standards in the Act are contained in paragraph 36A of Schedule 4, paragraph 49 of Part I of Schedule 9 and paragraph 18B of Part I of Schedule 9A*. The equivalent references in the Order are in paragraph 36A of Schedule 4, paragraph 49 of Part I of Schedule 9 and paragraph 18B of Part I of Schedule 9A.

8 Directors of companies incorporated under the Companies Acts are required by the Act to prepare accounts that give a true and fair view of the state of affairs of the company, and where applicable the group, at the end of the financial year and of the profit or loss of the company or the group for the financial year.

9 The Consultative Committee of Accountancy Bodies (CCAB) is committed to promoting and supporting compliance with accounting standards by its member bodies and by their members, whether as preparers or auditors of financial information.

10 The Councils of the CCAB bodies therefore expect their members who assume responsibilities in respect of financial statements to observe accounting standards. The Councils have agreed that:

(a) where this responsibility is evidenced by the association of members' names with such financial statements in the capacity of directors or other officers, other than auditors, the onus will be on them to ensure that the existence and purpose of accounting standards are fully understood by fellow directors and other officers. Members should also use their best endeavours to ensure that accounting standards are observed and that significant departures found to be necessary are adequately disclosed and explained in the financial statements.

****Editor's note:*** *Also paragraph 56 of the new Schedule 9A inserted by the Companies Act 1985 (Insurance Companies Accounts) Regulations 1993 (S.I. 1993 No. 3246).*

(b) where members act as auditors or reporting accountants, they should be in a position to justify significant departures to the extent that their concurrence with the departures is stated or implied. They are not, however, required to refer in their report to departures with which they concur, provided that adequate disclosure has been made in the notes to the financial statements.

The CCAB bodies, through appropriate committees, may enquire into apparent failures by their members to observe accounting standards or to ensure adequate disclosure of significant departures. **11**

The Board notes the continuing application of previously adopted SSAPs in the Republic of Ireland through their on-going promulgation by the Institute of Chartered Accountants in Ireland (ICAI). It further notes ICAI's intention of maintaining close liaison with the Board on promulgating, with appropriate modifications for legal differences, FRSs for application in the Republic of Ireland. The objective of the Board and ICAI is a regime of accounting standards common to both the United Kingdom and the Republic of Ireland. **12**

SCOPE AND APPLICATION OF ACCOUNTING STANDARDS

Accounting standards are applicable to financial statements of a reporting entity that are intended to give a true and fair view of its state of affairs at the balance sheet date and of its profit or loss (or income and expenditure) for the financial period ending on that date. Accounting standards need not be applied to immaterial items. **13**

Accounting standards should be applied to United Kingdom and Republic of Ireland group financial statements (including any amounts relating to overseas entities that are included in those financial statements). Accounting standards are not intended to apply to financial statements of overseas entities prepared for local purposes. **14**

Where accounting standards prescribe information to be contained in financial statements, such requirements do not override exemptions from disclosure given by law to, and utilised by, certain types of entity. **15**

COMPLIANCE WITH ACCOUNTING STANDARDS

Accounting standards are authoritative statements of how particular types of transaction and other events should be reflected in financial statements and accordingly compliance with accounting standards will normally be necessary for financial statements to give a true and fair view. **16**

In applying accounting standards it is important to be guided by the spirit and reasoning behind them. The spirit and reasoning are set out in the individual FRSs and are based on the Board's Statement of Principles for Financial Reporting. **17**

The requirement to give a true and fair view may in special circumstances require a departure from accounting standards. However, because accounting standards are **18** formulated with the objective of ensuring that the information resulting from their application faithfully represents the underlying commercial activity, the Board envisages that only in exceptional circumstances will departure from the requirements of an accounting standard be necessary in order for financial statements to give a true and fair view.

19 If in exceptional circumstances compliance with the requirements of an accounting standard is inconsistent with the requirement to give a true and fair view, the requirements of the accounting standard should be departed from to the extent necessary to give a true and fair view. In such cases informed and unbiased judgement should be used to devise an appropriate alternative treatment, which should be consistent with the economic and commercial characteristics of the circumstances concerned. Particulars of any material departure from an accounting standard, the reasons for it and its financial effects should be disclosed in the financial statements. The disclosure made should be equivalent to that given in respect of departures from specific accounting provisions of companies legislation.

20 The Financial Reporting Review Panel (the Review Panel) and the Department of Trade and Industry have procedures for receiving and investigating complaints regarding the annual accounts of companies in respect of apparent departures from the accounting requirements of the Act, including the requirement to give a true and fair view.* The Review Panel will be concerned with material departures from accounting standards, where as a result the accounts in question do not give a true and fair view, but it will also cover other departures from the accounting provisions of the Act. The Review Panel is empowered by regulations made under the Act to apply to the court for a declaration or declarator that the annual accounts of a company do not comply with the requirements of the Act and an order requiring the directors of the company to prepare revised accounts†. The Department of Trade and Industry has similar powers.

THE PUBLIC SECTOR

21 The prescription of accounting requirements for the public sector in the United Kingdom is a matter for the Government. Where public sector bodies prepare annual reports and accounts on commercial lines, the Government's requirements may or may not refer specifically either to accounting standards or to the need for the financial statements concerned to give a true and fair view. However, it can be expected that the Government's requirements in such cases will normally accord with the principles underlying the Board's pronouncements, except where in the particular circumstances of the public sector bodies concerned the Government considers these principles to be inappropriate or considers others to be more appropriate.

22 In the Republic of Ireland accounting standards will normally be applicable to reporting entities in the public sector as such entities are either established under

**Similar provisions exist for receiving and investigating complaints regarding the annual accounts of companies in respect of apparent departure from the accounting requirements of the Order.*

†The Review Panel does not operate in the Republic of Ireland.

companies legislation or are established under special legislation which requires them to produce financial statements which give a true and fair view.

THE ISSUE OF A FINANCIAL REPORTING STANDARD

Topics that become the subject of FRSs are identified by the Board either from its own research or from external sources, including submissions from interested parties. 23

When a topic is identified by the Board as requiring the issue of an FRS the Board commissions its staff to undertake a programme of research and consultation. This programme involves consideration of and consultation on the relevant conceptual issues, existing pronouncements and practice in the United Kingdom, the Republic of Ireland and overseas and the economic, legal and practical implications of the introduction of particular accounting requirements. 24

When the issues have been identified and debated by the Board a discussion draft is normally produced and circulated to parties who have registered their interest with the Board. When the issues require a more discursive treatment a discussion paper may be published instead. The purpose of either of these documents is to form a basis for discussion with parties particularly affected by, or having knowledge of, the issues raised in the proposals. An exposure draft of an accounting standard (a Financial Reporting Exposure Draft or FRED) is then published to allow an opportunity for all interested parties to comment on the proposals and for the Board to gauge the appropriateness and level of acceptance of those proposals. 25

The exposure draft is refined in the light of feedback resulting from the period of public exposure. There may follow another period of public or selective exposure prior to the issue of an FRS. Although the Board weighs carefully the views of interested parties, the ultimate content of an FRS must be determined by the Board's own judgement based on research, public consultation and careful deliberation about the benefits and costs of providing the resulting information. 26

APPLICABILITY OF AN ACCOUNTING STANDARD TO TRANSACTIONS ENTERED INTO BEFORE THE STANDARD WAS ISSUED

When a new accounting standard is issued the question arises whether its provisions should be applied to transactions which took place prior to the promulgation of the standard. The general policy of the Board is that the provisions of accounting standards should be applied to all material transactions irrespective of the date at which they are entered into. This is because exemption of certain transactions leads to similar transactions being accounted for differently in the same set of accounts, and can also hinder the comparison of the accounts of one entity with another. 27

In a few instances, application of the provisions of accounting standards to past transactions will entail a considerable amount of work and may result in information which is difficult for the user of accounts to interpret. In such a case, in drafting the 28 standard, the Board will consider incorporating an exclusion for transactions which took place prior to the promulgation of the standard.

29 In some instances, a new standard may have unforeseen consequences where financial statements are used to monitor compliance with contracts and agreements. The most widespread example is the covenants contained in banking and loan agreements, which may impose limits on measures such as net worth or gearing as shown in the borrower's financial statements.

30 The Board considers that the developing nature of accounting requirements is a long-established fact that would be known to the parties when they entered into the agreement. It is up to the parties to determine whether the agreement should be insulated from the effects of a future accounting standard or, if not, the manner in which it might be renegotiated to reflect changes in reporting rather than changes in the underlying financial position.* The Board, therefore, has no general policy of exempting transactions occurring before a specific date from the requirements of new accounting standards.

EARLY ADOPTION OF FINANCIAL REPORTING EXPOSURE DRAFTS†

31 An exposure draft is issued for comment and is subject to revision. Until it is converted into an accounting standard the requirements of any existing accounting standards that would be affected by proposals in the exposure draft remain in force.

32 Some companies or other reporting entities may wish to provide additional information reflecting proposals in an exposure draft. In the Board's view there are two ways that this can be achieved:

(a) insofar as the information does not conflict with existing accounting standards, it could be incorporated in the financial statements. It should be remembered, however, that the proposals may change before forming part of an accounting standard and the consequences of a change to the proposals should be considered.

(b) the information could be provided in supplementary form.

REVIEWS OF ACCOUNTING STANDARDS

33 Accounting standards are issued against the background of a business environment that evolves over time. The Board is, therefore, receptive to comments on accounting standards, recognising that, for some, a substantial period may be needed before their effectiveness can be judged, while in other cases there may be special reasons why an earlier review is necessary. However, the Board believes that it will normally be appropriate to allow new accounting standards a period in which to become established before commencing a process of formal post-issue review.

**The British Bankers' Association has indicated that it does not believe that problems arising from breaches in covenants consequent upon changes in accounting policies will occur frequently in practice.*

†Similar considerations apply to discussion documents issued by the Board.

ACCOUNTING STANDARDS AND THE LEGAL FRAMEWORK

In its debates on any accounting topic the Board initially develops its views by considering how its principles of accounting apply to the possible accounting options available for that topic. However, in deciding what is the most appropriate treatment the Board must also consider the environment in which its standards are to be applied. The legislation with which reporting entities must comply forms an important part of that environment. Accordingly, FRSs are drafted in the context of current United Kingdom and Republic of Ireland legislation and European Community Directives with the aim of ensuring consistency between accounting standards and the law. **34**

The status of accounting standards under United Kingdom legislation is addressed in the Opinion by Miss Mary Arden QC* 'The true and fair requirement', which is published as an appendix to this Foreword. **35**

INTERNATIONAL ACCOUNTING STANDARDS

FRSs are formulated with due regard to international developments. The Board supports the International Accounting Standards Committee in its aim to harmonise international financial reporting. As part of this support an FRS contains a section explaining how it relates to the International Accounting Standard (IAS) dealing with the same topic. In most cases, compliance with an FRS automatically ensures compliance with the relevant IAS. Where the requirements of an accounting standard and an IAS differ, the accounting standard should be followed by entities reporting within the area of application of the Board's accounting standards. **36**

WITHDRAWAL OF EXPLANATORY FOREWORD TO STATEMENTS OF STANDARD ACCOUNTING PRACTICE

The 'Explanatory Foreword' to SSAPs, issued by the ASC in May 1975 and revised in May 1986, is superseded by this Foreword and is accordingly withdrawn. **37**

******Now the Honourable Mrs Justice Arden.*

Appendix

Accounting Standards Board
The true and fair requirement

OPINION

1 This Opinion is concerned with the effect of recent changes in the law on the relationship between accounting standards and the requirement in Sections 226 and 227 of the Companies Act 1985 (as amended) that accounts drawn up in accordance with the Companies Act 1985 give a true and fair view of the state of affairs of the company, and where applicable the group, at the end of the financial year in question and of the profit or loss of the Company or group for that financial year. (I shall call this requirement 'the true and fair requirement'). As is well known, the true and fair requirement is overriding. Thus both sections provide that where in special circumstances compliance with the requirements of the Act as to the matters to be included in the accounts would be inconsistent with the true and fair requirement there must be a departure from those requirements to the extent necessary to give a true and fair view (sections 226(5) and 227(6)). The meaning of the true and fair requirement, as it appeared in earlier legislation, was discussed in detail in the Joint Opinions which I wrote in 1983 and 1984 with Leonard Hoffmann Q.C. (now the Right Hon. Lord Justice Hoffmann).

2 As stated in those Opinions, the question whether accounts satisfy the true and fair requirement is a question of law for the Court. However, while the true and fair view which the law requires to be given is not qualified in any way, the task of interpreting the true and fair requirement cannot be performed by the Court without evidence as to the practices and views of accountants. The more authoritative those practices and views, the more ready the Court will be to follow them. Those practices and views do not of course stand still. They respond to such matters as advances in accounting and changes in the economic climate and business practice. The law will not prevent the proper development of the practices and views of accountants but rather, through the process of interpretation, will reflect such development.

3 Up to August 1990 the responsibility for developing accounting standards was discharged by the Accounting Standards Committee ('the ASC'). Since August 1990 that responsibility has been discharged by the Accounting Standards Board ('the Board'). The Foreword to Accounting Standards approved by the Board describes in particular the circumstances in which accounts are expected to comply with accounting standards. For this purpose the key paragraph is paragraph 16, which provides

> 'Accounting standards are authoritative statements of how particular types of transaction and other events should be reflected in financial statements and accordingly compliance with accounting standards will normally be necessary for financial statements to give a true and fair view.'

The Foreword also describes the extensive process of investigation and consultation which precedes the issue of a standard and explains that the major accountancy bodies expect their members to observe accounting standards and may enquire into apparent failures by their members to observe standards or ensure adequate disclosure of departures from them.

What is the role of an accounting standard? The initial purpose is to identify proper accounting practice for the benefit of preparers and auditors of accounts. However, because accounts commonly comply with accounting standards, the effect of the issue of standards has also been to create a common understanding between users and preparers of accounts as to how particular items should be treated in accounts and accordingly an expectation that save where good reason exists accounts will comply with applicable accounting standards. **4**

The Companies Act 1989 now gives statutory recognition to the existence of accounting standards and by implication to their beneficial role in financial reporting. This recognition is achieved principally through the insertion of a new section (Section 256) into the Companies Act 1985 and of a new disclosure requirement into Schedule 4 to that Act. Section 256 provides: **5**

> '256. (1) In this Part 'accounting standards' means statements of standard accounting practice issued by such body or bodies as may be prescribed by regulations.
>
> (2) References in this Part to accounting standards applicable to a company's annual accounts are to such standards as are, in accordance with their terms, relevant to the company's circumstances and to the accounts.
>
> (3) The Secretary of State may make grants to or for the purposes of bodies concerned with –
> (a) issuing accounting standards,
> (b) overseeing and directing the issuing of such standards, or
> (c) investigating departures from such standards or from the accounting requirements of this Act and taking steps to secure compliance with them.
>
> (4) Regulations under this section may contain such transitional and other supplementary and incidental provisions as appear to the Secretary of State to be appropriate.'

In addition the notes to financial statements prepared under Schedule 4 must now comply with the following new requirement*:

> '36A. It shall be stated whether the accounts have been prepared in accordance with applicable accounting standards and particulars of any material departure from those standards and the reasons for it shall be given.'

Another significant change brought about by the 1989 Act is the introduction of a **6**

****This requirement also applies to group accounts drawn up under Schedule 4A. In addition the accounts of banking and insurance companies and groups drawn up under Schedules 9 and 9A must make the same disclosure. There is an exemption for small and medium-sized companies and for certain small and medium-sized groups.***

procedure whereby the Secretary of State or a person authorised by him may ask the Court to determine whether annual accounts comply with inter alia the true and fair requirement (Section 245B of the Companies Act 1985). The Financial Reporting Review Panel ('the Review Panel') has been authorised by the Secretary of State for this purpose. By agreement with the Department of Trade and Industry the ambit of the Review Panel is normally public and large private companies, with the Department exercising its powers in other cases.

7 The changes brought about by the Companies Act 1989 will in my view affect the way in which the Court approaches the question whether compliance with an accounting standard is necessary to satisfy the true and fair view requirement. The Court will infer from Section 256 that statutory policy favours both the issue of accounting standards (by a body prescribed by regulation) and compliance with them: indeed Section 256(3)(c) additionally contemplates the investigation of departures from them and confers power to provide public funding for such purpose. The Court will also in my view infer from paragraph 36A of Schedule 4 that (since the requirement is to disclose particulars of non-compliance rather than of compliance) accounts which meet the true and fair requirement will in general follow rather than depart from standards and that departure is sufficiently abnormal to require to be justified. These factors increase the likelihood, to which the earlier Joint Opinions referred, that the Courts will hold that in general compliance with accounting standards is necessary to meet the true and fair requirement.

8 The status of accounting standards in legal proceedings has also in my view been enhanced by the changes in the standard-setting process since 1989. Prior to the Companies Act 1989 accounting standards were developed by the ASC, which was a committee established by the six professional accountancy bodies who form the Consultative Committee of Accountancy Bodies ('the CCAB') and funded by them. The standard-setting process was reviewed by a committee established by the CCAB under the chairmanship of Sir Ron Dearing CB. The report of that Committee (the Dearing Report), which was published in 1988 and is entitled The Making of Accounting Standards, contained a number of recommendations, including recommendations leading to what are now paragraph 36A and Section 245B and the further recommendation that the standard-setting body should be funded on a wider basis. As a result of the implementation of these recommendations the standard-setting body no longer represents simply the views of the accountancy profession. Its members are appointed by a committee drawn from the Council of the Financial Reporting Council Limited ('the FRC'). The Council includes representatives of the Government, representatives of the business and financial community and members of the accountancy profession. Moreover, the Board is now funded, via the FRC, jointly by the Government, the financial community and the accountancy profession.

9 The statements referred to in Section 256 are of *standard* accounting practice. Parliament has thus recognised the desirability of standardisation in the accountancy field. The discretion to determine the measure of standardisation is one of the matters left to the Board. By definition, standardisation may restrict the availability of particular accounting treatments. Moreover the Act does not require that the practices

required by a standard should necessarily be those prevailing or generally accepted at the time.

As explained in the earlier Joint Opinions in relation to statements of standard accounting practice, the immediate effect of the issue of an accounting standard is to create a likelihood that the court will hold that compliance with that standard is necessary to meet the true and fair requirement. That likelihood is strengthened by the degree to which a standard is subsequently accepted in practice. Thus if a particular standard is generally followed, the court is very likely to find that accounts must comply with it in order to show a true and fair view. The converse of that proposition, that non-acceptance of a standard in practice would almost inevitably lead a court to the conclusion that compliance with it was not necessary to meet the true and fair requirement, is not however the case. Whenever a standard is issued by the Board, then, irrespective of the lack in some quarters of support for it, the court would be bound to give special weight to the opinion of the Board in view of its status as the standard-setting body, the process of investigation, discussion and consultation that it will have undertaken before adopting the standard and the evolving nature of accounting standards. **10**

The fact that paragraph 36A envisages the possibility of a departure from an 'applicable accounting standard' (in essence, any relevant standard: see section 256(2), above) does not mean that the Companies Act permits a departure in any case where the disclosure is given. The departure must have been appropriate in the particular case. If the Court is satisfied that compliance with a standard is necessary to show a true and fair view in that case, a departure will result in a breach of the true and fair requirement even if the paragraph 36A disclosure is given. **11**

Experience shows that from time to time and for varying reasons deficiencies in accounting standards appear. Following a recommendation in the Dearing Report, the Board has established a sub-committee called the Urgent Issues Task Force ('the UITF') to resolve such issues on an urgent basis in appropriate cases. The members of the UITF include leading members of the accountancy profession and of the business community. The agenda of the UITF is published in advance to allow for public debate. The UITF'S consensus pronouncements (contained in abstracts) represent the considered views of a large majority of its members. When the UITF reaches its view, it is considered by the Board for compliance with the law and accounting standards and with the Board's future plans. If an abstract meets these criteria the Board expects to adopt it without further consideration. It will then be published by the Board. The expectation of the CCAB, the Board and the profession is that abstracts of the UITF will be observed. This expectation has been borne out in practice. Accordingly in my view, the Court is likely to treat UITF abstracts as of considerable standing even though they are not envisaged by the Companies Acts. This will lead to a readiness on the part of the Court to accept that compliance with abstracts of the UITF is also necessary to meet the true and fair requirement. **12**

The Joint Opinions were particularly concerned with the effect of standards on the concept of true and fair. The approach to standards taken in the Joint Opinions is **13** consistent with the approach of the Court in *Lloyd Cheyham v. Littlejohn* [1987] BCLC 303 at 313. In that case Woolf J. (as he then was) held that standards of the ASC were 'very strong evidence as to what is the proper standard which should be adopted'.

14 As regards the concept of true and fair, I would emphasise the point made in the Joint Opinions that the true and fair view is a dynamic concept. Thus what is required to show a true and fair view is subject to continuous rebirth and in determining whether the true and fair requirement is satisfied the Court will not in my view seek to find synonyms for the words 'true' and 'fair' but will seek to apply the concepts which those words imply.

15 It is nearly a decade since the Joint Opinions were written. Experience and legislative history since then have both illustrated the subtlety and evolving nature of the relationship between law and accounting practice. Accounting standards are now assured as an authoritative source of the latter. In consequence it is now the norm for accounts to comply with accounting standards. I would add this. Just as a custom which is upheld by the courts may properly be regarded as a source of law, so too, in my view, does an accounting standard which the court holds must be complied with to meet the true and fair requirement become, in cases where it is applicable, a source of law in itself in the widest sense of that term.

Mary Arden

Erskine Chambers
Lincoln's Inn
21st April 1993

[SSAP 1]
Accounting for associated companies

(Issued January 1971; amended August 1974; revised April 1982; amended December 1990)

Contents

Accounting for associated companies

The provisions of this statement of standard accounting practice should be read in conjunction with the (Explanatory) Foreword to accounting standards *and need not be applied to immaterial items. The provisions apply to financial statements prepared under the historical cost convention and to financial statements prepared under the current cost convention.*

Part 1 – Explanatory note

Statement of Standard Accounting Practice 1 'Accounting for the Results of Associated Companies' (SSAP 1) was issued in January 1971 to introduce a standard accounting treatment for investments in companies, the policies of which, although they are not subsidiaries of the investing company, are subject to significant influence by the investing company. **1**

It is generally accepted accounting practice for a company not to take credit in its own (i.e. non-consolidated) profit and loss account and balance sheet for its share of the profits of other companies which have not been declared as dividends. The view is taken that the inclusion of undistributed profits would ignore the separate legal status of the entities concerned and, as regards the investing company, be contrary to the practice of not taking credit for investment income until it is received or receivable. **2**

However, where a company conducts an important part of its business through the medium of other companies, the mere disclosure of dividend income (or mere inclusion of dividend income alone) from these companies is unlikely to be sufficient to give adequate information regarding the sources of their income and the manner in which their funds are being employed. **3**

At one time such operations were usually carried out through the medium of subsidiary companies. It was for this reason that companies legislation required the preparation of group accounts, normally in the form of consolidated accounts. At the time of the original SSAP there had been two important developments. One was the growing practice of companies to conduct parts of their business through other companies (frequently consortium or joint venture companies) in which they had a substantial but not a controlling interest. The other was the importance which investors had come to attach to earnings per share and the price/earnings ratio. To ensure that the investing company's financial statements as a whole gave adequate information and provided a total of earnings from which the most useful ratios could be calculated, it was considered necessary that the coverage of consolidated financial statements should be extended to include (within the framework of the existing law) the share of earnings or losses of companies which were defined as associated companies. **4**

This approach recognised a difference in principle between the nature of investments in **5** associated companies (as defined in SSAP 1) and other forms of trade investment. The essence of the distinction was that an investing company actively participates in the commercial and policy decisions of its associated companies; it thus has a measure of direct responsibility for the return on its investment, and should account for its stewardship accordingly. However, it will not normally seek to exert direct management influence over the operating policy of other companies in which it invests and should continue to deal with them in accordance with traditional accounting methods.

6 The broad concept underlying the accounting treatment of the results of associated companies was the adoption in modified form of the consolidation procedures used for subsidiary companies. It followed from this that the investing company's share of associated companies' profits and losses would be reflected in its consolidated profit and loss account, and its share of their post-acquisition retained profits or accumulated deficits would be reflected in its consolidated balance sheet, though not in its own balance sheet as a legal entity. This is generally referred to as the equity method of accounting.

7 As part of its normal programme of reviewing standards the Accounting Standards Committee (ASC) has reconsidered the principles contained in the first edition of SSAP 1.

8 This SSAP continues the basic principles and requirements of the original SSAP. However, as part of the review ASC has incorporated some changes both in the definition of an associated company and in the presentation of the information involved. The presentation requires separate disclosure of the goodwill component.

9 This SSAP is intended to apply to companies incorporated under the Companies Acts. The principles laid down in it are, nevertheless, applicable to financial statements of any entity, whether incorporated or not, which invests in another entity or entities.

10 In some cases, partnerships or other non-corporate joint ventures can have features which justify accounting for a proportionate share of individual assets and liabilities as well as profits or losses.

Part 2 – Definition of terms

11 A *company* includes any enterprise which comes within the scope of statements of standard accounting practice. In particular, references to investments in companies include not only investments in corporate enterprises but can include investments in non-corporate joint ventures and consortia.

12 A *group* comprises a holding company and its subsidiaries.

13 An *associated company* is a company not being a subsidiary of the investing group or company in which:

(a) [*withdrawn*]

(b) the interest of the investing group or company is for the long term [. . .] and, having regard to the disposition of the other shareholdings, the investing group or company is in a position to exercise a significant influence over the company in which the investment is made.

Significant influence over a company essentially involves participation in the financial and operating policy decisions of that company (including dividend policy) but not necessarily control of those policies. Representation on the board of directors is indicative of such participation, but will neither necessarily give conclusive evidence of it nor be the only method by which the investing company may participate in policy decisions.

Where the interest of the investing group or company amounts to 20 per cent or more of the equity voting rights of a company, it should be presumed that the investing group or company has the ability to exercise significant influence over that company unless it can clearly be demonstrated otherwise. For example, there may exist one or more other large shareholdings which prevent the exercise of such influence. **14**

Where the interest of the investing group or company amounts to less than 20 per cent of the equity voting rights of a company it should be presumed that the investing group or company does not have the ability to exercise significant influence unless it can clearly demonstrate otherwise. Unless there are exceptional circumstances, this demonstration should include a statement from the company in which the investment is made that it accepts that the investing group or company is in a position to exercise significant influence over it. **15**

Where different companies in a group hold shares in a company, the investment in that company should be taken as the aggregate of the holdings of the investing company together with the whole of those of its subsidiaries but excluding those of its associates in determining whether or not significant influence is presumed to exist. **16**

[*Withdrawn*] **17**

Part 3 – Standard accounting practice

BASES OF ACCOUNTING FOR ASSOCIATED COMPANIES

Income from investments of a company or its subsidiaries in associated companies should be brought into account on the following bases: **18**

(a) *In the investing company's own financial statements:* dividends received and receivable.

(b) *In the investing group's consolidated financial statements (or the equivalent prepared in accordance with paragraphs 24 and 35 below):* the investing group's share of profits less losses of associated companies.

These bases need not be applied to interests in partnerships or non-corporate joint ventures where such arrangements have features which justify accounting for a proportionate share of individual assets and liabilities as well as profits or losses. Associated companies should be accounted for in accordance with the Companies Act 1985 as amended in 1989 (the Act). The Act should be applied by referring to the Interim Statement – Consolidated Accounts issued by the Accounting Standards Board and dated December 1990.*

PROFIT AND LOSS ACCOUNT ITEMS

19 *Profit before tax:* The investing group should include in its consolidated financial statements the aggregate of its share of before-tax profits less losses of associated companies. This item should be shown separately and suitably described.

20 *Taxation:* The tax attributed to the share of profits of associated companies should be disclosed separately within the group tax charge in the consolidated financial statements.

21 *Extraordinary items:* The investing group's share of aggregate extraordinary items dealt with in the associated companies' financial statements should be included with the group's extraordinary items to the extent that the group's share of the items involved would be classified, on the basis of the criteria set out in FRS 3 'Reporting Financial Performance' as extraordinary in the context of the financial statements of the investing group. Where that share is material in the context of the group's results it should be disclosed separately from extraordinary items arising from companies belonging to the group.

22 *Net profit retained by associated companies:* The investing group's share of aggregate net profits less losses retained by associated companies should be shown separately in the financial statements of the investing group.

23 Other items. The investing group should not include its share of associated companies' items such as turnover and depreciation in the aggregate amounts of these items disclosed in its consolidated financial statements. If the results of one or more associated companies are so material in the context of the financial statements of the investing group that more detailed information about them would assist in giving a true and fair view, this information should be given by separate disclosure of the total turnover of the associated companies concerned, their total depreciation charges, their total profits less losses before taxation and the amount of such profits less losses attributable to the investing group. In judging materiality regard should be had not merely to the group's share of the net profit of an associated company but also to the scale of its operations in relation to those of the group.

24 An investing company which does not prepare consolidated financial statements should show the information required by paragraphs 19 to 23 of this SSAP by preparing a separate profit and loss account or by adding the information in supplementary form to its own profit and loss account unless the investing company is exempt from preparing consolidated financial statements, or would be exempt, if it had

Editor's note: *The relevant extract is reproduced following this SSAP.*

subsidiaries. Information about the associated companies should be reported in such a way that the investing company's share of the profits of its associated companies is not treated as realised for the purposes of the Companies Act 1985. (References in this SSAP to investing groups and consolidated financial statements are to be taken as embracing this information in the case of investing companies showing results of their associated companies in this way.)

BALANCE SHEET ITEMS

Investing company's interests in associated companies: Unless shown at a valuation, the amount at which the investing company's interests in associated companies should be shown in the investing company's own financial statements is the cost of the investment less any amounts written off. **25**

Investing group's interests in associated companies: The amount at which the investing group's interests in associated companies should be shown in the consolidated balance sheet is the total of: **26**

(a) the investing group's share of the net assets other than goodwill of the associated companies stated, where possible, after attributing fair values to the net assets at the time of acquisition of the interest in the associated companies, and
(b) the investing group's share of any goodwill in the associated companies' own financial statements, together with
(c) the premium paid (or discount) on the acquisition of the interests in the associated companies in so far as it has not already been written off or amortised.

Item (a) should be disclosed separately but items (b) and (c) may be shown as one aggregate amount.

Loans to associated companies: The total of loans to associated companies from the group should be separately disclosed in the consolidated financial statements. **27**

Loans from associated companies: The total of loans from associated companies to the group should be separately disclosed in the consolidated financial statements. **28**

Trading balances: Balances arising from unsettled normal trading transactions between the associated companies and the investing group should be included under current assets or liabilities as appropriate, with separate disclosure if material in the context of the financial statements of the investing group. **29**

Other items: More detailed information about the associated companies' tangible and intangible assets and liabilities should be given if the interests in the associated companies are so material in the context of the financial statements of the investing group that more detailed information about them would assist in giving a true and fair view. In judging materiality, regard should be had not merely to the net carrying amount of the investment in an associated company, but also to the scale of its operations in relation to those of the group. **30**

Accumulated reserves: The investing group's share of the post-acquisition accumulated **31** reserves of associated companies and any movements therein should be disclosed in the consolidated financial statements. In arriving at the amount to be disclosed, it will also be necessary to take account of and disclose movements on associated companies' reserves which have not arisen from amounts passing through the profit and loss account, for example surpluses on revaluation of fixed assets. If the accumulated reserves of associated companies overseas would be subject to further tax on distribution, this should be made clear.

32 *Permanent impairment in value:* Where there has been permanent impairment in the value of any goodwill (including any premium paid) attributable to an investment in an associated company, it should be written down, and the amount written off in the accounting period separately disclosed. Because an impairment in the value of the underlying net assets would normally be reflected in the books of the associated company, further provision against the investing group's share of these net assets should not usually be necessary.

33 *Deficiency of net assets:* Where an associated company has a deficiency of net assets but is still regarded as a long-term investment it will usually be supported by its shareholders (either by way of loan or by way of an agreement, either formal or informal, to support it). In these circumstances, the investing group should reflect its share of the deficiency of net assets in its consolidated financial statements.

34 *Investment in an unincorporated entity:* Where an investment is made in an unincorporated entity, a liability could arise which would be in excess of that resulting from taking account only of the investing group's share of net assets of the associated company (e.g., as a result of joint and several liability in a partnership). In such circumstances it may be necessary to consider whether it would be prudent either to include an additional provision, or to recognise a contingent liability for this excess.

35 Except where it is exempt from preparing consolidated accounts, an investing company which does not prepare consolidated financial statements should show the information required by paragraphs 25 to 34 of this SSAP by preparing a separate balance sheet or by adding the information in supplementary form to its own balance sheet.

INCLUSION OF THE RESULTS OF ASSOCIATED COMPANIES IN THE CONSOLIDATED FINANCIAL STATEMENTS OF THE INVESTING GROUP

36 The financial statements used for the purpose of including the results of associated companies should be either coterminous with those of the investing group or made up to a date which is either not more than six months before, or shortly after, the date of the financial statements of the investing group. In relation to associated companies which are listed on a recognised stock exchange, only published financial information should be disclosed in the financial statements of the investing group.

37 Before incorporating the results of an associated company based on financial statements issued before completion of those of the investing group, care should be taken to

ensure that later information has not materially affected the view shown by the financial statements of the associated company. If financial statements not coterminous with those of the investing group are used and the effect is material the facts and the dates of year-ends should be disclosed.

Where the interest of the investing group or company is in any company other than a subsidiary or a proportionately consolidated joint venture and the investing group or company holds 20 per cent or more of the equity voting rights of that company but does not account for that company as an associated company, details of the accounting treatment adopted, and the reason for doing so, should be stated by way of a note to the financial statements. In those cases where disclosure of the reason would be harmful to the business, the directors may omit the information, after consultation with their auditors, (in a comparable manner to that permitted by the Companies Acts for subsidiaries where the disclosure would be harmful to the business except that the Secretary of State's approval would not be required in this case). Conversely, where the investing group or company holds less than 20 per cent of the equity voting rights of a company but accounts for that company as an associate, the basis on which significant influence is exercised should be stated. **38**

ACCOUNTING ADJUSTMENTS

Wherever the effect is material, adjustments similar to those adopted for the purpose of presenting consolidated financial statements should be made to exclude from the investing group's consolidated financial statements such items as unrealised profits on stocks transferred to or from associated companies and to achieve reasonable consistency with the accounting policies adopted by the investing group. **39**

RESTRICTIONS ON DISTRIBUTION

If there are significant restrictions on the ability of an associated company to distribute its retained profits (other than those shown as non-distributable) because of statutory, contractual or exchange control restrictions, the extent of the restrictions should be indicated. **40**

MINORITY INTERESTS

Where the investment in an associated company is held by a subsidiary in which there are minority interests, the minority interests shown in the consolidated financial statements of the group should include the minority share of the subsidiary's interest in the results and net assets of the associated company. **41**

INVESTMENTS BY ASSOCIATED COMPANIES

Where an associated company itself has subsidiary or associated companies, the results and net assets to be dealt with in the investing group's consolidated financial statements are its attributable proportion of the results and net assets of the group (including the **42** appropriate proportion of the results and net assets of its associated companies) of which the associated company is the holding company.

LOSS OF STATUS AS ASSOCIATED COMPANY

43 When an investment in a company ceases to fall within the definition of an associated company, it should be stated in the consolidated balance sheet of the investing group at the carrying amount under the equity method at that date. However, the carrying value should be adjusted if dividends are subsequently paid out of profits earned prior to the change of status. Provision should be made against the investment if there has been any impairment in value.

EFFECTIVE DATE OF ACQUISITION OR DISPOSAL

44 The effective date for both acquisition and disposal of an interest, or any portion of an interest, in an associated company should be the earlier of:

(a) the date on which the consideration passes; or
(b) the date on which an offer becomes unconditional.

This applies even if the acquiring company has the right under the agreement to share in the profits of the acquired business from an earlier date.

TREATMENT OF ASSOCIATED COMPANIES IN CURRENT COST ACCOUNTS

45 Investments in associated companies should be shown in the investing group's current cost consolidated balance sheet as in paragraph 26 of this SSAP, except that the figure for net assets, other than goodwill, should be based on current costs, or the directors' best estimate thereof. The figures for goodwill, being the investing group's share of goodwill in the associated companies' own financial statements and any premium arising on the acquisition of interests in the associated companies, should be the same as in the historical cost balance sheet, provided that fair values were attributed to the other assets at the dates of each acquisition.

46 The investing group's current cost consolidated profit and loss account should include either the investing group's share of the current cost profits less losses of the associated companies, stated before tax but after interest and the associated companies' separate gearing adjustments, or the directors' best estimate thereof.

47 The investing group's gearing adjustment should be calculated by applying the gearing ratio, calculated from the investing group's current cost consolidated balance sheet, to the total of the investing group's current cost adjustments including an adjustment for the associated companies. The adjustment for the associated companies should be the investing group's share of the current cost adjustments, including gearing, of the associated companies.

48 Where the associated companies do not themselves prepare current cost accounts and as a result the investing group includes information based on directors' best estimates, this fact should be disclosed.

DISCLOSURE OF PARTICULARS OF ASSOCIATED COMPANIES

The names of the principal associated companies should be disclosed in the financial **49**
statements of the investing group showing for each of these associated companies:

(a) the proportion of the number of the issued shares of each class held by the investing group; and
(b) an indication of the nature of its business.

CORRESPONDING AMOUNTS

On first introducing the amended standard method of accounting set out in this SSAP **50**
the corresponding amounts for the preceding period should be appropriately stated on a comparable basis.

DATE FROM WHICH EFFECTIVE

The amended method of accounting for associated companies set out in this SSAP **51**
should be adopted as soon as possible and regarded as standard in respect of financial statements relating to accounting periods starting on or after 1 January 1982.

Parts 4, 5 and 6

[*Withdrawn*]

Extract from ASB interim statement*

(Issued December 1990)

THIS EXTRACT REFERS TO CHANGES TO SSAP 1 'ACCOUNTING FOR ASSOCIATED COMPANIES' TO REMOVE INCONSISTENCIES WITH THE 1985 ACT AS AMENDED.

The remainder of the Interim Statement was superseded by FRS 2 'Accounting for subsidiary undertakings' (effective in respect of consolidated financial statements relating to periods ending on or after 23 December 1992). The paragraphs not superseded remain in force and are detailed on the following pages.

***Editor's note:** The amendments to SSAP 1 did not apply to companies registered in the Republic of Ireland. However, following the issue of the European Communities (Companies: Group Accounts) Regulations 1992 (which implemented the EC Seventh Directive in the Republic) the amendments are now relevant to such companies.*

Extract from ASB interim statement

Part 1 – Guidance on interpretation of the Act

JOINT VENTURES

The Act introduces the term 'joint venture' for the first time into company law. Schedule 4A.19 describes a joint venture and permits a joint venture that is neither a body corporate nor a subsidiary to be dealt with in the consolidated accounts by the method of proportional consolidation. In the Act a joint venture is essentially an undertaking jointly managed by one undertaking included in the consolidation with one or more undertakings not included in the consolidation. The Act uses 'joint management' to describe something which could in fact more aptly be described as joint control. The Act's provisions do not require the involvement of the joint venturers in the day-to-day operation of the venture's business nor do they exclude from the definition of a joint venture an undertaking which is managed on a day-to-day basis by a single operator. The Board considers that the general description of a joint venture in the Act can usefully be supplemented by a definition which identifies those key characteristics of a joint venture that distinguish it from other kinds of undertaking. 32

Definition of a joint venture

A joint venture is an undertaking by which its participants expect to achieve some common purpose or benefit. It is controlled jointly by two or more venturers. Joint control is the contractually agreed sharing of control. 33

Part 2 – Changes to SSAP 1 – 'Accounting for associated companies'

Not reproduced as all the changes have been incorporated in the text of SSAP 1. 38

Appendix

Commentary on Part 1 – Guidance on interpretation of the Act

JOINT VENTURES

A9 The comments received supported the need for an accounting standard to define a joint venture. The Board has drafted its guidance on the meaning of 'joint venture' in the light of comment received. In particular the ED50 definition was criticised for implying that the existence of a joint venture agreement was a necessary condition for an undertaking to be a joint venture. It also seemed to suggest that participants had to have been involved in the set up of the undertaking if that undertaking was to be taken as their joint venture. Thus the definition might not have covered the interests of those who did not participate in the venture until it was established. The definition of a joint venture offered in this guidance is closer to that of the IASC proposals than the ED50 definition.

A10 The Board has not issued interim guidance on the accounting treatment of joint ventures under the Act. The comments revealed no consensus on how joint ventures should be treated. This is also an area where the Act conflicts with the preferred treatments proposed by several commentators. The International Accounting Standards Committee is soon to publish its standard on the treatment of joint ventures*. The Board reserves its opinion on how joint ventures should be treated until it has the time to consider this as part of its full review of consolidated accounts.†

Commentary on Part 2 – Changes to SSAP 1

A13 Where SSAP 1 uses the terms 'joint ventures', 'partnerships' and 'consortia' these references are dropped as the Act now refers only to associated undertakings or joint ventures. The Act requires undertakings which are associated undertakings to be equity accounted. 'Associated undertaking' is defined in the Act not to include non-corporate joint ventures where the option to use proportional consolidation has been taken (paragraphs 10, 14, 15, 18 and 38 of SSAP 1).

A14 The changes made to paragraph 13 of SSAP 1 arise mainly as a result of the way 'associated undertaking' is defined in the Act. The definition is set out in Schedule 4A.20 and broadly provides that an associated undertaking is one where the investing undertaking has a participating interest and exercises a significant influence.

A15 Paragraph 17 of SSAP 1 is withdrawn. The term 'associated company' is now out of date so that restrictions on its use are meaningless.

***Editor's note:** *IAS 31 'Financial Reporting of Interests in Joint Ventures' was published in January 1991.*

†***Editor's note:*** *The ASB Discussion Paper 'Associates and Joint Ventures' considers the issues.*

Paragraph 19 of SSAP 1 gives an example of the heading under which the results of associated undertakings should be recorded. This does not comply with the Act so the reference is withdrawn. **A16**

When SSAPs 1 and 14* were revised or published wholly owned subsidiaries were the only companies which were not required to prepare group accounts The Act has now extended the exemptions from preparing group accounts so that a different phrase is now required to denote exempt companies (paragraphs 24, 35 of SSAP 1 and paragraph 20 of SSAP 14*). **A17**

In paragraph of SSAP 1 the reference of the Department of Trade has been updated to the Secretary of State. **A18**

Part 4 and Part 5 (paragraphs 63–64) of SSAP 1 and Part 4 and Section A of Part 5 of SSAP 14* give the legal requirements in Great Britain and Northern Ireland. These have been withdrawn in full as they are now out of date and bringing them up to date would require extensive changes. This affects the drafting of paragraph 49 of SSAP 1. Part 6 of SSAP 1 and SSAP 14* deals with compliance with international statements and has also been withdrawn as the International Accounting Standard referred to, IAS3 'Consolidated Financial Statements', has now been superseded†. In SSAP 14* this necessitates withdrawing the paragraph referring to IAS3 from the introductory passage. **A23**

****Editor's note:** SSAP 14 has been superseded by FRS 2 'Accounting for Subsidiary Undertakings'.*

*†**Editor's note:** IAS 3 was superseded by IAS 27 'Consolidated Financial Statements and Accounting for Investments in Subsidiaries' and IAS 28 'Accounting for Investments in Associates'.*

[SSAP 2]
Disclosure of accounting policies

(Issued November 1971)

Contents

***Editor's note:** The equivalent international accounting standard is IAS 1 'Disclosure of Accounting Policies'.*

Disclosure of accounting policies

It is fundamental to the understanding and interpretation of financial accounts that those who use them should be aware of the main assumptions on which they are based. The purpose of the statement which follows is to assist such understanding by promoting improvement in the quality of information disclosed. It seeks to achieve this by establishing as standard accounting practice the disclosure in the financial accounts of clear explanations of the accounting policies followed in so far as these are significant for the purpose of giving a true and fair view. The statement does not seek to establish accounting standards for individual items; these will be dealt with in separate statements of standard accounting practice issued from time to time.

Part 1 – Explanatory note

FUNDAMENTAL ACCOUNTING CONCEPTS, ACCOUNTING BASES AND ACCOUNTING POLICIES

In accounting usage terms such as 'accounting principles', 'practices', 'rules', 'conventions', 'methods', or 'procedures' have often been treated as interchangeable.* For the purpose of this statement it is convenient to distinguish between *fundamental accounting concepts*, *accounting bases* and *accounting policies*. 1

Fundamental accounting concepts are here defined as broad basic assumptions which underlie the periodic financial accounts of business enterprises. It is expedient to single out for special mention four in particular: (a) the 'going concern' concept, (b) the 'accruals' concept, (c) the 'consistency' concept and (d) the 'prudence' concept.† The use of these concepts is not necessarily self-evident from an examination of accounts, but they have such general acceptance that they call for no explanation in published accounts and their observance is presumed unless stated otherwise. They are practical rules rather than theoretical ideals and are capable of variation and evolution as accounting thought and practice develop, but their present generally accepted meanings are restated in paragraph 14 below. 2

Accounting bases are the methods which have been developed for expressing or applying fundamental accounting concepts to financial transactions and items. By their nature accounting bases are more diverse and numerous than fundamental concepts, since they have evolved in response to the variety and complexity of types of 3

In this series 'accounting practices' has been adopted as a generic term to encompass all aspects of financial accounting methods and presentation.

†It is emphasised that it is not the purpose of this statement to develop a basic theory of accounting. An exhaustive theoretical approach would take an entirely different form and would include, for instance, many more propositions than the four fundamental concepts referred to here. It is, however, expedient to recognise them as working assumptions having general acceptance at the present time.

business and business transactions, and for this reason there may justifiably exist more than one recognised accounting basis for dealing with particular items.

4 *Accounting policies* are the specific accounting bases judged by business enterprises to be most appropriate to their circumstances and adopted by them for the purpose of preparing their financial accounts.

PARTICULAR PROBLEMS IN APPLICATION OF THE FUNDAMENTAL CONCEPTS

5 The main difficulty in applying the fundamental accounting concepts arises from the fact that many business transactions have financial effects spreading over a number of years. Decisions have to be made on the extent to which expenditure incurred in one year can reasonably be expected to produce benefits in the form of revenue in other years and should therefore be carried forward, in whole or in part; that is, should be dealt with in the closing balance sheet, as distinct from being dealt with as an expense of the current year in the profit and loss account because the benefit has been exhausted in that year.

6 In some cases revenue is received for goods or services the production or supply of which will involve some later expenditure. In this case a decision must be made regarding how much of the revenue should be carried forward, to be dealt with in subsequent profit and loss accounts when the relevant costs are incurred.

7 All such decisions require consideration of future events of uncertain financial effect, and to this extent an element of commercial judgement is unavoidable in the assessment.

8 Examples of matters which give rise to particular difficulty are: the future benefits to be derived from stocks and all types of work in progress at the end of the year; the future benefits to be derived from fixed assets, and the period of years over which these will be fruitful; the extent to which expenditure on research and development can be expected to produce future benefits.

PURPOSE AND LIMITATIONS OF ACCOUNTING BASES

9 In the course of practice there have developed a variety of accounting bases designed to provide consistent, fair and as nearly as possible objective solutions to these problems in particular circumstances; for instance bases for calculating such items as depreciation, the amounts at which stocks and work in progress are to be stated, and deferred taxation.

10 Accounting bases provide an orderly and consistent framework for periodic reporting of a concern's results and financial position, but they do not, and are not intended to, substitute for the exercise of commercial judgement in the preparation of financial reports. Where a choice of acceptable accounting bases is available judgement must be exercised in choosing those which are appropriate to the circumstances and are best

suited to present fairly the concern's results and financial position; the bases thus adopted then become the concern's accounting policies. The significance of accounting bases is that they provide limits to the area subject to the exercise of judgement, and a check against arbitrary, excessive or unjustifiable adjustments where no other objective yardstick is available. By definition it is not possible to develop generalised rules for the exercise of judgement, though practical working rules may be evolved on a pragmatic basis for limited use in particular circumstances. Broadly, the longer a concern's normal business cycle – the period between initiation of business transactions and their completion – the greater the area subject to judgement and its effect on periodic financial accounts, and the less its susceptibility to close regulation by accounting bases. These limitations to the regulating powers of accounting bases must be recognised.

SIGNIFICANCE OF DISCLOSURE OF ACCOUNTING POLICIES

In circumstances where more than one accounting basis is acceptable in principle, the accounting policy followed can significantly affect a concern's reported results and financial position and the view presented can be properly appreciated only if the policies followed in dealing with material items are also explained. For this reason adequate disclosure of the accounting policies is essential to the fair presentation of financial accounts. As accounting standards become established through publication of statements of standard accounting practice, the choice of accounting bases regarded as generally available will diminish, but it has to be recognised that the complexity and diversity of business renders total and rigid uniformity of bases impracticable. 11

The items with which this statement is mainly concerned are those which are subject to the exercise of judgement as to how far they should be dealt with in the profit and loss account for the period under review or how far all or part should be carried forward in the balance sheet as attributable to the operations of future periods. The determination of the annual profit or loss of nearly every business substantially depends on a systematic approach to a few material items of this type. For the better appreciation of the view they give, annual accounts should include a clear explanation of the accounting policies followed for dealing with these few key items (some examples of which are given in paragraph 13 below). The intention and spirit of this statement are that management should identify those items of the type described which are judged material or critical for the purpose of determining and fully appreciating the company's profit or loss and its financial position, and should make clear the accounting policies followed for dealing with them. 12

EXAMPLES OF MATTERS FOR WHICH DIFFERENT ACCOUNTING BASES ARE RECOGNISED

Significant matters for which different accounting bases are recognised and which may have a material effect on reported results and financial position include: 13

- depreciation of fixed assets
- treatment and amortisation of intangibles such as research and development expenditure, patents and trademarks

- stocks and work in progress
- long-term contracts
- deferred taxation
- hire-purchase or instalment transactions
- leasing and rental transactions
- conversion of foreign currencies
- repairs and renewals
- consolidation policies
- property development transactions
- warranties for products or services.

This list is not exhaustive, and may vary according to the nature of the operations conducted.

Part 2 – Definition of terms

14 *Fundamental accounting concepts* are the broad basic assumptions which underlie the periodic financial accounts of business enterprises. At the present time the four following fundamental concepts (the relative importance of which will vary according to the circumstances of the particular case) are regarded as having general acceptability:

(a) the 'going concern' concept: the enterprise will continue in operational existence for the foreseeable future. This means in particular that the profit and loss account and balance sheet assume no intention or necessity to liquidate or curtail significantly the scale of operation;

(b) the 'accruals' concept: revenue and costs are accrued (that is, recognised as they are earned or incurred, not as money is received or paid), matched with one another so far as their relationship can be established or justifiably assumed, and dealt with in the profit and loss account of the period to which they relate; provided that where the accruals concept is inconsistent with the 'prudence' concept (paragraph (d) below), the latter prevails. The accruals concept implies that the profit and loss account reflects changes in the amount of net assets that arise out of the transactions of the relevant period (other than distributions or subscriptions of capital and unrealised surpluses arising on revaluation of fixed assets). Revenue and profits dealt with in the profit and loss account are matched with associated costs and expenses by including in the same account the costs incurred in earning them (so far as these are material and identifiable);

(c) the 'consistency' concept: there is consistency of accounting treatment of like items within each accounting period and from one period to the next;

(d) the concept of 'prudence': revenue and profits are not anticipated, but are recognised by inclusion in the profit and loss account only when realised in the form either of cash or of other assets the ultimate cash realisation of which can be assessed with reasonable certainty; provision is made for all known liabilities (expenses and losses) whether the amount of these is known with certainty or is a best estimate in the light of the information available.

Accounting bases are the methods developed for applying fundamental accounting concepts to financial transactions and items, for the purpose of financial accounts, and in particular (a) for determining the accounting periods in which revenue and costs should be recognised in the profit and loss account and (b) for determining the amounts at which material items should be stated in the balance sheet. **15**

Accounting policies are the specific accounting bases selected and consistently followed by a business enterprise as being, in the opinion of the management, appropriate to its circumstances and best suited to present fairly its results and financial position. **16**

Part 3 – Standard accounting practice

DISCLOSURE OF ADOPTION OF CONCEPTS WHICH DIFFER FROM THOSE GENERALLY ACCEPTED

If accounts are prepared on the basis of assumptions which differ in material respects from any of the generally accepted fundamental concepts defined in paragraph 14 above, the facts should be explained. In the absence of a clear statement to the contrary, there is a presumption that the four fundamental concepts have been observed. **17**

DISCLOSURE OF ACCOUNTING POLICIES

The accounting policies (as defined in paragraph 16 above) followed for dealing with items which are judged material or critical in determining profit or loss for the year and in stating the financial position should be disclosed by way of note to the accounts. The explanations should be clear, fair, and as brief as possible. **18**

DATE FROM WHICH EFFECTIVE

The accounting practices set out in this statement should be adopted as soon as possible and regarded as standard in respect of reports relating to accounting periods starting on or after 1st January 1972. **19**

[SSAP 3] Earnings per share

(Issued February 1972; revised August 1974; amended October 1992)

Contents

Earnings per share

The original Statement of Standard Accounting Practice on Earnings Per Share (SSAP 3) was issued in February 1972.

Although little change is needed in the basic definition of Earnings Per Share (Part 2) or in the standard accounting practice (Part 3), other parts of the statement have been brought up to date to take account of:

(a) *The change in the basis of taxation in the United Kingdom from the former system of corporation tax to the imputation system;*

(b) *The issue by the Councils of the bodies participating in the Accounting Standards Steering Committee of a number of statements of accounting practice; in particular SSAP 8* The treatment of taxation under the imputation system in the accounts of companies.

The Council of the Stock Exchange states in note 28 of the listing agreement that it will 'expect the accounts of listed companies to be drawn up in accordance with the standards approved by these accountancy bodies'. This requirement to apply the accounting standard on earnings per share is extended by note 6 of the listing agreement to the computation of the figure of earnings per share to be shown in preliminary profits announcements for the year or other full accounting period.*

This statement is intended to apply to the audited accounts of listed companies. The circumstances of smaller unlisted companies and the problems of computation (particularly when a company is financed by interest-free loans from directors) are often such that an earnings per share figure would not be meaningful.

Part 1 – Explanatory Note

The original call for a standard accounting practice for the disclosure of earnings per share was based on the increasing use of the price-earnings ratio as a standard stock market indicator. Despite the complication introduced by the imputation system of corporation tax and the limitation of dividends by Government regulation in the United Kingdom, price-earnings ratios remain one of the most commonly used stock market indicators. Although they are not strictly comparable because of differences between one country's tax system and another's, they are, nevertheless, used on a world-wide basis. 1

The continued use of price-earnings ratios requires that the earnings per share on which that ratio is based should be calculated and disclosed on a comparable basis as between one company and another and as between one financial period and another, so far as this is possible. 2

***Editor's note:** *Superseded by para 12.42(a) of the Listing Rules of the London Stock Exchange.*

3 As between one company and another, the main problem arising from the imputation system of corporation tax is the treatment of irrecoverable Advance Corporation Tax (ACT)* After the transitional period, only a small proportion of listed companies is likely to have irrecoverable ACT (or unrelieved overseas tax arising from a dividend) included in their tax charge for the year. These companies will mainly be those whose earnings arise overseas, or who have large capital allowances for corporation tax, such as the oil, mining, plantation and shipping companies. The calculation of earnings per share when there is irrecoverable ACT is considered in paragraphs 7 to 9.

4 One of the features of the change from the former system to the imputation system of corporation tax is that, whereas before April 1973 earnings after corporation tax were available to cover gross dividends before deduction of income tax, the earnings after corporation tax under the new system are available to cover the actual cash dividends payable to the shareholders. The transitional arrangements also give rise to problems of comparison.

5 In calculating the earnings for the equity shareholders it is not the former gross dividend but the amount of the dividend declared and payable to the preference shareholders, which falls to be deducted from the profit after tax, since, under the imputation system, post-tax profits are available to cover cash dividends.

6 Before calculating earnings per share under the new system, it is necessary to examine carefully the charge for taxation to be deducted in arriving at the earnings figure. The tax charge will always include some elements which are constant, in that they will not vary with the proportion of the profit distributed by way of dividend; the charge may however include other elements which do vary according to the amount of profit distributed and which would be absent if no distributions were made. These components may be classified as follows:

Constant
Corporation tax on income.
Tax attributable to dividends received.
Overseas tax unrelieved because the rate of overseas tax exceeds the rate of UK corporation tax.

Variable
Irrecoverable ACT.
Overseas tax unrelieved because dividend payments restrict the double tax credit available.

7 Two alternative methods of computing earnings per share under the imputation system have been propounded. One would take account of all the elements of the taxation charge listed above, both constant and variable – this is called the 'net basis'. The other would recognise only the constant elements, and because it seeks to arrive at what the earnings would be if the distributions were nil, it is called the 'nil basis'. It can be

**Recoverable and Irrecoverable ACT are defined in SSAP No. 8 Part 2.*

expected that most companies, in normal circumstances, will not incur either of the variable elements of taxation, so that for them calculations on the net basis and the nil basis will produce the same result. The companies where the two methods are most likely to produce divergent figures are those which have income taxed overseas, a significant proportion of which is distributed.

The advantage of the nil basis is that it produces a figure of earnings which is not dependent on the level of distribution, and so provides an indicator of one company's performance more closely comparable with that of another. The argument which is preferred is that the net basis takes account of all the relevant facts, including the additional tax liabilities inherent in the dividend policy pursued by the company, for which the directors should no less be accountable to shareholders. It is considered therefore that quoted companies should report in their accounts earnings per share primarily on net basis. **8**

Where, however, there is material difference between earnings per share calculated on the net basis and on the nil distribution basis, it is most desirable that the latter also be shown although the disclosure requirements in respect of the treatment of taxation in accounts* will enable this earnings per share on a nil basis to be calculated by the user. **9**

Part 2 – Definition of terms

EARNINGS PER SHARE

The profit in pence attributable to each equity share, based on the profit (or in the case of a group the consolidated profit of the period after tax, minority interests and extraordinary items and after deducting preference dividends, and other appropriations in respect of preference shares, divided by the number of equity shares in issue and ranking for dividend in respect of the period. **10**

NET BASIS OF CALCULATING EARNINGS PER SHARE

In determining earnings per share on the net basis, the charge for taxation used in determining earnings includes: **11**

(a) any irrecoverable advance corporation tax (ACT);
(b) any unrelieved overseas tax arising from the payment or proposed payment of dividends.

NIL DISTRIBUTION BASIS OF CALCULATING EARNINGS PER SHARE

In determining earnings per share on the nil basis, the charge for taxation used in determining earnings generally excludes (a) and (b) above (except in so far as these arise in respect of preference dividends). **12**

SSAP No. 8. *'The treatment of taxation under the imputation system in the accounts of companies.'

Part 3 – Standard accounting practice

APPLICABLE TO LISTED COMPANIES

13 This accounting standard shall apply to companies having a listing on a recognised stock exchange for any class of equity, other than companies claiming exemption from the disclosure requirements under Part III of Schedule 2 of the Companies Act 1967*.

14 In the audited accounts of such listed companies, the earnings per share should be shown on the face of the profit and loss account on the net basis both for the period under review and for the corresponding previous period. (The desirability of showing also the earnings per share on the nil distribution basis where materially different from those on the net basis is emphasised in paragraph 9.)

15 The basis of calculating earnings per share should be disclosed, either in the profit and loss account or in a note thereto. In particular, the amount of the earnings and the number of equity shares used in the calculation should be shown.

16 Where a company has at the balance sheet date contracted to issue further shares after the end of the period, or where it has already issued shares which will rank for dividend later, the effect may be to dilute future earnings per share. In addition, therefore, to the basic earnings per share, as set out above, the fully diluted earnings per share should be shown on the face of the profit and loss account of quoted companies in the following circumstances:

(a) where the company has issued a separate class of equity shares which do not rank for any dividend in the period under review, but which will do so in the future;
(b) where the company has issued debentures or loan stock (or preference shares) convertible into equity shares of the company;
(c) where the company has granted options or issued warrants to subscribe for equity shares of the company.

In each case:

(i) the basis of calculation of fully diluted earnings per share should be disclosed;
(ii) the fully diluted earnings per share need not be given unless the dilution is material. Dilution amounting to 5 per cent or more of the basic earnings per share is regarded as material for this purpose;
(iii) fully diluted earnings per share for the corresponding previous period should not be shown unless the assumptions on which it was based still apply;
(iv) equal prominence should be given to basic and fully diluted earnings per share wherever both are disclosed.

***Editor's note:** *Superseded by Schedules 9 and 9A to the Companies Act 1985 (banking and insurance companies and groups).*

DATE FROM WHICH EFFECTIVE

The disclosure of earnings per share became an accounting standard in respect of accounts relating to periods starting on or after 1st January 1972. This standard has been revised to take into account the imputation system of corporation tax which was introduced with effect from 6th April 1973. **17**

APPLICATION IN REPUBLIC OF IRELAND

[*Withdrawn.*]* **18**

[*Withdrawn.*]* **19**

***Editor's note:** *See para 1.4 of the Preface to Appendix 3 to SSAP 8.*

Appendix 1

This appendix is for general guidance and does not form part of the statement of standard accounting practice.

Guidelines for the determination of earnings per share

Primary considerations

PRELIMINARY

1 In simple terms, the earnings per share figure is calculated by apportioning the total amount earned for the equity share capital in a financial period over the number of shares in issue and ranking for dividend in respect of that period.

EARNINGS FOR EQUITY

2 The amount earned for equity should be the profit (or, in the case of a group, the consolidated profit) of the period after tax, minority interests and extraordinary items and after deducting preference dividends and other appropriations in respect of preference shares. It would include the earnings of associated companies – see Statement of Standard Accounting Practice *Accounting for associated companies*, issued April 1982.

PREFERENCE DIVIDENDS

3 Under the imputation system, the preference dividend has ceased to be the gross dividend but is now the cash amount declared and payable to the shareholder. This is the amount to be deducted from the profit after tax in calculating earnings per share.

4 Where the preference shares are cumulative, the dividend for the period should be taken into account, whether or not it has been earned or declared. Subject to this, arrears of preference dividend paid during the year should be ignored. In the case of a non-cumulative dividend the deduction should be the amount of the preferential dividend paid or proposed.

5 The fixed part of the dividend on participating preference shares should be treated in the same way as a preference dividend. If the participating element is limited (e.g., maximum 10 per cent) the whole dividend for the period may be deducted. If it is unlimited, then the appropriate proportion of the earnings for the period to allow for the participating element should be deducted before arriving at the earnings for the ordinary shares.

LOSSES

Where a loss is incurred or the amount earned for equity is a negative figure, the earnings per share should be determined in the normal manner and the result shown as a loss per share. 6

Where the tax charge is reduced by losses brought forward, the tax charge for the year shown in the profit and loss account (rather than a notional tax charge) should be used in the calculation of earnings per share accompanied by an adequate explanation of the effects of the incidence of tax relief on earnings per share for the year under review and for the preceding year. 7

SINKING FUND

Transfers to a loan redemption reserve or to a sinking fund (even though supported by a corresponding transfer of cash) merely divide the profits between those available for immediate distribution and those distributable later; they do not reduce the earnings of the period, and should not be deducted in calculating the earnings of the period. 8

CORRESPONDING AMOUNTS FOR THE PREVIOUS PERIOD

Earnings per share for the corresponding previous period should be shown. 9

EQUITY SHARE CAPITAL

Where there is only one class of equity share capital ranking for dividend, the calculation of earnings per share should be based on the number of such shares in issue during the period. Where there is more than one class of equity shares or where some of the shares are not fully paid, the earnings should be apportioned over the different classes of shares in accordance with their dividend rights or other right to participate in profits. 10

SUBSEQUENT CHANGES IN CAPITAL

Where there has been a change in the capital structure after the accounting date but before the preliminary announcement of the results of the period, the earnings per share shown in the profit and loss account should not take this into account; however, it is desirable that the effect on the basic earnings per share of any capitalisation issue, share split, or bonus element inherent in a rights issue should be disclosed. 11

Summary

Earnings per share should be calculated by apportioning the earnings [(that is the profit (or, in the case of a group, the consolidated profit of the period after taxation, minority interests and extraordinary items and after deducting preference dividends and other 12 appropriations in respect of preference shares – see paragraph 2 above)] over the number of equity shares in issue and ranking for dividend during the period. A simple example is given below.

EXAMPLE 1

Simple capital structure

A *Capital structure*
Issued share capital:
£500,000 in 10 per cent (now 7 per cent + tax credit)* cumulative preference shares of £1 (issued before 6th April, 1973), £1,000,000 in ordinary shares of 25p = 4,000,000 shares

	Year ended 31st December	
B *Trading results*	*Year 2*	*Year 1*
Profit after tax	£535,000	£435,000

Assumptions
No change in the issued share capital during the two years

C *Calculation of earnings per share*	*Year 2*	*Year 1*
Profit after tax	535,000	435,000
Less Preference dividend	35,000	35,000
Earnings	500,000	400,000
Number of ordinary shares	4,000,000	4,000,000

D *Illustration of presentation in the profit and loss account*	Year ended 31st December	
	Year 2	Year 1
Earnings per ordinary share of 25 p	12.5p	10p

Note. The calculation of earnings per share is based on earnings of £500,000 (Year 1 £400,000) and four million ordinary shares in issue throughout the two years ended 31st December, Year 2.

Treatment of changes in equity share capital

13 Where further equity shares have been issued during the financial year, they will probably have been issued by one of the following methods:

***See paragraph 18 of SSAP 8 'Accounting for corporation tax under the imputation system.'**

Each of these circumstances is likely to affect the method of determining the earnings per share and the effect is summarised below.

ISSUE AT FULL MARKET PRICE

Most issues for cash in this country are in the form of rights issues rather than at full market price. If, however, new equity shares have been issued either for cash at full market price or as consideration for the acquisition of an asset the earnings should be apportioned over the average number of shares ranking for dividend during the period weighted on a time basis. **14**

CAPITALISATION ISSUE

Where new equity shares have been issued by way of capitalisation during the period, the earnings should be apportioned over the number of shares ranking for dividend after the capitalisation. The corresponding figures for all earlier periods should be adjusted accordingly. Similar considerations apply where equity shares are split into shares of smaller nominal value. **15**

SHARE EXCHANGE

Where shares (ranking for dividend) or loan stock have been issued during the period as consideration for shares in a new subsidiary, it should be assumed that, for the purpose of calculating the earnings per share, these securities were issued on the first day of the period for which the profits of the new subsidiary are included in the earnings of the group. **16**

RIGHTS ISSUE AT LESS THAN FULL MARKET PRICE

Earnings per share for prior years: Where equity shares are issued by way of rights during the period it is recommended that the factor for adjustment of past earnings per share after a rights issue be based on the closing price* on the last day of quotation of the shares cum rights. The factor is therefore: **17**

$$\frac{\text{Theoretical EX RIGHTS price}}{\text{Actual CUM RIGHTS price on the last day of quotation cum rights}}$$

***i.e., the official middle market quotation published on the following day.*

Where a rights issue is made during the year under review, the earnings per share for the previous year, and for all earlier years, will need to be adjusted by the factor, calculated as above, to correct for the bonus element in the rights issue.

18 *Earnings per share for the year in which a rights issue is made:* For the current year in which a rights issue is made it would be undesirable to split the earnings into two periods, one before the rights issue and one after this event. It is necessary to adjust the weighted average share capital by taking the proportion of the capital in issue before the rights issue, applying to this figure the reciprocal of the factor set out above, i.e.,

$$\frac{\text{actual cum rights price}}{\text{theoretical ex rights price}}$$ and adding the proportion in issue after the rights issue.

Fully diluted earnings per share

INTRODUCTION

19 The earnings per share calculations considered up to this point have been based on either the weighted average share capital ranking for dividend in the period or, in the case of a capitalisation issue, the equity share capital ranking for dividend at the financial year-end.

20 Where a listed company has outstanding:

a separate class of equity shares which do not rank for dividend in the period but will do so in the future (see paragraph 29 below); or

debentures or loan stock (or preference shares) convertible into equity shares of the company (see paragraph 30 below); or

options or warrants to subscribe for equity shares of the company (see paragraph 31 below);

the company has entered into obligations which may dilute the earnings per share in the future. In these circumstances, in addition to the basic earnings per share, the fully diluted earnings per share should be calculated and shown on the face of the profit and loss account in accordance with paragraph 16 of Part 3 and paragraphs 22 to 28 below.

21 In each of these cases, full information as to the rights of the holders (existing shareholders, convertible stockholders, preference shareholders or holders of options or warrants) should be set out in the accounts.

22 Depending on the terms of the conversion rights or the options to subscribe, it is possible that the calculation of an earnings per share figure, based on the assumption that these rights or options had been exercised at the beginning of the period, would result in increasing the earnings per share above the basic figure. In these circumstances, it is likely that the conversion rights or options would not be exercised. The resultant figure (i.e., increased earnings per share rather than diluted earnings per share) should not be shown if it is in excess of the basic earnings per share.

The fully diluted earnings per share need not be given if the dilution is not material, in which event that fact should be stated. Dilution amounting to 5 per cent or more of the basic earnings per share is regarded as material for this purpose. **23**

The fully diluted earnings per share should not be shown when the basic earnings per share is a negative figure (i.e., a loss). **24**

Since the fully diluted earnings per share is concerned with future dilution, a corresponding amount for the previous period may not be meaningful; it should not be shown unless the assumptions on which it was based are still applicable. **25**

Where the dilution is material and the full diluted earnings per share is shown, the basis of calculation should be disclosed. **26**

A listed company may, in any period, have more than one type of convertible debenture or loan stock (or preference shares), in issue with differing conversion rights, or may also have issued shares to rank in a future period or have granted options or warrants to subscribe. In this event, the fully diluted earnings per share should take into account only those 'convertibles' or shares or options or warrants which would have a diluting effect on the earnings per share and should disregard those which have no such diluting effect. **27**

Wherever fully diluted earnings per share is disclosed in addition to the basic earnings per share, they should both be given equal prominence. **28**

ANOTHER CLASS OF EQUITY SHARE RANKING FOR DIVIDEND IN THE FUTURE

Where a listed company has in issue a class of equity shares* not yet ranking for dividend but which will do so in the future (by conversion or otherwise), in addition to the basic earnings per share (calculated on the equity shares ranking for all or any dividends in respect of the period), the fully diluted earnings per share should be calculated on the assumption that this class of shares ranked for dividend from the beginning of the period (or such later date as they were issued). **29**

CONVERTIBLE SECURITIES

Where a company has convertible loan stock in issue at any time during the period, in addition to the basic earnings per share, the fully diluted earnings per share should be calculated on the assumption that the maximum number of new equity shares had been issued on conversion and that this conversion had taken place on the first day of the **30**

******'New' shares of the same class as existing shares, which are separately quoted for a time, only because they are transferable in a different form or because they rank for a later (e.g., final) but not for an earlier (e.g., interim) dividend in respect of the period under review, should not be treated as a separate class of shares.*

period (or on the date of issue of the convertible loan stock if later). The earnings for the period should be adjusted by adding back the assumed saving of interest on the stock so converted, net of corporation tax.

OPTIONS OR WARRANTS TO SUBSCRIBE

31 Where a listed company has granted options or issued warrants to subscribe for equity shares of the company, in addition to the basic earnings per share, the fully diluted earnings per share should be calculated on the assumption that the maximum number of new shares had been issued under the terms of the options or warrants and that these had been exercised on the first day of the period (or the date of issue if later). The earnings for the period should be adjusted on the basis that the proceeds of subscription had been invested in 2½ per cent Consolidated Stock on the first day of the period at the closing price of the previous day.

EXCEPTIONS

32 In the circumstances dealt with in paragraphs 29 to 31 above fully diluted earnings per share should be shown on the face of the profit and loss account subject to the exceptions stated in paragraphs 22 to 25 above.

FINAL CONVERSION OR SUBSCRIPTION DURING THE YEAR

33 Where the convertible loan stock has been finally converted during the year (unless it was converted on the first day of the year and the shares issued have, therefore, ranked for dividend for the full year), it will still be necessary to show the fully diluted earnings per share in the accounts for the year in which that final conversion took place.

34 Similar considerations apply on final subscriptions in the case of options or warrants to subscribe.

Appendix 2

This appendix is for general guidance and does not form part of the statement of standard accounting practice.

Financial statistics in the historical summary

In order to present a fair comparison over the period of the historical summary the basic earnings per share figures will need to be adjusted for subsequent changes in capital on the basis set out in the three following paragraphs. The resultant figures should be described as the adjusted earnings per share and should be set out separately from the other financial data which is not so adjusted, e.g., in a separate box. **1**

ADJUSTMENTS FOR CAPITALISATION ISSUES

Where new equity shares have been issued by way of capitalisation of reserves during any financial year, or where shares have been split into shares of a lower nominal value, the earnings per share for all earlier years will need to be adjusted by the appropriate factor, i.e., the number of equity shares before the capitalisation divided by the number of such shares after the capitalisation. **2**

ADJUSTMENTS FOR RIGHTS ISSUES

Where the equity shares have been issued by way of rights in any financial year, the earnings per share for all earlier years should be adjusted by the factor set out in paragraph 17 of Appendix 1 of this statement. **3**

CUMULATIVE ADJUSTMENT

Where there is more than one capitalisation or rights issue, both these factors will operate cumulatively. **4**

DIVIDENDS PER SHARE

Where there have been capitalisation or rights issues in the period covered by the summary a straight record of the equity dividends actually paid would not, however, be comparable with the adjusted earnings per share. It is therefore suggested that a record of the equity dividends should be set out in the form of pence per share, the dividends being adjusted by the same factors for capitalisation and rights issues (set out in paragraphs 2 to 4 above) as the earnings per share. This record should cover the same period, being described as the adjusted equity dividends, and should be set alongside the adjusted basic earnings per share (e.g., in the box referred to in paragraph 1). **5**

EQUITY DIVIDEND COVER

Dividend cover will normally be found by dividing earnings by dividends under the imputation system of taxation but this simple relationship will not always apply, since **6** the payment of additional dividends may involve the company in the payment of further taxation either in the United Kingdom or overseas. It is the theoretical maximum dividend, after allowing for such additional taxation, which should then be divided by the actual dividend to give the cover.

[SSAP 4]
Accounting for government grants

(Issued April 1974; revised July 1990)

Contents

Accounting for government grants

The provisions of this statement of standard accounting practice should be read in conjunction with the (Explanatory) Foreword to accounting standards *and need not be applied to immaterial items.*

Part 1 – Explanatory note

INTRODUCTION

Government assistance takes many forms, including grants, equity finance, subsidised loans and advisory assistance. This statement deals with the accounting treatment and disclosure of government grants and other forms of government assistance. It is also indicative of best practice for accounting for grants and assistance from other sources. 1

Government grants are made in order to persuade or assist enterprises to pursue courses of action which are deemed to be socially or economically desirable. The range of grants available is very wide and changes regularly, reflecting changes in government policy. More significantly different grants tend to be given on different terms as to the eligibility, manner of determination, manner of payment and conditions to be fulfilled. While this statement has been written in the context of grants available at the time of its preparation, it is intended that it will be equally applicable to other grants that may be created in the future. 2

For the purposes of this statement, the term 'government' is defined widely. Thus, it includes not only the national government and all of the various tiers of local and regional government of any country, but also government agencies and 'non-departmental public bodies' (or quangos). It also includes the Commission of the European Communities and other EC bodies, together with other international bodies and agencies. 3

BASIC CONCEPTS

The 'accruals' concept requires that revenue and costs are accrued, matched with one another so far as their relationship can be established or justifiably assumed, and dealt with in the profit and loss account of the period to which they relate. Government grants should therefore be recognised in the profit and loss account so as to match them with the expenditure towards which they are intended to contribute. 4

The 'prudence' concept requires that revenue and profits are not anticipated, but are recognised by inclusion in the profit and loss account only when realised in the form either of cash or of other assets the ultimate cash realisation of which can be established with reasonable certainty. Accordingly, government grants should not be recognised in 5 the profit and loss account until the conditions for their receipt have been complied with and there is reasonable assurance that the grant will be received.

6 In many cases, the grant-making body has the right to recover all or part of a grant paid if the enterprise has not complied with the conditions under which the grant was made. On the assumption that the enterprise is a going concern, the application of the prudence concept does not normally require postponement of the recognition of the grant in the profit and loss account solely because there is a possibility that it might have to be repaid in the future. The enterprise should consider regularly whether there is a likelihood of a breach of the conditions on which the grant was made. If such a breach has occurred, or appears likely to occur, and it is probable that some grant will have to be repaid, provision should be made for the liability.

7 The treatment for taxation purposes of government grants varies according to the terms of the grant and the particular statute or regulation under which it is made. At one extreme, some grants are free of all tax; at the other, some are taxed as income on receipt. It is sometimes suggested that because grants are taxed as income on receipt they are intended to be regarded as income and should be credited to the profit and loss account as they are received. However, the treatment of an item for tax purposes does not necessarily determine its treatment for accounting purposes, and immediate recognition in the profit and loss account may result in an unacceptable departure from the principle that government grants should be matched with the expenditure towards which they are intended to contribute. Any timing differences that may arise between a tax charge and the recognition of the corresponding credit in the profit and loss account should be dealt with in accordance with SSAP 15 'Accounting for deferred tax'.

ESTABLISHING THE RELATIONSHIP BETWEEN GRANTS RECEIVED AND EXPENDITURE

8 The matching of grants received and expenditure is straightforward if the grant is made as a contribution towards specified items of expenditure (whether capital, revenue or a particular combination) and is described as such.

9 Difficulties arise where the terms of the grant do not specify precisely the expenditure it is intended to meet, but use such phrases as 'to assist with a project' or 'to encourage job creation', or where the basis of calculation is related to two or more criteria (for example the capital expenditure incurred and the number of jobs created). In these circumstances, it is usually appropriate to consider the circumstances which give rise to the payment of instalments of the grant. If the grant is paid when evidence is produced that certain expenditure has been incurred, the grant should be matched with that expenditure. If the grant is paid on a different basis, it will usually be paid on the achievement of a non-financial objective, such as the creation of a specified number of new jobs; in these circumstances, the grant should be matched with the identifiable costs of achieving that objective, for example the cost of creating and, if applicable, maintaining for the required period the specified new jobs.

10 In some cases, there may be persuasive evidence that the actual expenditure towards

which the grant is intended to contribute differs from the expenditure that forms the basis of payment. Such evidence may be contained in the formal application for the grant and subsequent correspondence and negotiation with the grant-making body. Where such evidence exists and is sufficiently persuasive, it is appropriate to match the grant received with the identified expenditure and this approach should be preferred to that outlined in the previous paragraph. For example, a discretionary grant might be given 'to assist with a project', with instalments of the grant being payable on the production of evidence that specific capital expenditure had been incurred; but it might be clear from correspondence that the grant had been made as a contribution to other costs as well, such as the provision of working capital or the meeting of initial training costs.

Where a grant is paid on the achievement of a non-financial objective, the costs of **11** achieving that objective must be identified or estimated on a reasonable basis. For example, if a grant is given on condition that jobs are created and maintained for a minimum period, the grant should be matched with the cost of providing jobs for that period, taking due account of the incidence of the costs incurred. As the costs of job creation will often be higher in the early stages of a project, because of start-up costs and the fact that a significant element of wage costs will initially be non-productive, the matching principle may require that an equivalent, higher proportion of the grant should be recognised in the earlier periods.

RECOGNITION OF GRANTS IN THE PROFIT AND LOSS ACCOUNT

Once the relationship between the grant and the related expenditure has been estab- **12** lished, the recognition of the grant in the profit and loss account will follow. The grant should be recognised in the same period as the related expenditure.

In certain circumstances, government grants may be given for the immediate financial **13** support or assistance of an enterprise or for the reimbursement of costs previously incurred, without conditions regarding the enterprise's future actions or a requirement to incur further costs. Government grants may also be given to finance the general activities of an enterprise over a specified period or to compensate for a loss of income; in some instances, the extent of these grants may be such as to constitute a major source of income for the enterprise. Grants that are payable on this basis should be recognised in the profit and loss account of the period in respect of which they are paid or, if they are not stated to be paid in respect of a specified period, in the profit and loss account of the period in which they become receivable.

Where an enterprise is required to repay a government grant, either in whole or **14** in part, the full amount to be repaid, after taking into account any unamortised deferred income relating to the grant, should be charged to the profit and loss account immediately it becomes repayable. Where appropriate, the repayment should be dealt with in accordance with FRS 3 'Reporting Financial Performance' as an exceptional item.

BALANCE SHEET TREATMENT OF GRANTS

15 The application of this statement may result in part or all of a grant that has been received not being recognised immediately in the profit and loss account. Any unrecognised amounts should normally be included in the balance sheet as deferred income. Where a grant is made as a contribution towards expenditure on fixed assets, there are two possible balance sheet treatments, both of which result in the grant being matched with the related expenditure in the profit and loss account. These are:

(a) to treat the amount of the grant as deferred income which is credited to the profit and loss account by instalments over the expected useful economic life of the related asset on a basis consistent with the depreciation policy; or

(b) to deduct the amount of the grant from the purchase price or production cost of the related asset, with a consequent reduction in the annual charge for depreciation.

It is considered that both treatments are acceptable and are capable of giving a true and fair view. However, the CCAB has received Counsel's opinion that paragraphs 17 and 26 of Schedule 4 to the Companies Act 1985 have the effect of prohibiting enterprises to which the legislation applies from accounting for grants made as a contribution towards expenditure on fixed assets by deducting the amount of the grant from the purchase price or production cost of the related asset.

16 Where a government grant takes the form of a transfer of non-monetary assets, the amount of the grant is the fair value of the assets transferred.

DISCLOSURE

17 The financial statements should disclose the accounting policy adopted in respect of government grants in terms which make clear the method or methods adopted. The period or periods over which grants are credited to the profit and loss account should be disclosed insofar as this is practicable given the number and variety of grants that are being received. Normally, it will be sufficient to give a broad indication of the future periods in which grants already received will be recognised in the profit and loss account.

18 Where the results for the period have been affected materially by amounts credited in respect of government grants, and/or where the results of future periods are expected to be affected materially by the recognition in the profit and loss account of grants already received, it is important for an understanding of the financial statements that the effects on the results or the financial position of the enterprise should be disclosed.

19 Government assistance to an enterprise may also be given in a form other than grants, for example consultancy and advisory services, subsidised loans and credit guarantees. Where such assistance has had a material effect on the results for the period, the nature and, where measurable, the effects of the assistance should be disclosed.

20 Under SSAP 18 'Accounting for contingencies' potential liabilities to repay grants should only be provided for to the extent that repayment is probable. A material contingent loss not so provided for should be disclosed, except where the possibility of repayment is remote.

Part 2 – Definition of terms

Government includes government and inter-governmental agencies and similar bodies whether local, national or international. 21

Government grants are assistance by government in the form of cash or transfers of assets to an enterprise in return for past or future compliance with certain conditions relating to the operating activities of the enterprise. 22

Part 3 – Standard accounting practice

Subject to paragraph 24 of this statement, government grants should be recognised in the profit and loss account so as to match them with the expenditure towards which they are intended to contribute. In the absence of persuasive evidence to the contrary, government grants should be assumed to contribute towards the expenditure that is the basis for their payment. To the extent that grants are made as a contribution towards specific expenditure on fixed assets, they should be recognised over the expected useful economic lives of the related assets. Grants made to give immediate financial support or assistance to an enterprise or to reimburse costs previously incurred should be recognised in the profit and loss account of the period in which they become receivable. Grants made to finance the general activities of an enterprise over a specific period or to compensate for a loss of current or future income should be recognised in the profit and loss account of the period in respect of which they are paid. 23

The foregoing requirements are subject to the proviso that a government grant should not be recognised in the profit and loss account until the conditions for its receipt have been complied with and there is reasonable assurance that the grant will be received. 24

Where the recognition in the profit and loss account of part or all of a grant that has been received is deferred, the amount so deferred should be treated as deferred income. To the extent that the grant is made as a contribution towards expenditure on a fixed asset, in principle it may be deducted from the purchase price or production cost of that asset. The CCAB has received Counsel's opinion, however, that the option to deduct government grants from the purchase price or production cost of fixed assets is not available to companies governed by the accounting and reporting requirements of the Companies Act 1985, as outlined in paragraph 34. 25

Grants relating to leased assets in the accounts of lessors should be accounted for in accordance with the requirements of SSAP 21 'Accounting for leases and hire purchase contracts'. 26

Potential liabilities to repay grants either in whole or in part in specified circumstances 27 should only be provided for to the extent that repayment is probable. The repayment of a government grant should be accounted for by setting off the repayment against any unamortised deferred income relating to the grant. Any excess should be charged immediately to the profit and loss account.

DISCLOSURE

28 The following information should be disclosed in the financial statements:

(a) the accounting policy adopted for government grants;
(b) the effects of government grants on the results for the period and/or the financial position of the enterprise;
(c) where the results of the period are affected materially by the receipt of forms of government assistance other than grants, the nature of that assistance and, to the extent that the effects on the financial statements can be measured, an estimate of those effects.

29 Potential liabilities to repay grants in specified circumstances should, if necessary, be disclosed in accordance with paragraph 16 of SSAP 18 'Accounting for contingencies'.

TRANSITIONAL PROVISIONS

30 Any adjustments arising as a result of a change in accounting policy to comply with the requirements of this statement should be accounted for as a prior year adjustment in accordance with FRS 3 'Reporting Financial Performance'.

DATE FROM WHICH EFFECTIVE

31 The accounting practices set out in this statement should be adopted as soon as possible. They should be regarded as standard accounting practice in respect of financial statements relating to accounting periods beginning on or after 1 July 1990.

Part 4 – Legal requirements in Great Britain and Northern Ireland

References are to the Companies Act 1985 and the Companies (Northern Ireland) Order 1986.

32 The balance sheet formats in Schedule 4 require that accruals and deferred income should be shown either under the heading 'Creditors' or separately as 'Accruals and deferred income'. This is relevant to the disclosure of deferred income in relation to government grants. (Standard paragraph 25).

33 Paragraph 12 of Schedule 4 requires that the amount of any item shall be determined on a prudent basis and, in particular, that only profits realised at the balance sheet date shall be included in the profit and loss account. (Paragraph 91 of the Schedule defines

realised profits in relation to a company's accounts as 'such profits of the company as fall to be treated as realised profits for the purposes of those accounts in accordance with principles generally accepted with respect to the determination for accounting purposes of realised profits at the time when those accounts are prepared'.) (Standard paragraph 24)

Paragraph 17 of Schedule 4 requires that, subject to any provision for depreciation or diminution in value, the amount to be included in the balance sheet in respect of any fixed asset shall be its purchase price or production cost. Paragraph 26(1) states that the purchase price of an asset shall be determined by adding to the actual price paid any expenses incidental to its acquisition. The CCAB has received Counsel's opinion that these paragraphs have the effect of prohibiting enterprises to which the legislation applies from accounting for grants made as a contribution towards expenditure on fixed assets by deducting the amount of the grant from the purchase price or production cost of the related asset. (Standard paragraph 25) **34**

Paragraph 50 (2) of Schedule 4 provides that 'The following information shall be given with respect to any other contingent liability not provided for: **35**

(a) the amount or estimated amount of that liability;
(b) its legal nature; and
(c) whether any valuable security has been provided by the company in connection with that liability and if so, what'. (Standard paragraph 29)

Part 5 – Legal requirements in the Republic of Ireland

References are to the Companies (Amendment) Act 1986 and the Schedule to that Act unless otherwise stated.

Note 8 to the balance sheet formats in the Schedule provides that government grants included in the item 'Accruals and deferred income' must be shown separately in a note to the accounts if not shown separately in the balance sheet. However, Note 8 does not impose an obligation to include government grants under 'Accruals and deferred income' and such grants may, therefore, be placed under a separate heading. This separate heading is often placed between liabilities and share capital/reserves. If a new heading is adopted (using Section 4(12)), the requirement under Note 8 to have a separate mention of the amount is not applicable. (Standard paragraph 25) **36**

Section 5(c) of the Act requires that the amount of any item shall be determined on a prudent basis and, in particular, that only profits realised at the balance sheet date shall be included in the profit and loss account. (Paragraph 72 of the Schedule defines realised profits in relation to a company's accounts as 'such profits of the company as fall to be treated as realised profits for the purposes of those accounts in accordance with principles generally accepted with respect to the determination for accounting purposes of realised profits at the time when those accounts are prepared'.) (Standard paragraph 24) **37**

Paragraph 5 of the Schedule requires that, subject to any provision for depreciation or **38** diminution in value, the amount to be included in respect of any fixed asset shall be its purchase price or production cost. Paragraph 14(1) states that the purchase price of an asset shall be determined by adding to the actual price paid any expenses incidental to its acquisition. The CCAB has received legal opinion that the equivalent paragraphs in UK legislation have the effect of prohibiting enterprises to which the legislation applies from accounting for grants made as a contribution towards expenditure on fixed assets by deducting the amount of the grant from the purchase price or production cost of the related asset. (Standard paragraph 25)

39 Paragraph 36(2) of the Schedule provides that 'The following information shall be given with respect to any other contingent liability not provided for:

(a) the amount or estimated amount of that liability;
(b) its legal nature; and
(c) whether any valuable security has been provided by the company in connection with that liability and if so, what'. (Standard paragraph 29)

40 The Companies (Amendment) Act 1983, Section 40 requires the convening of an extraordinary general meeting not later than 28 days from the earliest day on which it is known to a director of the company that its net assets have fallen to half or less of the company's called-up share capital (that a 'financial situation' exists). The 1983 Act also extends the reporting duties of auditors by requiring auditors to state whether in their opinion there existed at the balance sheet date a 'financial situation' in the context of Section 40 which would require the convening of an extraordinary general meeting. For the purpose of calculating the net assets of the company, the term 'liability' should be taken to include not only creditors, but also provisions for liabilities and charges, accruals and deferred income. Government grants treated as deferred income should, therefore, be regarded as a liability for the purposes of calculating net assets under Section 40.

Part 6 – Compliance with International Accounting Standard No.20 'Accounting for Government Grants and Disclosure of Government Assistance'

41 The requirements of International Accounting Standard No.20 'Accounting for Government Grants and Disclosure of Government Assistance' accord very closely with the content of the United Kingdom and Irish Accounting Standard No.4 (Revised) 'Accounting for government grants' and accordingly compliance with SSAP 4 (Revised) will ensure compliance with IAS 20 in all material respects.

[SSAP 5]
Accounting for value added tax

(Issued April 1974)

This statement seeks, by presenting a standard accounting practice, to achieve uniformity of accounting treatment of VAT in financial statements.

Part 1 – Explanatory note

GENERAL

VAT is a tax on the supply of goods and services which is eventually borne by the final consumer but collected at each stage of the production and distribution chain. As a general principle, therefore, the treatment of VAT in the accounts of a trader should reflect his role as a collector of the tax and VAT should not be included in income or in expenditure whether of a capital or of a revenue nature. There will however be circumstances, as noted below, in which a trader will himself bear VAT and in such circumstances the accounting treatment should reflect that fact. 1

PERSONS NOT ACCOUNTABLE FOR VAT

Persons not accountable for VAT will suffer VAT on inputs. For them VAT will increase the cost of all goods and services to which it applies and should be included in such costs. In particular, the VAT on fixed assets should be added to the cost of the fixed assets concerned. 2

ACCOUNTABLE PERSONS WHO ALSO CARRY ON EXEMPTED ACTIVITIES

In the case of persons who also carry on exempted activities there will be a residue of VAT, which will fall directly on the trader and which will normally be arrived at by division of his activities as between taxable outputs (including zero-rated) and those which are exempt. In such cases, the principle that such VAT will increase the costs to which it applies and should be included in such costs will be equally applicable. Hence the appropriate portion of the VAT allocable to fixed assets should, if irrecoverable, be added to the cost of the fixed assets concerned and the proportion allocable to other items should, if practicable and material, be included in such other items. In some cases, for example where financial and VAT accounting periods do not coincide, an estimate may be necessary. 3

NON-DEDUCTIBLE INPUTS

All traders will bear tax in so far as it relates to non-deductible inputs (for example, motor-cars, other than for resale, and certain business entertaining expenses). Such tax 4 should therefore be included as part of the cost of those items. A similar situation exists in the Republic of Ireland where traders dealing in products such as motor-cars, radios and television sets will bear some non-deductible VAT on the input cost of these items.

AMOUNTS DUE TO OR FROM THE REVENUE AUTHORITIES

5 The net amount due to or from the revenue authorities in respect of VAT should be included as part of debtors or creditors and will not normally require separate disclosure.

CAPITAL COMMITMENTS

6 The estimated amount of capital commitments should include the appropriate amount, if any, of irrecoverable VAT.

COMPARISONS

7 Where it has been customary for purchase tax (or sales taxes in the Republic of Ireland) to be included in turnover, it may be desirable in the initial years of VAT to disclose the turnover of periods in which such tax applied both gross and net of tax so as to assist in comparisons. In some cases, for example retailers, it may not be possible to ascertain the amount of purchase tax (or sales taxes) included in turnover; in those cases an explanatory note will be desirable. Where customs or excise duties are included in turnover and such duties are reduced to take account of VAT, an explanatory note may be necessary.

Part 2 – Standard accounting practice

TURNOVER

8 Turnover shown in the profit and loss account should exclude VAT on taxable outputs*. If it is desired to show also the gross turnover, the VAT relevant to that turnover should be shown as a deduction in arriving at the turnover exclusive of VAT.

IRRECOVERABLE VAT

9 Irrecoverable VAT allocable to fixed assets and to other items disclosed separately in published accounts should be included in their cost where practicable and material.

DATE FROM WHICH EFFECTIVE

10 The accounting practices set out in this statement should be adopted as soon as possible and regarded as standard in respect of accounting periods starting on or after 1st January 1974.

Editor's note: *Section 262(1) of the Companies Act 1985 defines 'turnover' in relation to a company.*

[SSAP 8]

The treatment of taxation under the imputation system in the accounts of companies*

(Issued August 1974; Appendix 3 added December 1977)

Contents

***Editor's note:** *TR 805 (issued 1990 and reproduced in Part 9 of this volume) draws attention in paras 2.5 to 2.9 to certain taxation references which are incorrect, arising from changes in tax legislation since SSAP 8 was issued.*

The treatment of taxation under the imputation system in the accounts of companies

The imputation system of company taxation started in the United Kingdom in April 1973 and in the Republic of Ireland in 1976. The purpose of this statement is to establish a standard treatment of taxation in company accounts, with particular reference to advance corporation tax and 'mainstream' corporation tax. This Statement has been prepared for use when the imputation system of corporation tax is fully implemented. It does not deal in detail with the problems arising in the transitional periods, which should be resolved in the light of the principles herein.

In order to obviate the need to amend the statement whenever there are changes in the rates of taxation the following have been assumed:

(a) corporation tax – 50 per cent;
(b) advance corporation tax – three-sevenths of the amount of qualifying distributions.

The small companies rate should be substituted where warranted by the circumstances.

The application of this statement to companies subject to taxation in the Republic of Ireland is dealt with in Appendix 3. (*December 1977*)

Part 1 – Explanatory note

INTRODUCTION

The principal features of the imputation system of corporation tax are broadly as follows. Corporation tax is charged at a single rate on a company's income whether distributed or undistributed; in the absence of a dividend the whole of the tax is payable on a date which may be a year or more* after the end of the relevant accounting period. When in an accounting period a company makes a distribution to shareholders, it does not withhold income tax from the payment, but is required to make an advance payment of corporation tax (ACT). This ACT will normally be set off against the company's total liability for corporation tax on its income (but not on its chargeable gains) of the same accounting period. The resultant net liability is known as the mainstream corporation tax. The charge for corporation tax therefore comprises the mainstream corporation tax and the ACT. From the paying company's point of view the concept of 'gross' dividends and the deduction of income tax at source therefrom has disappeared. However, an individual shareholder receiving the dividend is chargeable to tax on an amount of income equivalent to the dividend plus the imputed tax credit. This tax credit (generally equivalent to the ACT paid by the company) will 1

***Editor's note:** *Now nine months.*

discharge the basic rate liability to income tax of a United Kingdom resident or would in certain circumstances be recoverable. For corporate shareholders the concept of franked investment income continues.

2 The ACT set off against the final corporation tax bill is effectively restricted to 30 per cent (assuming a 50 per cent tax rate) of the company's taxable income. Any ACT thereby unrelieved (i.e., ACT on a distribution which together with the related ACT is in excess of taxable income) can be carried back for two years or forward without time limit (but cannot be set against corporation tax on income arising before 1st April 1973)*.

3 The main accounting problems arising from the imputation system are:

(a) the treatment in the profit and loss account of outgoing dividends and the related ACT;
(b) determining the recoverability of ACT;
(c) the treatment of irrecoverable ACT and of unrelieved overseas tax arising from the payment or proposed payment of dividends;
(d) the treatment in the balance sheet of taxation liabilities, recoverable ACT and dividends;
(e) the treatment of franked investment income.

DIVIDENDS AND THE RELATED ACT

4 The treatment in the profit and loss account of outgoing dividends and the related ACT, is concerned with whether ACT should be treated as part of the cost of the dividend or whether it should be treated as part of tax on the company's profits. The right of a company to deduct income tax from dividends no longer applies. Whatever percentage or per-share dividend is declared, that is the amount which the company will pay to its members. The fact that the dividend will carry a tax credit is a matter affecting the recipient rather than the company's method of accounting for the dividend. Accordingly it is considered appropriate that dividends should be shown in the profit and loss account at the amount paid or payable to the shareholders and that neither the related ACT nor the imputed tax credit should be treated as part of the cost of the dividend. It follows that the charge for taxation in the profit and loss account should embrace the full amount of corporation tax, and not merely the mainstream liability.

RECOVERABILITY OF ACT

5 ACT is primarily recovered by being set off against the corporation tax on the income of the year in which the related distribution is made. In the case of dividends paid during the year under review, the taxable income of that year and of the two previous years will normally be available to absorb the relief. Where a proposed dividend is to be paid in the following year, then the related ACT falls to be set off against the corporation tax on the taxable income of the year of payment of the proposed dividend

***Editor's note:** *See paragraph 2.6 of TR 805 reproduced in Part 9.*

and in default of that, against the taxable income of the year under review or of the year previous to that. In both cases ACT can be carried forward indefinitely if necessary. In each year there is an overriding restriction on the use of ACT for set off, by reference to the taxable income of that year*.

For accounting purposes it is necessary to decide whether recovery of the ACT is reasonably certain and foreseeable or whether it should be written off in the profit and loss account. If the taxable income of the year under review and the amounts available from the preceding year or years are insufficient to cover the ACT, then recoverability of ACT will depend on the extent to which income is earned in future periods in excess of dividends paid or on the existence of a deferred taxation account of adequate size (see paragraph 7). Although the relief remains available indefinitely it will be prudent to have regard only to the immediate and foreseeable future; how long this future period should be will depend upon the circumstances of each case, but it is suggested that where there is no deferred taxation account it should normally not extend beyond the next accounting period. 6

Where a deferred taxation account is maintained, the attitude to recoverability may be different. The balance on the deferred taxation account usually represents an amount which will be released to profit and loss account over the life of related fixed assets. Unrelieved ACT is available to offset against future taxable profits for an indefinite period. There is thus a similarity between unrelieved ACT and the balance on the deferred taxation account and it is therefore reasonable to regard unrelieved ACT as being available for deduction from the amount at which the deferred taxation account is stated in the accounts. Only a proportion of the balance on the account (at the rates assumed 30 per cent of the amount on which the credit balance of the account has been calculated) can be used for this purpose: this is the extent to which ACT can be set off against the corporation tax liability. It should be noted, however, that to the extent to which the deferred taxation account represents deferred chargeable gains, it is not available for this purpose. 7

IRRECOVERABLE ACT

Any irrecoverable ACT (i.e., ACT the recoverability of which is not reasonably certain and foreseeable) should be written off in the profit and loss account in which the related dividend is shown. 8

There are two differing views on the presentation in the profit and loss account of irrecoverable ACT written off. One view is that irrecoverable ACT should be treated as part of the tax charge upon the company to be deducted in arriving at profits after tax; the other that the irrecoverable ACT, being a cost stemming from the payment of a dividend, should be treated as an appropriation like the dividend itself. Of the two methods the first is supported as the appropriate accounting treatment because unrelieved ACT constitutes tax upon the company or group, as opposed to tax on the shareholders, and is not an appropriation of profits. It is appreciated however that some readers or analysts of accounts may wish for their purposes to regard 9

***Editor's note:** *See paragraph 2.7 of TR 805 reproduced in Part 9.*

irrecoverable ACT in some other manner. The amount of irrecoverable ACT should therefore be separately disclosed if material.

10 Irrecoverable ACT should be treated as part of the tax on ordinary activities.

UNRELIEVED OVERSEAS TAX

11 Although for tax purposes unrelieved overseas tax cannot be carried forward, the accounting treatment of unrelieved overseas tax arising from the payment of a dividend is similar to that of irrecoverable ACT. This matter is dealt with more fully in Appendix 2.

FRANKED INVESTMENT INCOME

12 The concept of franked investment income established under earlier tax systems is continued under the imputation system. Franked investment income comprises the amount of a qualifying distribution received from another UK resident company with the addition of the related tax credit. The net amount can be redistributed to shareholders of the recipient company without payment of ACT and the related tax credit remains attached from the viewpoint of the shareholder.

13 There are several possible methods of dealing with franked investment income in accounts. The two main possibilities are:

(a) to bring into the profit and loss account the cash amount received or receivable (i.e., excluding the tax credit); or

(b) to bring in the amount of the franked investment income (i.e., including the tax credit, an equivalent amount then being treated as part of the charge for taxation).

The first method would involve treating the income either as an item of profit before taxation, or as an addition to the profit after taxation – both alternatives are open to objection. The second method would allow recognition of the income both at the pre-tax and at the after-tax stage in a way which is consistent with other elements of profit, and is therefore adopted as the standard accounting practice.

MAINSTREAM CORPORATION TAX

14 Apart from ACT the dates of payments of corporation tax under the new system remain as before. Depending on the date to which a company makes up its accounts, the balance sheet should contain either (a) one liability for mainstream corporation tax, being that on the profit of the year, or (b) two liabilities. In the latter case they will be the mainstream corporation tax on the profits of the previous year payable within nine months of the balance sheet date, and mainstream corporation tax for the year under review payable twelve months later than the above liability. These liabilities should be separately disclosed, under current liabilities or otherwise as appropriate. If they are not shown under current liabilities, the due date of payment should be stated.

ACT

ACT on dividends paid will either have been paid by the balance sheet date or will be due for payment shortly afterwards. Where the ACT is regarded as recoverable then it will normally be deducted from the full corporation tax charge based on the profit of the period in arriving at the mainstream corporation tax liability shown in the balance sheet. **15**

In the case of dividends proposed but not paid at the balance sheet date, the related ACT will become due for payment within about three months of the dividend itself, and should be shown as a current liability. The right of set off, however (assuming the ACT is regarded as recoverable), will not arise for at least twenty-one months from the balance sheet date. This right is, therefore, in the nature of a deferred asset, and should be shown as such on the balance sheet, unless there is a deferred tax account from the balance of which the amount may be deducted. **16**

If ACT on dividends paid or proposed is treated as irrecoverable (see paragraphs 8 to 10) there is no corresponding asset to be dealt with in the balance sheet. **17**

PREFERENCE SHARES

Any dividend right established before 6th April 1973 at a gross rate or a gross amount was reduced by the Finance Act 1972, Schedule 23, paragraph 18* to seven-tenths of its former rate or amount. Steps should therefore be taken to distinguish, for example a 10 per cent preference share issued before 6th April 1973, on which the dividend is now 7 per cent, from such a preference share issued after that date. A change in the basic rate of income tax and a corresponding change in the rate of ACT would not affect this once-for-all 'netting down'. Thus a former 10 per cent preference share may in the future yield, with related tax credit, either more or less than 10 per cent on nominal value. The new rate of dividend on preference shares† should therefore be incorporated in the description of the shares in the balance sheet, e.g.: **18**

	Authorised	Issued
100,000 10 per cent (now 7 per cent + tax credit) preference shares of £1	£100,000	£100,000

APPENDICES

Certain accounting considerations arising from the imputation system of corporation tax are considered to be supplementary to the main purpose of this statement. These considerations have been dealt with as follows: **19**

**Subsequent changes in the rate of ACT have varied the rate of tax credit but not the amount of the cash divided payable to shareholders.*

†Including participating preference and preferred ordinary shares where the former rate of dividend forms part of the title.

Appendix 1 Examples of the taxation items to be disclosed.

Appendix 2 Further practical points:
(a) unrelieved overseas tax;
(b) earnings and dividends in the historical summary.

Part 2 – Definition of terms

RECOVERABLE ACT

20 The amount of the ACT paid or payable on outgoing dividends paid and proposed which can be:
(a) set off against a corporation tax liability on the profits of the period under review or of previous periods; or
(b) properly set off against a credit balance on deferred tax account; or
(c) expected to be recoverable taking into account expected profits and dividends – normally those of the next accounting period only.

IRRECOVERABLE ACT

21 ACT paid or payable on outgoing dividends paid and proposed other than recoverable ACT.

Part 3 – Standard accounting practice

PROFIT AND LOSS ACCOUNT

22 The following items should be included in the taxation charge in the profit and loss account and, where material, should be separately disclosed:
(a) the amount of the United Kingdom corporation tax specifying:
(i) the charge for corporation tax on the income of the year (where such corporation tax includes transfers between the deferred taxation account and the profit and loss account these should be separately disclosed where material);
(ii) tax attributable to franked investment income;
(iii) irrecoverable ACT;
(iv) the relief for overseas taxation;
(b) the total overseas taxation, relieved and unrelieved, specifying that part of the unrelieved overseas taxation which arises from the payment or proposed payment of dividends.

23 If the rate of corporation tax is not known for the whole or part of the period covered by the accounts, the latest known rate should be used and disclosed.

Outgoing dividends should not include either the related ACT or the attributable tax credit. **24**

Incoming dividends from United Kingdom resident companies should be included at the amount of cash received or receivable plus the tax credit. **25**

BALANCE SHEET

Dividends proposed (or declared and not yet payable) should be included in current liabilities, without the addition of the related ACT. The ACT on proposed dividends (whether recoverable or irrecoverable) should be included as a current tax liability. **26**

If the ACT on proposed dividends is regarded as recoverable, it should be deducted from the deferred tax account if such an account is available for this purpose. In the absence of a deferred taxation account ACT recoverable should be shown as a deferred asset. **27**

Where the title of a class of preference shares (or participating or preferred ordinary shares) issued before 6th April 1973, includes a fixed rate of dividend, the new rate of dividend should be incorporated in the description of the shares in the balance sheet. **28**

DATE FROM WHICH EFFECTIVE FOR COMPANIES SUBJECT TO TAXATION IN THE UNITED KINGDOM

The accounting practices set out in this statement should be adopted as soon as possible and regarded as standard in respect of financial statements relating to accounting periods beginning on or after 1st January 1975. **29**

DATE FROM WHICH EFFECTIVE FOR COMPANIES SUBJECT TO TAXATION IN THE REPUBLIC OF IRELAND

The accounting practices set out in Appendix 3 relating to companies subject to taxation in the Republic of Ireland should be regarded as standard in respect of financial statements relating to accounting periods beginning on or after 1st January 1978. **30**

Appendix 1

This appendix is for general guidance and does not form part of the statement of standard accounting practice.

This example indicates one method of showing (by way of note) the taxation items required to be disclosed under the Companies Act 1967* and Part 3 of this standard. In simple cases taxation may be dealt with entirely within the profit and loss account.

	£'000
Corporation tax on income at × per cent (including £b transferred to/from deferred taxation account)	a
Less relief for overseas taxation	c
	d
Overseas taxation†	e
Tax credit on UK dividends received	f
Irrecoverable advance corporation tax	g
	H

***Editor's note:** Now Companies Act 1985.*

† Including £J arising from the payment of dividends (see paragraphs 1 and 2 of Appendix 2)

Appendix 2

This appendix is for general guidance and does not form part of the statement of standard accounting practice.

Further practical points

UNRELIEVED OVERSEAS TAX*

1 If the rate of overseas tax on the overseas income of a UK company exceeds the rate of UK mainstream corporation tax thereon, then part of the overseas tax will be unrelieved. If the company pays all or part of a dividend out of its overseas income (i.e., if it pays a dividend which, together with the related ACT is substantially in excess of its, or its group's, taxable UK income) then the ACT on the dividend paid out of overseas income will not be available for the purpose of calculating overseas tax credit. Thus, the payment of a dividend in these circumstances may give rise to unrelieved tax (depending on the rate of overseas tax) but this unrelieved tax, unlike the irrecoverable ACT, is not available for carry forward.

2 Following the same reasoning as applied to the accounting treatment of irrecoverable ACT, unrelieved overseas tax which arises from an outgoing dividend should be treated as part of the tax charge to be deducted in arriving at profits after tax. The amount should be separately disclosed, if material.

EARNINGS AND DIVIDENDS IN THE HISTORICAL SUMMARY

3 The change to the imputation system destroyed the comparability, as between one period and another, of many of the figures in the historical records. For example, earnings were formerly available to cover gross dividends before deduction of income tax, but under the imputation system they are now available to cover the actual cash dividends payable to the preference or equity shareholders. Hence, in calculating earnings for equity under the imputation system, preference dividends should be deducted at the amount declared and payable to the shareholders – not at the former gross amount.

4 In general, it is likely to be either impracticable or unsatisfactory to attempt to adjust profits earned under one system of taxation to another tax system. Furthermore, if a company had been taxed differently, it might have taken different financial decisions. Most of the items in the historical summary should therefore be left as originally published.

***Editor's note:** *See paragraph 2.9 of TR 805 reproduced in Part 9.*

5 Figures such as earnings and dividends based on the old system of taxation should, however, be carefully distinguished from those based on the new system. It may be helpful to describe dividends paid under the old system of taxation as 'gross dividends' to distinguish them from dividends paid under the new system.

6 The transitional period, which may cover more than one accounting year, presents particular problems. It would usually be preferable (where practicable) to show an overlap with the figures calculated both ways for the straddling period, or alternatively to indicate in some other manner the points where comparability has been destroyed by a change in the system of taxation (i.e., 1965 and 1973). Figures relating to earlier periods can then be shown entirely on the old basis with subsequent figures being entirely on the new basis.

7 To calculate the gross dividends for the straddling year (for the purposes of historical summaries only) any dividends relating to that year paid on or after 6th April 1973 may be increased by the amount of the appropriate tax credits and added to any dividends paid before 6th April 1973. To calculate the equivalent 'new' dividends from gross dividends, the gross dividends may be reduced by 30 per cent.

Appendix 3

(This appendix was added in December 1977 and revised in 1988)

Appendix 3 contains the statement of standard accounting practice for application to companies subject to taxation in the *Republic of Ireland.*

Preface

1.1 This revision of the appendix is issued following the introduction of advance corporation tax (ACT) in the Republic of Ireland.

1.2 This statement is based on taxation legislation in force up to and including the Finance Act 1987.

1.3 In order to obviate the need to amend this statement whenever there are changes in the rates of taxation the following have been assumed:

(a) corporation tax – 50%
(b) advance corporation tax – 35/65ths of the amount of qualifying distributions.

1.4 The computation of earnings per share on a net basis is now relevant in the Republic of Ireland. For this purpose the principle enunciated in SSAP 3 should be applied (except paragraphs 18 and 19 which no longer have effect).

Part 1 – Explanatory note

INTRODUCTION

The principal features of the imputation system of corporation tax are broadly as follows. Corporation tax is charged at a single rate on a company's profits whether distributed or undistributed; the whole of the tax is generally payable six months after the end of the relevant accounting period. Where a company makes a distribution it is required to make an advance payment of corporation tax. This ACT paid and not repaid will normally be set off against the company's liability for corporation tax on its income (but not on its chargeable gains) of the accounting period in which the distribution is made. An individual shareholder receiving a dividend is chargeable to income tax on an amount of income equivalent to the dividend plus the imputed tax credit. This tax credit will discharge the equivalent amount of income tax of a Republic of Ireland resident or is, in certain circumstances, recoverable. For corporate shareholders, the concept of franked investment income continues. 1

Any unrelieved ACT (known in the legislation as surplus ACT) can be carried back against any corporation tax payable in respect of accounting periods ending within the 12 months prior to the period in which the ACT liability arises or forward without 2 time-limit for set off against the company's corporation tax liability on income. A carry-back claim must be made within two years of the end of the accounting period in which the distribution is made.

3 The main accounting problems arising from the imputation system are:

(a) the treatment in the profit and loss account of outgoing dividends and related ACT;
(b) determining the recoverability of ACT;
(c) the treatment of irrecoverable ACT arising from the payment or proposed payment of dividends;
(d) the treatment of any unrelieved overseas tax;
(e) the treatment of franked investment income;
(f) the balance sheet treatment of taxation liabilities, recoverable ACT and dividends;
(g) the title of preference shares.

Each of these matters is dealt with below.

DIVIDENDS AND THE RELATED ACT

4 The treatment in the profit and loss account of outgoing dividends and related ACT, is concerned with whether ACT should be treated as part of the cost of the dividend or whether it should be treated as part of tax on the company's profits. Whatever percentage or per-share dividend is declared, that is the amount which the company will pay to its members. The fact that the dividend will carry a tax credit is a matter affecting the recipient rather than the company's method of accounting for the dividend. Accordingly, it is considered appropriate that dividends should be shown in the profit and loss account at the amount paid or payable to the shareholders and that neither the related ACT nor the imputed tax credit should be treated as part of the dividend. It follows that the charge for taxation in the profit and loss account should embrace the full amount of corporation tax and not merely the reduced liability after ACT set off.

RECOVERABILITY OF ACT

5 ACT is primarily recovered by being set off against the corporation tax on the income of the year in which the distribution is made. In the case of dividends paid during the year under review, the corporation tax on the income of that year and of accounting periods ended in the previous year may be available to absorb the ACT. Where a proposed dividend is to be paid in the following year, then the related ACT falls to be set off against the corporation tax on the taxable income of the year of payment of the proposed dividend, and failing that against the corporation tax on the income of the year under review. Any surplus can be carried forward as outlined in paragraph 2 above.

6 For accounting purposes it is necessary to decide whether recovery of the ACT is reasonably certain and foreseeable, or whether it should be written off in the profit and

loss account. If the corporation tax on the income of the year under review and the amounts available from the preceding year are insufficient to cover the ACT, then recoverability of ACT will depend on the extent to which corporation tax payable in future periods is in excess of ACT on dividends paid and proposed or on the existence of a deferred taxation account of adequate size. Although the relief remains available indefinitely, it will be prudent to have regard only to the immediate and foreseeable future; how long this future period should be will depend upon the circumstances of each case, but where there is no deferred taxation account it should not normally extend beyond the next accounting period.

The approach to be adopted to recoverable ACT should be consistent with SSAP 15 **7**
(revised) paragraphs 31 and 32 which read as follows:

> 31 Debit balances arising in respect of advance corporation tax on dividends payable or proposed at the balance sheet date should be carried forward to the extent that it is foreseen that sufficient corporation tax will be assessed on the profits or income of the succeeding accounting period, against which the advance corporation tax is available for offset.
>
> 32 Debit balances arising in respect of advance corporation tax other than on dividends payable or proposed at the balance sheet date should be written off unless their recovery is assured beyond reasonable doubt. Such recovery will normally only be assured where the debit balances are recoverable out of corporation tax arising on profits or income of the succeeding accounting period, without replacement by equivalent debit balances.

It should be noted that paragraph 31 dealing with payable or proposed dividends permits ACT carry forward with replacement by an equivalent debit balance whereas paragraph 32 dealing with paid dividends does not.

The more stringent standard applying to paid dividends is justified since one would **8**
normally expect the ACT on dividends paid to be set off against the current year's corporation tax liability. Carrying forward the ACT for set off against the following year's tax liability amounts to a second opportunity for set-off which could create a revolving backlog of unrecovered ACT. The carry forward is allowed where the backlog can be cleared in the following year – otherwise it is not permitted.

On the other hand for dividends proposed the first possible set-off is against the **9**
following year's tax liability. In the event of inadequacy of the following year's liability the more stringent condition will be applied in the year subsequent to the following year when ACT carry forward is then being considered.

Where there is a provision for deferred taxation on income, the attitude to recoverabil- **10**
ity will be different. The balance on the deferred taxation account represents an amount of corporation tax which is expected to be payable in the future. Unrelieved ACT is available to off set against future corporation tax on income for an indefinite period. It is therefore reasonable to regard unrelieved ACT as being available for deduction from the amount at which the deferred taxation account is stated in the

accounts. It should be noted, however, that to the extent to which the deferred taxation account represents deferred chargeable gains, it is not available for this purpose.

IRRECOVERABLE ACT

11 Any irrecoverable ACT (i.e., ACT the recoverability of which is not reasonably certain and foreseeable) should be written off in the profit and loss account in which the related dividend is shown, or in the first subsequent period in which ACT, which was previously regarded as recoverable, is considered to have become irrecoverable.

12 There are two differing views on the presentation in the profit and loss account of irrecoverable ACT written off. One view is that irrecoverable ACT should be treated as part of the tax charge upon the company to be deducted in arriving at profits after tax; the other that the irrecoverable ACT being a cost stemming from the payment of a dividend should be treated as an appropriation like the dividend itself. Of the two methods the first is supported as the appropriate accounting treatment because unrelieved ACT constitutes tax upon the company or group, as opposed to tax on the shareholders and is not an appropriation of profits. It is appreciated, however, that some readers or analysts of accounts may wish for their purposes to regard irrecoverable ACT in some other manner. The amount of irrecoverable ACT should therefore be separately disclosed if material.

13 Irrecoverable ACT should be treated as part of the tax on ordinary activities.

UNRELIEVED OVERSEAS TAX

14 Unrelieved overseas tax cannot be carried forward for tax purposes. The accounting treatment of unrelieved overseas tax is similar to that of irrecoverable ACT.

FRANKED INVESTMENT INCOME

15 Franked investment income comprises the amount of a distribution received from another Irish resident company with the addition of the related tax credit. The net amount can usually be redistributed to shareholders of the recipient company without payment of ACT, and the related tax credit remains attached from the viewpoint of the shareholder.

16 There are several possible methods of dealing with franked investment income in accounts. The two main possibilities are:

(a) to bring into the profit and loss account the cash amount received or receivable (i.e. excluding the tax credit) or

(b) to bring in the amount of the franked investment income i.e. including the tax credit, an equivalent amount then being treated as part of the charge for taxation.

The first method would involve treating the income either as an item of profit before taxation, or as an addition to the profit after taxation – both alternatives are open to objection. The second method would allow recognition of the income both at the pre-tax and after tax stages in a way which is consistent with other elements of profit, and is therefore adopted as the standard accounting practice.

Where franked investment income includes a tax credit at less than the normal amount, due to export sales relief, manufacturing relief or Shannon exemption, the income should be grossed up at the rate of the imputed tax credit which would itself be shown as a component of the tax charge in the accounts. If the amount of franked investment income from manufacturing, export sales or Shannon exempt sources is material, it is recommended that the amount of relief should be disclosed in the financial statements. 17

BALANCE SHEET TREATMENT OF TAXATION LIABILITIES AND ACT

In most cases the balance sheet will contain one liability of corporation tax, being that on the profit of the year which is generally payable within six months of the end of the accounting period and thus shown as a current liability. In some cases Corporation Tax may be payable more than 12 months after the balance sheet date. Liabilities should be shown as current or non-current as appropriate. If shown as non-current the due date(s) of payment or periods over which payment is due should be stated. 18

ACT on dividends paid will be due for payment six months after the end of the accounting period in which the distribution is made. Where this ACT can be set off against corporation tax on the income of the year under review and the income of the preceding year, no separate liability for ACT should be shown (ACT being covered by the corporation tax liability); if this is not possible, the ACT should be shown as a separate current liability. 19

In the case of dividends proposed but not paid at the balance sheet date, the related ACT will become due for payment eighteen months after the end of the accounting period and should be shown as a separate non-current liability. Where the provision for corporation tax on the income of the period under review, as reduced by ACT on dividends paid, exceeds the liability for ACT on dividends proposed, no separate liability need be recorded for ACT on dividends proposed. 20

Where ACT is regarded as recoverable (see paragraphs 5–10) the amount should be shown as a non-current asset where it is not expected to be recovered within a year, or, where there is a deferred tax account, the amount should be debited to that account to the extent that the balance on that account represents tax on income. 21

Where ACT is regarded as irrecoverable (see paragraphs 11–13) the amount should be charged to profit and loss account. Where there is a substantial contingent asset in the form of irrecoverable ACT written off, the disclosure of the existence of this asset should be considered in the light of SSAP 18. 22

PREFERENCE SHARES

Any dividend right established before April 6, 1976 at a gross rate or a gross amount is reduced (by Section 178 of Corporation Tax Act 1976 as amended by Section 28 of 23

Finance Act 1978) to such an amount as would, with the tax credit, amount to the original gross rate. Steps should therefore be taken to distinguish, for example a 10% preference share issued before April 6, 1976 on which the dividend is now at a rate which, together with the tax credit, would amount to 10%. A change from year to year in the rate of tax credit used in the formula will affect this 'netting down' but not the gross rate. For example, a change in the rate of tax credit from 30% to 35% means the gross rate of 10% remains unchanged but its composition changes from net 7% plus tax credit 3% to net 6.5% plus tax credit 3.5%. The description of these shares in the balance sheet should show that the gross rate includes a tax credit. The 'netted down' rate of dividend applicable in the year in question on pre-1976 preference shares should therefore be incorporated in the description of the shares in the balance sheet e.g.

	Authorised	Issued
100,000 10% (including tax credit) preference shares of IR£1	IR£100,000	IR£100,000

NOTE: At the balance sheet date the composition of the gross dividend was 3.5% tax credit and 6.5% net dividend

'Preference' shares include participating preference shares and preferred ordinary shares issued prior to April 6, 1976 where the rate of dividend forms part of the title by which the share is described.

24 Where companies have claimed manufacturing relief, the Finance Act 1980, Sections 45–46, contains special provision relating to the tax credit attaching to distributions. Broadly speaking distributions must first be made from the pool of profits, called the 'primary fund', that have benefited from manufacturing relief. Such distributions have reduced tax credit attached to them of 1/18 of the distribution. In the interests of informative reporting, disclosure of the amount of the 'primary fund' is recommended.

LEGAL REQUIREMENTS

25 Attention is drawn to the requirements of Companies (Amendment) Act 1986 and, in particular, to paragraphs 32(1) (b) and (c), 33 and 40 of the Schedule.

Part 2 – Definition of terms

RECOVERABLE ACT

26 The amount of the ACT paid or payable on outgoing dividends paid and proposed:

(a) which can be properly set off against a credit balance on deferred tax account, or
(b) which can be recovered against the corporation tax liability on the income of any accounting period up to and including the period under review, or
(c) which cannot be set off or recovered under (a) or (b) above but
   (i) where relating to a dividend paid in the period under review or in a previous period, can be set off against the expected corporation tax liability on the

income of the subsequent period without replacement by an equivalent debit balance.

(ii) Where relating to a dividend payable in the subsequent period, can be set off against the expected corporation tax liability on the income of that period.

Recoverable ACT includes any ACT meeting this definition notwithstanding it has been written off previously as irrecoverable.

IRRECOVERABLE ACT

ACT paid or payable on outgoing dividends paid and proposed other than recoverable ACT. 27

Part 3 – Standard accounting practice

PROFIT AND LOSS ACCOUNT

The following items should be included in the taxation charge or credit in the profit and loss account and, where material, should be separately disclosed: 28

(a) the amount of corporation tax specifying:
   (i) the charge or credit for corporation tax on the income of the year;
   (ii) transfers between the deferred taxation account and the profit and loss account;
   (iii) the relief for overseas taxation.
(b) the total overseas taxation relieved and unrelieved;
(c) tax attributable to franked investment income;
(d) irrecoverable ACT (specifying the basis of the charge);
(e) ACT previously written off as irrecoverable now recovered or regarded as recoverable (specifying the basis of the credit).

Material adjustments in respect of previous periods should be disclosed. Where a company benefits from export sales relief, manufacturing relief or Shannon exemption this should be disclosed together with the dates of expiry of the relief. Where the tax charge is materially affected by timing differences not provided for, this should be disclosed.

The rate of corporation tax used should be disclosed. If the rate of corporation tax is not known for the whole or part of the period covered by the accounts the latest known rate should be used. 29

Outgoing dividends should not include either the related ACT or the attributable tax credit. However, the tax credit attaching to dividends paid or proposed should be disclosed in the notes to the accounts. 30

Incoming dividends from Republic of Ireland resident companies should be included in profit before taxation at the amount of cash received or receivable plus the tax credit. 31

BALANCE SHEET

32 Dividends proposed (or declared and not yet payable) should be included in current liabilities, without the addition of the related ACT.

33 Where ACT on dividends paid in the accounting period under review is exceeded by provisions for corporation tax on the income of the accounting period under review and/or the preceding accounting period(s) (against which that ACT can be set), no separate liability for this ACT should be recorded as ACT would not result in any increase in the overall tax liability. To the extent that this ACT exceeds such provisions it should be provided for as a separate current liability.

34 Where ACT on both dividends paid and dividends proposed in the accounting period under review is exceeded by the provision for corporation tax on the income of that period no separate liability needs to be recorded for ACT on the proposed dividends because the fact that the current period's corporation tax is available to discharge the subsequent period's ACT ensures that the ACT on the proposed dividends will not result in any increase in the overall tax liability. To the extent that ACT on dividends proposed exceeds the corporation tax provision, as reduced by ACT on dividends paid, it should be provided for as a separate non-current liability.

35 If a separate liability for ACT has to be provided for under paragraphs 33 and/or 34 above, the corresponding asset which arises if this ACT is regarded as recoverable should be deducted from any provision for deferred taxation on income in the balance sheet and, to the extent that such provision is inadequate to cover it, the recoverable ACT should be shown as a current or non-current asset as appropriate. At each subsequent balance sheet date, the recoverability of this asset should be re-assessed. If the ACT for which a separate liability has to be provided for under paragraphs 32 and/or 33 above is not regarded as recoverable, the provision for the liability should be created by a charge to profit and loss account for irrecoverable ACT (see paragraph 28(d) above).

36 Where the title of a class of preference shares (or participating preference or preferred ordinary shares) issued before April 6, 1976 includes a fixed rate of dividend, the fact that the rate in the title now includes a tax credit should be indicated in the description of the shares in the balance sheet or notes to the balance sheet. The composition of the gross rate at the balance sheet date between net dividend and the tax credit should also be disclosed.

DATE FROM WHICH EFFECTIVE FOR COMPANIES SUBJECT TO TAXATION IN THE REPUBLIC OF IRELAND

37 The accounting practices set out in this Statement should be regarded as standard in respect of financial statements relating to accounting periods beginning on or after January 1, 1988 and earlier adoption is encouraged.

Appendix

This appendix is for general guidance and does not form part of the Statement of Standard Accounting Practice.

1 PROFIT AND LOSS ACCOUNT

This example indicates one method of showing (by way of note to the profit and loss account) the taxation items required to be disclosed under the Companies (Amendment) Act 1986 and Part 3 of this standard. In simple cases, taxation may be dealt with entirely within the profit and loss account.

	IR£
Corporation tax on income at 50% (including £b transferred to/from deferred taxation account)	a
Less relief for overseas taxation	c
	d
Overseas taxation	e
Tax credit on Republic of Ireland dividends received	f
Irrecoverable advance corporation tax (explain basis)	g
	h

Note: The taxation charge has been reduced by IR£x in respect of export sales relief/manufacturing relief/Shannon exemption. Export sales relief expires on April 5, 1990; no relief may be claimed for any accounting period or part of a period commencing after that date.

2 BALANCE SHEET

(a) Paragraph 33 refers to the treatment of ACT on dividends paid as a current liability. Under the formats in the Schedule (the Schedule) to the Companies (Amendment) Act 1986 such ACT may be classified as follows:

Format 1	C8
Format 2	C8

(b) Paragraph 34 refers to the treatment of ACT on proposed dividends as a non-current tax liability. Such ACT may be classified in the Schedule formats as follows:

Format 1	F8
Format 2	C8 but including the ACT in the amounts falling due after more than one year.

(c) Paragraph 35 refers to the treatment of recoverable ACT as a current or non-current asset as appropriate. Such ACT may be classified in the Schedule formats as follows:

Format 1	BII
Format 2	BII

with non-current ACT recoverable being included in the amount falling due after more than one year.

[SSAP 9]
Stocks and long-term contracts

(Issued May 1975; Part 6 added August 1980; revised September 1988)

Contents

Stocks and long-term contracts

The provisions of this statement of standard accounting practice should be read in conjunction with the (Explanatory) Foreword to accounting standards *and need not be applied to immaterial items.*

Part 1 – Explanatory note

STOCKS

The determination of profit for an accounting year requires the matching of costs with related revenues. The cost of unsold or unconsumed stocks will have been incurred in the expectation of future revenue, and when this will not arise until a later year it is appropriate to carry forward this cost to be matched with the revenue when it arises; the applicable concept is the matching of cost and revenue in the year in which the revenue arises rather than in the year in which the cost is incurred. If there is no reasonable expectation of sufficient future revenue to cover cost incurred (e.g., as a result of deterioration, obsolescence or a change in demand) the irrecoverable cost should be charged to revenue in the year under review. Thus, stocks normally need to be stated at cost, or, if lower, at net realisable value. 1

The comparison of cost and net realisable value needs to be made in respect of each item of stock separately. Where this is impracticable, groups or categories of stock items which are similar will need to be taken together. To compare the total realisable value of stocks with the total cost could result in an unacceptable setting off of foreseeable losses against unrealised profits. 2

In order to match costs and revenue, 'costs' of stocks should comprise that expenditure which has been incurred in the normal course of business in bringing the product or service to its present location and condition. Such costs will include all related production overheads, even though these may accrue on a time basis. 3

The methods used in allocating costs to stocks need to be selected with a view to providing the fairest possible approximation to the expenditure actually incurred in bringing the product to its present location and condition. For example, in the case of retail stores holding a large number of rapidly changing individual items, stock on the shelves has often been stated at current selling prices less the normal gross profit margin. In these particular circumstances this may be acceptable as being the only practical method of arriving at a figure which approximates to cost. 4

NET REALISABLE VALUE

5 Net realisable value is the estimated proceeds from the sale of items of stock less all further costs to completion and less all costs to be incurred in marketing, selling and distributing directly related to the items in question.

REPLACEMENT COST

6 Items of stock have sometimes been stated in financial statements at estimated replacement cost where this is lower than net realisable value. Where the effect is to take account of a loss greater than that which is expected to be incurred, the use of replacement cost is not regarded as acceptable. However, in some circumstances (e.g., in the case of materials, the price of which has fluctuated considerably and which have not become the subject of firm sales contracts by the time the financial statements are prepared) replacement cost may be the best measure of net realisable value. Also, where a company adopts the alternative accounting rules of the Companies Act 1985, items of stock may be stated at the lower of current replacement cost and net realisable value.

LONG-TERM CONTRACTS

7 Separate consideration needs to be given to long-term contracts. Owing to the length of time taken to complete such contracts, to defer recording turnover and taking profit into account until completion may result in the profit and loss account reflecting not so much a fair view of the results of the activity of the company during the year but rather the results relating to contracts that have been completed in the year. It is therefore appropriate to take credit for ascertainable turnover and profit while contracts are in progress in accordance with paragraphs 8 to 11 below.

8 Companies should ascertain turnover in a manner appropriate to the stage of completion of the contracts, the businesses and the industries in which they operate.

9 Where the business carries out long-term contracts and it is considered that their outcome can be assessed with reasonable certainty before their conclusion, the attributable profit should be calculated on a prudent basis and included in the accounts for the period under review. The profit taken up needs to reflect the proportion of the work carried out at the accounting date and to take into account any known inequalities of profitability in the various stages of a contract. The procedure to recognise profit is to include an appropriate proportion of total contract value as turnover in the profit and loss account as the contract activity progresses. The costs incurred in reaching that stage of completion are matched with this turnover, resulting in the reporting of results that can be attributed to the proportion of work completed.

10 Where the outcome of long-term contracts cannot be assessed with reasonable certainty before the conclusion of the contract, no profit should be reflected in the profit and loss account in respect of those contracts, although, in such circumstances, if no loss is expected it may be appropriate to show as turnover a proportion of the total contract value using a zero estimate of profit.

If it is expected that there will be a loss on a contract as a whole, all of the loss should be recognised as soon as it is foreseen (in accordance with the prudence concept). Examples of how this can be achieved are given in Appendix 3. Initially, the foreseeable loss will be deducted from the work in progress figure of the particular contract, thus reducing it to net realisable value. Any loss in excess of the work in progress figure should be classified as an accrual within 'Creditors' or under 'Provisions for liabilities and charges' depending upon the circumstances. Where unprofitable contracts are if such magnitude that they can be expected to utilise a considerable part of the company's capacity for a substantial period, related administration overheads to be incurred during the period to the completion of those contracts should also be included in the calculation of the provision for losses. **11**

DISCLOSURE IN FINANCIAL STATEMENTS

A suitable description of the amount at which stocks (excluding long-term contract balances) are stated in financial statements would be 'at lower of cost and net realisable value.' **12**

In the case of long-term contracts: **13**

(a) long-term contract balances classified under the balance sheet heading of 'Stocks' are stated at total costs incurred, net of amounts transferred to the profit and loss account in respect of work carried out to date, less foreseeable losses and applicable payments on account. A suitable description in the financial statements would be 'at net cost, less foreseeable losses and payments on account.'
(b) cumulative turnover (i.e., the total turnover recorded in respect of the contract in the profit and loss accounts of all accounting periods since inception of the contract) is compared with total payments on account. If turnover exceeds payments on account an 'amount recoverable on contracts' is established and separately disclosed within debtors. If payments on account are greater than turnover to date, the excess is classified as a deduction from any balance on that contract in stocks, with any residual balance in excess of cost being classified with creditors.

In order to give an adequate explanation of the affairs of the company, the accounting policies followed in arriving at the amount at which stocks and long-term contracts are stated in the financial statements should be set out in a note. Where differing bases have been adopted for different types of stocks and long-term contracts, the amount included in the financial statements in respect of each type will need to be stated. **14**

FURTHER PRACTICAL CONSIDERATIONS

The basic considerations which must be taken into account in determining cost and net realisable value in relation to stocks and long-term contracts are set out in Parts 2 and 3 of this statement. The majority of problems which arise in practice in determining these amounts result from considerations which are relevant to particular businesses and are not of such universal application that they can be the subject of a statement of standard **15** accounting practice. Accordingly, Appendix 1 sets out in more detail some general guidelines which may be of assistance in determining cost and net realisable value and in identifying those situations in which net realisable value is likely to be less than cost. Appendix 1 also sets out considerations which need to be borne in mind in calculating the amount of profit to be taken into account in respect of long-term contracts.

Part 2 – Definition of terms

16 Stocks comprise the following categories:

(a) goods or other assets purchased for resale;
(b) consumable stores;
(c) raw materials and components purchased for incorporation into products for sale;
(d) products and services in intermediate stages of completion
(e) long-term contract balances; and
(f) finished goods.

17 *Cost* is defined in relation to the different categories of stocks as being that expenditure which has been incurred in the normal course of business in bringing the product or service to its present location and condition. This expenditure should include, in addition to cost of purchase (as defined in paragraph 18), such costs of conversion (as defined in paragraph 19) as are appropriate to that location and condition.

18 *Cost of purchase* comprises purchase price including import duties, transport and handling costs and any other directly attributable costs, less trade discounts, rebates and subsidies.

19 *Cost of conversion* comprises:

(a) costs which are specifically attributable to units of production, e.g., direct labour, direct expenses and sub-contracted work;
(b) production overheads (as defined in paragraph 20);
(c) other overheads, if any, attributable in the particular circumstances of the business to bringing the product or service to its present location and condition.

20 *Production overheads:* Overheads incurred in respect of materials, labour or services for production, based on the normal level of activity, taking one year with another. For this purpose each overhead should be classified according to function (e.g., production, selling or administration) so as to ensure the inclusion, in cost of conversion, of those overheads (including depreciation) which relate to production, notwithstanding that these may accrue wholly or partly on a time basis.

21 *Net realisable value:* The actual or estimated selling price (net of trade but before settlement discounts) less:

(a) all further costs to completion; and
(b) all costs to be incurred in marketing, selling and distributing.

22 *Long-term contract:* A contract entered into for the design, manufacture or construction of a single substantial asset or the provision of a service (or of a combination of assets or services which together constitute a single project) where the time taken substantially to complete the contract is such that the contract activity falls into different accounting periods. A contract that is required to be accounted for as long-term by this accounting standard will usually extend for a period exceeding one year. However, a duration exceeding one year is not an essential feature of a long-term contract. Some contracts with a shorter duration than one year should be accounted for as long-term contracts if they are sufficiently material to the activity of the period that not to record turnover and attributable profit would lead to distortion of the period's turnover and results such that the financial statements would not give a true and fair view, provided that the policy is applied consistently within the reporting entity and from year to year.

Attributable profit: That part of the total profit currently estimated to arise over the duration of the contract, after allowing for estimated remedial and maintenance costs and increases in costs so far as not recoverable under the terms of the contract, that fairly reflects the profit attributable to that part of the work performed at the accounting date. (There can be no attributable profit until the profitable outcome of the contract can be assessed with reasonable certainty.) **23**

Foreseeable losses: Losses which are currently estimated to arise over the duration of the contract (after allowing for estimated remedial and maintenance costs and increases in costs so far as not recoverable under the terms of the contract). This estimate is required irrespective of: **24**

(a) whether or not work has yet commenced on such contracts;
(b) the proportion of work carried out at the accounting date;
(c) the amount of profits expected to arise on other contracts.

Payments on account: All amounts received and receivable at the accounting date in respect of contracts in progress. **25**

Part 3 – Standard accounting practice

STOCKS

The amount at which stocks are stated in periodic financial statements should be the total of the lower of cost and net realisable value of the separate items of stock or of groups of similar items. **26**

Stocks should be sub-classified in the balance sheet or in the notes to the financial statements so as to indicate the amounts held in each of the main categories in the standard balance sheet formats (as adapted where appropriate) of Schedule 4 to the Companies Act 1985, Schedule 4 to the Companies (Northern Ireland) Order 1986 and, in the Republic of Ireland, the Schedule to the Companies (Amendment) Act 1986. **27**

LONG-TERM CONTRACTS

28 Long-term contracts should be assessed on a contract by contract basis and reflected in the profit and loss account by recording turnover and related costs as contract activity progresses. Turnover is ascertained in a manner appropriate to the stage of completion of the contract, the business and the industry in which it operates.

29 Where it is considered that the outcome of a long-term contract can be assessed with reasonable certainty before its conclusion, the prudently calculated attributable profit should be recognised in the profit and loss account as the difference between the reported turnover and related costs for that contract.

30 Long-term contracts should be disclosed in the balance sheet as follows:

(a) the amount by which recorded turnover is in excess of payments on account should be classified as 'amounts recoverable on contracts' and separately disclosed within debtors;
(b) the balance of payments on account (in excess of amounts (i) matched with turnover; and (ii) offset against long-term contract balances) should be classified as payments on account and separately disclosed within creditors;
(c) the amount of long-term contracts, at costs incurred, net of amounts transferred to costs of sales, after deducting foreseeable losses and payments on account not matched with turnover, should be classified as 'long-term contract balances' and separately disclosed within the balance sheet heading 'Stocks.' The balance sheet note should disclose separately the balances of:
    (i) net cost less foreseeable losses; and
    (ii) applicable payments on account;
(d) the amount by which the provision or accrual for foreseeable losses exceeds the costs incurred (after transfers to cost of sales) should be included within either provisions for liabilities and charges or creditors as appropriate.

31 Consequent upon the application of this revised standard, the corresponding amounts in the financial statements will need to be restated on a comparable basis.

STATEMENT OF ACCOUNTING POLICIES

32 The accounting policies that have been applied to stocks and long-term contracts, in particular the method of ascertaining turnover and attributable profit, should be stated and applied consistently within the business and from year to year.

DATE FROM WHICH EFFECTIVE

33 The accounting practices set out in this statement should be adopted as soon as possible and regarded as standard in respect of financial statements relating to accounting periods beginning on or after 1 July 1988.

Part 4 – Note on legal requirements in Great Britain and Northern Ireland

All paragraph references unless otherwise indicated are to Schedule 4 to the Companies Act 1985 and Schedule 4 to the Companies (Northern Ireland) Order 1986.

Paragraph 22 requires that, under the historical cost accounting rules, 'the amount to be included in respect of any current asset shall be its purchase price or production cost.' Paragraph 23(1) provides for the inclusion of the asset at net realisable value if lower than purchase price or production cost. **34**

Paragraph 90 [paragraph 89 of Schedule 4 to the Companies (Northern Ireland) Order 1986] provides that 'the purchase price of any asset ... includes any consideration (whether in cash or otherwise) given by the company in respect of that asset.' Counsel's opinion, obtained by the ASC, has indicated that one purpose of this paragraph is to enable debtors to be stated at face value, that is, at amounts which include a profit element, and that this does not conflict with paragraph 22. **35**

Paragraph 26 requires expenses incidental to the acquisition of an asset to be included in the purchase price. It also requires the inclusion of directly attributable production overheads in the production cost of an asset and permits the inclusion of overheads which are only indirectly attributable to the production of an asset and interest on borrowed capital. In cases where interest is included the fact must be stated and the amount of interest included must be disclosed in a note to the financial statements. Paragraph 26 also prohibits the inclusion of distribution costs. **36**

Paragraph 27 allows the following methods for valuation of stocks (but requires that the method chosen must be one which appears to the directors to be appropriate in the circumstances of the company): **37**

(a) the method known as 'first in, first out' (FIFO);
(b) the method known as 'last in, first out' (LIFO);
(c) a weighted average price; and
(d) any other method similar to any of the methods mentioned above.

This standard requires the use of a method which provides a fair approximation to the expenditure actually incurred. The use of some of the methods allowed by paragraph 27 of the Schedule will not meet this requirement. **38**

In particular, the use of the LIFO method can result in the reporting of current assets at amounts that bear little relationship to recent costs. This may result in not only a significant misstatement of balance sheet amounts but also a potential distortion of current and future results. This places a special responsibility on the directors to be assured that the circumstances of the company require the adoption of such a valuation method in order for the accounts to give a true and fair view. **39**

Paragraph 27(3) requires a company to state in a note to the accounts the difference between the replacement cost of stocks and their book amount – as determined by 37(a) to (d) above – where this difference is material. **40**

41 It is further provided in paragraph 27(5) that if the most recent actual purchase price or production cost before the balance sheet date appears to the directors of the company to constitute a more appropriate standard of comparison, then that amount may be used as a surrogate for replacement cost.

42 Paragraph 31(5) provides that, where a company adopts the alternative accounting rules, 'stocks may be included at their current cost.'

43 Paragraph 89 [paragraph 88 of Schedule 4 to the Companies (Northern Ireland) Order 1986] provides that provisions are amounts 'retained as reasonably necessary for the purpose of providing for any liability or loss which is either likely to be incurred, or certain to be incurred but uncertain as to amount or as to the date on which it will arise.'

44 Paragraph 91* [paragraph 90 of Schedule 4 to the Companies (Northern Ireland) Order 1986] declares that realised profits are 'such profits of a company as fall to be treated as realised profits for the purposes of those accounts in accordance with principles generally accepted with respect to the determination for accounting purposes of realised profits.' It is a 'generally accepted principle' that it is appropriate to recognise profit on long-term contracts when the outcome can be assessed with 'reasonable certainty.' The principle of recognising profit on long-term contracts under this standard, therefore, does not contravene this paragraph.

Part 5 – Note on legal requirements in the Republic of Ireland

45 The legal requirements in Great Britain and Northern Ireland are mirrored, in respect of the Republic of Ireland, in the Schedule to the Companies (Amendment) Act 1986. The following table indicates the corresponding paragraphs in respect of all the references contained in Part 4 of this statement.

Schedule 4 to the Companies Act 1985	*Schedule 4 to the Companies (Northern Ireland) Order 1986*	*The Schedule to the Companies (Amendment) Act 1986*
Paragraph 22	Paragraph 22	Paragraph 10
Paragraph 23(1)	Paragraph 23(1)	Paragraph 11(1)
Paragraph 26	Paragraph 26	Paragraph 14
Paragraph 27	Paragraph 27	Paragraph 15†
Paragraph 27(4)	Paragraph 27(4)	Paragraph 15(4)
Paragraph 27(5)	Paragraph 27(5)	Paragraph 15(5)
Paragraph 31(5)	Paragraph 31(5)	Paragraph 19(5)
Paragraph 89	Paragraph 88	Paragraph 70

***Editor's note:** *Now section 262(3).*

†There is no provision for the LIFO method of stock valuation in paragraph 15 of the Schedule to the Companies (Amendment) Act 1986.

Paragraph 90	Paragraph 89	Paragraph 71
Paragraph 91	Paragraph 90	Paragraph 72

Part 6 – Compliance with International Accounting Standard No. 2 'Valuation and presentation of inventories in the context of the historical cost system' and No. 11 'Accounting for construction contracts'

The requirements of International Accounting Standard No. 2 'Valuation and presentation of inventories in the context of the historical cost system' and International Accounting Standard No. 11 'Accounting for construction contracts'* accord very closely with the content of the United Kingdom and Irish Accounting Standard No. 9 (Revised) 'Stocks and long-term contracts' and accordingly compliance with SSAP 9 will ensure compliance with both IAS 2 and IAS 11 in all material respects. 46

***Editor's note:** *Revised versions of IAS 2 'Inventories' and IAS 11 'Construction Contracts' were issued in November 1993.*

Appendix 1

This appendix is for general guidance and does not form part of the statement of standard accounting practice.

Further practical considerations

Many of the problems involved in arriving at the amount at which stocks and long-term contracts are stated in financial statements are of a practical nature rather than resulting from matters of principle. This appendix discusses some particular areas in which difficulty may be encountered.

THE ALLOCATION OF OVERHEADS

1 Production overheads are included in cost of conversion (as defined in Part 2) together with direct labour, direct expenses and sub-contracted work. This inclusion is a necessary corollary of the principle that expenditure should be included to the extent to which it has been incurred in bringing the product 'to its present location and condition' (paragraph 17 of part 2). However, all abnormal conversion costs (such as exceptional spoilage, idle capacity and other losses) which are avoidable under normal operating conditions need for the same reason, to be excluded.

2 Where firm sales contracts have been entered into for the provision of goods or services to customer's specification, overheads relating to design, and marketing and selling costs incurred before manufacture, may be included in arriving at cost.

3 The costing methods adopted by a business are usually designed to ensure that all direct material, direct labour, direct expenses and sub-contracted work are identified and charged on a reasonable and consistent basis but problems arise on the allocation of overheads which must usually involve the exercise of personal judgement in the selection of an appropriate convention.

4 The classification of overheads necessary to achieve this allocation takes the function of the overhead as its distinguishing characteristic (e.g., whether it is a function of production, marketing, selling or administration), rather than whether the overhead tends to vary with time or with volume.

5 The costs of general management, as distinct from functional management, are not directly related to current production and are, therefore, excluded from cost of conversion and, hence, from the cost of stocks and long-term contracts.

6 In the case of smaller organisations whose management may be involved in the daily administration of each of the various functions, particular problems may arise in practice in distinguishing these general management overheads. In such organisations the cost of management may fairly be allocated on suitable bases to the functions of production, marketing, selling and administration.

Problems may also arise in allocating the costs of central service departments, the allocation of which should depend on the function or functions that the department is serving. For example the accounts department will normally support the following functions: 7

(a) production – by paying direct and indirect production wages and salaries, by controlling purchases and by preparing periodic financial statements for the production units;
(b) marketing and distribution – by analysing sales and by controlling the sales ledger;
(c) general administration – by preparing management accounts and annual financial statements and budgets, by controlling cash resources and by planning investments.

Only those costs of the accounts department that can reasonably be allocated to the production function fall to be included in the cost of conversion.

The allocation of overheads included in the valuation of stocks and long-term contracts needs to be based on the company's normal level of activity, taking one year with another. The governing factor is that the cost of unused capacity should be written off in the current year. In determining what constitutes 'normal' the following factors need to be considered: **8**

(a) the volume of production which the production facilities are intended by their designers and by management to produce under the working conditions (e.g., single or double shift) prevailing during the year;
(b) the budgeted level of activity for the year under review and for the ensuing year;
(c) the level of activity achieved both in the year under review and in previous years.

Although temporary changes in the load of activity may be ignored, persistent variation should lead to revision of the previous norm.

Where management accounts are prepared on a marginal cost basis, it will be necessary to add to the figure of stocks so arrived at, the appropriate proportion of those production overheads not already included in the marginal cost. **9**

The adoption of a conservative approach to the valuation of stocks and long-term contracts has sometimes been used as one of the reasons for omitting selected production overheads. In so far as the circumstances of the business require an element of prudence in determining the amount at which stocks and long-term contracts are stated, this needs to be taken into account in the determination of net realisable value and not by the exclusion from cost of selected overheads. **10**

METHODS OF COSTING

It is frequently not practicable to relate expenditure to specific units of stocks and long-term contracts. The ascertainment of the nearest approximation to cost gives rise to two problems: **11**

(a) the selection of an appropriate method for relating costs to stocks and long-term contracts (e.g., job costing, batch costing, process costing, standard costing);

(b) the selection of an appropriate method for calculating the related costs where a number of identical items have been purchased or made at different times (e.g., unit cost, average cost or FIFO).

12 In selecting the methods referred to in paragraphs 11(a) and (b) above, management must exercise judgement to ensure that the methods chosen provide the fairest practicable approximation to cost. Furthermore, where standard costs are used they need to be reviewed frequently to ensure that they bear a reasonable relationship to actual costs obtaining during the period. Methods such as base stock and LIFO are not usually appropriate methods of stock valuation because they often result in stocks being stated in the balance sheet at amounts that bear little relationship to recent cost levels. When this happens, not only is the presentation of current assets misleading, but there is potential distortion of subsequent results if stock levels reduce and out of date costs are drawn into the profit and loss account.

13 The method of arriving at cost by applying the latest purchase price to the total number of units in stock is unacceptable in principle because it is not necessarily the same as actual cost and, in times of rising prices, will result in the taking of a profit which has not been realised.

14 One method of arriving at cost, in the absence of a satisfactory costing system, is the use of selling price less an estimated profit margin. This is acceptable only if it can be demonstrated that the method gives a reasonable approximation of the actual cost.

15 In industries where the cost of minor by-products is not separable from the cost of the principal products, stocks of such by-products may be stated in accounts at their net realisable value. In this case the costs of the main products are calculated after deducting the net realisable value of the by-products.

THE DETERMINATION OF NET REALISABLE VALUE

16 The initial calculation of provisions to reduce stocks from cost to net realisable value may often be made by the use of formulae based on predetermined criteria. The formulae normally take account of the age, movements in the past, expected future movements and estimated scrap values of the stock, as appropriate. Whilst the use of such formulae establishes a basis for making a provision which can be consistently applied, it is still necessary for the results to be reviewed in the light of any special circumstances which cannot be anticipated in the formulae, such as changes in the state of the order book.

17 Where a provision is required to reduce the value of finished goods below cost, the stocks of the parts and sub-assemblies held for the purpose of the manufacture of such products, together with stocks on order, need to be reviewed to determine if provision is also required against such items.

18 Where stocks of spares are held for sale, special consideration of the factors in paragraph 16 of this appendix will be required in the context of:

(a) the number of units sold to which they are applicable;
(b) the estimated frequency with which a replacement spare is required;
(c) the expected useful life of the unit to which they are applicable.

Events occurring between the balance sheet date and the date of completion of the financial statements need to be considered in arriving at the net realisable value at the balance sheet date (e.g., a subsequent reduction in selling prices). However, no reduction falls to be made when the realisable value of material stocks is less than the purchase price, provided that the goods into which the materials are to be incorporated can still be sold at a profit after incorporating the materials at cost price. 19

THE APPLICATION OF NET REALISABLE VALUE

The principal situations in which net realisable value is likely to be less than cost are where there has been: 20

(a) an increase in costs or a fall in selling price;
(b) physical deterioration of stocks;
(c) obsolescence of products;
(d) a decision as part of a company's marketing strategy to manufacture and sell products at a loss;
(e) errors in production or purchasing.

Furthermore, when stocks are held which are unlikely to be sold within the turnover period normal in that company (i.e., excess stocks), the impending delay in realisation increases the risk that the situations outlined in (a) to (c) above may occur before the stocks are sold and needs to be taken into account in assessing net realisable value.

LONG-TERM CONTRACTS

In ascertaining costs of long-term contracts it is not normally appropriate to include interest payable on borrowed money. However, in circumstances where sums borrowed can be identified as financing specific long-term contracts, it may be appropriate to include such related interest in cost, in which circumstances the inclusion of interest and the amount of interest so included should be disclosed in a note to the financial statements. 21

In some businesses, long-term contracts for the supply of services or manufacture and supply of goods exist where the prices are determined and invoiced according to separate parts of the contract. In these businesses the most appropriate method of reflecting profits on each contract is usually to match costs against performance of the separable parts of the contract, treating each such separable part as a separate contract. In such instances, however, future revenues from the contract need to be compared with future estimated costs and provision made for any foreseen loss. 22

Turnover (ascertained in a manner appropriate to the industry, the nature of the contracts concerned and the contractual relationship with the customer) and related 23 costs should be recorded in the profit and loss account as contract activity progresses. Turnover may sometimes be ascertained by reference to valuation of the work carried out to date. In other cases, there may be specific points during a contract at which individual elements of work done with separately ascertainable sales values and costs can be identified and appropriately recorded as turnover (e.g., because delivery or customer acceptance has taken place). This accounting standard does not provide a definition of turnover in view of the different methods of ascertaining it as outlined above. However, it does require disclosure of the means by which turnover is ascertained.

24 In determining whether the stage has been reached at which it is appropriate to recognise profit, account should be taken of the nature of the business concerned. It is necessary to define the earliest point for each particular contract before which no profit is taken up, the overriding principle being that there can be no attributable profit until the outcome of a contract can reasonably be foreseen. Of the profit which in the light of all the circumstances can be foreseen with a reasonable degree of certainty to arise on completion of the contract, there should be regarded as earned to date only that part which prudently reflects the amount of work performed to date. The method used for taking up such profit needs to be consistently applied.

25 In calculating the total estimated profit on the contract, it is necessary to take into account not only the total costs to date and the total estimated further costs to completion (calculated by reference to the same principles as were applied to cost to date) but also the estimated future costs of rectification and guarantee work, and any other future work to be undertaken under the terms of the contract. These are then compared with the total sales value of the contract. In considering future costs, it is necessary to have regard to likely increases in wages and salaries, to likely increases in the price of raw materials and to rises in general overheads, so far as these items are not recoverable from the customer under the terms of the contract.

26 Where approved variations have been made to a contract in the course of it and the amount to be received in respect of these variations has not yet been settled and is likely to be a material factor in the outcome, it is necessary to make a conservative estimate of the amount likely to be received and this is then treated as part of the total sales value. On the other hand, allowance needs to be made for foreseen claims or penalties payable arising out of delays in completion or from other causes.

27 The settlement of claims arising from circumstances not envisaged in the contract or arising as an indirect consequence of approved variations is subject to a high level of uncertainty relating to the outcome of future negotiations. In view of this, it is generally prudent to recognise receipts in respect of such claims only when negotiations have reached an advanced stage and there is sufficient evidence of the acceptability of the claim in principle to the purchaser, with an indication of the amount involved also being available.

The amounts to be included in the year's profit and loss account will be both the appropriate amount of turnover and the associated costs of achieving that turnover, to the extent that these amounts exceed corresponding amounts recognised in previous years. The estimated outcome of a contract which extends over several accounting years will nearly always vary in the light of changes in circumstances and for this reason the result of the year will not necessarily represent the proportion of the total profit on the contract which is appropriate to the amount of work carried out in the period; it may also reflect the effect of changes in circumstances during the year which affect the total profit estimated to accrue on completion.

Appendix 2

This appendix is for general guidance and does not form part of the statement of standard accounting practice.

Glossary of terms

The use of the following terms in describing the accounting policies adopted in arriving at the amount at which stocks and long-term contracts are stated in financial statements should be restricted in conformity with the definitions given to each. Where these definitions are inapplicable, alternative expressions should be used and explained.

1 *Average cost:* The calculation of the cost of stocks on the basis of the application to the unit of stocks on hand of an average price computed by dividing the total cost of units by the total number of such units. This average price may be arrived at by means of a continuous calculation, a periodic calculation or a moving periodic calculation.

2 *Base stock:* The calculation of the cost of stocks on the basis that a fixed unit value is ascribed to a predetermined number of units of stock, any excess over this number being valued on the basis of some other method. If the number of units in stock is less than the predetermined minimum, the fixed unit value is applied to the number in stock.

3 *Completed long-term contract:* A long-term contract on which no further work, apart from maintenance work, is expected to take place.

4 *Current cost* of stock is the lower of:

(a) its net current replacement cost; and
(b) its net realisable value.

5 *FIFO (first in, first out):* The calculation of the cost of stocks on the basis that the quantities in hand represent the latest purchases or production.

6 *LIFO (last in, first out):* The calculation of the cost of stocks on the basis that the quantities in hand represent the earliest purchases or production.

7 *Replacement cost:* The cost at which an identical asset could be purchased or manufactured.

8 *Standard cost:* The calculation of the cost of stocks on the basis of periodically predetermined costs calculated from management's estimates of expected levels of costs and of operations and operational efficiency and the related expenditure.

9 *Unit cost:* The cost of purchasing or manufacturing identifiable units of stocks.

Appendix 3

This appendix is for general guidance and does not form part of the statement of standard accounting practice.

Long-term contracts: further consideration of financial statement presentation

The classification of an 'amount recoverable on contracts' within debtors is a somewhat unfamiliar concept which needs careful consideration. **1**

The determination of the point at which ownership of completed work passes from the contractor to the customer is a complex matter of legal form and industry practice. **2**

An 'amount recoverable on contracts' may not have the contractual status of a debtor in strict legal form. However, it is well established under the accruals concept of revenue and cost recognition that this should not preclude debtors and creditors from being recorded, where this is necessary to reflect the substance of a transaction. **3**

An essential test for an 'amount recoverable on contracts' to be recorded as an asset is that it should be realisable. This applies equally whether the balance is classified as a debtor or as an element of work in progress. **4**

An 'amount recoverable on contracts' represents an excess of the value of work carried out to date (which has been recorded as turnover) over cumulative payments on account. The amount and realisability of the balance therefore depend on the value of work carried out being ascertained appropriately. The balance arises as a derivative of this process of contract revenue recognition and is directly linked to turnover. In substance, it represents accrued revenue receivable and has the attributes of a debtor. **5**

Accordingly, the standard concludes that 'amounts recoverable on contracts' should be classified as debtors, although separate disclosure is prescribed. Counsel's opinion obtained by the ASC confirms that 'amounts recoverable on contracts' should be classified under 'Debtors' and cannot be classified under 'Stocks.' **6**

In determining the amounts at which long-term contracts should be included in the financial statements, contracting activity should be reviewed on an individual contract by contract basis. The following example illustrates the process of applying the principles set out in the standard to long-term contracts. **7**

Project Number

	1	*2*	*3*	*4*	*5*	*Balance Sheet Total*	*Profit & Loss Account*
Recorded as turnover – being value of work done	145	520	380	200	55		1,300
Cumulative payments on account	(100)	(600)	(400)	(150)	(80)		
Classified as amounts recoverable on contracts	45			50		95DR	
Balance (excess) of payments on account		(80)	(20)		(25)		
Applied as an offset against long-term contract balances – see below		60	20		15		
Residue classified as payments on account		(20)	–		(10)	(30)CR	
Total costs incurred	110	510	450	250	100		
Transferred to cost of sales	(110)	(450)	(350)	(250)	(55)		(1,215)
	–	60	100		45		
Provision/accrual for foreseeable losses charged to cost of sales				(40)	(30)		(70)
		60	100		15		
Classified as provision/accrual for losses				(40)		(40)CR	
Balance (excess) of payments on account applied as offset against long-term contract balances		(60)	(20)		(15)		
Classified as long-term contract balances		–	80		–	80DR	
Gross profit or loss on long-term contracts	35	70	30	(90)	(30)		15

PROJECT 1

Profit and Loss Account – cumulative

Included in turnover	145
Included in cost of sales	(110)
Gross profit	35

Balance Sheet

The amount to be included in debtors under 'amounts recoverable on contracts' is calculated as follows:

Cumulative turnover	145
LESS: Cumulative payments on account	(100)
Included in debtors	45

In this case, all the costs incurred to date relate to the contract activity recorded as turnover and are transferred to cost of sales, leaving a zero balance in stocks.

NB If the outcome of the contract could not be assessed with reasonable certainty, no profit would be recognised. If no loss is expected, it may be appropriate to show as turnover a proportion of the total contract value using a zero estimate of profit.

PROJECT 2

Profit and Loss Account – cumulative

Included in turnover	520
Included in cost of sales	(450)
Gross profit	70

Balance sheet

As cumulative payments on account are greater than turnover there is a credit balance, calculated as follows:

Cumulative turnover	520
LESS: Cumulative payments on account	(600)
Excess payments on account	(80)

This credit balance should firstly be offset against any debit balance on this contract included in stocks and then any residual amount should be classified under creditors as a payment received on account as follows:

Total cost incurred to date	510
LESS: Cumulative amounts recorded as cost of sales	(450)
	60

LESS: Excess payments on account (above)	(80)
Included in creditors	(20)

The amount to be included in stocks is zero and the credit balance of 20 is classified as a payment received on account and included in creditors.

The balance sheet note on stocks should disclose separately the net cost of 60 and the applicable payments on account of 60.

PROJECT 3
Profit and Loss Account – cumulative

Included in turnover	380
Included in the cost of sales	(350)
Gross profit	30

Balance sheet
As with Project 2, cumulative payments on account are greater than turnover and there is a credit balance calculated as follows:

Cumulative turnover	380
LESS: Cumulative payments on account	(400)
Excess payments on account	(20)

This credit balance should firstly be offset against any debit balance on this contract included in stocks and the residual amount, if any, should be classified under creditors as a payment received on account.

The amount to be included in stocks under long-term contract balances is calculated as follows:

Total costs incurred to date	450
LESS: Cumulative amounts recorded as costs of sales	(350)
	100
LESS: Excess payments on account (above)	(20)
Included in long-term contract balances	80

The balance sheet note on stocks should disclose separately the net cost of 100 and the applicable payments on account of 20.

PROJECT 4

Profit and Loss Account – cumulative

Included in turnover	200
Included in cost of sales	(290)
Gross loss	(90)

Balance sheet

The amount to be included in debtors under 'amounts recoverable on contracts' is calculated as follows:

Cumulative turnover	200
LESS: Cumulative payments on account	(150)
Included in debtors	50

The amount to be included as a provision/accrual for foreseeable losses is calculated as follows:

Total costs incurred to date	250
LESS: Transferred to cost of sales	(250)
Foreseeable losses on contract as a whole	(40)
	(290)
Classified as provision/accrual for foreseeable losses	(40)

Note that the credit balance of 40 is not offset against the debit balance of 50 included in debtors.

PROJECT 5

Profit and Loss Account – cumulative

Included in turnover	55
Included in cost of sales	(85)
Gross loss	(30)

Balance Sheet

As cumulative payments on account are greater than turnover there is a credit balance, calculated as follows:

Cumulative turnover	55
LESS: Cumulative payments on account	(80)
Excess payments on account	(25)

The credit balance should firstly be deducted from long-term contract balances (after having deducted foreseeable losses) and the residual balance included in creditors under payments received on account as follows:

Total costs incurred to date	100
LESS: Transferred to cost of sales	(55)
Foreseeable losses on contract as a whole	(30)
	(85)
	15
LESS: Excess payments on account (above)	(25)
Included in creditors	(10)

The balance sheet note on stocks should disclose separately the net cost of 15 and the applicable payments on account of 15.

[SSAP 12]
Accounting for depreciation

(Issued December 1977; amended November 1981; revised January 1987)

Contents

Accounting for Depreciation

The provisions of this statement of standard accounting practice should be read in conjunction with the (Explanatory) Foreword to accounting standards *and need not be applied to immaterial items.*

Part 1 – Explanatory note

Fixed assets are those assets which are intended for use on a continuing basis in the enterprise's activities. This statement deals with the depreciation of fixed assets (other than investment properties, goodwill, development costs and investments), including the depreciation of amounts capitalised in respect of finance leases. 1

Virtually all fixed assets have finite useful economic lives. In order for the financial statements to reflect properly all the costs of the enterprise it is necessary for there to be a charge against income in respect of the use of such assets. This charge is referred to as depreciation (or amortisation in the case of leasehold property). 2

Depreciation is the measure of the wearing out, consumption or other reduction in the useful economic life of a fixed asset, whether arising from use, effluxion of time or obsolescence through technological or market changes. Depreciation should be allocated so as to charge a fair proportion of cost or valuation of the asset to each accounting period expected to benefit from its use. 3

4

The assessment of depreciation, and its allocation to accounting periods, involves the consideration of three factors:

(a) the carrying amount of the asset (whether cost or valuation);
(b) the length of the asset's expected useful economic life to the business of the enterprise, having due regard to the incidence of obsolescence; and
(c) the estimated residual value of the asset at the end of its useful economic life in the business of the enterprise.

Where an asset is carried at historical cost, the carrying amount is either the cost of acquisition or, in the case of a self-constructed asset, the cost of its production. It has, however, become increasingly common for enterprises to revalue their fixed assets, in particular freehold and leasehold property, and to incorporate these revalued amounts in their financial statements. This gives useful and relevant information to users of accounts. This statement does not prescribe how frequently assets should be revalued but, where a policy of revaluing assets is adopted, the valuations should be kept up to date. 5

An asset's useful economic life may be: 6

(a) pre-determined, as in the case of a lease;

(b) directly governed by extraction or consumption, as in the case of a mine;
(c) dependent on its physical deterioration through use or effluxion of time;
(d) reduced by economic or technological obsolescence.

7 The useful economic lives of assets should be reviewed regularly and, when necessary, revised. Such a review would normally be undertaken at least every five years, and more frequently where circumstances warrant it. Realistic estimation and regular review of asset lives should result in there being few fully depreciated assets still in economic use. The omission of depreciation on such assets should not be sufficiently material to impair the true and fair view.

8 There is a range of acceptable depreciation methods. Management should select the method regarded as most appropriate to the type of asset and its use in the business so as to allocate depreciation as fairly as possible to the periods expected to benefit from the asset's use. Although the straight line method is the simplest to apply, it may not always be the most appropriate.

9 It is not appropriate to omit charging for the depreciation of an asset on the grounds that its current market value is greater than its net book amount. If account is taken of such increased value by writing up the net book amount of a fixed asset, then an increased charge for depreciation will become necessary.

Part 2 – Definition of terms

10 *Depreciation* is the measure of the wearing out, consumption or other reduction in the useful economic life of a fixed asset whether arising from use, effluxion of time or obsolescence through technological or market changes.

11 The *useful economic life* of an asset is the period over which the present owner will derive economic benefits from its use.

12 *Residual value* is the realisable value of the asset at the end of its useful economic life, based on prices prevailing at the date of acquisition or revaluation, where this has taken place. Realisation costs should be deducted in arriving at the residual value.

13 *Recoverable amount* is the greater of the net realisable value of an asset and, where appropriate, the amount recoverable from its further use.

Part 3 – Standard accounting practice

SCOPE

14 This statement applies to all fixed assets other than:

(a) investment properties, which are dealt with in SSAP 19 'Accounting for investment properties';

(b) goodwill, which is dealt with in SSAP 22 'Accounting for goodwill';
(c) development costs, which are dealt with in SSAP 13 'Accounting for research and development'; and
(d) investments.

ACCOUNTING TREATMENT

Provision for depreciation of fixed assets having a finite useful economic life should be made by allocating the cost (or revalued amount) less estimated residual value of the assets as fairly as possible to the periods expected to benefit from their use. The depreciation methods used should be the ones which are the most appropriate having regard to the types of asset and their use in the business. **15**

The accounting treatment in the profit and loss account should be consistent with that used in the balance sheet. Hence, the depreciation charge in the profit and loss account for the period should be based on the carrying amount of the asset in the balance sheet, whether historical cost or revalued amount. The whole of the depreciation charge should be reflected in the profit and loss account. No part of the depreciation charge should be set directly against reserves. Supplementary depreciation, namely that in excess of the depreciation based on the carrying amount of the assets, should not be charged in the profit and loss account. This does not, however, preclude the appropriation of retained profits to, for example, a reserve specially designated for replacement of fixed assets. **16**

It is essential that asset lives are estimated on a realistic basis. Identical asset lives should be used for the calculation of depreciation both on a historical cost basis and on any bases that reflect the effects of changing prices. **17**

The useful economic lives of assets should be reviewed regularly and, when necessary, revised. The allocation of depreciation to accounting periods involves the exercise of judgement by management in the light of technical, commercial and accounting considerations and, accordingly, requires regular review. When, as a result of experience or of changed circumstances, it is considered that the original estimate of the useful economic life of an asset requires revision, the effect of the change in estimate on the results and financial position needs to be considered. Usually, when asset lives are reviewed regularly, there will be no material distortion of future results or financial position if the net book amount is written off over the revised remaining useful economic life. Where, however, future results would be materially distorted, the adjustment to accumulated depreciation should be recognised in the accounts in accordance with FRS 3 'Reporting Financial Performance' as an exceptional item included under the same statutory format heading as the ongoing depreciation charge. The nature and amount of the adjustment should be disclosed. **18**

If at any time there is a permanent diminution in the value of an asset and the net book amount is considered not to be recoverable in full (perhaps as a result of obsolescence or a fall in demand for a product), the net book amount should be written down immediately to the estimated recoverable amount, which should then be written off **19** over the remaining useful economic life of the asset. If at any time the reasons for making such a provision cease to apply, the provision should be written back to the extent that it is no longer necessary.

20 In the case of an asset that has not been revalued, provisions for permanent diminution in value of an asset (and any reversals) should be charged (credited) in the profit and loss account for the period. (This paragraph does not discuss the treatment of provisions for permanent diminution in value in the case of previously revalued assets.)

21 A change from one method of providing depreciation to another is permissible only on the grounds that the new method will give a fairer presentation of the results and of the financial position. Such a change does not, however, constitute a change of accounting policy; the net book amount should be written off over the remaining useful economic life, commencing with the period in which the change is made.

22 Where it is an enterprise's policy to include some or all of its fixed assets in the financial statements at revalued amounts, the charge for depreciation of such assets should be based on the revalued amounts and the remaining useful economic lives. Depreciation charged prior to the revaluation should not be written back to the profit and loss account, except to the extent that it relates to a provision for permanent diminution in value which is subsequently found to be unnecessary.

23 Freehold land does not normally require a provision for depreciation, unless it is subject to depletion by, for example, the extraction of minerals. However, the value of freehold land may be adversely affected by considerations such as changes in the desirability of its location and in these circumstances it should be written down.

24 Buildings are no different from other fixed assets in that they have a limited useful economic life, albeit usually significantly longer than that of other types of assets. They should, therefore, be depreciated having regard to the same criteria.

DISCLOSURE

25 The following should be disclosed in the financial statements for each major class of depreciable asset:

(a) the depreciation methods used;
(b) the useful economic lives or the depreciation rates used;
(c) total depreciation charged for the period; and
(d) the gross amount of depreciable assets and the related accumulated depreciation.

26 Where there has been a change in the depreciation method used, the effect, if material, should be disclosed in the year of change. The reason for the change should also be disclosed.

27 Where assets have been revalued, the effect of the revaluation on the depreciation charge should, if material, be disclosed in the year of revaluation.

DATE FROM WHICH EFFECTIVE

The accounting and disclosure requirements set out in this statement should be adopted as soon as possible and regarded as standard in respect of financial statements relating to accounting periods beginning on or after 1 January 1987. **28**

Part 4 – Note on legal requirements in the United Kingdom and the Republic of Ireland

UNITED KINGDOM

Paragraphs 30–33 relate to companies, which, in Great Britain, prepare their accounts in accordance with sections 228 and 230* of the Companies Act 1985 or, in Northern Ireland, prepare them in accordance with articles 236 and 238 of the Companies (Northern Ireland) Order 1986. References to 'the Schedule' are to Schedule 4 to the Companies Act 1985 and Schedule 4 to the Companies (Northern Ireland) Order 1986. **29**

Paragraph 1(1) of the Schedule requires that fixed assets be shown in the balance sheet under the headings of intangible assets, tangible assets and investments. Further specified subdivisions within those headings are also required. **30**

Under paragraph 17 of the Schedule the initial carrying amount of any fixed asset must be its purchase price or production cost. A company may, however, avail itself of the alternative accounting rules in Part II Section C of the Schedule under which intangible fixed assets, other than goodwill, my be included at their current cost and tangible fixed assets may be included at market value (as the date of the last valuation) or at their current cost. **31**

Where a fixed asset has a limited useful economic life, paragraph 18 of the Schedule requires that its cost less estimated residual value be reduced by provisions for depreciation so as to write it off systematically over its useful economic life. If the alternative accounting rules are followed, under paragraph 32(1) of the Schedule, the starting point for calculating depreciation is the current cost or market value. Provision must also be made for any permanent diminution in the value of a fixed asset (paragraph 19(2) of the Schedule) but where such a provision is no longer considered to be necessary, paragraph 19(3) of the Schedule requires that it be written back. Disclosure must be made, either on the face of the profit and loss account or in the notes (paragraphs 1(1) and 3(4) of the Schedule), of the depreciation charge and any charge or credit in respect of provisions for diminution in value. **32**

The following additional information must also be disclosed (paragraph 42 of the Schedule). **33**

(a) For each fixed asset balance sheet heading:

***Editor's note:** *Now sections 226 and 227.*

(i) the cost or revalued amount at the beginning and end of the year;
(ii) movements in respect of revaluations, acquisitions, disposals and transfers;
(iii) the accumulated depreciation at the beginning and end of the period and movements in respect of the depreciation charge for the year, disposals of fixed assets and any other adjustments.

(b) Where fixed assets are accounted for using the alternative accounting rules paragraph 33 of the Schedule requires disclosure of the comparable amounts determined under the historical cost accounting rules or the difference between these amounts and those shown in the balance sheet.

(c) Where fixed assets are carried at revalued amounts paragraph 43 of the Schedule requires disclosure of the years of the valuations, the values given in those years and, for assets valued during the financial year, the names or qualifications of the valuers and the valuation bases used.

REPUBLIC OF IRELAND

Accounts under the Companies Act 1963

34 Paragraphs 35–39 below relate to companies which prepare their accounts in compliance with sections 149 and 152 of the Companies Act 1963. References to 'the Schedule' are to the Sixth Schedule to that Act.

35 Paragraph 4 of the Schedule requires that reserves, provisions, liabilities and fixed and current assets be classified under headings appropriate to the company's business, fixed assets being distinguished from current assets. In addition the method of arriving at the amount of fixed assets must be disclosed.

36 Under paragraph 5(1) of the Schedule the amount of the fixed assets must be the difference between the cost (or valuation) and the accumulated provisions in respect of depreciation and diminution in value. This does not apply to goodwill, patents or trademarks.

37 Disclosure is required, under paragraph 5(3) of the Schedule, of the total cost (or valuation) of fixed assets and the total depreciation or amounts written off.

38 Paragraph 12(a) of the Schedule requires disclosure of the profit and loss account charge in respect of depreciation, renewals or diminution in value of fixed assets.

39 If depreciation or replacement of fixed assets is provided for by some method other than a depreciation charge or provision for renewals or is not provided for at all, paragraph 14(2) of the Schedule requires disclosure of the method or the fact that no provision has been made.

Accounts prepared under the Companies (Amendment) Act 1986

40 Paragraphs 41–44 relate to companies which prepare their accounts in compliance with section 3 of the Companies (Amendment) Act 1986 ('the 1986 Act'). References to 'the Schedule' are to the Schedule to that Act

Section 4 of the Act and Part I of the Schedule require that fixed assets be shown in the balance sheet under the headings of intangible assets, tangible assets and financial assets. Further specified sub-divisions within these headings are also required. **41**

Under paragraph 5 of the Schedule the initial carrying amount of any fixed asset must be its purchase price or production cost. A company may, however, avail itself of the alternative accounting rules in Part III of the Schedule under which intangible fixed assets, other than goodwill, may be included at their current cost and tangible fixed assets may be included at market value (as at the date of the last valuation) or at their current cost. **42**

Where a fixed asset has a limited useful economic life, paragraph 6 of the Schedule requires that its cost less estimated residual value may be reduced by provisions for depreciation so as to write it off systematically over its useful economic life. If the alternative accounting rules are followed, under paragraph 20(1) of the Schedule, the starting point for calculating depreciation is the current cost or market value. Provision must also be made for any permanent diminution in the value of a fixed asset (paragraph 7(2) of the Schedule) but where such a provision is no longer considered to be necessary, paragraph 7(3) of the Schedule requires that it be written back. Disclosure must be made, either on the face of the profit and loss account or in the notes (Section 4(1) and (6) of the 1986 Act), of the depreciation charge and any charge or credit in respect of provisions for permanent diminution in value. **43**

The following additional information must also be disclosed (paragraph 29 of the Schedule). **44**

(a) For each fixed asset balance sheet heading:
   (i) the cost or revalued amount at the beginning and end of the year;
   (ii) movements in respect of revaluations, acquisitions, disposals and transfers;
   (iii) the accumulated depreciation at the beginning and end of the period and movements in respect of the depreciation charge for the year, disposals of fixed assets and any other adjustments.

(b) Where fixed assets are accounted for using the alternative accounting rules paragraph 21 of the Schedule requires disclosure of the comparable amounts determined under the historical cost accounting rules or the difference between these amounts and those shown in the balance sheet.

(c) Where fixed assets are carried at revalued amounts, paragraph 30 of the Schedule requires disclosure of the years of the valuations, the values given in those years and, for assets valued during the financial year, the names or qualifications of the valuers and the valuation bases used.

Part 5 – Compliance with International Accounting Standard No. 4 'Depreciation Accounting'

45 Compliance with the requirements of this statement will automatically ensure compliance with International Accounting Standard No. 4 'Depreciation Accounting' so far as assets within the scope of this statement are concerned.

[SSAP 13]
Accounting for research and development

(Issued December 1977; revised January 1989)

Contents

Accounting for research and development

The provisions of this statement of standard accounting practice should be read in conjunction with the (Explanatory) Foreword to accounting standards *and need not be applied to immaterial items.*

Part 1 – Explanatory note

BASIC CONCEPTS

The accounting policies to be followed in respect of research and development expenditure must have regard to the fundamental accounting concepts including the 'accruals' concept by which revenue and costs are accrued, matched and dealt with in the period to which they relate and the 'prudence' concept by which revenue and profits are not anticipated but are recognised only when realised in the form either of cash or of other assets the ultimate cash realisation of which can be established with reasonable certainty. It is a corollary of the prudence concept that expenditure should be written off in the period in which it arises unless its relationship to the revenue of a future period can be established with reasonable certainty. 1

THE DIFFERENT TYPES OF RESEARCH AND DEVELOPMENT EXPENDITURE

The term 'research and development' is currently used to cover a wide range of activities, including those in the services sector. The definitions of the different types of research and development used in this statement are based on those used by the Organisation for Economic Co-operation and Development for the purposes of collecting data world-wide. 2

Classification of expenditure is often dependent on the type of business and its organisation. However, it is generally possible to recognise three broad categories of activity, namely pure research, applied research and development. The definitions of the individual categories are set out in Part 2. 3

The dividing line between these categories of expenditure is often indistinct and particular expenditure may have characteristics of more than one category. This is especially so when new products or services are developed through research and development to production, when the activities may have characteristics of both development and production. 4

Research and development activity is distinguished from non-research activity by the presence or absence of an appreciable element of innovation. If the activity departs 5 from routine and breaks new ground it should normally be included; if it follows an established pattern it should normally be excluded.

6 Examples of activities that would normally be included in research and development are:

(a) experimental, theoretical or other work aimed at the discovery of new knowledge, or the advancement of existing knowledge;
(b) searching for applications of that knowledge;
(c) formulation and design of possible applications for such work;
(d) testing in search for, or evaluation of, product, service or process alternatives;
(e) design, construction and testing of pre-production prototypes and models and development batches;
(f) design of products, services, processes or systems involving new technology or substantially improving those already produced or installed;
(g) construction and operation of pilot plants.

7 Examples of activities that would normally be excluded from research and development would include:

(a) testing analysis either of equipment or product for purposes of quality or quantity control;
(b) periodic alterations to existing products, services or processes even though these may represent some improvement;
(c) operational research not tied to a specific research and development activity;
(d) cost of corrective action in connection with break-downs during commercial production;
(e) legal and administrative work in connection with patent applications, records and litigation and the sale or licensing of patents;
(f) activity, including design and construction engineering, relating to the construction, relocation, rearrangement or start-up of facilities or equipment other than facilities or equipment whose sole use is for a particular research and development project;
(g) market research.

THE ACCOUNTING TREATMENT OF RESEARCH AND DEVELOPMENT

8 Expenditure incurred on pure and applied research can be regarded as part of a continuing operation required to maintain a company's business and its competitive position. In general, no one particular period rather than any other will be expected to benefit and therefore it is appropriate that these costs should be written off as they are incurred. Expenditure on pure or applied research may not be treated as an asset (Companies Act 1985, Schedule 4, paragraph 3(2)(c)).

9 The development of new products or services is, however, distinguishable from pure and applied research. Expenditure on such development is normally undertaken with a reasonable expectation of specific commercial success and of future benefits arising from the work, either from increased revenue and related profits or from reduced costs. On these grounds it may be argued that such expenditure, to the extent that it is recoverable, should be deferred to be matched against the future revenue.

It will only be practicable to evaluate the potential future benefits of development expenditure if: 10

(a) there is a clearly defined project; and
(b) the related expenditure is separately identifiable.

The outcome of such a project would then need to be examined for: 11

(a) its technical feasibility; and
(b) its ultimate commercial viability considered in the light of factors such as:
    (i) likely market conditions (including competing products or services);
    (ii) public opinion;
    (iii) consumer and environmental legislation.

Furthermore a project will be of value: 12

(a) only if further development costs to be incurred on the same project, together with related production, selling and administrative costs, will be more than covered by related revenues; and
(b) adequate resources exist, or are reasonably expected to be available, to enable the project to be completed and to provide any consequential increases in working capital.

The elements of uncertainty inherent in the considerations set out in paragraphs 11 and 12 are considerable. There will be a need for different persons with different types of judgement to be involved in assessing the technical, commercial and financial viability of the project. Combinations of the possible differing assessments which they might validly make can produce different assessments of the existence and amounts of future benefits. 13

If these uncertainties are viewed in the context of the concept of prudence, the future benefits of most development projects would be too uncertain to justify carrying the expenditure forward. Nevertheless, in certain industries it is considered that there are a number of major development projects that satisfy the stringent criteria set out in paragraphs 10 to 12. Accordingly, when the expenditure on development projects is judged on a prudent view of available evidence to satisfy these criteria, it may be carried forward and amortised over the period expected to benefit. 14

At each accounting date the unamortised balance of development expenditure should be examined project by project to ensure that it still fulfils the criteria in paragraphs 10 to 12. Where any doubt exists as to the continuation of those circumstances the balance should be written off. 15

Fixed assets may be acquired or constructed in order to provide facilities for research and/or development activities. The use of such fixed assets usually extends over a 16 number of accounting periods and accordingly they should be capitalised and written off over their useful life. The depreciation so written off should be included as part of the expenditure on research and development and disclosed in accordance with SSAP 12.

EXCEPTIONS

17 Where companies enter into a firm contract:

(a) to carry out development work on behalf of third parties on such terms that the related expenditure is to be fully reimbursed, or

(b) to develop and manufacture at an agreed price calculated to reimburse expenditure on development as well as on manufacture,

any such expenditure which has not been reimbursed at the balance sheet date should be dealt with as contract work-in-progress.

18 Expenditure incurred in locating and exploiting oil, gas and mineral deposits in the extractive industries does not fall within the definition of research and development used in this accounting standard. Development of new surveying methods and techniques as an integral part of research on geological phenomena should, however, be included in research and development.

DISCLOSURE

19 While there are uncertainties inherent in research and development projects, such activities are important in forming a view of a company's future prospects. Detailed disclosure raises considerable problems of definition and the disclosure requirements of this standard are therefore limited to:

(a) accounting policy as required by SSAP 2;

(b) disclosure of the total amount of research and development expenditure charged in the profit and loss account, distinguishing between the current year's expenditure and amounts amortised from deferred expenditure;

(c) the movements on deferred development expenditure during the year.

20 Having regard to the problems of definition and disclosure referred to above, the scope of disclosure required under paragraph 19(b) is (except in the case of Republic of Ireland companies) restricted in effect to companies which are public limited companies, or special category companies*, or subsidiaries of such companies, or which exceed by a multiple of 10 the criteria for defining a medium-sized company under the Companies Act 1985.

***Editor's note:** Now banking and insurance companies.*

Part 2 – Definition of terms

The following definition is used for the purpose of this statement:

Research and development expenditure means expenditure falling into one or more of the following broad categories (except to the extent that it relates to locating or exploiting oil, gas or mineral deposits or is reimbursable by third parties either directly or under the terms of a firm contract to develop and manufacture at an agreed price calculated to reimburse both elements of expenditure): **21**

(a) *pure (or basic) research:* Experimental or theoretical work undertaken primarily to acquire new scientific or technical knowledge for its own sake rather than directed towards any specific aim or application;

(b) *applied research:* Original or critical investigation undertaken in order to gain new scientific or technical knowledge and directed towards a specific practical aim or objective;

(c) *development:* Use of scientific or technical knowledge in order to produce new or substantially improved materials, devices, products or services, to install new processes or systems prior to the commencement of commercial production or commercial applications, or to improving substantially those already produced or installed.

Part 3 – Standard accounting practice

SCOPE

This standard applies to all financial statements intended to give a true and fair view of the financial position of profit or loss, but, except in the case of Republic of Ireland companies (see paragraphs 45 and 46), the provisions set out in paragraph 31 regarding the disclosure of the total amounts of research and development charged in the profit and loss account need not be applied by an entity that: **22**

(a) is not a public limited company or a special category company* (as defined by Section 257 of the Companies Act 1985)† or a holding company that has a public limited company or a special category company as a subsidiary; and

(b) satisfies the criteria, multiplied in each case by 10, for defining a medium-sized company under Section 248‡ of the Companies Act 1985, as amended from time

***Editor's note:** *Now banking and insurance companies as defined in section 744 of the Companies Act 1985.*

† There is no exact equivalent of 'special category companies' in the Republic of Ireland. The Sixth Schedule to the 1963 Act refers to 'special classes of company' which include banking, discount and assurance companies but not shipping companies.

‡ ***Editor's note:*** *Now section 247.*

to time by statutory instrument and applied in accordance with the provisions of Section 249* of the Act.†

ACCOUNTING TREATMENT

23 The cost of fixed assets acquired or constructed in order to provide facilities for research and development activities over a number of accounting periods should be capitalised and written off over their useful lives through the profit and loss account.

24 Expenditure on pure and applied research (other than that referred to in paragraph 23) should be written off in the year of expenditure through the profit and loss account.

25 Development expenditure should be written off in the year of expenditure except in the following circumstances when it may be deferred to future periods:

(a) there is a clearly defined project, and
(b) the related expenditure is separately identifiable, and
(c) the outcome of such a project has been assessed with reasonable certainty as to:
  (i) its technical feasibility, and
  (ii) its ultimate commercial viability considered in the light of factors such as likely market conditions (including competing products), public opinion, consumer and environmental legislation, and
(d) the aggregate of the deferred development costs, any further development costs, and related production, selling and administration costs is reasonably expected to be exceeded by related future sales or other revenues, and
(e) adequate resources exist, or are reasonably expected to be available, to enable the project to be completed and to provide any consequential increases in working capital.

26 In the foregoing circumstances development expenditure may be deferred to the extent that its recovery can reasonably regarded as assured.

27 If an accounting policy of deferral of development expenditure is adopted, it should be applied to all developmental projects that meet the criteria in paragraph 25.

28 If development costs are deferred to future periods, they should be amortised. The amortisation should commence with the commercial production or application of the product, service, process or system and should be allocated on a systematic basis to each accounting period, by reference to either the sale or use of the product, service, process or system or the period over which these are expected to be sold or used.

***Editor's note:** *Now section 247.*

†Equivalent legal references.

Great Britain	Northern Ireland	Republic of Ireland
Companies Act 1985	*Companies (Northern Ireland) Order 1986*	*Companies (Amendment) Act 1986*
Section 248 } (Now section 247)	Article 256 (as amended)	Section 8
Section 249 } (Now section 247)	Article 257	Section 9 Companies Act 1963
Section 257 (Now section 744)	Article 265	Sixth Schedule, paragraph 23

Deferred development expenditure for each project should be reviewed at the end of each accounting period and where the circumstances which have justified the deferral of the expenditure (paragraph 25) no longer apply, or are considered doubtful, the expenditure, to the extent to which it is considered to be irrecoverable, should be written off immediately project by project. 29

DISCLOSURE

The accounting policy on research and development expenditure should be stated and explained. 30

The total amount of research and development expenditure charged in the profit and loss account should be disclosed, analysed between the current year's expenditure and amounts amortised from deferred expenditure. 31

Movements on deferred development expenditure and the amount carried forward at the beginning and the end of the period should be disclosed under intangible fixed assets in the balance sheet. 32

DATE FROM WHICH EFFECTIVE

The accounting and disclosure requirements set out in this statement should be adopted as soon as possible and regarded as standard in respect of financial statements relating to accounting periods beginning on or after 1 January 1989. 33

Part 4 – Note on legal requirements in Great Britain and Northern Ireland

All paragraph references unless otherwise indicated are to the Companies Act 1985 and the Companies (Northern Ireland) Order 1986.

Paragraph 3(1) of Schedule 4 enables any items required to be shown in a company's balance sheet or profit and loss account to be shown in greater detail than required by the format adopted. 34

Paragraph 3(2)(c) of Schedule 4 provides that a company's balance sheet or profit and loss account may include an item representing or covering the amount of any asset or liability, income or expenditure not otherwise covered by any of the items listed in the accounts format adopted. Cost of research shall not be treated as an asset in any company's balance sheet. 35

Paragraph 19(1) of Schedule 4 does not allow provision to be made for a temporary diminution in value other than for a fixed asset investment. 36

Paragraph 19(2) of Schedule 4 requires provision for diminution in value to be made in respect of any fixed asset which has diminished in value if the reduction is expected to be 37 permanent (whether its useful economic life is limited or not) and the amount to be included in respect of it to be reduced accordingly. Any such provisions not shown in the profit and loss account shall be disclosed (either separately or in aggregate) in a note to the accounts.

38 Paragraph 19(3) requires that where the reasons for which any provision was made have ceased to apply to any extent, then the provision shall be written back to the extent that it is no longer necessary. Any amounts written back in accordance with this sub-paragraph which are not shown in the profit and loss account shall be disclosed (either separately or in aggregate) in a note to the accounts.

39 Paragraph 20(1) of Schedule 4 requires that notwithstanding that an item in respect of development costs is included under fixed assets in the balance sheet formats set out in Part 1 of Schedule 4, an amount may only be included in a company's balance sheet in respect of development costs in special circumstances.

40 Paragraph 20(2) of Schedule 4 requires that if any amount is included in a company's balance sheet in respect of development costs the following information shall be given in a note to the accounts:

(a) the period over which the amount of those costs originally capitalised is being or is to be written off; and
(b) the reasons for capitalising the development costs in question.

41 Paragraph 6(c) of Schedule 7 requires the Directors' Report to contain an indication of the activities (if any) of the company and its subsidiaries in the field of research and development.

42 Section 269(2)(b) of the Companies Act 1985 on the treatment of development costs requires that where the unamortised development expenditure carried forward is not treated as a realised loss when determining distributable reserves, the notes to the financial statements shall disclose:

(a) the fact that the amount of the unamortised development expenditure is not to be treated as a realised loss for the purposes of calculating distributable profits; and
(b) the circumstances that the directors relied upon to justify their decision not to treat the unamortised development expenditure as a realised loss.

Part 5 – Note on legal requirements in the Republic of Ireland

References are to the Companies (Amendment) Act 1986 and to the Schedule to that Act unless otherwise stated.

43 Section 4(5) of the Act enables any items required to be shown in a company's balance sheet or profit and loss account to be shown in greater detail than required by the format adopted.

44 Section 4(12) of the Act provides that the balance sheet, or profit and loss account, of a company may include an item representing or covering the amount of any asset or liability or income or expenditure not otherwise covered by any of the items listed in the format adopted but that costs of research shall not be treated as assets in the balance sheet of a company.

Paragraph 43(4) of the Schedule requires the amount expended on research and development in the financial year, and any amount committed in respect of research and development in subsequent years, to be stated. **45**

Paragraph 43(5) of the Schedule provides that where, in the opinion of the directors, the disclosure of any information required by Paragraph 43(4) would be prejudicial to the interests of the company, that information need not be disclosed, but the fact that any such information has not been disclosed shall be stated. **46**

Paragraph 7(1) of the Schedule does not allow provision to be made for a temporary diminution in value other than for a fixed asset investment. **47**

Paragraph 7(2) of the Schedule requires provision for diminution in value to be made in respect of any fixed asset which has diminished in value if the reduction is expected to be permanent (whether its useful economic life is limited or not) and the amount to be included in respect of it shall be reduced accordingly. Any such provisions which are not shown in the profit and loss account shall be disclosed (either separately or in aggregate) in a note to the accounts. **48**

Paragraph 7(3) of the Schedule requires that where the reasons for which any provision was made have ceased to apply to any extent, then the provision should be written back to the extent that it is no longer necessary. Any amounts written back in accordance with this sub-paragraph which are not shown in the profit and loss account shall be disclosed (either separately or in aggregate) in a note to the accounts. **49**

Paragraph 8(1) of the Schedule requires that notwithstanding that an item in respect of development costs is included under fixed assets in the balance sheet formats set out in Part 1 of the Schedule, an amount may only be included in a company's balance sheet in respect of development costs in special circumstances. **50**

Paragraph 8(2) of the Schedule requires that if any amount is included in a company's balance sheet in respect of development costs, the following information shall be given in a note to the accounts: **51**

(a) the period over which the amount of those costs originally capitalised is being or is to be written off, and
(b) the reasons for capitalising the development costs in question.

Section 13(c) of the Act requires the Directors' Report to contain an indication of the activity, if any, of the company and its subsidiaries, if any, in the field of research and development. **52**

Section 45A of the Companies (Amendment) Act 1983 on the treatment of **53** development costs, provides that where development costs are shown in a company's accounts any amount shown as an asset in respect of those costs shall be treated as a realised loss for the purpose of determining profits available for distribution. This provision does not apply to any part of that amount representing an unrealised profit made on revaluation of these costs; nor does it apply if:

(a) there are special circumstances justifying the directors of the company concerned in deciding that the amount mentioned in respect thereof in the company's accounts shall not be treated as a realised loss, and

(b) the note to the accounts required by paragraph 8(2) of the Schedule states that the amount is not to be so treated and explains the circumstances relied upon to justify the decision of the directors to that effect.

Part 6 – Compliance with International Accounting Standard No. 9 'Accounting for research and development activities'

54 The requirements of International Accounting Standard No. 9 'Accounting for research and development activities'* accord very closely with the content of the United Kingdom and Irish Accounting Standard No. 13 (Revised) 'Accounting for research and development' and accordingly compliance with SSAP 13 (Revised) will ensure compliance with IAS 9 in all material aspects.

***Editor's note:** *A revised version of IAS 9 was issued in November 1993.*

[SSAP 15]
Accounting for deferred tax

(Issued October 1978; revised May 1985; amended December 1992)

Contents

Accounting for deferred tax

The provisions of this statement of standard accounting practice should be read in conjunction with the (Explanatory) Foreword to accounting standards *and need not be applied to immaterial items.*

Part 1 – Explanatory note

SCOPE

This statement is concerned with accounting for tax on profits and surpluses which are recognised in the financial statements in one period but assessed in another. It thus relates primarily to deferred corporation tax and income tax in the United Kingdom and in the Republic of Ireland and, insofar as the principles are similar, to overseas taxes on profits payable by UK and Irish enterprises or their subsidiaries. 1

A number of other taxes, including value added tax, petroleum revenue tax and some overseas taxes, are not assessed directly on profits for an accounting period and are therefore not addressed specifically in this statement. For such taxes, enterprises should generally follow the principle underlying this statement, that deferred tax should be provided to the extent that it is probable that a liability or asset will crystallise but not to the extent that it is probable that a liability or asset will not crystallise. 2

BACKGROUND

The amount of tax payable on the profits of a particular period often bears little relationship to the amount of income and expenditure appearing in the financial statements. This results from the different basis on which profits are arrived at for the purpose of tax computations as opposed to the basis on which profits are stated in financial statements. 3

The different basis of arriving at profits for tax purposes derives from two main sources. Firstly, certain types of income are tax-free and certain types of expenditure are disallowable, giving rise to 'permanent differences' between taxable and accounting profits. Permanent differences also arise where there are tax allowances or charges with no corresponding amount in the financial statements. Secondly, there are items which are included in the financial statements of a period different from that in which they are dealt with for tax purposes, giving rise to 'timing differences'; thus revenue, gains, expenditure and losses may be included in financial statements either earlier or later than they enter into the computation of profit for tax purposes. 4

Extraordinary items, prior year adjustments and movements on reserves are not included in profit or loss on ordinary activities but may also have an impact on the total tax payable. 5

BASIS OF PROVISION

6 There are three principal bases for computing deferred tax.

7 The first is called 'nil provision' or 'flow through' and is based on the principle that only the tax payable in respect of a period should be charged in that period. No provision for deferred tax would therefore be made. Those who hold this view argue that any tax liability arises on taxable profits, not accounting profits, and therefore consider that it is necessary to provide tax only on taxable profits. Further, any liability arising on timing differences will depend on the incidence of future taxable profits and may therefore be difficult to quantify.

8 A basis radically different from nil provision is 'full provision', sometimes called 'comprehensive allocation'. This is based on the principle that financial statements for a period should recognise the tax effects, whether current or deferred, of all transactions occurring in that period.

9 An advantage of either of these bases is that the amounts involved can be precisely quantified. However, a crucial disadvantage is that they can lead to a purely arithmetical approach, in which certainty of calculation is given precedence over a reasoned assessment of what the tax effects of transactions will actually be.

10 The effect of timing and other differences on tax charges in relation to reported profits would be of little significance if taxation were not regarded as relevant to the performance of the enterprise for the period, and hence the only accepted indicator of performance were to be the result before tax. However, the result after tax is also widely regarded as an important indicator of performance and this will be distorted by accounting for deferred tax where it is probable that a liability or asset will not crystallise, or by failing to account for deferred tax where it is probable that a liability or asset will crystallise.

11 So far as the balance sheet is concerned, the amount of shareholders' funds and its relationship with the amount of funds from other sources may similarly be distorted by accounting for deferred tax where it is probable that a liability or asset will not crystallise, or by failing to account for deferred tax where it is probable that a liability or asset will crystallise.

12 A third basis is 'partial provision', which requires that deferred tax should be accounted for in respect of the net amount by which it is probable that any payment of tax will be temporarily deferred or accelerated by the operation of timing differences which will reverse in the foreseeable future without being replaced. Partial provision recognises that, if an enterprise is not expected to reduce the scale of its operations significantly, it will often have what amounts to a hard core of timing differences so that the payment of some tax will be permanently deferred. On this basis, deferred tax has to be provided only where it is probable that tax will become payable as a result of the reversal of timing differences. Because it is based on an assessment of what will actually be the position, partial provision is preferable to the other bases described above.

PENSIONS AND OTHER POST-RETIREMENT BENEFITS

Paragraph 32A permits preparers of financial statements, where they consider it appropriate in their particular circumstances, to use the same recognition criteria for the deferred tax implications of pensions and other post-retirement benefits as in accounting for the obligations to provide those benefits. **12A**

Where an enterprise is contemplating the recognition of a deferred tax asset that is permitted by paragraph 32A in respect of a provision for pensions or other post-retirement obligations it should be noted that the normal rules regarding the recoverability of assets are applicable. **12B**

METHOD OF COMPUTATION

There are two principal methods of computation. The first is the deferral method, under which the tax effects of timing differences are calculated using the tax rates current when the differences arise. No adjustments are made subsequently if tax rates change. Reversals are accounted for using the tax rates in force when the timing differences originated, although in practice the effects of reversals and new timing differences are sometimes accounted for as one item. Those who support this method recognise that, when tax rates change, this method will not give an indication of the amount of tax payable or recoverable. Any deferred tax balance will therefore be a deferred tax credit or charge rather than a liability or asset. When tax rates change there is no need to revise the deferred tax already provided. Thus the tax charge or credit for the period relates solely to that period and is not distorted by any adjustments relating to prior periods. **13**

The other method is the liability method, under which deferred tax provisions are calculated at the rate at which it is estimated that tax will be paid (or recovered) when the timing differences reverse. Usually the current tax rate is used as the best estimate, unless changes in tax rates are known in advance. As a result, deferred tax provisions are revised to reflect changes in tax rates. Thus the tax charge or credit for the period may include adjustments of accounting estimates relating to prior periods. The deferred tax provision represents the best estimate of the amount which would be payable or recoverable if the relevant timing differences reversed. **14**

The liability method is the method consistent with the aim of partial provision, which is to provide the deferred tax which it is probable will be payable or recoverable. **15**

METHOD OF PRESENTATION

It is generally accepted that, however they have been calculated, tax effects should be shown in financial statements separately from the items or transactions to which they relate. An alternative would be to treat the tax effects of timing differences as integral parts of the revenue or expenditure, assets, provisions or liabilities to which they relate, rather than showing them separately. This 'net of tax' method recognises that the value of assets and liabilities is affected by tax considerations, in particular tax deductibility. **16**

On the other hand, it fails to distinguish between a transaction and its tax consequences and therefore should not be used in financial statements.

Part 2 – Definition of terms

17 *Deferred tax* is the tax attributable to timing differences.

18 *Timing differences* are differences between profits or losses as computed for tax purposes and results as stated in financial statements, which arise from the inclusion of items of income and expenditure in tax computations in periods different from those in which they are included in financial statements. Timing differences originate in one period and are capable of reversal in one or more subsequent periods.

19 A loss for tax purposes which is available to relieve future profits from tax constitutes a timing difference.

20 The revaluation of an asset (including an investment in an associated or subsidiary company) will create a timing difference when it is incorporated in the balance sheet, insofar as the profit or loss that would result from realisation at the revalued amount is taxable, unless disposal of the revalued asset and of any subsequent replacement assets would not result in a tax liability, after taking account of any expected rollover relief.

21 The retention of earnings overseas will create a timing difference only if:

(a) there is an intention or obligation to remit them; and
(b) remittance would result in a tax liability after taking account of any related double tax relief.

22 *Financial statements* are balance sheets, profit and loss accounts, statements of source and application of funds, notes and other statements, which collectively are intended to give a true and fair view of financial position and profit or loss.

23 The *liability method* is a method of computing deferred tax whereby it is calculated at the rate of tax that it is estimated will be applicable when the timing differences reverse. Under the liability method deferred tax not provided is calculated at the expected long-term tax rate.

Part 3 – Standard accounting practice

GENERAL

24 Deferred tax should be computed under the liability method.

25 Tax deferred or accelerated by the effect of timing differences should be accounted for to the extent that it is probable that a liability or asset will crystallise.

26 Tax deferred or accelerated by the effect of timing differences should not be accounted for to the extent that it is probable that a liability or asset will not crystallise.

The assessment of whether deferred tax liabilities or assets will or will not crystallise should be based upon reasonable assumptions. 27

The assumptions should take into account all relevant information available up to the date on which the financial statements are approved by the board of directors, and also the intentions of management. Ideally this information will include financial plans or projections covering a period of years sufficient to enable an assessment to be made of the likely pattern of future tax liabilities. A prudent view should be taken in the assessment of whether a tax liability will crystallise, particularly where the financial plans or projections are susceptible to a high degree of uncertainty or are not fully developed for the appropriate period (see paragraph 52). 28

The provision for deferred tax liabilities should be reduced by any deferred tax debit balances arising from separate categories of timing differences and any advance corporation tax which is available for offset against those liabilities (see Appendix paragraphs 16 and 17). 29

Deferred tax net debit balances should not be carried forward as assets, except to the extent that they are expected to be recoverable without replacement by equivalent debit balances (see Appendix paragraphs 13–15). 30

Debit balances arising in respect of advance corporation tax on dividends payable or proposed at the balance sheet date should be carried forward to the extent that it is foreseen that sufficient corporation tax will be assessed on the profits or income of the succeeding accounting period, against which the advance corporation tax is available for offset. 31

Debit balances arising in respect of advance corporation tax other than on dividends payable or proposed at the balance sheet date should be written off unless their recovery is assured beyond reasonable doubt. Such recovery will normally be assured only where the debit balances are recoverable out of corporation tax arising on profits or income of the succeeding accounting period, without replacement by equivalent debit balances. 32

Notwithstanding the other requirements of this Statement of Standard Accounting Practice, either the full provision basis or the partial provision basis may be used in accounting for the deferred tax implications of pensions and other post-retirement benefits accounted for in accordance with SSAP 24 'Accounting for pension costs' and UITF 6 'Accounting for post-retirement benefits other than pensions'. The policy adopted should be disclosed. 32A

PROFIT AND LOSS ACCOUNT

Deferred tax relating to the ordinary activities of the enterprise should be shown separately as a part of the tax on profit or loss on ordinary activities, either on the face of the profit and loss account or in a note. 33

Deferred tax relating to any extraordinary items should be shown separately as part of 34 the tax on extraordinary items, either on the face of the profit and loss account or in a note.

35 The amount of any unprovided deferred tax in respect of the period should be disclosed in a note, analysed into its major components.

36 Adjustments to deferred tax arising from changes in tax rates and tax allowances should normally be disclosed separately as part of the tax charge for the period.

BALANCE SHEET

37 The deferred tax balance, and its major components, should be disclosed in the balance sheet or notes.

38 Transfers to and from deferred tax should be disclosed in a note.

39 Where amounts of deferred tax arise which relate to movements on reserves (e.g., resulting from the expected disposal of revalued assets) the amounts transferred to or from deferred tax should be shown separately as part of such movements.

40 The total amount of any unprovided deferred tax should be disclosed in a note, analysed into its major components.

41 Where the potential amount of deferred tax on a revalued asset is not shown because the revaluation does not constitute a timing difference under paragraph 20, the fact that it does not constitute a timing difference and that tax has therefore not been quantified should be stated.

42 Where the value of an asset is shown in a note because it differs materially from its book amount, the note should also show the tax effects, if any, that would arise if the asset were realised at the balance sheet date at the noted value.

GROUPS

43 Where a company is a member of a group, it should, in accounting for deferred tax, take account of any group relief which, on reasonable evidence, is expected to be available and any charge which will be made for such relief. Assumptions made as to the availability of group relief and payment therefor should be stated.

44 Deferred tax in respect of the remittance of overseas earnings should be accounted for in accordance with the provisions of this statement. Where deferred tax is not provided on earnings retained overseas, this should be stated.

DATE FROM WHICH EFFECTIVE

The accounting practices set out in this statement should be adopted as soon as possible and regarded as standard in respect of financial statements relating to accounting periods beginning on or after 1 April 1985.* **45**

Part 4 – Note on legal requirements in Great Britain

RELATIVE TO FINANCIAL STATEMENTS PREPARED IN COMPLIANCE WITH THE REQUIREMENTS OF SECTIONS 228 AND 230 OF THE COMPANIES ACT 1985†

The references to 'the Schedule' below are to Schedule 4 to the Companies Act 1985. Format references are to the formats in paragraph 8 of the Schedule: **46**

Deferred tax provisions should be included in the balance sheet under the heading 'Provisions for liabilities and charges' as part of the provision for 'Taxation, including deferred taxation' (balance sheet format 1–I, 2, format 2 – liabilities B, 2). Paragraph 89 of the Schedule describes provisions for liabilities or charges as 'any amount retained as reasonably necessary for the purpose of providing for any liability or loss which is either likely to be incurred, or certain to be incurred but uncertain as to the amount or as to the date on which it will arise'. **47**

The amount of any provisions for taxation other than deferred taxation has to be stated (paragraph 47 of the Schedule). Taking this requirement together with that referred to in paragraph 47 above, the balance of deferred tax will be ascertainable as the remaining figure. Tax provisions are distinguished from tax liabilities falling due within, or after more than, one year, which are shown separately under creditors in the balance sheet (balance sheet format 1–E, 8 and H, 8, format 2 – liabilities C, 8 and note 9 on the balance sheet format). **48**

Paragraph 46(1) of the Schedule requires the information set out in paragraph 46(2) of the Schedule to be given where any amount is transferred to any provisions for liabilities and charges or from any provision for liabilities and charges, except where the transfer is for the purpose for which the provision was established. The information required in paragraph 46(2) of the Schedule is: **49**

'(a) the amount of the reserves or provisions as at the date of the beginning of the financial year and as at the balance sheet date respectively;

***Editor's note:** The amendment in December 1992 (the insertion of paragraphs 12A, 12B and 32A) became effective immediately.*

*†**Editor's note:** Now sections 226 and 227.*

(b) any amounts transferred to or from the reserves or provisions during that year; and

(c) the source and application respectively of any amounts so transferred.'

50 Any deferred tax carried forward as an asset should be included under the heading of 'Prepayments and accrued income' either within 'Current Assets/Debtors', if it is current, or separately under main heading D. In the former case, any amount falling due after more than one year should be shown separately (note 5 on the balance sheet formats).

51 In determining the aggregate amount of deferred tax, this statement requires deferred tax debit balances to be matched with deferred tax liabilities against which they will be able to be offset. This is in accordance with paragraph 14 of the Schedule as individual deferred tax debit balances and liabilities which can be offset for tax purposes are not separate items, which under paragraph 5 of the Schedule cannot be offset but are elements of an aggregate deferred tax asset or liability.

52 The amount of any item has to be determined on a prudent basis. In particular, all liabilities and losses which have arisen or are likely to arise in respect of the financial year to which the accounts relate or a previous financial year have to be taken into account (paragraph 12 of the Schedule).

53 Paragraph 50(2) of the Schedule requires information to be given with respect to the amount or estimated amount of any contingent liability not provided for, its legal nature and any valuable security provided. The ASC has obtained legal advice to the effect that unprovided deferred tax is a contingent liability, except where the prospect of it becoming payable is so remote that it does not amount to a contingent liability at all.

54 Where a company is a member of a group, any contingent deferred tax liability on behalf of other members of the group has to be shown separately in the financial statements of any company which has undertaken the commitment, analysed between amounts in respect of any subsidiary and amounts in respect of any holding company or fellow subsidiary (paragraph 50(6) of the Schedule).

55 The tax treatment of amounts credited or debited to the revaluation reserve has to be disclosed (paragraph 34(4) of the Schedule).

56 The basis on which the charge for United Kingdom tax is computed has to be stated (paragraph 54(1) of the Schedule). Particulars are required of any special circumstances affecting the tax liability for the financial year or succeeding financial years (paragraph 54(2) of the Schedule).

57 Paragraph 54(3) of the Schedule requires the amounts shown under the items 'tax on profit or loss on ordinary activities' and 'tax on extraordinary profit or loss', to be analysed between:

(a) United Kingdom corporation tax, before and after any double tax relief;

(b) United Kingdom income tax; and
(c) overseas tax.

Deferred tax is not specifically referred to in the profit and loss account formats. However, this statement requires any deferred tax to be separately shown as part of the tax on profit or loss on ordinary activities or of the tax on extraordinary profit or loss, as appropriate, either on the face of the profit and loss account or in a note.

RELATIVE TO FINANCIAL STATEMENTS PREPARED IN COMPLIANCE WITH THE REQUIREMENTS OF SECTIONS 258 AND 259 OF THE COMPANIES ACT 1985*

Sections 258 and 259 of the Companies Act 1985* are applicable to some banking, insurance and shipping companies and their holding companies, as laid down in section 257 of the Act. The references to 'the Schedule' below are to Schedule 9 to the Companies Act 1985. **58**

Paragraph 9 of the Schedule requires that any amount set aside to prevent undue fluctuation in charges for taxation should be disclosed. If any of that sum is used for another purpose, that fact has to be disclosed together with the amount (paragraph 13(14) of the Schedule). **59**

Paragraph 13(7) of the Schedule requires the general nature of all contingent liabilities not provided for to be stated and, where practicable, the aggregate amount or estimated amount of those liabilities, if it is material. The ASC has obtained legal advice to the effect that unprovided deferred tax is a contingent liability, except where the prospect of it becoming payable is so remote that it does not amount to a contingent liability at all. **60**

Paragraph 14(1)(c) of the Schedule requires the tax charge to be analysed between: **61**

(a) United Kingdom corporation tax, before and after any double tax relief;
(b) United Kingdom income tax; and
(c) overseas tax.

There is no requirement in the Schedule for deferred tax to be disclosed separately in the profit and loss account or the notes thereto. However, this statement requires any deferred tax to be shown separately, distinguishing between deferred tax on profit or loss on ordinary activities and deferred tax on extraordinary profit or loss, either on the face of the profit and loss account or in a note.

The basis on which the charge for United Kingdom taxation is computed has to be stated (paragraph 18(3) of the Schedule). Particulars are required of any special circumstances affecting the liability for the financial year or succeeding financial years (paragraph 18(4) of the schedule). **62**

***Editor's note:** *Now sections 255 and 255A and no longer applicable to shipping companies. Paragraphs 58 to 62 of this SSAP are no longer applicable. The legal requirements for banking companies and groups are set out in Schedule 9 (as amended) to the Companies Act 1985. The legal requirements for insurance companies and groups are set out in Schedule 9A (as amended).*

Part 5 – Note on legal requirements and other matters in Ireland*

NORTHERN IRELAND

63 The legal requirements described in Part 4, paragraphs 47 to 57, apply equally to Northern Ireland by virtue of Schedule 6 to the Companies Act (Northern Ireland), 1960, as inserted by Article 3 of The Companies (Northern Ireland) Order 1982. The Schedule references are the same except for paragraph 89 (paragraph 47 above) and paragraph 34(4) (paragraph 55 above), for which the equivalent references in Northern Ireland are paragraphs 88 and 34(5) respectively.

64 The legal requirements described in Part 4, paragraphs 59 to 62, apply equally to Northern Ireland by virtue of Schedule 6A to the Companies Act (Northern Ireland), 1960 as renumbered by Article 3 of The Companies (Northern Ireland) Order 1982. Schedule 6A is applicable to some banking, insurance and shipping companies and their holding companies as laid down in Schedule 2 to The Companies (Northern Ireland) Order 1982. The equivalent references in Northern Ireland are set out below:

SSAP	*GB*	*NI*
59	9	7A
59	13(14)	11(8A)
60	13(7)	11(5)
61	14(1)(c)	12(1)(c)
62	18(3)	14(3)
62	18(4)	14(3A)

REPUBLIC OF IRELAND

65 The references to 'the Schedule' below are to the Sixth Schedule to the Companies Act, 1963, which sets out general provisions as to the balance sheet and profit and loss account of companies registered in the Republic of Ireland.

66 Paragraph 4 of the Schedule requires that liabilities shall be classified under headings appropriate to the company's business. Amounts set aside to meet future tax liabilities or for tax equalisation (deferred tax) purposes shall be treated as provisions but separately indicated.

67 Paragraph 11(4) of the Schedule requires the general nature of contingent liabilities not provided for and, where practicable, the aggregate amount or estimated amount of those liabilities to be shown. Paragraph 11(9) of the Schedule requires to be shown the basis on which the amount, if any, set aside for taxation on profits is computed.

68 Paragraph 12(c) of the Schedule requires to be shown the amount of the charge for income tax and other taxation on profits including income tax and other taxation

**Editor's note:* *TR 805 issued in 1990 and reproduced in Part Nine contains an annex which updates the legal references in Northern Ireland and the Republic of Ireland.*

payable outside the State on profits and distinguishing where practicable between income tax and other taxation.

Paragraph 14(3) of the Schedule requires to be shown the basis on which the charge for income tax and other taxation on profits, whether payable in or outside the State, is computed. **69**

Differences exist between United Kingdom law and Republic of Ireland law on advance corporation tax. Deferred tax is affected by advance corporation tax in the following respects: (a) the off-set of advance corporation tax against a deferred tax liability; and (b) the carry forward of a net debit balance on the deferred tax account represented by advance corporation tax. The general provisions of the statement in regard to these two matters will be applicable to Republic of Ireland companies with one exception. Because advance corporation tax is payable six months from the end of the accounting period in which the dividend is paid, it will be necessary to consider the possibility of offsetting an advance corporation tax liability against the asset representing advance corporation tax recoverable. If such an offset were probable the advance corporation tax recoverable would not be deducted from a deferred tax credit balance under paragraph 29 or recognised as a deferred tax debit balance under paragraphs 31 and 32. **70**

Certain Irish companies and branches of foreign companies are totally relieved of corporation tax or are subject to tax at reduced rates on profits arising from the export of manufactured goods and services (export sales relief and 'Shannon' relief). Where such companies have timing differences originating during the period of total relief or of reduced relief and it is probable that these difference will reverse after expiry of the relief period – or when the reduced rates no longer apply – and that a tax liability will crystallise, then provision should be made for taxation deferred. The amount of tax to be deferred in respect of such timing differences should be calculated by reference to the effective rate estimated to be applicable in the years of reversal. **71**

A reduced rate of corporation tax applies to companies in regard to income arising from the sale of goods manufactured in the Republic of Ireland. Under present legislation the relief is for sales made in periods up to December 31, 2000. In calculating deferred tax provisions where a reduced rate applies, similar considerations to those given in the preceding paragraphs should be taken into account. **72**

Part 6 – Compliance with International Accounting Standard No. 12 'Accounting for taxes on income'

Compliance with the requirements of Statement of Standard Accounting Practice No. 15 (revised) 'Accounting for deferred tax' will automatically ensure compliance with International Accounting Standard No. 12 'Accounting for taxes on income' so far as deferred tax is concerned.* **73**

***Editor's note:** *An exposure draft of a revised version of IAS12 was published in October 1994 (E49 'Income Taxes').*

Appendix

Note: This appendix is for guidance only and does not form part of the statement of standard accounting practice.

Deferred tax effects of current tax legislation in the United Kingdom and Republic of Ireland

INTRODUCTION

1 This appendix gives guidance on the accounting treatment of the tax effects of permanent and timing differences between taxable and accounting income resulting from current tax legislation in the United Kingdom and Republic of Ireland. It reflects legislation current as at May 1985 and will need to be amended when necessary to reflect changes in legislation.

2 The principal areas of difference are:

(a) permanent differences;
(b) timing differences;
(c) losses;
(d) items not included in profit or loss on ordinary activities; and
(e) advance corporation tax.

Items not included in profit or loss on ordinary activities are dealt with in paragraphs 34 and 39 of this statement and accordingly are not considered in this appendix.

PERMANENT DIFFERENCES

3 Examples of permanent differences are UK entertaining and fines (disallowable) and regional development grants and interest on tax repayments (tax free). Stock relief in the Republic of Ireland is effectively a permanent difference. These differences will not reverse in future periods and thus give rise to no tax effects in other periods.

TIMING DIFFERENCES

4 The combined effect of timing differences should be considered when attempting to assess whether a tax liability will crystallise, rather than looking at each timing difference separately. Paragraphs 27 and 28 of the standard indicate that reasonable assumptions, by reference to suitable financial plans or projections covering a period of years, are required when making this assessment. The period may be relatively short – say three to five years – where the pattern of timing differences is expected to be regular. However, it may need to be longer for an enterprise with an irregular pattern of timing differences. The length of the lives of the relevant assets and the enterprise's assumptions on growth in capital expenditure also affect the length of the period which needs to be considered.

A number of timing differences arise from the use of the receipts and payments basis for tax purposes and the accruals basis in financial statements. Examples of these and other timing differences are: 5

(a) interest receivable accrued in the accounting period, but taxed when received;
(b) dividends from foreign subsidiaries accrued in a period prior to that in which they arise for tax purposes;
(c) intra-group profits in stock deferred upon consolidation until realisation to third parties;
(d) interest or royalties payable accrued in the accounting period, but allowed when paid;
(e) pension costs accrued in the financial statements but allowed for tax purposes when paid or contributed at some later date;
(f) provisions for repairs and maintenance made in the financial statements but not allowed for tax purposes until the expenditure is incurred;
(g) bad debt provisions not allowed for tax purposes unless and until they become 'specific';
(h) provisions for revenue losses on closing down plants or for costs of reorganisation upon which tax relief is not obtained until the costs or losses are incurred; and
(i) revenue expenditure deferred in the financial statements, such as development or advertising, if it is allowed for tax purposes as it is incurred.

A number of these differences are 'short term' timing differences in that they can be identified with specific transactions and normally reverse in the accounting period following that in which they originated. Short term and other timing differences need to be considered together when attempting to assess whether a tax liability will crystallise. 6

ACCELERATED CAPITAL ALLOWANCES

Accelerated capital allowances are timing differences which arise from the availability of capital allowances in tax computations which are in excess of the related depreciation charges in financial statements. The reverse may also occur, whereby the depreciation charges in financial statements exceed the capital allowances available in tax computations. 7

In many businesses, timing differences arising from accelerated capital allowances are of a recurring nature and reversing differences are themselves offset, wholly or partially, or are exceeded, by new originating differences, thereby giving rise to continuing tax reductions or the indefinite postponement of any liability attributable to the tax benefits received. Thus an enterprise having a relatively stable or growing investment in depreciable assets can take tax relief year by year on capital expenditure. This tax relief may equal or exceed the additional tax which would otherwise have been payable in consequence of the reversal of the original timing differences through depreciation. Where for economic or other reasons a spasmodic or highly irregular pattern of capital allowances is forecast, a substantial period of time will need to be considered in attempting to assess whether a tax liability will crystallise. Where there is a declining availability of capital allowances, any originating timing differences will usually 8 reverse, and deferred tax should be provided unless it is probable for other reasons that no tax liability will crystallise.

REVALUATIONS OF FIXED ASSETS

9 When a fixed asset is revalued above cost a timing difference potentially arises in that, in the absence of rollover relief, tax on a chargeable gain may be payable if and when the asset is disposed of at its revalued amount. Where it is probable that a liability will crystallise, provision for the tax payable on disposal is required to be made out of the revaluation surplus, based on the value at which the fixed asset is carried in the balance sheet. Whether or not a liability will crystallise can usually be determined, in the absence of rollover relief, at the time the enterprise decides to dispose of the asset.

10 *Revaluations not incorporated in the accounts*

Paragraph 42 of the standard requires that, where the value of an asset is not incorporated in the balance sheet but is given elsewhere such as in a note, the tax effects, if any, which would arise if the asset was realised at the noted value should also be shown. This also applies where the value is given in the directors' report instead of in the notes.

11 *Rollover relief*

Rollover relief has the effect of deferring the reversal of the timing difference arising on the revaluation of an asset beyond the date of sale, or of creating a timing difference on the sale of an asset that has not been revalued, or a combination of the two. Where rollover relief has been obtained on the sale of an asset, with the 'base cost' of the replacement asset for tax purposes thereby being reduced, and the potential deferred tax has not been disclosed, the standard requires disclosure of the fact that the revaluation does not constitute a timing difference and that tax has therefore not been quantified, as it will not otherwise be evident from the accounts.

12 *Overseas assets*

Translation of the financial statements of overseas subsidiaries or associated companies is not regarded as creating a timing difference. Gains and losses arising on translation of an enterprise's own overseas assets (including investments in subsidiaries and associated companies) and liabilities may give rise to timing differences depending on whether or not the gains or losses have a tax effect.

LOSSES

13 Paragraph 30 of the standard requires that deferred tax assets, including those arising from losses, should be recognised only when they are expected to be recoverable without replacement by equivalent debit balances. Recovery may be affected, among other things, by the period of time for which losses are available to be carried forward for tax purposes.

14 Deferred tax relating to current trading losses may be treated as recoverable when:

(a) the loss results from an identifiable and non-recurring cause; and

(b) the enterprise, or predecessor enterprise, has been consistently profitable over a considerable period, with any past losses being more than offset by income in subsequent periods; and
(c) it is assured beyond reasonable doubt that future taxable profits will be sufficient to offset the current loss during the carry-forward period prescribed by tax legislation.

Deferred tax relating to capital losses may be treated as recoverable when: **15**

(a) a potential chargeable gain not expected to be covered by rollover relief is present in assets which have not been revalued in the financial statements to reflect that gain and which are not essential to the future operations of the enterprise; and
(b) the enterprise has decided to dispose of these assets and thus realise the potential chargeable gain; and
(c) the unrealised chargeable gain (after allowing for any possible loss in value before disposal) is sufficient to offset the loss in question, such that it is assured beyond reasonable doubt that a tax liability on the relevant portion of the chargeable gain will not crystallise.

ADVANCE CORPORATION TAXATION (ACT)

The minimum tax charge in the profit and loss account in any accounting period will **16** normally be the amount payable as ACT (net of any recovery) plus any amounts charged in respect of overseas tax. As noted in paragraph 7 of SSAP 8 'The treatment of tax under the imputation system in the accounts of companies', ACT which cannot be recovered out of the corporation tax liability on the income of the year but which is carried forward to be recovered out of the corporation tax liability on the income of future periods may, subject to certain limitations, be deducted from the deferred tax account. Where there is no balance on the deferred tax account or to the extent that the balance is insufficient for this purpose, consideration will need to be given as to whether the ACT is recoverable out of the corporation tax liability on the income of future periods.

It may be incorrect to carry forward an amount of ACT to offset an equal credit **17** amount of deferred tax. This is because ACT may only be carried forward at the basic rate of income tax on the gross amount of any distribution, to be set off against corporation tax at the full or small companies rates on the same gross amount of taxable income, excluding chargeable gains.*

***Editor's note:** *See para 2.10 of TR 805, reproduced in Part Nine.*

[SSAP 17]
Accounting for post balance sheet events

(Issued August 1980)

Contents

Accounting for post balance sheet events

The provisions of this statement of standard accounting practice should be read in conjunction with the (Explanatory) Foreword to Accounting Standards *and need not be applied to immaterial items. The provisions apply equally to financial statements prepared under the historical cost convention and to financial statements prepared under the current cost convention.*

Part 1 – Explanatory note

Events arising after the balance sheet date need to be reflected in financial statements if they provide additional evidence of conditions that existed at the balance sheet date and materially affect the amounts to be included. **1**

To prevent financial statements from being misleading, disclosure needs to be made by way of notes of other material events arising after the balance sheet date which provide evidence of conditions not existing at the balance sheet date. Disclosure is required where this information is necessary for a proper understanding of the financial position. **2**

A post balance sheet event for the purpose of this standard is an event which occurs between the balance sheet date and the date on which the financial statements are approved by the board of directors. It is not intended that the preliminary consideration of a matter which may lead to a decision by the board of directors in the future should fall within the scope of this standard. **3**

Events which occur after the date on which the financial statements are approved by the board of directors do not come within the scope of this standard. If such events are material the directors should consider publishing the relevant information so that users of financial statements are not misled. **4**

The process involved in the approval of financial statements by the directors will vary depending on the management structure and procedures followed in preparing and finalising financial statements. However, the date of approval will normally be the date of the board meeting at which the financial statements are formally approved, or in respect of unincorporated enterprises the corresponding date. In respect of group accounts, the date of approval is the date the group accounts are formally approved by the board of directors of the holding company. **5**

CLASSIFICATION OF POST BALANCE SHEET EVENTS

Events occurring after the balance sheet date may be classified into two categories: 'adjusting events' and 'non-adjusting events.' **6**

7 Adjusting events are events which provide additional evidence relating to conditions existing at the balance sheet date. They require changes in amounts to be included in financial statements. Examples of adjusting events are given in the appendix.

8 Some events occurring after the balance sheet date, such as a deterioration in the operating results and in the financial position, may indicate a need to consider whether it is appropriate to use the going concern concept in the preparation of financial statements. Consequently these may fall to be treated as adjusting events.

9 Non-adjusting events are events which arise after the balance sheet date and concern conditions which did not exist at that time. Consequently they do not result in changes in amounts in financial statements. They may, however, be of such materiality that their disclosure is required by way of notes to ensure that financial statements are not misleading. Examples of non-adjusting events which may require disclosure are given in the appendix.

10 Disclosure would be required of the reversal or maturity after the year end of transactions entered into before the year end, the substance of which was primarily to alter the appearance of the company's balance sheet. Such alterations include those commonly known as 'window dressing.'

11 There are certain post balance sheet events which, because of statutory requirements or customary accounting practice, are reflected in financial statements and so fall to be treated as adjusting events. These include proposed dividends, amounts appropriated to reserves, the effects of changes in taxation and dividends receivable from subsidiary and associated companies.

DISCLOSURE IN FINANCIAL STATEMENTS

12 Separate disclosure of adjusting events is not normally required as they do no more than provide additional evidence in support of items in financial statements.

13 In determining which non-adjusting events are of sufficient materiality to require disclosure, regard should be had to all matters which are necessary to enable users of financial statements to assess the financial position.

Part 2 – Definition of terms

14 *Financial statements* are balance sheets, profit and loss accounts, statements of source and application of funds, notes and other statements, which collectively are intended to give a true and fair view of financial position and profit or loss.

15 *Company* includes any enterprise which comes within the scope of statements of standard accounting practice.

16 *Directors* include the corresponding officers of organisations which do not have directors.

The date on which the financial statements are approved by the board of directors is the date the board of directors formally approves a set of documents as the financial statements. In respect of unincorporated enterprises, the date of approval is the corresponding date. In respect of group accounts, the date of approval is the date when the group accounts are formally approved by the board of directors of the holding company. **17**

Post balance sheet events are those events, both favourable and unfavourable, which occur between the balance sheet date and the date on which the financial statements are approved by the board of directors. **18**

Adjusting events are post balance sheet events which provide additional evidence of conditions existing at the balance sheet date. They include events which because of statutory or conventional requirements are reflected in financial statements. **19**

Non-adjusting events are post balance sheet events which concern conditions which did not exist at the balance sheet date. **20**

Part 3 – Standard accounting practice

Financial statements should be prepared on the basis of conditions existing at the balance sheet date. **21**

A material post balance sheet event requires changes in the amounts to be included in financial statements where: **22**

(a) it is an adjusting event; or
(b) it indicates that application of the going concern concept to the whole or a material part of the company is not appropriate.

A material post balance sheet event should be disclosed where: **23**

(a) it is a non-adjusting event of such materiality that its non-disclosure would affect the ability of the users of financial statements to reach a proper understanding of the financial position; or
(b) it is the reversal or maturity after the year end of a transaction entered into before the year end, the substance of which was primarily to alter the appearance of the company's balance sheet.

In respect of each post balance sheet event which is required to be disclosed under paragraph 23 above, the following information should be stated by way of notes in financial statements: **24**

(a) the nature of the event; and
(b) an estimate of the financial effect, or a statement that it is not practicable to make such an estimate.

The estimate of the financial effect should be disclosed before taking account of **25** taxation, and the taxation implications should be explained where necessary for a proper understanding of the financial position.

26 The date on which the financial statements are approved by the board of directors should be disclosed in the financial statements.

DATE FROM WHICH EFFECTIVE

27 The accounting practices set out in this statement should be adopted as soon as possible and regarded as standard in respect of financial statements relating to accounting periods beginning on or after 1st September 1980.

Part 4 – Compliance with International Accounting Standard No. 10 'Contingencies and events occurring after the balance sheet date'

28 The requirements of International Accounting Standard No. 10 'Contingencies and events occurring after the balance sheet date' concerning post balance sheet events accord very closely with the content of the United Kingdom and Irish Accounting Standard No. 17 'Accounting for post balance sheet events' and accordingly compliance with SSAP 17 will ensure compliance with IAS 10 in all material respects so far as post balance sheet events are concerned.

Appendix

This appendix is for general guidance and does not form part of the statement of standard accounting practice. The examples are merely illustrative and the lists are not exhaustive.

The examples listed distinguish between those normally classified as adjusting events and as non-adjusting events. However, in exceptional circumstances, to accord with the prudence concept, an adverse event which would normally be classified as non-adjusting may need to be reclassified as adjusting. In such circumstances, full disclosure of the adjustment would be required.

ADJUSTING EVENTS

The following are examples of post balance sheet events which normally should be classified as adjusting events:

(a) *Fixed assets:* The subsequent determination of the purchase price or of the proceeds of sale of assets purchased or sold before the year end.
(b) *Property:* A valuation which provides evidence of a permanent diminution in value.
(c) *Investments:* The receipt of a copy of the financial statements or other information in respect of an unlisted company which provides evidence of a permanent diminution in the value of a long-term investment.
(d) *Stocks and work in progress:*
    (i) The receipt of proceeds of sales after the balance sheet date or other evidence concerning the net realisable value of stocks.
    (ii) The receipt of evidence that the previous estimate of accrued profit on a long-term contract was materially inaccurate.
(e) *Debtors:* The renegotiation of amounts owing by debtors, or the insolvency of a debtor.
(f) *Dividends receivable:* The declaration of dividends by subsidiaries and associated companies relating to periods prior to the balance sheet date of the holding company.
(g) *Taxation:* The receipt of information regarding rates of taxation.
(h) *Claims.* Amounts received or receivable in respect of insurance claims which were in the course of negotiation at the balance sheet date.
(i) *Discoveries.* The discovery of errors or frauds which show that the financial statements were incorrect.

NON-ADJUSTING EVENTS

The following are examples of post balance sheet events which normally should be classified as non-adjusting events:

(a) *Mergers* and acquisitions.
(b) *Reconstructions* and proposed reconstructions.
(c) *Issues* of shares and debentures.
(d) *Purchases and sales of fixed assets* and investments.

(e) *Losses of fixed assets* or stocks as a result of a catastrophe such as fire or flood.
(f) *Opening new trading activities* or extending existing trading activities.
(g) *Closing a significant part of the trading activities* if this was not anticipated at the year end.
(h) *Decline in the value* of property and investments held as fixed assets, if it can be demonstrated that the decline occurred after the year end.
(i) *Changes in rates of foreign exchange.*
(j) *Government action*, such as nationalisation.
(k) *Strikes* and other labour disputes.
(l) *Augmentation of pension benefits.*

[SSAP 18]
Accounting for contingencies

(Issued August 1980)

Contents

Accounting for contingencies

The provisions of this Statement of Standard Accounting Practice should be read in conjunction with the (Explanatory) Foreword to Accounting Standards *and need not be applied to immaterial items. The provisions apply equally to financial statements prepared under the historical cost convention and to financial statements prepared under the current cost convention.*

Part 1 – Explanatory note

The term contingency used in this statement is applied to a condition which exists at the balance sheet date, where the outcome will be confirmed only on the occurrence or non-occurrence of one or more uncertain future events. It is not intended that uncertainties connected with accounting estimates should fall within the scope of this statement, for example the lives of fixed assets, the amount of bad debts, the net realisable value of inventories, the expected outcome of long-term contracts or the valuation of properties and foreign currency balances. 1

Contingencies existing at the balance sheet date should be taken into consideration when preparing financial statements. Estimates of the outcome and of the financial effect of contingencies should be made by the board of directors of the company. These estimates will be based on consideration of information available up to the date on which the financial statements are approved by the board of directors and will include a review of events occurring after the balance sheet date. As an example, in the case of a substantial legal claim against a company, the factors to be considered would include the progress of the claim at the date on which the financial statements are approved, the opinion of legal experts or other advisers and the experience of the company in similar cases. 2

The treatment of a contingency existing at the balance sheet date is determined by its expected outcome. In addition to accruals under the fundamental concept of prudence in SSAP 2 'Disclosure of accounting policies', contingent losses will be accrued in financial statements where it is probable that a future event will confirm a loss which can be estimated with reasonable accuracy at the date on which the financial statements are approved by the board of directors. 3

Existing conventions preclude contingent gains from being accrued in financial statements. The existence of a contingent gain should be disclosed only if it is probable that the gain will be realised. When the realisation of the gain becomes reasonably certain, then such a gain is not a contingency and accrual is appropriate. 4

Subject to paragraphs 3 and 4 above, a material contingency which is not accounted for under existing requirements should be disclosed by way of notes in order to ensure that financial statements do not present a misleading position. Such disclosures should 5 indicate the nature of the contingency, the uncertainties which are expected to affect the ultimate outcome and either a prudent estimate of the financial effect or a statement that it is not practicable to make such an estimate.

6 A contingency may be reduced or avoided because it is matched by a related counter-claim or claim by or against a third party. In such cases any accrual, or the amount to be disclosed in financial statements by way of notes, should be reduced by taking into account the probable outcome of the claim. However, the likelihood of success, and the probable amounts of the claim and the counter-claim, should be separately assessed, and separately disclosed where appropriate.

7 In disclosing the financial effect of a contingency, the amount should be stated before taking account of taxation, and the taxation implications of a contingency crystallising should be explained where necessary for a proper understanding of the financial position.

8 There are some contingencies where the possibility of the ultimate outcome having a material effect on the financial statements is so remote that disclosure could be misleading. This statement does not require disclosure of remote contingencies.

9 This statement should be read in conjunction with Part 4 – Note of legal requirements.

Part 2 – Definition of terms

10 *Financial statements* are balance sheets, profit and loss accounts, statements of source and application of funds, notes and other statements, which collectively are intended to give a true and fair view of financial position and profit or loss.

11 *Company* includes any enterprise which comes within the scope of statements of standard accounting practice.

12 *Directors* include the corresponding officers of organisations which do not have directors.

13 *The date on which the financial statements are approved by the board of directors* is the date the board of directors formally approves a set of documents as the financial statements. In respect of unincorporated enterprises, the date of approval is the corresponding date. In respect of group accounts, the date of approval is the date when the group accounts are formally approved by the board of directors of the holding company.

14 *Contingency* is a condition which exists at the balance sheet date, where the outcome will be confirmed only on the occurrence or non-occurrence of one or more uncertain future events. A contingent gain or loss is a gain or loss dependent on a contingency.

Part 3 – Standard accounting practice

In addition to amounts accrued under the fundamental concept of prudence in SSAP 2 'Disclosure of accounting policies', a material contingent loss should be accrued in financial statements where it is probable that a future event will confirm a loss which can be estimated with reasonable accuracy at the date on which the financial statements are approved by the board of directors. **15**

A material contingent loss not accrued under paragraph 15 above should be disclosed except where the possibility of loss is remote. **16**

Contingent gains should not be accrued in financial statements. A material contingent gain should be disclosed in financial statements only if it is probable that the gain will be realised. **17**

In respect of each contingency which is required to be disclosed under paragraphs 16 and 17 above, the following information should be stated by way of notes in financial statements: **18**

(a) the nature of the contingency;
(b) the uncertainties which are expected to affect the ultimate outcome; and
(c) a prudent estimate of the financial effect, made at the date on which the financial statements are approved by the board of directors; or a statement that it is not practicable to make such an estimate.

Where there is disclosure of an estimate of the financial effect of a contingency, the amount disclosed should be the potential financial effect. In the case of a contingent loss, this should be reduced by: **19**

(a) any amounts accrued; and
(b) the amounts of any components where the possibility of loss is remote.

The net amount only need be disclosed.

The estimate of the financial effect should be disclosed before taking account of taxation, and the taxation implications of a contingency crystallising should be explained where necessary for a proper understanding of the financial position. **20**

Where both the nature of, and the uncertainties which affect, a contingency in respect of an individual transaction are common to a large number of similar transactions, the financial effect of the contingency need not be individually estimated but may be based on the group of similar transactions. In these circumstances the separate contingencies need not be individually disclosed. **21**

DATE FROM WHICH EFFECTIVE

The accounting practices set out in this statement should be adopted as soon as possible and regarded as standard in respect of financial statements relating to accounting periods beginning on or after 1st September 1980. **22**

Part 4 – Note of legal requirements

23 Paragraph 11 (5) of Schedule 2 to the Companies Act 1967*, paragraph 11 (4) of Schedule 6 to the Companies Act 1963 (Republic of Ireland) and paragraph 11 (5) of Schedule 6 to the Companies (Northern Ireland) Act 1960 or when implemented paragraph 11 (5) of Schedule 2 to the Companies (Northern Ireland) Order 1978 require the following to be stated by way of note on, or in a statement or report annexed to, the balance sheet:

> 'The general nature of any other contingent liabilities not provided for and, where practicable, the aggregate amount or estimated amount of those liabilities, it if is material.'

Part 5 – Compliance with International Accounting Standard No. 10 'Contingencies and events occurring after the balance sheet date'

24 The requirements of International Accounting Standard No. 10 'Contingencies and events occurring after the balance sheet date' concerning contingencies accord very closely with the content of the United Kingdom and Irish Accounting Standard No. 18 'Accounting for contingencies' and accordingly compliance with SSAP 18 will ensure compliance with IAS 10 in all material respects so far as contingencies are concerned.

****Editor's note:** The current legal requirements in Great Britain are set out in para 50(2) of Schedule 4 to the Companies Act 1985 (for banking companies para 66(5) of Schedule 9 and for insurance companies para 70(2) of 'new' Schedule 9A or para 13(7) of the 'old' Schedule 9A).*

[SSAP 19]
Accounting for investment properties

(Issued November 1981; amended July 1994)

Contents

Accounting for investment properties

The provisions of this Statement of Standard Accounting Practice should be read in conjunction with the (Explanatory) Foreword to Accounting Standards. *The provisions apply equally to financial statements prepared under the historical cost convention and to financial statements prepared under the current cost convention. They need not be applied to immaterial items.*

Part 1 – Explanatory note

Under the accounting requirements of SSAP 12 'Accounting for depreciation', fixed assets are generally subject to annual depreciation charges to reflect on a systematic basis the wearing out, consumption or other loss of value whether arising from use, effluxion of time or obsolescence through technology and market changes. Under those requirements it is also accepted that an increase in the value of such a fixed asset does not generally remove the necessity to charge depreciation to reflect on a systematic basis the consumption of the asset. **1**

A different treatment is, however, required where a significant proportion of the fixed assets of an enterprise is held not for consumption in the business operations but as investments, the disposal of which would not materially affect any manufacturing or trading operations of the enterprise. In such a case the current value of these investments, and changes in that current value, are of prime importance rather than a calculation of systematic annual depreciation. Consequently, for the proper appreciation of financial position, a different accounting treatment is considered appropriate for fixed assets held as investments (called in this standard 'investment properties'). **2**

Investment properties may be held by a company which holds investments as part of its business such as an investment trust or a property investment company. **3**

Investment properties may be held by a company whose main business is not the holding of investments. **4**

Where an investment property is held on a lease with a relatively short unexpired term, it is necessary to recognise the annual depreciation in the financial statements to avoid the situation whereby a short lease is amortised against the investment revaluation reserve whilst the rentals are taken to the profit and loss account. **5**

This statement requires investment properties to be included in the balance sheet at open market value. The statement does not require the valuation to be made by qualified or independent valuers; but (in paragraph 12) calls for disclosure of the names or qualifications of the valuers, the bases used by them and whether the person making the valuation is an employee or officer of the company. However, where investment properties represent a substantial proportion of the total assets of a major enterprise (e.g., a listed company) the valuation thereof would normally be carried out: **6**

(a) annually by persons holding a recognised professional qualification and having recent post-qualification experience in the location and category of the properties concerned; and
(b) at least every five years by an external valuer.

Part 2 – Definition of terms

7 For the purposes of this statement, but subject to the exceptions in paragraph 8 below, an *investment property* is an interest in land and/or buildings:

(a) in respect of which construction work and development have been completed; and
(b) which is held for its investment potential, any rental income being negotiated at arm's length.

8 The following are exceptions from the definition:
(a) A property which is owned and occupied by a company for its own purposes is not an investment property.
(b) A property let to and occupied by another group company is not an investment property for the purposes of its own accounts or the group accounts.

Part 3 – Standard accounting practice

9 This statement does not apply to investment properties owned by charities.

10 Investment properties should not be subject to periodic charges for depreciation on the basis set out in SSAP 12 except for properties held on lease which should be depreciated on the basis set out in SSAP 12 at least over the period when the unexpired term is 20 years or less.

11 Investment properties should be included in the balance sheet at their open market value.

12 The names of the persons making the valuation, or particulars of their qualifications, should be disclosed together with the bases of valuation used by them. If a person making a valuation is an employee or officer of the company or group which owns the property this fact should be disclosed.

13 Subject to paragraph 14 below, changes in the market value of investment properties should not be taken to the profit and loss account but should be taken to the statement of total recognised gains and losses (being a movement on an investment revaluation reserve), unless a deficit (or its reversal) on an individual investment property is expected to be permanent, in which case it should be charged (or credited) in the profit and loss account of the period. In the special circumstances of investment companies as defined in companies legislation (as mentioned in paragraphs 31 and 66 of FRS 3 'Reporting Financial Performance') and of property unit trusts it may not be

appropriate to deal with such deficits in the profit and loss account. In such cases they should be shown only in the statement of total recognised gains and losses.

Paragraph 13 does not apply to the financial statements of: **14**

(a) insurance companies and groups (and consolidated financial statements incorporating such entities) where changes in the market value of investment properties (including those comprising assets of the long-term business) are included in the profit and loss account.
(b) pension funds where changes in the market value of investment properties are dealt with in the relevant fund account.

The carrying value of investment properties and the investment revaluation reserve should be displayed prominently in the financial statements. **15**

DATE FROM WHICH EFFECTIVE

The accounting and disclosure requirements in this statement should be adopted as soon as possible and regarded as standard in respect of financial statements relating to accounting periods starting on or after 1 July 1981.* **16**

Part 4 – Legal requirements in UK and Ireland

The application of this standard will usually be a departure, for the overriding purpose of giving a true and fair view, from the otherwise specific requirement of the law to provide depreciation on any fixed asset which has a limited useful economic life. In this circumstance there will need to be given in the notes to the accounts 'particulars of that departure, the reasons for it, and its effect'. UITF Abstract 7 'True and fair view override disclosures' gives guidance on the interpretation of this statutory requirement. **17**

In Great Britain paragraphs 19 and 32 of Schedule 4 (for banking companies and groups paragraphs 26 and 42 of Schedule 9) to the Companies Act 1985 set out the legal requirements relating to provisions for diminution in value that are expected to be permanent. In the case of insurance companies and groups reporting under the amended Schedule 9A to the Companies Act 1985 (introduced by SI 1993/3246) note 9 on the profit and loss account format and paragraph 29(7) of the Schedule set out the relevant statutory requirements. **18**

There are legal requirements similar to Schedule 4† in Northern Ireland (the Companies (Northern Ireland) Order 1986 Schedule 4 paragraphs 19 and 32 and **19**

***Editor's note:** *The amendment in July 1994 (revised paragraphs 13 and 14) became standard in respect of financial statements relating to accounting periods ending on or after 22 September 1994. Earlier adoption was encouraged but not required. The amendment noted that 'if an enterprise changes its presentation of revaluation deficits as a result of this amendment, the classification of reserves and comparative figures should be restated in accordance with FRS 3 'Reporting Financial Performance'.*

†**Editor's note:** *Also similar to Schedule 9.*

Schedule 9 paragraphs 26 and 42) and in the Republic of Ireland (the Companies (Amendment) Act 1986 (the Schedule paragraphs 7 and 20) and the European Communities (Credit Institutions: Accounts) Regulations 1992 (the Schedule paragraphs 26 and 42)). Requirements similar to the amended Schedule 9A are expected to be enacted in Northern Ireland and the Republic of Ireland.

[SSAP 20]
Foreign currency translation

(Issued April 1983)

Contents

Foreign currency translation

The provisions of this statement of standard accounting practice should be read in conjunction with the (Explanatory) Foreword to accounting standards *and need not be applied to immaterial items. The provisions apply to financial statements prepared under either the historical cost convention or the current cost convention.*

This statement sets out the standard accounting practice for foreign currency translation, but does not deal with the method of calculating profits or losses arising from a company's normal currency dealing operations; neither does it deal specifically with the determination of distributable profits.

Part 1 – Explanatory note

BACKGROUND

A company may engage in foreign currency operations in two main ways: 1

(a) Firstly, it may enter directly into business transactions which are denominated in foreign currencies; the results of these transactions will need to be translated into the currency in which the company reports.
(b) Secondly, foreign operations may be conducted through a foreign enterprise which maintains its accounting records in a currency other than that of the investing company; in order to prepare consolidated financial statements it will be necessary to translate the complete financial statements of the foreign enterprise into the currency used for reporting purposes by the investing company.

OBJECTIVES OF TRANSLATION

The translation of foreign currency transactions and financial statements should produce results which are generally compatible with the effects of rate changes on a company's cash flows and its equity and should ensure that the financial statements present a true and fair view of the results of management actions. Consolidated statements should reflect the financial results of and relationships as measured in the foreign currency financial statements prior to translation. 2

PROCEDURES

In this statement the procedures which should be adopted when accounting for foreign operations are considered in two stages, namely: 3

(a) the preparation of the financial statements of an individual company; and
(b) the preparation of consolidated financial statements.

THE INDIVIDUAL COMPANY STAGE

4 During an accounting period, a company may enter into transactions which are denominated in a foreign currency. The result of each transaction should normally be translated into the company's local currency using the exchange rate in operation on the date on which the transaction occurred; however, if the rates do not fluctuate significantly, an average rate for a period may be used as an approximation. Where the transaction is to be settled at a contracted rate, that rate should be used; where a trading transaction is covered by a related or matching forward contract, the rate of exchange specified in that contract may be used.

5 Once non-monetary assets, e.g., plant, machinery and equity investments, have been translated and recorded they should be carried in the company's local currency. Subject to the provisions of paragraph 30 concerning the treatment of foreign equity investments financed by foreign currency borrowings, no subsequent translations of these assets will normally need to be made.

6 At the balance sheet date monetary assets and liabilities denominated in a foreign currency, e.g., cash and bank balances, loans and amounts receivable and payable, should be translated by using the rate of exchange ruling at that date, or, where appropriate, the rates of exchange fixed under the terms of the relevant transactions. Where there are related or matching forward contracts in respect of trading transactions, the rates of exchange specified in those contracts may be used.

7 An exchange gain or loss will result during an accounting period if a business transaction is settled at an exchange rate which differs from that used when the transaction was initially recorded, or, where appropriate, that used at the last balance sheet date. An exchange gain or loss will also arise on unsettled transactions if the rate of exchange used at the balance sheet date differs from that used previously.

8 Exchange gains or losses arising on settled transactions in the context of an individual company's operations have already been reflected in cash flows, since a change in the exchange rate increases or decreases the local currency equivalent of amounts paid or received in cash settlement. Similarly, it is reasonably certain that exchange gains or losses on unsettled short-term monetary items will soon be reflected in cash flows. Therefore, it is normally appropriate, because of the cash flow effects, to recognise such gains and losses as part of the profit or loss for the year; they should be included in profit or loss from ordinary activities unless they arise from events which themselves would fall to be treated as extraordinary items, in which case they would be included as part of such items.

9 When dealing with long-term monetary items, additional considerations apply. Although it is not easy to predict what the exchange rate will be when a long-term liability or asset matures, it is necessary, when stating the liability or the asset in terms of the reporting currency, to make the best estimate possible in the light of the information available at the time; generally speaking translation at the year-end rate will provide the best estimate, particularly when the currency concerned is freely dealt in on the spot and forward exchange markets.

In order to give a true and fair view of results, exchange gains and losses on long-term monetary items should normally be reported as part of the profit or loss for the period in accordance with the accruals concept of accounting; treatment of these items on a simple cash movements basis would be inconsistent with that concept. Exchange gains on unsettled transactions can be determined at the balance sheet date no less objectively than exchange losses; deferring the gains whilst recognising the losses would not only be illogical by denying in effect that any favourable movement in exchange rates had occurred but would also inhibit fair measurement of the performance of the enterprise in the year. In particular, this symmetry of treatment recognises that there will probably be some interaction between currency movements and interest rates and reflects more accurately in the profit and loss account the true results of currency involvement. **10**

For the special reasons outlined above, both exchange gains and losses on long-term monetary items should be recognised in the profit and loss account. However, it is necessary to consider on the grounds of prudence whether the amount of the gain, or the amount by which exchange gains exceed past exchange losses on the same items, to be recognised in the profit and loss account should be restricted in the exceptional cases where there are doubts as to the convertibility or marketability of the currency in question. **11**

Gains or losses on exchange arising from transactions between a holding company and its subsidiaries, or from transactions between fellow subsidiaries, should normally be reported in the individual company's financial statements as part of the profit or loss for the year in the same way as gains or losses arising from transactions with third parties. **12**

THE CONSOLIDATED FINANCIAL STATEMENTS STAGE

The method used to translate financial statements for consolidation purposes should reflect the financial and other operational relationships which exist between an investing company and its foreign enterprises. **13**

In most circumstances the closing rate/net investment method, described in paragraphs 15 to 20, should be used and exchange differences accounted for on a net investment basis. However, in certain specified circumstances (see paragraphs 21 to 24) the temporal method should be used. **14**

THE CLOSING RATE/NET INVESTMENT METHOD

This method recognises that the investment of a company is in the net worth of its foreign enterprise rather than a direct investment in the individual assets and liabilities of that enterprise. The foreign enterprise will normally have net current assets and fixed assets which may be financed partly by local currency borrowings. In its day-to-day operations the foreign enterprise is not normally dependent on the reporting currency **15** of the investing company. The investing company may look forward to a stream of dividends but the net investment will remain until the business is liquidated or the investment disposed of.

16 Under this method the amounts in the balance sheet of a foreign enterprise should be translated into the reporting currency of the investing company using the rate of exchange ruling at the balance sheet date. Exchange differences will arise if this rate differs from that ruling at the previous balance sheet date or at the date of any subsequent capital injection (or reduction).

17 Amounts in the profit and loss account of a foreign enterprise should be translated at the closing rate or at an average rate for the accounting period. The use of the closing rate is more likely to achieve the objective of translation, stated in paragraph 2, of reflecting the financial results and relationships as measured in the foreign currency financial statements prior to translation. However, it can be argued that an average rate reflects more fairly the profits or losses and cash flows as they arise to the group throughout an accounting period. The use of either method is therefore permitted, provided that the one selected is applied consistently from period to period.

18 No definitive method of calculating the average rate had been prescribed, since the appropriate method may justifiably vary as between individual companies. Factors that will need to be considered include the company's internal accounting procedures and the extent of seasonal trade variations; the use of a weighting procedure will in most cases be desirable. Where the average rate used differs from the closing rate, a difference will arise which should be dealt with in reserves.

19 The results of the operations of a foreign enterprise are best reflected in the group profit and loss account by consolidating the net profit or loss shown in its local currency financial statements without adjustment (other than for normal consolidation adjustments). If exchange differences arising from the retranslation of a company's net investment in its foreign enterprise were introduced into the profit and loss account, the results from trading operations, as shown in the local currency financial statements, would be distorted. Such differences may result from many factors unrelated to the trading performance or financial operations of the foreign enterprise; in particular, they do not represent or measure changes in actual or prospective cash flows. It is therefore inappropriate to regard them as profits or losses and they should be dealt with as adjustments to reserves.

20 Although equity investments in foreign enterprises will normally be made by the purchase of shares, investments may also be made by means of long-term loans and inter-company deferred trading balances. Where financing by such means is intended to be , for all practical purposes, as permanent as equity, such loans and inter-company balances should be treated as part of the investing company's net investment in the foreign enterprise; hence exchange differences arising on such loans and inter-company balances should be dealt with as adjustments to reserves.

THE TEMPORAL METHOD

For most investing companies in the UK and Ireland foreign operations are normally carried out through foreign enterprises which operate as separate or quasi-independent entities rather than as direct extensions of the trade of the investing company. **21**

However, there are some cases in which the affairs of a foreign enterprise are so closely interlinked with those of the investing company that its results may be regarded as being more dependent on the economic environment of the investing company's currency than on that of its own reporting currency. In such a case the financial statements of the foreign enterprise should be included in the consolidated financial statements as if all its transactions had been entered into by the investing company itself in its own currency. For this purpose the temporal method of translation should be used; the mechanics of this method are identical with those used in preparing the accounts of an individual company, as stated in paragraphs 4 to 12. **22**

It is not possible to select one factor which of itself will lead a company to conclude that the temporal method should be adopted. All the available evidence should be considered in determining whether the currency of the investing company is the dominant currency in the economic environment in which the foreign enterprise operates. Amongst the factors to be taken into account will be: **23**

(a) the extent to which the cash flows of the enterprise have a direct impact upon those of the investing company;
(b) the extent to which the functioning of the enterprise is dependent directly upon the investing company;
(c) the currency in which the majority of the trading transactions are denominated;
(d) the major currency to which the operation is exposed in its financing structure.

Examples of situations where the temporal method may be appropriate are where the foreign enterprise: **24**

(a) acts as a selling agency receiving stocks of goods from the investing company and remitting the proceeds back to the company;
(b) produces a raw material or manufactures parts or sub-assemblies which are then shipped to the investing company for inclusion in its own products;
(c) is located overseas for tax, exchange control or similar reasons to act as a means of raising finance for other companies in the group.

THE TREATMENT OF FOREIGN BRANCHES

For the purpose of this statement, foreign operations which are conducted through a foreign branch should be accounted for in accordance with the nature of the business operations concerned. Where such a branch operates as a separate business with local finance, it should be accounted for using the closing rate/net investment method. Where the foreign branch operates as an extension of the company's trade and its cash flows have a direct impact upon those of the company, the temporal method should be used. **25**

AREAS OF HYPER-INFLATION*

26 Where a foreign enterprise operates in a country in which a very high rate of inflation exists it may not be possible to present fairly in historical cost accounts the financial position of a foreign enterprise simply by a translation process. In such circumstances the local currency financial statements should be adjusted where possible to reflect current price levels before the translation process is undertaken.

THE SPECIAL CASE OF EQUITY INVESTMENTS FINANCED BY FOREIGN BORROWINGS

27 Under the procedures set out in this statement, exchange gains or losses on foreign currency borrowings taken up by an investing company or foreign enterprise would normally be reported as part of that company's profit or loss from ordinary activities and would flow through into the consolidated profit and loss account.

28 Where an individual company has used borrowings in currencies other than its own to finance foreign equity investments, or where the purpose of such borrowings is to provide a hedge against the exchange risk associated with existing equity investments, the company may be covered in economic terms against any movement in exchange rates. It would be inappropriate in such cases to record an accounting profit or loss when exchange rates change.

29 Therefore, provided the conditions set out in this paragraph apply, the company may denominate its foreign equity investments in the appropriate foreign currencies and translate the carrying amounts at the end of each accounting period at the closing rates of exchange. Where investments are treated in this way, any resulting exchange differences should be taken direct to reserves and the exchange gains or losses on the borrowings should then be offset, as a reserve movement, against these exchange differences. The conditions which must apply are as follows:

(a) in any accounting period, exchange gains or losses arising on the borrowings may be offset only to the extent of exchange differences arising on the equity investments;
(b) the foreign currency borrowings, whose exchange gains or losses are used in the offset process, should not exceed, in the aggregate, the total amount of cash that the investments are expected to be able to generate, whether from profits or otherwise; and
(c) the accounting treatment adopted should be applied consistently from period to period.

30 Similarly, within a group, foreign borrowings may have been used to finance group investments in foreign enterprises or to provide a hedge against the exchange risk

***Editor's note:** *See also UITF Abstract 9 'Accounting for operations in hyper-inflationary economies'.*

associated with similar existing investments. Any increase or decrease in the amount outstanding on the borrowings arising from exchange movements will probably be covered by corresponding changes in the carrying amount of the net assets underlying the net investments (which would be reflected in reserves). Since in this case the group will be covered in economic terms against any movement in exchange rates, it would be inappropriate to record an accounting profit or loss when exchange rates change.

In the consolidated financial statements, therefore, subject to certain conditions, the **31** exchange gains or losses on such foreign currency borrowings, which would otherwise have been taken to the group profit and loss account, may be offset as reserve movements against exchange differences on the retranslation of the net investments. The conditions which must apply are as follows:

(a) the relationship between the investing company and the foreign enterprises concerned should be such as to justify the use of the closing rate method for consolidation purposes;

(b) in any accounting period, exchange gains or losses arising on foreign currency borrowings may be offset only to the extent of the exchange differences arising on the net investments in foreign enterprises;

(c) the foreign currency borrowings, whose exchange gains or losses are used in the offset process, should not exceed, in the aggregate, the total amount of cash that the net investments are expected to be able to generate, whether from profits or otherwise; and

(d) the accounting treatment adopted should be applied consistently from period to period.

Where the provisions of paragraph 29 have been applied in the investing company's **32** financial statements to a foreign equity investment which is neither a subsidiary nor an associated company, the same offset procedure may be applied in the consolidated financial statements.

Part 2 – Definition of terms

Financial statements are balance sheets, profit and loss accounts, statements of source **33** and application of funds, notes and other statements, which collectively are intended to give a true and fair view of the financial position and profit or loss.

Company includes any enterprise which comes within the scope of statements of **34** standard accounting practice.

An exempt company is one which: **35**

(a) is registered in Great Britain and does not prepare its accounts in accordance with either Sections 149 and 152 of the Companies Act 1948;* or

(b) is registered in Northern Ireland and is exempted from full disclosure by Part 3 of Schedule 6A to the Companies Act (Northern Ireland) 1960 as amended by the Companies (Northern Ireland) Order 1982; or

***Editor's note:** *Now sections 226 and 227 of the Companies Act 1985.*

(c) is registered in the Republic of Ireland and is exempted from full disclosure by Part 3 of Schedule 6 to the Companies Act 1963.

36 *A foreign enterprise* is a subsidiary, associated company or branch whose operations are based in a country other than that of the investing company or whose assets and liabilities are denominated mainly in a foreign currency.

37 *A foreign branch* is either a legally constituted enterprise located overseas or a group of assets and liabilities which are accounted for in foreign currencies.

38 *Translation* is the process whereby financial data denominated in one currency are expressed in terms of another currency. It includes both the expression of individual transactions in terms of another currency and the expression of a complete set of financial statements prepared in one currency in terms of another currency.

39 A company's *local currency* is the currency of the primary economic environment in which it operates and generates net cash flows.

40 An *exchange rate* is a rate at which two currencies may be exchanged for each other at a particular point in time; different rates apply for spot and forward transactions.

41 The *closing rate* is the exchange rate for spot transactions ruling at the balance sheet date and is the mean of the buying and selling rates at the close of business on the day for which the rate is to be ascertained.

42 A *forward contract* is an agreement to exchange different currencies at a specified future date and at a specified rate. The difference between the specified rate and the spot rate ruling on the date the contract was entered into is the discount or premium on the forward contract.

43 The *net investment* which a company has in a foreign enterprise is its effective equity stake and comprises its proportion of such foreign enterprise's net assets; in appropriate circumstances, intra-group loans and other deferred balances may be regarded as part of the effective equity stake.

44 *Monetary items* are money held and amounts to be received or paid in money and, where a company is not an exempt company, should be categorised as either short-term or long-term. Short-term monetary items are those which fall due within one year of the balance sheet date.

Part 3 – Standard accounting practice

45 When preparing the financial statements of an individual company the procedures set out in paragraphs 46 to 51 should be followed. When preparing consolidated financial statements, the procedures set out in paragraphs 52 to 58 should be followed.

INDIVIDUAL COMPANIES

Subject to the provisions of paragraphs 48 and 51 each asset, liability, revenue or cost arising from a transaction denominated in a foreign currency should be translated into the local currency at the exchange rate in operation on the date on which the transaction occurred; if the rates do not fluctuate significantly, an average rate for a period may be used as an approximation. Where the transaction is to be settled at a contracted rate, that rate should be used. Where a trading transaction is covered by a related or matching forward contract, the rate of exchange specified in that contract may be used. **46**

Subject to the special provisions of paragraph 51, which relate to the treatment of foreign equity investments financed by foreign currency borrowings, no subsequent translations should normally be made once non-monetary assets have been translated and recorded. **47**

At each balance sheet date, monetary assets and liabilities denominated in a foreign currency should be translated by using the closing rate or, where appropriate, the rates of exchange fixed under the terms of the relevant transactions. Where there are related or matching forward contracts in respect of trading transactions, the rates of exchange specified in those contracts may be used. **48**

All exchange gains or losses on settled transactions and unsettled short-term monetary items should be reported as part of the profit or loss for the year from ordinary activities (unless they result from transactions which themselves would fall to be treated as extraordinary items, in which case the exchange gains or losses should be included as part of such items). **49**

Exchange gains and losses on long-term monetary items should also be recognised in the profit and loss account; however, it is necessary to consider on the grounds of prudence whether, in the exceptional cases outlined in paragraph 11, the amount of the gain, or the amount by which exchange gains exceed past exchange losses on the same items to be recognised in the profit and loss account, should be restricted. **50**

Where a company has used foreign currency borrowings to finance, or provide a hedge against, its foreign equity investments and the conditions set out in this paragraph apply, the equity investments may be denominated in the appropriate foreign currencies and the carrying amounts translated at the end of each accounting period at closing rates for inclusion in the investing company's financial statements. Where investments are treated in this way, any exchange differences arising should be taken to reserves and the exchange gains or losses on the foreign currency borrowings should then be offset, as a reserve movement, against these exchange differences. The conditions which must apply are as follows: **51**

(a) in any accounting period, exchange gains or losses arising on the borrowings may be offset only to the extent of exchange differences arising on the equity investments;
(b) the foreign currency borrowings, whose exchange gains or losses are used in the offset process, should not exceed, in the aggregate, the total amount of cash that

the investments are expected to be able to generate, whether from profits or otherwise; and

(c) the accounting treatment adopted should be applied consistently from period to period.

CONSOLIDATED FINANCIAL STATEMENTS

52 When preparing group accounts for a company and its foreign enterprises, which includes the incorporation of the results of associated companies or foreign branches into those of an investing company, the closing rate/net investment method of translating the local currency financial statements should normally be used.

53 Exchange differences arising from the retranslation of the opening net investment in a foreign enterprise at the closing rate should be recorded as a movement on reserves.

54 The profit and loss account of a foreign enterprise accounted for under the closing rate/net investment method should be translated at the closing rate or at an average rate for the period. Where an average rate is used, the difference between the profit and loss account translated at an average rate and at the closing rate should be recorded as a movement on reserves. The average rate used should be calculated by the method considered most appropriate for the circumstances of the foreign enterprise.

55 In those circumstances where the trade of the foreign enterprise is more dependent on the economic environment of the investing company's currency than that of its own reporting currency, the temporal method should be used.

56 The method used for translating the financial statements of each foreign enterprise should be applied consistently from period to period unless its financial and other operational relationships with the investing company change.

57 Where foreign currency borrowings have been used to finance, or provide a hedge against, group equity investments in foreign enterprises, exchange gains or losses on the borrowings, which would otherwise have been taken to the profit and loss account, may be offset as reserve movements against exchange differences arising on the retranslation of the net investments provided that:

(a) the relationships between the investing company and the foreign enterprises concerned justify the use of the closing rate method for consolidation purposes;

(b) in any accounting period, the exchange gains and losses arising on foreign currency borrowings are offset only to the extent of the exchange differences arising on the net investments in foreign enterprises;

(c) the foreign currency borrowings, whose exchange gains or losses are used in the offset process, should not exceed, in the aggregate, the total amount of cash that the net investments are expected to be able to generate, whether from profits or otherwise; and

(d) the accounting treatment is applied consistently from period to period.

58 Where the provisions of paragraph 51 have been applied in the investing company's financial statements to a foreign equity investment which is neither a subsidiary nor an associated company, the same offset procedure may be applied in the consolidated financial statements.

DISCLOSURE

The methods used in the translation of the financial statements of foreign enterprises and the treatment accorded to exchange differences should be disclosed in the financial statements. **59**

The following information should also be disclosed in the financial statements: **60**

(a) for all companies, or groups of companies, which are not exempt companies, the net amount of exchange gains and losses on foreign currency borrowings less deposits, identifying separately:
   (i) the amount offset in reserves under the provisions of paragraphs 51, 57 and 58; and
   (ii) the net amount charged/credited to the profit and loss account;

(b) for all companies, or groups of companies, the net movement on reserves arising from exchange differences.

DATE FROM WHICH EFFECTIVE

The accounting and disclosure requirements set out in this statement should be adopted as soon as possible. They should be regarded as standard in respect of financial statements relating to accounting periods beginning on or after 1 April 1983. **61**

Part 4 – Legal requirements in UK and Ireland

Paragraphs 63 to 69 below apply to companies preparing accounts in compliance with Sections 149 and 152* of the Companies Act 1948 or with Sections 143 and 146 of the Companies Act (Northern Ireland) 1960. The references to the Schedule which follow are to Schedule 8† to the Companies Act 1948 (as inserted by Section 1 of the Companies Act 1981). References to the Schedule will also be to Schedule 6 to the Companies Act (Northern Ireland) 1960, as inserted by Article 3 of the Companies (Northern Ireland) Order 1982, when this is brought into operation on 1 July 1983. **62**

Paragraph 12 of the Schedule requires that the amount of any item shall be determined on a prudent basis and, in particular, that only profits realised at the balance sheet date shall be included in the profit and loss account. (Paragraph 90 of the Schedule‡ defines realised profits in relation to a company's accounts as 'such profits of the company as **63**

***Editor's note:** *Now sections 226 and 227 of the Companies Act 1985.*

†***Editor's note:** *Now Schedule 4 to the Companies Act 1985.*

‡***Editor's note:** *Now section 262(3) of the Companies Act 1985.*

fall to be treated as realised profits for the purposes of those accounts in accordance with principles generally accepted with respect to the determination for accounting purposes of realised profits at the time when those accounts are prepared').

64 Paragraph 15 of the Schedule permits a departure from paragraph 12 of the Schedule if it appears to the directors that there are special reasons for such a departure. Particulars of any departure, the reasons for it and its effect must be given in a note to the accounts.

65 For companies other than exempt companies, all exchange gains taken through the profit and loss account, other than those arising on unsettled long-term monetary items, are realised. For such companies the application of paragraph 50 of this statement may result in unrealised exchange gains on unsettled long-term monetary items being taken to the profit and loss account. In this statement the need to show a true and fair view of results, referred to in paragraph 10 above, is considered to constitute a special reason for departure from the principle under paragraph 15 of the Schedule.

66 This statement is based on the assumption that the process of translation at closing rates for the purposes of this statement does not constitute a departure from the historical cost rules under Section C of the Schedule nor does it give rise to a diminution in value of an asset under Section B of the Schedule.

67 Paragraph 58 (1) of the Schedule requires that, where sums originally denominated in foreign currencies are brought into the balance sheet or profit and loss account, the basis on which those sums have been translated into sterling shall be stated.

68 Part I of the Schedule lays down the choice of formats permitted for the presentation of accounts. Distinction is drawn between operating and other income and expense. For this reason it is necessary to consider the nature of each foreign exchange gain or loss and to allocate each accordingly. Gains or losses arising from trading transactions should normally be included under 'Other operating income or expense' while those arising from arrangements which may be considered as financing should be disclosed separately as part of 'Other interest receivable/payable and similar income/expense'. Exchange gains or losses which arise from events which themselves fall to be treated as extraordinary items should be included as part of such items.

69 Paragraph 46 of the Schedule requires the following information to be disclosed about movements on any reserve:

(a) the amount of the reserve at the date of the beginning of the financial year and as at the balance sheet date respectively;
(b) any amounts transferred to or from the reserve during that year; and
(c) the source and application respectively of any amounts so transferred.

70 Paragraphs 1 and 2 of Schedule 2 to the Companies Act 1981 permit certain companies to prepare accounts in compliance with Sections 149A and 152A of and Schedule 8A to the Companies Act 1948 instead of Sections 149 and 152 and Schedule 8.* Paragraph 11 (9) of Schedule 8A requires disclosure of the basis on which foreign currencies have been converted into sterling. Schedule 2 to the Companies (Northern Ireland) Order 1982 will permit similar companies registered in Northern Ireland to prepare accounts in accordance with Sections 143A and 146A of and Schedule 6A to the Companies Act (Northern Ireland) 1960 which require the same disclosure.

Similar legal requirements are expected to be enacted in the Republic of Ireland. **71**

Part 5 – Compliance with International Accounting Standard No. 21 'Accounting for the effects of changes in foreign exchange rates'

Compliance with the requirements of Statement of Standard Accounting Practice No. 20 'Foreign currency translation' will automatically ensure compliance with International Accounting Standard No. 21 'Accounting for the effects of changes in foreign exchange rates.'† **72**

***Editor's note:** *These requirements have been replaced by the special provisions for banking companies and groups in Schedule 9 to the Companies Act 1985 and for insurance companies and groups in Schedule 9A.*

*†**Editor's note:** A revised version of IAS21 was issued in November 1993.*

SSAP 21: Accounting for leases and hire purchase contracts

(Issued August 1984)

Foreword

Over the past few years, leasing has grown in importance such that it is now a major source of finance for industry in the UK. In consequence, the question of how to account for various types of lease has itself become important. SSAP 21 distinguishes finance leases from operating leases and sets out standard practice for each. It codifies accepted practice for some aspects of lease accounting and introduces a requirement for lessees to capitalise material finance leases – which a significant number of companies are doing already.

Why is a capitalisation requirement necessary? When a company is leasing a substantial amount of assets instead of buying them, the effect is that, unless the leased assets and obligations are capitalised, potentially large liabilities build up off balance sheet; equally, the leased assets employed are not reflected on the balance sheet. These omissions may mislead users of a company's accounts – both external users and the company's own management. SSAP 21 therefore requires assets held under finance leases and the related leasing obligations to be capitalised on a company's balance sheet.

Capitalisation of finance leases will be helpful in at least two respects: to external users of companies' accounts and for internal management purposes. External users may use a company's accounts when making investment or credit decisions. Capitalisation of assets held under finance leases results in a company's assets and obligations being more readily apparent than if leased assets and obligations are not recognised. The information provided by SSAP 21 should in this way enhance the usefulness of the accounts for decision-making purposes.

In the latter context, divisional managers may in some cases not be aware of or involved in the choice of finance for the assets which they use. Without capitalisation, the choice to lease instead of buy could result in a divisional manager's performance being assessed by reference to a misleading figure of capital employed, whilst at the group level assets (and obligations, and thus gearing) would be similarly understated. SSAP 21 removes these anomalies by requiring recognition on a balance sheet of the leased assets and related obligations.

It is sometimes argued that leased assets should not be recognised on a company's balance sheet as the company does not have legal title to the asset. Whilst it is true that a lessee does not have legal ownership of the leased asset, however, he has the right to use the asset for substantially the whole of its useful economic life. These rights are for most practical purposes equivalent to legal ownership. It has long been accepted that assets held under hire purchase contracts should be recognised on the balance sheet of the hirer of the asset. SSAP 21 extends this treatment to finance leasing; it recognises that whether an asset is owned, leased or held under a hire purchase contract, it represents an economic resource which is needed in the business and which the accounts ought to reflect in a consistent manner.

Detailed guidance notes are published separately from the attached standard. They are non-mandatory and their primary purpose is to recommend practical methods which will assist companies to comply with the standard.

Finally I would stress that the standard, like all accounting standards, need not be applied to immaterial items. Hence, it is only of relevance to companies engaged in a significant amount of leasing.

Ian Hay Davison, *Chairman*
Accounting Standards Committee

[SSAP 21]
Accounting for leases and hire purchase contracts

Contents

Accounting for leases and hire purchase contracts

The provisions of this Statement of Standard Accounting Practice should be read in conjunction with the (Explanatory) Foreword to Accounting Standards *and need not be applied to immaterial items. The provisions apply equally to financial statements prepared under the historical cost convention and to financial statements prepared under the current cost convention.*

This statement does not apply to lease contracts concerning the rights to explore for or to exploit natural resources such as oil, gas, timber, metals and other minerals. Nor does it apply to licensing agreements for items such as motion picture films, video recordings, plays, manuscripts, patents and copyrights.

Part 1 – Explanatory note

BACKGROUND

Leases and hire purchase contracts are means by which companies obtain the right to use or purchase assets. In the UK there is normally no provision in a lease contract for legal title to the leased asset to pass to the lessee. 1

A hire purchase contract has similar features to a lease except that under a hire purchase contract the hirer may acquire legal title by exercising an option to purchase the asset upon fulfilment of certain conditions (normally the payment of an agreed number of instalments). 2

Current tax legislation provides that in the normal situation capital allowances can be claimed by the lessor under a lease contract but by the hirer under a hire purchase contract. 3

Lessors fall into three broad categories. They may be companies, including banks and finance houses, which provide finance under lease contracts to enable a single customer to acquire the use of an asset for the greater part of its useful life; they may operate a business which involves the renting out of assets for varying periods of time probably to more than one customer; or they may be manufacturer or dealer lessors who use leasing as a means of marketing their products, which may involve leasing a product to one customer or to several customers. 4

As a lessor and lessee are both parties to the same transaction it is appropriate that the same definitions should be used and the accounting treatment recommended should ideally be complementary. However, this will not mean that the recorded balances in both financial statements will be the same because the taxation consequences and hence the pattern of cash flows will be different. 5

FORMS OF LEASE

6 Leases can appropriately be classified into finance leases and operating leases. The distinction between a finance lease and an operating lease will usually be evident from the terms of the contract between the lessor and the lessee.

7 An operating lease involves the lessee paying a rental for the hire of an asset for a period of time which is normally substantially less than its useful economic life. The lessor retains most of the risks and rewards of ownership of an asset in the case of an operating lease.

8 A finance lease usually involves payment by a lessee to a lessor of the full cost of the asset together with a return on the finance provided by the lessor. The lessee has substantially all the risks and rewards associated with the ownership of the asset, other than the legal title. In practice all leases transfer some of the risks and rewards of ownership to the lessee, and the distinction between a finance lease and an operating lease is essentially one of degree.

9 Sometimes, the lessor may receive part of his return in the form of a guarantee from an independent third party, in which case the lease may be a finance lease as far as the lessor is concerned, but not from the lessee's point of view.

10 Briefly, this standard requires that a finance lease should be capitalised by the lessee, that is, accounted for as the purchase of rights to the use and enjoyment of the asset with simultaneous recognition of the obligation to make future payments. A hire purchase is normally accounted for in a similar way. Under an operating lease, only the rental will be taken into account by a lessee.

11 The effect of a lease is to create a set of rights and obligations related to the use and enjoyment by the lessee of a leased asset for the term of the lease. Such rights constitute the rewards of ownership transferred under the lease to the lessee whilst the obligations, including in particular the obligation to continue paying rent for the period specified in the lease, constitute the risks of ownership so transferred. Where the rights and obligations of the lessee are such that his corresponding rewards and risks are, despite the absence of the ability to obtain legal title, substantially similar to those of an outright purchaser of the asset in question, the lease will be a finance lease.

12 Conceptually, what is capitalised in the lessee's accounts is not the asset itself but his rights in the asset (together with his obligation to pay rentals). However, the definition of a finance lease is such that a lessee's rights are for the practical purposes little different from those of an outright purchaser. Hence, it is appropriate that lessees should include these assets in their financial statements, but they should describe them as 'leased assets' to distinguish them from owned assets.

Part 2 – Definition of terms

13 *Company* includes any enterprise which comes within the scope of statements of standard accounting practice.

A *lease* is a contract between a lessor and a lessee for the hire of a specific asset. The lessor retains ownership of the asset but conveys the right to the use of the asset to the lessee for an agreed period of time in return for the payment of specified rentals. The term 'lease' as used in this statement also applies to other arrangements in which one party retains ownership of an asset but conveys the right to the use of the asset to another party for an agreed period of time in return for specified payments. **14**

A *finance lease* is a lease that transfers substantially all the risks and rewards of ownership of an asset to the lessee. It should be presumed that such a transfer of risks and rewards occurs if at the inception of a lease the present value of the minimum lease payments including any initial payment, amounts to substantially all (normally 90 per cent or more) of the fair value of the leased asset. The present value should be calculated by using the interest rate implicit in the lease (as defined in paragraph 24). If the fair value of the asset is not determinable, an estimate thereof should be used. **15**

Notwithstanding the fact that a lease meets the conditions in paragraph 15, the presumption that it should be classified as a finance lease may in exceptional circumstances be rebutted if it can be clearly demonstrated that the lease in question does not transfer substantially all the risks and rewards of ownership (other than legal title) to the lessee. Correspondingly, the presumption that a lease which fails to meet the conditions in paragraph 15 is not a finance lease may in exceptional circumstances be rebutted. **16**

An *operating lease* is a lease other than a finance lease. **17**

A *hire purchase contract* is a contract for the hire of an asset which contains a provision giving the hirer an option to acquire legal title to the asset upon the fulfilment of certain conditions stated in the contract. **18**

The *lease term* is the period for which the lessee has contracted to lease the asset and any further terms for which the lessee has the option to continue to lease the asset, with or without further payment, which option it is reasonably certain at the inception of the lease that the lessee will exercise. **19**

The *minimum lease payments* are the minimum payments over the remaining part of the lease term (excluding charges for services and taxes to be paid by the lessor) and: **20**

(a) in the case of the lessee, any residual amounts guaranteed by him or by a party related to him; or
(b) in the case of the lessor, any residual amounts guaranteed by the lessee or by an independent third party.

The *gross investment* in a lease at a point in time is the total of the minimum lease payments and any unguaranteed residual value accruing to the lessor. **21**

The *net investment* in a lease at a point in time comprises: **22**

(a) the gross investment in a lease (as defined in paragraph 21): *less*
(b) gross earnings allocated to future periods.

23 The *net cash investment* in a lease at a point in time is the amount of funds invested in a lease by a lessor, and comprises the cost of the asset plus or minus the following related payments or receipts:

(a) government or other grants receivable towards the purchase or use of the asset;
(b) rentals received;
(c) taxation payments and receipts, including the effect of capital allowances;
(d) residual values, if any, at the end of the lease term;
(e) interest payments (where applicable);
(f) interest received on cash surplus;
(g) profit taken out of the lease.

24 The *interest rate implicit in a lease* is the discount rate that at the inception of a lease, when applied to the amounts which the lessor expects to receive and retain produces an amount (the present value) equal to the fair value of the leased asset. The amounts which the lessor expects to receive and retain comprise (a) the minimum lease payments to the lessor (as defined in paragraph 20), plus (b) any unguaranteed residual value, less (c) any part of (a) and (b) for which the lessor will be accountable to the lessee. If the interest rate implicit in the lease is not determinable, it should be estimated by reference to the rate which a lessee would be expected to pay on a similar lease.

25 *Fair value* is the price at which an asset could be exchanged in an arm's length transaction less, where applicable, any grants receivable towards the purchase or use of the asset.

26 *Unguaranteed residual value* is that portion of the residual value of the leased asset (estimated at the inception of the lease), the realisation of which by the lessor is not assured or is guaranteed solely by a party related to the lessor.

27 *Finance charge* is the amount borne by the lessee over the lease term, representing the difference between the total of the minimum lease payments (including any residual amounts guaranteed by him) and the amount at which he records the leased asset at the inception of the lease.

28 *Gross earnings* comprise the lessor's gross finance income over the lease term, representing the difference between his gross investment in the lease (as defined in paragraph 21) and the cost of the leased asset less any grants receivable towards the purchase or use of the asset. Where a lessor selects option (b) of paragraph 41 the grants to be deducted should be the grossed-up amount.

29 The *inception of a lease* is the earlier of the time the asset is brought into use and the date from which rentals first accrue.

30 *Initial direct costs* are those costs incurred by the lessor that are directly associated with negotiating and consummating leasing transactions, such as commissions, legal fees, costs of credit investigations and costs of preparing and processing documents for new leases acquired.

Part 3 – Standard accounting practice

HIRE PURCHASE AND LEASING

Those hire purchase contracts which are of a financing nature should be accounted for on a basis similar to that set out below for finance leases. Conversely, other hire purchase contracts should be accounted for on a basis similar to that set out below for operating leases. **31**

ACCOUNTING BY LESSEES

A finance lease should be recorded in the balance sheet of a lessee as an asset and as an obligation to pay future rentals. At the inception of the lease the sum to be recorded both as an asset and as a liability should be the present value of the minimum lease payments, derived by discounting them at the interest rate implicit in the lease. **32**

In practice in the case of a finance lease the fair value of the asset will often be a sufficiently close approximation to the present value of the minimum lease payments and may in these circumstances be substituted for it. **33**

The combined benefit to a lessor of regional development and other grants together with capital allowances, which reduce tax liabilities, may enable the minimum lease payments under a finance lease to be reduced to a total which is less than the fair value of the asset. In these circumstances, the amount to be capitalised and depreciated should be restricted to the minimum lease payments. A negative finance charge should not be shown. **34**

Rentals payable should be apportioned between the finance charge and a reduction of the outstanding obligation for future amounts payable. The total finance charge under a finance lease should be allocated to accounting periods during the lease term so as to produce a constant periodic rate of charge on the remaining balance of the obligation for each accounting period, or a reasonable approximation thereto. **35**

An asset leased under a finance lease should be depreciated over the shorter of the lease term (as defined in paragraph 19) and its useful life. However, in the case of a hire purchase contract which has the characteristics of a finance lease, the asset should be depreciated over its useful life. **36**

The rental under an operating lease should be charged on a straight-line basis over the lease term, even if the payments are not made on such a basis, unless another systematic and rational basis is more appropriate. **37**

ACCOUNTING BY LESSORS

The amount due from the lessee under a finance lease should be recorded in the balance sheet of a lessor as a debtor at the amount of the net investment in the lease after making provisions for items such as bad and doubtful rentals receivable. **38**

39 The total gross earnings under a finance lease should normally be allocated to accounting periods to give a constant periodic rate of return to the lessor's **net cash investment** in the lease in each period. In the case of a hire purchase contract which has characteristics similar to a finance lease, allocation of gross earnings so as to give a constant periodic rate of return on the finance company's **net investment** will in most cases be a suitable approximation to allocation based on the net cash investment. In arriving at the constant periodic rate of return, a reasonable approximation may be made.

40 As an alternative to paragraph 39, an allocation may first be made out of gross earnings of an amount equal to the lessor's estimated cost of finance included in the net cash investment calculation, with the balance being recognised on a systematic basis.

41 Tax free grants which are available to the lessor against the purchase price of assets acquired for leasing should be spread over the period of the lease and may be dealt with either:

(a) by treating the grant as non-taxable income; or
(b) by grossing up the grant and including the grossed-up amount in arriving at the profit before tax.

Where treatment (b) is adopted, the lessor should disclose the amount by which the profit before tax and the tax charge have been increased as a result of grossing up such grants.

42 An asset held for use in operating leases by a lessor should be recorded as a fixed asset and depreciated over its useful life.

43 Rental income from an operating lease, excluding charges for services such as insurance and maintenance, should be recognised on a straight-line basis over the period of the lease, even if the payments are not made on such a basis, unless another systematic and rational basis is more representative of the time pattern in which the benefit from the leased asset is receivable.

44 Initial direct costs incurred by a lessor in arranging a lease may be apportioned over the period of the lease on a systematic and rational basis.

MANUFACTURER/DEALER LESSOR

45 A manufacturer or dealer lessor should not recognise a selling profit under an operating lease. The selling profit under a finance lease should be restricted to the excess of the fair value of the asset over the manufacturer's or dealer's cost less any grants receivable by the manufacturer or dealer towards the purchase, construction or use of the asset.

SALE AND LEASEBACK TRANSACTIONS

Accounting by the seller/lessee

In a sale and leaseback transaction which results in a finance lease any apparent profit or loss (that is, the difference between the sale price and the previous carrying value) should be deferred and amortised in the financial statements of the seller/lessee over the shorter of the lease term and the useful life of the asset. **46**

If the leaseback is an operating lease: **47**

(a) any profit or loss should be recognised immediately, provided it is clear that the transaction is established at fair value;

(b) if the sale price is below fair value, any profit or loss should be recognised immediately except that if the apparent loss is compensated by future rentals at below market price it should to that extent be deferred and amortised over the remainder of the lease term (or, if shorter, the period during which the reduced rentals are chargeable);

(c) if the sale price is above fair value, the excess over fair value should be deferred and amortised over the shorter of the remainder of the lease term and the period to the next rent review (if any).

Accounting by the buyer/lessor

A buyer/lessor should account for a sale and leaseback in the same way as he accounts for other leases, that is, using methods set out in paragraphs 38 to 45 above. **48**

DISCLOSURE BY LESSEES

The gross amounts of assets which are held under finance leases* together with the related accumulated depreciation should be disclosed by each major class of asset. The total depreciation allocated for the period in respect of assets held under finance leases should be disclosed by each major class of asset. **49**

The information required by paragraph 49 may, as an alternative to being shown separately from that in respect of owned fixed assets, be integrated with it such that the totals of gross amount, accumulated depreciation, net amount and depreciation allocated for the period for each major class of asset are included with similar amounts in respect of owned fixed assets. Where this alternative treatment is adopted, the net amount of assets held under finance leases* included in the overall total should be disclosed. The amount of depreciation allocated for the period in respect of assets held under finance leases* included in the overall total should also be disclosed. **50**

The amounts of obligations related to finance leases* (net of finance charges allocated **51**

****Including the equivalent information in respect of hire purchase contracts which have characteristics similar to that type of lease (see paragraph 31).***

to future periods) should be disclosed separately from other obligations and liabilities, either on the face of the balance sheet or in the notes to the accounts.

52 These net obligations under finance leases* should be analysed between amounts payable in the next year, amounts payable in the second to fifth years inclusive from the balance sheet date, and the aggregate amounts payable thereafter. This analysis may be presented either (a) separately for obligations under finance leases* or (b) where the total of these items is combined on the balance sheet with other obligations and liabilities, by giving the equivalent analysis of the total in which it is included. If the analysis is presented according to (a) above, a lessee may, as an alternative to analysing the net obligations, analyse the gross obligations, with future finance charges being separately deducted from the total.

53 The aggregate finance charges allocated for the period in respect of finance leases* should be disclosed.

54 Disclosure should be made of the amount of any commitments existing at the balance sheet date in respect of finance leases* which have been entered into but whose inception occurs after the year end.

55 The total of operating lease rentals* charged as an expense in the profit and loss account should be disclosed, analysed between amounts payable in respect of hire of plant and machinery and in respect of other operating leases.*

56 In respect of operating leases*, the lessee should disclose the payments which he is committed to make during the next year, analysed between those in which the commitment expires within that year, in the second to fifth years inclusive and over five years from the balance sheet date, showing separately the commitments in respect of leases of land and buildings and other operating leases*.

57 Disclosure should be made of the policies adopted for accounting for operating leases* and finance leases*.

DISCLOSURE BY LESSORS

58 The net investment in (i) finance leases and (ii) hire purchase contracts at each balance sheet date should be disclosed.

59 The gross amounts of assets held for use in operating leases*, and the related accumulated depreciation charges, should be disclosed.

60 Disclosure should be made of:

(a) the policy adopted for accounting for operating leases* and finance leases* and, in detail, the policy for accounting for finance lease income*;

(b) the aggregate rentals receivable in respect of an accounting period in relation to (i) finance leases* and (ii) operating leases*; and

**Including the equivalent information in respect of hire purchase contracts which have characteristics similar to that type of lease (see paragraph 31).*

(c) the cost of assets acquired, whether by purchase or finance lease*, for the purpose of letting under finance leases.*

DATE FROM WHICH EFFECTIVE FOR LESSORS AND FINANCE COMPANIES

The accounting practices set out in this statement should be adopted as soon as possible **61**
and regarded as standard for financial statements relating to accounting periods beginning on or after 1 July 1984 in respect of leases and hire purchase contracts (a) entered into on or after 1 July 1984 or (b) which have five years or more to run on 1 July 1984. If the provisions of this statement are not applied retroactively to all leases and hire purchase contracts existing at 1 July 1984, lessors and finance companies should disclose the amounts of gross earnings from finance leases and hire purchase contracts for the current year and the comparative period which have arisen under each of the principal bases used.

DATE FROM WHICH EFFECTIVE FOR LESSEES AND HIRERS

The accounting practices set out in this statement should be adopted by lessees and **62**
hirers as soon as possible and regarded as standard in respect of financial statements relating to accounting periods beginning on or after 1 July 1987. However, the disclosure requirements in paragraphs 52 and 54 to 57 should be regarded as standard in respect of financial statements relating to accounting periods beginning on or after 1 July 1984.

Part 4 – Legal requirements in Great Britain

Paragraph 50 (5) of Schedule 8† provides that 'Particulars shall also be given of any **63**
other financial commitments which:

(a) have not been provided for; and
(b) are relevant to assessing the company's state of affairs.'

Insofar as finance leases are capitalised by lessees, the obligations under finance leases are provided for in the accounts. This will not be the case to the extent that lessees take advantage of the delayed implementation of capitalisation as set out in paragraph 62.

Paragraph 53 (6) of Schedule 8† requires disclosure of the 'amount charged to revenue **64**
in respect of sums payable in respect of the hire of plant and machinery' (Standard, paragraphs 49, 50, 53 and 55 and guidance notes).

The balance sheet formats in Schedule 8† require that creditors falling due within one **65**
year should be shown separately from creditors falling due after more than one year (Standard, paragraph 52 and guidance notes).

Including the equivalent information in respect of hire purchase contracts which have characteristics similar to that type of lease (see paragraph 31).

*†**Editor's note:** Now Schedule 4 to the Companies Act 1985.*

66 The balance sheet formats in Schedule 8† provide that the 'amount falling due after more than one year shall be shown separately for each item included under debtors'. This is relevant to the disclosure of amounts receivable by a lessor (Standard, paragraph 58 and guidance notes).

Part 5 – Legal requirements in Ireland

NORTHERN IRELAND

67 The Schedule references in Part 4 (paragraphs 63 to 66) apply equally to Schedule 6 of the Companies Act (Northern Ireland) 1960, as inserted by Article 3 of the Companies (Northern Ireland) Order 1982.

REPUBLIC OF IRELAND

68 General provisions as to accounts are set out in the Sixth Schedule to the Companies Act 1963. There are no legal requirements in the Republic of Ireland similar to those outlined in Part 4.

Part 6 – Compliance with International Accounting Standard No. 17 'Accounting for leases'

69 The requirements of International Accounting Standard No. 17 'Accounting for leases' accord very closely with the content of the United Kingdom and Irish Accounting Standard No. 21 'Accounting for leases and hire purchase contracts' and accordingly compliance with SSAP 21 will ensure compliance with IAS 17 in all material respects.

†*Editor's note: Now Schedule 4 to the Companies Act 1985.*

Guidance Notes on SSAP 21: Accounting for leases and hire purchase contracts

(Issued August 1984)

These notes are for guidance only and do not form part of the statement of standard accounting practice.

Contents

INTRODUCTION

General

1 The statement of Standard Accounting Practice on Accounting for Leases and Hire Purchase Contracts sets out objectives and disclosure requirements. The primary purpose of the guidance notes is to recommend practical methods which will assist companies to comply with the standard. The guidance notes are not mandatory.

2 The aim in writing the guidance notes has been to cover the most common situations which will be met in practice. It is not possible to lay down methods which will cover all situations.

3 The guidance notes do not recognise the effect of the transitional provisions set out in paragraphs 61 and 62 of the standard. In the periods affected by these provisions different methods and disclosures may be required.

4 All references in the guidance notes to legal requirements are to the UK Companies Acts; the examples assume that companies are subject to Schedule 8, Companies Act 1948.*

5 The definitions of terms in the standard apply also to the guidance notes.

6 The effects of value added tax have been ignored in the guidance notes.

Materiality

7 The standard, in common with all standards, need not be applied to immaterial items. In this context, the relevant criterion is the size of the lease (or leases in aggregate, if more than one) in the context of the size of the lessee or lessor.

8 In deciding whether or not a lease is material, regard should be had to the effect which treating the lease according to the main requirements of the standard (e.g., capitalising it) would have on the financial statements as a whole. Thus, it may be necessary to consider the effect of (in this example) capitalisation on (a) total fixed assets, (b) total borrowings and obligations, (c) the gearing ratio and (d) the profit or loss for the year (as a result of the difference between charging the lease payment and charging the total of depreciation plus finance charge). If capitalisation of the lease would not have a material effect on any of these items, the lease need not be capitalised.

The simplified approach to accounting for small leases

9 Where a lease is material, the main provisions of the standard will need to be applied. Thus, a finance lease will need to be capitalised by a lessee. Similarly, a finance lease should be shown as a receivable by a lessor.

***Editor's note:** *Now Schedule 4 to the Companies Act 1985.*

However, Part I of these guidance notes describes the use of simplified methods for leases and suggests when they may be used. In particular, paragraphs 32 to 36 describe the simplified approach to lessee accounting whereby a lessee may use the straight-line method to write off finance charges under a finance lease. Part II discusses a number of methods of lessors' income recognition, including simplified methods (see, for example paragraphs 81, 95, 119 and 122). 10

Hire purchase and leasing

It is not intended that this standard should change the existing best practice for accounting for hire purchase contracts by either finance companies or hirers. 11

Most hire purchase contracts are of a financing nature. Generally, the option to purchase the asset is exercisable at below market value – often at a nominal amount – such that the hirer can be expected from the outset to take up the option. The standard therefore provides that such hire purchase contracts should be accounted for on a basis similar to that set out for finance leases. 12

Less commonly, there are found hire purchase contracts which are not of a financing nature. For example, the option to purchase may be exercisable at a relatively high price such that the hirer may not take it up. The standard therefore provides that such hire purchase contracts should be accounted for on a similar basis to that set out for operating leases. 13

Part I – Lessee accounting

INTRODUCTION

Part I explains the accounting requirements for lessees in the following sections: 14

	Paragraphs
A – General principles	15–19
B – The arithmetic of capitalising finance leases	20–47
C – Balance sheet presentation, note disclosure and legal requirements for lessees	48–63
D – Initial recording of the leased asset	64–68

A – GENERAL PRINCIPLES

A lessee should classify his leases in (a) operating leases and (b) finance leases, according to the definitions in paragraphs 15 to 17 of the standard. Additional guidance on lease classification may be found in paragraphs 133 to 138. 15

Operating leases

The right to use an asset or the obligation to pay rentals under an operating lease should not be recorded in the balance sheet but a lessee should disclose certain 16 information by way of note to the financial statements (see paragraphs 57 to 63). The rentals under an operating lease should be charged on a straight-line basis over the lease term, even if the payments are not made on such a basis, unless another systematic and rational basis is more appropriate. Thus, in situations such as rental holidays in which a lease has been arranged so that, for example, no payment is made in the first year (although the asset is in use during that year), the total rentals should be charged over the period in which the asset is in use.*

Finance leases

17 Under a finance lease the lessee acquires substantially all the benefits of the use of an asset for the greater part of its useful economic life and takes on substantially all of the risks associated with ownership. In economic substance it is similar to the purchase of an asset even though legal title to the asset remains with the lessor.

18 The risks of ownership of an asset include unsatisfactory performance, obsolescence and idle capacity. The benefits include the right to the unencumbered use of the asset over most of its useful economic life.

19 The two aspects of a finance lease should be recorded in the lessee's balance sheet. The right to use the asset should be capitalised and shown as a fixed asset. The obligation to pay rentals should be shown as a liability.

B – THE ARITHMETIC OF CAPITALISING FINANCE LEASES

20 The capitalisation of finance leases is now illustrated by means of numerical examples. Three methods of writing off finance charges are shown:

(a) the actuarial method;
(b) the 'Rule of 78' (or 'Sum of the Digits') method; and
(c) the straight-line method.

The standard (paragraph 35) provides that the 'total finance charge under a finance lease should be allocated to accounting periods during the lease term so as to produce a constant periodic rate of charge on the remaining balance of the obligation for each accounting period, or a reasonable approximation thereto'. Of the above three methods, the actuarial method gives the most accurate result.

Terms of the lease

21 The examples illustrated are based on the following lease:

> A lessee leases an asset on a non-cancellable lease contract with a primary term of five years from 1 January 1987. The rental is £650 per quarter payable in advance. The lessee has the right to continue to lease the asset after the end of the primary period for as long as he wishes at a peppercorn rent. In addition the lessee is required to pay all maintenance and insurance costs as they arise. The leased asset could have been purchased for cash at the start of the lease for £10,000.

***Editor's note:** *The last sentence has been superseded by UITF Abstract 12 'Lessee accounting for reverse premiums and similar incentives'.*

A lessee should, strictly, record a finance lease at the present value of the minimum lease payments (Standard, paragraph 32). However, for most practical purposes, it will be acceptable to record the leased asset at its fair value (Standard, paragraph 33). (The present value of the minimum lease payments in a finance lease will normally be at least 90% of the fair value of the leased asset.) The two approaches would produce different results where the lessor expects to benefit from a residual value which is not guaranteed by the lessee. In this example it is assumed for simplicity that the asset has no residual value at the end of the lease term. At the start of the lease, therefore, the lessee should capitalise the asset in his balance sheet at a cost of £10,000 and also record the obligation under the finance lease of £10,000 as a liability. Guidance on a more rigorous determination of the amount to be capitalised in respect of a leased asset is given in paragraphs 64 to 68. **22**

The minimum lease payments amount to 20 × £650 = £13,000. The total finance charges under the lease are therefore £3,000. **23**

The total finance charges should be allocated to accounting periods during the lease so as to produce a constant periodic rate of charge on the remaining balance of the obligation for each accounting period. This calculation is shown in Table 1. **24**

The actuarial method

TABLE 1

CALCULATION OF THE PERIODIC FINANCE CHARGE IN THE LEASE **25**

Period	*Capital sum at start of period*	*Rental paid*	*Capital sum during period*	*Finance charge (2.95% per quarter)**	*Capital sum at end of period*
	£	£	£	£	£
1/87	10,000	650	9,350	276	9,626
2/87	9,626	650	8,976	265	9,241
3/87	9,241	650	8,591	254	8,845
4/87	8,845	650	8,195	242	8,437
				1,037	
1/88	8,437	650	7,787	230	8,017
2/88	8,017	650	7,367	217	7,584
3/88	7,584	650	6,934	205	7,139
4/88	7,139	650	6,489	191	6,680
				843	

**The quarterly finance charge of 2.95% may be calculated in a number of ways: (a) by trial and error, (b) by financial pocket calculator or computer program, (c) by a mathematical formula, or (d) by reference to present value tables.*

1/89	6,680	650	6,030	178	6,208
2/89	6,208	650	5,558	164	5,722
3/89	5,722	650	5,072	150	5,222
4/89	5,222	650	4,572	135	4,707
				627	
1/90	4,707	650	4,057	120	4,177
2/90	4,177	650	3,527	104	3,631
3/90	3,631	650	2,981	88	3,069
4/90	3,069	650	2,419	71	2,490
				383	
1/91	2,490	650	1,840	54	1,894
2/91	1,894	650	1,244	37	1,281
3/91	1,281	650	631	19	650
4/91	650	650	–	–	–
				110	
		£13,000		£3,000	

26 The annual rental may therefore be apportioned between a finance charge and a capital repayment based on the figures in Table 1:

TABLE 2

APPORTIONMENT OF ANNUAL RENTALS – ACTUARIAL METHOD

	Finance charge	*Capital Repayment*	*Total rental*
	£	£	£
1987	1,037	1,563	2,600
1988	843	1,757	2,600
1989	627	1,973	2,600
1990	383	2,217	2,600
1991	110	2,490	2,600
	£3,000	£10,000	£13,000

27 The allocation of the finance charge to accounting periods by the actuarial method in Table 1 is not easy to calculate manually and it may be appropriate to use the rule of 78 or the straight-line method as an approximation. These are discussed in turn.

Rule of 78

The rule of 78 may normally be regarded as an acceptable approximation to the actuarial method; it works well provided that the lease term is not very long (say, not more than seven years) and interest rates are not very high. The calculations using the rule of 78 are as follows: **28**

TABLE 3

'RULE OF 78' CALCULATIONS

Period	*Number of rentals not yet due*			*Finance charge per annum*
			£	£
1/87	19		= 300	
2/87	18		= 284	
3/87	17		= 268	
4/87	16		= 253	
				1,105
1/88	15		= 237	
2/88	14		= 221	
3/88	13		= 205	
4/88	12		= 190	
				853
1/89	11		= 174	
2/89	10	÷ 190 × 3000	= 158	
3/89	9		= 142	
4/89	8		= 126	
				600
1/90	7		= 110	
2/90	6		= 95	
3/90	5		= 79	
4/90	4		= 63	
				347
1/91	3		= 47	
2/91	2		= 32	
3/91	1		= 16	
4/91	–		= –	
				95
	190*		£3,000	£3,000

This total may be calculated using the formula

$$\frac{n(n+1)}{2}$$ *where n is the number of periods in question.*

Hence in this case $n = 19$ *and* $\frac{19 \times 20}{2} = 190$.

29 The term 'Rule of 78' arose because, if finance charges are allocated over a one year period, months 1 to 12 when added together add up to 78. Here, the weights add up to 190.

30 In this example rentals are payable in advance. Hence the final payment is made on the first day of period 4/91, and no interest should be allocated to that period. If the rentals had been payable in arrears, then one unit of interest would have been chargeable to that period, and 20 units to period 1/87, with corresponding changes to the other periods.

31 Having calculated the finance charge as in paragraph 28 using the rule of 78, all the other calculations are continued in the same way as for the actuarial method.

The straight-line method

32 As noted above, and as can be seen in Table 5 below, the use of the rule of 78 results in a close approximation to the actuarial method. However, it may be appropriate in certain cases to use the straight-line method. This is the simplest of the methods illustrated. It does not attempt to produce a constant periodic rate of change, but if used in connection with a relatively small lease it may produce figures which in any year are not significantly different from those which would be produced by one of the other methods. What is a small lease will depend on the size of the company.

33 The calculations using the straight-line method are as follows. The finance charges under the lease should be apportioned on a straight-line basis over the period of the lease in which rentals are being paid:

£3,000 ÷ 5 = £600 per annum

34 The annual rental may be apportioned between the finance charge and the capital repayment as follows:

TABLE 4

APPORTIONMENT OF ANNUAL RENTALS – STRAIGHT-LINE METHOD

	Finance charge	*Capital repayment*	*Total rental*
	£	£	£
1987	600	2,000	2,600
1988	600	2,000	2,600
1989	600	2,000	2,600
1990	600	2,000	2,600
1991	600	2,000	2,600
	£3,000	£10,000	£13,000

35 The finance charges as calculated under the actuarial method, the rule of 78 and the straight-line method are compared below:

TABLE 5

COMPARISON OF FINANCE CHARGES

	Actuarial		*Rule of 78*		*Straight-line*	
	£	%	£	%	£	%
1987	1,037	34	1,105	37	600	20
1988	843	28	853	28	600	20
1989	627	21	600	20	600	20
1990	383	13	347	12	600	20
1991	110	4	95	3	600	20
	£3,000	100	£3,000	100	£3,000	100

Whether the straight-line method (or the rule of 78) provides a reasonable approximation to an accurate method depends on the facts of each case. Where a lease is small in relation to the size of the lessee, the difference between the methods may not be material.

It is sometimes argued that, in order to establish whether the straight-line method provides a reasonable approximation, it is necessary to calculate the finance charge allocation on two or more bases. This is not necessarily so. In some cases the *total* finance charges may not be material in which case the straight-line method may be used: there will be no need to compare the allocation under the straight-line method with that under any other method. **36**

Variation clauses

Where a lease contains an interest variation clause which adjusts the rental by reference to movements in Finance House base rate, or some other indicator, no adjustment need normally be made to the calculations, such as those in Table 1, which are carried out at the start of the lease. Any increase or reduction in rentals should be accounted for as an increase or reduction in finance charges in the period in which it arises. **37**

Where a lease contains a tax variation clause which adjusts the rental in order to protect the parties from the effects of tax changes, any increase or reduction in rentals should be accounted for as an increase or reduction in finance charges. Where the reduction in rentals exceeds the future finance charges, the excess should be applied to reduce future depreciation charges. **38**

Depreciation

The leased asset should be depreciated on a basis compatible with that adopted for assets which are owned. SSAP 12 'Accounting for depreciation' requires an asset to be depreciated by allocating the cost less estimated residual value of the asset as fairly as possible to the periods expected to benefit from its use. **39**

The period over which a leased asset should be depreciated is the shorter of (a) the lease **40** term and (b) the asset's useful life. The lease term is the primary period of the lease (i.e., the non-cancellable part) together with any secondary periods during which the lessee has the contractual right to continue to use the asset and which right, at the start of the lease, it is reasonable to expect him to exercise.

41 In this example the lessee estimates that the lease will be continued for a further two years after the end of the primary period so that he should depreciate the leased asset over seven years. This is the period over which he depreciates similar assets which he owns.

42 In most cases the residual value of leased assets at the end of the lease is likely to be small so that even where the lessee has the right to share in the ultimate residual value it is usual to assume for the purposes of establishing an appropriate depreciation charge that it will be nil. This will be the case whether the residual value takes the form of sale proceeds or a rebate of rentals.

43 In this example the lessee estimates that the asset will have a useful life of seven years and that the residual value will be nil. The annual depreciation charge on a straight-line basis is therefore:

$$£10,000 \div 7 = £1,429$$

44 In the case of a hire purchase contract which has the characteristics of a finance lease, it is expected from the outset that the hirer will take up the option to purchase. Hence, the asset should be depreciated over its useful life, regardless of the term of the hire contract.

Calculation of balance sheet values

45 The leased asset should be described in the balance sheet as 'Assets held under finance leases'. The liability should be described as 'Obligations under finance leases'. The net book value of the asset at the end of each year, if straight-line depreciation is used, will be:

TABLE 6

BALANCE SHEET VALUES – LEASED ASSETS

	Cost	*Accumulated depreciation*	*Net book value of assets held under finance leases*
	£	£	£
31.12.87	10,000 –	1,429 =	8,571
31.12.88	10,000 –	2,858 =	7,142
31.12.89	10,000 –	4,287 =	5,713
31.12.90	10,000 –	5,716 =	4,284
31.12.91	10,000 –	7,145 =	2,855
31.12.92	10,000 –	8,574 =	1,426
31.12.93	10,000 –	10,000 =	–

The obligations under finance leases (i.e., the capital element of future rentals payable) will be calculated as follows: 46

TABLE 7

BALANCE SHEET VALUES – LEASING OBLIGATIONS

	Obligations under finance leases outstanding at start of year	*Capital repayment*	*Obligations under finance leases outstanding at year end*
	£	£	£
31.12.87	10,000 –	1,563 =	8,437
31.12.88	8,437 –	1,757 =	6,680
31.12.89	6,680 –	1,973 =	4,707
31.12.90	4,707 –	2,217 =	2,490
31.12.91	2,490 –	2,490 =	–
31.12.92			
31.12.93			

(These figures assume that the actuarial method is being used. The capital repayments are taken from Table 2.)

Comparison of the balance sheet amounts of the capitalised leased asset

The figures in Tables 6 and 7 are compared below: 47

TABLE 8

LEASED ASSETS AND OBLIGATIONS

	NBV of assets held under finance leases	*Obligations under finance leases outstanding at year end*	*Difference*
	£	£	£
31.12.87	8,571 –	8,437 =	134
31.12.88	7,142 –	6,680 =	462
31.12.89	5,713 –	4,707 =	1,006
31.12.90	4,284 –	2,490 =	1,794
31.12.91	2,855 –	– =	2,855
31.12.92	1,426 –	– =	1,426
31.12.93	– –	– =	–

The differences shown in the third column do not appear separately on a balance sheet. They are timing differences which result from capitalising a lease, and are needed for the calculation of deferred tax (see paragraphs 171 to 173). Charging the total of depreciation and interest to the profit and loss account is likely to result in recognition of the total costs of a finance lease in a different pattern from that in which the rentals are paid and the tax allowances are received. In this example, the costs are recognised later because the asset is depreciated over seven years whereas the instalments are paid over five years. Hence the timing differences cause a temporary, reversing, increase in equity, which is reflected in the above table by asset values being temporarily higher than the obligations.

C – BALANCE SHEET PRESENTATION, NOTE DISCLOSURE AND LEGAL REQUIREMENTS FOR LESSEES

48 A finance lease will be shown in a lessee's balance sheet both as an asset and as an obligation. At the start of the lease the amount of the asset and the obligation will be the same but they are unlikely to be so in subsequent years. The obligation under the lease may be paid off before the asset is fully depreciated.

49 Schedule 8 to the Companies Act 1948* contains, inter alia, formats which must be followed by companies (except those subject to Schedule 8A†) in the presentation of their accounts. Leased assets and leasing obligations are not specifically mentioned in the formats, but paragraphs 3(1) and (2) of the 8th Schedule* provide that items may be shown in greater detail than required by the formats and that new items may be inserted for items not covered by the formats.

50 Assets held under finance leases are not legally owned by the lessee. (The same applies to assets subject to hire purchase contracts, until the purchase option is exercised.) The lessee's right is to use the asset, not to own it. Similarly, a lessee's obligations under a finance lease are not, from a legal point of view, debt but rather obligations under a bailment to hire. Therefore, in order to reflect this legal difference, assets held under finance leases and the related obligations should be described in such a way as to be distinguishable from owned assets and debt respectively.

51 The standard permits a company to aggregate the amounts which are required to be presented on a balance sheet or disclosed in notes in respect of (i) finance leases and (ii) hire purchase contracts which have characteristics similar to finance leases. It is expected that most companies will choose to combine the amounts.

52 Assets held under finance leases and hire purchase contracts should generally be integrated with owned fixed assets on a balance sheet. The analysis of fixed assets may be in one of two forms: either

(a) the notes to the accounts should contain details of the assets held under finance leases and hire purchase contracts, by class of asset; or

(b) the fixed assets note should analyse, by class of asset, the combined total of owned assets and assets held under finance leases and hire purchase contracts. In order to distinguish owned assets from non-owned assets, a note similar to the following should be shown:

'The net book value of fixed assets of £x includes an amount of £8,571 in respect of assets held under finance leases and hire purchase contracts'.

***Editor's note:** *Now Schedule 4 to the Companies Act 1985.*

*†**Editor's note:** Now Schedules 9 and 9A to the Companies Act 1985.*

Obligations under finance leases and hire purchase contracts should be analysed between those amounts payable within one year and those amounts payable in more than one year. These two amounts should be described, either on the face of the balance sheet or in the notes to the accounts, as 'Obligations under finance leases and hire purchase contracts' under the headings of 'Creditors: amounts falling due within one year' and 'Creditors: amounts falling due after more than one year' respectively. **53**

Alternatively, obligations under finance leases and hire purchase contracts may be combined with other items (for example, bank loans and overdrafts) under each of the 'Creditors' headings referred to in the preceding paragraph. **54**

The standard requires the amount of obligations under finance leases and hire purchase contracts falling due after more than one year, or the total in which it is included, to be further analysed as to amounts due in the second to fifth years inclusive from the balance sheet date and the aggregate amounts payable thereafter. **55**

Where the treatment in paragraph 54 is adopted, a note such as the following will comply with the disclosure requirements and with company law: **56**

Bank loans, overdrafts, obligations under finance leases and hire purchase contracts

These comprise:

Bank loans and overdrafts		20,000
Obligations under finance leases and hire purchase contracts (see paragraph 47)		8,437
		£28,437

The maturity of the above amounts is as follows:

Under one year		10,000
Over one year		
In the second to fifth years inclusive	12,500	
Over five years	5,937	
		18,437
		£28,437

The £10,000 should be included under the heading 'Creditors: amounts falling due within one year'; the £18,437 should be included under the heading 'Creditors: amounts falling due after more than one year'. (The Stock Exchange additionally requires listed companies to disclose the amount payable in the second year after the balance sheet date.)

Note disclosure – profit and loss account

57 Paragraph 53(6) of Schedule 8* to the Companies Act 1948 requires disclosure of the amount, if material, charged to revenue in respect of sums payable in respect of the hire of plant and machinery. To comply with this requirement it is necessary to disclose the amounts charged to revenue for operating leases and finance leases and hire purchase contracts. In the latter cases this would consist of depreciation and finance charges.

The following is an example of an appropriate note which combines these legal requirements with those of the standard (assuming that the company has a charge for each item):

Profit is stated after charging:	£
Depreciation of owned assets	a
Depreciation of assets held under finance leases and hire purchase contracts	b[1]
Interest payable – bank loans and overdrafts and other loans repayable within five years	c
Finance charges payable – finance leases and hire purchase contracts	d[2]
Hire of plant and machinery – operating leases	e[3]
Hire of other assets – operating leases	f[4]

(Note: amounts charged to revenue in respect of finance leases and hire purchase contracts are shown separately under the headings of depreciation (£b) and finance charges (£d) (total, £g.))

Notes:

1. This amount is required to be disclosed by paragraphs 49 and 50 of the standard as well as in compliance with paragraph 53(6) of Schedule 8.*
2. This amount is required to be disclosed by paragraph 53 of the standard as well as in compliance with paragraph 53(6) of Schedule 8.*
3. This amount is required to be disclosed by paragraph 55 of the standard as well as in compliance with paragraph 53(6) of Schedule 8.*
4. This is required to be disclosed by paragraph 55 of the standard. When added to the amount in the above line for hire of plant and machinery, it gives the total charge in respect of operating leases.

Disclosure of commitments under operating leases

58 In the case of operating leases, the standard requires a lessee to disclose, in addition to the amount charged in the year, the yearly amount of the payments to which he is committed at the year end (the annual commitment). This will not necessarily be the same as the amount paid in the year then ending as it will include a full year's rental for leases which have been taken out during the year and it will exclude rentals in respect of leases which terminated during the year. The annual payments to which he is commit-

***Editor's note:** *Now Schedule 4 to the Companies Act 1985.*

ted should be analysed between those in which the commitment expires within that year, in the second to fifth years inclusive and over five years from the balance sheet date. Leases of land and buildings are to be shown separately from other operating leases.

In the case of these disclosure requirements, materiality should be borne in mind. Thus if either the amounts for leases of land and buildings or for other leases are not material, the two categories may be aggregated. If the total is immaterial, no disclosure needs to be made. 59

A suggested note is set out below: 60

At 31 December 1987 the company had annual commitments under non-cancellable operating leases as set out below.

£000's	1987 *Land and Buildings*	1987 *Other*	1986 *Land and Buildings*	1986 *Other*
Operating leases which expire:				
within one year	30	100	25	90
in the second to fifth years inclusive	80	50	75	40
over five years	120	20	110	10
	230	170	210	140

The majority of leases of land and buildings are subject to rent reviews.

Other disclosures

SSAP 2 'Disclosure of accounting policies' already requires disclosure of the accounting policies followed for dealing with items which are judged material or critical in determining profit or loss for the year and in stating the financial position. The present standard does not change the need to give such information and therefore disclosure should be made of the policies adopted for capitalisation and depreciation of leased assets and for the recognition of finance charges, where material. 61

It may also be necessary, in order to show a true and fair view, to disclose information relevant to lease contracts or hire purchase contracts which is of particular significance to users of financial statements. This may include such items as: 62

(a) the nature of any contingent rentals such as those based on usage or sales;
(b) the nature of any contingent liability, for example costs which may arise at the end of the lease term.

Further, as with any other form of financing, it may be appropriate to disclose financial restrictions imposed by the lease or hire purchase agreement such as limitations on additional borrowing or further leasing.

63 The standard (paragraph 54) requires disclosure of the amount of any material commitments in respect of finance leases which have been entered into but whose inception occurs after the year end. This is analogous to the legal requirement in respect of capital commitments in paragraph 50(3)(a) of Schedule 8* to the Companies Act 1948.

D – INITIAL RECORDING OF THE LEASED ASSET

64 As noted in paragraph 22 above, strictly, a lessee should record a finance lease at the present value of the minimum lease payments. (The minimum lease payments comprise all payments guaranteed by the lessee including rentals and any residual value guaranteed by him.) However, the present value of the minimum lease payments in a finance lease will normally be at least 90% of the fair value of the leased asset. For most practical purposes therefore it will be acceptable to record the leased asset at its fair value.

65 There are two occasions on which the leased asset would not be recorded at fair value. The first is where both the fair value and the present value of the minimum lease payments are known and the fair value is found to be not a sufficiently close approximation to the present value. Such cases are likely to be rare, as, by definition, the two figures are likely to be within 10% of each other.

66 The second possibility would be where the fair value of the asset is not known. Whilst this would be unusual in the UK, it may occur, for example where the asset can be obtained from only one manufacturer and he will make it available only by way of a finance lease. In such a case, a lessee should follow the rule in paragraph 32 of the standard and record the finance lease at the present value of the minimum lease payments. The present value should be determined by reference to the interest rate implicit in a lease. This is defined in paragraph 24 of the standard; it should be noted in particular that if the interest rate implicit in a lease is not determinable, it should be estimated by reference to the rate which a lessee would be expected to pay on a lease of similar term and in respect of the same class of asset.

67 Set out below is an example of the procedure to be followed in the circumstances described in paragraph 66. Assume that a lessee has entered into a finance lease for an asset whose fair value he does not know. The minimum lease payments are five annual instalments of £2,500 each, payable in advance.

The lessee establishes that a typical implicit rate of interest for leases of this type is 11%. He therefore discounts the payments as follows:

***Editor's note:** Now Schedule 4 to the Companies Act 1985.*

TABLE 9
PRESENT VALUE CALCULATION

Year	*Discount factor*	*Payment*	*Present value*
0	1.000	2,500	2,500
1	0.901	2,500	2,252
2	0.812	2,500	2,030
3	0.731	2,500	1,828
4	0.659	2,500	1,647
	4.103		10,257

The asset should be recorded at £10,257, the balance of £2,243 (12,500−10,257) representing finance charges.

In some cases, there may be difficulties in deciding whether or not a lease is a finance lease, for example where the fair value of the asset is not known. Additional guidance on this and similar problems is given in paragraphs 133 to 138 and 180 to 181. **68**

Part II – Lessor accounting

INTRODUCTION

Part II explains the accounting requirements for lessors in the following sections: **69**

	Paragraphs
A – General principles	70–73
B – Finance leases – background considerations	74–87
C – The arithmetic of lessor accounting for finance leases	88–122
D – Balance sheet presentation, note disclosure and legal requirements for lessors	123–131

A – GENERAL PRINCIPLES

A lessor should classify his leases into (a) finance leases, and (b) operating leases. **70**

Under a finance lease a lessor retains legal title to an asset but passes substantially all the risks and rewards of ownership to the lessee in return for a stream of rentals. In substance, under a finance lease, the lessor provides finance and expects a return thereon. **71**

In the case of an operating lease the lessor retains both the legal title and the risks and rewards of ownership of the asset. It may not be possible to predict with certainty the future rentals and expenses, as they may be received and incurred under successive lease agreements with one or more parties; furthermore, the equipment may become obsolete, and changes in the level of economic activity may affect demand. In substance, under an operating lease the lessor is trading with the assets he leases. **72**

The lessor should account for leases in accordance with their economic substance. Hence, a finance lease should be accounted for on a basis similar to that for a loan, **73** rather than as a fixed asset subject to depreciation. Conversely, an operating lease should be accounted for by capitalising and depreciating the leased asset.

B – FINANCE LEASES – BACKGROUND CONSIDERATIONS

74 The standard deals, inter alia, with calculation of the carrying value of the finance lease receivables and with lessors' profit recognition. It requires the receivables to be carried on a balance sheet at an amount based on the net investment in the lease. Conversely, it requires that profit recognition should normally be based on the lessor's net *cash* investment.

75 The net investment in a lease is initially the cost of the asset to the lessor, less any government or other grants receivable (i.e., the fair value).

76 The rentals paid by the lessee should be apportioned by the lessor between (a) gross earnings (i.e., the lessor's interest earned) and (b) a repayment of capital.

77 Over the period of the lease the net investment in the lease (i.e., the carrying value of the receivables) will therefore be the fair value of the asset less those portions of the rentals which are apportioned as a repayment of capital.

78 For the purposes of profit recognition, however, the total gross earnings should normally be allocated to accounting periods to give a constant periodic rate of return on the lessor's net *cash* investment (NCI) in the lease in each period. (Paragraph 40 of the standard allows an alternative method, which is also partly based on NCI. This is described in paragraph 94 below.) The NCI is based on the funds which the lessor has invested in the lease. The amount of funds invested in a lease by a lessor is different from the net investment in the lease because there are a number of other cash flows which affect the lessor, in addition to those which affect net investment. In particular, tax cash flows are an important component of the NCI. The components of the NCI are listed in paragraph 23 of the standard.

79 Sometimes a lessor receives an amount which takes the form of a deposit or of non-recourse indebtedness. This amount may be received from the lessee and may in economic substance have the nature of an advance rental. It may be appropriate for the lessor to include such receipts and any repayments thereof in computing the net cash investment for the purpose of allocating gross earnings to accounting periods.

80 In the case of hire purchase, profit recognition should also, in principle, be based on net cash investment. However, since the capital allowances under a hire purchase contract accrue to the lessee, the finance company's net cash investment is often not significantly different from its net investment; hence allocation of gross earnings (i.e., finance charges) based on net investment will in most cases be a suitable approximation to allocation based on net cash investment.

81 The standard permits a reasonable approximation to be made in arriving at the constant periodic rate of return. Hence there are a number of different methods of profit recognition which may comply with the standard. Some of these methods are illustrated in the next section. However, other methods may be appropriate for use by lessors of any size where they provide a reasonable approximation to the methods described below. It may be appropriate for a lessor to use one of the methods specifically described for its large leases and a simplified method for other leases. What is a large lease will depend on the size of the company.

Initial direct costs are costs such as commissions and legal fees which are often incurred by lessors in negotiating and arranging a lease. The definition (standard, paragraph 30) is not intended to exclude salesperson's costs. Initial direct costs may be apportioned over the lease term on a systematic basis (or may be written off immediately). The same effect as apportioning the costs over the lease term may be achieved by either (a) treating the costs as a deduction from the total gross earnings before the latter are allocated to accounting periods or (b) recognising sufficient gross earnings in the first year to cover the costs. In the case of an operating lease initial direct costs may also either be written off immediately or be deferred and amortised over the lease term. **82**

In most finance leases the estimated residual values of leased assets will be small. They are usually left out of calculations to apportion income from the lease and are accounted for as they arise. Where estimated residual values are used in assessing the lessor's investment in a lease, the estimate should be reviewed regularly and any permanent reduction in the estimated residual value (net of any profits to be recognised later in the lease) should be recognised immediately by an appropriate charge in the profit and loss account. **83**

Where individual finance leases are for relatively small amounts, the administration costs in collecting the rentals may be significant. It may therefore be necessary to take them into account when determining an appropriate method of allocating the gross earnings. Failure to take administration costs into account in that manner could result in the recognition in a particular period of costs relating to a lease which exceed the gross earnings recognised in respect of the lease in that period. **84**

There will always be a degree of uncertainty about cash flows which are predicted for a number of years ahead. Factors about which there may be uncertainties include: **85**

(a) doubts about the ability of the lessee to fulfil his obligations under the lease;
(b) any term in the lease which suggests that the lease is cancellable without appropriate compensation for the lessor;
(c) doubts about the ability of the lessor to utilise capital allowances at the time he anticipated being able to do so at the start of the lease;
(d) material uncertainty about interest rates where the lessor is dependent on borrowed funds and the lease rentals are fixed;
(e) uncertainty concerning future tax changes in the territory where the lease is operative.

The treatment to be followed by the lessor will depend on the degree of uncertainty relating to cash flows. If the degree of uncertainty is not great, such that (a) collectibility of the minimum lease payments is reasonably assured and (b) there are no important uncertainties surrounding the amount of unreimbursable costs yet to be incurred by the lessor under the lease, then it will normally be appropriate to classify the lease as a finance lease. The necessity to make a provision for bad debts based on experience of **86** similar finance lease receivables would not preclude a lessor from classifying a lease as a finance lease. In such circumstances the lessor should in general not change the way in which he recognises gross earnings, but should make specific provisions for those cash flows about which the uncertainty exists, such as a provision for bad debts.

87 The degree of uncertainty of cash flows may however be such as to indicate that the lease does not have the characteristics of a finance lease and should more appropriately be accounted for as an operating lease.

C – THE ARITHMETIC OF LESSOR ACCOUNTING FOR FINANCE LEASES

88 There will in most cases be a close relationship between the initial evaluation of a lease and the way in which it is subsequently accounted for. Many lessors evaluate leases by using a method similar to that shown in Table 13 (see paragraph 109). In such an evaluation, the pricing of the rental determines the rate of return in each period. Hence, the manner in which the income is recognised is related to the original lease evaluation.

89 The general approach in the standard is to regard each rental receivable as partly gross earnings and partly a return of capital. A method has to be determined for making this allocation of each rental between the gross earnings and the capital repayment.

90 The total rentals receivable will be known in advance from the terms of the contract and the fair value of the asset will generally be known so that the gross earnings may be calculated.

91 The numerical examples are based on rates of tax and allowances which, according to indications at the time of writing (August 1984), will be in force from April 1986 onwards, that is, a 35% rate of corporation tax and 25% writing down allowances.

92 As already noted, the standard requires that gross earnings should normally be allocated to accounting periods so as to give a constant periodic rate of return (or a reasonable approximation thereto) on the lessor's net cash investment (NCI) in the lease in each period. This implies the use of a so-called 'after-tax' method such as:

(a) the actuarial method after tax; or
(b) the investment period method (IPM).

These methods are illustrated below. However, as shown in paragraphs 120 to 122 below, other methods may yield acceptable results.

93 The fact that these methods are known as 'after-tax' methods does not mean that they seek to allocate the profit after tax to accounting periods. Rather, the term means that the gross earnings are being allocated on a basis which takes into account the tax effect on cash flows – that is, the allocation is based on the NCI.

94 The standard (paragraph 40) also allows a lessor to adopt a method which involves making an allocation out of gross earnings of an amount equal to the lessor's estimated cost of finance included in the net cash investment calculation; the balance remaining after this allocation is then recognised on a systematic basis. For example, allocation of the profit after estimated finance costs on the rule of 78 basis has the merit, in the case of a lease providing for equal rentals at equal intervals, of relating profit recognition to the amount of outstanding future rentals, non-payment of which is one of the principal risks for the lessor. Since the cost of finance allocation is taken from the NCI calculation, it reflects the tax effects of cash flows, hence this method is also an 'after-tax' method.

The concept of earning a constant periodic rate of return on the net cash investment is commonly known as the investment period principle (IPP), of which the actuarial method after tax and the IPM are two of the most common methods. The actuarial method after tax is the most accurate method. The IPM is based on similar principles. Other methods have also been developed which attempt to produce the same constant periodic rate of return. They are not all illustrated here. If they come close to producing the constant periodic rate of return, then they can be used. **95**

The examples are based on a lease as follows: **96**

> The terms of the lease used in this example are the same as those set out in paragraph 21 and used in the lessee examples in Part 1. A lessor leases an asset to a lessee on a non-cancellable finance lease for five years from 1 January 1987. The rental is £650 per quarter payable in advance. The lessee pays all the maintenance and insurance costs as they arise. The cost of the asset is £10,000.
>
> The lessor obtains writing down allowances on the leased asset at the rate of 25%. The rate of corporation tax is 35%. The lessor's year end is 31 December and he pays or recovers tax nine months after the year end.

In the examples which follow, the lessor always needs funds to support the lease, that is, the lease does not generate a cash surplus. In other cases, a cash surplus may arise in certain periods, for example if the lessor buys the asset later in his accounting year, or where for other reasons tax allowances are receivable earlier in the lease. In these circumstances the lessor would use the surplus cash to invest and earn a return which would be attributed to the lease. Competition may force the lessor to take any interest earnings on surplus cash into account when fixing the rental. Any cash surplus would tend to arise late in the lease and so the estimate of interest earnings should be made on a conservative basis. It should be treated in the lease evaluations as set out in Tables 10 and 13 as the converse of interest paid. **97**

The actuarial method after tax

The actuarial method after tax is a method which recognises all significant cash flows which affect a lease. It apportions the gross earnings over the period of the lease to give a constant periodic rate of return on the net cash investment. The net cash investment in a lease at a point in time is the amount of funds invested in a lease by the lessor, and comprises the cost of the asset plus or minus the following related payments or receipts: **98**

(a) government or other grants receivable towards the purchase or use of the asset;
(b) rentals received;
(c) taxation payments and receipts including the effect of capital allowances;
(d) residual values, if any, at the end of the lease term less any estimated rebate of rental arising therefrom;

100 **TABLE 10**

ACTUARIAL METHOD AFTER TAX — NO INTEREST PAYMENTS

Period (3 months)	*Net cash investment at start of period*	*Cash flows in period (Note 1)*	*(Note 2)*	*Average net cash investment in period*	*Profit taken out of lease (2.06%) Note 3)*	*Net cash investment at end of period*
	£	£	£	£	£	£
1/87	–	(10,000)	650	(9,350)	(193)	(9,543)
2/87	(9,543)		650	(8,893)	(183)	(9,076)
3/87	(9,076)		650	(8,426)	(174)	(8,600)
4/87	(8,600)		650	(7,950)	(164)	(8,114)
			2,600		(714)	
1/88	(8,114)		650	(7,464)	(154)	(7,618)
2/88	(7,618)		650	(6,968)	(143)	(7,111)
3/88	(7,111)		650	(6,461)	(133)	(6,594)
4/88	(6,594)	(35)	650	(5,979)	(123)	(6,102)
			2,600		(553)	
1/89	(6,102)		650	(5,452)	(112)	(5,564)
2/89	(5,564)		650	(4,914)	(101)	(5,015)
3/89	(5,015)		650	(4,365)	(90)	(4,455)
4/89	(4,455)	(254)	650	(4,059)	(84)	(4,143)
			2,600		(387)	
1/90	(4,143)		650	(3,493)	(72)	(3,565)
2/90	(3,565)		650	(2,915)	(60)	(2,975)
3/90	(2,975)		650	(2,325)	(48)	(2,373)
4/90	(2,373)	(418)	650	(2,141)	(44)	(2,185)
			2,600		(224)	
1/91	(2,185)		650	(1,535)	(31)	(1,566)
2/91	(1,566)		650	(916)	(19)	(935)
3/91	(935)		650	(285)	(6)	(291)
4/91	(291)	(541)	650	(182)	(4)	(186)
			2,600		(60)	
1/92	(186)			(186)	(4)	(190)
2/92	(190)			(190)	(4)	(194)
3/92	(194)			(194)	(4)	(198)
4/92	(198)	198		–	–	–
					(12)	
		(10,000)	13,000		(1,950)	
		(1,050)				

(e) interest payments (where applicable);
(f) interest received on cash surplus (if any);
(g) profit taken out of the lease.

It is sometimes argued that the net cash investment need not be adjusted for profit taken out of the lease, but this assumes that all cash received is used to reduce the investment and ignores the fact that some of the cash will be used, for example, to meet indirect costs and pay dividends. Even if the surplus is not distributed or used to pay indirect costs, it should be regarded as unconnected with the lease. If the profit is not taken out of the lease, the level of cash needed to finance the lease and the interest charges are understated.

The calculations are illustrated in Tables 10 and 13. In Table 10, it is assumed for simplicity of illustration that the lessor has no interest cost. A more realistic way of making the allocation, where interest payable is introduced into the calculation, is illustrated in Table 13 (paragraph 109). **99**

Notes*: **100**

1. (a) The fair value of the asset is £10,000.
   (b) Tax at the rate of 35% is payable at the beginning of period 4 in each year. It is calculated on rentals less capital allowances. (Interest received which arises on any cash surplus would also be taxable). The figure of £(1,050) is the total of tax payments less recoveries.
   (c) In arriving at the figure of £198 of tax recoverable in period 4/92, it has been assumed that the lessor receives an allowance of the amount of expenditure – £2,372 – which is unrelieved after five years' writing down allowances have been claimed. This will be the case where the lessor sells the asset for its tax written down value and passes the proceeds to the lessee as a rebate of rentals; in this instance the allowance of £2,372 will take the form of tax relief on the rebate of rentals rather than a balancing allowance. (The sales proceeds and the rebate of rentals are not shown in the Table, as their net cash flow effect is nil.) In other circumstances, such as where the lessor continues to hold the asset, the tax written down value of £2,372 will remain part of a pool and will continue to attract a stream of allowances totalling £2,372 on a reducing balance basis into the indefinite future. In such circumstances, it may be appropriate for the lessor to make an adjustment in respect of the delay in receiving the allowances.
2. Rentals of £650 are payable in advance.
3. The profit taken out of the lease is calculated at 2.06% on the average net cash invested in each period until period 3/92, after which point the lessor no longer has funds invested in the lease. The calculations made to arrive at 2.06% will normally be carried out by financial institutions by computer program, but it can be attained by trial and error. The calculation is, initially, carried out ignoring the profit taken out of the lease and this will then leave a balance of surplus cash left over at the end which represents the approximate profit on the transaction.

By dividing the total profit by the total average net cash investment in the period, an approximate percentage is obtained. As the profit taken out of the lease each quarter

***Editor's note:** *to table 10.*

affects the average net cash investment in the following quarter, the net cash investment at the end of the whole transaction will not be zero until the percentage used is refined as in the above example to 2.06%.

101 The profit and loss accounts resulting from the cash flows in paragraph 100 are:

TABLE 11
PROFIT AND LOSS ACCOUNTS – NO INTEREST PAYMENTS

	1987	*1988*	*1989*	*1990*	*1991*	*1992*	Total
	£	£	£	£	£	£	£
Rental	2,600	2,600	2,600	2,600	2,600	–	13,000
Less capital repayment	(1,502)	(1,749)	(2,005)	(2,255)	(2,508)	19	(10,000)
Profit before tax (= gross earnings)	1,098	851	595	345	92	19	3,000
Taxation	(35)	(254)	(418)	(541)	198	–	(1,050)
	1,063	597	177	(196)	290	19	1,950
Deferred tax (see para. 174)	(349)	(44)	210	420	(230)	(7)	–
Net profit	£714	£553	£387	£224	£60	£12	£1,950
Average net cash investment in the period*:	8,655	6,718	4,697	2,718	729	142	
Gross earnings expressed as a % return on the average net cash investment in the period:	12.7%	12.7%	12.7%	12.7%	12.6%†	13.4%†	

102 Table 11 is constructed from the bottom line upwards. The net profit for each year is taken from Table 10. The rentals and tax payments and recoveries are also found in Table 10. The net profit figures should then be grossed up by the rate of tax of 35%, giving the profit before tax (e.g., £714 ÷ 0.65 = £1,098). The figures for deferred tax and capital repayments may then be found.

103 Table 11 is used to arrive at one figure only, namely the capital repayment in each year. In practice none of the other figures in the table will be used, as when financial statements are being drawn up actual figures will be used, i.e., it is not necessary to accumulate individual figures lease by lease for interest and tax; these will be calculated in total for a company.

These amounts may be derived from the column 'Average net cash investment in period' in Table 10, for example £(9,350 + 8,893 + 8,426 + 7,950) ÷ 4 = £8,655.

† Rounding error.

In Table 11 the effects of the five year lease contract spread over into six financial years. **104**
In fact the capital repayments for 1991 and 1992 may be added together for all practical purposes.

The capital repayments may be expressed in percentage terms: **105**

1987	*1988*	*1989*	*1990*	*1991/92*	*Total*
£1,502	£1,749	£2,005	£2,255	£2,489	£10,000
15%	17%	20%	23%	25%	100%

Using the method set out above, the percentages of the capital repayment by year may **106**
be calculated for any lease and, as long as tax and interest rates remain unchanged, the percentages so calculated may be applied to any other lease which possesses the same ratio of capital to rental payments and whose inception date is the same. Thus it is not always necessary to undertake a separate calculation for each individual lease.

The lessor's balance sheets would include the amounts shown below. The relevant **107**
disclosure requirements are described in paragraphs 123 to 131.

TABLE 12

BALANCE SHEETS – EXTRACTS

	1987	*1988*	*1989*	*1990*	*1991*	*1992*
	£	£	£	£	£	£
Assets: Net Investment in finance leases	8,498	6,749	4,744	2,489	(19)	–
Tax recoverable	–	–	–		198	–
Deferred tax	–	–	–	237	7	–
	£8,498	£6,749	£4,744	£2,726	£186	–
Liabilities:	349	393	183	–	–	–
Deferred tax						
Current tax	35	254	418	541	–	–
Cash deficit*	8,114	6,102	4,143	2,185	186	–
	£8,498	£6,749	£4,744	£2,726	£186	–

The actuarial method after tax – building in interest payments

Where a lessor borrows funds to finance his leases a more realistic reflection of his cash **108**
flows may be obtained by building into the cash flows in Table 10 payments of interest on his borrowings. The tax charges will of course alter as will the amount required to finance the lease in each period.

**These amounts represent the net cash investment (as referred to in paragraph 98 above). The cash deficits will not in practice appear as separate items on a balance sheet, but they represent the amount of funds invested in a lease by the lessor; this may be equity or debt or a mixture of the two.*

109 Table 10 may thus be re-stated as follows:

TABLE 13

ACTUARIAL METHOD AFTER TAX – BUILDING IN INTEREST PAYMENTS

Period (3 months)	*Net cash investment at start of period*	*Cash flows in period (Note 1)*	*(Note 2)*	*Average net cash investment in period*	*Interest paid (Note 3)*	*Profit taken out of lease (Note 4)*	*Net cash investment at end of period*
	£	£	£	£	£	£	£
1/87	–	(10,000)	650	(9,350)	(234)	(33)	(9,617)
2/87	(9,617)		650	(8,967)	(224)	(32)	(9,223)
3/87	(9,223)		650	(8,573)	(214)	(30)	(8,817)
4/87	(8,817)		650	(8,167)	(204)	(29)	(8,400)
			2,600		(876)	(124)	
1/88	(8,400)		650	(7,750)	(194)	(28)	(7,972)
2/88	(7,972)		650	(7,322)	(183)	(26)	(7,531)
3/88	(7,531)		650	(6,881)	(172)	(25)	(7,078)
4/88	(7,078)	272	650	(6,156)	(154)	(22)	(6,332)
			2,600		(703)	(101)	
1/89	(6,332)		650	(5,682)	(142)	(20)	(5,844)
2/89	(5,844)		650	(5,194)	(130)	(18)	(5,342)
3/89	(5,342)		650	(4,692)	(117)	(17)	(4,826)
4/89	(4,826)	(8)	650	(4,184)	(105)	(15)	(4,304)
			2,600		(494)	(70)	
1/90	(4,304)		650	(3,654)	(91)	(13)	(3,758)
2/90	(3,758)		650	(3,108)	(78)	(11)	(3,197)
3/90	(3,197)		650	(2,547)	(64)	(9)	(2,620)
4/90	(2,620)	(245)	650	(2,215)	(55)	(8)	(2,278)
			2,600		(288)	(41)	
1/91	(2,278)		650	(1,628)	(41)	(6)	(1,675)
2/91	(1,675)		650	(1,025)	(26)	(4)	(1,055)
3/91	(1,055)		650	(405)	(10)	(1)	(416)
4/91	(416)	(440)	650	(206)	(5)	(1)	(212)
			2,600		(82)	(12)	
1/92	(212)			(212)	(5)	(1)	(218)
2/92	(218)			(218)	(5)	(1)	(224)
3/92	(224)			(224)	(6)	(1)	(231)
4/92	(231)	226 }		1	(1)	–	–
		6 }			(17)	(3)	
		(10,000)	13,000		(2,460)	(351)	
		(189)					

Notes:

1. (a) The fair value of the asset is £10,000.
   (b) Tax is payable at the beginning of period 4 in each year. It is calculated on rentals, interest paid and capital allowances. (Interest received which arises on any cash surplus would also be taxable.) In period 4/92 the £6 is tax recoverable in 1993. The figure of £(189) is the total of tax payments less recoveries.
   (c) See note 1(c) to Table 10.
2. Rentals of £650 are payable in advance.
3. Interest paid is calculated at 2.5% per quarter on the average net cash investment in each period.
3. The profit taken out of the lease is calculated at 0.36% on the average net cash invested in each period until period 3/92. (For an explanation of how this is calculated, see note 3 to Table 10.)

Similarly, profit and loss accounts resulting from the cash flows in Table 13 are: **110**

TABLE 14

PROFIT AND LOSS ACCOUNTS – BUILDING IN INTEREST PAYMENTS

	1987	*1988*	*1989*	*1990*	*1991*	*1992*	*Total*
	£	£	£	£	£	£	£
Rental	2,600	2,600	2,600	2,600	2,600	–	13,000
Less capital repayment	(1,533)	(1,742)	(1,998)	(2,249)	(2,500)	22	(10,000)
Gross earnings	1,067	858	602	351	100	22	3,000
Interest	(876)	(703)	(494)	(288)	(82)	(17)	(2,460)
Profit before tax	191	155	108	63	18	5	540
Taxation	272	(8)	(245)	(440)	226	6	(189)
	463	147	(137)	(377)	244	11	351
Deferred tax (see para. 174)	(339)	(46)	207	418	(232)	(8)	–
Net profit	£124	£101	£70	£41	£12	£3	£351

This table is constructed in a manner similar to Table 11, as described in paragraph 102.

Where a lease contains interest variation clauses which adjust the rental by reference to movements in Finance House base rate, or some other indicator, no adjustment need normally be made to the calculations in paragraphs 109 and 110. Any increase or reduction in rentals should be accounted for as an increase or reduction in gross **111** earnings in the period in which it arises; this treatment will compensate for the additional finance cost incurred in the same period.

The investment period method

112 As referred to above, the investment period method is used by some leasing companies as an alternative to the actuarial method after tax.

113 The investment period method of accounting for finance leases allocates the gross earnings over that part of the lease in which the lessor has a net cash investment in proportion to the net cash investment at each interval.

114 Using the cash flows set out in paragraph 109 the allocation of gross earnings becomes:

TABLE 15

ALLOCATION OF GROSS EARNINGS UNDER IPM

Period	*Net cash investment at end of period**	*Gross earnings allocation*	*Total gross earnings for year*
	£	£	£
1/87	9,617	285	
2/87	9,223	274	
3/87	8,817	262	1,070
4/87	8,400	249	
1/88	7,972	236	
2/88	7,531	223	
3/88	7,078	210	857
4/88	6,332	188	
1/89	5,844	173	
2/89	5,342	158	
3/89	4,826	143	602
4/89	4,304	128	
1/90	3,758	111	
2/90	3,197	95	
3/90	2,620	78	352
4/90	2,278	68	
1/91	1,675	50	
2/91	1,055	31	
3/91	416	12	99
4/91	212	6	
1/92	218	6	
2/92	224	7	
3/92	231	7	20
4/92	–	–	
	£101,170	£3,000	£3,000

****Use of the average net cash investment figures from Table 13 would yield the same result as use of the end-of-period figures. The reason for this is that the interest paid and the profit taken out of the lease are both proportional to the average NCI; hence the closing NCI figures are also proportional to the average NCI.***

The allocation of gross earnings is calculated as follows:

$$1/87\ £9,617 \times \frac{3,000}{101,170} = £285$$

The same calculation is repeated for each period.

The profit and loss accounts resulting from Table 15 are as follows: 115

TABLE 16

PROFIT AND LOSS ACCOUNTS – INVESTMENT PERIOD METHOD

	1987	*1988*	*1989*	*1990*	*1991*	*1992*	*Total*
	£	£	£	£	£	£	£
Rental	2,600	2,600	2,600	2,600	2,600	–	13,000
Less capital repayment	(1,530)	(1,743)	(1,998)	(2,248)	(2,501)	20	(10,000)
Gross earnings	1,070	857	602	352	99	20	3,000
Interest	(876)	(703)	(494)	(288)	(82)	(17)	(2,460)
Profit before tax	194	154	108	64	17	3	540
Taxation	272	(8)	(245)	(440)	226	6	(189)
	466	146	(137)	(376)	243	9	351
Deferred tax	(340)	(46)	207	418	(232)	(7)	–
Net profit	£126	£100	£70	£41	£11	£2	£351

This table is constructed differently from Tables 11 and 14. Under the IPM, the allocation of the gross earnings is calculated as shown in Table 15. The capital repayment may therefore be found by subtraction. The figures for interest are the same as those in Tables 13 and 14. The profit before tax may be found by subtraction; note that the total is the same as in Table 14 but the allocation among the years is slightly different. The tax payable figures are the same as in Tables 13 and 14. The net profit is calculated as 65% of the profit before tax, and the deferred tax line is calculated as a balancing figure.

Hire purchase

As noted in paragraph 80, for hire purchase contracts, allocation of finance charges to accounting periods based on the net investment will in most cases be a suitable alternative to allocation based on net cash investment. The following two methods are therefore illustrated, using the rentals and other details set out in paragraph 21: 116

(a) the actuarial method before tax;
(b) the rule of 78.

The actuarial method before tax

117 In this example the finance charges of £3,000 on the hire purchase contract (i.e., total rentals receivable minus the cost of the asset) are apportioned over the period of the contract to give a constant periodic rate of return on the net investment. In this method, the effects of taxation are ignored in apportioning the finance charges (hence the description 'before tax'). Interest on borrowed funds is usually ignored in this method but may be taken into account.

118 The calculations are the same as in Tables 1 and 2 in paragraphs 25 and 26. The results are as follows:

TABLE 17

ACTUARIAL METHOD BEFORE TAX

	1987	*1988*	*1989*	*1990*	*1991*	*Total*
	£	£	£	£	£	£
Rentals receiveable	2,600	2,600	2,600	2,600	2,600	13,000
Less capital repayments	1,563	1,757	1,973	2,217	2,490	10,000
Finance charges	£1,037	£843	£627	£383	£110	£3,000
Average sum outstanding in the period	8,778	7,144	5,308	3,246	929	
Finance charges expressed as a % return on the average net investment in the period	11.8%	11.8%	11.8%	11.8%	11.8%	

The rule of 78

119 The calculations for apportioning the finance charge on the basis of the rule of 78 are the same as those shown in Table 3 in paragraph 28. For a hire purchase company it is particularly important to be aware that the rule of 78 has a tendency to front-load income, which tendency becomes more pronounced the higher finance charges are relative to the amount financed. Therefore, in the case of longer contracts (say, over seven years) the actuarial method before tax is preferred.

Comparison of methods

120 The allocation of gross earnings (or finance charges) under the methods described above may be compared as follows:

TABLE 18

COMPARISON OF GROSS EARNINGS ALLOCATION

	1987	*1988*	*1989*	*1990*	*1991*	*1992*	*Total*
	£	£	£	£	£	£	£
Actuarial method after tax (para. 110)	1,067	858	602	351	100	22	3,000
IPM (para. 115)	1,070	857	602	352	99	20	3,000
Actuarial method before tax (para. 118)	1,037	843	627	383	110	–	3,000
Rule of 78 (paras. 119 and 28)	1,105	853	600	347	95	–	3,000

A number of points may be noted from the above table. Under the assumption of 35% tax and 25% writing down allowances, the two after-tax methods give very similar results. The reason for this is that the lease never goes into surplus (see paragraph 109). If different assumptions are made about rates of tax and allowances, cash surpluses may arise in certain periods and in these circumstances the actuarial method after tax and the IPM yield different results. In the former method, the interest received on the cash surplus (the re-investment income) is brought back and recognised in the periods when the lessor has funds invested in the lease, rather than taken to income when it arises. Thus no profit is recognised in the periods when the lease is in surplus. Because of this effect, the lessor may be in an exposed position in this period in the event, for example, of early termination of the lease by the lessee. If this method is used, it may therefore be necessary to make an appropriate provision for early termination losses so that the net investment in the lease does not exceed the termination value at any time. Under the IPM, any re-investment income is recognised when it arises, that is, it is not brought back and recognised in the periods in which the lessor has funds invested in the lease. Thus, where cash surpluses arise, the IPM is more conservative than the actuarial method after tax. **121**

Depending on the materiality of the amounts involved, it may be appropriate under assumptions such as those used in the above numerical examples to use the actuarial method before tax and the rule of 78 to allocate gross earnings from finance leases, although these methods are primarily intended for use in allocating finance charges from hire purchase contracts. **122**

D – BALANCE SHEET PRESENTATION, NOTE DISCLOSURE AND LEGAL REQUIREMENTS FOR LESSORS

The standard requires disclosure of the net investment in (a) finance leases and (b) hire purchase contracts at each balance sheet date. The amounts should be described as receivables. Whereas in lessee accounting the figures in respect of leases and hire purchase contracts may be aggregated, in the case of lessors and finance companies the amounts in respect of each should be shown separately. **123**

For companies subject to Schedule 8* of the Companies Act 1948, the net investment in **124**

***Editor's note:** *Now Schedule 4 to the Companies Act 1985.*

finance leases and hire purchase contracts should be included in current assets under the heading 'Debtors' and described as 'finance lease receivables' and/or 'hire purchase receivables' as appropriate. It should be analysed in the notes to the accounts between those amounts receivable within one year and those amounts receivable thereafter.

125 A suitable form of disclosure would be:

BALANCE SHEET AS AT 31 DECEMBER 1987

Current assets		*1986*
Finance lease and hire purchase receivables	£1200	£1100

Note to the accounts:

1. The amounts receivable under finance leases and hire purchase contracts comprise:

Finance leases	900	820
Hire purchase contracts	300	280
	£1200	£1100

Included in the totals receivable is £900 (1986 £850) which falls due after more than one year.

126 The standard requires that the gross amounts (i.e., original cost or revaluation) and accumulated depreciation of assets held for use in operating leases should be disclosed. This information could be incorporated into tables showing the amounts for other fixed assets or could be shown as a separate table. It is recognised that, for banks, assets held for use in operating leases are different in nature from a bank's infrastructure (e.g., its own premises). Hence it may not be appropriate to combine assets held for use in operating leases with a bank's infrastructure for capital adequacy purposes.

127 Details of the accounting policies followed by lessors in respect of both operating leases and finance leases are required by the standard, as well as by SSAP 2, 'Disclosure of accounting policies'. This would include information on the depreciation policy for assets leased on operating leases. The standard places particular emphasis on detailed disclosure of the policy adopted for recognition of finance lease income by lessors. This might include items such as the basic method of income recognition (e.g., investment period method); the policies followed in respect of initial direct costs; and assumptions about tax rates and payment dates.

128 It may also be necessary in order to show a true and fair view to disclose information relating to leases and hire purchase contracts which is of particular significance to users of accounts. This may include: contingent liabilities; contingent rentals payable or receivable (e.g., rentals receivable on a hotel may be related to its profits and therefore the income in future years may fluctuate); or new-for-old guarantees given (e.g.. on computer leases).

Lessors' turnover

In the case of operating leases, a lessor's turnover should be the aggregate rentals receivable in respect of the accounting period. 129

In the case of finance leases, a lessor should disclose gross earnings as turnover. (This is analogous to 'interest receivable' in the case of a bank.) However, as this provides an incomplete measure of a lessor's activity, disclosure should also be made in the notes of the aggregate rentals receivable under finance leases and of the cost of assets acquired for letting under finance leases. 130

The term 'turnover', although used in the Companies Act formats, is not normally used in the leasing industry. Paragraph 3(3) of Schedule 8* to the Companies Act 1948 requires directors to adapt the headings used in the formats in any case where the special nature of a company's business requires such adaptation. It may therefore be appropriate to use a term such as 'gross earnings under finance leases'. 131

Part III – Problem areas

INTRODUCTION

Part III gives guidance on problem areas in accounting for leases as follows: 132

	Paragraphs
A – Lease definition and classification	133–138
B – Land and buildings	139–144
C – Leasing by manufacturers or dealers	145–149
D – Sale and leaseback transactions	150–160
E – Sub-leases and back-to-back leases	161–169
F – Deferred taxation	170–175
G – Regional development grants	176–181
H – Bad debts	182–185

A – LEASE DEFINITION AND CLASSIFICATION

The definition of a lease is contained in paragraph 14 of the standard. However, in practice there are a number of arrangements which may in substance be leases even though different terms are used to describe them. Whether such an arrangement falls within the definition of a lease is a question to be decided in the light of the facts of each case. For example, a bare-boat charter (a charter of a boat without a crew) will generally have the characteristics of a lease, and the terms of the charter will enable the parties to determine whether it is a finance lease or an operating lease. There are also other arrangements which would not normally be lease contracts (although in 133

***Editor's note:** *Now Schedule 4 to the Companies Act 1985.*

exceptional cases they could in substance be leases). An example of these other arrangements is where company A builds a plant on the basis that company B is obliged to buy sufficient of the output of the plant (whether or not B requires it) in order to give a full payout on the cost of the assets involved, together with a normal profit margin: such arrangements are sometimes called take-or-pay contracts or through-put agreements. In many cases such arrangements will in substance be more in the nature of long-term purchase/supply contracts than contracts 'for the hire of a specific asset . . . (under which) the lessor retains ownership of the asset but conveys the right to the use of the asset to the lessee for an agreed period of time in return for the payment of specified rentals' (standard, paragraph 14).

134 A finance lease is defined in paragraphs 15 and 16 of the standard. The definition in paragraph 15 involves considering whether substantially all the risks and rewards of ownership are transferred to the lessee; the presumption is that this transfer occurs if at the inception of the lease the present value of the minimum lease payments amounts to (normally) 90% or more of the fair value of the leased asset. An alternative way of considering whether substantially all the risks and rewards are transferred to the lessee and whether therefore the lease is a finance lease is to consider whether the present value of any amounts excluded from the minimum lease payments exceeds 10% of the fair value. The amounts excluded from the minimum lease payments are (a) in the case of a lessee, amounts (usually residual amounts) which are unguaranteed or which are guaranteed by a third party, and (b) in the case of a lessor, any unguaranteed residual value. Hence, if these amounts are (or are anticipated to be) insignificant, a finance lease may be indicated.

135 Exceptionally, it may not be practicable to determine the lease classification based on consideration of whether the present value of the minimum lease payments amounts to (normally) 90% or more of the fair value of the leased asset; equally, it may not be practicable to use the '10% approach' suggested above. In such a case, there may be other means of determining whether or not substantially all the risks and rewards of ownership of an asset are transferred to the lessee. For example, if a lessee has the use of an asset for the period in which substantially all the economic benefits can be derived from the asset, then a finance lease is indicated.

136 In considering the classification of leases, especially in difficult and marginal cases, the role of residual values is particularly important. Of the residual value of a leased asset (i.e., its value at the end of the lease term), some or the whole (a) may be guaranteed by the lessee to the lessor or (b) may be guaranteed to the lessor by a third party or (c) may be unguaranteed. That part of the residual value which is guaranteed by the lessee (or by a party related to him) is included in the lessee's minimum lease payments. As far as the lessor is concerned his minimum lease payments include any residual amounts guaranteed by the lessee or by an independent third party. Thus the amounts which a lessor expects to receive in relation to the lease may exceed the minimum lease payments which a lessee expects to make to the extent of (a) residual amounts guaranteed by a third party and/or (b) unguaranteed residual amounts. (Insuring residual values is equivalent to obtaining a third party guarantee.) Two examples may illustrate the effect of residual values on lease classification.

Consider first a lease of an asset which has a fair value of £3,900. The lessee is required to make three annual payments of £1,000 in advance. The lessor estimates that the asset will have a residual value of £1,500 at the end of the three years; the manufacturer guarantees to buy it back for £1,200. **137**

The minimum lease payments as far as the lessee is concerned are £3,000; from the lessor's point of view they are £4,200. The unguaranteed residual value (URV) is £300 (£1,500–£1,200). The interest rate implicit in the lease is that rate which equates the lessor's minimum lease payments (£4,200) and the URV (£300) to the fair value of £3,900. The expected cash flows are therefore:

	Lessee	Lessor
T = 0	1,000	1,000
T = 1	1,000	1,000
T = 2	1,000	1,000
T = 3	–	1,500
	£3,000	£4,500

In this instance it is clear even without performing any calculations that the lease is an operating lease for the lessee, because, even with a zero rate of interest, the minimum lease payments are less than 90% of the fair value. Similarly, the lease is a finance lease from the lessor's point of view because the URV is less than 10% of the fair value of the asset before discounting; when discounted the URV would be even smaller. The presence of a third party guarantee means that the two parties to the lease classify it in different ways. (This is recognised in paragraph 9 of the standard.) If there had been no third party guarantee the lease would have been an operating lease for both lessor and lessee.

Where the figures are different and the classification is not as obvious as in the above example, the implicit rate of interest should be calculated using one of the methods suggested in paragraph 24 of the standard.

A slightly different problem relating to residual values may be illustrated by means of a further example. **138**

> A lessee takes out a lease under which the total of his minimum lease payments approximately equals the fair value of the asset. The present value of the minimum lease payments will therefore be a smaller amount and the classification of the lease may appear borderline. In such a case the lessee should consider the substance of the transaction rather than the precise arithmetic of the 90% test. For example, the minimum lease payments may include a residual value which is guaranteed by the lessee. If this guaranteed value is in fact considerably less than the probable residual value of the leased asset, then it is likely that the lessor will sell the asset in the open market and the lessee will not be called on to pay the amount which he guaranteed. This would suggest that the lessor is trading in the asset rather than providing finance, and that the lease is an operating lease.

B – LAND AND BUILDINGS

139 Land and buildings which are subject to lease agreements should be accounted for using the same criteria as other assets.

140 Many leases of land and buildings are for only a small part of the useful life of the building and the lessee does not obtain the economic benefits of ownership arising, for example, from any increase in value. Moreover, since the leases usually provide for regular rent reviews, the rent payable is regularly brought up to current market rates and the lease thereby has the characteristics not of a financing arrangement but of the provision of a service. Most leases involving land and buildings would therefore be classified as operating leases.

141 There may, however, be instances when a lease of land and buildings has the characteristics of a financing arrangement and in such cases the lease would normally be classified as a finance lease. Examples might be: (a) a lease of a building with a relatively short useful life, for example a warehouse built to a customer's specification or a building with a specific use such as a battery house; or (b) certain leasebacks of office buildings in a sale and leaseback arrangement (see paragraphs 150 to 160).

142 As with all types of lease, it is important in deciding whether a lease of land and buildings is a finance lease or an operating lease to consider its characteristics, in particular to consider whether or not substantially all the risks and rewards of ownership of the land and buildings in question are transferred to the lessee. It should be noted that under the definition of a finance lease set out in paragraphs 15 and 16 of the standard, the classification which results from the application of the '90% formula' to the lease may be rebutted if the lease in question does not transfer substantially all the risks and rewards of ownership to the lessee; this may occur for example because of rent reviews which revert the principal rewards of ownership to the lessor.

143 In the context of land and buildings the term 'open market value' is commonly used for what is described elsewhere in this standard as 'fair value'.

144 Nothing in the standard precludes the recognition as a fixed asset of an amount paid in the form of a premium as consideration for a leasehold interest.

C – LEASING BY MANUFACTURERS OR DEALERS

145 Manufacturers or dealers may offer customers the choice of either buying or leasing an asset. The leases offered may be either finance leases or operating leases, and may be described by a variety of terms, including hire or rental agreements.

146 Where a manufacturer or dealer enters into an operating lease, no sale has been made and it is therefore not appropriate to recognise a selling profit when the asset is first leased. A manufacturer or dealer lessor should account for an operating lease in the same way as any other lessor.

147 When a manufacturer or dealer enters into a finance lease such transactions give rise to

two types of income: (a) the initial profit or loss at the start of the lease which is equivalent to the profit or loss resulting from an outright sale of the asset being leased, and (b) the finance charges (or gross earnings) over the period of the lease.

As the offer of a lease agreement is often influenced by a manufacturer's or dealer's marketing considerations, the pricing of the lease may not necessarily be based on the normal outright sale price. Hence the initial selling profit on a lease should be restricted to an amount which will enable the finance charges under the lease to be based on the rate of interest which, in the absence of such marketing considerations, the lessor would expect to charge the lessee. The rate of interest should take into account any tax benefits accruing to the lessor. **148**

Consider the following example. A manufacturer makes a machine which costs him £10,000. He normally sells the machine for £12,500 giving him a profit on the sale of £2,500. **149**

The manufacturer offers the machine on a five year finance lease with a rental of £687.50 payable quarterly in advance. Using the figures in Table 1, paragraph 25, this rental would justify a capital cost of £10,577 for the cost of the asset. (Using the implicit rate in Table 1 of 2.95% per quarter, a quarterly rental of £650 is equivalent to a capital cost of £10,000. Therefore a quarterly rental of £687.50 is equivalent to a capital cost of:

$$\text{£}10{,}000 \times \frac{687.50}{650.00} = \text{£}10{,}577).$$

That is, where the implicit rate is not known, an estimate thereof has to be used in order to calculate the capital cost. The manufacturer should therefore restrict his selling profit to £577 at the start of the lease. The balance of the profit arises as gross earnings over the period of the lease.

D – SALE AND LEASEBACK TRANSACTIONS

A sale and leaseback transaction takes place when an owner sells an asset and immediately re-acquires the right to use the asset by entering into a lease with the purchaser. **150**

Before dealing with the accounting for the sale and leaseback transaction itself, the carrying value of the asset in question should be reviewed. If the asset has suffered a permanent diminution in value below its carrying amount it should be written down immediately to its fair value. This is nothing to do with sale and leaseback specifically, but it is a step which should be taken so that the sale and leaseback accounting is not distorted. **151**

Once that first step has been taken, the asset will be carried at fair value, or less. It is then necessary to determine whether the leaseback is an operating lease or a finance lease. This should be decided according to the criteria for all leases as set out in paragraphs 15 to 17 of the standard. **152**

Finance leaseback

153 If the leaseback is a finance lease, the seller-lessee is in effect re-acquiring substantially all the risks and rewards of ownership of the asset. In other words, he never disposes of his ownership interest in the asset, and so it would not be correct to recognise a profit or loss in relation to an asset which (in substance) never was disposed of.

154 However, it is possible that a sale and leaseback resulting in a finance lease may be arranged on terms reflecting a higher or lower capital value than the book value of the asset (i.e., so as to reflect an *apparent* profit or loss). For example, an asset which has a carrying value of £70 may be sold at £120 and leased back on a finance lease. In such a case, the lease payments would (other things being equal) be higher than if the sale and leaseback had been arranged at carrying value. The standard therefore provides that the £50 apparent profit should be deferred and amortised (i.e., credited to income) over the lease term: this will have the effect of reducing the rentals – which are shown as interest and depreciation of the leased-back asset – to a level consistent with the previous carrying value of the asset. Where the asset is carried at below fair value, it may be appropriate to revalue it. If, in the same example, the fair value of the asset were £100, the asset could be revalued to that amount, and there would remain only £20 of apparent profit to be deferred and amortised over the lease term. The effect would then be to reduce the rentals to a level consistent with the fair value of the asset.

155 As an alternative to calculating the apparent profit and deferring and amortising that amount, the same result can be achieved by leaving the previous carrying value unchanged, setting up the amount received on sale as a creditor, and treating the lease payments partly as principal and partly as a finance charge. This treatment will reflect the substance of the transaction, namely that it represents the raising of finance secured on an asset which is held and not disposed of.

Operating leaseback

156 Conversely, if the leaseback is an operating lease, the seller-lessee has disposed of substantially all the risks and rewards of ownership of the asset, and so has realised a profit or loss on the disposal. Provided that the transaction is established at fair value, the profit or loss should be recognised. However, it is possible that a sale and leaseback transaction can be arranged at other than fair value. If the sale price is above fair value (paragraph 47(c) of the standard), the excess will not be genuine profit, but will arise solely because the operating lease rentals payable in the ensuing years will also be at above fair value. The standard therefore provides that the excess of sale price over fair value should not be recognised as profit in the year but should be credited to income, over the shorter of the remainder of the lease term and the period to the next rent review (if any), so as to reduce the rentals payable to a level consistent with the fair value of the asset.

157 This may be illustrated as follows:

Carrying value of asset	£70	Recognise profit on sale of £30
Fair value of asset	£100	
Sale price	£120	
Annual rental (for 5 years)	£28	

The excess of the sale price over fair value should be deferred and amortised (credited to income) over the non-cancellable period, i.e.:

$$\frac{120-100}{5} = £4 \text{ p.a.}$$

This credit will in effect reduce the rentals from £28 p.a. to £24 p.a.

The converse situation may also arise, namely that the sale price is below fair value (standard, paragraph 47(b)). This could arise for two reasons. First, the sale could simply be a bad bargain, for example because the seller-lessee needed to raise cash quickly. In that case any profit or loss should be recognised immediately. Second, the price may be artificially low so as to compensate for future rentals at below market price. Depending on the previous carrying value, either a profit or loss may arise. These cases are considered in turn. **158**

The following figures illustrate the case where a profit arises, even though the price is artificially low so as to compensate for future rentals at below market price: **159**

Carrying value	£70	Profit £10
Sale price	£80	
Fair value	£100	
Annual rental (5 years)	£20	

The profit of £10 should be recognised immediately, but the difference between £80 and £100 should not be recognised.

Conversely, an apparent loss may arise if the sale price is below the carrying value as well as being below fair value. This is illustrated as follows: **160**

Carrying value	£95	Apparent loss £15
Sale price	£80	
Fair value	£100	
Annual rental (5 years)	£20	

In such a case, provided the apparent loss is compensated by below market rentals, the loss should not be recognised but should be deferred and amortised so as to give the effect of increasing the rentals to a level consistent with a selling price of £95. The loss should be deferred and amortised (i.e., debited to income) over the remainder of the lease term (or, if shorter, the period during which the reduced rentals are chargeable).

E – SUB-LEASES AND BACK-TO-BACK LEASES

The main provisions of the standard and the other sections of these guidance notes deal principally with leases in which only two parties, the lessor and the lessee, are involved. However, some lease arrangements are more complex and involve three (or more) parties. There are many different types of arrangement and it is not possible to give guidance on all of them. In addition, there are variations in the terms used to describe **161** the leases and the parties to the lease. The notes in this section are intended therefore to give guidance on the general principles of three-party lease arrangements.

162 The three parties may be termed (a) the original lessor, (b) the intermediate party and (c) the ultimate lessee. In effect, the intermediate party may be both a lessee in the original lease and a lessor as regards the sub-lease.

163 Unless the original lease agreement is replaced by a new agreement, the accounting by the original lessor should not be affected by the fact that the intermediate party enters into a sub-lease.

164 The accounting by the intermediate party will depend on the structure of his arrangements with the original lessor and the ultimate lessee.

165 If the intermediate party's role is in substance that of a broker or an agent for transactions between the original lessor and the ultimate lessee such that there is no recourse to the intermediate party in the event of default, then the intermediate party should not include the asset or obligation in his balance sheet and should account for any income due to him on a systematic and rational basis. For example, a pure commission might be recognised immediately, whilst a guarantee fee might be spread over the period of risk. For both operating and finance leases, he should treat any contingent loss as required by SSAP 18.

166 Conversely, the intermediate party may enter into a lease with the original lessor, the terms of which require him to make payments to the lessor regardless of whether the ultimate lessee completes his payments. That is, the asset would be sub-leased by the intermediate party to the ultimate lessee, but the lease agreement between the original lessor and the intermediate party would remain in effect. If the original lease is a finance lease, the intermediate party should record his obligation thereunder. If the sub-lease is also a finance lease, the intermediate party should account for it as such; this will result in his showing an obligation under the original lease and a receivable under the sub-lease. If the sub-lease is an operating lease, the leased asset remains as a fixed asset. The principal differences which arise if the sub-lease is a finance lease as opposed to an operating lease are that the intermediate party (a) treats the asset as a receivable instead of a fixed asset and (b) recognises income according to finance lease principles.

167 The ultimate lessee should classify the sub-lease according to paragraphs 15 to 17 of the standard and account for it accordingly.

168 In the context of complex multi-party leases, paragraph 16 of the standard is particularly important. This paragraph permits the presumption that a lease should be classified as a finance lease to be rebutted if it can be clearly demonstrated that in the circumstances in question the lease does not transfer substantially all the risks and rewards of ownership to the lessee. This rebuttal can be relevant, for example, where there is a series of sub-leases which results in a series of partial interests in an asset with each party carrying a percentage of the total risks in return for a percentage of the total rewards.

Where the intermediate party is not relieved of his primary obligation under the original lease and where the sub-lease is a finance lease, it is sometimes thought that this results in the leased asset's being capitalised in the accounts of two companies. This is not the case. The asset is capitalised only in the books of the ultimate lessee. The remaining balances are in the nature of indebtedness between the parties. 169

F – DEFERRED TAXATION

The accounting requirements for dealing with deferred tax are set out in SSAP 15 'Accounting for deferred taxation'. The present standard in no way changes these requirements. It should be noted, however, that at the time of writing SSAP 15 is under review. 170

Lessee's deferred taxation

Where a lessee charges the full rental he pays as a tax expense in the year of payment, timing differences may arise. These differences may be either (a) to the extent that the depreciation and finance charge exceed or fall short of the rental on a finance lease or (b) to the extent of any deferral or accrual of the rental on an operating lease. The lessee should consider whether deferred tax needs to be provided on these timing differences. 171

The amounts in question in the example in Part 1 are those shown in column three of Table 8 in paragraph 47. 172

The timing difference described above will need to be considered together with all other timing differences which a lessee may experience and, unless the conditions set out in paragraphs 27 to 30 of SSAP 15* are met, a provision for deferred tax will be required. 173

Lessor's deferred taxation

It will be seen from paragraph 101 that capital allowances have a material impact on a lessor's position. If deferred tax were not provided by a lessor he would report profits in some periods and losses in others. 174

SSAP 15 requires that the total position of a company must be looked at and not just one contract. A lessor therefore needs to consider the likely pattern of future timing differences. For example, he may be able to decide not to provide for deferred tax because any reduction in leasing may be offset by increases of tax allowances in other areas. 175

***Editor's note:** *SSAP 15 was revised in 1985 and the current requirements are set out in paragraphs 24 to 30.*

G – REGIONAL DEVELOPMENT GRANTS

Lessors and RDGs

176 Leases which involve equipment on which a regional development grant (RDG) may be claimed need special consideration. The lessor may claim a grant (currently of 15% or 22%) towards the cost of purchasing an asset. The grant is not taxable and the lessor may also claim capital allowances on the full purchase price of the asset. The rentals charged to the lessee will reflect the benefit the lessor has obtained from both the RDG and the capital allowances. Unless any adjustments are made, the lessor's profit and loss account may show a loss before tax and a profit after tax from such a lease.

177 Some consider that presentation of a loss before tax and a profit after tax leads to difficulties in interpreting the accounts, and therefore prefer to adjust the profit and loss account by 'grossing up' the RDG by the rate of taxation to show it as a gross amount as if tax were payable on the grant.

178 The difference between the two approaches is illustrated in the following example. The figure shown represent the aggregate profit and loss accounts for all the years affected by the lease and, for simplicity, ignore interest.

TABLE 19

REGIONAL DEVELOPMENT GRANT PRESENTATION

	Actual transaction		*Adjusted presentation*	
	£	£	£	£
Rentals receivable over the lease term		750		750
Cost of asset	1,000		1,000	
Less RDG	220		338	
		780		662
Profit/(Loss) before tax		(30)		88
Taxation recoverable (payable)		87		(31)
Profit after tax		£57		£57

179 The standard permits either approach to be followed. If a company grosses up its RDGs, it should disclose the amount by which the profit before tax and the tax charge have been increased as a result of grossing up such grants.

Lessees and RDGs

180 In cases where the asset which is leased qualifies for an RDG the position of the lessee also calls for attention. In the example in paragraph 178 the net cost of the asset after allowing for the RDG is £780. The total rentals payable amount to £750 which is less than the net cost of the asset.

181 In these circumstances an appropriate way of dealing with the situation is to capitalise the asset at £750 and to assume that no finance charge is payable. The £750 would then be depreciated over the shorter of the lease term or the useful life of the asset. It is not considered appropriate to show a negative finance charge.

H – BAD DEBTS

Since a lessor's profit on a finance lease is assessed on the basis of the whole of the lease period, it is essential that bad debts resulting from the failure of the lessee to pay rentals throughout the period are taken into consideration. **182**

The level of bad debts will depend upon the type of business the lessor writes. In many instances bad debts will not be significant; in other instances they may be. **183**

As noted in paragraph 86, where a pattern of bad debt experience can be established, a lessor should make a provision for bad debts but this should not in general change the way in which he recognises gross earnings. **184**

Where there is a significant risk of bad debts, the carrying value of the leasing receivable should be determined having regard to the amount expected to be realised from the leased asset. For example, if it is likely that the asset will be re-possessed, the lessor may need to consider the amount which he will be able to recover through that route. As explained in paragraph 87 the bad debt risk may be sufficient to render classification as a finance lease inappropriate. **185**

Part IV – Leased assets and current cost accounting

INTRODUCTION

Part IV gives guidance on the procedures to be used for accounting for leased assets under SSAP 16 'Current cost accounting'. At the time of writing these guidance notes, SSAP 16 is under review.* However it remains in force until replaced. **186**

ACCOUNTING BY LESSEES

A lessee should record a finance lease in his balance sheet as an asset and as an obligation to pay future rentals. For CCA purposes the asset and the obligation should be considered separately. The lessee's asset forms part of his operating capability which should be maintained. **187**

The asset, which will be included amongst fixed assets in the lessee's balance sheet, should be restated at its value to the business on the basis suggested in the Guidance Notes on SSAP 16 'Current cost accounting'. The depreciation charge in each period should be based on current costs. **188**

The obligation to pay future rentals is equivalent to a borrowing and should be included in the calculation of the gearing adjustment for CCA purposes. **189**

***Editor's note:** *SSAP 16 was suspended in June 1985 and withdrawn in July 1988.*

190 In the example of lessee accounting given in Part I the amounts which have to be restated for CCA purposes in respect of the asset are shown in paragraph 45 and the obligations under finance leases which are to be taken into account in calculating the gearing adjustment are listed in paragraph 46.

191 The part of the rental under a lease which is apportioned as a finance charge should be included as part of the interest costs in the CCA profit and loss account. These amounts are given in paragraphs 26, 28, 34 and 35.

192 Rentals under an operating lease are charged to the profit and loss account and would not normally require adjustment for CCA purposes.

ACCOUNTING BY LESSORS

193 Assets held by lessors for use in operating leases should be restated for CCA purposes on the same basis as any other fixed asset. The lessor is trading in assets and it is appropriate that he maintains his operating capability in terms of the particular fixed assets he is using.

194 Where a lessor is engaged in finance leasing, the rentals he will receive will be fixed in money terms and he therefore has a monetary asset rather than a physical asset in his balance sheet. A monetary working capital adjustment relating to the finance lease receivables should therefore be made for CCA purposes.

[SSAP 22]
Accounting for goodwill

(Issued December 1984; revised July 1989)

Contents

Accounting for goodwill

The provisions of this statement of standard accounting practice should be read in conjunction with the (Explanatory) Foreword to accounting standards. *The standard need not be applied to immaterial items. The provisions apply to financial statements prepared under either the historical cost convention or the current cost convention.*

FRS 7 'Fair Values in Acquisition Accounting', published September 1994, supersedes paragraphs 14, 23, 27, 30 and 33 of this standard. Following publication of FRS 7, SSAP 22 is to be interpreted in the light of FRS 7; references to 'separable net assets' should be interpreted as 'identifiable assets and liabilities'.

FRS 6 'Acquisitions and Mergers', published September 1994, supersedes disclosure paragraphs 48–51; amended disclosure requirements are included in FRS 6.

Part 1 – Explanatory note

NATURE AND MEANING OF GOODWILL

It is usual for the value of a business as a whole to differ from the value of its separable net assets. The difference, which may be positive or negative, is described as goodwill. **1**

Goodwill is therefore by definition incapable of realisation separately from the business as a whole; this characteristic of goodwill distinguishes it from all other items in the accounts. Its other characteristics are that: **2**

(a) the value of goodwill has no reliable or predictable relationship to any cost which may have been incurred;
(b) individual intangible factors which may contribute to goodwill cannot be valued;
(c) the value of goodwill may fluctuate widely according to internal and external circumstances over relatively short periods of time; and
(d) the assessment of the value of goodwill is highly subjective.

Thus, any amount attributed to goodwill is unique to the valuer and to the specific point in time at which it is measured, and is valid only at that time, and in the circumstances then prevailing.

'Purchased goodwill' (positive or negative) is established when a business combination is accounted for as an acquisition; it includes goodwill arising on consolidation, and on the acquisition of an interest in an associated company* or of an unincorporated business. On the purchase of a company, the shares acquired are recorded at cost, being the fair value of the consideration given. For the purposes of consolidated accounts, the cost of the shares is allocated amongst the separable net assets acquired, with purchased goodwill emerging as the difference. Similar principles apply on the acquisition of an unincorporated business. **3**

**See paragraph 26(c) of SSAP 1 'Accounting for associated companies.'*

4 Goodwill can also be attributed to businesses which are not the subject of an acquisition (non-purchased goodwill, as defined in paragraph 29), in that as going concerns they are worth more (positive goodwill), or less (negative goodwill), than the sum of the fair values of their separable net assets. However, except when goodwill is evidenced by a purchase transaction, it is not an accepted practice to recognise it in financial statements.

5 There is no difference in character between purchased goodwill and non-purchased goodwill. However, the value of purchased goodwill, although arising from a subjective valuation of the business, is established as a fact at a particular point in time by a market transaction; this is not true of non-purchased goodwill.

THE ACCOUNTING TREATMENT OF PURCHASED GOODWILL

6 The standard requires that purchased goodwill should normally be eliminated from accounts by immediate write-off. (In this context, the term 'write-off' does not imply an equivalent actual loss of value – see paragraph 7 below). The principal reason for this is that immediate write-off of purchased goodwill is consistent with the accepted practice of not including non-purchased goodwill in accounts. Thus, if purchased goodwill is treated as an asset whilst non-purchased goodwill is not, a balance sheet does not present the total goodwill of a company (or group); it reflects only the purchased goodwill of the acquired business(es) at the date of acquisition, to the extent that it has not been written off.

7 The standard requires that the immediate write-off of purchased goodwill should be made against reserves, not as a charge in the profit and loss account. This is because (a) purchased goodwill is written off as a matter of accounting policy, that is, in order to achieve consistency of treatment with non-purchased goodwill, rather than because it has suffered a permanent diminution in value and (b) the write-off is not related to the results of the year in which the acquisition was made.

8 There will be cases wh.re the fair value of the separable net assets exceeds the value of the business as a whole. This difference is termed 'negative goodwill'. Negative goodwill, which is the mirror image of positive goodwill, should be credited to reserves. Where negative goodwill arises, the amounts allocated to the relevant separable net assets will need to be reviewed particularly carefully to ensure that the fair values ascribed to them are not overstated.

9 It is recognised that there is an alternative way of looking at positive goodwill. This is that, although goodwill is intangible, it is a reality, it exists and when a business is purchased the price paid includes an amount attributable to purchased goodwill; thus capital has been expended in exchange for an asset – goodwill – which should be recognised and treated in the same way as any other capital asset.

10 Whilst providing that companies should normally follow the preferred treatment of writing off goodwill immediately against reserves, the standard also allows a company to carry positive goodwill as an asset and to amortise it through the profit and loss account over its useful economic life.

Guidance on factors to be considered in determining the useful economic life of purchased goodwill is contained in Appendix 1. As the factors which affect the estimates of the useful economic life of purchased goodwill are likely to vary according to the different circumstances of different acquisitions, there is no requirement in the standard to select the same useful economic life for the goodwill arising on different acquisitions. **11**

It is envisaged that most companies will select the policy of elimination of goodwill immediately on acquisition and that only a limited number will select the policy of amortisation. There may, however, be cases where an individual company's circumstances require that it adopts different policies in relation to the goodwill which arises in different acquisitions; for example, a company may in general follow the preferred policy of immediate write-off but it may need to adopt the policy of amortising the goodwill on an unusually large acquisition because of the effect which immediate write-off would have on its reserves. **12**

GOODWILL AND SEPARABLE NET ASSETS

In deciding whether a particular asset falls into the category of separable net assets, the test is whether that asset could be identified and sold separately without disposing of the business as a whole. For example, an asset may be an essential part of a company's manufacturing operations, and it may be that the asset would be of very little value other than in its present use; but it could be sold separately or bought from its manufacturers, whereas goodwill could not be – it could only be either acquired or sold as part of the process of acquiring or selling the business as a whole. Separable net assets may include identifiable intangibles such as those specifically mentioned in the balance sheet formats in the Companies Act 1985, i.e. 'concessions, patents, licences, trade marks and similar rights and assets'; other examples include publishing titles, franchise rights and customer lists. (This list of examples is not intended to be comprehensive.) Identifiable intangibles such as these form part of the separable net assets which are recorded in an acquiring company's accounts at fair value, even if they were not recorded in the acquired company's accounts. **13**

When ascribing fair values to separable net assets at the time of an acquisition, a provision may be needed in respect of items which were taken into account in arriving at the purchase price, that is, anticipated future losses or costs of reorganisation. Where such provision is needed, it forms part of the liabilities which are set up at the time of the acquisition (see Appendix 3). Such a provision may be needed whether goodwill is positive or negative. **14***

***Editor's note:** *See preamble to SSAP 22 inserted by FRS 7.*

SPECIAL TYPES OF ASSET

15 Some property assets are valued on a basis which has regard to the trading potential which attaches to the property.* This trading potential is sometimes thought of as goodwill, but such a basis of valuation would normally exclude any goodwill which is personal to the present owner or management and which would not pass with the property on a sale with vacant possession. This practice is acceptable in certain limited categories of business. Where it is followed, the assets concerned should be disclosed separately and the notes to the accounts should make clear that this practice has been followed and that the amount at which the assets concerned are stated does not exceed their open market value,† having regard to the trading potential of the business. This treatment is not dealt with in Part 3 of the standard as it concerns the treatment of other assets, not of goodwill.

GOODWILL IN THE ACCOUNTS OF INDIVIDUAL ENTITIES AND HOLDING COMPANIES AND IN CONSOLIDATED ACCOUNTS

16 The standard requires that the amount to be attributed to purchased goodwill should be the difference between the fair value of the consideration given and the aggregate of the fair values of the separable net assets acquired. This applies equally to the accounts of an individual entity, to the accounts of a holding company and to consolidated accounts. However, the circumstances of each require separate consideration.

17 Where an individual entity acquires an unincorporated business, it will account for the cost of the business acquired by attributing fair values to the separable net assets it has acquired. If the fair value of the consideration given differs from the aggregate of the fair values of the separable net assets acquired, the difference will be purchased goodwill and it will be identified separately in the entity's accounting records. This purchased goodwill should then be eliminated from the accounts as set out in the standard.

18 Where a holding company acquires another company and merger accounting is not used, it will include in its own balance sheet the shares in the acquired company at cost, based on the fair value of the consideration given. From the point of view of the holding

**See the Royal Institution of Chartered Surveyors' Guidance Notes on the Valuation of Assets (2nd edition), Background Paper No. 7, 'Open market valuations having regard to trading potential'. Paragraph 2 of the Paper‡ notes that 'there are certain types of property designed or adapted for particular uses, which invariably change hands in the open market at prices based directly on trading potential for a strictly limited use. Examples of such properties which normally are sold as fully operational business units include hotels, public houses, cinemas, theatres, bingo clubs, gaming clubs, petrol filling stations, betting shops, specialised leisure and sporting facilities.'*

†*In the context of land and buildings the term 'open market value' is commonly used for what is described elsewhere in this standard as 'fair value.'*

‡**Editor's note:** *This is now paragraph 3 of Statement of Asset Valuation Practice No. 12.*

company, the separable net assets will be the shares in the acquired company, not the individual assets and liabilities of the acquired company. Since the fair value of the shares acquired will normally be equal to the fair value of the consideration given, no purchased goodwill will arise in the accounting records of the holding company. The standard does not require an adjustment to be made in the holding company's accounts to the carrying value of the shares in the acquired company in respect of any consolidation goodwill written off either in the group accounts or in the accounts of the subsidiary or associate, except to the extent that the carrying value of the investment in shares should be written down to reflect any permanent diminution in value.

On consolidation, the cost of the investment is attributed to the separable net assets of **19**
the acquired company – that is, the fixed and net current assets less long-term liabilities – by stating them at their fair values. Any difference between that total and the carrying value of the investment (i.e., the fair value of the purchase consideration) represents purchased goodwill arising on consolidation. This goodwill should then be eliminated from the accounts as set out in the standard.

EXPLANATORY NOTE ON ADDITIONAL DISCLOSURE

Paragraphs 47–53 of SSAP 22 require certain additional disclosures to be made when **20**
recording acquisitions and disposals. These are intended to improve the financial reporting of business combinations within the scope of this standard by enabling users of financial statements to gain a better appreciation of the business acquired and of the extent to which the results of the combined entity after an acquisition are attributable to trading performance as opposed to other factors, such as the disposal of part of the business or the release of unutilised provisions established when the business combination occurred. These additional disclosures will complement appropriate accounting treatments and not be a substitute for them.

The requirements include the disclosure of the fair value of the consideration. While **21**
this is a figure which could be calculated from the other disclosures already made in relation to acquisitions, it will be helpful to have it separately disclosed, particularly if the basis of calculation is given in those cases where the fair value could differ considerably according to the valuation method chosen.

The amount of purchased goodwill shown in the accounts may be different from that **22**
arising from an acquisition where, for example, the statutory provisions of the UK Companies Act 1985 relating to merger relief are applied and only the residual figure after application of merger relief is disclosed. This effective netting of goodwill against merger reserve without explicit mention in the financial statements can convey the misleading impression that the consideration for the purchase was less than was actually the case. To avoid this result, the amount of purchased goodwill arising on an acquisition should be shown in the year of acquisition in all cases.

When ascribing fair values to separable net assets at the time of an acquisition, **23***
adjustments may have to be made on consolidation to the book amount of assets and

***Editor's note:** *See preamble to SSAP 22 inserted by FRS 7.*

liabilities of the acquired company. Such adjustments may include revaluations; applying the acquiring group's accounting policies to the acquiree; making provisions; and recognising previously unrecorded assets such as intangible assets. Disclosure of details of the consolidation adjustments made and of movements on provisions related to acquisitions, analysed under the headings of paragraph 48, will provide valuable information to the user of financial statements on the acquisition itself and enables post-acquisition trading performance to be distinguished from the effects of, for example, the release of unutilised provisions. Appropriate disclosure will also help allay the concern expressed by some commentators that, in certain instances, profits may have benefited from provisions made at acquisition but which subsequently did not prove necessary.

24 The disclosure of the profit or loss on disposals of businesses, or business segments, previously acquired also enables post-combination trading performance to be separated from the effect of other factors. Some commentators have suggested that the disclosure of the profit or loss on disposal may not, on its own, provide sufficient information about the disposal in the absence of details of the extent to which attributable goodwill arising on the earlier acquisition has previously been written off to reserves. It is accepted that, where a reorganisation has taken place since an acquisition, an element of estimation may be required in determining the goodwill attributable to the disposal. However, it is not considered that the calculation problems are insurmountable, particularly where the goodwill is allocated on or soon after acquisition, in the knowledge that this information may be required later. For disposals of businesses, or business segments, acquired before the effective date of this standard, goodwill need not be attributed and disclosed where it would be impractical to do so but, in these circumstances, this fact should be disclosed. Although goodwill is defined in paragraph 26 by reference to the business as a whole, goodwill can be allocated over different business segments.

25 Enterprises that amortise goodwill are encouraged but not required to disclose earnings per share before goodwill amortisation in addition to following the present requirements of SSAP 3 (Revised) – Earnings per share. This will help the comparison of their results with those of enterprises which charge no amortisation for purchased goodwill on acquisition as they have written it off immediately against reserves. The basis on which the additional earnings per share figure has been calculated should be disclosed. It should be clearly stated that the additional calculation differs from that required by SSAP 3. Earnings per share on the SSAP 3 basis is required by SSAP 3 to be shown on the face of the profit and loss account.

Part 2 – Definition of terms

26 *Goodwill* is the difference between the value of a business as a whole and the aggregate of the fair values of its separable net assets.

27* *Separable net assets* are those assets (and liabilities) which can be identified and sold (or

***Editor's note:** *See preamble to SSAP 22 inserted by FRS 7.*

discharged) separately without necessarily disposing of the business as a whole. They include identifiable intangibles.

Purchased goodwill is goodwill which is established as a result of the purchase of a business accounted for as an acquisition. Goodwill arising on consolidation is one form of purchased goodwill. **28**

Non-purchased goodwill is any goodwill other than purchased goodwill. **29**

Fair value is the amount for which an asset (or liability) could be exchanged in an arm's length transaction. **30***

Useful economic life of purchased goodwill is the best estimate of the life of such goodwill at the date of purchase. **31**

Company, for the purpose of this standard, includes any enterprise or group which comes within the scope of statements of standard accounting practice. **32**

Acquisition adjustments are those accounting adjustments to the assets or liabilities of an acquired business made for any matters arising in consequence of or in anticipation of an acquisition. **33***

A *business segment* is a material and separately identifiable component of the business operations of a company or group whose activities, assets and results can be clearly distinguished from the remainder of the company's activities. A business segment will normally have its own separate product lines or markets. **34**

Part 3 – Standard accounting practice

GENERAL

No amount should be attributed to non-purchased goodwill in the balance sheets of companies or groups. **35**

The amount to be attributed to purchased goodwill should be the difference between the fair value of the consideration given and the aggregate of the fair values of the separable net assets acquired. **36**

The amount attributed to purchased goodwill should not include any value for separable intangibles. The amount of these, if material, should be included under the appropriate heading within intangible fixed assets in the balance sheet. **37**

Purchased goodwill should not be carried in the balance sheet of a company or group as a permanent item. **38**

Purchased goodwill (other than negative goodwill) should normally be eliminated from the accounts immediately on acquisition against reserves ('immediate write-off'). **39**

***Editor's note:** *See preamble to SSAP 22 inserted by FRS 7.*

40 Any excess of the aggregate of the fair values of the separable net assets acquired over the fair value of the consideration given (negative goodwill) should be credited directly to reserves.

41 Purchased goodwill (other than negative goodwill) may be eliminated from the accounts by amortisation through the profit and loss account in arriving at profit or loss on ordinary activities on a systematic basis over its useful economic life ('amortisation'). When this treatment is selected, the following points apply:

(a) Purchased goodwill should not be revalued. If there is a permanent diminution in value of purchased goodwill, it should be written down immediately through the profit and loss account to its estimated recoverable amount.
(b) The useful economic life should be estimated at the time of acquisition. It should not include any allowance for the effects of subsequent expenditure or other circumstances subsequently affecting the company since these would have the effect of creating non-purchased goodwill.
(c) The estimated useful economic life over which purchased goodwill is being amortised may be shortened but may not be increased.

42 Nothing in this standard precludes a company from using both the immediate write-off treatment and the amortisation treatment in respect of the goodwill which relates to different acquisitions, so long as the accounting policies provide for the elimination of goodwill on a basis consistent with the standard.

DISCLOSURE

43 The accounting policy followed in respect of goodwill should be explained in the notes to the accounts.

44 The amount of goodwill recognised as a result of any acquisitions during the year should be shown separately for each acquisition where material.

45 Where the amortisation treatment is selected, purchased goodwill should be shown as a separate item under intangible fixed assets in the balance sheet until fully written off. In addition, the following should be disclosed:

(a) the movement on the goodwill account during the year, showing the cost, accumulated amortisation and net book value of goodwill at the beginning and end of the year, and the amount of goodwill amortised through the profit and loss account during the year; and
(b) the period selected for amortising the goodwill relating to each major acquisition.

46 If the accounting treatment of goodwill existing at the date of introduction of the standard is different from the policy followed in respect of all other goodwill, that treatment and the amounts involved should be disclosed.

47 The fair value of the consideration and the amount of purchased goodwill arising on each acquisition during the period should be separately disclosed. Disclosure should identify the method of dealing with goodwill arising and whether it has been set off against merger reserve of other reserves or has been carried forward as an intangible asset (for the use of 'merger reserve' in relation to Republic of Ireland companies, see paragraph 65).

A table should be provided showing the book values, as recorded in the acquired company's books at the date of acquisition but before any acquisition adjustments, and the fair values of each major category of assets and liabilities acquired. An explanation of the reasons for differences between values should given for each major category of assets and liabilities and these adjustments should be analysed between: **48***

(i) revaluations;
(ii) provisions for future trading losses;
(iii) other provisions;

Any amounts that cannot be classified within (i)–(iii) above should be analysed between:

(iv) bringing accounting policies into line with those of the acquiring group;
(v) any other major item.

Movements on provisions related to acquisitions should be disclosed and analysed between the amounts used and the amounts released unused or applied for another purpose. Sufficient details should be given to identify the extent to which the provisions have proved unnecessary. **49***

Where the fair value of the assets and liabilities, or the consideration, can only be determined on a provisional basis at the end of the accounting period in which the acquisition took place, this should be stated and the reasons given. Where there are subsequent material adjustments to such provisional fair values, with a consequent adjustment to goodwill, those adjustments should be disclosed and explained. **50***

The disclosures required by paragraphs 47–50 should be made separately for each material acquisition and in aggregate for other acquisitions where these are material in total although not so individually. **51***

The following should be disclosed in respect of each material disposal of a previously acquired business or business segment: **52**

(a) the profit or loss on the disposal;
(b) the amount of purchased goodwill attributable to the business or business segment disposed of and how it has been treated in determining the profit or loss on disposal;†

****Editor's note:*** *Superseded by FRS 6, which is effective for business combinations first accounted for in financial statements relating to accounting periods commencing on or after 23 December 1994.*

†***Editor's note:*** *See also UITF Abstract 3 'Treatment of goodwill on disposal of a business'.*

(c) the accounting treatment adopted and the amount of the proceeds in situations where no profit or loss is recorded on a disposal because the proceeds have been accounted for as a reduction in the cost of the acquisition.

53 The provisions in paragraph 52 relating to goodwill on disposals should apply to all disposals where the relevant information is obtainable and in all cases where disposals relate to acquisitions made after the effective date for this section. Where, in relation to acquisitions prior to the effective date, it is impossible or impractical to ascertain the attributable goodwill on a disposal this should be stated and the reasons given.

DATE FROM WHICH EFFECTIVE

54 The accounting practices set out in this statement should be adopted as soon as possible. Except as stated in paragraph 55 below they should be regarded as standard accounting practice in respect of financial statements relating to accounting periods beginning on or after 1 January 1985.

55 The accounting practices set out in paragraphs 47–53 of this statement should be adopted as soon as possible and regarded as standard in respect of accounting periods beginning on or after 1 January 1989.

Part 4 – Legal requirements in Great Britain and Northern Ireland

References are to the Companies Act 1985 and the Companies (Northern Ireland) Order 1986.

GENERAL

56 Set out below is a summary of the main legal requirements which are directly relevant to goodwill in Great Britain. In each case a brief description of the point is given, together with the relevant Companies Act reference and a note of the paragraph(s) in the standard where the point is covered. It should be noted that in general these legal provisions apply to the accounts of both individual companies and groups. However, paragraphs 59 and 61 apply only to individual companies.

57 The accounting policy adopted by the company in respect of goodwill should be disclosed (4 Sch. 36; standard, paragraph 43).

58 The balance sheet formats in Schedule 4 require that purchased goodwill, to the extent that it has not been written off, should be shown under the heading of intangible fixed assets. Goodwill should be shown separately from other intangible assets such as patents, licences and trade marks (CA 1985 4 Sch. formats and note 3 to the balance sheet formats; standard, paragraphs 37 and 45).

59 If goodwill is treated as an asset (i.e., where it is not written off immediately), it should be amortised systematically over a period chosen by the directors (4 Sch. 21(2);

standard, paragraph 41). The period chosen should not exceed the useful economic life of the goodwill in question (4 Sch. 21(3); standard, paragraph 41). The period chosen and the reasons for choosing that period should be disclosed in a note (4 Sch. 21(4); standard, paragraph 45(b) and paragraph 4 of Appendix 1).

Goodwill may not be revalued (4 Sch. 31(1); standard, paragraph 41(a)). **60**

In the case of a permanent diminution in value of goodwill which is carried as an asset, a **61** provision should be made and the carrying amount of goodwill should be reduced accordingly. The provision should either be shown in the profit and loss account or disclosed in a note (4 Sch. 19(2); standard, paragraph 41(a)).

The movements on the goodwill account should be disclosed. The same level of **62** disclosure is required as for other fixed assets (CA 1985 4 Sch. 42; standard, paragraph 45(a)).

NOTE ON REALISED PROFITS

Realised profits are defined by paragraph 91* of Schedule 4 Companies Act 1985 **63** (paragraph 90 of Schedule 4 to the Companies (Northern Ireland) Order 1986) as being those which 'fall to be treated as realised profits ... in accordance with principles generally accepted with respect to the determination for accounting purposes of realised profits at the time when those accounts are prepared'. Appendix 2 gives guidance on the effect of accounting for goodwill on realised profits.

Part 5 – Legal requirements in the Republic of Ireland

The legal requirements in Great Britain and Northern Ireland are mirrored, in respect **64** of the Republic of Ireland, in the Schedule to the Companies (Amendment) Act 1986. The following table indicates the corresponding paragraphs in respect of all the references contained in Part 4 of this statement.

Schedule 4 to the Companies Act 1985	*Schedule 4 to the Companies (Northern Ireland) Order 1986*	*The Schedule to the Companies (Amendment) Act 1986*
Formats and note 3 to the balance sheet formats	Formats and note 3 to the balance sheet formats	Formats and note 2 to the balance sheet formats
Paragraph 19	Paragraph 19	Paragraph 7
Paragraph 21	Paragraph 21	Paragraph 9
Paragraph 31	Paragraph 31	Paragraph 19
Paragraph 36	Paragraph 36	Paragraph 24
Paragraph 42	Paragraph 42	Paragraph 31
Paragraph 91*	Paragraph 90	Paragraph 72

Editor's note: *Now section 262(3).*

65 No legislation equivalent to the merger relief in the Companies Act 1985 currently exists in the Republic of Ireland. Until such a time as equivalent legislation is enacted, no explicit relief from the requirement to establish a share premium account (section 62(1), Companies Act 1963) is available.

Part 6 – Compliance with International Accounting Standard No. 22 'Accounting for business combinations'

66 The requirements of International Accounting Standard No. 22 'Accounting for business combinations' which related to accounting for goodwill accord very closely with the content of the United Kingdom and Irish Accounting Standard No. 22 'Accounting for goodwill' and accordingly compliance with SSAP 22 will ensure compliance in all material respects with the requirements of IAS 22 which relate to accounting for goodwill.*

Editor's note: *A revised version of IAS 22 was issued in November 1993. This does not permit the immediate write-off of goodwill against reserves.*

Appendix 1

This appendix is for guidance only and does not form part of the statement of standard accounting practice.

FACTORS TO BE CONSIDERED IN DETERMINING THE USEFUL ECONOMIC LIFE OF PURCHASED GOODWILL

Where a company employs the amortisation treatment, it will need to determine the 1
useful economic life of the goodwill in respect of each acquisition. The useful economic life of goodwill is also relevant to the transfer from unrealised to realised reserves as referred to in paragraph 2 of Appendix 2. The useful economic life of purchased goodwill is the period over which benefits may reasonably be expected to accrue from that goodwill in the acquired company which existed and was identified at the time of acquisition. In the period following the acquisition, the value of the purchased goodwill is considered to diminish although it may be replaced by non-purchased goodwill. The total goodwill (purchased and non-purchased) may remain constant or may increase or decrease. However, in determining the useful economic life of purchased goodwill, the effects of subsequent expenditure or other circumstances affecting the company after the date of the acquisition should not be taken into account, since these would have the effect of creating non-purchased goodwill. The purchased goodwill whose useful life is being determined is only that which existed and was recognised at the time of acquisition.

There are a number of factors which may be relevant to a determination of the useful 2
economic life of purchased goodwill. These factors should be assessed at the time the acquisition was made, and include; expected changes in products, markets or technology; the expected period of future service of certain employees; and expected future demand, competition or other economic factors which may affect current advantages.

It is sometimes argued that the value of an investment at a given point in time can be 3
regarded as the present value of the future net cash flows from the investment. Consequently, the period of time during which returns can reasonably be anticipated from the investment would set an upper limit on the amortisation period. This factor may suggest a relatively short amortisation period such as the five years envisaged by the general rule of the EC 4th Directive. However, in implementing the 4th Directive, the UK took advantage of the Member State option to permit amortisation over a period exceeding five years, but not exceeding the useful economic life. The standard also provides for amortisation of goodwill over its useful economic life and, accordingly, it is inappropriate to indicate any maximum period in numerical terms.

It is not possible to specify general rules regarding the useful economic life over which 4
purchased goodwill should be amortised in any particular case, and it is likely that different useful economic lives will be selected for the goodwill arising on different acquisitions. Paragraph 45 of the standard requires, *inter alia*, disclosure of the amortisation period(s) selected in relation to major acquisitions. Further, as noted in paragraph 59, there is a legal requirement for disclosure of the reasons for choosing the

amortisation period. The amortisation period will generally have been selected because it represents the useful economic life of the goodwill and a statement to that effect would appear to satisfy the requirement.

Appendix 2

This appendix is for guidance only and does not form part of the statement of standard accounting practice.

EFFECT OF ELIMINATION OF GOODWILL ON REALISED PROFITS

Paragraph 63 of the standard sets out the legal definition of realised profits. This is relevant only in the case of an individual company. In the case of goodwill arising on consolidation, the distinction between realised and unrealised reserves is not relevant. Distributions are made from the profits of individual companies, not by groups, and hence the elimination of consolidation goodwill has no effect on the distributable profits of any company. 1

Where it is the policy of an individual company to eliminate goodwill against reserves immediately on acquisition, the question arises whether such elimination constitutes a reduction of realised reserves. To the extent that the goodwill is considered to have suffered an actual diminution in value, the write-off should be charged against realised reserves. In other cases, where goodwill is written off on acquisition as a matter of accounting policy, rather than because of an actual diminution in value, realised reserves should not be reduced immediately. However, the standard is based on the concept in the UK Companies Acts that purchased goodwill has a limited useful life so that ultimately its elimination must constitute a realised loss. It may in some circumstances (e.g., where a company lacks sufficient distributable reserves to cover the purchase cost of the goodwill) be appropriate to charge the elimination of goodwill initially to a suitable unrealised reserve, thereby spreading the effect of the elimination of goodwill on realised reserves over its useful life rather than impairing realised reserves immediately. The Accounting Standards Committee is advised by the Department of Trade and Industry that the restriction regarding the use of the revaluation reserve set out in paragraph 34(3) of Schedule 4 has the effect that this reserve should not be charged with the write-off of goodwill. A suitable unrealised reserve may exist as a result of the crediting to reserves of negative goodwill – see paragraph 3 below. To maintain parity of effect as regards distributable reserves with the amortisation method permitted by paragraph 41 of the standard, the amount written off should then be transferred from unrealised reserves to realised reserves so as to reduce realised reserves on a systematic basis in the same way as if the goodwill had been amortised. In case of doubt on the points in this paragraph, legal advice should be sought. 2

Where negative goodwill arises in the accounts of an individual company it should be credited initially to an unrealised reserve, from which it may be transferred to realised reserves in line with the depreciation or realisation of the assets acquired in the business combination which gave rise to the goodwill in question. On the introduction of this standard, amounts representing negative goodwill which arose on prior acquisitions may already have been credited to reserves. To the extent that the assets acquired have, on the introduction of this standard, been depreciated or realised, the relevant amount or reserves may be regarded as realised. 3

Appendix 3

This appendix is for guidance only and does not form part of the statement of standard accounting practice.

FAIR VALUE TABLE

1 The following example is given to indicate a format for the fair value table and adjustments required by paragraph 48. This example is neither exhaustive nor prescriptive but is for general guidance. In practice only material adjustments need be separately disclosed.

Fair value table
Acquisition – XYZ Ltd *Date* – 19.2.89

Consideration – 100,000 £1 ordinary shares were issued to acquire the following assets. The fair value of the consideration, using the mid-market price on 19.2.89 of £3.06, was £306,000 giving rise to goodwill of £100,000.

	Book value £000	*Revaluation* £000	*Provisions for trading losses* £000	*Other provisions* £000	*Accounting policy alignment* £000	*Other major items* £000	*Fair value to the group* £000
Fixed assets							
Intangible	—	—	—	—	—	80 [f]	80
Tangible	160	20 [a]	—	—	—	—	180
Investments	20	5 [b]	—	—	—	—	25
Current assets:							
Stock	40	—	(4) [c]	(5) [d]	(2) [e]	—	29
Debtors	35	—	—	—	—	—	35
Investments	10	—	—	—	—	—	10
Cash at bank	12	—	—	—	—	—	12
Total assets	277	25	(4)	(5)	(2)	80	371
Liabilities							
Provisions:							
Pensions	30	—	—	—	—	—	30
Taxation	45	—	—	—	—	10 [g]	55
Other	10	—	8 [c]	—	—	—	18
Creditors:							
Debenture	2	—	—	—	—	—	2
Bank Loans	15	—	—	—	—	—	15
Trade creditors	30	—	—	—	—	—	30
Other creditors	10	—	—	—	—	—	10
Accruals	5	—	—	—	—	—	5
Total liabilities	147	—	8	—	—	10	165
Net Assets	130	25	(12)	(5)	(2)	70	206

	Adjustments	Explanations
(i)	**Revaluations**	
	Note a	Increases in value of freehold properties since last revaluation in 1981.
	Note b	Increase in value of shares of USM investment since purchase in 1983.
(ii)	**Provisions for trading losses**	
	Note c	Losses expected to be incurred prior to closing down small tools division.
(iii)	**Other provisions**	
	Note d	Write-down following reassessment of realisable value of stock which is more than one year old.
(iv)	**Accounting policy alignments**	
	Note e	Change of stock valuation from weighted average cost to FIFO which is used by the group.
(v)	**Other major items**	
	Note f	Recognition of intangibles – relating to publishing titles and brands acquired.
	Note g	Adjustment to deferred tax arising from the incorporation of fair values.

The provisions of the revised SSAP 22 'Accounting for goodwill' retain the requirements of SSAP 22 as issued in December 1984, but with additional disclosure requirements (paragraphs 47–53) recommended by the ASC and approved by the Councils of the Consultative Committee of Accounting Bodies. Apart from the updating of the section on legal requirements and the removal of the paragraphs on transitional provisions and the treatment of existing goodwill, the original SSAP 22 'Accounting for goodwill' is unchanged. This limited revision is not intended to change for the present the accounting treatments required in the original standard. These treatments are currently the subject of fundamental review by the ASC in its work on Fair Value and Business Combinations.* While SSAP 22 and 23 are undergoing this review, the CCAB believes the additional disclosures that will now be required will assist users of financial statements in gaining a better appreciation of the financial position and changes in the financial position of a reporting company which makes a business acquisition or disposal.

The ASC intends to publish the results of its review of accounting for Business Combination later this year.

Editor's note: *This work culminated in the issue by the ASB in September 1994 of FRS 6 'Acquisitions and Mergers' and FRS 7 'Fair Values in Acquisition Accounting'.*

[SSAP 23]
Accounting for acquisitions and mergers*

(Issued April 1985)

Contents

****Editor's note:** SSAP 23 is superseded by FRS 6, which is effective for business combinations first accounted for in financial statements relating to accounting periods commencing on or after 23 December 1994.*

Accounting for acquisitions and mergers

The provisions of this statement of standard accounting practice should be read in conjunction with the (Explanatory) Foreword to accounting standards *and need not be applied to immaterial items. The provisions deal with financial statements prepared under either the historical cost convention or the current cost convention.*

Part 1 – Explanatory note

INTRODUCTION

This standard deals with accounting for business combinations, which arise when one or more companies become subsidiaries of another company. It deals only with accounting in group accounts and not with the accounting to be used in individual companies' own accounts; guidance on this latter point is provided in the appendix. Other standards which deal with related matters are FRS 2 'Accounting for subsidiary undertakings' and SSAP 22 'Accounting for goodwill.' 1

Two different methods have been developed to account for business combinations: acquisition accounting and merger accounting. In acquisition accounting the results of the acquired company are brought into the group accounts only from the date of acquisition. Assets acquired are stated at cost to the acquiring group. In merger accounting, conversely, the financial statements are aggregated and presented as if the combining companies had always been together. Accordingly, although the merger may have taken place part of the way through the year, the full year's results of both combining companies are reflected in the group accounts for the year, and corresponding amounts are presented on the same basis. 2

For the purposes of this standard, the main criterion employed to determine the appropriate method or methods of accounting is whether or not the combination is based principally on a share for share exchange. Merger accounting is considered to be an appropriate method of accounting when two groups of shareholders continue, or are in a position to continue, their shareholdings as before but on a combined basis. Acquisition accounting is therefore required when there is a transfer of the ownership of at least one of the combining companies, and substantial resources leave the group as consideration for that transfer. Conversely, when only limited resources leave the group, merger accounting may be used. 3

Paragraph 11(d) indicates that, for merger accounting to be available, the resources which leave the group should be restricted such that no more than 10% of the fair value of the consideration given for equity capital may be in a form other than equity, such as cash or loan stock. Similarly, no more than 10% of the fair value of the consideration given for voting non-equity capital may be in a form other than equity or voting non-equity. 4

DIFFERENCES BETWEEN ACQUISITION ACCOUNTING AND MERGER ACCOUNTING

5 There are a number of differences between acquisition accounting and merger accounting. The acquired company's assets and liabilities are included in the consolidated accounts at fair values in acquisition accounting but not in merger accounting. Hence, increased depreciation charges are likely to arise in acquisition accounting. Goodwill often arises in acquisition accounting but not in merger accounting. Differences which are sometimes described as goodwill can arise in merger accounting, such as where the nominal value of the shares issued exceeds the aggregate of the nominal value of the shares and the reserves of the other company, but these differences are not goodwill as defined in SSAP 22 as they are not based on the fair values of the consideration given and the separable net assets acquired; such differences should be adjusted against consolidated reserves.

Part 2 – Definition of terms

6 A *business combination* arises when one or more companies become subsidiaries of another company.

7 An *offer* is any offer made by or on behalf of a company ('the offeror') for shares in another company ('the offeree'). A number of separate offers constituting in substance a composite transaction is considered to be a single offer.

8 The provisions of this standard which are set out in relation to 'an offer' and the results thereof apply also to any scheme or arrangement having similar effect.

9 The *effective date of acquisition or merger* is the earlier of:

(a) the date on which the consideration passes; or
(b) the date on which an offer becomes or is declared unconditional.

This applies even if the acquiring company has the right under the agreement to share in the profits of the acquired business from an earlier date.

10 *Equity share capital* is as defined in section 744, Companies Act 1985, namely, 'in relation to a company, its issued share capital excluding any part of that capital which, neither as respects dividends nor as respects capital, carries any right to participate beyond a specified amount in a distribution.'

Part 3 – Standard accounting practice

CLASSIFICATION OF BUSINESS COMBINATIONS

11 A business combination may be accounted for as a merger if all of the following conditions are met:

(a) the business combination results from an offer to the holders of all equity shares and the holders of all voting shares which are not already held by the offeror; and
(b) the offeror has secured, as a result of the offer, a holding of (i) at least 90% of all equity shares (taking each class of equity separately) and (ii) the shares carrying at least 90% of the votes of the offeree; and
(c) immediately prior to the offer, the offeror does not hold (i) 20% or more of all equity shares of the offeree (taking each class of equity separately), or (ii) shares carrying 20% or more of the votes of the offeree; and
(d) not less than 90% of the fair value of the total consideration given for the equity share capital (including that given for shares already held) is in the form of equity share capital; not less than 90% of the fair value of the total consideration given for voting non-equity share capital (including that given for shares already held) is in the form of equity and/or voting non-equity share capital.

For the purposes of paragraph 11, any convertible stock outstanding at the time of the **12**
offer is not to be regarded as equity except to the extent that it is converted into equity as a result of and at the time of the business combination.

For the purposes of paragraph 11, 'offeror' includes the offeror's holding company or **13**
subsidiary or fellow subsidiary or its or their nominees.

The references in paragraph 11 to shares in the offeree which carry votes relate to full **14**
voting shares, rather than shares which carry votes only in special circumstances, for example when dividends are in arrears.

If a business combination does not meet all the conditions in paragraph 11, it should be **15**
accounted for as an acquisition.

ACQUISITION ACCOUNTING

Where a business combination is accounted for as an acquisition, the fair value of the **16**
purchase consideration should, for the purpose of consolidated financial statements, be allocated between the underlying net tangible and intangible assets other than goodwill, on the basis of the fair value to the acquiring company. Any difference between the fair value of the consideration and the aggregate of the fair values of the separable net assets including identifiable intangibles such as patents, licences and trade marks will represent goodwill, which should be accounted for in accordance with the provisions of SSAP 22.

In an acquisition, the results of the acquired company should be brought into the group **17**
accounts from the date of acquisition only.

MERGER ACCOUNTING

In merger accounting, it is not necessary to adjust the carrying values of the assets and **18**
liabilities of the subsidiary to fair value either in its own books or on consolidation. However, appropriate adjustments should be made to achieve uniformity of accounting policies between the combining companies.

19 In the group accounts for the period in which the merger takes place, the profits or losses of subsidiaries brought in for the first time should be included for the entire period without any adjustment in respect of that part of the period prior to the merger. Corresponding amounts should be presented as if the companies had been combined throughout the previous period and at the previous balance sheet date.

20 A difference may arise on consolidation between the carrying value of the investment in the subsidiary (which will normally be the nominal value of the shares issued as consideration plus the fair value of any additional consideration) and the nominal value of the shares transferred to the issuing company. Where the carrying value of the investment is less than the nominal value of the shares transferred, the difference should be treated as a reserve arising on consolidation. Where the carrying value of the investment is greater than the nominal value of the shares transferred, the difference is the extent to which reserves have been in effect capitalised as a result of the merger and it should therefore be treated on consolidation as a reduction of reserves.

DISCLOSURE

21 The following information should be disclosed in respect of all material **business combinations**, whether accounted for as acquisitions or mergers, in the financial statements of the acquiring or issuing company which deal with the year in which the combination takes place:

(a) the names of the combining companies;
(b) the number and class of the securities issued in respect of the combination, and details of any other consideration given;
(c) the accounting treatment adopted for the business combination (i.e., whether it has been accounted for as an acquisition or a merger); and
(d) the nature and amount of significant accounting adjustments by the combining companies to achieve consistency of accounting policies.

22 In respect of all material **acquisitions** during the year, the consolidated financial statements should contain sufficient information about the results of subsidiaries acquired to enable shareholders to appreciate the effect on the consolidated results. In addition, disclosure should be made of the date from which the results of major acquisitions have been brought into the accounts (that is, the effective date of those acquisitions).

23 In respect of all material **mergers**, the following information should be disclosed in the financial statements of the issuing company for the year in which the merger takes place:

(a) the fair value of the consideration given by the issuing company;
(b) an analysis of the current year's attributable profit before extraordinary items between that of before and that of after the effective date of the merger;
(c) an analysis of the attributable profit before extraordinary items of the current year up to the effective date of the merger and of the previous year between that of the issuing company and that of the subsidiary; and

(d) an analysis of extraordinary items so as to indicate whether each individual extraordinary item relates to pre- or post-merger events, and to which party to the merger the item relates.

APPLICABILITY TO VARIOUS STRUCTURES OF BUSINESS COMBINATION

The provisions in this standard, which are explained by reference to an acquiring or issuing company which issues shares as consideration for the transfer to it of shares in the other company, should also be read so as to apply to other arrangements which achieve similar results. Such arrangements would include those whereby a new holding company or new entity is formed and issues shares to the shareholders of two or more companies as consideration for the transfer to it of shares in both those companies. Whatever the nature of the arrangement, all the conditions in paragraph 11 should be complied with if merger accounting is to be adopted. **24**

DATE FROM WHICH EFFECTIVE

The accounting practices set out in this statement should be adopted as soon as possible and regarded as standard in respect of business combinations first accounted for in financial statements relating to accounting periods beginning on or after 1 April 1985. **25**

Part 4 – Legal requirements in Great Britain

Section 130(1), Companies Act 1985 (the '1985 Act') provides that 'if a company issues shares at a premium, whether for cash or otherwise, a sum equal to the aggregate amount or value of the premiums on those shares shall be transferred to an account called "the share premium account."' The provisions of the 1985 Act relating to the reduction of a company's share capital apply, with exceptions,as if the share premium account were part of its paid up share capital. **26**

Limited relief from the above ('merger relief') is given by sections 131 to 134 of the 1985 Act. **27**

Section 131 of the 1985 Act provides, *inter alia*, that subject to specified conditions, where an issuing company has secured at least a 90% equity holding in another company, section 130 does not apply to the premiums on shares included in the consideration. The relief is available only in respect of shares issued in the transaction which takes a holding to at least 90%, not of shares already held and which count towards the 90%. **28**

Section 132 of the 1985 Act gives relief from section 130 in respect of group reconstructions. **29**

Section 12 of the Companies Consolidation (Consequential Provisions) Act 1985 gives retrospective relief from section 130 in certain circumstances. **30**

31 Section 133(1) of the 1985 Act provides that the premium on any shares to which the relief in sections 131, 132 and 12 of the Acts referred to above applies, may also be disregarded in determining the amount at which any shares, or other consideration provided for the shares issued, is to be included in the offeror company's balance sheet.

32 Paragraph 75 of Schedule 4* to the 1985 Act contains certain disclosure requirements which apply when a company has entered into arrangements subject to merger relief under section 131(2) of the Act.

33 The standard is based on current UK and Irish law. Both countries are required to enact the provisions of the EC 7th Directive by 1 January 1988 for application to accounting periods beginning on or after 1 January 1990. The standard will be reviewed following enactment of that law. It appears that the major effect of the enactment of the Directive will be that, for merger accounting to be available, the arrangement should not include a cash payment exceeding 10% of the nominal value of the shares issued.† The term 'arrangement' appears to relate to the transaction which takes the holding to at least 90%.

Part 5 – Legal requirements in Northern Ireland

34 Section 56(1) of the Companies Act (Northern Ireland) 1960 is similar to section 130(1) of the Companies Act 1985 as set out in paragraph 26.

35 In Northern Ireland, legislation equivalent to the merger relief in the Companies Act 1985 has been introduced by the Companies (Northern Ireland) Order 1982. Articles 37 to 42 of the Order give relief from section 56(1) of the Companies Act (Northern Ireland) 1960; this relief is similar to that available under the Companies Act 1985.

Part 6 – Legal requirements in the Republic of Ireland

36 Section 62(1) of the Companies Act 1963 is similar to section 130(1) of the Companies Act 1985 as set out in paragraph 26.

37 No legislation equivalent to the merger relief in the Companies Act 1985 currently exists in the Republic of Ireland. Until such time as equivalent legislation is enacted, no explicit relief from section 62(1) is available.

38 However, section 149(5) of the Companies Act 1963 provides that, whilst in general,

***Editor's note:** Now paragraphs 10 and 29 of Schedule 5.*

*†**Editor's note:** The EC Seventh Directive was implemented in Great Britain by the Companies Act 1989. Paragraph 10(1)(c) of Schedule 4A to the Companies Act 1985 (as amended) introduced this condition for merger accounting.*

pre-acquisition profits of acquired subsidiaries may not be treated in the holding company's accounts as revenue profit, an exemption from that provision is available in that 'where the directors and auditors are satisfied and so certify that it would be fair and reasonable and would not prejudice the rights and interests of any person, the profits or losses attributable to any shares in a subsidiary may be treated in a manner otherwise than in accordance with this subsection.'

If the decision in *Shearer v Bercain* were followed in the Republic of Ireland, there is doubt as to the possible impact of the section 149(5) exemption referred to above. Accordingly, legal advice should be sought before implementing merger accounting in the Republic of Ireland. 39

Part 7 – Compliance with International Accounting Standard No. 22 'Accounting for Business Combinations'

The requirements of International Accounting Standard No. 22 'Accounting for business combinations' which relate to accounting for acquisitions and mergers, accord very closely with the content of the United Kingdom and Irish Accounting Standard No. 23 'Accounting for acquisitions and mergers' and accordingly compliance with SSAP 23 will ensure compliance with the requirements of IAS 22 which relate to accounting for acquisitions and mergers in all material respects.* 40

***Editor's note:** *A revised version of IAS 22 was issued in November 1993.*

Appendix

This appendix is for guidance only and does not form part of the statement of standard accounting practice.

ACCOUNTS OF THE HOLDING COMPANY

1 The standard deals only with the method of accounting to be used in group accounts. That is, it does not deal with the form of accounting to be used in the offeror's own accounts and does not restrict the rights available to the offeror under sections 131 to 134, Companies Act 1985. The normal treatment would be that the investment in the new subsidiary would be recorded by the offeror:

(a) in acquisition accounting, at cost, which will be the fair value of the consideration given; and

(b) in merger accounting, at the nominal value of the shares which it issues; where there is additional consideration in some form other than equity shares (or, where appropriate, other than voting non-equity; see paragraph 11(d)), the fair value of such additional consideration should be added to the nominal value of the shares issued.

2 Where the investment in the subsidiary is carried in the offerer's own accounts (rather than as a result of a consolidation adjustment) at the fair value of the consideration given and the fair value of any shares included in the consideration given exceeds their nominal value, the excess should, where relief is available under sections 131 to 134, Companies Act 1985, be credited to a separate merger reserve. Where such relief is not available, the excess should be credited to a share premium account.

3 Paragraph 15(5) of the old Schedule 8 to the Companies Act 1948 was amended in formulating what is now paragraph 19(5) of Schedule 9* to the Companies Act 1985 and does not appear in what is now Schedule 4 to the Companies Act 1985. As a result of these changes, where a dividend is paid to the acquiring or issuing company out of pre-combination profits, it would appear that it need not necessarily be applied as a reduction in the carrying value of the investment in the subsidiary. Such a dividend received should be applied to reduce the carrying value of the investment to the extent that it is necessary to provide for a diminution in value of the investment in the subsidiary as stated in the accounts of the issuing company. To the extent that this is not necessary, it appears that the amount received will be a realised profit in the hands of the issuing company.

4 Where the holding company records the cost of the subsidiary on the basis of the nominal value of shares issued in consideration, no further questions arise than those

****Editor's note:*** *Paragraph 19(5) of Schedule 9 was repealed by the Companies Act 1989.*

mentioned in paragraph 3 above. Where merger relief under the Companies Act 1985 is available, but the holding company records the investment at fair value (see paragraph 2 above), it will in some cases, as noted in paragraph 3, be necessary for the holding company to credit to the investment the dividends paid out of the subsidiary's pre-combination profits. In these circumstances, the question arises as to whether as a result of this treatment an equivalent amount of the merger reserve can legally be regarded as realised. No firm legal ruling on this is yet available.

[SSAP 24]
Accounting for pension costs

(Issued May 1988)

Contents

Accounting for pension costs

The provisions of this statement of standard accounting practice should be read in conjunction with the (Explanatory) Foreword to accounting standards *and need not be applied to immaterial items.*

Part 1 – Explanatory note

IMPORTANCE OF PENSION COSTS

The provision of a pension is part of the remuneration package of many employees. Pension costs form a significant proportion of total payroll costs and they give rise to special problems of estimation and of allocation between accounting periods. Accordingly, it is important that standard accounting practice exists concerning the recognition of such costs in the employers' financial statements. This statement deals with the accounting for, and the disclosure of, pension costs and commitments in the financial statements of enterprises that have pension arrangements for the provision of retirement benefits for their employees. 1

TYPES OF PENSION SCHEMES

Pension arrangements can take different forms. The employer may have a commitment arising from the contract of employment, the provision of pensions may have arisen from custom and practice or *ex gratia* arrangements may be made on a case by case basis. This Statement covers a scheme where an enterprise has entered into a commitment, whether legal, contractual, or implicit in the employer's actions, to provide pensions for its employees. It also addresses situations where *ex gratia* or discretionary payments are made in the absence of such a commitment. 2

Pension schemes to which this Statement applies may basically be divided into defined contribution schemes and defined benefit schemes. In a defined contribution scheme, the employer will normally discharge his obligation by making agreed contributions to a pension scheme and the benefits paid will depend upon the funds available from these contributions and investment earnings thereon. The cost to the employer can, therefore, be measured with reasonable certainty. A number of pension schemes in the United Kingdom and Ireland, including many smaller ones, are defined contributions schemes. 3

In a defined benefit scheme, however, the benefits to be paid will usually depend upon either the average pay of the employee during his or her career or, more typically, the final pay of the employee. In these circumstances, it is impossible to be certain in advance that the contributions to the pension scheme, together with the investment return thereon, will equal the benefits to be paid. The employer may have a legal 4 obligation to provide any unforeseen shortfall in funds or, if not, may find it necessary to meet the shortfall in the interests of maintaining good employee relations. Conversely, if a surplus arises the employer may be entitled to a refund of, or reduction in, contributions paid into the pension scheme. Thus, in this type of scheme the employer's commitment is generally more open than with defined contribution schemes and the final cost is subject to considerable uncertainty. The larger UK and Irish schemes are generally of the defined benefit kind and these cover the great majority of members of schemes.

5 Pension schemes may also be classified by the way in which they are financed, namely funded schemes or schemes where the benefits are paid directly by the employer. The same accounting principles apply to both types of scheme.

6 The trustees of a funded scheme may make use of the services of an insurance company – an approach that is particularly common amongst the smaller schemes. Insurance companies offer a wide variety of contracts, but, in the case of defined benefit schemes, these contracts are normally no more than investment management and administrative arrangements, possibly with life cover included, and do not relieve the employer of the responsibility to ensure that the scheme is adequately financed.

ACTUARIAL CONSIDERATIONS

7 In view of the very long-term nature of the pensions commitment, it is necessary to make use of actuarial calculations in determining the pension cost charge in respect of defined benefit schemes. In the case of defined contribution schemes there is no need for actuarial advice in order to establish the pension cost although such advice may be required for other purposes in connection with the operation of the scheme.

8 In defined benefit schemes, the choice of assumptions and the choice of valuation method can each have a major effect on the contribution rate calculated at each valuation. The choice of assumptions can be as significant as the choice of method.

9 The assumptions which the actuary must make in carrying out his valuation will be about matters such as future rates of inflation and pay increases, increases to pensions in payment, earnings on investments, the number of employees joining the scheme, the age profile of employees and the probability that employees will die or leave the company's employment before they reach retiring age. The actuary will view the assumptions as a whole; he will make assumptions which are mutually compatible, in the knowledge that , if experience departs from the assumptions made, the effects of such departures may well be offsetting, notably in the case of investment yields and increases in prices and earnings.

10 Most pension schemes undergo a formal actuarial valuation on a triennial basis. In such cases it is not intended that any special valuation exercise should be carried out by enterprises for the purpose of implementing this Statement for the first time.

11 The Councils of the Institute and Faculty of Actuaries published a paper in May 1986 entitled 'Pension Fund Terminology: specimen descriptions of commonly used valuation methods.' In addition, the Auditing Practices Committee has published an Audit Brief entitled 'The work of a pension scheme actuary.' This covers matters such as the valuation of defined benefit and defined contribution schemes, valuation assumptions and inter-professional co-operation. A glossary of pensions terminology for pension schemes has been published by The Pensions Management Institute and The Pensions Research Accountants Group.

THE FUNDING PLAN

The funding methods developed by actuaries are designed to build up assets in a **12**
prudent and controlled manner in advance of the retirement of the members of the scheme, in order that the obligations of the scheme may be met without undue distortion of the employer's cash flow. The actuary's main concern is that the present and estimated future contribution levels should be at least sufficient to provide security for the payment of the promised benefits.

A range of actuarial methods is available for determining the level of contributions **13**
needed to meet the liabilities of the pension scheme. Some methods will tend to lead to higher levels of funding in the scheme than others.

In practice, it is common for actuaries to aim at a level contribution rate, as a **14**
proportion of pensionable pay in respect of current service. The contribution rate thus determined depends on the particular actuarial method used and the assumptions made regarding new entrants to the scheme. In broad terms, in projecting a stable contribution rate, accrued benefits methods rely on the assumption that the flow of new entrants will be such as to preserve the existing average age of the work-force; prospective benefits methods, on the other hand, normally look only to the existing work-force and seek a contribution rate that will remain stable for that group despite its increasing age profile until the last member retires or leaves. In a mature scheme both types of method may in practice achieve stable contribution rates but the size of the fund under a prospective benefits method will tend to be larger than under an accrued benefits method because it is intended to cover the ageing of the existing work-force.

From time to time it may be necessary to improve the level of funding because of **15**
deficiencies (where these are not expected to be offset by future surpluses). This may be done by an increase in the ordinary annual rate of contribution or by additional special payments over a limited period. On occasion the employer may make additional lump sum contributions which have the effect of reducing his future liabilities, if to do so is convenient in the context of the financial policy of the employer's business. Conversely, a previously high level of funding may be lowered by reducing or interrupting the contributions if there is a surplus in the fund or in times of financial stringency for the company. However, whilst the financial position of the sponsoring employer may influence the pattern of funding it will not provide a satisfactory basis for determining the pension charge for the period.

THE ACCOUNTING OBJECTIVE

16 From the point of view of the employee a pension may be regarded as deferred remuneration; from the point of view of the employer it is part of the cost incurred in obtaining the employee's services. The accounting objective therefore requires the employer to recognise the cost of providing pensions on a systematic and rational basis over the period during which he benefits from the employees' services. Many companies have, until now, simply charged the contributions payable to the pension scheme as the pension cost in each accounting period. In future, in order to comply with this Statement, it will be necessary to consider whether the funding plan provides a satisfactory basis for allocating the pension cost to particular accounting periods.

DEFINED CONTRIBUTION SCHEMES

17 In the case of a defined contribution scheme the employer's obligation at any point in time is restricted to the amount of the contributions payable to date. The pension cost is, therefore, the amount of the contributions payable in respect of the particular accounting period.

DEFINED BENEFIT SCHEMES

18 The selection of the actuarial method and assumptions to be used in assessing the pension cost of a defined benefit scheme is a matter of judgement for the actuary in consultation with his client, taking account of the circumstances of the specific company and its work-force. This Statement requires that the actuarial valuation method and assumptions used for accounting purposes should satisfy the accounting objective. In order that full provision may be made over the employees' service lives for the expected costs of their pensions, the effect of expected future increases in earnings, including merit increases, up to the assumed retirement date or earlier date of withdrawal or death in service, should be recognised. Account will also need to be taken of expected future increases in deferred pensions and pensions in payment where the employer has an express or implied commitment to grant such increases. The calculation of benefit levels should be based on the situation most likely to be experienced and not on a contingent event not likely to occur. The actuarial method selected should be used consistently and should be disclosed. If there is a change of method this fact should be disclosed and the effect quantified. The actuarial assumptions and the actuarial method taken as a whole should be compatible and should lead to the actuary's best estimate of the cost of providing the pension benefits promised.

19 If the funding plan does not provide a satisfactory basis for determining the pension cost charge, separate actuarial calculations will be required.

REGULAR PENSION COST AND VARIATIONS IN COST

20 The total cost of pensions in a year can notionally be divided into the regular cost, which is the consistent ongoing cost recognised under the actuarial method used, and

variations from the regular cost. Where a stable contribution rate for regular contributions, expressed as a percentage of pensionable earnings, has been determined, that rate will provide an acceptable basis for calculating the regular cost under the stated accounting objective so long as it makes full provision for the expected benefits over the anticipated service lives of employees.

Variations from the regular cost may arise from: **21**

(a) experience surpluses or deficiencies;
(b) the effects on the actuarial value of accrued benefits of changes in assumptions or method;
(c) retroactive changes in benefits or in conditions for membership;
(d) increases to pensions in payment or to deferred pensions for which provision has not previously been made.

SPREADING VARIATIONS FROM REGULAR COST

Experience deficiencies or surpluses are part of the ongoing process of revising the estimate of the ultimate liabilities which will fall on the employer. Any effect on the cost should normally be taken into account by adjusting the current and future costs charged in the accounts and should not be treated as a prior year adjustment. **22**

In accordance with the accounting objective, the normal period over which the effect of material deficiencies or surpluses should be spread for accounting purposes is the expected remaining service lives of the current employees in the scheme after making suitable allowances for future withdrawals. A period representing the average remaining service lives of the current membership may be used if desired. This period, which will vary from scheme to scheme and from time to time, should be determined by the actuary. It would not be appropriate to credit or charge the entire surplus or deficiency against profits in one accounting period, except as provided in paragraphs 81 to 83. **23**

The only circumstances in which there may be a departure from the normal principle of spreading material surpluses or deficiencies as set out in paragraph 23 are summarised in this paragraph and in paragraph 29 below. The full conditions which must be satisfied before there may be a departure from the normal spreading requirements are set out in paragraphs 81 to 83. The circumstances referred to below represent situations that properly lie outside the actuarial assumptions and normal running of the scheme and, accordingly, are expected to arise infrequently. They are: **24**

(a) where there is a significant reduction in the number of employees covered by the company's and/or group's pension scheme arrangements;
(b) where, in the circumstances set out in paragraph 82, prudence requires a material deficiency to be recognised over a shorter period.

In many companies, there have been reorganisation programmes in recent years that have involved significant redundancies. These have often led to large non-reversing surpluses building up in related pension schemes. This Statement recognises that in such instances it would not be appropriate to spread the effect of the refund of such surpluses over the remaining service lives of the current employees in the scheme. **25**

26 In the circumstances set out in paragraph 24(a) a refund of a surplus, contributions holiday or reduction in contributions should be accounted for as it becomes receivable and should not be anticipated, that is, if it is agreed that contributions will be reduced for a period of years the reduction should be recognised on a year by year basis and not accumulated and reflected in the financial statements in the period the first reduction becomes effective. Where a reduction in the number of employees is related to an event such as the sale or termination of an operation, it is accepted that it may not be possible to apply the rule set out in this paragraph. This is because FRS 3 'Reporting Financial Performance' requires provisions consequent on the sale or termination of an operation to be made after taking account of future profits of the operation or the disposal of its assets. It may therefore not be appropriate to defer recognition of an associated pension cost or credit.

27 The exemption from the normal spreading principle relating to significant reductions in the total number of employees covered by a group's or company's pension arrangements does not cover situations where employees are transferred from one group scheme to another one.

28 As stated in paragraph 24(b), in strictly limited circumstances prudence may require that a material deficiency should be recognised over a period shorter than the expected remaining service lives of current employees in the scheme. A precondition of invoking this section is that significant additional contributions have had to be paid into the pension scheme. Furthermore, the additional payments should have been made as stated in paragraph 24 in respect of a major transaction or event outside the actuarial assumptions and normal running of the scheme. A possible example of such a situation would be where there had been a major mismanagement of a pension scheme's assets. However, it is emphasised that each situation must be judged on its particular merits.

29 Where a refund that is subject to deduction of tax in accordance with the provisions of the UK Finance Act 1986, or equivalent legislation, is made to the employer, the enterprise may depart from the normal spreading principle and instead recognise the refund in the period in which it occurs. The accounting treatment adopted in respect of such refunds should be disclosed.

CHANGES IN ASSUMPTIONS, VALUATION METHOD AND BENEFITS

30 The effect of changes in the assumptions or valuation method on the cost of providing for past service is analogous to an experience deficiency or surplus and should be accounted for in a similar way.

31 Retroactive changes in benefits and membership are decided upon currently and it is thus not appropriate to charge any part of the costs arising from these decisions as a prior year adjustment. Past service costs should normally be written off over the remaining service lives of the current employees.

32 Where a surplus in a pension fund is utilised to provide benefits for which the company had previously established a provision in its financial statements, the provision, to the

extent that it is no longer required, should be released over the estimated remaining service lives of the current employees.

INCREASES TO PENSIONS IN PAYMENT AND DEFERRED PENSIONS

Increases to pensions in payment up to a certain level may be specified in the rules of the pension scheme. Other increases may be granted in response to pensioners' needs and in the interests of continuing good industrial relations. In the United Kingdom, increases to deferred pensions, that is the prospective pensions of early leavers, are required by law to be made up to a specific level. **33**

Increases specified in the pension scheme rules or required by law will be taken into account in the actuarial assumptions. The cost will, therefore, be charged over the service lives of the employees. Any divergence between the assumptions and experience will be accounted for as an element of any overall experience deficiency or surplus. **34**

Other increases are, at least in form, discretionary at the time they are awarded; whether they are paid through the scheme or directly by the employer. Discretionary increases may be granted on the basis that the rules require there to be an annual review or because the employer has announced an intention to grant increases but no previous commitment has been made. The preferred treatment is for such increases, where they are likely to be granted on a regular basis, to be allowed for in the actuarial assumptions. They will then be recognised as part of the pension cost over the working lives of the beneficiaries. **35**

Once an increase has been awarded it is very unlikely that it will be withdrawn and so it should be regarded thereafter as part of the employer's commitments. Accordingly, this Statement provides that, if provision has not been made for the increase in the actuarial assumptions, the capitalised amount of the increase should be provided for in the period in which it is granted to the extent that it is not covered by a surplus. **36**

Where a non-recurring ('one-off') increase is granted which applies to the current period but will not affect pensions paid in future periods, it should be treated as purely *ex gratia* and its cost should be charged in the period in which it is granted to the extent that it is not covered by a surplus. **37**

Employers may occasionally grant *ex gratia* pensions to employees at the time of their retirement. An example would be a pension granted to a long-serving employee who for some reason had not been a member of the company's scheme and for whom the company decided to make provision. As with discretionary pension increases, the capital cost of any such *ex gratia* pensions should be charged in the period in which they are granted to the extent that they are not covered by a surplus. **38**

HYBRID SCHEMES

A few schemes are hybrid in nature combining features of defined contribution and defined benefit schemes. In such instances the rules or trust deed should be carefully **39** studied and the operation of the scheme in practice, or its proposed method of operation, taken into account when determining the appropriate accounting treatment. The accounting treatment adopted should be in accordance with the underlying substance of the scheme.

DISCOUNTING

40 By their nature actuarial valuations make allowance for interest so that future cash flows are discounted to their present value. Financial statements, however, normally include items at their face value without discounting them. The question of whether items should be discounted in financial statements is a general one and this Statement does not attempt to establish standard practice. Interest effects arising from short-term timing differences between the payment of contributions and the recognition of cost are not likely to be material and can be ignored. If the difference is long-term, the situation becomes akin to that arising in respect of an unfunded scheme. If a scheme is unfunded the provision for pension costs is assessed and reviewed on a discounted basis and adjusted each year by an amount comprising two elements: a charge for the year (equivalent to a contribution in a funded scheme) and interest on the unfunded liability.

FOREIGN SCHEMES

41 In principle, the pension costs charged in respect of all pension schemes included in group accounts should conform to the accounting objective and a consolidation adjustment should be made where the cost charged in the individual accounts of a group company does not do so.

42 No adjustment would normally be necessary in respect of UK and Irish schemes as the pension cost in the individual company accounts should already conform to the requirements of this Statement. On the other hand, in the case of foreign schemes, the commitment of the employer regarding the provision of pensions may be very different from that which is customary in the United Kingdom and Ireland so that it would be inappropriate to adjust the pension cost charged. In some cases, for example, the employer's obligation may be discharged by prescribed payments under a nationwide or industry-wide scheme with characteristics similar to those of the State scheme in the United Kingdom. In such cases charging the contributions payable will satisfy the requirements of this Statement.

43 In other instances the nature of the employer's commitment may be similar to that in the UK and Ireland and the different determination of the pension cost charge may be caused solely by different accounting policies. An adjustment to the charge would then be appropriate although it is recognised that it may sometimes be impractical to make such an adjustment because of the difficulties and cost of obtaining compatible actuarial valuations in order to be able to recalculate the pension charge in accordance with the full provisions of this Statement. In such circumstances while an adjustment to the charge is not mandatory it is encouraged and suitable disclosure should be made.

DEFERRED TAXATION

For many enterprises the pension cost charge for the period has in the past been equal to the contributions payable. Under the requirements of this Statement the charge in the financial statements could be different from the contributions payable if, for example, a deficiency on valuation is being spread forward in the financial statements over the estimated remaining service lives of current employees although an additional lump-sum payment has been paid into the pension fund. Since taxation relief is generally granted in respect of payments made to the pension fund, accounting for pension costs in the manner prescribed by this Statement may have deferred tax implications. Where these occur they should be accounted for in accordance with SSAP 15 (Revised) 'Accounting for Deferred Tax.' **44**

DISCLOSURES

Sufficient information should be disclosed to give the user of the financial statements a proper understanding of the impact of the pension arrangements on the group's and/or the company's financial statements. **45**

For a defined contribution scheme it will usually suffice to indicate the nature of the scheme and the amounts included in the profit and loss account and balance sheet. **46**

For a defined benefit scheme more extensive disclosures are needed because of the greater and more uncertain obligations of the employer. Disclosures required include the accounting policy, the actuarial valuation method and major actuarial assumptions adopted, the cost charged, with explanations of it, and certain actuarial valuation information. In view of the significant long-term variable commitment of the employer, the disclosures should not only relate to the amounts in the financial statements for the periods presented but should also give an indication of significant changes in future costs that are expected under the actuarial assumptions and method used. Examples of how a small company and a large group may satisfy the disclosure requirements are given in Appendix 1. **47**

As explained in paragraph 14, the effect of aiming for a level contribution rate varies according to the actuarial method used and the assumption made regarding new entrants. It is therefore necessary to disclose what assumption has been made in this regard unless it is immediately apparent from the disclosure of the actuarial method used. **48**

This statement requires the disclosure of an outline of the results of the most recent formal actuarial valuation or later review of the pension scheme on an ongoing basis. Specific disclosures to be made include the market value of scheme assets at the date of their valuation or review and the level of funding expressed in percentage terms. In certain instances it may be necessary to provide further information in order that details on the level of funding may be seen in their proper context. The level of funding and/or market values of scheme assets at the date of valuation or review may, for example, have subsequently changed markedly as a result of changes in general stock **49** market values or in the level of contributions paid into the pension scheme. In particular, it should be considered whether the figures disclosed relating to the last valuation or review need to be amplified by a discussion of changes that have occurred since that date.

50 Disclosure is also required of changes in the group and/or company's pension scheme arrangements where these have had, or will have, a material effect on the future cost of providing pensions.

51 Where a company or group has more than one scheme it will often be necessary to give information on a combined basis in order to keep the volume of disclosures within reasonable limits. However, it is important that the combined figures should provide a proper understanding of the impact of the pension arrangements on the group's and/or company's financial position.

GROUP SCHEMES

52 It is quite common for a number of companies within the same group to contribute to a single group scheme. With such schemes it is normally accepted that the same contribution rate, expressed as a percentage of payroll, should apply to the different member companies even though, if calculated on an individual company basis, the rate payable may vary between the employers within a group. This Statement permits the use of a common group rate for contributions payable by sponsoring employers. If a group scheme is in operation it may not be possible to estimate the pension obligations for which a particular group company is responsible and it would not be meaningful to provide information relating to the group as a whole in the subsidiary's financial statements. Provision is therefore made for reduced disclosure in the financial statements of subsidiary companies that are members of group schemes. The full details relating to the pension scheme should be disclosed in the financial statements of the holding company.

TRANSITIONAL PROVISIONS

53 When, on implementing this Statement for the first time, a cumulative adjustment arises in respect of prior years, this may either be dealt with in accordance with the other provisions of this Statement or accounted for in accordance with the provisions of FRS 3 'Reporting Financial Performance'. That is, the cumulative adjustment may, except as discussed below, be spread over the expected remaining service lives of current employees in the scheme or accounted for as a prior year adjustment. To the extent that the adjustment relates to a variation from regular cost that, in accordance with the provisions of paragraphs 81 and 82, would not be eligible to be spread over the remaining service lives it should be accounted for as a prior year item. (An example of such an adjustment would be one arising from a significant reduction in the number of employees covered by a company's pension scheme arrangements.) Similar considerations may also arise in respect of paragraphs 84 and 85 which deal with discretionary and *ex gratia* pension increases and *ex gratia* pensions. The cumulative adjustment should be calculated, as at the beginning of the accounting period in which this

Statement is first applied, as the actuarial value of the surplus or deficiency on an ongoing basis as adjusted by any existing provision for unfunded pension costs or any existing pensions prepayment. In order that enterprises do not have to undertake a special valuation exercise for the purposes of implementing this Statement, they may base the calculation of the cumulative adjustment on the results of the last actuarial valuation so long as it was carried out on a basis broadly consistent with the requirements of this Statement. In arriving at the adjustment any surplus or deficiency at the last valuation date should be adjusted to take account of any additional payments or reduced contributions made since that date as a consequence of it. It may also be necessary to make allowance for major changes affecting the pension scheme since the last valuation.

THE REPUBLIC OF IRELAND

The Republic of Ireland, unlike the United Kingdom, currently does not have any **54** legislative requirement for defined benefit pension schemes to be actuarially assessed and the actuarial profession's involvement with pension schemes has tended to be less than in the United Kingdom. Legislation is to be introduced based on the recommendations contained in the First Report of the National Pensions Board but the first actuarial valuation for a number of schemes will not take place until the beginning of the next decade. Accordingly, the provisions of paragraphs 77, 79 to 85 and 88(g) and 88(h) will not be mandatory for non-quoted companies registered in the Republic of Ireland in respect of the financial statements of periods commencing before 1 January 1993. Such companies are, however, encouraged to comply with the full requirements of this Statement as soon as possible.

The full requirements of this Statement will apply to companies registered in the **55** Republic of Ireland and quoted on the International Stock Exchange of the United Kingdom and the Republic of Ireland Limited from the same date as it applies to companies registered in the United Kingdom.

Part 2 – Definitions

Accrued benefits are the benefits for service up to a given point in time, whether the **56** rights to the benefits are vested or not. They may be calculated in relation to current earnings or projected final earnings.

An *accrued benefits method* of actuarial valuation is a valuation method in which the **57** actuarial value of liabilities relate at a given date to:

(a) the benefits, including future increases promised by the rules, for the current and deferred pensioners and their dependants; and
(b) the benefits which the members assumed to be in service on the given date will receive for service up to that date only.

Allowance may be made for expected increases in earnings after the given date, and/or for additional pension increases not promised by the rules. The given date may be a current or future date. The further into the future the adopted date lies, the closer the results will be to those of a prospective benefits valuation method.

58 The *average remaining service life* is a weighted average of the expected future service of the current members of the scheme up to their normal retirement dates or expected dates of earlier withdrawal or death in service. The weightings can have regard to periods of service, salary levels of scheme members and future anticipated salary growth in a manner which the actuary considers appropriate having regard to the actuarial method and assumptions used.

59 A *current funding level valuation* considers whether the assets would have been sufficient at the valuation date to cover liabilities arising in respect of pensions in payment, preserved benefits for members whose pensionable service has ceased and accrued benefits for members in pensionable service, based on pensionable service to and pensionable earnings at, the date of valuation including revaluation on the statutory basis or such higher basis as has been promised.

60 An *ex gratia pension* or *discretionary* or *ex gratia increase* in a pension is one which the employer has no legal, contractual or implied commitment to provide.

61 A *defined benefit scheme* is a pension scheme in which the rules specify the benefits to be paid and the scheme is financed accordingly.

62 A *defined contribution scheme* is a pension scheme in which the benefits are directly determined by the value of contributions paid in respect of each member. Normally the rate of contribution is specified in the rules of the scheme.

63 An *experience surplus or deficiency* is that part of the excess or deficiency of the actuarial value of assets over the actuarial value of liabilities, on the basis of the valuation method used, which arises because events have not coincided with the actuarial assumptions made for the last valuation.

64 A *funding plan* is the timing of payments in an orderly fashion to meet the future cost of a given set of benefits.

65 A *funded scheme* is a pension scheme where the future liabilities for benefits are provided for by the accumulation of assets held externally to the employing company's business.

66 The *level of funding* is the proportion at a given date of the actuarial value of liabilities for pensioners' and deferred pensioners' benefits and for members' accrued benefits that is covered by the actuarial value of assets. For this purpose the actuarial value of future contributions is excluded from the value of assets.

67 An *ongoing actuarial valuation* is a valuation in which it is assumed that the pension scheme will continue in existence and (where appropriate) that new members will be admitted. The liabilities allow for expected increases in earnings.

Past service is used in this Statement to denote service before a given date. It is often used, however, to denote service before entry into the pension scheme. **68**

Pensionable payroll/earnings are the earnings on which benefits and/or contributions are calculated. One or more elements of earnings (e.g., overtime) may be excluded, and/or there may be a reduction to take account of all or part of the state scheme benefits which the member is deemed to receive. **69**

A *pension scheme* is an arrangement (other than accident insurance) to provide pension and/or other benefits for members on leaving service or retiring and, after a member's death, for his/her dependants. **70**

A *prospective benefits method* of valuation is a valuation method in which the actuarial value of liabilities relates to: **71**

(a) the benefits for current and deferred pensioners and their dependants, allowing where appropriate for future pension increases; and
(b) the benefits that active members will receive in respect of both past and future service, allowing for future increases in earnings up to their assumed exit dates, and where appropriate for pension increases thereafter.

Regular cost is the consistent ongoing cost recognised under the actuarial method used. **72**

Part 3 – Standard accounting practice

SCOPE

This Statement applies where the employer has a legal or contractual commitment under a pension scheme or one implicit in the employer's actions, to provide, or contribute to, pensions for his employees. It also addresses discretionary and *ex gratia* increases in pensions and *ex gratia* pensions. The same principles apply irrespective of whether the scheme is funded or unfunded. **73**

This Statement applies to defined contribution schemes and defined benefit schemes. **74**

Although this Statement primarily addresses pensions, its principles may be equally applicable to the cost of providing other post-retirement benefits.* **75**

This Statement does not apply to either state social security contributions or redundancy payments. **76**

PENSION COST

The accounting objective is that the employer should recognise the expected cost of providing pensions on a systematic and rational basis over the period during which he **77**

***Editor's note:** *See UITF Abstract 6 'Accounting for post-retirement benefits other than pensions'.*

derives benefit from the employees' services. The ways in which this is to be achieved are detailed in paragraphs 78 to 92.

DEFINED CONTRIBUTION SCHEMES

78 For defined contribution schemes the charge against profits should be the amount of contributions payable to the pension scheme in respect of the accounting period.

DEFINED BENEFIT SCHEMES

79 For defined benefit schemes the pension cost should be calculated using actuarial valuation methods which are consistent with the requirements of this Statement. The actuarial assumptions and method, taken as a whole, should be compatible and should lead to the actuary's best estimate of the cost of providing the pension benefits promised. The method of providing for expected pension costs over the service lives of employees in the scheme should be such that the regular pension cost is a substantially level percentage of the current and expected future pensionable payroll in the light of the current actuarial assumptions.

80 Subject to the provisions of paragraphs 81 to 83, variations from the regular cost should be allocated over the expected remaining service lives of current employees in the scheme. A period representing the average remaining service lives may be used if desired.

81 The provisions of paragraph 80 should not be applied where, and to the extent that, a significant change in the normal level of contributions occurs because contributions are adjusted to eliminate a surplus or deficiency resulting from a significant reduction in the number of employees covered by the enterprise's pension arrangements. Where the significant reduction in the number of employees is related to the sale or termination of an operation, the associated pension cost or credit should be recognised immediately to the extent necessary to comply with the requirement of paragraph 18 of FRS 3 'Reporting Financial Performance'. In all other cases where there is a reduction in contributions arising from a significant reduction in employees the reduction of contributions should be recognised as it occurs. Amounts receivable may not be anticipated; for example, the full effect of a contribution holiday should not be recognised at the outset of the holiday, but rather spread over its duration.

82 In strictly limited circumstances prudence may require that a material deficit be recognised over a period shorter than the expected remaining service lives of current employees in the scheme. Such circumstances are limited to those where a major event or transaction has occurred which has not been allowed for in the actuarial assumptions, is outside the normal scope of those assumptions and has necessitated the payment of significant additional contributions to the pension scheme.

83 Where a refund that is subject to deduction of tax in accordance with the provisions of the UK Finance Act 1986, or equivalent legislation, is made to the employer, the enterprise may depart from the requirements of paragraph 80 and account for the surplus or deficiency in the period in which the refund occurs.

EX GRATIA PENSIONS AND DISCRETIONARY AND *EX GRATIA* PENSION INCREASES

Where *ex gratia* pensions are granted the capital cost, to the extent not covered by a surplus, should be recognised in the profit and loss account in the accounting period in which they are granted. **84**

Where allowance for discretionary or *ex gratia* increases in pensions is not made in the actuarial assumptions, the capital cost of such increases should, to the extent not covered by a surplus, be recognised in the profit and loss account in the accounting period in which they are initially granted. **85**

BALANCE SHEET

If the cumulative pension cost recognised in the profit and loss account has not been completely discharged by payment of contributions or directly paid pensions, the excess should be shown as a net pension provision. Similarly, any excess of contributions paid or directly paid pensions over the cumulative pension cost should be shown as a prepayment. **86**

DISCLOSURES

The following disclosures should be made in respect of a defined contribution scheme: **87**

(a) the nature of the scheme (i.e., defined contribution);
(b) the accounting policy;
(c) the pension cost charge for the period;
(d) any outstanding or prepaid contributions at the balance sheet date.

The following disclosures should be made in respect of a defined benefit scheme: **88**

(a) the nature of the scheme (i.e., defined benefit);
(b) whether it is funded or unfunded;
(c) the accounting policy and, if different, the funding policy;
(d) whether the pension cost and provision (or asset) are assessed in accordance with the advice of a professionally qualified actuary and, if so, the date of the most recent formal actuarial valuation or later formal review used for this purpose. If the actuary is an employee or officer of the reporting company, or of the group of which it is a member, this fact should be disclosed;
(e) the pension cost charge for the period together with explanations of significant changes in the charge compared to that in the previous accounting period;
(f) any provisions or prepayments in the balance sheet resulting from a difference between the amounts recognised as cost and the amounts funded or paid directly;
(g) the amount of any deficiency on a current funding level basis, indicating the action, if any, being taken to deal with it in the current and future accounting periods;
(h) an outline of the results of the most recent formal actuarial valuation or later formal review of the scheme on an ongoing basis. This should include disclosure of:

(i) the actuarial method used and a brief description of the main actuarial assumptions;
(ii) the market value of scheme assets at the date of their valuation or review;
(iii) the level of funding expressed in percentage terms;
(iv) comments on any material actuarial surplus or deficiency indicated by (iii) above;

(i) any commitment to make additional payments over a limited number of years;
(j) the accounting treatment adopted in respect of a refund made in accordance with the provisions of paragraph 83 where a credit appears in the financial statements in relation to it;
(k) details of the expected effects on future costs of any material changes in the group's and/or company's pension arrangements.

89 Where a company or group has more than one pension scheme disclosure should be made on a combined basis, unless disclosure of information about individual schemes is necessary for a proper understanding of the accounts. For the purposes of paragraph 88(g) above, however, a current funding level basis deficiency in one scheme should not be set off against a surplus in another.

GROUP SCHEMES

90 A subsidiary company which is a member of a group scheme should disclose this fact in its financial statements and disclose the nature of the group scheme indicating, where appropriate, that the contributions are based on pension costs across the group as a whole. Such a company is exempt from the disclosure requirements of paragraph 88(g) and (h) and should instead state the name of the holding company in whose financial statements particulars of the actuarial valuation of the group scheme are contained. This exemption only applies if the holding company is registered in the United Kingdom or the Republic of Ireland.

FOREIGN SCHEMES

91 Where, in respect of foreign operations, the employer has an obligation to provide pensions, the pension charge should reflect that obligation and, therefore, be dealt with in accordance with the requirements of this Statement. An adjustment on consolidation will be necessary where the charge is not already calculated in accordance with the basis set out in this Statement, unless the nature of the employer's commitment is very different from that which is customary in the United Kingdom and Ireland. It is recognised, however, that in some cases it may be impractical to make the adjustment because of the difficulties and cost of obtaining the necessary actuarial information. In such cases, the amount charged to the profit and loss account and the basis of the charge should, as a minimum, be disclosed in the consolidated financial statements.

TRANSITIONAL PROVISIONS

92 When, on implementing this Statement for the first time, a cumulative adjustment arises in respect of prior years this may either be dealt with in accordance with the other provisions of this Statement or accounted for in accordance with the provisions of FRS 3 'Reporting Financial Performance'. The way in which the transitional provisions have been applied should be disclosed in the financial statements for the period in which this Statement is first implemented.

DATE FROM WHICH EFFECTIVE

The accounting and disclosure requirements set out in this Statement should be adopted as soon as possible and, except in the case of certain companies registered in the Republic of Ireland as provided in paragraph 94, regarded as standard in respect of financial statements relating to accounting periods beginning on or after 1 July 1988. **93**

In the case of companies that are registered in the Republic of Ireland and not quoted on the International Stock Exchange of the United Kingdom and Ireland paragraphs 77, 79 to 85 and 88(g) and 88(h) should be adopted as soon as possible and regarded as standard in respect of financial statements relating to accounting periods beginning on or after 1 January 1993. The remainder of the required accounting practices and disclosures should be regarded as standard in respect of financial statements relating to accounting periods beginning on or after 1 July 1988. A cumulative adjustment that arises in respect of paragraph 84 on *ex gratia* pensions may either be dealt with in accordance with FRS 3 'Reporting Financial Performance' or allocated over the expected remaining service lives of current employees in the scheme. **94**

Part 4 – Legal requirements in Great Britain and Northern Ireland

References are to the Companies Act 1985 and the Companies (Northern Ireland) Order 1986.

Paragraph 50(4) of Schedule 4 requires a company to give details of any pension commitments provided for in the company's balance sheet and also of any such commitments for which no provision has been made. Particulars of pension commitments to past directors of the company must be disclosed separately. **95**

Paragraph 50(6)* of Schedule 4 requires that disclosure under paragraph 50(4) should separately include details of commitments undertaken on behalf of, or for the benefit of, any holding company or fellow subsidiary of the company and any subsidiary of the company. **96**

Paragraph 56(4) of Schedule 4 requires companies to disclose the total pension costs incurred in the year on behalf of all employees of the company, together with separate disclosure of social security costs incurred on their behalf. **97**

By virtue of paragraphs 61 and 68 of Schedule 4†, the above requirements also apply to group accounts. **98**

****Editor's note:*** *Now covered by paragraph 59 of Schedule 4.*

*†**Editor's note:** Now paragraph 1 of Schedule 4A.*

99 Banking, insurance and shipping companies are exempt from the above requirements of Schedule 4.*

100 Paragraph 28 of Schedule 5† requires companies to disclose the total amount of pension paid to directors or past directors, other than pensions funded substantially through a pension scheme. If they are so funded, the amount disclosed as emoluments has to include contributions to the scheme (paragraph 22).‡

Part 5 – Legal requirements in the Republic of Ireland

101 In this part references to companies legislation have been abbreviated as follows:

Companies Act 1963 – The 1963 Act

The Schedule to the Companies (Amendment) Act 1963 – The Schedule

102 Section 191 of the 1963 Act requires disclosure of the aggregate amount of directors' and past-directors' pensions, other than pensions under a scheme where contributions are substantially adequate for the maintenance of the scheme. The Section also requires disclosure of the aggregate amount of directors' emoluments; for the purpose of the section emoluments include contributions paid in respect of directors to any pension scheme.

103 Paragraph 36(4) of the Schedule requires disclosure of any pension commitments included in the company's balance sheet and any such commitments for which no provision has been made. Where any such commitment relates wholly or partly to pensions payable to past directors of the company, separate particulars shall be given of that commitment so far as it relates to such pensions.

104 Information required to be disclosed under paragraph 36(5) of the Schedule is as follows:

(a) the nature of every pension scheme operated by or on behalf of the company including information as to whether or not each scheme is a defined benefit scheme or a defined contribution scheme;

(b) whether each such scheme is externally funded or internally financed;

(c) whether any pension costs and liabilities are assessed in accordance with the advice of a professionally qualified actuary and, if so, the date of the most recent relevant actuarial valuation;

(d) whether, and if so where, any such actuarial valuation is available for public inspection.

***Editor's note:** *Similar requirements to those in Schedule 4 are now included in Schedule 9 for banking companies and Schedule 9A (effective 1995) for insurance companies.*

†**Editor's note:** *Now paragraph 7 of Schedule 6.*

‡**Editor's note:** *Now covered by paragraph 1(4)(c) of Schedule 6.*

Part 6 – Compliance with International Accounting Standard No. 19 'Accounting for Retirement Benefits in the Financial Statements of Employers'

Compliance with the requirements of this Statement will automatically ensure compliance with International Accounting Standard No. 19 'Accounting for Retirement Benefits in the Financial Statements of Employers.'* **105**

***Editor's note:** *A revised version of IAS 19 was issued in November 1993.*

Appendix

This appendix is for general guidance and does not form part of the statement of standard accounting practice.

EXAMPLES OF DISCLOSURES

(a) *Defined contribution scheme*
The company operates a defined contribution pension scheme. The assets of the scheme are held separately from those of the company in an independently administered fund. The pension cost charge represents contributions payable by the company to the fund and amounted to £500,000 (1986 £450,000). Contributions totalling £25,000 (1986 £15,000) were payable to the fund at the year-end and are included in creditors.

(b) *Defined benefit scheme*

(i) *Small company*
The company operates a pension scheme providing benefits based on final pensionable pay. The assets of the scheme are held separately from those of the company, being invested with insurance companies. Contributions to the scheme are charged to the profit and loss account so as to spread the cost of pensions over employees' working lives with the company. The contributions are determined by a qualified actuary on the basis of triennial valuations using the projected unit method.* The most recent valuation was as at 31 December 1987. The assumptions which have the most significant effect on the results of the valuation are those relating to the rate of return on investments and the rates of increase in salaries and pensions. It was assumed that the investment returns would be 9% per annum, that salary increases would average 7% per annum and that present and future pensions would increase at the rate of 4% per annum.

The pension charge for the period was £50,000 (1986 £48,000). This included £5,200 (1986 £5,000) in respect of the amortisation of experience surpluses that are being recognised over 10 years, the average remaining service lives of employees.

The most recent actuarial valuation showed that the market value of the scheme's assets was £1,200,000 and that the actuarial value of those assets represented 104% of the benefits that had accrued to members, after allowing for expected future increases in earnings. The contributions of the company and employees will remain at 11% and 5% of earnings respectively.

(ii) *Large group*
The group operates a number of pension schemes throughout the world. The major schemes, which cover 85% of scheme members, are of the defined benefit type. With the exception of the main scheme in Germany, the assets of the schemes are held in separate trustee administered funds.

**These and other actuarial funding methods are described in 'Pension Fund Terminology: specimen descriptions of commonly used valuation methods' issued by the Institute and Faculty of Actuaries.*

The total pension cost for the group was £2,050,000 (1986 £1,585,000) of which £300,000 (1986 £285,000) relates to the overseas schemes. The pension cost relating to the UK schemes is assessed in accordance with the advice of a qualified actuary using the attained age method.* The latest actuarial assessment of those schemes was as at 31 December 1985. The assumptions which have the most significant effect on the results of the valuation are those relating to the rate of return on investments and the rates of increase in salaries and pensions. It was assumed that the investment return would be 9% per annum, that salary increases would average 7% per annum and that present and future pensions would increase at a rate of 4% per annum. The cost has risen significantly as a result of the acquisition of ABC Limited at the beginning of the period and the resultant increase in group scheme members. Of the total cost, £350,000 (1986 £300,000) is attributable to amortisation of past service liabilities that are being written off over a ten-year period ending in 1988.

At the date of the latest actuarial valuation, the market value of the assets of the UK scheme was £32.1m and the actuarial value of the assets was sufficient to cover 85% of the benefits that had accrued to members, after allowing for expected future increases in earnings. This deficiency should be eliminated by 1991 at the current employer's contribution rate of 12% of pensionable earnings.

The element of the total pension cost relating to foreign schemes includes £280,000 (1986 £250,000) where the charge has been determined in accordance with local best practice and regulations in the Federal Republic of Germany.

A provision of £5,500,000 (1984, £5,000,000) is included in creditors, this being the excess of the accumulated pension cost over the amount funded. The major part of this provision relates to the unfunded German scheme.

**These and other actuarial funding methods are described in 'Pension Fund Terminology: specimen descriptions of commonly used valuation methods' issued by the Institute and Faculty of Actuaries.*

[SSAP 25]
Segmental reporting

(Issued June 1990)

Contents

Segmental reporting

The provisions of this statement of accounting practice should be read in conjunction with the (Explanatory) Foreword to accounting standards *and need not be applied to immaterial items.*

Part 1 – Explanatory note

PURPOSE OF SEGMENTAL INFORMATION

Many entities carry on several classes of business or operate in several geographical areas, with different rates of profitability, different opportunities for growth and different degrees of risk. It is not usually possible for the user of the financial statements of such an entity to make judgements about either the nature of the entity's different activities or their contribution to the entity's overall financial results unless the financial statements provide some segmental analysis of the information they contain. The purpose of segmental information is, therefore, to provide information to assist the users of financial statements: 1

(a) to appreciate more thoroughly the results and financial position of the entity by permitting a better understanding of the entity's past performance and thus a better assessment of its future prospects; and

(b) to be aware of the impact that changes in significant components of a business may have on the business as a whole.

This accounting standard should ensure as far as possible that the segmental information reported by an entity is disclosed on a consistent basis, year by year. However, caution should be exercised if comparing similar segments in different entities, because, in addition to any differences in accounting policies adopted, the basis of accounting for inter-segment sales or the treatment of common costs may not be consistent between entities. 2

SCOPE AND APPLICABILITY

This accounting standard contains provisions relating to the statutory segmental disclosure requirements contained in companies legislation in the United Kingdom and the Republic of Ireland. All companies are required to comply with these provisions. 3

This accounting standard also contains provisions relating to the disclosure of inter-segment turnover, geographical segment result, segment net assets, origin of turnover, and segmental information about associated undertakings, which are not required by companies legislation. These provisions apply to any entity that: 4

(a) is a public limited company or has a public limited company as a subsidiary; or

(b) is a banking or insurance company or group (as defined for the purposes of Part VII of the Companies Act 1985); or
(c) exceeds the criteria, multiplied in each case by 10, for defining a medium-sized company under Section 248 of the Companies Act 1985, as amended from time to time by statutory instrument.

However, a subsidiary that is not a public limited company or a banking or insurance company need not comply with these provisions if its parent provides segmental information in compliance with this accounting standard.

5 All entities are encouraged to apply the provisions of this accounting standard in all financial statements intended to give a true and fair view of the financial position and profit or loss.

6 Where, in the opinion of the directors, the disclosure of any information required by this accounting standard would be seriously prejudicial to the interests of the reporting entity, that information need not be disclosed; but the fact that any such information has not been disclosed must be stated. This repeats the exemption contained in paragraph 55(5) of Schedule 4 to the Companies Act 1985* in the wider context of this accounting standard.

DETERMINING REPORTABLE SEGMENTS

7 Information contained in financial statements can be segmented in two principal ways – by class of business and geographically. The Companies Act 1985 recognises both of these bases in paragraph 55 of Schedule 4, referring to the geographical areas as 'markets'. Paragraph 55 states that in analysing the source (in terms of either business or market) of turnover or profit or loss the directors should have regard to the manner in which the company's activities are organised. Paragraph 55 also states that it is for the directors to determine whether the company has carried on business of two or more classes or has supplied markets that differ substantially from each other and that where, in the opinion of the directors, the classes of business or the markets do not differ substantially from each other they may be treated as one.

8 In identifying separate reportable segments, the directors should have regard to the overall purpose of presenting segmental information (as set out in paragraph 1) and the need of the user of the financial statements to be informed where an entity carries on operations in different classes of business or in different geographical areas that:

(a) earn a return on investment that is out of line with the remainder of the business; or
(b) are subject to different degrees of risk; or
(c) have experienced different rates of growth; or
(d) have different potentials for future development.

***Throughout this statement of standard accounting practice, references to paragraph 55 of Schedule 4 to the Companies Act 1985 should be read in the Republic of Ireland as references to paragraph 41 of the Schedule to the Companies (Amendment) Act 1986.*

Each class of business or geographical segment that is significant to an entity as a whole should be identified as a reportable segment. For the purposes of this accounting standard a segment should normally be regarded as significant if: 9

(a) its third party turnover is ten per cent or more of the total third party turnover of the entity; or
(b) its segment result, whether profit or loss, is ten per cent or more of the combined result of all segments in profit or of all segments in loss, whichever combined result is the greater; or
(c) its net assets are ten per cent or more of the total net assets of the entity.

The directors should review the definitions of the segments annually and re-define them when appropriate. In doing so the directors should have regard to the fundamental objective of this accounting standard, which is to achieve, as far as possible, consistency and comparability between years. 10

CLASSES OF BUSINESS

A separate class of business is a distinguishable component of an entity that provides a separate product or service or a separate group of related products or services. 11

When deciding whether or not an entity operates in different classes of business, the directors should take into account the following factors: 12

(a) the nature of the products or services;
(b) the nature of the production processes;
(c) the markets in which the products or services are sold;
(d) the distribution channels for the products;
(e) the manner in which the entity's activities are organised;
(f) any separate legislative framework relating to part of the business, for example, a bank or an insurance company.

Although it is possible to identify certain characteristics that differentiate between classes of business, no single set of characteristics is universally applicable nor is any single characteristic determinative in all cases. Consequently, determination of an entity's classes of business must depend on the judgement of the directors. 13

GEOGRAPHICAL SEGMENTS

A geographical segment is a geographical area comprising an individual country or a group of countries in which an entity operates, or to which it supplies products or services. 14

A geographical analysis should help the user of the financial statements to assess the extent to which an entity's operations are subject to factors such as the following: 15

(a) expansionist or restrictive economic climates;
(b) stable or unstable political regimes;

(c) exchange control regulations;
(d) exchange rate fluctuations.

16 It is not practicable to define a method of grouping that will reflect all the differences between international business environments and that would apply to all entities. The selected grouping should reflect the purpose of presenting segmental information (as set out in paragraph 1) and the factors noted in paragraphs 8 and 15. Although geographical proximity may indicate similar economic trends and risks, this will not necessarily be the case.

INFORMATION TO BE DISCLOSED

General

17 The entity should define in its financial statements each reported class of business and geographical segment.

Turnover

18 The factors listed in paragraph 15 apply both to the geographical locations of the entity's operations and to the geographical locations of its markets. The user of the financial statements gains a fuller understanding of the entity's exposure to these factors, if turnover is disclosed according to both location of operations and location of markets. For the purposes of this accounting standard, origin of turnover is the geographical area *from* which products or services are supplied to a third party or another segment. Destination of turnover is the geographical area *to* which goods or services are supplied. Because disclosure relating to segment results and net assets will generally be based on location of operations, an analysis of turnover on the same basis will enable the user to match turnover, result and net assets on a consistent basis, and to relate all three to the perceived risks and opportunities of the segments. For these reasons this accounting standard requires the disclosure of sales by origin, but reporting entities should also disclose turnover by destination unless there is no material difference between the two. If there is no material difference, a statement to that effect is required.

19 Inter-segment sales and transfers are often a material part of the total turnover of the reportable segments and in such cases they should be analysed segmentally and shown separately. The geographical analysis of inter-segment turnover should be disclosed by origin. Analysis by destination usually has little or no value and would not normally be provided.

20 The Companies Act 1985 and the Companies (Northern Ireland) Order 1986 contain provisions exempting banking and insurance companies and groups from the requirement to disclose turnover in certain circumstances. In the Republic of Ireland, similar exemptions are extended to special classes of companies (banking, discount and insurance companies) under the Companies Act 1963. Certain other entities – for

example, building societies – are subject to different statutory rules from those applied to companies. Where turnover is not required by statute to be disclosed, it is not required by this accounting standard to be disclosed segmentally. The fact that such turnover has not been disclosed segmentally should be stated.

Segment result

The entity should disclose the result of each reportable segment before accounting for taxation, minority interests and extraordinary items. The geographical analysis of segment result should normally be based on the areas from which products or services are supplied. 21

In the majority of entities, different classes of business or geographical segments are financed by different proportions of interest-bearing debt and equity. The interest earned or incurred by individual segments is therefore a result of the entity's overall financial policy rather than a proper reflection of the results of the various segments. Consequently, comparisons of profit between segments or between different years for the same segment are likely to be meaningless if interest is included in arriving at the result. For these reasons, it will normally be appropriate for segment results to be disclosed before taking account of interest. However, where all or part of the entity's business is to earn and/or incur interest (as in the financial sector, for example), or where interest income or expense is central to the business (as in the contracting or travel businesses, for example), interest should normally be included in arriving at the segment result. 22

Common costs

Common costs are costs relating to more than one segment. They should be treated in the way that the directors deem most appropriate in pursuance of the objectives of segmental reporting. Entities may apportion some common costs for the purpose of internal reporting and, in such cases, it may be reasonable for such costs to be similarly apportioned for external reporting purposes. If the apportionment would be misleading, common costs should not be apportioned in the segmental disclosures but should be deducted from the total of the segment results. Costs that are directly attributable to individual reportable segments are not common costs for the purposes of this accounting standard and therefore should be allocated to those segments, irrespective of the fact that they may have been borne by a different segment or by the Head Office. 23

Segment net assets

The net assets of each reportable segment should be disclosed. In most cases these will be the non-interest bearing operating assets less the non-interest bearing operating liabilities. However, to the extent that the segment result is disclosed after accounting for interest as described in paragraph 22, the corresponding interest-bearing operating assets and liabilities should also be included. 24

Segment operating assets and liabilities may include assets and liabilities relating exclusively to one segment and also an allocated portion of assets and liabilities that 25 relate jointly to more than one segment. Assets and liabilities used jointly by more than one segment should be allocated to the segments on a reasonable basis. Assets and liabilities that are not used in the operations of any segment should not be allocated to segments. Operating assets of a segment should not normally include loans or advances to, or investments in, another segment unless interest therefrom has been included in arriving at the segment result on the basis set out in paragraph 22.

Associated undertakings

26 Sometimes associated undertakings form a significant part of a reporting entity's results or assets. In such circumstances the following information should be analysed segmentally and shown separately in the segmental report:

(a) the reporting entity's share of the profits or losses of associated undertakings before accounting for taxation, minority interests and extraordinary items; and
(b) the reporting entity's share of the net assets of associated undertakings (including goodwill to the extent that it has not been written off) stated, where possible, after attributing fair values to the net assets at the date of acquisition of the interest in each associated undertaking.

However, it is recognised that this information might be unobtainable or publication might be prejudicial to the business of the associate. In such circumstances the disclosure is not required but the reason for non-disclosure should be stated by way of note, together with a brief description of the omitted business or businesses.

27 For the purposes of this accounting standard, associated companies form a significant part of the reporting entity's results or assets if, in total, they account for at least 20% of the total result or 20% of the total net assets of the reporting entity.

General

28 The total of the amounts disclosed by segment should agree with the related total in the financial statements. If it does not, the reporting entity should provide a reconciliation between the two figures. Reconciling items should be properly identified and explained.

29 Comparative figures for the previous accounting period should be provided. If a change is made to the definitions of the segments or to the accounting policies that are adopted for reporting segmental information, the nature of the change should be disclosed. The reason for the change and the effect of the change should be stated. The previous year's figures should be restated to reflect the change.

Part 2 – Definition of terms

30 A *class of business* is a distinguishable component of an entity that provides a separate product or service or a separate group of related products or services.

31 A *geographical segment* is a geographical area comprising an individual country or group of countries in which an entity operates, or to which it supplies products or services.

Origin of turnover is the geographical segment from which products or services are supplied to a third party or to another segment. 32

Destination of turnover is the geographical segment to which products or services are supplied. 33

Part 3 – Standard accounting practice

If an entity has two or more classes of business, or operates in two or more geographical segments which differ substantially from each other, it should define its classes of business and geographical segments in its financial statements, and it should report with respect to each class of business and geographical segment the following financial information: 34

(a) turnover, distinguishing between (i) turnover derived from external customers and (ii) turnover derived from other segments;
(b) result, before accounting for taxation, minority interests and extraordinary items; and
(c) net assets.

The reporting entity should disclose the geographical segmentation of turnover by origin. It should also disclose turnover to third parties by destination or state where appropriate that this amount is not materially different from turnover to third parties by origin. Segment result will normally be disclosed before taking account of interest. However, where all or part of the entity's business is to earn and/or incur interest, or where interest income or expense is central to the business, interest should normally be included in arriving at the segment result. Net assets will normally be non-interest bearing operating assets less the non-interest bearing operating liabilities, but to the extent that the segment result is disclosed after accounting for interest the corresponding interest-bearing assets or liabilities should also be included.

When both parent and consolidated financial statements are presented, segmental information should be presented on the basis of the consolidated financial statements. 35

The reporting entity should disclose the following information segmentally in relation to its associated undertakings if these account for at least 20% of its total result or 20% of its total net assets: 36

(a) the entity's share of the results of associated undertakings before accounting for taxation, minority interests and extraordinary items; and
(b) the entity's share of the net assets of associated undertakings (including goodwill to the extent it has not been written off) stated, where possible, after attributing fair values to the net assets at the date of acquisition of the interest in each undertaking.

The segmental disclosure should be of the aggregate amounts of all associated undertakings for which the information is available and should be shown separately in the segmental report. However, this information need not be disclosed if it is unobtainable or publication would be prejudicial to the business of the associate. In such circumstances, the reason for non-disclosure should be stated by way of note, together with a brief description of the omitted business or businesses.

37 The total of the amounts disclosed by segment should agree with the related total in the financial statements. If it does not, the reporting entity should provide a reconciliation between the two amounts. Reconciling items should be properly identified and explained.

38 Comparative figures for the previous accounting period should be provided. If, however, on the first occasion on which an entity provides a segmental report the necessary information is not readily available, comparative figures need not be provided.

39 The directors should re-define the segments when appropriate. If a change is made to the definitions of the segments or to the accounting policies that are adopted for reporting segmental information, the nature of the change should be disclosed. The reason for the change and its effect should be stated. The previous year's figures should be re-stated to reflect the change.

40 This accounting standard contains provisions relating to the statutory segmental disclosure requirements contained in companies legislation in the United Kingdom and the Republic of Ireland. All companies are required to comply with these provisions.

41 This accounting standard also contains provisions relating to segmental disclosures which are not required by companies legislation.* These provisions apply to any entity that:

(a) is a public limited company or that has a public limited company as a subsidiary; or
(b) is a banking or insurance company or group (as defined for the purposes of Part VII of the Companies Act 1985); or
(c) exceeds the criteria, multiplied in each case by 10, for defining a medium-sized company under section 247† of the Companies Act 1985, as amended from time to time by statutory instrument.

However, a subsidiary that is not a public limited company or a banking or insurance

**Disclosures not required by the Companies Act 1985 are those set out in paragraphs 34(a)ii, 34(b) insofar as it relates to geographical segment result, 34(c), 34 insofar as it relates to origin of turnover, and 36.*

†Equivalent legal references:

Great Britain	Northern Ireland	Republic of Ireland
Companies Act 1985	*Companies (Northern Ireland) Order 1986*	*Companies (Amendment) Act 1986*
Section 247	Article 256 (as amended)	Section 8.

company need not comply with these provisions if its parent provides segmental disclosures in compliance with this accounting standard.

All other entities are encouraged to apply the provisions of this accounting standard in all financial statements intended to give a true and fair view of the financial position and profit or loss. 42

Where, in the opinion of the directors, the disclosure of any information required by this accounting standard would be seriously prejudicial to the interests of the reporting entity, that information need not be disclosed. The fact that any such information has not been disclosed must be stated. 43

Entities that are not required by statute to disclose turnover in their financial statements are not required by this accounting standard to disclose turnover segmentally. The fact that turnover has not been disclosed segmentally should be stated in the financial statements. 44

DATE FROM WHICH EFFECTIVE

The provisions of this statement of standard accounting practice should be adopted as soon as possible and regarded as standard in respect of financial statements relating to accounting periods beginning on or after 1 July 1990. 45

Part 4 – Legal and International Stock Exchange requirements in Great Britain and Northern Ireland

COMPANY LAW

All paragraph references, unless otherwise indicated, are to the Schedules to the Companies Act 1985 and the Companies (Northern Ireland) Order 1986.

Paragraph 55(1) of Schedule 4 requires all companies that, in the course of the financial year, have carried on business of two or more classes that (in the opinion of the directors) differ substantially from each other to state: 46

(a) a description of each class of business;
(b) the amount of turnover attributable to each class of business; and
(c) the amount of the profit or loss of the company before taxation that is, in the opinion of the directors, attributable to each class of business.

Paragraph 55(2) of Schedule 4 requires all companies that, in the course of the financial year, have supplied geographical markets that (in the opinion of the directors) differ substantially from each other to state the amount of the turnover attributable to each market. 47

Paragraph 55(3) of Schedule 4 provides that, in analysing the source (in terms of either classes of business or markets) of turnover or profit or loss for the purposes of 48 paragraph 55, the directors of the company shall have regard to the manner in which the company's activities are organised.

49 Paragraph 55(4) of Schedule 4 provides that, for the purposes of paragraph 55:

(a) classes of business which, in the opinion of the directors, do not differ substantially from each other shall be treated as one class;
(b) markets which, in the opinion of the directors, do not differ substantially from each other shall be treated as one market; and
(c) any amounts properly attributable to one class of business or to one market which are not material may be included in the amount stated in respect of another.

50 Paragraph 55(5) of Schedule 4 states that where, in the opinion of the directors, the disclosure of any information required by paragraph 55 would be seriously prejudicial to the interests of the company, that information need not be disclosed but the fact that any such information has not been disclosed must be stated.

51 Schedule 9 deals with the special provisions for banking and insurance companies and groups.* Paragraph 17 of Schedule 9† requires the following matters to be stated by way of note, if not otherwise shown:

(a) the turnover for the financial year, except in so far as it is attributable to the business of banking or discounting;
(b) if some or all of the turnover is omitted by reason of its being attributable to the business of banking or discounting, the fact that it is so omitted; and
(c) the method by which turnover stated is arrived at.

52 Paragraph 17(5) of Schedule 9‡ provides that a company should not be subject to the requirements of paragraph 17 if it is neither a parent company nor a subsidiary undertaking and the turnover which, apart from sub-paragraph 17(5), would be required to be stated does not exceed £1 million.

53 Schedule 10 deals with the directors' report where accounts are prepared in accordance with the special provisions for banking or insurance companies or groups.§ Paragraph 2 provides that where a company prepares group accounts in accordance with the special provisions and, in the course of the financial year to which the accounts relate, the group has carried on business of two or more classes (other than banking or discounting of a class prescribed for the purpose of paragraph 17(2) of that Schedule) that in the opinion of the directors differ substantially from each other, there shall be contained in the directors' report a statement of:

***Editor's note:** *Schedule 9 as amended deals with banking companies and groups; paragraph 76 requires analysis of specified income items by geographical market. Schedule 9A deals with insurance companies and groups; paragraph 75 of the new Schedule 9A inserted by SI 1993 No 3246 requires certain analysis by class of business.*

†**Editor's note:** *See now paragraph 17, as amended, of old Schedule 9A.*

‡**Editor's note:** *Now old Schedule 9A.*

§**Editor's note:** *Schedule 10 deals only with Directors' Reports where accounts are prepared in accordance with old Schedule 9A for insurance companies or groups.*

(a) the proportions in which the turnover for the financial year (so far as stated in the consolidated accounts) is divided amongst those classes (describing them); and
(b) as regards business of each class, the extent or approximate extent (expressed in money terms) to which, in the opinion of the directors, the carrying on of business of that class contributed to, or restricted, the profit or loss of the company for that year (before taxation).

Classes of business which, in the opinion of the directors, do not differ substantially from each other, are to be treated as one class.

INTERNATIONAL STOCK EXCHANGE

The International Stock Exchange of the United Kingdom and the Republic of Ireland Ltd sets out its requirements for segmental information in the 'Admission of Securities to Listing'.* Section 5, Chapter 2, paragraph 21(c) of that publication requires: **54**

> 'a geographical analysis of both net turnover and contribution to trading results of those trading operations carried on by the company (or group) outside the United Kingdom and the Republic of Ireland'.

No analysis of the contribution to trading results is required unless the contribution to profit or loss from a specific area is 'abnormal' in nature. 'Abnormal' is defined as substantially out of line with the normal ratio of profit to turnover. **55**

Part 5 – Legal and International Stock Exchange requirements in the Republic of Ireland

COMPANY LAW

All paragraph references, unless otherwise indicated, are to the Schedule to the Companies (Amendment) Act 1986.

Paragraph 41(1) requires all companies that, in the course of the financial year, have carried on business of two or more classes that (in the opinion of the directors) differ substantially from each other to state: **56**

(a) a description of each class of business; and
(b) the amount of turnover attributable to each class of business.

Paragraph 41(2) requires all companies that, in the course of the financial year, have supplied geographical markets that (in the opinion of the directors) differ substantially from each other, to state the amount of the turnover attributable to each market. **57**

Paragraph 41(3) provides that, in analysing the source (in terms of either classes of business or markets) of turnover, the directors of the company shall have regard to the manner in which the company's activities are organised. **58**

Editor's note: *These requirements have been deleted as they are now covered by SSAP25.*

59 Paragraph 41(4) provides that, for the purposes of paragraph 41:

(a) classes of business which, in the opinion of the directors, do not differ substantially from each other shall be treated as one class;
(b) markets which, in the opinion of the directors, do not differ substantially from each other shall be treated as one market; and
(c) any amounts properly attributable to one class of business or to one market which are not material may be included in the amount stated in respect of another.

60 Paragraph 41(5) states that where, in the opinion of the directors, the disclosure of any information required by paragraph 41 would be seriously prejudicial to thc interests of the company, that information need not be disclosed but the fact that any such information has not been disclosed must be stated.

61 Banking, discount and insurance companies are regarded as special classes of companies and as such come within Part III of the Sixth Schedule to the Companies Act 1963 which exempts them from the disclosure requirements of the Schedule to the Companies (Amendment) Act 1986.

62 The International Stock Exchange of the United Kingdom and the Republic of Ireland Ltd sets out its requirements for segmental information in the 'Admission of Securities to Listing'. Section 5, Chapter 2, paragraph 21(c) of that publication requires:

> 'a geographical analysis of both net turnover and contribution to trading results of those trading operations carried on by the company (or group) outside the United Kingdom and the Republic of Ireland'.

63 No analysis of the contribution to trading results is required unless the contribution to profit or loss from a specific area is 'abnormal' in nature. 'Abnormal' is defined as substantially out of line with the normal ratio of profit to turnover.

Part 6 – Compliance with International Accounting Standard No.14 'Reporting Financial Information by Segment'

64 Compliance with the requirements of this accounting standard will ensure compliance with IAS 14 in all material respects, except in the following circumstances.

(a) This accounting standard does not require the basis of inter-segment pricing to be disclosed. This information must be disclosed in order to comply with IAS 14.
(b) This accounting standard requires the disclosure of segment 'net assets', whereas IAS 14 refers to 'assets employed'. However, as stated in paragraph 34, net assets will normally be the non-interest bearing operating assets less the non-interest bearing operating liabilities, and in those cases net assets will not be materially different from assets employed.
(c) This accounting standard gives the following exemptions which do not appear in IAS 14.
    (i) An entity need not disclose segmental information if disclosure would be seriously prejudicial to its interests.

(ii) An entity that is not required by statute to disclose turnover is not required to disclose turnover segmentally.

(iii) A subsidiary that is not a public limited company or a banking or insurance company need not make the segmental disclosures required by this accounting standard if its parent does so.

Appendix: Illustrative segmental report

This Appendix is for general guidance only and does not form part of the Statement of Standard Accounting Practice

	CLASSES OF BUSINESS							
	Industry A		Industry B		Other industries		Group	
	1990 £000	1989 £000	1990 £000	1989 £000	1990 £000	1989 £000	1990 £000	1989 £000
TURNOVER								
Total sales	33,000	30,000	42,000	38,000	26,000	23,000	101,000	91,000
Inter-segment sales	(4,000)	–	–	–	(12,000)	(14,000)	(16,000)	(14,000)
Sales to third parties	29,000	30,000	42,000	38,000	14,000	9,000	85,000	77,000
PROFIT BEFORE TAXATION								
Segment profit	3,000	2,500	4,500	4,000	1,800	1,500	9,300	8,000
Common costs							300	300
Operating profit							9,000	7,700
Net interest							(400)	(500)
							8,600	7,200
Group share of the profits before taxation of associated undertakings	1,000	1,000	1,400	1,200	–	–	2,400	2,200
Group profit before taxation							11,000	9,400
NET ASSETS								
Segment net assets	17,600	15,000	24,000	25,000	19,400	19,000	61,000	59,000
Unallocated assets							3,000	3,000
							64,000	62,000
Group share of the net assets of associated undertakings	10,200	8,000	8,800	9,000	–	–	19,000	17,000
Total net assets							83,000	79,000

	GEOGRAPHICAL SEGMENTS									
	United Kingdom		North America		Far East		Other		Group	
	1990 £000	1989 £000	1990 £000	1989 £000	1990 £000	1989 £000	1990 £000	1989 £000	1990 £000	1989 £000
TURNOVER										
Turnover by destination										
Sales to third parties	34,000	31,000	16,000	14,500	25,000	23,000	10,000	8,500	85,000	77,000
Turnover by origin										
Total sales	38,000	34,000	29,000	27,500	23,000	23,000	12,000	10,500	102,000	95,000
Inter-segment sales	–	–	(8,000)	(9,000)	(9,000)	(9,000)	–	–	(17,000)	(18,000)
Sales to third parties	38,000	34,000	21,000	18,500	14,000	14,000	12,000	10,500	85,000	77,000
PROFIT BEFORE TAXATION										
Segment profit	4,400	2,900	2,500	2,300	1,800	1,900	1,000	900	9,300	8,000
Common costs									300	300
Operating profit									9,000	7,700
Net interest									(400)	(500)
									8,600	7,200
Group share of the profit before taxation of associated undertakings	950	1,000	1,450	1,200	–	–	–	–	2,400	2,200
Group profit before taxation									11,000	9,400
NET ASSETS										
Segment net assets	16,000	15,000	25,000	26,000	16,000	15,000	4,000	3,000	61,000	59,000
Unallocated assets									3,000	3,000
									64,000	62,000
Group share of the net assets of associated undertakings	8,500	7,000	10,500	10,000	–	–	–	–	19,000	17,000
Total net assets									83,000	79,000

Unallocated assets consist of assets at the Group's head office in London amounting to £2.4 million (1989 £2.5 million) and at the Group's regional office in Hong Kong amounting to £0.6 million (1989 £0.5 million).

[FRS 1]
Cash flow statements

(Issued September 1991)

Contents

Editor's note: Review of FRS 1

On 24 March 1994 the ASB announced a review of FRS 1 and invited suggestions for improving any aspect of the standard, indicating that it would be particularly interested in receiving comments on the following issues:

- the definition of cash and cash equivalents and the treatment of short-term investments;
- the format of the cash flow statement and, in particular, whether changes in presentation could assist understanding of the statement, for example by providing a reconciliation to net debt;
- the classification of items in the cash flow statement and whether amounts should be shown gross or net or both; and
- the scope of the standard.

In its announcement, the ASB emphasised that there must be full compliance with the specific provisions of the FRS as they now stand unless and until the standard is amended.

Cash flow statements

SUMMARY

Financial Reporting Standard No. 1 — 'Cash Flow Statements' (the FRS) establishes standards for cash flow reporting. It supersedes Statement of Standard Accounting Practice No. 10 — 'Statements of Source and Application of Funds' (SSAP 10) and requires reporting entities which fall within its scope to prepare a cash flow statement as part of their financial statements setting out on a standard basis their cash generation and absorption for a period. The FRS sets out the required structure of the cash flow statement and minimum level of disclosure. **a**

The Statement of Principles for Financial Reporting being developed by the Accounting Standards Board (the Board) recognises that users of financial statements need information on the liquidity, viability and financial adaptability of the entity concerned. Deriving this information involves the user in making assessments of the future cash flows of the entity. Accruals accounting, used in producing profit and loss (or income and expenditure) accounts and balance sheets, adjusts cash flows to measure results for a period and this is the primary basis for projections. Nevertheless, long-term provisions and other allocations associated with accruals accounting need to be eliminated in order to reveal the leads and lags in historical cash flows, thereby improving understanding of a reporting entity's cash generating or cash absorption mechanisms and providing a basis for the assessment of future cash flows. **b**

In order to promote understanding and to help to achieve the objectives of cash flow reporting by securing the useful presentation of information, the FRS requires that individual cash flows should be classified under certain standard headings according to the activity that gave rise to them. The standard headings required in a cash flow statement are: **c**

operating activities;
returns on investments and servicing of finance;
taxation;
investing activities;and
financing.

In addition, the FRS requires that the cash flow statement should show a total giving the net cash inflow or outflow before financing. The FRS specifies particular cash flows to be separately reported under each of the standard headings apart from operating activities. Analysis of net cash flow from operating activities on the so-called 'direct method' is encouraged but not required.

In order to ensure that it reflects clearly the substance of a reporting entity's cash management, the cash flow statement deals with flows of cash equivalents as well as with cash flows. **d**

A reconciliation between the operating profit reported in the profit and loss (or income **e** and expenditure) account and the net cash flow from operating activities should be given as a note to the cash flow statement. This reconciliation should disclose separately the movements in stocks, debtors and creditors related to operating activities and other differences between cash flows and profits. A reconciliation of the amounts shown in the balance sheet of the reporting entity in respect of items reported within the financing section of the cash flow statement with the equivalent figures in the previous year's balance sheet, disclosing separately the movements resulting from cash flows, differences arising from changes in foreign currency exchange rates and other movements, should also be given as a note to the cash flow statement.

Small reporting entities

f The FRS exempts most small reporting entities from the requirement to include a cash flow statement as part of their financial statements. The exemption does not extend to public companies, banking companies, insurance companies, authorised persons under the Financial Services Act 1986, or members of a group containing one or more of the above mentioned entities.

Wholly owned subsidiary undertakings

g A wholly owned subsidiary undertaking of a parent undertaking established under the law of a member State of the European Community is exempt from the requirements of the FRS if:

(i) the parent undertaking publishes, in English, consolidated financial statements which include the subsidiary undertaking concerned, drawn up in accordance with United Kingdom or Republic of Ireland companies legislation or the EC Seventh Company Law Directive; and
(ii) those consolidated financial statements include a consolidated cash flow statement dealing with the cash flows of the group; and
(iii) that cash flow statement gives sufficient information to enable a user of the financial statements to derive the totals of the amounts required to be shown under each of the standard headings set out in the FRS.

OBJECTIVE

1 The objective of the FRS is to require reporting entities falling within its scope to report on a standard basis their cash generation and cash absorption for a period. To this end reporting entities are required to provide a primary financial statement analysing cash flows under the standard headings of 'operating activities', 'returns on investments and servicing of finance', 'taxation', 'investing activities' and 'financing', disclosed in that sequence, in order to assist users of the financial statements in their assessment of the reporting entity's liquidity, viability and financial adaptability. The objective of the standard headings is to ensure that cash flows are reported in a form that highlights the significant components of cash flow and facilitates comparison of the cash flow performance of different businesses.

DEFINITIONS

The following definitions shall apply for the purposes of this FRS and in particular the statement of standard accounting practice set out in paragraphs 7 to 46.

Cash	Cash in hand and deposits repayable on demand with any bank or other financial institution. Cash includes cash in hand and deposits denominated in foreign currencies.	**2**
Cash equivalents	Short-term, highly liquid investments which are readily convertible into known amounts of cash without notice and which were within three months of maturity when acquired; less advances from banks repayable within three months from the date of the advance. Cash equivalents include investments and advances denominated in foreign currencies provided that they fulfil the above criteria.	**3**
Cash flow	An increase or decrease in an amount of cash or cash equivalent resulting from a transaction.	**4**
Companies Act 1985	Companies Act 1985 as amended by the Companies Act 1989.	**5**
Companies (Northern Ireland) Order 1986	Companies (Northern Ireland) Order 1986 as amended by the Companies (Northern Ireland) Order 1990 and the Companies (NO. 2) (Northern Ireland) Order 1990.	**6**

STATEMENT OF STANDARD ACCOUNTING PRACTICE

The statement of standard accounting practice set out in paragraphs 7 to 46 of the FRS should be read together with the Objective of the FRS as stated in paragraph 1, the definitions set out in paragraphs 2 to 6 and also the Foreword to Accounting Standards and the Statement of Principles for Financial Reporting issued from time to time by the Board.

The Explanation section of the FRS, set out in paragraphs 48 to 84, shall be regarded as part of the statement of standard accounting practice insofar as it assists in interpreting that statement.

7 Reporting entities falling within the scope of paragraph 8 of the FRS are required to provide as a primary statement within the reporting entity's financial statements a cash flow statement drawn up in accordance with the standard accounting principles set out in paragraphs 9 to 46 of the FRS.

Scope

8 This FRS applies to all financial statements intended to give a true and fair view of the financial position and profit or loss (or income and expenditure) except those of entities that are:

(a) companies incorporated under the Companies Acts and entitled to the exemptions available in Sections 246 to 249 of the Companies Act 1985* for small companies when filing accounts with the Registrar of Companies; or
(b) entities which would have come under category (a) above had they been companies incorporated under companies legislation; or
(c) wholly owned subsidiary undertakings of a parent undertaking which is established under the law of a member State of the European Community where
    (i) the parent undertaking publishes, in English, consolidated financial statements which include the subsidiary undertaking concerned, drawn up in accordance with United Kingdom or Republic of Ireland companies legislation or the EC Seventh Company Law Directive; and
    (ii) those consolidated financial statements include a consolidated cash flow statement dealing with the cash flows of the group; and
    (iii) that cash flow statement gives sufficient information to enable a user of the financial statements to derive the totals of the amounts required to be shown under each of the standard headings set out in this FRS; or
(d) Building Societies, as defined by the Building Societies Act 1986 in the United Kingdom and by the Building Societies Act 1989 in the Republic of Ireland, but

**The equivalent references in Northern Ireland legislation are Sections 254 to 257 of the Companies (Northern Ireland) Order 1986.*

The equivalent references in Republic of Ireland legislation are Sections 8, 9, 10 and 12 of the Companies (Amendment) Act 1986.

only so long as they are required by law to prepare as part of their financial statements a statement of source and application of funds in a prescribed format*; or

(e) mutual life assurance companies.

The cash flow statement provided with group financial statements should reflect the cash flows of the group. 9

Insurance companies, other than mutual life assurance companies to which the FRS does not apply, should include the cash flows of their long-term life, pensions and annuity businesses only to the extent that the cash flows are those of the insurance company itself rather than cash flows of the long-term funds. 10

Preparation of cash flow statements

The cash flow statement should include all the reporting entity's inflows and outflows of cash and cash equivalents except those movements within cash and cash equivalents that result from the purchases and sales for cash or cash equivalents of holdings which form part of that entity's cash equivalents. Transactions which do not result in cash flows of the reporting entity should not be reported in the cash flow statement. 11

Format for cash flow statements

The cash flow statement should list the inflows and outflows of cash and cash equivalents for the period classified under the following standard headings: 12

operating activities;
returns on investments and servicing of finance;
taxation;
investing activities; and
financing

in that order and showing a total for each standard heading and a total of the net cash inflow or outflow before financing. Examples of formats for cash flow statements are provided in the illustrative examples annexed to the FRS.

Classification of cash flows

The cash flow statement should disclose separately, where material, the individual categories of cash flows under the standard headings set out in paragraphs 15 to 30 except in the extremely rare circumstances where this presentation would not be a fair representation of the activities of the reporting entity. In such cases informed judgement should be used to devise an appropriate alternative treatment. The cash flow classifications may be subdivided further to give a fuller description of the activities of the reporting entity or to provide segmental information. 13

Where a cash flow is not specified in the categories set out in paragraphs 15 to 30 below then it should be shown under the most appropriate standard heading. 14

***Editor's note:** *No change in the law on this has yet been made.*

Classification of cash flows by standard heading

Operating activities

15 Cash flows from operating activities are in general the cash effects of transactions and other events relating to operating or trading activities. Net cash flow from operating activities represents the net increase or decrease in cash and cash equivalents resulting from the operations shown in the profit and loss account in arriving at operating profit.

16 Operating cash flows may be reported in the cash flow statement on a net or gross basis.

17 A reconciliation between the operating profit (for non- financial companies normally profit before interest) reported in the profit and loss account and the net cash flow from operating activities should be given as a note to the cash flow statement. This reconciliation should disclose separately the movements in stocks, debtors and creditors related to operating activities and other differences between cash flows and profits.

Returns on investments and servicing of finance

18 'Returns on investments and servicing of finance' are receipts resulting from the ownership of an investment and payments to providers of finance excluding those items required by paragraphs 15 and 24 to 30 to be classified under operating, investing or financing activities.

19 Cash inflows from returns on investments and servicing of finance include:

(a) interest received, including any related tax recovered;
(b) dividends received (disclosing separately dividends received from equity accounted entities), net of any tax credits.

20 Cash outflows from returns on investments and servicing of finance include:

(a) interest paid (whether or not the charge is capitalised), including any tax deducted and paid to the relevant tax authority;
(b) dividends paid, excluding any advance corporation tax;
(c) the interest element of finance lease rental payments.

Taxation

21 The cash flows included under the heading taxation are cash flows to or from taxation authorities in respect of the reporting entity's revenue and capital profits. Cash flows in respect of other taxation, including payments and receipts in respect of Value Added Tax, other sales taxes, property taxes and other taxes not assessed on the profits of the reporting entity should be dealt with as set out in paragraphs 34 and 35 of this FRS.

22 Taxation cash inflows include cash receipts from the relevant tax authority of tax rebates, claims or returns of overpayments.

23 Taxation cash outflows include cash payments to the relevant tax authority of tax, including payments of advance corporation tax and purchases of certificates of tax deposit.

Investing activities

The cash flows included in investing activities are those related to the acquisition or disposal of any asset held as a fixed asset or as a current asset investment (other than assets included within cash equivalents). **24**

Cash inflows from investing activities include: **25**

(a) receipts from sales or disposals of fixed assets;
(b) receipts from sales of investments in subsidiary undertakings net of any balances of cash and cash equivalents transferred as part of the sale;
(c) receipts from sales of investments in other entities with separate disclosure of divestments of equity accounted entities;
(d) receipts from repayment or sales of loans made to other entities by the reporting entity or of other entities' debt (other than cash equivalents) which were purchased by the reporting entity.

Cash outflows from investing activities include: **26**

(a) payments to acquire fixed assets;
(b) payments to acquire investments in subsidiary undertakings net of balances of cash and cash equivalents acquired;
(c) payments to acquire investments in other entities with separate disclosure of investments in equity accounted entities;
(d) loans made by the reporting entity and payments to acquire debt of other entities (other than cash equivalents).

Financing

Financing cash flows comprise receipts from or repayments to external providers of finance of amounts in respect of principal amounts of finance. **27**

Financing cash inflows include: **28**

(a) receipts from issuing shares or other equity instruments;
(b) receipts from issuing debentures, loans, notes and bonds and from other long and short-term borrowings (other than those included within cash equivalents).

Financing cash outflows include: **29**

(a) repayments of amounts borrowed (other than those included within cash equivalents);
(b) the capital element of finance lease rental payments;
(c) payments to re-acquire or redeem the entity's shares;
(d) payments of expenses or commissions on any issue of shares, debentures, loans, notes, bonds or other financing.

30 The amounts of any finance cash flows received from or paid to equity accounted entities should be disclosed separately.

Exceptional and extraordinary items

31 Where cash flows relate to items that are classed as exceptional items in the profit and loss account these exceptional cash flows should be shown under the appropriate standard headings, according to the nature of each item. Sufficient disclosure of the nature of cash flows relating to exceptional items should be given in a note to the cash flow statement to allow a user of the financial statements to gain an understanding of the effect on the reporting entity's cash flows of the underlying transactions.

32 Where cash flows relate to items that are classed as extraordinary items in the profit and loss account these extraordinary cash flows should be shown separately under the appropriate standard headings, according to the nature of each item. In the extremely rare circumstances where it is inappropriate to include a cash flow relating to an extraordinary item under one or more of the standard headings within the cash flow statement the cash flows should be shown within a separate section in the cash flow statement.

33 Sufficient disclosure of the nature of cash flows relating to extraordinary items should be given in a note to the cash flow statement to allow a user of the financial statements to gain an understanding of the effect on the reporting entity's cash flows of the underlying transactions.

Value Added Tax and other taxes

34 Cash flows should be shown net of any attributable Value Added Tax or other sales tax unless the tax is irrecoverable by the reporting entity. The net movement on the amount payable to, or receivable from, the taxing authority should be allocated to cash flows from operating activities unless a different treatment is more appropriate in the particular circumstances concerned. In circumstances where sales taxes paid by the reporting entity are irrecoverable cash flows should be shown gross by including the associated sales tax unless this is impracticable, in which case the irrecoverable tax should be included under the most appropriate standard heading.

35 Taxation cash flows excluding those in respect of the reporting entity's revenue and capital profits and Value Added Tax, or other sales tax, should be included within the cash flow statement under the same standard heading as the cash flow which gave rise to the taxation cash flow, unless a different treatment is more appropriate in the particular circumstances concerned.

Foreign currencies

36 Where a portion of a reporting entity's business is undertaken by a foreign entity, the cash flows of that entity are to be included in the cash flow statement on the basis used for translating the results of those activities in the profit and loss account of the reporting entity.

Hedging transactions

Cash flows that result from transactions undertaken to hedge another transaction should be reported under the same standard heading as the transaction that is the subject of the hedge. **37**

Groups

A group cash flow statement should only deal with flows of cash and cash equivalents external to the group. Accordingly, cash flows that are internal to the group should be eliminated in the preparation of the group cash flow statement. Dividends paid to any minority interests should be reported under the heading returns on investments and servicing of finance, and disclosed separately. **38**

The cash flows of any entity which is equity accounted in consolidated financial statements should only be included in the group cash flow statement to the extent of the actual cash flows between the group and the entity concerned. **39**

Acquisitions and disposals

Where a group acquires or disposes of a subsidiary undertaking, the amounts of cash and cash equivalents paid or received in respect of the consideration should be shown net of any cash and cash equivalent balances transferred as part of the purchase or sale of the subsidiary undertaking. In addition, a note to the cash flow statement should show a summary of the effects of acquisitions and disposals indicating how much of the consideration comprised cash and cash equivalents and the amounts of cash and cash equivalents transferred as a result of the acquisitions and disposals. **40**

Where a subsidiary undertaking joins or leaves a group during a financial year the cash flows of the group should include the cash flows of the subsidiary undertaking concerned for the same period as that for which the group's profit and loss account includes the results of the subsidiary undertaking. **41**

Material effects on amounts reported under each of the standard headings reflecting the cash flows of a subsidiary undertaking acquired or disposed of in the period should be disclosed, as far as practicable, as a note to the cash flow statement. This information need only be given in the financial statements for the period in which the acquisition or disposal occurs. **42**

Major non-cash transactions

Material transactions not resulting in movements of cash or cash equivalents of the reporting entity should be disclosed in the notes to the cash flow statement if disclosure is necessary for an understanding of the underlying transactions. **43**

Reconciliation with balance sheet figures

The movements in cash and cash equivalents and the items shown within the financing section of the cash flow statement should be reconciled to the related items in the **44** opening and closing balance sheets for the period. The reconciliations should disclose separately for cash and cash equivalents and for financing items the movements resulting from cash flows, differences arising from changes in foreign currency exchange rates (those relating to the retranslation of any opening balances of cash and cash equivalents and financing items and those resulting from the translation of the cash flows of foreign entities at exchange rates other than the year end rate) and other movements. Where several balance sheet amounts or parts thereof have to be combined to permit a reconciliation, sufficient detail should be shown to enable the movements to be understood. Possible formats for such reconciliations are provided in the illustrative examples annexed to the FRS.

Comparative figures

45 Comparative figures should be given for all items in the cash flow statement and such notes thereto as are required by the FRS.

Date from which effective

46 The accounting practices set out in this FRS should be adopted as soon as possible and regarded as standard in respect of financial statements relating to accounting periods ending on or after 23 March 1992.

Financial Reporting Standard No. 1 — 'Cash Flow Statements' was adopted by the unanimous vote of the nine members of the Accounting Standards Board.

Members of the Accounting Standards Board

David Tweedie	(Chairman)
Sir Bryan Carsberg	(Vice Chairman)
Allan Cook	(Technical Director)
Robert Bradfield	
Elwyn Eilledge	
Michael Garner	
Donald Main	
Roger Munson	
Graham Stacy	

COMPLIANCE WITH INTERNATIONAL ACCOUNTING STANDARDS

Compliance with the FRS ensures compliance with International Accounting Standard NO. 7 — 'Statement of Changes in Financial Position'. The FRS is also broadly in line with the exposure draft of a proposed International Accounting Standard — 'Cash Flow Statements' issued by the International Accounting Standards Committee in July 1991.* 47

***Editor's note:** IAS 7 was revised in 1992 and is now titled 'Cash Flow Statements'. It was developed from the exposure draft issued in July 1991.*

EXPLANATION

The need for cash flow information

48 Historical cash flow information may assist users of financial statements in making judgements on the amount, timing and degree of certainty of future cash flows; it gives an indication of the relationship between profitability and cash generating ability, and thus of the quality of the profit earned. In addition, analysts and other users of financial information often, formally or informally, develop models to assess and compare the present value of the future cash flows of entities. Historical cash flow information could be useful to check the accuracy of past assessments and indicate the relationship between the entity's activities and its receipts and payments.

49 A cash flow statement in conjunction with a balance sheet provides information on liquidity, viability and financial adaptability. The balance sheet provides information about an entity's financial position at a particular point in time including assets, liabilities and equity and their relationship with each other at the balance sheet date. The balance sheet is often used to obtain information on liquidity, but the information is incomplete for this purpose as the balance sheet is drawn up at a particular point in time.

50 A cash flow statement shows information about the reporting entity's cash flows in the reporting period, but this provides incomplete information for assessing future cash flows. Some cash flows result from transactions that took place in an earlier period and some cash flows are expected to result in further cash flows in a future period. Accordingly, cash flow statements should normally be used in conjunction with profit and loss accounts and balance sheets when making an assessment of future cash flows.

Cash instead of working capital

51 The Board believes that the information provided by a cash flow statement has the following advantages over that provided by a working capital based funds flow statement:

(a) Funds flow data based on movements in working capital can obscure movements relevant to the liquidity and viability of an entity. For example, a significant decrease in cash available may be masked by an increase in stock or debtors. Entities may, therefore, run out of cash while reporting increases in working capital. Similarly, a decrease in working capital does not necessarily indicate a cash shortage and a danger of failure;

(b) As cash flow monitoring is a normal feature of business life and not a specialised accounting technique, cash flow is a concept which is more widely understood than are changes in working capital;

(c) Cash flows can be a direct input into a business valuation model and, therefore, historical cash flows may be relevant in a way not possible for funds flow data;

(d) A funds flow statement is based largely on the difference between two balance sheets. It reorganises such data, but does not provide new data. The cash flow statement and associated notes required by the FRS may include data not disclosed in a funds flow statement.

Cash and cash equivalents

Entities often invest cash in excess of immediate needs in short-term highly liquid investments or borrow on a short-term basis to cover a peak in working capital requirements. Whether an entity's liquid resources comprise cash or a financial instrument that is readily convertible to a known amount of cash is largely irrelevant to users' assessments of liquidity and future cash flows. It is also irrelevant whether a cash flow results in a decrease in a cash balance or results in an increase in an overdraft or short-term bank loan. The Board, therefore, decided that a statement of cash flows should focus on the aggregate of cash and cash equivalents and that cash equivalents should be calculated net of short-term bank advances. **52**

Entities' cash management programmes vary in the range of short- to medium-term deposits and instruments which they manage as a cash or near cash portfolio. In adopting the definition of cash equivalents for the purposes of the FRS the Board distinguished between those deposits and instruments that are effectively available immediately at face value and those that are placed for a longer term and would consequently incur some price risk if they were to be utilised at an earlier date. Thus cash equivalents, apart from any offset of overdrafts and other short-term bank borrowings, must be highly liquid, convertible into known amounts of cash without notice and not have any significant risk of changes in value owing to changes in interest rates. **53**

The Board believes that a reasonable cut-off for cash equivalents is represented by a three month maturity threshold on the grounds that instruments within three months of maturity do not have any significant risk of changes in value due to changes in interest rates. The Board believes that the same cut-off point of three months should be used for bank borrowings. An investment purchased with more than three months to maturity does not become a cash equivalent when its remaining maturity is three months. Similarly, bank borrowings with a maturity of more than three months when drawn down do not become cash equivalents when their remaining maturity becomes three months because in these circumstances no transaction has taken place and it would be misleading to represent the approach of maturity as a cash flow. **54**

Some entities, particularly banks and other financial institutions, hold highly liquid financial instruments for investment or trading purposes and not as part of their cash management programme. The Board's definition of cash equivalents includes highly liquid instruments only if they had less than three months remaining to maturity when purchased. The Board believes that consistency between the cash flow statements of different reporting entities is desirable, as far as possible, and accordingly highly liquid instruments held by financial institutions for trading purposes should be included as part of their cash equivalents only if they fall within the definition of cash equivalents set out in paragraph 3.. **55**

Cash or net debt

56 The Board believes that the focus of the cash flow statement should be not only cash flows but also the movements in a reporting entity's net cash or debt position. By separating the servicing of finance from the movements in principal amounts of finance, by requiring a total giving the net cash inflow or outflow before financing and by requiring disclosure of movements in the reporting entity's financing, the Board believes that information on the movements in the net cash or debt position is given an appropriate degree of prominence. The Board has not specified the form of presentation of the change in cash and cash equivalents because the significance of this item may be expected to differ for individual reporting entities. The illustrative examples show two out of a number of possible forms of presentation.

Scope

57 The Board has examined the circumstances of small reporting entities and has exempted most of them from the requirement to include a cash flow statement as part of their financial statements. This exemption does not extend to public companies that have the powers under their constitutions to offer their shares or debentures to the public and may lawfully exercise that power, or to banking companies, insurance companies, authorised persons under the Financial Services Act 1986, or members of a group containing one or more of the above mentioned entities. The scope of the exemption may be restricted at a later date as part of a wider examination of the reporting requirements of small entities.

58 The Board believes that the small entities exemption is justified because the costs for small entities, which are often owner managed, of producing historical cash flow information in a highly standardised form are likely to be disproportionate to the benefits. The Board has restricted the definition so that entities that are authorised to hold public money or offer securities to the public are required to produce a cash flow statement. However, the Board encourages small reporting entities to include a cash flow statement as part of their financial statements if it would provide useful information to users of those financial statements and the benefits of doing so outweigh the costs of providing the information.

59 The Board recognises that trade and other creditors may be users of financial statements, but has taken into account the fact that small companies or groups of companies as defined by the Companies Act 1985 are able to take advantage of provisions in that Act allowing them to file abbreviated accounts with the Registrar of Companies. These abbreviated accounts need not include a cash flow statement or an equivalent, and thus the information would not necessarily be within the public domain.

60 The Board has examined and rejected the proposition that wholly owned subsidiary undertakings should have to include a cash flow statement as part of their financial statements. Wholly owned subsidiary undertakings are legal entities in their own right and thus have legal obligations to creditors. They are, however, often controlled and managed on a day-to-day basis by their parent and the group may have a centralised treasury or other cash/debt management operation which results in a wholly owned subsidiary undertaking's cash flow being wholly or partly dependent on the group's overall cash or funding position. In view of the fact that cash balances can be moved around a group rapidly, historical cash flow information of individual group companies is limited in the information that it can contribute to an assessment of future cash flows. Accordingly, the Board believes that a cash flow statement is not meaningful in relation to wholly owned subsidiary undertakings.

The Board has examined the proposition that a cash flow statement would not be **61** particularly useful in respect of financial institutions, particularly banks, insurance companies and building societies.

The main reasons advanced for these views in respect of banks are that a bank's cash is **62** its stock in trade and that more useful information would be given by a statement dealing with the capital resources available to the bank. The Board agrees that capital resources are an important indicator of the viability and financial adaptability of financial institutions, but also believes that a cash flow statement provides users of financial statements published by banks with useful information on the sources of cash and how it has been utilised and thus no exemption from the requirements of the FRS is given to banks.

The Board does, however, believe that the reporting of gross operating cash flows for a **63** bank would not provide a user of the bank's financial statements with useful information, because many of the gross operating cash flows are essentially cash flows originated as a result of a decision by third parties who hold deposits or have loans with the bank to move funds to or from their accounts with the bank and thus these cash flows are beyond the day-to-day control of the bank's management. However, the FRS allows reporting entities to report cash flows from operations on a net basis (ie. gross cash flows after deduction of other cash flows) and the Board believes that the reporting of net operating cash flows, together with cash flow information on a bank's investing and financing activities, provides useful information to users of the bank's financial statements. The illustrative examples annexed to the FRS include an example of a cash flow statement for a bank.

The main reason advanced for an exemption from the requirement to publish a cash **64** flow statement as part of financial statements of an insurance company is that the cash inflows for an insurance company, unlike those of a manufacturing company, relate to premiums which by their nature precede the cash outflows in respect of claims, sometimes by a long period of time, and thus a cash flow statement gives little information on the liquidity, viability and financial adaptability of an insurance company. However, the Board believes that cash flow statements are useful to users of insurance company financial statements because, if used in conjunction with profit and loss accounts and balance sheets, they can assist the user of the financial statements to obtain a rounded picture of financial performance, position and adaptability. Accordingly, no general exemption from the requirements of the FRS is given to insurance companies.

However, the Board believes that cash flows arising from 'long term assurance' **65** business (life, annuity and pensions) of an insurance company should not be dealt with in the cash flow statement except to the extent that the cash flows are those of the insurance company itself (eg. cash withdrawn from the long-term funds by the insurance company), rather than cash flows of the long-term funds. The Board believes that this presentation is appropriate, as the shareholders of an insurance company generally have restricted rights to any profits, and associated cash surpluses, made by the long-term funds. In addition, the Board believes that this presentation is consistent with the manner in which many insurance companies currently draw up their profit and loss accounts, balance sheets and statements of source and application of funds. The illustrative examples annexed to the FRS include an example of a cash flow statement for an insurance company. The same considerations apply to mutual life assurance companies that are owned by the policy holders and, accordingly, these companies are exempt from the requirements of the FRS.

66 Users of the financial statements of financial institutions, including insurance companies, may find it useful to have information on total liquid assets when making assessments of liquidity, viability and financial flexibility. In these circumstances the financial institutions concerned may wish to provide additional information on the amounts and flows of those liquid assets not dealt with in the cash flow statement. A possible way of presenting such information is set out in the notes to illustrative example 6 — 'XYZ Insurance Company Limited'.

67 Building Societies in the United Kingdom are required by Section 72(1)(C) of the Building Societies Act 1986 to prepare a statement of source and application of funds as part of their annual financial statements. The format of this statement, which is prescribed, is set out in Schedule 3 of the Building Societies (Accounts and Related Provisions) Regulations 1987. The equivalent requirement to prepare a statement of source and application of funds in Republic of Ireland legislation is set out in Section 77 of the Building Societies Act 1989. The Board believes that the cost to Building Societies of including a cash flow statement in addition to the statement of source and application of funds would outweigh the benefits to users of Building Society financial statements. Accordingly, Building Societies are exempt from the provisions of the FRS during the period that they are required by law to include a statement of source and application of funds in their financial statements in a separately prescribed format.

Classification of cash flows

68 The Board believes that, in order to promote understanding and to help achieve the objectives of cash flow reporting by presenting the information in a useful way, individual cash flows should be classified according to the activity which gave rise to them. In order to promote comparability amongst different entities the FRS prescribes certain standard headings. The standard headings to be identified in a cash flow statement are 'operating activities', 'returns on investments and servicing of finance', 'taxation', 'investing activities' and 'financing'. The Board believes that the totals of the amounts within each standard heading provide useful information for general comparison purposes. However, the significance of the components within each standard heading may vary from reporting entity to reporting entity and accordingly the FRS requires sub-division of the amounts shown under each standard heading. In order to provide users of cash flow statements with a standard set of information that they can use in their analyses the FRS specifies certain standard sub-divisions which should be separately disclosed, if material, but reporting entities are encouraged to disclose additional information relevant to their particular circumstances.

Reporting net cash flow from operating activities

The Board considered the respective merits of the so-called 'direct' and 'indirect' methods for reporting net cash flow from operating activities. The direct method shows operating cash receipts and payments (including, in particular, cash receipts from customers, cash payments to suppliers and cash payments to and on behalf of employees), aggregating to the net cash flow from operating activities. The indirect method starts with operating profit and adjusts it for non-cash charges and credits to reconcile it to the net cash flow from operating activities. **69**

The principal advantage of the direct method is that it shows operating cash receipts and payments. Knowledge of the specific sources of cash receipts and the purposes for which cash payments were made in past periods may be useful in assessing future cash flows. However, the Board does not believe at present that in all cases the benefits to users of this information outweigh the costs to the reporting entity of providing it and, therefore, has not required the information to be given. Nevertheless, in those circumstances where the benefits to users of the information given by the direct method outweigh the costs of providing it the Board encourages reporting entities to provide the relevant information. **70**

The principal advantage of the indirect method is that it highlights the differences between operating profit and net cash flow from operating activities. Many users of financial statements believe that such a reconciliation is essential to give an indication of the quality of the reporting entity's earnings. Some investors and creditors assess future cash flows by estimating future income and then allowing for accruals adjustments; thus information about past accruals adjustments may be useful to help estimate future adjustments. **71**

The Board believes that it is important that cash flow statements produced by different reporting entities are comparable as far as possible in the circumstances and thus believes that it should prescribe the outline format of the statement. Accordingly, the FRS requires the cash flow statement to show the net cash flow from operating activities, supplemented by a note reconciling this to the reporting entity's operating profit for the period. This reconciliation should not be given in the primary cash flow statement, in order to avoid confusing operating profit and the reconciling items with cash flows. The result is that reporting entities must give the information required by the indirect method, but may also give the information required by the direct method. **72**

Interest and dividend payments and receipts

The Board believes that the presentation of net cash flow from operating activities should not be affected by the capital structure of the reporting entity, that payments **73** resulting from the servicing of finance should be shown together and that the cash flow statement format should be consistent with the other primary statements including the profit and loss account wherever possible. Accordingly, interest and dividends paid are normally required to be classified under a separate heading entitled 'returns on investments and servicing of finance'. Cash flows in relation to interest rate hedging instruments such as interest rate swaps (other than those purchased or sold by a financial institution as part of its operating activities) should also be included under returns on investments and servicing of finance because these cash flows are equivalent to interest or are hedges of interest receipts or payments.

74 Interest and dividends received may result from investment activities, investment of cash and cash equivalents, or in some cases operating activities. The Board believes that, in general, interest received and paid should be shown in the same category within the cash flow statements, that dividends received should be shown under the same heading as interest and that the most appropriate category is returns on investments and servicing of finance. However, investment companies that show interest and dividends received in their profit and loss accounts prior to arriving at their operating profit should include interest and dividends received as part of their operating cash flows. Similarly banks that show interest received and paid in their profit and loss account prior to arriving at their operating profit should include interest received and paid as part of their operating cash flows and insurance companies that include interest and dividends received and certain interest paid in their profit and loss account prior to arriving at their operating profit should include the cash flows relating to those amounts as part of their operating cash flows.

Taxation

75 The taxation cash flows of a reporting entity in relation to revenue and capital profits may result from complex computations that are affected by the operating, investing and financing activities of an entity. The Board believes that it is not useful to divide taxation cash flows into constituent parts relating to the activities that gave rise to them because the apportionment will, in many cases, have to be made on an arbitrary basis. As taxation cash flows generally arise from activities in an earlier period, apportioning the taxation cash flows would not necessarily report the taxation cash flows along with the transactions that gave rise to them. In addition, the Board notes that a taxation cash flow is not normally a collection of individual cash inflows and outflows and thus analysing it in this manner would require preparers of financial statements to allocate individual cash flows over the standard headings and would not necessarily give information on the entity's underlying cash flows.

76 Accordingly, the Board believes that taxation cash flows in relation to revenue and capital profits should be disclosed in a separate section within the cash flow statement entitled taxation.

77 The existence of Value Added Tax (VAT), and other sales taxes raises the question of whether the relevant cash flows should be reported gross or net of the tax element and how the balance of tax paid to, or repaid by, the taxing authorities should be reported.

Generally sales taxes, including VAT, are payable by the ultimate consumer of the goods or services concerned. A business providing goods or services on which VAT is payable (even if at a zero rate) is generally able to reclaim the VAT incurred by it in providing those goods or services. However, businesses that make exempt supplies are unable to reclaim VAT. Between these two categories are partially exempt businesses that can reclaim part of the VAT incurred by them. **78**

The cash flows of an entity include VAT where appropriate and thus strictly the various elements of the cash flow statement should include VAT. However, this treatment does not take into account the fact that normally VAT is a short-term timing difference as far as the entity's overall cash flows are concerned and the inclusion of VAT in the cash flows may distort the allocation of cash flows to standard headings. In order to avoid this distortion and to show cash flows attributable to the reporting entity's activities, the Board believes that cash flows should be shown net of sales taxes and the net movement on the amount payable to, or receivable from, the taxing authority should be allocated to cash flows from operating activities unless a different treatment is more appropriate in the particular circumstances concerned. **79**

Taxation cash flows excluding those in respect of the reporting entity's revenue and capital profits and Value Added Tax, or other sales tax, should be included within the cash flow statement under the same standard heading as the cash flow that gave rise to the taxation cash flow unless a different treatment is more appropriate in the particular circumstances concerned. This presentation is consistent with the manner in which transactions are presented in profit and loss accounts and balance sheets. **80**

Investing activities

Investing activities are sometimes undertaken to maintain an entity's current level of operations and sometimes to expand or contract the level of operations. In addition investing activities may have consequential effects on operating activities, for example by creating a need for further working capital. The Board decided that criteria for distinguishing expenditure to expand the level of operations from expenditure to maintain the level of operations would vary from reporting entity to reporting entity and would distort the comparability provided by the standard headings. Similar problems arise in analysing changes in working capital. Reporting entities that find it useful to make such distinctions are encouraged to do so within the standard headings or by way of note. **81**

Hedging transactions

Entities may undertake hedging transactions that result in cash flows. Often the hedging transactions are carried out with investment instruments that would normally be reported as cash flows under investing activities or returns on investments and servicing of finance. However, reporting hedging cash flows separately from the transactions being hedged would not result in the cash flow statement accurately reflecting the commercial effect of the linked transactions. Accordingly, the Board believes that cash flows which result from transactions undertaken to hedge another transaction should be reported under the same standard heading as the transaction that is the subject of the hedge. **82**

Major non-cash transactions

83 Consideration for transactions may be in a form other than cash. The purpose of a cash flow statement is to report cash flows and non-cash transactions should, therefore, not be reported in a cash flow statement. However, to obtain a full picture of the alterations in financial position caused by the transactions for the period, separate disclosure of material non-cash transactions (such as a vendor placing, the exchange of major assets or the inception of a finance lease contract) is also necessary.

Identification with balance sheet figures

84 The amounts of cash and cash equivalents and amounts shown in the financing section of the cash flow statement should be reconciled to the related items in the opening and closing balance sheets for the period in order to facilitate the use of both cash flow and balance sheet information in assessing the liquidity, viability and financial adaptability of the reporting entity.

ILLUSTRATIVE EXAMPLES

These illustrative examples are for general guidance and do not form part of the Financial Reporting Standard. In particular, the analyses of net cash flows from operating activities under the direct method, the subtotalling in the reconciliation of operating profit to net cash flow from operating activity for a bank, and the disclosure of total liquid assets for an insurance company, shown in the examples in italics, are optional disclosures.

This section sets out examples of cash flow statements for six types of reporting entity. The examples, which are for illustrative purposes only, do not include comparative figures, except where they are required for a better understanding of the example.

1 Single company
2 Group, including equity accounted entities, with acquisitions and a disposal during the year
3 Property investment company
4 Investment company
5 Bank
6 Insurance company

ILLUSTRATIVE EXAMPLE 1 – SINGLE COMPANY

XYZ LIMITED
Cash flow statement for the year ended 31 March 1992

	£'000	£'000
Net cash inflow from operating activities		6,889
Returns on investments and servicing of finance		
Interest received	3,011	
Interest paid	(12)	
Dividends paid	(2,417)	
Net cash inflow from returns on investments and servicing of finance		582
Taxation		
Corporation tax paid (including advance corporation tax)	(2,922)	
Tax paid		(2,922)
Investing activities		
Payments to acquire intangible fixed assets	(71)	
Payments to acquire tangible fixed assets	(1,496)	
Receipts from sales of tangible fixed assets	42	
Net cash outflow from investing activities		(1,525)
Net cash inflow before financing		3,024
Financing		
Issue of ordinary share capital	211	
Repurchase of debenture loan	(149)	
Expenses paid in connection with share issues	(5)	
Net cash inflow from financing		57
Increase in cash and cash equivalents		3,081

Notes to the cash flow statement

RECONCILIATION OF OPERATING PROFIT TO NET CASH INFLOW FROM OPERATING ACTIVITIES 1

	£'000
Operating profit	6,022
Depreciation charges	893
Loss on sale of tangible fixed assets	6
Increase in stocks	(194)
Increase in debtors	(72)
Increase in creditors	234
Net cash inflow from operating activities	6,889

ANALYSIS OF CHANGES IN CASH AND CASH EQUIVALENTS DURING THE YEAR 2

	£'000
Balance at 1 April 1991	21,373
Net cash inflow	3,081
Balance at 31 March 1992	24,454

ANALYSIS OF THE BALANCES OF CASH AND CASH EQUIVALENTS AS SHOWN IN THE BALANCE SHEET 3

	1992 £'000	1991 £'000	Change in year £'000
Cash at bank and in hand	529	681	(152)
Short-term investments	23,936	20,700	3,236
Bank overdrafts	(11)	(8)	(3)
	24,454	21,373	3,081

ANALYSIS OF CHANGES IN FINANCING DURING THE YEAR 4

	Share capital £'000	Debenture loan £'000
Balance at 1 April 1991	27,411	156
Cash inflow/(outflow) from financing	211	(149)
Profit on repurchase of debenture loan for less than its book value		(7)
Balance at 31 March 1992	27,622	–

ILLUSTRATIVE EXAMPLE 2 — GROUP

XYZ GROUP PLC
Cash flow statement for the year ended 31 March 1992

	£'000	£'000
Operating activities		
Cash received from customers	*195,016*	
Cash payments to suppliers	*(109,225)*	
Cash paid to and on behalf of employees	*(56,434)*	
Other cash payments	*(12,345)*	
Net cash inflow from continuing operating activities	*17,012*	
Net cash outflow in respect of discontinued activities and reorganisation costs	*(990)*	
Net cash inflow from operating activities		16,022
Returns on investments and servicing of finance		
Interest received	508	
Interest paid	(2,389)	
Interest element of finance lease rentals payments	(373)	
Dividend received from associated undertaking	15	
Dividends paid	(2,606)	
Net cash outflow from returns on investments and servicing of finance		(4,845)
Taxation		
UK corporation tax paid	(2,880)	
Overseas tax paid	(7)	
Tax paid		(2,887)
Investing activities		
Purchase of tangible fixed assets	(3,512)	
Purchase of subsidiary undertakings (net of cash and cash equivalents acquired) (See note 7)	(18,221)	
Sale of plant and machinery	1,052	
Sale of business (See note 8)	4,208	
Sale of trade investment	1,595	
Net cash outflows in respect of unsuccessful takeover bid	(3,811)	
Net cash outflow from investing activities		(18,689)
Net cash outflow before financing		(10,399)

	£'000	£'000
Financing		
Issue of ordinary share capital	(49)	
New secured loan repayable in 1995	(1,091)	
New unsecured loan repayable in 1993	(1,442)	
New short-term loans	(2,006)	
Repayment of amounts borrowed	847	
Capital element of finance lease rental payments	1,342	
Net cash inflow from financing		(2,399)
Decrease in cash and cash equivalents		(8,000)
		(10,399)

Notes to the cash flow statement

1 RECONCILIATION OF OPERATING PROFIT TO NET CASH INFLOW FROM OPERATING ACTIVITIES

	£'000
Operating profit	20,249
Depreciation charges	3,158
Profit on sale of tangible fixed assets	(50)
Increase in stocks	(12,263)
Increase in debtors	(3,754)
Increase in creditors	9,672
Net cash inflow from continuing operating activities	17,012
Net cash outflow in respect of discontinued activities and reorganisation costs	(990)
Net cash inflow from operating activities	16,022

2 ANALYSIS OF CHANGES IN CASH AND CASH EQUIVALENTS DURING THE YEAR

	£'000
Balance at 1 April 1991	78
Net cash outflow before adjustments for the effect of foreign exchange rate changes	(8,000)
Effect of foreign exchange rate changes	(102)
Balance at 31 March 1992	(8,024)

3 ANALYSIS OF THE BALANCES OF CASH AND CASH EQUIVALENTS AS SHOWN IN THE BALANCE SHEET

	1992	1991	Change in year
	£'000	£'000	£'000
Cash at bank and in hand	1,041	1,279	(238)
Bank overdrafts	(9,065)	(1,201)	(7,864)
	(8,024)	78	(8,102)

ANALYSIS OF CHANGES IN FINANCING DURING THE YEAR 4

	Share capital (including premium) £'000	Loans and finance lease obligations £'000
Balance at 1 April 1991	10,334	7,589
Cash inflows from financing	49	2,350
Shares issued for non-cash consideration	9,519	
Loans and finance lease obligations of subsidiary undertakings acquired during the year	3,817	
Inception of finance lease contracts		2,845
Balance at 31 March 1992	19,902	16,601

[*Note to preparers of financial statements*

The disclosures set out below in respect of non-cash transactions may be combined with information disclosed elsewhere in the financial statements, eg. the disclosure in respect of subsidiary undertakings acquired during the year could be combined with the disclosures required by paragraph 13(5) of Schedule 4A to the Companies Act 1985.]

MAJOR NON-CASH TRANSACTIONS 5

(a) During the year the group entered into finance lease arrangements in respect of assets with a total capital value at the inception of the leases of £2,845,000.

(b) Part of the consideration for the purchases of subsidiary undertakings and the sale of a business that occurred during the year comprised shares and loan notes respectively. Further details of the acquisitions and the disposal are set out below:

PURCHASE OF SUBSIDIARY UNDERTAKINGS 6

	£'000
Net assets acquired	
Tangible fixed assets	12,194
Investments	1
Stocks	9,384
Debtors	13,856
Taxation recoverable	1,309
Cash at bank and in hand	1,439
Creditors	(21,715)
Bank overdrafts	(6,955)
Loans and finance leases	(3,817)
Deferred taxation	(165)
Minority shareholders' interests	(9)
	5,522
Goodwill	16,702
	22,224

Satisfied by	
Shares allotted	9,519
Cash	12,705
	22,224

The subsidiary undertakings acquired during the year contributed £1,502,000 to the group's net operating cash flows, paid £1,308,000 in respect of net returns on investments and servicing of finance, paid £522,000 in respect of taxation and utilised £2,208,000 for investing activities.

7 ANALYSIS OF THE NET OUTFLOW OF CASH AND CASH EQUIVALENTS IN RESPECT OF THE PURCHASE OF SUBSIDIARY UNDERTAKINGS

	£'000
Cash consideration	12,705
Cash at bank and in hand acquired	(1,439)
Bank overdrafts of acquired subsidiary undertakings	6,955
Net outflow of cash and cash equivalents in respect of the purchase of subsidiaries	18,221

8 SALE OF BUSINESS

	£'000
Net assets disposed of	
Fixed assets	775
Stocks	5,386
Debtors	474
	6,635
Loss on disposal	(1,227)
	5,408
Satisfied by	
Loan notes	1,200
Cash	4,208
	5,408

The business sold during the year contributed £200,000 to the group's net operating cash flows, paid £252,000 in respect of net returns on investments and servicing of finance, paid £145,000 in respect of taxation and utilised £209,000 for investing activities.

ILLUSTRATIVE EXAMPLE 3 — PROPERTY INVESTMENT COMPANY

XYZ PROPERTY INVESTMENTS LIMITED
Cash flow statement for the year ended 31 March 1992

	£m	£m
Operating activities		
Cash received from tenants	*263.8*	
Cash payments in respect of direct property costs	*(14.4)*	
Cash paid to and on behalf of employees	*(9.0)*	
Other cash payments	*(8.9)*	
Net cash inflow from operating activities		231.5
Returns on investments and servicing of finance		
Interest received	45.1	
Interest paid	(111.1)	
Dividends paid	(75.7)	
Net cash outflow from returns on investments and servicing of finance		(141.7)
Taxation		
Corporation tax paid	(55.3)	
Tax paid		(55.3)
Investing activities		
Purchase of property	(361.6)	
Sales of property	80.6	
Purchase of plant and machinery and fixtures & fittings	(1.2)	
Sale of plant and machinery and fixtures & fittings	0.1	
Other cash outflows from investing activities	(0.3)	
Net cash outflow from investing activities		(282.4)
Net cash outflow before financing		(247.9)
Financing		
Issue of ordinary share capital	(0.9)	
Issue of Convertible Bonds	(175.0)	
Issue of Unsecured Loan Notes	(3.9)	
Repayments of debenture stocks	11.9	
Amounts paid in respect of the expenses of the issues of Convertible Bonds and Unsecured Loan Notes	3.3	
Net cash inflow from financing		(164.6)
Decrease in cash and cash equivalents		(83.3)
		(247.9)

Notes to the cash flow statement

1 RECONCILIATION OF OPERATING PROFIT TO NET CASH INFLOW FROM OPERATING ACTIVITIES

	£m
Operating profit	241.1
Depreciation charges	1.5
Increase in debtors	(32.5)
Increase in creditors	21.0
Effect of other deferrals and accruals of operating activity cash flow	0.4
Net cash inflow from operating activities	231.5

2 ANALYSIS OF CHANGES IN CASH AND CASH EQUIVALENTS DURING THE YEAR

	£m
Balance at 1 April 1991	350.5
Net cash outflow	(83.3)
Balance at 31 March 1992	267.2

3 ANALYSIS OF THE BALANCES OF CASH AND CASH EQUIVALENTS AS SHOWN IN THE BALANCE SHEET

	1992 £m	1991 £m	Change in year £m
Cash at bank and in hand	0.4	3.4	(3.0)
Short-term deposits	266.8	347.1	(80.3)
	267.2	350.5	(83.3)

4 ANALYSIS OF CHANGES IN FINANCING DURING THE YEAR

	Share capital (including premium) £m	Loans including convertible bonds £m
Financing at 1 April 1991	503.7	1,113.5
Cash inflows from financing	0.9	167.0
Financing at 31 March 1992	504.6	1,280.5

ILLUSTRATIVE EXAMPLE 4 — INVESTMENT COMPANY

XYZ INVESTMENT COMPANY PLC

Cash flow statement for the year ended 31 March 1992

	£'000	£'000
Operating activities		
Cash received from investments	*9,491*	
Interest received	*2,870*	
Investment management fees paid	*(1,057)*	
Cash paid to and on behalf of directors	*(35)*	
Other cash payments	*(720)*	
Net cash inflow from operating activities		10,549
Returns on investments and servicing of finance		
Interest paid	(114)	
Dividends paid	(6,642)	
Net cash outflow from returns on investments and servicing of finance		(6,756)
Taxation		
UK corporation tax paid	(1,286)	
Overseas tax paid	(362)	
Total tax paid		(1,648)
Investing activities		
Purchase of investments	(149,770)	
Sales of investments	114,097	
Net cash outflow from investing activities		(35,673)
Net cash outflow before financing		(33,528)
Financing		
Issue of Equity Index Unsecured Loan Stock 2004	(60,000)	
Expenses paid in respect of the loan stock issue	1,162	
Net cash inflow from financing		(58,838)
Increase in cash and cash equivalents		25,310
		(33,528)

Notes to the cash flow statement

1 RECONCILIATION OF OPERATING PROFIT TO NET CASH INFLOW FROM OPERATING ACTIVITIES

	£'000
Income before interest payable and taxation	12,475
Increase in accrued income	(46)
Decrease in other debtors	243
Decrease in creditors	(23)
Tax on franked investment income included within income from UK companies	(2,100)
Net cash inflow from operating activities	10,549

2 ANALYSIS OF CHANGES IN CASH AND CASH EQUIVALENTS DURING THE YEAR

	£'000
Balance at 1 April 1991	10,359
Net cash inflow	25,310
Balance at 31 March 1992	35,669

3 CASH AND CASH EQUIVALENTS

The balance for cash and cash equivalents is shown in the balance sheet as 'Cash at bank and in hand' £35,669,000 (1991 – £10,359,000).

4 ANALYSIS OF CHANGES IN FINANCING DURING THE YEAR

	Share capital £'000	Loans including equity index loan stock £'000
Balance at 1 April 1991	55,902	476
Cash inflow from financing		60,000
Change in value of Equity Index Loan Stock		(253)
Balance at 31 March 1992	55,902	60,223

ILLUSTRATIVE EXAMPLE 5 — BANK

XYZ INTERNATIONAL BANK LIMITED
Cash flow statement for the year ended 31 March 1992

	£m	£m
Net cash inflow from operating activities		1,106.9
Returns on investments and servicing of finance		
Dividends received from associated undertakings	9.9	
Ordinary dividends paid	(57.2)	
Preference dividends paid	(10.4)	
Dividends paid to minority shareholders in subsidiary undertaking	(0.2)	
Net cash outflows from returns on investments and servicing of finance		(57.9)
Taxation		
Corporation tax paid	(73.8)	
Overseas tax paid	(14.2)	
Total tax paid		(88.0)
Investing activities		
Purchase of trade investments	(14.7)	
Sale of trade investments	5.7	
Investment in associated undertaking	(56.1)	
Sale of investment in associated undertaking	71.2	
Purchase of tangible fixed assets	(121.4)	
Sales of tangible fixed assets	40.1	
Net cash outflow from investing activities		(75.2)
Net cash inflow before financing		885.8
Financing		
Issue of ordinary share capital	(6.3)	
Repayments of loan capital	12.3	
Net cash outflow from financing		6.0
Increase in cash and cash equivalents		879.8
		885.8

Notes to the cash flow statement

1 RECONCILIATION OF OPERATING PROFIT TO NET CASH INFLOW FROM OPERATING ACTIVITIES

	£m
Operating profit	241.4
Increase in interest receivable and prepaid expenses	(161.2)
Increase in interest payable and accrued expenses	118.1
Provision for loan losses	20.8
Release of provisions against rescheduled country debt	(50.7)
Depreciation	53.2
Profit on sale of tangible fixed assets	(0.9)
Effect of other deferrals and accruals of operating activity cash flow	1.1
Net cash flow from trading activities	221.8
Net increase in deposits and commercial paper	2,542.8
Net increase in loans to customers	(1,419.1)
Net change in finance lease balances receivable	(241.2)
Decrease in securities held (other than those treated as investment activities)	39.9
Increase in collections on other banks	(18.7)
Net increase in placings with banks (repayable beyond 3 months)	(18.6)
Net cash inflow from operating activities	1,106.9

2 ANALYSIS OF CHANGES IN CASH AND CASH EQUIVALENTS DURING THE YEAR

	£m
Balance at 1 April 1991	6,322.9
Net cash inflow before adjustments for the effect of foreign exchange rate changes	879.8
Effect of foreign exchange rate changes	(142.3)
Balance at 31 March 199	7,060.4

3 ANALYSIS OF THE BALANCES OF CASH AND CASH EQUIVALENTS AS SHOWN IN THE BALANCE SHEET

	1992 £m	1991 £m	Change in year £m
Coin, bank notes and balances with central banks	912.5	736.9	175.6
Money at call and short notice	5,322.4	4,781.6	540.8
Marketable bills of exchange	562.5	584.8	(22.3)
Certificates of deposit	263.0	219.6	43.4
	7,060.4	6,322.9	737.5

The group is required to maintain balances with the Bank of England which, at 31 March 1992, amounted to £54 million (1991 — £43.3 million).

Certain subsidiary undertakings of the group are required by law to maintain average reserve balances with the Federal Reserve Bank in the United States of America. Such reserve balances amounted to $30.4 million at 31 March 1992 (1991 — $28.6 million).

ANALYSIS OF CHANGES IN FINANCING DURING THE YEAR **4**

	Share capital (including premium)	Loan capital
	£'000	£'000
Balance at 1 April 1991	435.3	1,248.1
Effect of foreign exchange differences		(115.7)
Cash inflow/(outflow) from financing	6.3	(12.3)
Other movements	(0.1)	
Balance at 31 March 1992	441.5	1,120.1

ILLUSTRATIVE EXAMPLE 6 — INSURANCE COMPANY

XYZ INSURANCE COMPANY LIMITED

Cash flow statement for the year ended 31 March 1992

	£m	£m
Operating activities		
Premiums received from customers	*2,410.8*	
Reinsurance premiums paid	*(400.3)*	
Claims paid	*(1,634.2)*	
Reinsurance receipts in respect of claims	*350.3*	
Cash received from long-term funds	*85.3*	
Cash paid to and on behalf of employees	*(127.5)*	
Interest received	*152.5*	
Dividends received	*166.3*	
Interest paid	*(22.0)*	
Other operating cash payments	*(656.8)*	
Net cash inflow from operating activities		324.4
Returns on investments and servicing of finance		
Interest paid	(20.0)	
Dividends paid	(79.2)	
Net cash outflow from returns on investments and servicing of finance		(99.2)
Taxation		
Corporation tax paid (including advance corporation tax)	(132.5)	
Tax paid		(132.5)
Investing activities		
Purchase of liquid investments (other than cash equivalents)	(382.1)	
Purchase of other investments (other than cash equivalents)	(50.0)	
Sale of liquid investments (other than cash equivalents)	363.8	
Sale of other investments (other than cash equivalents)	48.0	
Purchase of tangible fixed assets	(16.7)	
Net cash outflow from investing activities		(37.0)
Net cash inflow before financing		55.7
Financing		
Issue of ordinary share capital	6.1	
Repayment of long-term loan	(60.1)	
Net cash outflow from financing		(54.0)
Increase in cash and cash equivalents		1.7

Notes to the cash flow statement

RECONCILIATION OF OPERATING PROFIT TO NET CASH INFLOW FROM OPERATING ACTIVITIES 1

	£m
Operating profit	181.8
Depreciation charges	12.0
Increase in debtors	(90.4)
Increase in amount owed by long-term funds	(16.7)
Increase in unearned premiums	47.2
Increase in claims provisions	206.3
Increase in creditors	12.2
Tax on franked investment income included within operating income	(28.0)
Net cash inflow from operating activities	324.4

ANALYSIS OF CHANGES IN CASH AND CASH EQUIVALENTS AND OTHER LIQUID INVESTMENTS DURING THE YEAR 2

	Cash and cash equivalents	*Other liquid investments*	*Total*
Total	*£m*	*£m*	*£m*
Balance at 1 April 1991	23.7	*3,720.4*	*3,744.1*
Net cash inflow	1.7		*1.7*
Purchase of investments		*382.1*	*382.1*
Sale of investments		*(363.8)*	*(363.8)*
Change in market value		*331.3*	*331.3*
Balance at 31 March 1992	25.4	*4,070.0*	*4,095.4*

ANALYSIS OF THE BALANCES OF CASH AND CASH EQUIVALENTS AND OTHER LIQUID INVESTMENTS AS SHOWN IN THE BALANCE SHEET 3

	1992 £m	1991 £m	Change in year £m
Cash at bank and in hand	59.9	34.6	25.3
Bank overdrafts	(34.5)	(10.9)	(23.6)
Total cash and cash equivalents	25.4	23.7	1.7
Other liquid investments	4,070.0	3,720.4	349.6
	4,095.4	3,744.1	351.3

ANALYSIS OF CHANGES IN FINANCING DURING THE YEAR

	Share capital (including premium)	Long-term loan
	£m	£m
Financing at 1 April 1991	296.5	346.2
Cash inflow/(outflow) from financing	6.1	(60.1)
Financing at 31 March 1992	302.6	286.1

THE DEVELOPMENT OF THE STANDARD

This section does not form part of the Financial Reporting Standard.

Summary of the principal changes from Statement of Standard Accounting Practice NO. 10 — 'Statements of source and application of funds'

Statement of Standard Accounting Practice NO. 10 (SSAP 10), issued July 1975, sought to establish the practice of providing statements of source and application of funds as a part of audited financial statements and to lay down a minimum standard of disclosure in such statements. 1

The objective of the statement of source and application of funds required by SSAP 10 was to show the manner in which the operations of a reporting entity had been financed and in which its financial resources had been used. The information disclosed in the statement is essentially a rearrangement of the information given in the profit and loss (or income and expenditure) account and balance sheet. 2

SSAP 10 was drafted to allow preparers of accounts flexibility in the preparation of funds flow statements. It did not provide a definition of funds or set out a basic structure for a statement. It did, however, specify certain key information which was required to be given in the statement and also provided two examples for general guidance in an appendix, which did not form part of the statement of standard accounting practice. 3

The FRS requires reporting entities to report cash flows rather than accrual based funds flows and the basic structure of the cash flow statement is prescribed. 4

SSAP 10 applied to all financial statements intended to give a true and fair view of the financial position and profit or loss (or income and expenditure) other than those entities with turnover or gross income of less than £25,000 per annum although consideration was to be given to providing the statement for small entities whenever it was desirable. The FRS allows exemptions to a much larger number of reporting entities including most small reporting entities and wholly owned subsidiary undertakings. 5

SSAP 10 allowed the purchase or disposal of subsidiary undertakings to be dealt with either by showing the consideration paid or received as a separate item within the statement of source and application of funds or by reflecting the effects of the acquisition or disposal on the separate assets and liabilities dealt with in the statement. The FRS requires purchase or sales consideration (unless merger accounting is used) to be shown under investing activities and the method reflecting the effects on the separate assets and liabilities, the so-called 'line by line' method, is not permitted. 6

Summary of the principal changes from Exposure Draft NO. 54 — 'Cash flow statements'

The proposed Statement of Standard Accounting Practice set out in Exposure Draft No. 54 (ED54), issued in July 1990 by the ASC, sought to replace the statement of source 1 and application of funds required by SSAP 10 with a cash flow statement and to set out a general format for such a statement.

2 The requirements of the FRS have been based upon ED54 and the comments received on it together with the Board's own research, consultation and careful deliberation about the benefits and costs of providing the information. The vast majority of commentators on ED54 were supportive of the overall approach adopted. The principal differences in the requirements of the FRS and ED54 are set out below.

Scope

3 ED54 proposed that the standard should apply to all financial statements intended to give a true and fair view of the financial position and profit or loss (or income and expenditure) other than those entities that do not report under the Companies Act and which have turnover or revenue of less than £25,000 per annum. This scope, which allowed fewer exemptions than those allowed by SSAP 10, was criticised by some commentators, who believed that small companies and wholly owned subsidiary undertakings subsidiaries should be exempted in certain circumstances. The FRS allows exemptions from its requirements to a much larger number of reporting entities including most small reporting entities and wholly owned subsidiary undertakings.

Classification of cash flows

4 ED54 identified the same major classes of activity (ie. operating, investing and financing) as the FRS, but the FRS requires certain cash flows to be reported differently from the proposals contained in ED54 as explained in paragraphs 5 to 8 below. In addition the FRS requires cash flows arising from financing activities to be divided into two separate categories; cash flows resulting from movements of principal amounts of finance, and returns on investments and servicing of finance.

Reporting net cash flow from operating activities

5 ED54 considered two methods, direct and indirect, for reporting net cash flow from operating activities and allowed either method to be used. The Board notes that many users of financial statements require the reconciliation between operating profit and net cash flow from operating activities. Some respondents to ED54 stated that they believed that it would be costly to implement the direct method as they did not currently collect information in such a form directly from their accounting systems. Particular problems would be encountered by multinational groups implementing the direct method. Accordingly, the FRS allows the net cash flow from operating activities to be reported on a net or gross basis, but, in addition, a note to the cash flow statement should give a reconciliation between the reporting entity's operating profit and the net cash flow from operating activities. Thus reporting entities must give the information required by the indirect method, but may also give the information required by the direct method and the Board encourages reporting entities to give a breakdown of their cash flows under the direct method in those circumstances where the benefits to users of the information outweigh the costs of providing it.

Interest and dividend receipts and payments

ED54 required interest received and paid to be included under operating activities. However, there was no consensus in the comments on ED54 concerning the treatment of interest received and paid in a cash flow statement and in order to present the cash flow information in a useful way the FRS requires that interest received and paid should normally be shown under returns on investments and servicing of finance. **6**

ED54 drew a distinction between interest paid, which is contractual, and dividends paid, which are discretionary, although both are paid to providers of capital. It proposed that dividends paid be included under the reporting entity's financing activities and dividends received under operating activities. However, there was no consensus in the comments on ED54 concerning the treatment of dividends received and paid in a cash flow statement and in order to present cash flow information in a useful way that is consistent with the presentation of receipts and payments of interest the FRS does not make such a distinction and requires both dividends received and dividends paid to be shown under returns on investments and servicing of finance. **7**

Taxation

ED54 required taxation cash flows in relation to income and capital gains to be shown as operating activities unless material elements of the cash flows related to another activity, when an apportionment could be made. Many commentators on ED54 did not agree with this presentation, but preferred that taxation be disclosed separately within its own section in order to present the information in a more useful way or to avoid arbitrary apportionments. The Board agrees with these views and accordingly the FRS requires such cash flows to be shown in a separate section of the statement entitled 'taxation'. **8**

ED54 required cash flows to be disclosed inclusive of any attributable Value Added Tax, or other sales taxes, but the FRS requires cash flows to be reported net of any such taxes unless the tax is not recoverable by the reporting entity, when cash flows should normally include the irrecoverable tax. There was no consensus in the comments on ED54 on the treatment of Value Added Tax, although some commentators believed that problems would be encountered in the production and interpretation of tax inclusive cash flows. **9**

Cash or net debt

Many commentators on the exposure draft stated that they believed that a statement that analysed the movement in a reporting entity's net cash or debt position would be more useful than one which reported the movement in cash and cash equivalents alone. These commentators noted that the cash position of an entity must be considered along with obligations that the entity may have. The Board agrees with these comments, but believes that the main focus of the cash flow statement should still be cash flows. However, by splitting the servicing of finance from the movements in principal amounts of finance, requiring a total giving the net cash flow before financing and by requiring a reconciliation of the items within the financing section of the statement to **10** the opening and closing balance sheets the Board believes that the information required by these commentators is given.

[FRS 2]
Accounting for subsidiary undertakings

(Issued July 1992)

Contents

Accounting for subsidiary undertakings

SUMMARY

Financing Reporting Standard NO. 2 – 'Accounting for Subsidiary Undertakings' (the FRS sets out the conditions under which an undertaking that is the parent undertaking of other undertakings (its subsidiary undertakings) should prepare consolidated financial statements. The FRS also sets out the manner in which consolidated financial statements are to be prepared. The purpose of consolidated financial statements is to provide financial information about the economic activities of a group. The Companies Act 1985, as amended by the Companies Act 1989 (the amended Act is referred to as 'the Act') defines a parent undertaking and its subsidiary undertakings that together make up a group. The FRS adopts these definitions. a

The FRS supersedes Statement of Standard Accounting Practice NO. 14 — 'Group accounts' and the Board's 'Interim Statement: Consolidated Accounts', except for the following paragraphs of the Interim Statement: paragraphs 32 and 33, A9 and A10, on joint ventures and paragraphs 38, A13 – A18 and A23 dealing with the amendments to SSAP 1 'Accounting for Associated Companies'. b

The FRS applies to all parent undertakings. A parent undertaking that does not report under the Act should comply with the requirements of the FRS except to the extent that these are not permitted by any statutory framework under which the undertaking reports. c

A parent undertaking should prepare consolidated financial statements for its group in accordance with the standard accounting practice set out in the FRS unless it uses one of the exemptions permitted by the Act and set out in paragraph 21 of the FRS. d

The Act and the FRS exempt a parent undertaking from preparing consolidated financial statements if: e

(i) its group is small or medium-sized and not an ineligible group as defined in section 248; or
(ii) it is a wholly-owned or majority-owned subsidiary undertaking and its immediate parent undertaking is established under the law of a member state of the European Community. Exemption is conditional on compliance with certain further conditions in section 228; or
(iii) all of its subsidiary undertakings are permitted or required to be excluded from consolidation by section 229.

The consolidated financial statements should be prepared by consolidating financial information for the parent undertaking and all its subsidiary undertakings, except for any subsidiary undertakings that are to be excluded from consolidation by virtue of the requirements of the Act and the FRS. f

g A subsidiary undertaking is to be excluded from consolidation if:

(i) severe long-term restrictions substantially hinder the exercise of the parent undertaking's rights over the subsidiary undertaking's assets or management; or
(ii) the group's interest in the subsidiary undertaking is held exclusively with a view to subsequent resale and the subsidiary undertaking has not previously been consolidated; or
(iii) the subsidiary undertaking's activities are so different from those of other undertakings to be included in the consolidation that its inclusion would be incompatible with the obligation to give a true and fair view.

The Act permits rather than requires exclusion in cases (i) and (ii) above. The FRS requires exclusion in these circumstances because the same conditions that justify permitting exclusion also make consolidation inappropriate. In addition, the FRS requires the circumstances in which subsidiary undertakings are to be excluded from consolidation to be interpreted strictly. It is important that only those subsidiary undertakings whose consolidation would be inappropriate are excluded from consolidation so that consolidated financial statements reflect in full the resources, obligations and results of the group.

h The FRS requires additional disclosures for subsidiary undertakings excluded from consolidation and requires them to be accounted for as follows.

(i) Subsidiary undertakings excluded from consolidation because of severe long-term restrictions are to be treated as fixed asset investments. They are to be included at their carrying amount when the restrictions came into force, subject to any write down for permanent diminution in value, and no further accruals are to be made for profits or losses of those subsidiary undertakings, unless the parent undertaking still exercises significant influence. In the latter case they are to be treated as associated undertakings.
(ii) Subsidiary undertakings excluded from consolidation because they are held exclusively for resale and have not previously been consolidated are to be included as current assets at the lower of cost and net realisable value.
(iii) Subsidiary undertakings excluded from consolidation because of their different activities are to be accounted for using the equity method as required by the Act.

i Minority interests in total should be reported separately in the consolidated balance sheet and profit and loss account. When an entity becomes a subsidiary undertaking the assets and liabilities attributable to its minority interest should be included on the same basis as those attributable to the interest held by the parent and other subsidiary undertakings. The effect of this for an acquisition is that all the subsidiary undertaking's identifiable assets and liabilities are included at fair value as required by the Act. No goodwill should be attributed to the minority interest.

j Intra-group transactions may result in profits or losses being included in the book value of assets to be included in the consolidation; the FRS requires the elimination in full of any such profits or losses because, for the group as a whole, no profits or losses have arisen.

Uniform group accounting policies should generally be used in preparing the consolidated financial statements; in exceptional cases different policies may be used with disclosure. **k**

The financial statements of all subsidiary undertakings to be used in preparing consolidated financial statements should have the same financial year end and be for the same accounting period as those of the parent undertaking of the group. Where the financial year of a subsidiary undertaking differs from that of the parent undertaking of the group, interim financial statements for that subsidiary undertaking prepared to the parent undertaking's accounting date should be used. If this is impracticable, earlier financial statements of the subsidiary undertaking may be used, provided they are prepared for a financial year that ended not more than three months earlier. **l**

Changes in membership of a group occur on the date control passes, whether by a transaction or other event. Changes in the membership of the group during the period should be disclosed. **m**

When a subsidiary undertaking is acquired the FRS requires its identifiable assets and liabilities to be brought into the consolidation at their fair values at the date that undertaking becomes a subsidiary undertaking, even if the acquisition has been made in stages. When a group increases its interest in an undertaking that is already its subsidiary undertaking, the identifiable assets and liabilities of that subsidiary undertaking should be revalued to fair value and goodwill arising on the increase in interest should be calculated by reference to that fair value. This revaluation is not required if the difference between fair values and carrying amounts of the identifiable assets and liabilities attributable to the increase in stake is not material. **n**

The effect of consolidating the parent and its subsidiary undertakings may be that aggregation obscures useful information about the different undertakings and activities included in the consolidated financial statements. Parent undertakings are encouraged to give segmental analysis to provide readers of consolidated financial statements with useful information on the different risks and rewards, growth and prospects of the different parts of the group. The specification of such analysis, however, falls outside the scope of the FRS. **o**

The accounting practices set out in the FRS should be adopted as soon as possible and regarded as standard for periods ending on or after 23 December 1992, except for Republic of Ireland companies, who should regard it as standard after the date of application of the Irish legislation implementing the European Community Seventh Directive.* Such Irish companies should adopt the accounting practices in the FRS as soon as possible after the enactment of the implementing legislation. **p**

***Editor's note:** *Enacted in 1992. See paragraph 98 of this FRS.*

OBJECTIVE

1 The objective of this FRS is to require parent undertakings to provide financial information about the economic activities of their groups by preparing consolidated financial statements.* These statements are intended to present financial information about a parent undertaking and its subsidiary undertakings as a single economic entity to show the economic resources controlled by the group, the obligations of the group and the results the group achieves with its resources.†

**'Financial statements' is the term used in the FRS to mean the same as the term 'accounts' used in the Companies Acts.*

†The Companies Act 1985, as amended by the 1989 Act, contains detailed provisions relating to consolidated financial statements. The FRS considers the application of the Act and adds to its provisions where necessary.

DEFINITIONS

The following definitions apply for the purposes of the FRS and in particular the statement of standard accounting practice set out in paragraphs 18 to 56.

The terms defined below which are also defined in the Act have the same meaning in the FRS as in the Act, notwithstanding that in some cases the FRS definition is a summary or explanation rather than a repetition of the definition in the Act. The definitions should therefore be interpreted by reference to the full provisions of the Act. The marginal notes give the main references in the Act. References to sections and schedules are to those of the Act unless otherwise stated.

The Act:- **2**
Companies Act 1985 as amended by the Companies Act 1989.

Companies (Northern Ireland) Order 1986:- **3**
Companies (Northern Ireland) Order 1986 as amended by the Companies (Northern Ireland) Order 1990 and the Companies (No 2) (Northern Ireland) Order 1990.

Consolidated financial statements:- **4**
The financial statements of a group prepared by consolidation.

Consolidation:- **5**
The process of adjusting and combining financial information from the individual financial statements of a parent undertaking and its subsidiary undertaking to prepare consolidated financial statements that present financial information for the group as a single economic entity.

Control:- **6**
The ability of an undertaking to direct the financial and operating policies of another undertaking with a view to gaining economic benefits from its activities.

Dominant influence:- **7**
Influence that can be exercised to achieve the operating and financial policies desired by the holder of the influence, notwithstanding the rights or influence of any other party.

[*From 10ASch4(1)*]

(a) In the context of paragraph 14(c) and section 258(2)(c) *the right to exercise a dominant influence* means that the holder has a right to give directions with respect to the operating and financial policies of another undertaking with which its directors are obliged to comply, whether or not they are for the benefit of that undertaking.

[*FRS defining phrase used in s258(4)(a)*]

(b) *The actual exercise of dominant influence* is the exercise of an influence that achieves the result that the operating and financial policies of the undertaking influenced are set in accordance with the wishes of the holder of the influence and for the holder's benefit whether or not those wishes are explicit. The actual exercise of dominant influence is identified by its effect in practice rather than by the way in which it is exercised.

8 *Equity method:-*
A method of accounting for an investment that brings into the consolidated profit and loss account the investor's share of the investment undertaking's results and that records the investment in the consolidated balance sheet at the investor's share of the investment undertaking's net assets including any goodwill arising to the extent that it has not previously been written off.

9 *Group:-*
A parent undertaking and its subsidiary undertakings. [*From s262*]

10 *Interest held on a long-term basis:-* [FRS *defining phrase used in s260*]
An interest which is held other than *exclusively with a view to subsequent resale.*

11 *Interest held exclusively with a view to subsequent resale:-* [FRS *defining phrase used in s229(3)(c)*]

(a) An interest for which a purchaser has been identified or is being sought, and which is reasonably expected to be disposed of within approximately one year of its date of acquisition; or
(b) an interest that was acquired as a result of the enforcement of a security, unless the interest has become part of the continuing activities of the group or the holder acts as if it intends the interest to become so.

12 *Managed on a unified basis:-* [FRS *defining phrase used in s258(4)(b)*]
Two or more undertakings are managed on a unified basis if the whole of the operations of the undertakings are integrated and they are managed as a single unit. Unified management does not arise solely because one undertaking manages another.

13 *Minority interest in a subsidiary undertaking:-* [*From 4ASch 17*]
The interest in a subsidiary undertaking included in the consolidation that is attributable to the shares held by or on behalf of persons other than the parent undertaking and its subsidiary undertakings.

14 *Parent undertaking and subsidiary undertaking:-* [*From s258 and 10ASch*]
An undertaking is the parent undertaking of another undertaking (a subsidiary undertaking) if any of the following apply.

(a) It holds a majority of the voting rights in the undertaking. [*From s258(2)(a)*]
(b) It is a member of the undertaking and has the right to appoint or

[From s258(2)(b) and 10ASch3] remove directors holding a majority of the voting rights at meetings of the board on all, or substantially all, matters.

(c) It has the right to exercise a dominant influence over the undertaking:

[From s258(2)(c) and 10ASch4] (i) by virtue of provisions contained in the undertaking's memorandum or articles; or

(ii) by virtue of a control contract. *[From 10ASch4(2)]* The control contract must be in writing and be of a kind authorised by the memorandum or articles of the controlled undertaking. It must also be permitted by the law under which that undertaking is established.

[From s258(2)(d)] (d) It is a member of the undertaking and controls alone, pursuant to an agreement with other shareholders or members, a majority of the voting rights in the undertaking.

[From s258(4)] (e) It has a participating interest in the undertaking and:

(i) it actually exercises a dominant influence over the undertaking; or

(ii) it and the undertaking are managed on a unified basis.

[From s258(5)] (f) A parent undertaking is also treated as the parent undertaking of the subsidiary undertakings of its subsidiary undertakings.

[From s258(3)] For the purpose of section 258 [parent and subsidiary undertakings] an undertaking shall be treated as a member of another undertaking:

(i) if any of its subsidiary undertakings is a member of that undertaking; or

(ii) if any shares in that other undertaking are held by a person acting on behalf of the parent undertaking or any of its subsidiary undertakings.

[From 10ASch9] Any shares held, or powers exercisable, by a subsidiary undertaking should be treated as held or exercisable by its parent undertaking.

[From s260] *Participating interest:-* 15

An interest held by an undertaking in the shares of another undertaking which it holds on a long-term basis for the purpose of securing a contribution to its activities by the exercise of control or influence arising from or related to that interest.

(a) A holding of 20% or more of the shares of an undertaking shall be presumed to be a participating interest unless the contrary is shown.

(b) An interest in shares includes an interest which is convertible into an interest in shares, and includes an option to acquire shares or any interest which is convertible into shares.

(c) An interest held on behalf of an undertaking shall be treated as held by that undertaking.

16 *Undertaking:-* [*From s259*]
A body corporate, a partnership or an unincorporated association carrying on a trade or business with or without a view to profit.

17 *Voting rights in an undertaking:-* [*From 10ASch2(1)*]
Rights conferred on shareholders in respect of their shares or, in the case of an undertaking not having a share capital, on members, to vote at general meetings of the undertaking on all, or substantially all, matters. Schedule 10A deals with the attribution of voting rights in certain circumstances.

STATEMENT OF STANDARD ACCOUNTING PRACTICE

The statement of standard accounting practice set out in paragraphs 18 to 56 of the FRS should be read in the context of the Objective of the FRS as stated in paragraph 1, the definitions set out in paragraphs 2 to 17 and also of the Foreword to Accounting Standards and the Statement of Principles for Financial Reporting currently in issue.

In the statement of standard accounting practice marginal notes give the main references to the Act. If no marginal reference is given the requirement is that of the FRS alone. The statement of standard accounting practice should be interpreted by reference to the full provisions of the Act notwithstanding that the statement summarises certain provisions of the Act. References to sections and schedules are to those of the Act unless otherwise stated.

The Explanation section of the FRS, set out in paragraphs 59 to 94, shall be regarded as part of the statement of standard accounting practice in so far as it assists in interpreting that statement.

Scope

This standard applies to all parent undertakings that prepare the financial statements described below, whether or not they report under the Act. Parent undertakings that prepare consolidated financial statements intended to give a true and fair view of the financial position and profit or loss (or income and expenditure) of their group should prepare such statements in accordance with the requirements of the FRS. A parent undertaking that uses one of the exemptions from preparing consolidated financial statements (described in paragraph 21) but prepares individual financial statements intended to give a true and fair view of its own financial position and profit or loss (or income and expenditure) should include the statement required by paragraph 22. The FRS does not otherwise deal with the individual financial statements of a parent undertaking. **18**

Parent undertakings that do not report under the Act should comply with the requirements of the FRS, and of the Act where referred to in the FRS, except to the extent that these requirements are not permitted by any statutory framework under which such undertakings report. **19**

Consolidated financial statements

Preparation of consolidated financial statements

20 A parent undertaking should prepare consolidated financial statements for its group unless it uses one of the exemptions set out in paragraph 21. [s227, s228 and s248]

Exempt parent undertakings

21 A parent undertaking is exempt from preparing consolidated financial statements for its group on any one of the following grounds.

(a) The group is small or medium-sized and is not an ineligible group as defined in section 248. A group is ineligible if any of its members is a public company, a banking institution, an insurance company or an authorised person under the Financial Services Act 1986. [s248]

(b) The parent undertaking is a wholly-owned subsidiary undertaking and its immediate parent undertaking is established under the law of a member state of the European Community. Exemption is conditional on compliance with certain further conditions set out in section 228(2). A parent undertaking is not exempt if any of its securities is listed on a stock exchange in any European Community country. [s228]

(c) The parent undertaking is a majority-owned subsidiary undertaking and meets all the conditions for exemption as a wholly-owned subsidiary undertaking set out in section 228(2) as well as the additional conditions set out in section 228(1)(b). [s228]

(d) All of the parent undertaking's subsidiary undertakings are permitted or required to be excluded from consolidated by section 229. (The conditions of exclusion of section 229 are more fully described in paragraph 25 and are elaborated on in paragraphs 76 to 78.) [s229(5)]

22 The Act sets out disclosure requirements for parent companies not required to prepare consolidated financial statements. In addition to providing this information, a parent undertaking making use of an exemption from preparing consolidated financial statements should state that its financial statements present information about it as an individual undertaking and not about its group. This statement should include or refer to a note giving the grounds on which the parent undertaking is exempt from preparing consolidated financial statements, as required by Schedule 5 paragraph 1(4). [s231 and 5Sch Part 1]

Undertakings to be included in the consolidation

23 As required by the Act, the consolidated financial statements should include the parent undertaking and all its subsidiary undertakings, [s229(1)] except those that are required to be excluded under the conditions set out in paragraph 25 below.

Disproportionate expense and undue delay

[FRS *allows s229(3)(b) exclusion only where the undertaking is not material*]

24 Neither disproportionate expense nor undue delay in obtaining the information necessary for the preparation of consolidated financial statements can justify excluding from consolidation subsidiary undertakings that are individually or collectively material in the context of the group.

Subsidiary undertakings to be excluded from consolidation

[*s229(3)&(4)*]

25 The exclusions required by this paragraph are based on the exclusions permitted or required by section 229(3) and (4). A subsidiary undertaking should be excluded from consolidation where:

[FRS *requires exclusion permitted by s229(3)(a)*]

(a) severe long-term restrictions substantially hinder the exercise of the rights of the parent undertaking over the assets or management of the subsidiary undertaking. The rights referred to are those by reason of which the parent undertaking is defined as such under section 258 and in the absence of which it would not be the parent undertaking; or

[FRS *requires exclusion permitted by s229(3)(c)*]

(b) the interest in the subsidiary undertaking is held exclusively with a view to subsequent resale (as defined in paragraph 11) and the subsidiary undertaking has not previously been consolidated in group accounts prepared by the parent undertaking; or

[*s229(4)*]

(c) the subsidiary undertaking's activities are so different from those of other undertakings to be included in the consolidation that its inclusion would be incompatible with the obligation to give a true and fair view. It is exceptional for such circumstances to arise and it is not possible to identify any particular contrast of activities where the necessary incompatibility with the true and fair view generally occurs. The Act provides that exclusion on the grounds of different activities does not apply 'merely because some of the undertakings are industrial, some commercial and some provide services, or because they carry on industrial or commercial activities involving different products or provide different services'.

[s231 and 5Sch15(4)]

26 As required by the Act, subject to the conditions and exemptions of section 231, the names of any subsidiary undertakings excluded from the consolidation and the reasons why they have been excluded should be given.

Accounting for excluded subsidiary undertakings

Severe long-term restrictions

27 A subsidiary undertaking excluded on the grounds set out in paragraph 25(a) [severe long-term restrictions] should be treated as a fixed asset investment. If restrictions were in force at its acquisition date, the subsidiary undertaking should be carried initially at cost; if restrictions came into force at a later date, the subsidiary undertaking should be carried at a fixed amount calculated using the equity method at that date. While the restrictions are in force, no further accruals should be made for the profits or losses of that subsidiary undertaking, unless the parent undertaking still exercises a significant influence over it. If this is the case, it should treat the subsidiary undertaking as an associated undertaking using the equity method. The carrying amount of subsidiary undertakings subject to severe long-term restrictions should be reviewed and written down for any permanent diminution in value. In assessing diminution in value, each subsidiary undertaking should be considered individually. Any intra-group amounts due from subsidiary undertakings excluded on the grounds of severe long-term restrictions should also be reviewed and written down, if necessary.

28 When the severe restrictions cease and the parent undertaking's rights are restored, the amount of the unrecognised profit or loss that accrued during the period of restriction for that subsidiary undertaking should be separately disclosed in the consolidated profit and loss account of the period in which control is resumed. Similarly, any amount previously charged for permanent diminution that needs to be written back as a result of restrictions ceasing should be separately disclosed.

Held exclusively with a view to subsequent resale

29 A subsidiary undertaking that is excluded from consolidation on the grounds set out in paragraph 25(b) [held exclusively with a view to subsequent resale] should be recorded in the consolidated financial statements as a current asset at the lower of cost and net realisable value.

Different activities [*4ASch 18*]

30 A subsidiary undertaking excluded on the grounds set out in paragraph 25(c) [different activities] should be recorded in the consolidated financial statements as required by the Act.

Disclosures for subsidiary undertakings excluded from consolidation [*s231 and 5Sch 15–20*]

31 In addition to the disclosures required by Schedule 5, subject to section 231, the following information should be given in the consolidated financial statements for subsidiary undertakings not included in the consolidation:

(a) particulars of the balances between the excluded subsidiary undertakings and the rest of the group;
(b) the nature and extent of transactions of the excluded subsidiary undertakings with the rest of the group;
(c) for an excluded subsidiary undertaking carried other than by the equity method, any amounts included in the consolidated financial statements in respect of:
   (i) dividends received and receivable from that undertaking; and
   (ii) any write-down in the period in respect of the investment in that undertaking or amounts due from that undertaking;
(d) for subsidiary undertakings excluded because of different activities, the separate financial statements of those undertakings. Summarised information may be provided for undertakings that individually, or in combination with those with similar operations, do not account for more than 20% of any one or more of operating profits, turnover or net assets of the group. The group amounts should be measured by including all excluded subsidiary undertakings.

Disclosures for excluded subsidiary undertakings in general apply to individual excluded subsidiary undertakings. However, if the information about excluded subsidiary undertakings is more appropriately presented for a sub-unit of the group comprising more than one excluded subsidiary undertaking, the disclosures may be made on an aggregate basis. Any individual sub-unit for these disclosures is to include only subsidiary undertakings excluded under the same subsection of section 229. Individual disclosures should be made for any excluded subsidiary undertaking, including its sub-group where relevant, that alone accounts for more than 20% of any one or more of operating profits, turnover or net assets of the group. The group amounts should be measured by including all excluded subsidiary undertakings. **32**

Disclosures for principal subsidiary undertakings

[*s231 and 5Sch Part II*] In addition to the disclosures required by Schedule 5, and, like those, subject to the exemptions and conditions of section 231, the following should be shown for each subsidiary undertaking whose results or financial position principally affects the figures in the consolidated financial statements: **33**

(a) the proportion of voting rights held by the parent and its subsidiary undertakings; and
(b) an indication of the nature of its business.

Disclosure of the basis of dominant influence

34 Where an undertaking is a subsidiary undertaking only because its parent undertaking has a participating interest in it and actually exercises a dominant influence over it, the consolidated financial statements should disclose the basis of the parent undertaking's dominant influence in addition to the disclosures required, subject to section 231, by Schedule 5 paragraph 15(5). [*s231 and 5Sch15(5)*]

Minority interests

35 The consolidated balance sheet should show separately the aggregate of the capital and reserves attributable to minority interests at the end of the period under 'Minority interests' in accordance with Schedule 4A paragraph 17(2). This amount represents the aggregate share of net assets or liabilities of subsidiary undertakings included in the consolidation that are attributable to the minority interests. [*4ASch17(2)*]

36 The consolidated profit and loss account should show separately the aggregate of profit or loss on ordinary activities for the period attributable to the minority interests under 'Minority interests' in accordance with Schedule 4A paragraph 17(3). Any extraordinary profit or loss attributable to minority interests should be shown separately in accordance with Schedule 4A paragraph 17(4). [*4ASch17(3) & (4)*]

37 Profits or losses arising in a subsidiary undertaking should be apportioned between the controlling and minority interests in proportion to their respective interests held over the period in which the profits or losses arose. Where the losses in a subsidiary undertaking attributable to the minority interest result in its interest being one in net liabilities rather than net assets, the group should make provision to the extent that it has any commercial or legal obligation (whether formal or implied) to provide finance that may not be recoverable in respect of the accumulated losses attributable to the minority interest.

38 Whether the assets and liabilities of a subsidiary undertaking are included at fair values or adjusted carrying amounts,* those attributable to the minority interest should be included on the same basis as

**Where the acquisition method of accounting is to be used in consolidating a subsidiary undertaking, Schedule 4A paragraph 9 requires the identifiable assets and liabilities of the undertaking acquired to be included in the consolidation at their fair values as at the date of acquisition.*

Where the merger method of accounting is to be used, Schedule 4A paragraph 11 requires the assets and liabilities of the subsidiary undertaking to be consolidated at the amounts at which they stand in that undertaking's financial statements, subject to any adjustments authorised or required by the Act.

those attributable to the interests held by the parent and its other subsidiary undertakings. However, goodwill arising on acquisition should only be recognised with respect to the part of the subsidiary undertaking that is attributable to the interest held by the parent and its other subsidiary undertakings. No goodwill should be attributed to the minority interest.

Consolidation adjustments

Intra-group transactions

[FRS requirement in relation to 4ASch 6. The Act allows partial elimination but the FRS requires elimination in full]

To the extent that they are reflected in the book value of assets to be included in the consolidation, profits or losses on any intra-group transactions should be eliminated in full. Amounts in relation to debts and claims between undertakings included in the consolidation should also be eliminated. The elimination of profits or losses relating to intra-group transactions should be set against the interests held by the group and the minority interest in respective proportion to their holdings in the undertaking whose individual financial statements recorded the eliminated profits or losses. All profits or losses on transactions that would be eliminated if they were between undertakings included in the consolidation should also be eliminated if one party is a subsidiary undertaking excluded because of its different activities (paragraph 25(c)). **39**

Accounting policies

[4ASch 3(1)] Subject to paragraph 41 below, uniform group accounting policies should be used for determining the amounts to be included in the consolidated financial statements, if necessary by adjusting for consolidation the amounts which have been reported by subsidiary undertakings in their individual financial statements. **40**

[4A Sch 3(2)] In exceptional cases, different accounting policies may be used. Where the directors of the parent undertaking depart from the Act's general requirement to use the same group accounting rules to value or otherwise determine the assets and liabilities to be included in the consolidated financial statements, Schedule 4 paragraph 3(2) requires disclosure of the particulars, which should include the different accounting policies used. **41**

Accounting periods and dates

The financial statements of all subsidiary undertakings to be used in preparing the consolidated financial statements should, wherever practicable, be prepared to the same financial year end and for the same accounting period as those of the parent undertaking of the group. **42**

43 Where the financial year of a subsidiary undertaking differs from that of the parent undertaking of the group, interim financial statements should be prepared to the same date as those of the parent undertaking of the group for use in the preparation of the consolidated financial statements. If it is not practicable to use such interim financial statements, the financial statements of the subsidiary undertaking for its last financial year should be used, providing that year ended not more than three months before the relevant year end of the parent undertaking of the group. In this case any changes that have taken place in the intervening period that materially affect the view given by the group's financial statements should be taken into account by adjustments in the preparation of the consolidated financial statements. [*FRS preference of alternatives permitted by 4ASch2(2)*]

44 The following information should be given for each subsidiary undertaking which is included in the consolidated financial statements on the basis of information prepared to a different date or for a different accounting period from that of the parent undertaking of the group: [*Subject to s231, 5Sch19 requires disclosures for different financial year ends*]

(a) the name of the subsidiary undertaking;
(b) the accounting date or period of the subsidiary undertaking; and
(c) the reason for using a different accounting date or period for the subsidiary undertaking.

Changes in composition of a group

Date of changes in group membership

45 The date for accounting for an undertaking becoming a subsidiary undertaking is the date on which control of that undertaking passes to its new parent undertaking. This date is the date of acquisition for Schedule 4A paragraph 9 or the date of merger. The date for accounting for an undertaking ceasing to be a subsidiary undertaking is the date on which its former parent undertaking relinquishes its control over that undertaking.

Ceasing to be a subsidiary undertaking

46 When an undertaking ceases to be a subsidiary undertaking during a period, the consolidated financial statements for that period should include the results of that subsidiary undertaking up to the date that it ceases to be a subsidiary undertaking and any gain or loss arising on that cessation, to the extent that these have not been already provided for in the consolidated financial statements.

47 The gain or loss directly arising for the group on an undertaking ceasing to be its subsidiary undertaking is calculated by comparing the carrying amount of the net assets of that subsidiary undertaking attributable to the group's interest before the cessation with any remaining carrying amount attributable to the group's interest after the cessation together with any proceeds received. The net assets compared should include any related goodwill not previously written off through the profit and loss account.* This calculation of gain or loss applies whether the cause of the undertaking ceasing to be a subsidiary undertaking is a direct disposal, a deemed disposal or other event.

[4ASch 15] In addition to the disclosures required by Schedule 4A paragraph 15, the consolidated financial statements should give the name of any material undertaking that has ceased to be a subsidiary undertaking in the period, showing any ownership interest retained. Where any material undertaking has ceased to be a subsidiary undertaking other than by the disposal of at least part of the interest held by the group, the circumstances should be explained. **48**

Becoming or ceasing to be a subsidiary undertaking other than by a purchase or exchange of shares

Where an undertaking has become or ceased to be a subsidiary undertaking other than as a result of a purchase or exchange of shares, the circumstances should be explained in a note to the consolidated financial statements. **49**

Changes in stake

Acquiring a subsidiary undertaking in stages

[4ASch 9] Schedule 4A paragraph 9 requires that the identifiable assets and liabilities of a subsidiary undertaking be included in the consolidation at fair value at the date of its acquisition, that is, the date it becomes a subsidiary undertaking. This requirement is also applicable where the group's interest in the undertaking that becomes a subsidiary undertaking is acquired in stages. **50**

Increasing an interest held in a subsidiary undertaking

When a group increases its interest in an undertaking that is already its subsidiary undertaking, the identifiable assets and liabilities of that subsidiary undertaking should be revalued to fair value and goodwill arising on the increase in interest should be calculated by reference to those fair values. This revaluation is not required if the difference between net fair values and carrying amounts of the assets and liabilities attributable to the increase in stake is not material. **51**

****Editor's note:** *See also UITF abstract 3 'Treatment of goodwill on disposal of a business'.*

Reducing an interest held in a subsidiary undertaking

52 Where a group reduces its interest in a subsidiary undertaking, it should record any profit or loss arising calculated as the difference between the carrying amount of the net assets of that subsidiary undertaking attributable to the group's interest before the reduction and the carrying amount attributable to the group's interest after the reduction together with any proceeds received. The net assets compared should include any related goodwill not previously written off through the profit and loss account. Where the undertaking remains a subsidiary undertaking after the disposal, the minority interest in that subsidiary undertaking should be increased by the carrying amount of the net identifiable assets that are now attributable to the minority interest because of the decrease in the group's interest. No amount for goodwill that arose on acquisition of the group's interest in that subsidiary undertaking should be attributed to the minority interest.

Distributions

Restrictions on distribution

53 Where significant statutory, contractual or exchange control restrictions on distributions by subsidiary undertakings materially limit the parent undertaking's access to distributable profits, the nature and extent of the restrictions should be disclosed.

Tax on the accumulated reserves of overseas subsidiary undertakings

54 The extent to which deferred tax has been accounted for in respect of future remittances of the accumulated reserves of overseas subsidiary undertakings should be disclosed. Where deferred tax has not been provided in respect of all the accumulated reserves of overseas subsidiary undertakings the reason for not fully providing should be given.

Date from which effective

55 The accounting practices set out in this statement should be adopted as soon as possible and regarded as standard in respect of consolidated financial statements relating to periods ending on or after 23 December 1992 except for those companies considered below. The accounting practices in this statement should be adopted by Republic of Ireland companies as soon as possible after the enactment of the Irish legislation implementing the European Community Seventh Directive and

regarded as standard in respect of consolidated financial statements for periods specified in the date of application of that legislation.*

Withdrawal of SSAP 14 'Group accounts' and 'Interim Statement: Consolidated Accounts'

56 [*Not reproduced as all changes have been reflected in the material reproduced in this volume.*]

Financial Reporting Standard NO. 2 'Accounting for Subsidiary Undertakings' was adopted by the unanimous vote of the nine members of the Accounting Standards Board

Members of the Accounting Standards Board

David Tweedie (Chairman)
Allan Cook (Technical Director)
Robert Bradfield
Sir Bryan Carsberg
Elwyn Eilledge
Michael Garner
Donald Main
Roger Munson
Graham Stacy

****Editor's note:*** *See paragraph 98 of this FRS. The date of application is accounting periods beginning on or after 1 September 1992.*

COMPLIANCE WITH INTERNATIONAL ACCOUNTING STANDARDS

57 Compliance with the FRS ensures compliance with International Accounting Standard NO. 27 – 'Consolidated Financial Statements' (IAS 27) except that IAS 27 does not have an exclusion from consolidation for a subsidiary undertaking based on the grounds that its activities are dissimilar from those of other undertakings to be included in the consolidation. The exclusion for different activities is an exclusion required by statute. As explained in the FRS, this is expected to apply only exceptionally when the inclusion of a subsidiary undertaking would not be compatible with the obligation to give a true and fair view.

58 The IASC has issued E45 'Proposed Statement – Business Combinations' which includes proposals to implement its harmonisation programme. E45 proposes as the benchmark treatment that, when an entity becomes a subsidiary undertaking and is not wholly owned, minority interests should be measured at the pre-acquisition carrying amounts of their attributable identifiable assets and liabilities. The FRS requires the minority interests to be measured at their proportion of the amount at which the identifiable assets and liabilities are included in the consolidation; for an acquisition this is fair value at that date. This treatment is proposed by the IASC as an allowed alternative.*

****Editor's note:*** *E45 has been superseded by a revised version of IAS 22 'Business Combinations'. This includes as standard the E45 proposals referred to in this paragraph.*

EXPLANATION

The purpose of consolidated financial statements

For a variety of legal, tax and other reasons undertakings generally choose to conduct their activities not through a single legal entity but through several undertakings under the ultimate control of the parent undertaking of that group. For this reason the financial statements of a parent undertaking by itself do not present a full picture of its economic activities or financial position. Consolidated financial statements are required in order to reflect the extended business unit that conducts activities under the control of the parent undertaking. 59

The legal background to the FRS

In the United Kingdom the preparation of consolidated financial statements for companies is governed by the Act and the Companies (Northern Ireland) Order 1986. These implement in their respective jurisdictions the provisions of the European Community Seventh Directive. The FRS is drafted to be consistent with the Act, supplementing it with guidance on its application and additional requirements where necessary. The definitions and statement of standard accounting practice contain marginal notes that give references to the Act where these are relevant. Any differences in the application of the FRS in Northern Ireland are explained in the sections setting out the legal provisions in that jurisdiction (paragraph 97). The application of the FRS in the Republic of Ireland is explained in the section on the legal requirements in the Republic of Ireland (paragraph 98). 60

Parent undertakings not subject to the Act

The FRS is drafted in terms derived from the Act but applies to all parent undertakings that prepare financial statements intended to give a true and fair view. A parent undertaking not subject to the Act should comply with the requirements of the FRS, and of the Act where referred to in the FRS, except to the extent that these requirements are not permitted by any statutory framework under which the undertaking reports. By reference to the Act, which in most cases accords with requirements the FRS might otherwise introduce itself in respect of such undertakings, the FRS achieves a single set of requirements relating to the preparation of consolidated financial statements both for companies that report under the Act and for other undertakings. 61

The relationship between the legal background and accounting principles

The accounting concept that underlies the presentation of consolidated financial statements for a group as a single economic entity is summarised in the definition of control in paragraph 6. Although the definitions of parent and subsidiary undertakings in the Act are founded mainly on the accounting concept of control, section 258 uses a list of tests rather than relying on control directly to determine which undertakings are parent and subsidiary undertakings. In the main the effect of applying the tests in the Act is the same as using a criterion based directly on the accounting concept of control. However, in some cases the tests of the Act may either fail to identify as a subsidiary 62 undertaking one that is controlled by another undertaking or identify as a subsidiary undertaking one that is not controlled by its parent undertaking. In other cases section 258 may identify more than one undertaking as the parent undertaking of the same subsidiary undertaking. Where more than one undertaking is thereby identified as a parent of one subsidiary undertaking, not more than one of those parents can have control as defined in paragraph 6.

63 In practice such apparent differences between the effects of applying the Act and the standard can generally be resolved by taking into account the following factors:

(a) the existence of a quasi subsidiary (paragraph 64); or
(b) the existence of severe long-term restrictions on the rights of the parent undertaking (paragraph 65); or
(c) the existence of a joint venture agreement, whether formal or informal (paragraphs 66 and 67).

64 Undertakings that are directly or indirectly controlled by another undertaking and are sources of benefit to that other, but do not qualify according to the tests in the Act as subsidiary undertakings, are described as 'quasi subsidiaries'. The definition and treatment of quasi subsidiaries are not dealt with in this standard.*

65 The Act allows a subsidiary undertaking to be excluded from consolidation if the parent undertaking suffers severe long-term restrictions that substantially hinder the exercise of its rights over the assets or management of the subsidiary undertaking. Paragraph 78(c) discusses severe long-term restrictions further.

66 The control that identifies undertakings as parent and subsidiary undertakings should be distinguished from shared control, for example, as in a joint venture. It is the parent undertaking's sole control of its subsidiary undertakings that gives it access to its subsidiary undertakings' resources. The parent undertaking extends its economic activities through its subsidiary undertakings using their assets and liabilities in a similar way to its own. The ability of an undertaking that shares control to direct the operating and financial policies of the undertaking in which control is shared is circumscribed by the need to take account of the wishes of the other parties that share control. An undertaking identified as a parent by section 258 that shares control over its subsidiary undertaking may be suffering from severe long-term restrictions, as discussed in paragraph 78(c), in relation to the undertaking in which it shares control.

67 Where the tests of the Act identify more than one undertaking as the parent of one subsidiary undertaking it is likely that they have shared control and, therefore, their interests in the subsidiary undertaking are in effect interests in a joint venture and should be treated accordingly. Alternatively, one or more of the undertakings identified under the Act as a parent undertaking may exercise a non-controlling but significant influence over its subsidiary undertaking, in which case it would be more appropriate to treat that subsidiary undertaking in the same way as an associated undertaking rather than to include it in the consolidation.

At the time of issue of the FRS, the Board is in the course of developing a separate standard dealing inter alia with quasi subsidiaries. [Editor's note:** Now FRS 5 'Reporting the Substance of Transactions.]*

Identifying parent and subsidiary undertakings

Parent and subsidiary undertakings are defined in the FRS by applying the provisions of section 258, which are repeated in an abbreviated form in paragraph 14 of the FRS. In addition, the FRS defines some of the phrases that are used in the Act to define undertakings that are parent or subsidiary undertakings. Paragraphs 69–74 below consider some of the terms used. 68

Dominant influence

The Act uses 'dominant influence' as a key phrase in two of the conditions of section 258 that identify parent and subsidiary undertakings. 69

Section 258(2)(c) identifies an undertaking as a parent undertaking if it has the right to exercise a dominant influence over another undertaking: 70

(a) by virtue of provisions contained in the undertaking's memorandum or articles; or
(b) by virtue of a control contract.

Schedule 10A paragraph 4(1) states that for the purposes of sub-section 258(2)(c) 'an undertaking shall not be regarded as having the right to exercise a dominant influence over another undertaking unless it has a right to give directions with respect to the operating and financial policies of that other undertaking which its directors are obliged to comply with whether or not they are for the benefit of that other undertaking'. This forms the basis of the definition set out in paragraph 7(a) of the FRS. In the United Kingdom directors are bound by a common law duty to act in the best interests of their company. For this reason there may, in some cases, be a risk that accepting a right to exercise dominant influence, as here defined, would be in breach of the above duty.

In a second reference to dominant influence, section 258(4)(a) identifies an undertaking as the subsidiary undertaking of another (its parent undertaking) if that other has a participating interest in it and actually exercises a dominant influence over it. Schedule 10A paragraph 4(3) provides that the definition of the 'right to exercise a dominant influence' for the purposes of section 258(2)(c) shall not affect the construction of 'actually exercises a dominant influence' in section 258(4)(a). The FRS defines 'actual exercise of dominant influence', as the exercise of an influence that achieves the result that the operating and financial policies of the undertaking influenced are set in accordance with the wishes of the holder of the influence and for its benefit (whether or not those wishes are explicit). 71

As indicated in paragraph 7(b) of the FRS, the actual exercise of dominant influence is identified by its effect in practice rather than the means by which it is exercised. The effect of the exercise of dominant influence is that the undertaking under influence implements the operating and financial policies that the holder of the influence desires. Thus a power of veto or any other reserve power that has the necessary effect in practice can form the basis whereby one undertaking actually exercises a dominant influence over another. However, such powers are likely to lead to the holder actually exercising 72 a dominant influence over an undertaking only if they are held in conjunction with other rights or powers or if they relate to the day-to-day activities of that undertaking and no similar veto is held by other parties unconnected to the holder. The full circumstances of each case should be considered, including the effect of any formal or informal agreements between the undertakings, to decide whether or not one undertaking actually exercises a dominant influence over another. Commercial relationships such as that of supplier, customer or lender do not of themselves constitute dominant influence.

73 A parent undertaking may actually exercise its dominant influence in an interventionist or non-interventionist way. For example, a parent undertaking may set directly and in detail the operating and financial policies of its subsidiary undertaking or it may prefer to influence these by setting out in outline the kind of results it wants achieved without being involved regularly or on a day-to-day basis. Because of the variety of ways that dominant influence may be exercised evidence of continuous intervention is not necessary to support the view that dominant influence is actually exercised. Sufficient evidence might be provided by a rare intervention on a critical matter. Once there has been evidence that one undertaking has exercised a dominant influence over another, then the dominant undertaking should be assumed to continue to exercise its influence until there is evidence to the contrary. However, it is still necessary for the preparation of the consolidated financial statements to examine the relationship between the undertakings each year to assess any evidence of change in status that may have arisen.

Managed on a unified basis

74 Section 258(4)(b) identifies an undertaking as a parent undertaking of another undertaking (its subsidiary undertaking) if it has a participating interest in that other undertaking and they are managed on a unified basis. Undertakings are managed on a unified basis if the whole of the operations of the undertakings are integrated and they are managed as a single unit. Unified management does not arise solely because one undertaking manages another because this may not fulfil the condition that the operations of the undertakings are integrated.

Preparation of consolidated financial statements

75 The requirements of the FRS apply to all parent undertakings that prepare consolidated financial statements intended to give a true and fair view of the financial position and profit or loss of the group. In giving such a view the same accounting principles apply in general to consolidated financial statements as would apply to the financial statements of a single entity. Parent undertakings should comply with the requirements of the FRS in preparing consolidated financial statements giving a true and fair view, even if the parent undertaking is not specifically required to prepare consolidated financial statements.

Exclusion of subsidiary undertakings from consolidation

76 The Act requires that all the subsidiary undertakings of a parent undertaking are to be included in the consolidated financial statements for that group, subject to the exceptions permitted or required by section 229(2)–(4). The circumstances in which the Act permits or required a subsidiary undertaking to be excluded from consolidation are the following:

Permissive exclusions

(a) 'if its inclusion is not material for the purpose of giving a true and fair view; but two or more undertakings may be excluded only if they are not material taken together'; or

(b) 'where the information necessary for the preparation of group accounts cannot be obtained without disproportionate expense or undue delay'; or

(c) 'where severe long-term restrictions substantially hinder the exercise of the rights of the parent company over the assets or management of that undertaking'; or

(d) 'where the interest of the parent company is held exclusively with a view to subsequent resale and the undertaking has not previously been included in consolidated group accounts prepared by the parent company';

Required exclusion

(e) 'where the activities of one or more subsidiary undertakings are so different from those of other undertakings to be included in the consolidation that their inclusion would be incompatible with the obligation to give a true and fair view'.

Within this statutory framework, the FRS elaborates on the conditions for exclusion set **77**
out in the Act so that these identify, as far as possible, only those undertakings, defined as subsidiary undertakings by section 258, that are not controlled by their parent undertaking in a way that would in principle justify consolidation. This gives effect to the Board's view that a parent undertaking should consolidate all those undertakings that are its subsidiary undertakings unless there are circumstances that make consolidation inappropriate. Under the circumstances set out in paragraph 78(c) and (d) below, the FRS requires the parent undertaking to exclude a subsidiary undertaking because the same conditions that justify permitting exclusion of a subsidiary undertaking also make consolidation of that undertaking inappropriate. Exclusion from consolidation is not the only way of clarifying the effect on the group of the circumstances affecting some of its subsidiary undertakings; exclusion should only be used exceptionally. In many cases circumstances, such as restrictions or activities with special risks, are better dealt with by disclosure, for example by giving additional segmental information, rather than by exclusion from consolidation of the subsidiary undertakings concerned.

In order to help preparers identify the exceptional cases where it is inappropriate to **78**
consolidate a subsidiary undertaking, the exclusions allowed or required by section 229(2)–(4) are discussed below.

Materiality

(a) The FRS deals only with material items. Thus this ground for exclusion requires no special mention in the FRS. The Act only allows exclusion for two or more subsidiary undertakings if they are not material taken together.

Disproportionate expense and undue delay

(b) In principle neither expense nor delay can justify excluding from consolidation subsidiary undertakings that are individually or collectively material in the context of the group.

Severe long-term restrictions

(c) Restrictions are only relevant to justify the exclusion of a subsidiary undertaking from consolidation if the restrictions substantially hinder the exercise of the rights of the parent undertaking over the assets or management of the subsidiary undertaking. The rights affected must be those by reason of which the undertaking holding them is the parent undertaking and without which it would not be the parent undertaking. Severe long-term restrictions justify excluding a subsidiary undertaking from consolidation only where the effect of those restrictions is that the parent undertaking does not control its subsidiary undertaking. Severe long-term restrictions are identified by their effect in practice rather than by the way in which the restrictions are imposed. For example, a subsidiary undertaking should not be excluded because restrictions are threatened or because another party has the power to impose them unless such threats or the existence of such a power has a severe and restricting effect in practice in the long term on the rights of the parent undertaking. Generally, restrictions are dealt with better by disclosure than by non-consolidation. However, the loss of the parent undertaking's control over its subsidiary undertaking resulting from severe long-term restrictions would make it misleading to include that subsidiary undertaking in the consolidation. Where a subsidiary undertaking is subject to an insolvency procedure in the United Kingdom, control over that undertaking may have passed to a designated official (for example, an administrator, administrative receiver or liquidator) with the effect that severe long-term restrictions are in force. A company voluntary arrangement does not necessarily lead to loss of control. In some overseas jurisdictions even formal insolvency procedures may not amount to loss of control.

Interest held exclusively with a view to subsequent resale

(d) This exclusion applies only to those undertakings that have never formed a continuing part of group activities and have not previously been included in consolidated financial statements prepared by the parent undertaking. Paragraph 11 defines the two sets of circumstances in which an interest in a subsidiary undertaking is considered to be held exclusively with a view to subsequent resale. The first set of circumstances (paragraph 11(a)) depends on an immediate intention to sell and the expectation of a sale within approximately one year. An interest for which a sale is not completed within a year of its acquisition may still fulfil the conditions of paragraph 11(a) if, at the date the accounts are signed, the terms of the sale have been agreed and the process of disposing of that interest is substantially complete. The second set of circumstances (paragraph 11(b)) depends on the way in which the interest was acquired, that is, whether it was acquired as a result of the enforcement of a security. The provisions of Schedule 10A paragraph 8(b) may be relevant in determining whether such an interest has been acquired. This paragraph provides that rights attached to shares held as a security are to be treated as held by the person providing the security, where the shares are held in connection with the granting of loans as part of normal business activities and, apart from the right to exercise them to preserve the value of the security or to realise it, the rights are exercisable only in the interests of the provider of the security.

Different activities

(e) The key feature of this exclusion is that it refers only to a subsidiary undertaking whose activities are so different from those of other undertakings included in the consolidation that to include that subsidiary undertaking in the consolidation would be incompatible with the obligation to give a true and fair view. Cases of this sort are so exceptional that it would be misleading to link them in general to any particular contrast of activities. For example, the contrast between Schedule 9 and 9A companies (banking and insurance companies and groups) and other companies or between profit and not-for-profit undertakings is not sufficient of itself to justify non-consolidation. The different activities of undertakings included in the consolidation can better be shown by presenting segmental information rather than by excluding from consolidation the subsidiary undertakings with different activities.

Treatment of excluded subsidiary undertakings

Severe long-term restrictions

(a) Where severe long-term restrictions are in force so that a subsidiary undertaking is no longer under the control of its parent undertaking, that subsidiary undertaking should not be consolidated. From the date severe long-term restrictions come into force and until they are lifted, the subsidiary undertaking subject to the restrictions should be excluded from consolidation and treated instead as a fixed asset investment. If restrictions are in force when the subsidiary undertaking is acquired, it should be carried initially at cost; if restrictions came into force at a later date, the subsidiary undertaking should be carried at a fixed amount calculated using the equity method as at the date the restrictions came into force. If, in spite of severe long-term restrictions, the parent undertaking retains significant influence over a subsidiary undertaking, the investment should be treated as an associated undertaking using the equity method. Because severe long-term restrictions may give rise to diminutions in value, the FRS requires the value of the excluded subsidiary undertaking to be reviewed to assess whether any permanent diminution in value has occurred. Any intra-group amounts due from such excluded subsidiary undertakings may also be affected by severe long-term restrictions, particularly if the restrictions extend to remittances. These balances should also be reviewed and provision made as necessary. **79**

Held exclusively for resale

(b) A subsidiary undertaking held exclusively for resale and not previously included in the consolidated financial statements of the parent undertaking does not form part of the continuing activities of the group. Although the parent undertaking (as identified by section 258 and paragraph 14 of the FRS) may control such a subsidiary undertaking, its control is temporary and is not used to deploy the underlying assets and liabilities of that subsidiary undertaking as part of the continuing group's activities for the benefit of the parent undertaking of the group. The subsidiary undertaking is therefore excluded from consolidation and the temporary nature of the parent undertaking's interest is recognised by carrying it as a current asset at the lower of cost and net realisable value.

Difference activities make consolidated incompatible with giving a true and fair view

(c) Even where a subsidiary undertaking's activities are, exceptionally, so different from those of other undertakings included in the consolidation that its consolidation is not compatible with the obligation to give a true and fair view, that subsidiary undertaking contributes to the wealth and performance of the group. The net assets and results of such a subsidiary undertaking should, therefore, be reflected in the consolidated financial statements and, because it is inappropriate to do this by consolidation, the equity method should be used instead. The use of the equity method is required by Schedule 4A paragraph 18. The FRS also requires separate financial statements for such excluded subsidiary undertakings to accompany the consolidated financial statements so that the information given is complete and fully reflects the different types of assets and liabilities used in the activities of the group as a whole.

Intra-group guarantees re excluded subsidiary undertakings

(d) Liabilities to third parties of one group member guaranteed by another are themselves included in the consolidated financial statements so that intra-group guarantees do not normally require disclosure. Guarantees in respect of subsidiary undertakings excluded from consolidation have to be treated in the same way as guarantees given by members of the group to third parties because, in these cases, the intra-group guarantees relate to liabilities that are not included gross in the consolidated financial statements.

Minority interests

80 Despite the title 'Minority interests', there is in principle no upper limit to the proportion of shares in a subsidiary undertaking which may be held as a minority interest while the parent undertaking still qualifies as such under section 258 of the Act (described in paragraph 14 of the FRS). The amounts reported in the consolidated balance sheet and profit and loss account for the minority interests indicate the extent to which the assets and liabilities and profits and losses of subsidiary undertakings included in the consolidation are attributable to shareholders other than the parent or its other subsidiary undertakings. The effect of the existence of minority interests on the returns to investors in the parent undertaking is best reflected by presenting the net identifiable assets attributable to minority interests on the same basis as those attributable to group interests. Using the same basis for including group assets and liabilities, irrespective of the extent to which they are attributable to the minority interest, presents the assets and liabilities on a consistent basis for the group as a whole.

81 The FRS requires that losses be attributed to the minority interest in a loss making subsidiary undertaking, regardless of whether or not this leads to a debit balance for the minority interest; to do otherwise would obscure the comparison between the assets and liabilities and results attributable to the minority interest and those attributable to the group interests both during the periods when the accumulated losses accrue and afterwards, if these are then made good by later profits. Accumulated losses of subsidiary undertakings do not of themselves necessarily require funding by the parent undertaking and a debit balance for minority interests represents net liabilities attributable to the shares held by the minorities in that subsidiary undertaking rather than a debt due from them. The group should provide for any commercial or legal obligation (whether formal of implied) to provide finance that may not be recoverable in respect of the accumulated losses attributable to the minority interests. Provisions of this sort would include the minorities' share of any liability guaranteed by the group, or any liability that the group itself would be likely to settle for commercial or other reasons, if the subsidiary undertaking could not do so itself. Any provision made with respect to minority debit balances should be set directly against the minority interest amount in the profit and loss account and the balance sheet.

The FRS requires that the goodwill arising on acquisition of a subsidiary undertaking **82**
that is not wholly owned should be recognised only in relation to the group's interest and that none should be attributed to the minority interest. Although it might be possible to estimate by extrapolation or valuation an amount of goodwill attributable to the minority when a subsidiary undertaking is acquired, this would in effect recognise an amount for goodwill that is hypothetical because the minority is not a party to the transaction by which the subsidiary undertaking is acquired.

Consolidation adjustments and intra-group transactions

Presenting information about the economic activities of the group as a single economic **83**
entity in consolidated financial statements requires adjustment for intra-group transactions of the amounts reported in the individual financial statements of the parent and its subsidiary undertakings. Intra-group transactions may result in a profit or loss that is included at least temporarily in the book value of group assets. To the extent that such assets are still held in the undertakings included in the consolidation at the balance sheet date, the related profits or losses recorded in the individual financial statements have not arisen for the group as a whole and must therefore be eliminated from group results and asset values. The elimination should be in full, even where the transactions involve subsidiary undertakings with minority interests. Transactions between undertakings included in the consolidation deal with the assets and liabilities that are wholly within the group's control, even if they are not wholly owned. From the perspective of the group as a single entity no profit or loss arises on intra-group transactions because no increase or decrease in the group's net assets has occurred. Where there are subsidiary undertakings excluded from consolidation because of their different activities, transactions with those subsidiary undertakings, which would be eliminated if they related wholly to subsidiary undertakings included in the consolidation, should also be eliminated. Profits or losses arising on transactions with undertakings excluded from consolidation because they are held exclusively with a view to subsequent re-sale or because of severe long-term restrictions need not be eliminated, except to the extent appropriate where significant influence is retained and the subsidiary undertaking is

treated as an associated undertaking. However, it is important to consider whether it is prudent to record any profit arising from transactions with subsidiary undertakings excluded on these grounds.

Changes in composition of a group

84 The date on which an undertaking becomes or ceases to be another undertaking's subsidiary undertaking marks the point at which a new accounting treatment for that undertaking is applied. The relevant date is the date on which control passes and paragraph 45 of the FRS is framed in these terms. This date should also be the one on which an undertaking begins or ceases to qualify as a parent or subsidiary undertaking under section 258. The date on which control passes is a matter of fact and cannot be backdated or otherwise altered.

85 Where control is transferred by a public offer, the date control is transferred is the date the offer becomes unconditional, usually as a result of a sufficient number of acceptances being received. For private treaties, the date control is transferred is generally the date an unconditional offer is accepted. Where an undertaking becomes or ceases to be a subsidiary undertaking as a result of the issue or cancellation of shares, the date control is transferred is the date of issue or cancellation. The date that control passes may be indicated by the acquiring party commencing its direction of the operating and financial policies of the acquired undertaking or by changes in the flow of economic benefits. The date on which the consideration for the transfer of control is paid is often an important indication of the date on which a subsidiary undertaking is acquired or disposed of. However, the date the consideration passes is not conclusive evidence of the date of the transfer of control because this date can be set to fall on a date other than that on which control is transferred, with compensation for any lead or lag included in the consideration. Consideration may also paid in instalments.

86 An undertaking may cease to be a subsidiary undertaking as a result of the parent undertaking losing control over it because of changes in the rights it holds or in those held by another party in that subsidiary undertaking. A parent undertaking may also lose control of its subsidiary undertaking because of changes in some other arrangement that gave it control without there being any change in the former parent undertaking's holding in its former subsidiary undertaking. For example, control may pass if there is a change in voting rights or in how these are allocated. In these circumstances neither a gain nor a loss accrues in the consolidated financial statements, unless there is a payment for the transfer of control, because there is no change in the net assets attributable to the group's holding in the former subsidiary undertaking. The assets and liabilities of the former subsidiary undertaking should cease to be consolidated but should be shown instead as an associated undertaking or investment as appropriate.

87 An undertaking usually ceases to be a subsidiary undertaking because the group reduces its proportional interest in that undertaking. The reduction of the group's interest may result from its directly disposing of part of the interest it holds or from a deemed disposal. Any reduction in the group's proportional interest other than by a direct disposal is a deemed disposal. Disposals and deemed disposals may give rise to profits or losses for the group, which should be calculated as set out in paragraph 47. There may be other losses or gains that arise for the group as a result of an undertaking ceasing to be a subsidiary undertaking. These are not part of the direct gain or loss described here but may need to be provided for, if they are quantifiable, or otherwise disclosed to show the full effect of the cessation. Deemed disposals may arise where the group's interest in a subsidiary undertaking is reduced, inter alia:

(a) because the parent undertaking and its group do not take up their full allocation of rights in a rights issue; or
(b) because the parent undertaking and its group do not take up their full share of scrip dividends while other equity holders in that subsidiary undertaking take up some, at least, of their share; or
(c) because another party has exercised its options or warrants; or
(d) because the subsidiary undertaking has issued shares to parties other than the parent undertaking and its group.

Changes in stake

When an undertaking is first consolidated, its identifiable assets and liabilities are initially brought into the consolidation at their fair values at the date of its acquisition as a subsidiary undertaking (the acquisition method of accounting as provided by Schedule 4A paragraph 9). Where a subsidiary undertaking is acquired in stages, its net identifiable assets and liabilities are to be included in the consolidation at their fair values on the date it becomes a subsidiary undertaking, rather than at the date of the earlier purchases. Using other methods to compute the amounts to be included in the consolidation would fail to give a full picture of the assets and liabilities acquired that now comprise part of the group's resources. **88**

The effect of the Schedule 4A paragraph 9 method of acquisition accounting is to treat as goodwill, or negative goodwill, the whole of the difference between, on the one hand, the fair value, at the date an undertaking becomes a subsidiary undertaking, of the group's share of its identifiable assets and liabilities and, on the other hand, the total acquisition cost of the interests held by the group in that subsidiary undertaking. This applies even where part of the acquisition cost arises from purchases of interests at earlier dates. In the generality of cases this method provides a practical means of applying acquisition accounting because it does not require retrospective assessments of the fair values of the identifiable assets and liabilities of the acquired undertaking. In special circumstances, however, not using fair values at the dates of earlier purchases, while using an acquisition cost part of which relates to earlier purchases, may result in accounting that is inconsistent with the way the investment has been treated previously and, for that reason, may fail to give a true and fair view. For example, an undertaking that has been treated as an associated undertaking by a group may then be acquired by that group as a subsidiary undertaking. Using the method required by Schedule 4A paragraph 9 to calculate goodwill on such an acquisition has the effect that the group's share of profits or losses and reserve movements of its associated undertaking becomes reclassified as goodwill (usually negative goodwill). A similar problem may arise where the group has substantially restated its investment in an undertaking that subsequently becomes its subsidiary undertaking. For example, where a provision has been made **89** against such an investment for permanent diminution in value, the effect of applying the Schedule 4A paragraph 9 method of acquisition accounting would be to increase reserves and create an asset (goodwill). In the rare cases where the Schedule 4A paragraph 9 calculation of goodwill would be misleading, goodwill should be calculated as the sum of goodwill arising from each purchase of an interest in the relevant undertaking adjusted as necessary for any subsequent diminution in value. Goodwill arising on each purchase should be calculated as the difference between the cost of that purchase and the fair value at the date of that purchase of the identifiable assets and liabilities attributable to the interest purchased. The difference between the goodwill calculated on this method and that calculated on the method provided by the Act is shown in reserves. Section 227(6) sets out the disclosures required in cases where the statutory requirement is not applied.*

90 Where a group increases its stake in an undertaking that is already its subsidiary undertaking the consideration paid may not be equal to the fair value of the identifiable assets and liabilities previously attributed to the minority and now acquired from the minority. If the assets and liabilities were not revalued to fair values before calculating the goodwill arising on the change in stake, then the difference between the consideration paid and the relevant proportion of the carrying value of net assets acquired would be made up in part of goodwill and in part of changes in value. The FRS requires that the assets and liabilities of the subsidiary undertaking be revalued to fair value at the date of the increase in stake unless the difference between the fair values and the carrying amounts of the share of net assets acquired is not material.

91 Where the group decreases its stake in an undertaking whether or not it continues to be a subsidiary undertaking, a profit or loss generally arises. Consolidated financial statements are prepared from the perspective of investors in the parent undertaking of the group. Where the group disposes of part of its interest in a subsidiary undertaking it transacts directly with third parties and a profit or loss for the group arises and is reported in the consolidated financial statements. This can be contrasted with the treatment of intra-group transactions where no profit or loss arises for the group as a whole because the transaction involves only undertakings included in the consolidation and under common control and does not directly involve any third party.

Distributions

92 SSAP 15 'Accounting for deferred tax' states that the retention of earnings overseas will create a timing difference only if:

(a) there is an intention or obligation to remit them; and
(b) remittance would result in a tax liability after taking account of any related double tax relief.

It also requires that, where deferred tax is not provided on earnings retained overseas, this should be stated. In addition this FRS requires disclosure of the extent to which deferred tax has been accounted for in respect of future remittances of the accumulated reserves of overseas subsidiary undertakings. Where deferred tax has not been

***Editor's note:** *See also UITF abstract 7 'True and Fair View Override Disclosures'.*

provided for in full, the reason for not providing fully should be given, for example, that the amounts are considered to be permanently re-invested overseas and are not intended to be remitted.

Disclosures

The FRS refers to the disclosure requirements of the Act and, where appropriate, adds further disclosure requirements of its own. By referring to certain of the disclosure requirements in the Act in the text of the statement of standard accounting practice the FRS extends these disclosure requirements to parent undertakings not subject to the Act. Requirements of the Act are identified by section or schedule numbers; reference to the Act itself is necessary to ascertain the full disclosures required. **93**

Segmental information

Segmental information has a particular importance in group financial reporting. The aggregation and adjustments required to consolidate financial information for the parent undertaking and its subsidiary undertakings may obscure information about the different undertakings and activities included in the consolidated financial statements. The information about the separate group activities that may be obscured by consolidation can be restored by giving information about the group on a segmental basis. Parent undertakings should consider how to provide segmental information for their group, indicating the different risks and rewards, growth and prospects of the different parts of the group and treating the requirements of SSAP 25 'Segmental reporting' as a minimum rather than a limit to disclosure. Two examples of how segmental information could supplement consolidated financial statements are given below. **94**

Segmentation rather than exclusion for certain subsidiary undertakings

(a) Where the FRS discusses excluding subsidiary undertakings from consolidation, it stresses the importance of the completeness of the information presented in the consolidated financial statements. Thus, where subsidiary undertakings engage in different activities or are subject to certain restrictions that are not such as to require exclusion from consolidation under the FRS, the most complete picture is presented by consolidating the subsidiary undertakings concerned and giving additional information or by identifying the assets, liabilities and results attributable to undertakings engaging in those activities or subject to those restrictions.

Minority interests

(b) Users of consolidated financial statements who are interested in assessing the effect of the existence of minority interests in certain parts of the group on the expected returns to investors in the parent undertaking may find it helpful to have information showing the amounts attributable to the minority interest in different group segments.

NOTE OF LEGAL REQUIREMENTS

Legal requirements in Great Britain

References are to the Companies Act 1985 as amended by the Companies Act 1989.

Readers should refer to the Act itself for an understanding of the relevant points of law. This section lists only the main sections in the Act containing provisions in relation to subsidiary undertakings. The provisions of the Act are not considered further here because they are dealt with in the many references to the Act in the other sections of the FRS.

Main sections of the Companies Act

95 The main sections of the Companies Act containing provisions relating to the preparation of consolidated financial statements are the following.

Section 227	'Duty to prepare group accounts'
Section 228	'Exemption for parent companies included in accounts of larger group'
Section 229	'Subsidiary undertakings included in the consolidation'
Section 230	'Treatment of individual profit and loss account where group accounts prepared'
Section 231	'Disclosure required in notes to accounts: – related undertakings'
Section 248	'Exemption for small and medium-sized groups'
Section 249	'Qualification of group as small or medium-sized'
Section 258	'Parent and subsidiary undertakings'
Section 259	'Meaning of "undertaking" and related expressions'
Section 260	'Participating interests'
Section 262	'Minor definitions'
Section 262A	'Index of defined expressions'
Schedule 4A *(All paragraphs)*	'Form and Content of Group Accounts'
Schedule 5 *(All paragraphs)*	'Disclosure of Information: Related Undertakings'
Schedule 10A *(All paragraphs)*	'Parent and Subsidiary Undertakings: supplementary provisions'

Disclosure requirements

96 The following sections and paragraphs give the main disclosure requirements of the Act with respect to consolidated financial statements.

Section 227(4)–(6)
Section 228(2)
Section 231
Schedule 4A – Paragraphs 3, 4, 13, 14, 15, 17

Schedule 5 – 'Disclosure of Information: Related Undertakings'
Part I – 'Companies not Required to Prepare Group Accounts'
Part II – 'Companies Required to Prepare Group Accounts'

Legal requirements in Northern Ireland

The legal requirements in Northern Ireland are very similar to those in Great Britain. The following table shows the Articles and Schedules in the Companies (Northern Ireland) Order 1986 which correspond to the legal references in paragraphs 95–96 above. 97

Companies Act 1985 (as amended)	*The Companies (Northern Ireland) Order 1986 (as amended)*
Section 227	Article 235
Section 228	Article 236
Section 229	Article 237
Section 230	Article 238
Section 231	Article 239
Section 248	Article 256
Section 249	Article 257
Section 258	Article 266
Section 259	Article 267
Section 260	Article 268
Section 262	Article 270
Section 262A	Article 270A
Schedules	
Sched 4A (*all paragraphs*)	Sched 4A (*all paragraphs*)
Sched 5 (Parts I & II) (*all paragraphs*)	Sched 5 (Parts I & II) (*all paragraphs*)
Sched 10A (*all paragraphs*)	Sched 10A (*all paragraphs*)

LEGAL REQUIREMENTS IN THE REPUBLIC OF IRELAND

The principal legislation is contained in the European Communities (Companies: Group Accounts) Regulations **1992** ('the Regulations'), SI No 201 of 1992, which implement the EC Seventh Directive. The Regulations amend certain group accounts related provisions in the Companies Acts **1963–1990** and also apply provisions in that legislation to group accounts. 98

This section is not a summary of all the legal provisions related to group accounts. It gives a listing of the contents of the Regulations and the Irish equivalent for UK legal references.

Readers are advised to refer to the Regulations for an understanding of relevant legal points.

European Communities (Companies: Group Accounts) Regulations – contents:

Regulation 1	Citation, commencement, and construction
Regulation 2	Application
Regulation 3	Interpretation
Regulation 4	Subsidiary undertaking – definition
Regulations 5 & 6	Requirement to present group accounts
Regulations 7–9	Exemptions from requirement to present group accounts
Regulations 10–12	Exclusions from consolidation
Regulations 13 & 14	General provisions in relation to group accounts
Regulation 15	Format of accounts
Regulation 16	Group balance sheet and group profit and loss account
Regulations 17 & 18	Acquisition and merger accounting
Regulations 19 & 20	The acquisition method of accounting
Regulations 21 & 22	The merger method of accounting
Regulation 23	Acquisition of a group
Regulations 24–26	Methods of consolidation
Regulation 27	Changes in composition of a group
Regulations 28–31	Valuation
Regulation 32	Joint ventures
Regulations 33 & 34	Associated undertakings – equity method of accounting
Regulation 35	Participating interest
Regulations 36–40	Publication of information
Regulation 41	Offences
Regulations 42–45	Amendments to the Companies (Amendment) Act 1986
Schedule	
Part 1 Paragraphs 1–10	Amendments to the Schedule to the Companies (Amendment) Act 1986
Part 2 paragraphs 11–23	Information required by way of notes to the group accounts

Table of equivalent legal references in the Republic of Ireland:

References in text

FRS 2	GB REFERENCE	ROI REFERENCE
Summary		
para a	Companies Act 1985 as amended by the Companies Act 1989 ('the Act')	The Companies Acts 1963–1990 and the European Communities (Companies: Group Accounts) Regulations 1992 ('the Regulations')
para e	section 228	Regulations 8 & 9
	section 229	Regulations 10–12
	section 248	Regulations 6 & 7

para p	–	The date of application is accounting periods beginning on or after 1st September 1992

Statement of Standard Accounting Practice

para 7a	section 258(2)(c)	Regulation 4(1)(b)
para 14	section 258	Regulation 4
para 21a	section 248	Regulations 6 & 7
para 21b	section 228(2)	Regulation 8
para 21c	section 228(1)(b)	Regulation 8
para 21d	section 229	Regulations 10–12
para 22	Companies Act Schedule 5 Part 1	Regulation 8(3)(d)
para 25	section 229(3) and (4)	Regulations 11 & 12
para 25a	section 258	Regulation 4
para 26	section 231	Companies (Amendment) Act 1989, section 16
para 31	section 231 and Schedule 5	Companies (Amendment) Act 1986, section 16
para 32	section 229	Regulations 11 & 12
para 33	section 231	Companies (Amendment) Act 1986, section 16
para 34	section 231 Schedule 5, 15(5)	–
para 35	Schedule 4A 17(2)	Regulations, Schedule para 8
para 36	Schedule 4A 17(3) 17(4)	Regulations, Schedule para 9
para 41	Schedule 4A para 3(2)	Regulation 29(3)
para 45	Schedule 4A para 9	Regulation 19
para 48	Schedule 4A para 15	Regulation 27
para 50	Schedule 4A para 9	Regulation 19
para 55	-	The date of application is accounting periods beginning on or after 1st September 1992

Explanation

para 62	section 258	Regulation 4
para 66	section 258	Regulation 4
para 68	section 258	Regulation 4
para 69	section 258	Regulation 4
para 70	section 258(2)(c)	Regulation 4(1)(b)
	Schedule 10A para 4(1)	Regulation 4(5)
para 71	section 258(4)(a)	Regulation 4(1)(c)(i)
	Schedule 10A para 4(3)	Regulation 4(7)
	section 258(2)(c)	Regulation(1)(a)(ii)
para 74	section 258(4)(b)	Regulation 4 (1)(c)(ii)
para 76	section 229(2)–(4)	Regulations 10–12
para 77	section 258	Regulation 4
para 78	section 229(2)–(4)	Regulation 10–12
para 80	section 258	Regulation 4

para 84	section 258	Regulation 4
para 88	section 258	Regulation 4
para 89	Schedule 4A para 9	Regulations 19–20
	section 227(6)	Regulation 14(3)
	section 258	Regulation 4

References in footnotes:

FRS 2	ROI REFERENCE
para 1**	European Communities (Companies: Group Accounts) Regulations 1992
para 38*	Regulation 19(2) — Acquisitions Regulation 22(2) — Mergers

References in margins:

FRS 2	ROI REFERENCE
para 7a	Regulation 4(5)
para 7b	No Irish equivalent
para 10	No Irish equivalent
para 11	Regulation 11(c)
Para 12	Regulation 4(1)(c)(ii)
para 13	Regulation Schedule 8(2)
para 14	Regulation 4
para 14a	Regulation 4(1)(a)(i)
para 14b	Regulation 4(1)(a)(ii) &4(2)
para 14c	Regulation 4(1)(b)
para 14c(ii)	Regulation 4(1)(b)(ii)
para 14d	Regulation 4(1)(a)(iii)
para 14e	Regulation 4(1)(c)
para 14f	Regulation 4(1)(d)
para 15	Regulation 35
para 16	Regulation 3(1)
para 17	Regulation 3(4)
para 20	Regulation 5(1)
para 21a	Regulations 5 & 6
para 21b	Regulations 8 & 9
para 21c	Regulations 8 & 9
para 21d	Regulation 10 & 11
para 23	Regulation 5(2)
para 24	Regulation 11(b)
para 25	Regulations 11 & 12
para 25a	Regulation 11(a)

FRS 2	ROI REFERENCE
para 25b	Regulation 11(c)
para 25c	Regulation 12(1)
para 26	Companies (Amendment) Act 1986, section 16
para 30	Regulation 12(1)
para 31	Companies (Amendment) Act 1986, section 16
para 33	Companies (Amendment) Act 1986, section 16
para 34	–
para 35	Regulation Schedule para 8
para 36	Regulation Schedule para 9 (1–3)
para 39	Regulations specify that elimination should only refer to 'undertakings dealt with in the Group Accounts', ie the FRS goes further than the Regulations
para 40	Regulations refer to uniform valuation methods
para 43	Regulation 26(2)
para 44	No Irish equivalent
para 46	No Irish equivalent

THE DEVELOPMENT OF THE STANDARD

This section does not form part of the Financial Reporting Standard

History of the FRS

Statement of Standard Accounting Practice NO. 14 (SSAP 14) 'Group Accounts', issued September 1978, dealt with the presentation of group accounts for a group of companies. The practice of preparing group accounts for companies and their subsidiaries had been well established in the United Kingdom and Ireland since 1947. However, the issue of International Accounting Standard NO. 3 'Consolidated Financial Statements' made it desirable for there to be a domestic standard on the subject. **i**

SSAP 14 was drafted to accord with relevant provisions of the Companies Acts then in force. At that time the Companies Acts did not include detailed rules regarding the preparation of group accounts. **ii**

SSAP 14 defined a holding company and a subsidiary company by reference to the legal definitions current at that time. The terms now used are 'parent undertaking' and 'subsidiary undertaking' which are defined in the Companies Act 1985, as amended by the Companies Act 1989 (the Act). The Act now contains new provisions on group accounts to implement the European Community Seventh Company Law Directive with the result that the requirements of SSAP 14 are no longer entirely consistent with current legislation. **iii**

The need to revise SSAP 14 for changes in the law has provided an opportunity to conduct a thorough review of the standard. This was undertaken initially by the Accounting Standards Committee whose proposals were issued as ED 50 'Consolidated accounts' in June 1990. The Accounting Standards Board issued the 'Interim Statement: Consolidated Accounts' in December 1990, to give timely guidance on how certain provisions of the Act were to be interpreted in the preparation of consolidated accounts. The Interim Statement also made the changes to SSAP 14 'Group Accounts' that were required as a consequence of the statutory changes. The issue of the FRS by the Accounting Standards Board completes the review process. **iv**

Summary of the principal changes from Statement of Standard Accounting Practice NO. 14 – 'Group Accounts'

SSAP 14 defined a company as a subsidiary of another 'if, but only if, **v**

(a) that other either:
 (i) is a member of it and controls the composition of its board of directors; or
 (ii) holds more than half in nominal value of its equity share capital; or
(b) the first mentioned company is a subsidiary of any company which is that other's subsidiary, and it otherwise comes within the terms of section 154 of the Companies Act 1948' (now repealed).

The FRS defines a parent undertaking and a subsidiary undertaking in the same way as the Act using a set of conditions that are based on whether one undertaking controls another. These are set out in paragraph 14 of the FRS.

vi The FRS requires a parent undertaking not making use of an exemption to prepare consolidated financial statements for its group. SSAP 14 exceptionally allowed alternative forms of group reporting if the resulting group accounts were considered to give a fairer view of the financial position of the group as a whole than would consolidated financial statements.

vii SSAP 14 exempted from the obligation to prepare group accounts only holding companies that were wholly owned subsidiaries not otherwise required by law to prepare group accounts. The FRS follows the Act in allowing other exemptions from preparing consolidated financial statements. A parent undertaking is in general exempt from the requirement to prepare consolidated financial statements if its group is a small or medium-sized one; or if it is wholly or majority-owned by an undertaking established under the law of a member state of the European Community; or if all its subsidiary undertakings fall within the exclusions from consolidation.

viii The circumstances in which subsidiary undertakings are to be excluded from the consolidation have changed in certain respects from those in SSAP 14.

(a) SSAP 14 required a subsidiary to be excluded from consolidation if its activities were so dissimilar from those of other companies within the group that its consolidation would be misleading and information would be better provided by presenting financial statements for the excluded subsidiary separate from the financial statements for the rest of the group. The FRS requires a subsidiary undertaking to be excluded from consolidation if, exceptionally, its activities are so different from other subsidiary undertakings included in the consolidation that its inclusion in the consolidation would be incompatible with the obligation to give a true and fair view.

(b) SSAP 14 required a subsidiary to be excluded from consolidation if the holding company held more than half of the subsidiary's equity share capital but either: (a) it did not own share capital carrying more than half the votes; or (b) contractual or other restrictions were imposed on its ability to appoint the majority of the board of directors. Although the FRS does not have the same exclusion, the FRS will in most cases have the same practical effect because (a) an undertaking is a subsidiary undertaking if another undertaking holds a majority of its voting rights and (b) exclusion is required where severe long-term restrictions substantially hinder the rights of the parent undertaking over the assets or management of its subsidiary undertaking.

(c) SSAP 14 required exclusion from consolidation of a subsidiary where control was intended to be temporary. The FRS requires consolidation where one undertaking controls another and, therefore, has not based exclusion on control being temporary. However, it does require exclusion from consolidation of a subsidiary undertaking held exclusively with a view to resale which has not previously been consolidated. This condition for exclusion is more restrictive than the temporary control test.

SSAP 14 required that the consolidated financial statements should contain sufficient information about material subsidiaries acquired or sold to enable shareholders to appreciate the effect on the consolidated results. There are now specific disclosure requirements in the law, as well as in accounting standards in respect of acquisitions, and the general SSAP 14 requirement is not repeated in the FRS. In addition FRS 1 'Cash Flow Statements' contains a requirement to show the cash flow effects of acquisitions and disposals. ix

SSAP 14 sets out the effective date of acquisition or disposal as the earlier of the date on which consideration passes or the date on which an offer becomes or is declared unconditional. This is replaced in the FRS by a single triggering date which is the date control of the undertaking passes. This date is a matter of fact and cannot be backdated or otherwise altered. x

SSAP 14 required that debit balances for the minority interests should only be recognised in the balance sheet if there was a binding obligation on minority shareholders to make good losses incurred which they were able to meet. The FRS requires minority interests to be debited in full with their share of any loss whether or not this results in a debit balance, subject to the need for a provision discussed below. A debit for minority interests does not represent a liability of the minority shareholders and it may be misleading to refer to their being obliged to make good losses. The group should make provision to the extent that it has any commercial or legal obligation (whether formal or implied) to provide finance that may not be recoverable in respect of the accumulated losses attributable to minority interests. xi

Summary of the principal changes from the Board's 'Interim Statement: Consolidated Accounts'

In December 1990 the Board issued the 'Interim Statement: Consolidated Accounts' to give timely guidance on the application of certain provisions of the new Act to the preparation of consolidated financial statements. The Interim Statement dealt mainly with the interpretation of the new phrases used in the conditions that identified parent and subsidiary undertakings and with the exclusions from consolidation permitted or required by the Act for certain subsidiary undertakings. Although the drafting has changed to fit the format of an accounting standard, the FRS incorporates the guidance given by the Interim Statement except in the following areas. xii

(a) Dominant influence is now defined without explicit reference to control although the effect of dominant influence is the same as control.
(b) The explanation dealing with subsidiary undertakings whose activities are so different that consolidation is incompatible with the obligation to give a true and fair view now states explicitly that the contrast between Schedule 9 and 9A companies and other companies or between profit and not-for-profit undertakings is not sufficient of itself to justify non consolidation.
(c) The Interim Statement defined a joint venture. The FRS deals only with accounting for subsidiary undertakings leaving joint ventures as a separate project.

Summary of the principal changes from Exposure Draft NO. 50 – 'Consolidated accounts'

xiii Exposure Draft NO. 50 (ED 50) 'Consolidated accounts' was issued in June 1990 by the Accounting Standards Committee. It proposed standard accounting practice for the preparation of consolidated accounts covering both accounting for subsidiary undertakings and accounting for associated undertakings and joint ventures. The FRS deals only with accounting for subsidiary undertakings in consolidated financial statements. The Board is engaged in another project considering accounting for associated undertakings and joint ventures.

xiv The Explanatory Note in ED 50 considered the purpose of consolidated accounts, the basis of consolidation and the meaning of control. The FRS deals only briefly in its explanation section with the conceptual background to financial reporting for groups. The conceptual basis of consolidated financial statements and consideration of the group as a reporting entity are to be considered by the Board in the chapter of its Statement of Principles dealing with the boundaries of the reporting entity.

xv ED 50 used the terms 'subsidiary', 'parent' and 'enterprise' in line with earlier accounting standards. Commentators on its proposals considered that it would be more appropriate to use the terminology of the Act on which the FRS is based. The FRS now refers to 'subsidiary undertaking', 'parent undertaking' and 'undertaking'. However, in line with the Board's other published work, the FRS uses 'financial statements' instead of 'accounts' as used in the Act.

xvi ED 50 proposed definitions for the phrases used in the Act in the criteria for identifying parent and subsidiary undertakings. The FRS elaborates on these definitions in the light of the comments received on the ED. The general thrust of the definitions remains the same but the following changes are worth noting:

(a) 'Dominant influence' is no longer defined in terms of control but by its ability to achieve the operating and financial policies desired by the holder of the influence, notwithstanding the rights or influence of any other party. The actual exercise of dominant influence is identified by its effect in practice rather than the way in which it is exercised. The effect of dominant influence is the same as the effect of control.

(b) The role of reserve powers and powers of veto in the actual exercise of dominant influence has been clarified.

xvii ED 50 proposed that a parent undertaking using an exemption from preparing consolidated accounts should make additional disclosures if its individual financial statements alone were not sufficient to give a true and fair view of its financial position. ED 50 noted that in some cases such additional information might better be presented by providing consolidated financial statements for the whole group. This proposal attracted adverse comment because, in certain circumstances, its effect would be to take away an exemption given by the Act. The FRS requires a parent undertaking using an exemption to state that its financial statements present information about it as an individual undertaking and not about its group. Parent undertakings using any of the exemptions should also make the disclosures set out in Schedule 5 Part 1 of the Companies Act.

ED 50 proposed definitions for the phrases used in the Act to set the conditions under which a subsidiary undertaking was permitted or required to be excluded from consolidation. As a result of the comments received the guidance of the FRS on how these conditions are to be interpreted has changed slightly from that given in ED 50 although the emphasis remains on interpreting these conditions restrictively. The main changes are set out below. **xviii**

(a) *Interests held exclusively with a view to subsequent resale.* A second part has been added bringing acquisitions as a result of the enforcement of a security within the definition of interests held exclusively with a view to subsequent resale unless the subsidiary undertaking has become part of the continuing activities of the group or the holder acts as if it intends the interest to become so.
(b) *Activities so different that consolidation would be incompatible with the obligation to give a true and fair view.* ED 50 proposed that such an incompatibility could arise only from consolidating a Schedule 9 or 9A company with non Schedule 9 or 9A companies. Several commentators considered that a requirement not to consolidate Schedule 9 and 9A companies with others might result in a loss of useful and comparable information on group activities as a whole. Linking incompatibility with the true and fair view to issues relating to the format in which financial statements were presented was considered unsatisfactory. The FRS, therefore, stresses that the key feature of this exclusion is that including a given subsidiary undertaking in the consolidation is incompatible with the obligation to give a true and fair view. The FRS notes that this incompatibility will be so exceptional in practice that it would be misleading to associate it with any particular contrast of activities. For example, the contrasts between Schedule 9 or 9A companies and other companies or between profit and not-for-profit undertakings would not of themselves be sufficient to justify nonconsolidation.

ED 50 followed SSAP 14 and proposed that losses should only be debited to minority interests where they resulted in a debit balance if there was a binding and reliable obligation on the minority to make good any such losses. The FRS's treatment for the minority's share of losses is explained in paragraph xi above. **xix**

ED 50 proposed dropping the requirement of SSAP 14 (paragraph 18) that appropriate adjustments should be made to the consolidated financial statements for any abnormal transactions in the intervening period between the end of the period of a subsidiary and the later one of the group. Commentators considered that some disclosure of this sort would be useful. The FRS requires that, where a subsidiary undertaking's financial year end differs from that of the parent undertaking, the consolidated financial statements should be prepared using interim financial statements or, only if this is impracticable, its financial statements for its last financial year ending not more than three months before that of the group's parent undertaking. In this latter case adjustment is required for changes in the intervening period that materially affect the view given by the consolidated financial statements. **xx**

xxi ED 50 proposed that the effective date of acquisition or disposal be the earlier of:

(a) the date on which the consideration passes; or
(b) the date at which an offer becomes or is declared unconditional; or
(c) the date of such other event at which control is gained or ceases to exist.

The FRS now sets the date of changes in membership of the group as the date that control passes. The Explanation (paragraphs 84 and 85) considers the transactions and events that indicate when control passes.

xxii ED 50 proposed that its requirement to include the appropriate proportion of the results of a subsidiary undertaking that has been disposed of should be subject to the requirements of SSAP 6 'Extraordinary items and prior year adjustments' (paragraphs 11–14) dealing with the disposal of a segment. The FRS does not refer to SSAP 6 and requires that the consolidated profit and loss account should include the results of a subsidiary undertaking up to the date of its disposal. The Board is proposing to supersede SSAP 6 with an FRS developed from FRED 1 'The Structure of Financial Statements – Reporting of Financial Performance'.*

xxiii The FRS has dropped the proposed requirement of ED 50 in respect of disposals to disclose the amount of purchased goodwill attributable to business or business segments disposed of and how that goodwill has been treated in determining the profit or loss on disposal. These disclosures are still required by paragraph 52(b) of SSAP 22 'Accounting for goodwill'. The treatment of goodwill on disposal is set out in paragraph 47, which requires that the net assets disposed of include any related goodwill not previously written off through the profit and loss account.

xxiv In response to criticism of the ED 50 proposals, the FRS changes the treatment for increases in stake in a subsidiary undertaking. ED 50 did not propose to require a revaluation to fair value on an increase in stake, and, consequently, the goodwill balance arising could have consisted of an amount relating to revaluation of net identifiable assets as well as goodwill. The FRS requires that the goodwill should be calculated by revaluing the subsidiary undertaking's assets and liabilities to fair value at the date of the change in stake, unless the difference between fair values and carrying amounts is not material.

***Editor's note:** *This became FRS 3 'Reporting Financial Performance'.*

[FRS 3]
Reporting financial performance

(Issued October 1992; amended June 1993)

Contents

Reporting financial performance

Summary

a Financial Reporting Standard No. 3 'Reporting Financial Performance' (the FRS) introduces: changes to the format of the profit and loss account; a note of historical cost profits and losses; a statement of total recognised gains and losses; and a reconciliation of movements in shareholders' funds. The FRS supersedes Statement of Standard Accounting Practice No. 6 (Revised) 'Extraordinary items and prior year adjustments' (SSAP 6), amends SSAP 3 'Earnings per share' and makes consequential changes to a number of other accounting standards.

b A layered format is to be used for the profit and loss account to highlight a number of important components of financial performance:

(i) results of continuing operations (including the results of acquisitions);
(ii) results of discontinued operations;
(iii) profits or losses on the sale or termination of an operation, costs of a fundamental reorganisation or restructuring and profits or losses on the disposal of fixed assets; and
(iv) extraordinary items.

The thrust of this approach can be illustrated diagramatically as follows:

Continuing	*Discontinued*
Normal operations	Normal operations
The items listed in b(iii) above	The items listed in b(iii) above

Extraordinary items — being unusual items outside ordinary activities

c In presenting the profit and loss account the following requirements should be observed:

(i) The analysis between continuing operations, acquisitions (as a component of continuing operations) and discontinued operations should be disclosed to the level of operating profit (which for non-financial reporting entities is normally profit before income from shares in group undertakings). The analysis of turnover and operating profit is the minimum disclosure required in this respect on the face of the profit and loss account.
(ii) All exceptional items, other than those in (iii) below, should be included under the

statutory format headings to which they relate. They should be separately disclosed by way of note or, where it is necessary in order that the financial statements give a true and fair view, on the face of the profit and loss account.

(iii) The following items, including provisions in respect of such items, should be shown separately on the face of the profit and loss account after operating profit and before interest:
- profits or losses on the sale or termination of an operation;
- costs of a fundamental reorganisation or restructuring; and
- profits or losses on the disposal of fixed assets.

(iv) Extraordinary items should be disclosed.

d Earnings per share should be calculated on the profit attributable to equity shareholders of the reporting entity, after accounting for minority interests, extraordinary items, preference dividends and other appropriations in respect of preference shares. Where a reporting entity wishes to present an additional earnings per share calculated on another level of earnings the additional indicator should be presented on a consistent basis over time and, wherever disclosed, reconciled to the amount required by the FRS. Such a reconciliation should list the items for which an adjustment is being made and disclose their individual effect on the calculation. The earnings per share required by the FRS should be at least as prominent as any additional version presented and the reason for calculating the additional version should be explained.

e The note of historical cost profits and losses is a memorandum item, thc primary purpose of which is to present the profits or losses of reporting entities that have revalued assets on a more comparable basis with those of entities that have not. It is an abbreviated restatement of the profit and loss account which adjusts the reported profit or loss, if necessary, so as to show it as if no asset revaluations had been made. Unless the historical cost information is unavailable, the note is required whenever there is a material difference between the result as disclosed in the profit and loss account and the result on an unmodified historical cost basis; it should be presented immediately following the profit and loss account or the statement of total recognised gains and losses.

f The statement of total recognised gains and losses is a primary financial statement that enables users to consider all recognised gains and losses of a reporting entity in assessing its overall performance. It, therefore, includes the profit or loss for the period together with all other movements on reserves reflecting recognised gains and losses attributable to shareholders. The statement is not intended to reflect the realisation of gains recognised in previous periods nor does it deal with transfers between reserves, which should continue to be shown in the notes to the financial statements.

g The reconciliation of movements in shareholders' funds brings together the performance of the period, as shown in the statement of total recognised gains and losses, with all the other changes in shareholders' funds in the period, including capital contributed by or repaid to shareholders.

h Prior period adjustments should be accounted for by restating the comparative figures for the preceding period in the primary statements and notes and adjusting the opening balance of reserves for the cumulative effect. The cumulative effect of the adjustments should also be noted at the foot of the statement of total recognised gains and losses of the current period. The effect of prior period adjustments on the results for the preceding period should be disclosed where practicable.

The accounting practices set out in the FRS should be adopted as soon as possible and i
regarded as standard in respect of financial statements relating to accounting periods ending on or after 22 June 1993.

Objective

1 The objective of the FRS is to require reporting entities falling within its scope to highlight a range of important components of financial performance to aid users in understanding the performance achieved by a reporting entity in a period and to assist them in forming a basis for their assessment of future results and cash flows.

Definitions

The following definitions apply for the purposes of the FRS and in particular the statement of standard accounting practice set out in paragraphs 12 to 33.

2 *Ordinary activities:-*
Any activities which are undertaken by a reporting entity as part of its business and such related activities in which the reporting entity engages in furtherance of, incidental to, or arising from, these activities. Ordinary activities include the effects on the reporting entity of any event in the various environments in which it operates, including the political, regulatory, economic and geographical environments, irrespective of the frequency or unusual nature of the events.

3 *Acquisitions:-*
Operations of the reporting entity that are acquired in the period.

4 *Discontinued operations:-*
Operations of the reporting entity that are sold or terminated and that satisfy all of the following conditions.

(a) The sale or termination is completed either in the period or before the earlier of three months after the commencement of the subsequent period and the date on which the financial statements are approved.
(b) If a termination, the former activities have ceased permanently.
(c) The sale or termination has a material effect on the nature and focus of the reporting entity's operations and represents a material reduction in its operating facilities resulting either from its withdrawal from a particular market (whether class of business or geographical) or from a material reduction in turnover in the reporting entity's continuing markets.
(d) The assets, liabilities, results of operations and activities are clearly distinguishable, physically, operationally and for financial reporting purposes.

Operations not satisfying all these conditions are classified as continuing.

5 *Exceptional items:-*
Material items which derive from events or transactions that fall within the ordinary activities of the reporting entity and which individually or, if of a similar type, in aggregate, need to be disclosed by virtue of their size or incidence if the financial statements are to give a true and fair view.

Extraordinary items:- 6
Material items possessing a high degree of abnormality which arise from events or transactions that fall outside the ordinary activities of the reporting entity and which are not expected to recur. They do not include exceptional items nor do they include prior period items merely because they relate to a prior period.

Prior period adjustments:- 7
Material adjustments applicable to prior periods arising from changes in accounting policies or from the correction of fundamental errors. They do not include normal recurring adjustments or corrections of accounting estimates made in prior periods.

Total recognised gains and losses:- 8
The total of all gains and losses of the reporting entity that are recognised in a period and are attributable to shareholders.

Companies Act 1985:- 9
The Companies Act 1985 as amended by the Companies Act 1989.

Companies (Northern Ireland) Order 1986:- 10
The Companies (Northern Ireland) Order 1986 as amended by the Companies (Northern Ireland) Order 1990 and the Companies (No. 2) (Northern Ireland) Order 1990.

Companies (Amendment) Act 1986:- 11
The Republic of Ireland Companies (Amendment) Act 1986 as amended by the Companies Act 1990 and by the European Communities (Companies: Group Accounts) Regulations 1992 (*the* 1992 *Regulations*).

Statement of standard accounting practice

The statement of standard accounting practice set out in paragraphs 12 to 33 of the FRS should be read in the context of the Objective of the FRS as stated in paragraph 1, the definitions set out in paragraphs 2 to 11 and also of the foreword to Accounting Standards and the Statement of Principles for Financial Reporting currently in issue.

The Explanation section of the FRS, set out in paragraphs 35 to 66, shall be regarded as part of the statement of standard accounting practice insofar as it assists in interpreting that statement.

Scope

12 The FRS applies to all financial statements intended to give a true and fair view of a reporting entity's financial position and profit or loss (or income and expenditure). Every such reporting entity should apply the requirements of the FRS except to the extent that these requirements are not permitted by the statutory framework (if any) under which the entity reports.

PROFIT AND LOSS ACCOUNT

13 All gains and losses recognised in the financial statements for the period should be included in the profit and loss account or the statement of total recognised gains and losses. Gains and losses may be excluded from the profit and loss account only if they are specifically permitted or required to be taken directly to reserves by this or other accounting standards or, in the absence of a relevant accounting standard, by law.

Continuing and discontinued operations

14 The aggregate results of each of continuing operations, acquisitions (as a component of continuing operations) and discontinued operations should be disclosed separately. The results of acquisitions included in continuing operations should not include those that are also discontinued in the same period. The minimum disclosure required down to the operating profit level on the face of the profit and loss account in respect of continuing operations, acquisitions and discontinued operations is the analysis of turnover and operating profit (which for non-financial reporting entities is normally profit before income from shares in group undertakings). The analysis between continuing operations, acquisitions (as a component of continuing operations) and discontinued operations of each of the other statutory profit and loss account format items between turnover and operating profit should be given by way of note where not shown on the face of the profit and loss account. In those circumstances where a reporting entity presents allocations of interest or tax between continuing and discontinued operations, the method and underlying assumptions used in making the allocations should be disclosed.

15 Where an acquisition, or a sale or a termination, has a material impact on a major business segment this should be disclosed and explained.

Acquisitions

Where it is not practicable to determine the post-acquisition results of an operation to the end of the current period, an indication should be given of the contribution of the acquisition to the turnover and operating profit of the continuing operations in addition to the information required by the Companies Act 1985*. If an indication of the contribution of an acquisition to the results of the period cannot be given, this fact and the reason should be explained. **16**

Discontinued operations

Only income and costs directly related to discontinued operations should appear under the heading of discontinued operations. Reorganisation or restructuring of continuing operations resulting from a sale or termination should be treated as part of continuing operations. **17**

The consequences of a decision to sell or terminate an operation

If a decision has been made to sell or terminate an operation, any consequential provisions should reflect the extent to which obligations have been incurred that are not expected to be covered by the future profits of the operation or the disposal of its assets. This principle requires that the reporting entity should be demonstrably committed to the sale or termination. This should be evidenced, in the former case, by a binding sale agreement and, in the latter, by a detailed formal plan for termination from which the reporting entity cannot realistically withdraw. The provision should cover only (a) the direct costs of the sale or termination and (b) any operating losses of the operation up to the date of sale or termination, in both cases, after taking into account the aggregate profit, if any, to be recognised in the profit and loss account from the future profits of the operation or disposal of its assets. Unless the operation qualifies as a discontinued operation in the period under review, the write down of assets and any provisions should appear in the continuing operations category. In the subsequent period when the operation does qualify as discontinued, the provisions should be used to offset the results of the operation in the discontinued category. The related disclosure in that subsequent period, however, should be to show the results of the discontinued operation under each of the statutory format headings with the utilisation of the provision analysed as necessary between the operating loss and the loss on sale or termination of the discontinued operation and disclosed on the face of the profit and loss account immediately below the relevant items. **18**

**Companies Act 1985 Schedule 4A* paragraph 13. The equivalent reference in Northern Ireland legislation is the Companies (Northern Ireland) Order 1986 Schedule 4A paragraph 13.

The nearest equivalent reference in the Republic of Ireland is the 1992 Regulations section 27 which sets out a general requirement for disclosure in the case of changes in the composition of a group.

Exceptional items

19 All exceptional items, other than those included in the items listed in paragraph 20, should be credited or charged in arriving at the profit or loss on ordinary activities by inclusion under the statutory format headings to which they relate. They should be attributed to continuing or discontinued operations as appropriate. The amount of each exceptional item, either individually or as an aggregate of items of a similar type, should be disclosed separately by way of note, or on the face of the profit and loss account if that degree of prominence is necessary in order to give a true and fair view. An adequate description of each exceptional item should be given to enable its nature to be understood.

20 The following items, including provisions in respect of such items, should be shown separately on the face of the profit and loss account after operating profit and before interest, and included under the appropriate heading of continuing or discontinued operations:

(a) profits or losses on the sale or termination of an operation;
(b) costs of a fundamental reorganisation or restructuring having a material effect on the nature and focus of the reporting entity's operations; and
(c) profits or losses on the disposal of fixed assets.
In calculating the profit or loss in respect of the above items consideration should only be given to revenue and costs directly related to the items in question.

When the net amount of (a) or (c) above is not material, but the gross profits or losses are material, the relevant heading should still appear on the face of the profit and loss account with a reference to a related note analysing the profits and losses. Relevant information regarding the effect of these items on the taxation charge and, in the case of consolidated financial statements, any minority interests should both be shown in a note to the profit and loss account. As a minimum the related tax and the minority interest should both be shown in aggregate, but if the effect of the tax and minority interests differs for the various categories of items further information should be given, where practicable, to assist users in assessing the impact of the different items on the net profit or loss attributable to shareholders. The taxation effects of these items are also referred to in paragraphs 23 and 24.

Profit or loss on the disposal of an asset

21 The profit or loss on the disposal of an asset should be accounted for in the profit and loss account of the period in which the disposal occurs as the difference between the net sale proceeds and the net carrying amount, whether carried at historical cost (less any provisions made) or at a valuation.

Extraordinary items

22 Any extraordinary profit or loss should be shown separately on the face of the profit and loss account, after the profit or loss on ordinary activities after taxation but before deducting any appropriations such as dividends paid or payable and, in the case of

consolidated financial statements, after the figure for minority interests. The amount of each extraordinary item should be shown individually either on the face of the profit and loss account or in a note and an adequate description of each extraordinary item should be given to enable its nature to be understood. The tax on extraordinary profit or loss and, in the case of consolidated financial statements, the extraordinary profit or loss attributable to minority shareholders should be shown separately as a part of the extraordinary item either on the face of the profit and loss account or in a note. Any subsequent adjustments to the tax on extraordinary profit or loss in future periods should be shown as an extraordinary item.

Taxation

Any special circumstances that affect the overall tax charge or credit for the period, or that may affect those of future periods, should be disclosed by way of note to the profit and loss account and their individual effects quantified. Such disclosures should include any special circumstances affecting the tax attributable to the items specified in paragraph 20. The effects of a fundamental change in the basis of taxation should be included in the tax charge or credit for the period and separately disclosed on the face of the profit and loss account. 23

The tax on items of the type listed in paragraph 20 or on an extraordinary profit or loss should be determined by computing the tax on the profit or loss on ordinary activities as if the items did not exist, and comparing this notional tax charge with the tax charge on the profit or loss for the period (after extraordinary items). Any additional tax charge or credit (including deferred tax) arising should be attributed to the items. If there are items in both groups in the same period, the tax on the items combined should be calculated then apportioned between the two groups in relation to their respective amounts, unless a more appropriate basis of apportionment is available. If a more appropriate basis is adopted the method of apportionment should be disclosed. 24

EARNINGS PER SHARE

Paragraph 10 of SSAP 3 concerning the definition of earnings per share is withdrawn and replaced by the following paragraph: 25

> '10 The profit in pence attributable to each equity share, based on the profit (or in the case of a group the consolidated profit) of the period after tax, minority interests and extraordinary items and after deducting preference dividends and other appropriations in respect of preference shares, divided by the number of equity shares in issue and ranking for dividend in respect of the period.'

If an additional earnings per share calculated at any other level of profit is presented it should be presented on a consistent basis over time and, wherever disclosed, reconciled to the amount required by the FRS. Such a reconciliation should list the items for which an adjustment is being made and disclose their individual effect on the calculation. The earnings per share required by the FRS should be at least as prominent as any additional version presented and the reason for calculating the additional version should be explained. The reconciliation and explanation should appear adjacent to the earnings per share disclosure, or a reference should be given to where they can be found.

NOTE OF HISTORICAL COST PROFITS AND LOSSES

26 Where there is a material difference between the result as disclosed in the profit and loss account and the result on an unmodified historical cost basis, a note of the historical cost profit or loss for the period should be presented. Where full historical cost information is unavailable or cannot be obtained without unreasonable expense or delay, the earliest available values should be used. The note of the historical cost profit or loss should include a reconciliation of the reported profit on ordinary activities before taxation to the equivalent historical cost amount and should also show the retained profit for the financial year reported on the historical cost basis. The note should be presented immediately following the profit and loss account or the statement of total recognised gains and losses.

STATEMENT OF TOTAL RECOGNISED GAINS AND LOSSES

27 A primary statement should be presented, with the same prominence as the other primary statements, showing the total of recognised gains and losses and its components. The components should be the gains and losses that are recognised in the period insofar as they are attributable to shareholders*.

RECONCILIATION OF MOVEMENTS IN SHAREHOLDERS' FUNDS

28 A note should be presented reconciling the opening and closing totals of shareholders' funds of the period.

PRIOR PERIOD ADJUSTMENTS

29 Prior period adjustments should be accounted for by restating the comparative figures for the preceding period in the primary statements and notes and adjusting the opening balance of reserves for the cumulative effect. The cumulative effect of the adjustments should also be noted at the foot of the statement of total recognised gains and losses of the current period. The effect of prior period adjustments on the results for the preceding period should be disclosed where practicable.

COMPARATIVE FIGURES

30 Comparative figures should be given for all items in the primary statements and such notes thereto as are required by the FRS. The comparative figures in respect of the profit and loss account should include in the continuing category only the results of those operations included in the current period's continuing operations.

**As explained in UITF* Abstract 3 and paragraphs 6 and 7 of SSAP 22 'Accounting for goodwill', the immediate write-off to reserves of purchased goodwill is not a recognised loss.

INVESTMENT COMPANIES

Investment companies as defined in companies legislation should include in the profit and loss account only profits available for distribution. 31

INSURANCE BUSINESSES

The requirements of paragraphs 13 and 21 do not apply to the financial statements of insurance companies or insurance groups as defined in companies legislation* for the gains or losses arising on the holding or disposal of investments. Additionally, the requirements of paragraphs 13 and 21 do not apply to consolidated financial statements to the extent they include insurance companies or insurance groups. 31A

DATE FROM WHICH EFFECTIVE

The accounting practices set out in the FRS should be adopted as soon as possible and regarded as standard in respect of financial statements relating to accounting periods ending on or after 22 June 1993. 32

WITHDRAWAL OF SSAP 6 AND AMENDMENT OF OTHER STATEMENTS

[*Not reproduced as all changes have been reflected in the material reproduced in this volume.*]

Financial Reporting Standard No. 3 'Reporting Financial Performance' was adopted by a vote of eight of the nine members of the Accounting Standards Board. Mr Bradfield dissented. His dissenting view is set out on pages 458 to 459.

Members of the Accounting Standards Board

David Tweedie (Chairman)

Allan Cook (Technical Director)

Robert Bradfield

Sir Bryan Carsberg

Elwyn Eilledge

Michael Garner

Donald Main

Roger Munson

Graham Stacy

**Companies Act 1985 Section 744 and Section 255A(5).*

The equivalent legislation in Northern Ireland is the Companies (Northern Ireland) Order 1986 Article 2 and Article 263A(5).

The equivalent legislation in the Republic of Ireland is the Companies (Amendment) Act 1986 Section 2(3) and the European Communities (Companies: Group Accounts) Regulations 1992 regulation 6(2)(g).

Compliance with international accounting standards

34 The requirements of the FRS are consistent with International Accounting Standard 5 'Information to be Disclosed in Financial Statements' and International Accounting Standard 8 'Unusual and Prior Period Items and Changes in Accounting Policies'. The FRS is also consistent with the exposure draft of a proposed revised International Accounting Standard—'Extraordinary Items, Fundamental Errors and Changes in Accounting Policies' issued by the International Accounting Standards Committee in July 1992.*

***Editor's note:** *A revised version of IAS 8, now titled 'Net profit or loss for the period, fundamental errors and changes in accounting policies', was issued in November 1993. This is based on the exposure draft issued in July 1992.*

Explanation

COMPONENTS OF FINANCIAL PERFORMANCE

The many parts of a reporting entity's activities exhibit features which differ in stability, risk and predictability, indicating a need for the separate disclosure of components of financial performance in the profit and loss account and in the statement of total recognised gains and losses. The disclosure of these components is designed to facilitate understanding of the performance achieved in a period and to assist users in deciding on the extent to which past results are useful in helping to assess potential future results. A component, of whatever nature, should be shown separately if it has a special significance for the assessment of some aspect of performance. **35**

The total of all recognised gains and losses attributable to shareholders of a reporting entity includes the following components: **36**

(a) profit or loss before the deduction of dividends;
(b) adjustments to the valuation of assets; and
(c) differences in the net investment in foreign enterprises arising from changes in foreign currency exchange rates.

The profit and loss account and statement of total recognised gains and losses are intended to present all the entity's gains and losses recognised in a particular period. Profit or loss of a period focuses on what a reporting entity earns for its output (revenue) and what it sacrifices to obtain that output (expenses). Gains and losses may be excluded from the profit and loss account only if they are specifically permitted or required to be taken directly to reserves by this or other accounting standards or, in the absence of a relevant accounting standard, by law. For example, a gain on the revaluation of a fixed asset should be reflected directly in the statement of total recognised gains and losses of the period in which the revaluation takes place. The realisation, or part realisation, of such a gain on the sale of the asset in a subsequent period is not itself a gain of that later period but, rather, confirmation of a gain that had already occurred by the time of the revaluation. Consequently, the gain or loss on the disposal of the asset is to be calculated as the difference between the net sale proceeds and the net carrying amount. **37**

PROFIT AND LOSS ACCOUNT

Continuing and discontinued operations

The objective of reporting separately the results of continuing operations, acquisitions (as a component of continuing operations) and discontinued operations is to assist users, first, in assessing the financial performance of these aspects of a reporting entity's operations and, secondly, in forming a basis for the assessment of future income. Separate presentation assists analysis of the significance of the part of a reporting entity's operations that has ceased and of new operations that have been acquired. The various aspects of the definition and requirements regarding discontinued operations are explained in paragraphs 41 to 44. In respect of acquisitions, the requirement is to **38** disclose their post-acquisition results for the period in which the acquisition occurs. In some circumstances it may also be useful to users for the results of acquisitions for the first full financial year for which they are a part of the reporting entity to be disclosed in the notes.

39 The FRS requires each of the statutory profit and loss account headings between turnover and operating profit to be analysed between continuing operations, acquisitions (as a component of continuing operations) and discontinued operations. For non-financial reporting entities operating profit is normally profit before income from shares in group undertakings, although in certain cases income from associated undertakings or from other participating interests may be considered to be part of operating profit. In order to avoid too much data on the face of the profit and loss account, the minimum disclosure required there in respect of continuing operations, acquisitions and discontinued operations is the analysis of turnover and operating profit. A similar analysis is required between continuing and discontinued operations for the items specifically required to be disclosed by paragraph 20; where practicable this analysis should identify, either on the face of the profit and loss account or in the notes, the amounts arising in respect of acquisitions.

40 The analysis in respect of continuing operations, acquisitions and discontinued operations is required only to the profit before interest level because interest payable is often a reflection of a reporting entity's overall financing policy, involving both equity and debt funding considerations on a group wide basis, rather than an aggregation of the particular types of finance allocated to individual segments of the reporting entity's operations. Any allocation of interest would involve a considerable degree of subjectivity, that could leave the user uncertain as to the relevance and reliability of the information. If a reporting entity wishes to provide such an allocation, the FRS requires that the method and underlying assumptions used in making the allocation be disclosed.

Discontinued operations

41 The FRS requires operations to be classified as discontinued when the sale or termination is completed either in the period or before the earlier of three months after the commencement of the subsequent period and the date on which the financial statements are approved. Only the results of operations up to the balance sheet date should be included; operations in the subsequent period should be included in the results of that period, separately classified as discontinued if material. Any income and costs associated with a sale or termination that has not been completed are to be included in the continuing category. In some cases it may be appropriate to disclose separately in a note to the profit and loss account the results of operations which although not discontinued are in the process of discontinuing, but they should not be classified as discontinued.

42 To be included in the category of discontinued operations, a sale or termination must have a material effect on the nature and focus of the reporting entity's operations and represent a material reduction in its operating facilities resulting either from its withdrawal from a particular market (whether class of business or geographical) or from a material reduction in turnover in its continuing markets. The nature and focus of a reporting entity's operations refers to the positioning of its products or services in their markets including the aspects of both quality and location. For example, if a hotel company which had traditionally served the lower end of the hotel market sold its existing chain and bought luxury hotels then, while remaining in the business of managing hotels, the group would be changing the nature and focus of its operations. A similar situation would arise if the same company were to sell its hotels in, say, the United States of America and buy hotels in Europe. The regular sales and replacements of material assets which are undertaken by a reporting entity as part of the routine maintenance of its portfolio of assets should not be classified as discontinuances and acquisitions. In the example, the sale of hotels and the purchase of others within the same market sector and similar locations would be treated as wholly within continuing operations.

To be classified as discontinued a sale or termination should have resulted from a strategic decision by the reporting entity either to withdraw from a particular market (whether class of business or geographical) or to curtail materially its presence in a continuing market (i.e. 'downsizing'). The sale or termination of a component of a reporting entity's operations which is undertaken primarily in order to achieve productivity improvements or other cost savings is a part of that entity's continuing operations and the effects of the sale or termination should be included under that heading. **43**

To be classified as discontinued, the assets, liabilities, results of operations and activities of an operation must be clearly distinguishable, physically, operationally and for financial reporting purposes. If the financial results of a sold or terminated operation are not identifiable separately from the accounting records or to a material extent can only be derived through making allocations of income or expenses, then the operation cannot be classified as a discontinued operation. For example, a manufacturing facility that is closed down but which lacks an external market price for its output cannot be classified as a discontinued operation. **44**

The consequences of a decision to sell or terminate an operation

Paragraph 18 sets out the principle underlying the establishment of provisions as a consequence of a decision to sell or terminate an operation. This principle focuses on the fact that an obligation arises at the point when the reporting entity becomes demonstrably committed to the sale or termination. Evidence of the commitment might be the public announcement of specific plans, the commencement of implementation, or other circumstances effectively obliging the reporting entity to complete the sale or termination. A binding contract entered into after the balance sheet date may provide additional evidence of asset values and commitments at the balance sheet date. In the case of an intended sale for which no legally binding sale agreement exists, no obligation has been entered into by the reporting entity; accordingly, provisions for the direct costs of the decision to sell and for future operating losses should not be made. In accordance with normal practice, however, any permanent diminutions in asset values should be recorded. **45**

Exceptional items

46 Exceptional items are defined in paragraph 5. They are an inherent part of the normal activities of a reporting entity and are included in the computation of profit or loss on ordinary activities but, because of their exceptional size or incidence, require separate disclosure to explain the performance of a period. Exceptional items may arise from a variety of sources and for larger or more complex businesses they are likely to occur in one form or another in most periods. They should not be aggregated on the face of the profit and loss account under one heading of exceptional items but, rather, each should be included within its natural statutory format heading or paragraph 20 category and separately disclosed in accordance with the requirements of paragraphs 19 and 20. The nature of exceptional items makes it necessary to distinguish exceptional profits from exceptional losses, in the notes if not on the face of the profit and loss account. The profits or losses on the disposal of fixed assets in paragraph 20 (c) are not intended to include profits and losses that are in effect no more than marginal adjustments to depreciation previously charged. In any references to profit or loss as including or excluding exceptional items, an explanation should be given of the relevance of their inclusion or exclusion (as the case may be) in the context of considering the results of the period or assessing maintainable earnings.

47 Exceptional items may occur in either continuing or discontinued operations and need to be identified individually as belonging to one or other category. In showing the amount of each exceptional item, individual items or groups of a similar type of item should not be combined if separately they relate to continuing and to discontinued operations.

Extraordinary items

48 Extraordinary items are defined in paragraph 6. Extraordinary items should be shown on the face of the profit and loss account before deducting any appropriations such as dividends paid or payable and, in the case of consolidated financial statements, after the figure for minority interests. Extraordinary items are extremely rare as they relate to highly abnormal events or transactions that fall outside the ordinary activities of a reporting entity and which are not expected to recur. In view of the extreme rarity of such items no examples are provided. Items falling into the category of exceptional in accordance with the terms of the FRS cannot, by definition, be extraordinary.

49 The FRS follows companies legislation in requiring the tax on extraordinary profit or loss and, in the case of consolidated financial statements, the minority shareholders' interest in an extraordinary profit or loss, to be shown separately.

Taxation

50 Companies legislation requires disclosure in the notes of the details of any special circumstances that affect any liability to taxation, whether for the financial year in question or for future years, and whether in respect of profits, income or capital gains. Such special circumstances could include, for example, the effect on the tax charge of losses whether utilised or carried forward. This disclosure can be useful in

understanding the period's charge or credit in respect of taxation, particularly when there are items of the type specified in paragraph 20. It is recognised that analysing an entity's total taxation charge between component parts of its result for a period can involve arbitrary allocations that tend to become less meaningful the more components there are. However, in respect of items such as disposal profits or losses the tax can often be identified with the exceptional item concerned and the relationship between the profit or loss and the attributable tax may be significantly different from that in respect of operating profits or losses. In such circumstances it is relevant to identify the tax charge or credit more specifically. Disclosure of special circumstances can also be useful in assessing likely future amounts of taxation. Therefore, the FRS requires that the notes should not only disclose the existence of any special circumstances but should also quantify their individual effects.

The application of the fundamental accounting concept of consistency requires that the **51**
tax effects of an extraordinary item should themselves be treated as extraordinary. This principle would apply even where an extraordinary item and its tax effects are recognised in different periods, such as where the tax relief in respect of an extraordinary loss is not recognised until it is utilised in a subsequent period.

EARNINGS PER SHARE

It is not possible to distil the performance of a complex organisation into a single **52**
measure. Undue significance, therefore, should not be placed on any one such measure which may purport to achieve this aim. To assess the performance of a reporting entity during a period all components of its activities must be considered. For this reason and to provide a starting point for analysis, the FRS requires earnings per share to be calculated on profit attributable to equity shareholders of the reporting entity. If preparers wish to highlight any other version of earnings per share, they are required to provide an explanation of the particular significance they are attaching to that version and to itemise and quantify the adjustments they are making to the earnings per share required by the FRS.

SEGMENTAL REPORTING

It is important for a thorough understanding of the results and financial position of a **53**
reporting entity that the impact of changes on material components of the business should be highlighted. To assist in this objective, if an acquisition, a sale or a termination has a material impact on a major business segment the FRS requires that this impact should be disclosed and explained.

NOTE OF HISTORICAL COST PROFITS AND LOSSES

The note of historical cost profits and losses is a memorandum item that is an **54**
abbreviated restatement of the profit and loss account adjusting the reported profit or loss, if necessary, so as to show it as if no asset revaluations had been made. Adjustments are made for such items as:

(a) gains recognised in prior periods in the statement of total recognised gains and losses and realised in the current period; for example, the difference between the profit on the disposal of an asset calculated on depreciated historical cost and that calculated on a revalued amount; and
(b) the difference between an historical cost depreciation charge and the depreciation charge calculated on the revalued amount included in the profit and loss account of the period.

55 Two reasons for disclosing the profit or loss for a period on the unmodified historical cost basis of accounting are commonly cited. The first is, that for as long as discretion exists on the timing or scale of revaluations included in financial statements, the unmodified historical cost basis will give the reported profits or losses of different reporting entities on a more comparable basis. The second is the wish of certain users to assess the profit or loss on sale of assets based on their historical cost, rather than, as the FRS requires, on their revalued carrying amount. In acknowledgement of these concerns, the Board has made the provision of a note of historical cost profits and losses a requirement of the FRS in those circumstances where there is a material difference between the result as disclosed in the profit and loss account and the result on an unmodified historical cost basis. Where full historical cost information is unavailable or cannot be obtained without unreasonable expense or delay, the earliest available values should be used. The note of historical cost profits and losses should be presented immediately following the profit and loss account or the statement of total recognised gains and losses. In consolidated financial statements, the profit and loss account figure for minority interests should be amended for the purposes of this note to reflect the adjustments made where they affect subsidiary companies with a minority interest. For the purpose of paragraph 26 the following are not deemed to be departures from the historical cost convention: (a) adjustments necessarily made to cope with the impact of hyper-inflation on foreign operations and (b) the practice of market makers and other dealers in investments of marking to market where this is an established industry practice.

STATEMENT OF TOTAL RECOGNISED GAINS AND LOSSES

56 The range of important components of financial performance which the FRS requires reporting entities to highlight would often be incomplete if it stopped short at the profit and loss account, since certain gains and losses are specifically permitted or required by law or an accounting standard to be taken directly to reserves. An example is an unrealised gain, such as a revaluation surplus on fixed assets. It is necessary to consider all gains and losses recognised in a period when assessing the financial performance of a reporting entity during that period. Accordingly, the FRS requires, as a primary statement, a statement of total recognised gains and losses to show the extent to which shareholders' funds have increased or decreased from all the various gains and losses recognised in the period. It follows from this perspective that the same gains and losses should not be recognised twice (for example, a holding gain recognised when a fixed asset is revalued should not be recognised a second time when the revalued asset is sold).

Statements of total recognised gains and losses contribute further to the purposes of financial reporting by: 57

(a) combining information about operating and related performance with other aspects of a reporting entity's financial performance; and
(b) providing information (jointly with the other primary statements) that is useful for assessing the return on investment in a reporting entity.

If a reporting entity has no recognised gains or losses other than the profit or loss for the period a statement to this effect immediately below the profit and loss account will satisfy the requirement of paragraph 27.

Where there is a material recognised movement between the amount attributable to different classes of shareholders which does not affect total shareholders' funds an explanatory footnote to the statement may be appropriate. An example might be an appropriation of profit to accrue a premium on redemption of preference shares. 58

RECONCILIATION OF MOVEMENTS IN SHAREHOLDERS' FUNDS

The profit and loss account and the statement of total recognised gains and losses reflect the performance of a reporting entity in a period. There are, however, other changes in shareholders' funds that can also be important in understanding the change in the financial position of the entity. The purpose of the reconciliation of movements in shareholders' funds is to highlight those other changes. If included as a primary statement, the reconciliation should be shown separately from the statement of total recognised gains and losses. 59

PRIOR PERIOD ADJUSTMENTS

The majority of items relating to prior periods arise mainly from the corrections and adjustments which are the natural result of estimates inherent in accounting and more particularly in the periodic preparation of financial statements. They are dealt with in the profit and loss account of the period in which they are identified and their effect is stated where material. They are not exceptional or extraordinary merely because they relate to a prior period; their nature will determine their classification. Prior period adjustments, that is prior period items which should be adjusted against the opening balance of retained profits or reserves, are rare and limited to items arising from changes in accounting policies or from the correction of fundamental errors. 60

Estimating future events and their effects requires the exercise of judgement and will require reappraisal as new events occur, as more experience is acquired or as additional information is obtained. Because a change in estimate arises from new information or developments, it should not be given retrospective effect by a restatement of prior periods. Sometimes a change in estimate may have the appearance of a change of accounting policy and care is necessary to avoid confusing the two. 61

62 It is a fundamental accounting concept that there is consistency of accounting treatment within each accounting period and from one period to the next. A change in accounting policy may therefore be made only if it can be justified on the grounds that the new policy is preferable to the one it replaces because it will give a fairer presentation of the result and of the financial position of a reporting entity. It is a characteristic of a change in accounting policy that it is the result of a choice between two or more accounting methods. Therefore it does not arise from the adoption or modification of an accounting method necessitated by transactions or events that are clearly different in substance from those previously occurring. Following a change in accounting policy, the amounts for the current and corresponding periods should be restated on the basis of the new policies. The cumulative adjustments should also be noted at the foot of the statement of total recognised gains and losses of the current period and included in the reconciliation of movements in shareholders' funds of the corresponding period in order to highlight for users the effect of the adjustments.

63 In exceptional circumstances it may be found that financial statements of prior periods have been issued containing errors which are of such significance as to destroy the true and fair view and hence the validity of those financial statements. The corrections of such fundamental errors and the cumulative adjustments applicable to prior periods have no bearing on the results of the current period and they are therefore not included in arriving at the profit or loss for the current period. They are accounted for by restating prior periods, with the result that the opening balance of retained profits will be adjusted accordingly, and highlighted in the reconciliation of movements in shareholders' funds. As the cumulative adjustments are recognised in the current period, they should also be noted at the foot of the statement of total recognised gains and losses of the current period.

COMPARATIVE FIGURES

64 Comparative figures should be given for all items in the primary statements and such notes thereto as are required by the FRS. To aid comparison, the comparative figures in respect of the profit and loss account should be based on the status of an operation in the financial statements of the period under review and should, therefore, include in the continuing category only the results of those operations included in the current period's continuing operations. The comparative figures appearing under the heading 'continuing operations' may include figures which were shown under the heading of acquisitions in that previous period; no reference need be made to the results of those acquisitions, since they are not required to be presented separately in the current year. Where, however, information on acquisitions is provided voluntarily in respect of the first full year, it may be helpful to provide comparative figures for those acquisitions. Similarly, the comparative figures for discontinued operations will include both amounts relating to operations discontinued in the previous period and amounts relating to operations discontinued in the period under review, which in the previous period would have been included as part of continuing operations. The analysis of comparative figures between continuing and discontinued operations is not required on the face of the profit and loss account.

INVESTMENT COMPANIES

The FRS is based on the view that the profit and loss account for the period should include and show separately all gains and losses which are recognised in that period, except for those which are specifically permitted or required by this or other accounting standards to be taken directly to reserves or, in the absence of a relevant accounting standard, specifically permitted or required by law to be taken directly to reserves. This is a concept which applies to all types of reporting entity, although the precise form of presentation of the results of financial performance will vary between types of reporting entity. **65**

Investment companies as defined in section 266 of the Companies Act 1985* (Companies Act investment companies) have special legal provisions regarding the recording of unrealised capital losses, with the result that their profit and loss accounts are not comparable with those of other reporting entities. In the case of such investment companies all recognised gains and losses of a capital nature should be shown only in the statement of total recognised gains and losses leaving the profit and loss account to be confined to profits available for distribution. **66**

The equivalent legislation in Northern Ireland is Article 274 of the Companies (Northern Ireland) Order 86. The equivalent legislation in the Republic of Ireland is section 47 of the Companies (Amendment) Act 1993.

Note on legal requirements

GREAT BRITAIN

General

67 The requirements of Schedules 4 and 4A to the Companies Act 1985* relating to the form and content of company and group financial statements set out formats for the profit and loss account allowing some flexibility in certain circumstances in the manner in which the information is presented. The provisions of the FRS supplement those legal requirements, while remaining within their bounds.

Disclosure

68 Companies Act 1985 Schedule 4 paragraph 54

'(1) The basis on which the charge for United Kingdom corporation tax and United Kingdom income tax is computed shall be stated.
(2) Particulars shall be given of any special circumstances which affect liability in respect of taxation of profits, income or capital gains for the financial year or liability in respect of taxation of profits, income or capital gains for succeeding financial years.'

69 Companies Act 1985 Schedule 4A paragraph 13

'(1) The following information with respect to acquisitions taking place in the financial year shall be given in a note to the accounts.'
'(4) The profit or loss of the undertaking or group acquired shall be stated—
(a) for the period from the beginning of the financial year of the undertaking or, as the case may be, of the parent undertaking of the group, up to the date of the acquisition, and
(b) for the previous financial year of that undertaking or parent undertaking;

and there shall also be stated the date on which the financial year referred to in paragraph (a) began.'

70 Companies Act 1985 Schedule 4A paragraphs 15 and 16

'15 Where during the financial year there has been a disposal of an undertaking or group which significantly affects the figures shown in the group accounts, there shall be stated in a note to the accounts—
(a) the name of that undertaking or, as the case may be, of the parent undertaking of that group, and
(b) the extent to which the profit or loss shown in the group accounts is attributable to profit or loss of that undertaking or group.

The requirements relating to banking and insurance companies and groups are set out in Schedule 9 to the Companies Act 1985 [Editor's note:** Insurance companies are now Schedule 9A.].*

16 The information required by paragraph 13, or ... 15 above need not be disclosed with respect to an undertaking which—

(a) is established under the law of a country outside the United Kingdom, or
(b) carries on business outside the United Kingdom,

if in the opinion of the directors of the parent company the disclosure would be seriously prejudicial to the business of that undertaking or to the business of the parent company or any of its subsidiary undertakings and the Secretary of State agrees that the information should not be disclosed.'

Definition

Companies Act 1985 section 266 **71**

'(1) In section 265 "investment company" means a public company which has given notice in the prescribed form (which has not been revoked) to the registrar of companies of its intention to carry on business as an investment company, and has since the date of that notice complied with the requirements specified below.

(2) Those requirements are—

(a) that the business of the company consists of investing its funds mainly in securities, with the aim of spreading investment risk and giving members of the company the benefit of the results of the management of its funds,
(b) that none of the company's holdings in companies (other than those which are for the time being in investment companies) represents more than 15 per cent. by value of the investing company's investments,
(c) that distribution of the company's capital profits is prohibited by its memorandum or articles of association,
(d) that the company has not retained, otherwise than in compliance with this Part, in respect of any accounting reference period more than 15 per cent. of the income it derives from securities.'

NORTHERN IRELAND

Schedules 4 and 4A of the Companies (Northern Ireland) Order 1986 are similar to Schedules 4 and 4A of the Companies Act 1985 as referred to in paragraph 67. **72**

Paragraph 54 of Schedule 4 of the Companies (Northern Ireland) Order 1986 is similar to paragraph 54 of Schedule 4 of the Companies Act 1985 as set out in paragraph 68. **73**

Paragraphs 13, 15 and 16 of Schedule 4A of the Companies (Northern Ireland) Order 1986 are similar to paragraphs 13, 15 and 16 of Schedule 4A of the Companies Act 1985 as set out in paragraphs 69 and 70. **74**

Article 274 of the Companies (Northern Ireland) Order 1986 is similar to section 266 of the Companies Act 1985 as set out in paragraph 71. **75**

REPUBLIC OF IRELAND

76 The Schedule of the Companies (Amendment) Act 1986 is similar to Schedule 4 of the Companies Act 1985 as referred to paragraph 67.

77 Paragraph 40 of the Schedule of the Companies (Amendment) Act 1986 is similar to paragraph 54 of Schedule 4 of the Companies Act 1985 as set out in paragraph 68.

78 Section 27 of the 1992 Regulations sets out a general requirement for disclosure in the case of changes in the composition of a group. There are no specific equivalents to paragraphs 13(4) 15 and 16 of Schedule 4A of the Companies Act 1985 as set out in paragraphs 69 and 70.

79 Section 47 of the Companies (Amendment) Act 1983 is similar to section 266 of the Companies Act 1985 as set out in paragraph 71.

Illustrative examples

These illustrative examples are for general guidance and do not form part of the Financial Reporting Standard. The best form of the disclosure will depend on individual circumstances.

The example on pages 452 to 456 includes two profit and loss accounts along with a statement of total recognised gains and losses, a note of historical cost profits and losses, a reconciliation of movements in shareholders' funds and certain related notes. The following matters should also be noted:

The entity is a group of companies.

The group has made acquisitions and disposals of operations during the year under review.

In this example there is no extraordinary item. However, the positioning of such an item on the face of the profit and loss account is shown although in practice the caption would not appear if no extraordinary items existed.

The profit and loss account examples include the disclosure of earnings per share numbers and a pro forma reconciliation statement for adjusted earnings per share numbers is also shown.

The profit and loss account examples have been prepared using Format 1* as contained in Schedule 4 of the Companies Act 1985. Equivalent information should be shown if any of the other statutory formats are used.

The example on page 457 is one of a Companies Act Investment company.

**The equivalent legislation in Northern Ireland is Format 1 in Schedule 4 of the Companies (Northern Ireland) Order 1986.*

The equivalent legislation in the Republic of Ireland is Format 1 in the Schedule to the Companies (Amendment) Act 1983.

Profit and loss account example 1

	1993 £million	1993 £million	1992 as restated £million
Turnover			
Continuing operations	550		500
Acquisitions	50		
	600		
Discontinued operations	175		190
		775	690
Cost of sales		(620)	(555)
Gross profit		155	135
Net operating expenses		(104)	(83)
Operating profit			
Continuing operations	50		40
Acquisitions	6		
	56		
Discontinued operations	(15)		12
Less 1992 provision	10		
		51	52
Profit on sale of properties in continuing operations		9	6
Provision for loss on operations to be discontinued			(30)
Loss on disposal of discontinued operations	(17)		
Less 1992 provision	20		
		3	
Profit on ordinary activities before interest		63	28
Interest payable		(18)	(15)
Profit on ordinary activities before taxation		45	13
Tax on profit on ordinary activities		(14)	(4)
Profit on ordinary activities after taxation		31	9
Minority interests		(2)	(2)
[Profit before extraordinary items]		29	7
[Extraordinary items] (included only to show positioning)		–	–
Profit for the financial year		29	7
Dividends		(8)	(1)
Retained profit for the financial year		21	6
Earnings per share		**39p**	**10p**
Adjustments [to be itemised and an adequate description to be given]		Xp	Xp
Adjusted earnings per share [Reason for calculating the adjusted earnings per share to be given]		Yp	Yp

Profit and loss account example 2

	Continuing operations 1993	Acquisitions 1993	Discontinued operations 1993	Total 1993	Total 1992 as restated
	£million	*£million*	*£million*	*£million*	*£million*
Turnover	550	50	175	775	690
Cost of sales	(415)	(40)	(165)	(620)	(555)
Gross profit	135	10	10	155	135
Net operating expenses	(85)	(4)	(25)	(114)	(83)
Less 1992 provision			10	10	
Operating profit	50	6	(5)	51	52
Profit on sale of properties	9			9	6
Provision for loss on operations to be discontinued					(30)
Loss on disposal of discontinued operations			(17)	(17)	
Less 1992 provision			20	20	
Profit on ordinary activities before interest	59	6	(2)	63	28
Interest payable				(18)	(15)
Profit on ordinary activities before taxation				45	13
Tax on profit on ordinary activities				(14)	(4)
Profit on ordinary activities after taxation				31	9
Minority interests				(2)	(2)
[Profit before extraordinary items]				29	7
[Extraordinary items] (included only to show positioning)				-	-
Profit for the financial year				29	7
Dividends				(8)	(1)
Retained profit for the financial year				21	6
Earnings per share				**39p**	**10p**
Adjustments [to be itemised and an adequate description to be given]				Xp	Xp
Adjusted earnings per share				Yp	Yp

[Reason for calculating the adjusted earnings per share to be given]

Statement of total recognised gains and losses

	1993	1992 as restated
	£million	*£million*
Profit for the financial year	29	7
Unrealised surplus on revaluation of properties	4	6
Unrealised (loss)/gain on trade investment	(3)	7
	30	20
Currency translation differences on foreign currency net investments	(2)	5
Total recognised gains and losses relating to the year	28	25
Prior year adjustment (as explained in note x)	(10)	
Total gains and losses recognised since last annual report	18	

Note of historical cost profits and losses

	1993	1992 as restated
	£million	*£million*
Reported profit on ordinary activities before taxation	45	13
Realisation of property revaluation gains of previous years	9	10
Difference between a historical cost depreciation charge and the actual depreciation charge of the year calculated on the revalued amount	5	4
Historical cost profit on ordinary activities before taxation	59	27
Historical cost profit for the year retained after taxation, minority interests, extraordinary items and dividends	35	20

Notes to the financial statements

Note required in respect of profit and loss account example 1

	1993			1992 (as restated)		
	Continuing	**Discontinued**	**Total**	**Continuing**	**Discontinued**	**Total**
	£million	*£million*	*£million*	*£million*	*£million*	*£million*
Cost of sales	455	165	620	385	170	555
Net operating expenses						
Distribution costs	56	13	69	46	5	51
Administrative expenses	41	12	53	34	3	37
Other operating income	(8)	0	(8)	(5)	0	(5)
	89	25	114	75	8	83
Less 1992 provision	0	(10)	(10)			
	89	15	104			

The total figures for continuing operations in 1993 include the following amounts relating to acquisitions: cost of sales £40 million and net operating expenses £4 million (namely distribution costs £3 million, administrative expenses £3 million and other operating income £2 million).

Note required in respect of profit and loss account example 2

	1993			1992		
	Continuing	**Discontinued**	**Total**	**Continuing**	**Discontinued**	**Total**
	£million	*£million*	*£million*	*£million*	*£million*	*£million*
Turnover				500	190	690
Cost of sales				385	170	555
Net operating expenses						
Distribution costs	56	13	69	46	5	51
Administrative expenses	41	12	53	34	3	37
Other operating income	(8)	0	(8)	(5)	0	(5)
	89	25	114	75	8	83
Operating profit				40	12	52

The total figure of net operating expenses for continuing operations in 1993 includes £4 million in respect of acquisitions (namely distribution costs £3 million, administrative expenses £3 million and other operating income £2 million).

Reconciliation of movements in shareholders' funds

	1993 *£million*	**1992 as restated** *£million*
Profit for the financial year	29	7
Dividends	(8)	(1)
	21	6
Other recognised gains and losses relating to the year (net)	(1)	18
New share capital subscribed	20	1
Goodwill written-off	(25)	
Net addition to shareholders' funds	15	25
Opening shareholders' funds (originally £375 million before deducting prior year adjustment of £10 million)	365	340
Closing shareholders' funds	380	365

Reserves

	Share premium account *£million*	**Revaluation reserve** *£million*	**Profit and loss account** *£million*	**Total** *£million*
At beginning of year as previously stated	44	200	120	364
Prior year adjustment			(10)	(10)
At beginning of year as restated	44	200	110	354
Premium on issue of shares (nominal value £7 million)	13			13
Goodwill written-off			(25)	(25)
Transfer from profit and loss account of the year			21	21
Transfer of realised profits		(14)	14	0
Decrease in value of trade investment		(3)		(3)
Currency translation differences on foreign currency net investments			(2)	(2)
Surplus on property revaluations		4		4
At end of year	57	187	118	362

Note: Nominal share capital at end of year £18million (1992 £11million)

Companies Act investment company

Profit and loss account

	1993 £million	1992 £million
Revenue	35	30
Expenses	(11)	(10)
	24	20
Interest payable	(5)	(7)
Profit on ordinary activities before taxation	19	13
Tax on profit on ordinary activities	(4)	(3)
Profit on ordinary activities after taxation	15	10
Minority interests	(1)	(1)
Profit available for distribution	14	9
Dividends	(13)	(8)
Transfer to revenue reserves	1	1

Statement of total recognised gains and losses

	1993 £million	1992 £million
Capital profit on investments		
Realised gains and losses	52	70
Unrealised gains and losses	138	75
	190	145
Tax	(16)	(22)
Minority interest	(1)	(4)
	173	119
Unrealised surplus on revaluation of tangible fixed assets	4	2
Capital surplus for the year	177	121
Revenue profit available for distribution	14	9
Total recognised gains and losses for the year	191	130
Distributable profits		
Revenue profit available for distribution	14	9
Dividends	(13)	(8)
Transfer to distributable reserves	1	1
Non-distributable profits		
Transfer to non-distributable reserves	177	121
	178	122

Dissenting view

Mr Bradfield dissents from the FRS because he fears that it could frequently produce misleading measures of performance. He notes that it emphasises the components of pre-tax profit, which are now to include the results of business disposals. Shareholders will attach a different level of significance to each of these components—profits from trading being the most important in assessing the underlying performance. However, the FRS ignores, so far as the face of the profit and loss account is concerned, the often material impact in the eyes of shareholders of tax, minority interests and the issue of further shares on each of these components. Here, he believes, the FRS meets neither its own objective nor the intent of many passages in the Board's Statement of Principles.

Under the FRS, the results from trading and business disposals are shown as separate components of profit before tax but are combined thereafter. Information on the tax and minority interests relating to disposals is required, where practicable, to be given in the notes. However, there is no requirement to identify the disposals component of 'profit before tax', 'profit after tax and minorities' or 'earnings per share'. Under SSAP 6, which the FRS replaces, business disposal profits were excluded from all these measures.

Business disposal profits reflect internally generated goodwill often accrued over many years, together with an element of inflation; they are different in kind from the trading results of the year. Pending realisation, they constitute a hidden reserve. They may attract little tax and rarely contain a minority interest. By contrast, Mr Bradfield notes, it is the magnitude and quality of the earnings from trading, after tax and minority interests, that are the focus of attention for the shareholder as he uses the financial statements to assess the continuity of the source of dividends.

Mr Bradfield believes it imperative that users should clearly see the effects of tax and minorities on trading results attributable to shareholders. If, in an international group of companies, the pre-tax trading profits in a low tax regime were to fall and those in a high tax regime were to rise by an identical amount, the shareholder would be materially worse off. SSAP 6 clearly displayed this decline; the FRS serves only to mask it.

Mr Bradfield notes that increasing tax and minority interests can convert an improvement in trading profit, from one year to the next, into a decline in profit attributable to shareholders. Also, where both disposal profits and losses arise, a modest pre-tax result from disposals can be transformed into a substantial after-tax result. Superimposing these elements of profit, as opposed to displaying them separately, may create a reassuring facade which will hide the underlying trend from many users of accounts. If, in addition, there has been a rights issue or an acquisition for shares, users will be left without a single indicator of whether the entity has done well or badly. SSAP 6, when faithfully applied, coped with all these situations.

In Mr Bradfield's view, such outcomes conflict with many of the qualities of financial statements referred to in chapter 2 of the draft Statement of Principles ('The Objective of Financial Statements and Qualitative Characteristics of Financial Information').

These qualities include:

> 'comparability', whereby 'users must be able to compare the financial statements of an enterprise over time to identify trends in its financial ... performance' (paragraph 34); and
>
> 'understandability', whereby information should be 'readily understandable by users' (paragraph 38).

Furthermore, Mr Bradfield believes that the main sub-totals from 'profit before taxation on ordinary activities' downwards impart no useful information to the user. They therefore conflict with the twin primary characteristics of 'relevance' (paragraph 23) and 'reliability' (paragraph 26); in the latter case because of failure to 'represent faithfully the effect of the transactions and other events' (paragraph 28). Mr Bradfield therefore believes that the FRS will fail to meet the reasonable expectations of users of financial statements.

Mr Bradfield has suggested some alternative routes for the FRS. One would require each of the headings 'profit before tax', 'profit after tax and minorities' and 'earnings per share' to be analysed into two parts: one from trading and one from disposals. This remains an option open to preparers. He believes that it would enable individual profit and loss accounts, five year summaries and summary financial statements to present helpful and realistic pictures that accord with users' expectations of financial reporting.

The development of the Standard

GENERAL

i SSAP 6, which is superseded by FRS 3, was originally issued in 1974 and was based on the 'all-inclusive' concept of profit. It was revised as recently as 1986, but, in spite of a number of improvements that were included, there remained significant problems with its interpretation in practice, particularly in respect of the variety of treatments of apparently similar events as either ordinary or extraordinary items in the profit and loss account. The 1986 revision had not achieved the objective of narrowing the differences and variety of accounting practice in this area and calls for change had been heard from users of financial statements as well as from many preparers and auditors involved with the problem.

ii The Board responded by proposing a major change to the presentation of financial performance both in the profit and loss account itself and for items passing through reserves. Its initial proposals were issued in a discussion draft in April 1991 and these were developed in Financial Reporting Exposure Draft 1 'The Structure of Financial Statements—Reporting of Financial Performance' (FRED 1) published in December 1991.

iii The FRS has retained the essential features of FRED 1, in particular the shift of emphasis from a single performance indicator. The Board believes that the performance of complex organisations cannot be summarised in a single number and has therefore adopted an 'information set' approach that highlights a range of important components of performance. This approach inevitably means that financial statements will sometimes appear more complex than under the former standard. However, it is widely accepted that certain totals in the profit and loss account, such as profit before tax and earnings per share, have been used too simplistically and have obscured the significance of relevant underlying components of financial performance. The presentation and disclosure requirements of the FRS should provide a framework which will facilitate the analysis and interpretation of the various aspects of performance.

iv Under the previous SSAP 6 approach, the inconsistencies underlying earnings per share (calculated before extraordinary items) were not clearly evident to users of financial statements and automatic reliance was often placed on the resultant numbers without there being sufficient awareness of the subjective judgements of the preparers in what was included or excluded. In future earnings per share will be all-inclusive with the result that significant variations from one period to another or the absence of expected variations, whatever the cause, will demand some explanation. Earnings per share will tend to be more volatile than under SSAP 6, because, for example, they will include all business disposal profits and losses, but, as indicated above, there was, in any event, significant inconsistency in how SSAP 6 was applied in practice. Moreover, the FRS permits preparers of financial statements to present additional versions of earnings per share provided that (a) the assumptions on which they are based are explicitly disclosed, (b) the reasons for presenting the additional versions are explained and (c) there is consistency in the approach adopted. It is recognised that users may develop methods to calculate and publish an adjusted earnings per share of individual reporting entities on the basis of an independent assessment of financial statements. The FRS should facilitate such assessments by requiring the provision of a range of relevant information.

It will be for users to identify particular components that they consider of significance in varying circumstances. This is a feature of the information set approach. For the reasons stated above, it will not be appropriate under FRS 3 (any more than it was in practice under SSAP 6) for users to pay particular attention to any 'headline' number on the face of the profit and loss account or statement of total recognised gains and losses without considering the number's composition. Using the information required by the FRS either on the face of the financial statements or in the notes, users should adapt any headline number to give the performance measure required. The Board considers that the FRS is an important step forward in providing the requisite information to users in a form designed to assist a more mature understanding and analysis of financial performance. Where summarised or highlighted information is presented, (such as a preliminary announcement) it will be the responsibility of the presenters of such information to emphasise the particular components of performance which are of significance in their specific circumstances. v

PRINCIPAL CHANGES FROM FRED 1

The consequences of a decision to sell or terminate an operation

FRED 1 did not address the making of provisions in respect of operations that are to be discontinued in future periods. In response to comments received, this issue has been addressed in the FRS. vi

Exceptional items

In the light of the proposed severe restrictions on what should be categorised as extraordinary, FRED 1 proposed that a material profit or loss on the sale or termination of an operation should always be shown on the face of the profit and loss account. The FRS has extended this disclosure to two other items—costs of a fundamental reorganisation or restructuring having a material effect on the nature and focus of the reporting entity's operations and profits or losses on the disposal of fixed assets. FRED 1 also proposed that the tax and minority interest attributable to a profit or loss on sale or termination should be shown in a note. In view of the additional items required to be shown on the face of the profit and loss account by the FRS, the Board has given further thought to the question of attributable tax and minority interests and has added paragraphs requiring as a minimum that the aggregate tax and minority interest related to these three items should be disclosed. Preparers should provide further information, where practicable and relevant, identifying the tax and minority interest related to individual categories of these items, in order to assist users in assessing the impact of individual items on the net profit or loss attributable to shareholders. vii

A concern was expressed by respondents to FRED 1 about exceptional items and the prominence they were to be given. In summary, the view was that exceptional items viii should not be transferred to a single heading of 'exceptional', because profit before exceptional items could then become the focus of financial statement presentations, with the implication that no exceptional items are expected in the future. To meet this concern the FRS requires all exceptional items (other than three specific types of item) to be included in the income or expense heading to which they relate.

Revenue investment (discretionary expenditure)

ix The discussion draft introduced the concept of discretionary expenditure. Users of financial statements had encouraged the Board to require disclosure of expenses that are incurred largely for the benefit of future periods and that can therefore be varied by material amounts without affecting current revenues. The draft sought to do this by including a definition along these lines and amplifying it by reference to common examples of such expenses, viz., research and development expense, training, advertising and major maintenance.

x In FRED 1 the concept of discretionary expenditure was developed and in the process the name 'discretionary expenditure' was changed to 'revenue investment'. More detailed guidance was given as to what should be included under this heading and a minimum disclosure requirement was proposed. This was for the disclosure, where material, of the charges to the profit and loss account of the period in respect of research and development, training, advertising and major maintenance and refurbishment. A requirement for an explanation of all material changes between the current and prior period in the level of revenue investment was also proposed.

xi These revenue investment proposals failed to attract support in the context of the proposed accounting standard, and the Board therefore concluded that they should not be pursued by that means. The Board remains of the view that appropriate disclosures of this kind can be of assistance to users of financial statements but in the light of the responses to FRED 1 concluded that the concept can best be developed within the Board's proposals for an Operating and Financial Review to support a company's annual report—i.e. as part of a wider discussion of a company's performance. The Board's decision on the FRED 1 proposal on revenue investment does not in any way affect the existing requirements of SSAP 13—'Accounting for research and development' and the Companies Act 1985 regarding the disclosure of research and development activities.

Reconciliation of movements in shareholders' funds

xii Several respondents to FRED 1, in commenting on the statement of total recognised gains and losses, suggested it should be extended to provide a complete reconciliation of the movements in shareholders' funds. The Board agreed that changes in shareholders' funds other than those included in the statement of total recognised gains and losses can also be important in understanding the change in the financial position of a reporting entity and concluded that this additional information should be required in a reconciliation of movements in shareholders' funds. In order not to divert attention from the components of performance of the total of recognised gains and losses for the period, it specified that if included as a primary statement, the reconciliation should be shown separately from the statement of total recognised gains and losses.

Financial Reporting Standard 4 is set out in paragraphs 1–67.

The Statement of Standard Accounting Practice set out in paragraphs 18–67 should be read in the context of the Objective as stated in paragraph 1 and the definitions set out in paragraphs 2–17 and also of the Foreword to Accounting Standards and the Statement of Principles for Financial Reporting currently in issue.

The Application Notes specify how some of the requirements of FRS 4 are to be applied to transactions that have certain features.

The Explanation set out in paragraphs 68–102 and the Application Notes shall be regarded as part of the Statement of Standard Accounting Practice insofar as they assist in interpreting that statement.

Appendix III 'The development of the FRS' reviews considerations and arguments that were thought significant by members of the Board in reaching the conclusions on FRS 4. The Board adopted the FRS on the basis of the overall considerations; individual members gave greater weight to some factors than to others.

[FRS 4]
Capital instruments

(Issued December 1993)

Contents

Appendix I – Note on legal requirements

Appendix II – Compliance with international accounting standards

Appendix III – The development of the FRS

Capital instruments

Summary

Financial Reporting Standard 4 'Capital Instruments' requires capital instruments to be presented in financial statements in a way that reflects the obligations of the issuer. The FRS prescribes methods to be used to determine the amounts to be ascribed to capital instruments and their associated costs and specifies relevant disclosures. a

The amount of shareholders' funds attributable to equity and non-equity interests is to be disclosed. In consolidated financial statements a similar analysis of minority interests is to be disclosed. If any capital instrument other than shares contains an obligation to transfer economic benefits, it is to be classified as a liability. Convertible debt is to be displayed separately from other liabilities. The key distinctions may be summarised as follows: b

Item	Analysed between	
Shareholders' funds	Equity interests	Non-equity interests
Minority interests in subsidiaries	Equity interests in subsidiaries	Non-equity interests in subsidiaries
Liabilities	Convertible liabilities	Non-convertible liabilities

The direct costs incurred in connection with the issue of capital instruments should be deducted from the proceeds of the issue. This treatment applies only to those costs that can be demonstrated to relate directly to the instrument in question. Other costs are to be charged as expenses when incurred. c

The finance costs associated with liabilities and non-equity shares are to be allocated to periods at a constant rate based on the carrying amount. The amount to be attributed to these instruments initially is the net amount of the issue proceeds. The finance cost for a period is added to the carrying amount and payments deducted from it. In the case of a redeemable instrument this will result in the carrying amount at the time it is redeemed being equal to the amount payable at that time. d

The FRS applies to all reporting entities whose financial statements are intended to give a true and fair view, irrespective of size or ownership. e

The requirements of the FRS apply to all transactions and to all instruments irrespective of the date at which they are issued. f

Financial Reporting Standard 4
Objective

1 The objective of this FRS is to ensure that financial statements provide a clear, coherent and consistent treatment of capital instruments, in particular as regards the classification of instruments as debt, non-equity shares or equity shares; that costs associated with capital instruments are dealt with in a manner consistent with their classification, and, for redeemable instruments, allocated to accounting periods on a fair basis over the period the instrument is in issue; and that financial statements provide relevant information concerning the nature and amount of the entity's sources of finance and the associated costs, commitments and potential commitments.

Definitions

The following definitions shall apply in this FRS and in particular in the Statement of Standard Accounting Practice set out in paragraphs 18–67.

Capital instruments:- 2
All instruments that are issued by reporting entities as a means of raising finance, including shares, debentures, loans and debt instruments, options and warrants that give the holder the right to subscribe for or obtain capital instruments. In the case of consolidated financial statements the term includes capital instruments issued by subsidiaries except those that are held by another member of the group included in the consolidation.

Companies Act 1985:- 3
The Companies Act 1985 as amended by the Companies Act 1989.

Companies (Northern Ireland) Order 1986:- 4
The Companies (Northern Ireland) Order 1986 as amended by the Companies (Northern Ireland) Order 1990 and the Companies (No 2) (Northern Ireland) Order 1990.

Companies (Amendment) Act 1986:- 5
The Republic of Ireland Companies Acts 1963–1990 and the European Communities (Companies: Group Accounts) Regulations 1992.

Debt:- 6
Capital instruments that are classified as liabilities.

Equity shares:- 7
Shares other than non-equity shares.

Finance costs:- 8
The difference between the net proceeds of an instrument and the total amount of the payments (or other transfers of economic benefits) that the issuer may be required to make in respect of the instrument.

Investment companies:- 9
Investment companies as defined in section 266 of the Companies Act 1985, or in section 274 of the Companies (Northern Ireland) Order 1986, or in section 47(3) of the Companies (Amendment) Act 1983.

Issue costs:- 10
The costs that are incurred directly in connection with the issue of a capital instrument, that is, those costs that would not have been incurred had the specific instrument in question not been issued.

Net proceeds:- 11
The fair value of the consideration received on the issue of a capital instrument after deduction of issue costs.

12 *Non-equity shares:-*
Shares possessing any of the following characteristics:

(a) any of the rights of the shares to receive payments (whether in respect of dividends, in respect of redemption or otherwise) are for a limited amount that is not calculated by reference to the company's assets or profits or the dividends on any class of equity share.
(b) any of their rights to participate in a surplus in a winding up are limited to a specific amount that is not calculated by reference to the company's assets or profits and such limitation had a commercial effect in practice at the time the shares were issued or, if later, at the time the limitation was introduced.
(c) the shares are redeemable either according to their terms, or because the holder, or any party other than the issuer, can require their redemption.

13 *Participating dividend:-*
A dividend (or part of a dividend) on a non-equity share that, in accordance with a company's memorandum and articles of association, is always equivalent to a fixed multiple of the dividend payable on an equity share.

14 *Share:-*
Share in the share capital of the reporting company (or, in the context of consolidated financial statements, the holding company of a group), including stock.

15 *Shareholders' funds:-*
The aggregate of called up share capital and all reserves, excluding minority interests.

16 *Term (of a capital instrument):-*
The period from the date of issue of the capital instrument to the date at which it will expire, be redeemed, or be cancelled.

If either party has the option to require the instrument to be redeemed or cancelled and, under the terms of the instrument, it is uncertain whether such an option will be exercised, the term should be taken to end on the earliest date at which the instrument would be redeemed or cancelled on exercise of such an option.*

If either party has the right to extend the period of an instrument, the term should not include the period of the extension if there is a genuine commercial possibility that the period will not be extended.

17 *Warrant:-*
An instrument that requires the issuer to issue shares (whether contingently or not) and contains no obligation for the issuer to transfer economic benefits.

***Editor's note:** *See also UITF Abstract 11 'Capital instruments: issuer call options'.*

Statement of standard accounting practice

SCOPE

Financial Reporting Standard 4 applies to all financial statements intended to give a true and fair view of a reporting entity's financial position and profit or loss (or income and expenditure) for a period. The terminology used in this statement will be appropriate for those reporting entities that are companies. Entities other than companies should adapt the terminology as appropriate. **18**

The FRS applies to accounting for capital instruments by entities that issue them. It does not address accounting for investments in capital instruments issued by other entities. **19**

The scope of the FRS includes capital instruments denominated in a foreign currency. However, the FRS does not address the translation of foreign currency amounts relating to such instruments into the reporting currency or the accounting for foreign exchange differences arising from such translations. **20**

The requirements of the FRS apply to all capital instruments with the following exceptions: **21**

(a) warrants issued to employees under employee share schemes;
(b) leases, which should be accounted for in accordance with SSAP 21;
(c) equity shares issued as part of a business combination that is accounted for as a merger.

In applying the requirements of the FRS, capital instruments that are issued at the same time in a composite transaction should be considered together. They should be accounted for as a single instrument unless they are capable of being transferred, cancelled or redeemed independently of each other. **22**

CLASSIFICATION OF CAPITAL INSTRUMENTS

All capital instruments should be accounted for in the balance sheet within one of the following categories: **23**

- liabilities,
- shareholders' funds,
- in the case of consolidated financial statements, minority interests.

Capital instruments (other than shares, which are addressed at paragraphs 37–45 below) should be classified as liabilities if they contain an obligation to transfer economic benefits (including a contingent obligation to transfer economic benefits). Capital instruments that do not contain an obligation to transfer economic benefits should be reported within shareholders' funds. **24**

DEBT

Convertible debt

25 Conversion of debt should not be anticipated. Convertible debt should be reported within liabilities and the finance cost should be calculated on the assumption that the debt will never be converted. The amount attributable to convertible debt should be stated separately from that of other liabilities.

26 When convertible debt is converted, the amount recognised in shareholders' funds in respect of the shares issued should be the amount at which the liability for the debt is stated as at the date of conversion. No gain or loss should be recognised on conversion.

Carrying amount and allocation of finance costs

27 Immediately after issue, debt should be stated at the amount of the net proceeds.

28 The finance costs of debt should be allocated to periods over the term of the debt at a constant rate on the carrying amount. All finance costs should be charged in the profit and loss account, except in the case of investment companies, which are addressed in paragraph 52.

29 The carrying amount of debt should be increased by the finance cost in respect of the reporting period and reduced by payments made in respect of the debt in that period.

30 Accrued finance costs may be included in accruals rather than in the carrying amount of debt to the extent that the finance costs have accrued in one accounting period and will be paid in cash in the next. Any such accrual should be included in the carrying amount of the debt for the purposes of calculating finance costs and gains and losses arising on repurchase or early settlement.

31 Where the amount of payments required by a debt instrument is contingent on uncertain future events such as changes in an index, those events should be taken into account in the calculation of the finance costs and the carrying amount once they have occurred.

Repurchase of debt

32 Gains and losses arising on the repurchase or early settlement of debt should be recognised in the profit and loss account in the period during which the repurchase or early settlement is made.

The maturity of debt

33 An analysis of the maturity of debt should be presented showing amounts falling due:

(a) in one year or less, or on demand;
(b) between one and two years;

(c) between two and five years; and
(d) in five years or more.

The maturity of debt should be determined by reference to the earliest date on which the lender can require repayment. 34

Where committed facilities are in existence at the balance sheet date that permit the refinancing of debt for a period beyond its maturity, the earliest date at which the lender can require repayment should be taken to be the maturity date of the longest refinancing permitted by a facility in respect of which all the following conditions are met: 35

(a) The debt and the facility are under a single agreement or course of dealing with the same lender or group of lenders.
(b) The finance costs for the new debt are on a basis that is not significantly higher than that of the existing debt.
(c) The obligations of the lender (or group of lenders) are firm: the lender is not able legally to refrain from providing funds except in circumstances the possibility of which can be demonstrated to be remote.
(d) The lender (or group of lenders) is expected to be able to fulfil its obligations under the facility.

Where the maturity of debt is assessed by reference to that of refinancing permitted by facilities in accordance with paragraph 35, the amounts of the debt so treated, analysed by the earliest date on which the lender could demand repayment in the absence of the facilities, should be disclosed. 36

SHARES AND WARRANTS

Shares and warrants should be reported as part of shareholders' funds. In the period in which shares or warrants are issued, the net proceeds should be reported in the reconciliation of movements in shareholders' funds. 37

The balance sheet should show the total amount of shareholders' funds. 38

Where shares are repurchased or redeemed, shareholders' funds should be reduced by the value of the consideration given. 39

The analysis of shareholders' funds

Shareholders' funds should be analysed between the amount attributable to equity interests and the amount attributable to non-equity interests. The amount of shareholders' funds attributable to equity interests is the difference between total shareholders' funds and the total amount attributable to non-equity interests. The amount attributable to non-equity interests is the aggregate of amounts relating to all classes of non-equity shares and warrants for non-equity shares. 40

The amount attributable to non-equity shares within the analysis of shareholders' funds and the allocation of finance costs

41 Immediately after the issue of a non-equity instrument the amount of non-equity shareholders' funds attributable to it should be the net proceeds of the issue. This amount should be increased by the finance costs in respect of the period and reduced by dividends or other payments made in respect of the instrument in that period.

42 The finance costs for non-equity shares should be calculated on the same basis as the finance costs for debt set out in paragraphs 27–31 above.

43 Where the entitlement to dividends in respect of non-equity shares is calculated by reference to time, the dividends should be accounted for on an accruals basis except in those circumstances (for example where profits are insufficient to justify a dividend and dividend rights are non-cumulative) where ultimate payment is remote. All dividends should be reported as appropriations of profit.

44 Where the finance costs for non-equity shares are not equal to the dividends the difference should be accounted for in the profit and loss account as an appropriation of profits.

Equity shares and warrants

45 The net proceeds from the issue of equity shares and warrants for equity shares should be credited direct to shareholders' funds. The amount attributed to equity shares or warrants should not be subsequently adjusted to reflect changes in the value of the shares or warrants.

46 When a warrant is exercised, the amount previously recognised in respect of the warrant should be included in the net proceeds of the shares issued.

47 When a warrant lapses unexercised, the amount previously recognised in respect of the warrant should be reported in the statement of total recognised gains and losses.

Scrip dividends

48 Where shares are issued (or proposed to be issued) as an alternative to cash dividends, the value of such shares should be deemed to be the amount receivable if the alternative of cash had been chosen. Where the number of shareholders who will elect to receive the shares is uncertain, the whole amount should be treated as a liability to pay cash dividends.

SHARES ISSUED BY SUBSIDIARIES

49 Shares issued by subsidiaries (other than shares held by companies within the group) should be accounted for in consolidated financial statements as liabilities if the group taken as a whole has an obligation to transfer economic benefits in connection with the shares, for example where another member of the group has given a guarantee of payments to be made in respect of the shares. In all other cases they should be reported as minority interests.

The amount of minority interests shown in the balance sheet should be analysed between the aggregate amount attributable to equity interests and amounts attributable to non-equity interests. **50**

The amounts attributed to non-equity minority interests and their associated finance costs should be calculated in the same manner as those for non-equity shares. The finance costs associated with such interests should be included in minority interests in the profit and loss account. **51**

INVESTMENT COMPANIES

Investment companies may include the finance costs in respect of capital instruments and any gains or losses recognised in accordance with paragraph 32 in the statement of total recognised gains and losses to the extent that these items relate to capital. The amount so treated should be disclosed within the statement, and the accounting policy for determining the allocation of finance costs between revenue and capital should be stated. **52**

DISCLOSURES

The disclosures required by the following paragraphs should be made in addition to those required by paragraphs 25, 33, 36, 38, 40, 50 and 52 above. **53**

Where the disclosures required by paragraphs 25, 40 and 50 of convertible debt, non-equity interests in shareholders' funds and non-equity interests in minority interests are given in the notes to the financial statements rather than on the face of the balance sheet, the relevant caption on the face of the balance sheet should state that convertible debt or non-equity interests (as the case may be) are included. **54**

Disclosures relating to shares

An analysis should be given of the total amount of non-equity interests in shareholders' funds relating to each class of non-equity shares and series of warrants for non-equity shares. **55**

A brief summary of the rights of each class of shares should be given. This should include the following: **56**

(a) the rights to dividends;
(b) the dates at which the shares are redeemable and the amounts payable in respect of redemption;
(c) their priority and the amounts receivable on a winding up;
(d) their voting rights.

This information will usually make clear why a class of share has been classified as equity or non-equity, but, if necessary, additional information should be given to explain the classification. Where rights vary according to circumstances, these circumstances and the variation should be described.

57 The disclosure required by paragraph 56 need not be given for equity shares that have all the following features:

(a) no right to dividends other than those that may be recommended by the directors;
(b) no redemption rights;
(c) unlimited right to share in the surplus remaining on a winding up after all liabilities and participation rights of other classes of shares have been satisfied;
(d) one vote per share.

58 Where warrants or convertible debt are in issue that may require the company to issue shares of a class that is not currently in issue the information set out in paragraph 56 should be given in respect of that class.

59 The aggregate dividends for each class of share should be disclosed including the total amount in respect of each of: dividends on equity shares; participating dividends; and other dividends on non-equity shares. Any other appropriation of profit in respect of non-equity shares should also be disclosed. Where there are amounts relating to non-equity shares and the above information is not given on the face of the profit and loss account the relevant caption should make clear that such amounts are included.

Disclosures relating to minority interests

60 The minority interests charge in the profit and loss account should be analysed between equity and non-equity minority interests.

61 Where there are non-equity minority interests a description should be given of any rights of holders of the shares against other group companies.

Disclosures relating to debt

62 In respect of convertible debt, details of the dates of redemption and the amount payable on redemption should be disclosed. The number and class of shares into which the debt may be converted and the dates at or periods within which the conversion may take place should be stated. It should also be stated whether conversion is at the option of the issuer or at that of the holder.

63 A brief description should be given of the legal nature of any instrument included in debt where it is different from that normally associated with debt, for example where the debt is subordinated or where the obligation to repay is conditional. Where amounts are included in debt that represent instruments in respect of which the amount payable, or the claim that would arise on a winding up, is significantly different from that at which the instrument is stated in the financial statements, that amount should be stated. This information may be summarised and need not be given for each individual instrument.

Gains and losses arising on the repurchase or early settlement of debt should be disclosed in the profit and loss account as separate items within or adjacent to 'interest payable and similar charges'. **64**

General

Where the brief summaries required by paragraphs 56, 58, 61, 62 or 63 cannot adequately provide the information necessary to understand the commercial effect of instruments, that fact should be stated in the accounts together with particulars of where the relevant information may be obtained. The principal features of the instruments should, in any event, be stated. **65**

DATE FROM WHICH EFFECTIVE

The accounting practices set out in the FRS should be regarded as standard in respect of financial statements relating to accounting periods ending on or after 22 June 1994. Earlier adoption is encouraged but not required. **66**

WITHDRAWAL OF UITF ABSTRACT 1 AND ABSTRACT 8

The FRS supersedes UITF Abstract 1 and Abstract 8. **67**

Explanation

CAPITAL INSTRUMENTS

The definition of capital instruments, given in paragraph 2, includes all kinds of shares and debt instruments as well as options and warrants to obtain such instruments. It characterises capital instruments as a means of raising finance: an instrument may be within the definition whether or not the consideration given for its issue takes the form of cash. Capital instruments may take the form of contracts between two parties (for example a borrower and its bank) as well as an issue of transferable securities. **68**

IDENTIFICATION OF DISTINCT CAPITAL INSTRUMENTS

In order to apply the requirements of the FRS it is necessary to determine whether instruments issued at the same time should be accounted for individually or not. Accounting for the individual instruments is required by paragraph 22 if (and only if) the instruments are capable of being transferred, cancelled or redeemed independently of each other. For example, if debt and warrants are issued simultaneously and the warrants can be transferred, cancelled or redeemed independently of the debt, the two components should be accounted for separately. It would be necessary in such a case to apportion the proceeds of the issue to each component. **69**

THE CLASSIFICATION OF CAPITAL INSTRUMENTS

70 The FRS contains requirements for determining whether capital instruments should be accounted for as liabilities. Special considerations, discussed at paragraphs 82–87 below, arise in connection with shares of the entity and these requirements accordingly do not apply to them.

71 The FRS requires capital instruments to be accounted for as liabilities if they contain an obligation to transfer economic benefits (paragraph 24). The most common example of such an obligation is the requirement to make cash payments to the holder of the instrument, but an obligation to transfer other kinds of property would also cause the instrument to be classified as a liability. The payments may be described in various ways, for example as interest, or as an amount payable on redemption: how the obligation is described is not relevant to the classification of the instrument.

72 If a capital instrument contains an obligation for the issuer to transfer economic benefits to another party it should be classified as debt even if the obligation is contingent. For example an instrument that gives the holder the right to require either the transfer of cash or the issue of an equity share imposes an obligation on the issuer and should therefore be classified as a liability. The only obligations to transfer economic benefits that should not be taken into account are those that would not be considered in accordance with the going concern concept, that is, those that would arise only on the insolvency of the issuer and, where the issuer is expected to be able to comply with covenants on loan and similar agreements, those that would follow a breach of those covenants.

THE TERM OF DEBT

73 The FRS requires debt and non-equity interests to be accounted for by allocating finance costs over the term of the instrument at a constant rate. The term of the instrument is usually self-evident but where either party has the option to extend the term, or to require the instrument to be redeemed early, such options should be carefully evaluated. If there is an option for early redemption, the term should be taken to end on the earliest date the option could be exercised, unless there is no genuine commercial possibility that the option will be exercised. The term should not include any period for which the instrument might be extended unless such an extension is virtually certain at the time the instrument is issued: that is, there is no genuine commercial possibility that the period will not be extended.

74 In evaluating the commercial possibilities of options, it should be assumed that the parties will act in accordance with their economic interests. A severe deterioration in the creditworthiness of the issuer should not be anticipated, but should be taken into account when it occurs. For example, in the case of a zero coupon bond, the return to the lender consists entirely of the amount received at maturity. If the lender under such an instrument had the right to require early redemption, but on exercise of that right he would receive only the original issue price, it would be unrealistic to assume that he would exercise it unless the issuer's creditworthiness deteriorated to a significant extent. The term of such a bond would therefore normally be taken to extend to its final maturity.

FINANCE COSTS

The FRS requires finance costs to be recognised at a constant rate on the carrying amount of debt. In some instances the nominal yield on the debt will not be materially different from the amount required by the FRS to be recognised and in these circumstances calculations will not be necessary in order to derive the information required by the FRS. 75

The FRS also requires all finance costs to be charged in the profit and loss account. However, the FRS does not prohibit the capitalisation of finance costs as part of the cost of an asset by way of a simultaneous transfer from the profit and loss account that is separately disclosed. 76

THE MATURITY OF DEBT

The FRS requires the maturity of debt to be assessed according to the earliest date on which the lender could demand repayment, taking account of facilities granted by the same lender before the balance sheet date that may permit the refinancing of the debt. For example, a bank loan may fall due three months after the balance sheet date but the borrower may have obtained a commitment from the bank before the balance sheet date to provide a further loan for the same amount for a further three years. In such a case, providing the conditions required by the FRS are met, the debt would be included in the analysis of the maturity of debt as falling due between two and five years from the balance sheet date. 77

The restriction to facilities provided by the same lender or group of lenders ensures that the facility and the borrowings in question are related. It is also consistent with the requirements of companies legislation*. For this purpose lenders should be regarded as part of the same group if they are parties to the same agreement or course of dealing, even if it is not always the same members of the group who participate in individual financings entered into under that agreement or in the course of dealing. This may be the case for some multi-option facilities. However, under commercial paper arrangements funds are raised from lenders who are not parties to an agreement that provides for finance beyond the maturity of existing indebtedness. The maturity of such arrangements should therefore be taken to be that of the existing debt, even if there is an agreement with other lenders to refinance the debt if fresh commercial paper cannot be issued. 78

An increase in the price of debt is as significant as its refinancing: for this reason the FRS requires the maturity of borrowings to be assessed by reference to borrowings under related facilities only where the finance costs for the new debt are not on a basis that is 79

**Companies Act 1985, Schedule 4 paragraph 85. The equivalent legislation in Northern Ireland is the Companies (Northern Ireland) Order 1986, Schedule 4 paragraph 84, and in the Republic of Ireland is the Companies (Amendment) Act 1986, the Schedule paragraph 67.*

significantly higher than that of the existing debt. Where the cost of finance under a facility is determined by reference to a base rate (such as LIBOR) a change in that base rate should not be regarded as an increase in the level of finance costs for this purpose.

80 It would be right to have regard to facilities only if there are objective grounds for believing that the lender will fulfil its commitment. The FRS therefore requires that the facilities must be committed and that there must be no circumstances expected or likely that would either permit the lender to refrain from providing new borrowings or prevent it from providing them. The expectation that the new borrowings will be available, if required, must have existed at the balance sheet date and be reviewed in the light of any post balance sheet events to ensure that it remains reasonable on the date the financial statements are approved by the directors.

81 Particular care should be taken in considering the circumstances in which the lender may refrain from providing new borrowings. If these circumstances are described in a way that may be interpreted subjectively – for example if further finance may be withheld if the borrower's financial condition suffers an 'adverse change' and that term is not further defined – it will be unsafe to rely on borrowings under the facility being available. For that reason, the FRS requires that it can be demonstrated that any circumstances that would enable the lender to withhold finance are remote.

SHARES AND WARRANTS

82 The FRS requires all shares to be reported within shareholders' funds. Warrants are also required to be reported within shareholders' funds since, by definition, they do not contain an obligation to transfer economic benefits.

83 Certain kinds of shares have features that make them economically similar to debt. Nonetheless, the requirement to classify capital instruments as debt if they contain an obligation to transfer economic benefits does not apply to shares. The legal status of shares is well established and understood and there are specific conditions in UK and Irish legislation that have to be satisfied if any payment is made in respect of them. In addition, the balance sheet formats prescribed by companies legislation require called up share capital to be stated separately from liabilities.

84 The FRS requires shareholders' funds to be analysed to show the amount relating to equity and non-equity interests. The definition of non-equity shares is widely drawn, so that any right to a dividend or to a redemption payment that is for a limited amount will have the effect that the shares will be considered non-equity shares, irrespective of the other rights they may enjoy.

85 It is possible that in rare circumstances shares will be classified as non-equity shares in accordance with the requirements of the FRS even though they fall within the definition of equity share capital contained in companies legislation. If this situation arises further explanation would be required to clarify the position.

As financial statements are usually prepared on a going concern basis, rights of shares to participate on a winding up do not usually affect the accounting for the shares. But if winding up is foreseeable when shares are issued, the limitation of rights has a commercial effect. Such a circumstance could arise, for example, where a group raises finance by way of an issue of shares of a special purpose subsidiary with a pre-determined life. For this reason the definition requires that a limitation on the rights to participate on a winding up is taken into account only where, at the date it was introduced, it was likely that it would have a commercial effect in practice. **86**

Shares that the issuer may or will be required to redeem are classed as non-equity shares, since they do not form part of the residual interest in the company. Furthermore, since the amount payable in respect of redemption must be fixed prior to redemption, the rights of the shares in respect of redemption will be restricted. **87**

SHARES ISSUED BY SUBSIDIARIES

Usually, where subsidiaries have shares in issue that are not held by another company in the group they are reported in the consolidated financial statements within minority interests but in some cases they are required by the FRS to be reported within liabilities, that is, as debt. **88**

Consolidated financial statements are prepared on the basis that the undertakings included in the consolidation form a single entity ('the group'). Therefore, where a subsidiary has shares in issue it is necessary to look at the effect on the group as a whole when the consolidated financial statements are being prepared and to consider the rights attaching to the shares in conjunction with any agreements to which other group companies are a party. For example, if another company in the group has provided guarantees in respect of dividends or redemption, or has undertaken to purchase the shares in the event of the subsidiary failing to make the expected payments, the group as a whole will be unable to avoid the transfer of economic benefits irrespective of the financial condition of the subsidiary: accordingly the issue will constitute a liability of the group and should be reported as such. This will also be the case where the shares are issued by a subsidiary incorporated in a jurisdiction where it cannot avoid paying dividends or amounts in respect of redemption even if there are insufficient profits, in which case funds would have to be provided by other group companies. **89**

Particular care is necessary in assessing the effect of subordinated guarantees given by group companies in respect of shares issued by subsidiaries, as the degree of subordination varies widely. The intent of some such guarantees is that the rights of the holder of the shares against the group are the same as those of the holder of preference shares of the parent. All the rights and remedies of the holders of the subsidiary undertaking's shares against group companies should be considered and the shares should be reported as liabilities unless it is clear that the intended equivalence of the rights to **90** those attaching to preference shares of the parent is actually attained. If it is, the shares should be reported as non-equity minority interests.*

91 Where it is determined that it is appropriate to report shares issued by subsidiaries in consolidated financial statements within minority interests rather than as a liability, it is necessary to determine whether they represent an equity interest or a non-equity interest. Companies legislation† requires the balance sheet to show as minority interests the amount of capital and reserves attributable to shares in subsidiary undertakings included in the consolidation held by or on behalf of persons other than the parent company and its subsidiary undertakings. Where the shares are equity shares the relevant amount of minority interests will be the proportionate share of net identifiable assets. If the shares are non-equity shares the amount of capital and reserves attributable to the shares will correspond to the amount determined by the requirements of the FRS: that is the net proceeds plus recognised finance costs less payments made.

ISSUE COSTS

92 The FRS requires issue costs, as defined, to be accounted for as a reduction in the proceeds of a capital instrument. Such costs are not assets as defined in the Board's draft Statement of Principles because they do not provide access to any future economic benefits.

93 In the case of shares, issue costs are integral to a transaction with owners and for this reason the FRS requires them to be taken into account in determining the net proceeds that are reported in the reconciliation of movements in shareholders' funds. They should not be disclosed in the statement of total recognised gains and losses.

94 In the case of most debt instruments, the issuer has the use of funds during the life of the instrument, and in return pays interest. The benefit obtained from the issue costs is reflected in the interest expense: indeed, issue costs are in some cases economically indistinguishable from a discount on issue. Issue costs are therefore appropriately accounted for as an adjustment to the amount of the liability, which effectively results in their being charged over the life of the instrument. If it became clear that the instrument would be redeemed early, then the amortisation of the issue costs and any discount on issue would have to be accelerated.

95 Where the life of an instrument is indeterminate, the benefit of the issue costs is reflected in terms of the financing indefinitely. In such a case, the issue costs are therefore not

**Even if the rights of the holders of shares in a subsidiary against all companies in a group are equivalent to those of holders of a class of shares in the parent, the precise means by which those rights will be enforced, if the need arises, will differ. There will also inevitably be a risk that future events will show that the presumed equivalence does not exist. For these reasons, it would never be right to show shares issued by a subsidiary within the shareholders' funds of the group.*

†Companies Act 1985, Schedule 4A paragraph 17. The equivalent legislation in Northern Ireland is the Companies (Northern Ireland) Order 1986, Schedule 4A paragraph 17, and in the Republic of Ireland is European Communities (Companies: Group Accounts) Regulations 1992, the Schedule, paragraph 8.)

taken to the profit and loss account until such time as the instrument is redeemed or cancelled.

Care should be taken in the determination of the amount that falls to be treated as issue costs to avoid the danger of overstating finance costs over the life of the instrument in question. For this reason, the definition of issue costs is deliberately restrictive. The definition does not admit costs of researching and negotiating sources of finance or of ascertaining the suitability or feasibility of particular instruments, nor allocations of internal costs that would have been incurred had the instrument not been issued: for example management remuneration. The costs incurred in connection with a financial restructuring or renegotiation also do not qualify as issue costs; such costs relate to previous sources of finance and not to any instrument that may be issued following the restructuring or renegotiation. Costs that do not qualify as issue costs should be written off to the profit and loss account as incurred. **96**

The requirement of the FRS that issue costs are reflected in the amounts charged to the profit and loss account over the term of a capital instrument is not intended to prohibit the subsequent charging of issue costs to the share premium account by means of a transfer between reserves. The amounts that may be charged to the share premium account are determined by the requirements of companies legislation. **97**

INVESTMENT COMPANIES

Paragraph 52 of the FRS permits investment companies (provided certain conditions are met) to deal with some gains and costs relating to capital instruments in the statement of total recognised gains and losses rather than in the profit and loss account. This exemption has been included in view of the requirements of companies legislation that such companies distinguish revenue and capital and distribute as dividends a large proportion of their revenue and none of their capital. If special provisions were not included in respect of investment companies, the introduction of the FRS might result in inequitable consequences: for example, in the case of split capital investment trusts the distribution of returns as between one class of shareholder and another might be changed in a way that was contrary to the previous expectations of the shareholders and the company. The Board is considering whether guidance on accounting by investment companies, including the distinction between revenue and capital, is required. **98**

SCRIP DIVIDENDS

The FRS requires that where scrip dividends are issued or proposed the value of shares issued or to be issued should be taken to be the amount of the cash dividend. Where, as is often the case, a scrip dividend takes the legal form of a bonus issue of shares, the appropriation should be written back as a reserve movement, and appropriate amounts transferred between reserves and share capital to reflect the capitalisation of reserves. **99**

DISCLOSURE REQUIREMENTS

100 The FRS requires non-equity interests in shareholders' funds, non-equity interests in minority interests, and convertible debt to be disclosed separately from amounts relating to equity interests and non-convertible debt respectively. Because these distinctions have fundamental implications for the forecasting of future cash flows, they are extremely important and in many cases where such instruments are in issue it will be necessary for this information to be given on the face of the balance sheet. In the assessment of materiality in connection with convertible securities, consideration should be given not only to their carrying amount but also to the implications of conversion. In some cases, however, on grounds of materiality, this information may be disclosed in the notes to the financial statements rather than on the face of the balance sheet. Where this is the case, paragraph 54 requires that the caption on the face of the balance sheet should indicate that the balance sheet total includes non-equity interests or convertible debt. Similarly, paragraph 59 requires the captions used in the profit and loss account to indicate the existence of non-equity interests the details of which are disclosed only in the notes.

101 There is a presumption that amounts included in debt relate to conventional borrowing agreements. As this may not always be the case, paragraph 63 requires a brief description of the obligations and legal arrangements relating to any debt that are different from those usually associated with debt. This would apply, for example, to subordinated debt, to non-recourse debt and to those shares issued by subsidiary undertakings that are classified as debt in accordance with the FRS.

102 Although the FRS does not require the disclosure of the market values of capital instruments, such information may be useful to users of financial statements as it provides an insight into the economic burden represented by the debt. Where information on market values would assist users, its disclosure should be considered.

Application notes

These Application Notes specify how some of the requirements of FRS 4 are to be applied to transactions that have certain features. However, the Notes are not an exhaustive guide to all the requirements that may be relevant and should therefore be read in conjunction with the FRS itself.

Capital instruments may have a combination of features and accordingly more than one Note may be relevant to a single capital instrument.

The illustrations shown in the shaded areas are provided as an aid to understanding and shall not be regarded as part of the Statement of Standard Accounting Practice.

Contents

Auction Market Preferred Shares ('AMPS')

Features

AMPS are preference shares that are entitled to dividends determined in accordance with an auction process in which a panel of investors participates, the shares being transferred at a fixed price to the investor who will accept the lowest dividend. If the auction process fails — for example because no bids are received — the shares remain in the ownership of the former holder and the dividend is increased to a rate, known as the default rate, that is calculated in accordance with a prescribed formula. (This default rate may change if there is any change in the credit rating of the issuer.) In some cases dividends may be passed at the option of the issuer and in any event will not be paid by a

UK company if there are insufficient distributable profits. If the dividend is not paid the holders of the AMPS do not obtain any additional rights, for example to demand redemption. AMPS are redeemable at the option of the issuer, usually at the issue price.

Analysis and required accounting

As AMPS are shares, dividends cannot be paid in respect of them except out of distributable profits, nor can they be redeemed unless the redemption is financed out of distributable profits or by a fresh issue of shares. Because they are redeemable at a fixed amount, and because the dividend rights are limited, AMPS constitute non-equity shares.

In accordance with the requirements of the FRS, AMPS should be reported within shareholders' funds as non-equity shares and included in the amount attributable to non-equity shares (paragraph 40). The finance cost for each period should be the dividend rights accruing in respect of the period.

Capital contributions

Features

Capital contributions are sometimes made by a holding company to its wholly-owned subsidiary in order to provide the finance necessary for the subsidiary where it is not desired that this should be by way of debt and there would be adverse consequences (for example, tax consequences) arising from a subscription for new shares. Whilst a capital contribution enhances the value of the holding company's investment in its subsidiary, there is no requirement for the subsidiary to bear any servicing cost, nor can it be required to repay the contribution.

Analysis and required accounting

From the standpoint of the subsidiary, a capital contribution does not contain an obligation to transfer economic benefits. In accordance with paragraph 24 of the FRS it should be reported within shareholders' funds. In the year in which the capital contribution is made, it should be reported in the reconciliation of movements in shareholders' funds.

Convertible capital bonds

Features

The detailed provisions of convertible capital bonds vary but the following are typical. Convertible capital bonds are debt instruments on which interest is paid periodically, issued by a special purpose subsidiary incorporated outside the UK. Prior to maturity they may be exchanged for shares of the subsidiary which, at the option of the bondholder, are either immediately redeemed or immediately exchanged for ordinary shares of the parent. The bonds and payments in respect of the shares of the subsidiary are guaranteed by the parent. The parent has the right to issue convertible redeemable preference shares of its own in substitution for the bonds should it wish to do so.

Analysis and required accounting

From the standpoint of the subsidiary, convertible capital bonds are clearly debt since the obligation to pay interest is an obligation to transfer economic benefits. In addition, paragraph 25 of the FRS requires that conversion of debt should not be anticipated. In the subsidiary's financial statements the bonds should therefore be accounted for as debt.

From the standpoint of the group they are also liabilities. Even though the parent has the option to issue convertible preference shares in substitution for the bonds, the requirements of paragraph 25 of the FRS again entail that such conversion should not be anticipated. Whilst non-equity shares have a particular legal status that justifies their inclusion in shareholders' funds, this does not justify reporting within shareholders' funds an instrument that does not have that status and may never be converted into one that does.

Since the liabilities are convertible, the amount attributable to convertible capital bonds should be included in the amount of convertible debt, which should be stated separately from other liabilities.

Convertible debt with a premium put option

Features

Convertible debt with a premium put option contains an option for the holder to demand redemption (either at the maturity of the debt or at some earlier date) for an amount that is in excess of the amount originally received for the debt. At the time the debt is issued, it is uncertain whether the debt will be converted before the redemption option may be exercised, and hence whether the premium on redemption will be paid.

Analysis and required accounting

The premium put option provides a higher guaranteed return to the holder of the debt than would be received on identical debt without such a put option. Often this higher return corresponds to that which the holder would have expected to receive on non-convertible debt. The holder's decision as to whether to exercise the option will depend on the relative values of the shares to which he would be entitled on conversion and the cash receivable, including the premium, on exercise of the option.

In accordance with the definition of the term of an instrument contained in paragraph 16 of the FRS, the term of convertible debt with a premium put option should be considered to end on the earliest date at which the holder has the option to require redemption. The premium payable on exercise of the premium put option falls to be included in the calculation of the finance costs for the debt.

On conversion, in accordance with paragraph 26 of the FRS, the proceeds of the shares issued should be deemed to be the carrying amount of the debt, including accrued premium, immediately prior to conversion.

Convertible debt with enhanced interest

Features

As an alternative to the premium put structure discussed above, convertible debt may contain an undertaking that the interest will be increased at a date in the future. At the time the debt is issued, it is uncertain whether the debt will be converted before the enhanced interest is payable.

Analysis and required accounting

The enhanced rate of interest increases the guaranteed return to the holder. Often this higher return corresponds to that which the holder would have expected to receive on non-convertible debt. The holders' decision as to whether to convert the debt will take into account the interest forgone by such a decision.

In accordance with the definitions set out in paragraphs 8 and 16 of the FRS, the interest for the full term of the convertible debt should be taken into account in the allocation of finance costs, which should be allocated at a constant rate in accordance with paragraph 28.

Illustration

Convertible debt is issued on 1 January 2000 for £1,000 and is redeemable at the same amount on 31 December 2014. It carries interest of £59 a year (a nominal rate of 5.9 per cent) for the first five years, after which the rate rises to £141 a year (a nominal rate of 14.1 per cent).

In order to comply with paragraph 28 of the FRS the finance costs should be allocated to accounting periods at the rate of 10 per cent a year. The movements on the carrying amount over the term of the debt would be as follows:

Year ending	*Balance at beginning of year*	*Finance costs for year (10%)*	*Cash paid during year*	*Balance at end of year*
	£	£	£	£
31.12.2000	1,000	100	(59)	1,041
31.12.2001	1,041	104	(59)	1,086
31.12.2002	1,086	109	(59)	1,136
31.12.2003	1,136	113	(59)	1,190
31.12.2004	1,190	119	(59)	1,250
31.12.2005	1,250	125	(141)	1,234
31.12.2006	1,234	124	(141)	1,217
31.12.2007	1,217	122	(141)	1,198

31.12.2008	1,198	120	(141)	1,177
31.12.2009	1,177	118	(141)	1,154
31.12.2010	1,154	116	(141)	1,129
31.12.2011	1,129	113	(141)	1,101
31.12.2012	1,101	110	(141)	1,070
31.12.2013	1,070	107	(141)	1,036
31.12.2014	1,036	105*	(141 + 1,000)	—

Debt issued with warrants

Features

Debt is sometimes issued with warrants. The issue is often made for the par value of the debt and the debt will be redeemed at the same amount. The warrants and the debt are capable of being transferred separately.

Analysis and required accounting

In accordance with paragraph 22 of the FRS, the proceeds of the issue should be allocated between the debt and the warrants. As a result, the amount of the proceeds deemed to relate to the debt will be less than par value. The discount on issue should be treated as finance costs and apportioned to accounting periods so that the total finance costs on the debt will have a constant relationship to the outstanding obligation.

Accounting for warrants is specified at paragraphs 45–47 of the FRS.

Illustration

Debt and warrants are issued together for £1,250. The debt is redeemable at the same amount. The term of the debt is five years from 1 January 2000 and it carries interest at 4.7 per cent (£59 a year). It is determined (for example by reference to the market values for the debt and the warrants immediately after issue) that the fair value of the debt and the warrants are respectively £1,000 and £250.

The debt would initially be recognised at £1,000. The finance cost of the debt is the difference between the payments required by the debt which total £1,545 ((5 × £59) + £1,250) and the deemed proceeds of £1,000, that is, £545. In order to allocate these costs over the term of the debt at a constant rate on the carrying amount (as required by paragraph 28 of the FRS) they must be allocated at the rate of 10 per cent. The movements on the carrying amount of the debt over its term would be as follows:

**Increased by £1 rounding difference*

Year ending	Balance at beginning of year	Finance costs for year (10%)	Cash paid during year	Balance at end of year
	£	£	£	£
31.12.2000	1,000	100	(59)	1,041
31.12.2001	1,041	104	(59)	1,086
31.12.2002	1,086	109	(59)	1,136
31.12.2003	1,136	113	(59)	1,190
31.12.2004	1,190	119	(1,250 + 59)	—

Deep discount bonds

Features

Deep discount bonds are bonds that carry a low nominal rate of interest and accordingly are issued at a discount to the value at which they will be redeemed. In the extreme case where no interest at all is payable they are sometimes referred to as zero coupon bonds.

Analysis and required accounting

The cost to the borrower of issuing a deep discount bond comprises the discount on issue as well as any interest payments. It is clear that deep discount bonds represent liabilities of the issuer since they contain an obligation to make cash payments. In accordance with the definition of 'finance costs' in paragraph 8 of the FRS the finance costs will constitute the difference between the net proceeds and the total payments that the issuer may be required to make in respect of the instrument. In accordance with paragraph 28 of the FRS the finance costs will be allocated to periods at a constant rate on the carrying amount, with the result that the carrying amount of the bond immediately prior to redemption will equate to the amount at which it is to be redeemed. The discount should not be treated as an asset.

Accounting for a deep discount bond is illustrated above in connection with debt issued with warrants.

Income bonds

Features

The distinctive feature of income bonds is that interest is payable only in the event that the issuer has sufficient reported profits (after allowing for interest on other kinds of debt) to make the payment. If profits are insufficient the issuer is not in default and no additional rights accrue to the holder of the bond, although interest payments may be cumulative. Income bonds must be redeemed by the issuer at a fixed amount on a specific date.

Analysis and required accounting

The requirement to redeem the bonds is an obligation to transfer economic benefits. The bonds must therefore be accounted for as a liability as required by paragraph 24 of the FRS. Even if the issuer were not required to redeem the bonds, they would still be classed as a liability, because of the obligation to pay interest. The fact that the obligation to pay is dependent on the existence of profits makes the obligation contingent, but it does not remove the obligation.

Index linked loans

Features

Sometimes loan agreements do not state a specific amount for the payments: instead they include a formula to be used for their calculation. For example, in the case of floating rate loans, the amount of periodic payments of interest will be calculated by reference to a base rate—e.g. LIBOR + 2 per cent.

Another example is that of index linked loans which may be redeemable at the principal amount multiplied by an index.

Analysis and required accounting

Paragraph 31 requires that finance costs contingent on uncertain events such as changes in an index should be adjusted to reflect those events only once they have occurred. The effect is that the initial carrying amount will take no account of those events but the carrying amount at each subsequent balance sheet date will be recalculated to take account of the changes occurring in that reporting period. The resulting change in carrying amount is accounted for as an increase or decrease in finance costs for the period.

Illustration

A loan of £1,250 is issued on 1 January 2000 on which interest of 4 per cent (£50) is paid annually and the principal amount is repayable based on an index. The balance at the end of each year is found by multiplying the original principal amount by the index at the end of the year: the change in the amount is treated as additional finance costs.

Year ending	*Balance at beginning of year*	*Finance costs for year (10%)*	*Cash paid during year*	*Balance at end of year*	*Index at end of year*
	£	£	£	£	
31.12.2000	1,250	125	(50)	1,325	106
31.12.2001	1,325	100	(50)	1,375	110
31.12.2002	1,375	75	(50)	1,400	112
31.12.2003	1,400	150	(50)	1,500	120
31.12.2004	1,500	175	(1,625 + 50)	—	130

Limited recourse debt

Features

Sometimes debt is raised on terms that the lender's recourse is limited. Although the borrower is expected to meet the obligations of the debt out of his general resources, in the event of default the lender can obtain repayment only by enforcing his rights against the particular security that is identified in the loan agreement. If the proceeds of the security are insufficient to repay the loan, the lender must bear the loss and has no further rights against the borrower.

Analysis and required accounting

Limited recourse debt constitutes an obligation on the part of the borrower to repay, and hence should be accounted for as a liability*. The borrower will normally have all the benefits of the security (including the right to receive the sale proceeds) and will have to meet the obligation to repay the debt in order to preserve these rights. Although if the security declines in value the borrower may possibly be able to elect to hand it over to the lender and thus avoid any further liability in respect of the debt, such an eventuality would be unusual, and therefore should not be reflected in the accounting until such time as the asset is transferred.

Limited recourse debt is one of the kinds of debt envisaged in paragraph 63 of the FRS in that its legal nature differs from that usually associated with debt. A brief description of its nature should be given. An illustration of such disclosure is set out below.

Illustration of disclosures

'The limited recourse debt of £XXX is secured on the company's investment in an industrial warehouse at Allington Industrial Estate, Barsetshire, which has a market and book value of £YYY. In the event of non-payment of the interest or principal on this debt, the lenders have the right to require the sale of the property and will be paid all the sale proceeds up to the amount of the debt but have no other rights against the company.'

Participating preference shares

Features

Participating preference shares are similar to other familiar kinds of preference shares except that they are entitled, in addition to a fixed dividend for each accounting period, to a proportion of the dividends paid on equity shares.

The Board's project on reporting the substance of transactions addresses the limited circumstances in which non-recourse finance should be accounted for using a linked presentation. (Editor's note: See FRS 5.*)*

Analysis and required accounting

Because participating preference shares contain an entitlement to share in profits that is of a restricted amount and has priority over the other classes of shares, they are non-equity shares in accordance with the definition in paragraph 12 of the FRS and their interest in shareholders' funds should be presented in the balance sheet within the aggregate amount attributable to non-equity shares as required by paragraph 40. The fixed and participating elements of the dividend will be disclosed separately as required by paragraph 59.

Perpetual debt

Features

Perpetual debt is debt in respect of which the issuer has neither the right nor the obligation to repay the principal amount of the debt. Usually, interest is paid at a constant rate, or at a fixed margin over a benchmark rate such as LIBOR.

Analysis and required accounting

Sometimes it is suggested that as the principal amount will never be repaid there is no need for the balance sheet to reflect a liability in respect of the debt. However, the obligation to pay interest is an obligation to transfer economic benefits and hence the instrument is a liability. As there are no repayments of principal the burden of this liability never diminishes.

The FRS is based on the principle that debt should be accounted for having regard to all the payments required by the debt, irrespective of their legal description, in the determination of the appropriate finance charge and capital repayment for each accounting period. In the case of perpetual debt where interest is paid at a constant rate, or at a fixed margin over a benchmark, the correct finance charge will be equal to the coupon payable for each period. Hence no part of the repayments will reduce the carrying amount and the debt will always be shown at the amount of net proceeds. If the amount of the claim that would arise on a winding up is different from the carrying amount of the debt, it should be stated in accordance with paragraph 63.

Repackaged perpetual debt

Features

Sometimes perpetual debt is issued that carries interest at a relatively high rate for a number of years ('the primary period'), and then bears no further interest, or only a nominal amount. As the debt cannot be required to be redeemed, its value after the primary period has expired is negligible and, in practice, there will usually be arrangements to transfer it to a party friendly to the issuer or to enable the issuer to elect, in effect, to redeem the debt for a token amount.

Analysis and required accounting

The substance of such an arrangement is that the debt is repaid over the primary period. The payments required by the debt should be apportioned between a finance charge for each accounting period and the effective reduction of the principal amount. It would be necessary to make full disclosure of the arrangement in the financial statements.

The finance costs of the debt (as defined in paragraph 8 of the FRS) will be the difference between the net proceeds and the payments which the issuer is required to make. This will be allocated to periods over the primary period at a constant rate on the carrying amount, as required by paragraph 28 of the FRS.

Illustration

On 1 January 2000 a company borrows £1,250 which is stated to be irredeemable and to carry interest of 16.275 per cent for the first ten years after which no further payments are required. The annual payments would be £203. The substance of the arrangement is that the ten payments of £203 would repay the amount borrowed and the finance charge would be allocated using a rate of 10 per cent. The accounting would be as follows:

Year ending	*Balance at beginning of year*	*Finance costs for year (10%)*	*Cash paid during year*	*Balance at end of year*
	£	£	£	£
31.12.2000	1,250	125	(203)	1,172
31.12.2001	1,172	117	(203)	1,086
31.12.2002	1,086	108	(203)	991
31.12.2003	991	99	(203)	887
31.12.2004	887	88	(203)	772
31.12.2005	772	77	(203)	646
31.12.2006	646	64	(203)	507
31.12.2007	507	50	(203)	354
31.12.2008	354	35	(203)	186
31.12.2009	186	17*	(203)	—

Stepped interest bonds

Features

The stated rate of interest payable in respect of stepped interest bonds increases progressively over the period of issue.

**Reduced by £1 rounding difference*

Analysis and required accounting

In the case of stepped interest bonds, the stated rate of interest for each accounting period does not reflect the true economic cost of borrowing in any period during the time the bond is outstanding, since low rates of interest in one period are compensated for by higher rates in another.

Under the requirements of paragraph 28 of the FRS the pattern of the interest payments does not affect the allocation of finance costs. The payments required by the debt should be apportioned between a finance charge for each accounting period at a constant rate on the outstanding obligation and a reduction of the carrying amount. The effect of this accounting on a stepped interest bond is that the overall effective interest cost will be charged in each accounting period: an accrual will be made in addition to the cash payments in earlier periods and will reverse, partially offsetting the higher cash payments, in later periods. It would be necessary to make full disclosure of the arrangement in the financial statements.

Illustration

A loan of £1,250 is entered into on 1 January 2000 under which interest is payable according to the following schedule:

Year ending	*Rate of interest (as a percentage of nominal account)*	*Amount of interest*
		£
31.12.2000	6.0	75
31.12.2001	8.0	100
31.12.2002	10.0	125
31.12.2003	12.0	150
31.12.2004	16.4	205

The overall effective rate can be found to be 10 per cent. The movement on the loan over its period in issue would be as follows:

Year ending	*Balance at beginning of year*	*Finance costs for year (10%)*	*Cash paid during year*	*Balance at end of year*
	£	£	£	£
31.12.2000	1,250	125	(75)	1,300
31.12.2001	1,300	130	(100)	1,330
31.12.2002	1,330	133	(125)	1,338
31.12.2003	1,338	134	(150)	1,322
31.12.2004	1,322	133	(1,250 + 205)	—

Subordinated debt

Features

Subordinated debt is debt under which the rights of the lender are not as great as those of other creditors of the issuer. The methods of subordination vary widely. For example, one method is for subordinated debt to be repaid only when certain conditions are met, which are intended to ensure that the interests of other creditors are not impaired by the repayment. Another method of subordination is a prohibition on repayment of the debt whilst other creditors remain unpaid.

Analysis and required accounting

Irrespective of the means of subordination that is used, the lender on subordinated terms does not forgo the right to be repaid: he simply accepts that under certain conditions repayment will be postponed. It follows that, despite the subordination, the company has an obligation to repay (that is, an obligation to transfer economic benefits) and therefore subordinated debt should be accounted for as a liability.

Subordinated debt is one of the kinds of debt envisaged in paragraph 63 of the FRS in that its legal nature differs from that usually associated with debt. A brief description of its nature should be given. An illustration of such disclosure is set out below.

Illustration of disclosures

'The only event of default in relation to the subordinated debt is non-payment of principal or interest. The only remedy available to the holders of the subordinated debt in the event of default is to petition for the winding up of the company. In a winding up no amount will be paid in respect of the subordinated debt until all other creditors have been paid in full.'

Adoption of FRS 4 by the Board

Financial Reporting Standard 4—'Capital Instruments' was approved for issue by the eight members of the Accounting Standards Board.

David Tweedie	(Chairman)
Allan Cook	(Technical Director)
Robert Bradfield	
Ian Brindle	
Sir Bryan Carsberg	
Michael Garner	
Donald Main	
Graham Stacy	

Appendix I

Note on legal requirements

1 The following note sets out certain of the requirements of the law relating to accounting for capital instruments and, where necessary, explains the relationship between the requirements of the FRS and the legal requirements.

GREAT BRITAIN

Presentation of shareholders' funds

2 Paragraph 40 of the FRS requires the aggregate amount of shareholders' funds to be analysed between the amount attributable to equity interests and the amount attributable to non-equity interests. It is envisaged that this analysis will be presented as supplementary to the information required by the Companies Act 1985 (the amounts of called up share capital, share premium account, revaluation reserve, other reserves (with a sub-analysis of this amount) and profit and loss account). The FRS does not require any of the individual components of shareholders' funds to be analysed between equity and non-equity interests.

3 Sections 130–133 of the Companies Act 1985 contain requirements for amounts to be taken to the share premium account and for the application of that account. The FRS does not contain any requirements concerning the amounts to be taken to the share premium account or called up share capital and therefore does not conflict with these requirements of the law. For example, nothing in the FRS affects the availability of merger relief under section 131 of the Act.

Minority interests

4 Paragraph 1 of Schedule 4A to the Companies Act 1985 requires group accounts to be prepared as if the group were a single company. Paragraph 17 of that Schedule requires the amount of capital and reserves attributable to shares in consolidated subsidiary undertakings held by persons other than the parent company or other group companies to be shown under minority interests. Paragraph 49 of the FRS addresses the interaction of those requirements where the shareholder of a subsidiary has other rights against group companies, for example under a guarantee given by a parent. It requires the accounting to reflect such an obligation, by recognising a liability in respect of it. Where this accounts entirely for the arrangement there will be no amount remaining that represents an interest in the capital and reserves of the subsidiary.

Discount on issue and premium on redemption

5 Paragraph 24 of Schedule 4 to the Companies Act 1985 permits the excess of the amount repayable on a debt over the consideration received to be treated as an asset.

As this treatment is not, however, mandatory, the FRS, which, in accordance with its principles, requires a different treatment, is not in conflict with the Act.

Paragraph 3(2) of Schedule 4 to the Companies Act 1985 prohibits treating the expenses of and commission on any issue of shares or debentures as an asset. 6

Maturity of debt

Paragraph 85 of Schedule 4 to the Companies Act 1985 requires a loan to be treated as falling due for repayment on the earliest date on which the lender could require repayment if he exercised all options and rights available to him. The requirements of the FRS are consistent with this requirement. 7

Other requirements

Schedule 4 to the Companies Act 1985 also requires the following information to be disclosed: 8

(a) In respect of shares (paragraph 38(1))
  (i) the authorised share capital; and
  (ii) where there are shares of more than one class, the number and aggregate nominal value of shares of each class allotted.

(b) In the case of allotted redeemable shares (paragraph 38(2))
  (i) the earliest and latest dates on which the company may redeem them;
  (ii) whether redemption is mandatory, or is at the option of either the company or the shareholder; and
  (iii) whether any (and, if so, what) premium is payable on redemption.

(c) Where the company has allotted any shares during the year (paragraph 39)
  (i) the reason for the allotment;
  (ii) the classes of shares allotted; and
  (iii) in respect of each class of shares, the number allotted, their aggregate nominal value and the consideration received by the company.

(d) In respect of contingent rights to the allotment of further shares (such as options to subscribe or rights relating to the conversion of shares or securities) the following information (paragraph 40)
  (i) the number, description and amount of the shares involved;
  (ii) the period during which the right is exercisable; and
  (iii) the price to be paid for the shares allotted.

(e) Where the company has issued any debentures during the year (paragraph 41(1))
  (i) the reason for making the issue;
  (ii) the classes of debentures issued; and
  (iii) in respect of each class of debentures, the amount issued, and the consideration received by the company.

(f) Particulars of any redeemed debentures which the company has power to reissue (paragraph 41(2)).

(g) Where debentures are held by a nominee or trustee for the company, the nominal amount and the amount at which the debentures are stated in the accounting records (paragraph 41(3)).

(h) In respect of each item under creditors (paragraph 48)
  (i) the total amount that is not repayable by instalments and is not due for repayment within five years of the balance sheet date;
  (ii) the total amount that is repayable by instalments, some of which fall due beyond five years from the balance sheet date, disclosing separately the amount that falls due beyond five years. (This is not required for amounts that are included in a category of creditors falling due within one year);
  (iii) the terms of repayment and interest on each debt details of which are given under (i) or (ii) above; or, if this would result in a statement of excessive length, a general indication of the terms of payment or repayment and the rates of interest; and
  (iv) the total amount in respect of which any security has been given, and an indication of the nature of the security.

(i) In respect of dividends and reserve transfers
  (i) the profit and loss account must show the amounts set aside to or withdrawn from reserves and the aggregate amount of any dividends paid and proposed (paragraph 3(7));
  (ii) the aggregate amount which is recommended for distribution by way of dividend (paragraph 51(3)); and
  (iii) the amount of any arrears of fixed cumulative dividends on any class of the company's shares, and the period for which they are in arrears (paragraph 49).

(j) The amount of interest on or similar charges in respect of each of (paragraph 53(2))
  (i) bank loans and overdrafts, and other loans which are not repayable by instalments and fall due within five years of the balance sheet date;
  (ii) bank loans and overdrafts, and other loans which are repayable by instalments the last of which falls due for payment within five years of the balance sheet date;
  (iii) other loans.

(k) The amount of convertible loans shall be shown separately from other debenture loans (note (7) on the balance sheet formats).

Banking and insurance companies and groups

9 Schedule 4 to the Companies Act 1985 does not apply to banking and insurance companies and groups. Requirements equivalent to those of Schedule 4 for banking companies and groups are contained in Schedule 9 (as amended by the Companies Act 1985 (Bank Accounts) Regulations 1991); those for insurance companies and groups are contained in Schedule 9A to the Companies Act 1985, which is expected to be amended shortly by the Companies Act 1985 (Insurance Companies Accounts) Regulations.*

***Editor's note:** *Issued December 1993 (SI 1993 No 3246).*

NORTHERN IRELAND

The Companies (Northern Ireland) Order 1986 requires similar information in respect of share capital and reserves to that required by the Companies Act 1985, as referred to in paragraph 2 above. 10

Articles 140–143 of the Companies (Northern Ireland) Order 1986 are similar to sections 130–133 of the Companies Act 1985, referred to in paragraph 3 above. 11

Schedules 4 and 4A to the Companies (Northern Ireland) Order 1986 are similar to Schedules 4 and 4A to the Companies Act 1985. 12

Schedule 9 to the Companies (Northern Ireland) Order 1986, as amended by the Companies (1986 Order) (Bank Accounts) Regulations (Northern Ireland) 1992 is similar to Schedule 9 to the Companies Act 1985 (as amended by the Companies Act 1985 (Bank Accounts) Regulations 1991). Schedule 9A to the Companies (Northern Ireland) Order 1986, which is expected to be amended shortly, is similar to Schedule 9A to the Companies Act 1985. 13

REPUBLIC OF IRELAND

The Companies (Amendment) Act 1986 requires similar information in respect of share capital and reserves to that required by the Companies Act 1985, as referred to in paragraph 2. 14

Section 62 of the Companies Act 1963 is similar to section 130 of the Companies Act 1985. There are no requirements in the legislation of the Republic of Ireland equivalent to sections 131–133 of the Companies Act 1985. 15

The following table shows the references to the requirements of legislation of the Republic of Ireland which correspond to the provisions of Schedule 4A to the Companies Act 1985 mentioned above. 16

Companies Act 1985 Schedule 4A paragraph 1

European Communities (Companies: Group Accounts) Regulations paragraph 15

Companies Act 1985 Schedule 4A paragraph 17

European Communities (Companies: Group Accounts) Regulations, the Schedule paragraphs 8–9.

The following table shows the references to the requirements of legislation of the Republic of Ireland which correspond to the provisions of Schedule 4 to the Companies Act 1985 mentioned above. 17

Great Britain: Companies Act 1985 Schedule 4	*Republic of Ireland: Companies (Amendment) Act 1986 Schedule (unless otherwise stated)*
Paragraph 3(2)	Section 4(12)
3(7)	Section 4(15)
24	Paragraph 12
38(1)	26(1)
38(2)	26(2)
39	27
40	No equivalent
41(1)	28(1)
41(2)	28(2)
41(3)	28(3)
48	34
49	35
51(3)	37(3)
53(2)	39(2)
85	67
Note (7) on the balance sheet formats	Note (5) on the balance sheet formats

18 Schedule 6 to the Companies Act 1963, as amended by the European Communities (Credit Institutions: Accounts) Regulations 1992 is similar to Schedule 9 to the Companies Act 1985 (as amended by the Companies Act 1985 (Bank Accounts) Regulations 1991). Schedule 6 to the Companies Act 1963, insofar as it relates to insurance companies, is expected to be amended shortly to implement the EC Insurance Accounts Directive.

Appendix II – Compliance with international accounting standards

The requirements of the FRS are consistent with existing International Accounting Standards. However, the International Accounting Standards Committee ('IASC') has issued an exposure draft (E40) that is a draft of a proposed standard on Financial Instruments.

The principal areas where the proposals of the IASC exposure draft and the FRS are at variance are:

(a) The IASC exposure draft proposes that certain preferred shares, for example those where the holder has the right to require redemption, should be accounted for as liabilities. For the reasons given in paragraphs 5–6 of Appendix 111, the FRS requires all shares to be reported within shareholders' funds.

(b) The IASC exposure draft proposes that the proceeds of instruments that have both liability and equity rights should be allocated between the component parts. For the reasons given in paragraphs 14–18 of Appendix 111, the FRS requires such instruments to be accounted for wholly as a liability.

The IASC has announced that a revised exposure draft, E48, Financial Instruments will be published on 1 January 1994. It is not expected that the proposals of E48 will differ from those of E40 in respect of the above matters.*

***Editor's note:** The published E48 proposals do not differ.*

Appendix III – The development of the FRS

1 The Board undertook the development of an FRS on accounting for capital instruments in view of the increasing number and variety of capital instruments that have been introduced in recent years. Accounting for some of the new instruments has not always been uniform, and a variety of arguments have been advanced to justify differing treatments. Some of these arguments have called into question methods of accounting for capital instruments that have been used for many years and had previously appeared uncontroversial. The central issues that required resolution were the criteria to be used to determine whether a capital instrument represents debt or equity and the treatment of instruments such as convertible debt that will or may be exchanged for other instruments.

2 The contents of the FRS are closely based on the proposals contained in FRED 3 'Accounting for Capital Instruments' which was issued in December 1992. In turn, the proposals in that FRED were based on those set out in the Board's Discussion Paper 'Accounting for Capital Instruments' which was published in December 1991. The considerations that the Board found persuasive in framing the principal proposals in the frs are summarised in paragraphs 3–23 below. Paragraphs 24–44 summarise the principal comments made by respondents to the FRED and discuss consequent modifications to the proposals of the FRED that have been made in response to those comments.

The rationale of the FRS

The distinction between debt and equity

3 The Board's draft Statement of Principles defines a liability as follows:

> Liabilities are an entity's obligations to transfer economic benefits as a result of past transactions or events.

4 Thus the criterion used in the FRS to determine whether a capital instrument represents a liability is whether it contains an obligation to transfer economic benefits.

5 This criterion is not, however, used to determine the accounting for a company's shares. Shares have a distinct legal status reflected *(inter alia)* in the limitations imposed by companies legislation on the circumstances in which payments may be made in respect of them. It is also impossible to classify shares as liabilities within the constraints of the statutory formats for the balance sheet.

6 Although there are practical and legal difficulties in classifying shares as liabilities, another distinction—that between equity and non-equity shares—is practicable and is of great significance in assessing the financial position of the company. Equity shares represent the residual interest in a company. They have no claim on the company's assets that ranks prior to any other claim, but obtain the exclusive right to any increase in the net assets. Therefore the FRS requires the interests of equity shareholders in the

company to be stated prominently, clearly distinguished from those of shares that have any element of priority. Priority requires some limitation in the amount to which priority attaches, and so the definition of 'non-equity shares' focuses on limitation of rights.

As explained in paragraphs 88–91 of the Explanation, it is sometimes the case that shares issued by subsidiaries, when considered in the context of the group, are liabilities of the group. Where this is the case, the FRS requires them to be accounted for as liabilities. In other cases, the FRS proposes that an analysis be presented of minority interests between the amount attributable to equity and non-equity interests. This analysis is similar to that of shareholders' funds and is required for the same reasons. **7**

Warrants

When a company issues warrants its only obligation is to issue shares at a fixed price, if so required by the holder. **8**

The price paid for a warrant can be thought of as part of the subscription price for a share that may (or may not) be issued at a future date. For this reason, the FRS requires warrants to be reported within shareholders' funds. **9**

Once the warrant expires unexercised the amount paid for the warrant accrues to the benefit of the shareholders. For this reason, the FRS requires that on the expiry of a warrant the amount previously recognised in shareholders' funds be recognised in the statement of total recognised gains and losses. Showing the gain in that statement rather than in the profit and loss account is consistent with the role of the statement of total recognised gains and losses as providing a summary of changes in total reserves. **10**

The Board acknowledges that the subject of warrants raises wider issues than are dealt with in the FRS. In particular, it is sometimes argued that, when the amount paid on exercise of warrants is lower than the fair value of the shares issued, there is an additional, implicit consideration that needs to be reflected in the financial statements. If this view is accepted, the question arises whether the estimate of fair value for this purpose should be made as at the issue date of the warrants or as at the exercise date. **11**

Another view of warrants, which is that of a minority of the Board, is that, in substance, they are transactions with owners. Those who subscribe to this view would disagree with the proposal of the FRS that where a warrant lapses unexercised the amount previously recognised should be reported in the statement of total recognised gains and losses as they consider that that statement should not be affected by capital transactions between owners and the company. The Board rejected this view as it considers that the warrant holders are not owners of the company; the issue of warrants that are not subsequently exercised therefore represents a gain that should be reflected in the statement of total recognised gains and losses. **12**

The problem involves conceptual and practical issues requiring research and consultation that the Board believes would be better conducted as a separate project. The FRS, therefore, excludes from its scope warrants and share options issued under employee **13** share schemes, which are the most common example of warrants giving rise to these wider issues. If and when the Board addresses these issues it will also review the definition and treatment of warrants specified in this FRS.

Convertible instruments

14 There are a number of possible approaches to the accounting for convertible debt, but the most usual is to report it as a liability. Although this is uncontroversial where conversion is uncertain or unlikely, it is sometimes argued that where conversion is probable convertible debt should be reported outside liabilities.

15 The FRS, however, requires convertible debt to be reported within liabilities irrespective of the probability of future conversion. This is because the balance sheet is a record of the financial position of the company at a point in time, rather than a forecast of future events. (This is not, of course, to deny that financial statements may be useful in forming an assessment of future events.) There are difficulties with the idea that convertible debt should be classified according to the probability of conversion, notably in specifying how the probability of conversion should be judged, whether convertible debt should be reclassified if the probability of conversion changes, and whether the interest on convertible debt that is not reported as a liability should be deducted in arriving at profit before taxation.

16 One of the criticisms of reporting convertible debt as a liability is that it ignores the equity rights that are inherent in an issue of convertible debt. Two methods of accounting that attempt to address this are 'split accounting' and 'the imputed interest method'.

17 The IASC's exposure draft E40 proposes that split accounting should be required for convertible debt. Under this method the proceeds of an issue of convertible debt are allocated between two components: the equity rights, and the liability. Because the amount at which the liability is initially recognised is reduced, compared with more conventional accounting, the reported finance charges over the term of the debt are increased, and would normally be similar to those that would arise on an issue of non-convertible debt. The overall accounting effect is similar to that of an issue of debt issued with warrants as illustrated in the Application Notes.

18 The Discussion Paper illustrated 'split accounting' and 'the imputed interest method' and sought respondents' views on them, although it did not propose that these methods should be required. The FRED also sought respondents' views on methods of accounting for convertible debt. The majority of the respondents who addressed the issue agreed that these methods should not be required, giving as their reasons complexity and subjectivity.

Accounting for debt and non-equity interests

19 The FRS requires finance costs to be allocated to periods at a constant rate of interest on the outstanding amount. This method reflects the fact that finance costs are a function of the amount outstanding and the passage of time. It is also a familiar method because it is already required by SSAP 21 to be used by lessees to account for their obligations under finance leases.

A minority of the Board believes that the method by which the FRS requires finance costs to be allocated can result in significant distortions, for example where long-term debt is issued at a time when interest rates are expected to change significantly. For this reason, the minority takes the view that the FRS should at least have permitted finance costs to be spread by reference to the term structure of interest rates implicit in the terms of the financing. The Discussion Paper discussed this method and also methods based on the market values of liabilities. They were rejected mainly on grounds of subjectivity and complexity. The Discussion Paper also rejected the allocation of finance costs on a straight line basis because it does not reflect the relationship between finance costs and the amount outstanding. **20**

Scope of the FRS

Although the FRS applies to the majority of capital instruments, certain exclusions have been made. **21**

The FRS does not deal with accounting for warrants and options issued to employees under employee share schemes, for the reasons explained at paragraphs 8–13 above. **22**

Equity shares issued as part of a business combination that is accounted for as a merger, and leases have been excluded from the scope of the FRS as the Board did not wish to reconsider accounting for business combinations or for leases as part of the development of this FRS. The Board issued FRED 6 'Acquisitions and Mergers' in May 1993 and expects to issue an FRS on that subject in due course. The Board has not yet determined whether it will reconsider accounting for leases. **23**

MATTERS CONSIDERED IN THE LIGHT OF RESPONSES TO THE FRED

Most of the respondents to the FRED agreed with its principal proposals. The following paragraphs describe those points on which respondents expressed concern and, where appropriate, explain the Board's reasons for the changes from the proposals of the FRED. **24**

Consistency between FRS 4 and 'Reporting the Substance of Transactions'

Several respondents expressed concern that the proposals in FRED 3 seemed to be inconsistent with those contained in FRED 4 'Reporting the Substance of Transactions'. They contrasted the objective of FRED 4 that transactions should be accounted for in accordance with their substance, with the proposals of FRED 3 which, in their view, suggested that the legal form of capital instruments rather than their substance should determine how they were accounted for. Examples that were cited included the proposal that convertible debt should be reported as a liability until such time as it is actually converted, irrespective of the probability of conversion. Some **25** respondents suggested that if conversion was probable, the substance of the instrument was that of equity.

26 The Board noted that convertible debt typically contains an obligation to make payments in respect of interest up to the time of conversion and that this alone would be sufficient to justify reporting it as a liability. More fundamentally, however, it concluded that, even where conversion is probable, this does not affect the substance of the relationship prevailing between the issuer and the holder of convertible debt prior to conversion which is that of debtor and creditor. Although FRED 4 states that exercise of an option should be assumed where there is no genuine commercial possibility that the option will not be exercised, it will not typically be the case that the option to convert debt is of this kind, given the volatile changes that affect companies and hence the value of their equity. Although conversion of convertible debt is sometimes probable, it is not usually certain. Furthermore, the legal nature of the relationship between the issuer and the holder of the debt has important economic consequences: for example in the case of a deterioration in the financial condition of the issuer the holder of convertible debt has a much more valuable set of legal rights to secure recovery of his investment than a shareholder. Indeed in some cases this may be why the investor has chosen to make his investment in the form of convertible debt. The Board therefore concluded that requiring convertible debt to be accounted for as a liability was faithful both to its economic substance and to its legal form.

27 Another proposal that respondents considered to require accounting that was inconsistent with the substance of an instrument was that non-equity shares should be reported within shareholders' funds rather than as a liability. The Board's reasons for not requiring non-equity shares to be reported as liabilities are explained at paragraphs 5 and 6 above. The Board takes the view that whilst some non-equity shares may have characteristics of liabilities, the clear distinction of the amount attributable to such shares from equity shareholders' funds ensures that the amount of equity shareholders' funds is clearly stated and alerts the user to the existence of non-equity shares, the characteristics of which may need to be analysed carefully.

Disclosure requirements

28 Most respondents agreed with the items for which FRED 3 proposed disclosure, and accordingly they have largely been retained in the FRS. Several respondents, however, disagreed with the proposals of the FRED that certain distinctions should be drawn on the face of the primary financial statements, which they considered excessive; in their view making this disclosure in this way could make the accounts more difficult to understand.

29 As stated in paragraph 100 of the Explanation, the Board believes that the items for which separate disclosure on the face of the balance sheet was proposed are important, and that such disclosure will be necessary in many cases. Although the Board does not agree with respondents that disclosure on the face of the primary financial statements will often result in excessive detail, it decided that it would be adequate for the FRS to leave it to the discretion of preparers as to where this information was best given in their particular circumstances, provided that in making a decision they bear in mind the fundamental requirement for the accounts to give a true and fair view and that, if the information is given in the notes, that fact is indicated on the face of the primary financial statements.

The FRS does not retain the requirement proposed in the FRED to disclose the accounting policy used for capital instruments. The Board agreed with respondents that disclosure of this was already required by SSAP 2 and, in the case of companies that prepare their accounts in accordance with Schedule 4, by paragraph 36 of that Schedule. 30

Another disclosure requirement that was proposed in the FRED but has not been retained in the FRS is that of the market value of debt and non-equity shares, where such a value could be readily ascertained. Such a disclosure is useful to users of financial statements as it provides an insight into the economic burden represented by the debt. However, respondents, and some Board members, objected to this requirement on the grounds that the disclosure might be misleading; for example, it might imply that a company would be able to take advantage of short-term changes in the value of its debt when it was not, in fact, able to do so. The information might also be considered to be of limited usefulness as the market value disclosure would often be given for only part of a company's total exposure. In particular it is beyond the scope of the FRS to develop similar disclosure requirements for off balance sheet instruments. The Board concluded that it would not be appropriate to require disclosure of market values at this time, but that it should be encouraged, and that the desirability of such disclosure would be considered in the Board's future work in conjunction with that of other standard-setting bodies. 31

The requirement to disclose participating dividends separately from other dividends on non-equity shares has been introduced to meet the concern that a division of dividends simply into equity and non-equity failed properly to reflect the fact that participating dividends are directly linked to the dividend on equity shares. 32

Maturity of liabilities

The FRS retains the proposal of the FRED that in general the maturity of debt should be assessed by reference to its contractual maturity and that a departure from this should be made only where the same lender (or group of lenders) has agreed to provide a further loan on substantially the same terms as the existing debt. 33

The Board carefully considered the views expressed by respondents who pointed out that commercial paper (which is a form of short-term debt) is frequently reported as long-term because the issuer holds back-up facilities that would permit its refinancing. Under the proposals of the FRED commercial paper would be reported as short-term notwithstanding the back-up facilities because the facility is not granted by the lender but by another party and because the rate of interest on the debt permitted by the facility is greater than that payable on the commercial paper. The considerations that influenced the Board in reaching its decision are summarised below. 34

The Board noted that issuers who regard commercial paper as a long-term source of 35 funds normally expect to be able to refinance commercial paper by further issues of commercial paper. The purpose of the back-up facility is to provide funds in the event that further commercial paper cannot be issued, a circumstance that may arise either for reasons specific to the issuer or because of events of a more general nature. Although the possibility of an issuer's not being able to issue commercial paper may be remote in the larger markets for such paper, this is not necessarily the case where commercial paper is issued in smaller markets. As noted above, the borrowings that the issuer may make under a back-up facility are not similar to borrowings under commercial paper. The Board does not therefore consider that such facilities could reasonably be regarded as an extension of the indebtedness created by the commercial paper; rather they are arrangements entered into to safeguard the issuer from the remote possibility that it may be unable to finance the redemption of commercial paper from a fresh issue or from other sources. The Board was also aware that it was sometimes suggested that back-up facilities might not be available in the circumstances where fresh commercial paper cannot be issued.

36 The analysis of maturity that is secured by the requirements of the frs indicates the time at which new borrowings may have to be entered into. This is important information for users of accounts because entering into new borrowings causes the price and other terms of the borrowings to change. The Board noted that, given the range of financial instruments that are now available, no single analysis will provide all the information that a user of financial statements may require. It considers, however, that the most objective and relevant basis for financial reporting is that which is founded on the actual instruments in issue, rather than one which reports the combined effect of various arrangements that may not always be intrinsically linked, which consequently may obscure the underlying financial flexibility. The Board noted that its statement on the Operating and Financial Review encourages companies to give a narrative discussion of their capital structure and liquidity. The Review provides an opportunity to explain the company's overall financial structure and how the instruments reflected in the accounts integrate with other instruments and facilities for the execution of its financial policy.

37 The Board also noted that the Companies Act requires that *"A loan is treated as falling due for repayment . . . on the earliest date on which the lender could require repayment . . . if he exercised all options and rights available to him."* (Companies Act 1985, Schedule 4 paragraph 85). The Board takes the view that the requirements of the FRS are consistent with that requirement, but that alternatives favoured by respondents might not be.

Repurchase of debt

38 The FRS includes requirements in respect of repurchase of debt, which was not specifically addressed in the FRED. The subject was addressed in Abstract 8 of the Board's Urgent Issues Task Force, issued in March 1993. The requirements of the FRS are substantially the same as those of the Abstract.

39 The FRS requires gains and losses arising on the repurchase or other settlement of debt to be recognised at that time and not deferred, for example over the period of the original borrowing. This requirement is based on the view that the finance cost reported by an entity should normally reflect only its current borrowing arrangements, and not be influenced by any previous borrowings that have now been terminated.

UITF 8 included two exceptions to the requirement for immediate recognition of a gain or loss arising on the repurchase of debt. The first prohibited a gain or loss being recognised where the agreement to repurchase the debt was coupled with its re-financing on substantially the same terms; the second prohibited a gain or loss being recognised where the repurchase was not at fair value and the shortfall or excess was compensated for by other terms of the transactions. As explained in FRED 4 'Reporting the Substance of Transactions', the substance of such a series of transactions should be determined by viewing the series as a whole. Accordingly, gains and losses on such linked transactions should be recognised only where justified by a change in the substance of the entity's assets and liabilities. **40**

Renegotiation of debt

In response to comments made on the FRED, the Board considered whether the FRS should address the accounting for the renegotiation of debt, that is the agreement by a creditor to a reduction or a deferral of payments due under the debt with the effect that the borrower's obligations are significantly reduced. **41**

The question arises in such circumstances whether the concession should be recognised as a gain at the time it is granted or whether its effect should be spread over the remaining period of the debt as a reduction in finance charges. Deferral of the recognition of the effect of a renegotiation can have the result that an agreement that has significant economic consequences is not reported in the period in which those consequences arise and that liabilities and finance costs for subsequent periods are shown at amounts that do not properly represent the agreement then in force. The Board therefore concluded that in principle the gain should be recognised in the period in which renegotiation is concluded. Proposals to that effect were published in July 1993. **42**

A further question is whether, in recognising the gain and determining the subsequent finance costs, the accounting should be based on the market values prevailing at the time of renegotiation or whether the revised payments should be discounted at the rate inherent in the original debt. The Board's proposals were that the market values prevailing at the time of the renegotiation should be used, as this would result in the carrying amount of the debt following the renegotiation and finance costs for subsequent periods that reflected the economic circumstances that prevailed at the time of renegotiation. Several respondents objected to this aspect of the proposals, pointing out that if (as would often be the case in practice) fair values had to be estimated by a process of discounting, it seemed wrong to use a relatively high rate reflecting the distressed circumstances of the borrower, since this would increase the recorded gain. The Board also noted that the IASC was preparing a revised exposure draft on Financial Instruments that differed from its original exposure draft on this point in that it proposed the use of the original inherent rate. **43**

In the light of these concerns, the Board concluded that the FRS should not address accounting for renegotiation of debt. The Board will continue to monitor the developments of the IASC project and may re-address the issue at a later date. **44**

Financial Reporting Standard 5 is set out in paragraphs 1–39.

The Statement of Standard Accounting Practice set out in paragraphs 11–39 should be read in the context of the Objective as stated in paragraph 1 and the definitions set out in paragraphs 2–10 and also of the Foreword to Accounting Standards and the Statement of Principles for Financial Reporting currently in issue.

The Application Notes specify how some of the requirements of FRS 5 are to be applied to transactions that have certain features.

The Explanation set out in paragraphs 40–103 and the Application Notes shall be regarded as part of the Statement of Standard Accounting Practice insofar as they assist in interpreting that statement.

Appendix III 'The development of the FRS' reviews considerations and arguments that were thought significant by members of the Board in reaching the conclusions on FRS 5.

[FRS 5]
Reporting the substance of transactions

(Issued April 1994; amended December 1994)

Contents

Adoption of FRS 5 by the Board

Appendices

Reporting the substance of transactions

Summary

GENERAL

Financial Reporting Standard 5 'Reporting the Substance of Transactions' requires an entity's financial statements to report the substance of the transactions into which it has entered. The FRS sets out how to determine the substance of a transaction (including how to identify its effect on the assets and liabilities of the entity), whether any resulting assets and liabilities should be included in the balance sheet, and what disclosures are appropriate. The FRS also contains some provisions in respect of how transactions should be reported in the profit and loss account and the cash flow statement. **a**

The FRS will not change the accounting treatment and disclosure of the vast majority of transactions. It will mainly affect those more complex transactions whose substance may not be readily apparent. The true commercial effect of such transactions may not be adequately expressed by their legal form and, where this is the case, it will not be sufficient to account for them merely by recording that form. **b**

Transactions requiring particularly careful analysis will often include features such as – **c**

(i) the party that gains the principal benefits generated by an item is not the legal owner of the item,
(ii) a transaction is linked with others in such a way that the commercial effect can be understood only by considering the series as a whole, or
(iii) an option is included on terms that make its exercise highly likely.

The FRS sets out principles that will apply to all transactions. In addition, there are five Application Notes that describe the application of the FRS to transactions with certain features: consignment stock; sale and repurchase agreements; factoring; securitised assets; and loan transfers. The Application Notes need not be referred to in all cases. At the start of each Note there is a 'Features' section that may serve as a quick reference point to determine whether further study is required. In addition, each Note concludes with a table summarising its main provisions. **d**

Identification and recognition of the substance of transactions

A key step in determining the substance of any transaction is to identify whether it has given rise to new assets or liabilities for the entity and whether it has increased or decreased the entity's existing assets or liabilities. Assets are, broadly, rights or other access to future economic benefits controlled by an entity; liabilities are, broadly, an entity's obligations to transfer economic benefits. **e**

The future economic benefits inherent in an asset are never completely certain in **f** amount; there is always some risk that the benefits will turn out to be greater or less than expected. Whether the entity gains or suffers from such variations in benefits is evidence of whether it has an asset.

g The definition of a liability requires an obligation to transfer benefits. Evidence that an entity has such an obligation is given if there is some circumstance in which the entity is unable to avoid an outflow of benefits.

h Once identified, an asset or liability should be recognised (ie included) in the balance sheet, provided that there is sufficient evidence that an asset or liability exists, and the asset or liability can be measured at a monetary amount with sufficient reliability.

i Following its recognition, an asset may be affected by a subsequent transaction. Where the transaction does not significantly alter the entity's rights to benefits or its exposure to risks, the entire asset should continue to be recognised. Conversely, where the transaction transfers to others all significant rights to benefits and all significant exposure to risks, the entity should cease to recognise the asset in its entirety. Finally, in other cases where not all significant benefits and risks have been transferred, it may be appropriate to amend the description or monetary amount of an asset and, where necessary, recognise a liability for any obligations it has assumed.

Linked presentation for certain non-recourse finance arrangements

j A special form of presentation, termed a 'linked presentation', should be used for certain non-recourse finance arrangements. This presentation shows, on the face of the balance sheet, the finance deducted from the gross amount of the item it finances. It should be used where, although the entity has significant rights to benefits and exposure to risks relating to a specific item, the item is financed in such a way that the maximum loss the entity can suffer is limited to a fixed monetary amount. For use of a linked presentation it is necessary that both –

(i) the finance will be repaid only from proceeds generated by the specific item it finances (or by transfer of the item itself) and there is no possibility whatsoever of a claim on the entity being established other than against funds generated by that item (or the item itself), and

(ii) there is no provision whatsoever whereby the entity may either keep the item on repayment of the finance or re-acquire it at any time.

Disclosure of the substance of transactions

k Adequate disclosure of a transaction is important to an understanding of its commercial effect. For most transactions, the disclosures currently required will be sufficient for this purpose. However, where the nature of any recognised asset or liability differs from that of items usually found under the relevant balance sheet heading, the differences should be explained. Furthermore, to the extent that a transaction has not resulted in the recognition of assets or liabilities, disclosure may nevertheless be required in order to give an understanding of its commercial effect.

Quasi-subsidiaries

Sometimes assets and liabilities are placed in an entity (a 'vehicle') that is in effect controlled by the reporting entity but does not meet the legal definition of a subsidiary. Where the commercial effect for the reporting entity is no different from that which would result were the vehicle a subsidiary, the vehicle will be a 'quasi-subsidiary'. **l**

The FRS requires the assets, liabilities, profits, losses and cash flows of any quasi-subsidiary to be included in the consolidated financial statements of the group that controls it in the same way as if they were those of a subsidiary. However, where a quasi-subsidiary is used to finance a specific item in such a way that the provisions of paragraph j above are met from the point of view of the group, the assets and liabilities of the quasi-subsidiary should be included in consolidated financial statements using the linked presentation described in paragraph j. **m**

Disclosure is required, in summary form, of the financial statements of quasi-subsidiaries. **n**

Financial Reporting Standard 5

OBJECTIVE

The objective of this FRS is to ensure that the substance of an entity's transactions is reported in its financial statements. The commercial effect of the entity's transactions, and any resulting assets, liabilities, gains or losses, should be faithfully represented in its financial statements. **1**

DEFINITIONS

The following definitions shall apply in this FRS and in particular in the Statement of Standard Accounting Practice set out in paragraphs 11–39.

Assets:- **2**
Rights or other access to future economic benefits controlled by an entity as a result of past transactions or events.

Control in the context of an asset:- **3**
The ability to obtain the future economic benefits relating to an asset and to restrict the access of others to those benefits.

Liabilities:- **4**
An entity's obligations to transfer economic benefits as a result of past transactions or events.

Risk:- **5**
Uncertainty as to the amount of benefits. The term includes both potential for gain and exposure to loss.

6 *Recognition:-*
The process of incorporating an item into the primary financial statements under the appropriate heading. It involves depiction of the item in words and by a monetary amount and inclusion of that amount in the statement totals.

7 *Quasi-subsidiary:-*
A quasi-subsidiary of a reporting entity is a company, trust, partnership or other vehicle that, though not fulfilling the definition of a subsidiary, is directly or indirectly controlled by the reporting entity and gives rise to benefits for that entity that are in substance no different from those that would arise were the vehicle a subsidiary.

8 *Control of another entity:-*
The ability to direct the financial and operating policies of that entity with a view to gaining economic benefit from its activities.

9 *Subsidiary:-*
A subsidiary undertaking as defined by companies legislation.

10 *Companies legislation:-*

(a) In Great Britain, the Companies Act 1985;
(b) in Northern Ireland, the Companies (Northern Ireland) Order 1986; and
(c) in the Republic of Ireland, the Republic of Ireland Companies Acts 1963–1990 and the European Communities (Companies: Group Accounts) Regulations 1992.

Statement of standard accounting practice

SCOPE

11 Subject to paragraph 12, Financial Reporting Standard 5 applies to all transactions of a reporting entity whose financial statements are intended to give a true and fair view of its financial position and profit or loss (or income and expenditure) for a period. In the FRS, the term 'transaction' includes both a single transaction or arrangement and also a group or series of transactions that achieves or is designed to achieve an overall commercial effect.

12 The following are excluded from the scope of the FRS, unless they are a part of a transaction that falls within the scope of the FRS:

(a) forward contracts and futures (such as those for foreign currencies or commodities);
(b) foreign exchange and interest rate swaps;
(c) contracts where a net amount will be paid or received based on the movement in a price or an index (sometimes referred to as 'contracts for differences');
(d) expenditure commitments (such as purchase commitments) and orders placed, until the earlier of delivery or payment; and
(e) employment contracts.

Where the substance of a transaction or the treatment of any resulting asset or liability falls not only within the scope of this FRS but also directly within the scope of another FRS, a Statement of Standard Accounting Practice ('SSAP'), or a specific statutory requirement governing the recognition of assets or liabilities, the standard or statute that contains the more specific provision(s) should be applied. 13

GENERAL

The substance of transactions

A reporting entity's financial statements should report the substance of the transactions into which it has entered. In determining the substance of a transaction, all its aspects and implications should be identified and greater weight given to those more likely to have a commercial effect in practice. A group or series of transactions that achieves or is designed to achieve an overall commercial effect should be viewed as a whole. 14

Quasi-subsidiaries

Where the entity has a quasi-subsidiary, the substance of the transactions entered into by the quasi-subsidiary should be reported in consolidated financial statements. 15

THE SUBSTANCE OF TRANSACTIONS

Identifying assets and liabilities

To determine the substance of a transaction it is necessary to identify whether the transaction has given rise to new assets or liabilities for the reporting entity and whether it has changed the entity's existing assets or liabilities. 16

Evidence that an entity has rights or other access to benefits (and hence has an asset) is given if the entity is exposed to the risks inherent in the benefits, taking into account the likelihood of those risks having a commercial effect in practice. 17

Evidence that an entity has an obligation to transfer benefits (and hence has a liability) is given if there is some circumstance in which the entity is unable to avoid, legally or commercially, an outflow of benefits. 18

Where a transaction incorporates one or more options, guarantees or conditional provisions, their commercial effect should be assessed in the context of all the aspects and implications of the transaction in order to determine what assets and liabilities exist. 19

Recognition of assets and liabilities

Where a transaction results in an item that meets the definition of an asset or liability, that item should be recognised in the balance sheet if – 20

(a) there is sufficient evidence of the existence of the item (including, where appropriate, evidence that a future inflow or outflow of benefit will occur), and
(b) the item can be measured at a monetary amount with sufficient reliability.

Transactions in previously recognised assets

Continued recognition of an asset in its entirety

21 Where a transaction involving a previously recognised asset results in no significant change in –

(a) the entity's rights or other access to benefits relating to that asset, or
(b) its exposure to the risks inherent in those benefits,

the entire asset should continue to be recognised. In particular this will be the case for any transaction that is in substance a financing of a previously recognised asset, unless the conditions for a linked presentation given in paragraphs 26 and 27 are met, in which case such a presentation should be used.

Ceasing to recognise an asset in its entirety

22 Where a transaction involving a previously recognised asset transfers to others –

(a) all significant rights or other access to benefits relating to that asset, and
(b) all significant exposure to the risks inherent in those benefits,

the entire asset should cease to be recognised.

Special cases

23 Paragraphs 21 and 22 deal with most transactions affecting items previously recognised as assets. In other cases where there is a significant change in the entity's rights to benefits and exposure to risks but the provisions of paragraph 22 are not met, the description or monetary amount relating to an asset should, where necessary, be changed and a liability recognised for any obligations to transfer benefits that are assumed. These cases arise where the transaction takes one or more of the following forms:

(a) a transfer of only part of the item in question;
(b) a transfer of all of the item for only part of its life; and
(c) a transfer of all of the item for all of its life but where the entity retains some significant right to benefits or exposure to risk.

24 In the special cases referred to in paragraph 23, where the amount of any resulting gain or loss is uncertain, full provision should be made for any probable loss but recognition of any gain, to the extent it is in doubt, should be deferred. In addition, where the uncertainty could have a material effect on the financial statements, this fact should be disclosed in the notes to the financial statements.

The meaning of 'significant'

In applying paragraphs 21–23 above and paragraph 26 below, 'significant' should be judged in relation to those benefits and risks that are likely to occur in practice, and not in relation to the total possible benefits and risks. 25

Linked presentation for certain non-recourse finance arrangements

Where a transaction involving an item previously recognised as an asset is in substance a financing – and therefore meets the condition of paragraph 21 regarding no significant change in the entity's access to benefits or exposure to risks – but the financing 'ring-fences' the item such that – 26

(a) the finance will be repaid only from proceeds generated by the specific item it finances (or by transfer of the item itself) and there is no possibility whatsoever of a claim on the entity being established other than against funds generated by that item (or the item itself),
(b) there is no provision whatsoever whereby the entity may either keep the item on repayment of the finance or re-acquire it at any time, and
(c) all of the conditions given in paragraph 27 are met,

the finance should be shown deducted from the gross amount of the item it finances on the face of the balance sheet within a single asset caption (a 'linked presentation'). The gross amounts of the item and the finance should be shown on the face of the balance sheet and not merely disclosed in the notes to the financial statements. A linked presentation should also be used where an item that is financed in such a way that all of the above three conditions are met has not been recognised previously as an asset.

A linked presentation should be used only where all of the following are met: 27

(a) the finance relates to a specific item (or portfolio of similar items) and, in the case of a loan, is secured on that item but not on any other asset of the entity;
(b) the provider of the finance has no recourse whatsoever, either explicit or implicit, to the other assets of the entity for losses and the entity has no obligation whatsoever to repay the provider of finance;
(c) the directors of the entity state explicitly in each set of financial statements where a linked presentation is used that the entity is not obliged to support any losses, nor does it intend to do so;
(d) the provider of the finance has agreed in writing (in the finance documentation or otherwise) that it will seek repayment of the finance, as to both principal and interest, only to the extent that sufficient funds are generated by the specific item it has financed and that it will not seek recourse in any other form, and such agreement is noted in each set of financial statements where a linked presentation is used;
(e) if the funds generated by the item are insufficient to pay off the provider of the finance, this does not constitute an event of default for the entity; and
(f) there is no provision whatsoever, either in the financing arrangement or otherwise, whereby the entity has a right or an obligation either to keep the item upon

repayment of the finance or (where title to the item has been transferred) to re-acquire it at any time. Accordingly:

(i) where the item is one (such as a monetary receivable) that directly generates cash, the provider of the finance will be repaid out of the resulting cash receipts (to the extent these are sufficient); or

(ii) where the item is one (such as a physical asset) that does not directly generate cash, there is a definite point at which either the item will be sold to a third party and the provider of the finance repaid from the proceeds (to the extent these are sufficient) or the item will be transferred to the provider of the finance in full and final settlement.

Where all of these conditions hold for only part of the finance, a linked presentation should be used for only that part. In such cases, the maximum future payment that the reporting entity could make (other than from funds generated by the specific item being financed) should be excluded from the amount deducted on the face of the balance sheet.

28 In respect of an arrangement for which a linked presentation is used, profit should be recognised on entering into the arrangement only to the extent that the non-returnable proceeds received exceed the previous carrying value of the item. Thereafter, any profit or loss deriving from the item should be recognised in the period in which it arises. The net profit or loss recognised in each period should be included in the profit and loss account and separate disclosure of its gross components should be given in the notes to the financial statements.

Offset

29 Assets and liabilities should not be offset. Debit and credit balances should be aggregated into a single net item where, and only where, they do not constitute separate assets and liabilities, ie where, and only where, all of the following conditions are met:

(a) The reporting entity and another party owe each other determinable monetary amounts, denominated either in the same currency, or in different but freely convertible currencies. For this purpose a freely convertible currency is one for which quoted exchange rates are available in an active market that can rapidly absorb the amount to be offset without significantly affecting the exchange rate;

(b) The reporting entity has the ability to insist on a net settlement. In determining this, any right to insist on a net settlement that is contingent should be taken into account only if the reporting entity is able to enforce net settlement in all situations of default by the other party; and

(c) The reporting entity's ability to insist on a net settlement is assured beyond doubt. It is essential that there is no possibility that the entity could be required to transfer economic benefits to another party whilst being unable to enforce its own access to economic benefits. For this to be the case it is necessary that the debit balance matures no later than the credit balance. It is also necessary that the reporting entity's ability to insist on a net settlement would survive the insolvency of the other party.

Disclosure of the substance of transactions

Disclosure of a transaction in the financial statements, whether or not it has resulted in assets or liabilities being recognised or ceasing to be recognised, should be sufficient to enable the user of the financial statements to understand its commercial effect. **30**

Where a transaction has resulted in the recognition of assets or liabilities whose nature differs from that of items usually included under the relevant balance sheet heading, the differences should be explained. **31**

QUASI-SUBSIDIARIES

Identification of quasi-subsidiaries

In determining whether another entity (a 'vehicle') gives rise to benefits for the reporting entity that are in substance no different from those that would arise were the vehicle a subsidiary, regard should be had to the benefits arising from the net assets of the vehicle. Evidence of which party gains these benefits is given by which party is exposed to the risks inherent in them. **32**

In determining whether the reporting entity controls a vehicle regard should be had to who, in practice, directs the financial and operating policies of the vehicle. The ability to prevent others from directing those policies is evidence of control, as is the ability to prevent others from enjoying the benefits arising from the vehicle's net assets. **33**

Where the financial and operating policies of a vehicle are in substance predetermined, contractually or otherwise, the party possessing control will be the one that gains the benefits arising from the net assets of the vehicle. Evidence of which party gains these benefits is given by which party is exposed to the risks inherent in them. **34**

Accounting for quasi-subsidiaries

Subject to paragraph 37, the assets, liabilities, profits, losses and cash flows of a quasi-subsidiary should be included in the group financial statements of the group that controls it in the same way as if they were those of a subsidiary. Where an entity has a quasi-subsidiary but no subsidiaries and therefore does not prepare group financial statements, it should provide in its financial statements consolidated financial statements of itself and the quasi-subsidiary, presented with equal prominence to the reporting entity's individual financial statements. **35**

Paragraph 35 should be applied by following the requirements regarding the preparation of consolidated financial statements set out in companies legislation and in FRS 2 'Accounting for Subsidiary Undertakings'. However, quasi-subsidiaries should be excluded from consolidation only where the interest in the quasi-subsidiary is held **36**

exclusively with a view to subsequent resale* and the quasi-subsidiary has not previously been included in the reporting entity's consolidated financial statements.

37 Where a quasi-subsidiary holds a single item or a single portfolio of similar items and the effect of the arrangement is to finance the item in such a way that the provisions of paragraphs 26 and 27 are met from the point of view of the group, the quasi-subsidiary should be included in consolidated financial statements using a linked presentation.

Disclosure of quasi-subsidiaries

38 Where one or more quasi-subsidiaries are included in consolidated financial statements, this fact should be disclosed. A summary of the financial statements of each quasi-subsidiary should be provided in the notes to the financial statements, unless the reporting entity has more than one quasi-subsidiary of a similar nature, in which case the summary may be given on a combined basis. These summarised financial statements should show separately each main heading in the balance sheet, profit and loss account, statement of total recognised gains and losses and cash flow statement for which there is a material item, together with comparative figures.

DATE FROM WHICH EFFECTIVE

39 Subject to paragraph 39A, the accounting practices set out in the FRS should be regarded as standard in respect of financial statements relating to accounting periods ending on or after 22 September 1994. Earlier adoption is encouraged but not required.

39A (a) The requirements of paragraph 29 in so far as they relate to balances arising either from insurance broking transactions or, for insurers (including Lloyd's syndicates), from insurance transactions placed through brokers, and

(b) The accounting practices set out in the FRS, in so far as they relate to financial reinsurance included in the accounts of Lloyd's syndicates drawn up to 31 December 1993,

should be regarded as standard in respect of financial statements relating to accounting periods ending on or after 22 September 1996. Where, in accordance with the previous sentence, the accounting practices set out in the FRS are not applied for accounting periods ending on or after 22 September 1994, this fact and, where available, a quantification of the effect should be disclosed.

Explanation

SCOPE

40 The scope of the FRS, as set out in paragraph 11, extends to all kinds of transactions, subject only to the exclusions given in paragraph 12. Most transactions are straightforward, giving rise to a number of standard rights and obligations with the result that their substance and commercial effect are readily apparent. Applying established

**As defined in FRS 2, paragraph 11.*

accounting practices will be sufficient to ensure that the substance of such transactions is properly reported in the financial statements, without the need to refer to the FRS.

Conversely, applying established accounting practices may not be sufficient to portray the substance of more complex transactions whose commercial effect may not be readily apparent. For such transactions it will be necessary to refer to the FRS in order to ensure that their substance is correctly identified and properly reported. **41**

Exclusions from the FRS

Paragraph 12 excludes from the FRS certain contracts for future performance except where they are merely a part of a transaction (or of a group or series of transactions) that falls within the FRS. For example, an interest rate swap forming part of a securitisation would fall to be considered under the FRS in relation to its role in the securitisation. Conversely, an interest rate swap that was no more than a part of an entity's overall treasury management activities would fall outside the scope of the FRS. **42**

Other standards

The FRS sets out general principles relevant to reporting the substance of all transactions. Other accounting standards, the Application Notes of the FRS and companies legislation apply general principles to particular transactions or events. It follows that where a transaction falls within the scope of both the FRS and another accounting standard or statute, whichever contains the more specific provisions should be applied. Nevertheless, the specific provisions of any standard or statute should be applied to the substance of the transaction and not merely to its legal form and, for this purpose, the general principles set out in FRS 5 will be relevant. **43**

Pension obligations are an example of an item falling within the scope of both FRS 5 and another standard, the latter being SSAP 24 'Accounting for pension costs'. As SSAP 24 contains the more specific provisions on accounting for pension obligations and does not require consolidation of pension funds, such funds should not be consolidated as quasi-subsidiaries. FRS 5, however, contains the more specific provisions in respect of certain other transactions that may take place between an entity and its pension fund, for example a sale and repurchase agreement relating to one of the entity's properties. **44**

The relationship between SSAP 21 'Accounting for lease and hire purchase contracts' and FRS 5 is particularly close. In general, SSAP 21 contains the more specific provisions governing accounting for stand-alone leases that fall wholly within its parameters, although the general principles of the FRS will also be relevant in ensuring that leases are classified as finance or operating leases in accordance with their substance. However, for some lease arrangements, and particularly for those that are merely one element of a larger arrangement, the FRS will contain the more specific provisions. An example is a sale and leaseback arrangement where there is also an option for the seller/lessee to repurchase the asset; in this case the provisions of Application Note B are more specific than those of SSAP 21. **45**

THE SUBSTANCE OF TRANSACTIONS

General principles

46 Paragraph 14 of the FRS sets out general principles for reporting the substance of a transaction. Particularly for more complex transactions, it will not be sufficient merely to record the transaction's legal form, as to do so may not adequately express the commercial effect of the arrangements. Notwithstanding this caveat, the FRS is not intended to affect the legal characterisation of a transaction, or to change the situation at law achieved by the parties to it.

Features of more complex transactions

47 Transactions requiring particularly careful analysis will often include features such as –

(a) the separation of legal title to an item from rights or other access to the principal future economic benefits associated with it and exposure to the principal risks inherent in those benefits*,
(b) the linking of a transaction with others in such a way that the commercial effect can be understood only by considering the series as a whole, or
(c) the inclusion of options or conditions on terms that make it highly likely that the option will be exercised or the condition fulfilled.

(a) Separation of legal title from benefits and risks

48 A familiar example of the separation of legal title from benefits and risks is a finance lease. Another is goods sold under reservation of title. In both cases, the location of legal title will not normally be expected to have a commercial effect in practice. Thus the party having the benefits and risks relating to the underlying property should recognise an asset in its balance sheet even though it does not have legal title. Arrangements involving the separation of legal title from benefits and risks are dealt with in detail in Application Note B.

(b) Linking of transactions

49 The linking of two or more transactions extends the possibilities for separating legal title from benefits and risks. A sale of goods linked with a commitment to repurchase may leave the original owner with the principal benefits and risks relating to the goods if the repurchase price is set at the costs, including interest, incurred by the other party in holding the goods. In such a case, application of the FRS will result in the transaction being accounted for as a financing rather than a sale, showing the asset and a corresponding liability on the balance sheet of the original owner.

**For ease of reading, 'rights or other access to future economic benefits' are frequently referred to hereafter as 'rights to benefits' or 'benefits', and 'exposure to the risks inherent in those benefits' is frequently referred to hereafter as 'exposure to risks' or 'risks'.*

(c) Inclusion of options

Some sale transactions are accompanied by an option, rather than a commitment, for either the original owner to repurchase or the buyer to resell. Often the commercial effect of such an arrangement is that an economic penalty (such as the forgoing of a profit) would be suffered by the party having the option if it failed to exercise it. Some transactions incorporate both a put option for the buyer and a call option for the original owner, in such a way that it will almost certainly be in the commercial interests of one of the parties to exercise its option (as for example where both options have the same exercise price and are exercisable on the same date). In such cases, there will be no genuine commercial possibility that the original owner will fail to repurchase the item and application of the FRS will again result in the transaction being accounted for as a financing rather than a sale. **50**

Assessing commercial effect by considering the position of other parties

Whatever the substance of a transaction, it will normally have commercial logic for each of the parties to it. If a transaction appears to lack such logic from the point of view of one or more parties, this may indicate that not all related parts of the transaction have been identified or that the commercial effect of some element of the transaction has been incorrectly assessed. **51**

It follows that in assessing the commercial effect of a transaction, it will be important to consider the position of all of the parties to it, including their apparent expectations and motives for agreeing to its various terms. In particular, where one party to the transaction receives a lender's return but no more (comprising interest on its investment perhaps together with a relatively small fee), this indicates that the substance of the transaction is that of a financing. This is because the party that receives a lender's return is not compensated for assuming any significant exposure to loss other than that associated with the creditworthiness of the other party, nor is the other party compensated for giving up any significant potential for gain. **52**

Identifying assets and liabilities

In accounting terms, the substance of a transaction is portrayed through the assets and liabilities, including contingent assets and liabilities, resulting from or altered by the transaction. A key step in reporting the substance of any transaction is therefore to identify its effect on the assets and liabilities of the entity. **53**

Assets – control of access to benefits

The definition of an asset requires that access to future economic benefits is controlled by the entity. Access to future economic benefits will normally rest on a foundation of legal rights, although legally enforceable rights are not essential to secure access. Control is the means by which the entity ensures that the benefits accrue to itself and not to others. Control can be distinguished from management (ie the ability to direct the use of an item that generates the benefits) and, although the two often go together, this need not be so. For example, the manager of a portfolio of securities does not have **54** control of the securities, as he does not have the ability to obtain the economic benefits associated with them. Such control rests with his appointer who has delegated to the manager the right to take day-to-day decisions about the composition of the portfolio.

Assets – risk

55 The future economic benefits inherent in an asset are never completely certain in amount; there is always the possibility that the actual benefits will be greater or less than those expected, or will arise sooner or later than expected. For instance, the value of stocks may rise or fall as market conditions change; foreign currency balances may become worth more or less because of exchange rate movements; debtors may default or be slow in paying. This uncertainty regarding the eventual benefit is referred to as 'risk', with the term encompassing both an upside element of potential for gain and a downside element of exposure to loss.

56 The entity that has access to the benefits will usually also be the one to suffer or gain if these benefits turn out to be different from those expected. Hence, evidence of whether an entity has access to benefits (and hence has an asset) is given by whether it has the risks inherent in those benefits.

Liabilities – obligations to transfer benefits

57 The definition of liabilities requires an obligation to transfer economic benefits. Whilst most obligations are legally enforceable, a legal obligation is not a necessary condition for a liability. An entity may be commercially obliged to adopt a certain course of action that is in its long-term best interests in the widest sense, even if no third party can legally enforce that course. As illustrated in paragraph 50 above, the prospect of a commercial or economic penalty if a certain action is not taken may negate a legal right to refrain from taking that action.

58 The notion of obligation implies that the entity is not free to avoid an outflow of resources. Where there is some circumstance in which the entity is unable to avoid such an outflow whether for legal or commercial reasons, it will have a liability. However, in accordance with SSAP 18 'Accounting for contingencies' if the entity's obligation is contingent on the occurrence of one or more uncertain future events (as under a stand-alone guarantee given by the entity) its liability may not be recognised.

Options

59 On its own, an option to acquire an item of property in the future represents a different asset from ownership of the property itself. For example, when an option to purchase shares at a future date is acquired, the only asset is the option itself; the asset 'shares' will be acquired only on exercise of the option. Similarly, an unconditional obligation is not the same as a contingent commitment to assume such an obligation at another party's option. Although both are liabilities, they are different liabilities and if recognised in the balance sheet their descriptions will be different.

Where an option is part of a more complex transaction, it may not necessarily represent a separate asset or liability of the type discussed in paragraph 59. For example, an option may serve, in conjunction with the other aspects of the transaction, to give one party access to the future benefits arising from an item of property without legal ownership. Alternatively the terms of an option, together with other aspects of the overall transaction, may in effect create an unconditional obligation even though the legal obligation is expressed as being conditional on the exercise of the option. Options of this kind should be accounted for by considering the substance of the transaction as a whole. **60**

In determining the substance of a transaction incorporating options, in accordance with paragraph 14, greater weight must be given to those aspects and implications more likely to have a commercial effect in practice. This will involve considering the extent to which there is a genuine commercial possibility that the option will be exercised or, alternatively, that it will not be exercised. In extreme cases, there will be no genuine commercial possibility that the option will be exercised, in which case the existence of that option should be ignored; alternatively, there will be no genuine commercial possibility that an option will fail to be exercised, in which case its future exercise should be assumed. For example, a transaction may be structured in such a way that the cost of exercising an option will almost inevitably be lower (or, alternatively, higher) than the benefits obtained from its exercise. As another example, there may be a combination of put and call options such that it will almost certainly be in the commercial interests of one or other party to exercise its option. In both these cases, the substance of the overall transaction is that the parties have outright, and not optional or conditional, obligations and access to benefits. In less extreme cases, further analysis will be required. It may be necessary to consider the true commercial objectives of the parties and the commercial rationale for the inclusion of such options in the transaction. This may reveal either that the parties in substance have outright obligations and access to benefits, or, alternatively, that the parties' obligations and access to benefits are genuinely optional or conditional. **61**

In assessing the commercial effect of an option, all the terms of the transaction and the circumstances of the parties that are likely to be relevant during the exercise period of the option should be taken into account. It should be assumed that each of the parties will act in accordance with its economic interests. Any actions that the parties would take only in the event of a severe deterioration in liquidity or creditworthiness should not be anticipated but should be taken into account only when such a deterioration occurs (for example, when creditworthiness has declined because of the prospect of imminent cash flow difficulties). **62**

Guarantees and conditional provisions

Paragraphs 59–62 should also be applied to guarantees and other conditional provisions. The commercial effect of such provisions should in all cases be determined in the context of the overall transaction. **63**

Recognition of assets and liabilities

64 Once it appears from analysis of a transaction that an asset or liability has been acquired or assumed by an entity, it is necessary to apply various recognition tests to determine whether the asset or liability should be included in the balance sheet.

65 The general criteria set out in paragraph 20* require that an asset or liability should be recognised only where it can be measured with 'sufficient' reliability. The effect of prudence is that less reliability of measurement is acceptable when recognising items that involve decreases in equity (eg increases in liabilities) than when recognising items that do not (eg increases in assets). It follows that, particularly for liabilities, where a reasonable estimate of the amount of an item is available, the item should be recognised.

Transactions in previously recognised assets

66 Following its recognition, an asset may be affected by a subsequent transaction and it will be necessary to consider whether, as a result of the transaction, the description or monetary amount of the asset needs to be changed. In this regard paragraphs 21–28 and 67–88 will apply.

Continued recognition of an asset in its entirety

67 Paragraph 21 requires that where there is no significant change in the entity's rights to benefits, its previously recognised asset should continue to be recognised. In the same way, the entity will continue to have an asset where its exposure to the risks inherent in the benefits of the asset is not significantly altered. Even if the proceeds generated by the asset are directed in the first instance to another party, provided the entity gains or suffers from all significant changes in those proceeds it should be regarded as having the benefits of the asset and should continue to recognise it. For example, a 'sale' of debts with recourse to the seller for all bad debts and provision for the seller to pay a finance charge that reflects the speed of payment by debtors leaves the seller with all significant risks relating to the debts (the risks being the speed of payment and the degree of non-payment). This is so even if actual cash receipts are collected directly by the buyer and only a net surplus or deficit settled with the seller. In such cases the seller would continue to recognise an asset equal in amount to the debts, although the transfer of legal title would be disclosed.

68 Thus, under paragraph 21, it will not be appropriate to cease to recognise any part of an asset where the transaction entered into is in substance a financing of that asset, even if the financing is without recourse. Such financing transactions leave the entity with those rights to benefits and exposures to risks (including potential for gain) that are likely to have a commercial effect in practice, as well as creating a liability to repay the finance. The only exception to this is non-recourse finance arrangements that meet the conditions for a linked presentation given in paragraphs 26–27. Although such

**These criteria are drawn from Chapter 4 of the Board's draft Statement of Principles.*

arrangements are in substance financings, their particular features are such that a linked presentation is required to portray all the effects of the arrangement. This is explained further in paragraphs 76–80 below.

Ceasing to recognise an asset in its entirety

Conversely, paragraph 22 requires that where a transaction transfers to others all significant rights to benefits and all significant exposure to risks that relate to a previously recognised asset, the entire asset should cease to be recognised. An example would be a sale of debts for a single non-returnable cash payment. **69**

Special Cases

Paragraphs 21 and 22 deal with the great majority of transactions affecting previously recognised assets. However, in other cases there may be a significant change in the entity's rights to benefits and exposure to risks but not a complete transfer of all significant benefits and risks. In such cases, it will be necessary to consider whether the description or monetary amount of the asset needs to be changed and also whether a liability needs to be recognised for any obligations assumed or risks retained. These special cases arise where the transaction takes one or more of the following forms: **70**

(a) a transfer of only part of the item in question;
(b) a transfer of all of the item for only part of its life; and
(c) a transfer of all of the item for all of its life but where the entity retains some significant right to benefits or exposure to risk.

(a) Transfer of only part of an item

Transfer of part of an item that generates benefits may occur in one of two ways. The most straightforward is where a proportionate share of the item is transferred. For example, a loan transfer might transfer a proportionate share of a loan (including rights to receive both interest and principal), such that all future cash flows, profits and losses arising on the loan are shared by the transferee and transferor in fixed proportions. A second, less straightforward way of transferring a part of an item arises where the item comprises rights to two or more separate benefit streams, each with its own risks. A part of the item will be transferred where all significant rights to one or more of those benefit streams and associated exposure to risks are transferred whilst all significant rights to the other(s) are retained. An example would be a 'strip' of an interest-bearing loan into rights to two or more different cash flow streams that are payable on different dates (for instance 'interest' and 'principal'), with the entity retaining rights to only one of those streams (for instance 'principal'). In both these cases, the entity would cease to recognise the part of the original asset that has been transferred by the transaction, but would continue to recognise the remainder. A change in the description of the asset might also be required. **71**

(b) Transfer of an item for only part of its life

Paragraph 23 also applies to a transaction that transfers all of an item that generates benefits for only part of its life. Provided that the entity's access to benefits and **72** exposure to risks following the transaction are both significantly different from those it had before the transaction, the description or monetary amount of the asset previously recognised would need to be changed. For example, an entity may sell an item of property but agree to repurchase it in a substantially depreciated form (as for example where the item will be used for most of its life by the buyer). In this case the entity's original asset has changed from being the original item of property to a residual interest in that item and, in addition, the entity has assumed a liability of its obligation to pay the repurchase price. Sale and repurchase agreements are dealt with further in Application Note B.

(c) Transfer of an item for all of its life with some benefit or risk retained

73 Finally, paragraph 23 applies to a transaction that transfers an item that generates benefits for all of its life, but leaves the entity with significant rights to benefits or exposure to risks relating to that item. Whilst control has passed to the transferee, the retention of significant rights to benefits or exposure to risks has the result that the transaction fails to meet the conditions in paragraph 22 for ceasing to recognise an asset in its entirety. For example, an entity may sell an investment in a subsidiary with the consideration including an element of deferred performance-related consideration. Provided that significant rights to benefits and exposure to risks associated with the subsidiary have passed to the buyer (as will be the case where the deferred consideration is only a portion of the subsidiary's profits arising in only a limited period), both the description and the monetary amount of the asset will need to be changed. This reflects the fact that the asset is no longer an investment in a subsidiary but rather is a debtor for the performance-related consideration (although, under the provisions of SSAP 18, the debtor may be measured at nil and therefore not recognised but merely disclosed). As another example, an entity may sell equipment subject to a warranty in respect of the condition of the equipment at the time of sale, or subject to a guarantee of its residual value. This would normally transfer all significant rights to benefits and some significant exposure to risks to the buyer (these being those arising from the equipment's future use and resale), but leave the seller with some significant risk in the form of obligations relating to the equipment's future performance or residual value. The seller would therefore cease to recognise the equipment as an asset, but would recognise a liability for its warranty obligation or guarantee (with the liability being accounted for in accordance with the provisions of SSAP 18).

Measurement and profit recognition

74 In any of the above three classes of transaction, there arises the issue of how to measure the change in the entity's assets or liabilities and any resulting profit or loss. This measurement process requires that the previous carrying value of the asset is apportioned into an amount relating to those benefits and risks disposed of and an amount relating to those retained. In some cases, measurement will be relatively easy; for instance this might be the case where a proportionate share of the original asset is retained as described in paragraph 71 above or where there are similar and frequent transactions in liquid and freely accessible markets. In other cases, measurement may be more difficult with the result that the amount of any gain or loss is uncertain. In such cases, in accordance with the provisions of SSAP 18, paragraph 24 requires a prudent approach to be adopted, with full provision being made for any probable loss but recognition of any gain, to the extent it is in doubt, being deferred.

The meaning of 'significant'

In applying paragraphs 21–23 and 26 it may be necessary to determine whether certain rights to benefits or exposure to risks are 'significant'. When this is done, greater weight should be given to what is likely to have a commercial effect in practice. In particular, whether any retained risk is 'significant' should be judged not against the total possible variation in benefits, but against that variation which is likely to occur in practice. For instance, if for a portfolio of debts of 100, bad debts are expected to be 2 and the debts are sold with recourse to the entity for bad debts of up to 5, the seller will have retained all significant risk of non-payment. Thus the debts would continue to be recognised in their entirety (unless the conditions for a linked presentation are met). **75**

Linked presentation for certain non-recourse finance arrangements

General principles

Sometimes an entity finances an item on terms that the provider of the finance has recourse to only the item it has financed and not to the entity's other assets. It is sometimes argued that the effect of such arrangements is that the entity no longer has an asset in respect of the item, nor does it have a liability for the finance. For the purpose of determining the appropriate accounting treatment, non-recourse finance arrangements can be classified into two types. **76**

Separate presentation of an asset and liability

The first type of arrangement is where, although in the event of default the provider of the finance can obtain repayment only by enforcing its rights against the specified item, the entity retains rights to all the benefits generated by the item and can repay the finance from its general resources in order to preserve those rights. In such a case the entity has both an asset (its access to all the benefits generated by the item) and a liability (its obligation to repay the finance) and they should be included in the balance sheet in the normal way. **77**

Linked presentation

The second type of non-recourse finance arrangement is where the finance will be repaid only from benefits generated by the specified item. Although the entity has rights to any surplus benefits remaining after repayment of the finance, it has no right or obligation to keep the item or to repay the finance from its general resources. In these cases the entity does not have an asset equal to the gross amount of the item (as it does not have access to all the future benefits generated by it), nor a liability for the full **78** amount of the finance (as the financier will be repaid only from benefits generated by the specific item and not from benefits generated by any other assets of the entity). However, the entity does retain rights to those benefits and exposure to those risks that are likely to have a commercial effect in practice – ie the significant benefits and risks. It is retention of the significant benefits and risks that distinguishes this type of non-recourse financing from the transactions described in paragraph 23 that transfer a part of an asset. Where there is no transfer of significant benefits and risks the transaction is in substance a financing arrangement and the other party would usually receive a lender's return and no more. Conversely, the transactions described in paragraph 23 involve a transfer of significant benefits and risks. Indications of such transactions are where the other party has rights to benefits greater than those associated with a lender's return and has corresponding exposure to some significant risk.

79 For example, assume an entity transfers title to a portfolio of high quality debts of 100 in exchange for non-returnable proceeds of 90. The entity cannot be required to repay these non-returnable proceeds in any circumstance or in any form, nor can it be required to make any other payment in respect of the debts. In addition, the entity retains rights to a further sum (calculated as 10 less any bad debts and a finance charge) whose amount depends on whether and when the debtors pay. In this situation the entity does not have a liability for the non-returnable proceeds of 90 (as it can never be required to repay them except out of cash generated by the debts portfolio), nor an asset of 100 (as the first 90 of benefits generated by the debts must be passed to the transferee). However, the entity does have a new asset in its rights to future benefits of up to 10, which depends principally on the performance of the entire portfolio of 100. If any one debt proves to be completely bad or if all debts prove to be partly bad, the entity bears the entire loss (subject to the ceiling of 10) as its future cash receipts are reduced accordingly. Although it has transferred catastrophe risk (of benefits being less than 90), the entity has retained all the variation in benefits likely to occur in practice – ie the significant benefits and risks. The catastrophe risk that is transferred is not significant since, although the potential losses involved are large in absolute terms, it is extremely unlikely that such losses will occur in practice.

80 For this type of arrangement, a special presentation (a 'linked presentation') is required to give a true and fair view of the entity's position. This presentation involves giving additional information on the face of the balance sheet about the entity's new net asset (of 10 in the above example). In the above example, the linked presentation would be as follows:

Debts subject to financing arrangements:	
Debts (after providing for expected bad debts of 1)	99
Less: non-returnable amounts received	(90)
	9

This linked presentation shows both that the entity retains significant benefits and risks relating to all the debts, and that the claim of the provider of the finance is limited strictly to the funds generated by them.

Detailed conditions for use of a linked presentation

A linked presentation is appropriate only where the commercial effect for the entity is that the item is being sold but the sale process is not yet complete. Thus there must be no doubt whatsoever that the claim of the provider of the finance is limited strictly to funds generated by the specific item it finances. It must be clear that there is no legal, commercial or other obligation under which the entity may fund any losses (from whatever cause) on the items being financed or transfer any economic benefits (apart from those generated by the item). In addition, the entity must have no right or obligation to repay the finance from its general resources, to keep the item on repayment of the finance or to re-acquire it in the future. These principles are reflected in the detailed conditions for use of a linked presentation set out in paragraph 27. **81**

Condition 27(a) requires that the finance relates to a specific item or group of similar items. A linked presentation should not be used where the finance relates to two or more items that are not part of a portfolio, or to a portfolio containing items that would otherwise be shown under different balance sheet captions. Similarly, a linked presentation should not be used where the finance relates to any kind of business unit, or for items that generate the funds required to repay the finance only by being used in conjunction with other assets of the entity. The item must generate the funds required to repay the finance either by unwinding directly into cash (as in the case of a debt), or by its sale to a third party. **82**

Conditions 27(b)–(e) require that there is no recourse and no other condition (legal, commercial or other) that could result in the entity supporting losses, from whatever cause, on the items being financed (or, as discussed in the next paragraph, supporting such losses beyond a fixed monetary ceiling). Recourse could take a number of forms, for instance: an agreement to repurchase non-performing items or to substitute good items for bad ones; a guarantee given to the provider of the finance or any other party (of performance, proceeds or other support); a put option under which items can be transferred back to the entity; a swap of some or all of the amounts generated by the item for a separately determined payment; or a penalty on cancelling an ongoing arrangement such that the entity bears the cost of any items that turn out to be bad. Normal warranties given in respect of the condition of the item at the time the non-recourse finance arrangement is entered into would not breach this condition; however, warranties relating to the condition of the item in the future or to its future performance would do so. **83**

If there is partial recourse for losses up to a fixed monetary ceiling, a linked presentation may still be appropriate in respect of that part of the finance for which there is no recourse. However, where the entity provides any kind of open-ended guarantee (ie one that does not have a fixed monetary ceiling) a linked presentation should not be used. An example of such an open-ended guarantee would be a guarantee of completion provided by a property developer. **84**

The following example illustrates the effect of partial recourse. An entity transfers title to a portfolio of debts of 100 (for which expected bad debts are 4) in return for proceeds of 95 plus rights to a future sum whose amount depends on whether and when debtors **85** pay. In addition, there is recourse to the entity for the first 10 of any losses. Assuming the conditions set out in paragraphs 26–27 are met, the arrangement would be presented as follows:

Debts subject to financing arrangements:	
Gross debts (after providing for bad debts)	96
Less: non-returnable proceeds	(85)
	11

The remaining 10 of the finance would be included within liabilities.

86 Condition 27(f) requires there to be no provision for the entity to repurchase the item being financed. For instance, where legal title to the item has been transferred, a linked presentation should not be used to the extent that one party has a put or a call option to effect repurchase, or where there is an understanding between the parties that the item will be re-acquired in the future.

Profit or loss recognition and presentation

87 Where a linked presentation is used, profits or losses should be recognised in the period in which they arise so as to reflect the fact that the entity continues to gain or suffer from the performance of the underlying gross item. For example, on entering into the arrangement, a gain will arise only to the extent that the non-returnable proceeds received exceed the previous carrying value of the item. In subsequent periods, a gain (or loss) will arise to the extent that the income from the item exceeds (or falls short of) the amounts due to the provider of finance in respect of that period. Finally, any gain resulting from an onward sale of the item to a third party will arise only in the period in which the onward sale occurs.

88 Where a linked presentation is adopted in the balance sheet, normally it will be sufficient for only the net amount of any income or expense recognised in each period to be included in the profit and loss account, with the gross components being disclosed by way of note. However, the gross components should be shown on the face of the profit and loss account by using a linked presentation where the effect of the arrangement on the performance of the entity is so significant that to include merely the net amount of income or expense within the captions shown on the face of the profit and loss account would not be sufficient to give a true and fair view.

Offset

89 Offsetting is the process of aggregating debit and credit balances and including only the net amount in the balance sheet. In order to present the commercial effect of transactions, it is necessary that any separate assets and liabilities that result are not offset.

90 Offset is permissible, and indeed necessary, between related debit and credit balances that are not separate assets and liabilities as defined in the FRS. For this to be the case, it is necessary that all of the conditions given in paragraph 29 are met, such that there is no possibility that the entity could be required to pay another party and later find it was unable to obtain payment itself. In this respect, the requirement in condition (c) in paragraph 29 that the debit balance matures no later than the credit balance will be met if, at its own discretion, the reporting entity can ensure that result by accelerating the maturity of the debit balance or deferring the maturity of the credit balance. Where the reporting entity or the other party is a group, particular care must be taken to ensure that the reporting entity, through its constituent legal entities, can insist on a net settlement of the amounts to be offset in all situations of default and that this ability would survive the insolvency of any of the separate legal entities that constitute the other party.

Where the conditions for a linked presentation given in paragraphs 26–27 are met, **91** the entity's asset is the net amount. Such a presentation does not constitute offset of an asset and a liability; rather it is the provision of additional information about an asset (which is the net amount), necessary in order to give a true and fair view.

Disclosure of the substance of transactions

Paragraph 30 requires that disclosure of a transaction should be sufficient to enable the **92** user of the financial statements to understand its commercial effect. For the vast majority of transactions this involves no more than those disclosures currently required. However, this may not be sufficient to portray fully the commercial effect of more complex transactions, in which case further information will need to be disclosed.

Assets and liabilities resulting from more complex transactions will not necessarily be **93** exactly the same as those resulting from more straightforward transactions. The greater the differences the greater the need for disclosure. For example, certain assets may not be available for use as security for liabilities of the entity; or certain liabilities, whilst not qualifying for the linked presentation set out in paragraphs 26–27 may, in the event of default, be repayable only to the extent that the assets on which they are secured yield sufficient benefits. **94**

Even where a transaction does not result in any items being recognised in the balance sheet, the need for disclosure should still be considered. The transaction may give rise to guarantees, commitments or other rights and obligations which, although not sufficient to require recognition of an asset or liability, require disclosure in order that the financial statements give a true and fair view.

QUASI-SUBSIDIARIES

Identification of quasi-subsidiaries

An entity may directly control access to future economic benefits or may control such **95** access through the medium of another entity, normally a subsidiary. Control through the medium of another entity is of such widespread significance that it underlies the statutory definition of a subsidiary undertaking and is reflected in the requirement for the preparation of consolidated accounts. However, such control is not confined to cases where another entity is a subsidiary as defined in statute. 'Quasi-subsidiaries' are sometimes established by arrangements that give as much effective control over another entity as if that entity were a subsidiary.

Benefits

96 In deciding whether or not an entity is a quasi-subsidiary, access to the whole of the benefit inflows arising from its gross assets and responsibility for the whole of the benefit outflows associated with its liabilities are not the key considerations. In practice, many subsidiaries do not give rise to a possible benefit outflow for their parent of an amount equal to their gross liabilities – indeed, the limiting of benefit outflows in the event of losses occurring may have been a factor for the parent in establishing a subsidiary. In addition, as the liabilities of a subsidiary have a prior claim on its assets, the parent will not have access to benefit inflows of an amount equal to those gross assets. For this reason, it is necessary to focus on the benefit flows associated with the net assets of the entity. Often evidence of where these benefits lie is given by which party stands to suffer or gain from the financial performance of the entity – ie which party has the risks inherent in the benefits.

Control

97 Control is the means by which one entity determines how the assets of another entity are employed and by which the controlling entity ensures that the resulting benefits accrue to itself and not to others. Control may be evidenced in a variety of ways depending on its basis (eg ownership or other rights) and the way in which it is exercised (interventionist or not). Control includes the ability to restrict others from directing major policies, but a power of veto will not of itself constitute control unless its effect is that major policy decisions are taken in accordance with the wishes of the party holding that power. One entity will not control another where there is a third party that has the ability to determine all major issues of policy.

98 In some cases, arrangements are made for allocating the benefits arising from the activities of an entity such that active exercise of control is not necessary. The party or parties who will gain the benefits (and bear their inherent risks) are irreversibly specified in advance. No party has direct control in the sense of day-to-day direction of the entity's financial and operating policies, since all such matters are predetermined. In such cases, control will be exercised indirectly via the arrangements for allocating the benefits and it will be necessary to look at the effects of those arrangements to establish which party has control. It follows that, for the reasons set out in paragraph 96 above, the party possessing control will be the one that gains the benefits arising from the net assets of the entity.

Accounting for quasi-subsidiaries

99 In essence, consolidation is founded on the principle that all the entities under the control of the reporting entity should be incorporated into a single set of financial statements. Applying this principle has the result that the assets, liabilities, profits, losses and cash flows of any entity that is a quasi-subsidiary should be included in

group financial statements in the same way as if they were those of a member of the statutory group (this is referred to below as 'inclusion of a quasi-subsidiary in group financial statements').

The entities that constitute a group are determined by companies legislation. Companies legislation also requires that where compliance with its provisions would not be sufficient to give a true and fair view, the necessary additional information shall be given in the accounts or in a note to them* . Inclusion of a quasi-subsidiary in group financial statements is necessary in order to give a true and fair view of the group as legally defined and thus constitutes provision of such additional information. **100**

Companies legislation and FRS 2 'Accounting for Subsidiary Undertakings' permit or require subsidiaries to be excluded from consolidation in certain circumstances. However, as inclusion of a quasi-subsidiary in group financial statements is required in order that those financial statements give a true and fair view of the group, these exclusions are generally not appropriate for a quasi-subsidiary. The following considerations are relevant. **101**

(a) An immaterial quasi-subsidiary is outside the scope of this FRS, which need not be applied to immaterial items.
(b) Where severe long-term restrictions substantially hinder the exercise of the rights of the reporting entity over the assets or management of another entity, the reporting entity will not have the control necessary for the definition of a quasi-subsidiary to be met. Where the financial and operating policies of another entity are predetermined, this affects the manner in which control of that entity is exercised, but does not preclude the entity from being a quasi-subsidiary.
(c) Disproportionate expense or undue delay in obtaining information justifies excluding a quasi-subsidiary only if it is immaterial.
(d) Where there are significant differences between the activities of a quasi-subsidiary and those of the group that controls it, these should be disclosed. However, the quasi- subsidiary should nevertheless be included in the consolidation in order that the group financial statements present a true picture of the extent of the group's activities.

It is appropriate to exclude a quasi-subsidiary from consolidation only where the interest in the quasi-subsidiary is held exclusively with a view to subsequent resale and the quasi-subsidiary has not previously been included in the reporting entity's consolidated financial statements. In determining if this exclusion is appropriate in a particular instance, reference should be made to FRS 2.

Some arrangements for financing an item on a non-recourse basis involve placing the item and its finance in a quasi-subsidiary as a means of 'ring-fencing' them. Where, as a result, the conditions of paragraphs 26 and 27 are met from the point of view of the **102**

**In Great Britain section 227(5) of the Companies Act 1985. Equivalent references for Northern Ireland and the Republic of Ireland are given in paragraphs 5 and 6 respectively of Appendix I 'Note on legal requirements'.*

group as legally defined, the item and its finance should be included in the group financial statements by using a linked presentation. As noted above, the inclusion of a quasi-subsidiary in group financial statements forms additional information, necessary in order to give a true and fair view of the group as legally defined – the quasi-subsidiary is not part of that group. Where an item and its finance are effectively ring-fenced in a quasi-subsidiary, a true and fair view of the position of the group is given by presenting them under a linked presentation. In this situation, the group does not have an asset equal to the gross amount of the item, nor a liability for the full amount of the finance. However, where the item and its finance are similarly ring-fenced in a subsidiary, a linked presentation may not be used. This is because the subsidiary is part of the group as legally defined – hence the item and its finance, being an asset and a liability of the subsidiary, are respectively an asset and liability of the group. The subsidiary would be consolidated in the normal way in accordance with companies legislation and a linked presentation would not be used (unless a linked presentation were appropriate in the subsidiary's individual financial statements).

Disclosure of quasi-subsidiaries

103 When one or more quasi-subsidiaries are included in the consolidated financial statements of a statutory group, companies legislation requires the fact that such additional information has been included, and the effect of its inclusion, to be clearly disclosed*.

****In Great Britain section 227 of the Companies Act 1985. Equivalent references for Northern Ireland and the Republic of Ireland are given in paragraphs 5 and 6 respectively of Appendix I 'Note on legal requirements'.***

Application notes

These Application Notes specify how the requirements of FRS 5 are to be applied to transactions that have certain features. For such transactions, observance of the Notes will normally be sufficient to ensure compliance with the requirements of FRS 5.

The tables and illustrations shown in the shaded areas are provided as an aid to understanding and shall not be regarded as part of the Statement of Standard Accounting Practice.

It is not intended that the accounting treatment determined by FRS 5 or the terminology used in the Application Notes should change the situation at law achieved by the parties. Accordingly, it is not intended that the legal effectiveness of any transfer should be affected.

Contents

APPLICATION NOTE A – CONSIGNMENT STOCK

NB: Although this Application Note is drafted in terms of the motor trade it applies equally to similar arrangements in other industries.

Features

Consignment stock is stock held by one party (the 'dealer') but legally owned by another (the 'manufacturer'), on terms that give the dealer the right to sell the stock in the normal course of its business or, at its option, to return it unsold to the legal owner. The stock may be physically located on the premises of the dealer, or held at a car compound or other site nearby. The arrangement has a number of commercial advantages for both parties: the dealer is able to hold or have faster access to a wider range of stock than might otherwise be practicable; the manufacturer can avoid a build-up of stock on its premises by moving it closer to the point of sale; and both benefit from the greater sales potential of the arrangement. A1

The main features of a consignment stock arrangement are as follows: A2

(a) The manufacturer delivers goods to the dealer, but legal title does not pass until one of a number of events takes place, eg the dealer has held the goods for a specified period, adopts them by using them as demonstration models, or sells them to a third party. Until such a crystallising event, the dealer is entitled to return the goods to the manufacturer or the manufacturer is able to require their return or insist that they are passed to another dealer.
(b) Once legal title passes, the transfer price becomes payable by the dealer. This price may be fixed at the date goods are delivered to the dealer, it may vary with the period between delivery and transfer of title, or it may be the manufacturer's list price at the date of transfer of title.
(c) The dealer may also be required to pay a deposit to the manufacturer, or to pay the latter a display or financing charge. This deposit or charge may be fixed for a period (eg one year) or may fluctuate. Its amount is usually set with reference to the dealer's past sales of the manufacturer's goods or to average or actual holdings of consignment stock. It may (or may not) bear interest. In some cases, a finance company will pay the deposit or charge to the manufacturer and will charge interest thereon to the dealer.
(d) Other terms of the arrangement will usually cover items such as inspection and access rights of the manufacturer, and responsibility for damage, loss or theft and related insurance. These are usually of minor importance in determining the accounting treatment.

ANALYSIS

A3 The purpose of the analysis below is to determine whether, at any particular time, the dealer has an asset in the stock and a corresponding liability to pay the manufacturer for it. To this end, it is necessary to identify whether the dealer has access to the benefits of the stock and exposure to the risks inherent in those benefits. From the dealer's perspective, the principal benefits and risks of consignment stock are as follows:

Benefits:
(i) the future cash flows from sale to a third party and the right to retain items of stock in order to achieve such a sale;
(ii) insulation from changes to the transfer price charged by the manufacturer for its stock (eg because the manufacturer has increased its list price); and
(iii) the right to use the stock (eg as a demonstration model) by adopting it.

Risks:
(i) the risk of being compelled to retain stock that is not readily saleable or is obsolete, resulting in no sale or a sale at a reduced price; and
(ii) the risk of slow movement, resulting in increased costs of financing and holding the stock and an increased risk of obsolescence.

Paragraphs A5–A10 show how the various features of a consignment stock agreement will determine where the above benefits and risks lie. The stock should be included on the dealer's balance sheet where the dealer has access to its principal benefits and bears the principal risks inherent in those benefits.

In determining the substance of an agreement, it will be necessary to look at all its features and give greater weight to those that are more likely to have a commercial effect in practice. In addition, it will be necessary to consider the interaction between the features and to evaluate the arrangement as a whole. **A4**

Manufacturer's right of return (benefit (i))

The dealer's access to the benefits of the stock will be constrained by any right of the manufacturer to require goods to be returned or transferred to another dealer. The likely commercial effect of this constraint should be assessed. For instance, if a high proportion of the consignment stock is returned or transferred without compensation, this indicates that the stock is not an asset of the dealer. Conversely, if the dealer is able to resist requests made by the manufacturer for transfers and in practice actually does so, or in practice the manufacturer compensates the dealer for agreeing to transfer stock in accordance with the manufacturer's wishes, this indicates that the stock is an asset of the dealer. **A5**

Dealer's right of return (risk (i))

If the dealer has a right to return stock without payment of a penalty, it will not bear obsolescence risk. This indicates that the dealer has neither the asset 'stock', nor a liability to pay the manufacturer for it. Again, the likely commercial effect of any such right of return and the significance of obsolescence risk should be considered. If the right of return is exercised frequently or the manufacturer regularly provides a significant incentive (such as a price discount or a free extension to the consignment period) to persuade the dealer not to return stock where it would otherwise do so, this indicates that the stock is not an asset of the dealer. Conversely, if the dealer either has no right to return stock, or in practice does not exercise its right or is charged a significant penalty for doing so, this indicates that the dealer bears the principal risks relating to the stock and the stock is an asset for it. In such cases the dealer will also have a corresponding liability (legal or commercial) to pay for the stock. **A6**

Stock transfer price and deposits (benefit (ii), risk (ii))

Whether the dealer is insulated from changes in the prices charged by the manufacturer for its stock depends on how the stock transfer price is determined. Where the price is based on the manufacturer's list price at delivery, then the manufacturer is unable to pass on any subsequent price changes, which indicates that the stock became an asset of the dealer at the date of delivery. Conversely, if the price charged to the dealer is the manufacturer's list price at the date of the transfer of legal title, this indicates that the stock remains an asset of the manufacturer until legal title is transferred. **A7**

The stock transfer price will also affect the incidence of slow movement risk and who bears the variable cost of financing the stock until sold. In a simple arrangement where there is no deposit and stock is supplied for a fixed price that is payable by the dealer only when legal title is transferred it will be clear that the manufacturer bears the slow movement risk. The manufacturer will bear the slow movement risk wherever the transfer price is not determined by reference to the length of time for which stock is held **A8** (such as where the transfer price is the manufacturer's list price at either delivery or transfer of legal title). Conversely, if in the same basic arrangement, the price to be paid by the dealer increases by a factor that varies with the time the stock is held and approximates to commercial interest rates, then it will be equally clear that the dealer bears the slow movement risk. This may be so even where the financing element of the price charged to the dealer is based on average past movements of stocks held by that dealer (eg for administrative convenience), or is levied in another form (eg a display charge).

A9 The existence of a deposit complicates the analysis. The main question to be answered is whether the effect of the deposit is that the dealer, rather than the manufacturer, bears variations in the stock financing costs that are due to slow movement. For example, this could be achieved by a substantial, interest-free deposit whose amount is related to levels of stock held by the dealer. Alternatively, a finance company might advance the deposit to the manufacturer and charge interest thereon (in whatever form) to the dealer.

Dealer's right to use the stock (benefit (iii))

A10 Whilst a right for the dealer to use the stock in its business will not, of itself, be sufficient to make the stock an asset of the dealer, the exercise of the right will usually have this effect. Such exercise will usually cause the transfer of legal title to the dealer and give rise to an unconditional obligation for it to pay the manufacturer.

Required accounting

Substance of the transaction is that the stock is an asset of the dealer

A11 Where it is concluded that the stock is in substance an asset of the dealer, the stock should be recognised as such on the dealer's balance sheet, together with a corresponding liability to the manufacturer. Any deposit should be deducted from the liability and the excess classified as a trade creditor. The notes to the financial statements should explain the nature of the arrangement, the amount of consignment stock included in the balance sheet and the main terms under which it is held, including the terms of any deposit.

Substance of the transaction is that the stock is not an asset of the dealer

A12 Where it is concluded that the stock is not in substance an asset of the dealer, the stock should not be included on the dealer's balance sheet until the transfer of title has crystallised. Any deposit should be included under 'other debtors'. The notes to the financial statements should explain the nature of the arrangement, the amount of consignment stock held at the year-end, and the main terms under which it is held, including the terms of any deposit.

Table

Indications that the stock is not an asset of the dealer at delivery	**Indications that the stock is an asset of the dealer at delivery**
Manufacturer can require the dealer to return stock (or transfer stock to another dealer) without compensation, or Penalty paid by the dealer to prevent returns/transfers of stock at the manufacturer's request.	Manufacturer cannot require dealer to return or transfer stock, or Financial incentives given to persuade dealer to transfer stock at manufacturer's request.
Dealer has unfettered right to return stock to the manufacturer without penalty and actually exercises the right in practice.	Dealer has no right to return stock or is commercially compelled not to exercise its right of return.
Manufacturer bears obsolescence risk, eg: - obsolete stock is returned to the manufacturer without penalty; or - financial incentives given by manufacturer to prevent stock being returned to it (eg on a model change or if it becomes obsolete).	Dealer bears obsolescence risk, eg: - penalty charged if dealer returns stock to manufacturer; or - obsolete stock cannot be returned to the manufacturer and no compensation is paid by manufacturer for losses due to obsolescence.
Stock transfer price charged by manufacturer is based on manufacturer's list price at date of transfer of legal title.	Stock transfer price charged by manufacturer is based on manufacturer's list price at date of delivery.
Manufacturer bears slow movement risk, eg: - transfer price set independently of time for which dealer holds stock, and there is no deposit.	Dealer bears slow movement risk, eg: - dealer is effectively charged interest as transfer price or other payments to manufacturer vary with time for which dealer holds stock; or - dealer makes a substantial interest-free deposit that varies with the levels of stock held.

APPLICATION NOTE B – SALE AND REPURCHASE AGREEMENTS

NB: For ease of reading the parties to a sale and repurchase agreement are referred to below as 'seller' and 'buyer', notwithstanding that analysis of the transaction in accordance with this Application Note may result in the seller continuing to show an asset on its balance sheet.

Features

B1 Sale and repurchase agreements are arrangements under which assets are sold by one party to another on terms that provide for the seller to repurchase the asset in certain circumstances. A similar commercial effect may be achieved by arrangements under which one party holds an asset on behalf of another: although such arrangements are not sale and repurchase agreements, a similar analysis is appropriate and these are therefore covered by this Application Note.

B2 The main features of a sale and repurchase agreement will usually be:

(a) the sale price – this may be market value or another agreed price (analysed in paragraph B9);
(b) the nature of the repurchase provision – this may be: an unconditional commitment for both parties; an option for the seller to repurchase (a call option); an option for the buyer to resell to the seller (a put option); or a combination of put and call options; (analysed in paragraphs B10–B12);
(c) the repurchase price – this may: be fixed at the outset; vary with the period for which the asset is held by the buyer; or be the market price at the time of repurchase. It may also be designed to permit the buyer to recover incidental holding costs (eg insurance) if these do not in fact continue to be met by the seller; (analysed in paragraphs B13–B14); and
(d) other provisions, including where appropriate: for the seller to use the asset whilst it is owned by the buyer; for determining the time of repurchase; or for remarketing the asset if it is to be sold to a third party; (analysed in paragraphs B15–B18).

Analysis

Overview of basic principles

B3 The purpose of the analysis is to determine both whether the seller has an asset (and what is the nature of that asset), and whether the seller has a liability to repay the buyer some or all of the amounts received from the latter.

B4 In a straightforward case, the substance of a sale and repurchase agreement will be that of a secured loan – ie the seller will retain all significant rights to benefits relating to the original asset and all significant exposure to the risks inherent in those benefits and will have a liability to the buyer for the whole of the proceeds received. For example, this would be the case where the seller has in effect an unconditional commitment to repurchase the original asset from the buyer at the sale price plus interest. The seller should account for this type of arrangement by showing the original asset on its balance sheet together with a liability for the amounts received from the buyer.

B5 In certain more complex cases, it may be determined that a sale and repurchase agreement is not in substance a financing transaction and that the seller retains access to only some of the benefits of the original asset and retains only some of their inherent risks. Where this is so, in accordance with paragraph 23, the description or monetary amount of the original asset should be changed and a liability recognised for any obligation to transfer benefits that is assumed. It will also be necessary to give full disclosure of these more complex arrangements in the notes to the financial statements.

The substance of the arrangement may be more readily apparent if the position of both buyer and seller are considered, together with their apparent expectations and motives for agreeing to its various terms. In particular, where the substance is that of a secured loan, the buyer will require that it is assured of a lender's return on its investment and the seller will require that the buyer earns no more than this return. Thus whether or not the buyer earns such a return is an important indicator of the substance of the transaction. **B6**

Benefits and risks

The analysis that follows shows how the features set out in paragraph b2 may result in the seller having a liability to the buyer or in the seller retaining rights to some or all of the benefits of the original asset and exposure to some or all of the risks inherent in those benefits. These benefits and risks will usually include some or all of the following: **B7**

Benefits:
(i) the benefit of any expected increase in the value of the asset; and
(ii) benefits arising from use or development of the asset.

Risks:
(i) the risk of an unexpected variation (adverse or favourable) in the value of the asset;
(ii) the risk of obsolescence; and
(iii) where repurchase is not at a set date, the risk of a variation in the cost of financing the asset because of the variable period between sale and repurchase.

In analysing any specific agreement in practice, it will be necessary to look at all the features of the agreement and give greater weight to those that are more likely to have a commercial effect in practice. In addition, it will be necessary to consider the interaction between the features in order to determine the substance of the arrangement as a whole. **B8**

Feature (a) – Sale price

A sale price of other than the market value of the asset at the time of sale indicates that some benefit and risk have been retained by the seller, such that the seller has an asset (either the original asset or a new one) or a liability to the buyer. Even where the sale price is the asset's market value, the seller may nevertheless have an asset or a liability since the other terms of the arrangement may result in the seller retaining significant benefits and risks. **B9**

Feature (b) – Nature of repurchase provision

1. Commitment

B10 Any type of unconditional commitment for the seller to repurchase will give rise to both a liability and an asset for the seller: the liability being the seller's commitment to pay the repurchase price; and the asset being continued access to some or all of the benefits of the original asset that forms the subject of the sale and repurchase agreement. The price at which repurchase will occur and the other provisions of the arrangement will determine the exact nature of the seller's asset; these are dealt with in paragraphs B13–B18 below.

B11 There may in effect be a commitment to repurchase even without a strict legal obligation. In particular, this will be the case where there is an option (or a combination of options) on terms that leave no genuine commercial possibility that the option will fail to be exercised. For example, the exercise price of a call option may be set at a significant discount to expected market value, the seller may need the asset to use on an ongoing basis in its business, or the asset may provide in effect the only source of the seller's future sales. Unwritten understandings between the parties may also result in a commercial commitment for the seller to repurchase even in the absence of a strict legal obligation. Such a commitment is more likely to exist where the buyer's business does not usually involve it in taking on risks of a kind associated with the asset.

2. Put and call options

B12 In some cases the seller may have a call option to repurchase the asset but have no commitment to do so, or the buyer may have a put option to transfer the asset back to the seller without the seller having an equivalent right to insist on repurchase. It will be important to determine why the parties have agreed to such a one-sided option and to assess the commercial effect of the option with regard to all aspects of the arrangement, including whether the seller has a commercial need to repurchase the asset. This analysis may reveal that, in substance, there is a commitment to repurchase as discussed above. Conversely, such an analysis may reveal that the buyer assumes significant benefits and risks relating to the original asset, indicating that the seller has neither the original asset, nor a liability for the option's exercise price. In such a case, where the seller holds a call option it will have a new asset in the form of the option itself; where the buyer has a put option, the seller will have a contingent liability to the buyer for the exercise price of the option (contingent on the buyer exercising its option). In both cases, the seller's new asset or liability should be recognised or disclosed, on a prudent basis, following the principles set out in SSAP 18 'Accounting for contingencies'.

Feature (c) – Repurchase price and provision for a lender's return

B13 In the most straightforward case, the repurchase price will be the sum of the original sale price, plus any major costs incurred by the buyer and a lender's return (comprising interest on the sale price and costs incurred by the buyer, perhaps with a relatively small fee), but no more. In this case, even if the repurchase provision takes the form of an option, the repurchase price indicates that the substance of the transaction is that of a secured loan, with the benefits and risks of the asset remaining with the seller. This is because the buyer is not compensated for assuming any significant exposure to loss, nor is the seller compensated for giving up any significant potential for gain, thus indicating that the transaction is, in substance, a financing. It will be necessary to look at the arrangement as a whole to establish whether the buyer receives a lender's return since the means of providing it will vary. For example, it may be achieved by lease or other regular payments, licence fees, adjustment to the original sales price or the calculation of the repurchase price.

Conversely, if the buyer is not assured of a lender's return, this indicates that some benefit and risk have been passed to the buyer such that the seller has not retained the original asset. The seller may, nevertheless, have a different asset (and a corresponding liability). For example, if a manufacturer sells equipment but agrees to repurchase it in a substantially different form towards the end of its economic life, the manufacturer has both a liability (to pay the repurchase price) and an asset (the equipment as at the repurchase date). **B14**

Feature (d) – Other provisions

1. Ability to use the asset

Whilst the ability of the seller to determine the use of the original asset does not, of itself, result in the substance of the transaction being that of a secured loan, it will usually indicate this is so. Continued use of the asset by the seller may indicate that it has a commercial obligation to repurchase even if it has no legal obligation to do so, for instance if there is a commercial need for the seller to repurchase or an expectation that it will do so. **B15**

Where the seller continues to use the asset in its business by entering into a sale and leaseback transaction, the provisions of both SSAP 21 'Accounting for leases and hire purchase contracts' and this Application Note will be relevant. Where, in the terms of this Application Note, the substance of the transaction is that of a secured loan, it will be structured so that no significant benefits or risks are passed to the buyer, with the rentals and other lease payments providing the buyer with a lender's return. Thus, in the terms of SSAP 21, 'substantially all the risks and rewards of ownership' of the asset will remain with the seller, the leaseback will be classified as a finance lease, and the transaction will be accounted for as the raising of finance secured on the asset. If, on the other hand, the leaseback is in substance an operating lease, the transaction will be accounted for as a sale of the original asset. **B16**

2. Profits or losses on a sale of the asset to a third party

In some cases, the seller may retain access to any increase in the value of the asset via provisions that pass to it substantially all of any profit arising on a sale by the first buyer to a third party (subject to the buyer receiving a lender's return). In addition the buyer may be protected from risk of loss, for instance by the seller being obliged to reimburse the whole or part of any loss on a sale to a third party, or the original sale price being such that losses are unlikely to occur in practice. The substance of such an arrangement is that of a secured loan. **B17**

3. Use of special entities ('vehicles')

B18 Some cases may involve a sale to a special entity (a 'vehicle') that is partly or wholly financed by a party other than the seller (eg a financial institution). In such a case, the seller will usually retain access to any increase in the value of the asset and, where relevant, the benefits from its use, via a right either to repurchase the asset or, in the event that the seller does not repurchase, to receive the majority of any profits from a future sale to a third party. In addition, the seller may provide protection against loss to the other investors in the vehicle, eg by providing a subordinated loan to the vehicle that acts as a cushion to absorb any losses or by guaranteeing the value of the asset in the event that it is sold on to a third party. Such provisions are clear indications that the substance of the transaction is that of a secured loan. Where the terms of the arrangement taken as a whole mean that the investors in the vehicle are reasonably assured of recovering their original investment and earning a lender's return (but no more) thereon, the substance of the transaction will be that of a secured loan.

Required accounting

Substance of the transaction is that of a secured loan

B19 Where the substance of the transaction is that of a secured loan, the seller should continue to recognise the original asset and record the proceeds received from the buyer as a liability. Interest – however designated – should be accrued. The carrying amount of the asset should be reviewed and provided against if necessary. The notes to the financial statements should describe thc principal features of the arrangement, including the status of the asset and the relationship between the asset and liability.

B20 Where the transaction is a sale and leaseback, no profit should be recognised on entering into the arrangement and no adjustment made to the carrying value of the asset. As stated in the guidance notes to SSAP 21, this represents the substance of the transaction, "namely the raising of finance secured on an asset that continues to be held and that is not disposed of".

Substance of the transaction is that the seller has a different asset

B21 Where the seller has a new asset or liability (for example, merely a call option to repurchase the original asset), it should recognise or disclose that new asset or liability on a prudent basis in accordance with the provisions of SSAP 18. In particular, the seller should recognise (and not merely disclose) a liability for any kind of unconditional obligation it has entered into. Where doubts exist regarding the amount of any gain or loss arising, full provision should be made for any expected loss but recognition of any gain, to the extent that it is in doubt, should be deferred until it is realised. The notes to the financial statements should describe the main features of the arrangement, including: the status of the asset; the relationship between the asset and the liability; and the terms of any provision for repurchase (including any options) and of any guarantees.

Table

Indications of sale of original asset to buyer (nevertheless, the seller may retain a different asset)	**Indications of no sale of original asset to buyer (secured loan)**
	Sale price does not equal market value at date of sale.
No commitment for seller to repurchase asset, eg: - call option where there is a real possibility the option will fail to be exercised.	Commitment for seller to repurchase asset, eg: - put and call option with the same exercise price; - either a put or a call option with no genuine commercial possibility that the option will fail to be exercised; or - seller requires asset back to use in its business, or asset is in effect the only source of seller's future sales.
Risk of changes in asset value borne by buyer such that buyer does not receive solely a lender's return, eg: - both sale and repurchase price equal market value at date of sale/purchase.	Risk of changes in asset value borne by seller such that buyer receives solely a lender's return, eg: - repurchase price equals sale price plus costs plus interest; - original purchase price adjusted retrospectively to pass variations in the value of the asset to the seller; - seller provides residual value guarantee to buyer or subordinated debt to protect buyer from falls in the value of the asset.
Nature of the asset is such that it will be used over the life of the agreement, and seller has no rights to determine its use. Seller has no rights to determine asset's development or future sale.	Seller retains right to determine asset's use, development or sale, or rights to profits therefrom.

Illustrations

Illustration 1

A, a house-builder, agrees with B, a bank, to sell to B some of the land within its land bank. The arrangements surrounding the sale are as follows:

(a) the sales price will be open market value as determined by an independent surveyor;
(b) B grants A the right to develop the land at any time during B's ownership, subject to its approval of the development plans, which approval shall not be unreasonably withheld; for this right, A pays all the outgoings on the land plus an annual fee of 5 per cent of the purchase price;
(c) B will maintain a memorandum account in respect of the land for the purpose of determining the price to be paid by A should A ever re-acquire the land or any adjustments necessary to the original purchase price. In this account will be entered the purchase price, any expenses incurred by B in relation to the transaction, a sum added quarterly (or on the sale by B of the land) calculated by reference to B's base lending rate plus 2 per cent applied to the daily balance on the account; and from the account will be deduced any annual fees paid by A to B;
(d) B grants A an option to acquire the land at any time within the next five years; the acquisition price is to be the balance on the memorandum account at the time of exercising the option;
(e) A grants B an option to require it to repurchase the land at any time within the next five years, the price to be the balance on the memorandum account at that time;
(f) on the expiry of five years from the date of acquiring the land, B will offer it for sale generally; and at any time prior to that it may with the consent of A offer the land for sale; and
(g) in the event of B selling the land to a third party, the proceeds of sale shall be deducted from the memorandum account maintained by B and the balance on the account shall be settled between A and B in cash, as a retrospective adjustment of the price at which B originally purchased the land from A.

The commercial effect of the above arrangement is that of a secured loan. A continues to bear all significant benefits and risks relating to the land, retains control of its development, and bears all resulting gains and losses (via either exercise of its call option, or adjust to the purchase price on sale of the land to a third party). This latter feature also gives rise to a liability for A to repay the whole of the sale proceeds received from B. In addition, B is assured of a lender's return (and no more): whilst the regular payments by A to B to secure the right to develop the land are not sufficient to provide this, B's return is guaranteed through the operation of the memorandum account and its role in determining the option price on a resale.

Illustration 2

This illustration is similar to the first but makes use of V, a vehicle company, and a subordinated loan to effect the purchase. A agrees with B (the bank) and V to sell land within its land bank to V. Relevant terms are as follows:

(a) the sale price is open market value;
(b) B grants V a loan of 60 per cent of the market value to effect the purchase, with A providing V with a subordinated loan of the balance of the consideration. B's loan bears interest at the bank's base rate plus 2 per cent: A's loan bears interest

at 10 per cent. All payments of interest and capital on A's loan are subordinated to all sums due to B in any period;

(c) V grants A the right to develop the land at any time during V's ownership, subject to its approval. For this right, A pays V a market rental on the land. If this is less than the interest payable on V's loan from B, then A will advance the amount of the shortfall as an addition to its subordinated loan;

(d) V grants A an option to acquire the land at any time within the next five years, at a price equal to the original sales price plus any incidental costs incurred by V;

(e) on the expiry of five years from the date of acquiring the land, V will offer it for sale generally, and at any time before then may with the consent of A offer the land for sale; and

(f) in the event of V selling the land, to the extent that the proceeds of sale and any other cash accumulated in V exceed any sums due to B and A under the terms of their respective loans, an immediate payment shall be made to A as a retrospective adjustment of the price at which V originally purchased the land from A.

In this illustration, the substance of the transaction is that of a secured loan. A continues to bear all significant benefits and risks relating to the land, it continues to have the ability to develop it and access to the whole of any profits from its future sale. In addition, the subordinated loan from A provides a cushion to absorb losses on the disposal of the land by the vehicle; this ensures that all foreseeable losses accrue to A and thus protects the position of the bank. In practice, such subordinated loans are often sufficiently large to make any loss by the bank through a loss in value of the land extremely remote. Where this is not the case or there is no subordinated loan, the necessary protection may be provided through put options – such as are incorporated within Illustration 1 – which enable the buyer to require the seller to repurchase the asset. Where the substance of the transaction is that of a secured loan, the buyer will require that the terms of the arrangement taken as a whole mean it is reasonably assured of receiving return of the purchase price and any costs it incurs plus a lender's return (but no more) on its investment.

APPLICATION NOTE C – FACTORING OF DEBTS

NB: For ease of reading the parties to a factoring agreement are referred to in this Application Note as 'seller' and 'factor', notwithstanding that analysis of the transaction in accordance with this Application Note may result in the seller continuing to show the factored debts as an asset on its balance sheet.

Features

Factoring of debts is a well established method of obtaining finance, sales ledger administration services, or protection from bad debts. The principal features of a factoring arrangement are as follows: C1

(a) Specified debts are transferred to the factor (usually by assignment). The transfer may be of complete debtor balances or of all invoices relating to named debtors (perhaps subject to restrictions on the amount that will be accepted from any one debtor).

(b) The factor offers a credit facility that permits the seller to draw up to a fixed percentage of the face value of the debts transferred. Normally these advances are repaid as and when the underlying debts are collected, often by paying the money that is collected into a specially nominated bank account for the benefit of the factor.

(c) The factor may also offer a credit protection facility (or insurance cover). This will limit or eliminate the extent to which the factor has recourse to the seller for debts that are in default.

(d) The factor may administer the sales ledger of the seller. Where such a service is provided, the factor becomes responsible for collecting money from debtors and pursuing those that are slow in paying. In such cases the fact that debts have been factored is likely to be disclosed to the seller's customers; this may not be necessary in other circumstances.

C2 On the transfer of debts, the factoring charges levied on the seller will be set by the factor with reference to expected collections from the debtors and any credit protection services provided (sales ledger administration services are usually invoiced separately). These charges may be fixed at the outset or subject to adjustment at a later date to reflect actual collections; they may be payable immediately or on some future date.

Analysis

Overview of basic principles

C3 The purpose of the analysis below is to determine the appropriate accounting treatment in the seller's financial statements. There are three possible treatments:

(a) to remove the factored debts from the balance sheet and show no liability in respect of any proceeds received from the factor ('derecognition');

(b) to show the proceeds received from the factor deducted from the factored debts on the face of the balance sheet within a single asset caption (a 'linked presentation'); or

(c) to continue to show the factored debts as an asset, and show a corresponding liability within creditors in respect of the proceeds received from the factor (a 'separate presentation').

C4 In order to determine the appropriate accounting treatment, it is necessary to answer two questions:

(a) whether the seller has access to the benefits of the factored debts and exposure to the risks inherent in those benefits (referred to below as 'benefits and risks'); and

(b) whether the seller has a liability to repay amounts received from the factor.

Where the seller has transferred all significant benefits and all significant risks relating to the debts, and has no obligation to repay the factor, derecognition is appropriate; where the seller has retained significant benefits and risks relating to the debts but there is absolutely no doubt that its downside exposure to loss is limited, a linked presentation should be used; and in all other cases a separate presentation should be adopted.

Benefits and risks

The main benefits and risks relating to debts are as follows: **C5**

Benefits:
(i) the future cash flows from payment by the debtors.

Risks:
(i) slow payment risk; and
(ii) credit risk (the risk of bad debts).

Analysis of benefits

At first glance it may appear that the factor has access to the cash flows from payments by debtors. This may be particularly so if the money that is collected is to be paid direct to the factor (or into a specially nominated bank account for its benefit). However, it may actually be the seller that benefits from payments by debtors, these payments merely representing the primary source from which the factor will be repaid. In particular, where the seller has an obligation to repay any sums received from the factor on or before a set date regardless of the level of collections from the underlying debts, it is clear that the seller has the benefit of payments by debtors, exposure to their inherent risks and a liability to the factor. Such an arrangement should be accounted for by using a separate presentation. Conversely, where the seller receives a single non-returnable cash payment from the factor and the only future payments to be made are by the seller passing to the factor all and any payments from debtors as and when paid, the seller will both have transferred the benefits and risks of the factored debts and have no obligation to repay amounts received from the factor. **C6**
This latter arrangement would qualify for derecognition.

Considering the benefits in isolation will not normally enable a clear decision to be made on the appropriate accounting treatment for a factoring. The cash flows may appear similar in both of the above arrangements – an initial cash inflow for the seller followed by a later cash outflow (or a sacrifice of a cash inflow that would otherwise occur). For this reason, the risks (both upside potential for gain and downside exposure to loss) are more significant than the benefits. **C7**

Slow payment risk: credit facility

The first main risk associated with non-interest bearing debts is slow payment risk (including the upside potential from prompt payment by debtors). Where the finance cost charged by the factor is essentially a fixed sum determined at the time the transfer is made, the factor will bear the risk of slow payment; where it varies to reflect the speed of collection of the debts subsequently, the seller will bear that risk. Close attention to the arrangements and to their commercial effect in practice may be necessary to determine whether a variable finance cost falls upon the seller since it may take various forms, **C8** including a bonus for early settlement, or a retrospective adjustment to the purchase price.

Credit risk: credit protection facility

C9 Credit risk is the other main risk associated with trade debts. If there is no recourse to the seller for bad debts, the factor will bear this risk; if there is full recourse, the seller will bear it. Furthermore, as non-payment is merely the ultimate form of slow payment, where credit risk is retained by the seller, the latter will normally also bear at least some risk of slow payment. For example, where the arrangement takes the form of the seller repurchasing debts that remain outstanding after a given time, the seller bears the slow payment risk beyond this time as well as bearing the credit risk.

Administration arrangements and service-only factoring

C10 For the purpose of deciding upon the appropriate accounting treatment, the administration arrangements will not be directly significant (provided they are on an arm's length basis, and for a fee that is commensurate with the service provided). In a service-only factoring arrangement, where the factor administers the sales ledger but cash is received no earlier than if the debts had not been factored, the seller retains access to the benefits of the debts and exposure to their inherent risks. Thus such an arrangement should be accounted for by using a separate presentation.

Derecognition

C11 Derecognition (ie ceasing to recognise the factored debts in their entirety) is appropriate only where the seller retains no significant benefits and no significant risks relating to the factored debts.

C12 Whilst the commercial effect of any particular transaction should be assessed taking into account all its aspects and implications, the presence of all of the following indicates that the seller has not retained significant benefits and risks, and derecognition is appropriate:

(a) the transaction takes place at an arm's length price for an outright sale;

(b) the transaction is for a fixed amount of consideration and there is no recourse whatsoever, either implicit or explicit, to the seller for losses from either slow payment or non-payment. Normal warranties given in respect of the condition of the debts at the time of the transfer (eg a warranty that goods have been delivered or that the borrower's credit limit had not been breached at the time of granting him credit) would not breach this condition. However, warranties relating to the condition of the debts in the future or to their future performance (eg that debtors will not move into arrears in the future) would breach the condition. Other possible forms of recourse are set out in paragraph 83; and

(c) the seller will not benefit or suffer in any way if the debts perform better or worse than expected. This will not be the case where the seller has a right to further sums from the factor which vary according to the future performance of the debts (ie according to whether or when the debtors pay). Such sums might take the form of deferred consideration, a retrospective adjustment to the purchase price, or rebates of certain charges; they include all forms of variable finance cost.

Where any of the above three features is not present, this indicates that the seller has retained benefits and risks relating to the factored debts and, unless these are insignificant, either a separate presentation or a linked presentation should be adopted. **C13**

Whether any benefit and risk retained are 'significant' should be judged in relation to those benefits and risks that are likely to occur in practice, and not in relation to the total possible benefits and risks. For example, if for a portfolio of factored debts of 100, expected bad debts are 5 and there is recourse to the seller for credit losses of up to 10, significant risk will have been retained (as the seller would bear losses of up to twice those expected to occur). Accordingly, in this example, derecognition would not be appropriate and either a linked presentation or a separate presentation should be used. The terms of any roll-over provisions and their effect in practice require careful consideration since these may result in the seller continuing to bear significant risk where, at first sight, it appears that the arrangements do not have this effect. For example, the pricing of future transfers may be adjusted to reflect recent slow payment or bad debt experience and there may be a significant disincentive (eg a penalty) for the seller to cancel the arrangement. This may result in the seller continuing to bear significant risk, albeit disguised as revised charges for debts factored subsequently. **C14**

Linked presentation

A linked presentation will be appropriate where, although the seller has retained significant benefits and risks relating to the factored debts, there is absolutely no doubt that its downside exposure to loss is limited to a fixed monetary amount. A linked presentation should be used only to the extent that there is both absolutely no doubt that the factor's claim extends solely to collections from the factored debts, and no provision for the seller to re-acquire the debts in the future. The conditions that need to be met in order for this to be the case are set out in paragraph 27 and explained in paragraphs 81–86. When interpreting these conditions in the context of a factoring arrangement the following points apply: **C15**

condition (a) (specified assets) –

a linked presentation should not be used where the debts that have been factored cannot be separately identified.

condition (d) (that the factor agrees in writing there is no recourse, and such agreement is noted in the financial statements) –

the inclusion of an appropriate statement in the factoring agreement will meet the first part of this condition.

Where debts are factored on an ongoing basis, the arrangements for terminating the agreement must be carefully analysed in order to ensure that the conditions for a linked presentation are met. It will be necessary that, although the factor does not take on any new debts, it continues to bear losses on debts already factored and is not able to transfer them back to the seller. Where this is not the case, there remains the possibility **C16** that the factor will return debts that it suspects to be bad by terminating the arrangement. In such a case the seller's exposure to loss is not limited, and a separate presentation should be adopted.

Separate presentation

C17 Where the seller has retained significant benefits and risks relating to the debts and the conditions for a linked presentation are not met, a separate presentation should be adopted.

Required accounting

Derecognition

C18 Where the seller has retained no significant benefits and risks relating to the debts and has no obligation to repay amounts received from the factor, the debts should be removed from its balance sheet and no liability shown in respect of the proceeds received from the factor. A profit or loss should be recognised, calculated as the difference between the carrying amount of the debts and the proceeds received.

Linked presentation

C19 Where the conditions for a linked presentation are met, the proceeds received, to the extent they are non-returnable, should be shown deducted from the gross amount of the factored debts (after providing for bad debts, credit protection charges and any accrued interest) on the face of the balance sheet. An example is given in illustration 2 below. The interest element of the factor's charges should be recognised as it accrues and included in the profit and loss account with other interest charges. The notes to the financial statements should disclose: the main terms of the arrangement; the gross amount of factored debts outstanding at the balance sheet date; the factoring charges recognised in the period, analysed as appropriate (eg between interest and other charges); and the disclosures required by conditions (c) and (d) in paragraph 27.

Separate presentation

C20 Where neither derecognition nor a linked presentation is appropriate, a separate presentation should be adopted, ie a gross asset (equivalent in amount to the gross amount of the debts) should be shown on the balance sheet of the seller within assets, and a corresponding liability in respect of the proceeds received from the factor should be shown within liabilities. The interest element of the factor's charges should be recognised as it accrues and included in the profit and loss account with other interest charges. Other factoring costs should be similarly accrued and included in the profit and loss account within the appropriate caption. The notes to the financial statements should disclose the amount of factored debts outstanding at the balance sheet date.

Table

Indications that derecognition is appropriate (debts are not an asset of the seller)	**Indications that a linked presentation is appropriate**	**Indications that a separate presentation is appropriate (debts are an asset of the seller)**
Transfer is for a single, non-returnable fixed sum.	Some non-returnable proceeds received, but seller has rights to further sums from the factor (or vice versa) whose amount depends on whether or when debtors pay.	Finance cost varies with speed of collection of debts, eg: - by adjustment to consideration for original transfer; or - subsequent transfers priced to recover costs of earlier transfers
There is no recourse to the seller for losses.	There is either no recourse for losses, or such recourse has a fixed monetary ceiling.	There is full recourse to the seller for losses.
Factor is paid all amounts received from the factored debts (and no more). Seller has no rights to further sums from the factor.	Factor is paid only out of amounts collected from the factored debts, and seller has no right or obligation to repurchase debts.	Seller is required to repay amounts received from the factor on or before a set date, regardless of timing or amounts of collections from debtors.

Illustrations

Illustration 1 – Factoring with recourse (separate presentation)

Company S enters into a factoring arrangement with F, with the following principal terms:

(a) S will transfer (by assignment) all its trade debts to F, subject only to credit approval by F and a limit placed on the proportion of the total that may be due from any one debtor;

(b) F administers S's sales ledger and handles all aspects of collection of the debts in return for an administration charge at an annual rate of 1 per cent, payable monthly, based upon the total debts factored at each month-end;

(c) S may draw up to 70 per cent of the gross amount of debts factored and outstanding at any time, such drawings being debited in the books of F to a factoring account operated by F for S;

(d) weekly, S assigns and sends copy invoices to F as they are raised. F sends statements to debtors, following up all overdue invoices by telephone or letter;
(e) F credits collections from debtors to the factoring account, and debits the account monthly with interest calculated on the basis of the daily balances on the account using a rate of base rate plus 2 per cent. Thus this interest charge varies with the amount of finance drawn by S under the finance facility from F, the speed of payment of the debtors and the base rate;
(f) any debts not recovered after 90 days are reassigned to S for an immediate cash payment, which is credited to the factoring account;
(g) F pays for all other debts, less any advances and interest charges made, 90 days after the date of their assignment to F, and debits the payment to the factoring account; and
(h) on termination of the agreement the balance on the factoring account is settled in cash.

The commercial effect of the above arrangements is that, although the debts have been legally transferred to F, the benefits and risks are retained by S. S continues to bear the slow payment risk as the interest charged by F varies with the speed of payment by the debtors; S continues to bear all of the credit risk as it must pay for any debts not recovered after 90 days, and it therefore has unlimited exposure to loss. In addition, S in effect has an obligation to repay amounts received from F on or before a set date regardless of the levels of collections from the factored debts – either out of collections from debtors on the day they pay, or from its general resources after 90 days, whichever is the earlier. Thus a separate presentation should be adopted.

Illustration 2 – Factoring without recourse (linked presentation)

S enters into an agreement with F with the following principal terms:

(a) S will transfer (by assignment) to F such trade debts as S shall determine, subject only to credit approval by F and a limit placed on the proportion of the total that may be due from any one debtor. F levies a charge of 0.15 per cent of turnover, payable monthly, for this facility;
(b) S continues to administer the sales ledger and handle all aspects of collection of the debts;
(c) S may draw up to 80 per cent of the gross amount of debts assigned at any time, such drawings being debited in the books of F to a factoring account operated by F for S;
(d) weekly, S assigns and sends copy invoices to F as they are raised;
(e) S is required to bank the gross amounts of all payments received from debts assigned to F direct into an account in the name of F. Credit transfers made by debtors direct into S's own bank account must immediately be paid to F;
(f) F credits such collections from debtors to the factoring account, and debits the account monthly with interest calculated on the basis of the daily balances on the account using a rate of base rate plus 2.5 per cent. Thus this interest charge varies with the amount of finance drawn by S under the finance facility from F, the speed of payment of the debtors and base rate;

(g) F provides protection from bad debts. Any debts not recovered after 90 days are credited to the factoring account, and responsibility for their collection is passed to F. A charge of 1 per cent of the gross value of all debts factored is levied by F for this service and debited to the factoring account;
(h) F pays for the debts, less any advances, interest charges and credit protection charges, 90 days after the date of purchase, and debits the payment to the factoring account; and
(i) on either party giving 90 days' notice to the other, the arrangement will be terminated. In such an event, S will transfer no further debts to F, and the balance remaining on the factoring account at the end of the notice period will be settled in cash in the normal way.

The commercial effect of this arrangement is that, although the debts have been legally transferred to F, S continues to bear significant benefits and risks relating to them. S continues to bear slow payment risk as the interest charged by F varies with the speed of collections of the debts. Hence, the gross amount of the debts should continue to be shown on its balance sheet until the earlier of collection and transfer of all risks to F (ie 90 days). However, S's maximum downside loss is limited since any debts not recovered after 90 days are in effect paid for by F, which then assumes all slow payment and credit risk beyond this time. Thus, even for debts that prove to be bad, S receives some proceeds.* Hence, assuming the conditions given in paragraphs 26 and 27 are met, a linked presentation should be adopted. The amount deducted on the face of the balance sheet should be the lower of the proceeds received and the gross amount of the debts less all charges to the factor in respect of them. In the above example, for a debt of 100 this latter amount would be calculated at 100 less the credit protection fee of 1 and the maximum finance charge (calculated for 90 days at base rate plus 2.5 per cent). Assuming the proceeds received of 80 are lower than this, and accrued interest charges at the year-end are 2, the arrangement would be shown as follows:

Current Assets

Stock		x
Debts factored without recourse:		
Gross debts (after providing for credit protection fee and accrued interest)	97	
less: non-returnable proceeds	(80)	
		17
Other debtors		x

In addition, the non-returnable proceeds of 80 would be included within cash and the profit and loss account would include both the credit protection expense of 1 and the accrued interest charges of 2.

For a debt of 100 that subsequently proves to be bad, the proceeds received would be 100, less the credit protection fee of 1, less an interest charge calculated for 90 days at base rate plus 2.5%.

APPLICATION NOTE D – SECURITISED ASSETS

Features

D1 Securitisation is a means by which providers of finance fund a specific block of assets rather than the general business of a company. The assets that have been most commonly securitised in the UK are household mortgages. Other receivables such as credit card balances, hire purchase loans and trade debts are sometimes securitised, as are non-monetary assets such as property and stocks. This Application Note applies to all kinds of assets.

D2 The main features are generally as follows:

(a) The assets to be securitised are transferred by a company (the 'originator') to a special purpose vehicle (the 'issuer') in return for an immediate cash payment. Additional deferred consideration may also be payable.

(b) The issuer finances the transfer by the issue of debt, usually tradeable loan notes or commercial paper (referred to below as 'loan notes'). The issuer is usually thinly capitalised and its shares placed with a party other than the originator – charitable trusts have often been used for this purpose – with the result that the issuer is not classified as a subsidiary of the originator under companies legislation. In addition, the major financial and operating policies of the issuer are usually predetermined by the agreements that constitute the securitisation, such that neither the owner of its share capital nor the originator has any significant continuing discretion over how it is run.

(c) Arrangements are made to protect the loan noteholders from losses occurring on the assets by a process termed 'credit enhancement'. This may take the form of third party insurance, a third party guarantee of the issuer's obligations or an issue of subordinated debt (perhaps to the originator); all provide a cushion against losses up to a fixed amount.

(d) The originator is granted rights to surplus income (and, where relevant, capital profits) from the assets – ie to cash remaining after payment of amounts due on the loan notes and other expenses of the issuer. The mechanisms used to achieve this include: servicing or other fees; deferred sale consideration; 'super interest' on amounts owed to the originator (eg subordinated debt); dividend payments; and swap payments.

(e) In the case of securitised debts, the originator may continue to service the debts (ie to collect amounts due from borrowers, set interest rates etc). In this capacity it is referred to as the 'servicer' and receives a servicing fee.

(f) Cash accumulations from the assets (eg from mortgage redemptions) are reinvested by the issuer until loan notes are repaid. Any difference between the interest rate obtained on reinvestments and that payable on the loan notes will normally affect the originator's surplus under (d) above. The terms of the loan notes may provide for them to be redeemed as assets are realised, thus minimising this reinvestment period. Alternatively, cash accumulations may be invested in a 'guaranteed investment contract' that pays a guaranteed rate of interest (which may be determined by reference to a variable benchmark rate such as LIBOR) sufficient to meet interest payments on the loan notes. Another alternative, used particularly for short-term debts arising under a facility (eg credit card balances), is a provision for cash receipts (here from card repayments) to be reinvested in similar assets (eg new balances on the same credit card accounts). This reinvestment in similar assets will occur for a specified period only, after which time cash accumulations will either be used to redeem loan notes or be reinvested in other more liquid assets until loan notes are repaid.

(g) In certain circumstances, for example if tax changes affect the payment of interest to the noteholders or if the principal amount of loan notes outstanding declines to a specified level, the issuer may have an option to buy back the notes. Such repurchase may be funded by the originator, in which case the originator will re-acquire the securitised assets.

From the originator's standpoint, the effect of the arrangement is usually that it continues to obtain the benefit of surplus income (and, where relevant, capital profits) from the securitised assets and bears losses up to a set amount. Usually, however, the originator is protected from losses beyond a limited amount and has transferred catastrophe risk to the issuer. **D3**

Analysis

The purpose of the analysis is to determine the following: **D4**

(a) the appropriate accounting treatment in the originator's individual company financial statements. There are three possible treatments:
  (i) to remove the securitised assets from the balance sheet and show no liability in respect of the note issue, merely retaining the net amount (if any) of the securitised assets less the loan notes as a single item ('derecognition');
  (ii) to show the proceeds of the note issue deducted from the securitised assets on the face of the balance sheet within a single asset caption (a 'linked presentation'); or
  (iii) to show an asset equivalent in amount to the gross securitised assets within assets, and a corresponding liability in respect of the proceeds of the note issue within creditors (a 'separate presentation');
(b) the appropriate accounting treatment in the issuer's financial statements. Again there are three possible treatments: derecognition, a linked presentation or a separate presentation; and
(c) the appropriate accounting treatment in the originator's group accounts. This involves issues of:
  (i) whether the issuer is a subsidiary or (more usually) a quasi-subsidiary of the originator such that it should be included in the originator's group accounts; and
  (ii) where the issuer is a quasi-subsidiary, whether a linked presentation should be adopted in the originator's consolidated accounts.

Each of these is considered in more detail below.

(a) Originator's individual accounts

Overview of basic principles

D5 The principles for determining the appropriate accounting treatment in the originator's individual company financial statements are similar to those applied in both Application Note C – 'Factoring of debts' and in Application Note E – 'Loan transfers'. It is necessary to establish what asset and liability (if any) the originator now has, by answering two questions:

(a) whether the originator has access to the benefits of the securitised assets and exposure to the risks inherent in those benefits (referred to below as 'benefits and risks') and

(b) whether the originator has a liability to repay the proceeds of the note issue.

Where the originator has transferred all significant benefits and risks relating to the securitised assets and has no obligation to repay the proceeds of the note issue, derecognition is appropriate; where the originator has retained significant benefits and risks relating to the securitised assets but there is absolutely no doubt that its downside exposure to loss is limited, a linked presentation should be used; and in all other cases a separate presentation should be adopted.

D6 The benefits and risks relating to securitised assets will depend on the nature of the particular assets involved. In the case of interest bearing loans, the benefits and risks are described in paragraph E6 of Application Note E – 'Loan transfers'.

Derecognition

D7 Derecognition (ie ceasing to recognise the securitised assets in their entirety) is appropriate only where the originator retains no significant benefits and no significant risks relating to the securitised assets.

D8 Whilst the commercial effect of any particular transaction should be assessed taking into account all its aspects and implications, the presence of all of the following indicates that the originator has not retained significant benefits and risks, and derecognition is appropriate:

(a) the transaction takes place at an arm's length price for an outright sale;

(b) the transaction is for a fixed amount of consideration and there is no recourse whatsoever, either implicit or explicit, to the originator for losses from whatever cause. Normal warranties given in respect of the condition of the assets at the time of the transfer (eg in a mortgage securitisation, a warranty that no mortgages are in arrears at the time of transfer, or that the income of the borrower at the time of granting the mortgage was above a specified amount) would not breach this condition. However, warranties relating to the condition of the assets in the future or to their future performance (eg that mortgages will not move into arrears in the future) would breach the condition. Other possible forms of recourse are set out in paragraph 83; and

(c) the originator will not benefit or suffer if the securitised assets perform better or worse than expected. This will not be the case where the originator has a right to further sums from the vehicle that vary according to the eventual value realised for the securitised assets. Such sums could take a number of forms, for instance deferred consideration, a performance-related servicing fee, payments under a swap, dividends from the vehicle, or payments from a reserve fund.

Where any of these three features is not present, this indicates that the originator has retained benefits and risks relating to the securitised assets and, unless these are insignificant, either a separate presentation or a linked presentation should be adopted.

Whether any benefit and risk retained are 'significant' should be judged in relation to those benefits and risks that are likely to occur in practice, and not in relation to the total possible benefits and risks. Where the profits or losses accruing to the originator are material in relation to those likely to occur in practice, significant benefit and risk will be retained. For example, if for a portfolio of securitised assets of 100, expected losses are 0.5 and there is recourse to the originator for losses of up to 5, the originator will have retained all but an insignificant part of the downside risk relating to the assets (as the originator bears losses of up to ten times those expected to occur). Accordingly, in this example, derecognition will not be appropriate and either a linked presentation or a separate presentation should be used. **D9**

Linked presentation

A linked presentation will be appropriate where, although the originator has retained significant benefits and risks relating to the securitised assets, there is absolutely no doubt that its downside exposure to loss is limited to a fixed monetary amount. A linked presentation should be used only to the extent that there is both absolutely no doubt that the noteholders' claim extends solely to the proceeds generated by the securitised assets, and there is no provision for the originator to re-acquire the securitised assets in the future. The conditions that need to be met in order for this to be the case are set out in paragraph 27 and explained in paragraphs 81–86. When interpreting these conditions in the context of a securitisation the following points apply: **D10**

condition (a) (specified assets) –
a linked presentation should not be used where the assets that have been securitised cannot be separately identified. Nor should a linked presentation be used for assets that generate the funds required to repay the finance only by being used in conjunction with other assets of the originator;

condition (d) (agreement in writing that there is no recourse; such agreement noted in the financial statements) –
where the noteholders have subscribed to a prospectus or offering circular that clearly states that the originator will not support any losses of either the issuer or the noteholders, the first part of this condition will be met. Provisions that give the noteholders recourse to funds generated by both the securitised assets themselves and third party credit enhancement of those assets would also not breach this condition;

condition (f) (no provision for the originator to repurchase assets) –

where there is provision for the originator to repurchase only part of the securitised assets (or otherwise to fund the redemption of loan notes by the issuer), the maximum payment that could result should be excluded from the amount deducted on the face of the balance sheet. Where there is provision for the issuer (but not the originator) to redeem loan notes before an equivalent amount has been realised in cash from the securitised assets, a linked presentation may still be appropriate provided there is no obligation (legal, commercial or other) for the originator to fund the redemption (eg by repurchasing the securitised assets).

D11 These conditions should be regarded as met notwithstanding the existence of an interest rate swap agreement between the originator and the issuer, provided all the following conditions are met:

(a) the swap is on arm's length market-related terms and the obligations of the issuer under the swap are not subordinated to any of its obligations under the loan notes;
(b) the variable interest rate(s) that are swapped are determined by reference to publicly quoted rates that are not under the control of the originator;
(c) at the time of transfer of the assets to the issuer, the originator had hedged exposures relating to these assets (either individually or as part of a larger portfolio) and entering into the swap effectively restores the hedge position left open by their transfer. Thereafter, where the hedging of the originator's exposure under the swap requires continuing management, any necessary adjustments to the hedging position are made on an ongoing basis. This latter requirement will be particularly relevant where any prepayment risk involved cannot be hedged exactly.

The conditions for a linked presentation should also be regarded as met notwithstanding the existence of an interest rate cap agreement between the originator and the issuer provided that, in addition to all the above conditions being met, the securitisation was entered into before 22 September 1994.

D12 In the case of securitisations of revolving assets that arise under a facility (eg credit card balances), a careful analysis of the mechanism for repaying the loan notes is required in order to establish whether or not conditions (b) and (f) in paragraph 27 are met. For such assets, the loan notes are usually repaid from proceeds received during a period of time (referred to as the 'repayment period'). The proceeds received in the repayment period will typically comprise both repayments of securitised balances existing at the start of the repayment period and repayments of balances arising subsequently (for example arising from new borrowings in the repayment period on the credit card accounts securitised). In order that the conditions for a linked presentation are met, it is necessary that loan notes are repaid only to the extent that there have been, in total, cash collections from securitised balances existing at the start of the repayment period equal to the amount repaid on the loan notes. This is necessary in order to ensure that the issuer is allocated its proper share of any losses.

D13 It will also be necessary to analyse carefully any provisions that enable the originator to transfer additional assets to the issuer in order to establish whether or not conditions (b) and (f) in paragraph 27 are met. To the extent that the originator is obliged to replace poorly performing assets with good ones, there is recourse to the originator and a linked presentation should not be used. However, where there is merely provision for the originator to add new assets to replace those that have been repaid earlier than expected (and thus to 'top up' the pool in order to extend the life of the securitisation), the conditions for a linked presentation may still be met. For a linked presentation to be used, it is necessary that the addition of new assets does not result in either the originator being exposed to losses on the new or the old assets, or in the originator re-acquiring assets. Provided these features are present, the effect is the same as if the noteholders were repaid in cash and they immediately reinvested that cash in new assets, and a linked presentation may be appropriate.

Separate presentation

Where the originator has retained significant benefits and risks relating to the securitised assets and the conditions for a linked presentation are not met, the originator should adopt a separate presentation. **D14**

Multi-originator programmes

There are some arrangements where one issuer serves several originators. The arrangement may be structured such that each originator receives future benefits based on the performance of a defined portfolio of assets (typically those it has transferred to the issuer and continues to service or use). For instance, in a mortgage securitisation, the benefits accruing to any particular originator may be calculated as the interest payments received from a defined portfolio of mortgages, less costs specific to that portfolio (eg insurance premiums, payments for credit facilities), less an appropriate share of the funding costs of the issuer. The effect is that each originator bears significant benefits and risks of a defined pool of mortgages, whilst being insulated from the benefits and risks of other mortgages held by the issuer. Thus each originator should show that pool of mortgages for which it has significant benefits and risks on the face of its balance sheet, using either a linked presentation (if the conditions for its use are met) or a separate presentation. **D15**

(b) Issuer's accounts

The principles set out in paragraphs D5–D15 for the originator's individual financial statements also apply to the issuer's financial statements. In a securitisation, the issuer usually has access to all future benefits from the securitised assets (in the case of mortgages, to all cash collected from mortgagors) and is exposed to all their inherent risks. Hence, derecognition will not be appropriate. In addition, the noteholders usually have recourse to all the assets of the issuer (these may include the securitised assets themselves, the benefit of any related insurance policies or credit enhancement, and a small amount of cash). In this situation, the issuer's exposure to loss is not limited, and use of a linked presentation will not be appropriate. Thus the issuer should usually adopt a separate presentation. **D16**

(c) Originator's group financial statements

D17 Assuming a separate presentation is used in the issuer's financial statements but not in those of the originator, the question arises whether the relationship between the issuer and the originator is such that the issuer should be included in the originator's group financial statements. The following considerations are relevant:

(a) Where the issuer meets the definition of a subsidiary, it should be consolidated in the normal way by applying the relevant provisions of companies legislation and FRS 2. Where the issuer is not a subsidiary, the provisions of this FRS regarding quasi-subsidiaries are relevant.

(b) In order to meet the definition of a quasi- subsidiary, the issuer must give rise to benefits for the originator that are in substance no different from those that would arise were the entity a subsidiary. This will be the case where the originator receivesthe future benefits arising from the net assets of the issuer (principally the securitised assets less the loan notes). It is not necessary that the originator could face a possible benefit outflow equal in amount to the issuer's gross liabilities. Strong evidence of whether this part of the definition is met is whether the originator stands to suffer or gain from the financial performance of the issuer.

(c) The definition of a quasi-subsidiary also requires that the issuer is directly or indirectly controlled by the originator. Usually securitisations exemplify the situation described in paragraphs 34 and 98, in that the issuer's financial and operating policies are in substance predetermined (in this case under the various agreements that constitute the securitisation). Where this is so, the party possessing control will be the one that has the future benefits arising from the issuer's net assets.

D18 It follows that it should be presumed that the issuer is a quasi-subsidiary where either of the following is present:

(a) the originator has rights to the benefits arising from the issuer's net assets, ie to those benefits generated by the securitised assets that remain after meeting the claims of noteholders and other expenses of the issuer. These benefits may be transferred to the originator in a number of forms, as described in paragraph D2(d); or

(b) the originator has the risks inherent in these benefits. This will be the case where, if the benefits are greater or less than expected (eg because of the securitised assets realising more or less than expected), the originator gains or suffers.

D19 In general, where an issuer's activities comprise holding securitised assets and the benefits of its net assets accrue to the originator, the issuer will be a quasi-subsidiary of the originator. Conversely, the issuer will not be a quasi-subsidiary of the originator where the owner of the issuer is an independent third party that has made a substantial capital investment in the issuer, has control of the issuer, and has the benefits and risks of its net assets.

D20 Where the issuer is a quasi-subsidiary of the originator, the question arises whether a linked presentation should be adopted in the originator's group financial statements. It follows from paragraph 37 that where the issuer holds a single portfolio of similar assets, and the effect of the arrangement is to ring-fence the assets and their related finance in such a way that the provisions of paragraphs 26 and 27 are met from the point of view of the group, a linked presentation should be used.

Required accounting

Originator's individual financial statements

Derecognition

Where the originator has retained no significant benefits and risks relating to the securitised assets and has no obligation to repay the proceeds of the note issue, the assets should be removed from its balance sheet, and no liability shown in respect of the proceeds of the note issue. A profit or loss should be recognised, calculated as the difference between the carrying amount of the assets and the proceeds received. **D21**

Linked presentation

Where the conditions for a linked presentation are met, the proceeds of the note issue (to the extent they are non-returnable) should be shown deducted from the securitised assets on the face of the balance sheet within a single asset caption. Profit should be recognised and presented in the manner set out in paragraphs 28 and 87–88. The following disclosures should be given: **D22**

(a) a description of the assets securitised;
(b) the amount of any income or expense recognised in the period, analysed as appropriate;
(c) the terms of any options for the originator to repurchase assets or to transfer additional assets to the issuer;
(d) the terms of any interest rate swap or interest rate cap agreements between the issuer and the originator that meet the conditions set out in paragraph D11;
(e) a description of the priority and amount of claims on the proceeds generated by the assets, including any rights of the originator to proceeds from the assets in addition to the non-recourse amounts already received;
(f) the ownership of the issuer; and
(g) the disclosures required by conditions (c) and (d) in paragraph 27.

Where an originator uses a linked presentation for several different securitisations that all relate to a single type of asset (ie all the assets, if not securitised, would be shown within the same balance sheet caption), these may be aggregated on the face of the balance sheet. However, securitisations of different types of asset should be shown separately. In addition, details of each material arrangement should be provided in the notes to the financial statements, unless they are on similar terms and relate to a single type of asset, in which case they may be disclosed in aggregate. **D23**

Separate presentation

Where neither derecognition nor a linked presentation is appropriate, a separate presentation should be adopted, ie a gross asset (equal in amount to the gross amount **D24** of the securitised assets) should be shown on the balance sheet of the originator within assets, and a corresponding liability in respect of the proceeds of the note issue shown within liabilities. No gain or loss should be recognised at the time the securitisation is entered into (unless adjustment to the carrying value of the assets independent of the securitisation is required). Disclosure should be given in the notes to the financial statements of the gross amount of assets securitised at the balance sheet date.

Issuer's financial statements

D25 The requirements set out in paragraphs D21–D24 for the originator's individual financial statements also apply to the issuer's financial statements. For the reasons set out in paragraph D16, in most cases the issuer will be required to adopt a separate presentation, in which case the provisions of paragraph D24 will apply.

Originator's consolidated financial statements

D26 Where the issuer is a quasi-subsidiary of the originator, its assets, liabilities, profits, losses and cash flows should be included in the originating group's consolidated financial statements. Where the provisions of paragraph D20 are met, a linked presentation should be applied in the consolidated financial statements and the disclosures required by paragraphs D22 and D23 should be given; in all other cases a separate presentation should be used and the disclosure required by paragraph D24 should be given.

Table

Indications that derecognition is appropriate (securitised assets are not assets of the originator)	**Indications that a linked presentation is appropriate**	**Indications that a separate presentation is appropriate (securitised assets are assets of the originator)**
Originator's individual financial statements		
Transaction price is arm's length price for an outright sale	Transaction price is not arm's length price for an outright sale.	Transaction price is not arm's length price for an outright sale.
Transfer is for a single, non-returnable fixed sum.	Some non-returnable proceeds received, but originator has rights to further sums from the issuer, the amount of which depends on the performance of the securitised assets.	Proceeds received are returnable, or there is a provision whereby the originator may keep the securitised assets on repayment of the loan notes or re-acquire them.

There is no recourse to the originator for losses.	There is either no recourse for losses, or such recourse has a fixed monetary ceiling.	There is or may be full recourse to the originator for losses, eg: - originator's directors are unable or unwilling to state that it is not obliged to fund any losses; - noteholders have not agreed in writing that they will seek repayment only from funds generated by the securitised assets.
Originator's consolidated financial statements		
Issuer is owned by an independent third party that made a substantial capital investment, has control of the issuer, and has the benefits and risks of its net assets.	Issuer is a quasi-subsidiary of the originator, but the conditions for a linked presentation are met from the point of view of the group.	Issuer is a subsidiary of the originator.

APPLICATION NOTE E – LOAN TRANSFERS

NB: In this Application Note, the following terminology is used:

(a) the 'lender' is the party that has rights to principal and interest under the original loan agreement, and is purporting to transfer them;
(b) the 'transferee' is the party purporting to acquire the loan, and includes a new lender (in a novation), an assignee and a sub-participant;
(c) the 'borrower' is the party that has obligations to make payments of principal and interest under the original loan agreement; and
(d) references to the transfer of a 'loan' or 'loans' apply equally to the transfer of both a single loan and a portfolio of loans.

Features

This Application Note deals with the transfer of interest-bearing loans to an entity other than a special purpose vehicle. The main features of a loan transfer are as follows: E1

(a) Specified loans are transferred from a lender to a transferee by one of the methods set out in paragraph E2 below, in return for an immediate cash payment. The transfer may be of the whole of a single loan, part of a loan, or of all or part of a portfolio of similar loans.
(b) Payments of principal and interest collected from borrowers are passed to the

transferee (either direct or via the lender). In some cases, there may be a difference between amounts received from borrowers and those passed to the transferee (the lender retaining or making up the difference), or if a borrower fails to make payments when due, the lender may nevertheless make payments to the transferee.

E2 Loans cannot be 'sold' in the same way as tangible assets. However, there are three methods by which the benefits and risks of a loan can be transferred:

Novation: The rights and obligations under the loan agreement are cancelled and replaced by new ones whose main effect is to change the identity of the lender. Although rights can be transferred by other means, novation is the only method of transferring obligations (eg to supply funds under an undrawn loan facility) with the consequent release of the lender.

Assignment: Rights (to principal and interest), but not obligations, are transferred to a third party (the 'assignee'). There are two types of assignment: statutory assignment, which must relate to the whole of the loan and where notice in writing must be given to the borrower and other obligors (eg a guarantor); and equitable assignment, which may relate to only part of a loan and which does not require notice to the borrower. Both types are subject to equitable rights arising before notice is received. For example, a right of set-off held by the borrower against the lender will be good against the assignee for any transactions undertaken before the borrower receives notice of the assignment.

Sub-participation: Rights and obligations are not formally transferred but the lender enters into a non-recourse back-to-back agreement with a third party, the 'sub participant', under which the latter deposits with the lender an amount equal to the whole or part of the loan and in return receives from the lender a share of the cash flows arising on the loan.

E3 The terms of a loan transfer will usually not be identical to those of the original loan, and a gain or loss will arise for the lender. This gain or loss may occur in one of two ways: first, if all future payments made by the borrower (and only such payments) are to be passed to the transferee, the consideration for the transfer will differ from the carrying amount of the loan and the lender's gain or loss will be realised in cash immediately. Alternatively, the consideration for the transfer may be set equal to the carrying amount of the loan, and the amounts to be paid by the borrower and those to be passed on to the transferee will differ. In this case, the lender's gain or loss will be the net present value of this difference and will be realised in cash over the term of the loan.

Analysis

Overview of basic principles

E4 The purpose of the analysis is to determine the appropriate accounting treatment in the financial statements of the lender. There are three possible treatments:

(a) to remove the loan (or a part of it) from the balance sheet and show no liability in respect of the amounts received from the transferee ('derecognition');

(b) to show the amounts received from the transferee deducted from the loan on the face of the balance sheet within a single asset caption (a 'linked presentation'); or
(c) to continue to show the loan as an asset, and show a corresponding liability within creditors in respect of the amounts received from the transferee (a 'separate presentation').

The principles to be applied to determine the appropriate accounting treatment are similar to those applied in both Application Note D – 'Securitised assets' relating to individual (rather than consolidated) financial statements and in Application Note C – 'Factoring of debts'. It is necessary to answer two questions: E5

(a) whether the lender has access to the benefits of the loans and exposure to the risks inherent in those benefits (referred to below as 'benefits and risks'); and
(b) whether the lender has a liability to repay the transferee.

Where the lender has transferred all significant benefits and risks relating to the loans and has no obligation to repay the transferee, derecognition is appropriate (this would be the case where all future cash flows from borrowers – but only those cash flows – are passed to the transferee as and when received). Where the lender has retained significant benefits and risks relating to the loans but there is absolutely no doubt that its downside exposure to loss is limited, a linked presentation should be used (this is likely to be rare for a loan transfer). In all other cases a separate presentation should be adopted.

Benefits and risks

The main benefits and risks relating to loans are as follows: E6

Benefits:
(i) the future cash flows from payments of principal and interest.

Risks:
(i) credit risk (the risk of bad debts);
(ii) slow payment risk;
(iii) interest rate risk (the risk of a change in the interest rate paid by the borrower. Included in this risk is a form of basis risk, ie the risk of a change in the interest rate paid by the borrower not being matched by a change in the interest rate paid to the transferee);
(iv) reinvestment/early redemption risk (the risk that, where payments from the loans are reinvested by the lender before being paid to the transferee, the rate of interest obtained on the reinvested amounts is above or below that payable to the transferee); and
(v) moral risk (the risk that the lender will feel obliged, because of its continued association with the loans, to fund any losses arising on them).

Analysis of benefits

At first sight it may appear that the transferee has access to the cash collected from borrowers. However, as set out in more detail in paragraphs c6 and c7, the cash flows E7 may appear similar even where different accounting treatments are appropriate and considering the benefits in isolation will not normally enable a clear decision to be made. Rather, it is necessary to determine which party is exposed to the risks relating to the loans (both upside potential for gain and downside exposure to loss).

Analysis of risks

E8 The benefit of cash payments of principal and interest are subject to the five risks outlined in paragraph E6. The first of these, credit risk, will be borne by the lender to the extent there is recourse to it for bad debts; if there is no such recourse, the transferee will bear the credit risk.

E9 The second risk, slow payment, will be borne by the party that suffers (or benefits) if borrowers pay later (or earlier) than expected. If amounts are passed to the transferee only when received from the borrower, the transferee will bear this risk; if the lender pays amounts to the transferee regardless of whether it has received an equivalent payment from the borrower, the lender will bear it.

E10 Interest rate risk will be borne by the lender where the interest it receives from the borrower and payments it makes to the transferee are not directly related*. Where any changes in the interest rate charged to the borrower are passed on to the transferee after a short administrative delay, the lender may not bear significant interest rate risk; however, where any delays are significant the lender will bear significant risk.

E11 The lender will bear reinvestment risk where payments received from the borrower are not immediately passed on to the transferee but are reinvested by the lender for a period. An exception would be where the transferee is entitled to all of any interest actually earned (but no more) on the amounts reinvested by the lender.

E12 The final risk is moral risk. For either derecognition or a linked presentation to be appropriate, the lender must have taken all reasonable precautions to eliminate this risk such that it will not feel obliged to fund any losses. This will include ensuring that the arrangements for servicing the loans reflect the standards of commercial behaviour expected of the lender.

Derecognition

E13 Derecognition (ie ceasing to recognise the loans in their entirety) is appropriate only where the lender retains no significant benefits and no significant risks relating to the loans. In determining whether any benefit and risk retained are 'significant', greater weight should be given to what is more likely to have a commercial effect in practice.

E14 The three possible methods of transferring the benefits and risks relating to a loan are described in paragraph E2; each may result in derecognition in appropriate cases:

(a) A novation (ie the replacement of the original loan by a new one with the

**'Directly related' in this context means that either the interest rates paid and received are both fixed, or the two rates are tied to the same external rate eg LIBOR.*

consequent release of the lender) will usually transfer all significant benefits and risks, provided that there are no side agreements that leave benefits and risks with the lender.

(b) An assignment (ie the transfer of the rights to principal and interest that constitute the original loan, whilst not transferring any obligations) may also transfer all significant benefits and risks, provided that, in addition to there being no side agreements that leave benefits and risks with the lender, there are no unfulfilled obligations (eg to supply additional funds in the event of a restructuring of the loan) and any doubts regarding intervening equitable rights are satisfied.

(c) A sub-participation (ie the entering into an additional non-recourse back-to-back agreement with the sub-participant rather than the transfer of any of the rights or obligations that constitute the original loan itself) may also transfer all significant benefits and risks, provided that the lender's obligation to pay amounts to the transferee eliminates its access to benefits from the loans but extends only to those benefits. Thus the sub-participant must have a claim on all specified payments from the loans but on only those payments, and there must be no possibility that the lender could be required to pay amounts to the sub-participant where it has not received equivalent payments from the borrower.* Where this is the case, the loans no longer constitute an asset of the lender, nor does the deposit placed by the sub-participant represent a liability; it will therefore be appropriate to derecognise the loans. Particular attention should be paid to the effect of the borrower asking for a rescheduling. The lender may, for commercial reasons, wish to agree to a rescheduling plan, whereas the sub participant may simply look to the lender for compensation if it is not repaid. Where the lender has an obligation (legal, commercial or other) to provide such compensation, derecognition will not be appropriate.

Whilst the commercial effect of any particular transaction should be assessed taking into account all its aspects and implications, the presence of all of the following indicates that the lender has not retained significant benefits and risks, and derecognition is appropriate: **E15**

(a) the transaction takes place at an arm's length price for an outright sale;

(b) the transaction is for a fixed amount of consideration and there is no recourse whatsoever, either implicit or explicit, to the lender for losses from whatever cause. Normal warranties given in respect of the condition of the loans at the time of the transfer (eg a warranty that no loan was in arrears at the time of transfer) would not breach this condition. However, warranties relating to the condition of the loans in the future or to their future performance (eg that loans will not move into arrears in the future) would breach the condition. Other possible forms of recourse are set out in paragraph 83; and

(c) the lender will not benefit or suffer in any way if the loans perform better or worse than expected. This will not be the case where the lender has a right to further sums that vary according to the future performance of the loans (ie according to whether or when borrowers pay, or according to the amounts borrowers pay).

**Where only part of the payments due under the original loan are eliminated in this way, it may be appropriate to derecognise only part of the original loan. This is addressed in paragraphs* E19 and E20 below.

Such sums might take the form of an interest differential, deferred consideration, a performance-related servicing fee or payments under a swap.

Where any of these three features is not present, this indicates that the lender has retained benefits and risks relating to the loan and, unless these are insignificant, either a separate presentation or a linked presentation should be adopted.

E16 Whether any benefit and risk retained are 'significant' should be judged in relation to those benefits and risks that are likely to occur in practice, and not in relation to the total possible benefits and risks. Where the profits or losses accruing to the lender are material in relation to those likely to occur in practice, significant benefit and risk will be retained, such that derecognition will not be appropriate and either a linked presentation or a separate presentation should be used.

Linked presentation

E17 A linked presentation will be appropriate where, although the lender has retained significant benefits and risks relating to the loans, there is absolutely no doubt that its downside exposure to loss is limited to a fixed monetary amount. A linked presentation should be used only to the extent that there is both absolutely no doubt that the transferee's claim extends solely to cash collected from the loans, and no provision for the lender to keep or re-acquire the loans by repaying the transferee. The conditions that need to be met in order for this to be the case are set out in paragraph 27 and explained in paragraphs 81–86.

Separate presentation

E18 Where the lender retains significant benefits and risks relating to the loans and the conditions for a linked presentation are not met, a separate presentation should be adopted.

Transfers of part of a loan

E19 In some cases the amount received by the lender from the transferee represents only part of the original loan. As explained in paragraph 71, where the effect of the arrangement is that a part of the loan is transferred, derecognition of that part will be appropriate. This will be the case where each party has a proportionate share of all future cash collected from the loan (and of related profits and losses). For example, were the transferee to be entitled to 40 per cent of any cash flows from payments of both principal and interest as and when paid by the borrower (ie it does not receive cash if such payments are not made), the lender should cease to recognise 40 per cent of the loan. Conversely, if the lender bears losses in preference to the transferee and thus retains significant risk relating to the loans, derecognition of any part of them is not appropriate. For example, were the transferee to have first claim on any cash flows arising from a portfolio of loans with the lender's share acting as a cushion to absorb any losses, the lender should continue to show the gross amount of the whole portfolio on the face of its balance sheet (although if the conditions for a linked presentation are met, it should be used).

In other cases, the entire principal amount of a loan may be funded by the transferee, but there may be a difference between the interest payments due from the borrower and those the lender has agreed to pass on to the transferee. In such cases derecognition of a part of the original loan may still be appropriate provided that the lender's interest differential does not result in it bearing significant risks relating to the loan. For instance, if the lender's interest differential is fixed and is in substance no more than a fee for originating or administering the loan, derecognition will be appropriate. Conversely, if the lender's interest differential varies depending on the performance of the loan (as where it acts as a cushion to absorb losses or the lender bears interest rate risk), either a separate presentation or a linked presentation should be used. A linked presentation should be used only where the lender's maximum loss is capped, as might be the case where a variable rate loan is funded by a fixed rate one (if the lender's maximum loss is capped at the fixed interest payments due to the transferee). However, a linked presentation should not be used where the lender's maximum loss is not capped, as will be the case where a fixed rate loan is funded by a variable rate one, or where a loan in one currency is funded by a loan in another. The principles in this paragraph apply equally where the transferee funds only part of the principal amount of the original loan. **E20**

Administration arrangements

Whether or not the lender continues to administer the loans is not, of itself, relevant to deciding upon the appropriate accounting treatment. However, the administration arrangements may affect where certain benefits and risks lie. For instance, where the lender's servicing fee is not an arm's length fee for the services provided, this indicates it has retained significant benefits and risks relating to the loans. **E21**

Required accounting

Derecognition

Where the lender has retained no significant benefits and risks relating to the loans and has no obligation to repay the transferee, the loans should be removed from its balance sheet and no liability shown in respect of the amounts received from the transferee. A profit or loss may arise for the lender in the two ways set out in paragraph E3. Where the profit or loss is realised in cash it should be recognised, calculated as the difference between the carrying amount of the loans and the cash proceeds received. Where, however, the lender's profit or loss is not realised in cash and there are doubts as to its amount, full provision should be made for any expected loss but recognition of any gain, to the extent it is in doubt, should be deferred until cash has been received. **E22**

Linked presentation

Where the conditions for a linked presentation are met, the proceeds received, to the extent they are non-returnable, should be shown deducted from the gross amount of the loans on the face of the balance sheet. Profit should be recognised and presented as set out in paragraphs 28 and 87–88. The notes to the financial statements should **E23** disclose: the main terms of the arrangement; the gross amount of loans transferred and outstanding at the balance sheet date; the profit or loss recognised in the period, analysed as appropriate; and the disclosures required by conditions (c) and (d) in paragraph 27.

Separate presentation

E24 Where neither derecognition nor a linked presentation is appropriate, a separate presentation should be adopted, ie a gross asset (equivalent in amount to the gross amount of the loans) should be shown on the balance sheet of the lender within assets, and a corresponding liability in respect of the amounts received from the transferee should be shown within creditors. No gain or loss should be recognised at the time of the transfer (unless adjustment to the carrying value of the loan independent of the transfer is required). The notes to the financial statements should disclose the amount of loans subject to loan transfer arrangements that are outstanding at the balance sheet date.

Table

Indications that derecognition is appropriate (off lender's balance sheet)	Indications that a linked presentation is appropriate	Indications that a separate presentation is appropriate (on lender's balance sheet)
Transfer is for a single, non-returnable fixed sum.	Some non-returnable proceeds received, but lender has rights to further sums whose amount depends on whether or when the borrowers pay.	The proceeds received are returnable in the event of losses occurring on the loans.
There is no recourse to the lender for losses from any cause.	There is either no recourse for losses, or such recourse has a fixed monetary ceiling.	There is full recourse to the lender for losses.
Transferee is paid all amounts received from the loans (and no more), as and when received. Lender has no rights to further sums from the loans or the transferee.	Transferee is paid only out of amounts received from the loans, and lender has no right or obligation to repurchase them.	Lender is required to repay amounts received from the transferee on or before a set date, regardless of the timing or amount of payments by the borrowers.

Adoption of FRS 5 by the board

Financial Reporting Standard 5 – 'Reporting the Substance of Transactions' was approved for issue by the nine members of the Accounting Standards Board.

David Tweedie	(Chairman)
Allan Cook	(Technical Director)
Robert Bradfield	
Ian Brindle	
Sir Bryan Carsberg	
Michael Garner	
Raymond Hinton	
Donald Main	
Graham Stacy	

Appendix I
Note on legal requirements

Great Britain
References are to the Companies Act 1985.

Group accounts

1 Definitions of 'parent undertaking' and 'subsidiary undertaking' are set out and explained in section 258 and Schedule 10A.

2 Other provisions of the Companies Act relevant to the preparation of consolidated accounts are given in paragraphs 95 and 96 of FRS 2 'Accounting for Subsidiary Undertakings'.

3 *The requirement to show a true and fair view*

Section 227 provides the following:

"(1) If at the end of a financial year a company is a parent company the directors shall, as well as preparing individual accounts for the year, prepare group accounts.

(2) Group accounts shall be consolidated accounts comprising –

(a) a consolidated balance sheet dealing with the state of affairs of the parent company and its subsidiary undertakings, and

(b) a consolidated profit and loss account dealing with the profit or loss of the parent undertaking and its subsidiary undertakings.

(3) The accounts shall give a true and fair view of the state of affairs as at the end of the financial year, and the profit or loss for the financial year, of the undertakings included in the consolidation as a whole, so far as concerns members of the company.

(4) A company's group accounts shall comply with the provisions of Schedule 4A as to the form and content of the consolidated balance sheet and consolidated profit and loss account and additional information to be provided by way of notes to the accounts.

(5) Where compliance with the provisions of that Schedule, and the other provisions of this Act, as to the matters to be included in a company's group accounts or in the notes to those accounts, would not be sufficient to give a true and fair view, the necessary additional information shall be given in the accounts or in a note to them.

(6) If in special circumstances compliance with any of those provisions is inconsistent with the requirement to give a true and fair view, the directors shall depart from that provision to the extent necessary to give a true and fair view.

Particulars of any such departure, the reasons for it and its effect shall be given in a note to the accounts."

Section 255A(5) states that, in the case of a banking or insurance company, the references to the provisions of Schedule 4A in section 227(5) and (6) shall be read as references to those provisions as modified by Part II of Schedule 9.

Offset

The Companies Act contains the following provisions relating to offset: 4

Schedule 4 paragraph 5 (an identical requirement for banking companies and groups is contained in Schedule 9 paragraph 5)

> 'Amounts in respect of items representing assets or income may not be offset against amounts in respect of items representing liabilities or expenditure (as the case may be), or vice versa.'

Schedule 4 paragraph 14 (an identical requirement for banking companies and groups is contained in Schedule 9 paragraph 21)

> 'In determining the aggregate amount of any item the amount of each individual asset or liability that falls to be taken into account shall be determined separately.'

Northern Ireland

The legal requirements in Northern Ireland are identical to those in Great Britain. In particular: 5

Article 266 of and Schedule 10A to the Companies (Northern Ireland) Order 1986 are identical to section 258 of and Schedule 10A to the Companies Act 1985 as referred to in paragraph 1 above.

Other provisions of companies legislation relevant to the preparation of consolidated accounts, as referred to in paragraph 2 above, are given in paragraph 97 of FRS 2 'Accounting for Subsidiary Undertakings'.

Articles 235 and 263A(5) of the Companies (Northern Ireland) Order 1986 are identical to sections 227 and 255A(5) respectively of the Companies Act 1985 as referred to in paragraph 3 above.

Paragraphs 5 and 14 of Schedule 4 to the Companies (Northern Ireland) Order 1986 are identical to paragraphs 5 and 14 of Schedule 4 to the Companies Act 1985 as referred to in paragraph 4 above.

Republic of Ireland

The legal requirements in the Republic of Ireland are similar to those in Great Britain. In particular: 6

Regulation 4 of the European Communities (Companies: Group Accounts) Regulations 1992 is similar to section 258 of and Schedule 10A to the Companies Act 1985 as referred to in paragraph 1 above.

Other provisions of companies legislation relevant to the preparation of consolidated accounts, as referred to in paragraph 2 above, are given in the insert replacing paragraph 98 of FRS 2 'Accounting for Subsidiary Undertakings'.

Regulations 5, 13 and 14 of the European Communities (Companies: Group Accounts) Regulations 1992 are similar to section 227 of the Companies Act 1985 as referred to in paragraph 3 above. As regards banks, section 5(1) of the European Communities (Credit Institutions: Accounts) Regulations 1992 is similar to section 255A(5) of the Companies Act 1985 as referred to in paragraph 3 above. Pending implementation of the EC Insurance Accounts Directive (91/674 EC) there is no legislation similar to section 255A(5) for insurance companies.

Sections 4(11) and 5(e) of the Companies (Amendment) Act 1986 are similar to paragraphs 5 and 14 of Schedule 4 to the Companies Act 1985 as referred to in paragraph 4 above.

Appendix II
Compliance with International Accounting Standards

There is no International Accounting Standard on this subject. The International Accounting Standards Committee (IASC) has issued a 'Framework for the Preparation and Presentation of Financial Statements'. The definitions of assets and liabilities set out in the FRS and the principles underlying it are similar in all material respects to those set out in the IASC's Framework. However, neither International Accounting Standards nor the Framework currently envisage use of a linked presentation for certain non-recourse finance as required by paragraphs 26–28 of the FRS.

Appendix III
The development of the FRS

General

1 The problems of what is commonly referred to as 'off balance sheet financing' became evident during the 1980s. In that period, a number of complex arrangements were developed that, if accounted for in accordance with their legal form, resulted in accounts that did not report the commercial effect of the arrangement. In particular, concern grew over arrangements for financing a company's operations in such a way that, if the arrangement were accounted for merely by recording its legal form, the finance would not be shown as a liability on the balance sheet.

2 At the same time, there was rapid innovation in financial markets. New arrangements for financing assets were developed, the accounting for which was not immediately obvious. An example of one such arrangement is securitisation, whereby an asset and its non-recourse finance are tightly ring-fenced using a separate vehicle company.

3 These developments raised fundamental questions about the nature of assets and liabilities and when they should be included in the balance sheet. Questions were also raised about the accounting for some transactions that had been used by businesses for many years. For example, some queried whether factoring should be accounted for as a secured loan rather than as a sale of debts.

4 The FRS has been developed to address these issues and to deal with the problems caused by the misleading effects that 'off balance sheet financing' can have on the accounts. As that term indicates, the most widely recognised effect is the omission of liabilities from the balance sheet. However, the assets being financed, as well as the finance itself, are excluded, with the result that both the resources of the entity and its financing are understated. There may also be important effects on the profit and loss account. For instance, a profit may be reported on a 'sale' that is, in substance, a secured loan. As another example, what is in substance a finance charge may be either omitted from the profit and loss account altogether or described as some other kind of expense. All of these effects make it harder for the reader of the accounts to assess the true economic position of the reporting entity because they obscure the true extent and nature of its borrowings, its assets and the results of its activities.

5 The Board believes that financial statements should represent faithfully the commercial effects of the transactions and other events they purport to represent. This requires transactions to be accounted for in accordance with their substance and not merely their legal form, since the latter may not fully indicate the commercial effect of the arrangements entered into.

History of documents issued

TR 603

6 The first authoritative document to address this issue was Technical Release 603 (TR 603) – 'Off Balance Sheet Financing and Window Dressing', issued in December 1985

by the Institute of Chartered Accountants in England and Wales. The main provision of this short, preliminary document was that, in determining the accounting treatment of transactions, their economic substance rather than their mere legal form should be considered.

ED 42

TR 603 was followed by ED 42 'Accounting for special purpose transactions', which was issued in March 1988 by the Accounting Standards Committee (ASC). ED 42 took a general approach, providing guidance that could be applied to a variety of situations, rather than specifying detailed rules for specific transactions. It proposed that assets and liabilities arising from off balance sheet transactions be included in the balance sheet rather than merely disclosed in the notes. For this purpose, ED 42 described the essential characteristics of assets and liabilities. It also proposed that 'controlled non-subsidiaries' should be consolidated as if they were subsidiaries as legally defined. The definition of a controlled non-subsidiary was substantially the same as that of a quasi-subsidiary given in FRS 5. 7

ED 49

ED 49 'Reflecting the substance of transactions in assets and liabilities' was issued by the ASC in May 1990. ED 49 responded to the comments received on ED 42 as well as certain changes in the law. The ED continued to take a general approach, proposing analysis of the substance of transactions by reference to the essential characteristics of assets and liabilities. It also continued to propose that controlled non-subsidiaries should be consolidated in group accounts, although these vehicle entities were renamed 'quasi subsidiaries'. The main changes from ED 42 were: the inclusion, for the first time, of general recognition tests; the inclusion of Application Notes specifying how the draft standard was to be applied to five specific transaction types (including securitisation and factoring) – these were included at the specific request of commentators to ED 42 and their inclusion was later supported by the majority of commentators to ED 49; and the addition of guidance on identifying control. 8

Bulletin 15

Respondents to ED 49 raised, inter alia, the concern that the treatment it proposed for factoring was inconsistent with that proposed for securitisation. This led the Accounting Standards Board to review the accounting for securitisation and, in October 1991, to issue proposals (in Bulletin 15) under which most securitised assets would be shown on the balance sheet, the arrangement being accounted for as a secured loan. This was on the grounds that, in most securitisations, the originating entity retains significantly all of the profits from the securitised assets. Although the entity has strictly limited its exposure to losses on those assets, the same is true for other non-recourse finance arrangements and for limited liability subsidiaries, where it is accepted that assets and liabilities should be reported gross. 9

The respondents to Bulletin 15 were divided on whether securitisations should be accounted for on balance sheet as a secured loan, or off balance sheet as a sale. Views on both sides of the argument were strongly held, reflecting different beliefs about the 10 primary purpose of the balance sheet. Those who favoured securitisations being accounted for on balance sheet believed that the primary use of the balance sheet is in assessing the amounts, timing and certainty of future cash flows. In their view, the total resources that underlie these future cash flows (and on which income will be earned in the future) should be shown on one side of the balance sheet, and the means by which they are financed should be shown on the other. They also pointed out that typically, the originating entity continues to gain significantly all the profits from the securitised assets and to be exposed to all those losses likely to occur in practice.

11 Those respondents who favoured securitisations being accounted for as a sale and therefore off balance sheet believed that the primary use of the balance sheet is in assessing the maximum possible loss to which the entity is exposed. They thought that the accounting treatment of securitisations (and perhaps other forms of non-recourse finance) should concentrate on showing that the originating entity has a limited downside exposure to loss, and that only a net asset of the amount to which the entity is exposed should be presented.

12 The Board debated in detail the issues raised by the respondents and also consulted numerous interested parties. It concluded that users of accounts need to know both the entity's gross resources and finance (as these determine the size of its future income) and the net amount of these (as this is the maximum loss the entity can suffer). Hence the Board developed a new kind of presentation – a 'linked presentation' – under which the finance is deducted from the gross securitised assets on the face of the balance sheet. This presentation shows the gross resources that underlie the business (and on which income will be earned in the future), yet highlights that the entity has a strictly limited exposure to loss.

FRED 4

13 Finally, in February 1993, the Board issued FRED 4 'Reporting the Substance of Transactions'. This carried through the general principles set out in ED 49 with only two major changes. The first was the introduction of proposals for a linked presentation for certain forms of non-recourse finance (including securitisations), as described above. These proposals attracted general support and are retained in the FRS with only one minor change which is described in paragraphs 29–32 below.

14 The only other major change from ED 49 was the inclusion of detailed criteria for when items may be offset in accounts. These prohibited offset of amounts denominated in different currencies or bearing interest on different bases, on the grounds that, for two items to be offset, they must exactly eliminate one another. Such elimination would not be present where the items were in different currencies or bore interest on different bases, because of the currency or interest rate risk that was present. It was therefore proposed that the two items should not be offset but should be reported as separate assets and liabilities. This proposal has been modified in the FRS, in the light of comments received, as described below.

15 Other, less significant changes from ED 49 were: the inclusion of definitions of assets and liabilities as opposed to a description of their 'essential characteristics' (these definitions are drawn from the Board's draft Statement of Principles); the provision of more guidance on accounting for transactions with options; the inclusion, for the first time, of criteria for when assets should cease to be recognised; the introduction of a distinction between control of an asset and control of another entity; and changes to some of ED 49's recognition tests, including removing the proposal that recognition be based on a 'reasonable accounting analogy'.

Matters considered in the light of responses to FRED 4

Most of the respondents to FRED 4 agreed with its principal proposals and these have been largely retained in the FRS. The following paragraphs describe those points on which respondents expressed concern and, where appropriate, explain, with reasons, the changes the Board has made to the proposals of FRED 4 or the Board's reasons for not adopting a change. **16**

Complexity of the FRS

Several respondents expressed concern that FRED 4 was complex and difficult to understand. In part, this complexity stemmed from the inclusion of proposals for a linked presentation as set out above. Another reason for the FRED being difficult to understand was its general approach of specifying principles applicable to all transactions rather than detailed rules for specific situations. Whilst this general approach was supported, there was concern that the resulting principles appeared somewhat abstract and difficult to comprehend on a first reading. **17**

To meet these concerns, the structure and drafting of the FRED have been reviewed and, where possible, simplified. In addition, the Explanation section to the FRS gives examples where appropriate. However, the Board believes this is a complex area that cannot be reduced to a few simple rules without the danger of over-simplification. Indeed, simple rules, mechanically applied, would result in accounts that do not report substance. **18**

Offset

As noted above, FRED 4 proposed prohibiting offset of amounts denominated in different currencies or bearing interest on different bases but asked for comments on this prohibition. The majority of those who commented favoured either allowing or requiring offset of such items. Their reasons included: that the balance sheet does not, in general, show currency or interest rate exposures, hence grossing up the items does not necessarily allow a better assessment of these risks; that the currency or interest rate risk may be hedged such that the risk portrayed by grossing up may, in fact, no longer exist; that given freely accessible and liquid foreign exchange markets, monetary items in different currencies can be regarded as being freely convertible, and essentially a single item; and that the balance sheet should focus on portraying credit risk since users expect to get information about credit risk from the balance sheet, but not about currency or interest rate risks. A majority of the Board is persuaded by these arguments and, accordingly, the FRS requires offset of amounts denominated in different currencies or bearing interest on different bases provided that certain criteria are met. **19**

20 The Board also considered whether it should require disclosure of amounts in different currencies or bearing interest on different bases that have been offset. Such disclosure would allow the user to draw up a balance sheet incorporating all items that do not exactly eliminate one another. However, such a balance sheet would give only part of the information needed to assess the entity's exposure to currency and interest rate risk. For a full assessment, it would be necessary to disclose the currency and interest rate profile of all recognised assets and liabilities as well as the effects of 'off balance sheet' instruments such as swaps and options. The Board decided that it was not yet in a position to specify comprehensive disclosure of such risks and that to require disclosures that gave only partial information on currency and interest rate risk would be potentially misleading. Accordingly, the FRS does not require disclosure of amounts that have been offset.

21 FRED 4 also proposed prohibiting offset where the right to settle net was contingent (for example on the counterparty going into liquidation). This was on the basis that as such contingent rights could not have been exercised at the balance sheet date, they should not be reflected in the assets and liabilities reported at that date. After reviewing the comments on this issue, the Board decided that provided: (a) the right to settle net can be invoked in all situations of default; and (b) the entity's debit balance matures no later than its credit balance, the amounts should be offset. This is because in such a situation there is no possibility that the entity could be required to pay out its credit balance without first having recovered its debit balance.

22 Finally, FRED 4 did not propose the approach taken in US and certain other overseas accounting standards that require for offset that the reporting entity intends to settle net; FRED 4 required merely that the reporting entity has the ability to do so. The reason FRED 4 did not propose this approach is that the intended manner of settlement is essentially a matter of administrative convenience and does not affect the economic position of the parties. This reasoning was supported by commentators and, accordingly, the conditions given in the FRS for offset are not based on the intent of the reporting entity.

Ceasing to recognise assets

23 FRED 4 contained criteria for when assets should cease to be recognised. These required both that no significant access to benefits was retained and that any risk retained was immaterial. Commentators were particularly concerned over the second of these conditions: for instance that it might require continued recognition of an asset sold with a residual value guarantee or of a subsidiary sold with deferred performance-related consideration.

24 As a result, the FRS distinguishes three types of transactions. The first is transactions that transfer all significant rights to benefits relating to an asset and all significant exposures to the risks inherent in those benefits. For such transactions, the asset should cease to be recognised in its entirety. Conversely, where a transaction transfers no significant rights to benefits relating to an asset or no significant exposures to their inherent risks, the asset should continue to be recognised in its entirety. The third type of transaction comprises those special cases where not all significant benefits and risks have been transferred, but it is necessary to amend the description or monetary amount of the original asset or to recognise a new liability for any obligations assumed. Examples of this third type of transaction are given in paragraphs 71–73.

Contracts for future performance

For the avoidance of doubt, the Board decided that contracts for future performance, **25**
such as swaps, forward contracts and purchase commitments, should be removed from the scope of the FRS, except where they are merely a part of a transaction (or of a connected series of transactions) that falls within the FRS. The accounting for such contracts is a complex area that requires further research and consultation before an FRS dealing with their accounting could be issued.

Options

FRED 4's approach to options and the new guidance it contained were generally **26**
supported. However, the comments revealed some uncertainty over the approach to be taken to options for which there is a genuine commercial possibility both that the option will be exercised and that it will not be exercised, but the transaction is structured such that one or other outcome is significantly more likely. The FRS provides that the commercial effect of an option should be assessed in the context of all the aspects and implications of the transaction. It also explains that it may be necessary to consider the true commercial objectives of the parties and the commercial rationale for the inclusion of the option in the transaction in order to establish whether the parties' rights and obligations are, in substance, optional or conditional or, alternatively, outright.

Finally, for the avoidance of doubt, the FRS emphasises that, in assessing the commer- **27**
cial effect of an option, all the terms of the transaction and the circumstances of the parties that are likely to be relevant during the exercise period of the option should be taken into account – and not just conditions existing at the balance sheet date.

Linked presentation for subsidiaries

The FRS carries through the proposal in FRED 4 that where an item and its non-recourse **28**
finance are 'ring-fenced' in a quasi-subsidiary in such a way that the conditions for a linked presentation are met from the point of view of the group, the quasi-subsidiary should be included in consolidated financial statements using a linked presentation. However, if in a similar arrangement the item and its finance are held by a subsidiary, a linked presentation may not be used. In this case, the subsidiary is part of the group as legally defined: hence the item and its finance, being an asset and liability of the subsidiary, are respectively an asset and a liability of the group and companies legislation requires them to be shown in consolidated accounts in the normal way. Some respondents argued that the commercial effect is the same regardless of whether the vehicle is a subsidiary or a quasi-subsidiary, and hence the same accounting treatment should be adopted. However, companies legislation does not permit this. In legal terms, the inclusion of a quasi-subsidiary constitutes the provision of *additional* information about the group as legally defined and thus a quasi-subsidiary may be included in any way necessary to give a true and fair view of that group. However, a

subsidiary is *part of* the group as legally defined and companies legislation requires the subsidiary to be consolidated in the normal way.

The use of swaps in securitisations

29 The Board was asked to clarify whether, in a securitisation, an interest rate swap or an interest rate cap between an originator and an issuer would restrict use of a linked presentation. FRED 4 required, as does the FRS, that, for a linked presentation, there must be 'no recourse whatsoever' to the originator and 'no possibility whatsoever of a claim being established on the entity [ie the originator] other than against funds generated by that item [ie the securitised assets]'. These provisions would prohibit use of a linked presentation where there is an interest rate swap or an interest rate cap between the originator and the issuer.

30 However, the argument was put to the Board that an exception to this principle was appropriate because the risks are often hedged by the originator as part of its normal hedging activities and thus payments to the issuer under the swap or cap would not represent a net loss to the originator. In many cases, the originator will have hedged any interest rate (and related) risks relating to the securitised assets prior to the securitisation, with the result that the securitisation opens up a gap in the originator's hedging portfolio by removing a hedged asset without removing its hedge. The most natural way to close this gap is for the issuer and the originator to enter into an interest rate swap or cap. Such a swap or cap will also be advantageous to the issuer by providing it with a hedge of the difference in the interest rate received on its newly acquired assets and that paid on its loan notes. It was also stated that, in the case of an interest rate swap (although not in the case of an interest rate cap), the issuer is currently unable to enter into a suitable swap with a third party as there is currently no market for such swaps in the UK (principally because the swap would require an amortising amount of principal to reflect actual repayments of the securitised assets).

31 The Board believes, as a matter of principle, that a linked presentation should be permitted only where there is no recourse whatsoever to the originator and accordingly should not be permitted where there is an interest rate swap or cap between the originator and the issuer. However, it decided with reluctance and as a pragmatic and provisional response to the issue, to permit use of a linked presentation in the originator's accounts notwithstanding the presence of an interest rate swap between the originator and the issuer in a securitisation provided certain strict criteria are met. (These are set out in paragraph D11.) In reaching this decision, the Board took into account the interaction of its decision with the present framework for regulating banks. The Board was also swayed by the fact that there is currently no market for such swaps in the UK and hence the issuer is unable to enter into a suitable swap with anyone other than the originator. For interest rate caps, the Board decided to give a similar concession but to restrict it to those securitisations in existence prior to 22 September 1994 since the availability of a suitable market for interest rate caps means there is no need for future transactions of this kind to be undertaken with the originator. The FRS also requires disclosure of interest rate swaps and caps between the originator and the issuer where a linked presentation is used.

The Board's decision with respect to interest rate swaps represents an interim measure and will be reviewed in the light of developments in securitisations and of progress made in the Board's forthcoming project on derivatives. 32

Disclosures of derecognised assets

Three of the Application Notes to FRED 4 contained specific disclosure requirements in respect of derecognised assets. Commentators generally thought these requirements were excessive, and they have not been retained in the FRS. 33

Financial Reporting Standard 6 is set out in paragraphs 1–39.

The Statement of Standard Accounting Practice set out in paragraphs 4–39 should be read in the context of the Objective as stated in paragraph 1 and the definitions set out in paragraphs 2–3 and also of the Foreword to Accounting Standards and the Statement of Principles for Financial Reporting currently in issue.

The Explanation set out in paragraphs 40–89 shall be regarded as part of the Statement of Standard Accounting Practice insofar as it assists in interpreting that statement.

Appendix III 'The development of the FRS' reviews considerations and arguments that were thought significant by members of the Board in reaching the conclusions on FRS 6.

[FRS6]
Acquisition and mergers

(Issued September 1994)

Contents

Acquisitions and mergers

SUMMARY

Financial Reporting Standard 6 'Acquisitions and Mergers' sets out the circumstances in which the two methods of accounting for a business combination – acquisition accounting and merger accounting – are to be used. a

Acquisition accounting regards the business combination as the acquisition of one company by another; the identifiable assets and liabilities of the company acquired are included in the consolidated balance sheet at their fair value at the date of acquisition, and its results included in the profit and loss account from the date of acquisition. The difference between the fair value of the consideration given and the fair values of the net assets of the entity acquired is accounted for as goodwill. b

Merger accounting, on the other hand, treats two or more parties as combining on an equal footing. It is normally applied without any restatement of net assets to fair value, and includes the results of each for the whole of the accounting period. Correspondingly, it does not reflect the issue of shares as an application of resources at fair value. The difference that arises on consolidation does not represent goodwill but is deducted from, or added to, reserves. c

The FRS requires acquisition accounting to be used for any business combination where a party can be identified as having the role of an acquirer, since this method of accounting reflects the application of resources by the acquirer and the net assets acquired. d

Merger accounting is restricted to, and required for, those business combinations where the use of acquisition accounting would not properly reflect the true nature of the combination. A merger is a business combination in which, rather than one party acquiring control of another, the parties come together to share in the future risks and benefits of the combined entity. It is not the augmentation of one entity by the addition of another, but the creation of what is effectively a new reporting entity from the parties to the combination. e

A combination meets the definition of a merger only if it satisfies the five criteria set out in paragraphs 6–11 of the FRS. These criteria relate to: f

1. the way the roles of each party to the combination are portrayed;
2. the involvement of each party to the combination in the selection of the management of the combined entity;
3. the relative sizes of the parties to the combination;
4. whether shareholders of the combining entities receive any consideration other than equity shares in the combined entity;

5 whether shareholders of the combining entities retain an interest in the performance of only part of the combined entity.

g Where a combination meets these criteria, acquisition accounting is not permitted as this method would not fairly present the effect of the combination.

h The FRS also contains provisions for applying merger accounting to mergers effected by the creation of a new holding company, and also to certain group reconstructions where acquisition accounting may not be appropriate.

i The FRS contains disclosure requirements applying to business combinations accounted for by using merger accounting so that the transition from separate entities to the merged entity can be understood; and further disclosure requirements, replacing those in SSAP 22 'Accounting for goodwill', for business combinations accounted for by using acquisition accounting, so that the effect of the acquisition can be understood.

Financial Reporting Standard 6

OBJECTIVE

1 The objective of this FRS is: to ensure that merger accounting is used only for those business combinations that are not, in substance, the acquisition of one entity by another but the formation of a new reporting entity as a substantially equal partnership where no party is dominant; to ensure the use of acquisition accounting for all other business combinations; and to ensure that in either case the financial statements provide relevant information concerning the effect of the combination.

DEFINITIONS

2 The following definitions shall apply in this FRS and in particular in the Statement of Standard Accounting Practice set out in paragraphs 4–39.

Acquisition:

A business combination that is not a merger.

Business combination:

The bringing together of separate entities into one economic entity as a result of one entity uniting with, or obtaining control over the net assets and operations of, another.

Equity shares:

Shares other than non-equity shares.

Group reconstruction:

Any of the following arrangements:

(a) the transfer of a shareholding in a subsidiary undertaking from one group company to another;

(b) the addition of a new parent company to a group;
(c) the transfer of shares in one or more subsidiary undertakings of a group to a new company that is not a group company but whose shareholders are the same as those of the group's parent;
(d) the combination into a group of two or more companies that before the combination had the same shareholders.

Merger:

A business combination that results in the creation of a new reporting entity formed from the combining parties, in which the shareholders of the combining entities come together in a partnership for the mutual sharing of the risks and benefits of the combined entity, and in which no party to the combination in substance obtains control over any other, or is otherwise seen to be dominant, whether by virtue of the proportion of its shareholders' rights in the combined entity, the influence of its directors or otherwise.

Non-equity shares:

Shares possessing any of the following characteristics:
(a) any of the rights of the shares to receive payments (whether in respect of dividends, in respect of redemption or otherwise) are for a limited amount that is not calculated by reference to the company's assets or profits or the dividends on any class of equity share;
(b) any of their rights to participate in a surplus in a winding up are limited to a specific amount that is not calculated by reference to the company's assets or profits and such limitation had a commercial effect in practice at the time the shares were issued or, if later, at the time the limitation was introduced;
(c) the shares are redeemable, either according to their terms or because the holder, or any party other than the issuer, can require their redemption.

References to companies legislation mean: **3**

(a) in Great Britain, the Companies Act 1985;
(b) in Northern Ireland, the Companies (Northern Ireland) Order 1986; and
(c) in the Republic of Ireland, the Companies Acts 1963–90 and the European Communities (Companies: Group Accounts) Regulations 1992.

STATEMENT OF STANDARD ACCOUNTING PRACTICE

The marginal notes give the main references to the Companies Act 1985 in Great Britain. For the equivalent references in companies legislation in Northern Ireland and the Republic of Ireland see Appendix I.

SCOPE

4 Financial Reporting Standard 6 applies to all financial statements that are intended to give a true and fair view of a reporting entity's financial position and profit or loss (or income and expenditure) for a period. Although the FRS is framed in terms of an entity becoming a subsidiary undertaking of a parent company that prepares consolidated financial statements, it also applies where an individual company or other reporting entity combines with a business other than a subsidiary undertaking.

USE OF MERGER ACCOUNTING

5 A business combination should be accounted for by using merger accounting if:

(a) the use of merger accounting for the combination is not prohibited by companies legislation; and *[4A Sch 10]*

(b) the combination meets all the specific criteria set out in paragraphs 6–11 below and thus falls within the definition of a merger.

Acquisition accounting should be used for all other business combinations, except as provided in paragraphs 13 and 14.

Criteria for determining whether the definition of a merger is met

6 *Criterion 1* – No party to the combination is portrayed as either acquirer or acquired, either by its own board or management or by that of another party to the combination.

7 *Criterion 2* – All parties to the combination, as represented by the boards of directors or their appointees, participate in establishing the management structure for the combined entity and in selecting the management personnel, and such decisions are made on the basis of a consensus between the parties to the combination rather than purely by exercise of voting rights.

8 *Criterion 3* – The relative sizes of the combining entities are not so disparate that one party dominates the combined entity by virtue of its relative size.

9 *Criterion 4* – Under the terms of the combination or related arrange-

ments, the consideration received by equity shareholders of each party to the combination, in relation to their equity shareholding, comprises primarily equity shares in the combined entity; and any non-equity consideration, or equity shares carrying substantially reduced voting or distribution rights, represents an immaterial proportion of the fair value of the consideration received by the equity shareholders of that party. Where one of the combining entities has, within the period of two years before the combination, acquired equity shares in another of the combining entities, the consideration for this acquisition should be taken into account in determining whether this criterion has been met.

For the purpose of paragraph 9, the consideration should not be taken to include the distribution to shareholders of: **10**

(a) an interest in a peripheral part of the business of the entity in which they were shareholders and which does not form part of the combined entity; or
(b) the proceeds of the sale of such a business, or loan stock representing such proceeds.

A peripheral part of the business is one that can be disposed of without having a material effect on the nature and focus of the entity's operations.

Criterion 5 – No equity shareholders of any of the combining entities retain any material interest in the future performance of only part of the combined entity. **11**

For the purposes of paragraphs 6–11 above any convertible share or loan stock should be regarded as equity to the extent that it is converted into equity as a result of the business combination. **12**

Group reconstructions

A group reconstruction may be accounted for by using merger accounting, even though there is no business combination meeting the definition of a merger, provided: **13**

[4A Sch 10] (a) the use of merger accounting is not prohibited by companies legislation;
(b) the ultimate shareholders remain the same, and the rights of each such shareholder, relative to the others, are unchanged; and
(c) no minority's interest in the net assets of the group is altered by the transfer.

Combination effected by using a new parent company

Where a combination is effected by using a newly formed parent company to hold the shares of each of the other parties to a combi- **14** nation, the accounting treatment depends on the substance of the business combination being effected: that is, whether a combination of the entities other than the new parent company would have been an acquisition or a merger. If the combination would have been an acquisition, one entity can be identified as having the role of an acquirer. This acquirer and the new parent company should first be combined by using merger accounting; then the other parties to the business combination should be treated as acquired by this combined company by using the acquisition method of accounting. On the other hand, where the substance of the business combination effected by a new parent company is a merger, the new parent company and the other parties should all be combined by using merger accounting.

Applicability to various structures of business combination

15 The provisions of the FRS, which are explained by reference to an acquirer or issuing entity that issues shares as consideration for the transfer to it of shares in the other parties to the combination, should also be read so as to apply to other arrangements that achieve similar results.

MERGER ACCOUNTING

16 With merger accounting the carrying values of the assets and liabilities of the parties to the combination are not required to be adjusted to fair value on consolidation, although appropriate adjustments should be made to achieve uniformity of accounting policies in the combining entities. *[4A Sch 11]*

17 The results and cash flows of all the combining entities should be brought into the financial statements of the combined entity from the beginning of the financial year in which the combination occurred, adjusted so as to achieve uniformity of accounting policies. The corresponding figures should be restated by including the results for all the combining entities for the previous period and their balance sheets for the previous balance sheet date, adjusted as necessary to achieve uniformity of accounting policies.

18 The difference, if any, between the nominal value of the shares issued plus the fair value of any other consideration given, and the nominal value of the shares received in exchange should be shown as a movement on other reserves in the consolidated financial statements. Any existing balance on the share premium account or capital redemption reserve of the new subsidiary undertaking should be brought in by being shown as a movement on other reserves. These movements should be shown in the reconciliation of movements in shareholders' funds.

Merger expenses are not to be included as part of this adjustment, but should be charged to the profit and loss account of the combined entity at the effective date of the merger, as reorganisation or restructuring expenses, in accordance with paragraph 20 of FRS 3 'Reporting Financial Performance'. **19**

ACQUISITION ACCOUNTING

[4A Sch 9] Business combinations not accounted for by merger accounting should be accounted for by acquisition accounting. Under acquisition accounting, the identifiable assets and liabilities of the companies acquired should be included in the acquirer's consolidated balance sheet at their fair value at the date of acquisition. The results and cash flows of the acquired companies should be brought into the group accounts only from the date of acquisition. The figures for the previous period for the reporting entity should not be adjusted. The difference between the fair value of the net identifiable assets acquired and the fair value of the purchase consideration is goodwill, positive or negative*. **20**

DISCLOSURE

Acquisitions and mergers

[4A Sch 13(2)] The following information in respect of all business combinations occurring in the financial year, whether accounted for as acquisitions or mergers, should be disclosed in the financial statements of the acquiring entity or, in the case of a merger, the entity issuing shares: **21**

(a) the names of the combining entities (other than the reporting entity);
(b) whether the combination has been accounted for as an acquisition or a merger;
(c) the date of the combination.

Mergers

In respect of each business combination accounted for as a merger, other than group reconstructions falling within paragraph 13, the following information should be disclosed in the financial statements of the combined entity for the period in which the merger took place: **22**

[Extension of 4A Sch 13(4)] (a) an analysis of the principal components of the current year's profit and loss account and statement of total recognised gains and losses into

**The date of acquisition and the acquisition of a subsidiary undertaking in stages are dealt with in FRS 2, paragraphs 45, 50 84–85 and 88–89.*

(i) amounts relating to the merged entity for the period after the date of the merger, and

(ii) for each party to the merger, amounts relating to that party for the period up to the date of the merger.

(b) an analysis between the parties to the merger of the principal components of the profit and loss account and statement of total recognised gains and losses for the previous financial year; *[Extension of 4A Sch 13(4)]*

(c) the composition and fair value of the consideration given by the issuing company and its subsidiary undertakings; *[4A Sch 13(3)]*

(d) the aggregate book value of the net assets of each party to the merger at the date of the merger;

(e) the nature and amount of significant accounting adjustments made to the net assets of any party to the merger to achieve consistency of accounting policies, and an explanation of any other significant adjustments made to the net assets of any party to the merger as a consequence of the merger; and *[4A Sch 13(6)]*

(f) a statement of the adjustments to consolidated reserves resulting from the merger. *[4A Sch 13(6)]*

The analysis of the profit and loss account in (a) and (b) above should show as a minimum the turnover, operating profit and exceptional items, split between continuing operations, discontinued operations and acquisitions; profit before taxation; taxation and minority interests; and extraordinary items.

Acquisitions

23 The disclosure requirements for business combinations accounted for as acquisitions apply as follows:

(a) those in paragraphs 24–35 are required for each material acquisition; and, with the exception of those in paragraph 35, should also be given for other acquisitions in aggregate;

(b) the additional disclosure requirements in paragraph 36 apply to substantial acquisitions as defined in paragraph 37.

24 The composition and fair value of the consideration, given by the acquiring company and its subsidiary undertakings should be disclosed. The nature of any deferred or contingent purchase consideration should be stated, including, for contingent consideration, the range of possible outcomes and the principal factors that affect the outcome. *[4A Sch 13(3)]*

25 A table should be provided showing, for each class of assets and liabilities of the acquired entity: *[4A Sch 13(5)]*

(a) the book values, as recorded in the acquired entity's books immediately before the acquisition and before any fair value adjustments;

(b) the fair value adjustments, analysed into

(i) revaluations
(ii) adjustments to achieve consistency of accounting policies, and
(iii) any other significant adjustments,

giving the reasons for the adjustments; and

(c) the fair values at the date of acquisition.

The table should include a statement of the amount of purchased goodwill or negative goodwill arising on the acquisition.

In the table required by paragraph 25, provisions for reorganisation and restructuring costs that are included in the liabilities of the acquired entity, and related asset write-downs, made in the twelve months up to the date of acquisition should be identified separately. **26**

Where the fair values of the identifiable assets or liabilities, or the purchase consideration, can be determined only on a provisional basis at the end of the accounting period in which the acquisition took place, this should be stated and the reasons given. Any subsequent material adjustments to such provisional fair values, with corresponding adjustments to goodwill, should be disclosed and explained. **27**

As required by FRS 3, in the period of acquisition the post-acquisition results of the acquired entity should be shown as a component of continuing operations in the profit and loss account, other than those that are also discontinued in the same period; and where an acquisition has a material impact on a major business segment this should be disclosed and explained. **28**

Where it is not practicable to determine the post-acquisition results of an operation to the end of the period of acquisition, an indication should be given of the contribution of the acquired entity to the turnover and operating profit of the continuing operations. If an indication of the contribution of an acquired entity to the results of the period cannot be given, this fact and the reason should be explained. **29**

Any exceptional profit or loss in periods following the acquisition that is determined using the fair values recognised on acquisition should be disclosed in accordance with the requirements of FRS 3, and identified as relating to the acquisition. **30**

The profit and loss account or notes to the financial statements of periods following the acquisition should show the costs incurred in those periods in reorganising, restructuring and integrating the acquisition. Such costs are those that: **31**

(a) would not have been incurred had the acquisition not taken place; and
(b) relate to a project identified and controlled by management as

part of a reorganisation or integration programme set up at the time of acquisition or as a direct consequence of an immediate post-acquisition review.

32 Movements on provisions or accruals for costs related to an acquisition should be disclosed and analysed between the amounts used for the specific purpose for which they were created and the amounts released unused.

33 In accordance with FRS 1, the cash flow statement should show the amounts of cash and cash equivalents paid in respect of the consideration, net of any cash and cash equivalents balances transferred as part of the acquisition. In addition, a note to the cash flow statement should show a summary of the effects of acquisitions indicating how much of the consideration comprised cash and cash equivalents and the amounts of cash and cash equivalents transferred as a result of the acquisition.

34 In accordance with FRS 1, material effects on amounts reported under each of the standard headings reflecting the cash flows of the acquired entity in the period should be disclosed, as far as is practicable, as a note to the cash flow statement. This information need be given only in the financial statements for the period in which the acquisition occurs.

35 For a material acquisition, the profit after taxation and minority interests of the acquired entity should be given for: *[4A Sch 13(4)]*

(a) the period from the beginning of the acquired entity's financial year to the date of acquisition, giving the date on which this period began; and
(b) its previous financial year.

Substantial acquisitions

36 For acquisitions meeting the conditions set out in the next paragraph, the following information should be disclosed in the financial statements of the combined entity for the period in which the acquisition took place: *[Extension of 4A Sch 13(4)]*

(a) the summarised profit and loss account and statement of total recognised gains and losses of the acquired entity for the period from the beginning of its financial year to the effective date of acquisition, giving the date on which this period began; this summarised profit and loss account should show as a minimum the turnover, operating profit and those exceptional items falling within paragraph 20 of FRS 3; profit before taxation; taxation and minority interests; and extraordinary items;
(b) the profit after tax and minority interests for the acquired entity's previous financial year.

This information should be shown on the basis of the acquired entity's accounting policies prior to the acquisition.

The disclosures in paragraph 36 should be given for each business combination accounted for by using acquisition accounting where: **37**

(a) for listed companies, the combination is a Class 1 or Super Class 1 transaction under the Stock Exchange Listing Rules;
(b) for other entities, either
   (i) the net assets or operating profits of the acquired entity exceed 15 per cent of those of the acquiring entity, or
   (ii) the fair value of the consideration given exceeds 15 per cent of the net assets of the acquiring entity;

and should also be made in other exceptional cases where an acquisition is of such significance that the disclosure is necessary in order to give a true and fair view. For the purposes of (b) above, net assets and profits should be those shown in the financial statements for the last financial year before the date of the acquisition; and the net assets should be augmented by any purchased goodwill eliminated against reserves as a matter of accounting policy and not charged to the profit and loss account.

DATE FROM WHICH EFFECTIVE

The accounting practices set out in the FRS should be regarded as standard in respect of business combinations first accounted for in financial statements relating to accounting periods commencing on or after 23 December 1994. Earlier adoption is encouraged but not required. **38**

WITHDRAWAL OF SSAP 23 AND AMENDMENT OF SSAP 22

The FRS supersedes SSAP 23 'Accounting for acquisitions and mergers' and paragraphs 48–51 of SSAP 22 'Accounting for goodwill'. **39**

Explanation

INTRODUCTION

40 Two different methods have been used to account for business combinations: merger accounting and acquisition accounting.

41 In merger accounting the financial statements of the parties to the combination are aggregated, and presented as though the combining entities had always been part of the same reporting entity. Accordingly, although the merger may have taken place part of the way through the financial year, the results of the combining entities for the full financial year are reflected in the group accounts for the period and corresponding amounts are presented on the same basis. The accounting policies of the combining entities are adjusted to achieve uniformity, but the assets and liabilities need not be adjusted to reflect fair values at the date of the combination. Under merger accounting, a difference may arise on consolidation between the nominal value of the shares issued, taken together with the fair value of any other consideration, and the aggregate of the nominal values of the shares received in exchange. Such difference is not goodwill, as it does not result from the difference between the fair value of the consideration and the fair value of the identifiable net assets. It should be shown as a movement on consolidated reserves. Any share premium accounts and capital redemption reserves of the new subsidiary undertaking are not preserved as such in the consolidated accounts, since they do not relate to the share capital of the reporting entity, but are brought in by being shown as a movement on other reserves.

42 In acquisition accounting the results of the acquired company are brought into the group accounts only from the date of acquisition. The identifiable assets and liabilities acquired are included at fair value in the consolidated accounts and are therefore stated at their cost to the acquiring group. The fair value of the consideration given is set against the aggregate fair value of the net identifiable assets acquired and any resulting balance is goodwill, if positive, or else a negative consolidation difference called negative goodwill.*

43 The fact that a particular business combination does not meet the criteria for merger accounting, and is thus accounted for by using acquisition accounting, does not preclude the acquirer from obtaining merger relief in its individual accounts under the provisions of section 131 of the Companies Act 1985 if the requirements of that section are met. In such cases, in the consolidated accounts, acquisition accounting is applied in the normal way: goodwill is still calculated by comparing the fair value of the shares issued, rather than their nominal or recorded value, with the fair value of the net assets acquired; and any resulting excess over the nominal value of the shares issued, taken together with the fair value of any other consideration, is shown, not as share premium, but as a separate reserve.

**The treatment of such balances is dealt with in SSAP 22 'Accounting for goodwill' and is the subject of a current ASB project.*

DEFINITION OF A MERGER AND AN ACQUISITION

A merger is a rare type of business combination in which two or more parties come together for the mutual sharing of benefits and risks arising from the combined businesses, in what is in substance an equal partnership, each sharing influence in the new entity. No party can be regarded as acquiring control over another, or becoming controlled by another; and the reporting entity formed by the combination must be regarded as a new entity rather than the continuation of one of the combining entities, enlarged by its having obtained control over the others. **44**

An acquisition is defined as any business combination that is not a merger. In many acquisitions, the shareholders of the acquired party do not have a continuing interest in the combined entity, but instead sell their shareholdings for cash or other non-equity consideration. Even where all parties in an acquisition retain an interest in the combined entity, the parties do not come together on equal terms; one party has a greater degree of influence than the others, and is seen as acquiring the other entities in exchange for a share in the combined entity. An acquisition is therefore a transaction that is, in substance, the application of resources by the acquiring entity to obtain control of one or more other entities, by the payment of cash, transfer of other assets, the incurring of a liability or the issue of shares. **45**

The legal form of a business combination will normally be for one company to acquire shares in one or more others. This fact does not make that company an acquirer in the sense discussed above. Similarly, the question of whether the combined entity should be regarded as a new reporting entity is not affected by whether or not a new legal entity has been formed to acquire shares in others. **46**

RATIONALE FOR MERGER ACCOUNTING

In a merger, no party to the combination can be properly regarded as obtaining control over the other; rather, the parties to the combination join together on an equal footing to form a combined enterprise for their mutual benefit. **47**

For such mergers it is misleading to account for the combination as the application of resources by one party to obtain control over the other, since this assumes a distinction in the roles of the parties that does not reflect reality. Furthermore, it is only the legal structure of the combination that would determine which party would be treated under acquisition accounting as the acquirer, and thus determine the party whose net assets would be treated as being acquired and whose goodwill would be recognised. **48**

A merger is a true mutual sharing of the benefits and risks of the combined entity. Therefore the joint history of the entities that have combined will be relevant to the combined group's shareholders. This record will be provided by merger accounting because it treats the separate businesses as though they were continuing as before, only now jointly owned and managed. If acquisition accounting were to be used, it would focus artificially on only one of the parties to the combination, which would lead to a discontinuity in information reported on the combined entity. **49**

50 Thus the concept of a merger is of a partnership or pooling of interests, where all the parties to the combination participate in the combined businesses of the merged entity on substantially equal terms; and where the substance of the arrangement is such that the reporting entity cannot be regarded as merely being enlarged by the acquisition of the other entities, but must be considered as effectively a new reporting entity.

51 In a business combination that qualifies as a merger, expenses of the combination are similar in nature to expenses of a fundamental reorganisation or restructuring, and should be charged to the profit and loss account for the period in which the merger occurred, shown as an exceptional item in accordance with paragraph 20 of FRS 3. This is not intended to prohibit the subsequent charging of issue costs to the share premium account by means of a transfer between reserves.

RATIONALE FOR ACQUISITION ACCOUNTING

52 The acquisition of another entity is a transaction by which an entity seeks to increase the assets under its control. Acquisition accounting is appropriate for most business combinations since it reflects in the financial statements the application of resources by one party to the combination in order to obtain control of the other, represented by the fair value of the net assets over which control is obtained together with goodwill.

53 The profits of the acquired company are brought into account only from the date of the combination and the history of the group is seen as the history of the acquirer with occasional additions when it acquires other entities.

DECIDING WHETHER A BUSINESS COMBINATION IS A MERGER OR AN ACQUISITION

54 The FRS requires that to determine whether a business combination meets the definition of a merger, it should be assessed against certain specified criteria; failure to meet any of these criteria indicates that the definition was not met and thus that merger accounting is not to be used for the combination.

55 Individually these tests are insufficient to define the intangible quality of a true merger, and may appear arbitrary. Nevertheless, taken as a whole, they provide a reasonable basis for determining whether a particular business combination meets the definition of a merger and thus should be accounted for by using merger accounting.

56 In applying the criteria, it is necessary to consider the substance and not just the form of the arrangements, and to take account of all relevant information related to the combination. It is important to have regard to the transaction as a whole, including any related arrangements that are connected with the business combination either because they are entered into in contemplation of that combination or because they are part of

the process by which that combination is effected. The vast majority of business combinations will be acquisitions and only in rare circumstances will a combination fulfil all the detailed conditions for it to be treated as a merger.

Parties to the combination

For the purposes of assessing whether a combination is a merger meeting the criteria, the parties to the combination are considered as comprising not solely the business of each entity that is combining but also the management of the entity and the body of its shareholders. **57**

Merger accounting is not appropriate for a combination where one of the parties results from a recent divestment by a larger entity, because the divested business will not have been independent for a sufficient period to establish itself as being a party separate from its previous owner. Only once the divested business has established a track record of its own can it be considered as a party to a merger. However, a party to a combination may divest itself of a peripheral part of its business before the combination (or as part of the arrangements for the combination) and still meet the criteria for merger accounting. **58**

Where a party to the combination is not a company with share capital, the conditions applying to equity shares should be interpreted as applying to those elements of its capital structure that allocate rights to profits and control. **59**

Criterion 1 – role of the parties

An essential feature of a merger is that it represents a genuine combining of the interests of the parties; such a genuine combination of interests cannot exist if one party portrays itself, or another party, as having a dominant role as an acquirer or the subservient role of being acquired. **60**

Where the terms of a share-for-share exchange indicate that one party has paid a premium over the market value of the shares acquired, this is evidence that that party has taken the role of an acquirer unless there is a clear explanation for this apparent premium other than its being a premium paid to acquire control. **61**

The circumstances surrounding the transaction may provide evidence to indicate the nature of a business combination. The following, while not individually conclusive, would need to be considered: the form by which the combination was achieved, the plans for the combined entity's future operations (for example, whether any closures or disposals related more to one party than another), and the proposed corporate image (such as the name, logo and the location of the headquarters and principal operations). Where a publicly quoted company is a party to a business combination, the content of communications with its shareholders is likely also to be relevant in determining the substance of the transaction. **62**

Criterion 2 – dominance of management

63 An essential feature of the genuine combination of interests underlying the definition of a merger is that all parties to the combination are involved in determining the management of the combined entity and reach a consensus on the appropriate structure and personnel; if decisions can be reached only by the exercise of majority voting rights against the wishes of one of the parties to the merger, or if one party clearly dominates this process, this indicates that the combination is not a genuine pooling of interests. However, this does not preclude the possibility of all, or most, of the management team of the combined entity coming from only one of the parties, provided that this clearly reflects the wishes of the others.

64 In applying this test, it is necessary to consider not only the formal management structure of the combined entity, but also the identity of all persons involved in the main financial and operating decisions and the way in which the decision-making process operates in practice within the combined entity.

65 Normally the management of the combined entity would contain representatives of each of the combining parties. Where the senior management structure and personnel of the combined entity are essentially those of one of the combining parties, this criterion will not have been met unless it is clear that all the parties to the merger genuinely participated in the decision.

66 In applying this test it is necessary to consider only the decisions made in the period of initial integration and restructuring at the time of the combination; but both the short-term effects and expected long-term consequences of decisions made in this period need to be considered.

Criterion 3 – relative size of the parties

67 Where one party is substantially larger than the other parties it would be presumed that the larger party can or will dominate the combined undertaking. This will not be consistent with treating such a business combination as a merger as the combined entity will not be a substantially equal partnership.

68 A party would be presumed to dominate if it is more than 50 per cent larger than each of the other parties to the combination, judged by reference to the ownership interests; that is, by considering the proportion of the equity of the combined entity attributable to the shareholders of each of the combining parties. However, this presumption may be rebutted if it can be clearly shown that there is no such dominance; other factors, such as voting or share agreements, blocking powers or other arrangements, can mean that a party to the combination has more influence, or conversely less influence, than is indicated by its relative size. Circumstances that rebut the presumption of dominant influence based on relative sizes would need to be disclosed and explained.

Criterion 4 – non-equity consideration

69 Criterion 4 is concerned with the extent to which equity shareholders of the combining entities receive any consideration other than equity shares (as defined in paragraph 2

above) in the combined entity. Cash, other assets, loan stock and preference shares are all examples of non-equity consideration.

As stated in the note on legal requirements (Appendix I), companies legislation provides that one of the conditions for merger accounting is that the fair value of any consideration other than the issue of equity shares (as defined in companies legislation) did not exceed 10 per cent of the nominal value of the equity shares issued. Criterion 4 requires a further condition to be met, that all but an immaterial proportion of the fair value of the consideration received must be in the form of equity shares (as defined in paragraph 2); this definition of equity, which is that adopted in FRS 4 'Capital Instruments', is narrower than that of companies legislation, and is used to avoid the possibility of criterion 4 being met by the use of shares that, although within the statutory definition of equity, have characteristics that are closer to non-equity. 70

The FRS requires that all arrangements made in conjunction with the combination must be taken into account. Equity shareholders will be considered to have disposed of their shareholding for cash where any arrangement is made in connection with the combination that enabled them to exchange or redeem the shares they received in the combination for cash (or other non-equity consideration); for example, a vendor placing or similar arrangement should be treated as giving rise to non-equity consideration. However, a normal market selling transaction, or privately arranged sale, entered into by a shareholder is not made in conjunction with the combination and does not prevent the criterion being met. 71

A business combination may not be accounted for as a merger if a material part of the consideration that the issuing entity offers the equity shareholders in the other parties is in the form of shares with substantially reduced rights. Such an offer would be contrary to the concept that a merger is the mutual sharing in risks and rewards of the combined entity. Some adjustment to the rights attaching to the shares held by the non-issuing entities' shareholders may be compatible with the combination being a merger, as business combinations result from a negotiating process where different pre-existing rights have to be reconciled. Whether any change in the rights of one group of shareholders is sufficient to prevent that business combination being treated as a merger will depend on the facts in any individual case, taking into account such matters as what rights shareholders originally had, the total arrangement negotiated, time limits and whether any new restrictions apply equally to all sets of shareholders. In determining whether equity shares with reduced rights have been issued, both rights to vote and rights to distributions attaching to the shares would need to be taken into account. If any of these individual rights were significantly reduced or circumscribed the combination would fail to fulfil this condition. 72

If one entity has acquired an interest in another in exchange for non-equity consideration, or equity shares with significantly reduced rights, within the two years before those entities combined, such consideration should be regarded as part of the consideration for the combination for the purpose of determining whether this criterion is met. 73

Sometimes a peripheral part of the business of one of the combining parties will be excluded from the combined entity. The FRS states that shares in the peripheral 74 business, or the proceeds of sale of the business, that are distributed to the shareholders of that party to the combination as part of the arrangements for the combination are not to be counted as part of the consideration for the purposes of this criterion.

Criterion 5 – minorities etc

75 Criterion 5 is concerned with a party retaining an interest in only part of the combined entity. The concept of a merger is that the participants enter into a mutual sharing of the risks and rewards of the whole of the new entity, including the pooled future results of the combined entity. This concept is incompatible with certain participants having a preferential interest in one part of the combined entity. This criterion would not, therefore, be met if the share of the equity in the combined entity allocated to the shareholders of one of the parties to the combination depended to any material extent on the post-combination performance of the business, or any part of it, formerly controlled by that party.

76 This criterion would similarly not be met where earn-outs or similar performance-related schemes are included in the arrangements to effect a merger. The test is also failed if there is any material minority (defined by companies legislation as 10 per cent) of shareholders left in one of the combining parties that have not accepted the terms of the combination offer.

77 However, the criterion would not necessarily be invalidated by an arrangement whereby the allocation of consideration between the shareholders of the combining parties depended on the determination of the eventual value of a specific liability or asset contributed by one of the parties – such as the eventual outcome of a claim against one of the parties, or the eventual sales value of a specific asset owned by one of the parties – as opposed to the future operating performance of that party.

GROUP RECONSTRUCTIONS

78 In addition to mergers as defined above, merger accounting may also be appropriate for a group reconstruction, provided that the relative rights of the ultimate shareholders are not altered. Such reconstructions include not only the transfer of shares in a subsidiary undertaking within a group, but also arrangements such as the introduction of a new holding company, the splitting off of one or more subsidiary undertakings, as in some demergers, where a separate group is formed, and the bringing together into a new group of two or more companies that were previously under common ownership. Acquisition accounting would require the restatement at fair value of the assets and liabilities of the company transferred, and the recognising of goodwill, which is likely to be inappropriate in the case of a transaction that does not alter the relative rights of the ultimate shareholders.

79 Where a minority interest exists, merger accounting is permitted only for those group reconstructions that do not change the interest of the minority in the net assets of the group. Thus the transfer of a subsidiary undertaking within a subgroup that has a minority shareholder may qualify for merger accounting; but acquisition accounting must be used for the transfer of a subsidiary undertaking out of, or into, such a subgroup. If a minority has effectively acquired, or disposed of, rights to part of the net assets of the group, the FRS requires the transfer to be accounted for by using acquisition accounting rather than merger accounting.

DISCLOSURE

The disclosure requirements in the FRS cover and supplement those in companies legislation. **80**

Mergers

With merger accounting the financial statements of the combined entity are drawn up by combining the results of the combining entities for the whole of the financial year in which the merger occurred. Users, particularly those who have been assessing the parties to the combination as separate businesses, may require information on the financial performance of the individual parties. The FRS therefore requires an analysis of the profit and loss account and statement of total recognised gains and losses into pre- and post-merger amounts; and a further analysis of the pre-merger amounts between each of the parties to the merger. An analysis between the parties of the preceding financial year is also required. However, it is not necessary, where revaluation gains or losses have been recognised as a result of a valuation at the year-end, to obtain further valuations at the date of the merger in order to apportion the gains or losses between pre- and post-merger periods. **81**

Group reconstructions that are accounted for by using merger accounting are exempted from the disclosure requirements in the FRS, but must still give the information required by companies legislation. **82**

Acquisitions

The disclosure requirements of the FRS provide information about the resources applied in acquisitions, the net assets acquired and the effects on the consolidated financial statements of the acquiring group. Separate presentation of the results of acquisitions assists analysis of the significance of new operations that have been acquired. In some circumstances it may also be useful to users for the results of acquisitions for the first full financial year for which they are a part of the reporting entity to be disclosed in the notes. **83**

Paragraph 23 of the FRS requires the disclosures in paragraphs 24–35 to be given for each material acquisition, and those in paragraphs 24–34 to be given for other acquisitions in aggregate. Materiality must be judged by whether the information relating to the acquisition might reasonably be expected to influence decisions made by the users of general purpose financial statements. Paragraph 36 applies further disclosure requirements to certain substantial acquisitions. **84**

In order to give a true and fair view of post-acquisition financial performance, **85** paragraph 30 of the FRS requires disclosure of exceptional profits or losses determined using fair values recognised on an acquisition. Examples include profits or losses on the disposal of acquired stocks where the fair values of stocks sold lead to abnormal trading margins after the acquisition; the release of provisions in respect of an acquired loss-making long-term contract that the acquirer makes profitable; and the realisation of contingent assets or liabilities at amounts materially different from their attributed fair values. In accordance with the requirements of FRS 3, exceptional items would be included in the profit and loss account format headings to which they relate, and would be disclosed by way of note, or on the face of the profit and loss account if necessary to give a true and fair view.

86 FRS 3 requires the profits or losses on the post-acquisition sale or termination of an operation, or on the disposal of fixed assets, to be shown in the profit and loss account below operating profit. Post-acquisition integration, reorganisation and restructuring costs, including provisions in respect of them, would, if material, be reported as exceptional items; but only if the restructuring is fundamental, having a material effect on the nature and focus of the enlarged group's operations, would the costs be shown below operating profit as an item falling under paragraph 20 of FRS 3. Paragraph 31 of FRS 6 requires that costs of reorganising, restructuring and integration that relate to an acquisition, whether relating to a fundamental restructuring or not, should be shown separately from other exceptional items.

87 The costs of reorganising, restructuring and integrating an acquired entity may extend over more than one period. For major acquisitions, therefore, management may wish to state in the notes to the financial statements the nature and amount of such costs expected to be incurred in relation to the acquisition (including asset write-downs), indicating the extent to which they have been charged to the profit and loss account. If part of these costs relate to asset write-downs (beyond any impairments recognised in adjusting to fair values on the acquisition) it may be useful to distinguish these from cash expenditure. An illustrative example of how such information might be shown is included as Appendix IV to the FRS.

Substantial acquisitions

88 Where an acquisition has been made that has a substantial effect on the consolidated results of the acquiring entity, additional disclosures are required to enable the user to assess the effect of the acquisition on the consolidated results. Although control over the acquired entity is obtained only at the date of acquisition, in most cases it is a continuing business that is acquired, and information on the results for the period up to the date of acquisition is relevant to the user. For acquisitions that meet the size tests in paragraph 37, the FRS therefore requires the disclosure of the results of the acquired entity for the part of its financial year up to the date of the acquisition, and for its previous financial year. Since neither of these periods will necessarily be twelve months, their commencing dates should also be indicated.

89 Several components of the pre-acquisition results are required to be shown for the part of the acquired entity's financial year up to the date of acquisition, since this period may be particularly relevant to an understanding of the post-acquisition results and may not otherwise be publicly reported. Equivalent information for the preceding financial year is likely to be of less relevance, and the disclosure requirement is limited to profit after tax and minority interests. The FRS requires this information to be given on the basis of the acquired entity's accounting policies before the acquisition; in some cases, the management of the acquiring entity may consider it helpful in explaining the impact of the acquisition to give, in addition, the same information restated onto the basis of the acquiring entity's accounting policies.

Adoption of FRS 6 by the board

Financial Reporting Standard 6 – 'Acquisitions and Mergers' was approved for issue by the eight members of the Accounting Standards Board.

Sir David Tweedie (Chairman)

Allan Cook (Technical Director)

Robert Bradfield

Ian Brindle

Michael Garner

Raymond Hinton

Donald Main

Graham Stacy

Appendix I
Note on legal requirements

GREAT BRITAIN

References are to the Companies Act 1985

Merger accounting

1 The Companies Act describes the acquisition method of accounting (Schedule 4A paragraph 9) and the merger method of accounting (Schedule 4A paragraph 11). Schedule 4A paragraph 10 lays down the conditions that must be met if a business combination is to be accounted for as a merger. The conditions are:

(a) that at least 90 per cent of the nominal value of the relevant shares (those with unrestricted rights to participate both in distributions and in the assets on liquidation) in the undertaking acquired is held by or on behalf of the parent company and its subsidiary undertakings;
(b) that the proportion referred to in (a) was attained pursuant to an arrangement providing for the issue of equity shares by the parent company or one or more of its subsidiary undertakings;
(c) that the fair value of any consideration other than the issue of equity shares given pursuant to the arrangement by the parent company and its subsidiary undertakings did not exceed 10 per cent of the nominal value of the equity shares issued; and
(d) that adoption of the merger method of accounting accords with generally accepted accounting principles or practice.

2 Where a group is acquired, the Companies Act requirements described in the previous paragraph also apply. References to shares of the undertaking acquired are to be construed as references to the shares of the acquired group's parent and references to the assets and liabilities, income and expenditure, and capital and reserves of the undertaking acquired are to be construed as references to the same elements of the group acquired, after making the necessary set-off and adjustments required for the consolidated accounts (Schedule 4A paragraph 12).

Disclosures

3 The following information shall be given in a note to the accounts for all business combinations taking place in the financial year:

(a) the names of the entities involved;
(b) whether the combination has been accounted for by the acquisition or merger method of accounting (Schedule 4A paragraph 13(2)).

4 In addition, for any business combination that significantly affects the figures shown in the group accounts, the following further information shall be given:

(a) the composition and fair value of the consideration for the acquisition given by the parent and its subsidiary undertakings (Schedule 4A paragraph 13(3));
(b) the profit or loss of the undertaking or group acquired for the period up to the date of the acquisition from the beginning of the financial year of that undertaking or group, and for the previous financial year of that undertaking or group. The date on which this financial year began should also be stated (Schedule 4A paragraph 13(4)).

Where the acquisition method of accounting has been adopted, the book values immediately prior to acquisition and fair values at the date of acquisition of each class of assets and liabilities of the acquired entity shall be stated in tabular form, including a statement of the amount of any goodwill or negative consolidation difference arising on the acquisition, together with an explanation of any significant adjustments made (Schedule 4A paragraph 13(5)). **5**

Where the merger method of accounting has been adopted, an explanation shall be given of any significant adjustments made in relation to the amounts of the assets and liabilities of the undertaking or group acquired, together with a statement of any resulting adjustment to the consolidated reserves (including the restatement of opening consolidated reserves) (Schedule 4A paragraph 13(6)). **6**

None of the information required by paragraph 13 of Schedule 4A to the Act need be disclosed for an undertaking which: **7**

(a) is established under the law of a country outside the United Kingdom; or
(b) carries on business outside the United Kingdom

if, in the opinion of the directors of the parent company, the disclosure would be seriously prejudicial to the business of that undertaking or to the business of the parent company or any of its subsidiary undertakings and the Secretary of State agrees that the information should not be disclosed (Schedule 4A paragraph 16).

Share premium and merger relief

Section 130(1) of the Companies Act provides that if a company issues shares at a premium, whether for cash or otherwise, a sum equal to the aggregate amount or value of the premiums on those shares should be transferred to an account called the share premium account. The provisions of the Companies Act relating to the reduction of a company's share capital apply, with exceptions, as if the share premium account were part of its paid-up share capital. **8**

Limited relief from the above ('merger relief') is given by sections 131–134. **9**

Section 131 of the Companies Act provides, inter alia, that, subject to specified conditions, where an issuing company has secured at least a 90 per cent equity holding in another company, section 130 does not apply to the premium on shares issued in the transaction which takes the holding in that other company to at least 90 per cent. **10**

Section 133(1) provides that the premium on any shares to which the relief in sections **11**

131 and 132 of the Companies Act applies may also be disregarded in determining the amount at which any shares, or other consideration provided for the shares issued, are to be included in the offeror company's balance sheet.

12 The Companies Act requires the disclosure of additional information where merger relief is taken. Schedule 5 paragraphs 10 and 29 refer respectively to companies that are not obliged to prepare group accounts and those that are. They apply to arrangements attracting merger relief, that is, where a company allots shares in consideration for the issue, transfer or cancellation of shares in another body corporate ('the other company') in circumstances such that section 131(2) (merger relief) applies to the premiums on the shares.

13 If the company makes such an arrangement during the financial year, the following information shall be given:

(a) the name of the other company;
(b) the number, nominal value and class of shares allotted;
(c) the number, nominal value and class of shares in the other company issued, transferred or cancelled; and
(d) particulars of the accounting treatment adopted in the consolidated accounts in respect of the issue, transfer or cancellation.

14 In addition, for companies that are required to prepare group accounts Schedule 5 paragraph 29(2) requires the disclosure of particulars of the extent to which and manner in which the profit or loss for the financial year shown in the consolidated accounts is affected by any profit or loss of the other company, or any of its subsidiary undertakings, that arose before the time of the arrangement.

Accounts of the parent company

15 The FRS deals only with the method of accounting to be used in group accounts; it does not deal with the form of accounting to be used in the acquiring or issuing company's own accounts and in particular does not restrict the reliefs available under sections 131–133 of the Companies Act.

16 Where a dividend is paid to the acquiring or issuing company out of pre-combination profits, it would appear that it need not necessarily be applied as a reduction in the carrying value of the investment in the subsidiary undertaking. Such a dividend received should be applied to reduce the carrying value of the investment to the extent necessary to provide for a diminution in value of the investment in the subsidiary undertaking as stated in the accounts of the parent company. To the extent that this is not necessary, it appears that the amount received will be a realised profit in the hands of the parent company.

NORTHERN IRELAND

17 The legal requirements in Northern Ireland are similar to those in Great Britain. The following table shows the references to the Companies (Northern Ireland) Order 1986 that correspond to the marginal references in the FRS and the legal references in paragraphs 1–16 above.

Great Britain: the Companies Act 1985	Northern Ireland: the 1986 Order
Merger accounting	
Schedule 4A paragraphs 9–12	Schedule 4A paragraphs 9–12
Disclosures	
Schedule 4A paragraph 13	Schedule 4A paragraph 13
Schedule 4A paragraph 16	Schedule 4A paragraph 16
Share premium and merger relief	
Sections 130–134	Articles 140–144
Schedule 5 paragraph 10	Schedule 5 paragraph 10
Schedule 5 paragraph 29	Schedule 5 paragraph 29

REPUBLIC OF IRELAND

The following table shows the references to the European Communities (Companies: Group Accounts) Regulations 1992 and the Companies Act 1963 that correspond to the marginal references in the FRS and the legal references in paragraphs 1–16 above. 18

Great Britain: the Companies Act 1985	Republic of Ireland: the 1992 Regulations
Merger accounting	
Schedule 4A paragraph 9	Paragraph 19
Schedule 4A paragraph 10	Paragraph 21
Schedule 4A paragraph 11	Paragraph 22
Schedule 4A paragraph 12	Paragraph 23

Disclosures

Schedule 4A paragraph 13(2)	The Schedule paragraph 12(2)
Schedule 4A paragraph 13(3)-13(6)	No exact equivalent; paragraph 27 of the 1992 Regulations states that if the composition of the undertakings dealt with in the group accounts has changed significantly in the course of a financial year, the group accounts must include information that makes the comparison of successive sets of group accounts meaningful.
Schedule 4A paragraph 16	No equivalent

Share premium and merger relief

Section 130	Companies Act 1963 section 62
Sections 131–134	No equivalent
Schedule 5 paragraph 10	No equivalent
Schedule 5 paragraph 29	No equivalent

Merger relief in the Republic of Ireland

19 As there is currently no legislation equivalent to merger relief in the Republic of Ireland, no explicit relief from the requirement of section 69(1) of the Companies Act 1963 to establish a share premium account is available.

20 However, section 149(5) of the Companies Act 1963 provides that, whilst, in general, pre-acquisition profits of acquired subsidiaries may not be treated in the holding company's accounts as revenue profit, an exemption from that provision is available in that, where the directors and auditors are satisfied and so certify that it would be fair and reasonable and would not prejudice the rights and interests of any person, the profits or losses attributable to any shares in a subsidiary may be treated in a manner otherwise than in accordance with that subsection.

21 The possible need for legal advice in relation to the application of section 149(5) to merger accounting should be considered before merger accounting is applied to Republic of Ireland companies.

Appendix II
Compliance with International Accounting Standards

The requirements of the FRS are consistent with International Accounting Standard 22 'Business Combinations' (revised 1993), except for the provision in paragraph 13 of that standard relating to reverse acquisitions, which is incompatible with companies legislation in the UK and the Republic of Ireland.

Appendix III
The development of the FRS

HISTORY

Before the Companies Act 1981

1 Although some use was made of merger accounting in the UK before the Companies Act 1981, and indeed an exposure draft of an accounting standard, ED 3, was published (in 1971), there was concern that the share premium provisions of the Companies Act 1948 might be interpreted so as to prohibit the use of merger accounting. This view was confirmed by the decision in *Shearer v Bercain* in 1980.

The Companies Act 1981 and SSAP 23

2 The Companies Act 1981 introduced the concept of merger relief, removing the legal obstacle to merger accounting. Following this, the Accounting Standards Committee (ASC) issued an exposure draft, ED 31, converted into an accounting standard, SSAP 23 'Accounting for acquisitions and mergers', in 1985.

3 SSAP 23 based its concept of a merger on whether or not the arrangements for the combination resulted in material resources leaving the group. This concept was supported by four criteria defining the circumstances in which merger accounting was permitted:

(a) the business combination results from an offer to the holders of all equity shares and the holders of all voting shares that are not already held by the offeror; and
(b) the offeror has secured, as a result of the offer, a holding of (i) at least 90 per cent of all equity shares (taking each class of equity separately) and (ii) the shares carrying at least 90 per cent of the votes of the offeree; and
(c) immediately prior to the offer, the offeror does not hold (i) 20 per cent or more of all equity shares of the offeree (taking each class of equity separately) or (ii) shares carrying 20 per cent or more of the votes of the offeree; and
(d) not less than 90 per cent of the fair value of the total consideration given for the equity share capital (including that given for shares already held) is in the form of equity share capital; not less than 90 per cent of the fair value of the total consideration given for voting non-equity share capital (including that given for shares already held) is in the form of equity and/or voting non-equity share capital.

4 Note, however, that merger accounting remained optional even if these criteria were met.

The EC Seventh Directive and the Companies Act 1989

5 The EC Seventh Company Law Directive introduced more stringent requirements to be met before merger accounting was permitted. The conditions of the Directive were

implemented in Great Britain, with some additional provisions, by the Companies Act 1989, as amendments to the Companies Act 1985. These conditions are:

(a) that at least 90 per cent of the nominal value of the relevant shares (those with unrestricted rights to participate both in distributions and in the assets on liquidation) in the undertaking acquired is held by or on behalf of the parent company and its subsidiary undertakings;
(b) that the proportion referred to in (a) was attained pursuant to an arrangement providing for the issue of equity shares by the parent company or one or more of its subsidiary undertakings;
(c) that the fair value of any consideration other than the issue of equity shares given pursuant to the arrangement by the parent company and its subsidiary undertakings did not exceed 10 per cent of the nominal value of the equity shares issued; and
(d) that adoption of the merger method of accounting accords with generally accepted accounting principles or practice.

In requiring compliance with generally accepted accounting principles, the Companies Act clearly acknowledged that merger accounting would not be appropriate for all business combinations that met the first three conditions. **6**

The comparison, in condition (c), with the nominal value of shares issued is also noteworthy. The nominal value is of no economic significance. In contrast, the corresponding condition (d) of SSAP 23 refers to the fair value of the equity shares issued. **7**

Limiting the use of merger accounting – the ED 48 proposals

ED 48 was issued by the ASC in February 1990 in response to widespread concern that the SSAP 23 conditions were too readily circumvented. It proposed to limit the use of merger accounting to a very restricted class of combinations that could be regarded as 'true' mergers. These were to be defined as a combination that was effectively an equal partnership between the combining parties, where no party saw itself as either an acquirer or an acquiree. In addition, there had to be continuing involvement from the management of each of the parties in the combined entity; and the parties were to be of broadly equal size. Any minority not accepting the merger offer was not to exceed 10 per cent, and no material consideration other than equity shares was permitted. **8**

ED 48 then proposed that merger accounting would be required, and not merely permitted, for all combinations meeting these conditions (although, as a practical matter, it has been suggested that it would be relatively easy for merging parties to ensure that one of the conditions was not met, without fundamentally altering the commercial substance of the transaction, if they did not wish to use merger accounting and thus for practical purposes the option to use acquisition accounting might be seen to remain). **9**

Although respondents to ED 48 were generally in agreement with its proposals, there was criticism of the conditions for merger accounting, in particular of their subjective **10** nature, which, it was expected, would give rise to difficulties in applying them consistently.

International Accounting Standards

11 The merger concept underlying ED 48 is similar to that proposed for a 'uniting of interests' in the International Accounting Standard 22, revised in 1993, although that standard does not develop tests for identifying when a combination is a merger. IAS 22 defines a uniting of interests as:

> 'a business combination in which the shareholders of the combining enterprises combine control over the whole, or effectively the whole, of their net assets and operations to achieve a continuing mutual sharing in the risks and benefits attaching to the combined entity such that neither party can be identified as the acquirer.'

FRED 6

12 In considering the application of merger accounting, the Board was concerned by the apparent choice available in many cases between acquisition and merger accounting, and that two business combinations with very similar economic substance could be accounted for in different ways, with substantial differences in reported results and balance sheets not only for the financial year in which the combination occurred but for several years thereafter. The Board also found it difficult to identify any theoretical basis to justify the use of merger accounting for the wide range of business combinations for which it was then permissible.

13 In issuing FRED 6, the Board therefore adopted the intention of ED 48, of narrowing the use of merger accounting.

14 No major changes were proposed, but the Board sought to remove subjectivity where possible. The approach of the FRED was based on the belief that merger accounting should be applied to only a few rare instances of business combinations that were properly regarded as mergers, and that the vast majority of business combinations were more appropriately accounted for as acquisitions.

15 The definition of a merger was redrafted, but its intent was unchanged. The definition of an acquisition was amended to make it clear that all combinations were either mergers or acquisitions.

16 The six conditions under which merger accounting would have been permitted by ED 48 were redrafted as five criteria, as follows:

Criterion 1 – redrafted form of ED 48 condition (a).

Criterion 2 – amended form of ED 48 condition (b), acknowledging that to require the board of a merged entity to have equal participation from each of the parties to the merger might prevent the parties to the merger from choosing the management they considered most appropriate; and might lead to too much focus on the numerical representation of each party on the new board at the expense of considering where the real decision taking influence lay.

Criterion 3 – redrafted form of ED 48 condition (e).

Criterion 4 – redrafted form of ED 48 condition (c).

Criterion 5 – redrafted form of ED 48 conditions (d) and (f), reducing these to a more general principle.

Disclosure

The disclosure requirements proposed by ED 48 were extended to require analysis into pre-combination and post-combination periods of several items in the profit and loss account, and the statement of total recognised gains and losses, rather than focusing solely on profit after tax and extraordinary items. **17**

MATTERS CONSIDERED IN THE LIGHT OF RESPONSES TO FRED 6

A large majority of the respondents to FRED 6 agreed with the proposals it contained, and these are accordingly unchanged. The following paragraphs describe those points on which respondents expressed concern and explain whether or not a change was made and the Board's reasoning for its decision. **18**

Disclosure requirements on an acquisition

The full disclosure requirements proposed in the FRED relating to the pre-combination results of the parties to a merger, and the acquired entity in an acquisition, were supported by a majority of respondents, and particularly by users of accounts. Concern was expressed, however, at the practical difficulties in obtaining this information relating to acquisitions, and many preparers of financial statements questioned whether such disclosures were, in practice, of value to users. **19**

The Board has therefore reconsidered the extent of the disclosures required in respect of the acquired company, and has made three main relaxations in the requirements: **20**

(a) less detailed analysis of the results of the acquired company up to the date of acquisition is now required;
(b) only the profit after tax and minority interests for its previous financial year is now required to be shown; and
(c) fuller disclosure is now required only for substantial acquisitions, defined as being 'Class 1' or 'Super Class 1' where the acquirer is a listed company, or in excess of 15 per cent of net assets or profits for others.

The FRS now states that this information is to be given using the accounting policies of the acquired company, instead of being restated using the acquirer's accounting policies.

Some respondents suggested that it would be more helpful for all disclosure **21** requirements relating to acquisitions to be consolidated into one standard. The Board has accordingly included in this FRS the proposed disclosure requirements set out in FRED 7 (which were based on those in SSAP 22), amended to take account of responses made to that FRED. It has also incorporated references to the disclosure requirements relating to acquisitions in FRS 1 and FRS 3, unchanged other than to make it clear that the disclosures should be made separately for each material acquisition, and for other acquisitions in aggregate.

Disclosure requirements on a merger

22 The Board concluded that, in the case of a merger, no relaxation of the proposed disclosures was appropriate. Because of the continuing involvement of management of both parties to the merger, the practical difficulties would be less, and the likely significance of the merger to the shareholders would make it desirable to provide fuller information. Although it was argued that analysing pre-merger results among the parties was in some sense contrary to the concept of merger accounting, in that the financial statements were drawn up on the basis that the parties had always been merged, the Board took the view that full information on the combining parties separately was important to an understanding of the combined entity.

Definitions and criteria for merger accounting

23 The definitions of mergers and acquisitions, and the criteria for merger accounting, were generally agreed as appropriate by respondents, and only minor drafting changes have been made. Criterion 4 has been amended to make clear the effect of an entity disposing of part of its business prior to the combination.

Group reconstructions

24 There was general agreement with the proposed use of merger accounting in group reconstructions, but some respondents requested that this should be more widely available. The Board has therefore agreed to widen the definition of group reconstructions, provided minority rights are unaffected, to include situations where a new holding company is created; where a 'horizontal group' of companies under common ownership become a group under the companies legislation definition; and where a part of a group is transferred to a new company, not part of the group but owned by the same shareholders as the group.

Merger expenses

25 The FRED proposed that merger expenses should be charged to the profit and loss account. Although a majority of respondents supported this proposal, there was significant support for deducting such costs from reserves, in a way similar to the costs of issuing an equity instrument under FRS 4. The Board believes, however, that there is a fundamental difference between the costs of issue of an equity instrument, which raises new capital, from which the costs may sensibly be deducted, and the costs of a merger, which does not raise new capital, but which requires an expenditure of

resources that should therefore be charged to the profit and loss account. The Board has clarified that these costs should be shown as an exceptional item in accordance with paragraph 20 of FRS 3.

Demergers

Several respondents suggested that the FRS should deal with the accounting issues arising on demergers as well. However, the Board took the view that such issues as arise on a demerger are unrelated to those of business combinations, and should not be dealt with in the same FRS (although the restructuring that takes place on a demerger may fall within the group restructuring provisions of this FRS). **26**

Alternative view – prohibiting the use of merger accounting

The Preface to the FRED set out an alternative view, that the use of merger accounting should be prohibited (other than for certain group reconstructions). This alternative view attracted little support; most commentators thought that mergers, although rare, were a separate class of business combination for which merger accounting should be available. The Board has, accordingly, not proceeded with that proposal. **27**

Appendix IV
Illustrative example of disclosure of reorganisation and integration costs

This example is provided as an aid to understanding and does not form part of the Financial Reporting Standard.

Paragraph 87 of the Explanation suggests that, for major acquisitions, management may wish to include in the notes to the financial statements the amount of reorganisation and other costs to be incurred in relation to the acquisition. The following example indicates one way in which this optional information might be presented. The best form of the disclosure will depend on individual circumstances.

COSTS OF REORGANISING AND INTEGRATING ACQUISITIONS

	Acquisition of European business (note (a))	Other acquisitions	TOTAL
	£ million	£ million	£ million
Announced but not charged as at the previous year-end	–	25	25
Announced in relation to acquisitions during the year	170	–	170
Adjustments to previous years' estimates	–	(5)	(5)
	170	20	190
Charged in the year			
– operating profit	55	12	67
– elsewhere	65	–	65
	120	12	132
Announced but still to be charged at 31 December 1995	50	8	58

Note (a): Acquisition of European business

		£ million
Cost of acquisition		400
Reorganisation and integration expenditure announced		
Fundamental restructuring:		
– withdrawal from existing US business and related redundancies	65	
Other items (to be charged to operating profit):		
– other redundancy costs	75	
– re-branding and redesign costs	30	
Announced reorganisation and integration costs as shown in above table		170
Total investment		570

In addition to the £120 million expenditure shown in the above table, reorganisation and integration costs charged during the year include £30 million in respect of write-downs to fixed assets consequent on the closure of the XYZ plant.

Financial Reporting Standard 7 is set out in paragraphs 1–31.

The Statement of Standard Accounting Practice set out in paragraphs 4–31 should be read in the context of the Objective as stated in paragraph 1 and the definitions set out in paragraphs 2–3 and also of the Foreword to Accounting Standards and the Statement of Principles for Financial Reporting currently in issue.

The Explanation set out in paragraphs 32–85 shall be regarded as part of the Statement of Standard Accounting Practice insofar as it assists in interpreting that statement.

Appendix III 'The development of the FRS' reviews considerations and arguments that were thought significant by members of the Board in reaching the conclusions on FRS 7. The views of the member who dissented are set out in Appendix IV.

[FRS7]
Fair values in acquisition accounting

(Issued September 1994)

Contents

Fair values in acquisition accounting

Summary

GENERAL

a Financial Reporting Standard 7 'Fair Values in Acquisition Accounting' sets out the principles of accounting for a business combination under the acquisition method of accounting. Companies legislation requires the identifiable assets and liabilities of the acquired entity to be included in the consolidated financial statements of the acquirer at their fair values at the date of acquisition. The difference between these and the cost of acquisition is recognised as goodwill or negative goodwill. The results of the acquired entity are included in the profit and loss account of the acquiring group from the date of acquisition.

FAIR VALUES OF IDENTIFIABLE ASSETS AND LIABILITIES

b The assets and liabilities recognised in the allocation of fair values should be those of the acquired entity that existed at the date of acquisition. They should be measured at fair values that reflect the conditions at the date of the acquisition.

c The liabilities of the acquired entity should not include provisions for future operating losses. Changes in the assets and liabilities resulting from the acquirer's intentions or from events after the acquisition should be dealt with as post-acquisition items. Similarly, costs of reorganisation and integrating the business acquired, whether they relate to the acquired entity or the acquiring group, should be dealt with as post-acquisition costs and do not affect the fair values at the date of acquisition.

d Fair values should be based on the value at which an asset or liability could be exchanged in an arm's length transaction. The fair value of monetary items should take into account the amounts expected to be received or paid and their timing.

e Unless they can be measured at market value, the fair values of non-monetary assets will normally be based on replacement cost, but should not exceed their recoverable amount as at the date of acquisition. The recoverable amount reflects the condition of the assets on acquisition but not any impairments resulting from subsequent events. The FRS specifies the methods for determining fair values of individual categories of assets and liabilities.

INVESTIGATION PERIOD AND GOODWILL ADJUSTMENTS

f The identification and valuation of assets and liabilities acquired should be completed, if possible, by the date on which the first post-acquisition financial statements of the acquirer are approved by the directors. If it has not been possible to complete the investigation of fair values by that date, provisional valuations should be made; these should be amended if necessary in the next financial statements with a corresponding adjustment to goodwill.

COST OF ACQUISITION

g The cost of acquisition is the amount of cash or cash equivalents paid and the fair value of other purchase consideration given by the acquirer, together with the expenses of the acquisition. The FRS explains the methods used to determine the amounts to be ascribed to constituent parts of the purchase consideration.

h Where the payment of consideration for an acquisition is to be made after the date of acquisition, reasonable estimates of the amounts expected to be paid should be included in the cost of acquisition at their present values.

Financial Reporting Standard 7

OBJECTIVE

1 The objective of this FRS is to ensure that when a business entity is acquired by another, all the assets and liabilities that existed in the acquired entity at the date of acquisition are recorded at fair values reflecting their condition at that date; and that all changes to the acquired assets and liabilities, and the resulting gains and losses, that arise after control of the acquired entity has passed to the acquirer are reported as part of the post-acquisition financial performance of the acquiring group.

DEFINITIONS

2 The following definitions shall apply in this FRS and in particular in the Statement of Standard Accounting Practice set out in paragraphs 4–31.

Acquisition:

A business combination that is accounted for by using the acquisition method of accounting.

Business combination:

The bringing together of separate entities into one economic entity as a result of one entity uniting with, or obtaining control over the net assets and operations of, another.

Date of acquisition:

The date on which control of the acquired entity passes to the acquirer. This is the date from which the acquired entity is accounted for by the acquirer as a subsidiary undertaking under FRS 2 'Accounting for Subsidiary Undertakings'.

Fair value:

The amount at which an asset or liability could be exchanged in an arm's length transaction between informed and willing parties, other than in a forced or liquidation sale.

Identifiable assets and liabilities:

The assets and liabilities of the acquired entity that are capable of being disposed of or settled separately, without disposing of a business of the entity.

Recoverable amount:

The greater of the net realisable value of an asset and, where appropriate, the value in use.

Value in use:

The present value of the future cash flows obtainable as a result of an asset's continued use, including those resulting from the ultimate disposal of the asset.

References to companies legislation mean: **3**

(a) in Great Britain, the Companies Act 1985;
(b) in Northern Ireland, the Companies (Northern Ireland) Order 1986; and
(c) in the Republic of Ireland, the Companies Acts 1963–90 and the European Communities (Companies: Group Accounts) Regulations 1992.

Statement of Standard Accounting Practice

SCOPE

Financial Reporting Standard 7 applies to all financial statements that are intended to give a true and fair view of a reporting entity's financial position and profit or loss (or income and expenditure) for a period. Although the FRS is framed in terms of the acquisition of a subsidiary undertaking by a parent company that prepares consolidated financial statements, it also applies where an individual company or other reporting entity acquires a business other than a subsidiary undertaking. **4**

DETERMINING THE FAIR VALUES OF IDENTIFIABLE ASSETS AND LIABILITIES ACQUIRED

Principles of recognition and measurement on an acquisition

The identifiable assets and liabilities to be recognised should be those of the acquired entity that existed at the date of the acquisition. **5**

The recognised assets and liabilities should be measured at fair values that reflect the conditions at the date of the acquisition. **6**

Application of the principles

As a consequence of the above principles, the following do not affect fair values at the date of acquisition and therefore fall to be treated as post-acquisition items: **7**

(a) changes resulting from the acquirer's intentions or future actions;
(b) impairments, or other changes, resulting from events subsequent to the acquisition;

(c) provisions or accruals for future operating losses or for reorganisation and integration costs expected to be incurred as a result of the acquisition, whether they relate to the acquired entity or to the acquirer.

8 The application of these principles to specific classes of asset and liability is detailed in paragraphs 9–22 below. Subject to those paragraphs, fair values should be determined in accordance with the acquirer's accounting policies for similar assets and liabilities.

Tangible fixed assets

9 The fair value of a tangible fixed asset should be based on:

(a) market value, if assets similar in type and condition are bought and sold on an open market; or
(b) depreciated replacement cost, reflecting the acquired business's normal buying process and the sources of supply and prices available to it.

The fair value should not exceed the recoverable amount of the asset.

Intangible assets

10 Where an intangible asset is recognised, its fair value should be based on its replacement cost, which is normally its estimated market value.

Stocks and work-in-progress

11 Stocks, including commodity stocks, that the acquired entity trades on a market in which it participates as both a buyer and a seller should be valued at current market prices.

12 Other stocks, and work-in-progress, should be valued at the lower of replacement cost and net realisable value. Replacement cost is for this purpose the cost at which the stocks would have been replaced by the acquired entity, reflecting its normal buying process and the sources of supply and prices available to it – that is, the current cost of bringing the stocks to their present location and condition.

Quoted investments

13 Quoted investments should be valued at market price, adjusted if necessary for unusual price fluctuations or for the size of the holding.

Monetary assets and liabilities

14 The fair value of monetary assets and liabilities, including accruals and provisions, should take into account the amounts expected to be received or paid and their timing.

Fair value should be determined by reference to market prices, where available, by reference to the current price at which the business could acquire similar assets or enter into similar obligations, or by discounting to present value.

Contingencies

Contingent assets and liabilities should be measured at fair values where these can be determined. For this purpose reasonable estimates of the expected outcome may be used. **15**

Business sold or held exclusively with a view to subsequent resale

Where an interest in a separate business of the acquired entity is sold as a single unit within approximately one year of the date of acquisition, the investment in that business should be treated as a single asset for the purposes of determining fair values. Its fair value should be based on the net proceeds of the sale, adjusted for the fair value of any assets or liabilities transferred into or out of the business, unless such adjusted net proceeds are demonstrably different from the fair value at the date of acquisition as a result of a post-acquisition event. This treatment should be applied to any business operation, whether a separate subsidiary undertaking or not, provided that its assets, liabilities, results of operations and activities are clearly distinguishable, physically, operationally and for financial reporting purposes, from the other assets, liabilities, results of operations and activities of the acquired entity. **16**

Where the business has not been sold by the time of approval of the first financial statements after the date of acquisition, the fair value of the interest in the business should be based on the estimated net proceeds of the sale, provided: **17**

(a) a purchaser has been identified or is being sought; and
(b) the disposal is reasonably expected to occur within approximately one year of the date of the acquisition.

The interest in the business or, if it is not a separate subsidiary undertaking, in the assets of the business, should be shown within current assets. When the sale price is subsequently determined, the original estimate of fair value should be adjusted to reflect the actual sale proceeds.

If the subsidiary undertaking or business operation is not, in fact, sold within approximately one year of the acquisition, it should be consolidated normally with fair values attributed to the individual assets and liabilities as at the date of acquisition, and corresponding adjustments to goodwill. **18**

Pensions and other post-retirement benefits

The fair value of a deficiency or, to the extent that it is reasonably expected to be realised, a surplus in a funded pension or other post-retirement benefits scheme, or accrued obligations in an unfunded scheme, should be recognised as a liability or an asset of the acquiring group. **19**

Changes in pension or other post-retirement arrangements following an acquisition **20** should be accounted for as post-acquisition items and should be dealt with in accordance with the requirements of the standard concerned with pension costs.

Deferred taxation

21 Deferred tax assets and liabilities recognised in the fair value exercise should be determined by considering the enlarged group as a whole.

22 The benefit to the group of any tax losses attributable to an acquired entity at the date of acquisition should be recognised in accordance with the requirements of the standard concerned with deferred tax.

Investigation period and goodwill adjustments

23 The recognition and measurement of assets and liabilities acquired should be completed, if possible, by the date on which the first post-acquisition financial statements of the acquirer are approved by the directors.

24 If it has not been possible to complete the investigation for determining fair values by the date on which the first post-acquisition financial statements are approved, provisional valuations should be made; these should be amended, if necessary, in the next financial statements with a corresponding adjustment to goodwill.

25 Any necessary adjustments to those provisional fair values and the corresponding adjustment to purchased goodwill should be incorporated in the financial statements for the first full financial year following the acquisition. Thereafter, any adjustments, except for the correction of fundamental errors, which should be accounted for as prior period adjustments, should be recognised as profits or losses when they are identified.

DETERMINING THE COST OF ACQUISITION

26 The cost of acquisition is the amount of cash paid and the fair value of other purchase consideration given by the acquirer, together with the expenses of the acquisition as described in paragraph 28. Where a subsidiary undertaking is acquired in stages, the cost of acquisition is the total of the costs of the interests acquired, determined as at the date of each transaction.

27 Where the amount of purchase consideration is contingent on one or more future events, the cost of acquisition should include a reasonable estimate of the fair value of amounts expected to be payable in the future. The cost of acquisition should be adjusted when revised estimates are made, with consequential corresponding adjustments continuing to be made to goodwill until the ultimate amount is known.

28 Fees and similar incremental costs incurred directly in making an acquisition should, except for the issue costs of shares or other securities that are required by FRS 4 'Capital Instruments' to be accounted for as a reduction in the proceeds of a capital instrument, be included in the cost of acquisition. Internal costs, and other expenses that cannot be directly attributed to the acquisition, should be charged to the profit and loss account.

DISCLOSURES

The disclosures that should be made relating to an acquisition are set out in paragraphs 21 and 23–37 of FRS 6 'Acquisitions and Mergers'. 29

DATE FROM WHICH EFFECTIVE

The accounting practices set out in the FRS should be regarded as standard in respect of business combinations first accounted for in financial statements relating to accounting periods commencing on or after 23 December 1994. Earlier adoption is encouraged but not required. 30

AMENDMENT OF SSAP 22

The FRS supersedes paragraphs 14, 23, 27, 30 and 33 of SSAP 22 'Accounting for goodwill'. 31

The following preamble is inserted in SSAP 22 before the Explanatory note:

"FRS 7 'Fair Values in Acquisition Accounting', published September 1994, supersedes paragraphs 14, 23, 27, 30 and 33 of this standard. Following publication of FRS 7, SSAP 22 is to be interpreted in the light of FRS 7; references to 'separable net assets' should be interpreted as 'identifiable assets and liabilities'.

FRS 6 'Acquisitions and Mergers', published September 1994, supersedes disclosure paragraphs 48–51; amended disclosure requirements are included in FRS 6."

Explanation

INTRODUCTION

The FRS is consistent with the requirements of companies legislation regarding the acquisition method of accounting. It sets out principles for identifying the assets and liabilities of an acquired entity and determining their fair values, and for determining the cost of acquisition. 32

Under the acquisition method of accounting, the identifiable assets and liabilities acquired are recognised at their fair values as at the date of acquisition, and the difference between these and the cost of acquisition is accounted for as goodwill or negative goodwill. 33

DETERMINING THE FAIR VALUES OF IDENTIFIABLE ASSETS AND LIABILITIES ACQUIRED

Existing assets and liabilities of the acquired entity

The identifiable assets and liabilities over which the acquirer obtains control are those representing rights to future economic benefits and obligations to transfer economic 34 benefits, including contingent rights and obligations, of the acquired entity that were in existence before the date of acquisition.

35 The identifiable assets and liabilities may include items that were not previously recognised in the financial statements of the acquired entity. These include assets and liabilities that are not normally recognised in accounts where no acquisition is involved, because other accounting standards preclude their immediate recognition. Examples are:

(a) pension surpluses or deficiencies identified on an acquisition that are otherwise recognised over several financial years in an entity's financial statements, in accordance with the requirements of SSAP 24 'Accounting for pension costs';
(b) contingent assets that may be assigned a value on acquisition, but cannot otherwise be recognised in financial statements because SSAP 18 'Accounting for contingencies' precludes the recognition of a contingent gain until realisation becomes reasonably certain.

36 The examples given above are included in the identifiable assets and liabilities because when an acquisition is made it is necessary to identify and recognise, so far as possible, all assets and liabilities acquired, provided they can be reliably valued. If this is not done, the reporting of post-acquisition performance is distorted by changes in assets and liabilities not being recognised in the correct period. The usual accounting practice, for example, of deferring recognition of contingent assets, does not apply, because the recognition of an acquired asset represents the expectation that the amounts expended on its acquisition will be recovered; it does not anticipate a future gain. It is, however, necessary to review the recoverable amounts of such assets to ensure that provision is made for any probable losses.

37 Certain contingent assets and liabilities that crystallise as a result of the acquisition would also be recognised, provided that the underlying contingency was in existence before the acquisition. An example is where the acquired entity has previously entered into a contract that contains a clause under which obligations are triggered in the event of a change of ownership.

38 Identifiable liabilities include items such as onerous contracts and commitments that existed at the time of acquisition, whether or not the corresponding obligations were recognised as liabilities in the financial statements of the acquired entity. When an acquisition is made, provisions for liabilities would be recognised as identifiable liabilities only if such commitments had been made by the acquired entity before the date of acquisition. In the case of business closure decisions made by the acquired entity before the date of acquisition, the principles for recognising consequential provisions are set out in FRS 3 'Reporting Financial Performance', which states that obligations are incurred when there is a detailed formal plan for termination from which the entity cannot realistically withdraw*.

**FRS 3, paragraph 18.*

Exclusion of post-acquisition costs

The FRS does not permit provisions for future losses or for reorganisation costs expected to be incurred as a result of the acquisition to be included as liabilities acquired: they are not liabilities of the acquired entity as at the date of acquisition. As an example, if the acquirer decides to close a factory of the acquired entity as a measure to integrate the combined operations, this is a post-acquisition event. Only if the acquired entity was already committed to this course of action, and unable realistically to withdraw from it, would it be regarded as pre-acquisition. Similarly, if the acquirer undertakes a reorganisation to integrate the acquired operation or to improve its efficiency, this is also a post-acquisition event. **39**

Where provisions for future costs were made by an acquired entity shortly before an acquisition took place, for example during the course of negotiations with the acquirer, it would be necessary to pay particular attention to the circumstances in order to determine whether obligations were incurred by the acquired entity before the acquisition. Only if the acquired entity was demonstrably committed to the expenditure whether or not the acquisition was completed would it have a liability at the date of acquisition. If obligations were incurred by the acquired entity as a result of the influence of the acquirer, it would be necessary to consider whether control of the acquired entity had been transferred at an earlier date and, consequently, whether the date of acquisition under the requirements of FRS 2 'Accounting for Subsidiary Undertakings' pre-dated such commitments*. Under paragraph 26 of FRS 6 'Acquisitions and Mergers', disclosure is required of provisions made by the acquired entity within the twelve months preceding the date of acquisition. **40**

Measurement of identifiable assets and liabilities

Most acquisitions are not made on the basis of individual transactions in assets and liabilities. The acquisition transaction does not itself determine the values attributed to each asset and liability acquired and for this reason companies legislation and accounting standards require a fair value exercise to determine initial carrying amounts of assets and liabilities on an acquisition. **41**

Although the FRS contains specific requirements for determining fair values of different classes of assets and liabilities, the concept of fair value underlying the specific rules is the value at which the asset, or liability, could be exchanged in an arm's length transaction between informed and willing parties. **42**

Where similar assets are bought and sold on a readily accessible market, the market price will represent the fair value. Where quoted market prices are not available, market prices can often be estimated, either by independent valuations, or valuation **43**

**Under paragraph 45 of FRS 2 the date of acquisition may be indicated by the acquiring entity commencing its direction of the operating and financial policies of the acquired undertaking or by changes in the flow of economic benefits.*

techniques such as discounting estimated future cash flows to their present values. In some cases, where quoted market prices are not available, subsequent sales of acquired assets may provide the most reliable evidence of fair value at the time of the acquisition.

44 Where a fair value is based on a market price, it is important to ensure that such price is appropriate to the circumstances of the acquired business. For example, it may be possible to obtain a price for secondhand plant and machinery of the type used in the business, but the secondhand market may deal in very small volumes; or the items may not be identical in terms of the ability to obtain maintenance or technical support from the manufacturer or for the machinery to be customised to the requirements of the business. In general, unless the acquired business is genuinely able to consider the purchase of secondhand equipment as a viable alternative to purchasing direct from the manufacturer, the fair value of plant and machinery is more appropriately determined from the replacement cost of an equivalent new asset, depreciated where appropriate to reflect its age and condition.

45 The fair value attributed to an asset should not exceed the value the business is able to recover from the asset, either from its disposal or, in the case of a fixed asset, by continuing to use the asset. Where the fair value is based on a market price, the net realisable value will be similar to the fair value, differing only by costs of realisation and the dealer's margin. However, where the fair value is based on depreciated replacement cost or cost of manufacture, the net realisable value and, in the case of a fixed asset, the value in use will also need to be considered.

46 Both net realisable value and value in use at the time of the acquisition are unaffected by the acquirer's intentions for the future use of the asset. Net realisable value represents the amount for which the business would be able to sell the asset, whether or not such sale is intended. Similarly, the value in use of a fixed asset at the time of the acquisition depends, not on the intended use, but on the most profitable possible use of the asset.

Impaired assets

47 Where the replacement cost of an acquired asset is not recoverable in full (owing, for example, to lack of profitability, under-utilisation or obsolescence), the fair value is the estimated recoverable amount. The FRS requires that a valuation at recoverable amount should reflect the condition of the asset on acquisition but not any impairments resulting from subsequent events.

48 Where acquired assets that had not been impaired before acquisition are disposed of after acquisition for a reduced price (for example, as part of a post-acquisition reorganisation of the enlarged group), any losses resulting from their disposal would be treated as post-acquisition losses, ie attributed to the reorganisation, and would not reduce the fair values as at the date of acquisition.

49 In some cases recoverable amount can be determined only by considering as a whole a group of assets that are used jointly, rather than by attempting to determine the recoverable amount of each identifiable asset in that group. Aggregation in such cases serves to facilitate the attribution of cash flows to the assets that help to generate them.

Tangible fixed assets

Where reliable market values are obtainable – for example, for quoted investments and certain types of property – fair value would be based on current market values of similar assets. As explained in paragraph 44 above, for many types of fixed asset – for example most plant and machinery, and specialised properties specific to the business – fair value is represented by gross replacement cost reduced by depreciation to take account of the age and condition of the asset. Depreciation rates need to reflect estimated asset lives and residual amounts used by the acquirer for similar types of asset; otherwise, without there being any change in the asset's use or intended use, the first post-acquisition profit and loss account would reflect the adjustment from the previous management's depreciation rate to the acquirer's depreciation rate. **50**

For certain assets it is not easy to determine current replacement cost; neither is it possible to estimate the value of the future services that an asset can provide through its continued use, because of the inherent subjectivity of such a valuation. In such circumstances the historical cost of the asset updated by the use of price indices may be the most reliable means of estimating replacement cost. Where prices have not changed materially it would be acceptable to use a carrying value based on historical cost as a reasonable proxy for fair value. **51**

Stocks and work-in-progress

Where stocks are replaced by purchasing in a ready market – for example, commodities and dealing stocks – to which the acquired entity has access, fair value is represented by market value. Where there is no ready market for a category of stocks – for example, most manufactured stocks – fair value is represented by the current cost to the acquired company of reproducing the stocks. **52**

The FRS requires account to be taken of the way the acquired business purchased or manufactured the stocks. For example, for a business purchasing in wholesale markets the replacement cost would be the wholesale price; and the replacement cost of finished goods of a manufacturer will be the current cost of manufacture, not the cost of buying in finished goods from another manufacturer. Although this replacement cost takes account of the effects of input price changes during the period the stocks are held, no addition would be made for unrealised profit that would not normally be recognised in the acquired entity until the stocks are sold. **53**

The current cost of manufacture for finished goods and work-in-progress would be based on current standard costs where these are employed. In practice, where there is a short manufacturing cycle, replacement cost may not be materially different from historical cost. **54**

For long-term, maturing stocks, replacement cost would be based on market values if stocks at similar stages of completion are regularly traded in the market. In other cases, **55** where such market transactions do not occur because either there is no market or the market is very thin, and where it is difficult to find replacement cost because replacement would be impossible in the short term, a surrogate for replacement cost may be found in the historical cost of bringing the stocks to their present location and condition, including an amount representing an interest cost in respect of holding the stock.

56 For long-term contracts, SSAP 9 'Stocks and long-term contracts' requires turnover and cost of sales to be recognised as the contract progresses, and attributable profit to be recognised prudently as it is earned. For this reason, no adjustments to book values would be required to such contracts, other than adjustments that would normally result from assessing the outcome of the contract under SSAP 9, or reflecting the changeover to the acquirer's accounting policies.

57 In estimating the net realisable value of stocks, an acquirer may reach a judgement about the value of slow-moving or redundant stocks that differs from that of the management of the acquired entity. However, any material write-down of the carrying value of stocks in the acquired entity's books before or at the time of the acquisition would need to be justified by the circumstances of the acquired entity before acquisition. If exceptional profits appear to have been earned on the realisation of stocks after the date of the acquisition, it will be necessary to re-examine the fair values determined on acquisition as required by paragraphs 23–25 of the FRS and, if necessary, to make an adjustment to these values and a corresponding adjustment to goodwill. If, alternatively, the profit is attributable to post-acquisition events it should be disclosed as an exceptional item as required by paragraph 30 of FRS 6.

Quoted investments

58 The fair value of quoted investments will normally be their market price. However, it may be necessary to adjust the market price to allow for short-term fluctuations or, in the case of large holdings, to reflect either a lower realisable value representing the difficulties of disposal or a higher value for a holding representing a substantial voting block.

Monetary assets and liabilities

59 Most short-term monetary assets and liabilities, including trade debtors and creditors, would be recognised at amounts expected to be received or paid on settlement or redemption.

60 The fair values of certain long-term monetary items may, however, be materially different from their book values. One example is where an acquired entity is carrying material amounts of long-term debt at fixed rates that do not reflect current borrowing rates. The fair value will be greater or lower than book value depending on the direction of changes in interest rates since the debt was issued. Another example is a material long-term debtor where the delay in settlement is not compensated by an interest charge reflecting current market rates.

61 The FRS requires monetary items to be stated at fair values where these are materially different from book values. Where the monetary item is a quoted security, its fair value is normally its market price. The fair values of other monetary items may be determined by considering the current terms on which a similar monetary asset or liability could be acquired or assumed, or by discounting to their present values the total amounts expected to be received or paid. The choice of interest rate to be applied to long-term borrowings would be affected by current lending rates for an equivalent term, the credit standing of the issuer and the nature of any security. For long-term debtors (after any necessary provisions have been made) the interest rate would be based on current lending rates.

The differences between fair values arrived at by discounting and the total amounts receivable or payable in respect of the relevant items represent discounts or premiums on acquisition that would be dealt with in the financial statements of the acquiring group as interest income or expense – that is, by allocation to accounting periods over the term of the monetary items at a constant rate based on their carrying amounts. **62**

Where debt instruments issued by the acquired company are quoted, market values at the date of acquisition would be used instead of present values. However, in cases where a reduced pre-acquisition market value of an acquired entity's debt reflected the market's perception that it was at risk of being unable to fulfil its repayment obligations, the reduction would not be recognised in the fair value allocation if the debt was expected to be repaid at its full amount. **63**

Contingencies

The value attributed to a contingent asset or liability needs to reflect the best estimate of the likely outcome; otherwise the post-acquisition profit and loss account will reflect the change from the previous management's estimate to the acquirer's estimate, without any related event or change in circumstances. In rare cases where a commitment or a contingent asset is of a kind that is normally assumed or acquired in an arm's length transaction (for example, underwriting commitments), its fair value would reflect the market price for such transactions. **64**

Business sold or held exclusively with a view to subsequent resale

Where the acquisition of a group of companies includes a subsidiary undertaking or a discrete business operation that has been sold, or is expected to be sold, as a single unit within approximately a year of the acquisition it is appropriate to treat the investment in this business as a single asset, and to assign a single fair value to the whole investment rather than assign individual fair values to the various assets and liabilities that are included in the operation to be sold. The asset the group acquires is regarded as the investment in the subsidiary undertaking or business operation, rather than the individual items; and the actual net realised value will normally provide the most reliable evidence of fair value at the date of acquisition. One effect of this treatment is that goodwill is effectively apportioned between the part of the acquired group that is to be kept and the part sold, with the result that no further adjustment to write off the goodwill relating to the business disposed of, to comply with UITF Abstract 3 'Treatment of goodwill on disposal of a business', would be necessary. Where the effect is **65** material, the net proceeds would be discounted to obtain their present value at the date of acquisition (taking into account any distribution of profits from the business). The principle explained in paragraph 85 below for attributing expenses to the cost of an acquisition would also apply to the costs of disposals.

66 Where the disposal has not been completed at the time of the first financial statements after the acquisition, the fair value is based on the estimated sales proceeds. Any initial estimate of fair value would normally be adjusted to actual net realised value within the period allowed for completing the investigation of fair values, with the change being adjusted against goodwill.

67 Such intended disposals would neither have been previously consolidated by the acquirer, nor have formed a continuing part of the activities of the acquiring group. In these circumstances, for an interest in a subsidiary undertaking, companies legislation* permits, and FRS 2 requires, the interest to be recognised as a current asset in the acquirer's consolidated accounts. The results of its operations during the holding period are excluded from the profit and loss account of the acquiring group.

68 The FRS requires the same principles of valuation to be applied to disposals of other business operations that are not subsidiary undertakings. Therefore, for example, the assets of a division held for resale would be shown as a single separately described current asset.

69 In the following circumstances it would be appropriate to estimate separately fair values at the acquisition date and to record a post-acquisition profit or loss on disposal:

(a) the acquirer has made a material change to the acquired business before disposal;
(b) specific post-acquisition events occur during the holding period that materially change the fair value of the business from the fair value estimated at the date of acquisition; or
(c) the disposal is completed at a reduced price for a quick sale.

Pensions and other post-retirement benefits

70 The FRS requires that where an acquired entity sponsors a defined-benefit pension scheme, or a defined-benefit post-retirement scheme other than a pension scheme, the allocation of fair values should include an asset in respect of a surplus in a funded scheme and a liability in respect of a deficiency in a funded scheme or accrued obligations relating to an unfunded scheme. These assets or liabilities are in substitution for existing prepayments or provisions that have accumulated in the accounts of the acquired entity under the requirements of SSAP 24.

71 The fair value attributed to a surplus in a funded scheme would be determined by taking into account not only the actuarial surplus of the fund, but also the extent to which the surplus could be realised in cash terms, by way of reduction of future contributions or otherwise, and the timescale of such potential realisations.

In Great Britain, the Companies Act 1985, section 229(3)(c); in Northern Ireland, the Companies (Northern Ireland) Order 1986, Article 237(3)(c); and in the Republic of Ireland the European Communities (Companies: Group Accounts) Regulations 1992, Regulation 11(c).

This treatment differs from the normal requirements of SSAP 24, which in many circumstances do not permit the immediate recognition of assets and liabilities in respect of surpluses or deficiencies, but require them to be recognised systematically over the average remaining service lives of the employees in the scheme. Whilst SSAP 24 is primarily concerned with the allocation of pension costs to a company's profit and loss account on a continuing basis over several financial years, accounting for an acquisition transaction necessitates the recognition in the acquirer's group accounts of all assets and liabilities of the acquired entity identified at the date of acquisition. A pension asset, however, would be recognised only insofar as the acquired entity or the acquirer was able to benefit from the existing surplus. **72**

The valuation of the pension fund surplus or deficit depends on several assumptions: interest rates, inflation and investment returns; the likely turnover of staff; and future salary increases; and the acquirer would apply its own judgement in determining these assumptions. However, the FRS requires changes in pension or other post-retirement arrangements following an acquisition to be accounted for as post-acquisition items. An example is the cost of improvements to benefits granted to members of an acquired scheme as part of a policy of harmonising remuneration packages in the enlarged group. This treatment is consistent with accounting for any changes stemming from the acquisition that affect the pension arrangements of the acquirer's own workforce, and has the effect of treating changes in pension arrangements on the same basis as the realignment of any other aspects of remuneration. The cost of post-acquisition changes to pension and other post-retirement arrangements would be dealt with in accordance with the requirements of SSAP 24 relating to variations in pension cost. **73**

Deferred taxation

Deferred tax has to be determined on a group basis; at the end of the accounting period in which the acquisition occurred, the enlarged group's deferred tax provision will be calculated as a single amount, on assumptions applicable to the group. To determine the deferred tax of the acquired company at the date of acquisition using different assumptions from those applying to the group as a whole would result in the post-acquisition profit and loss account reflecting the change from one set of assumptions to another, rather than any real change in the circumstances of the group. **74**

The benefit to the group of any tax losses in an acquired entity at the date of acquisition would be recognised on acquisition in accordance with the requirements of SSAP 15 'Accounting for deferred tax'. The losses would therefore be treated as timing differences, and would be recognised as reductions in deferred tax liabilities (if any), with any remainder recognised as deferred tax assets provided that the criteria for recognition specified in SSAP 15 are met. Application of these principles may result in deferred tax assets that were previously unrecognised in the acquired entity's financial statements being recognised on acquisition. If the criteria for the recognition of the benefits of tax losses in the group financial statements are not met as at the date of acquisition or within the permitted period for completing the fair value exercise, the benefits (if any) will be recognised in post-acquisition periods when the criteria are met, and any necessary disclosure required by paragraph 23 of FRS 3 will be given. **75**

DETERMINING THE COST OF ACQUISITION

Fair values of the components of the purchase consideration

76 In order to apply the requirements of the FRS, it is necessary to determine the fair values of the constituent parts of the purchase consideration. The purchase consideration may comprise:

(a) cash or other monetary items, including the assumption of liabilities by the acquirer;
(b) capital instruments issued by the acquirer, including shares, debentures, loans and debt instruments, share warrants and other options relating to the securities of the acquirer; or
(c) non-monetary assets, including securities of another entity.

Cash and other monetary consideration

77 Where the purchase consideration is in the form of cash or other monetary assets given or liabilities assumed, its fair value is normally readily determinable as the amount paid or payable in respect of the item. When settlement of cash consideration is deferred, fair values are obtained by discounting to their present value the amounts expected to be payable in the future. The appropriate discount rate is the rate at which the acquirer could obtain a similar borrowing, taking into account its credit standing and any security given.

Capital instruments

78 Where shares (and other capital instruments) issued by the acquirer are quoted on a ready market, the market price on the date of acquisition would normally provide the most reliable measure of fair value. Where control is transferred by a public offer, the relevant date is the date on which the offer or, where there is a series of revised offers, the successful offer becomes unconditional, usually as a result of a sufficient number of acceptances being received. Where, owing to unusual fluctuations, the market price on one particular date is an unreliable measure of fair value, market prices for a reasonable period before the date of acquisition, during which acceptances could be made, would need to be considered.

79 Where securities issued by the acquirer are not quoted or, if they are quoted, the market price is unreliable owing, for example, to the lack of an active market in the quantities involved, it would be necessary to make a valuation of those securities. The fair value would be estimated by taking into account items such as:

(a) the value of similar securities that are quoted;
(b) the present value of the future cash flows of the instrument issued;
(c) any cash alternative to the issue of securities; and
(d) the value of any underlying security into which there is an option to convert.

Where it is not possible to value the consideration given by any of the above methods, the best estimate of its value may be given by valuing the entity acquired.

Non-monetary consideration

Where the purchase consideration takes the form of non-monetary assets, fair values would be determined by reference to market prices, estimated realisable values, independent valuations, or other available evidence. **80**

Contingent consideration

The terms of an acquisition may provide that the value of the purchase consideration, which may be payable in cash, shares or other securities at a future date, depends on uncertain future events, such as the future performance of the acquired company. An example is an 'earn-out', where consideration payable to the vendor takes the form of an initial payment, together with further payments based on a multiple of future profits of the acquired company. By its nature, the fair value of such contingent consideration cannot be determined precisely at the date of acquisition. The FRS requires that the cost of acquisition should include a reasonable estimate of its fair value. Where it is not possible to estimate the total amounts payable with any degree of certainty, at least those amounts that are reasonably expected to be payable would be recognised. Initial estimates would be revised as further and more certain information becomes available. **81**

Where contingent consideration is to be satisfied by the issue of shares, there is no obligation to transfer economic benefits and, accordingly, amounts recognised would be reported as part of shareholders' funds, for example as a separate caption representing shares to be issued. In the analysis of shareholders' funds, amounts would be attributed to equity and non-equity interests depending on the nature of the shares to be issued, in accordance with FRS 4 'Capital Instruments'. When the shares are issued, appropriate transfers would be necessary between any amounts then held in shareholders' funds in respect of their issue and called up share capital and share premium. **82**

If the acquirer can satisfy part of the consideration by the issue of shares or the payment of cash at its option, this part of the future consideration is not a liability because there is no obligation to transfer economic benefits. Consequently, the expected future consideration would be accounted for as a credit to shareholders' funds as explained in paragraph 82 above until an irrevocable decision regarding the form of consideration has been taken. If, however, the vendor has the right to demand cash or shares, the expected future consideration represents an obligation to the vendor and would be accounted for as a liability until the shares are issued or the cash is paid. **83**

Acquisition agreements may require payments to be made in various forms, for example as non-competition payments or as bonuses to the vendors who continue to work for the acquired company. In such circumstances, it is necessary to determine whether the substance of the agreement is payment for the business acquired, or an expense such as compensation for services or profit sharing. In the first case the expected payments would be accounted for as contingent purchase consideration; in the other case the payments would be treated as expenses of the period to which they relate. **84**

Acquisition expenses

85 Acquisition expenses to be treated as part of the cost of acquisition include incremental costs such as professional fees paid to merchant banks, accountants, legal advisers, valuers and other consultants. Such expenses exclude any allocation of costs that would still have been incurred had the acquisition not been entered into – for example, the costs of maintaining an acquisitions department or management remuneration; such costs would be charged to the profit and loss account as incurred. Expenses of issuing shares and other capital instruments that qualify as issue costs as defined in FRS 4 would be dealt with in accordance with the requirements of that standard. Such expenses are not added to the cost of acquisition.

Adoption of FRS 7 by the Board

Financial Reporting Standard 7 – 'Fair Values in Acquisition Accounting' was approved for issue by a vote of seven of the eight members of the Accounting Standards Board. Mr Main dissented. His dissenting view is set out in Appendix IV.

Members of the Accounting Standards Board

Sir David Tweedie (Chairman)

Allan Cook (Technical Director)

Robert Bradfield

Ian Brindle

Michael Garner

Raymond Hinton

Donald Main

Graham Stacy

Appendix I
Note on Legal Requirements

GREAT BRITAIN

References are to the Companies Act 1985

The Companies Act describes the acquisition method of accounting in Schedule 4A paragraph 9: 1

(a) The identifiable assets and liabilities of the undertaking acquired shall be included in the consolidated balance sheet at their fair values as at the date of acquisition. The 'identifiable' assets or liabilities of the undertaking acquired mean the assets or liabilities that are capable of being disposed of or discharged separately, without disposing of a business of the undertaking (Schedule 4A paragraph 9(2)).

(b) The income and expenditure of the undertaking acquired shall be brought into the group accounts only as from the date of the acquisition (Schedule 4A paragraph 9(3)).

(c) There shall be set off against the acquisition cost of the interest in the shares of the undertaking held by the parent company and its subsidiary undertakings the interest of the parent company and its subsidiary undertakings in the adjusted capital and reserves of the undertaking acquired. The resulting amount if positive shall be treated as goodwill, and if negative as a negative consolidation difference (Schedule 4A paragraph 9(4)-(5)).

(d) The 'acquisition cost' is defined as the amount of any cash consideration and the fair value of any other consideration, together with such amount (if any) in respect of fees and other expenses of the acquisition as the company may determine; and 'the adjusted capital and reserves' of the undertaking acquired are defined as the capital and reserves at the date of the acquisition after adjusting the identifiable assets and liabilities of the undertaking to fair values as at that date (Schedule 4A paragraph 9(4)).

Share premium and merger relief

Section 130(1) of the Act provides that if a company issues shares at a premium, whether for cash or otherwise, a sum equal to the aggregate amount or value of the premiums on those shares should be transferred to an account called the share premium account. The provisions of the Act relating to the reduction of a company's share capital apply, with exceptions, as if the share premium account were part of its paid-up share capital. 2

Limited relief from the above ('merger relief') is given by sections 131–134. 3

Section 131 provides, inter alia, that, subject to specified conditions, where an issuing company has secured at least a 90 per cent equity holding in another company, section 130 does not apply to the premium on shares issued in the transaction that takes the holding in that other company to at least 90 per cent. 4

Section 133(1) provides that the premium on any shares to which the relief in sections 5

131 and 132 applies may also be disregarded in determining the amount at which any shares or other consideration provided for the shares issued is to be included in the offeror company's balance sheet.

Share premium and fair value

6 Shares forming part of the consideration are valued at their fair value for the purposes of computing acquisition cost and goodwill under paragraph 9(4) of Schedule 4A. By contrast, the value of the share premiums arising on the shares issued, for the purposes of section 130, is based on the value to the issuing company of the consideration it has received. Where these values are different, or where (if the merger relief provisions apply) the premiums are disregarded, the cost of investment in the parent company's books will be different from the cost of acquisition for the purposes of paragraph 9(4). In such circumstances the difference should form a separate element of consolidated reserves, and does not form part of goodwill.

NORTHERN IRELAND

7 The legal requirements in Northern Ireland are very similar to those in Great Britain. The following table shows the references to the Companies (Northern Ireland) Order 1986 that correspond to the legal references in paragraphs 1–6 above.

Great Britain	*Northern Ireland*
Schedule 4A paragraph 9	Schedule 4A paragraph 9
Sections 130–134	Articles 140–144

REPUBLIC OF IRELAND

8 The following table shows the references to the European Communities (Companies: Group Accounts) Regulations 1992 and the Companies Act 1963 that correspond to the legal references in paragraphs 1–6 above.

Great Britain	*Republic of Ireland*
Schedule 4A paragraph 9	Regulation 19
Section 130	Companies Act 1963 section 62
Sections 131–134	No equivalent

Appendix II
Compliance with International Accounting Standards

The International Accounting Standards Committee (IASC) has issued a revised standard IAS 22 'Business Combinations'. The principal areas where the revised IAS 22 and the FRS are at variance* are as follows. First, the revised IAS 22 requires that fair values of identifiable assets and liabilities acquired in an acquisition should be determined by reference to their intended use by the acquirer. The FRS requires the identifiable assets and liabilities to be recorded at their fair values as at the date of acquisition. Secondly, certain adjustments that would be treated as fair value adjustments under the revised IAS 22, for example those for additional liabilities recognised to reflect an acquirer's different intentions regarding an acquisition, would be accounted for as post-acquisition items under the FRS.

The Board's reasons for adopting proposals that differ from those of the IASC's revised IAS 22 are set out in Appendix III, at paragraphs 15–16 and 27–28.

Appendix III
The development of the FRS

GENERAL AND HISTORY

1 The principle of attributing fair values in consolidated financial statements to the assets and liabilities of newly acquired subsidiaries has been recognised in UK accounting standards for many years and, since 1989, in companies legislation.

SSAP 14

2 SSAP 14 'Group accounts', which was published in 1978, required the purchase consideration for the acquisition of a subsidiary to be allocated between the underlying net tangible and intangible assets other than goodwill on the basis of the fair value to the acquiring company. The standard gave no guidance on how to determine fair values.

SSAP 22

3 SSAP 22 'Accounting for goodwill', issued in 1984, gave limited guidance on how to identify the assets and liabilities of an acquired business that should be regarded as separable from the purchased goodwill arising on the acquisition. It also sanctioned the practice that had evolved of adjusting the fair values ascribed to the separable net assets acquired to include provisions for anticipated future losses or costs of reorganisation. Such provisions were permitted to be recognised in the fair value exercise if the future losses or costs were taken into account in arriving at the purchase price.

4 Subsequently, however, concern among users began to emerge over the extent to which the use of provisions could potentially be hidden or abused. The Accounting Standards Committee (ASC) took action to address these concerns by amending SSAP 22 to include some specific disclosure requirements relating to the fair value exercise. The revised SSAP 22, published in 1989, required disclosure of adjustments made to the book values of the assets and liabilities of an acquired business, analysed into revaluations and provisions. It also required disclosure of movements on provisions related to acquisitions, analysed into the amounts used and the amounts released unused or applied for another purpose. At the same time as SSAP 22 was being amended, the ASC was developing an accounting standard on fair value accounting (see paragraph 6 below).

Companies Act 1989

5 The Companies Act 1989 introduced a new Schedule 4A to the Companies Act 1985, which set out rules regarding the form and content of consolidated financial statements. The Act requires that, in accounting for the acquisition of a subsidiary, the

subsidiary's identifiable assets and liabilities must be included in the consolidated balance sheet at their fair values as at the date of acquisition. There is no guidance in the Act on how to determine the fair values of assets and liabilities acquired.

ED 53

The ASC issued a discussion paper in 1988, followed in 1990 by an exposure draft, ED 53 'Fair value in the context of acquisition accounting'. ED 53 contained proposals for determining fair values of assets and liabilities identified in an acquisition, for dealing with anticipated reorganisation costs and for valuing the consideration given for an acquisition. **6**

ED 53 proposed that fair values should be determined from the perspective of the acquiring company, based on circumstances at the date of acquisition. Its proposals for dealing with acquisition provisions did not permit provision to be made for future trading losses of acquired businesses but did, however, continue to permit provisions for reorganisation costs to be made as fair value adjustments if there was a clearly defined programme of reorganisation that had been costed in reasonable detail and there was evidence that the acquirer took account of the plans and costs in formulating the offer. **7**

ASB Discussion Paper

In April 1993, the Board published a Discussion Paper, 'Fair values in acquisition accounting'. The Board adopted much of the work of the ASC in framing its proposals, but concluded that a different approach to the recognition of liabilities was necessary to address a number of issues, including those raised in responses to ED 53. A theme common to several of the commentators' responses had been that the basic principles underlying ED 53's approach had not been properly developed and in particular that the exposure draft had failed to rationalise its conclusions on key issues such as the recognition of reorganisation and future loss provisions. **8**

The Discussion Paper contained proposals that attempted to draw a clear distinction of principle between recording the elements of the purchase transaction, including accounting for the pre-acquisition assets and liabilities of the acquired business, and the items that should fall into the post-acquisition period. The proposals would have precluded provisions both for future losses in acquired businesses and, as a departure from ED 53, for reorganisation costs following an acquisition from being included as fair value adjustments. The principal reasons for proposing such a radical change to existing practices were threefold: **9**

(a) the proposals for dealing with the recognition of anticipated future losses and reorganisation costs were consistent with the Board's draft Statement of Principles regarding the recognition of liabilities;
(b) the proposals were consistent with the philosophy behind the 'information set' approach in FRS 3 'Reporting Financial Performance' in respect of presenting the financial effects of post-acquisition activities, including reorganisation of acquired businesses;

(c) to meet users' concerns on perceived scope for abuse; it was doubtful whether an alternative approach of developing a standard founded on enhanced disclosure of acquisition provisions, supplemented by specific and probably arbitrary rules on cut-off between pre- and post-acquisition items would prove as effective in the long term as an approach built on the Board's draft Statement of Principles.

FRED 7

10 FRED 7 was published in December 1993. It retained the essential features of the proposals in the Discussion Paper, while refining and clarifying them to take account of the comments received.

11 Views on the proposal in the Discussion Paper that all costs of reorganising acquired businesses should be treated as charges to post-acquisition profits had been divided, with a small majority in favour of the proposed treatment. Support had been strongest among user groups, who generally welcomed the transparency of the proposals in providing a proper basis for analysing the financial consequences of acquisition activities. Opposition had been voiced by many – although by no means all – preparers, who argued that the proposals belied the reality of the way acquisitions are handled because they failed to reflect the fact that the cost of an acquisition and subsequent, directly related expenditure are the product of a single investment decision. As an example, many commentators had argued that the costs incurred in the immediate post-acquisition period to implement a business plan to reorganise an acquisition were probably discrete and significant and were an integral part of the investment appraisal process; such costs, they contended, should not be reported in the group's trading results. The purchase and integration of a subsidiary, in their eyes, was in substance a single capital transaction, despite the fact that some elements might be revenue in form.

12 The Board set out in FRED 7 the basis for its conclusions on the proposed treatment of post-acquisition reorganisation costs. The main arguments, which are equally applicable to the FRS, are summarised as follows.

(a) The proposals were made in the context of the fundamental changes to the disclosure of financial performance that were introduced by FRS 3. If a company incurs material revenue expenditure to improve future profitability, the costs are normally charged to the profit and loss account. FRS 3 and the Operating and Financial Review both provide the facility for proper disclosure and explanation of the resulting volatility in the reported results. The Board believed that all such expenditure should be treated similarly, whether it related to a reorganisation following an acquisition or to a reorganisation of an ongoing business. It would be left to investment analysis to assess the benefit to an entity of a reorganisation.

(b) The proposals in respect of the recognition of liabilities were consistent with the Board's draft Statement of Principles. The approach rested on whether there was an obligation in the acquired entity at the acquisition date. The Board recognised that, where an acquisition was made, the acquirer might have taken into account additional costs to reorganise the operations of the combining entities and such costs might have been factored into the investment decision and the amount of purchase consideration to be offered. However, it did not follow that these costs should be deemed to increase the liabilities of the acquired entity existing at the acquisition date.

(c) The proposals, which required reorganisations related to acquisitions to be treated on the same footing as any other reorganisations, set out principles that avoided the need to define cut-off points between items to be included in the fair value exercise and items to be recognised in the post-acquisition period, which would have been difficult to achieve. Framing an alternative approach on the basis of the acquirer's intentions at the time of the acquisition would, in the Board's opinion, have led to artificial distinctions being drawn not only between the treatment of reorganisations affecting the acquired business and consequential changes in the existing business of the acquirer, but also between reorganisations that were planned at the time of acquisition and those that occurred later.

Many commentators had argued that the 'acquirer's perspective' should be retained as a principle for attributing fair values to the assets and liabilities acquired. They had contended that because the purchase consideration was based on the acquirer's assessment of the fair value of the acquired entity and its underlying assets and liabilities, it followed that the allocation of the purchase consideration should also be based on the acquirer's perspective. **13**

The Board is of the view that under its draft Statement of Principles, management intent is not a sufficient basis for recognising changes to an entity's assets and liabilities. It is events, not intentions for future actions, that increase or decrease an entity's assets or liabilities. When intentions are translated into actions that commit the entity to particular courses of action, the accounting should then reflect any obligations or changes in assets that arise from those actions. In relation to acquisition accounting, the Board concluded that events of a post-acquisition period that resulted in the recognition of additional liabilities or the impairment of existing assets of an acquired entity should be reported as events of that period rather than of the pre-acquisition period. **14**

Some commentators expressed concern that the proposals for precluding any reorganisation provisions as fair value adjustments were more restrictive than the requirements in the USA or International Accounting Standards. They urged the Board to go no further than to achieve consistency with US GAAP which, although not permitting provisions for future losses of acquired companies to be recognised as fair value adjustments, would allow adjustments to be made to take account of management intentions in the valuation of acquired assets, including, for example, provisions in respect of the intended closure of facilities in the acquired entity that are duplicated in the enlarged group. **15**

In developing FRED 7, the Board took into account the fact that US GAAP in this area considerably pre-dates the development of the present framework of general accounting concepts in the USA, as well as the IASC framework and the UK draft Statement of Principles, which are similar. The Board took the view that its proposals were consistent with the conceptual frameworks that had been developed elsewhere and, in particular, noted that the principle of accounting for obligations rather than management intentions was gaining greater acceptance internationally. **16**

MATTERS CONSIDERED IN THE LIGHT OF RESPONSES TO FRED 7

17 The following paragraphs refer to comments made by respondents to FRED 7, and explain with reasons the changes the Board has made to the proposals of the FRED or the Board's reasons for rejecting arguments for changes. Individual Board members gave greater weight to some factors than to others.

Reorganisation provisions

18 FRED 7 proposed that the identifiable assets and liabilities recognised in the fair value exercise should be those of the acquired entity that existed at the date of acquisition, and should include provisions neither for future operating losses nor for reorganisation and integration costs expected to be incurred as a result of the acquisition.

19 This proposal met with outright support from institutional investors, analysts and users of accounts; substantial support from accountancy firms and accountancy bodies; and strong, though not unanimous, opposition from preparers of accounts.

20 The main arguments raised by respondents opposed to the proposals in the FRED are summarised below, together with the Board's response to the arguments.

Commercial reality

21 It was argued that the FRED ignored the commercial reality of the transaction, namely that the acquirer's management takes the reorganisation and integration costs into account in its 'project plan' for the acquisition, and regards these costs as part of the 'investment'; they should therefore be treated as akin to additional consideration. Furthermore, it was argued, under the FRED's proposals the acquisition of a poorly organised business that is then reorganised by the acquirer gives a different accounting result from the acquisition of an equivalent but well-organised business that is not in need of reorganisation.

22 Of those who preferred the status quo on reorganisation provisions, most agreed that the existing situation was unsatisfactory and that tighter definitions and controls were needed; in particular, there was little support for continuing to allow provisions to be made for future losses of the acquired business, and most agreed that there should be rules to restrict the use of reorganisation provisions made as fair value adjustments.

23 The Board has carefully reconsidered the arguments against its proposals, which reiterated the arguments raised by a majority of preparers against the proposals in the Discussion Paper. The Board recognises the strength of feeling held in some quarters against this aspect of its proposals, which changes long-standing accounting practice. It has also balanced these views with those of user and other groups who supported the proposals. While not discounting the reasons or rationale underlying the position of those opposed to its proposals, the Board decided that it should develop an FRS on the basis of the proposals in FRED 7. It believes that this FRS will lead to clearer and more consistent reporting than has been the case under existing practices. Furthermore, the

Board remains of the view that the approach adopted in the FRS is more soundly based on principle than would be an alternative approach that sought to improve existing standards by addressing disclosure issues and developing detailed rules that had the principal objective of constraining reorganisation provisions solely in order to prevent abuse.

Without repeating all the arguments underlying the Board's position as set out in FRED 7, the Board reaffirms that the principles in the FRS for determining the fair values of the assets and liabilities of the acquired entity adhere closely to the Board's draft Statement of Principles in respect of the recognition of assets and liabilities, and to the philosophy behind FRS 3 (complemented by the Operating and Financial Review) for reporting financial performance and other gains and losses. **24**

The FRS, therefore, follows the principle (as set out in the draft Statement of Principles) that identifiable liabilities are limited to obligations of the acquired entity that existed at the date of acquisition and, consequently, other changes should fall into the post-acquisition period. The Board recognises that rationalisation expenditures, whether to improve or to integrate part of the business following an acquisition, are undertaken because they are expected to result in lasting and long-term benefits. However, in the Board's view this does not justify the effective capitalisation of that expenditure as goodwill, irrespective of whether it was planned at the time of the acquisition or whether the plans were formulated after the acquisition took place. **25**

The Board also takes the view that the acquisition of a well-organised company is a different transaction from the acquisition of a company in need of reorganisation, and there is no reason why the two transactions should result in the same accounting outcome. In one case the acquirer is reporting the acquisition of a business whose previous management ran it efficiently; in the other, the acquirer is reporting the acquisition of a less efficient business and the subsequent expenditure intended to improve it. In the first case, the success of the business was apparent before the acquirer agreed to buy it; in the second, the value of the reorganisation expenditure will be judged subsequently by the increase in profitability of the acquired business that is achieved. **26**

International competitiveness and international GAAP

It was suggested by some respondents that the FRED's approach, by being stricter in some respects than the corresponding provisions of accounting standards in other countries (in particular, US GAAP and the International Accounting Standard) would damage the competitiveness of UK companies. Conversely, others have argued that the existing flexible accounting practices in the UK have encouraged UK companies to overpay for acquisitions compared with foreign companies. The Board takes the view that accounting standards should be neutral as to economic effect. Therefore, the FRS seeks to provide greater clarity in the reporting of acquisition activities. The more transparent accounting resulting from the FRS and from other accounting reforms that the Board has undertaken should contribute to sound economic decisions. **27**

The Board carefully considered the international harmonisation issue during the **28** development of FRED 7. As noted in paragraph 16 above, the Board believes that the FRS is consistent with the conceptual frameworks that have been adopted by various standard-setting bodies.

'Socio-economic' consequences

29 Some respondents also claimed that acquirers will be less willing to acquire companies in need of reorganisation, thus allowing inefficient management to remain and preventing rationalisation that is beneficial to the economy as a whole. However, the Board notes that the cash flow effect of a transaction is the same whichever accounting treatment is adopted.

Understandability of financial statements

30 Several preparers of accounts suggested that the reporting of acquisitions would be more difficult to understand, because the full cost to the acquirer will not be clear and the post-acquisition results will be distorted by reorganisation and integration costs. However, users who responded were unanimous that the FRED's proposals would provide them with clearer and more informative information on acquisitions.

31 In response to those commentators who argued that the financial statements should be capable of showing the full cost of the investment in an acquisition, including the intended costs of post-acquisition reorganisation, the FRS has introduced a recommendation that the planned reorganisation expenditure relating to the acquisition should be disclosed in the notes to the financial statements (see paragraph 40 below).

Anti-avoidance measures

32 There was concern that the requirements of the FRS could be circumvented by collusion between the vendor and the acquirer, resulting for example in the vendor entering into obligations to restructure the business on the instructions of the acquirer before the formal transfer of control.

33 The Discussion Paper had proposed that any reorganisation provisions made by the vendor in the six months before the acquisition should be treated as post-acquisition; however, this was generally regarded as unnecessarily draconian and was omitted from the FRED.

34 The FRS deals with the issue in three ways. First, it emphasises that provisions should be included in the balance sheet of the acquired company at the date of acquisition only if that entity had a commitment from which it could not realistically withdraw whether or not the acquisition had been completed. Secondly, it draws attention to the possibility that the effective transfer of control took place at an earlier date than the formal transfer of shares. Thirdly, there is an additional disclosure requirement (included in FRS 6) for any provisions for reorganisation made by the acquired company within 12 months before the date of acquisition to be shown separately in the 'fair value table'.

Conclusion

The Board gave careful consideration to the arguments of those opposed to the proposals in the FRED, and acknowledged the strength of feeling particularly among many preparers of accounts. However, it concluded that the arguments put forward were essentially those it had already addressed in coming to its initial views expressed in the Discussion Paper and FRED 7. Moreover, where the arguments concern the understandability of financial statements, due regard must be given to the views of the professional users of accounts – in particular, the institutional investors and analysts, who were fully in support of the proposals. 35

Other issues

'Acquirer's perspective'

Several respondents (including both some of those who supported the FRED's approach to reorganisation provisions as well as some of those who opposed it) argued that the fair values should be determined from the 'acquirer's perspective'. However, the Board took the view that this term had no single clear meaning, and might be interpreted to indicate that fair values should take into account the decisions of the acquirer taken after the acquisition. For this reason, the Board has avoided using the term in the FRS, but has added more specific descriptions of the extent to which the acquirer's estimates and perceptions are taken into account in determining fair values. The concept of fair value underlying these specific rules remains, however, the value at which the asset, or liability, could be exchanged in an arm's length transaction between informed and willing parties. This concept is independent of the particular circumstances of either the acquirer or the acquired business. 36

Disclosure of provisions for reorganisation costs

Several respondents were concerned that, if reorganisation and similar costs relating to an acquisition were reported in the profit and loss account in accordance with the provisions of FRS 3, such costs might be reported as a deduction from the results of acquisitions, or as part of continuing activities; or, if they related to a fundamental reorganisation of the acquiring entity, as an exceptional item outside operating profit. Users might therefore find it difficult to ascertain the total costs relating to acquisitions. Instead, they proposed that a new category of exceptional item should be defined, to include all costs of reorganisation, restructuring and integration relating to an acquisition, that would not form part of operating profit. 37

The Board concluded that this alternative proposal would confuse different kinds of costs relating to acquisitions, some of which might properly be excluded from operating profit but others of which were just as much an operating cost as the costs of routinely reorganising an existing part of the business. Furthermore, the introduction of a new class of exceptional item would lead to considerable difficulties of definition, as in many cases it was difficult to draw a clear distinction between costs relating to the acquisition, and similar costs relating to the acquirer's existing business that might well still have been incurred had the acquisition not taken place. 38

39 The Board therefore decided against introducing a new class of exceptional item. FRS 6, which now includes all disclosure requirements relating to acquisitions, sets out in paragraph 86 how the requirements of FRS 3 apply to costs relating to acquisitions.

40 In addition, paragraph 87 of FRS 6 suggests that management may wish to show, in a note to the financial statements, the total expenditure announced in relation to reorganisation and integration of acquisitions, together with the expenditures charged in the profit and loss account in the period and the further amount expected to be incurred. This would provide users with a clear statement of the total costs involved with the acquisition, and companies would be able to add what further explanation and discussion of the figures they think appropriate.

Pension surpluses

41 The FRED proposed that an actuarial surplus or deficit on a pension scheme operated by the acquired company should be recognised as an asset or liability on acquisition. Many respondents thought it imprudent to carry such a surplus as an asset, as it was often uncertain whether it could be realised. They therefore proposed that, whilst provision should still be made for a deficit, a surplus should not be recognised as an asset.

42 The Board has reconsidered the issue, and concluded that, although recognition of a surplus is consistent with the principles on which the FRS is based, it is important that the fair value attributed to such a surplus is justified. The FRS therefore requires the fair value of a surplus to be determined taking into account the extent to which, and timescale over which, the surplus is reasonably expected to be realised, normally in the form of reductions in future contributions.

43 The Board is currently reviewing the existing accounting standard on pension costs, SSAP 24. However, the Board decided that to omit reference to pension surpluses and deficits in the FRS, or to require fair values to be based on the assets or liabilities recognised by the acquired company in its own accounts under SSAP 24, might result in the omission of significant assets and liabilities and subsequent misstatement of profits of the enlarged group.

Acquisition expenses

44 The FRED proposed that the amount of incidental expenses that fall to be treated as an addition to the cost of acquisition should be restricted to incremental costs that would not have been incurred had the acquisition not taken place, and did not permit the capitalisation of internal costs even where they might be directly related to the acquisition. This proposal was consistent with the revised IAS 22 and US GAAP, and took a deliberately restrictive view to avoid the danger of overstating the cost of acquisition.

45 An alternative view is that the incremental cost approach is anomalous where the equivalent services, such as legal advice or acquisition search and investigation services, are provided by in-house departments rather than by external advisers or consultants.

There was substantial support from respondents for each view. The Board concluded that the difficulty of defining 'incremental' for in-house facilities might lead to excessive costs being capitalised, with the resulting overstatement of profits. This outweighed the possible anomalies that might arise. The proposals in the FRED have accordingly been carried through to the FRS. 46

Discounting

The FRED proposed that monetary assets and liabilities should be discounted to present value where they were materially different from nominal amounts. Although this was supported, a substantial minority of respondents were concerned over the introduction of discounting on a piecemeal basis, applying only to assets and liabilities of an acquisition, rather than as part of a more general application of discounting to all assets and liabilities. 47

The Board has reaffirmed its view that monetary assets and liabilities acquired in an acquisition should be included at their fair value at the time of the acquisition; this fair value will depend on the estimated amounts and timing of payments, and, in the case of long-term items not bearing interest at current market rates, may be materially different from their face value or nominal value. Significant distortions to reported profits may arise if such items are not included at their fair value. Discounting is an established and widely used valuation technique, and is one method of arriving at an estimate of fair value. The Board notes that this treatment is also consistent with the revised IAS 22 and with US GAAP. 48

Appendix IV
Dissenting view

1 Mr Main dissents from the FRS because of its treatment of the costs an acquiring company incurs to convert an acquired entity into the business unit it envisaged when making the acquisition. He was content at the exposure draft stage to let the proposal go forward in order to elicit a public response. However, he has found his concern reinforced by comments received and therefore feels unable to vote for the FRS.

2 Mr Main believes that it is very rare for a company to acquire another without intending to make changes to the acquired business to enable it to operate efficiently. Such changes may include, on the one hand, investment in, and reorganisation of, the assets being acquired to enable products or services to be provided efficiently, and, on the other hand, reductions of excessive manpower, buildings or equipment to enable an adequate profit to be earned.

3 Mr Main believes that the need for such changes and the likely cost of executing them are invariably known to the acquirer at the time the acquisition is made, and that the normal practice of management when considering a proposed acquisition for approval is to aggregate the acquisition price with these costs of bringing the acquired entity into a state acceptable to the buyer, in order to arrive at the investment total against which the expected earnings are judged.

4 The requirements of the FRS will prevent a company from recognising in the financial statements at the time of acquisition the costs of the intended changes. It is only when such costs are committed irrevocably that they are to be included in the financial statements, and even then, to the extent that these costs are not capital expenditure, they cannot be included as part of the investment cost of the acquisition.

5 For these reasons the financial statements will, in his view, be misleading and fail to provide accountability for the transactions that have taken place.

6 Mr Main supports the view expressed by many commentators on the Discussion Paper and exposure draft, as set out in paragraphs 11 and 21 of 'The development of the FRS' (Appendix III), that the costs of an acquisition and subsequent directly related expenditure are the product of a single investment decision; and that the purchase and integration of a subsidiary are in substance a single capital transaction. He believes that the opposition to this view by certain commentators reflected less an endorsement of the principles underlying the FRS than a reaction to perceived abuses in previous practice, including the making of excessive acquisition provisions to cover future trading losses and types of expenditure whose relationship to the acquisition was remote. He would summarise the responses to the exposure draft on this point as follows:

(a) from preparers of accounts: overwhelming opposition;

(b) from users: acceptance, because they want to know the amount of post-acquisition provisions (which he considers to be a valid point), but a view that they would ignore the amounts charged against profits (indicating that they do not regard such charges as a proper reduction of profit);

(c) from auditors: acceptance, because it can be very difficult at times to pass judgement on directors' decisions as to the proper capital provision for post- acquisition costs.

Mr Main believes that the concerns over past abuses could be met, without overturning long-standing practice, by a standard that provided a stricter definition of what costs should be permitted to be included in acquisition provisions, together with more detailed note disclosure of the provisions made. Provisions would be restricted to costs to be incurred within twelve months of the acquisition, and would exclude any costs relating to the acquiring entity's own activities. Provisions for future losses would also be prohibited. Notes to the financial statements would be required to disclose the separate elements of the provisions involved and the actual expenditure subsequently charged against the provisions. Surplus provisions would be required to be adjusted against goodwill rather than be released to the profit and loss account. He believes that the disclosure requirements in the related FRS 6 would provide sufficient information on the effects of an acquisition without the need for the radical change in practice introduced in FRS 7. **7**

Mr Main believes that his alternative would ensure that: **8**

(a) the total cost of the acquisition investment decision would be reflected clearly in the financial statements;
(b) accountability could be measured; and
(c) the potential for abuse would be removed and auditors would have a clear standard against which the contents of the provision could be judged.

Part Three

Statements by the Accounting Standards Board

Operating and financial review

(Issued July 1993)

This Statement is designed as a formulation and development of best practice; it is intended to have persuasive rather than mandatory force and is not an accounting standard. In the interests of good financial reporting its use is commended by the Hundred Group of Finance Directors and the London Stock Exchange.

Preface by the Financial Reporting Council

The Financial Reporting Council considers that, with the increasing complexity of many businesses, there is a growing need for annual reports to include an objective discussion that analyses and explains the main features underlying the results and financial position. Many companies already include reviews that go a long way towards achieving this aim, and the FRC believes that the ASB's Statement has an important role to play in assisting directors in developing these reviews, and in encouraging other major companies to emulate the achievements of the best. The FRC therefore welcomes the ASB Statement, and within the framework of necessary commercial confidentiality, invites the directors of all listed companies, and other major corporations, to follow its spirit.

Introduction

Many listed companies' annual reports already include detailed and penetrating reviews of operations and financing. This Statement, developed from the ASB's earlier Discussion Paper of April 1992, is voluntary and not an accounting standard but aims to build on the foundations of existing best practice by providing a framework within which directors can discuss the main factors underlying the company's financial performance and position.

An Operating and Financial Review (OFR) would include a discussion and interpretation of the business, the main factors, features as well as uncertainties that underlie it and the structure of its financing. Although it is a report on the year under review, not a forecast of future results, it should nevertheless draw out those aspects of the year under review that are relevant to an assessment of future prospects. It would therefore give users of the annual report a more consistent foundation on which to make investment decisions regarding the company.

CONFIDENTIALITY

Directors will naturally be concerned to ensure that the benefits to the users of the annual report of particular disclosures, and, in competitive capital markets, the consequent benefit to the company, outweigh the potential commercial damage to the business from the disclosure of sensitive information to competitors. Accordingly, the emphasis in this Statement is on discussion of matters of significance to the business as a whole, and it is expected that in most cases directors will be able to provide a reasonably comprehensive and informative OFR whilst avoiding disclosures of a confidential or sensitive nature.

SCOPE

This Statement has been drafted with listed companies in mind, but is also applicable to other large corporations where there is a legitimate public interest in their financial statements. The detailed guidance is particularly relevant to major corporations who are better placed to lead the way in developing this form of communication with shareholders. Other listed companies, especially smaller ones or those operating in specialized or highly competitive industries, are urged to follow the spirit of the Statement and use their best endeavours to adapt the detailed guidance to their own circumstances.

The operating and financial review

1 The Operating and Financial Review (OFR) is a framework for the directors to discuss and analyse the business's performance and the factors underlying its results and financial position, in order to assist users to assess for themselves the future potential of the business.

2 Directors are encouraged to develop the presentation of their OFR in a way that best complements the format of their annual report as a whole. The proposals are not intended to result in the duplication of information already provided in the annual report. It is for each company's directors to decide whether to deal with the matters addressed in this Statement in a separate, stand-alone section, or by incorporating them within the structure of one or more other sections such as a chief executive's report. If the latter course is adopted, care should be taken to ensure that the combination of OFR information with other material does not obscure its impact or impair the balance and objectivity envisaged by this Statement.

ESSENTIAL FEATURES OF AN OFR

3 The essential features of an OFR are as follows:

- it should be written in a clear style and as succinctly as possible, to be readily understandable by the general reader of annual reports, and should include only matters that are likely to be significant to investors;
- it should be balanced and objective, dealing even-handedly with both good and bad aspects;
- it should refer to comments made in previous statements where these have not been borne out by events;
- it should contain analytical discussion rather than merely numerical analysis;

- it should follow a 'top-down' structure, discussing individual aspects of the business in the context of a discussion of the business as a whole;
- it should explain the reason for, and effect of, any changes in accounting policies;
- it should make it clear how any ratios or other numerical information given relate to the financial statements;
- it should include discussion of:
  - trends and factors underlying the business that have affected the results but are not expected to continue in the future; and
  - known events, trends and uncertainties that are expected to have an impact on the business in the future.

In discussing trends and uncertainties, the OFR should explain their significance to the business; but it is not intended that the OFR should necessarily include a forecast of the outcome of such uncertainties; nor is it suggested that the OFR should contain anything of the nature of a profit forecast. **4**

In some cases, the directors may conclude that a proper discussion of some aspect of the business would require disclosure of confidential or commercially sensitive information, where they consider the potential damage to the company to be greater than the benefits of disclosure. Where the directors decide not to disclose such information, the OFR should ensure that the user is not misled by a discussion that is no longer complete and balanced. **5**

Detailed guidance

The following sections indicate how the general principles set out above can be developed, covering two main areas, the operating review and the financial review. In applying this guidance, directors should consider what matters are of significance in the circumstances of their business. **6**

The detailed guidance should not be regarded as a comprehensive list of all matters that might be relevant, nor are all items listed relevant to all businesses. The OFR should focus on those matters that are of greatest significance to that business. **7**

OPERATING REVIEW

The principal aim of the operating review is to enable the user to understand the dynamics of the various lines of business undertaken—that is, the main influences on the overall results, and how these interrelate. Thus the OFR needs to identify and explain the main factors that underlie the business, and in particular those which either have varied in the past or are expected to change in the future. **8**

Operating results for the period

The OFR should discuss the significant features of operating performance for the period covered by the financial statements, covering all aspects of the profit and loss **9** account to the level of profit on ordinary activities before taxation, and focusing on the overall business and on those segments or other divisions that are relevant to an understanding of the performance as a whole. This should cover changes in the industry or the environment in which the business operates, developments within the business, and their effect on the results. Examples are:

- changes in market conditions;
- new products and services introduced or announced;
- changes in market share or position;
- changes in turnover and margins;
- changes in exchange rates and inflation rates;
- new activities, discontinued activities and other acquisitions and disposals.

10 In the case of material acquisitions, the discussion should comment on the extent to which the expectations at the time of acquisition have been realised. Where a seasonal business has been acquired in the period under review, and the results of the acquisition consolidated are not indicative of those for a full year, this should be indicated.

11 The discussion should cover any other special factors that have affected the results for the period under review; this includes influences whose effect cannot be quantified, as well as specific 'exceptional items'.

Dynamics of the business

12 The OFR should also discuss the main factors and influences that may have a major effect on future results, whether or not they were significant in the period under review. This would include a discussion identifying the principal risks and uncertainties in the main lines of business, together with a commentary on the approach to managing these risks and, in qualitative terms, the nature of the potential impact on results. Examples of matters that may be relevant, depending on the nature of the business, are:

- scarcity of raw materials;
- skill shortages and expertise of uncertain supply;
- patents, licences or franchises;
- dependence on major suppliers or customers;
- product liability;
- health and safety;
- environmental protection costs and potential environmental liabilities;
- self insurance;
- exchange rate fluctuations;
- rates of inflation differing between costs and revenues, or between different markets.

Although some items of this nature will be referred to in the contingent liabilities note within the financial statements, to which reference may be made in the OFR, the discussion should cover a wider range of risks and uncertainties relating to the business.

Investment for the future

Users of annual reports are interested in the extent to which the directors have sought to maintain and enhance future income or profits. The OFR should therefore discuss the business's main activities in this area. This would include activities and expenditure of the period under review which are intended wholly or partly to enhance future profitability and which can be varied, at the discretion of management, over a relatively wide range without significantly affecting current trading. **13**

Capital expenditure is a particularly important element, because of both the amounts involved and the long lead time in implementing projects. The OFR should discuss the current level of capital expenditure together with planned future expenditure (both committed, and authorised but not committed). This discussion should indicate the overall level of expenditure, the major business segments and geographical areas accounting for material elements of the total, and the major projects involved. **14**

Information should also be given on the likely benefits expected from capital expenditure. This should cover both those benefits arising in the period under review as a result of previous expenditure, and the future benefits expected. **15**

In addition to capital expenditure, many other activities and expenditure can be regarded, to a greater or lesser extent, as a form of investing in the future. By their very nature, the definition of such items will vary from one business to another, and particularly from one industry to another. Furthermore, it is often difficult to split such expenditure between that benefiting the current accounting period and that benefiting future periods; nor is the level of activity always measured meaningfully by the expenditure involved. Thus the absolute level of expenditure is less relevant to the user than the impact on current reported profitability of changes in the levels of such activities and expenditure, the potential effect on future earnings of these changes, and management policies in these areas. **16**

Examples of such activities and expenditure for the enhancement of future profits include: **17**

- marketing and advertising campaigns;
- training programmes;
- refurbishment and maintenance programmes;
- pure and applied research which may lead to potential new products and services;
- development of new products and services;
- technical support to customers.

The OFR should discuss the nature of the business's activities in these areas, with particular emphasis on changes in the level of activity and management policy, and should also refer to the benefits expected from such activities. **18**

Profit for the financial year, total recognised gains and losses and shareholders' perspective

19 The OFR should discuss the overall return attributable to shareholders, in terms of dividends and increases in shareholders' funds, commenting on the contributions from the operating performance of the various business units and on other items reported as part of total recognised gains and losses.

20 This discussion should comment on the significant gains and losses that were previously simply accounted for as reserve movements and are now given prominence in the statement of total recognised gains and losses. For many businesses, especially those that are wholly or partly investment businesses, unrealised gains and losses that are recognised in the statement of total recognised gains and losses form an essential component of the overall performance for the year, and should be discussed as such.

Profit for the financial year, dividends and earnings per share

21 The OFR should include a commentary on the comparison between profit for the financial year and dividends, both in total and in per share terms, indicating the directors' overall dividend policy. Other measures of earnings per share which, as permitted by FRS 3, the directors have shown in the profit and loss account—for example, as providing a more useful indication of future trends should also be discussed.

Accounting policies

22 In applying accounting policies, it is sometimes necessary for directors to make subjective judgements and relatively arbitrary allocations which may have very significant effects on the reported results. Many of these are a consequence of the need to report within the arbitrary timescale of a financial year the results of transactions whose life extends for a considerable period beyond the financial year. Whilst to refer to all subjective areas would be confusing, the OFR should indicate and explain any subjective judgements to which the financial statements are particularly sensitive.

FINANCIAL REVIEW

23 The principal aim of this section of the OFR is to explain to the user of the annual report the capital structure of the business, its treasury policy and the dynamics of its financial position—its sources of liquidity and their application, including the implications of the financing requirements arising from its capital expenditure plans.

24 The discussion should concentrate on matters of significance to the position of the business as a whole. It should be a narrative commentary, supported by figures where these assist understanding of the policies and their effect in practice. The following paragraphs indicate specific matters that should be addressed where these are important to an understanding of the business.

Capital structure and treasury policy

The OFR should contain a discussion of the capital structure of the business, in terms of maturity profile of debt, type of capital instruments used, currency, and interest rate structure. This should include comments on relevant ratios such as interest cover and debt/equity ratios. **25**

The discussion should state the capital funding and treasury policies and objectives. These will cover the management of interest rate risk, the maturity profile of borrowings, and the management of exchange rate risk. The OFR should also discuss the implementation of these policies in the period under review, in terms of: **26**

- the manner in which treasury activities are controlled;
- the currencies in which borrowings are made and in which cash and cash equivalents are held;
- the extent to which borrowings are at fixed interest rates;
- the use of financial instruments for hedging purposes;
- the extent to which foreign currency net investments are hedged by currency borrowings and other hedging instruments.

The purpose and effect of major financing transactions undertaken up to the date of approval of the financial statements should be explained. **27**

The effect of interest costs on profits and the potential impact of interest rate changes should be discussed. **28**

Taxation

Where the overall tax charge is significantly different from a 'standard' tax charge (i.e., the normal UK tax rate applied to the profit before taxation), the main components of the reconciliation between the actual and 'standard' tax charges should be discussed. **29**

Funds from operating activities and other sources of cash

The cash generated from operations and other cash inflows during the period under review should be discussed, commenting on any special factors that influenced these. **30**

Although segmental analysis of profit may be indicative of the cash flow generated by each segment, this will not always be so—for example, because of fluctuations in capital expenditure. Where segmental cash flows are significantly out of line with segmental profits this should be indicated and explained. **31**

Current liquidity

The business's liquidity at the end of the period under review should be discussed. This should include comment on the level of borrowings at the end of the period under review, the seasonality of borrowing requirements, indicated by the peak level of borrowings during that period, and the maturity profile of both borrowings and committed borrowing facilities. **32**

33 Reference should be made to the funding requirements for capital expenditure commitments and authorisations.

34 The discussion should refer to any restrictions on the ability to transfer funds from one part of the group to meet the obligations of another part of the group, where these represent, or might foreseeably come to represent, a significant restraint on the group. Such constraints would include exchange controls and taxation consequences of transfers.

35 Where the business has entered into covenants with lenders which could have the effect of restricting the use of credit facilities, and negotiations with the lenders on the operation of these covenants are taking place or are expected to take place, this fact should be indicated in the OFR. Where a breach of a covenant has occurred or is expected to occur, the OFR should give details of the measures taken or proposed to remedy the situation.

Going concern

36 The Cadbury Report Code of Best Practice* proposed that directors of listed companies should state in the annual report their opinion that the company is a going concern, and the Report recommended that the accountancy bodies, together with representatives of listed companies, should develop guidance on the form such confirmation should take. Subject to what such guidance says when available, the going concern confirmation may appropriately be made as part of the OFR discussion of financial position.†

Balance sheet value

37 The OFR could also give a commentary on strengths and resources of the business whose value is not reflected in the balance sheet (or only partially shown in the balance sheet). Such items could include brands and similar intangible items. Where considered appropriate, the value of such items, and increases or decreases in their value, could be discussed. It is not intended that an overall valuation of the business be given, nor, in the case of listed companies, for net asset value to be reconciled to market capitalisation.

STATEMENT OF COMPLIANCE

38 As this is a statement of voluntary best practice, directors are not expected to include in the annual report any formal confirmation that they have complied with the principles set out in this Statement, although the inclusion of some comment on the extent to which the Statement has been followed may be helpful to the user. Where it is implied, through the use of the words 'operating and financial review' or otherwise, that the directors have endeavoured to follow these principles, they should signal any fundamental departure from them.

**Report of the Committee on the Financial Aspects of of Corporate Governance – December 1992*

† Guidance on 'Going concern and financial reporting' was issued in November 1994. Paragraph 43 states that the disclosure by directors should be located in the OFR.

The application of UITF abstracts

(Issued December 1992)

At its last meeting the Urgent Issues Task Force discussed the practical application of Abstracts. As with accounting standards it is important when applying UITF Abstracts to be guided by the spirit and reasoning, as set out in the individual Abstracts, so as to achieve their underlying purpose. Abstracts are intended to be as concise as the nature of a particular topic being dealt with allows and not to be detailed rule-books dealing with every conceivable circumstance. 1

As an example of the unsatisfactory application of an Abstract the Task Force has noted the way that a small minority of companies have applied UITF 3 'Treatment of goodwill on disposal of a business; Two approaches have been noted, as follows: 2

(a) The first approach has been to present the goodwill debit* in the profit and loss account separately from, rather than as a part of, the profit or loss on disposal. Although UITF 3 requires the disclosure of the goodwill component should be included *as part of* the profit or loss on disposal, and not distanced from it as a separate item. Where the item is presented as two components there should be, in addition, a single sub-total showing the profit or loss on disposal. It follows that a caption such as 'loss on sale of subsidiary' should not be used to describe an item that does not take account of related goodwill.

(b) The second approach concerns the corresponding release in the accounts of the goodwill previously eliminated against reserves at the time of the acquisition giving rise to the goodwill. In some cases, this has been done by crediting, in the profit and loss account, before the deduction of dividends, an amount equal to the goodwill component of the profit or loss on disposal. The Task Force believes that, while it is acceptable to show that dividends are paid out of accumulated reserves, this should not be done in a way that implies (e.g. by the striking of a sub-total) that profit for the period is calculated after crediting the goodwill release.

Regarding (b) above the ASB wishes to emphasise (as footnoted in FRS 3) that the immediate elimination of goodwill against reserves is not a recognised loss, and therefore would appear in the reconciliation of movements in shareholders' funds, but not in the profit and loss account or in the statement of total recognised gains or losses. Similarly the credit adjustment arising on a disposal should also be shown in the reconciliation of movements in shareholders' funds, but not in the profit and loss account for the year (unless it is extended to include a full appropriation account) or in the statement of total recognised gains and losses. 3

**This statement assumes positive rather than negative goodwill.*

Part Four

UITF Abstracts

Foreword to UITF abstracts

(Issued February 1994)

Contents

Foreword to UITF abstracts

INTRODUCTION

1 This Foreword explains the authority, scope and application of the 'UITF Abstracts' issued by the Accounting Standards Board (ASB) that set out the consensus reached by its Urgent Issues Task Force (UITF) on particular issues. The composition and procedures of the UITF are set out in the Appendix to this Foreword.

2 The UITF's main role is to assist the ASB with important or significant accounting issues where there exists an accounting standard or a provision of companies legislation* (including the requirement to give a true and fair view) and where unsatisfactory or conflicting interpretations have developed or seem likely to develop. In such circumstances it operates by seeking a consensus as to the accounting treatment that should be adopted. Such a consensus is reached against the background of the ASB's declared aim of relying on principles rather than detailed prescription.

3 The UITF forms its view as to the appropriate accounting treatment for any particular issue within the framework of the law and the principles established in the accounting standards and other statements issued or adopted by the ASB. It also has due regard to international developments.

4 Given the standing of the UITF's membership, the ASB normally expects to accept the UITF's consensus, subject only to the ASB's overriding duty to ensure that nothing is done that conflicts with the law, accounting standards, or the ASB's present or future policy or plans. The rules of procedure have been designed accordingly.

AUTHORITY OF UITF ABSTRACTS

5 The establishment of the UITF and its aim of avoiding the development of unsatisfactory or conflicting interpretations of law or accounting standards have the strong support of the Consultative Committee of Accountancy Bodies (CCAB). The Councils of the CCAB bodies expect their members who assume responsibilities in respect of financial statements to observe UITF Abstracts until they are replaced by accounting standards or otherwise withdrawn by the ASB. The Councils have agreed that:

(a) where this responsibility is evidenced by the association of members' names with such financial statements in the capacity of directors or other officers other than auditors, the onus will be on them to ensure that the existence and purpose of UITF

**References to companies legislation are to: in Great Britain, the Companies Act 1985; in Northern Ireland, the Companies (Northern Ireland) Order 1986; and in the Republic of Ireland, the Companies Acts 1963–90 and the European Communities (Companies: Group Accounts) Regulations 1992.*

Abstracts are fully understood by fellow directors and other officers. Members should also use their best endeavours to ensure that UITF Abstracts are observed and that any significant departures found to be necessary are adequately disclosed and explained in the financial statements.

(b) where members act as auditors or reporting accountants, they should be in a position to justify significant departures to the extent that their concurrence with the departures is stated or implied. They are not, however, required to refer in their report to departures with which they concur, provided that adequate disclosure has been made in the notes to the financial statements.

The CCAB bodies, through appropriate committees, may enquire into apparent failures by their members to observe UITF Abstracts or to ensure adequate disclosure of significant departures. **6**

The UITF notes the intention of the Institute of Chartered Accountants in Ireland of maintaining close liaison with the UITF on promulgating, with appropriate modifications for legal differences, UITF Abstracts for application in the Republic of Ireland. **7**

SCOPE AND APPLICATION OF UITF ABSTRACTS

Directors of companies incorporated under companies legislation are required to prepare accounts that give a true and fair view of the state of affairs of the company, and where applicable the group, at the end of the financial year and of the profit or loss of the company or group for the financial year. **8**

UITF Abstracts are applicable to financial statements of a reporting entity that are intended to give a true and fair view of its state of affairs at the balance sheet date and of its profit or loss (or income and expenditure) for the financial period ending on that date. UITF Abstracts need not be applied to immaterial items. Nothing in the UITF Abstracts is to be construed as amending or overriding the accounting standards or other statements adopted or issued by the ASB. **9**

As with accounting standards it is important when applying UITF Abstracts to be guided by the spirit and reasoning behind them. The spirit and reasoning are set out in the individual UITF Abstracts (and are based on the ASB's Statement of Principles for Financial Reporting). UITF Abstracts are intended to be as concise as the nature of a particular topic allows rather than detailed rules dealing with every conceivable circumstance. **10**

UITF Abstracts should be applied to United Kingdom and Republic of Ireland group financial statements (including any amounts relating to overseas entities that are included in those financial statements). UITF Abstracts are not intended to apply to financial statements of overseas entities prepared for local purposes. **11**

Where UITF Abstracts prescribe information to be contained in financial statements, such requirements do not override exemptions from disclosure given by law to, and utilised by, certain types of entity. **12**

COMPLIANCE WITH UITF ABSTRACTS

13 UITF Abstracts should be regarded as part of the corpus of practices forming the basis for determining what constitutes a true and fair view and should be read in conjunction with accounting standards. UITF Abstracts consequently may be taken into consideration by the Financial Reporting Review Panel (the Review Panel) in deciding whether financial statements call for review.

14 In the United Kingdom, the Review Panel and, in Great Britain the Department of Trade and Industry, in Northern Ireland the Department of Economic Development, have procedures for receiving and investigating complaints regarding the annual accounts of companies in respect of apparent departures from the accounting requirements of companies legislation including the requirement to give a true and fair view. The Review Panel is authorised under the legislation to apply to the court for a declaration or declarator that the annual accounts of a company do not comply with the statutory requirements and an order requiring the directors of the company to prepare revised accounts. The Department of Trade and Industry and the Department of Economic Development have similar powers.*

15 The requirement to give a true and fair view may in special circumstances require a departure from UITF Abstracts. However, because UITF Abstracts are formulated with the objective of ensuring that the information resulting from their application faithfully represents the underlying commercial activity, the ASB envisages that only in exceptional circumstances will departure from the requirements of a UITF Abstract be necessary in order for the financial statements to give a true and fair view.

16 If in exceptional circumstances compliance with the requirements of a UITF Abstract is inconsistent with the requirement to give a true and fair view, the requirements of the UITF Abstract should be departed from to the extent necessary to give a true and fair view. In such cases informed and unbiased judgement should be used to devise an appropriate alternative treatment, which should be consistent with the economic and commercial characteristics of the circumstances concerned. Particulars of any material departure from a UITF Abstract, the reasons for it and its financial effects should be disclosed in the financial statements. The disclosure made should be equivalent to that given in respect of departures from specific accounting provisions of companies legislation.

APPLICABILITY OF A UITF ABSTRACT TO TRANSACTIONS ENTERED INTO BEFORE THE ABSTRACT WAS ISSUED

17 When a new UITF Abstract is issued the question arises whether its provisions should be applied to transactions that took place before the promulgation of the Abstract. The

**In the Republic of Ireland the Department of Enterprise and Employment has powers to investigate generally the affairs of companies. The Review Panel does not operate in the Republic of Ireland.*

general policy of the ASB is that the provisions of UITF Abstracts should apply to all material transactions irrespective of the date at which they are entered into. The reasons for this policy are set out more fully in paragraphs 27–30 of the 'Foreword to Accounting Standards'. All references in those paragraphs to 'accounting standards' should in the present context be read as references to 'UITF Abstracts'.

UITF ABSTRACTS AND THE LEGAL FRAMEWORK

The status of UITF Abstracts in United Kingdom legislation is addressed in the Opinion by Miss Mary Arden QC* 'The true and fair requirement', which is published as an appendix to the 'Foreword to Accounting Standards' and should be read in conjunction with this Foreword. **18**

DISSEMINATION AND IMPLEMENTATION

The UITF Abstracts are made publicly available by the ASB for the guidance of users, preparers and auditors of financial information. They include a discussion of the matter, the accounting issues identified, reference sources, and a summary of the UITF's deliberations, and clearly indicate what conclusion has been reached. **19**

If the UITF is unable to reach a consensus, or if a consensus is not ratified by the ASB, an explanation of the circumstances will be published. **20**

A UITF Abstract takes effect from the effective date in the published Abstract, and is thereafter to be regarded as accepted practice in the area in question. Accordingly, all reporting entities will be expected to conform to it, if necessary by changing previously adopted accounting policies, unless the consensus explicitly states otherwise. **21**

Now the Honourable Mrs Justice Arden.

Appendix
Composition and procedures of the UITF

COMPOSITION

A1 The UITF is a committee of the ASB comprising a number of people of standing in the field of financial reporting. Its purpose is to enlist the experience and influence of its members to assist the ASB in its task of establishing and improving standards of financial accounting and reporting, for the benefit of users, preparers and auditors of financial information.

A2 The UITF consists of up to sixteen members experienced in the technicalities of financial reporting. The membership includes:

eight senior representatives from the eight largest accounting firms;

one member from a medium-sized or small accounting firm;

four members from industry or commerce; and

up to three further members chosen on a personal basis.

A3 The ASB may adjust the size and composition of the UITF from time to time.

A4 All members are appointed for two-year periods. Membership is personal. Each member may have a named alternate for his period of office; the alternate may attend and vote at any meetings that the member is unable to attend. If neither the member nor his named alternate is able to attend, another alternate may attend, but does not have the right to vote.

A5 The Chairman of the UITF is appointed from the members of the ASB. In the initial period the Chairman is the Chairman of the ASB.

A6 Members of the ASB are free to attend UITF meetings and have the right to speak, but do not have the right to vote.

A7 If in his view it would assist the conduct of business, the Chairman may invite others to attend UITF meetings as observers.

ADMISSION OF ITEMS TO THE AGENDA

A8 Auditors and companies are invited to refer substantial new issues to the UITF where there is doubt about the most appropriate accounting treatment leading to a true and fair view and it is important that a standard treatment should be established before a precedent is set by practice.

A9 The Councils of the CCAB bodies invite their members to raise for possible consideration by the UITF any substantial accounting issues of general concern that arise in connection with the preparation and audit of financial statements. In raising such issues members should not disclose information of a confidential nature either directly or by implication to anyone likely to be aware of the background.

The UITF will not consider any issue that the ASB indicates falls within its own agenda unless specifically requested to do so by the ASB. **A10**

CONSULTATION

The UITF deals with urgent and emerging issues, which necessarily means that it is not possible to follow a normal consultation and due process procedure. The ASB therefore takes special measures to publicise the matters on the UITF's agenda. Preliminary decisions reached by the UITF are circulated for comment to all recipients for the ASB Bulletin. **A11**

QUORUM

A quorum for the UITF is at least eleven voting members or their named alternates. **A12**

VOTING

A consensus will have been attained where not more than two voting members of the UITF, or their named alternates, present at the meeting dissent from the treatment proposed as the appropriate accounting practice for the matter in question. **A13**

A member of the UITF is expected to support any vote of his alternate and to agree to be bound by it. **A14**

The Chairman has no vote. **A15**

RATIFICATION BY THE ASB

As indicated in paragraph 4 of the 'Foreword to UITF Abstracts', the ASB will normally expect to accept the UITF's consensus and will not separately consider the issue. However, the ASB retains the right to decline to accept any consensus that it believes is contrary to law or to its extant or intended accounting standards. Where such a situation arises the ASB will set out its views to the UITF in writing for consideration as soon as practicable thereafter with the objective if possible of achieving a mutually acceptable solution. **A16**

UITF abstract 3: Treatment of goodwill on disposal of a business

(Issued December 1991)

THE ISSUE

In consolidated accounts, the question arises how the profit or loss on disposal of a previously acquired business should be determined where goodwill arising on its acquisition has previously been eliminated against reserves in accordance with the preferred treatment recommended by SSAP 22. 1

The following simple example illustrates the problem. 2

- A subsidiary was purchased for £500m, of which £150m was attributed to the fair value of net assets acquired. The remaining £350m was therefore attributed to goodwill and was eliminated against group reserves on consolidation.
- In a subsequent accounting period, when the consolidated carrying value of the subsidiary's net assets remains at £150m, the subsidiary is resold for £400m.

The issue is which of the following results the group should record on disposal:

(a) a profit of £250m (proceeds of £400m less carrying value of the subsidiary's net assets after the elimination of goodwill, £150m); or

(b) a loss on disposal of £100m (proceeds of £400m less cost of business sold, £500m, being the carrying value of the subsidiary's net assets, £150m, together with purchased goodwill of £350m previously eliminated against reserves).

Existing accounting and disclosure requirements are given in SSAPs 14* and 22. SSAP 22 (paragraph 52) states that for each material disposal of a previously acquired business or business segment, there should be disclosed: 3

> 'the amount of purchased goodwill attributable to the business or business segment disposed of and how it has been treated in determining the profit or loss on disposal'.

SSAP 22 does not provide any measurement rule.

SSAP 14 (paragraph 31) states that the consolidated profit or loss on disposal of a subsidiary is the difference between the proceeds of the sale and the holding company's share of its net assets together with any premium (less any amounts written off) or discount on acquisition. SSAP 14 has been interpreted as requiring the profit or loss on disposal to be calculated as the difference between sale proceeds and net assets excluding goodwill previously eliminated against reserves. However, SSAP 14 was 4

***Editor's note:** *SSAP 14 was replaced by FRS 2 in 1992.*

issued long before SSAP 22 was developed, when it was common practice to carry purchased goodwill in the balance sheet.*

5 SSAP 22 comments on the treatment of eliminating or 'writing-off' purchased goodwill immediately to reserves. Paragraph 6 states: 'In this context, the term 'write-off' does not imply an equivalent actual loss of value'. Paragraph 7 states that the write-off should not be a charge in the profit and loss account because 'purchased goodwill is written off as a matter of accounting policy, that is, in order to achieve consistency of treatment with non-purchased goodwill, rather than because it has suffered a permanent diminution in value'.

6 The issue relates to each material disposal of a previously acquired business, subsidiary or associated undertaking where the goodwill attributable has been eliminated against reserves and has not previously been charged in the profit and loss account. In view of the current uncertainty regarding the most appropriate approach in the light of existing accounting standards, and pending the development of a revised standard on accounting for goodwill, the Task Force issues the following consensus.

UITF CONSENSUS†

7 The Task Force reached a consensus that the amount included in the consolidated profit or loss account in respect of the profit and loss on disposal of a previously acquired business, subsidiary or associated undertaking should be determined by including, if material, the attributable amount of purchased goodwill where it has previously been eliminated against reserves as a matter of accounting policy and has not previously been charged in the profit and loss account.

8 In the view of the Task Force, this treatment is necessary in order to prevent purchased goodwill that has been eliminated against reserves from bypassing the profit and loss account completely.

9 The Task Force considered the supplementary question whether the amount of goodwill brought into the calculation of the profit or loss on disposal should be the gross attributable amount has been eliminated against reserves or whether there should be an adjustment for any notional amortisation during the period of ownership. The Task Force concluded that, if there has previously been no charge in the profit and loss account in respect of the premium paid on acquisition, the gross attributable amount should be brought into the calculation. This treatment similarly is to ensure that none of the attributable goodwill bypasses the profit and loss account.

10 This consensus requires the amount of purchased goodwill attributable to the business disposed of and included in the calculation of the profit or loss on disposal to be

***Editor's note:** *SSAP 14 was replaced by FRS 2 in 1992. Paragraph 47 of FRS 2 reflects the consensus reached in this abstract.*

†**Editor's note:** *See also the ASB statement on the application of UITF abstracts, reproduced in Part Three.*

separately disclosed as a component of the profit or loss on disposal, either on the face of the profit and loss account or in a note to the financial statements.

The Task Force recognises that in some cases a practical problem may arise in identifying goodwill attributable to disposals. However, it considers that the disclosure requirements of both the Companies Act 1985 and SSAP 22 relating respectively to (a) the cumulative amount of goodwill written off, net of goodwill attributable to disposals, and (b) goodwill attributable to businesses disposed of, effectively require companies to maintain records that would normally enable an appropriate estimate or apportionment to be made of the purchased goodwill attributable to disposals. Nevertheless, there may be cases where it is genuinely impractical to make a reasonable estimate of the purchased goodwill attributable to a disposal, for example, where a disposal relates to a business that was part of a group acquired many years ago and subsequently restructured. Accordingly, in those cases where it is not possible to ascertain the goodwill attributable to a business disposed of, or to make a reasonable apportionment of the goodwill recognised in the original acquisition, this fact and the reason should be explained. (The transitional provisions of SSAP 22 and the Companies Act 1985 contain similar provisions regarding their respective disclosure requirements for acquisitions made before the requirements came into effect.) **11**

The principles set out above in respect of disposals also apply to closures of businesses and to negative goodwill. **12**

In order to ensure consistency of treatment, comparative figures for preceding years should be restated where applicable. **13**

DATE FROM WHICH EFFECTIVE

The accounting treatment required by this consensus should be adopted in financial statements relating to accounting periods ending on or after 23rd January 1992, but earlier adoption is encouraged. **14**

REFERENCES

Statement of Standard Accounting Practice 14 – Group accounts.*

Statement of Standard Accounting Practice 22 – Accounting for goodwill.

Companies Act 1985 – Paragraph 14 of Schedule 4A; (paragraphs 4 and 58(2) of Schedule 4).

Northern Ireland – Companies (Northern Ireland) Order 1986 – Paragraph 14 of Schedule 4A; paragraphs 4 and 58(2) of Schedule 4.

Republic of Ireland – Companies (Amendment) Act 1986 – Section 4(8)–(10); paragraph 44(2) of the Schedule.

***Editor's note:** *SSAP 14 was replaced by FRS 2 in 1992.*

ACCOUNTING STANDARDS BOARD OPINION ON RELATIONSHIP WITH FRED 1*

The Accounting Standards Board has developed proposals for a Financial Reporting Standard to reform the structure of the profit and loss account. Financial Reporting Exposure Draft 1 (FRED 1), 'The structure of financial statements – Reporting of financial performance', was issued by the Board in December 1991. FRED 1 proposes that financial statements should include an additional primary financial statement, a statement of total recognised gains and losses. Its purpose is to highlight those changes in a reporting entity's net assets in a period resulting from gains and losses which are recognised in the financial statements, other than those resulting from capital contributed by or repaid to shareholders. The Task Force considered that it would be helpful for the Board to clarify the inter-relationship of this consensus with the treatment of purchased goodwill in the context of FRED 1. In this respect, the Board confirms that it does not consider purchased goodwill eliminated against reserves on acquisition and, consequently, any reinstatement of such goodwill on disposal, to be a recognised loss or gain. This view is consistent with SSAP 22 (see paragraph 5 above). Accordingly, the elimination and reinstatement of goodwill would not be included in the statement of total recognised gains and losses.

***Editor's note:** Now FRS 3 'Reporting Financial Performance' (see footnote to paragraph 27).*

UITF abstract 4: Presentation of long-term debtors in current assets

(Issued July 1992)

THE ISSUE

Both for liabilities and for debtors the Companies Act requires a distinction to be drawn between the amounts payable or receivable within one year and those due to be settled or received after more than one year. Although the distinction is disclosed in the notes for each of the items forming part of debtors, (including prepayments and accrued income if included in debtors), unlike in the case of liabilities it is not required to be carried through to the total of current assets nor to the significant Format 1 sub-total of net current assets (liabilities). 1

In consequence, there is a certain imbalance between the items that the formats require to be classified under current assets or current liabilities. For example, a pension fund surplus (to the extent recognised in the balance sheet) could give rise to a prepayment forming part of net current assets (liabilities), whereas a deficiency would normally be shown as a provision under long-term liabilities. In some cases the period expected to be required for recovery of such an asset may be considerable, perhaps in excess of ten years. Other examples of long-term debtor items include much of the trade debtors of lessors and deferred consideration in respect of the sale of an investment or other fixed asset. 2

UITF CONSENSUS

In most cases it will be satisfactory to disclose the size of debtors due after more than one year in the notes to the accounts. There will be some instances, however, where the amount is so material in the context of the total net current assets that in the absence of disclosure of debtors due after more than one year on the face of the balance sheet readers may misinterpret the accounts. The Task Force have agreed that, in such circumstances, the amount should be disclosed on the face of the balance sheet. 3

DATE FROM WHICH EFFECTIVE

The disclosure required by this consensus should be adopted in financial statements relating to accounting periods ending on or after 23 August 1992, but earlier adoption is encouraged. 4

REFERENCES

Companies Act 1985 and Companies (Northern Ireland) Order 1986 – Schedule 4 Balance Sheet Formats 1 and 2 including notes 5 and 6.

Republic of Ireland – Companies (Amendment) Act 1986, the Schedule, Balance Sheet Formats 1 and 2 including note 4.

Statement of Standard Accounting Practice 21—Accounting for leases and hire purchase contracts.

Statement of Standard Accounting Practice 24—Accounting for pension costs.

International Accounting Standard 13—Presentation of Current Assets and Current Liabilities.

UITF abstract 5: Transfers from current assets to fixed assets

(Issued July 1992)

THE ISSUE

The Companies Act 1985 defines a fixed asset as one intended for use on a continuing basis in the company's activities and any which are not intended for such use are current assets (section 262(1)CA 1985). Where at a date subsequent to its original acquisition a current asset is retained for use on a continuing basis in the company's activities it becomes a fixed asset and the question arises as to the appropriate transfer value. An example is a property which is reclassified from trading properties to investment properties. 1

Of particular concern is the possibility that companies could avoid charging the profit and loss account with write-downs to net realisable value arising on unsold trading assets. This could be done by transferring the relevant assets from current assets to fixed assets at above net realisable value, as a result of which any later write down might be debited to revaluation reserve. 2

This abstract deals only with situations where current assets are included in the balance sheet at the lower of cost and net realisable value under paragraphs 22 and 23 of Schedule 4 to the Companies Act 1985. 3

The timing of the transfer of current assets to fixed assets should reflect the timing of management's change of intent and should not be backdated (for example to the start of the financial year). Since the date of the management decision is unlikely to correspond with the balance sheet date at which a full review of carrying values would be made, consideration must be given to the appropriate amounts at which such assets should be transferred at the time of transfer. 4

UITF CONSENSUS

The Task Force reached a consensus that where assets are transferred from current to fixed, the current asset accounting rules should be applied up to the effective date of transfer, which is the date of management's change of intent. Consequently the transfer should be made at the lower of cost and net realisable value, and accordingly an assessment should be made of the net realisable value at the date of transfer and if this is less than its previous carrying value the diminution should be charged in the profit and loss account, reflecting the loss to the company while the asset was held as a current asset. 5

Whether assets are transferred at cost or at net realisable value in accordance with paragraph 5 above, fixed asset accounting rules will apply to the assets subsequent to the date of transfer. In cases where the transfer is at net realisable value, the asset 6 should be accounted for as a fixed asset at a valuation (under the alternative accounting rules of the Act) as at the date of the transfer; at subsequent balance sheet dates it may or may not be revalued, but in either event the disclosure requirements appropriate to a valuation should be given.

DATE FROM WHICH EFFECTIVE

7 The accounting treatment required by this consensus should be adopted in financial statements relating to accounting periods ending on or after 23 December 1992, but earlier adoption is encouraged. In order to ensure consistency of treatment, corresponding amounts for preceding years should be restated where applicable.

REFERENCES

Companies Act 1985 Section 222(1) and Schedule 4 paragraphs 17 to 19, 22 to 23, 30 to 34 and 43.

Northern Ireland—Companies (Northern Ireland) Order 1986, articles 229(1) and 270(1) and Schedule 4 paragraphs 17 to 19, 22 to 23, 30 to 34 and 43.

Republic of Ireland—Companies Act 1990 section 202(1) and the Companies (Amendment) Act 1986, the Schedule paragraphs 5 to 7, 10 to 11, 18 to 22, 30 and 60.

FRS 3 'Reporting Financial Performance'—paragraph 13.

Statement of Standard Accounting Practice 9—'Stocks and long-term contracts—paragraph 26.

Statement of Standard Accounting Practice 19—'Accounting for investment properties—paragraphs 11 and 13.

NOTE ON LEGAL REQUIREMENTS

The Task Force has been advised by leading Counsel that assets can be treated as having been transferred from current assets to fixed assets at a value equal to the lower of cost and net realisable value. Counsel indicated that the above advice is based on the assumption that where the transfer takes place at net realisable value, the asset will be accounted for as a fixed asset as at the date of transfer in accordance with the accounting rules in Schedule 4 to the Companies Act (that is, included at a current value rather than historical cost).

UITF abstract 6: Accounting for post-retirement benefits other than pensions

(Issued November 1992)

THE ISSUE

As well as providing pensions for their employees, some employers also provide post-retirement health care or other benefits. Although these arrangements are still relatively rare in the UK, they are common in some other countries, notably the United States. UK holding companies with overseas subsidiaries may therefore have to consider the question of accounting for them in their group accounts even if they have no material obligations in the UK. 1

Statement of Standard Accounting Practice No. 24 – 'Accounting for pension costs' (SSAP 24) does not deal specifically with benefits other than pensions, but does state in paragraph 75: 2

> 'Although this Statement primarily addresses pensions, its principles may be equally applicable to the cost of providing other post-retirement benefits'.

In July 1989, the Accounting Standards Committee (ASC) issued Technical Release 756 (TR756) which stated that the above extract from SSAP 24 was not binding, but was indicative only. TR756 further said that until the ASC produced a Statement on accounting for other post-retirement benefits, there was no obligation to apply the principles of SSAP 24 to such benefits, although companies might consider it appropriate to do so. 3

Since the issue of TR756, an accounting standard has been published in the United States which addresses the accounting for post-retirement benefits other than pensions (FAS106). FAS106 requires a change from the practice of accounting for these benefits on a cash basis to accounting on an accruals basis. Following the issue of FAS106 it is appropriate for the Task Force to review the conclusion reached in TR756, which is superseded by this consensus. 4

UITF CONSENSUS

The Task Force reached a consensus that, as a matter of principle, post-retirement benefits other than pensions are liabilities, which, in accordance with the accruals and prudence concepts of SSAP 2 and the Companies Act, should be recognised in financial statements. Such benefits share many of the characteristics of pensions and the principles of SSAP 24 are applicable to their measurement and disclosure. 5

The Task Force recognised, however, that the measurement of such obligations poses difficulties additional to those which apply in the case of pensions. Also in some cases employers are engaged in negotiations which may affect significantly the extent of the obligations. For these reasons the Task Force has decided to allow a transitional period 6 before it becomes mandatory to apply SSAP 24 principles to the measurement of all post-retirement benefits, although earlier application is encouraged. In the meantime this consensus also requires disclosure relating to the obligations as described in paragraph below if SSAP 24 principles are not adopted.

7 Where a UK parent undertaking has US subsidiaries which are governed by the requirements of FAS106, they will already have measured the cost of the benefits for that purpose. FAS106 discusses the subject in considerable detail and it may therefore also provide a useful source of guidance for non-US schemes. Whilst methods already adopted for accounting for pension costs under SSAP 24 are generally to be utilised, measurement in accordance with FAS106, including use of the transitional 20 year spreading option, will be deemed to satisfy SSAP 24 principles for full provision.

8 When employers change their accounting policy in order to account for post-retirement benefits other than pensions in terms of SSAP 24 they should deal with the cumulative cost relating to previous years in accordance with paragraph 92 of SSAP 24. This permits the unprovided obligation to be recognised either by means of a prior year adjustment in accordance with FRS 3 or by spreading it forward over the expected remaining service lives of current employees. The transitional method chosen should be disclosed.

9 When employers have adopted a SSAP 24 basis of accounting for post-retirement benefits other than pensions (which, as indicated in paragraph 7, includes a FAS106 basis) they should make disclosures in relation to them equivalent to those required in respect of pension schemes under SSAP 24. These should include details of any important assumptions which are specific to the measurement of such benefits, such as the assumed rate of inflation in the cost of providing the benefits. Material balance sheet provisions for post-retirement benefits other than pensions should be distinguished from other provisions in the notes to the accounts.

10 Even if it is not recognised as a liability, an obligation to meet post-retirement benefits constitutes a financial commitment which requires to be disclosed in terms of paragraph 50(5) of Schedule 4 to the Companies Act 1985. Employers who have not yet provided for post-retirement benefits other than pensions under SSAP 24 principles should give the following disclosures where the cost of meeting such benefits is expected to be material:

- a general description of the nature of the benefits to which employees are entitled and the approximate number of employees eligible to receive them;
- an estimate of the liability (i.e., the provision that would appear in the balance sheet if the obligation was recognised) or a statement why no reliable estimate can be made;
- a statement as to whether or not the employer expects the costs of meeting the liability to attract taxation relief when they are paid and if so an estimate of the amount of such relief, where practicable;
- the amount of expense recognised in the period in relation to these benefits. On a pay as you go basis this may be substantially less than the amount which would be

recognised on an accruals basis, and if the difference is likely to be material this fact should be indicated; and

- the accounting policy applied in relation to post- retirement benefits other than pensions.

DATE FROM WHICH EFFECTIVE

SSAP 24 principles should be applied in relation to all post-retirement benefits in financial statements relating to accounting periods ending on or after 23 December 1994. Where employers have not yet applied SSAP 24 to post-retirement benefits other than pensions they should give the disclosures required by paragraph 10 of this consensus in their financial statements relating to accounting periods ending on or after 23 December 1992. Earlier adoption is encouraged in both cases. **11**

REFERENCES

Companies Act 1985 and Companies (Northern Ireland) Order 1986 Schedule 4, paragraph 50(5).

Republic of Ireland—Companies (Amendment) Act 1986, the Schedule paragraph 36(3).

Statement of Standard Accounting Practice No. 2—'Disclosure of Accounting Policies' (SSAP 2).

Financial Reporting Standard No. 3—'Reporting Financial Performance' (FRS 3).

Statement of Standard Accounting Practice No. 24—'Accounting for pension costs' (SSAP 24).

The Accounting Standards Committee—Technical Release 756 FASB Statement of Financial Accounting Standards No. 106—Employers' Accounting for post-retirement benefits other than pensions FAS106.

NOTE ON DEFERRED TAX IMPLICATIONS

SSAP 24 indicates that where timing differences arise in respect of pension costs they should be accounted for in accordance with SSAP 15. However a number of commentators have pointed out that SSAPs 15 and 24 use different criteria for the recognition of profit and loss account charges and related assets and liabilities. This problem is particularly exacerbated in practice in the case of post-retirement benefits other than pensions, which are generally unfunded. In recognition of the difficulties the requirements of this abstract, if taken together with those of SSAP 15, could cause, the Accounting Standards Board has decided to propose a limited amendment to SSAP 15. This would permit the use of either the full provision basis or the partial provision basis in accounting for the deferred tax implications of pensions and other post-retirement benefits accounted for in accordance with SSAP 24 and UITF 6, pending a comprehensive review of SSAP 15 that will take place in due course. An exposure draft for this proposed amendment has been issued.*

Editor's note: SSAP 15 was formally amended, as proposed in the exposure draft, in December 1992.

UITF abstract 7: True and fair view override disclosures

(Issued December 1992)

THE ISSUE

1 The Companies Act 1985, as amended ('the Act') provides, both for individual company accounts and for group accounts, that if in special circumstances compliance with any of the provisions of the Act as to the matters to be included in a company's accounts (or notes thereto) is inconsistent with the requirement to give a true and fair view of the state of affairs and profit or loss, the directors shall depart from that provision to the extent necessary to give a true and fair view. Where this true and fair view override is used the Act requires that 'particulars of any such departure, the reasons for it and its effect shall be given in a note to the accounts'. The Act gives no further elaboration of this requirement.

2 The objectives of this disclosure requirement are to highlight instances where there are departures from specific rules in the act and to provide the reader of the accounts with information on the position had the normal rules in the Act been applied. This is necessary in order to assist in achieving the equivalence of information available in respect of companies not only in the UK and Ireland but throughout the European Community.

3 The interpretation of the requirement in practice has varied and there has been a tendency for some companies to understate rather than emphasise the significance of what they have done. In some cases it has not been clear from the notes to the accounts whether the directors consider that they have departed from a specific statutory rule and that the true and fair view override is being invoked.

UITF CONSENSUS

4 The Task Force reached a consensus that in cases where the true and fair view override is being invoked this should be stated clearly and unambiguously. To this end the statutory disclosure requirement should be interpreted as follows:

(a) 'Particulars of any such departure'—a statement of the treatment which the Act would normally require in the circumstances and a description of the treatment actually adopted;

(b) 'the reasons for it'—a statement as to why the treatment prescribed would not give a true and fair view;

(c) 'its effect'—a description of how the position shown in the accounts is different as a result of the departure, normally with quantification, except (i) where quantification is already evident in the accounts themselves (an example of which might be a presentation rather than a measurement matter, such as an adaptation of the headings in the Act's format requirements not covered by paragraph 3(3) of Schedule 4), or (ii) whenever the effect cannot reasonably be quantified, in which case the directors should explain the circumstances.

5 Where a departure continues in subsequent financial statements, the disclosures should be made in all such subsequent statements, and should include corresponding amounts for the previous year.

6 Where a departure affects only the corresponding amount, the disclosures required by this abstract should be given for those corresponding amounts.

7 The disclosures required by this abstract should either be included, or cross-referenced, in the note required under paragraph 36A of Schedule 4 (re compliance with accounting standards and particulars of any material departure from those standards and the reasons for it).

8 The expression 'particulars of any such departure, the reasons for it and its effect' is also used in paragraph 15 of Schedule 4 and paragraph 22 of Schedule 9 (both relating to departure from the specified statutory accounting principles)* and paragraph 3(2) of Schedule 4A use of inconsistent accounting rules for an undertaking included in group accounts). The interpretation of the expression given in this abstract is also applicable to these cases.

DATE FROM WHICH EFFECTIVE

9 The interpretation required by this abstract should be adopted in financial statements relating to accounting periods ending on or after 23 December 1992.

REFERENCES

Companies Act 1985, sections 226(5) and 227(6), Schedule 4 paragraphs 15 and 36A, Schedule 4A paragraph 3(2) and Schedule 9 paragraph 22.

Northern Ireland—Companies (Northern Ireland) Order 1986 articles 234(5) and 235(6), Schedule 4 paragraphs 15 and 36A and Schedule 4A paragraph 3(2), and Companies (1986 Order) (Banks Accounts) Regulations (NI) 1992 (SR 1992/258), Schedule 1 paragraph 22.

Republic of Ireland—Companies (Amendment) Act 1986 sections 3(1) (d)—(e), and 6, and European Communities (Companies: Group Accounts) Regulations 1992 regulations 14(3)—(4) and 29 (2)—(3), and European Communities (Credit Institutions: Accounts) regulations 1992 (SI No.294 of 1992), the Schedule, Chapter 2, paragraph 22. There is no equivalent reference to paragraph 36A of Schedule 4 to the Act.

Editor's note: *Paragraph 19 of the new Schedule 9A also refers to departures from the specified statutory accounting principles.*

UITF abstract 9: Accounting for operations in hyper-inflationary economies

(Issued June 1993)

THE ISSUE

SSAP 20 'Foreign currency translation' states that 'where a foreign enterprise operates in a country in which a very high rate of inflation exists it may not be possible to present fairly in historical cost accounts the financial position of a foreign enterprise simply by a translation process. In such circumstances the local currency financial statements should be adjusted where possible to reflect current price levels before the translation process is undertaken'. However there is some uncertainty as to when and how this guidance should be applied in practice. 1

The overriding requirement to give a true and fair view of the profit or loss and state of affairs can be considered to require appropriate adjustments to be made where significant distortions arise from very high rates of inflation ('hyper-inflation'). Because it is a common condition, users of financial statements have developed tolerance for some inflation and in varying degrees allow for it in their analyses. The distortions caused by hyper-inflation may in practice be diluted by the relative rates of inflation in the reporting country and in other countries where the reporting entity operates, when taken together with the relative size of the operations in hyper-inflationary economies in the context of the reporting group. 2

The question of what constitutes hyper-inflation is necessarily judgmental. International Accounting Standard No.29 'Financial Reporting in Hyperinflationary Economies' describes a number of characteristics of the economic environment of a country which indicate hyper-inflation (see the Appendix to this Abstract). Failure to adjust for hyper-inflation before application of the SSAP 20 closing rate/net investment method of translation produces a significant debit to group reserves, whilst at the same time inflated profits are included in the group profit and loss account (whether from high interest income on deposits in a rapidly depreciating local currency or from trading operations at what could be considered unrealistically high profitability). 3

Methods adopted to eliminate distortions caused by hyper-inflation need to take account of the following factors: 4

(a) the lack of reliable and timely inflation indices in a number of hyper-inflationary economies can pose a major practical problem to adjusting local currency financial statements;
(b) it is necessary to have regard to the particular local circumstances as these can vary significantly between countries in terms of how real profitability should be measured.

UITF CONSENSUS

5 The Task Force reached a consensus that adjustments are required where the distortions caused by hyper-inflation are such as to affect the true and fair view given by the group financial statements. In any event adjustments are required where the cumulative inflation rate over three years is approaching, or exceeds, 100% and the operations in the hyper-inflationary economies are material.

6 The Task Force considered that the following two methods of eliminating the distortions were consistent with SSAP20 and therefore acceptable:

(a) adjusting the local currency financial statements to reflect current price levels before the translation process is undertaken, as suggested in paragraph 26 of SSAP 20. This includes taking any gain or loss on the net monetary position through the profit and loss account.

(b) using a relatively stable currency (which would not necessarily be sterling) as the functional currency (i.e., the currency of measurement) for the relevant foreign operations. For example in certain businesses operating in Latin American territories the US dollar acts effectively as the functional currency for business operations. The functional currency would in effect be the 'local currency' as defined in paragraph 39 of SSAP 20. In such circumstances, if the transactions are not recorded initially in that stable currency, they must first be remeasured into that currency by applying the temporal method described in SSAP 20 (but based on the dollar or other stable currency rather than sterling). The effect is that the movement between the original currency of record and the stable currency is used as a proxy for an inflation index.

7 If neither of the above methods is considered appropriate for material operations, then the reasons should be stated and alternative methods to eliminate the distortions should be adopted.

8 Where group operations in areas of hyper-inflation are material in the context of group results or net assets, the accounting policy adopted to eliminate the distortions of such inflation should be disclosed.

DATE FROM WHICH EFFECTIVE

9 The accounting treatment required by this consensus should be adopted in financial statements relating to accounting periods ending on or after 23 August 1993, but earlier adoption is encouraged. In order to ensure consistency of treatment, corresponding amounts for preceding years should be restated where applicable.

REFERENCES

Statement of Standard Accounting Practice 20—Foreign Currency Translation—paragraphs 26, 39 and 55.

International Accounting Standard 29—Financial Reporting in Hyper-inflationary Economies.

Appendix

Extract from IAS 29 'Financial Reporting in Hyper-inflationary Economies'

'3 This Statement does not establish an absolute rate at which hyperinflation is deemed to arise. It is a matter of judgement when restatement of financial statements in accordance with this Statement becomes necessary. Hyperinflation is indicated by characteristics of the economic environment of a country which include, but are not limited to, the following:

(a) the general population prefers to keep its wealth in nonmonetary assets or in a relatively stable foreign currency. Amounts of local currency held are immediately invested to maintain purchasing power;
(b) the general population regards monetary amounts not in terms of the local currency but in terms of a relatively stable foreign currency. Prices may be quoted in that currency;
(c) sales and purchases on credit take place at prices that compensate for the expected loss of purchasing power during the credit period, even if the period is short;
(d) interest rates, wages and prices are linked to
(a) price index; and
(e) the cumulative inflation rate over three years is approaching, or exceeds, 100%'.

UITF abstract 10: Disclosure of directors' share options

(Issued September 1994)

THE ISSUE

Introduction

The UITF has considered present practice for reporting the granting and exercise of share options in the light of the statutory and other requirements for the disclosure of directors' emoluments and options. 1

Legal and other considerations

The reporting of directors' share options falls for consideration under several separate legal requirements: 2

(a) In Great Britain paragraph 1(4) (d) of Schedule 6 to the Companies Act 1985 ('the Act') states that the aggregate emoluments disclosable under section 232 include 'the estimated money value of any other benefits ... otherwise than in cash.' Paragraph 11(1) of Schedule 6 to the Act provides that 'the amounts to be shown for any financial year ... are the sums receivable in respect of that year (whenever paid) or in the case of sums not receivable in respect of a period, the sums paid during that year'.

(b) As regards individual directors, paragraphs 3(1) and 4(3) of Schedule 6 to the Act require the separate disclosure of the aggregate emoluments of the chairman and of the highest paid director, if not the chairman; paragraph 4(2) requires the inclusion of the emoluments of all directors in bands and paragraph 5 provides for the inclusion of the estimated money value of any other benefits in these disclosures.

(c) Section 325 of the Act requires every company to maintain a register which as regards options to subscribe for shares or debentures includes details for each director and his or her immediate family, of the date of grant, the period in which exercisable, the consideration for the grant (or if no consideration, that fact), the number of shares or debentures involved, the price to be paid and, on exercise, the numbers of shares or debentures acquired under option. The register is open to inspection. Paragraph 2B of Schedule 7 to the Act requires for each director that the information in the register as regards the number of shares or debentures in the company or its subsidiaries in respect of which the right was *granted* or *exercised* during the year, be given in the directors' report or by way of note to the company's accounts. Some companies are now giving the prices at which such options are granted or exercised, but this is not actually required by the law.

As regards listed and USM companies, paragraph 12.43(k) of The Listing Rules and The Unlisted Securities Market Rules of the London Stock Exchange require for each director disclosure of the total interests including options, distinguishing between beneficial and non-beneficial interests, in the directors' report as at the end of each year and until a date not more than one month prior to the circulation of the annual report. 3

4 The Report of the Committee on The Financial Aspects of Corporate Governance ('the Cadbury Report') states at paragraph 4.40 that 'The overriding principle in respect of board remuneration is that of openness. Shareholders are entitled to a full and clear statement of directors' present and future benefits, and of how they have been determined.' The Code of Best Practice promulgated by the Committee states at paragraph 3.2 that 'There should be full and clear disclosure of directors' total emoluments and those of the chairman and highest-paid UK director, including pension contributions and stock options. Separate figures should be given for salary and performance-related elements and the basis on which performance is measured should be explained.' This recommendation was intended to respond to the growing disquiet in many circles that reporting practices did not adequately reflect management remuneration.

Discussion

5 While it is generally accepted that the grant of an option is a 'benefit', many consider that the attribution of a meaningful estimated money value to an option at the date of grant can be very difficult. The difficulties of valuation stem from the fact that for most companies, valuation would require the use of theoretical models which become even more complicated and subjective when the rights under the option are contingent on future performance or other factors. Further, directors' options are by their nature an element of directors' compensation for the period between grant and exercise since such options are non-transferable and generally require continued employment to some date in the future. It can therefore be argued that, subject to the specific terms of any particular scheme, any value that may be attributed to options should be apportioned over the period during which the conditions have to be fulfilled, on the basis that the value is 'earned' and receivable in respect of the years within the period even though 'paid' at some other date. If this view were to be adopted, it would follow that some form of annual disclosure during that period would be appropriate.

6 As regards the disclosures required in the directors' report or by way of note to the accounts of directors' options, the UITF notes that current law and the London Stock Exchange do not explicitly require the aggregate number of directors' options by price nor the option prices applicable to each director to be disclosed.

7 As a result of the foregoing, few companies in the past have disclosed the option prices applicable to directors' options in total or the prices applicable to individual directors. However, the UITF notes that partly in response to the recommendations in the Cadbury Report for a move to more 'openness' in corporate reporting, a growing number of companies are providing expanded disclosures on options.

8 The principal concern of users appears to be that the current interpretation of present statutory requirements does not provide sufficient information about directors individually. The option prices pertaining to directors' options as a group are included with the information relating to the aggregate shares under option whose disclosure is required by paragraph 40 of Schedule 4 to the Act, which will include options granted under employee incentive schemes; the exercise price and periods applicable to individual directors are not generally disclosed.

UITF Consensus

The UITF believes that the grant of an option in the company's shares should be treated as giving rise to a benefit under the Act which should be included in the aggregate of directors' remuneration. However, given the practical difficulties of attributing a meaningful estimated money value to an option at the date of grant, and differing views on whether and if so how to apportion any benefit over time, the UITF has concluded that it is not presently practicable for it to specify an appropriate valuation method for options as a benefit in kind. **9**

Nevertheless, to reflect the conclusion that options should be treated as giving rise to a benefit, the UITF has reached a consensus that for all companies information concerning the option prices applicable to individual directors, together with market price information at the year-end and at the date of exercise, should be disclosed. This would be a practicable way of providing improved disclosures regarding directors' share options that would be consistent with the recommendations of the Cadbury Report referred to in paragraph 4 above. Such disclosures are illustrated in the Appendix. The UITF has received legal advice that the disclosures suggested in the Appendix, other than for each individual director the number of options granted or exercised during the year, cannot be construed as being necessary to meet the legal requirements set out in paragraph 2 above and consequently, while recommended by the UITF, they are not mandatory. **10**

References

Great Britain – Companies Act 1985 sections 232 and 325, Schedule 4 paragraph 40, Schedule 6 paragraphs 1(4), 3(1), 4(2) and (3), 5 and 11(1) and Schedule 7 paragraph 2B.

Northern Ireland – Companies (Northern Ireland) Order 1986 articles 240 and 333, Schedule 4 paragraph 40, Schedule 6 paragraphs 1(4), 3(1), 4(2) and (3), 5 and 11(1) and Schedule 7 paragraph 2B.

Republic of Ireland – Companies Act 1963 section 191 and Companies Act 1990 sections 59 and 63.

The Listing Rules of the London Stock Exchange paragraph 12.43(k)

The report of the Committee on the Financial Aspects of Corporate Governance (the Cadbury Report) paragraph 4.40 and paragraph 3.2 of the Code of Best Practice.

Appendix

SUGGESTED DISCLOSURES FOR DIRECTORS' SHARE OPTIONS

A1. Full information for each director as set out below. If this information would, for a particular company, be excessive in length, a more concise disclosure would be a satisfactory alternative. This is also considered further in paragraph A3 below.

(a) the number of shares under option at the end of the year* and at the beginning of the year (or date of appointment if later)

(b) the number of options
  (i) granted†
  (ii) exercised†
  (iii) lapsed unexercised during the year

(c) the exercise prices

(d) the dates from which the options may be exercised

(e) the expiry dates

(f) the cost of the options (if any)

(g) for any options exercised during the year, the market price of the shares at the date of exercise

(h) a concise summary of any performance criteria conditional upon which the options are exercisable.

Where directors have options exercisable at different prices and/or different dates then separate figures for items (a) to (g) above would be given for each exercise price and/or date combination. The market price of the shares at the end of the year, together with the range during the year (high and low), which provides an indication of the volatility of the company's share price, would also be disclosed.

A2. The information above might appear as:

	Number of options				**Exercise price**	**Market price at date of exercise**	**Date from which exercis-able**	**Expiry date**
Directors [names]		**During the year**						
	At 01.01.93	**Granted**	**Exercised**	**At 31.12.93**				
A	100	–	(100)	–	50p	130p	–	–
B	100	–	–	100	50p	–	31.12.92	31.12.99
	–	50	–	50	120p	–	31.12.95	31.12.02
C	200	–	(100)	100	50p	120p	31.12.92	31.12.99
D	100	–	–	100	150p	–	31.12.94	31.12.01
	–	50	–	50	120p	–	31.12.95	31.12.02

****required by paragraph 12.43(k) of the Listing Rules of the London Stock Exchange***

†required by the Companies Act 1985

No options lapsed during the year. The market price of the shares at 31.12.93 was 140p and the range during 1993 was 106p to 142p.

A3. As mentioned in paragraph A1, information set out in accordance with the above for a particular company might be excessive in length because of the number of directors and the number of different options granted at different times. A more concise disclosure, using weighted average exercise prices for each director, would be a satisfactory alternative, although some additional disclosure may be necessary. Thus if any options are 'out of the money' (ie the exercise price exceeds the market price of the underlying shares), they would need to be distinguished from 'in the money' options (ie the exercise price is below the market price of the underlying shares). Also, unusually large individual items may need to be noted to prevent misleading conclusions being drawn from an average (taking account of when such options are exercisable). This more concise approach would involve disclosure of the following:

(a) total shares under option at the beginning and end of the year for each director, with appropriate weighted average exercise prices applicable to shares under option at the end of the year;

(b) full details of any movements during the year (covering options granted and lapsed during the year with disclosure of the exercise price and options exercised in the year disclosing the exercise price and the share price at date of exercise).

Where concise rather than full disclosure is adopted a reference should be made to the fact that the company's Register of Directors' Interests (which is open to inspection) contains full details of directors' shareholdings and options to subscribe.

UITF abstract 11: Capital instruments: issuer call options

(Issued September 1994)

THE ISSUE

The terms of a capital instrument sometimes include an issuer call option, that is, a right of the issuer (but not the investor) to redeem the instrument early, usually on the payment of a premium. Such an option is included primarily to preserve the financial flexibility of the issuer. The question arises as to the appropriate accounting for an instrument that includes an issuer call option following the issue of FRS 4 'Capital instruments'. 1

FRS 4 requires the finance costs of debt and non-equity shares to be charged in the profit and loss account and allocated to periods over the term of the instrument at a constant rate on the carrying amount. Finance costs are defined as 'The difference between the net proceeds of an instrument and the total amount of the payments (or other transfers of economic benefits) that the issuer may be required to make in respect of the instrument' (paragraph 8). However, paragraph 16 states that 'If either party has the option to require the instrument to be redeemed or cancelled and, under the terms of the instrument, it is uncertain whether such an option will be exercised, the term should be taken to end on the earliest date at which the instrument would be redeemed or cancelled on exercise of such an option.' The Explanation of FRS 4 states that this is the case 'unless there is no genuine commercial possibility that the option will be exercised' (paragraph 73). This could be construed as requiring the accounting to be based on the assumption that the call option will be exercised and hence that the premium will be paid. Nevertheless, except in the special circumstances envisaged in paragraph 5 below, the amount payable under an issuer call option is not a payment 'that the issuer may be required to make in respect of the instrument' (part of the definition of 'finance costs' quoted above). 2

FRS 4 also contains a requirement that 'Gains and losses arising on the repurchase or early settlement of debt should be recognised in the profit and loss account in the period during which the repurchase or early settlement is made' (paragraph 32). Further, FRS 4 requires that where shares are redeemed, shareholders' funds should be reduced by the value of the consideration given (paragraph 39). 3

Issuers of instruments should not have to account for possible payments that they are not obliged to make, and may very well elect not to make. Payment of a premium on exercise of an issuer call option is a cost that stems directly from the decision to exercise the option and may therefore fairly be reported in the period in which exercise takes place. 4

Issuer call options as contemplated in this Abstract do not include those cases where 5 the effective rate of interest (or the margin above a base rate by which interest is calculated) increases after the date at which the option is exercisable. In these cases the exercise price may be deemed to compensate the investor for forgoing such increased interest.

UITF CONSENSUS

6 The Task Force reached a consensus that where an instrument includes a call option that can be exercised only by the issuer, the payment required on exercise of that option does not form part of the finance costs of the instrument in accordance with the requirements of FRS 4 'Capital Instruments'. In the case of debt, the gain or loss arising on any repurchase or early settlement will reflect the amount payable on exercise. In the case of shares, the amount payable on exercise will be used to reduce the amount of shareholders' funds.

7 The Task Force noted that in the case of an instrument with an issuer call option exercise of which is uncertain, the term of the instrument, as defined in paragraph 16 of FRS 4, would end on the date that the option was exercisable.

8 The Task Force agreed that, in accordance with paragraph 16 of FRS 4, this consensus should apply only to genuine options, and would not therefore apply to cases where, under the terms of the instrument, it was clear that the issuer would be commercially obliged to exercise its call option. An example of such a case would be where the terms of a debt instrument give the issuer the 'option' of early redemption but it is clear from the outset that in all conceivable circumstances it would be advantageous to the issuer to exercise the option rather than allow the debt to remain in issue.

9 The Task Force also agreed that the consensus should not apply to those cases described in paragraph 5 above. The Task Force agreed that in those cases, 'the total amount of the payments ... that the issuer may be required to make in respect of the instrument' must include the amount payable on exercise of the option.

DATE FROM WHICH EFFECTIVE

10 The accounting treatment required by this abstract should be adopted in financial statements relating to accounting periods ending on or after 23 October 1994, but earlier adoption is encouraged.

REFERENCES

Financial Reporting Standard 4 – Capital Instruments – paragraphs 8, 16, 32, 39 and 73.

UITF abstract 12: Lessee accounting for reverse premiums and similar incentives

(Issued December 1994)

THE ISSUE

Arrangements regarding an operating lease may include incentives for the lessee to sign the lease. Such incentives may take various forms, such as an up-front cash payment to the lessee (a reverse premium), a rent-free period or a contribution to certain lessee costs (such as fitting out or relocation), but are not limited to these examples. The question arises as to how such incentives should be accounted for in the accounts of the lessee. This Abstract does not deal with lessor accounting. 1

Although SSAP 21 'Accounting for leases and hire purchase contracts' does not deal specifically with accounting for reverse premiums, paragraph 37 requires operating lease rentals to be charged 'on a straight-line basis over the lease term, even if the payments are not made on such a basis, unless another systematic and rational basis is more appropriate'. In addition, paragraph 16 of the Guidance Notes on SSAP 21 states that 'in situations such as rental holidays in which a lease has been arranged so that, for example, no payment is made in the first year (although the asset is in use during that year), the total rentals should be charged over the period in which the asset is in use'. (Neither SSAP 21 nor the Guidance Notes specifically address the situation where rentals are periodically reviewed.) 2

The accruals concept in SSAP 2 'Disclosure of accounting policies' is also relevant because the existence of an up-front incentive creates a presumption that the subsequent rental levels, even though they may be termed 'market rate', are above the level required to attract a tenant in the market current at the time. In effect the lessor may have structured the overall market return to be expected from the lease in a way that accords with the cash flow needs of the lessee. The accruals concept suggests that any up-front payment received by the lessee should be spread to match the extra cost inherent in the subsequent rental level. 3

There is a view that the form of an up-front payment should determine the appropriate accounting treatment; for example, a contribution stated to be towards fitting-out costs (which in other circumstances may be incurred directly by the lessor) should be matched against those costs and thus effectively spread over the period such costs are amortised by the lessee. However, a lessor's main objective is to obtain a market rent for the property in question in the state it is in when the lease is agreed and he has no interest in how a lessee spends any up-front payments made. A lessor may agree an arrangement whereby contributions paid to the lessee match the cash flow effects of costs incurred by the lessee and this of course will be reflected in the cash flow statements of the lessee. However, the profit and loss account needs to reflect the true effective rental for which the premises have been obtained irrespective of the particular cash flow arrangements agreed between the parties. The accounting treatment should be similar however the form of an arrangement is structured. Because of the inevitable 4 inter-relationship between rental levels and any incentives provided, the underlying substance of any leasing arrangement is that the lessor exchanges the use of an asset for a specified period for a net amount of money. The accounting periods in which this net amount is recognised by the lessee should not be affected by the form of the arrangement.

5 Similar arguments regarding the commercial reality of the overall transaction apply to incentives such as contributions to relocation costs or to start-up costs when building up business in a new outlet. Incentives may also take a form other than a contribution to costs, for example an assumption of liabilities, such as rentals under an old lease which would otherwise fall to be a vacant property, or the gift of an asset, such as the lessor's bearing directly all the costs of fitting out to the lessee's specification. Regardless of the nature of the incentive to sign the lease a similar accounting treatment should apply.

6 This Abstract does not deal with incentives to surrender leases; however, such incentives should be examined to determine whether in substance the incentive relates to the new lease, particularly where the offer of the incentive is linked to an arrangement to vacate a property under lease from a different lessor. Such consideration should take into account the market rentals applicable to the old and new leases. If it is determined that the incentive, or part thereof, relates in substance to the new lease, the provisions of this Abstract apply.

7 The application of a 'spreading forward' accounting treatment for an incentive requires a determination to be made as to the future period over which the benefit should be recognised. Frequently leases provide for periodic reviews whereby the rental can be adjusted to the prevailing market rate; if it is believed that the need for the incentive arises from a temporary dip in the market, then the incentive should be spread over the period to the first review date at which the rental being paid can reasonably be expected to have come into line with the relevant market rate. In other circumstances, for example where the rent is set by reference to factors or formulae other than the relevant true market rates, the incentive should be spread over the full lease term.

UITF CONSENSUS

8 The Task Force reached a consensus on a standard treatment that, whatever form they may take, benefits received and receivable by a lessee, as an incentive to sign the lease, should be spread by the lessee on a straight-line basis over the lease term or, if shorter than the full lease term, over the period to the review date on which the rent is first expected to be adjusted to the prevailing market rate. Where, exceptionally, the presumption can be rebutted that an incentive (however structured) is in substance part of the lessor's market return another systematic and rational basis may be used, with disclosure of the following:

(a) an explanation of the specific circumstances that render the standard treatment specified by this Abstract misleading,

(b) a description of the basis used and the amounts involved, and
(c) a note of the effect on the result for the current and corresponding period of any departure from the standard treatment.

If in exceptional circumstances another method of spreading is considered more accurately to adjust the rents paid to the prevailing market rate, that method may be used, with the same disclosures as detailed in (a), (b) and (c) of paragraph 8. **9**

This Abstract supersedes that part of the guidance given in paragraph 16 of the Guidance Notes on SSAP 21 which suggests that the total rentals should be charged 'over the period in which the asset is in use'. **10**

DATE FROM WHICH EFFECTIVE

The accounting practices set out in this Abstract should be adopted for financial statements relating to accounting periods ending on or after 23 December 1994 (including corresponding amounts for the immediately preceding period) in respect of lease agreements commencing in the current or the preceding accounting period. Adoption in respect of earlier lease agreements is permitted but not required.

REFERENCES

Statement of Standard Accounting Practice 21 – Accounting for leases and hire purchase contracts – paragraph 37.

Guidance Notes on SSAP 21 paragraph 16.

Statement of Standard Accounting Practice 2 – Disclosure of accounting policies – paragraph 14.

Part Five

Relevant announcements by the Financial Reporting Review Panel

Disclosure of accounting policies — effect of introduction of paragraph 36A of Schedule 4 to the Companies Act 1985

(Issued January 1992)

To clarify a possible uncertainty the Financial Reporting Review Panel has taken legal advice about the effect of paragraph 36A of Schedule 4 to the Companies Act 1985 (introduced by the Companies Act 1989) on the accounting policy disclosure requirements of paragraph 36 of Schedule 4.

The legal advice confirms that the requirements of the two paragraphs are separate and distinct. Thus the inclusion in the notes to the accounts of a statement that the accounts have been prepared in accordance with applicable accounting standards, required by paragraph 36A, does not satisfy the requirement in paragraph 36 to state the accounting policies of the company. This is so both with respect to a policy which a company chooses to adopt and with respect to a policy that a company is compelled to adopt by virtue of the application of an accounting standard.

As regards the requirements of paragraph 36 itself, to satisfy them there must be a brief statement of each relevant accounting policy but that statement may either be in the accounts themselves or in the notes to the accounts.

Paragraph 36 does not require disclosure of accounting policies which are immaterial in the context of the accounts in question.

Press notice

Annual accounts statement of compliance with accounting standards: Review Panel Chairman reports progress (FRRP PN 8)

(Issued June 1992)

Since July 1991 the Review Panel has written to 240 listed companies who had failed to comply with the Companies Act requirement to disclose whether their accounts have been prepared in accordance with applicable accounting standards. A parallel letter was sent to the auditors of the company in question. In each case the directors concerned have confirmed that applicable accounting standards have been complied with, or have explained the reasons for any departures, and have given the Panel an assurance that their company's accounts will in future contain the statement required by the Act.

Mr Edwin Glasgow QC, Chairman of the Review Panel, said 'I believe that this initiative has been well worthwhile. A statement of a company's compliance with accounting standards, or disclosure of the particulars and reasons for any departures from standards, is an essential requirement of the legislation and is of vital interest to the users of the accounts in question'.

Continuing, Mr Glasgow added: 'It is important not only that the statement is made, but also that it is made clearly and unambiguously. In particular where there is a departure from accounting standards the particulars and the reasons for the departure need to be included either as part of the compliance statement itself or by the compliance statement containing a specific cross-reference to the Note in which the particulars and reasons for the departure are given. Statements such as 'except where the directors consider a departure necessary' or 'except where indicated below' do not meet the requirements'.

NOTES TO EDITORS

1. The legislative requirements in question are paragraph 36A of Schedule 4 and paragraph 18B of Schedule 9 to the Companies Act 1985. These provisions were inserted into the 1985 Act by paragraph 7 of Schedule 1 and paragraph 4 of Schedule 7 to the Companies Act 1989. Small and medium-sized companies (as defined by the Act) are exempt from these provisions.

2. The Financial Reporting Review Panel, which operates under the aegis of the Financial Reporting Council, is authorised by the Secretary of State for Trade and Industry for the purposes of section 245B of the Companies Act 1985. Thus the role of the Panel is to examine departures from accounting requirements of the Companies Act 1985 and if necessary to seek an order from the Court to remedy them. The Panel's main concern will be with an examination of material departures from accounting

standards with a view to considering whether the accounts in question nevertheless meet the statutory requirement to give a true and fair view.

3. The Chairman of the Panel is Edwin Glasgow QC and the Deputy Chairman, Michael Renshall CBE. There are 20 Panel members. When considering individual cases the Panel operates by means of Groups of 5 or more members.

Part Six

Statements of Recommended Practice

INTRODUCTORY NOTE

The ASC developed and issued two SORPs, 'Pension scheme accounts' and 'Accounting by charities', together with an Explanatory foreword to SORPs. These were not adopted by the ASB, but as they have not yet been replaced they are reproduced in this volume. (A revised SORP on charities is expected to be issued in summer 1995 – see the final paragraph of this note.) Although the recommendations in the SORP 'Accounting by charities' are applicable to charities of any size, the ASC believed that small charities would welcome some amplification and illustration of the recommendations. It therefore published a guide 'Accounting by charities: a guide for the smaller charity'. This is reproduced after SORP 2. In addition, as at 31 July 1990, the date the ASC retired, the following SORPs had been 'franked' by the ASC:

	Issuing body	*Issued*
Disclosures about oil and gas exploration and production activities	OIAC	April 1986
Accounting for oil and gas exploration and development activities	OIAC	December 1987
Accounting for abandonment costs	OIAC	June 1988

(These SORPs are available from:
Oil Industry Accounting Committee
Enterprise Oil plc
5 Strand
London WC2N 5HU.)

Accounting for securities by banks	BBA/IBF	July 1990

(This SORP is available from:
British Bankers' Association
10 Lombard Street
London EC3V 9EL

and

Irish Bankers Federation
Nassau House
Nassau Street
Dublin 2.)

Accounting for insurance business	ABI	May 1990

(This SORP is available from:
Association of British Insurers
51 Gresham Street
London EC2V 7HQ.)

The ASC also franked two SORPs on local authority accounting and one on accounting in UK universities, but these have been superseded respectively by the Code of Practice on Local Authority Accounting in Great Britain issued in 1993 and the SORP on Accounting in Higher Education Institutions (see below).

Statements of Recommended Practice

The ASB announced in 1990 that it would not issue its own SORPs. In the event that the ASB's own authority is required to standardise practice within a specialised industry, the ASB's preference is to issue an industry standard. The policy statement for the development of SORPs issued by the ASB in 1990 was updated in 1994 and this is reproduced after this note. In essence the ASB's approach is to satisfy itself that any industry body developing a proposed SORP is balanced and representative and conducts the development of its proposals with due process. The ASB does not attempt to vet the proposal in detail, but will issue a 'negative assurance statement' where it is satisfied that the proposal has been properly developed and does not appear to contain any fundamental points of principle that are unacceptable in the context of current accounting practice or to conflict with existing or proposed accounting standards.

Under these arrangements eight SORPs have so far been issued:

	Issuing body	*Issued*
Accounting for various financing, revenue and other transactions of oil and gas exploration and production companies	OIAC	January 1991
(Available from: Oil Industry Accounting Committee, Enterprise Oil plc, 5 Strand, London WC2N 5HU.)		
Authorised Unit Trust Schemes	IMRO	April 1991
(Available from: Investment Management Regulatory Organisation, Broadwalk House, 5 Appold St, London EC2A 2LL.)		
Off-balance sheet instruments and other commitments and contingent liabilities	BBA/IBF	November 1991
Advances	BBA/IBF	September 1992
Segmental reporting	BBA/IBF	January 1993

(Available from:
British Bankers' Association
10 Lombard Street
London EC3V 9EL

and

Irish Bankers Federation
Nassau House
Nassau Street
Dublin 2.)

Code of Practice on Local Authority Accounting in Great Britain	CIPFA/ LASAAC	September 1993

(Available from:
The Chartered Institute of Public
Finance and Accountancy
3 Robert Street
London WC2N 6BH.)

Note: Certain amendments to the Code were approved in March 1995.

Accounting by Registered Housing Associations	NFHA/ SFHA/ WFHA	February 1994

(Available from:
National Federation of Housing Associations
175 Gray's Inn Road
London WC1X 8UP.)

Accounting in Higher Education Institutions	CVCP	June 1994

(Available from:
Committee of Vice-Chancellors and Principals of
the Universities of the United Kingdom
29 Tavistock Square
London WC1H 9EZ.)

Work is currently in progress on the development of SORPs for:

(a) Investment trust companies. An exposure draft of a proposed SORP was published in April 1995 – available from:

Association of Investment Trust Companies
Durrant House
8–13 Chiswell Street
London
EC1Y 4YY

(b) Lessors

Work is also in progress on updating existing SORPs covering:

(c) Charities. A final draft of a revised SORP was issued by the Charity Commission in February 1995 to accompany the consultation draft of the regulations to be issued under Part VI of the Charities Act 1993. The authoritative version of the revised SORP is intended to be published in summer 1995 when the regulations have been finalised and it will supersede the ASC SORP on 'Accounting by charities' issued in 1988.
(d) The insurance business. An exposure draft of a revised SORP to supersede the ABI SORP issued in 1990 is due to be published shortly.
(e) Authorised unit trust schemes.
(f) Pension schemes.

Policy for the development of Statements Of Recommended Practice (SORPs)

(Issued by Accounting Standards Board October 1990; revised June 1994)

The Accounting Standards Board (ASB), in order to retain a degree of control over the contents of SORPs, whilst at the same time minimising the commitment of its time and resources, has adopted the following policy in respect of SORPs:

The ASB will not issue its own SORPs. If the ASB's own authority is required to standardise practice within a specialised industry, the ASB will issue an industry standard. **1**

The ASB will consider addressing separately any pressing matters ofgeneral concern. **2**

Franked SORPs will no longer be issued, but the ASB will recognise bodies for the purpose of issuing SORPs. Guidelines for determining whether a body is suitable to be recognised are set out in Attachment 1. **3**

ASB-recognised bodies must, as a condition of recognition, agree to abide by the ASB's code of practice in producing SORPs. The code of practice is set out in Attachment 2. **4**

SORPs issued by ASB-recognised bodies will include a negative assurance statement outlining the limited nature of the review the ASB has undertaken and confirming, or otherwise, that the SORP does not appear to contain any fundamental points of principle that are unacceptable in the context of current accounting practice or to conflict with any existing or currently contemplated accounting standard. A pro-forma negative assurance statement is set out in Attachment 3. **5**

For exposure drafts the ASB will not provide negative assurance but in appropriate circumstances will require a statement to be included indicating areas of overlap with its own work and any reservations that it would find necessary to make if the material were carried through to a final SORP. **6**

The ASB has appointed committees to advise it on whether to recognise bodies that wish to develop SORPs and on whether the ASB's statement of negative assurance should be given in respect of individual proposed SORPs. The committees include independent industry experts and are serviced by the ASB's technical staff and secretariat. The committees will monitor adherence to the code of practice and ensure that the ASB is fully apprised of any issues of fundamental importance. The committees will not be required to undertake a comprehensive review of a proposed SORP but only what is necessary to enable the ASB to make a negative assurance statement. **7**

No mention should be made of the ASB in the document, other than in its own negative assurance statement, without prior written approval from the ASB. **8**

Guidelines for the approving of recognised bodies

1 The sector or industry represented by the body should be of significant size.

2 The body should be representative of the whole or a major part of the sector or industry.

3 The body should share the ASB's aim of advancing and maintaining accounting standards in the public interest.

4 The body must agree to abide by the ASB's code of practice for the development of SORPs. The due process to be followed by the body is particularly important and should include wide consultation. The list of entities to be invited to comment would normally include member bodies of the CCAB, the major accountancy firms, the CBI and the Government.

Code of practice for recognised bodies

Admission to the Board's agenda

1 It is the responsibility of the ASB-recognised body to seek approval from the ASB before beginning a new SORP project. It should be recognised that rather than authorise the development of a SORP, the ASB may address urgent issues of general concern separately or decide to issue an industry standard.

2 The SORP should aim to go some way towards narrowing areas of difference of accounting within the sector or industry by indicating, as far as possible, preferred accounting treatments.

Membership of working parties

3 Drafting of the SORP should be undertaken or supervised by a working party of the ASB-recognised body that is representative of the sector or industry concerned, includes some outside representation on behalf of the wider public interest and has its own technical accounting support. Membership of the working party should be notified in advance to the ASB.

4 Each ASB-recognised body should inform the ASB when membership of its working party changes, so that the ASB may ensure that the working party remains representative of the sector or industry and maintains appropriate outside representation.

Due process

5 Preparation of the SORP should involve wide consultation within the sector or industry and appropriate publicity outside it. In particular, before publishing the final SORP, the ASB-recognised body should publish for public comment either an exposure draft or a statement of intent or both.

Liaison with the ASB

It is the responsibility of the ASB-recognised body to identify potential divergences from accounting standards and inform the ASB of them at an early stage. **6**

All exposure drafts and final SORPs should be presented to the relevant ASB committee for comment before publication. At each pre-publication stage sufficient time should be given to the committee to allow any necessary changes to be determined and incorporated. **7**

The ASB will wish to be satisfied that public comments have been appropriately invited, weighed and considered. Before publishing the SORP the ASB-recognised body should provide the ASB committee with a summary or analysis of the main comments and an indication of how they have been dealt with, in sufficient time to allow any necessary changes to be incorporated. **8**

It is the responsibility of the ASB-recognised body to monitor the SORPs it has issued, including those franked by the former Accounting Standards Committee, in order to identify any divergences from new accounting standards as they are issued and to notify the ASB of any such divergences. It is in the interest of the ASB-recognised body and its constituency that the possibility of such divergences should be signalled to the ASB at the earliest possible stage. **9**

The ASB requires the unrestricted right to reproduce any SORP in full without being subject to any financial charge. **10**

The ASB's statement

Each ASB-recognised body should agree to include the ASB's negative assurance statement in a prominent place in its SORPs and to make no other reference to the ASB without prior written approval from the ASB. **11**

In issuing a negative assurance statement on a particular SORP, the ASB in no way guarantees that it will not in time produce a subsequent pronouncement that will supersede, and may contradict, that SORP. **12**

For exposure drafts the ASB will not provide negative assurance but in appropriate circumstances will require a statement to be included indicating areas of overlap with its own work and any reservations that it would find necessary to make if the material were carried through to a final SORP. **13**

Pro-forma negative assurance statement

The statement below would be used in those cases where the ASB has no reservations about the SORP. Qualified statements would amend the pro-forma accordingly to explain the substance and extent of the disagreement with the recognised body.

'The Accounting Standards Board (ASB)

The ASB has approved the XYZ Association (the Association) for the purpose of issuing recognised Statements of Recommended Practice (SORPs). This arrangement requires the XYZ Association to follow the ASB's code of practice for the production and issuing of SORPS.

The code of practice provides the framework to be followed by the Association for the development of SORPs, but does not entail a detailed examination of the proposed SORP by the ASB. However, a review of limited scope is performed.

On the basis of its review, the ASB has concluded that the SORP has been developed in accordance with the ASB's code of practice and does not appear to contain any fundamental points of principle that are unacceptable in the context of current accounting practice or to conflict with any existing or currently contemplated accounting standard.'

Explanatory Foreword to SORPs

(Issued by the Accounting Standards Committee in May 1986)

INTRODUCTION

Statements of Recommended Practice ('SORPs') are developed in the public interest and set out current best accounting practice. The primary aims in issuing SORPs are to narrow the areas of difference and variety in the accounting treatment of the matters with which they deal and to enhance the usefulness of published accounting information. SORPs are issued on subjects on which it is not considered appropriate to issue an accounting standard at the time. **1**

SORPs may be developed and issued by the Accounting Standards Committee ('ASC'). Alternatively, they may be developed and, after approval and franking by the ASC, issued by an 'industry' group which is representative of the industry concerned for the purpose of developing SORPs specific to that industry and is recognised as such by the ASC. Such SORPs are referred to as 'franked SORPs'. (The term 'industry' is intended to refer to specific industries or sectors, including parts of the public sector.) **2**

Before approving and franking a franked SORP, the ASC will have reviewed the proposed statement and the procedures involved in its development. **3**

The ASC or the appropriate industry group may also develop and issue appendices to, and guidance notes on, SORPs. **4**

AUTHORITY

SORPs are issued with the authority of the ASC or the industry group concerned after approval and franking by the ASC. A statement at the beginning of each SORP will explain who has issued the document. **5**

The approval of the Councils of the governing bodies of the ASC (i.e., The Institute of Chartered Accountants in England and Wales, The Institute of Chartered Accountants of Scotland, The Institute of Chartered Accountants in Ireland, The Chartered Association of Certified Accountants, The Institute of Cost and Management Accountants and the Chartered Institute of Public Finance and Accountancy) is not sought prior to the issue of a SORP. **6**

STATUS

Unlike accounting standards, SORPs are not mandatory on members of the governing bodies of the ASC. It follows that entities which do not follow a SORP are not obliged by the ASC or, normally, by its governing bodies to disclose the fact or the nature of any departure. **7**

SCOPE

8 The scope of each SORP is set out in the text of the SORP itself.

RELATIONSHIP WITH ACCOUNTING STANDARDS

9 The authority, scope and application of accounting standards and the obligation of members of the governing bodies of the ASC to observe them or justify departures from them are set out in the *Explanatory Foreword* to accounting standards.

10 SORPs will always take account of the principles laid down in accounting standards. They can never be taken as authority to depart from the requirements imposed by accounting standards, nor to extend the scope of accounting standards to include entities or circumstances which are otherwise excluded from specific accounting standards or accounting standards in general.

11 It is recognised in the *Explanatory Foreword* to accounting standards that it would be impracticable for accounting standards to cater for all situations. In applying a modified or alternative treatment it is important to have regard to the spirit of and reasoning behind any relevant accounting standards. The recommendations contained in SORPs will always have regard to this spirit and reasoning. They may, therefore, be indicative of the treatment which should be adopted in a situation not specifically catered for by accounting standards.

FUTURE DEVELOPMENTS

12 Methods of accounting evolve and alter in response to changes in the environment, developments in business and financial practice and accounting thought. From time to time, therefore, existing SORPs, including franked SORPs, may be reviewed and, where appropriate, amended, withdrawn or replaced.

[SORP 1]
Pension scheme accounts

(Issued by the Accounting Standards Committee in May 1986)

Contents

Pension scheme accounts

This Statement of Recommended Practice ('SORP') sets out recommendations, intended to represent current best practice, on the form and contents of the accounts of pension schemes. It also explains the context in which it has been assumed the accounts will be placed.

The provisions of this statement should be read in conjunction with the Explanatory Foreword to *SORPs. Although SORPs are not mandatory, entities falling within their scope are encouraged to follow them and to state in their accounts that they have done so. They are also encouraged to disclose any departure from the recommendations and the reason for it. The provisions need not be* ***applied to immaterial items.***

Part 1 – Explanatory note

INTRODUCTION

The objectives of a pension scheme's annual report are to inform members and other users as to: 1

(a) the general activity, history and development of the scheme;
(b) the transactions of the scheme and the size of its fund;
(c) the progress of the scheme towards meeting its potential liabilities and obligations to members; and
(d) the investment policy and performance of the scheme.

To be of value to the users, this information should be provided on a timely basis.

In order to achieve these objectives and to present a balanced report on the pension scheme as a whole, the annual report should be made available as soon as possible after the accounting date and should comprise: 2

(a) A trustees' report. This is primarily a review of, or comment on:
  (i) membership statistics and major changes in benefits, constitution or legal requirements;
  (ii) the financial development of the scheme as disclosed in the accounts;
  (iii) the actuarial position of the scheme as disclosed in the actuary's statement; and
  (iv) the investment policy and performance of the scheme, including details of any delegation of investment management responsibilities by the trustees.
(b) Accounts: These are a stewardship report, designed to give a true and fair view of the financial transactions of the scheme during the accounting period and of the disposition of its net assets at the period end. An auditor's report on the accounts should be attached if the accounts have been audited.
(c) An actuary's statement: This is a statement by an actuary based on his investi-

gation into, and report on, the ability of the current fund of the pension scheme to meet accrued benefits and the adequacy of the fund and future contribution levels to meet promised benefits when due.

(d) An investment report: Investment policy and performance are important aspects of the stewardship function and accordingly the trustees' report in amplification of the accounts should contain or have appended additional information on investments held and investment income earned and comment on investment policy and performance.

3 As explained in paragraph 2, the information required of the investment report may instead be included in the trustees' report. The accounts and the actuary's statement are, however, two separate expert reports, having fundamentally different objectives. The former is a record of the origin and current size and disposition of the fund and the latter is a statement based on an investigation into, and report on, the present and future ability of the scheme to meet the accrued and prospective obligations to its members. These two reports require to be read in conjunction with each other, but neither should form a part of, or be subsumed into, the other.

FORM AND CONTEXT IN WHICH THE ACCOUNTS APPEAR

4 The form and context in which the accounts appear can have a significant effect on the overall message conveyed to the reader. It is therefore important that the separate components of the annual report are consistent with each other and do not omit any information which could affect the view given by the annual report as a whole. For example, the trustees' report's review of the financial development of the scheme should be both a fair review and consistent with the accounts. Similarly, the accounts should be presented in conjunction with an actuary's statement which comments comprehensively on the adequacy of the current fund and funding policy.

5 It is suggested, therefore, that when preparing pension scheme accounts one must consider the contents of the remainder of the annual report in order to ensure that the accounts are not submitted to members and employers in a misleading form or context.

FUNDAMENTAL ACCOUNTING CONCEPTS AND MATERIALITY

6 The recommendations contained in this statement should be considered in conjunction with the fundamental accounting concepts described in SSAP 2 'Disclosure of accounting policies' and should be applied only after taking into account the materiality of the item or matter involved.

LEGISLATION

7 Legislation designed to regulate certain aspects of pension schemes is being enacted in Great Britain and Northern Ireland. This legislation will impose on most schemes constituted in Great Britain or Northern Ireland a requirement that they prepare annual reports which include a set of accounts. The legislation will also set out in some

detail requirements on the form and contents of the accounts and the principles to be applied in preparing them. As a consequence, some of the recommendations contained in this statement are also expected to be embodied in legislation. This is dealt with further in Part 5.

TERMINOLOGY

Although this statement adopts the terms 'revenue account', 'net assets statement' and 'movement of funds statement', alternative terminology may be equally acceptable. The word 'company' is used in this statement to represent any incorporated or unincorporated entity. The statement is intended to be applied to schemes in the United Kingdom and the Republic of Ireland. However, for simplicity, it adopts terms such as 'UK investments' and 'sterling' rather than using phrases such as 'investments in assets domiciled at home' and 'local currency'. **8**

Part 2 – Definition of terms

The *accruals concept* is a concept of accounting whereby revenues and costs are recognised as they are earned or incurred (not as money is received or paid) and matched with one another so far as their relationship can be established or justifiably assumed. **9**

Added years is a form of provision of additional benefits whereby a member is promised benefit for a period in excess of that which would otherwise be taken into account in calculating the pension benefit. **10**

Additional voluntary contributions are the contributions (over and above the regular contributions, if any, required from a member by the scheme rules) which a member elects to pay in order to secure additional benefits. **11**

An *associated company* is a company, not being a subsidiary of the investing group or company, in which: **12**

(a) the interest of the investing group or company is effectively that of a partner in a joint venture or consortium and the investing group or company is in a position to exercise a significant influence over the company in which the investment is made; or

(b) the interest of the investing group or company is for the long term and is substantial and, having regard to the disposition of the other shareholdings, the investing group or company is in a position to exercise a significant influence over the company in which the investment is made.

The *closing rate of exchange* is the exchange rate for spot transactions ruling at the accounting date and is the mean of the buying and selling rates at the close of business on that day. **13**

Concentration of investment arises when a significant proportion of the assets of the **14** scheme is invested in one company and any connected companies and persons, or in one property. For the purpose of this definition, an investment includes:

(a) an interest in shares and securities of a company;
(b) mortgages on real property owned by a company or person;
(c) freeholds and leaseholds owned by the scheme's trustees and effectively leased directly to a company or person; and
(d) loans made to a company or person.

15 *A pension scheme is a *fully insured* scheme when the trustees have effected an insurance contract in respect of each member which guarantees benefits corresponding at all times to those promised under the rules.

16 A *fund* of a pension scheme is the net assets held on behalf of the scheme by the trustees for the purpose of meeting benefits when they become due.

17 *The *members* of a pension scheme are all employees and former employees entitled to a benefit from the scheme.

18 *A *money purchase* scheme is a pension scheme in which the benefits are directly determined by the value of contributions paid in respect of each member.

19 *Movement of funds statement* is the term used in this statement of recommended practice to describe the reconciliation of the movement in the net assets of the scheme during the accounting period when it is presented as a separate statement within the accounts.

20 The *net assets* of the scheme are its assets and its liabilities other than those for pensions and other benefits falling due after the date of the accounts.

21 *Net assets statement* is the term used in this statement of recommended practice to describe a summary of the net assets of a pension scheme presented as part of the accounts.

22 A *pension scheme* is an arrangement (other than for accident insurance) to provide pension and/or other benefits for members on leaving service or retiring and, possibly, after a member's death, for his or her dependants.

23 *Quoted securities* are, for the purposes of this statement, securities for which an established market exists and market prices are readily available. Any other security is an unquoted security.

24 *Revenue account* is the term used in this statement of recommended practice to describe a summary of the financial additions to, and withdrawals from, the fund of a pension scheme presented as part of the accounts.

25 *Self investment* is investment of all or part of a scheme's assets in the business of the

Definition taken from 'Pensions Terminology — A Glossary for Pension Schemes' published by PMI/PRAG in 1984.

scheme employer and any connected companies and persons. For the purpose of this definition, investment includes all investment set out in (a) to (d) of paragraph 14 and, in addition, includes money currently due to the scheme but held by the employer or any connected companies or persons, such as employer and employee contributions.

* A *state scheme premium* is a payment which may be made when either the pension scheme or a member of it ceases to be contracted out, in return for which the state scheme will provide the equivalent of the whole or a part of the guaranteed minimum pension, i.e., the statutory minimum pension which a pension scheme must provide as one of the conditions of contracting out under the Social Security Pensions Act 1975. **26**

Subsidiary company: A company is a subsidiary of another if, but only if, **27**

(a) that other either:
 (i) is a member of it and controls the composition of its board of directors; or
 (ii) holds more than half in nominal value of its equity share capital; or
(b) the first mentioned company is a subsidiary of any company which is that other's subsidiary.

Term insurance is a form of life insurance which provides a lump sum on death before a fixed future date. **28**

Part 3 – Recommended practice

SCOPE

The recommendations contained in this statement are intended to be applicable to all pension schemes constituted in the United Kingdom or the Republic of Ireland other than: **29**

(a) those which have only one member at the accounting date; and
(b) those which are unfunded, i.e., those under which benefits are paid directly by the employer and no provision is made for future liabilities by setting aside assets under trusts.

As such, the scope of this statement is intended to include, *inter alia*: **30**

(a) schemes which are fully insured and which may not, therefore, have any assets to disclose in the net assets statement; and
(b) schemes which are money purchase schemes and which may, therefore, have no need for an actuary's statement.

PRIMARY ADDRESSEES

The primary addressees of the accounts of a pension scheme are the members, the dependants of deceased former members and the participating employers. **31**

***Definition taken from 'Pensions Terminology — A Glossary for Pension Schemes' published by PMI/PRAG in 1984.**

BASIS OF ACCOUNTING

32 The accounts should normally be prepared on the basis of the accruals concept.

33 All the assets and liabilities of the scheme at the period end should be included in the net assets statement in order to show the current size and disposition of the fund. The only exceptions to this are:

(a) the liabilities to pay pensions and other benefits in the future, which will be reported upon separately in the actuary's statement (see paragraphs 43 to 45);
(b) insurance policies purchased to match the pension obligations of specific individual members (see paragraphs 61 and 62); and
(c) additional voluntary contributions separately invested from the assets of the principal scheme (see paragraphs 63 and 64).

34 The carrying amount of investments should be the market value at the date of the net assets statement, where such a value is available, or else at the trustees' estimate thereof. This is dealt with further in paragraphs 46 to 54.

35 The carrying amount of all other assets and liabilities recognised in the net assets statement should be based on normal accounting conventions.

CONTENT OF ACCOUNTS

36 The accounts and notes thereto should comprise:

(a) a revenue account which discloses the magnitude and character of the financial additions to, and withdrawals from, the fund during the accounting period;
(b) a net assets statement which discloses the size and disposition of the net assets of the scheme at the period end; and
(c) a reconciliation of the movement in the net assets of the scheme to the revenue account. This reconciliation may be shown as a separate statement (i.e., a 'movement of funds statement') or alternatively it may be incorporated into the revenue account or the net assets statement.

37 The revenue account, net assets statement, movement of funds statement (if any), and notes to the accounts should contain as a minimum the items set out in Part 4 of this statement.

38 Corresponding amounts should be disclosed. The accounting period will usually be one year in duration. If this is not the case for both the current and corresponding periods, this fact should be clearly stated.

39 The accounts should contain such additional information as is necessary to give a true and fair view of the financial transactions of the scheme for the accounting period and of the disposition of its net assets at the period end. This will include, for example, information about capital commitments, post balance sheet events and contingencies (other than future liabilities to pay pensions and related outgoings).

ACCOUNTING POLICIES

The accounting policies followed in dealing with items which are judged material or critical in accounting for or reporting on the transactions and net assets of the scheme should be explained in the notes to the accounts. The explanations should be clear, fair and as brief as possible. **40**

The following are examples of some areas where it will be appropriate to disclose the accounting policies adopted: **41**

(a) the policies adopted in applying the accruals concept to significant categories of income and expenditure, such as contributions, investment income, transfer values and benefits;
(b) the bases adopted for the valuation of assets;
(c) the basis of foreign currency translation;
(d) the treatment of interest on property developments; and
(e) the bases adopted for accounting for investments in subsidiary and associated companies.

It is a fundamental accounting concept that there is consistency of accounting treatment within each accounting period and from one period to the next. A change in accounting policy should not be made unless it can be justified on the ground that the new policy is preferable to the one it replaces because it will give a fairer presentation of the transactions and of the disposition of the net assets of the scheme. When changes are made they should be disclosed, along with the reasons for making the change. If the effect is material it should be accounted for as a prior year adjustment by restating the opening balance of the fund and the corresponding amounts. **42**

ACTUARIAL POSITION

The responsibility for reviewing the adequacy of the funding arrangements made to meet expected pensions and other benefits from the fund lies with the actuary to the scheme. This responsibility will normally be discharged by the preparation of an actuary's report which, although usually addressed to the trustees, is also made available to the members. A statement by the actuary based on this report forms a separate component of the annual report. **43**

An actuary's report will often not be prepared annually, and, when it is prepared, it will not necessarily coincide with the date of the annual report and accounts. Accordingly, the actuary will often provide an interim or supplementary statement explaining whether he is aware of any changes in circumstances or necessary changes in assumptions which would indicate that his previous statement could not, if prepared at the current date, be made. **44**

The accounts should refer to the actuary's statement by way of a note. This note might take the following form: **45**

'The accounts summarise the transactions and net assets of the scheme. They do not take account of liabilities to pay pensions and other benefits in the future. The actuarial position of the fund, which does take account of such liabilities, is dealt with in the statement by the actuary on pages 00 to 00 of the annual report and these accounts should be read in conjunction therewith.'

If the actuary's report is not recent and the actuary's statement has not been updated by an interim or supplementary statement, the above wording may need to be amended.

VALUATION OF INVESTMENTS

46 Investments should be included in the net assets statement at their market value at the date of the net assets statement, where such a value is available, or else at the trustees' estimate thereof. The carrying amount of the principal categories of investment should be arrived at by applying the valuation bases set out below in paragraphs 48 to 54. The bases adopted should be disclosed in the notes to the accounts.

47 Any significant restrictions affecting the ability of the scheme to realise its investments at the accounting date at all or at the value at which they are included in the accounts should be disclosed in a note to the accounts. This will include, for example, legal or contractual restrictions on the surrender of units (e.g., managed funds) or material penalties which would have been suffered if they had been surrendered at the accounting date. It will not include the inherent difficulties in disposing of a large investment.

48 Securities quoted in the UK should be valued at the mid-point of the quotations in the Stock Exchange Daily Official List or at similar recognised market values.

49 Other securities quoted overseas should similarly be valued at middle market prices from overseas stock exchanges translated at closing rates of exchange.

50 Unquoted securities (including venture capital funds where appropriate) should be valued by the trustees.

51 Investments which are held in units should be valued at the average of the unit bid and offer prices at the accounting date. For some unitised funds, offer prices are regularly quoted but bid prices are not. In such circumstances, a basis such as reducing the offer price by an amount which takes account of the specific circumstances is likely to give a suitable valuation. Where unit bid and offer prices are both not available or have otherwise not been used, the basis adopted in arriving at an estimate of market value should be disclosed.

52 Financial futures, options, and forward currency positions should be included or provided for at market value, where such market value is available. If it is not available, a trustees' valuation should be used.

53 Freehold and leasehold property should be included in the net assets statement at open market value. Guidance on this matter is given in Appendix 1 to this statement. The name, or employing firm, and qualification of the valuer should be stated. If the valuer is an employee of the scheme or the participating employers this fact should be stated.

If practicable, long-term insurance policies should be valued using a premium valuation method. Where there are difficulties in obtaining this value, however, the latest value established by the actuary for the assessment of the discontinuance position, adjusted by subsequent additions to and withdrawals from the policy, will usually be satisfactory. Guidance on this matter is given in Appendix 2 to this statement. **54**

ACCOUNTING FOR ASSOCIATED AND SUBSIDIARY COMPANIES

Pension schemes may have investments in associated or subsidiary companies. These companies will be either investment-holding companies or trading companies. The associated companies may include joint ventures such as managed funds or pooled investments. **55**

In principle, such investments should be accounted for as follows: **56**

(a) the results, assets and liabilities of subsidiary companies should by consolidated with the transactions, assets and liabilities of the scheme. For investment-holding subsidiaries the basis of this consolidation will usually be a proportional consolidation on a line-by-line basis; for other subsidiaries it will be a single-line equity method of accounting;
(b) investments in associated companies which are joint ventures should be treated in the same way as investments in subsidiary companies; and
(c) investments in associated companies which are not joint ventures should be treated in the same way as ordinary investments by including them in the net assets statement at market value and including only dividends received and receivable in the revenue account.

Where consolidated accounts are prepared, they may be the only accounts of the scheme; there is no need to produce separate 'entity' accounts. The consolidation bases to be used are explained more fully in paragraphs 57 to 60 below.

It will usually be appropriate to include in the scheme's accounts, on a line-by-line basis, a proportion of the results, assets and liabilities of subsidiary investment-holding companies based on the percentage equity shareholding of the scheme in the companies. **57**

However, if the pension scheme in effect has an interest or obligation in respect of the whole of the results, assets or liabilities of a subsidiary company, for example because it has agreed to acquire or indemnify the minority interests, it will be appropriate to consolidate the whole of the company's results, assets and liabilities and include the minority shareholders' interest in the net assets statement. **58**

Uniform group accounting policies should be followed by a pension scheme in preparing its consolidated accounts. For example, investments held by investment-holding subsidiary companies should be included in the consolidated accounts at market value. Where such group accounting policies are not adopted by a subsidiary, adjustments should be made in preparing the consolidated accounts. **59**

The scheme's investment in trading subsidiary companies should be included in the net **60** assets statement at market value. Although the same principles as in paragraphs 57 and 58 should be applied in determining the proportion of the net result of such companies which should be included in the scheme's revenue account, this proportion should be included on a single line rather than line-by-line as for investment-holding companies. The unrealised gains arising from the revaluation to market value of investments in trading subsidiaries should be treated in exactly the same way as those on other investments.

ACCOUNTING FOR LONG-TERM INSURANCE POLICIES

61 If long-term insurance policies are purchased which match, and fully guarantee, the pension obligations of the scheme in respect of specific individual members, the acquisition costs of the policy should be treated as the cost of discharging the obligations at the time of purchase. Such a policy should not be included in the net assets statement of the scheme.

62 All other long-term insurance policies should be included in the net assets statement.

ACCOUNTING FOR ADDITIONAL VOLUNTARY CONTRIBUTIONS ('AVCs')

63 Where AVCs are made to purchase added years or additional defined benefits within the provisions for benefits under the principal scheme, they should be included as contributions receivable from members in the scheme's revenue account and the assets acquired with them should be included in the net assets statement.

64 Where AVCs are separately invested in such a way that the proceeds from the investment determine the benefit to the members, they should be disclosed separately from the transactions and net assets of the fund but accounted for within the accounts of the scheme or the notes thereto.

DISCLOSURE ITEMS

65 If there is any self-investment in excess of 5% of the value of the net assets of the scheme, then this should be disclosed in a note to the accounts, together with details of the nature and value of the investment involved.

66 Where there is a concentration of investment (other than in UK Government securities) which exceeds 5% of the value of the net assets of the scheme, then this should be disclosed in a note to the accounts, together with details of the amount and nature of the investment and the company involved.

67 Where insurance policies form a material part of the net assets of the scheme, the main characteristics relevant to the overall investment policy, for instance whether the policies are with or without profits, should be disclosed.

INVESTMENT REPORT

This statement assumes that the annual report includes a report which contains a greater analysis of the investment portfolio and income than is disclosed in the accounts. This analysis will often include: **68**

(a) analysis of investments by industrial sector;
(b) analysis of investments by geographical sector;
(c) details of the ten or twenty largest investments;
(d) details of investments which represent 5% or more of any class of shares of any company; and
(e) details of the extent to which properties are subject to rent reviews.

The totals shown in any such report should be reconciled to the amounts shown in the accounts. **69**

Part 4 – Format of accounts

The accounts of a pension scheme, and the notes thereto, should contain the items listed below where they are material. These lists are not intended to be recommendations on either the layout or the order of these items. **70**

REVENUE ACCOUNT

1. Contributions receivable:
   - 1.1 from employers:
     - 1.1.1 normal;
     - 1.1.2 additional;
   - 1.2 from members:
     - 1.2.1 normal;
     - 1.2.2 additional voluntary (see paragraphs 63 and 64);
   - 1.3 transfers in:
     - 1.3.1 group transfers in from other schemes;
     - 1.3.2 individual transfers in from other schemes.
2. Investment income:
   - 2.1 income from fixed interest securities;
   - 2.2 dividends from equities;
   - 2.3 income from index-linked securities;
   - 2.4 income from managed or unitised funds;
   - 2.5 net rents from properties. Any material netting-off should be separately disclosed;
   - 2.6 interest on cash deposits;
   - 2.7 share of profits/losses of trading subsidiary companies and joint ventures.
3. Other income:
   - 3.1 claims on term insurance policies;
   - 3.2 any other category of income which does not naturally fall into the above classification, suitably described and analysed where material.

4. Benefits payable:
   4.1 pensions;
   4.2 commutation of pensions and lump sum retirement benefits;
   4.3 death benefits;
   4.4 payments to and on account of leavers:
      4.4.1 refunds of contributions;
      4.4.2 state scheme premiums;
      4.4.3 purchase of annuities to match preserved benefits;
      4.4.4 group transfers out to other schemes;
      4.4.5 individual transfers out to other schemes.
5. Other payments:
   5.1 premiums on term insurance policies;
   5.2 any other category of expenditure which does not naturally fall into the above classification, suitably described and analysed where material.
6. Administrative and other expenses borne by the scheme, with suitable analysis where material.

   Where the administrative expenses are borne directly by a participating employer, that fact should be disclosed.

NET ASSETS STATEMENT

7. Investment assets:
   7.1 fixed interest securities (analysed between public sector and other);
   7.2 equities;
   7.3 index-linked securities;
   7.4 managed funds (analysed between property and other);
   7.5 unit trusts (analysed between property and other);
   7.6 trading subsidiary companies and joint ventures;
   7.7 freehold and leasehold property;
   7.8 cash deposits;
   7.9 insurance policies;
   7.10 other investments, such as works of art;
   7.11 debtors and creditors in respect of investment transactions where these form part of the net assets available for investment within the investment portfolio;
   7.12 other assets and liabilities directly connected with investment transactions (e.g., financial futures, options and forward dealings in currencies and, where appropriate, tax recoverable).

   Investments should be further analysed between 'UK' and 'foreign' and between 'quoted' and 'unquoted', and freehold and leasehold property should be further analysed between 'short leasehold' and 'other'.
8. Fixed assets held primarily for reasons other than investment potential.
9. Long-term borrowings:
   9.1 sterling; and
   9.2 foreign currency.
10. Current assets and liabilities:
    10.1 contributions due from employer;
    10.2 unpaid benefits; and

10.3 other current assets and liabilities (other than liabilities to pay pensions and other benefits in the future).

RECONCILIATION OF THE MOVEMENT IN THE NET ASSETS OF THE SCHEME

11. The reconciliation of the movement in the net assets of the scheme may be incorporated into the revenue account or net assets statement, or alternatively be shown as a separate statement. Whichever method of presentation is adopted it should clearly disclose:
   11.1 opening net assets of the scheme;
   11.2 net new money invested, per revenue account;
   11.3 change in market value of investments (realised and unrealised); and
   11.4 closing net assets of the scheme.

The amount of sales and of purchases of investments should be disclosed either within one of the accounting statements referred to in paragraph 70 or elsewhere in the notes. 71

Part 5 – Note on legal requirements in Great Britain, Northern Ireland and the Republic of Ireland

GREAT BRITAIN AND NORTHERN IRELAND

Legislation designed to regulate certain aspects of pension schemes, including the periodic preparation of annual reports, is being enacted in Great Britain, and is contained within the Social Security Act 1985 and the Regulations being made under the Act.* Corresponding legislation for Northern Ireland is expected to be contained in the Social Security (Northern Ireland) Order 1985 and the Regulations being made under that Order. 72

As well as imposing on the trustees the requirement to prepare annual reports, the legislation will include detailed requirements on the form and content of the annual report, including the accounts. These requirements will provide a framework for the accounting for, and reporting on, the transactions, assets and liabilities of pension schemes. The legislation is expected to require the accounts of pension schemes to give a true and fair view of the financial transactions of the scheme during the period and of the disposition of its net assets at the period end. 73

The legislation is also expected to require the inclusion as a note to the accounts of a statement explaining whether or not the accounts have been prepared in accordance with Parts 2 to 4 of this Statement of Recommended Practice and, if not, giving particulars of material differences. 74

The recommendations contained in this Statement of Recommended Practice, which 75

***Editor's note:** The Occupational Pension Schemes (Disclosure of Information) Regulations (SI 1986 No. 1046 as amended).*

are expected to be consistent with the forthcoming legislation in all respects, provide guidance on best practice in complying with the legislation. However, the recommendations deal with some aspects of pension scheme accounting not expected to be dealt with in the legislation (for example, accounting for associated and subsidiary companies) and they go further than the legislation is expected to go in some respects. Examples of respects in which they go further include:

(a) the scope of the recommendations. As explained in paragraph 29, the recommendations are intended to be applicable to all pension schemes other than one-member schemes and unfunded schemes. The accounting requirements of the legislation are expected to apply to all occupational pension schemes other than one-member schemes, unfunded schemes, and public service schemes. 'Occupational pension scheme' is expected to be more narrowly defined than this statement's 'pension scheme'; and

(b) the disclosure required in respect of self-investment and concentration of investment. The definitions and terminology which are expected to be adopted in respect of these disclosures are not the same as those adopted in this statement. Consequently, whilst the minimum disclosure recommended in respect of these disclosures is (with the exception of the treatment of UK Government securities in paragraph 66 of this statement) expected to be sufficient to comply with legislation, the reverse will not necessarily be the case.

REPUBLIC OF IRELAND

76 There is no equivalent legislation to the Social Security Act 1985 or the Social Security (Northern Ireland) Order 1985 enacted in, or planned for, the Republic of Ireland.

77 Nevertheless, as this statement is complete in itself and does not rely on legislation in any way, its provisions are suitable for application to schemes operating in the Republic of Ireland.

78 Paragraph 26 of this statement refers to the Social Security Pensions Act 1975. This is Great Britain legislation and, whilst there is equivalent legislation in Northern Ireland (the Social Security Pensions (Northern Ireland) Order 1975), there is no equivalent in the Republic of Ireland. Consequently, the term defined ('state scheme premium') is not relevant in the context of schemes constituted in the Republic of Ireland.

79 Paragraph 27 of this statement adopts a definition of subsidiary company based on the statutory definitions given in the Companies Act 1985 and the Companies Act (Northern Ireland), 1960, as inserted by Article 3 of The Companies (Northern Ireland) Order 1982. However, the Companies Act 1963 (Republic of Ireland) gives a slightly different definition, in that a company in which the holding company holds more than half of the shares carrying voting rights, as distinct from more than half of the equity share capital, is also included. Such companies will normally come within the definition of paragraph 27 because holding more than half of the shares with voting rights will be equivalent to controlling the composition of the board of directors.

Appendix 1

This appendix does not form part of the statement of recommended practice.

Valuation of freehold and leasehold properties held as investments

Paragraph 53 of the statement recommends that freehold and leasehold property should be valued annually at open market value for inclusion in the accounts. The annual valuation of all such properties by external, qualified valuers may be expensive and time-consuming with no commensurate benefit. This appendix is intended to provide guidance on the matter.

Although a valuation of properties should be undertaken annually, it need not necessarily be by a qualified or independent valuer. It will usually be acceptable to have a valuation carried out by a qualified valuer at regular intervals, with an appraisal and, if necessary, update of this valuation carried out by the trustees during the intervening years. 1

The regularity with which the valuation should be carried out by a qualified valuer, and the possible involvement of independent valuers, depends, to some extent, on the proportion of assets held in the form of properties. In the absence of unusual circumstances a valuation by a qualified valuer should be undertaken every five years. 2

In order to ensure that the trend of the movement in market values is not distorted unnecessarily by carrying out such valuations every five years it may be appropriate to undertake them on a rolling basis, with a proportion of the total property portfolio being valued by a qualified valuer each year. 3

Appendix 2

This appendix does not form part of the statement of recommended practice.

Valuation of long-term insurance policies

The statement recommends that all investments of the pension scheme, including long-term insurance policies (other than policies referred to in paragraph 61), should be included in the net assets statement at market value. The market value of long-term insurance policies is not readily ascertainable, hence a basis of valuation which is consistent with that adopted for other assets (i.e., a middle-market price) and which is practicable should be used.

1 The main methods of valuing long-term insurance policies are as follows:

(i) surrender value;
(ii) assignment value;
(iii) value determined for an insurance company's own actuarial valuation;
(iv) premium value: This is an estimate of a single premium to purchase the payments at present secured under the policies;
(v) modified premium value: Although the premium value does not represent a middle-market price, it can be made similar by excluding the loadings made by the insurer in premium rating for initial expenses, such as issue expenses, brokerage and stamp duty. This 'modified premium value' is lower than the premium value;
(vi) valuation for actuarial assessment of the discontinuance position; and
(vii) valuation for actuarial assessment of the future contribution rate.

2 Surrender value is the value at which the insurer is prepared to buy back the policy and is consequently a realisable value. The surrender value quoted by the insurance company will depend on many factors unrelated to the policy's worth in normal circumstances, such as the willingness of the insurance company to buy the policy and the need to realise assets. Surrender value will therefore be the relevant valuation basis only if it is likely that the policy will be surrendered.

3 An assignment value is also a realisable value. Assignment of pension policies is unusual and the assignment value involved will be a matter of negotiation on each occasion. As such, it will be neither appropriate nor practicable to use such values for accounting purposes unless the policy is to be assigned.

4 The value determined by an insurance company for its own internal purposes will have been calculated on different assumptions and for different purposes than a valuation for use in pension scheme accounts. It will not, therefore, reflect the market value of the policy.

5 Premium value and modified premium value are replacement costs. There may be practical problems in trying to determine these values when certain policy benefits could not be purchased in their existing form, for example those under long established with-profits policies. When premiums are continuing under annual premium contracts the estimated single premium should be such as would, together with the contractual future premiums, purchase the same policy benefits.

A valuation for the actuarial assessment of the discontinuance position should be directly comparable to the market values attributed to other assets. **6**

A valuation for the actuarial assessment of the future contribution rate will, like the value referred to in 4, have been based on different assumptions from those usually adopted in determining market value. **7**

All of these methods are likely to produce different values. Surrender value, assignment value, the value determined by an insurance company for its own internal purposes and the value established by the actuary for the assessment of the future contribution rate will generally not be consistent with middle-market values. Premium value or modified premium value is most closely akin to middle-market value and should, therefore, be used. Where this is impractical, the carrying amount should be based on the value established by the actuary for the assessment of the discontinuance position. **8**

Such actuarial valuations should be undertaken at least every three years. In the interim years the value determined by the latest actuarial valuation should be adjusted to take account of additions to and withdrawals from the policy. **9**

These actuarial values are based on different principles from those on which premium values and modified premium values are based. Consequently they will not necessarily give comparable results. Although arguments can be advanced in favour of the use of actuarial values rather than premium values or vice versa, either of these bases will, as long as it is consistently applied, provide a satisfactory valuation for use in the accounts. **10**

[SORP 2]
Accounting by charities

(Issued by the Accounting Standards Committee in May 1988)

Contents*

***Editor's note:** As a revised Statement of Recommended Practice on 'Accounting by Charities' is being developed by the Charity Commission, the text of SORP 2 and the Guide for the Smaller Charity do not refer to any changes in requirements since these documents were issued. The revised SORP is due to be published in the summer of 1995 (a draft was issued in February 1995).*

Accounting by charities

This Statement of Recommended Practice sets out recommendations on the way in which a charity should report annually on the resources entrusted to it and the activities it undertakes.

Although the recommendations are not mandatory, charities are encouraged to follow them and to state in their accounts that they have done so. They are also encouraged to disclose any departure from the recommendations and the reason for it. The recommendations need not be applied to immaterial items.

The recommendations contained in this statement of recommended practice go beyond the requirements of the Charities Act 1960 and the Charities Act 1985 and have been welcomed by the Charity Commission. Accounts prepared in accordance with these recommendations will therefore be acceptable for filing with the Charity Commission and, if necessary, with the appropriate local authority.

Part 1 – Explanatory note

INTRODUCTION

The purpose of a charity's annual report is to provide timely and regular information on the charity, enabling the user of the report to gain an understanding of the charity's operations and achievements and a full and proper appreciation of the charity's transactions during the period and of its position at the period end. This statement of recommended practice sets out recommendations on the form and content of the annual report and on the way in which the accounts contained in the report should be prepared. **1**

The Accounting Standards Committee's purpose in setting out these recommendations is to help improve the quality of financial reporting by charities. It also wishes to provide assistance to those who are responsible for the preparation of charities' annual reports and accounts. The Accounting Standards Committee hopes that the recommendations will assist in reducing the current diversity in accounting practice and presentation although the intention is not to try to standardise them. **2**

Universities are not included within the scope of the recommendations. That apart, the statement is intended to be applicable to all charities in the United Kingdom and the Republic of Ireland, regardless of their constitution, size or complexity. However, it is recognised that some of the recommendations may not be applicable to all charities because of the nature of the particular charity or because of the limited classes or size of the transactions or assets involved. Nevertheless, the full recommendations have been given in this statement, leaving discretion to the trustees of each charity to apply the recommendations according to the character of their charity and the significance of the figures involved. **3**

4 The Accounting Standards Committee has issued 'Accounting by charities: A guide for the smaller charity' in order to assist the trustees of small charities in exercising this discretion.

INTERPRETATION OF FINANCIAL INFORMATION ON CHARITIES

5 Charities are highly disparate in character, so any comparison of the financial information they produce must be undertaken with care, even if the charities involved seem to be homogeneous. Also it is important to note that, when interpreting the income and expenditure account of a charity, the amount by which income exceeds expenditure, or expenditure exceeds income, in any one year is not usually a measure of performance or efficiency and does not usually provide an indication of the charity's future needs. Similarly, the balance sheet is not necessarily a measure of the wealth of the charity.

6 This statement recommends that a review and explanation of the accounts be provided in the annual report. It is important that reference be made to this review and explanation by those seeking to interpret the accounts correctly.

SIMPLIFIED REPORTING

7 It has been assumed in preparing this statement that a full annual report is to be prepared and that it will include a full set of accounts. However, some charities include simplified accounts in their annual report or include extracts from their annual report in other publications. As the form of such documents will vary considerably depending on the purpose for which they have been prepared, it is not practicable to include detailed recommendations on their preparation in this statement. However, some general principles which ought to be followed are set out below.

(a) Regardless of the intended circulation of any simplified report, a full annual report should always be produced. Details of how this full report can be obtained should be given in the simplified report.
(b) Simplified accounts should carry a statement explaining that they are not the full accounts and that they are not audited.
(c) Simplified accounts should be a fair summary of the full accounts. This means that they should contain information on both the income and expenditure account and the balance sheet and that they should be based on the principles set out in this statement.

Part 2 – Definition of terms

8 A *charity* is any institution established for charitable purposes only. Where the institution is involved in more than one activity, operates more than one fund, or is not centralised into one unit of operation, the term is used in this statement to incorporate

all those activities and funds which fall within the scope of a single governing instrument (or instruments supplemental to the main instrument) and any further endowments held within the terms of the original instrument.

A *fund* is a pool of unexpended resources, held and maintained separately from other pools because of the circumstances in which the resources were originally received or the way in which they have subsequently been treated. A fund will be one of two kinds: a restricted fund or an unrestricted fund. (The terms 'fund' and 'funds' are used in the statement in this specialised way except when used in the phrases 'fund-raising' and 'statement of source and application of funds'.) **9**

Restricted funds are funds subject to specific conditions, imposed by the donor* and binding on the trustees. They represent unspent restricted income and/or assets to which restrictions as to their use apply. **10**

A *permanent endowment* is a particular form of restricted fund in that the fund must be held permanently, although its constituent assets may change from time to time. **11**

A *designated fund* is a particular form of unrestricted fund, consisting of amounts of unrestricted funds which have been allocated or designated for specific purposes by the charity itself. The use of designated funds for their designated purpose will remain at the discretion of the trustees. **12**

Administration expenses comprise the costs which are not incurred directly on any of the charitable activities or projects of the charity and which are not incurred on fund-raising activities or publicity. Administration expenses will include a proper allocation of items of expenditure involving more than one cost category (e.g. administration expenses, fund-raising expenses etc.), but should not include any apportionment of costs which belong to other cost categories. **13**

Fund-raising expenses comprise the costs incurred by a charity in inducing others to make voluntary contributions to it. They will also include a proper allocation of items of expenditure involving more than one cost category (e.g. administration expenses, fund-raising expenses etc.), but should not include any apportionment of costs which belong to other cost categories. **14**

Part 3 – Recommended practice

THE SCOPE OF THE RECOMMENDATIONS

These recommendations are intended to be applicable to all charities other than universities. Any departure from the recommendations should be disclosed and explained in the annual report. **15**

****The conditions may alternatively be imposed not by the donor but by the trusts relating to the donation. For example, if a donation is made in response to a special appeal, its use will be restricted to the purpose of the appeal, notwithstanding the fact that the donor did not impose any restriction on its use.***

THE ANNUAL REPORT

Activities and funds to be reported on

16 The annual report of a charity should contain information on all the activities and funds of the charity and its non-autonomous branches. If a charity has some branches which are autonomous and which are therefore not dealt with in the report, this fact should be explained.

17 In order for the user to gain a full appreciation of the scope of a charity's activities, the annual report should also provide information on charities which are connected with the reporting charity and on its subsidiary and associated companies. Recommendations on the provision of this information are set out in paragraphs 70 to 73.

18 Funds held by a charity as custodian trustee will not usually fall within the scope of the annual report. Nevertheless, an indication of the extent to which the charity acts as a custodian trustee will need to be provided when explaining the charity's unquantifiable charitable work and the level of its administration expenses incurred.

The content of the annual report

19 The annual report should contain:

(a) legal and administrative details. These details will provide background information on the constitution of the charity. Paragraph 21 sets out the information which should usually be disclosed;
(b) a trustees' report or equivalent statement. This report should, as explained in paragraph 22, include a description of the charity and how it operates and a commentary on the figures shown in the accounts; and
(c) the accounts and notes thereto and, if the accounts have been audited, the auditors' report on them. The accounts are a report, expressed in financial terms, on the activities and resources of the charity. Paragraph 24 describes the accounts in detail, and the remainder of this statement sets out recommendations on their preparation.

Although it has been assumed in this statement that the legal and administrative details, the trustees' report, and the accounts will form three separate parts of the annual report, it is recognised that some or all of the legal and administrative details could just as easily be provided in the trustees' report or in the notes to the accounts.

Responsibility for preparing the annual report

20 The trustees are responsible for the preparation of the annual report and therefore for the form and content of the accounts. They should discharge this responsibility by formally approving and adopting the report. The trustees' report and balance sheet should be signed by at least two trustees on behalf of all of them in order to show this approval. The date of approval should also be disclosed.

LEGAL AND ADMINISTRATIVE DETAILS

The legal and administrative details provided in the annual report should include the following information: 21

(a) an indication of the nature of the governing instrument or legal status of the charity. If applicable, the charity registration number and the company registration number should also be provided;
(b) the names of the trustees and their nominating body (or other method of appointment or election), the names of the members of any management committee and the names of the principal officers of the charity;
(c) the principal or registered address of the charity;
(d) the names and addresses of any other relevant organisations or persons. This may include the names and addresses of those acting as bankers, solicitors, auditors, and investment or other advisers;
(e) details of any restrictions in the way in which the charity can operate. This should include details of any limitations in the trustees' powers of investment including, for example, any restrictions imposed by the Trustee Investments Act 1961.

THE TRUSTEES' REPORT

The trustees' report is the main narrative section of the annual report. It should contain: 22

(a) an explanation of the objectives of the charity and a description of the way in which the charity is organised. The policies that have been adopted in order to try to achieve these objectives should also be explained. If there have been any significant changes in the objectives, organisation or policies since the last report, this should also be made clear. The purpose of this part of the report is to explain what the charity is trying to achieve and how it is going about it;
(b) a review of the development, activities and achievements of the charity during the year. This review should bring the reader up-to-date on the charity's progress and achievements. It should also explain the important events which have occurred during the year and how the charity has responded to them. It will be in this part of the report that information enabling the reader to judge the effectiveness of the charity will usually be provided;
(c) a review of the transactions and financial position of the charity, and an explanation of the salient features of the accounts. This review should enable the reader to appreciate the significance of any surpluses or deficits disclosed in the accounts and the purposes for which the charity's assets are being held. It will also put the charity's current financial position in the context of its future plans and commitments, particularly with regard to on-going items of expenditure, projects not yet completed and obligations not yet met. The purpose of this part of the report is to help ensure that the accounts are properly interpreted.

Other information which, if not included in the accounts, could usefully be provided in the trustees' report includes details of voluntary help, donations-in-kind and other intangible income received during the accounting period (see paragraph 36), an 23 indication of the extent to which the charity is dependent upon certain donors and, if the charity was set up to undertake a specific project, cumulative figures on progress of the project.

THE ACCOUNTS

24 The accounts are a report in financial terms on the activities and resources of the charity. They should comprise:

(a) an income and expenditure account that shows the resources made available to the charity and the expenditure incurred by the charity during the period;
(b) a balance sheet that shows the assets, liabilities and funds of the charity. The balance sheet (or its notes, see (f) below) should also provide some indication of how the funds may or, because of restrictions imposed by donors, must be utilised;
(c) a statement of source and application of funds that shows the flow of cash through the charity. However, as explained more fully in paragraph 64, there may be circumstances in which such a statement is neither necessary nor helpful. If this is the case, the statement should not be prepared;
(d) an explanation of the accounting policies used to prepare the accounts;
(e) details of the movement on, and position of, the various funds of the charity; and
(f) other notes which explain or expand upon the information contained in the accounting statements referred to above or which provide other useful information. This will include notes which show an analysis of the figures in the accounts and notes which explain the relationships between the figures.

The corresponding amounts for the previous accounting period should be given for figures disclosed in the accounts or in the notes to the accounts. The duration of the current and corresponding accounting periods should also be shown.

ACCOUNTING FOR SEPARATE FUNDS

25 Most charities will hold unrestricted funds. Some may also hold one or more restricted funds, some of which may be permanent endowment funds. Appendix I explains in detail the legal position as regards transactions involving these various funds. To summarise, the position is as follows.

(a) The assets and liabilities representing the various funds of the charity need to be distinguished in the accounting records so that it is known which assets and liabilities are held in which funds.
(b) Realised and unrealised profits and losses on assets held in a particular fund form part of that fund. Similarly, provisions for depreciation or for a permanent fall in value of an asset form part of the fund in which the asset is held.
(c) Income generated from assets held in a particular fund may be subject to donor-imposed restrictions as to its use or the fund to which it belongs. However, where this is not the case the income will be unrestricted income.

Accounting for permanent endowment funds

Permanent endowment funds represent the capital of a charity. A consequence of this is that increases and decreases in the amount of the permanent endowment funds should not be dealt with in the income and expenditure account, but should instead be taken directly to the relevant permanent endowment fund in the balance sheet. A note to the accounts should disclose all movements on permanent endowment funds. **26**

Income derived from assets held within a permanent endowment fund may be subject to donor-imposed restrictions as to its use or the fund to which it belongs. However, where this is not the case the income will be unrestricted income: it will not form part of the permanent endowment fund. It should therefore be included in the income and expenditure account in the normal way. **27**

Accounting for other funds

The treatment of movements on all other funds should not be affected by the type of fund involved. This means, for example, that restricted income and unrestricted income received at the same time should be included in the income and expenditure account at the same time. Similarly, expenditure out of restricted funds should be included no sooner or later than expenditure made at the same time out of unrestricted funds. **28**

The accounts and notes should provide information on the charity's fund structure and on the significance of each of the major fund balances. There are a number of different ways in which this information could be presented. For example, the accounts could consist of a single set of accounting statements with columnar or note analysis. On the other hand, separate sets of statements could be produced for each major fund. The trustees should decide on the presentation to be adopted. In doing so, they should take into account the complexity of the funds structure and the need to avoid confusion between the movements on the various funds.* **29**

Whatever the presentation adopted, the accounts or notes should contain a reconciliation of the total opening funds of the charity to the total closing funds, showing the income less expenditure figure from the income and expenditure account and details of all other movements on the funds during the period. This reconciliation should be analysed between the major funds of the charity. The amount of each major fund should be analysed between the amount that is realised and the amount that is unrealised. The nature and purpose of each major fund should also be disclosed. **30**

References in the remainder of the statement to 'the income and expenditure account', 'the balance sheet' and 'the statement of source and application of funds' should be taken to be references to all income and expenditure accounts, balance sheets and statements of source and application of funds prepared by the charity.

31 When disclosing details of movements on the major funds, transfers should be shown separately from allocations to designated funds. Furthermore:

(a) material transfers and allocations of income received to designated funds should be separately disclosed, without aggregation or netting off, and should be accompanied by a narrative explanation of the nature and objective of the transfer or allocation;
(b) transfers and allocations should, if they are to be included in the income and expenditure account, be shown separately from, and beneath a subtotal of, the income and expenditure for the period.

ACCOUNTING POLICIES

32 In order to understand the accounts it is essential that they are accompanied by an explanation of the basis on which they have been prepared. The accounting policies adopted for dealing with material items should therefore be explained in the notes to the accounts. These explanations should be clear, fair, and as brief as possible.

33 Examples of the accounting policies which should be explained include the policies adopted in the following areas:

(a) the capitalisation and depreciation of fixed assets;
(b) commitments not yet met and the use of designated funds;
(c) determining the amounts at which assets are included in the balance sheet;
(d) donations, legacies and other forms of voluntary income;
(e) grants payable and receivable;
(f) identifying the items to be included within administration expenses, fund-raising expenses, and publicity expenses;
(g) investment income;
(h) netting off of expenses and related income;
(i) realised and unrealised gains and losses on investments and fixed assets;
(j) stock;
(k) subscriptions for life membership.

Where a charity is involved in specialised activities, such as research, it is particularly important that the accounting policies adopted to account for these activities are explained.

34 The accounting policies should be consistently applied throughout the period and from one period to the next. A change in accounting policy should not be made unless the new policy will give a fairer presentation of the transactions or financial position of the charity than the one it replaces. Any change in accounting policy should be disclosed. If the effect of such a change is material, it should be accounted for by restating the opening balance of the fund or funds involved. The corresponding amounts for the previous period should also be adjusted. Any such restatements should be disclosed and explained.

VOLUNTARY INCOME

Voluntary income consists of all incoming resources (whether in the form of cash or other assets or in kind) other than incoming resources received for permanent endowment, government and similar grants, investment income and gains, and payments received for services or goods. **35**

A charity may receive assistance in the form of donated facilities, voluntary help of beneficial loan arrangements. Such assistance is generally referred to as 'intangible income' or 'donations-in-kind'. Although some intangible income could be included in the income and expenditure account, it will usually be more appropriate to deal with it in the notes to the accounts or in the trustees' report – particularly as its value will often be impossible to quantify. The information disclosed in respect of such income should be sufficient to give a reasonable appreciation of the benefit derived from it. **36**

The value of all other voluntary income should be included in the income and expenditure account as soon as it is prudent and practicable to do so. This will usually be when the income is received. Paragraphs 38 to 44 expand upon this general principle. This means, for example, that all legacies (other than those received for permanent endowment) should be included in full in the income and expenditure account as soon as they are received. **37**

Restricted income

As explained in paragraph 28, the fact that income is restricted should not affect the manner in which it is accounted for in the income and expenditure account or the timing of its recognition as income. The one exception to this rule is when the restrictions imposed are so onerous that it is impossible to use the income in the way intended. In such circumstances the income should be carried forward in the balance sheet under the heading 'deferred restricted income' and the restrictions involved explained. **38**

Donated assets

Incoming resources in the form of donated assets should usually be included in the income and expenditure account as soon as they are received. The amount at which they should be included should be a reasonable estimate of their value to the charity. The basis of valuation should be disclosed. This treatment is appropriate regardless of whether the assets were donated for use, sale or distribution. **39**

On occasion it may not be practicable to ascertain the value of assets received, in which case their receipt should instead be disclosed in a note to the accounts. If it later becomes practicable to ascertain a value for them, this value should be included in the income and expenditure account as income at the date of valuation. For example, if an asset cannot be valued at the date of receipt but is later sold, the sale proceeds should be included as income at the date of sale. If the amount of assets included in income in a period other than the period of receipt is significant, this fact should be reported and the amounts involved disclosed. **40**

Cash collections

41 When income has been collected for a charity but has not been received by it by the end of the accounting period, an estimate of the amount not received should in theory be included in the income and expenditure account. Similarly, when some of the charity's income is in collection containers at public premises at the period end, an estimate of the amount in the containers should in theory be included as income. However, because of the practical difficulties which will often be involved, it is not necessary to include such estimates in the income and expenditure account. Whatever treatment is adopted to account for such income should be applied consistently and disclosed.

Life subscriptions

42 Life subscriptions purchase for the subscriber facilities or benefits extending over a number of years. In theory a proportion of each subscription received should be allocated to each of the periods for which it is anticipated the subscription will apply. However, rather than undertake lengthy calculations to estimate the appropriate period to use, it is acceptable to use an approximation, perhaps based on the relationship between the amount of the annual subscription and the amount of the life subscription. The period used should be disclosed.

Grants receivable

43 Government and similar grants should be dealt with in accordance with the terms of the grant. Grants made towards the cost of acquiring a fixed asset should be taken to income and expenditure account over the useful life of the asset concerned (see paragraphs 51 to 55, which deal with accounting for fixed assets). The amount of the grant still to be taken to income and expenditure account should be shown on the balance sheet as a deferred credit or, where appropriate, included in the relevant fund balance.

44 If a grant is to be received after the expenditure to which it relates, a best estimate of the amount to be received should be included in the income and expenditure account.

GAINS AND LOSSES ON INVESTMENTS AND FIXED ASSETS

45 A realised or unrealised gain or loss arising on an asset will form part of the fund in which the asset involved is (or, in the case of an asset disposed of, was) held.

Realised gains and losses

46 Realised gains and losses on the disposal of investments should either be:

(a) included in the income and expenditure account, in which case they should be disclosed separately from other income; or
(b) disclosed in the statement of investment gains (an example of which is shown in Appendix 2) and then added to or deducted from the appropriate fund in the balance sheet. Statements of investment gains should be disclosed on the face of the accounts, not in the notes.

Realised gains and losses on the disposal of fixed assets should be included in the income and expenditure account and, if material, disclosed separately from other income. 47

Unrealised gains and losses

As explained in paragraph 68, investments may be carried in the balance sheet at cost or at market value. Where they are carried at cost, there will be no unrealised gains or losses to account for, except in the case of a permanent diminution in value (see paragraph 69). Where they are carried at market value, unrealised gains and losses will arise. Such gains and losses should be accounted for in a manner which is consistent with realised gains and losses on investments; in other words, if realised gains and losses on investments are included in the income and expenditure account, unrealised gains and losses on investments should be as well. 48

Similarly, unrealised gains or losses will arise if fixed assets are included in the balance sheet at revalued amounts (see paragraph 68). Such gains and losses should not be included in the income and expenditure account: they should be added to or deducted from the appropriate fund in the balance sheet. 49

OTHER INCOME

If a charity carries out trading activities, the income should be accounted for in accordance with the normal accounting rules for profit-oriented entities. If a charity charges for services which it provides, the charges should be recognised as income in the income and expenditure account as they are earned. For example, if a service is provided over a period of time, the income involved should be recognised over the period of service and not over the period in which the payment is received. 50

ACCOUNTING FOR FIXED ASSETS

Capitalisation of fixed assets

All expenditure on the acquisition, production or installation of fixed assets and all receipts of fixed assets by way of gift should be capitalised and included in the balance sheet. This general principle is not affected by the source of finance used to pay for the fixed asset, or the source of finance likely to be used to pay for any future replacement of the asset. 51

(a) Expenditure on the acquisition, production or installation of fixed assets should be capitalised at the amount expended.
(b) Fixed assets received by way of gift should be capitalised at the value at which the gift was included in income (see paragraph 39).
(c) Fixed assets being capitalised some time after being acquired, for example as a result of a change in accounting policy, should similarly be capitalised at original cost or at the value at which the gift was included in income. However, if neither of these amounts are ascertainable, a reasonable estimate of the asset's current value to the charity should be used.

For the remainder of this statement all of these valuation bases will be referred to as 'cost'.

52 The only exception to this general principle is that a charity need not capitalise a fixed asset which is either:

(a) inalienable (in other words a fixed asset which the charity is prohibited from disposing of) or historic (such as a monument or statue); or
(b) for which neither a cost nor a market value is available. This should be an extremely rare occurrence: it will usually be possible to determine a reasonable estimate of its cost or value without incurring significant expenditure.

A summary of the fixed assets not included in the balance sheet but still in use should be given in the notes to the accounts. These summary details should be sufficient to enable the reader to appreciate the age and scale of fixed assets not included on the balance sheet.

Revaluation of fixed assets

53 If a charity revalues some or all of its fixed assets, this fact, together with the date and bases of valuation, should be stated in the notes to the accounts. In the year of valuation, the names and qualifications of the persons responsible for making the valuation should also be disclosed.

Depreciation of fixed assets

54 Most fixed assets depreciate, that is wear out, get consumed or otherwise suffer a reduction in their useful life through use, the passing of time or obsolescence. Fixed assets which have a finite useful life should be depreciated. Fixed assets which have an indefinite useful life, such as freehold land, should not be depreciated. This means that:

(a) fixed assets with finite useful lives should be included in the balance sheet at cost (or, if revalued, at a revalued amount) less an appropriate provision for depreciation; and
(b) fixed assets with an indefinite useful life should be included at cost (or, if revalued, at a revalued amount).

55 If a fixed asset is revalued its depreciation should be based on the revalued amount, the residual value and remaining useful life of the asset at the date of revaluation.

OTHER EXPENDITURE AND COSTS

56 All expenditure should be included in the income and expenditure account as soon as it is incurred. The only exception to this is expenditure incurred to acquire assets, that is, expenditure on the acquisition, production or installation of fixed assets, expenditure on stock items, expenditure on the acquisition of investments, advance expenditure or prepayments. Expenditure incurred to acquire assets should be carried forward in the balance sheet.

Expenditure is not incurred until consideration for the expenditure has passed, in other words until something is received in exchange for the expenditure. However, in the case of expenditure and grants relating directly to charitable activities an exchange is usually not involved. Where there is no exchange, the expenditure or grant should be recognised in the income and expenditure account when its payment becomes due. An implication of this is that commitments which extend beyond the end of the accounting period and grants which fall to be paid in future accounting periods should be charged in future income and expenditure accounts. (See also paragraphs 74 and 75). **57**

THE INCOME AND EXPENDITURE ACCOUNT

Presentation

The income and expenditure should be analysed in a manner appropriate to the charity. This analysis should enable the user of the accounts to gain a proper appreciation of the principal elements of the income and expenditure of the charity, but should not be excessively detailed. The following items should be shown separately in the analysis: **58**

(a) realised and unrealised gains and losses on investments (if included in the income and expenditure account) and, if material, realised gains and losses on the disposal of fixed assets;
(b) fund-raising expenses;
(c) publicity expenses;
(d) administration expenses; and
(e) expenditure and grants relating directly to charitable activities.

Administration expenses, fund-raising expenses and publicity expenses

It is not practicable to produce precise definitions of 'administration expenses', 'fund-raising expenses' and 'publicity expenses' or to set out detailed guidance, applicable to all charities, on what expenditure should be included within each heading. The following principles should however be applied. **59**

(a) Items of expenditure which involve more than one cost category, for example some administration expenses and some expenditure relating directly to charitable activities, should be allocated on a rational basis to the cost categories involved.
(b) Expenditure incurred on activities falling directly within one cost category should not be apportioned to any other cost category.

The absence of precise definitions or detailed guidance means that each charity should develop principles for cost allocation suitable to its own circumstances. These principles should be applied consistently. A full description of the items included within each category and of the principles adopted should be disclosed. **60**

Netting off

A minimum of 'netting off' of income and expenditure and of assets and liabilities should take place. However, if a charity has received income from, and incurred **61** expenses on, special fund-raising events or activities, it may occasionally be more informative to include only the net figure in the income and expenditure account. Where netting off takes place, the reason for it and, whenever practicable, the 'gross' figures should be disclosed in the notes.

Tax credits on income

62 Income received after deduction of tax at source and income received by deed of covenant should be grossed up for the tax recoverable and this gross figure included in the income and expenditure account. The tax recoverable should be shown as a debtor until the charity recovers the amount involved.

THE STATEMENT OF SOURCE AND APPLICATION OF FUNDS

63 The purpose of the statement of source and application of funds is to show the movement of cash through the charity. Some charities believe information on their cash transactions to be more meaningful than information on their income and expenditure because, for example, they are funded on the basis of their cash needs or because their investment activity is directed primarily towards making the proceeds of sales available for charitable purposes. Where this is the case the statement of source and application of funds may be given greater prominence than the income and expenditure account.

64 On the other hand, there may be circumstances in which the preparation of a statement of source and application of funds is neither necessary to give full disclosure of information nor helpful in enabling the user to understand the charity's activities. For example, charities that operate on a cash basis and consequently have no significant assets or liabilities will find that the statement will be similar to their income and expenditure account. In such circumstances, the statement need not be included in the accounts.

65 Where a statement of source and application of funds is prepared:

(a) the analysis of the cash movements and the use of figures which have been netted-off should follow the same principles as those adopted for the income and expenditure account (see paragraphs 35 to 44, and 61); and

(b) the statement should be reconcilable to the income and expenditure account and the balance sheet.

THE BALANCE SHEET

Presentation

66 The assets of a charity should be analysed in the balance sheet between fixed assets, investments (including investment properties), and current assets; and the liabilities should be analysed between current and long-term liabilities. In addition, the assets and liabilities should be analysed in a way that enables the reader to gain a proper appreciation of their spread and character. The example set of accounts in Appendix 2 illustrates what this might entail.

The total amount of the assets less liabilities of a charity should be analysed between its major funds. **67**

(a) Wherever possible it should be made clear which assets and liabilities form part of restricted funds, particularly permanent endowment funds. Where this is not practicable, the notes should provide an indication as to whether or not sufficient resources are held in an appropriate form to enable the funds concerned to be applied in accordance with the restrictions imposed. For example, if a charity has a fund which is to be spent in the near future, it should be made clear in the notes whether or not the assets held in the fund are short-term assets.

(b) Where funds have been divided into wider and narrower ranges under the powers given to trustees by the Trustee Investments Act 1961, the accounts or notes should indicate the investments allotted to each range.

The amounts at which assets and liabilities are included in the balance sheet

Except as explained in paragraph 69, the assets and liabilities of a charity should be included in the balance sheet at the following amounts: **68**

(a) fixed assets at cost (or valuation) less an appropriate provision for depreciation;
(b) investments at cost or market value. If the investments are included in the balance sheet at cost, the market value should be disclosed in the notes to the accounts;
(c) current assets at the lower of cost and net realisable value; and
(d) liabilities at their settlement value.

If an asset suffers a permanent loss (or diminution) in value, the amount at which the asset is carried in the balance sheet should be reduced to the asset's current value by a provision. Where this provision should be charged will depend on the circumstances involved. **69**

(a) If the asset involved is an investment, the provision should be charged to the same place as realised and unrealised losses on investments (see paragraphs 45 to 48).

(b) If the asset involved is a fixed asset, the provision should be charged to the income and expenditure account to the extent that it is not covered by a previous gain on revaluation of that asset. To the extent that it is covered by a previous gain, the provision should be used to reduce the gain by deducting it from the appropriate fund in the balance sheet.

In determining whether any asset has suffered a permanent loss, gains in the value of other assets should not be taken into account.

CONNECTED CHARITIES

A charity may be connected with other charities. It will usually be possible to identify whether charities are connected by considering whether they have common trustees, unity of administration, and common, parallel or related objects and activities. **70**

If the reporting charity is connected to other charities, information about the other charities' activities and resources should be included in its annual report. This information should include: **71**

(a) particulars of the connected charities, including principal contact addresses and the nature of the relationship between the charities; and
(b) particulars of any material transactions between the charities.

One way in which the relevant information could be given is by aggregating the accounts of the charity with those of its connected charities. If aggregated accounts are prepared, the basis on which they have been prepared should be disclosed. Separate accounts for the reporting charity should still be prepared.

SUBSIDIARY AND ASSOCIATED COMPANIES

72 A charity may have one or more subsidiary companies.

(a) The activities of a subsidiary may not be fundamentally different from those of the charity. For example, the subsidiary may be an investment-holding company; it might be concerned solely or largely with fund-raising; or it might be the vehicle used to undertake the charitable activities of the charity. If a charity has such a subsidiary or subsidiaries, it should prepare consolidated accounts for itself and its subsidiary or subsidiaries. Separate accounts for the charity itself should still be prepared.
(b) If a subsidiary undertakes activities which are fundamentally different from those of the charity, for example if it is a trading company, it will not be appropriate to consolidate its accounts with those of the charity. Instead, the investment in the subsidiary should be treated in the same way as other investments are treated. A summary of the transactions, assets and liabilities of the subsidiary, together with an explanation of its activities and their relevance to the charity, should be disclosed in the notes to the accounts. As an alternative to providing a summary of its subsidiary's transactions, assets and liabilities, the charity may if it wishes include the accounts of the subsidiary within its annual report.

73 A charity may have one or more associated companies. Investments in associated companies should be treated in the same way as investments in subsidiaries undertaking activities which are fundamentally different from those of the charity (see paragraph 72).

OTHER DISCLOSURE ITEMS

Commitments and designated funds

74 Particulars of all material commitments in respect of specific charitable projects, whether they are legally binding or not, should be disclosed in the accounts. These particulars should include the amounts involved, when the commitments are likely to be met, and the movements on commitments previously reported. Particulars of all other material legally binding commitments should also be disclosed.

75 Commitments can be dealt with either by disclosing them in a note to the accounts or by using designated funds to represent committed unrestricted funds. If designated funds are used, they should be disclosed separately from restricted funds and appropriately described.

Guarantees given by the charity, and the conditions under which liabilities might arise as a result of guarantees, should be disclosed in a note to the accounts. **76**

Loans and other liabilities

If loans or other liabilities are secured on the assets of a charity then this fact, along with details of the security, should be disclosed in the notes to the accounts. The existence of charges against assets should be disclosed in a similar manner. **77**

The amount and interest and repayment terms of all inter-fund loans should be disclosed in the notes to the accounts. **78**

Information relating to transactions with trustees and to employees of the charity

Particulars, including the amounts involved, of any transaction, contract or other arrangement between a charity and any of its employees or trustees, or persons connected with them, should be disclosed in the notes to the accounts if the transaction, contract or other arrangement is likely to be significant to the user of the accounts. Employees' contracts of employment are an example of contracts which will not usually be significant to the user. **79**

Particulars of any relevant connection of the trustees or officers of a charity (for example, as trustees or officers of charities with which the reporting charity works) should also be disclosed. **80**

If some or all of the trustees have received remuneration from the charity or have been reimbursed by the charity for expenses which they have incurred, this fact and the amounts involved should be disclosed in the notes to the accounts. An indication of the type of expenses reimbursed should also be provided. If no remuneration was paid or no expenses reimbursed, this should be reported. **81**

The total emoluments (i.e. remuneration and benefits-in-kind) paid to employees during the accounting period and the average number of employees during the period should be disclosed in the notes to the accounts. **82**

Part 4 – Notes on legal requirements in the United Kingdom and the Republic of Ireland

A charity constituted in the United Kingdom or the Republic of Ireland may, by virtue of its constitution or activities, be subject to a range of statutory reporting requirements. Some of the more commonly encountered requirements are referred to below. Although the recommendations contained in this statement are intended to represent best practice there may be circumstances in which they conflict with some of the **83** statutory requirements imposed on a charity. This statement cannot overrule such requirements.

84 The recommendations do not incorporate every statutory reporting requirement that may be imposed on a particular charity. For example, an incorporated charity would be required to provide certain additional disclosures and analyses in the notes to the accounts and would also be required to prepare a directors' report containing specified information. Compliance with the recommendations contained in this statement will therefore not necessarily mean that all the statutory reporting requirements that may be imposed on a charity have been met.

ENGLAND AND WALES

Charities Act 1960

85 All charities in England and Wales must comply with the financial reporting requirements of the Charities Act 1960 and the Charities (Statement of Account) Regulations, 1960 ('the 1960 legislation'). This legislation requires charities to keep proper accounting records to enable them to prepare consecutive statements of account. These statements of account should consist of an income and expenditure account relating to a period of not more than fifteen months and a balance sheet relating to the end of that period. Each statement of account should contain:

(a) particulars of the charity's assets at the balance sheet date, distinguishing between assets forming part of the permanent endowment and other assets. These particulars should include the names of the persons in whom the assets are vested;
(b) the approximate amount of the charity's liabilities at that date;
(c) the amount of the receipts during the period, classified according to the nature of the receipt and distinguishing between receipts forming part of the permanent endowment and other receipts; and
(d) the amount of the payments made during the period, classified according to the nature of the payment and distinguishing between payments made out of the permanent endowment and other payments.

86 All charities having permanent endowments, other than 'expected charities', must automatically send to the Commissioners each year a statement of account. All charities, other than 'exempt charities', must send statements of account to the Commissioners on request.

87 The format in which the income and expenditure account and balance sheet should be prepared, and the accounting policies which should be adopted in preparing them, are not specified in the legislation. Although the Charity Commission provide charities with standard forms for the preparation of statements of account, alternative formats can be used as long as the information provided meets the requirements of the legislation.

Charities Act 1985

All local charities whose sole or primary object is the relief of poverty, other than exempt charities (as defined in the 1960 legislation) and ecclesiastical charities, must send statements of account prepared in accordance with the 1960 legislation to the 'appropriate local authority'. **88**

Companies Act 1985

Many charities are incorporated as limited companies and, as a consequence, are required to follow the reporting requirements set out in the Companies Act 1985 ('the 1985 Act'). In essence, this Act requires all incorporated charities to prepare, in respect of each accounting period, and file an income and expenditure account, a balance sheet, various notes, a directors' report and an auditors' report. If, at the end of the accounting period, the charity has one or more subsidiaries, then group accounts should also be prepared and filed. The accounts of the charity and its group are required to show a true and fair view and, except where it is not consistent with the showing of a true and fair view, should comply with the detailed requirements set out in Schedule 4 to the 1985 Act. **89**

Schedule 4 sets out the formats in which the income and expenditure account and balance sheet should usually be prepared. These formats, and the income and expenditure account formats in particular, are not wholly appropriate for the income and expenditure accounts of charities. It is therefore normally necessary to take advantage of paragraph 3(3) of Schedule 4, which allows the formats to be adapted in respect of items to which an Arabic number has been assigned to reflect the special nature of a charity's operations. **90**

Although Schedule 4 requires the disclosure of certain information not referred to in this statement, the statement's recommendations, with the following exceptions, are consistent with the Schedule's requirements: **91**

(a) In paragraph 61 it is recognised that, although the netting off of income and expenditure will usually be inappropriate, it may occasionally be acceptable. Schedule 4, paragraph 5 states that no material netting off of separate items should take place.
(b) In paragraph 66 it is recommended that the assets of a charity be analysed between fixed assets, investments, and current assets. Schedule 4 requires assets to be analysed between fixed assets and current assets. Fixed assets and current assets are designated by capital letters in the balance sheet formats. They cannot, therefore, be adapted under paragraph 3(3). However, provided that all the investments are fixed assets it should be possible to satisfy both the Companies Act formats and the recommendations of the SORP.

SCOTLAND

Although the Companies Act 1985 extends to incorporated charities constituted in Scotland, there is no equivalent legislation to the Charities Act 1960 or the Charities **92**

Act 1985 in Scotland. This means that, whilst incorporated charities have to prepare and file an income and expenditure account, balance sheet and various notes in respect of each accounting period, unincorporated charities constituted in Scotland are not required by law to prepare accounts.

NORTHERN IRELAND

Charities Act 1964

93 In Northern Ireland charities are governed by the Charities Act [Norther Ireland] 1964. However, this Act requires neither registration nor the preparation or filing of accounts.

Companies (Northern Ireland) Order 1986

94 The Companies (Northern Ireland) Order 1986 is the Northern Ireland legislation equivalent to the Companies Act 1985. The references to the Companies Act 1985 in paragraphs 89 to 91 should therefore also be taken to be references to the 1986 Order.

REPUBLIC OF IRELAND

Charities Acts 1961 and 1973

95 In the Republic of Ireland charities are governed by the Charities Acts 1961 and 1973. Neither of these Acts requires charities to register or to prepare and submit accounts.

Companies (Amendment) Act 1986

96 The Companies (Amendment) Act 1986 ('the 1986 Act') is the Republic of Ireland legislation equivalent to the Companies Act 1985. The 1986 Act references that are equivalent to those given in paragraphs 89 to 91 are as follows:

The 1985 Act	*The 1986 Act*
Schedule 4	The Schedule
Paragraph 3(3) of Sch 4	Section 4 (13)

Appendix 1 – The funds of a charity

The purpose of this appendix is to explain the legal position as regards the various funds of a charity and the implications this has for the way in which the funds are accounted for.

THE TYPES OF FUNDS A CHARITY MIGHT HAVE

A charity's funds can be categorised into restricted funds and unrestricted funds. Restricted funds are funds subject to specific conditions, imposed by the donor, or the trusts under which the donation was made, and binding on the trustees. All other funds are unrestricted funds, which means that as long as they are used in pursuance of the charity's objectives and in a way which is consistent with the charity's charitable status, their use is at the complete discretion of the trustees. 1

THE NEED TO DISTINGUISH BETWEEN THE ASSETS AND LIABILITIES HELD IN DIFFERENT FUNDS

If a profit is made on the disposal of an asset, the profit will form part of the fund in which the asset was held. An unrealised profit on an asset will also form part of the fund in which the asset is held. Similarly, realised and unrealised losses and provisions for depreciation and for the permanent diminution in value of an asset reduce the fund in which the asset is (or, in the case of a realised loss, was) held. In order to ensure that profits, losses and provisions are added to or deducted from the correct fund, it is therefore essential to know which assets and liabilities are held in which fund. 2

The trustees of a charity will be in breach of trust if they use restricted income in a way which is not consistent with the restrictions imposed. To this end it is essential that items of income and expenditure are added to, or deducted from, the appropriate fund. It is also important for the trustees to ensure that the assets and liabilities held in a fund are consistent with the fund type: if a fund which, because of donor restrictions, must be used in the short-term is represented by assets which can only be utilised in the long-term, there is a real possibility that the charity will not be able to meet the restrictions. 3

INCOME DERIVED FROM ASSETS HELD BY THE CHARITY

Although profits arising on the disposal of an asset will form part of the fund in which the asset was held, this will not necessarily be the case with income derived from the asset. Unless the terms on which the asset was donated make it clear that an alternative treatment should be adopted, income derived from an asset already held by the charity will be unrestricted income, even if the asset is held in a permanent endowment fund. 4

PERMANENT ENDOWMENT FUNDS

5 One particular type of restricted fund is known as a permanent endowment fund. Permanent endowment funds must be held indefinitely. This does not however necessarily mean that the assets held in the permanent endowment fund cannot be disposed of – although the terms of the endowment might prohibit this. What it does mean is that the permanent endowment fund cannot be used to make payments to others, and the assets making up the permanent endowment fund cannot be given away. Furthermore, if an asset that is held as part of a permanent endowment fund is disposed of, its place in the fund must be taken by the assets received in exchange.

6 As explained above, if a profit is made on the disposal of an asset held in a permanent endowment fund, the profit will become part of the permanent endowment and the amount of the fund will increase. The other means by which permanent endowment funds will be increased will be by receiving incoming resources received for permanent endowment (whether in the form of new permanent endowment funds or additions to existing ones) and by recognising unrealised gains on assets held in permanent endowments. On the other hand, income derived from assets held within a permanent endowment fund does not affect the amount of permanent endowment unless either the terms of the original endowment require it to do so or the Charity Commission so order.

7 Similarly, a loss made on the disposal of an asset held in a permanent endowment fund will result in the amount of the fund being decreased. Such losses are in fact the only transactions which can reduce the amount of the permanent endowment. Provisions for the depreciation of assets held in permanent endowment funds or for the permanent diminution in value of assets held in permanent endowment funds, and unrealised losses recognised in the accounts in respect of assets held in permanent endowment funds are the only other means by which a permanent endowment fund can be reduced.

8 Permanent endowment funds, because of their permanence, are tantamount to being the capital of the charity. The statement of recommended practice recognises this by recommending that increases and decreases in the amount of permanent endowment funds are not dealt with in the income and expenditure account.

Appendix 2 – Example set of accounts

INCOME AND EXPENDITURE ACCOUNT
YEAR ENDED 31 DECEMBER 1987

				15 months ended 31.12.86
	£	£	£	£
Income				
Donations and gifts		7,920		8,942
Legacies		3,416		19,761
Covenanted income		15,600		15,500
Voluntary income		26,936		44,203
Grants received		2,793		2,749
Investment income		414		481
		30,143		47,433
Indirect expenditure				
Fund-raising expenses	782		656	
Publicity expenses	534		412	
Administration expenses	1,236		1,471	
		2,552		2,539
Income less indirect expenditure		27,591		44,894
Direct charitable expenditure		30,479		41,684
Income less expenditure		(2,888)		3,210

STATEMENT OF INVESTMENT GAINS
YEAR ENDED 31 DECEMBER 1987

	1987	*15 months ended 31.12.86*
	£	£
Realised gains on disposal of investments	1,463	912
Change in unrealised gains/(losses) on investments	(1,212)	361
Net investment gains	251	1,273

The income and expenditure account and statement of investment gains should be read in conjunction with the reconciliation and analysis of movements on the funds shown on page . . .

BALANCE SHEET AS 31 DECEMBER 1987

		1987		*1986*
	£	£	£	£
Fixed assets		5,461		5,698
Investments		3,913		4,561
Current assets				
Stock	671		631	
Debtors	483		886	
Cash at bank and in hand	816		361	
	1,970		1,878	
Current liabilities	421		216	
Net current assets		1,549		1,662
		10,923		11,921
Long-term liabilities		(248)		(225)
		10,675		11,696
Funds				
Permanent endowment funds		1,850		234
Other restricted funds		8,357		5,911
Unrestricted funds		468		5,551
		10,675		11,696

The balance sheet should be read in conjunction with the reconciliation and analysis of movements on the funds shown on page . . .

RECONCILIATION AND ANALYSIS OF MOVEMENTS ON THE FUNDS FOR THE YEAR ENDED 31 DECEMBER 1987

	Unrestricted funds			*Restricted funds* (excluding endowment funds)				Total	*Permanent endowment funds*
	General	*Designated*	*Total*	*Core*	*India*	*Africa*	*Total*		
	£	£	£	£	£	£	£	£	£
Income	22,038	–	22,038	–	7,112	993	8,105	30,143	–
Indirect expenditure	(1,636)	–	(1,636)	–	(822)	(94)	(916)	(2,552)	–
	20,402	–	20,402	–	6,290	899	7,189	27,591	–
Opening value of funds	938	4,100	5,038	1,513	3,631	1,280	6,424	11,462	234
Funds available for use	21,340	4,100	25,440	1,513	9,921	2,179	13,613	39,053	–
New permanent endowment fund	–	–	–	–	–	–	–	1,020	
Net investment gains	–	–	–	201	50	–	251	251	596
Charitable expenditure	(15,674)	(7,911)	(23,585)	–	(4,753)	(2,141)	(6,894)	(30,479)	–
	5,666	(3,811)	1,855	1,714	5,218	38	6,970	8,825	1,850
Transfers	(1,387)	–	(1,387)	1,387	–	–	1,387	–	–
Designations	(4,235)	4,235	–	–	–	–	–		
	44	424	468	3,101	5,218	38	8,357	8,825	1,850

EXTRACTS FROM NOTES

[NB Although the accounts would normally be accompanied by a full set of notes, only extracts from the notes are included here. The extracts shown illustrate some of the more important or more complex of the recommended disclosures. The notes should be cross referenced to the accounts.]

Fixed assets

	Motor vehicles	*Fixtures and fittings*	*Total*
Cost	£	£	£
Opening balance at 1 January 1987	7,531	1,100	8,631
Additions	2,980	–	2,980
Disposals	(2,329)	–	(2,329)
Closing balance at 31 December 1987	8,182	1,100	9,282
Accumulated depreciation			
Opening balance at 1 January 1987	2,383	550	2,933
Charge for the year	2,359	275	2,634
Depreciation on disposals	(1,746)	–	(1,746)
Closing balance at 31 December 1987	2,996	825	3,821
Net book value			
At 31 December 1987	5,186	275	5,461
At 1 January 1987	5,148	550	5,698

ANALYSIS OF FUND BALANCES BETWEEN THE NET ASSETS

	Unrestricted funds	*Restricted funds* (excluding permanent endowment funds)				*Permanent endowment funds*	*Total Funds*
		Core	*India*	*Africa*	*Total*		
	£	£	£	£	£	£	£
Fixed assets	–	–	4,106	–	4,106	1,355	5,461
Investments	–	3,101	279	38	3,418	495	3,913
Net current assets	716	–	833	–	833	–	1,549
Long term liabilities	(136)	–	–	–	–	–	(136)
Provisions	(112)	–	–	–	–	–	(112)
	468	3,101	5,218	38	8,357	1,850	10,675
Represented by:							
Realised amounts	468	2,435	5,188	38	7,661	1,619	9,748
Unrealised amounts	–	666	30	–	696	231	927
	468	3,101	5,218	38	8,357	1,850	10,675

Commitments

(a) Charitable commitments

As explained in accounting policy note ... , commitments for specific charitable projects are dealt with by making allocations to designated funds. Therefore, as the reconciliation and analysis of movements on the funds shows, the commitments of the charity in respect of such projects are as follows:

	1987	*1986*
	£	£
Commitments at the beginning of the period	4,100	796
Additional commitments entered into	4,235	8,213
Commitments met	(7,911)	(4,909)
Commitments at the end of the period	424	4,100

It is expected that the commitments outstanding at the period-end will all be met in 1988.

(b) Other commitments

In addition to the commitments referred to above, the charity has entered into the following legally-binding commitments:

	1987	*1986*
	£	£
For the purchase of motor vehicles	5,921	2,980

Subsidiary companies

The charity has a subsidiary, ShopCo Ltd, which undertakes trading activities. As these activities are fundamentally different from the activities of the charity, consolidated accounts have not been prepared. ShopCo Ltd operates three shops, located in various parts of the country. It purchases ornaments and artefacts from manufacturers and sells them to the public. The profits earned are passed to the charity by means of a deed of covenant; a fact which is referred to in the company's publicity material. Two trustees of the charity sit on the board of ShopCo Ltd but receive no remuneration for doing so. A summary of ShopCo Ltd's transactions and financial position is set out below.

(a) Profit and loss account	*1987*	*1986*
	£	£
Turnover	72,149	68,163
Cost of sales	43,637	40,611
Gross profit	28,512	27,552
Selling costs	9,361	8,800
Administration costs	3,461	3,013
Profit before deed of covenant	15,690	15,739
Deed of covenant	15,600	15,500
Profit before taxation	90	239
Taxation	–	–
Retained profit for the financial year	90	239

(b) Balance sheet		
Current assets		
Stock	9,239	12,576
Cash in hand and at bank	1,610	(311)
	10,849	12,265
Creditors: amounts due within one year		
Trade creditors	840	2,346
	10,009	9,919
Represented by:		
Share Capital	10,000	10,000
Profit and loss account	9	(81)
	10,009	9,919

Connected charities

The trustees of the charity are also the trustees of the Pollington Charity, a charity with which the charity shares administration facilities. Whilst the charity provides assistance and comfort to those being treated for cancer, the Pollington Charity makes grants to persons researching into cures for cancer. From time to time, loans on commercial terms may be made by one of the charities to the other, although there were no such loans outstanding at the year-end. There are no other transactions between the charities. A summarised set of accounts, in which the accounts of the charity and the Pollington charity have been aggregated, are set out below:

(a) Income and expenditure account

	1987 £	*1986* £
Voluntary income	34,631	57,351
Grants received	33,961	31,621
Investment income	1,321	1,012
	69,913	89,984
Indirect expenditure	7,264	6,982
	62,649	83,002
Direct charitable expenditure	60,192	73,139
Income less expenditure	2,457	9,863

(b) Statement of investment gains

Realised gains	2,651	1,101
Change in unrealised gains	381	1,312
Net investment gains	3,032	2,413

(c) Balance sheet

Fixed assets	5,461	5,698
Investments	28,140	24,163
Current assets	4,136	2,011
Current liabilities	(4,596)	(6,035)
Long-term liabilities	(248)	(225)
	32,893	25,612
Permanent endowment funds	6,211	4,419
Other restricted funds	10,487	9,321
Unrestricted funds	16,195	11,872
	32,893	25,612

The Pollington charity can be contacted at the following address: ... (Not shown)

Accounting by charities: a guide for the smaller charity

(Issued by the Accounting Standards Committee in May 1988)

Contents

Accounting by charities: a guide for the smaller charity

Preface

The Accounting Standards Committee has now published Statement of Recommended Practice No.2 *Accounting by charities* containing its recommendations on the way in which charities should account for and report on their activities and resources. Although the recommendations are applicable to charities of any size, the Committee believes that small charities would welcome some amplification and illustration of the recommendations. It has therefore published this guide.

The guidance provided is intended to be consistent with the Committee's recommendations. However, while a number of illustrations and examples of recommended practices in use have been provided, it is not practicable to deal with every possible circumstance which might arise: the aim has been to cover the situations most commonly encountered by small charities. As a result, some of the recommendations are not dealt with in the guide and others are dealt with in an apparently simplified way. Therefore, although the Committee believes the guide will provide satisfactory guidance to most small charities in most situations, the statement of recommended practice should be referred to if unusual circumstances arise.

Neither the recommendations nor the guide are mandatory. They are however intended to represent current best accounting practice and charities are encouraged to follow them. If a charity has any doubts about how to apply the recommendations or guidance, it is suggested that it seeks professional advice.

1 – Introduction

THE NEED TO PROVIDE FINANCIAL INFORMATION

All charity trustees are accountable under trust law for the resources they receive. This duty of accountability is reinforced by the Charities Act 1960 and by other Acts of Parliament, the result being that all charities are required to prepare financial reports (or 'statements of account') on their transactions, assets, liabilities and funds. 1.1

THE FORM AND CONTENT OF THESE FINANCIAL REPORTS

For most charities the form and content of these reports is not prescribed in detail. For example, although the Charity Commission provides newly-registered charities with standard forms* for the preparation of the statements of account required by the Charities Act 1960, these forms are not mandatory: the Commission will accept alternative formats as long as the information provided meets the Act's requirements. 1.2

**Copies of these forms re reproduced in Appendix II.*

1.3 Most legislation refers to the need to produce what are described in this guide as an income and expenditure account and a balance sheet. (Chapter 2 explains what is meant by these terms and what their preparation entails.) However, although the income and expenditure account and balance sheet ('the accounts') will provide a lot of useful information, they will rarely provide sufficient information to enable the reader to understand the financial affairs of the charity. In particular, if accounts are not accompanied by explanations, it is difficult to assess the information provided in its proper context. In any case, it is often much more informative to write about certain events or achievements than it is to try to portray them with figures. For this reason the accounts should be accompanied by information explaining what the charity is trying to achieve and how it is going about doing it. This will usually entail providing various legal and administrative details and a 'trustees' report. As this package of information – the accounts, the legal and administrative details and the trustees' report – is usually produced every twelve months, it is referred to in this guide as the 'annual report'.

1.4 It should be remembered that, while a charity will be fulfilling a legal obligation in preparing its accounts, in preparing its annual report it will be fulfilling an obligation to communicate effectively with those who have an interest in the charity. For some small and probably local charities it may be that much of this information can be more effectively communicated by means of an oral presentation at a general meeting. If this is the case, it may be possible to omit some of the information referred to in this guide.

LEGAL AND ADMINISTRATIVE DETAILS

1.5 The purpose in giving legal and administrative details is to provide background information on the constitution and structure of the charity and to explain who is involved in its running. It should also provide essential contact names and addresses. The actual information provided will vary from charity to charity. Example 1 illustrates the information which a typical small charity might provide.

Example 1

Legal and administrative details of a typical small charity

The Ewechester Homes Fund

The Ewechester Homes Fund was incorporated as a company limited by guarantee (company registration number 9327298) on 2 June 1958. The company was registered with the Charity Commission (registration number 265436) on 25 June 1958 as a charity whose purpose is to provide accommodation and care to the elderly of Ewechester.

Address of charity:	The Manor Elsberry Common Ewechester	Telephone Number: 03-139 3465

Addresses of homes run by the charity:	The Manor Elsberry Common Ewechester	Telephone Number: 03-139 3465
	Rose Gardens 15 Ewechester Fall Ewechester	Telephone Number: 03-139 4344
Trustees:	Col R J Cribbs F A Fredericks (Chairman) R C Murray A W Netherby T N Peters C T Richards Miss S M St C Shaw R T Taylor (Honorary Treasurer) P Elliott (Secretary)	The trustees are appointed at the annual general meeting of the charity, details of which can be found in the accompanying leaflet.

Sub-Committees:

The Manor Home Sub-Committee:	Mrs P Durey, D Ellis, D Goodwin, D Hart, R Hill, T N Peters (Chairman) and L Powell
The Rose Gardens Home Sub-Committee:	R Bailey, K Bodkin, Mrs B Clarke, M Eakin, R C Murray (Chairman), P Smith and D Walton
Finance and fund-raising Sub-Committee:	Mrs E Baker, J Butler, J Gollan, J Mirandha, S Martin, R T Taylor (Chairman) and D Turnidge

Bankers:	Rutland Bank 29 Station Road Ewechester	Auditors:	R Clifton & Co The Gables Hollingbrook Road Ewechester

Donations should be sent to Peter Elliott at Ewechester Homes Fund Ltd, The Manor, Elsberry Common, Ewechester. Cheques should be crossed and made payable to Ewechester Homes Fund Ltd.

THE TRUSTEES' REPORT

The trustees' report is probably the most important section of an annual report. It sets the tone for the annual report, putting the other information into context, and provides one of the main means by which a charity can assist its image and enhance its credibility. In general the trustees' report should: **1.6**

(a) explain the objectives of the charity, so that the reader understands what the charity is trying to achieve;
(b) describe the policies and structure or organisation of the charity, so that the reader understands how the charity is going about meeting its objectives;
(c) review the activities and achievements of the charity during the period, so that the reader is brought up-to-date on the events which have taken place during the period and how the charity has responded to these events;
(d) provide a commentary on the accounts by reviewing the transactions and financial position and explaining the salient features of the accounts. This commentary should be designed to help the reader to interpret the accounts correctly.

1.7 In addition, the trustees' report will also attempt to explain various qualitative points which cannot adequately be quantified in the accounts. It will for example provide:

(a) details of voluntary help and other donations in-kind received during the year;
(b) an indication of the extent to which the charity is dependent upon certain donors;
(c) details of the purposes for which the charity's assets are being held;
(d) details of the charity's future plans and commitments, particularly with regard to ongoing items of expenditure, projects not yet completed and obligations not yet met.

If the charity was set up to undertake a single, specific project, details of progress on the project should also be provided.

2 – Form and content of the accounts

GENERAL PRINCIPLES

2.1 The purpose of the accounts of a charity is to report on the transactions that the charity has undertaken during the period and the assets, liabilities and funds that the charity holds at the end of the period. In other words, the accounts report on what a charity has received, what it has spent, what it holds, what it owes, and how it is financed.

2.2 The accounts should be comprehensible and informative: they should not be misleading, confusing or obscure. Therefore, when preparing accounts the following basic rules should be borne in mind.

(a) Keep things simple. Most readers of charity accounts are not experts in reading accounts. It is important therefore that the accounts are as clear and concise as possible. Accounts can be difficult enough to understand without complex accounting treatments being used.
(b) Be consistent. Nothing causes confusion more than the inconsistent treatment of like items.
(c) Keep things factual. The accounts should reflect what has happened to the charity during the period. Even when the accounts are to be used to attract donations, they should not be manipulated in order to show a picture which is attractive but incorrect.

(d) Straightforward explanations of the salient features of the accounts must be provided if the accounts are to communicate their message effectively. For example:
   (i) if the nature and purpose of the various funds of the charity are not explained, the reader may not understand why the charity is not spending more money on charitable activities;
   (ii) if the accounting treatments adopted in preparing the accounts are not explained, the accounts will be almost useless;
   (iii) if the principal figures in the accounts are not adequately explained, they may be misinterpreted – sometimes to the charity's cost.

(e) The accounts should concentrate on the most important figures; they should avoid excessive detail. If all items, however small, are shown separately in the accounts, the charity's message may well be lost under a myriad of detail. Furthermore if the trustees have a choice between using a recommended but rather complex accounting treatment for a low-value item and using some other simpler treatment, the simpler treatment should usually be chosen. There is nothing to be gained by, for example, capitalising* insignificant amounts of capital expenditure* .

RESPONSIBILITY FOR PREPARING THE ACCOUNTS

It is the trustees who are responsible for the accounts of their charity, regardless of who prepares the accounts initially. They should therefore formally approve the accounts. The accounts should be signed by at least two trustees, on behalf of all the trustees, as evidence of this approval. 2.3

THE CONTENT OF THE ACCOUNTS

The accounts should consist of a statement of transactions (from now on referred to as an 'income and expenditure account') and a statement of assets, liabilities and funds (a 'balance sheet'). These statements should be accompanied by notes which amplify the information provided in the statements or which provide other useful information. 2.4

Income and expenditure account

The income and expenditure account of a charity should show the income made available to the charity and the expenditure which it incurred during the accounting period. Chapters 3 and 4 explain what is meant by the terms 'income' and 'expenditure'. They also explain how different types of income and expenditure should be dealt with in the income and expenditure account. 2.5

It is not satisfactory to show a single figure for income and a single figure for expenditure without providing any further analysis. The reader of the accounts needs to appreciate the spread and character of the income and expenditure of the charity, so income and expenditure need to be suitably analysed. This is discussed further in Chapters 3 and 4. In addition, Appendix I provides some examples of the form which an income and expenditure account might take. 2.6

**'Capitalising' and 'capital expenditure' are discussed in paragraph 4.5 of Chapter 4.*

2.7 Income and expenditure should as far as practicable be disclosed gross in the income and expenditure account. In other words, items of income and of expenditure should usually be shown separately – they should not normally be set off against each other. This does not mean that a charity should not draw attention in the notes to relationships which exist between items of income and items of expenditure. In fact, this will often be helpful to the reader.

2.8 However, sometimes netted-off figures are the only figures available to a charity for certain events. (Coffee mornings are a typical example of where this is often the case.) In addition, for special fund-raising events it may very occasionally be more helpful to net off the income earned from the event against the cost of holding it. (An example of when this might be the case is a special fund-raising event which is very expensive but which also raises very significant amounts of money.) Whatever the cause, where netting off takes place, the reason for the 'netting off' and, whenever practicable, the 'gross' figures should be disclosed in the notes to the accounts.

Balance sheet

2.9 The balance sheet of a charity should show the charity's assets, liabilities, and funds. Chapter 5 discusses the preparation of the balance sheet and the analysis of balance sheet items. In addition, Appendix I provides some examples of the form which the balance sheet might take.

Notes to the accounts

2.10 As mentioned in paragraph 2.4 above, the income and expenditure account and balance sheet should be accompanied by various notes. The purpose of these notes is:

(a) to provide explanatory information about the figures included in the accounts. This will include the disclosure of the accounting policies used to prepare the accounts (see paragraphs 2.14 and 2.15 below) and analyses of figures shown in the accounts; and

(b) to provide other information relevant to the charity's transactions and financial position. This will include, for example, details of the charity's commitments and of how the charity's assets must, because of the various restrictions imposed, or may be utilised.

ACCOUNTING FOR THE DIFFERENT FUNDS OF A CHARITY

2.11 A charity may hold a number of separate funds. For example, it may hold:

(a) restricted funds. Restricted funds are funds subject to specific conditions (usually imposed by the donor) binding on the trustees;

(b) permanent endowment funds. These funds are a particular form of restricted fund which must be held permanently – although the assets held in the fund can usually be changed from time to time;

(c) unrestricted funds. These are funds which are not subject to restrictions as to their use. Some charities identify a particular type of unrestricted fund, a designated fund, separately from other unrestricted funds. A designated fund consists of funds which the trustees have earmarked for specific purposes. The use of designated funds is therefore one means of keeping track of the charity's commitments.

In order for the reader to appreciate the structure of a charity's activities and finances, it is essential that the nature and purpose of each of its major funds are disclosed. **2.12**

Transactions which result in an increase or decrease in permanent endowment funds will not be accounted for in the same way as other transactions. (The accounting treatment of increases and decreases in permanent endowment funds is discussed in paragraphs 3.3 to 3.5 of Chapter 3 and paragraph 4.14 of Chapter 4). In most other respects, however, the existence of different funds will not affect the accounting treatment adopted. **2.13**

DISCLOSURE OF ACCOUNTING POLICIES

It is essential that the main accounting treatments or policies adopted in preparing the accounts are explained in the notes to the accounts in sufficient detail to enable the reader to understand and interpret the accounts. This will usually include explaining: **2.14**

(a) how each principal type of income (for example, donations, legacies, covenanted income etc.) has been dealt with in the income and expenditure account;
(b) how legal and other commitments entered into in respect of future charitable expenditure have been dealt with in the accounts;
(c) how it has been decided which expenditure should be treated as administration expenses, fund-raising expenses and publicity expenses;
(d) how capital expenditure and donated fixed assets have been dealt with in the accounts;
(e) instances in which income has been netted off against the expenditure;
(f) the amount at which assets are included in the balance sheet;
(g) whether profits and losses arising on the disposal of investments have been dealt with in the income and expenditure account or in the statement of investment gains.

Example 2 illustrates a typical statement of accounting policies. (Most of these accounting policies are discussed in detail in the chapters which follow. Readers may therefore find it preferable to refer to Example 2 only after having studied the remainder of this guide.)

The importance of consistency was referred to earlier in this chapter. It is particularly important that the accounting policies chosen are applied consistently throughout the accounting period and in successive periods. However, if the trustees believe it essential to change an accounting policy, the change should be highlighted and explained, and its effect should be quantified. **2.15**

Example 2

Statement of accounting policies

Voluntary income

1. Voluntary income is received in cash by way of donations and gifts, legacies, occasional flag collection days and special fund-raising events involving local and national celebrities.
   (a) Cash donations, gifts and legacies are included in full in the income and expenditure account as soon as they are received.
   (b) Cash collected during flag days is included in the income and expenditure account as soon as it is received by the Honorary Treasurer. This will usually be within seven days of the flag day.
   (c) Cash collected at special fund-raising events is included in the income and expenditure account after deducting the expenditure incurred directly in staging the event. Note ** shows the amount of cash collected at such events and the expenditure incurred in staging the events separately.
2. In addition, the charity receives help and support in the form of voluntary assistance in its two homes and donations of food and other goods.
   (a) Voluntary help is not included in the accounts. However, the extent of volunteer help received is explained in Note ** to the accounts.
   (b) Donations of food and other goods are generally included in the income and expenditure account when they are received at their estimated market value at the time. However, it is considered informative to value some of the goods received. These goods are not included in the accounts, but are referred to in Note **.

Investment income

3. Dividends are included in the income and expenditure account when they are declared at an amount which includes the tax credit recoverable from the Inland Revenue.
4. Bank interest is included in the income and expenditure account on receipt.

Expenditure

5. All expenditure, other than that which has been capitalised (see accounting policy notes 6 and 7 below), is included in the income and expenditure account. The value of purchase invoices received before the year-end but not paid until after the year-end has also been included in the income and expenditure account. The value of purchase invoices received after the year-end in respect of expenditure incurred before the year-end was insignificant and has therefore not been included in the income and expenditure account.

Fixed assets

6. The charity's two elderly peoples homes and its offices are included in the balance

sheet at cost less provisions for depreciation. Provisions for depreciation are in each case based on an estimated useful life of fifty years.

7. Other fixed assets whose original cost (or, if donated, value at the date of receipt) was more than £500 have been capitalised and depreciated over the following periods:

Furniture	5 years
Office equipment	3 years
Medical equipment	Between 3 and 5 years

Investments and investment gains and losses

8. Stocks and shares quoted on the London Stock Exchange are included in the balance sheet at their market value at the year-end. The differences between this market value and the original cost of the investments are, with the exception of those differences arising on investments held in permanent endowment funds (see accounting policy note 10 below), disclosed in the statement of investment gains and transferred from there to the balance sheet. No unquoted investments are held.

9. Profits and losses arising on the disposal of investments are not included in the income and expenditure account. Instead, those profits and losses arising on investments other than those held in permanent endowment funds are disclosed in the statement of investment gains and transferred from there to the balance sheet. Profits and losses arising on the disposal of investments held in permanent endowment funds are dealt with in the manner described in accounting policy Note 10.

Permanent endowment funds

10. Transactions and other events which increase or decrease the amount of the permanently endowed funds are not dealt with in the income and expenditure account. Instead they are take directly to the balance sheet. The movements involved are disclosed in Note **.

---

3 – Income

GENERAL PRINCIPLES

All resources coming into a charity are income and should be included in the income and expenditure account. The only exceptions to this are: 3.1

(a) incoming resources in the form of donations-in-kind (see paragraph 3.15 below);
(b) increases in permanent endowment funds (see paragraphs 3.3 to 3.5 below); and
(c) profits on the disposal of investments (see paragraph 3.17 below).

Income should be included in the income and expenditure account as soon as its receipt becomes due. For most voluntary income, this will be when it is received. The only 3.2

exceptions to this involve certain types of restricted income (see paragraph 3.7 below) and certain donated assets (see paragraph 3.13 below).

PERMANENT ENDOWMENT FUNDS

3.3 Incoming resources in the form of new permanent endowment funds or additions to existing permanent endowment funds are not income and should not be included in the income and expenditure account. Instead, they should be dealt with by increasing the amount of the permanent endowment funds shown in the balance sheet. A note to the accounts should show all the movements on permanent endowment funds during the period – an example of this note is given in Example 3 – and the trustees' report should usually comment on these movement.

Example 3

Movements on permanent endowment funds during the year

	Mary Cox Fund £	*Gina Bond Fund* £	*Albert Gee Fund* £	*Total* £
Balances at the beginning of the year	15,051	3,912	–	18,963
New permanent endowments	–	–	14,821	14,821
Additions to previous endowments	–	592	316	908
Investment gains less losses	2,111	(491)	–	1,620
Balance at the end of the year	17,162	4,013	15,137	36,312

3.4 A profit arising on the disposal of an asset held in a permanent endowment fund also represents an increase in permanent endowment funds and should therefore be dealt with in the manner described in paragraph 3.3. Other gains on assets held in permanent endowment funds should be similarly treated.

3.5 However, income received from an asset held in a permanent endowment fund does not represent an addition to the permanent endowment fund unless the terms of the deed relating to the endowment state otherwise. Instead, such income should be dealt with in the same way as any other investment income (see paragraph 3.16).

RESTRICTED INCOME

When making donations, donors may specify the way in which their donations are to be used. Such income is known as 'restricted income'. Usually the charity will be able to comply with the donor's wishes or 'restrictions', although occasionally there may be some doubt about the matter. Donations which cannot be used in the way the donor intended must, unless the donor can be persuaded to change his restrictions, be returned. **3.6**

If it is likely that the charity will be able to comply with the donor's wishes, the income should be included in the income and expenditure account as soon as it is received. However, if it is possible that the donation will have to be returned unused, they should not be included in the income and expenditure account until the conditions imposed are either met or become less onerous. In the meantime the donations should be shown in the balance sheet and described as 'deferred restricted income'. Example 4 provides an illustration of this treatment. **3.7**

Example 4

The treatment of income subject to onerous restrictions

Extract from the balance sheet ...

	£
CURRENT LIABILITIES	
Creditors	10,926
Deferred restricted income (see note 8)	5,112

Note 8 – Deferred restricted income

This balance is in respect of income received subject to restrictions which the charity may not be able to meet. The restriction imposed is that the income should only be used to provide assistance to the residents of the Harlyn Sheltered Housing Development. The governing instrument of the charity states that its activities should be limited to the inhabitants of Ewechester. As the Harlyn Sheltered Housing Development is not in Ewechester, it is possible that the income will have to be returned, unused, to the donor.

CASH DONATIONS, GIFTS AND LEGACIES

Cash donations, gifts and legacies should be included in the income and expenditure account in full as soon as they are received. (The references in this paragraph and the two which follow to including items in the income and expenditure account are not appropriate for increases in permanent endowment funds or for deferred restricted income.) **3.8**

Cash collections

3.9 In order to include all cash collections in the income and expenditure account in full as soon as they are received, it would be necessary to estimate cash held in collection containers at public premises and other cash collected but not yet received centrally. This will sometimes be difficult to do. However, it will usually be acceptable to include only those amounts received centrally. The treatment adopted should be explained in the accounting policy notes.

Covenanted income

3.10 Income received by deed of covenant is usually received after deduction of tax: the tax deducted being recoverable from the Inland Revenue. Covenanted income should be included in the income and expenditure account on receipt at an amount which includes both the amount received and the amount of tax recoverable. The tax recoverable should also be included in the balance sheet as a debtor until it is received.

NON-CASH DONATIONS, GIFTS AND LEGACIES

3.11 Non-cash donations, gifts and legacies fall into two categories: those involving the receipt of non-cash assets ('donated assets') and those involving the use or provision of services at a price below cost or even at nil cost ('donations-in-kind'). (The references in this paragraph and the five which follow to including items in the income and expenditure account are not appropriate for increases in permanent endowment funds or deferred restricted income.)

Donated assets

3.12 Donated assets should wherever possible be included in the income and expenditure account as soon as they are received, regardless of whether they are intended for use, distribution or resale. The amount at which they are included should be an estimate of their market value at the date of receipt.

3.13 Sometimes it will be difficult or costly to estimate the market value of a donated asset at the date of receipt. Where this is the case, the asset's receipt should be referred to in a note to the accounts (see Example 5). If it later becomes practicable to assign a value to the asset, a value should be assigned and this value should be included in the income and expenditure account of the period in which the asset was valued. (If, as a result of this practice, a significant amount of the income included in the income and expenditure account relates to assets received in previous years, it will usually be helpful to disclose this fact and the amounts involved.)

3.14 It may be that it will never become practicable to value some donated assets. These assets will therefore never appear in the income and expenditure account.

Example 5

Donated assets which cannot easily be valued

Note**

The charity receives a number of non-cash donations, mainly in the form of food and second-hand clothing and furniture. Although most of these donations have been dealt with in the income and expenditure account, the following donated assets have been omitted from income because of the difficulty in valuing them.

16	Second-hand beds
3	Second-hand sofas
8	Second-hand televisions
500lbs	of assorted clothing

Donations-in-kind

The charity may receive significant amounts of assistance in the form of donated or below-cost facilities, voluntary help, beneficial loan arrangements or other 'donations-in-kind'. No attempt need be made to value these donations for accounting purposes. Instead, the extent of the support received should be explained either in the notes to the accounts or in the trustees' report. Example 6 illustrates the form such an explanation might take. **3.15**

Example 6

Donations-in-kind explained

In addition to the amounts included in the accounts, the charity benefited from almost 2,000 hours of volunteer help during the year, most of which came in the form of direct assistance in caring for the elderly. We could not continue to provide our current level of support to the elderly without this gratefully received assistance.

INVESTMENT INCOME

A charity may also receive dividend, interest or rental income. Such income should be included in the income and expenditure account as it is received, unless: **3.16**

(a) the amounts involved are very significant, in which case dividend income should be recognised when it is declared, and the interest and rental income should be recognised over the period in which it is earned; or

(b) the income has been earned on assets held in permanent endowment funds and the terms of the deed relating to the endowment state that the income forms part of the endowment, in which case the income should be treated as an increase in permanent endowment funds (see paragraph 3.3 above).

PROFIT ON DISPOSAL OF INVESTMENTS

3.17 When a charity sells an investment, a profit or loss will arise. Such a profit or loss may be either included in the income and expenditure account (in which case it should be disclosed separately from other income or expenditure) or transferred directly to the appropriate fund in the balance sheet (in which case the amount involved should be disclosed in a statement of investment gains). Whichever method is used should be used consistently and explained in the accounting policies note. (Profits on disposal of investments held in permanent endowments are, as explained in paragraph 3.4, not dealt with in the same way as other disposal profits.)

3.18 Statements of investment gains, an example of which is given in Example 7, should be included on the same page as, or immediately after, the income and expenditure account.

Example 7

The statement of investment gains

	£
Realised gains on disposal of investments	1,463
Change in unrealised gains/(losses) on investments	(1,212)
Net investment gains	251

ANALYSIS OF INCOME IN THE ACCOUNTS

3.19 As was mentioned in Chapter 2, it is not satisfactory to show a single figure for income in the income and expenditure account without there being further analysis in the notes. Income should be analysed in a way that enables the reader to appreciate the spread and character of the income involved, although this analysis should not be excessively detailed.

3.20 It will usually be appropriate to show investment income separately from the other income included in the income and expenditure account. Realised and unrealised gains and losses on disposal of fixed assets and investments (to the extent that they are included in the income and expenditure account at all) should also be shown separately. That apart however, the analysis will need to be tailored to the needs of the charity involved. It might for example be appropriate to analyse income by reference to its source. This may be particularly helpful in the case of local charities or of charities which are dependent upon certain donors. On the other hand, an indication of the type of income – donations, legacies, covenants, investment income etc – will also be useful, particularly when the charity is dependent upon certain types of income. Example 8 illustrates how the income of a typical charity might be analysed.

Example 8

Analysis of the income of a typical charity

Extract from the income and expenditure account . . .

	£	£
INCOME		
Legacies	23,621	
Covenanted income	15,911	
Other cash donations	49,216	
Other donated assets	5,633	
		94,381
Dividend income received	1,219	
Bank interest received	63	
		1,282
Net gains on the disposal of fixed assets	39	
Net gains on the disposal of investments	621	
		660
Total income		96,323

Extracts from the notes to the accounts

LEGACIES

The income received in the form of legacies was received from Mrs Elsa Doran deceased.

OTHER CASH DONATIONS

The sources of the other cash donations were as follows:

Flag days	28,318
Fosse Way School jumble sales	5,236
Collection containers	11,549
Coffee mornings	4,113
	49,216

4 – Expenditure

GENERAL PRINCIPLES

4.1 All expenditure should be included in the income and expenditure account. The only exception to this involves significant amounts of expenditure incurred to purchase assets (see paragraphs 4.4 to 4.9 below).

4.2 Expenditure should be included in the income and expenditure account as soon as it is incurred. As long as the charity has no significant amounts of purchase invoices unpaid at the year-end and is not invoiced for any significant amounts in arrears or in advance, this will be equivalent to including items of expenditure in the income and expenditure account only when they are paid.

4.3 In addition to such expenditure, it may also be necessary to charge depreciation (see paragraphs 5.8 to 5.11) and losses on the disposal of investments (see paragraphs 4.15 and 4.16) in the income and expenditure account.

EXPENDITURE INCURRED TO PURCHASE ASSETS

4.4 Expenditure incurred to purchase an asset or assets will consist mainly of expenditure on the purchase of fixed assets (that is asset such as buildings and equipment) and expenditure on the purchase of investments (that is assets such as stocks and shares). Such expenditure should not be included in the income and expenditure account immediately. Instead it should be included in the balance sheet and only released into the income and expenditure account as the asset involved is used up or disposed of.

Expenditure on the purchase of fixed assets

4.5 Expenditure incurred on the purchase of a fixed asset is often referred to as 'capital expenditure'. Significant amounts of capital expenditure should be included in the balance sheet (that is, 'capitalised') under the heading 'fixed assets' and appropriately analysed. (The analysis of fixed assets is dealt with in Chapter 5). Insignificant amounts of capital expenditure should not be capitalised, but should instead be included in the income and expenditure account along with other expenditure.

4.6 Expenditure incurred to purchase an asset should if capitalised be released into the income and expenditure account over the useful life of the fixed asset so that, by the end of the asset's life, the whole of the expenditure will have been charged against income. This is achieved by making provisions for depreciation and charging them in the income and expenditure account. Depreciation is explained more fully in Chapter 5.

Expenditure incurred to purchase investments

4.7 Expenditure incurred to purchase an investment should be included in the balance sheet under the heading 'investments' and appropriately analysed. (The analysis of investments and other recommendations on the treatment of investments are discussed in Chapter 5.)

When the investment is sold, the difference between the sale proceeds and the cost of the investment will represent the profit or loss on disposal. (Paragraphs 3.4 and 3.17 deal with profits arising on the disposal of investments. Paragraphs 4.15 and 4.16 deal with losses.) **4.8**

As explained more fully in paragraph 5.15, it may also be necessary to reduce the amount at which an investment is shown in the balance sheet if there has been a permanent fall in its market value. **4.9**

EXPENDITURE OUTSTANDING AT THE YEAR-END

The income and expenditure account is intended to show the amount of expenditure incurred during the year, and not merely the amount paid. Nevertheless, as long as the charity does not have a significant amount of purchase invoices unpaid at the year-end, it will usually be acceptable to include only those invoices actually paid in the income and expenditure account. However, if significant amounts of unpaid invoices exist, it will be necessary to include in the income and expenditure account both invoices paid during the year and invoices unpaid at the year-end. **4.10**

Some expenditure is invoiced in arrears. For example, it is quite common for hire charges on equipment to be invoiced only at the end of the hire period. It may therefore be the case that the charity will receive goods or services before the year-end, but will not receive the related invoice until after the year-end. If, at the year-end the amount of uninvoiced goods and services received is significant, it will be necessary to include a charge for the uninvoiced amounts in the income and expenditure account. **4.11**

A liability or creditor balance will need to be included in the balance sheet in respect of unpaid invoices and amounts not invoiced at the year-end. This balance will be eliminated when the amounts are paid. **4.12**

AMOUNTS PAID IN ADVANCE

Similarly, a charity may from time to time make payments in respect of goods or services before they have been received (that is, before the expense has been incurred). For example, it is common to pay for annual insurance by means of a single premium at the beginning of the insurance year. At the beginning of the year therefore, the whole of the premium will have been paid in advance. Three months later, only nine-twelfths of it will have been paid in advance. **4.13**

If the amount of payments made in advance is significant at the year-end, the amounts involved should be excluded from the income and expenditure account and instead included in the balance sheet (described as 'prepayments'). When the expense is incurred, the payments should be released from the balance sheet and included in the income and expenditure account. **4.14**

LOSSES ON DISPOSAL OF INVESTMENTS

4.15 Losses on the disposal of investments held in permanent endowment funds decrease the amount of the permanent endowment funds. Decreases in permanent endowment funds should be dealt with in the same way as increases in permanent endowment funds (see paragraphs 3.3 and 3.4).

4.16 Losses on the disposal of other investments should be dealt with in the same way as profits on the disposal of such investments (see paragraphs 3.17 and 3.18).

ANALYSIS OF EXPENDITURE IN THE ACCOUNTS

4.17 Expenditure included in the income and expenditure account should, like income, be analysed in a way that enables the reader to understand how the charity's income has been spent. The exact form this analysis will take will depend on the circumstances of each charity. For some charities it will be preferable to analyse the expenditure by cost category (i.e. 'salaries', 'rent' etc.). For other charities, an analysis of expenditure by cost centre (i.e. 'cost of running Old Manor home' etc.) may be more useful. (Appendix I sets out some examples of what the analysis might look like.)

4.18 Whatever the analysis, it is important that fund-raising expenses, administration expenses and publicity expenses be shown separately from each other and from expenditure and grants relating directly to charitable activities.

5 – Assets, liabilities and funds

GENERAL PRINCIPLES

5.1 All assets, liabilities and funds* of a charity should, with the exception of certain fixed assets (see paragraphs 5.7 and 5.8) be included in its balance sheet.

5.2 Assets should be included in the balance sheet at either cost or revalued amount (see paragraph 5.19), subject to the possible need to reduce the cost or revalued amount for accounting purposes by a provision for a permanent reduction in the value of the asset (see paragraph 5.16). Liabilities should be included at their face value, that is, the amount at which they will be settled.

5.3 The assets and liabilities included in the balance sheet should be analysed to show the various types of assets and liabilities held and, for example, whether the balances be

**The term 'funds' is used in this guide to mean accumulated unspent income. A fund will be represented by assets and liabilities.*

long-term or short-term balances. In addition, the total funds of the charity should be analysed between the various funds involved and it should be made clear which assets and liabilities are held in which fund. (These various analyses are considered further below.)

ASSETS

An asset is, broadly speaking, something which will be of value or use to the charity in the future. A charity will come to acquire an asset in one of two ways. It may purchase it – the treatment of such 'capital expenditure' was considered in Chapter 4. Alternatively, the asset may be donated – the treatment of income received in the form of donated assets was considered in Chapter 3. 5.4

Assets shown in the balance sheet should be analysed between fixed assets, investments and current assets. 5.5

(a) Fixed assets are assets held for use over the coming years. They are the long-term assets of the charity. Examples of fixed assets include land and buildings, plant and machinery, office equipment and motor vehicles.
(b) Investments are assets held for the income or capital gain that arises directly from them. Some investments are held for the long-term, others for the short-term. Examples of investments include stocks and shares and investment properties.
(c) Current assets are assets held for use, disposal or turning into cash in the short-term (i.e. the next twelve months). Examples of current assets include cash and bank balances, prepayments and donated items held for resale or distribution.

FIXED ASSETS

All fixed assets should usually be included in the balance sheet, regardless of whether they were purchased by the charity or donated to it, and regardless of whether they will eventually be replaced and, if they will, how their replacement will be financed. 5.6

There are however two exceptions to this principle. A fixed asset need not be included on the balance sheet if either: 5.7

(a) neither a cost nor market value for the fixed asset is available. For example, a fixed asset may have been purchased some years ago but not capitalised at the time. If there is no record of the purchase cost and if the fixed asset's current market value cannot be satisfactorily estimated, it is not necessary to include the fixed asset in the balance sheet. If a fixed asset was donated to the charity and a satisfactory value for the asset could not be determined at the time of receipt or subsequently, it would again not be necessary to include the fixed asset in the balance sheet; or
(b) the fixed asset is either an historic asset (such as a silver chalice) or is inalienable.

A summary of the fixed assets not included in the balance sheet but still in use should be provided in the notes to the accounts. An example of such a summary, and the information that it should provide, is given in Example 9. 5.8

Example 9

Fixed assets not shown on the balance sheet

In addition to the fixed assets included in the balance sheet, the charity owns and continues to have use of a number of other fixed assets. These assets have not been included in the balance sheet, primarily because, when they were donated to the charity, the trustees did not believe that the cost of valuing them was commensurate with the benefit derived from including them in the balance sheet.

The most significant of the fixed assets involved are:

(a) Three acres of land adjoining the site of The Manor Home. No planning permission has as yet been sought for this land, which was donated to the charity in 1982 in order to provide a site for our planned remedial and convalescence centre.

(b) Two second-hand coaches. One of these coaches was donated in 1974, the other in 1985.

Depreciating fixed assets

5.9 As mentioned in Chapter 4, it may be necessary to make provision for the depreciation of some or all of the fixed assets. Most fixed assets have a finite useful life and therefore wear out, get consumed or simply become obsolescent. The length of the useful life will depend very much on the circumstances involved. The coaches referred to in Example 9, for example, will probably have a useful life of 15 to 20 years. On the other hand, some transport or agricultural vehicles used overseas are used in conditions which make it reasonable to write them off over one year. All fixed assets which have a finite useful life – that is, depreciate – should have provisions for depreciation made against them. Fixed assets which do not depreciate – an example of which is land – should not be depreciated.

5.10 The purpose of charging depreciation is to allocate capitalised expenditure to the income and expenditure accounts of the periods which will benefit from the capital expenditure. For example, if a machine that is expected to last for 10 years is bought, the aim should be to include one tenth of the cost of the machine in each income and expenditure account for the next 10 years. To illustrate this, assume, that the machine was bought for £8,000.

(a) The £8,000 will be capitalised and shown in the balance sheet as a fixed asset.

(b) The £8,000 will be depreciated so as to include one-tenth of the expenditure (i.e. £800) in each of the next 10 income and expenditure accounts.

(c) This means that at the end of year three, for example, the machine will be shown in the balance sheet at £5,600 (i.e. £8,000 – (3 × 800)).

(d) At the end of the tenth year, the whole of the capital expenditure will have been charged to the income and expenditure account: the asset will be included in the balance sheet at a nil amount.

5.11 As illustrated above, provisions for depreciation should be included in the income and expenditure account and used to reduce the amount at which the assets are carried in the balance sheet. This means that fixed assets will be included in the balance sheet at one of the following amounts: cost less accumulated depreciation; the value of the asset at the date the asset was donated less accumulated depreciation; or a revalued amount less accumulated depreciation. (Revaluations are considered in paragraph 5.19 below.)

Example 10 illustrates the information which should be disclosed in respect of depreciation. Other disclosure aspects are illustrated in Example 11. **5.12**

Example 10

The depreciation accounting policy note

Fixed assets are depreciated over their estimated useful lives. Equal amounts of depreciation are charged to each period in the life of the asset. The lives involved are as follows:

Buildings	25 years
Motor vehicles	5 years
Equipment	10 years

The total amount of fixed assets included in the balance sheet should be analysed, usually in the notes to the accounts, between the types of fixed assets involved (for example, buildings, motor vehicles and equipment). The notes should also provide details of the movements on the fixed asset figure since the last balance sheet. Example 11 illustrates a typical fixed asset note. **5.13**

INVESTMENTS

All investments should be included in the balance sheet, regardless of whether they were purchased or donated. Purchased investments should be included at either cost or a revalued amount and donated investments should be included at either their value at the time they were donated or a revalued amount. Revaluations are considered in paragraph 5.19 below. However, if the market value of an investment falls, the amount at which it is included in the balance sheet may need to be reduced (even if the investment is otherwise shown at cost). This is discussed further in paragraph 5.16. **5.14**

The investments figure in the balance sheet should be analysed between the various types of investment involved. This will include, for example, analysing 'stocks and shares' into equity and fixed interest securities and identifying securities quoted on a stock exchange separately from those which are not. **5.15**

Reductions in the market value of investments

The market value of each investment of a charity will vary over time. This market value may be less than the amount at which the investment is carried in the balance sheet. If it **5.16** is not expected that the market value will permanently be less than the balance sheet amount, it can, for accounting purposes, be ignored. However, if it appears likely to be permanent then it should be recognised (even if the investments are otherwise being carried at cost) by reducing the amount at which the investment is shown in the balance sheet in the market value and by charging the amount of the reduction in the income and expenditure account.

CURRENT ASSETS

5.17 All significant current assets should usually be included in the balance sheet and appropriately analysed. However, as explained in Chapter 3, it may not be practicable to value certain donated assets on receipt or, occasionally, at all, in which case it will not be possible to include them in the balance sheet. The existence of such assets should be referred to in the notes.

5.18 The amount at which current assets should be carried in the balance sheet will be as follows:

(a) Cash and bank balances – at the amount of the balances.
(b) Prepayments – at the amount prepaid.
(c) Debtors – at the amount receivable in respect of the debt.
(d) Items held for resale or distribution – at cost or, if donated, at their value at the date they were donated.

Example 11

Typical fixed asset note

	Freehold land and buildings	*Office equipment*	*Motor vehicles*	*Total*
	£	£	£	£
Cost				
Opening balance	100,000	5,236	8,000	113,236
Additions at cost	–	2,512	–	2,512
Cost of disposals	–	–	(8,000)	(8,000)
Closing balance	100,000	7,748	–	107,748
Accumulated depreciation				
Opening balance	10,000	2,618	6,000	18,618
Depreciation charge for year	2,000	700	1,000	3,700
Depreciation on assets disposed of	–	–	(7,000)	(7,000)
Closing balance	12,000	3,318	–	15,318
*Net book value**				
Opening	90,000	2,618	2,000	94,618
Closing	88,000	4,430	–	92,430

*[*i.e. cost less accumulated depreciation]*

REVALUATIONS OF ASSETS

A charity may estimate the current market value of some or all of its assets and use these values, rather than cost (or, if donated, value at the date of donation) in the balance sheet. The use of revalued amounts in this way means that the balance sheet provides a more up-to-date picture of the resources held by the charity. If revalued amounts are used, this should be explained in the accounting policies note. 5.19

If investments are not included in the balance sheet at current market value, then this amount should instead be disclosed in the notes to the accounts. For quoted securities, the mid-market value should be used. For other investments, an estimate of the likely market value should be used. 5.20

If items are included in the balance sheet at market value, surpluses and deficits on revaluation (so-called 'unrealised gains and losses') will arise. Unrealised gains and losses on investments should be dealt with in the accounts in the same way as profits and losses on the disposal of investments (so-called 'realised profits and losses'). (The treatment of disposals of investments is dealt with in Chapter 3). However, in the case of fixed assets, realised profits and losses should be included in the income and expenditure account while unrealised profits and losses should be taken directly to the balance sheet. 5.21

LIABILITIES

All significant liabilities incurred by the year-end should be included in the balance sheet. Liabilities are not incurred in respect of charitable expenditure until the payment date. 5.22

A charity's liabilities may include, for example: 5.23

(a) unpaid bills received before the year-end;
(b) expenditure incurred before the year-end for which bills were not received until after the year-end;
(c) bank overdrafts and loans.

Liabilities should be analysed in the balance sheet between current liabilities (i.e. amounts payable in the twelve months following the year end) and non-current, or long-term, liabilities. Long-term liabilities should be further analysed in the notes by showing separately the amount payable within five years and the amount payable after five years. 5.24

A liability may be secured on one or more of the charity's assets. Similarly, the charity 5.25

may have accepted a charge on some of its assets in respect of one or more of its liabilities. The existence of such securities or charges, and details of the assets involved, should be disclosed in the notes to the accounts.

FUNDS

5.26 As explained in Chapter 2, a charity may hold a number of different, and completely separate, funds. The funds of a charity fall into two categories: restricted and unrestricted. Restricted funds can be further classified between permanent endowment funds and other restricted funds. Some charities classify their unrestricted funds between designated funds and other unrestricted funds.

Example 12

Analysing assets and liabilities between funds

1. Extract from the balance sheet
The total net assets of the charity are represented by:

	£
Restricted funds:	
Fazackerly permanent endowment fund	63,921
The James Sessions restricted fund	15,213
Other restricted funds	11,119
	90,253
Unrestricted funds	78,163
	168,416

2. Extract from the notes to the accounts
Note** Assets and liabilities held in each fund

	Fazackerly permanent endowment fund	*James Sessions restricted fund*	*Other restricted funds*	*Unrestricted funds*	*Total funds*
	£	£	£	£	£
Fixed assets	63,921	9,281	2,162	27,779	103,142
Investments	–	–	3,126	42,611	45,737
Current assets	–	6,540	5,832	26,384	38,756
Current liabilities	–	(608)	–	(18,611)	(19,219)
	63,921	15,213	11,119	78,163	168,416

5.27 Increases and decreases in permanent endowment funds should not be treated in the same way as increases and decreases in other funds. That apart, the accounting treatment used should not differentiate between the funds involved. In other words, a legacy involving a restricted fund (other than a permanent endowment fund) should be dealt with in exactly the same way as a legacy involving an unrestricted fund, and expenditure made out of a restricted fund (other than a permanent endowment fund) should be dealt with in the same way as expenditure made out of an unrestricted fund.

This does not mean however that there is no need to keep track of which funds are involved in which transactions. It is essential that accounting records are maintained in sufficient detail to enable the trustees to ensure that income is used for the purpose for which it is intended. It is also essential that the following points of law are noted. **5.28**

(a) A realised or unrealised profit or loss arising on an asset will form part of the fund in which the asset is held. Similarly any provision for the depreciation of an asset or for the permanent fall in value of an asset will form part of the fund in which the asset is held.
(b) On the other hand income generated from an asset will be unrestricted income unless the terms on which the charity holds the asset dictate otherwise. This will be the case even if the asset is held in a permanent endowment fund.

It will also be essential to ensure that the assets and liabilities held in each of the funds are consistent with the purpose of the funds. For example, assets of a long-term nature should not be held in a short-term fund. The total net assets of the charity (that is, total assets less total liabilities) should therefore be analysed between the various funds held, and an indication of the types of assets and liabilities held within each fund should be provided. Example 12 illustrates how this might be done. **5.29**

6 – Sundry matters

DISCLOSURE OF ADDITIONAL INFORMATION

In addition to the information referred to already in this guide, it may be necessary to disclose various other pieces of information. The exact information involved will depend on the circumstances and activities of the charity involved, although the guiding principle should be to disclose everything the reader needs to understand the financial affairs of the charity. In addition to the information referred to elsewhere in this guide, the information provided will usually include: **6.1**

(a) the total amounts of remuneration paid to the trustees and to the employees, the average number of employees during the year, and details of the total amount of trustees' expenses reimbursed by the charity and the types of expenses involved; and
(b) details of the charity's future charitable or legal commitments. These details should include the amounts involved and when the commitments are likely to be met.

Appendix I, which contains full example sets of accounts, illustrates the manner in which this information can usefully be disclosed. It also provides other examples of information which may need to be disclosed. **6.2**

COMPARATIVE INFORMATION

6.3 When reading accounts it is usually helpful if, alongside the current year's figures, comparative information is provided. In most cases the most useful comparison to make will be with the previous year's figures (so-called 'corresponding amounts') for the same items.

6.4 It may be that the current year's figures are significantly different to those for the previous year. This is not a reason to do without comparatives – it means that further explanation is necessary.

LEGAL REQUIREMENTS

6.5 At the beginning of this guide it was explained that all charity trustees are accountable under trust law for the resources which they receive and that this duty of accountability is reinforced by various Acts of Parliament. It is essential that the trustees are fully aware of their legal observations in respect of annual reports and other matters. Attention is therefore drawn to paragraphs 84 to 87 of the Statement of Recommended Practice, which summarise some of the more commonly encountered legal requirements concerning the preparation of annual reports and accounts. If necessary, the trustees should also seek professional advice.

Appendix I – Example sets of accounts

INTRODUCTION

1. This appendix contains the following examples:

Example 1: A skeleton set of accounts for a charity which raises its own funds and then spends them on a range of charitable activities.
Example 2: A skeleton set of accounts for an endowed grant-making charity.
Example 3: A skeleton set of accounts for a non-endowed grant-making charity.
Example 4: The Ewechester Homes Fund accounts.

2. It should be noted that the purpose of these examples is to illustrate how different types of charity might report their activities and financial position. The purpose is not to prescribe standard formats or to imply that the formats in the examples given are necessarily better than any other.

EXAMPLE 1

3. Set out below are a skeleton set of accounts (in other words, accounts without any analysis or notes) for a charity which raises its own funds and then spends them on a range of activities. Such a charity will often have a number of different funds, so the tables shown in paragraphs 6 and 7 are essential to provide information about the movements on the different funds. It should be noted that what appears from a first glance at the income and expenditure account to be unspent income for the year turns out, from a review of the table shown in paragraph 7, to be income which has been spent on charitable fixed assets.

The grouping and order of items within the income and expenditure account is also worth noting: voluntary income is shown separately from investment income, and direct charitable expenditure is shown separately from indirect expenditure. This charity has chosen to show a sub-total for funds raised less cost of raising them.

4. INCOME AND EXPENDITURE ACCOUNT

	£	£
Donations	14,325	
Legacies	8,163	
Cash collections	11,321	
Voluntary income	33,809	
Fund-raising expenses	4,236	
Voluntary income less fund-raising expenses		29,573
Dividends	701	
Net profits on disposal of investments	523	
		1,224
		30,797
Administration expenses	2,161	
Publicity expenses	1,136	
		3,297
		27,500
Charitable expenditure		11,123
Income less expenditure		16,377
Accumulated funds at the beginning of the year		3,213
Accumulated funds at the end of the year		19,590

5. BALANCE SHEET

Fixed assets		16,321
Investments		1,200
Current assets	2,421	
Current liabilities	(226)	
		2,195
Long-term liabilities		(126)
		19,590
Restricted fund – A		16,321
– B		1,041
Unrestricted fund		2,228
		19,590

6. ANALYSIS OF MOVEMENTS OF FUNDS

	Restricted funds A	Restricted funds B	Unrestricted funds	Total
Voluntary income	16,321	7,727	9,761	33,809
Fund-raising expenses	–	(1,229)	(3,007)	(4,236)
Investment gains	–	111	1,113	1,224
Indirect expenses	–	–	(3,297)	(3,297)
	16,321	6,609	4,570	27,500
Opening funds	111	2,313	789	3,213
	16,432	8,922	5,359	30,713
Charitable expenditure	(111)	(7,881)	(3,131)	(11,123)
Closing funds	16,321	1,041	2,228	19,590

7. ANALYSIS OF BALANCE SHEET ITEMS BY FUND

	Restricted funds A	Restricted funds B	Unrestricted funds	Total
Fixed assets	16,321	–	–	16,321
Investments	–	623	577	1,200
Net current assets	–	418	1,777	2,195
Long-term liabilities	–	–	(126)	(126)
	16,321	1,041	2,228	19,590

EXAMPLE 2

8. This example deals with an endowed grant-making charity, in other words a charity which uses the income earned on its permanent endowment funds to make grants. This is a fairly simple type of charity, and its accounts reflect this fact.

9. INCOME AND EXPENDITURE ACCOUNT

	£
Investment income	15,213
Administration expenses	(891)
	14,322
Undistributed income from previous periods	1,115
Total amount available for distribution	15,437
Grants made in the period	(15,215)
Undistributed income carried forward	222

10. BALANCE SHEET

Investments	190,101
Current assets – cash	222
	190,323

Permanent endowment funds	190,101
Unrestricted fund	222
	190,323

The notes to the balance sheet would explain that the permanent endowment funds consist entirely of investments and that the unrestricted fund consists entirely of cash.

EXAMPLE 3

11. This example shows the accounts of a non-endowed grant-making charity. The charity raises income from a variety of sources. Some of this income is immediately paid out in grants. Most however is invested, the intention being to pay grants out of the income earned on the investments. A two column income and expenditure account is used to show this separation of income.

12. INCOME AND EXPENDITURE ACCOUNT

	General fund	*Designated fund*
Donations	7,345	–
Legacies	16,135	–
Cash collections	8,169	–
Voluntary income	31,649	–
Investment income	11,236	–
Income for the year	42,885	–
Indirect expenditure	(4,111)	–
	38,774	–
Opening funds	–	91,632
Charitable expenditure	(13,436)	–
Allocations to designated funds	(25,138)	25,138
	200	116,770
Investment gains	–	7,910
	200	124,680

13. BALANCE SHEET

Investments	124,321
Net current assets – cash	359
	124,680
Designated funds	124,480
General (unrestricted) funds	200
	124,680

Appendix II – Charity commission forms

As explained in paragraph 1.2, the Charity Commission provides all newly-registered charities with some standard forms for the preparation of the statements of account required by the Charities Act 1960. There are two types of form:

Form AC(A) – for use by small charities with incomes of £500 a year or less

Form AC(B) – for use by larger charities.

These forms are reprinted on the pages which follow. Copies are available free of charge from the Charity Commission, 14 Ryder Street, London SW1Y 6AH.

It should be noted that the use of these forms is not mandatory: accounts prepared in different formats will be equally acceptable to the Charity Commission as long as they contain the information required by the 1960 Act.

CHARITY COMMISSION AC(A)

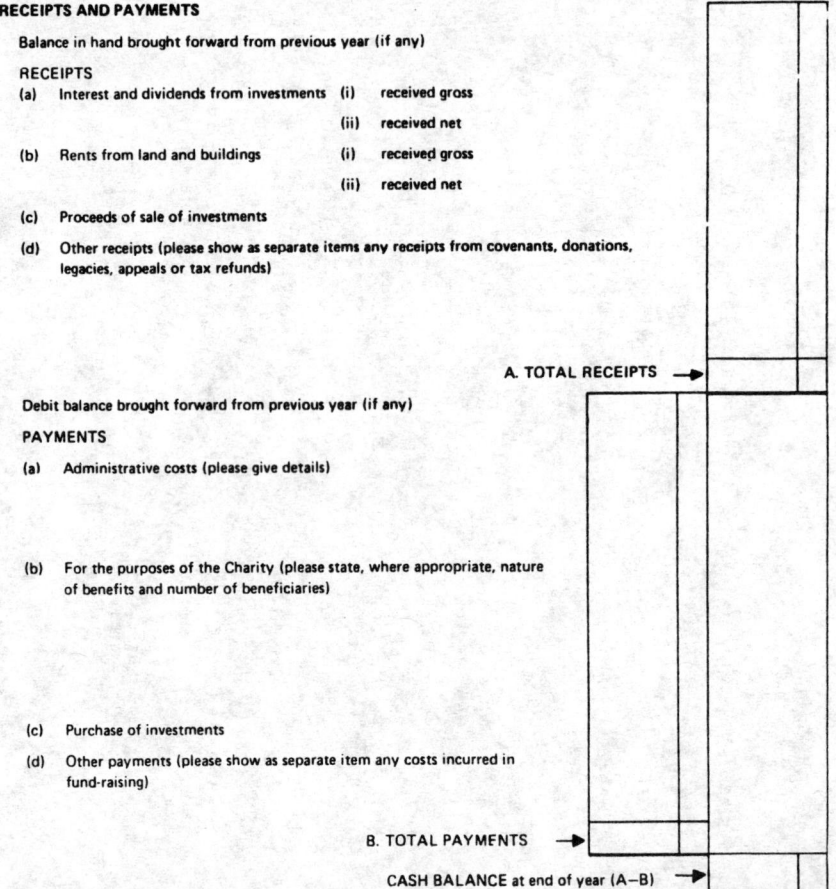

STATEMENT OF ACCOUNT – to be sent to the Charity Commissioners pursuant to section 8 of the Charities Act 1960

NAME OF CHARITY: PLACE:

COUNTY: CHARITY COMMISSION REFERENCE NO:

STATEMENT OF ACCOUNT for year ending:

1. **PARTICULARS OF TRUSTEES*** as at end of financial year:

Name	Address	Occupation

* i.e. those who control and manage the Charity, whether trustees, governors, committee of management, etc.

2. **RECEIPTS AND PAYMENTS**

Balance in hand brought forward from previous year (if any)

RECEIPTS

(a) Interest and dividends from investments (i) received gross

(ii) received net

(b) Rents from land and buildings (i) received gross

(ii) received net

(c) Proceeds of sale of investments

(d) Other receipts (please show as separate items any receipts from covenants, donations, legacies, appeals or tax refunds)

A. TOTAL RECEIPTS →

Debit balance brought forward from previous year (if any)

PAYMENTS

(a) Administrative costs (please give details)

(b) For the purposes of the Charity (please state, where appropriate, nature of benefits and number of beneficiaries)

(c) Purchase of investments

(d) Other payments (please show as separate item any costs incurred in fund-raising)

B. TOTAL PAYMENTS →

CASH BALANCE at end of year (A–B) →

3. **MONEY OWING TO THE CHARITY** at end of year (please give details)

MONEY OWING BY THE CHARITY at end of year (please give details)

4. **ASSETS OF THE CHARITY** Please insert letter 'P' in second column to indicate those assets which represent permanent endowment of the Charity

(a) Land and buildings used for the purposes of the Charity

Names in which held or vested if different from trustees named above

(b) Land and buildings held as an investment to produce income for the Charity

(c) Other investments (stocks, shares, etc)

(d) Rentcharges or similar fixed payments charged on land:

Description of property charged	Name and address of owner (or agent) making payment	Amount of charge

(e) Cash (at Bank and in hand)

5. **CHANGES IN ASSETS DURING YEAR**

(i) Acquired: Description	Cost	(ii) Disposed of: Description	Net proceeds

6. **TRUSTEES' CERTIFICATE**

I/We declare that the foregoing Statement of Account is correct.

Signed:

on behalf of the Trustees

Date:

7. **AUDITOR'S REPORT** (if auditor appointed)

Signature of Auditor(s):

Date:

This Statement of Account is forwarded by:

Name:

Address:

Bas 70152/1/1866 10m 7/79 TP

AC(B)

CHARITY COMMISSION

STATEMENT OF ACCOUNT

(To be sent to the Charity Commissioners pursuant to section 8 of the Charities Act 1960)

NAME OF CHARITY:

PLACE:

COUNTY: **CHARITY COMMISSION REFERENCE NO:**

STATEMENT OF ACCOUNT for year ending:

Section 1. **PARTICULARS OF TRUSTEES*** as at end of financial year

Name	Address	Occupation

*i.e. those who control and manage the Charity, whether trustees, governors, directors, committee of management, etc.

NOTES ON SECTIONS 2 AND 3

The Charities (Statements of Account) Regulations 1960 (SI 1960 No. 2425) prescribe the information to be included in statements of account forwarded to the Commissioners. The Regulations stipulate among other things that receipts and payments shall be classified according to their nature, and that receipts forming part of, and payments made out of, permanent endowment shall be distinguished in the accounts from other kinds of receipts and payments. **"Permanent endowment" is property of the Charity which may not be expended as income.**

Section 2 should show all receipts and payments which are not of a capital nature. These will be mainly receipts and payments relating to the day to day operations of the Charity; and

Section 3 should show only receipts and payments of capital, if any, distinguishing between capital which represents permanent endowment (column (a)) and capital which may be expended (column (b)).

To make the distinction between Sections 2 and 3 clear, any receipts which represent *income* from capital (eg dividends from stocks and shares or rent from the letting of land and buildings), or payments which represent *maintenance and upkeep costs* in respect of land and buildings held as capital (eg repairs, insurance, etc.) should be shown in Section 2 : only transactions which represent *movements of capital* should be recorded in Section 3.

Section 2. NON-CAPITAL RECEIPTS AND PAYMENTS

RECEIPTS

		Year ended 19	Previous year
Interest and dividends from investment	(i) received gross		
	(ii) received net		
Rents from land and buildings	(i) received gross		
	(ii) received net		
Rent charges			
Covenants	(i) received gross		
	(ii) received net		
Tax refunds on dividends, rents and covenants			
Donations			
Legacies			
Fund-raising receipts (gross)			
Grants from Government or Local Authorities	(please give details)		
Bank interest			
Other receipts (please give details)			
TOTAL	A		

Section 2. (Cont.)

PAYMENTS		Year ended 19	Previous year 19
(a) Property	(i) Rent		
	(ii) Rates		
	(iii) Insurance		
	(iv) Maintenance, repairs, etc.		
	(v) Other items (please give details)		
(b) Administration	(i) Staff salaries and wages		
	(ii) Office overheads (heating, lighting, etc.)		
	(iii) Printing, stationery, postage and telephone		
	(iv) Professional fees (please give details)		
	(v) Other management costs		
(c) Fund-raising costs (including wages, office overheads, printing etc.)			
(d) For the purposes of the Charity (please classify under appropriate heads and, where relevant, state nature of benefits and number of beneficiaries; if beneficiaries are institutions, please name them)			
(e) Other payments (please give details)			
TOTAL	B		
Excess of receipts over payments (A–B)	C		
or Excess of payments over receipts (B–A)	D		

Section 3. CAPITAL RECEIPTS AND PAYMENTS

		Year ended 19 (a) Permanent capital	(b) Non-permanent capital	Previous year
RECEIPTS				
Proceeds of sale of: (i) investments				
(ii) land and buildings held to produce income				
(iii) land and buildings used for the purposes of the Charity				
Legacies				
Loans received by the Charity (please give details)				
Repayments of sums lent or deposited by the Charity				
Other receipts of capital (please give details)				
TOTAL	E			
PAYMENTS				
Purchases of: (i) investments				
(ii) land and buildings to produce income				
(iii) land and buildings for use for the purposes of the Charity				
Loans or deposits made by the Charity				
Loans repaid by the Charity (please give details)				
Other payments of capital (please give details)				
TOTAL	F			
Excess of receipts over payments (E–F)	G			
or Excess of payments over receipts (F–E)	H			

Section 4. SUMMARY OF RECEIPTS AND PAYMENTS

Reconciling Sections 2 and 3 with the Charity's cash and bank balances

		Year ended 19	Previous year
Cash at bank and in hand at beginning of year (if any)			
Excess of receipts over payments for the year (if any) on:			
Non-capital (Section 2C)			
Capital (Section 3G)			
SUB-TOTAL	I		
Excess of payments over receipts for the year (if any) on:			
Non-capital (Section 2D)			
Capital (Section 3H)			
Bank overdraft at beginning of year (if any)			
SUB-TOTAL	J		
Cash at Bank and in hand (I–J)			
or			
Bank overdraft less cash in hand (J–I) at end of year			

Section 5. MONEY OWING TO OR BY THE CHARITY AT END OF YEAR

	Year ended 19	Previous year
1. Money owing to the Charity		
Income tax recoverable – claimed for year(s) 19		
– not yet claimed		
Loans granted by Charity, less repayments received to date* (please give details)		
Other money owing to the Charity (please give details)		
TOTAL		
2. Money owing by the Charity		
Money borrowed by the Charity and not yet repaid* (please give details)		
Other money owing by the Charity (please give details)		
TOTAL		

*Include any loans already shown in Sections 2 and 3

Section 6. ASSETS OF CHARITY AT END OF YEAR

Notes: (i) Please insert letter 'P' in the second column to indicate those assets which represent permanent endowment.
(ii) Please state whether land is leasehold or freehold, and the area (if known).

A. LAND AND BUILDINGS

Description		Name in which vested
(i) Used for the purposes of the Charity		
(ii) Held as an investment to produce income for the Charity		

B. INVESTMENTS (stocks and shares and other investments including mortgages)

		Names in which held

C. RENTCHARGES or similar fixed payments charged on land

Description of property charged	Name and address of owner (or agent) making payment	Amount of charge		

D. CASH (at Bank and in hand)			

E. OTHER ASSETS (motor vehicles, caravans, etc.)

Section 7. REPORT OF THE TRUSTEES (Please summarise the activities of the Charity during the year and comment on the overall financial position of the Charity at the end of the year).

Signed by: on behalf of the Trustees.

Section 8. TRUSTEES' CERTIFICATE

I/We declare that the foregoing Statement of Account is correct

Signed: Date:

Section 9. AUDITOR'S REPORT (if auditors appointed)

Signature of auditor(s): Date:

Occupation or qualification:

This statement of account is forwarded by:

Name:

Address:

Glossary of useful terms

1. The *accounting period* is the period from the balance sheet date for the previous accounts to the balance sheet date for the current accounts. The period will usually be twelve months.
2. *Administration expenses* comprise the costs which are not incurred directly on any of the charitable activities or projects of the charity and which are not incurred on fund-raising activities or publicity. Administration expenses will include a proper allocation of items of expenditure involving more than one cost category (e.g. administration expenses, fund-raising expenses etc.), but should not include any apportionment of costs which belong to other cost categories.
3. *Annual report* is the term used in this guide for the report which charities prepare annually and make available to interested parties. It normally contains some legal and administrative information, one or more narrative sections (for example a trustees' report) and accounts.
4. A *balance sheet* is an accounting statement which shows the financial position (that is the assets, liabilities and funds) of the charity as at the balance sheet date.
5. The *balance sheet date* is the date as at which the balance sheet was prepared. It is sometimes also referred to as the year-end.
6. *Capitalised expenditure* is expenditure that has been incurred in acquiring a fixed asset and has consequently been included in the balance sheet under heading 'fixed assets'.
7. A *charity* is any institution established for charitable purposes only. Where the institution is involved in more than one activity, operates more than one fund, or is not centralised into one unit of operation, the term is used in this statement to incorporate all those activities and funds which fall within the scope of a single governing instrument (or instruments supplemental to the main instrument) and any further endowments held within the terms of the original instrument.
8. *A current asset* is an asset which is expected to be disposed of, utilised or realised within twelve months of the balance sheet date.
9. A *current liability* is a liability which is expected to be met within twelve months of the balance sheet date.
10. A *designated fund* is a particular form of unrestricted fund, consisting of amounts of unrestricted funds which have been allocated or designated for specific purposes by the charity itself. The use of designated funds for their designated purpose will remain at the discretion of the trustees.
11. *Excepted charity* means a charity which is excepted by order or regulations from certain requirements of the Charities Act 1960, as defined in Section 45(6) of that Act (e.g. certain voluntary schools, various religious charities and some service charities).
12. *Exempt charity* means a charity comprised in the second schedule to the Charities Act 1960, in other words, certain universities and colleges, the British Museum, the Church Commissioners and registered industrial, provident and friendly societies.
13. A *fund* is a pool of unexpended resources, held and maintained separately from other pools because of the circumstances in which the resources were originally received or the way in which they have subsequently been treated. A fund will be

one of two kinds: a restricted fund or an unrestricted fund. (The terms 'fund' and 'funds' are used in the statement in this specialised way except when used in the phrases 'fund-raising' and 'statement of source and application of funds'.)

14. *Fund-raising expenses* comprise the costs incurred by a charity in inducing others to make voluntary contributions to it. They will also include a proper allocation of items of expenditure involving more than one cost category (e.g. administration expenses, fund-raising expenses etc.), but should not include any apportionment of costs which belong to other cost categories.
15. A *fixed asset* is an asset which is intended for use on a continuing basis in the charity's activities.
16. An *income and expenditure account* is an accounting statement which shows the transactions of the charity during the accounting period.
17. A *permanent endowment* is a particular form of restricted fund in that the fund must be held permanently, although its constituent assets may change from time to time.
18. *Restricted funds* are funds subject to specific conditions, imposed by the donor and binding on the trustees. They represent unspent restricted income and/or assets to which restrictions as to their use apply. The conditions may alternatively be imposed not by the donor but by the trusts relating to the donation. For example, if a donation is made in response to a special appeal, its use will be restricted to the purpose of the appeal, notwithstanding the fact that the donor did not impose any restriction on its use.

Index

Part Seven

Exposure Drafts in Issue

[ASC ED 51]
Accounting for fixed assets and revaluations

(Issued May 1990)

Contents

PREFACE

Introduction

1.1 This exposure draft sets out the relationship between this statement and other existing and proposed statements of standard accounting practice that deal with accounting for specific fixed assets, in particular, investment properties, leases and hire purchase contracts accounted for as fixed assets and intangible fixed assets.

Recognition

1.2 The exposure draft establishes criteria to be satisfied if a fixed asset is to be recognised on an enterprise's balance sheet.

Cost

1.3 Guidance is given on establishing the purchase price or production cost of a fixed asset and on identifying the commencement and conclusion of the period of production. The requirements dealing with determining the cost of fixed assets represent generally accepted practice.

Capitalisation of borrowing costs

1.4 It is proposed that enterprises should be allowed to choose whether they capitalise borrowing costs on projects that take a substantial period of time to bring into use for their intended purpose. However, once the enterprise has adopted a policy to capitalise such costs or not, the policy must be applied consistently to all eligible fixed assets. The exposure draft includes requirements on determining, where applicable, the amount of interest costs that may be capitalised by an enterprise.

Permanent diminutions

1.5 The exposure draft defines permanent diminutions, discusses how they can arise and sets out the accounting treatment which should be followed when they arise.

Valuations

1.6 The inclusion of some fixed assets in the balance sheet at a valuation in accounts prepared under the historical cost convention is a controversial issue. The alternative approaches available and the reasons why it has been decided to propose that enterprises should be permitted to carry selected assets at a valuation so long as the valuations are kept up-to-date and carried out in the structured form prescribed in this exposure draft are discussed in the Explanatory note.

1.7 This proposed statement of standard accounting practice includes requirements on various matters relating to valuations, including the definition of a class of fixed assets (since enterprises adopting a valuation policy must apply it on a class by class basis), the frequency of valuation (i.e., open market value or depreciated replacement cost), the necessary attributes of a valuer, accounting for the disposal of revalued assets and the use of the revaluation reserve.

Transitional provisions

The transitional provisions deal with the application of the exposure draft to enterprises that have undertaken occasional revaluations of some of their fixed assets in the past but which may not wish to follow the structured form of valuation proposed in this document. They also set out the date by which enterprises opting to include land and buildings at a valuation would be required to have their first valuation or review in accordance with the requirements of this proposed statement of standard accounting practice. Lastly, they explain how enterprises should account for changes in accounting policies that would be likely to arise from implementing this proposed statement. **1.8**

Comments

Comments are welcome on the exposure draft and, in particular, on the issues raised below. **1.9**

Capitalisation of borrowing costs

Should enterprises be given the option to decide whether to capitalise borrowing costs on major capital projects? Should capitalisation be optional, excluded or mandatory? (paragraph 73) **1.10**

Valuations

Do commentators agree that: **1.11**

(a) it is not appropriate to require that some or all of an enterprise's fixed assets must be carried at a valuation in accounts prepared under the historical cost convention?
(b) that it is not practicable to prohibit the carrying of selected fixed assets at a valuation?
(c) that it is preferable, if permitting fixed assets to be carried at a valuation, to require this to be done in a structured fashion? (paragraphs 29 to 35)

Should enterprises adopting a valuation policy be required to apply that policy to fixed assets on a class by class basis? Is the proposed method of identifying classes appropriate? (paragraphs 53 and 81) **1.12**

Do commentators agree that assets carried at a valuation should normally be carried at their open market value? Is it agreed that depreciated replacement cost is acceptable as a substitute for open market value where it is not practicable to determine an open market value for a particular fixed asset? (paragraphs 58 and 82) **1.13**

Do commentators support the requirements to have valuations of land and buildings performed, or the basis of valuation reviewed, by an external valuer? (paragraphs 63, 87 and 88) **1.14**

Exposure Drafts in issue

1.15 Is it agreed that, in the case of fixed assets carried at a valuation, the profit or loss on disposal, as well as the amount of any permanent diminutions, should be determined by reference to the revalued carrying amount? (paragraphs 79 and 80)

1.16 Do commentators agree that transfers should be made between the revaluation reserve and the profit and loss account reserve in the manner prescribed in this exposure draft? (paragraphs 93 to 98).

Disclosures

1.17 Are the proposed disclosure requirements acceptable? Are there any further requirements that commentators consider should be added? Are there any requirements that should be deleted? (paragraphs 99 to 108)

1.18 Should enterprises that are not carrying land and buildings at a valuation be required to disclose in a note to the accounts the market value of their land and buildings if this is materially different from the carrying amount?

Transitional provisions

1.19 Are the transitional provisions satisfactory? Are there any other issues which should be covered by them? (paragraphs 109 to 111)

Small companies

1.20 Do commentators agree that the requirements of this proposed statement of standard accounting practice should be applied to all enterprises and that it would not be appropriate to exempt small companies, as defined by ASC, from any of them?

Appendices

1.21 Are the appendices useful? Should they be retained in the standard?

Accounting for fixed assets and revaluations

The provisions of this statement of standard accounting practice should be read in conjunction with the (Explanatory) Foreword to accounting standards *and need not be applied to immaterial items.*

Part 1 – Explanatory note

Introduction

A fixed asset is defined in this statement of standard accounting practice as an asset that: 1

(a) is held by an enterprise for use in the production or supply of goods and services, for rental to others or for administrative purposes and may include items held for the maintenance or repair of such assets; and
(b) has been acquired or constructed with the intention of being used on a continuing basis; and
(c) is not intended for sale in the ordinary course of business.

Fixed assets often comprise a substantial proportion of an enterprise's total assets and their accounting treatment is, therefore, an important element in the presentation of its financial position. In addition, determining whether expenditure has led to the creation of an asset or whether it constitutes a charge to the profit and loss account can have a significant effect on an enterprise's results for the period. 2

This statement of standard accounting practice provides a general framework within which enterprises should account for their fixed assets. Other statements of standard accounting practice cover some specific matters relating to fixed assets, namely SSAP 4 'The accounting treatment of government grants'; SSAP 12 (Revised) 'Accounting for depreciation'; SSAP 13 (Revised) 'Accounting for research and development'; SSAP 19 'Accounting for investment properties'; SSAP 21 'Accounting for leases and hire purchase contracts' and SSAP 22 (Revised) 'Accounting for goodwill'. Future statements are planned on accounting for investments; the use of fair value in the context of acquisition accounting and accounting for intangible fixed assets. 3

The relationship between this statement and those other statements dealing with specific matters relating to fixed assets is addressed in this document. In general, this statement applies to all fixed assets other than fixed asset investments, which are intended to be the subject of a separate statement, development expenditure and goodwill. However, the statement contains exemptions from particular requirements in relation to investment properties, leases and hire purchase contracts accounted for as fixed assets, and intangible fixed assets. Generally, the exemptions from the requirements of this statement apply where the matter under consideration is dealt with in the statement specifically relating to the asset concerned. The frequency of valuation of 4 investment properties is, for example, covered in SSAP 19 'Accounting for investment properties' and, thus, investment properties are not required to follow the requirements on this issue set out in this statement.

Issues covered

5 The following are among the issues covered by this statement:

(a) the recognition of fixed assets;
(b) determining the cost of fixed assets;
(c) the capitalisation of borrowing costs;
(d) enhancement costs;
(e) permanent diminutions in value;
(f) the disposal of fixed assets;
(g) the carrying of fixed assets at a valuation;
(h) the application of the revaluation reserve.

The recognition of fixed assets

6 All fixed assets that qualify for recognition should be included in an enterprise's balance sheet. The IASC Framework for the Preparation and Presentation of Financial Statements which the ASC has recognised as a set of guidelines to assist in its work of developing and revising accounting standards, defines an asset as a resource controlled by the enterprise as a result of past events and from which future economic benefits are expected to flow to the enterprise. This statement indicates that an item that meets the definition of an asset should be recognised when:

(a) it is probable that any future economic benefits associated with the asset will flow to or from the enterprise; and
(b) the asset has a cost and, where carried at a valuation, a value that can be measured with reliability.

7 Just as it is important that all fixed assets that qualify for recognition should be included in the balance sheet, so it is equally important to users of financial statements that fixed assets should only be recognised when they do so qualify. Furthermore, when included in the balance sheet they should be properly described, that is included as part of the appropriate item.

8 In certain circumstances judgement is required to determine whether a larger object should be recognised as a separate asset or as part of another asset. For example, rather than treat an aircraft and its engines as a single unit it may be better to treat the engines as a separate unit if it is likely that their useful life will be shorter than that of the aircraft as a whole or that they will be moved from one aircraft to another.

The cost of fixed assets

9 For the purpose of this statement, the cost of a fixed asset under the historical cost convention is its purchase price or the expenditure incurred in its production together

with, in either case, the expenditure incurred in bringing the fixed asset to working condition for its intended use at its intended location.

The types of expenditure that are eligible or required to be included in the purchase price or production cost and certain considerations relating to the period of production are discussed in this statement and an illustrative list of expenditures frequently included in the purchase price or production cost of particular types of fixed asset is contained in Appendix 1. **10**

Administrative and other general overheads should not be included as part of the cost of a fixed asset unless they can be reasonably attributed to its purchase or to bringing it to its working condition. **11**

In certain businesses, especially those operating in the extractive and primary industries, major items of plant have long commissioning periods. This statement requires that where commissioning costs are incurred they should cease to be capitalised when the fixed asset starts to be used in, or to be available for use in, commercial production. If the commissioning process involves the plant being operated at less than normal capacity for a time it is reasonable to capitalise relevant resultant expenditure during this running-in period. **12**

If the period of construction of the asset is longer than expected a distinction should be drawn between additional construction time which was not anticipated but which it was essential to incur if the fixed asset was to be brought to working condition and delays resulting from inefficiencies. As an example, time required to resolve unforeseen technical complications arising from the installation of equipment using new technology would constitute unexpected construction time. **13**

Costs arising from inefficiencies include those costs arising from temporary idle capacity, industrial disputes or other similar causes. In determining whether such inefficiencies have occurred, regard should be had, when possible, to a comparison with the cost of equivalent purchased assets or, if an enterprise makes similar assets for sale in the normal course of business, to the cost of producing equivalent assets for sale. Incremental borrowing costs arising from inefficiencies should not be capitalised. **14**

Capitalisation of borrowing costs

Arguments can be advanced both for and against the capitalisation of borrowing costs as part of the cost of fixed assets taking a substantial period of time to be brought into use for their intended purpose. **15**

The following arguments favour capitalisation: **16**

(a) borrowing costs form part of the total costs incurred in bringing a fixed asset into use for its intended purpose. If a fixed asset takes a substantial time to complete, borrowing costs will be incurred and, if they are, they should be capitalised;
(b) failure to capitalise borrowing costs, where incurred, will mean that an enterprise's performance will appear to be different depending upon whether it has constructed fixed assets during the period or has acquired similar ones;

(c) capitalisation leads to similar fixed assets being accounted for in a like way in the balance sheet which results in a greater degree of comparability between the costs of self-constructed fixed assets and those of acquired ones because when a fixed asset is acquired the purchase price will normally reflect the borrowing costs incurred by the enterprise that has constructed it.

17 The main arguments against capitalisation include the following:

(a) it is illogical to treat financing costs as a period expense in normal circumstances, then to treat them as a direct cost of an asset during its period of construction and to revert to treating them as a period expense once the asset is complete even though financing costs are probably continuing to be incurred in respect of the asset;
(b) borrowing costs are generally incurred to support the whole of the activities of the enterprise. Any attempt to associate borrowing costs with a particular fixed asset will often be arbitrary;
(c) capitalisation of borrowing costs results in similar fixed assets having different carrying amounts depending on the method of financing adopted by the enterprise concerned. An enterprise with a large proportion of equity capital will generally carry its fixed assets at a lower amount than a highly leveraged enterprise.

18 The arguments for and against capitalisation are finely balanced and as a result this statement allows enterprises to decide whether or not to capitalise their borrowing costs on fixed assets that take a substantial period of time to bring into service. The requirements that are applicable to those enterprises that do capitalise borrowing costs aim to ensure that a consistent capitalisation policy is adopted within the enterprise, that through disclosure the impact of capitalisation on the results and financial position of the enterprise are understood and that there is comparability between enterprises capitalising borrowing costs.

Enhancement costs

19 Expenditure on improvements to a fixed asset should be capitalised and added to the gross carrying amount of the asset. It should be distinguished from expenditure on repairs that should be charged to the profit and loss account. Expenditure should only be capitalised if it increases the expected future benefits from the existing fixed asset beyond its previously assessed standard of performance. Examples of such future benefits include:

(a) a significant prolongation of the fixed asset's useful life beyond that conferred by repairs and maintenance;
(b) an increase in its capacity;
(c) a substantial improvement in the quality of output or a reduction in previously assessed operating costs; or
(d) a substantial increase in the open market value of the fixed asset.

20 Adaption works to buildings, carried out to meet the enterprise's requirements, will often qualify for capitalisation as enhancement costs.

Permanent diminutions

A fixed asset should not be carried in the balance sheet at more than its recoverable amount unless it is expected that a diminution in the recoverable amount to below its carrying amount will reverse in the foreseeable future. The recoverable amount is the amount recoverable from the further use of a fixed asset and its subsequent disposal. In determining this amount regard should be had to the enterprise's future intentions concerning the fixed asset. If it intends to continue to use the fixed asset, the recoverable amount will be the amount derived from its future use and ultimate disposal, whereas if it plans to sell it immediately the recoverable amount will be the estimated net realisable value. **21**

If there has been a permanent diminution in the amount recoverable from a fixed asset to below its carrying amount, the sum required to write down the carrying amount should be charged to the profit and loss account in the period in which the diminution occurs or is first perceived. **22**

To avoid a permanent diminution being absorbed into a revaluation surplus or deficit and hence debited to the revaluation reserve, a permanent diminution should be deemed to have occurred before any downwards revaluation during the period. **23**

A permanent diminution is caused by an irreversible change in circumstances including, but not limited to, the following: **24**

(a) significant technological developments;
(b) physical damage;
(c) structural changes in external economic conditions leading to reduced demand for the output produced by the fixed asset;
(d) a change in the law or the environment relating to the fixed asset.

A permanent diminution may arise from an event affecting the fixed asset itself, such as fire destroying part of a factory which is inadequately insured, or from an event linked to the physical environment in which the fixed asset operates. Alternatively, a permanent diminution may result from a fall in the amount recoverable from further use of the fixed asset because a technologically superior fixed asset which is more cost effective has been developed for the same purpose. **25**

When considering the effects of events giving rise to permanent diminutions it may also be necessary to have regard to the impact on the depreciation of the asset concerned. A significant technological development may, for example, not only reduce the expected amount recoverable from future use but may also lead to the fixed asset being replaced earlier than planned. Matters relating to depreciation are dealt with in SSAP 12 (Revised) 'Accounting for depreciation'. **26**

The purpose of valuations

Carrying fixed assets at a valuation in financial statements prepared under the historical cost convention is not a solution to the problem of reflecting the effects of changing **27** prices on an enterprise in its financial statements. The ASC Handbook on 'Accounting for the effects of changing prices' indicates that, of the variety of ways in which enterprises can evaluate and report on the effects of changing prices, it is considered most appropriate for companies to disclose information about the current year's result and financial position on the basis of current cost asset valuation using either the operating or financial capital maintenance concept and the nominal pound as the unit of measurement.

28 Nearly all enterprises in the United Kingdom and the Republic of Ireland currently prepare their main financial statements under the historical cost convention but they are encouraged to provide valuation-based information about their fixed assets in the notes to the financial statements as part of a supplementary statement on the effects of changing prices on their business.

29 This statement deals, however, with the practical issues of the carrying of selected fixed assets at a valuation within financial statements prepared under the historical cost convention. It permits fixed assets to be carried at a valuation in balance sheets prepared under the historical cost convention provided that the valuations are kept up-to-date and carried out within the framework laid down. The primary focus is on open market values, retaining a practice that has existed for many years.

30 Under the historical cost convention, and similarly the current cost convention, balance sheets are not intended to be statements of value of the enterprise as a going concern. Internally generated goodwill is, for example, not recognised on the balance sheet and acquired goodwill cannot be revalued upwards after acquisition. Up-to-date information on the value of an enterprise's fixed assets can nevertheless provide useful information to users of the financial statements.

31 Those in favour of permitting the incorporation of valuations into the balance sheet consider that they provide useful information to users of financial statements and that recognition of the valuations in the balance sheet enables performance ratios measuring the effectiveness with which capital has been employed to be calculated more satisfactorily.

32 Those in favour of requiring fixed assets to be carried only at historical cost consider that to allow selective revaluations in financial statements prepared under the historical cost convention undermines the integrity of that system, by departing from the nominal capital maintenance concept in a fairly arbitrary fashion, and allows the reporting enterprise too much discretion over their reported results and financial position. Proponents of these views consider that a statement of standard accounting practice on accounting for fixed assets should either require fixed assets to be carried at their historical cost amounts with revaluations prohibited or, failing that, should not include any requirements on the revaluation of fixed assets since they will inevitably lack conceptual justification. If it is necessary to provide information on the market value of particular fixed assets where this is markedly different from the depreciated historical cost figure, supporters of a strict historical cost system believe that this is best done by inclusion of the relevant information in the notes to the financial statements.

The position adopted in this statement of standard accounting practice is that, because financial statements are conventionally prepared on the historical cost basis, it is not considered appropriate to require the carrying of some or all of an enterprise's fixed assets at a valuation in historical cost accounts but, at the same time, it is regarded as impractical to seek to prohibit the carrying of any fixed assets at a valuation. Hence, it is proposed that fixed assets should continue to be permitted to be carried at a valuation. **33**

In the United Kingdom and the Republic of Ireland it is principally land and buildings that have been carried at a valuation. If valuations were to be prohibited, this would either involve requiring fixed assets presently included at a valuation to be restated at their historical cost or accepting, given the long life of most fixed assets included at a valuation, that financial statements would continue to show some fixed assets at cost and others at an out-of-date valuation for a considerable period. Neither of these outcomes is considered desirable. **34**

The requirements in this statement concerning valuations are designed to improve comparability in the way enterprises undertake valuations and to provide the necessary information to enable the performance and financial position of enterprises carrying some or all of their fixed assets at a valuation to be reliably compared with those of enterprises carrying all their fixed assets at historical cost. **35**

Structured revaluations

A carrying amount based on a valuation is regarded as a substitution for the historical cost figure. It is considered that it should be used in place of the historical cost amount for matters such as calculating depreciation, determining the profit or loss on disposal and determining whether there has been a permanent diminution in value. For each class of fixed assets, once the enterprise has decided whether performance and financial position are to be assessed on the basis of historical cost or revalued amounts the decision should be applied in a consistent manner. It is not, for example, considered appropriate to calculate depreciation on a fixed asset by reference to the revalued amount while profit and loss on disposal is determined by reference to its historical cost. **36**

The usefulness of valuation-based information about fixed assets to users of financial statements is limited when the valuations are not kept up-to-date. It is also important that valuations are carried out in a systematic fashion in order to avoid distortions that may otherwise arise. Accordingly, this statement lays down requirements on the frequency and method of valuation, the selection of fixed assets for valuation and on who should undertake valuations. **37**

When enterprises present information about the value of their fixed assets by way of note only, they are encouraged to apply the principles of this statement of standard accounting practice. **38**

Frequency of valuations

39 The requirements relating to the frequency of revaluations are designed to ensure that, where assets are carried at a valuation, the valuations are kept up-to-date. Therefore, the carrying amount of fixed assets may only be based on a valuation recognised in previous financial statements if this is not materially different from the value at the balance sheet date. In addition, as a minimum, enterprises are required to revalue fixed assets carried at a valuation at least once every five years.

Determining the class

40 Normally fixed assets included within a single item in the financial statements will constitute a class for the purposes of this statement. However, if classification of fixed assets has been based on distinctions other than the nature or function of the asset in the enterprise it will be necessary to consider whether a single item constitutes the whole of a class. In particular, this statement requires that assets in one geographical location should not be able to be carried at a valuation whilst similar ones in another location are carried at their historical cost. It would also not be acceptable for fixed assets shown as a single item in the financial statements to form part of more than one class of fixed assets.

Open market value and depreciated replacement cost

41 Although the historical cost convention has its shortcomings, particularly in failing to reflect the effects of changing prices, one of its strengths is that the amounts at which assets and liabilities are stated strongly exhibit the characteristic of reliability, that is the carrying amount can be determined with a high degree of certainty and can generally be verified because it is based on actual past transactions. Thus judgemental subjectivity is minimised.

42 The use of open market value in determining the carrying amount of fixed assets that are included at a valuation maintains, as far as possible, the characteristic of objectivity associated with historical cost amounts. This statement of standard accounting practice requires that fixed assets should normally be valued on the basis of their open market value. The open market value should reflect their value in their existing use except where the enterprise is committed to changing the use of a fixed asset and has obtained all the necessary consents to do so (such as planning consent) in which case the asset should be carried at its open market value in its alternative use. As enterprises are required to value all assets in a particular class, if they value any in the class, they are permitted to carry fixed assets at depreciated replacement cost as a substitute for open market value when it is not practicable to obtain an open market value.

43 An open market valuation will normally be obtainable in the case of land and buildings but the depreciated replacement cost basis may have to be used for specialised land and buildings such as oil refineries, power stations and dock installations or land and building located in particular geographical areas for special reasons or of such a size, design or arrangement as would make it impossible for the valuer to arrive at an open market value.

Qualified valuers

As the carrying amounts of fixed assets included in the balance sheet at a valuation are not based on actual transactions undertaken by the enterprise, the credibility of the financial statements depends upon the valuations being carried out by valuers with relevant qualifications and with experience of valuing fixed assets of a similar nature. This statement therefore requires valuations, whether internal or external, to be carried out by qualified valuers. Additionally, valuations of land and buildings, the fixed assets most frequently carried at a valuation, are required to be carried out by an external valuer except where an enterprise has an internal property department with a substantial number of qualified valuers, in which case a valuation by internal valuers will be acceptable provided that the basis of valuation is reviewed by an external valuer. **44**

The revaluation reserve

The object of this statement of standard accounting practice concerning the application of the revaluation reserve is that the balance on the reserve relating to fixed assets should equal not more than the sum of the unrealised and uncapitalised amounts arising from the revaluation of fixed assets that are still being used by the enterprise. **45**

To enable the users of financial statements to determine what the profit for the period would have been if the enterprise had carried all its fixed assets at historical cost, transfers made from the revaluation reserve to the profit and loss account reserve in respect of fixed assets carried at a valuation should be clearly identified in the financial statements. The transfer should include an amount in respect of the difference between depreciation calculated on the historical cost of revalued fixed assets and depreciation based on their revalued carrying amounts. Similarly, when a permanent diminution in the carrying amount of a fixed asset carried at a valuation occurs, a transfer of any amount in the revaluation reserve relating to that asset should be made to the profit and loss account reserve up to the amount of the permanent diminution. **46**

Revaluation surpluses and deficits arising within a class of fixed assets should be netted off within the revaluation reserve; if this results in a deficit on the reserve at the end of the accounting period, the deficit should, on grounds of prudence, be eliminated by means of a charge to the profit and loss account for the period. **47**

On disposal of a revalued fixed asset, any amount remaining in the revaluation reserve relating to that asset should be transferred to the profit and loss account reserve. In normal circumstances this will be equal to the difference between the profit or loss on disposal based on the depreciated historical cost and that based on the net revalued amount though this will not be the case if there is not an adequate balance on the revaluation reserve to enable the transfer to be made. Such a situation could arise if part of the revaluation reserve had been capitalised. **48**

Transitional provisions

The transitional provisions recognise that some enterprises that have previously undertaken valuations may not wish to do so under the more defined structure set out **49** in this statement, particularly if such valuations have only been recognised in the financial statements on an occasional or infrequent basis. Accordingly, if an enterprise had not revalued any of its fixed assets in the five years prior to its first implementation of this statement, it may continue to include them in the balance sheet at their carrying amount at the date of first implementation, less subsequent depreciation, and, where applicable, provisions for diminutions in value. If an enterprise does not come within the scope of this exemption it should account for fixed assets carried at a valuation in accordance with the requirements of this statement or restate them at historical cost.

50 In order that enterprises should have sufficient time to prepare for the external valuations or reviews required by this statement they do not need to undertake, where applicable, their first such valuation or review until three years after they first implement this statement, or longer if their last valuation occurred within two years of that date. Enterprises whose present policy is to include certain fixed assets at a valuation are encouraged, however, to undertake valuations in accordance with the requirements of this statement before the latest due date.

51 When implementing this statement for the first time, enterprises are not required to apply the provisions of SSAP 6 (Revised) 'Extraordinary items and prior year adjustments'* concerning changes in accounting policies since in many of the areas in which such changes are likely to occur, for example in accounting for fixed assets carried at a valuation, it would not often be practicable to restate prior year figures. Moreover the costs incurred in doing so would usually be far greater than the benefits derived by users of the financial statements from the information provided. Enterprises are required, however, to quantify the effect of adopting the new policies on the profit and loss account for the period in which the policies are first applied.

Part 2 – Definition of terms

52 *Borrowing costs* are financial costs incurred by the enterprise in connection with the borrowing of funds. They comprise interest, the amortisation of discounts or premiums arising on the issue of debt securities, loan fees and gains and losses on foreign currency differences relating to borrowed funds to the extent that they are regarded as an adjustment to interest costs.

53 *A class of fixed assets* is a category of fixed assets having a similar nature or function in the business of the enterprise and which comprises one or more items each of which is shown in the financial statements as a single item without further subdivision. For the purpose of this definition, subdivision by reference to the geographical location of fixed assets should be ignored.

54 *Costs arising from inefficiencies* include costs arising from temporary idle capacity, industrial disputes or other similar causes and resultant incremental borrowing costs.

55 The *depreciated replacement cost* of a fixed asset is the gross replacement cost of the

***Editor's note:** *Now superseded by FRS 3 'Reporting Financial Performance'.*

fixed asset, that is the current cost of replacing its service potential with a new asset, less depreciation based on that cost and on the age of the asset.

The *fair value* of a fixed asset is the amount for which it could be exchanged in an arm's-length transaction. **56**

A *fixed asset* is an asset that: **57**

(a) is held by an enterprise for use in the production or supply of goods and services, for rental to others, or for administrative purposes and may include items held for the maintenance or repair of such assets;
(b) has been acquired or constructed with the intention of being used on a continuing basis; and
(c) is not intended for sale in the ordinary course of business.

The *open market value* of a fixed asset is the best price at which the enterprise's interest in the asset might reasonably be expected to be sold at the date of the valuation, assuming: **58**

(a) a willing seller;
(b) a reasonable period in which to negotiate the sale, taking into account the nature of the asset and the state of the market;
(c) that values will remain static during this period;
(d) that the asset will be freely exposed to the open market; and
(e) that no account will be taken of any additional bid by a purchaser with a special interest.

A *permanent diminution* in the value of a fixed asset is a diminution in the amount recoverable from its future use and subsequent disposal which is not expected to reverse in the foreseeable future. **59**

The *production cost* of a fixed asset is the total of: **60**

(a) the price of raw materials and consumables used and directly attributable costs incurred by the enterprise in bringing the fixed asset to working condition for its intended use at its intended location;
(b) an appropriate proportion of production overheads incurred during the production period that can reasonably be attributed to the fixed asset; and
(c) attributable borrowing costs, if the fixed asset took a substantial period of time to bring into use for its intended purpose and if it is the enterprise's policy to capitalise such costs.

Production overheads are overheads incurred in respect of materials, labour or services based on the normal level of activity of the enterprise, taking one year with another. For this purpose, each overhead should be classified according to function (e.g., production, selling or administration) so as to ensure the inclusion in the cost of construction of those overheads (including depreciation) which relate to construction, notwithstanding that these may accrue wholly or partly on a time basis. **61**

The *purchase price* of a fixed asset is the actual price paid plus any directly attributable **62** cost of bringing the fixed asset to working condition for its intended use at its intended location.

63 A *valuer* may be either an external valuer or an internal valuer for the purposes of this statement, where:

- an *external valuer* is a qualified valuer who is not an internal valuer and who has no significant direct or indirect financial interest in the enterprise or group of which it forms part;
- an *internal valuer* is a qualified valuer who is an officer or employee of the enterprise, or the group of which it forms part, but has no other significant financial interest in the enterprise or group;
- a *qualified valuer* is a valuer with relevant qualifications and post-qualification experience and with knowledge of valuing fixed assets of a similar nature.

Part 3 – Proposed standard accounting practice

SCOPE

64 The provisions of this statement of standard accounting practice do not apply to fixed asset investments, which are intended to be the subject of a separate statement, to development expenditure or to goodwill.

65 Except where stated to the contrary, the provisions of this statement of standard accounting practice apply to all other fixed assets.

RECOGNITION

66 A fixed asset should be recognised on an enterprise's balance sheet when:

(a) it is probable that any future economic benefits associated with the asset will flow to the enterprise; and
(b) the asset has a cost, and where carried at a valuation, a value that can be measured with reliability.

COST

67 Fixed assets should be included in the financial statements at their purchase price or production cost as appropriate (except to the extent that they are carried at a valuation in accordance with the requirements of this statement), less any provisions for depreciation and permanent diminutions in value.

68 Costs arising from inefficiencies should not be included in the production cost of a fixed asset.

69 The following rules apply in determining the purchase price or production cost of a fixed asset:

(a) the capitalisation of costs should not commence until there is reasonable probability that the project will be undertaken, or has been undertaken, and is expected to be successfully completed;
(b) when the construction of a fixed asset is completed in parts and each part is capable of being used commercially whilst construction continues on the other parts, capitalisation of costs on each part should cease when it is completed;
(c) when costs are incurred in commissioning a fixed asset, capitalisation of costs should cease when the fixed asset starts to be used in, or is available for us in, commercial production.

In consolidated financial statements, the cost of a fixed asset should not include any intra-group profit or loss. **70**

When a number of fixed assets are acquired at the same time and an individual purchase price has not been attributed to each asset, the purchase price should be allocated to the fixed assets acquired on the basis of their fair value. This paragraph does not apply to the purchase of shares as part of a business combination. **71**

Paragraphs 67 to 70 do not apply to investment properties or to leases or hire purchase contracts accounted for as fixed assets. **72**

CAPITALISATION OF BORROWING COSTS

An enterprise that incurs borrowing costs in financing expenditure on a fixed asset that takes a substantial period of time to bring into use for its intended purpose should adopt a policy of either consistently capitalising borrowing costs or not capitalising them for all qualifying fixed assets. **73**

When an enterprise has adopted a policy of capitalising borrowing costs, the following requirements apply: **74**
(a) borrowing costs should be capitalised as part of the cost of an asset by applying an appropriate capitalisation rate to expenditures on the acquisition, construction or production of a fixed asset that requires a substantial period of time to bring into use for its intended purpose;
(b) the capitalisation rate should be determined by relating the borrowing costs incurred in financing expenditure on fixed assets during a period to the borrowings outstanding during that period;
(c) notwithstanding paragraph 74(b) above, when a borrowing can be associated with expenditures on the acquisition, construction or production of specific assets, the borrowing costs capitalised should be determined on the basis of the actual borrowing costs incurred on that borrowing;
(d) the amount of borrowing costs capitalised during a period should not exceed the total amount of borrowing costs incurred by the enterprise in that period. In consolidated financial statements, this limitation should be applied to the consolidated amount of borrowing costs;
(e) notional borrowing costs should not be capitalised.

75 **If an enterprise changes its accounting policy on the capitalisation of borrowing costs it should ensure that a consistent policy on capitalisation is applied before and after the change in relation to fixed assets which are in the course of construction at the time of the change.**

ENHANCEMENT COSTS

76 **Costs incurred in relation to a fixed asset after its initial purchase or production should be capitalised only to the extent that they increase the expected future benefits to the enterprise from the existing fixed asset beyond its previously assessed standard of performance. The cost of any such enhancements should be added to the gross carrying amount of the fixed asset concerned.**

EXCHANGE OF FIXED ASSETS

77 **When a fixed asset is acquired in exchange for a similar fixed asset that has a similar use in the same type of business and which has a similar fair value, the cost of the fixed asset acquired should be measured at the net carrying amount of the fixed asset given up and adjusted for any balancing payment or receipt of cash or other consideration.**

78 **Except in the circumstances set out in paragraph 77 above, when a fixed asset is acquired in exchange or part exchange for another fixed asset the cost of the fixed asset acquired should be measured at its fair value. The difference between the net carrying amount of the fixed asset given in the exchange and the fair value of the asset acquired should be accounted for in the profit and loss account of the period in which the exchange took place.**

PERMANENT DIMINUTIONS

79 **When there is a permanent diminution in the value of a fixed asset to below its carrying amount, whether carried at historical cost or a valuation, such a diminution should be recognised in the profit and loss account for the period in which it occurs or is first perceived. A permanent diminution should be deemed to have occurred before any revaluation during the same accounting period.**

DISPOSALS

80 **On disposal of a fixed asset, the difference between the net disposal proceeds and the net carrying amount, whether carried at historical cost or a valuation, should be accounted for in the profit and loss account for the period in which the disposal occurs.**

VALUATIONS

81 **For each class of fixed assets, the directors of an enterprise should determine whether it is their accounting policy to carry that class at cost or a valuation.**

When a fixed asset is carried at a valuation, the carrying amount should represent the open market value of the fixed asset except in circumstances in which it is not practicable to determine an open market value in which case the depreciated net replacement cost of the fixed asset concerned should be used in the valuation. **82**

The results of a valuation should initially be reflected in the financial statements of the period to which it relates. **83**

A fixed asset should not be included in the balance sheet at a valuation undertaken more than five years previously. **84**

Subject to paragraph 84 above, a class of fixed assets may be carried at a valuation recognised in previous financial statements, less subsequent depreciation and, where applicable, provisions for permanent diminutions in value, if the directors of the enterprise have reasonable grounds for believing that the value of the class of fixed assets at the balance sheet date is not materially different from that shown in the financial statements. **85**

Subject to the overriding requirements of paragraphs 84 and 85 above, fixed assets in a particular class may be revalued on a rolling basis in a systematic and rational manner. **86**

When land and buildings are carried at a valuation, the carrying amount should be based on a valuation by an external valuer except in the circumstances set out in paragraph 88 below. **87**

When an enterprise has an internal property department with a substantial number of qualified valuers, the carrying amount of land and buildings may be based on a valuation by an internal valuer so long as the basis of valuation has been subject to review by an external valuer. **88**

The carrying amount of fixed assets, other than land and buildings, that are carried at a valuation may be based on a valuation either by an internal valuer or by an external valuer. **89**

Paragraphs 82 to 89 do not apply to investment properties. **90**

Paragraph 82 does not apply to intangible fixed assets. **91**

THE REVALUATION RESERVE

In so far as it relates to fixed assets, the balance on the revaluation reserve should at any time equal not more than the sum of unrealised and uncapitalised amounts in respect of fixed assets being carried at a valuation and which are currently being used by the enterprise. **92**

When a permanent diminution occurs in the carrying amount of a revalued fixed asset, any amount in the revaluation reserve relating to that asset should be transferred to the profit and loss account reserve, up to the amount of the permanent diminution. In the **93** rare circumstances that there is a reversal of a permanent diminution previously charged to the profit and loss account, an amount equal to the increase in the carrying amount should be credited to the revaluation reserve; a similar amount (not exceeding the amount previously charged to the profit and loss account) should then be transferred from the revaluation reserve to the profit and loss account for the period.

94 Subject to paragraph 79, when a fixed asset is valued the difference between the revalued amount and the depreciated carrying amount immediately prior to the valuation should be credited or debited to the revaluation reserve and should not be taken to the profit and loss account for the period.

95 If at the end of the accounting period a debit balance arises on the revaluation reserve in respect of fixed assets, this should be eliminated by means of a charge to the profit and loss account for the period as additional depreciation.

96 A transfer should be made each period from the revaluation reserve to the profit and loss account reserve of an amount equal to the difference between depreciation for the period calculated on the basis of the historical cost of fixed assets carried at a valuation and the actual depreciation charge based on the revalued amounts in respect of those fixed assets.

97 When a fixed asset carried at a revalued amount is disposed of, any amount in the revaluation reserve relating to it should be transferred to the profit and loss account reserve.

98 There should be no transfers to and from the revaluation reserve in respect of fixed assets other than those referred to in this statement of standard accounting practice.

DISCLOSURES

Capitalisation of borrowing costs

99 The following should be disclosed:

(a) where relevant, the enterprise's policy concerning the capitalisation of borrowing costs on fixed assets that take a substantial period of time to bring into use for their intended purpose;

(b) if borrowing costs have been capitalised, the interest payable in the period before adjustments in respect of the capitalisation of borrowing costs; the amount of borrowing costs capitalised in the period in respect of each class of fixed assets and the interest charge, net of the amount capitalised, included in the profit and loss account for the period.

Fixed assets carried at a valuation

100 When an enterprise has adopted a policy of carrying certain classes of fixed assets at a valuation it should indicate which classes are so carried. If it is the policy of the enterprise not to carry any classes of fixed assets at a valuation this should be stated.

The following should be disclosed for each class of fixed assets carried at a valuation: **101**

(a) the date of the last valuation;
(b) the basis of the valuation (i.e., open market value, depreciated replacement cost) and whether it was carried out by an internal or external valuer;
(c) where the rolling method of valuation has been used for a class of fixed assets, this should be disclosed and the method explained;
(d) the gross historical cost and aggregate depreciation calculated on the historical cost basis.

When land and buildings are carried at a valuation by an internal valuer, the nature of the review by the external valuer should be described. **102**

In the period in which a valuation is carried out, the names of the valuers and details of their qualifications should be given. **103**

When a class of fixed assets is carried at an amount used in a previous set of financial statements on the grounds that the directors consider the value at the balance sheet date is not materially different to that earlier valuation, this fact should be stated. **104**

Other disclosures

Details of transfers to and from the revaluation reserve should be clearly disclosed and explained. **105**

The amounts of any permanent diminutions charged to the profit and loss account during the period should be disclosed and the reasons for them explained. **106**

The amount of any reversals of permanent diminutions credited to the profit and loss account for the period should be disclosed and the reasons for them explained. **107**

The way in which the transitional provisions have been applied should be explained. **108**

TRANSITIONAL PROVISIONS

When an enterprise which is carrying some fixed assets at a valuation has not revalued them in the five years prior to its implementation of this statement of standard accounting practice, it may continue to carry them at their carrying amount at the time it implements this statement (less subsequent depreciation and, where applicable, provisions for permanent diminutions in value) without applying the requirements of this statement to them provided that such fixed assets are clearly identified as not being at a valuation carried out in accordance with the requirements of this statement. **109**

When an enterprise that has adopted a revaluation policy is required by this statement to have a valuation or review by an external valuer of some or all of its fixed assets, the first valuation or review should take place not more than five years after the date of the previous valuation or three years after the enterprise first implements this statement of standard accounting practice, whichever is the later. **110**

111 When an enterprise implements this statement of standard accounting practice for the first time it is not required to restate the corresponding figures in the profit or loss account or the balance sheet that are affected by any consequential changes in accounting policies but it should quantify the effect of adopting the new policies on the profit and loss account for the period.

DATE FROM WHICH EFFECTIVE

112 The accounting and disclosure requirements set out in this statement of standard accounting practice should be adopted as soon as possible and regarded as standard in respect of financial statements relating to accounting periods beginning on or after [date to be inserted after exposure].

Part 4 – Note on legal requirements in Great Britain

113 The legal requirements set out below and in the corresponding sections on Northern Ireland and the Republic of Ireland are intended to be a summary of current legal requirements. They do not seek to interpret the law or to provide authoritative guidance on it.

114 All references in this section are to Schedule 4 to the Companies Act 1985 unless otherwise stated.

Formats

115 The following headings relating to fixed assets are set out in the balance sheet formats (paragraph 8).

Formats 1 and 2

B Fixed assets

I. Intangible assets
 1. Development costs
 2. Concessions, patents, licences, trade marks and similar rights and assets
 3. Goodwill
 4. Payments on account

II. Tangible assets
 1. Land and buildings
 2. Plant and machinery
 3. Fixtures, fittings, tools and equipment
 4. Payments on account and assets in course of construction.

116 Items to which Arabic numbers are assigned in any of the formats may be combined in a company's accounts for any financial year if their individual amounts are not material to assessing the state of affairs or profit or loss of the company for that year or if the combination facilitates that assessment. Where items are combined the individual amounts of any items shall be disclosed in a note to the accounts (paragraph 3(4)).

General

In respect of every item shown in a company's balance sheet or profit and loss account, the corresponding amount for the financial year immediately preceding that to which the balance sheet or profit or loss account item relates shall also be shown (paragraph 4). **117**

Historical cost accounting

Except where the alternative accounting rules are applied, the amounts to be shown in respect of all items shown in a company's accounts shall be determined in accordance with the rules set out in paragraphs 119 to 127 below (paragraph 16). **118**

Subject to any provisions for depreciation or diminution in value, all fixed assets shall be included at their purchase price or production cost (paragraph 17). **119**

In the case of any fixed asset which has a limited useful economic life, its purchase price or production cost or, if applicable, this amount less its estimated residual value, shall be systematically depreciated so that it is written off over the period of the asset's useful economic life (paragraph 18). **120**

Provisions for diminution in value of a fixed asset shall be made if the reduction in its value is expected to be permanent. Any such provisions which are not shown in the profit and loss account shall be disclosed, separately or in aggregate, in a note to the accounts (paragraph 19). **121**

Where the reasons for any provisions for diminution in value have ceased to apply to any extent, the provision shall be written back to the extent that it is no longer necessary. Any such amounts written back which are not shown in the profit and loss account shall be disclosed, separately or in aggregate, in a note to the accounts (paragraph 19). **122**

Assets may be included under 'tangible assets' at a fixed quantity and value if their overall value is not material to assessing the company's state of affairs and their quantity, value and composition are not subject to material variation (paragraph 25). **123**

The purchase price of an asset shall comprise the actual price paid and any expenses incidental to its acquisition (paragraph 26). **124**

The production cost of an asset shall include the price of the raw materials and consumables used and the costs incurred by the company which are directly attributable to the production cost of that asset. In addition, the production cost may include the following to the extent that they relate to the period of production: **125**

(a) a reasonable proportion of the costs incurred by the company indirectly attributable to the production of that asset; and

(b) interest on capital borrowed to finance the production of that asset (paragraph 26).

126 Where interest is included in accordance with paragraph 125 above, the fact that the interest has been included and its amount should be disclosed in a note to the accounts (paragraph 26).

127 Where there is no record of the purchase price of production cost of any asset, or of any price, expenses or cost relevant for determining its purchase price or production cost (or if the records cannot be obtained without unreasonable expense or delay), its purchase price or production cost shall be taken to be the value ascribed to it in the earliest available record of its value on or after its acquisition or production by the company (paragraph 28).

Alternative accounting rules

128 Intangible assets, other than goodwill, may be included at their current cost (paragraph 31).

129 Tangible fixed assets may be included at a market value determined as at the date of their last valuation or at their current cost (paragraph 31).

130 When the alternative accounting rules are applied, the items affected and the basis of valuation adopted in determining the amounts in respect of each such item shall be disclosed in a note to the accounts (paragraph 33).

131 For each balance sheet item affected, either the comparable amounts determined according to the historical cost accounting rules or the differences between those amounts and the corresponding amounts shown in the balance sheet in respect of that item shall be shown separately in the balance sheet or in a note to the accounts (paragraph 33).

132 References to the comparable amounts in paragraph 131 above are references to:

(a) the aggregate amount to be shown in respect of that item if the historical cost accounting rules had been applied; and
(b) the related aggregate amount of the cumulative provisions for depreciation or diminution in value determined under those rules (paragraph 33).

Revaluation reserve

133 When the alternative accounting rules are applied, any profit or loss arising shall be credited or debited, as appropriate, to a separate reserve ('the revaluation reserve') (paragraph 34).

134 The amount of the revaluation reserve shall be shown in the company's balance sheet under a separate sub-heading in the position given for the item 'revaluation reserve' in the balance sheet formats but it need not be shown under that name (paragraph 34).

An amount may be transferred from the revaluation reserve: **135**

(a) to the profit and loss account, if the amount was previously charged to that account or represents realised profit, or
(b) on capitalisation (paragraph 34).

In paragraph 135 above, capitalisation, in relation to an amount standing to the credit of the revaluation reserve, means applying it in wholly or partly paying up unissued shares in the company to be allotted to members of the company as fully or partly paid shares (paragraph 34). **136**

The revaluation reserve shall not be reduced except as mentioned in paragraphs 135 and 136 above (paragraph 34). **137**

The treatment for taxation purposes of amounts credited or debited to the revaluation reserve shall be disclosed in a note to the accounts (paragraph 34). **138**

The accounting policies adopted by the company in determining the amounts to be included in respect of items shown in the balance sheet and in determining the profit or loss of the company shall be stated (including such policies with respect to the depreciation and diminution in value of assets) (paragraph 36). **139**

Information supplementing the balance sheet

The following information shall be given in respect of each item under the general heading of fixed assets and for the constituent parts where items separately identified in the formats are combined under a common heading: **140**

(a) the appropriate amounts in respect of that item at the beginning and end of the financial period;
(b) the effect on the amounts at which an item is shown due to:
  (i) any revision made during the year to the amount in respect of any assets included under that item;
  (ii) acquisitions during the year of any assets;
  (iii) disposals during the year of any assets;
  (iv) any transfers of assets to and from that item during the year (paragraph 42).

In paragraph 140 above, the appropriate amount is that determined in accordance with the historical cost or alternative accounting rules, whichever are applicable, leaving out of account any provisions for depreciation or diminution in value (paragraph 42). **141**

The following shall also be stated for each item dealt with under paragraph 140 above: **142**

(a) the cumulative amount of provisions for depreciation or diminution in value of assets as at the beginning and end of the financial year;
(b) the amount of any such provisions made in respect of the financial year;
(c) the amount of any adjustments made in respect of any such provisions during the year or in consequence of the disposal of any assets;
(d) the amount of any other adjustments made in respect of any such provisions during the year (paragraph 42).

143 Where any fixed assets of the company (other than listed investments) are included under any item in the company's balance sheet in accordance with the alternative accounting rules, the following information shall be given:

(a) the years (so far as they are known to the directors) in which the assets were severally valued and the several values; and
(b) in the case of assets that were valued during the financial year, the names of the persons who valued them or particulars of their qualifications for doing so and the basis of valuation used by them (paragraph 43).

144 The following shall be stated in respect of any amount shown under the item 'land and buildings' or where an amount relating to land and buildings is combined with other items:

(a) how much of that amount is attributable to land of freehold tenure and how much to land of leasehold tenure; and
(b) how much of that attributable to leasehold tenure relates to land held on long leases and how much to land held on short leases (paragraph 44).

145 In respect of every item stated in a note to the accounts, the corresponding amount for the financial year immediately preceding that to which the accounts relate shall also be stated. Where the corresponding amount is not comparable it shall be adjusted and particulars of the adjustment and the reasons for it shall be given. This requirement does not apply in respect of amounts stated in accordance with the provisions set out in paragraphs 140 and 142 above.

Directors' report

146 If significant changes in the fixed assets of the company or in any of its subsidiaries have occurred in the financial year, the report shall contain particulars of the changes (Schedule 7 paragraph 1).

147 If, in the case of interests in land, their market value (as at the end of the financial year) differs substantially from the amount at which they are included in the balance sheet, and the difference is, in the directors' opinion, of such significance as to require that the attention of members of the company or of holders of its debentures should be drawn to it, the report shall indicate the difference with such degree of precision as is practicable (Schedule 7 paragraph 1).

Part 5 – Note on legal requirements in Northern Ireland and the Republic of Ireland

148 In Northern Ireland the legal requirements relating to fixed assets are dealt with in Schedule 4, the Companies (Northern Ireland) Order 1986 and in the Republic of Ireland in the Companies (Amendment) Act 1986. The requirements are very similar to those in Great Britain. The following table indicates the corresponding paragraphs in respect of the references contained in Part 4 of this statement of standard accounting practice.

Companies Act 1985, Schedule 4	*Companies (Northern Ireland) Order 1986, Schedule 4*	*Companies (Amendment) Act 1986, Sections or paragraphs in the Schedule (Republic of Ireland)*
Formats		
paragraph 8	paragraph 8	paragraph 3
paragraph 3(4)	paragraph 3(4)	Section 4(6)–(7)
General		
paragraph 4	paragraph 4	Section 4(8)–(10)
Historical cost accounting		
paragraph 16	paragraph 16	paragraph 4
paragraph 17	paragraph 17	paragraph 5
paragraph 18	paragraph 18	paragraph 6
paragraph 19	paragraph 19	paragraph 7
paragraph 19	paragraph 19	paragraph 7
paragraph 25	paragraph 25	paragraph 13
paragraph 26	paragraph 26	paragraph 14
paragraph 26	paragraph 26	paragraph 14
paragraph 26	paragraph 26	paragraph 14
paragraph 28	paragraph 28	paragraph 16
Alternative accounting rules		
paragraph 31	paragraph 31	paragraph 19
paragraph 31	paragraph 31	paragraph 19
paragraph 33	paragraph 33	paragraph 21
paragraph 33	paragraph 33	paragraph 21
paragraph 33	paragraph 33	paragraph 21
Revaluation reserve		
paragraph 34	paragraph 34	paragraph 22
paragraph 34	paragraph 34	paragraph 22
paragraph 34	paragraph 34	paragraph 22
paragraph 34	paragraph 34	paragraph 22
paragraph 36	paragraph 36	paragraph 24
Information supplementing the balance sheet		
paragraph 42	paragraph 42	paragraph 29

Exposure Drafts in issue

paragraph 42	paragraph 42	paragraph 29
paragraph 42	paragraph 42	paragraph 29
paragraph 43	paragraph 43	paragraph 30
paragraph 44	paragraph 44	no equivalent
paragraph 58	paragraph 58	paragraph 44

Directors' report

Schedule 7 para 1	Schedule 7 para 1	no equivalent
Schedule 7 para 1	Schedule 7 para 1	no equivalent

Part 6 – Compliance with International Accounting Standard No. 16 'Accounting for property, plant and equipment' and International Accounting Standard No. 23 'Capitalisation of borrowing costs'.

149 Compliance with the requirements of this proposed statement of standard accounting practice and with relevant legal requirements will automatically ensure compliance with IAS16 'Accounting for property, plant and equipment' and with IAS23 'Capitalisation of borrowing costs in all material respects'.*

***Editor's note:** *Revised versions of IAS 16 and IAS 23 were issued in November 1993.*

Appendix 1

This appendix is for guidance only and does not form part of the proposed statement of standard accounting practice.

Expenditures to be included in purchase price or production cost

Land and buildings

The cost of buildings includes the purchase price (excluding the cost of the land) plus all charges incurred (e.g., on repairs, alterations and improvements) in bringing them into use for their intended purpose. **1**

If a building is constructed by the enterprise itself instead of being purchased, the capitalised amount should include the cost of work sub-contracted, the cost of materials, labour, supervision and other direct production overheads, and other incidental costs including professional fees. **2**

Overheads which are indirectly attributable to the production of the building may be included to the extent they relate to the period of production. **3**

Plant and machinery

The cost of plant and machinery includes the purchase price, freight, duty and installation costs. If machinery has to be operated for a time for the purpose of running it in and testing it, the costs of such work may be capitalised. Self-constructed plant and machinery will include labour, materials and appropriate production overheads. The costs of relocating machinery within a factory or to another location should not be capitalised. **4**

Fixtures, fittings, tool and equipment

This group of assets should include the cost of relatively permanent property, such as show-cases and counters, shelving, display fixtures, safes, office equipment and furniture. **5**

Tools may be divided into two classes: machine tools and hand tools. Machine tools are a part of the machine and should be capitalised. However, because they usually wear out much more rapidly than the machine and have to be replaced, they should be recorded separately from the machine. Hand tools, because of their short life, are similarly recorded in a separate tool account or written off in the year of purchase. Two bases of accounting for tools which are frequently used are (i) to make periodic counts and value them at cost less depreciation, and (ii) to value them at a fixed amount. **6**

The cost of computer equipment may include software costs. Because of the likelihood of rapid operating and technological changes, these costs are often expensed as incurred or, if capitalised, are written off over a short period of time. **7**

Payments on account and assets in course of construction

8 This heading should include deposits against delivery of fixed assets and payments made to contractors for work completed to date.

9 Although both balance sheet formats include a separate heading of 'Payments on account and assets in course of construction', in many cases the amounts involved are insufficiently material to justify separate disclosure and are included in the heading appropriate to the asset being acquired or constructed.

Appendix 2

This appendix is for guidance only and does not form part of the statement of standard accounting practice.

Valuations of land and buildings

This appendix includes extracts from Guidance Notes (GNs) and Background Papers (BPs) prepared by the Assets Valuation Standards Committee of the Royal Institution of Chartered Surveyors.* It does not, however, seek to provide authoritative guidance on the contents of Guidance Notes and Background Papers. Where necessary, readers should refer directly to these documents.

Valuations

Valuations, as with other exercises in the use of judgement, depend very largely on the assumptions and bases that are used in making them. A valuation for one purpose, such as insurance, may be entirely different from a valuation for another purpose, such as a forced sale. It is important, therefore, that whenever figures based on a valuation are used the basis of the valuation is clearly stated. 1

The acceptable bases, the circumstances in which they should be used and statements on other related matters are set out in relevant GNs. The material which follows is based upon the main principles of those GNs and the BPs. 2

Open market value

Valuations of land and buildings will normally be on the basis of open market value, which takes into account evidence of open market transactions in similar properties (GN1 'Principles to be observed in preparing asset valuations'). 3

'Open Market Value' means the best price at which an interest in the property might reasonably be expected to be sold at the date of the valuation assuming: 4

(a) a willing seller;
(b) a reasonable period in which to negotiate the sale taking into account the nature of the property and the state of the market;
(c) the values will remain static during that period;
(d) that the property will be freely exposed to the open market; and
(e) that no account will be taken of any additional bid by a purchaser with a special interest.

***Editor's note:** *Guidance Notes have been replaced by Statements of Asset Valuation Practice (SAVPs) and Background Papers by Information Papers (IPs). This appendix has not been updated for changes made since ED51 was published and readers are referred to the current edition of RICS 'Statements of Asset Valuation Practice and Guidance Notes'.*

5 Valuations of land and buildings may reflect either:

(a) the use of the property for the same or similar purposes as at the present time ('existing use'); or
(b) the prospective use of the property for other purposes ('alternative use').

6 If a valuer considers it appropriate to apply any qualifying words to 'Open Market Value', the meaning of those words should be discussed and agreed with the client before instructions are finally accepted. The valuer should incorporate the agreed meaning of the qualifying words in his report.

7 There are certain types of land and buildings designed or adapted for particular uses which change hands in the open market at prices based directly on trading potential for a strictly limited use. Examples include hotels, public houses and cinemas. The existing use value of these units will have regard to their trading potential. When such land and buildings are sold they are disposed of as fully operational business units.

8 Open market transactions which involve the sale of the category of land and buildings referred to in paragraph 7 above, can provide evidence of existing use valuation for balance sheet purposes. When analysing the prices paid for comparable properties and preparing a valuation of the subject property, the valuer will consider the trading accounts for previous years and compare with those of similar properties where these are available. In this way he can form an opinion on the future trading potential and level of turnover likely to be achieved.

9 The valuer will exclude (if necessary, by apportionment from a global figure) the value of furniture, tenant's fixtures and fittings, stock and goodwill which has been created in the business by the present owner. The value of the trading potential which flows from the property itself and the value of intangibles such as liquor licences will therefore be reflected.

10 The valuer should also exclude any turnover which would only be available to the present owner or management. He should, however, reflect any trading potential that might be realised in the hands of a more efficient operator and which flows from the property itself.

11 A number of background papers provide guidance on determining the open market value of land and buildings including BP1 'Existing use value', BP2 'Alternative use value' and BP7 'Open market valuations having regard to trading potential'.

Depreciation replacement cost

12 Where evidence of transactions in similar land and buildings does not exist, the value of assets for their existing use can be arrived at only on the basis of 'depreciated replacement cost' (DRC). The DRC basis requires an estimate of the open market value of the land in its existing use and an estimate of the new replacement cost of the buildings and other site works from which deductions are then made to allow for age, condition, functional obsolescence and other factors which result in the existing property being worth less than a new replacement.

Examples of the type of land and buildings to which the DRC basis may apply are: **13**

- oil refineries and chemical works where usually the buildings are no more than structure or cladding for highly specialised plant;
- power stations and dock installations where the buildings and site engineering works are related directly to the business of the owner and it is highly unlikely that they would have a value to anyone other than a company acquiring the undertaking;
- land and buildings located in particular geographical areas for special reasons or of such a size, design or arrangement as would make it impossible for the valuer to arrive at a conclusion as to value from the evidence of open market transactions.

In some cases, the DRC of an asset may exceed the value of the asset to the business, **14**
having regard to potential profitability to be derived from the total assets employed in the undertaking. As a result, management may intend not to replace the asset if it is destroyed. In such cases, the asset should be treated as if it had suffered a permanent diminution in value from its DRC and should be stated as its value to the business according to Schedule 4, paragraph 19(2) of the Companies Act, 1985.

An example of a value to the business valuation is where a business is making intensive, **15**
but not highly profitable, use of a specialised property and could not justify the acquisition of replacement facilities at full depreciated replacement cost, having regard to its profitability.

In the case of properties in public ownership and similar premises not occupied **16**
primarily for profit, where the test of adequate potential profitability is not available, DRC should be expressed as having regard to the prospect and viability of the continuance of the occupation.

BP3 'The depreciated replacement cost basis of valuation' provides guidance on factors **17**
to be taken into account in determining the gross replacement cost of a building and the deductions that should be made to allow for the quality of the property as existing.

Financial statements

GN10 'Asset valuations for incorporation in company accounts or directors' reports **18**
and other financial statements prepared under the historical cost convention' states that alternative use values of assets without which the business could not function have no relevance in financial statements prepared on the going concern basis.

Where companies whose financial statements have been prepared under the going **19**
concern basis are holding assets pending disposal, such assets should be included at their open market value which includes the potential for alternative use.

The alternative use basis may also be relevant to an overall appraisal of the company's **20**
situation and, where significantly higher than the value of the existing use, should be disclosed in the Directors' Report (Schedule 7, paragraphs 1(2) of the Companies Act 1985).

Exposure Drafts in issue

21 The depreciated replacement cost basis of valuation will be used under the historical cost convention in the case of certain specialised properties. Depreciated replacement cost must always be expressed by the valuer as subject to adequate potential profitability.

Valuation certification procedures

22 GN5 'The Valuation Certificate' recommends that the Valuation Certificate should cover, *inter alia*, the following matters:

(a) the date, purpose and basis of valuation;
(b) the name, address and qualifications of the valuer;
(c) all material information and assumptions used in the valuation, as set out in GN5; and
(d) caveats and non-publication clauses.

23 If a person making a valuation is an employee or officer of the company or group which owns the property, this fact should be disclosed.

Valuer's letter of consent

24 GN5 'The Valuation Certificate' recommends that the Valuation Certificate should contain a clause prohibiting publication without consent and that such consent should only be given when a final proof of the relevant document (e.g., annual accounts) is available. The consent should refer to a specimen annexed and should be signed as identification of what has been approved.

[ASC ED 55]

Accounting for investments

(Issued July 1990)

Contents *Paragraphs*

PREFACE

Introduction

1.1 The purpose of this exposure draft is to propose a standard accounting practice for the treatment of investments that identifies and measures an enterprise's investment performance and provides information about its investment activity, for the benefit of the users of financial statements. In this context, the exposure draft addresses issues concerning balance sheet measurement, income recognition and disclosure.

1.2 For the purposes of this statement, an investment is defined in general terms as 'an asset that is characterised by its ability to generate economic benefits in the form of distributions and/or appreciation in value'. The proposed statement further classifies investments into current asset investments and fixed (or long-term) asset investments, each of which is sub-divided into 'readily marketable investments' and other (ie non-readily marketable) investments. Different accounting treatments are prescribed for the different categories.

The need for an accounting standard

1.3 While the ASC accepts that in general the principles of accounting for investments are well understood and relatively uncontroversial, it considers that in the light of recent developments in the financial services industry there is a need for a statement on the important accounting and disclosure issues that have emerged, in particular in relation to the practice of 'marking to market'.

1.4 Moreover, in 1986 the International Accounting Standards Committee published International Accounting Standard No. 25, 'Accounting for Investments'. It is the policy of the CCAB to implement its support for IASs by incorporating their provisions within the body of UK and Irish SSAPs. While some aspects of IAS25 are dealt with in SSAP19 'Accounting for investment properties', the ASC recognised a need, in accordance with the CCAB's stated policy, to develop proposals for an accounting standard to deal with those aspects of IAS25 that relate to accounting for investments generally.

Scope of the proposed statement

1.5 The proposed statement is framed in general terms and, therefore, it does not prescribe particular accounting treatments for different types of investment. As such, it does not address specifically accounting for complex financial instruments or capital issues, or accounting for hedging transactions. Neither does it apply to investment properties, which are dealt with in SSAP19 'Accounting for investment properties.' While the proposed statement does not deal with accounting for investments in associated or subsidiary undertakings in group accounts, it does apply to the treatment of such investments in the accounts of the parent company. The proposed statement complements ED51 'Accounting for fixed assets and revaluations' and its provisions in respect of fixed asset investments are consistent with the requirements of that statement. It includes a number of cross-references to the provisions of ED51, in particular as they relate to revaluations and disposals of fixed asset investments.

The proposed statement applies to all enterprises to which SSAPs apply. In developing these proposals, the ASC considered whether different accounting treatments should be prescribed for particular industries or categories of investors, for example those enterprises involved in trading actively in investments, such as market makers and other financial institutions that deal in investments, whose investment performance will have a significant effect on the operating results for the period. However, given that the objective of all enterprises is to secure the best return possible on their investment, commensurate with the risk, the ASC believes that it is appropriate to prescribe an accounting treatment that provides the best measure of investment performance regardless of the level of an enterprise's investment activity. This approach is also consistent with the object of the ASC to narrow the differences of financial accounting and reporting treatment between enterprises. However, it does not preclude the development of specific guidance for particular groups of enterprises or industries in the form of Statements of Recommended Practice consistent with the principles of this statement, which may be franked by the ASC in due course. **1.6**

The ASC recognises, however, that its proposals may cause practical problems for particular categories of enterprise which currently do not distinguish between current and fixed asset investments in their financial statements or which otherwise adopt specialised accounting practices in respect of investments, for example insurance enterprises. The ASC would welcome specifically comments on whether such enterprises should be included in the scope of the proposed statement or, alternatively, what special provisions might be appropriate to cater for their particular needs. **1.7**

Proposed accounting treatment

For the most part, the proposed statement codifies current generally accepted accounting practice, but with one significant exception. This concerns the proposal that investments held as current assets that are 'readily marketable' should be 'marked to market'. The effect of this proposal is thus to extend current practice among market makers and other investment dealers to the generality of enterprises. Marking to market refers to the practice of carrying marketable securities in the balance sheet at their current market value and recognising all movements in their market value in the profit and loss account for the period, regardless of whether or not the investment has been sold. The ASC believes that in principle marking to market provides the most appropriate basis of accounting for investments for the following reasons: **1.8**

- marketable securities represent a store of liquidity and, hence, movements in their market value represent a realised profit or loss for the period and should be recognised as such in the profit and loss account, in accordance with the accruals concept;
- marking to market gives a better measure of management performance, since it reflects the movement in the value of investments under its control during the period;

- it provides the most objective means of measuring the financial effect of decisions taken to purchase, hold and sell investments during the period;
- it eliminates the scope for management to manipulate the reported results for the period through decisions on the timing of the disposal of investments;
- the market value of an investment is the attribute of the asset that is of most significance both to the management of the enterprise and to those interested in the results or accounts of an enterprise;
- carrying investments at market value also eliminates the anomaly of measuring identical assets at different amounts merely because they were acquired at different times.

1.9 The rationale for the ASC's decision to restrict the application of marking to market to readily marketable investments held as current assets is that any profit arising from an increase in the market value of an investment should be capable of being measured with reasonable certainty. This reflects the view that it is 'reliability of measurement' that underlies the concept of realisation and the determination of realised profit, rather than 'conversion into cash or other assets'. While it might be argued that this represents a departure from the prudence concept defined in SSAP2 'Disclosure of accounting polices', the principle that, in certain circumstances, holding gains constitute realised profits is similarly reflected in SSAP20 'Foreign currency translation'.

1.10 From this it follows that the value at which investments are included in the balance sheet must be capable of being determined objectively and that the investment is capable of being readily disposed of at the stated value. In other words, the investment must be a 'readily marketable investment', which the proposed statement defines as 'an investment for which an active market exists, which is both open and accessible, and for which a market value (or some other indicator from which a value may be calculated) is quoted openly'.

1.11 Conversely, to recognise as income gains that may not be capable of being crystallised in such a way would be imprudent. For this reason, 'other current asset investments', which are defined as 'current asset investments that are not readily marketable', should not be marked to market, but should instead be carried at the lower of original cost and net realisable value (or at current cost, with any increase or decrease in value being treated as a revaluation surplus or deficit, and taken to a revaluation reserve).

1.12 Similarly, fixed asset investments, the current market value of which is of less immediate relevance for measuring performance, as the management of the enterprise either does not intend or is unable to dispose of its holding to crystallise any appreciation in their value, should also not be marked to market (whether they are readily marketable or not), but carried at their original cost, less any provision for a permanent diminution in value. Alternatively, they may be carried at a current market valuation, with any increase or decrease in value being treated as a revaluation surplus or deficit, and taken to a revaluation reserve in accordance with the provisions of ED51 'Accounting for fixed assets and revaluations'. However, this proposed statement goes further than ED51 in requiring that, where fixed asset investments are carried at revalued amounts, the value should be kept up-to-date, ie they should be revalued annually.

The proposed statement defines a fixed asset investment as 'an investment that is intended to be held for use on a continuing basis in the activities of the enterprise'. The definition goes on to state that 'an investment may be classified as a fixed asset only where an intention to hold the investment for the long term can clearly be demonstrated or where there are restrictions as to the investor's ability to dispose of the investment'. It is intended that this definition should be restrictive, ie only where an investment satisfies these criteria should it be accounted for as a fixed asset investment. In all other cases, by default, investments should be accounted for as current asset investments. **1.13**

Determination of market value

The proposed statement identifies three bases for determining the market value of readily marketable securities, namely bid, offer, and mid-market price. It does not prescribe which of these price bases should be adopted. Enterprises will need to determine which basis is most appropriate in their particular circumstances, subject to the caveat that whatever basis is adopted should be applied consistently. **1.14**

The proposed statement recognises, however, that in certain circumstances the market price quoted may not be a reliable guide to the price at which an enterprise could expect to dispose of a holding. In particular, this may be the case where an investor has a holding which is of larger than normal size, relative to either the nominal amount of stock in issue or the proportion of stock that is actively traded, or where there is a forced sale. In such circumstances, an enterprise could not dispose of its entire holding without moving the market price and, therefore, it may be argued that it is not appropriate to mark to market such a holding, because the value at which it is carried in the balance sheet cannot be measured with a sufficient degree of certainty to justify taking any upward movement in its value to the profit and loss account as part of the realised profit for the period. The alternative approach, which is reflected in the proposed statement, is to require the holding to be marked to market by adjusting the quoted price to a level at which the amount of the gain to the balance sheet date can prudently be measured. One method by which this may be achieved is to carry such holdings at a value at which the entire holding could be disposed of at the balance sheet date. An alternative approach, which is adopted in this statement, is that the adjustment to the quoted price should be sufficient to reflect the amount that the enterprise could realistically expect to raise by disposing of the holding in the ordinary course of business. Subject to such an appropriate adjustment being made to its carrying value, the proposed statement would still require such a holding to be marked to market. **1.15**

Where fixed asset investments are to be carried at revalued amounts, they should be valued in accordance with ED51 'Accounting for fixed assets and revaluations'. **1.16**

Legal implications

In developing these proposals, the ASC has given careful consideration to whether the practice of marking to market can be reconciled with the financial accounting and reporting requirements of the Companies Act 1985. The ASC has concluded that, for those enterprises governed by this legislation, it would be necessary to invoke the true **1.17** and fair override provisions of the Act in order to comply with this proposed statement. These provisions require that in 'special circumstances' a company should depart from the specific requirements of Schedule 4 to the 1985 Act in order to give a true and fair view. That Schedule states that current assets shall be included in the balance sheet at the lower of their net realisable value and their purchase price or production cost, whereas this statement requires that readily marketable investments held as current assets should be carried at their current market value. Whilst the 'alternative accounting rules' in Schedule 4 would permit this balance sheet treatment, they would require any movement in the market value to be treated as a revaluation surplus or deficit and taken to the revaluation reserve, rather than being accounted for in the profit and loss account as part of the realised profit or loss for the period, as under marking to market.

1.18 The ASC believes that both the profit and loss account and balance sheet treatments which together comprise marking to market are necessary in order to show a true and fair view of the profit or loss for the period and of the state of affairs at the balance sheet date of an investing enterprise that holds readily marketable investments as current assets. Moreover, given that in practice only a limited number of enterprises are likely to hold material amounts of such investments, the ASC takes the view that the circumstances of these enterprises will be sufficiently 'special' to satisfy the criteria for invoking the true and fair override provisions of the 1985 Act. The ASC considers that it is much more doubtful whether enterprises subject to that Act which hold readily marketable investments as current assets in amounts which are not material can properly use the override. However, the Department of Trade and Industry has indicated to the ASC that, even if enterprises not holding material amounts are excluded, in its present view the 'special circumstances' necessary to invoke the true and fair override are not sufficiently closely defined in the exposure draft. Therefore, the proposals to codify and extend the existing limited practice of marking to market to the generality of companies holding significant amounts of readily marketable investments cannot be reconciled with the specific legal requirements affecting companies. The DTI suggested that the scope of these proposals should be narrowed in order to introduce the necessary special circumstances. For example, the scope should be restricted explicitly to particular enterprises, such as market makers and other dealers in investments, for which it would be justifiable to invoke the true and fair override. However, the ASC believes that it would be illogical to require some enterprises to use what it considers to be a less appropriate method of accounting for investments simply because their investment activity may be incidental to their main business. At this stage, the ASC has not sought formal legal opinion on this matter. Instead, the proposals are being published in their current form to gauge the views of commentators as to whether the treatment proposed by the ASC is considered sound in conceptual terms and acceptable in practice, as the basis on which any legal problems may be reviewed and resolved.

Taxation implications

1.19 The ASC has also been concerned that enterprises should not suffer any tax disadvantages through complying with the proposed statement, by being assessed for tax on profits representing the increase in the market value of readily marketable investments held as current assets that had not been crystallised. Accordingly, the ASC asked the Inland Revenue for its reaction to its draft proposals. In response, the Inland Revenue, while noting that it would be keeping the position under review 'in the light of developments in accepted accountancy practice and the rapidly changing circumstances of the financial sector', stated:

> 'on existing case law, however, we have no present intention of contending that those profits [ie holding gains on readily marketable investments held as current assets that are marked to market] would constitute chargeable profits for tax. In the same way, we would not accept that any losses recognised on the exposure draft basis should be treated as sustained or incurred for tax purposes. But if a taxpayer wished to be taxed on the basis that the realised profits or losses arising from the adoption of the mark to market basis for accounts purposes should be regarded as realised for tax purposes, then subject to the facts of any particular case, the Revenue would probably accept that basis provided that it was applied consistently thereafter'.

Comments are invited on any part of the exposure draft and, in particular, on the **1.20** following:

(a) do commentators agree with the ASC that marking to market provides the most appropriate basis of accounting for readily marketable investments held as current assets?
(b) do commentators think that marking to market should be extended to any other categories of investments?
(c) do commentators agree with the proposal to prescribe marking to market as standard accounting practice in respect of readily marketable investments held as current assets for the generality of enterprises to which SSAPs apply?
(d) do commentators agree that it is appropriate to mark to market holdings of larger than normal size? If it is considered appropriate, do commentators agree with the particular accounting treatment proposed?
(e) are the definitions set out in Part 2 of the exposure draft considered appropriate?
(f) is the guidance given on the determination of market value appropriate?
(g) do commentators agree with the proposal that where fixed asset investments are carried at revalued amounts they should be revalued annually?
(h) are the disclosure requirements considered appropriate?
(i) is the scope of the proposed statement appropriate? Should there be exemptions or special provisions for particular categories of enterprise with specialised accounting practices?

Accounting for investments

The provisions of this statement of standard accounting practice should be read in conjunction with the (Explanatory) Foreword to accounting standards *and need not be applied to immaterial items.*

Part 1 – Explanatory note

INTRODUCTION

Investments may take many different forms and be held for a variety of different reasons. Some investments may take the form of a debt instrument, representing a monetary amount due to the holder, usually bearing interest, which may be fixed or variable; others may take the form of a stake in another enterprise, such as an equity shareholding. Investments of this type represent financial rights conferred by the holding of a security, bond or certificate. Other forms of investment include physical assets, such as land and buildings, holdings of precious metals or other commodities, including perishable commodities, and works of art. Different investments will have different characteristics in terms of both the ease with which they can be converted into cash or other assets and the extent to which they are actively traded between enterprises and the nature of the market in them. 1

The nature and level of an enterprise's holding of investments and its volume of activity in buying, holding and selling investments will also differ between types of enterprises. For some enterprises, especially those in certain sectors of the financial services industry, such as market makers and other dealers in investments, investment activity represents the major part of the operations of the business and its investment performance will affect significantly its reported operating results. There are other enterprises, such as investment companies, whose sole business is the holding and management of a portfolio of investments for the longer term to provide income or capital growth for their members. For other commercial and industrial enterprises, investments may represent a store of liquid funds and their investment activity may be regarded as part of their treasury management function, intended to secure the best return on those funds and minimise their net borrowing costs. Investments may also be held for the purpose of hedging other transactions. In addition, an enterprise may hold an equity share in another enterprise in order to exercise a significant influence or control over the financial and operating policy decisions of that enterprise. Further, an investment may be held to cement a trading relationship or establish a trading advantage. 2

However, a characteristic of all investments is that they are intended to generate future economic benefit to the investing enterprise. Accordingly, the purpose of this proposed statement on accounting for investments is to prescribe the accounting treatments that best identify and measure an enterprise's investment performance and provide information about its investment activity. 3

DEFINITION OF AN INVESTMENT

4 The underlying characteristic of investments identified in paragraph 3 can be applied to *all* assets, as defined in the IASC 'Framework for the Preparation and Presentation of Financial Statements'. This inevitably causes problems in defining 'investments' for the purposes of this statement in such a way that excludes other assets used in the activities of the business, such as land and buildings, plant and equipment, and stock, all of which represent a commitment of resources by the enterprise. The problem is compounded by the fact that for different enterprises 'investments' may have the characteristics of other forms of assets. Thus, for an enterprise for which investment activity constitutes its 'core' business or a major part of its day to day operations, such as market makers and other dealers in securities, a trading portfolio of investments is analogous to stock.

5 In developing a statement on accounting for investments, however, there is an implicit assumption that an asset classified as an investment requires a different accounting treatment to that of other assets. This in turn implies that there is something inherent in the nature of an investment which distinguishes it from other assets. The ASC has considered this question and has identified the distinguishing characteristic of investments, as a category of assets, as being the particular way in which the economic benefits from investments arise. These benefits will arise in either or both of the following forms. They may be derived in the form of receipts by way of *distribution*, such as interest, royalties, dividends and rentals; in a wider sense, this would also cover the favourable trading terms secured by means of a trade investment. Also, they may be derived by way of *capital appreciation*, reflecting an increase in the exchange value of the investment during the period it is held by the enterprise. This characteristic is reflected in the definition of an investment adopted for the purposes of this statement. While other assets, such as freehold land and buildings, may also increase in value over time, they would only be treated as investments under this definition insofar as they are held specifically for that purpose, rather than for use in the operations of the business.

6 It can be argued that investments held by market makers or other dealers as 'stock' in order to make a profit in the course of their ordinary trading activities do not meet the above definition of an investment. However, the ASC considers that the asset that is being traded in such cases has the same underlying characteristics as it has when held either by the enterprise which sells an investment to the dealer or by the ultimate purchaser. Therefore, it is intended that investments held for trading purposes by market makers or other dealers should be accounted for in accordance with the proposed statement.

7 Whilst the ASC believes that investments as a category can thus be distinguished from other assets, it does not consider that a single, specific accounting treatment is appropriate for all investments so defined. Accordingly, for the purposes of this statement, investments should further be classified into current asset investments and fixed for long-term) asset investments. Within these sub-divisions, the ASC considers that it is only in the case of those investments classified as current assets that are readily marketable that the nature of the asset is such as to justify a specific accounting

treatment different to that of other assets. The basis for the distinction between current and fixed asset investments, and between readily marketable and other investments, and the reasons for prescribing a different accounting treatment for each particular class of investments are set out below.

In framing a definition of investments in general terms, the ASC has sought to avoid an approach which identifies specific types of investment, such as 'marketable securities', and prescribes a particular accounting treatment for each type. However, for illustrative purposes, the definition of investments adopted in this statement would include: shares; debentures; interest-bearing securities; loan stock; bonds and other debt instruments; warrants; options; commodities (other than those intended for consumption in the activities of the enterprise); futures contracts; or rights to subscribe for any of these. It must be emphasised that the above list is not intended to be exhaustive. **8**

SCOPE

It was noted in paragraph 2 above that the level of an enterprise's holding of investments and the volume of investment activity will differ between different types of enterprises. The ASC has considered whether different accounting treatments should be prescribed for particular industries or categories of investors, for example for application to enterprises involved in trading actively in investments, whose investment performance will have a significant effect on the operating results for the period. However, the proposed statement has been developed for application to *all* enterprises to which SSAPs apply, rather than to a defined group of enterprises or those within a particular industry. **9**

This principle reflects the fact that the objective of enterprises is to secure the best return possible on their investment, commensurate with the risk. The ASC believes that it is appropriate, therefore, to prescribe an accounting treatment that provides the best measure of investment performance regardless of the level of an enterprise's investment activity; it would be illogical to require some enterprises to use a less appropriate method of accounting for investments simply because their investment activity may be incidental to their main business. Accordingly, the ASC has concluded that neither the nature of the investing enterprise nor the level of its holdings or volume of investment activity should determine a particular accounting treatment. This approach is also consistent with the object of the ASC to narrow the differences of financial accounting and reporting treatment between enterprises. **10**

In practice, however, only a limited number of enterprises are likely to hold material amounts of readily marketable investments as current assets. These would include market makers and others involved in dealing actively in investments. The great majority of industrial and commercial enterprises that hold investments will hold them for the long term, as fixed assets. **11**

The development of a general accounting standard on this basis does not preclude the development of specific guidance for particular groups of enterprises or industries in the form of Statements of Recommended Practice consistent with the principles of this statement. **12**

13 The proposed statement does not apply to investment properties, which are dealt with in SSAP19 'Accounting for investment properties'. Neither does it address specifically accounting for complex financial instruments or capital issues, or accounting for hedging transactions. However, investments held for hedging purposes should not be accounted for in accordance with the proposed statement, except where this would not properly reflect the economic substance of the hedge. Similarly, the principles that underlie the accounting treatment of current asset investments are also applicable to current liabilities representing short positions held by market makers. While the proposed statement does not deal with accounting for investments in associated or subsidiary undertakings in group accounts, it does apply to the treatment of such investments in the accounts of the parent company.

'MARK TO MARKET'

14 In certain sectors of the financial services industry, particularly among those enterprises involved in trading actively in investments, it is a widely adopted accounting practice to account for marketable securities on a 'mark to market' basis. Marking to market refers to the practice of carrying such investments in the balance sheet at their current market value and recognising all changes in their market value in the profit and loss account for the period. Thus, all movements in the market value of an investment are accounted for in the profit and loss account regardless of whether or not the investment has been sold. It is argued that this practice is necessary in order to show a true and fair view of the operating results of such enterprises, because the increase in the market value of securities held to the balance sheet date represents a realised profit for the period. It also gives a better measure of management performance, since it reflects the movement in the value of securities under its control during the period. Other arguments that are advanced in support of the general application of this basis of accounting for investments are summarised below.

15 Marking to market provides the most objective means of measuring the financial effect of decisions taken to purchase, hold and sell investments during the period, in terms of both economic reality and consistency. Although gains and losses may not be crystallised at the balance sheet date, the economic reality is that they could have been, but the management of the enterprise has chosen not to do so. Consequently, the financial effects of the decision of management to buy and hold an investment, rather than dispose of it before the balance sheet date, should properly be reflected in the financial statements.

16 A corollary of this argument is that marking to market also eliminates the scope afforded to management under the alternative method of accounting for investments at the lower of cost and net realisable value to manipulate the reported results for the period through decisions on the timing of the disposal of investments.

17 The market value of an investment is the attribute of the asset that is of most significance both to the management of the enterprise and to those interested in the results or accounts of an enterprise. Carrying investments at market value also elim-

inates the anomaly of measuring identical assets at different amounts merely because they were acquired at different times.

The ASC has considered these arguments and has concluded that marking to market provides the appropriate basis of accounting for those investments that are both 'readily marketable' and held as current assets. **18**

READILY MARKETABLE INVESTMENTS

The principal consideration that underlies the ASC's proposed restriction on the application of marking to market to this class of investments is that any profit arising from an increase in the market value of an investment should be capable of being measured with reasonable certainty. This reflects the view that it is 'reliability of measurement' that underlies the concept of realisation and the determination of realised profit, rather than 'conversion into cash or other assets'. The principle that, in certain circumstances, holding gains constitute realised profits is similarly reflected in SSAP20 'Foreign currency translation', which requires exchange gains on foreign currency balances to be reported as part of the profit or loss for the period in accordance with the accruals concept, even if not converted into sterling. **19**

From this it follows that the value at which investments are included in the balance sheet must be capable of being determined objectively and that the investment is capable of being readily disposed of at the stated value. Together, these considerations require that there should be an active market in a particular investment, which is both open and accessible, and in which the prices at which investments are traded are known and openly quoted. Moreover, the price quoted should be a reliable indicator of the price at which a transaction may be effected. Where such conditions apply, the investment is a 'readily marketable investment'. The ASC recognises that in practice the meaning of the phrase 'readily marketable' may not be the same for different enterprises. Thus, because of differences in access to markets and the availability of quotations, an investment which may be deemed to be readily marketable when held by enterprises in certain parts of the financial services industry may not be so defined when held by other enterprises. Indeed, it may be argued that *all* investments held as current assets by, for example, market makers and banks are readily marketable and should be marked to market accordingly. **20**

A readily marketable investment may be classified as either a current asset investment or, in the limited circumstances defined below (see paragraph 24), a fixed asset investment. Where such investments are held as current assets, it is appropriate to regard any increases in their value as realised and such investments should be marked to market. However, where a readily marketable investment is held as a fixed asset investment, because the enterprise is restricted from disposing, or unwilling to dispose, of its holding to crystallise any appreciation in value, it is not appropriate to regard any increases in its market value as realised and, therefore, such investments should not be marked to market. **21**

CURRENT ASSET INVESTMENTS

22 Readily marketable investments held as current assets are proposed to be marked to market. They should be carried in the balance sheet at their current market valuation, and any increase or decrease in value in the period should be included in the profit and loss account as part of the results for the period, in accordance with the accruals concept.

23 Other (ie non-readily marketable) current asset investments will be carried at the lower of their original cost and net realisable value. In practice, because such investments are not readily marketable, they will normally be carried at cost, except where it is judged that there has been a diminution in the value of the investment. Alternatively, they may be carried at their current cost, if this can be determined. Where this applies, any increase in the carrying amount of the investment in the period cannot be regarded as realised profit, because these investments do not meet the criteria where by the amount of any gain can be measured with reasonable certainty. Accordingly, any increase should be treated as a revaluation surplus and taken to a revaluation reserve.

FIXED ASSET INVESTMENTS

24 In certain circumstances an investment may fall to be treated as a fixed asset. The definition of a fixed asset investment in Part 2 is based on the general definition of a fixed asset used in the Companies Act 1985, which is also adopted in ED51 'Accounting for fixed assets and revaluations'. In accordance with this definition, investments should only be classified as a fixed asset where an intention to hold the investment for the long term can clearly be demonstrated or where there are practical restrictions as to the investor's ability to dispose of them. This applies regardless of whether the investments are readily marketable or not. This category would thus comprise:

(a) equity shareholdings in or loans to subsidiaries and associates;
(b) investments arising from other trading relationships;
(c) investments that either cannot be disposed of or cannot be disposed of without a significant effect on the operations of the enterprise; and
(d) investments that are intended to be held for use on a continuing basis by enterprises whose objective is to hold a portfolio of investments to provide income and/or capital growth for their members.

25 Only where an investment satisfies the above criteria should it be accounted for as a fixed asset investment. The mere fact that an investment has been held for a lengthy period does not necessarily mean that it should be accounted for as a fixed asset. In all other cases, by default, investments (whether readily marketable or not) should be accounted for as current asset investments.

26 Because fixed asset investments are by definition held for the longer term, their current market value is of less immediate relevance for measuring performance, as the management of the enterprise either does not intend, or is unable, to secure that value by their disposal. For this reason, fixed asset investments should be carried at historical cost, less provision for impairment in their value. Alternatively, they may be carried at

current market valuation. Where this option is exercised it is not appropriate to account for any increase in the current value as a realised profit for the period. Instead, the amount of any increase should be accounted for as a surplus on revaluation and taken to a revaluation reserve. Where carried at revalued amounts, they should be accounted for in accordance with ED51 'Accounting for fixed assets and revaluations'.

However, where management decides to carry fixed asset investments at market value, this statement proposes an additional requirement that such valuation should be kept up-to-date. In other words, enterprises will not be permitted to carry fixed asset investments at a valuation that is neither current value nor original cost. This reflects the view that the only value of an investment that has relevance or meaning for users of financial statements, other than its original costs, is its *current* value. **27**

DETERMINATION OF THE MARKET VALUE OF READILY MARKETABLE SECURITIES

In practice, for readily marketable securities, there are two market valuations at any one time: the 'bid' price quoted by a market maker, at which an investor can expect to dispose of a holding, and the 'offer' price, which an investor can expect to pay to acquire a holding. A third price basis that may be used for valuation purposes as an alternative to either bid or offer is the mid-market price, ie the average of bid and offer prices as at the balance sheet date. In practice, however, the 'spread', or difference, between the bid and offer prices of a readily marketable investment will generally be relatively small. Accordingly, this statement does not prescribe which of these price bases should be adopted. Enterprises will need to determine which basis is most appropriate in their particular circumstances. Thus, for market makers and other dealers it may be appropriate to value 'long' positions at the bid price and 'short' positions at the offer price. For the generality of enterprises, the theoretically correct price basis to adopt will be that of bid price. However, in practice the mid-market price will normally be acceptable. Individual prices may be arrived at on the basis of either an average of the prices quoted by recognised market makers or the market price quoted on an investment exchange as at the balance sheet date. Whatever basis is adopted should be applied consistently. The market value of a portfolio of investments should be calculated on an individual investment basis. **28**

It should be recognised that the market price quoted is an average, often based on a specific size of transaction, and may not be a reliable guide to the price at which, in its particular circumstances, an enterprise could dispose of a specific holding. In particular, this may be the case where an investor has a holding which is of larger than normal size. In these circumstances, it could not dispose of its entire holding without moving the market price and, therefore, the quoted price will need to be adjusted to a level at which the amount of the gain to the balance sheet date can prudently be measured. **29**

In practice, an enterprise will choose between selling the entire holding all at once at a price below the quoted market price or incurring additional costs by releasing smaller tranches of stock on to the market over a period of time. It could be argued that the level at which holdings should be carried is that at which the entire holding could be **30** disposed of at the balance sheet date. The alternative approach, which is adopted in this statement, is that the adjustment to the quoted price should be sufficient to reflect the amount that the enterprise could realistically expect to raise by disposing of the holding in the ordinary course of business.

31 Market prices are predicated on a willing buyer-willing seller relationship. In the case of forced sales, the effective market price may be significantly less than the quoted price. Another factor that may affect the market price is the proportion of a particular line of stock that is effectively available for trading at a particular time. Thus, although a holding may not be large relative to the nominal amount of such stock in issue, it may represent a large proportion of the stock that is actively traded, for example because the majority of shares in an enterprise are held by major shareholders who are unlikely to sell in the foreseeable future. The amount at which investments are included in the balance sheet in such circumstances will need to be considered accordingly.

DETERMINATION OF COST

32 For the purposes of this statement, the cost of an investment includes all costs relating to its acquisition, including brokerages, fees and duties. It does not include financing costs that may be incurred while building up an investment. The cost of a portfolio of investments should be calculated on an individual investment basis.

33 If an investment is acquired, or acquired in part, for a non-cash consideration, its cost will equate to the fair value of the asset given up or securities issued in exchange. However, reference may instead be made to the fair value of the investment acquired, where this can more readily be determined.

34 When a security is acquired together with any unpaid accrued interest or fixed dividend entitlement, the cost of the investment is its purchase price, excluding the amount of accrued interest or dividend.

REDEEMABLE INTEREST-BEARING SECURITIES

35 Unless a redeemable interest-bearing security that is acquired at a premium or discount on its redemption value is to be carried at current cost or market value, the amount of the premium or discount, where material, should be amortised systematically over the period to redemption and subtracted from or added to the carrying amount of the security to determine its carrying amount as at the balance sheet date. Thereby, the carrying amount of the security will be adjusted progressively upwards or downwards to its redemption value over the period to redemption.

TRANSFERS OF INVESTMENTS BETWEEN CATEGORIES

36 In certain circumstances, subject to the criteria outlined in paragraph 24 above, it may be appropriate for an investment originally acquired as a current asset to be reclassified as a fixed asset investment. Alternatively, an enterprise may need to reclassify a fixed asset investment as a current asset, where it ceases to meet the criteria set out in paragraph 24.

This statement proposes that all transfers of readily marketable investments between categories should be made at the prevailing market value at the date of the transfer. This treatment reflects the economic reality of the transaction, which is that the enterprise could have sold its investment and repurchased it immediately at the same price, ie the prevailing market price at the time of the transfer. It has the further advantage that it ensures that an enterprise's reported investment performance cannot be manipulated, for example by anticipating or deferring holding losses on investments, by transferring them between categories. **37**

Where a readily marketable investment held as a current asset is to be reclassified as a fixed asset investment, the amount of any difference between the market value at the date of the transfer and its carrying amount should be treated as part of the ordinary profit for the period, as in the normal way under marking to market. Where a readily marketable investment held as a fixed asset is to be reclassified as a current asset, the difference between the market value and its carrying amount will reflect previously unrecognised movements in its value which may have accrued over a number of years and should, if material, be disclosed separately in the profit and loss account. **38**

Transfers of non-readily marketable investments, whether from fixed to current or vice versa, should be made at the carrying amount. **39**

In all cases, the decision to transfer an investment between categories should be formally documented in the internal records of the enterprise. Such documentation should specify the date on which the transfer was effected. **40**

RECOGNITION OF INVESTMENT INCOME IN THE PROFIT AND LOSS ACCOUNT

Interest, dividends and other income from investments should be recognised in the profit and loss account on an accruals basis. In the case of dividends receivable on equity securities, the amount due should be brought into account on the date the dividend is declared or, in the case of quoted securities, on the ex dividend date. However, it is also acceptable to recognise the dividend when it is actually received, where the effect of the difference is not material. A parent company may also recognise in its own profit and loss account dividends receivable from subsidiary undertakings which are declared after its balance sheet date, but before the preparation of its financial statements. **41**

When a redeemable interest-bearing security is accounted for in accordance with paragraph 35 above, the premium or discount should be amortised systematically over the period to redemption by a method which recognises the constant yield earned on the investment, or a reasonable approximation of it. In practice, a straight-line basis of amortisation will usually meet this requirement. **42**

Holding gains on readily marketable investments held as current investments, reflect- **43** ing an increase in their market value during the period, are a realised profit. As such, they should be brought into the profit and loss account as income from investments earned during the period, in accordance with the accruals concept. Any decline in their market value during the period should be recognised as a loss.

44 In the case of other current asset investments, where the net realisable value of a holding falls below its original cost, provision for the loss should be made immediately it becomes known. Similarly, provision should be made for a permanent diminution in value of fixed asset investments. Such provisions should be reversed if they are no longer necessary because of a change in circumstances.

45 Where investments are carried at revalued amounts, any such decline in value should be measured against the revalued amount. In the case of other current asset investments, such amounts should be charged to the profit and loss account, to the extent that they are not offset by any revaluation surplus previously credited to and retained in the revaluation reserve in respect of that investment. In the case of fixed asset investments, such amounts should be accounted for in accordance with ED51 'Accounting for fixed assets and revaluations'.

DISPOSALS OF INVESTMENTS

46 When a readily marketable investment held as a current asset is sold, the difference between the carrying amount and the proceeds of the sale will be recognised in the profit and loss account as income from investments in exactly the same way as holding gains earned during the period.

47 Upon the disposal of other current asset investments or fixed asset investments, the difference between the carrying amount and the sale proceeds will be recognised in the profit and loss account as the profit or loss on disposal. Where such investments are carried at revalued amounts, the profit or loss will be calculated by reference to the amount at the latest revaluation. Any changes in carrying amount previously credited or debited to and retained in the revaluation reserve in respect of that investment should be transferred to the profit and loss account as a movement on reserves. The ASC recognises, however, that it may not be appropriate for an investment company as defined in the Companies Act 1985 to take gains or losses on the disposal of investments to the profit and loss account, since it will be prohibited by its memorandum or articles of association from distributing capital profits, including those arising on the realisation of investments, which are credited to capital reserves.

48 When only part of an enterprise's holding of a particular investment that is held at cost is disposed of, the carrying amount of the part sold will be calculated on the basis of the average cost of the total holding.

49 Any unpaid accrued interest or fixed dividend entitlement reflected in the proceeds of the sale of an investment should be accounted for separately.

TRANSACTION DATE

All investment transactions should be accounted for as of the date when substantially all of the risks and rewards of ownership pass from the seller to the purchaser. This will generally be when the transaction becomes unconditional. 50

DISCLOSURE

The financial statements should disclose the accounting policies adopted in respect of investments, in terms which make clear the bases of valuation and the circumstances in which each is applied. 51

It is important for an understanding of the financial statements, in particular of the profit and loss account, that the extent to which an enterprise's result for the year has been affected by its investment performance should be disclosed. This facilitates comparison both between years and between one enterprise and another. Accordingly, where material, the amount of readily marketable investments held as current assets should be disclosed separately, together with the amount of income from such investments, including income from changes in their market value. 52

The amount of any profit or loss arising on disposal of fixed asset investments and the amount of any provision for a permanent diminution in value of fixed asset investments should also be disclosed separately. In certain circumstances, such amounts may need to be disclosed as an extraordinary item, according to the nature of the event that gave rise to the disposal or diminution in value, in accordance with SSAP6 'Extraordinary items and prior year adjustments'.* 53

Part 2 – Definition of terms

An *investment* is an asset that is characterised by its ability to generate economic benefits in the form of distributions and/or appreciation in value. 54

A *fixed asset investment* is an investment that is intended to be held for use on a continuing basis in the activities of the enterprise. An investment should be classified as a fixed asset only where an intention to hold the investment for the long term can clearly be demonstrated or where there are restrictions as to the investor's ability to dispose of the investment. 55

A *current asset investment* is an investment other than a fixed asset investment. 56

A *readily marketable investment* is an investment for which an active market exists, 57

***Editor's note:** *FRS 3 'Reporting Financial Performance', which has replaced SSAP 6, changed the requirements regarding the classification and presentation of such items.*

which is both open and accessible, and for which a market value (or some other indicator from which a value may be calculated) is quoted openly.

58 *Other current asset investments* are current asset investments that are not readily marketable.

Part 3 – Proposed standard accounting practice

SCOPE

59 This statement deals with accounting for investments in the financial statements of all enterprises to which SSAPs apply. It does not cover investment properties, which should be accounted for in accordance with SSAP19 'Accounting for investment properties'. It does not deal with accounting for investments in associated and subsidiary undertakings in group accounts, but it does apply to the treatment of such investments in the financial statements of the parent company. Investments held for hedging purposes should not be accounted for in accordance with this statement, where this would not properly reflect the economic substance of the hedge.

ACCOUNTING FOR INVESTMENTS

60 Readily marketable investments held as current assets should be included in the balance sheet at their current market value.

61 Where the size or nature of a holding is such that the market is not capable of absorbing it without a material effect on its quoted price, the current market price should be adjusted to reflect the proceeds that the enterprise could realistically expect to raise by disposing of the holding in the ordinary course of business.

62 Other current asset investments should be included in the balance sheet at the lower of their original cost and net realisable value, or at current cost.

63 Investments held as fixed assets should be carried at their original cost, less any provision for a permanent diminution in value. Alternatively, they may be carried at revalued amounts in accordance with ED51 'Accounting for fixed assets and revaluations.' Where carried at revalued amounts, they should be revalued annually.

64 When a security is acquired together with any unpaid accrued interest or fixed dividend entitlement, the cost of the investment is its purchase price, excluding the amount of accrued interest or dividend.

65 In determining the total amount of investments to be included in the balance sheet under a particular category, each individual investment should be accounted for separately.

66 Any increase or decrease in the market value of readily marketable investments held as current assets should be recognised in the profit and loss account of the period within

income from investments and included in the profit or loss for the year from ordinary activities.

Where other current asset investments are carried at current cost, any increase in value over the original cost should be treated as a revaluation surplus and credited to a revaluation reserve. Subsequent revaluations should be measured by reference to the previous revalued amount and the surplus or deficit arising on revaluation should be credited or debited to the revaluation reserve. Any deficit rising on revaluation that is not offset by mounts previously credited to and retained in the revaluation reserve in respect of that investment should be written off to the profit and loss account. **67**

Where fixed asset investments are carried at revalued amounts, they should be accounted for in accordance with ED51 'Accounting for fixed assets and revaluations'. Any increase in value over the original cost should be treated as a revaluation surplus and credited to a revaluation reserve. Subsequent revaluations should be measured by reference to the previous revalued amount and the surplus arising on revaluation should be credited to the revaluation reserve. Similarly, a temporary decline in value should be measured against the revalued amount and the deficit arising on revaluation should be debited to the revaluation reserve. A permanent diminution in value should be written off to the profit and loss account. **68**

On disposal of an investment, the difference between the net disposal proceeds and the carrying amount should be credited or debited to the profit and loss account. In the case of readily marketable investments held as current assets, this amount should be accounted for as income from investments and included in the profit or loss for the year from ordinary activities. In the case of other current asset investments and fixed asset investments, the difference should be accounted for as a profit or loss on disposal. In the case of other current asset investments carried at current cost and fixed asset investments carried at revalued amounts, the profit or loss on disposal should be calculated by reference to the latest valuation. Any net surplus on revaluation previously credited to and retained in the revaluation reserve in respect of that investment should be credited to the profit and loss account as a movement on reserves. **69**

Paragraph 69 does not apply in the case of fixed asset investments held by investment companies as defined in the Companies Act 1985. **70**

When only part of an enterprise's holding of a particular investment that is carried at cost is disposed of, the carrying amount will be calculated on the basis of the average cost of the total holding. **71**

Transfers of readily marketable investments between categories should be made at the current market value of the investment as at the date of the decision to effect the transfer, and should be accounted for as a disposal and repurchase. Transfers of non-readily marketable investments should be made at the carrying amount. **72**

Interest, dividends and other income from investments should be recognised in the profit and loss account as they become receivable. **73**

74 When a redeemable interest-bearing security that is acquired at a premium or discount on its redemption value is to be carried at an amount other than current cost or valuation, the amount of the premium or discount should be amortised systematically over the period to redemption by a method which recognises the constant yield earned on the investment and the carrying amount at which the investment is included in the balance sheet should be adjusted accordingly.

75 The profit and loss account should be charged with a provision for a reduction in the net realisable value of other current asset investments carried at the lower of cost and net realisable value or for a permanent diminution in value of fixed asset investments carried at cost, immediately it becomes known. Such provisions should be reversed if they are no longer necessary because of a change in circumstances.

76 An investment transaction should be accounted for as of the date on which substantially all of the risks and rewards of ownership pass from the seller to the purchaser.

DISCLOSURE

77 The following information should be disclosed in the financial statements:

(a) the accounting policies adopted in respect of investments;
(b) the amount of readily marketable investments held as current assets;
(c) the amount of income from readily marketable investments held as current assets, including income from changes in market value, distinguishing separately profits and losses arising on the transfer of investments between categories*;
(d) the amount of any profit or loss arising on the disposal of fixed asset investments; and
(e) the amount of any provision for a permanent diminution in value of fixed asset investments.

TRANSITIONAL PROVISIONS

78 Any adjustments arising as a result of a change in accounting policy to comply with the requirements of this statement should be accounted for in accordance with the provisions of SSAP6 'Extraordinary items and prior year adjustments'.†

DATE FROM WHICH EFFECTIVE

79 The accounting practices set out in this statement should be adopted as soon as possible. They should be regarded as standard accounting practice in respect of

******Those enterprises that are governed by the accounting and reporting requirements of the Companies Act 1985 which rely on the true and fair override provisions of the Act to comply with this proposed statement should also disclose the particulars of the departure from the provisions of Schedule 4, the reasons for it and its effects in a note to the accounts. (**Editor's note:** See also UITF abstract 7 'True and fair view override disclosures'.)*

*†**Editor's note:** Now FRS 3 'Reporting Financial Performance'.*

financial statements relating to accounting periods beginning on or after [date to be inserted after exposure].

Part 4 – Note of the legal requirements in Great Britain and Northern Ireland

References are to Schedule 4 to the Companies Act 1985 as amended and Schedule 4 to the Companies (Northern Ireland) Order 1986, unless otherwise stated.

The legal requirements for companies governed by the accounting and reporting requirements of the Companies Act 1985 as amended and Companies (Northern Ireland) Order 1986, derive from both the accounting rules and disclosure requirements relating to fixed and/or current assets generally, and the accounting rules and disclosure requirements relating specifically to investments. This note is concerned particularly with the latter requirements. **80**

ACCOUNTING PRINCIPLES

Paragraph 12(a) states that only profits realised at the balance sheet date shall be included in the profit and loss account, while paragraph 13 states that all income and charges relating to the financial year to which the accounts relate shall be taken into account without regard to the date of receipt or payment. Increases in the market value of readily marketable investments held as current assets are realised profits for the purposes of paragraph 12(a) and, therefore, are required to be accounted for in the profit and loss account in accordance with paragraph 13. **81**

HISTORICAL COST ACCOUNTING RULES

Paragraph 19 states that provision may be made for a diminution in value of a fixed asset investment and that the amount at which it is included in the balance sheet may be reduced accordingly; where the diminution in value is expected to be permanent, provision must be made. Such provisions must be disclosed. Where the reasons for which they were made have ceased to apply, they should be reversed to the extent that they are no longer necessary. **82**

Paragraph 23(1) states that current assets shall be included in the balance sheet at the lower of their net realisable value and their purchase price or production cost. This statement requires that readily marketable investments that are held as current assets should be included in the balance sheet at their current market value. This reflects the ASC's belief that such an accounting treatment is necessary in order to show a true and fair view of the state of affairs of the investing enterprise at the balance sheet date. 'In special circumstances', and 'to the extent necessary to give a true and fair view', such a departure from paragraph 23(1) is required by section 226(5) of the Act as amended, the 'true and fair override'. As stated in the Explanatory note, in practice only a limited number of enterprises are likely to hold material amounts of readily marketable **83** investments as current assets and the ASC believes that it can be argued that the circumstances of these enterprises will be such as to satisfy the criteria for invoking this provision of the Act. The Act requires that where the true and fair override is invoked, particulars of the departure from the provisions of Schedule 4, the reasons for it and its effect shall be given in a note to the accounts.*

84 Paragraph 27 sets out the different methods that may be adopted by the directors of a company to determine the carrying amount of any assets which are 'fungible assets' (including investments). Fungible assets are assets that are substantially indistinguishable one from another. The methods are: FIFO, LIFO, weighted average price and any other similar method. The method chosen must be one which appears to be appropriate in the circumstances of the company. If the amount at which the assets are included under the chosen method differs materially from the assets' 'replacement cost', the amount of the difference must be disclosed.

ALTERNATIVE ACCOUNTING RULES

85 Paragraph 31(4) states that investments classified as current assets may be included in the balance sheet at their current cost. Paragraph 31(3) states that fixed asset investments may be included either at a market value determined as at the date of their last valuation or at a value on any basis which appears to the directors to be appropriate in the circumstances of the company. If a basis other than market value is adopted, the method of valuation adopted and the reasons for adopting it must be disclosed in a note to the accounts.

NOTES TO THE ACCOUNTS

86 Paragraph 45 sets out the disclosure requirements in respect of both current and fixed asset investments. The following information is required to be disclosed:

(i) the amounts of 'listed' investments included in each category, divided between
 (a) those listed on a recognised stock exchange; and
 (b) other listed investments;

(ii) the aggregate market value of listed investments where this differs from the amount at which they are included in the financial statements;

(iii) both the market value and stock exchange value of any listed investment where it is included at market value and this is higher than the stock exchange value.

87 Paragraph 53(4) requires the amount of income from listed investments included in the profit and loss account to be disclosed.

ASSOCIATED AND SUBSIDIARY UNDERTAKINGS

88 Note(15) to the profit and loss account formats states that income and interest derived from group undertakings must be shown in the profit and loss account separately from income and interest derived from other sources.

***Editor's note:** *See also UITF abstract 7 'True and fair view override disclosures'.*

Schedule 5 to the Companies Act 1985 as amended sets out the information that is required to be disclosed in the financial statements of a parent company about its investments in associated and subsidiary undertakings. Part I of the Schedule sets out the detailed disclosure requirements for companies not required to prepare group accounts; Part II sets out those for companies that are required to prepare group accounts. **89**

INVESTMENT COMPANIES

Part V of Schedule 4 sets out special accounting provisions for investment companies, as defined in Paragraph 73. **90**

BANKING AND INSURANCE COMPANIES AND GROUPS

Banking and insurance companies, and groups that include such companies, are permitted to prepare accounts in accordance with Schedule 9, which sets out special provisions for the form and content of their accounts.* **91**

Part 5 – Note of the legal requirements in the Republic of Ireland

The legal requirements in the Republic of Ireland are similar to those applying in Great Britain and Northern Ireland. The following table indicates those paragraphs in the Companies (Amendment) Act 1986 and the Schedule thereto that correspond to those referred to in Part 4 of this statement. **92**

Companies Act 1985 as amended	*Companies (Amendment) Act 1986*
Section 226(5)	Section 3
Note (15) to the p & l account formats	Note (15) to the p & l account formats
Schedule 4:	
para 12(a)	Section 5(c)(i)
para 13	Section 5(d)
para 19	Schedule, para 7
para 23(1)	Schedule, para 11(1)
para 27	Schedule, para 15
paras 31(3) and (4)	Schedule, paras 19(3) and (4)
para 45	Schedule, para 31
para 53(4)	Schedule, para 39(4)
Part V	Schedule, Part VI
para 73	Schedule, para 58
Schedule 5	Section 16 & Schedule, paras 47–55
Schedule 9	*Companies Act 1963, Part III, Schedule 6*

***Editor's note:** *Insurance companies and groups are now covered by Schedule 9A.*

Part 6 – Compliance with International Accounting Standards

93 International Accounting Standard No. 25 'Accounting for Investments' requires current asset investments to be carried in the balance sheet at either market value or the lower of cost and market value. Increases or decreases in the carrying amounts of investments carried at market value should be either included in income or taken to owners' equity. Long-term investments may be carried at cost or revalued amounts. Increases in the carrying amounts of investments carried at revalued amounts should be credited to owners' equity as a revaluation surplus; decreases in the carrying amount should be charged to income to the extent that they are not offset by amounts previously credited to the revaluation surplus.

94 E32 on 'Comparability of Financial Statements' proposes certain revisions to IAS25. The proposed preferred treatment for current investments is that they should be carried at market value, with lower of cost or market as the allowed alternative; the proposed preferred treatment for long-term investments is that they should be carried at cost, with revalued amounts as the allowed alternative.

95 Compliance with the requirements of this statement will ensure compliance with IAS25 in all material respects. However, whereas IAS25 requires declines in value that are expected to be other than temporary of fixed asset investments carried at valuation to be written off to the profit and loss account only to the extent that they are not offset by amounts previously credited to and retained in the revaluation reserve in respect of that investment, this statement requires the full amount of such a decline to be written off to the profit and loss account. This departure is necessary to ensure compliance with ED51 'Accounting for fixed assets and revaluations'.

96 International Accounting Standard No. 27 'Consolidated Financial Statements and Accounting for Investments in Subsidiaries' and No. 28 'Accounting for Investments in Associates' permit investments in subsidiaries or associates in the separate financial statements of the parent to be either accounted for by the 'equity method' of accounting or carried at cost or revalued amounts in accordance with the parent's accounting policy for long-term investments. This proposed statement does not permit investments in subsidiaries or associates to be accounted for by the equity method of accounting.

97 The requirements of this statement are consistent with the recognition criteria set out in the International Accounting Standards Committee's 'Framework for the Preparation and Presentation of Financial Statements'.

Statement of Principles Chapters 1 and 2 The objective of financial statements & the qualitative characteristics of financial information

(Issued July 1991)

Contents

The objective of financial statements & the qualitative characteristics of financial information

PREFACE

The Accounting Standards Board (the Board) has issued this proposed statement as part of its work in developing a statement on the principles that underlie accounting and financial reporting. This draft proposes the text of the first chapters of that Statement of Principles. These chapters consider the objective of financial statements and the attributes that financial information should have to enable financial statements to fulfil their purpose. Such attributes are called qualitative characteristics. The Board intends to develop statements on the other principles underlying accounting and financial reporting. The topics to be covered in the Statement of Principles are set out in paragraph 5 of the Introduction. **i**

Much work has been published on the principles underlying accounting and financial reporting – notably in the USA by the Financial Accounting Standards Board (FASB), which carried out the pioneering work on a conceptual framework in the late 70's and early 80's. More recently the International Accounting Standards Committee (IASC) has published its 'Framework for the Preparation and Presentation of Financial Statements' which sets out the principles of accounting in an international context. The Canadian Institute of Chartered Accountants and the Australian Accounting Research Foundation jointly with the Australian Accounting Standards Review Board have also published statements on conceptual frameworks. **ii**

The conceptual statements above have started by considering the objective of financial statements and the qualitative characteristics of financial information. On these topics the various statements show a large measure of agreement. Any differences tend to be limited to matters of emphasis and drafting rather than matters of substance. **iii**

For these initial chapters, therefore, the Board proposes to use wherever possible the IASC text from 'Framework for the Preparation and Presentation of Financial Statements'. By using the same text wherever possible, the Board expresses its commitment to the IASC's work in promoting harmonisation in international accounting. The Board also considers that it would be unproductive to add its own form of words in areas where it both supports the IASC and finds that the IASC's statement adequately addresses issues relevant to the United Kingdom and the Republic of Ireland. The Board considers that the amount of work already undertaken on the objective of financial statements and the qualitative characteristics of financial information has had the result that the substantive issues raised by these topics are now well known. **iv**

INTRODUCTION

Purpose and status

1 This Statement of Principles sets out the concepts that underlie the preparation and presentation of financial statements for external users. The purpose of the Statement of Principles is to:

(a) assist the Board in the development of future accounting standards and in its review of existing accounting standards;
(b) assist the Board by providing a basis for reducing the number of alternative accounting treatments permitted by law and accounting standards;
(c) assist preparers of financial statements in applying accounting standards and in dealing with topics that do not form the subject of an accounting standard;
(d) assist auditors in forming an opinion whether financial statements conform with accounting standards;
(e) assist users of financial statements in interpreting the information contained in financial statements prepared in conformity with accounting standards; and
(f) provide those who are interested in the work of the Board with information about its approach to the formulation of accounting standards.

2 This Statement of Principles is not an accounting standard and hence does not define standards for any particular measurement or disclosure issue. Nothing in this Statement of Principles overrides any specific accounting standard.

3 The Board recognises that in a limited number of cases there may be a conflict between the Statement of Principles and an accounting standard. In those cases where there is a conflict, the requirements of the accounting standard prevail over those of the Statement of Principles. The Board will be guided by the Statement of Principles in the development of future standards and in its review of existing standards, so that the number of cases of conflict between the Statement of Principles and accounting standards will diminish over time.

4 The Statement of Principles may be revised from time to time based on the Board's experience of working with it.

Scope

5 The following topics give in outline the matters the Board will consider in developing a statement of principles;

(a) the objective of financial statements;
(b) the attributes of financial information that enable financial statements to fulfil their purpose;
(c) the elements that make up financial statements;
(d) when items arc to bc rccognised in financial statements;
(e) how net resources and performance and changes therein are to be measured;

(f) how items can best be presented in the financial statements;
(g) the principles underlying consolidation, equity accounting and proportional consolidation.

The Statement of Principles is concerned with general purpose financial statements (hereafter referred to as 'financial statements') including consolidated financial statements. Such financial statements are prepared and presented at least annually and are directed toward the common information needs of a wide range of users. Some of these users may require, and have the power to obtain, information in addition to that contained in the financial statements. Many users, however, have to rely on the financial statements as their major source of financial information and such financial statements should, therefore, be prepared and presented with their needs in view. Special purpose financial reports, for example, prospectuses and computations prepared for taxation purposes, are outside the scope of this Statement of Principles. Nevertheless, the Statement of Principles may be applied in the preparation of such special purpose reports where the requirements permit. **6**

Financial statements form part of the process of financial reporting. A complete set of financial statements at present consists of a balance sheet, profit and loss account and cash flow statement together with those notes and other statements and explanatory material that are specified as an integral part of the financial statements. The contents and titles of these primary financial statements are subject to change as a result of changes in accounting standards and the law. They may also include supplementary schedules and information based on or derived from, and expected to be read with, such statements. Such schedules and supplementary information may deal, for example, with financial information prepared to comply with the requirements of overseas stock exchanges On the other hand, although important constituents of financial reporting, such items as reports by directors, statements by the chairman, discussion and analysis by management and similar items that may be included in financial reports do not form part of financial statements for the purposes of this document. **7**

A reporting enterprise is an enterprise for which there are users who rely on the financial statements as their major source of financial information about the enterprise. The Statement of Principles applies to the financial statements of all commercial and industrial reporting enterprises, whether in the public or the private sectors. The application of accounting standards to the Public Sector is discussed more fully in the Foreword to Accounting Standards. This statement is drafted in terms of profit-oriented organisations but in general should be taken to apply also to not-for-profit organisations. The qualitative characteristics described in Chapter 2 apply equally to not-for-profit as to profit oriented organisations. Other parts of the Statement of Principles would need to be interpreted with certain changes of emphasis in applying them to not-for-profit organisations. The main changes would be: that users be extended to include members and contributors, resource providers, consumers/recipients of goods and services and review or oversight bodies; that information on compliance with covenants or any other restrictions on the funds would become important; and that the emphasis on the profit figure be replaced for not-for-profit **8** organisations by other performance measures, both financial and non-financial. Such considerations should be borne in mind when applying these principles to not-for-profit organisations.

Users and their information needs

9 The users of financial statements include present and potential investors, employees, lenders, suppliers and other trade creditors, customers, governments and their agencies and the public. They use financial statements to satisfy some of their different needs for information. These needs include the following:

(a) *Investors.* The providers of risk capital and their advisers are concerned with the risk inherent in, and return provided by, their investments. They need information to help them determine whether they should buy, hold or sell. They are also interested in information that enables them to assess the ability of the enterprise to pay dividends and that helps them to assess the performance of management.

(b) *Employees.* Employees and their representative groups are interested in information about the stability and profitability of their employers. They are also interested in information that enables them to assess the ability of the enterprise to provide remuneration, retirement benefits and employment opportunities.

(c) *Lenders.* Lenders are interested in information that enables them to determine whether their loans, and the interest attaching to them, will be paid when due.

(d) *Suppliers and other trade creditors.* Suppliers and other creditors are interested in information that enables them to determine whether amounts owing to them will be paid when due. Trade creditors are likely to be interested in an enterprise over a shorter period than lenders unless they are dependent upon the continuation of the enterprise as a major customer.

(e) *Customers.* Customers have an interest in information about the continuance of an enterprise, especially when they have a long-term involvement with, or are dependent on, the enterprise.

(f) *Government and their agencies.* Governments and their agencies are interested in the allocation of resources and, therefore, the activities of enterprises. They also require information in order to regulate the activities of enterprises, determine taxation policies and provide a basis for national income and similar statistics.

(g) *Public.* Enterprises affect members of the public in a variety of ways. For example, enterprises may make a substantial contribution to the local economy in many ways including the number of people they employ and their patronage of local suppliers. Financial statements may assist the public by providing information about the trends and recent developments in the prosperity of the enterprise and the range of its activities.

10 While all the information needs of these users cannot be met by financial statements, there are needs that are common to all users. In particular, they all have some interest in the financial position, performance and financial adaptability of the enterprise as a whole. As investors are providers of risk capital to the enterprise, the provision of financial statements that meet their needs will also meet most of the needs of other users that financial statements can satisfy. Awarding primacy to investors does not imply that other users are to be ignored. The information prepared for investors is useful as a

frame of reference for other users, against which they can evaluate more specific information that they may obtain in their dealings with the enterprise.

The management of an enterprise carries the responsibility for the preparation and presentation of the financial statements of the enterprise. Management is concerned with the form and content of financial statements because these are the prime means of communicating financial information on the enterprise to third parties. Management has access to additional management and financial information that helps it carry out its planning, decision-making and control responsibilities. Management has the ability to determine the form and content of such additional information to meet its own needs. The reporting of such information, however, is beyond the scope of this Statement of Principles. Nevertheless, the published financial statements should be based on the information used by management about the financial position, performance and financial adaptability of the enterprise. 11

Chapter 1 – The objective of financial statements

The objective of financial statements is to provide information about the financial position, performance and financial adaptability of an enterprise that is useful to a wide range of users in making economic decisions. 12

Financial statements prepared for this purpose meet the common needs of most users. However, financial statements do not provide all the information that users may need to make economic decisions since they largely portray the financial effects of past events and do not necessarily provide non-financial information. 13

Financial statements also show the results of the stewardship of management, that is, the accountability of management for the resources entrusted to it. Those users who wish to assess the stewardship of management do so in order that they may make economic decisions; these decisions may include, for example, whether to hold or sell their investment in the enterprise of whether to re-appoint or replace the management. 14

FINANCIAL POSITION, PERFORMANCE AND CASH FLOW

The economic decisions that are taken by users of financial statements require an evaluation of the ability of an enterprise to generate cash and of the timing and certainty of its generation. This ability ultimately determines, for example, the capacity of an enterprise to pay its employees and suppliers, meet interest payments, undertake necessary investment, repay loans and make distributions to its owners. Users are better able to evaluate this ability to generate cash if they are provided with information that focuses on the financial position, performance and cash flow of an enterprise. 15

The financial position of an enterprise is affected by the economic resources it controls, its financial structure, its liquidity and solvency, and its capacity to adapt to changes in the environment in which it operates. Information about the economic resources 16 controlled by the enterprise and its capacity in the past to manage these resources is useful in predicting the ability of the enterprise to generate cash in the future. Information about financial structure is useful in predicting future borrowing needs and how future profits and cash flows will be distributed among those with an interest in the enterprise; it is also useful in predicting how successful the enterprise is likely to be in raising further finance. Information about liquidity and solvency is useful in predicting the ability of the enterprise to meet its financial commitments as they fall due. Liquidity refers to the availability of cash in the near future after taking account of financial commitments over this period. Solvency refers to the availability of cash over the longer term to meet financial commitments as they fall due.

17 Information about the performance of an enterprise, in particular its profitability, is required to assess potential changes in the economic resources that it is likely to control in the future. Information about variability of performance is important in this respect. Information about performance is useful in predicting the capacity of the enterprise to generate cash flows from its existing resource base. It is also useful in forming judgements about the effectiveness with which the enterprise might employ additional resources.

18 Information concerning the cash flows of an enterprise is useful in providing the user with a basis to assess the ability of the enterprise to generate cash and the needs of the enterprise to utilise those cash flows.

19 Information about financial position is primarily provided in a balance sheet. Information about performance is primarily provided in a profit and loss account with a statement of movements in reserves. Information about financial adaptability is provided in the financial statements by a separate statement of cash flows and by appropriate disclosures for that enterprise in that and the other primary statements.

20 The component parts of the financial statements interrelate because they reflect different aspects of the same transactions or other events. Although each statement provides information that is different from the others, none is likely to serve only a single purpose or provide all the information necessary for particular needs of users. For example, a profit and loss account provides an incomplete picture of performance unless it is issued in conjunction with the balance sheet and the statement of cash flows.

21 The financial statements also contain notes and supplementary schedules and other information. For example, they may contain additional information that is relevant to the needs of users about the items in the balance sheet, profit and loss account and cash flow statement. They may include disclosures about the risks and uncertainties affecting the enterprise and any resources and obligations not recognised in the balance sheet. The notes to the financial statements form an integral part of the financial statements but supplementary information, often unaudited, is sometimes presented outside the financial statements.

Chapter 2 – Qualitative characteristics of financial statements

The IASC framework identifies four principal qualitative characteristics: understandability, relevance, reliability and comparability. The Board considers that all of these are important in determining how to provide users of financial statements with the most useful information. It believes, however, that a better insight can be gained by considering the interrelation between these characteristics and recognising that relevance and reliability are the key characteristics that any piece of financial information must have in order to be useful. Once information has been identified as relevant and reliable, that information will best be presented to users in a way that enhances comparability and that ensures that a reasonably diligent user will be able to understand it. This ordering of qualitative characteristics is shown in the chart opposite which also shows how these qualitative characteristics are inter-related.

Qualitative characteristics are the attributes that make the information provided in financial statements useful to users. The two primary qualitative characteristics are relevance and reliability. 22

PRIMARY CHARACTERISTICS

Relevance

To be useful, information must be relevant to the decision-making needs of users. Information has the quality of relevance when it influences the economic decisions of users by helping them evaluate past, present or future events or by confirming, or correcting, their past evaluations. Such evaluations may be influenced by the choice made of which aspects of an item to represent in financial statements (see paragraphs 28 and 29 below). 23

The **predictive** and **confirmatory roles** of information are inter-related. For example, information about the current level and structure of asset holdings has value to users when they endeavour to predict the ability of the enterprise to take advantage of opportunities and its ability to react to adverse situations. The same information plays a confirmatory role in respect of past predictions about, for example, the way in which the enterprise would be structured or the outcome of planned operations. 24

Information about financial position and past performance is frequently used as the basis for predicting future financial position and performance and other matters in which users are directly interested, such as dividend and wage payments, security price movements and the ability of the enterprise to meet its commitments as they fall due. To have predictive value, information need not be in the form of an explicit forecast. The ability to make predictions from financial statements is enhanced, however, by the manner in which information concerning past transactions and events is displayed. For example, the predictive value of the income statement is enhanced if unusual, abnormal and infrequent items of income or expense are separately disclosed. 25

THE QUALITATIVE CHARACTERISTICS OF ACCOUNTING INFORMATION

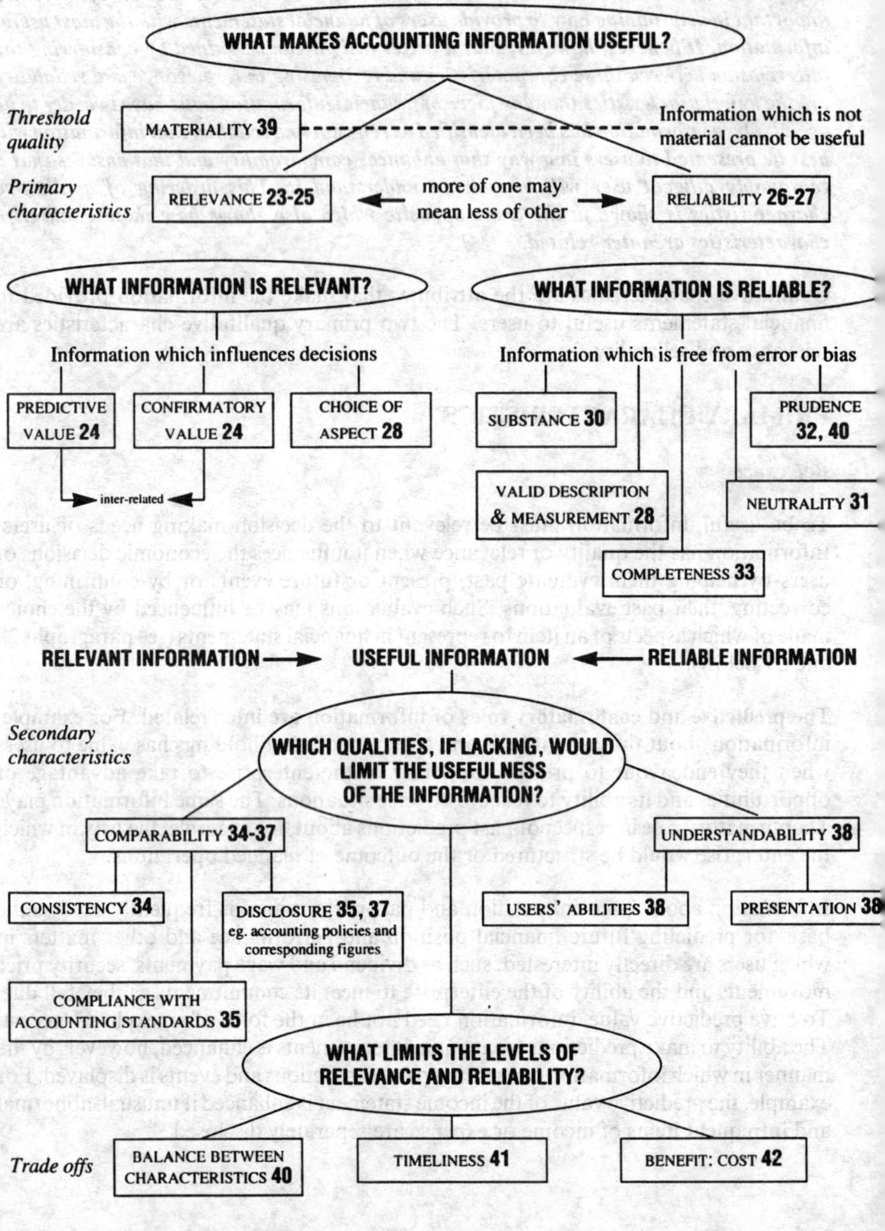

WHAT MAKES ACCOUNTING INFORMATION USEFUL?
Threshold quality
MATERIALITY 39
Information which is not material cannot be useful
Primary characteristics
RELEVANCE 23-25
more of one may mean less of other
RELIABILITY 26-27
WHAT INFORMATION IS RELEVANT?
WHAT INFORMATION IS RELIABLE?
Information which influences decisions
Information which is free from error or bias
PREDICTIVE VALUE 24
CONFIRMATORY VALUE 24
CHOICE OF ASPECT 28
SUBSTANCE 30
PRUDENCE 32, 40
inter-related
VALID DESCRIPTION & MEASUREMENT 28
NEUTRALITY 31
COMPLETENESS 33
RELEVANT INFORMATION
USEFUL INFORMATION
RELIABLE INFORMATION
Secondary characteristics
WHICH QUALITIES, IF LACKING, WOULD LIMIT THE USEFULNESS OF THE INFORMATION?
COMPARABILITY 34-37
UNDERSTANDABILITY 38
CONSISTENCY 34
DISCLOSURE 35, 37
eg. accounting policies and corresponding figures
USERS' ABILITIES 38
PRESENTATION 38
COMPLIANCE WITH ACCOUNTING STANDARDS 35
WHAT LIMITS THE LEVELS OF RELEVANCE AND RELIABILITY?
Trade offs
BALANCE BETWEEN CHARACTERISTICS 40
TIMELINESS 41
BENEFIT: COST 42

Reliability

To be useful, information must also be reliable. Information has the quality of reliability when it is free from material error and bias and can be depended upon by users to represent faithfully in terms of valid description that which it either purports to represent or could reasonably be expected to represent. **26**

Information may be relevant but so unreliable in nature or representation that its recognition in the financial statements may be potentially misleading. For example, if the validity and amount of a claim for damages under a legal action are disputed, it may be inappropriate for the enterprise to recognise the full amount of the claim in the balance sheet, although it may be appropriate to disclose the amount and circumstances of the claim. **27**

TO BE RELIABLE INFORMATION SHOULD HAVE THE FOLLOWING CHARACTERISTICS

Faithful representation

To be relevant and reliable information must represent faithfully the effect of the transactions and other events it either purports to represent or could reasonably be expected to represent. Thus, for example, a balance sheet should represent faithfully the effect of the transactions and other events that result in assets, liabilities and equity of the enterprise at the reporting date that meet the recognition criteria. Whether or not financial information is a faithful representation of what it purports to represent has a bearing on both the relevance and reliability of that piece of information. Faithful representation encompasses two distinct components of information: on the one hand, **valid description with freedom from error** and, on the other, the selection of which aspects of an item to represent. Valid description with freedom from error is an essential part of the reliability of information and this is the most important part of faithful representation. The **choice of aspect** affects the relevance of the information. **28**

Most financial information is subject to some risk of being less than a faithful representation of that which it purports to portray. This is not due to bias, but rather to inherent difficulties either in identifying the transactions and other events to be measured or in devising and applying measurement and presentation techniques that can convey messages that correspond with those transactions and events. In certain cases, the measurement of the financial effects of items could be so uncertain that enterprises generally would not recognise them in the financial statements. In other cases, however, it may be relevant to recognise items and to disclose the risk of error surrounding their recognition and measurement. **29**

SUBSTANCE

If information is to represent faithfully the transactions and other events that it purports to represent, it is necessary that they are accounted for and presented in accordance with their substance and economic reality and not merely their legal form. **30**

Exposure Drafts in issue

The substance of transactions and events is not always consistent with that which is apparent from their legal form, especially if that form is contrived. For example, an enterprise may dispose of an asset to another party in such a way that the documentation purports to pass legal ownership to that party; nevertheless, when the circumstances are looked at as a whole, it may be found that arrangements exist that ensure that the enterprise continues to enjoy the future economic benefits embodied in the asset, or to suffer the obligations of a liability. In such circumstances, the reporting of a sale would not be a valid description of the transaction entered into (if, indeed, there were a transaction).

Neutrality

31 To be reliable, the information contained in financial statements must be neutral, that is, free from bias. Financial statements are not neutral if, by the selection or presentation of information, they influence the making of a decision or judgement in order to achieve a predetermined result or outcome.

Prudence

32 The preparers of financial statements do, however, have to contend with the uncertainties that inevitably surround many events and circumstances, such as the collectability of debts, the probable useful life of plant and equipment and the number and magnitude of warranty claims that may occur. Such uncertainties are recognised by the disclosure of their nature and extent and by the exercise of prudence in the preparation of the financial statements. Prudence is the inclusion of a degree of caution in the exercise of the judgements needed in making the estimates required under conditions of uncertainty, such that assets or income are not overstated and liabilities or expenses are not understated. However, the exercise of prudence does not allow, for example, the creation of hidden reserves or excessive provisions, the deliberate understatement of assets or income, or the deliberate overstatement of liabilities or expenses, because the financial statements would not be neutral and, therefore, not have the quality of reliability.

Completeness

33 To be reliable, the information in financial statements must be complete within the bounds of materiality and cost. An omission can cause information to be false or misleading and thus unreliable and deficient in terms of relevance.

SECONDARY CHARACTERISTICS

After relevance and reliability, there are other characteristics that financial information should have. These secondary characteristics are comparability and understandability. Information lacking these qualities would be of limited usefulness, however relevant and reliable it was.

Comparability

User must be able to compare the financial statements of an enterprise over time to identify trends in its financial position and performance. Users must also be able to compare the financial statements of different enterprises to evaluate their relative financial position, performance and financial adaptability. Hence, the measurement and display of the financial effect of like transactions and other events must be carried out **in a consistent way** throughout an enterprise and over time for that enterprise and **in a consistent way** for different enterprises. **34**

An important implication of comparability is that users are **informed of the accounting policies** employed in preparation of the financial statements, any changes in those policies and the effects of such changes. Users need to be able to identify differences between the accounting policies for like transactions and other events used by the same enterprise from period to period and by different enterprises. **Compliance with accounting standards**, including the disclosure of the accounting policies used by the enterprise, helps to achieve comparability. **35**

The need for comparability should not be confused with mere uniformity and should not be allowed to become an impediment to the introduction of improved accounting standards. It is not appropriate for an enterprise to continue accounting in the same manner for a transaction or other event if the policy adopted is not in keeping with the qualitative characteristics of relevance and reliability. It is also inappropriate for an enterprise to leave its accounting policies unchanged when more relevant and reliable alternatives exist. **36**

Because users wish to compare the financial position, performance and changes in financial position of an enterprise over time, it is important that the financial statements show **corresponding information** for the preceding periods. **37**

Understandability

An essential quality of the information provided in financial statements is that it should **be presented in such a way that it is readily understandable** by users. For this purpose, **users are assumed to have a reasonable knowledge of business and economic activities and accounting and a willingness to study the information with reasonable diligence**. Information about complex matters that should be included in the financial statements because of its relevance to the economic decision-making needs of users should not be excluded merely on the grounds that it may be too difficult for certain users to understand. **38**

THRESHOLD QUALITY

A threshold quality is one that needs to be considered before considering the other qualities of that information. If any information does not pass the test of the threshold quality, it does not need to be considered further.

Materiality

39 Information is material if its omission or mis-statement could influence the economic decisions of users taken on the basis of the financial statements. Materiality depends on the size of the item or error judged in the particular circumstances of its omission or mis-statement, Thus, materiality provides a threshold or cut-off point rather than being a primary qualitative characteristic that information must have if it is to be useful.

TRADE-OFFS IN RELATION TO RELEVANT AND RELIABLE INFORMATION

The following paragraphs outline situations where more of one quality can only be achieved at a cost. This cost may be an actual cost or may be a reduction in the level of another quality.

Balance between qualitative characteristics

40 In practice a balancing, or trade-off, between qualitative characteristics is often necessary. Generally the aim is to achieve an appropriate balance among the characteristics in order to meet the objective of financial statements. The relative importance of the characteristics in different cases is a matter of judgement. For example, there is a potential conflict between the qualities of neutrality and prudence, both characteristics of reliability. Neutrality is freedom from bias. However, the application of prudence tends to result in a bias to reduce assets and profits and increase liabilities, losses and expenses. If the exercise of prudence in reporting financial information is not to amount to a loss of neutrality, prudence should be an attitude of mind denoting a careful assessment of all uncertainties and a vigilance to possible risks rather than a systematic measurement bias. Ideally the exercise of prudence results in a degree of scepticism about the results of uncertainty that exactly counteracts any tendency to optimism.

Timeliness

41 If there is undue delay in the reporting of information it may lose its relevance. Management may need to balance the relative merits of timely reporting and the provision of reliable information. To provide information on a timely basis it may often be necessary to report before all aspects of a transaction or other event are known, thus impairing reliability. Conversely, if reporting is delayed until all aspects are known, the information may be highly reliable but of little use to users who have had to make decisions in the interim. In achieving a balance between relevance and reliability, the overriding consideration, subject to any legal requirements on timing, is how best to satisfy the economic decision-making needs of users.

Benefit and cost

42 The balance between benefit and cost is a pervasive constraint rather than a qualitative characteristic. The benefits derived from information should exceed the cost of provid-

ing it. The evaluation of benefits and costs is, however, substantially a judgemental process. Furthermore, the costs do not necessarily fall on those users who enjoy the benefits. Benefits may also be enjoyed by users other than those for whom the information is prepared. For these reasons, it is difficult to apply a cost-benefit test in any particular case. Nevertheless, the Board in setting standards, as well as the preparers and users of financial statements, should be aware of this constraint.

TRUE AND FAIR VIEW

Financial statements are frequently described as giving a true and fair view of the financial position and performance of an enterprise. Although this Statement of Principles does not deal directly with this concept, the application of the principal qualitative characteristics and of the law and appropriate accounting standards should in all normal circumstances result in financial statements that convey what is generally understood as a true and fair view of such information. **43**

Appendix — the main changes to the IASC text

This note sets out the main changes that have been made to the IASC 'Framework for the Preparation and Presentation of Financial Statements'. The Board has also made a number of minor drafting changes. These are not described in this note, except where the changes made are significant to the meaning of the Statement. The changes are described in the order in which they appear in the text. **A1**

The Board has added a Preface setting out the background to the Statement of principles. The Preface explains why the Board considers it most effective to use the IASC text, 'Framework for the Preparation and Presentation of Financial Statements' as the base for this section. **A2**

The Board has added its own paragraph, paragraph 5, on the scope of the project for developing a Statement of Principles. This paragraph sets out the matters that the Board will consider in developing its Statement of Principles. **A3**

Paragraph 8 has been amended from the IASC text to refer to not-for-profit organisations as well as commercial enterprises. This paragraph also sets out the main changes that would need to be implemented if the text were to be changed explicitly for not-for-profit organisations. **A4**

Paragraph 10 has been changed. It preserves the primacy of investors as users of financial statements but explains more fully the reasons why catering for interests of investors will to a certain extent satisfy the needs of other users, particularly where those other users are interested in the entity as a whole. **A5**

The Board has dropped the section of the IASC text dealing with underlying assumptions, the accruals basis and the going concern concept. This section consisted of two paragraphs dealing respectively with the accruals basis and the going concern concept. **A6**

The underlying assumptions are neither part of the objective of financial reporting nor of the qualitative characteristics of such information. They are measurement conventions and arise from the application of the qualitative characteristics in accomplishing the objective of financial reporting. Thus they should not be discussed in a section dealing with the objective and qualitative characteristics of financial information.

A7 For Chapter 2 — Qualitative Characteristics of Financial Statements, the Board has developed a chart showing the qualitative characteristics of financial information and how these characteristics are related to each other. This chart is published alongside the text. The Board has also added an introductory paragraph to Chapter 2 explaining that, whereas the IASC identified four principal qualitative characteristics, understandability, relevance, reliability and comparability, the Board considers that there are only two primary characteristics, relevance and reliability. The chart attached to the text sets out the qualitative characteristics and their inter-relationships according to the Board's revised plan. The Board has, where necessary, added header sentences to the subsections on the qualitative characteristics to clarify the connection between the different characteristics so that these clearly tie in with the chart. Where component qualitative characteristics are mentioned but not given a separate heading, they are picked out in the text in bold.

A8 The discussion in Paragraph 28 does not agree completely with the IASC interpretation of faithful representation. The Board considers that faithful representation is most important as an element of reliability meaning valid description with freedom from error. Faithful representation, however, also has a role in contributing to the relevance of financial information. This can be described as selecting which aspects of an item to represent. The Board has thus added a note to the text describing faithful representation which divides faithful representation into these two component parts. Faithful representation still appears in the section discussing reliability as this is the more fundamental effect of this characteristic.

A9 The IASC 'framework' contains two paragraphs (29 and 30) discussing materiality. The Board has retained the second of these, which gives a concise and practical explanation of the concept, but has omitted the first, since the example discussed therein seems incomplete.

A10 In paragraph 40 the Board has added to the discussion of the need to seek a balance between qualitative characteristics an example citing the possible conflict between neutrality and prudence. Neutrality is defined as lack of bias, yet prudence applied consistently will result in a tendency to underestimate assets and profits and to overestimate liabilities costs and losses that might of itself constitute a bias.

Discussion Draft
Statement of Principles Chapter 3
The elements of financial statements

(Issued July 1992)

Contents

The elements of financial statements

INTRODUCTION

In this chapter the definitions of the elements of financial statements are set out and discussed. The elements are: 1

- assets
- liabilities
- equity
- gains
- losses
- contributions from owners
- distributions to owners.

These terms are logically related: assets and liabilities are mirror images of each other; equity is the difference between an entity's assets and its liabilities; gains and losses are respectively increases and decreases in equity other than those which relate to transactions with owners. The nature of the various elements and their interrelationship form the starting point for understanding what information can and should be communicated in financial statements. 2

The discussion of assets in this chapter is longer than that of the other elements of financial statements because they are the first elements to be addressed. Because the elements of financial statements are logically interrelated, much of that discussion is relevant to the other elements. It is not intended to suggest that assets are more fundamental than any other element: the discussion could have begun with any of the elements and then gone on to discuss the others. 3

Some users of financial statements emphasise the recognition of gains and losses and the need to match against revenue any related expenditure, in order to derive net gains for a period. They focus on the ability of the entity to generate outputs from its inputs – ie on the performance of the entity, and view balance sheet items as the residual of this process. Others emphasise the recognition of balance sheet items. They focus on the resources of the entity and on claims on those resources – ie on the wealth of the entity, and view net gains of a period as being the increase in net assets in that period, and hence derived from the balance sheet. Users need information about both the performance of the entity and its wealth. As gains and losses are defined in terms of changes in assets and/or liabilities, provided that the definitions of the elements given in this chapter are applied, the items recognised under both approaches will be the same. 4

The task of this chapter is the limited one of identifying the essential features which each of these elements of financial statements must possess; any item which does not fall within one of the definitions of elements should not be included in financial statements. But it does not follow that because an item falls within the definitions of an element it will be recognised in financial statements: for this to be the case it must also meet the recognition criteria disucssed in Chapter 4. 5

6 Nor does it follow that the characteristics which qualify an item as an element (or as a recognised element) in the financial statements will be those which will determine the basis of measurement. For example, as will be discussed shortly, the definition of an asset is based on the notion of future economic benefits, but it does not follow that the carrying value of assets should necessarily reflect a measurement of those future benefits. The measurement of assets and liabilities is discussed in Chapter 5.

ASSETS

7 Assets are defined as follows:

> Assets are rights or other access to future economic benefits controlled by an entity as a result of past transactions or events.

'Rights or other access'

8 Fundamental to the concept of assets is that an item which is an asset is so as a result not only of its inherent characteristics, but also by virtue of the relationship in which it stands to a reporting entity. Strictly speaking, it is not a particular item of property – such as a factory – which may be an asset of a particular entity; rather, it is the rights deriving from ownership or the other rights of occupation and use which constitute an asset.

9 Because it is the rights to items of property rather than the items of property themselves which are assets, the same item of property may be shared between various parties and each of these interests may be assets (or liabilities) of the respective parties.

10 Access to economic benefits may also derive from the ability to take part in an activity which will produce, or is expected to produce, economic benefits. For example, licences and permits may enable an entity to partake in such an activity which would not otherwise be possible, and therefore count as assets. The right to prevent another person from competing with the entity might also be an asset if it enhances the ability of the entity to carry out its business profitably.

'Future economic benefits'

11 Although in a purist sense economic benefits can be regarded as the ability to enjoy and consume goods or services, in the context of business activity they can be evidenced by the prospective receipt of cash. This is because cash provides command over resources in general, with the nature of the resources not specified. For the same reason cash itself represents a future economic benefit as opposed to a current one, and thus is an asset within the above definition.

12 The future receipt of cash flows can be directly associated with a debt receivable, and, at one further remove, with any item which may be sold.

13 Other assets provide economic benefits which are only indirectly related to the gener-

ation of cash flows. For example a factory provides the shelter (which would require the payment of rent were the factory not owned) within which goods are manufactured. Only when the goods are sold and the customer pays is the economic benefit resulting from the use of the factory realised in terms of cash flow. The ultimate cash realisation of the future economic benefits of some assets may be highly uncertain, although there is no significant doubt that an immediate benefit will be received. For example a facility might be constructed for use in an entity's research activities and have little alternative use. The ability to carry out research constitutes an immediate economic benefit which shows that the facility is an asset: like the factory, if the facility were needed but not owned a similar item of property would have to be rented. The uncertainty as to whether the research will in turn result in economic benefits in the form of cash flows to the entity does not in normal circumstances prejudice the facility's status as an asset, but it may affect its measurement.

'Controlled by the entity'

The definition of an asset requires that the access to the future economic benefits is controlled by the entity. 'Control', in this context, means the ability to obtain the economic benefits and to restrict the access of others, for example to those who pay. Where access to economic benefits is equally open to all parties – as, for example, in the case of public infrastructure which all may enjoy equally – none of these parties has an asset by virtue of such access. **14**

In many cases the entity will exercise its control by restricting access to all other parties so as to ensure that it receives the benefits itself: for example it will usually wish to be the sole recipient of the service potential of its plant and machinery. In other cases it will exercise its control by exchanging the future economic benefits for a payment from another party, as for example where the entity decides to sell a particular piece of plant which is surplus to requirements. **15**

'Past transactions or events'

The definition requires that the access to future economic benefits must result from past transactions or other events. Although it is most commonly transactions which give rise to assets, in some cases an event other than a transaction may give rise to an asset – for example the tortious act of another party may give rise to a claim for recompense. This part of the definition makes it clear that access to economic benefits which is obtained by an entity only after the relevant date is excluded from the notion of assets. For example, if a decision has been taken to order equipment there will be no asset (nor liability) before the order has been placed. An asset will only arise when the entity obtains the right to demand delivery of the equipment or the access to its service potential, which may be when the order is placed and accepted, or on delivery of the goods in question, depending on the terms applicable to the purchase. Sometimes arrangements are entered into which specify some of the terms on which certain kinds of transactions between the parties will be made but leave certain terms, such as the price for the goods, to be determined when an order is placed. The making of such a arrangement might not give rise to an asset (or liability) of either party, but the placing of an order under it would. **16**

17 Often where the asset is based on legal rights (for example where property is purchased or leased) it will be the entry into an enforceable contract which gives rise to the asset. In other cases it might be the performance of a service, for example where performance gives rise to a right to demand payment.

Relationship to legal form

18 Access to economic benefits can be obtained in various ways. Normally it is obtained by ownership of goods. This gives access to a number of future economic benefits, including the ability to use the goods in the production of other goods or in the provision of services and the ability to sell or exchange the goods or exploit their value by such means as pledging them as security for borrowing, or leasing them to others.

19 Sometimes similar access to economic benefits may be obtained without legal ownership. Use of goods may be obtained by leasing them. An option to acquire an item of property may provide an opportunity of benefiting (and suffering) from changes in the value of the item of property. In some of these cases the asset may be barely distinguishable in terms of financial commitment, opportunity for gain and risk of loss, from that obtained by ownership of the goods or property.

20 Ownership of securities gives access to future economic benefits in the form of dividends or other income and the amount receivable on sale or redemption. Rights against other parties which require them to make payments or render services are also examples of assets. Other kinds of legal rights which give access to economic benefits include the rights to the use of a patent or trademark and the rights enjoyed under licences or permits such as airlines' landing rights and milk quotas.

21 Ownership of an item of property or other rights are not necessary characteristics of assets and some assets do not rest on these. An entity may for example, have an asset (access to future economic benefits) as a result of past advertising which can be expected to result in increased sales (and hence profitability) at a future time. In such a case there is no item of property, nor is there a person who owes an obligation to the entity. It suffices that customers are expected to act in a way which will provide economic benefits to the entity. In examples such as this, issues of certainty and measurability are often more pronounced than in other examples of assets, but the access to future benefit is nonetheless an asset.

Uncertainty

22 The definition of an asset does not require certainty that the economic benefits to which an item grants access will accrue to the entity. All assets sometimes exhibit some degree of uncertainty that the future economic benefits will in fact accrue – physical property may be destroyed in a fire or other catastrophe and debtors may become insolvent. Even cash itself, because it is a surrogate for the ultimate economic benefit – the ability to enjoy and consume goods or services (see paragraph 11 above) – can exhibit similar uncertainty, for example in the presence of high rates of inflation or political instability. Nor is it necessary that the form in which economic benefits may flow to the entity is known: for example the ownership of a piece of plant may give rise to an asset even if it is not known whether the entity will use the plant for its entire economic life or will use

it for a shorter period and then sell it. Provided there is some possibility of access to some future benefit the definition of an asset is satisfied. However, the uncertainty that the benefit will accrue may be so great that the asset is not recognised, or the likely benefit may be so small that the asset will not be measured at a material amount. Issues of recognition and measurement are discussed in Chapters 4 and 5.

Relationship to cost

It is sometimes argued that the notion of an asset should be elucidated in terms of a deferred cost rather than a future benefit. However, it would never be correct to defer a cost except where there is an expectation of future benefit. Where a cost has been incurred it is a reasonable inference that current or future benefit was sought, but it does not follow that access to such benefits was obtained. If the charging to expense of a large, non-recurring cost results in the reported result for the period not being reliable guide to future profits, this apparent distortion may be met by additional disclosure rather than by postponing the expensing of part or all of the cost. It is also possible for assets to be obtained without a cost, for example where property is donated to the reporting entity. **23**

LIABILITIES

Liabilities are defined as follows: **24**

> Liabilities are an entity's obligations to transfer economic benefits as a result of past transactions or events.

Like the term 'asset', the term 'liability' characterises an item by virtue of its relationship to an entity. Hence, strictly, an item cannot be said to constitute a liability without reference (at least implicitly) to the entity of which it is a liability. **25**

Liabilities include creditors, accruals and some of the amounts referred to as provisions. Generally, the term 'creditors' is used to describe specific amounts owing to specific individuals and usually there is little uncertainty as to the timing of payments. 'Accruals' includes amounts which are due in respect of goods and services that have been received but which have not been invoiced or formally agreed with the supplier or provider. Those provisions which are liabilities are those items in accounts which reflect obligations incurred before the balance sheet date but in respect of which the precise amounts, timings or identity of the party to which payment will be made are uncertain. The term 'provision' is also generally used to refer to amounts used to reduce the carrying amount of assets, for example to reduce the face value of debtors to their recoverable amount, or to reduce fixed assets to their depreciated amounts: such provisions are not, of course, liabilities. **26**

Just as there are unrecognised assets, so there are unrecognised liabilities. Where the amount of a liability cannot be determined with any degree of reliability it may not be recognised but nonetheless a liability may exist. In some cases, it is difficult or impossible to determine whether or not a liability exists, as for example may be the case **27** where the entity is engaged in a dispute with another party. For practical purposes, the difference between a liability which is not recognised due to uncertainty and a claim which, because it is unfounded, does not represent a liability is unimportant: both situations are generally referred to as 'contingent liabilities'. Obligations which are not expected to result in a transfer of economic benefits – such as the guarantee of another entity's debt where the other entity is expected to remain solvent – are also liabilities, although they may not be recognised in financial statements.

'Obligations'

28 The definition requires that there be an obligation to transfer economic benefits. A legal obligation is a sufficient condition for a liability to exist since the beneficiary of the obligation can insist on the outflow of economic benefits in settlement, and in practice most liabilities are legal obligations.

29 But a legal obligation is not a necessary condition for a liability. For example, an entity may have a liability for taxation in relation to events which took place before the balance sheet date even though, as a matter of law, the tax does not constitute a liability until it is assessed, which may be considerably later. Commercial penalties may also be a substitute for legal commitments. For example, where an entity holds an option and failure to exercise it would expose the entity to severe commercial penalties, the exercise price under the option may represent a liability. That would be the case where the commercial penalty has the effect of negating the entity's legal right to refrain from such exercise. Another example of a liability existing in the absence of a legal commitment might be a provision for redundancy costs necessitated by the closure of a business unit that is already in progress.

30 The notion of an obligation implies that the entity is not free to avoid the outflow of resources. An entity may offer inducements to its creditors to accept settlement other than in the form which is contractually due, but it cannot insist that they accept such an offer. By contrast costs to be incurred in the future (for example, replacement or maintenance of plant) do not represent liabilities, unless the entity has an obligation to another party to incur the costs in question, or retains no discretion to avoid the expenditure. Such an obligation might arise under a contract for goods to be supplied or services performed.

'Transfer of economic benefits'

31 Outflows of economic benefits include the transfer of cash and any other kind of property. They also include the provision of a service, since no service can be provided except by the application of resources such as labour. Economic benefits can also be transferred by refraining from activities which would otherwise be profitable.

'Past transactions or events'

32 The definition requires that the obligation to transfer economic benefits must result from past transactions or events. In practice, it is most commonly transactions which give rise to liabilities. Simply making a decision to order equipment does not give rise to a liability even though once the decision is made it is probable that the entity will transfer economic benefits. A liability will only arise once the entity is obliged to give consideration for the equipment, which may be when the order is placed and accepted, or on delivery of the goods in question, depending on the terms applicable to the purchase. An example of a liability arising from an event other than a transaction is that of the imposition by a court of a penalty.

Sometimes it may be unclear which is the event which gives rise to the liability, for example whether the liability in respect of warranty claims should be deemed to arise when the warranty obligation is entered into (that is, usually, at the time the goods are sold) or when any product malfunction actually arises. It is the entering into the commitment which is the event which gives rise to a liability, since this is the time at which the entity assumes an obligation which may result in the future outflow of economic benefits, even if at that time the amount at which the liability is measured is small, or even nil. (It is usual to give details in notes to the accounts of any liabilities which have been included in the accounts at amounts much smaller than the amount of a possible future outflow of economic benefits.) Subsequent events (such as experience of the performance of the product) might show that the carrying amount needs to be revised to a greater or smaller amount, but they do not mark the inception or extinguishment of a liability. **33**

COMPLEMENTARY NATURE OF ASSETS AND LIABILITIES

Assets and liabilities are mirror images of each other. For example, a long term construction contract will be an asset if the economic benefit of receiving payment exceeds the obligations of a construction, but changes in the amount at which these are measured – for example as a result of changing estimates – may result in the contract becoming a liability. **34**

Normally items which represent reductions of inflows of economic benefits or outflows of economic benefits are treated as adjustments to the amount of the assets and liabilities which represent the inflows or outflows that are reduced. For example, if a credit note is given to a customer to recognise his dissatisfaction with goods supplied, the amount of the credit will usually be set against the amount due from the customer rather than reported as a separate liability. Equally a payment made on account of an agreed liability will usually be applied in a reduction of the reported amount of the liability rather than presented as a separate asset. **35**

However, in some cases where the asset and the liability in question are not reflected in the financial statements, a reduction in a future liability may be reported as an asset (and *vice versa*). For example, Advance Corporation Tax may not be recoverable except by offset against a future Corporation Tax liability, but may in some circumstances be reported as an asset. Similarly, rebates to which customers are entitled under a promotion may represent reductions of amounts receivable in future, rather than an obligation to make payments, for example if purchases in one accounting period beyond a certain threshold entitle the customer to reductions in the price of purchases in the next. The anticipated amount of such rebates may be shown as a liability, **36** although the obligation is not to transfer cash, but rather to accept a smaller amount of cash in settlement of future sales.

37 Assets and liabilities are also complementary in the sense that identifying a liability may lead to the identification of a corresponding asset (or vice versa). A call option held on an item of property, for example, is usually simply an asset in itself. But in some cases, as referred to in paragraph 29 above, the penalty for failing to exercise the option is so severe that the entity is commercially obliged to exercise the option. In such a case, the amount payable on exercise is a liability of the entity: if this is the case the asset is the right to receive the property.

OFFSETTING

38 It is sometimes unclear whether two or more items constitute separate assets and liabilities or whether they are a single item. For example, an entity may keep separate records relating to different kinds of transactions with another entity where that other entity is both a supplier and a customer. Whether two or more debit balances may be aggregated as a single debtor (or two or more credit balances may be aggregated as a single creditor) is frequently unimportant since all similar debtors are each generally presented in aggregate in financial statements in any case, as are all similar creditors. But it is only correct to aggregate a debit balance and a credit balance to form a net asset or liability in certain circumstances. This kind of aggregation is generally referred to as 'offsetting'. The circumstances in which offsetting is appropriate are considered in the following paragraphs.

39 Just as it may be convenient to maintain separate records of transactions with another entity, so it may be administratively convenient for these accounts to be settled separately when due. But it does not necessarily follow from the payment and receipt of the gross amounts at a later date that the underlying obligation at the balance sheet date was not to pay or receive a net amount. Thus the intent of the parties as to the means of settlement is not relevant to the question of whether offset is appropriate.

40 Offset is appropriate only where the entity has the ability to insist on settlement by paying the net amount (or by withholding any payment and requiring the other party to pay only the net amount), and such ability is assured. In such a case the liability of the entity, that is the obligation to transfer economic benefits, is only for the net amount.

41 Another circumstance which is necessary for offset to be appropriate is that the two items are of the same kind so that changes in the carrying amount of one will be mirrored by changes in that of the other. This is most likely to be the case where both items are monetary and expressed in the same currency. Where there is both the ability to insist on settlement by paying the net amount (as discussed above) and the items are of the same kind, the effect of the arrangement is that the access to economic benefit or obligation to transfer economic benefits relating to one item is negated by the other.

42 The condition that the ability to exercise the offset is assured will generally require that there be a legal right of offset (and that such rights would survive the insolvency of the

other party or parties), because otherwise the possibility would usually remain that the entity would be required to fulfil its obligation whilst being unable to enforce access to the economic benefits of the asset. A possible exception to the need for a legal right of offset in order to consider separate items to be a single asset or liability would be where an entity is able to transfer assets to another party which undertakes to discharge a liability of the entity and there is no risk that because of a failure by that party to honour its obligations the liability will revert to the entity. Such a transfer would have to be irrevocable. An example of such an arrangement might be that known as 'in-substance defeasance of debt' (which is not common in the United Kingdom).

Banks sometimes use non-recourse debt as a method effectively to transfer a loan, or **43** part of a loan, from one bank to another. These arrangements may achieve the effect of transferring the whole or a proportionate part of the benefits and risks attaching to the original loan. In both these cases, the original lender will have no asset in the loan or part of the loan transferred: any cash received from the customer that relates to the part transferred will not represent an economic benefit to the original lender, since it will be under an obligation to pass it on to the bank which provided the non-recourse finance. In the same way, the non-recourse finance does not represent a liability since there is no obligation whatsoever (either legal or commercial) to transfer economic benefits: any claim is only in respect of the loan or part of the loan transferred, which does not quality as an asset. In these circumstances, since all the benefits and obligations and the risks relating to them have been transferred, the items should be offset.*

EQUITY

Equity is defined as follows: **44**

> Equity is the ownership interest in the entity: it is the residual amount found by deducting all liabilities of the entity from all of the entity's assets.

Because of the residual nature of equity, it is the owners of a business who benefit from **45** all the increases in the entity's net assets. The owners' wealth may be increased even if a distribution to them is not made, because the funds not distributed will be retained for the benefit of the entity.

The owners of a business may share their rights to the equity in a variety of ways. For **46** example different owners (or groups of owners) may be entitled to a different share of the profits or of the assets remaining on a winding up. The shares of profits or assets may differ in relative amounts or in the manner in which they are calculated.

Sometimes equity interests in a company arise by the issue of instruments which give **47** the holder the right to obtain shares in the future. An example of such an instrument is a warrant to subscribe for shares. This gives the holder a right to demand the allotment of

The circumstances discussed in paragraph 43 do not include arrangements that leave the transferor with a significant part of the risks (of benefit or loss) likely to occur in practice. Such arrangements are addressed in the Board's project 'Reflecting the substance of transactions in assets and liabilities', which is in the course of development (Editor's note:** see now FRS 5).*

the shares to him, but does not require the entity to transfer economic benefits to him. Hence it is not within the definition of a liability.

48 The amount at which equity is shown in the balance sheet is dependent on the measurement of assets and liabilities. It would be coincidental for the aggregate amount of equity to correspond with the aggregate market value of the shares of the entity or the sum that could be raised by disposing of either the net assets on a piecemeal basis or the entity as a whole on a going concern basis.

49 Financial statements usually distinguish sources of equity. A distinction is made, for example, between equity which has resulted from the contributions made by owners and that which has resulted from other changes in net assets resulting from trading and other events. These divisions may in turn be analysed to show the differing nature of the ownership interests in the entity and to differentiate realised from unrealised profits.

50 The analysis of the equity of the entity may also usefully show the purposes to which reserves are intended to be applied or may legally be applied, which is frequently dependent on their sources.

51 Another component of the analysis of equity may be the cumulative amount of capital maintenance adjustments, that is, the amounts charged in arriving at profit to ensure that a given definition of capital is maintained. The nature of any such adjustment will depend on the concept of capital maintenance which has been adopted, as discussed further in Chapter 5. Such a capital maintenance adjustment forms part of the display of equity, and is not in itself one of the elements of financial statements.

GAINS AND LOSSES

52 Financial statements distinguish changes in equity resulting from transactions with owners from other changes in equity. The latter changes are referred to as gains and losses, which are defined as follows:

> Gains are increases in equity, other than those relating to contributions from owners.

> Losses are decreases in equity, other than those relating to distributions to owners.

53 All elements depend for their existence on flows of benefits to or from the entity. The interrelationship between the elements means that the recognition of a particular element (for example an asset), automatically requires the recognition of another element (for example a gain, a liability or a decrease in another asset). This interrelationship is reflected in the fact that the primary financial statements articulate; that is the primary statements present on a consistent basis different aspects of the effect on the entity of various past events. Hence the changes in the wealth of the entity (ie in net assets) depicted in the balance sheet are also reflected in its performance (ie in net gains of a period).

54 As used in this statement of principles 'gains' and 'losses' are broad terms including all changes in equity, other than those relating to transactions with owners. Various kinds of gains and losses may be distinguished, amongst the most fundamental of which are revenue gains and revenue losses, which are those gains and losses which are generally included in the profit and loss account of the entity.

Examples of revenue gains (commonly called 'revenue') include the amounts charged to customers for the supply of goods and the provision of services, and also the return on investments in the form of interest or dividends. These give rise to increases in equity either in cash or amounts receivable. Revenue losses (commonly called 'expenses') include such items as employment costs, and the consumption of property, plant and stock. **55**

Revenue gains and revenue losses are normally presented gross, that is, by aggregating under each revenue or expense head the (usually numerous) similar transactions that fit the description. Sometimes, however, a single significant event – such as the disposal of a major non-current asset – gives rise to a number of gains and losses, whose aggregate impact on the entity may be of more significance than the individual items. In such circumstances the net effect may be presented in the accounts and described as a 'gain' or 'loss' as the case may be. Another type of gains and losses is the effect on the assets and liabilities of the entity of changes in market values (to the extent such changes are recognised in accounts). As the various kinds of gains and losses have different significance for different purposes, they are often presented separately. The presentation of gains and losses in the profit and loss account and the statement of total recognised gains and losses is considered further in Chapters 4 and 6. **56**

When gains and losses are displayed in financial statements, a capital maintenance adjustment may be made in order to show the extent to which a net increase or decrease in equity represents a return in excess of that needed to maintain the capital of the business. The nature and amount of any such adjustment will depend on the concept of capital maintenance which has been adopted. Such a capital maintenance adjustment forms part of the display of gains and losses, and is not in itself one of the elements of financial statements. **57**

CONTRIBUTIONS FROM OWNERS AND DISTRIBUTIONS TO OWNERS

The remaining elements of financial statements are contributions from owners and distributions to owners. **58**

Contributions from owners are defined as follows: **59**

> Contributions from owners are increases in equity resulting from investments made by owners in their capacity as owners.

Owners most commonly make contributions in the form of cash, but contributions may also be made by transferring other forms of property or by accepting equity in satisfaction of liabilities. Owners may also make contributions by performing services: **60** even though such services may be charged immediately as an expense (for example, if the future economic benefits relating to them are uncertain), such services do represent an asset, and hence an increase in equity, for at least a short time.

61 Not all investments in an entity are contributions from owners. Where an investor purchases shares from another shareholder, for example, there will be no increase in equity (as equity is defined in this chapter) and hence such an investment does not constitute a contribution from owners.

62 The consideration for contributions received from owners is the granting of equity rights in the entity. There is a distinction between equity rights granted on a *pro rata* basis to the whole of the existing body of shareholders and those granted to any other group or individual. In the first case, there is no necessary connection between the value of the contribution made and that of any new equity rights granted: provided all pre-existing owners are treated equally, any apparent over or under-payment for new equity rights will be compensated by an equal increase or decrease in the value of their previous investment. In the second case, if the transaction is to be equitable as between new owners and pre-existing owners, it will be necessary that the value of the equity rights correspond to that of the contribution made. If the contribution received does not approximate to the fair value of the equity rights granted in exchange, the difference represents hidden consideration that needs to be reflected as a gain or loss to the entity.

63 Distributions to owners are defined as follows:

Distributions to owners are decreases in equity resulting from transfers made to owners in their capacity as owners.

64 Distributions to owners include the payment of dividends and the return of capital, for example where a company purchases its own shares. A bonus issue of shares however, does not result in a decrease of equity, and hence is not within the definition of distribution to owners.

65 Contributions from owners and distributions to them are only those transactions to which they are a party in their capacity as owners. The results of trading transactions with owners are gains or losses since they enter into such transactions not as owners, but in other capacities, for example that of customers or suppliers. It is possible, however, that a single transaction may combine both elements: for example, the sole owner of an entity may purchase property from the entity for a price less than its true value. Such a transaction would include a distribution to the owner (being the difference between the true value of the property and the price paid) as well as the consideration received for the disposal of the asset, both of which would need to be taken into account in determining the profit or loss on disposal.

Discussion Draft
Statement of Principles Chapter 4
The recognition of items in financial statements

(Issued July 1992)

Contents

Italics are used in this draft to highlight major themes. They are not necessarily intended to denote a superior status to the passages italicised.

The recognition of items in financial statements

1 – Introduction

Recognition is the process of incorporating an item into the primary financial statements. It involves depiction of the item in words and by a monetary amount and the inclusion of that amount in the statement totals. 1

The objective of financial statements is to provide information about the financial position, performance and financial adaptability of an entity that is useful to a wide range of users in making economic decisions. Primarily, this objective is met by recognising items in financial statements where those items meet certain criteria. 2

Items that satisfy the recognition criteria given below should be recognised in the appropriate statement(s). The loss of information resulting from the failure to recognise such items is not rectified by disclosure. However, recognition of an item does not preclude disclosure of further information about it where that improves understanding of the item. In addition, the notes to the financial statements should provide information about items that fail to meet the recognition criteria where knowledge of them is relevant to the users' understanding of the financial statements. 3

2 – The Features of Recognition

(A) GENERAL RECOGNITION CRITERIA

Recognition

An item should be recognised in financial statements if: 4

(a) the item meets the definition of an element of financial statements; and
(b) there is sufficient evidence that the change in assets or liabilities inherent in the item has occurred (including, where appropriate, evidence that a future inflow or outflow of benefit will occur); and
(c) the item can be measured at a monetary amount with sufficient reliability.

Chapter 3 sets out definitions of the elements (ie of assets, liabilities, equity, gains, losses, contributions from owners and distributions to owners): this chapter concentrates on whether or not an item that meets one of those definitions should be recognised. 5

Separability is not included in the recognition criteria, and a lack of separability does not disqualify an item from being recognised. Even where an item is inseparable from the entity, information about it may still be useful to users of financial statements. Hence, provided the criteria given above are met, the item still merits recognition. 6

Derecognition

7 The criteria for ceasing to recognise assets and liabilities (derecognition) are similar to those for recognition. *An item should cease to be recognised as an asset or liability (together with recognition of any consequent change in equity) if:*

(a) the item no longer meets the definition of the relevant element of financial statements; or

(b) there is no longer sufficient evidence that the entity has access to future economic benefits or an obligation to transfer economic benefits (including where appropriate, evidence that a future inflow or outflow of benefit will occur).

8 The majority of this chapter is a discussion of the above criteria. Prior to this discussion and in order to set it in context, paragraphs 9 to 20 describe the recognition process, and paragraphs 21 to 26 describe how uncertainty affects this process and gives rise to the need for recognition criteria.

(B) THE RECOGNITION PROCESS

What triggers recognition?

9 *Recognition is triggered where a past event indicates that there has been a measurable change in the assets or liabilities of the entity.* Because of the way equity, gains, losses, contributions from owners and distributions to owners are defined (as assets less liabilities, and increases or decreases in these), for the definition of any of the elements to be met there must have been a change in the entity's assets or liabilities – either the obtaining of a new asset or liability, or a change in (including the disposal of) an existing one.

10 *The event that triggers recognition must have occurred prior to the balance sheet date.* Financial statements attempt to capture in financial terms the effects on the entity of events occurring up to a certain date; they do not anticipate future events. Consequently, there must be some past event that triggers the recognition of a change in the entity's contemporary assets and liabilities, even though the measurement of this change may reflect views on the amount of benefits that will flow to or from the entity in the future. For example, if an item of stock is sold after the balance sheet date, this transaction is not recognised in the current reporting period. However, it may highlight a need to reduce the carrying value of the stock at the balance sheet date, by providing evidence of the monetary amount of the future benefits that were then recoverable from it.

11 *There are three classes of past events that may involve a measurable change in assets or liabilities and hence that may trigger recognition: transactions, contracts for future performance ('contracts'), and other events.*

(a) Transactions

12 *A transaction is a transfer of assets or liabilities to or from an external party.* Because they involve a transfer of assets or liabilities, both fully performed contracts and partly

performed contracts (to the extent performance has occurred) amount to transactions; whereas contracts where performance by all parties lies in the future do not. For example, both cash sales and credit sales are transactions, but the placing of an order with no payment being made is not. Although a transfer of assets or liabilities is required for a transaction, an exchange of assets or liabilities is not necessary – transactions include both exchange transactions and donations to or by the entity. Finally, an external party is required for a transaction – thus whilst the purchase of a fixed asset constitutes a transaction, use of the asset in the business of the entity does not.

(b) Contracts

A contract is an enforceable, but as yet unperformed, promise given to or by an external party to transfer assets and/or liabilities in the future. It includes both contracts where neither party has performed to any extent (eg a lease that takes effect after the year end where both delivery of the leased property and payment of the first rental have yet to occur), and the unperformed part of contracts where at least one party has partly performed, but both parties have something left to do under the contract (eg a lease that is part way through its term where the leased item must continue to be made available and future lease payments are still outstanding). However, performance by one party to a contract, whether by physical delivery, provision of services or payment, amounts to a transaction. Conversely, a mere decision to enter into a transfer of assets or liabilities in the future, but where no promise has yet been given to an external party, does not constitute a contract. **13**

(c) Other events

Other events are changes in assets and liabilities other than transactions and contracts. **14** Examples are changes in market prices, the elapse of time, the manufacture of goods, and decisions taken by third parties that affect the entity (eg decisions by government regarding taxation).

Once it is established that a transaction, contract or other event has occurred, it is **15** necessary to decide the nature of the items involved. *To the extent a past event has resulted in access to future economic benefits (or obligations to transfer economic benefits) assets (or liabilities) are recognised; to the extent that it has resulted in previously recognised access to future economic benefits (or obligations to transfer economic benefits) being transferred or ceasing to exist, assets (or liabilities) are derecognised; and to the extent that it has resulted in a flow of economic benefits in the current period, a gain or loss is recognised (unless the flow relates to a transaction with owners, in which case a contribution from owners or distribution to owners is recognised).* The same past event often results in the initial recognition of some assets and liabilities, the derecognition of others, and/or the recognition of a gain or loss (eg a sale of stock on credit results in the initial recognition of a debtor, ceasing to recognise the item of stock, and the recognition of a related gain or loss).

Recognition of assets and liabilities

16 *The recognition of assets and liabilities falls into three stages:*

(a) *initial recognition* (ie incorporation of an item into financial statements for the first time). Initial recognition is most commonly triggered by transactions or contracts (eg recognition of a fixed asset may be triggered by a purchase transaction or a lease contract), although occasionally other events result in initial recognition (as where the accidental pollution of the environment gives rise to the initial recognition of a liability);

(b) *subsequent remeasurement* (ie changing the monetary amount at which a previously recognised item is recorded). Following initial recognition, events may occur that affect the recognised item, and therefore it is necessary to test at intervals thereafter to see if the recorded amount needs to be changed. This second stage of subsequent remeasurement is triggered by other events (eg amortisation of a leasehold property may be triggered by the passage of time, and its revaluation may be triggered by a change in market prices); and

(c) *derecognition* (ie the removal from the financial statements of a previously recognised item). Finally, events may occur that mean recognition of an item is no longer appropriate. Derecognition is most often triggered by transactions or contracts (eg the sale of stock), although occasionally it will result from other events (eg the destruction of an asset in a fire).

Recognition of gains and losses

17 *At any stage in the recognition process, where a change in assets if not offset by an equal change in liabilities a gain or a loss will result (unless the change relates to a transaction with owners, in which case a contribution from owners or distribution to owners will be recognised). Gains and losses should be recognised either in the profit and loss account or in the statement of total recognised gains and losses.* Gains and losses by their nature are single period items, and the three stage process described above for assets and liabilities is not relevant to them. Whilst another event in a subsequent period may give rise to the recognition of a new gain or loss in that period, it will not give rise to the remeasurement or derecognition of a prior period's gain or loss.*

Measurement of recognised items

18 *Where initial recognition is triggered by a transaction, any asset acquired or liability assumed will be measured at the amount inherent in the transaction (ie the amount of assets or liabilities given or received as consideration).* Where initial recognition is triggered by a contract, as discussed in paragraph 34, each party will usually record an

**Although accounts of a period are subject to continuous revisions of judgements made in earlier periods, such revisions are normally accounted for as giving rise to a new gain or loss. As stated in chapter 6, it will normally only be useful to restate a prior period's gain or loss following the correction of a material fundamental error in the recognition of gains or losses or a change in an accounting policy that would have affected the disclosure of past results.*

asset and a liability of equal amount, measured with respect to the size of that party's obligation under the contract (although this amount may be ascertained by reference to the amount of any asset received).* There is a presumption that the transaction or contract is carried out at fair value; hence, in the absence of evidence to the contrary, any asset acquired or liability assumed will be measured at the value inherent in the transaction or contract, and no gain or loss will result in respect of this newly recognised item†.

Where a previously recognised item is disposed of or settled in a transaction, the item will again be measured at the amount inherent in the transaction (ie the amount of assets or liabilities received as consideration or given in settlement). If this is different from the carrying value of the asset or liability immediately prior to the transaction a gain or loss will arise. Similarly, where an item ceases to be recognised as a result of a contract, the gain or loss will be measured with respect to the size of the entity's obligation under the contract, taking particular care not to include any element of unearned future profit (see paragraphs 34 and 56 below). **19**

Following this description of the recognition process, paragraphs 21 to 26 deal with how uncertainty affects that process and results in the need for recognition criteria. The application of those criteria is then addressed in the remainder of the chapter. **20**

(C) THE EFFECT OF UNCERTAINTY

The recognition process described above does not deal with the effects of uncertainty. *The environment in which entities operate is inherently uncertain and for many past events there is either a lack of certainty that there has been a change in the entity's assets or liabilities, or a lack of certainty as to the monetary amount of the change. It is this lack of certainty that gives rise to recognition problems.* **21**

Chapter 2 states that in order for financial statements to provide useful information, they must be both relevant and reliable. Furthermore, it is often necessary to achieve a balance between these two primary qualitative characteristics: an item may be relevant in that it meets the definition of an element and is therefore likely to influence users' decisions, but to be useful the information also needs to exhibit valid description with freedom from error and hence be reliable. Valid description with freedom from error means both that the description of an item is a faithful representation of that item (its nature and existence), and that given the item's description, the monetary amount ascribed to it is a reasonably accurate one. The uncertainty inherent in the environment in which entities operate means complete reliability is unattainable. However, where there is a high degree of uncertainty recognition of an item may be misleading, and ultimately the level of uncertainty may become so great that recognition would cause the financial statements to cease to be useful. **22**

**Measurement problems that may arise (eg where recognition is triggered by a non-monetary transaction or contract or by other events) are discussed in paragraph 42.*

† Where a transaction or contract results in the disposal of a previously recognised item, a gain or loss will arise in respect of the item disposed of – for instance a sale of stock on credit will give rise to a recognised gain or loss on the item 'stock'. However, no gain or loss results in respect of the newly recorded debtor.

23 *Uncertainty is countered by evidence – the more evidence there is about an item and the better the quality of that evidence, the less uncertainty there will be over its existence, nature and measurement, and the more reliable the item will be.* Hence, the recognition criteria specify that an item should only be recognised if there is sufficient evidence about it. Evidence is required both that a change in the assets or liabilities of the entity has occurred (recognition criterion (b) – 'evidence of occurrence'); and of the monetary amount at which to measure the change (recognition criterion (c) – 'reliability of measurement').

24 *In dealing with uncertainty, prudence requires more persuasive evidence (of both occurrence and amount) for the recognition of items that result in an increase in equity than for the recognition of items that do not.* This is to ensure that assets and gains are not overstated, and liabilities and losses are not understated. *In addition, since profit as stated in the profit and loss account is used as a prime measure of performance, prudence requires particularly good evidence for the recognition of gains in the profit and loss account.* However, the exercise of prudence does not allow for the omission of assets or gains where there is sufficient evidence of occurrence and reliability of measurement, or for the inclusion of liabilities or losses where there is not. This would amount to the deliberate understatement of assets or gains, or the deliberate overstatement of liabilities or losses.

25 What constitutes sufficient evidence is a matter of judgement in the particular circumstances of each case: the evidence must be adequate, but need not be (and usually cannot be) conclusive. The nature of the evidence will vary from item to item; it will include all relevant information that becomes available up to the time when the financial statements are prepared and that relates to conditions existing at the balance sheet date. Evidence is provided primarily by past or present experience with the item itself or with similar items. This will include evidence provided by the event that triggers recognition (eg the cost of purchasing stock), past experience within a group of similar items (eg the levels of losses arising in the past on stock of different ages), and current information directly relating to the item (eg the current physical condition of items of stock, their current selling price, and current levels of orders for them). It will also include evidence provided by transactions of other entities in similar assets and liabilities. Where such transactions are frequent and the items traded are very similar to the one held by the entity (ie there is an efficient market in homogeneous items), the evidence will be strong and is likely to be sufficient for recognition; as the frequency of transactions decreases or differences between the items traded and the one held by the entity increase, the evidence will become less persuasive and is less likely to be sufficient for recognition.

26 The activities of an entity are a continuous process, and for many items there may be several events that could trigger recognition. For example, in a sale transaction there may be several major events in the sale process, each of which provides a different level of evidence of the existence and amount of a gain and an associated increase in assets: these could include completion of production; receipt of an order; delivery; and receipt of payment. Different points may provide sufficient evidence for recognition in different cases. Although deciding on the timing of recognition often involves the exercise of

judgement in the circumstances of a particular case, the recognition criteria given in paragraph 4 set out the general principles that are relevant. The remainder of this chapter explains the application of these criteria in more detail.

3 – The General Recognition Criteria Explained

CRITERION (A) – DEFINITIONS OF ELEMENTS

The elements and their interaction form the basis on which financial statements present relevant information in a structured manner – hence, *the first condition for recognition is that the item constitutes an element as defined in Chapter 3*. Reference should be made to that chapter for a full understanding of these definitions. 27

CRITERION (B) – EVIDENCE OF OCCURRENCE

The various past events that may trigger recognition (ie transactions, contracts and other events), by their nature provide differing degrees of persuasiveness that a change in assets or liabilities has occurred. 28

Transactions

A transaction, by definition, always involves an obvious change in the composition of the assets and liabilities of the entity. Hence *arm's length transactions provide conclusive evidence that a change in assets or liabilities has occurred (ie evidence of occurrence), and always call for recognition. However, transactions not at arm's length can give rise to recognition problems due to a lack of independence.* This often results in a need for additional disclosure about the transaction and, in the extreme, may result in the need to modify its recognition so as to represent faithfully the substance of the transaction. 29

Contracts

Contracts only provide sufficient evidence of occurrence where there is a 'firm commitment' – ie the obligation of the reporting entity resulting from the contract can be enforced by an external party (usually by another party to the contract) and the circumstances are such that the obligation will be enforced by the other party if necessary. For there to be a firm commitment, the contract must incorporate features such that the reporting entity is compelled (either commercially, or legally and practically) to perform the transfer. The contract feature that most commonly indicates a firm commitment is provision for a severe penalty on cancellation (ie a penalty so large that the entity would perform under the contract rather than incur it). However, the existence of a severe penalty is only one possible indication of a firm commitment, and it is neither necessary nor sufficient. 30

In addition, for a firm commitment to exist, it is necessary that the quantities to be supplied and amount to be paid under the contract can be determined. For example, an agreement to provide such goods in the future as a customer shall require on terms to be agreed would not merit recognition. 31

Where, as in most contracts, there is not such a firm commitment, there will be significant 32 *uncertainty over whether the necessary change in assets or liabilities has occurred, and hence insufficient evidence for recognition.* For instance, in most routine sale and purchase orders there will not be a firm commitment as the reporting entity is not compelled to perform the transfer: *inter alia* this will be indicated by the fact that the entity could cancel the contract without incurring a severe penalty. Even where the other party has the legal right to sue for performance or damages or to levy a penalty on cancellation, there may not be a firm commitment if it would not do so in practice because of cost/benefit considerations. For instance, some contracts between suppliers and their customers, or employers and their employees, incorporate penalty provisions that would not normally be invoked in the case of cancellation, as the costs of doing so (such as legal fees, loss of clientele, loss of customer/employee goodwill) exceed the benefits. Such contracts do not give rise to firm commitments and hence should not result in recognition.

33 Conversely, there is more likely to be a firm commitment where the other party would suffer substantial loss were the reporting entity to cancel the contract. For instance, contracts for major items or specialised products that are produced to order are more likely to give rise to a firm commitment – either on signing the contract or as goods are produced – than are routine orders for standard items. Even where there is no provision for a severe penalty to be paid on cancellation there may be a firm commitment if the other party could enforce the contract or sue for damages in a court of law and the scale of loss is such that it would actually do so.

34 *Where a contract gives rise to firm commitments for both parties they should recognise their respective obligations.* An example is a contract for the hire of an aircraft, where the contract covers a material period of time and carries a severe penalty on cancellation by either party that would be enforced in practice due to the contract's size. Here the aircraft owner should recognise its obligation by ceasing to recognise that part of its interest in the aircraft that it has agreed to pass to the hirer (and recognise an asset 'debtor'), and the hirer should recognise its obligation to pay future rentals (together with the corresponding asset 'rights to use aircraft'). Other examples of such contracts include long term contract work in progress, purchase commitments and take or pay contracts (ie contracts that oblige an entity to pay a fixed sum, which may be offset against any purchases made by that entity in the period)*.

35 *Contracts should be measured with respect to the size of the obligation, with the result that for sales contracts, gains will not generally arise.* Thus the elements recognised will usually be assets, liabilities and, if applicable, losses. Gains should not generally be recognised because until performance has occurred any gain will not be earned, the increase in assets resulting from the contract being matched by an increase in obligations (this is discussed further in paragraph 56). Thus, in the example above of a contract for the hire of an aircraft, the asset and liability recognised by the owner

**The application of the principle given in this paragraph is subject to the usual cost/benefit and materiality criteria. Its implementation in the form of an FRS would represent a major change from existing practice and will be considered by the Board as its work programme permits. In this regard it should also be noted that one of the stated aims of the Board is to take account of the desire of the financial community for evolutionary rather than revolutionary change, where appropriate.*

should exclude any profit element. The only exceptions to this are circumstances in which at the point the contract is entered into a gain is already earned, as for instance where the gain is not performance or time related and no other material event associated with it remains outstanding.

A reason often given for non-recognition of contracts is that, as performance lies in the future, recognition of a contract merely anticipates the future activities of the business, which are best reflected in future years' accounts. Whilst this is a valid reason for deferring the recognition of any unearned gain to a future period, it is not a valid reason for failing to recognise the assets and liabilities involved. The existence of a firm commitment means there is sufficient evidence that a change in the assets or liabilities of the entity has already occurred. The persuasiveness of the evidence is of the same order as if performance had occurred, and hence these contracts call for recognition in the same way as do transactions. 36

Other events

The nature of other events is such that they often provide less persuasive evidence of a change in the assets or liabilities of an entity than do transactions or contracts. Other events are of two types:- 37

(a) *other events that involve a change in the benefits associated with an asset or liability. Here there may be very persuasive evidence of occurrence.* For example the destruction of a factory as a result of a fire provides very strong evidence of a change in an asset or liability, as does the passage of time for items such as accrued interest where a change in benefits is time related;

(b) *other events that merely involve the revaluation of the flow of benefits associated with an asset or liability, but not a change in the benefit flows themselves.* Examples are a change in the value of a piece of land or a freehold property (apart from that due to any physical deterioration) where the benefits of occupation are unchanged but the monetary value of those benefits is affected by market price changes. *Here the nature of the event does not, of itself, provide clear evidence that a change in an asset or liability has occurred.* In such cases, evidence of occurrence and reliability of measurement amount to the same thing – ie evidence of a change in the monetary amount of an unchanged flow of benefits. *Hence, particular care must be taken to ensure the evidence is sufficient for recognition, especially where the recognition of a gain is involved.* Transactions by other parties in similar assets and liabilities may provide sufficient evidence of a change in value, but only if they are frequent and the assets and liabilities involved are sufficiently similar to that of the entity. For this reason, while such a potential change in value is a candidate for recognition, not all such changes are recognised. Whether or not a change is recognised will depend on the particular circumstances of each case: relevant considerations are the persuasiveness of the available evidence and the nature of the item (whether it increases or decreases equity).

In practice, these two types of other event may occur in the same period and they may be indistinguishable. For example, the monetary amount of a leasehold property may be affected both by the passage of time that reduces the benefits of occupation inherent 38 in the property (a type (a) event) and by changes in market prices (a type (b) event). In some instances, and particularly where the two types of other event provide different levels of evidence, they may be accounted for separately (eg a leasehold property may be both depreciated to reflect the passage of time and revalued to reflect a change in market prices). In other instances, it may be difficult to distinguish changes arising from each type of other event and it will be more practicable to account for them both together.

39 Decisions that affect the entity (whether taken by the entity itself or by an external party) are also other events. *A mere decision to enter into a transaction in a future period does not of itself provide sufficient evidence for recognition.* There will not be sufficient evidence of a change in the entity's assets or liabilities unless and until such time as the entity either enters into a transaction or the circumstances are such that it has a firm commitment. For example, a decision taken prior to the balance sheet date to purchase a fixed asset in the following period does not provide sufficient evidence for recognition, and its effect should not be anticipated by recognition in the current reporting of a possible future transaction or contract. However, future transactions may provide evidence that a previously unrecognised asset or liability existed at the balance sheet date, or evidence that the monetary amount of a previously recognised item had changed. For example, the payment of a taxation charge after the balance sheet date in respect of a previous period may provide evidence that a liability for the taxation existed at the balance sheet date, and the price at which an item of stock is sold after the balance sheet date may provide evidence of a decline in the net realisable value of stock prior to the balance sheet date.

CRITERION (C) – RELIABILITY OF MEASUREMENT

40 Reliability of measurement means that, for a given basis of measurement, different measurers of an item will arrive at amounts that are not materially different. *Reliability of measurement is affected by the amount of evidence available about two factors:-*

(i) the expression of the benefits inherent in the item in monetary terms, and
(ii) the size of these benefits (both the spread of possible levels of benefit and the chance of any particular level of benefit occurring).

For instance, in measuring a freehold property there may be frequent monetary transactions in similar properties that indicate a relatively narrow range of possible amounts (with an amount towards the middle of the range being significantly more likely than one at either extreme), and that provide a reliable means of expressing the benefits of the property in monetary terms. In this case different measurers will arrive at market based estimates of the monetary amount that are not materially different, and the property can be measured reliably. Conversely, a project to research a new chemical may have a wide range of possible outcomes ranging from zero benefit (if unsuccessful), through some benefit (if it results in a product for which there is only low demand) to a very high level of benefit (if it results in a unique product for which there is high demand), and until the research progresses there may be very little evidence of what the outcome will be. Also, there will usually be no direct market in similar research projects by which to translate these benefits into monetary terms. The monetary amount of this asset is much less certain, and different measurers may arrive at amounts that are materially different.

(i) The expression of an item in monetary terms

The amounts of some assets and liabilities (commonly referred to as monetary items) are fixed in terms of numbers of pounds sterling; this facilitates their expression in monetary terms*. However, for those monetary items which will not be paid in the near future, the future cash flows inherent in them need to be discounted in order to obtain their value at the balance sheet date. Discounting involves uncertainty as to what is the appropriate discount rate, and hence affects reliability of measurement.† As the effect of discounting is greater where payment of a cash flow is further away, short term monetary items can be expressed in monetary terms with more reliability than can long term ones. **41**

Some non-monetary items result either from an arm's length transaction for a monetary asset or liability, or from a firm contract that specifies a monetary amount to be paid in the future. These can be measured by reference to the monetary item; hence, on initial recognition and subject to any need for discounting, problems of their expression in monetary terms will not arise. However, those non-monetary items that result from barter transactions, barter contracts or other events can only be expressed in monetary terms by reference to monetary transactions in similar assets and liabilities. For such items, the ability to express them in monetary terms depends on both the frequency of monetary transactions in similar items, and on the extent of any differences between the items traded and the one held by the entity (including differences between the date of those transactions and the balance sheet date). **42**

(ii) Uncertainty over the size of benefits inherent in an item

Reliability of measurement means that the monetary amount of the recognised item under the stated measurement basis and description given is free from material error – it does not necessarily imply that the recognised item is free from material variation of possible future outcome. However, where there are a number of materially different possible outcomes, perhaps occurring at different times, different measurers may not agree on the amounts, timing and likelihood of the various outcomes and thus may arrive at amounts for the item that are materially different. Hence problems of reliability of measurement may arise unless either a means can be found of reducing the variability of outcome, or there is sufficient evidence about the item for different measurers to agree on the various possible outcomes and their likelihoods of occurrence. **43**

Where an item has several materially different outcomes, there are three means by which this variability of outcome can be overcome and a reliable measure with **44**

**The same principles apply where the amount of an item is similarly fixed in terms of another currency, provided there is an active market for that currency.*

†If the item bears interest at a variable market rate, assuming this rate is deemed to be the appropriate discount rate, the value of the item will equal its principal amount and these problems will not occur.

significantly less variability obtained. First, where the item has resulted from a recent arm's length transaction, the item can be measured at the transaction price (ie at 'historical cost') – it can reasonably be assumed that on initial recognition this is an appropriate measure of the various probabilities of the various possible levels of future benefit flow. Secondly, where there is no transaction price (eg on subsequent remeasurement or where a donation or barter transaction triggers initial recognition) but there is a reasonably efficient market for the item, a market based measure* can be used to measure it – here the market consensus over the amount of the benefits inherent in the item means the market based measure will have a low variability of outcome, and thus be a reliable measure. Finally, where the entity has a group of homogeneous but not identical items, the expected value of the entire group can be used† – provided the group is of a sufficient size the expected value will also have a low variability of outcome, and its use permits the group as a whole to be measured reliably.

45 Where none of the above three situations applies – ie the entity has a single item for which there is neither a reasonably efficient market nor a recent measurable transaction – it will not be possible to reduce the variability of outcome of the item by use of an appropriate measurement basis. In such instances, in order to give relevant information to users, a measure is required that enables users to form a view about the amounts, certainty and timing of future cash flows. Hence, a measure is required that takes account of all possible outcomes, and their respective likelihoods of occurrence. The expected value of future outcomes from continuing to hold the item is such a measure and, provided it can be ascertained with sufficient reliability, should be used.

46 For some items there will not be enough information available about the various possible outcomes and their respective likelihood of occurrence to arrive at a reasonably reliable expected value. In such a situation, if there is some minimum level of benefit flow that is reasonably assured, the item should be recognised at no less than the value of this minimum, and disclosure given of the range of other potential outcomes‡. If it is not possible to form a reasonable estimate of a minimum level of benefit flow, the item will not merit recognition. However, it will be necessary to disclose its existence and to describe the nature of the item and the uncertainty involved.

**In this context market based measures (also referred to as 'market prices') include replacement cost and net realisable value. What is the appropriate basis of measurement is the subject of Chapter 5.*

† Expected value is a weighted average of all possible outcomes, calculated using the probability of occurrence of an outcome as its weight. For a group of similar items, different items will have different outcomes, with the number of items having a particular outcome being related to the probability of that outcome. Hence, the expected value will represent a reasonable estimate of the monetary amount of the benefits associated with the entire group. For instance, in assessing the level of a bad debt provision, whilst it may be unlikely that any individual debt will prove to be bad, for a large population of receivables, some degree of non-payment is normally expected; hence a loss representing this expected reduction in economic benefits should be recognised. If each debt were to be considered individually and measured at its most likely outcome, each debtor might be judged more likely than not to pay, and hence no bad debt provision would be made. However, this clearly would not represent a reasonable measure of future economic benefits for the entire group.

‡ As discussed further in paragraph 50, the application of prudence may mean that a potential loss (and any related liability) subject to uncertainty of measurement should be recognised at an amount higher than this minimum.

Assessments of the probability of a future flow of economic benefits of a given level (and hence of expected value) are made on the basis of available evidence, and the principles given in paragraphs 24 to 26 are relevant. Such assessments may be based on evidence gained from past experience within a group of similar items (eg the probability and amount of warranty claims for a given product), or on evidence gained from current information directly relating to the item (eg the probability of a loan guarantee being called upon, based on the current financial standing of the borrower). In particular, the existence of a recent arm's length transaction involving the item, or of market prices reflecting transactions in very similar items, provides evidence that the probabilities of the various possible levels of future benefit flow can be appropriately measured at the monetary amount of the transaction or market price*. **47**

Where a number of materially different outcomes are represented by a single number this may create an impression of certainty of outcome that does not in fact exist. Hence, where the item is significant, clear disclosure is required; this should include the fact there is uncertainty of outcome, the range of possible outcomes, the basis of measurement and the principal factors that affect what the outcome will be. **48**

The use of reasonable estimates

The uncertainty inherent in the environment in which entities operate means that for many items there will not be complete reliability of measurement and the item will have to be estimated. *The use of reasonable estimates is a normal part of the preparation of financial statements and provided a reasonably reliable estimate can be made of the item it should be recognised.* **49**

Prudence has the effect that less reliability of measurement is required for the recognition of a loss than for a gain. Hence, where an estimate of an item is available but there are significant doubts as to the reliability, a loss should be recognised in circumstances where a gain subject to similar uncertainty would not be recognised until its amount is better evidenced. If despite some uncertainty as to the exact amount of the item it is reasonably assured that at least some minimum change in the entity's assets or liabilities has occurred, the change should be recognised at no less than the monetary amount of this minimum. In this latter situation, *applying prudence may also mean that a potential loss subject to uncertainty of measurement should be recognised at a higher amount than a potential gain subject to the same degree of uncertainty. The recognition of the gain should be restricted to an amount that is reasonably assured; the recognition of the loss should be at an amount that it is reasonably assured is sufficient.* **50**

Although the effect of prudence is that more reliability of measurement is required for the recognition of some items than for others, even for gains recognised in the profit and loss account the use of reasonable estimates may be appropriate. For example, the **51**

****This illustrates that, in practice, expected values are used intuitively when estimating the amount of an item. Expected value is the concept that underlies estimates based on previous experience, transaction prices and market prices.***

degree of completion of a long term contract, and the total gain currently expected to arise from the contract need to be estimated if any gain on the contract is to be recognised prior to its completion. Where a reasonable estimate can be made, the gain (often referred to as the 'attributable profit') may be recognised as the contract progresses, although in the face of uncertainty prudence dictates the amount of the gain recognised be restricted to a level that, given the available evidence, is reasonably assured.

52 Where, despite significant uncertainty relating to measurement of an item, the item is recognised at a reasonable estimate, disclosure is required of the degree of uncertainty surrounding the estimate and of significant assumptions used in arriving at it, in order that the information is useful for making economic decisions. Such disclosure is relevant in assessing both the timing and certainty of generation of future benefit flows, and also in assessing the stewardship of management. For example, the calculation of the pension charge for a defined benefits scheme depends on a number of assumptions, including future rates of inflation and pay increases, earnings on investments, the number of employees joining and leaving the scheme and mortality rates. Each of these may be subject to a high degree of uncertainty, and a reasonable estimate must be made. This uncertainty does not preclude the recognition of a pension charge, but disclosure of the key assumptions used significantly enhances the usefulness of the information.

4 – The Recognition Of Gains and Losses

(A) THE RECOGNITION OF GAINS

General Considerations

53 *The recognition of gains involves consideration of whether there is sufficient evidence that an increase in equity (ie in net assets) had occurred before the end of the reporting period. This is referred to as the gain being 'earned'.* Where a potential gain had not been earned at the end of a reporting period, it is not a gain of that period; hence it should not be recognised as a gain until the future period (if any) in which it becomes earned. Being earned is discussed further in paragraphs 56 and 57 below.

54 *Prudence requires stronger evidence for the recognition of gains than for the recognition of other items. Accordingly, the recognition of a gain requires strong evidence of both the existence and monetary amount of an increase in equity.*

Recognition of gains in the profit and loss account

55 As for all gains, gains recognised in the profit and loss account must have been earned – ie they must not belong to a future period. In addition, as profit as stated in the profit and loss account is used as a primary measure of performance, prudence requires particularly strong evidence (of both the existence and amount) of the gains that comprise it. Hence, *gains should only be recognised in the profit and loss account when, in addition to the general recognition criteria being met, the following are satisfied:-*

(a) the gain is earned – that is there is no material transaction, contract or other event that must occur before the change in the assets or liabilities of the entity inherent in the gain will have occurred; and

(b) the gain is realised – that is one of the following is met:-

(i) a transaction whose value is measurable with sufficient reliability has occurred. In addition, for a transaction involving an exchange, the assets or liabilities exchanged must be dissimilar or monetary; or

(ii) the gain results from a change in an asset or liability of a type not held for continuing use in the business, and the resultant asset or liability is readily convertible to known amounts of cash or cash equivalents; or

(iii) the gain results from a liability expiring, being cancelled or otherwise ceasing to exist.

(a) The Gain is Earned

The requirement that gains be earned ensures that revenue received in advance of performance does not give rise to the recognition of a gain, since until performance occurs the increase in assets resulting from the revenue will be matched by an increase in liabilities. For instance, an annual subscription for a monthly magazine received at the start of the subscription period is not earned until the entity produces and delivers the magazine – until that time the entity has a liability (in the form of an unfulfilled obligation to supply the magazine or to make a refund) of a monetary amount equal to the consideration received*. **56**

Some gains are earned over a period of time as performance occurs. For example, profit on a long term contract may be earned over several accounting periods as the contractor performs (this being the only material act outstanding). For shorter lived items that result from the entity's revenue generating activities, being earned often takes the form of a critical event having occurred (the critical event being the point in the operating cycle where the most important decision is taken or the most critical act performed); hence gains resulting from changes in the market price of commodity stock held by a trader could be earned if no significant marketing or selling effort is required. For items that represent remuneration from others for the use of the entity's resources and hence that accrue over time (eg royalties, interest, rents), being earned takes the form of the appropriate time having elapsed. For items where the entity has completed all it needs to do, but a third party still has some act to perform (eg sales contingent on acceptance by the buyer, sale or return), this third party action should be taken into account. **57**

(b) The Gain is Realised

The requirement that gains be realised ensures that recognition of a gain in the profit and loss account is restricted to items whose existence and amount is particularly well evidenced. This usually means that conversion into cash or cash equivalents must **58**

Paragraph 18 notes that where a transaction gives rise to the initial recognition of a liability there is a presumption that the transaction is carried out at fair value. Hence the liability assumed will initially be measured at the value inherent in the transaction and no gain or loss will arise.

either have occurred or be reasonably assured. Hence, in most cases, gains will not be recognised in the profit and loss account until evidenced by the more persuasive evidence of a transaction (eg a sale of goods). Changes in value may be caused by other events (eg the manufacture of goods, and possibly a change in the market price of those goods), but until evidenced by a transaction they are not normally recognised in the profit and loss account.* For instance, a holding gain on a freehold property should not be included in the profit and loss account as the entity still has to enter into a sale transaction, and until such a transaction occurs there is insufficient evidence of the gain for recognition in the profit and loss account.

59 Requirement b(i) in paragraph 55 has the result that a barter transaction may give rise to the recognition of a gain in the profit and loss account provided the transaction is sufficiently measurable. An example is the exchange of a freehold property for a readily disposable quantity of shares in a quoted company. The requirement that any items exchanged be dissimilar or monetary prohibits the recognition of a gain in the profit and loss account where, for example, one freehold property is swapped for an essentially equivalent one with a similar use in the business, as in this case no material change has occurred in the future benefits to which the entity has access.

60 Requirement b(ii) has the result that a gain may be recognised in the profit and loss account where no transaction has taken place provided certain strict criteria are met. In this context, 'known amounts' mean either

(a) evidenced by quoted prices available in an active market that can rapidly absorb the quantity held by the entity without significantly affecting the price; or
(b) the price is specified in a contract of exchange relating to the asset or liability in question, and there is no significant uncertainty relating to the amount of the item; for example uncertainty over the collectability of the item, the specified price, the amount of any related costs, or the extent of any returns.

61 Under this requirement the attributable profit on a long term contract may be realised (and hence recognised in the profit and loss account), as may gains on commodity stocks for which there is an active market and gains arising from the marking to market of readily marketable current asset investments. However, this requirement prohibits the recognition in the profit and loss account of gains on most stocks held by the entity (as there is not usually an active market with quoted prices – and they may not be earned as outlined above), and the recognition of a gain in the profit and loss account arising from an increase in the market value of most long term investments (as they are of a type held for continuing use in the business).

62 Requirement b(iii) states that a gain resulting from a liability that has ceased to exist should be recognised in the profit and loss account.† For example, the expiration of a

**Paragraph 60 sets out the limited circumstances in which such gains should be recognised in the profit and loss account. In addition, as discussed in paragraph 63 where such gains do not qualify for recognition in the profit and loss account, they may nevertheless qualify for recognition in the statement of total recognised gains and losses.*

†If a liability is repaid in a transaction criterion b(i) applies.

previously recognised liability under a guarantee given by the entity would result in a gain being recognised in the profit and loss account.

Gains or potential gains that fail the tests of being earned and realised may nevertheless meet the general recognition criteria. Such items should not be recognised in the profit and loss account. Where earned but not realised they should be included in the statement of total recognised gains and losses; an example is an unrealised holding gain on the revaluation of a property. Where not yet earned they do not represent a gain of the current period, hence their recognition as a gain should be delayed until such time as they are earned; an example is a magazine subscription received in advance of performance. **63**

(B) RECOGNITION OF LOSSES

The recognition of losses involves consideration of whether there is sufficient evidence that a decrease in equity (ie in net assets) had occurred before the end of the reporting period. Prudence dictates it should be assumed that any economic benefits acquired in the period or brought forward from a previous period have expired or been consumed in the current period (with the consequent recognition of a loss) unless there is evidence to the contrary – ie evidence that the item satisfies the criteria for the recognition of an asset. Similarly, prudence dictates it should be assumed that any expenditure incurred in the period results in a loss unless there is evidence either that it contributes to the generation of future benefits sufficient for the recognition of an asset, or that it reduces a previously recognised obligation to transfer benefits in the future sufficient for the derecognition or reduction of a liability. **64**

The process commonly referred to as 'matching' is, *inter alia*, a means of ensuring that where there is sufficient evidence that expenditure has resulted in access to future economic benefits, an asset is recorded until the period in which those benefits are consumed or expire – at which time a loss is recognised. Matching means that expenditure that has a direct association with the generation of specific gains should be recognised as a loss in the same period as the gains are recognised, rather than in the period in which the expenditure is incurred. However, the application of the matching concept does not allow the recognition of items in the balance sheet which do not meet the definition of assets, liabilities or equity. **65**

When expenditure results in economic benefits that arise over several accounting periods and the association of the expenditure with the generation of specific gains can be only broadly or indirectly determined, an asset should be recognised and subsequently expensed on a systematic basis over the periods in which the benefits arise. Where evidence of intermediate values of the item cannot be directly obtained with sufficient reliability, it may be reasonable to assume that the item declines in a systematic manner over its expected life. This process forms part of the accepted methods of dealing with uncertainty. As noted above, perfect certainty of measurement is not required for recognition, and assuming this process results in a reasonable estimate of the asset and loss, they may be recognised on this basis. However, periodic reviews are required of the recorded amount of the asset to ensure there is sufficient evidence that future benefits of not less than this amount will occur. **66**

67 Where expenditure has no association (direct or indirect) with the generation of specific gains in the future, it should be recognised as a loss in the period in which it is incurred. This will be the case when expenditure produces either no future economic benefits or future economic benefits that do not meet the recognition criteria for an asset. The recognition of a loss does not imply that management's intention in incurring the expenditure was other than to create economic benefit – it may be that the benefit has already occurred, or that there is insufficient evidence of future benefit to warrant recognition of an asset.

68 Additionally, a loss should be recognised when, and to the extent that, previously recognised assets have been reduced or eliminated, or cease to quality for recognition as assets. Finally, a loss should be recognised where a liability is incurred or increased without an equivalent increase in recognised assets, as for example where the elapse of time results in an increase in the monetary amount of a deep discounted bond (and the consequent accrual of interest).

5 – Derecognition

69 The criteria for derecognition of assets and liabilities are given in paragraph 7 above. They are similar to those for recognition.

CONDITION (A) – DEFINITION OF ELEMENTS

70 *Derecognition is appropriate where a past event has eliminated a previously recognised asset or liability.* Thus derecognition of an asset is appropriate where the rights or other access to future economic benefit that comprise the asset have been exercised, cancelled, have expired or otherwise ceased to exist, or where they have been transferred to others. Similarly, derecognition of a liability is appropriate where the obligations to transfer economic benefits that comprise the liability have been discharged, cancelled, have expired or otherwise ceased to exist, or where they have been transferred to others.

CONDITION (B) – EVIDENCE OF OCCURRENCE

71 *Derecognition should also occur where the expectation of a future benefit flow on which recognition was originally based is no longer sufficiently strong to support continued recognition.* Hence, derecognition of an asset is appropriate when due to a change in circumstances there is no longer any level of future benefit flow that is reasonably assured; derecognition of a liability is appropriate where it is reasonably assured no future flow of economic benefit will occur. In both instances the monetary measure of the item will be nil.

72 Whilst conceptually the elimination or transfer of an asset or liability (condition (a) above) is not the same as measurement at nil value due to insufficient evidence of a future benefit inflow or outflow (condition (b) above), the two have the same effect in financial statements – that of derecognition. For example, previously capitalised development costs in respect of a new product may cease to qualify for recognition as an asset if the introduction of an alternative product by a competitor means profitable future sales of the new product are not reasonably assured. Conceptually this is not the same as transferring the rights to exploit the new product, but nevertheless both result in derecognition.

Discussion Draft
Statement of Principles Chapter 5
Measurement in financial statements

(Issued March 1993)

Contents

Measurement in financial statements

INTRODUCTION

1 This chapter deals with the principles underlying the measurement of the elements of the balance sheet (assets, liabilities and equity) and of the components of the statements of financial performance* of a reporting entity.

2 The three elements of the balance sheet, and their relationship can be defined by the fundamental balance sheet identity, ie:

Assets, less liabilities = equity (capital).

It might seem to be an obvious statement that owners of equity have the residual claim on the net worth of the business, but it has important implications for the balance sheet and the statements of financial performance. The identity draws attention to the fact that the method of measuring assets and liabilities will determine the amount at which capital is measured. Moreover, if assets and liabilities are measured upon different bases, the residual term, equity, will be a hybrid measure whose significance is not immediately clear.

3 Capital does not measure the economic wealth of an entity because, in practice, the goodwill inherent in the equity is not fully reflected in the balance sheet and assets are not shown at current economic value. Similarly, 'total recognised gains and losses' does not measure the change in 'wealth' in a period as the statements of financial performance do not measure the changes in the entity's economic wealth but only those changes in net assets (other than injections or distributions of capital) recognised during the year.

4 Chapter 4 states that 'recognition is triggered where a past event indicates that there has been a measurable change in the assets or liabilities of the entity'. Gains and losses which are recognised broadly emerge either from transactions or from other events. In a simple trading entity, total recognised gains and losses would be determined by transactions and would be fully reflected in profit which compares the revenue derived from goods sold to the value of the assets consumed in producing that output. In more complex entities other events would lead to remeasurement of certain assets and liabilities and to the recognition of gains or losses which are of a different nature to profit. Such gains or losses are taken to reserves rather than the profit and loss account but nevertheless form part of the entity's total recognised gains and losses, ie:

Profits + other gains and losses = total recognised gains and losses.

5 Total recognised gains and losses can be derived either by considering each event or transaction affecting the entity individually (a 'transactions-based approach') or by considering the transactions in aggregate by comparing the opening and closing capital

**See chapter 6 – 'presentation of financial information'.*

of a period. Whichever approach is used, the same overall measure of the total recognised gains and losses of a period will result. In practice, accounting is transactions-based and does not simply compare opening and closing capital of a period to measure gains and losses. In addition, the transactions-based approach, unlike the aggregate approach, reveals the components of the changes in an entity's net assets during a period and gives users of financial statements important information in the form of a detailed breakdown of profit and other gains and losses. Such components of the gains and losses give users information about the quality of particular gains and losses and can indicate whether they are realised, relate to readily realisable assets or liabilities or relate to assets essential to the entity's operations which are unlikely to be sold.

6 Using the transactions-based approach, a coherent measure of total recognised gains and losses can only be made if profits are calculated by using a consistent basis for the value of the assets consumed to produce the output and a similar consistent basis is used to calculate the other gains and losses. Similarly, coherent measures of 'total recognised gains and losses' in aggregate can only be made if the opening and closing measures of net assets (capital) are measured on a consistent basis and are adjusted for any capital-introduced (such as subscriptions for shares in companies) and capital withdrawn (such as dividends paid by companies). The total of changes made to the value of assets and liabilities to ensure that a consistent measure is adopted is called the capital maintenance adjustment. Total recognised gains and losses are measured only after capital has been maintained.

7 Paragraphs 39 to 58 below discuss the influence of capital maintenance concepts on the measurement of profit and other gains and losses.

RECOGNITION

8 Chapter 4 – 'The recognition of items in financial statements' details the recognition process for assets and liabilities. This defines the following criteria for recognition:

(a) the item meets the definition of an element of financial statements; and
(b) there is sufficient evidence that the change in assets or liabilities inherent in the item has occurred (including, where appropriate, evidence that a future inflow or outflow of benefit will occur); and
(c) the item can be measured at a monetary amount with sufficient reliability.

9 Initial recognition most commonly occurs as a result of a transaction such as the purchase of an asset. The measurement method for first recognition, therefore, will typically be a cost based method. Thus assets and liabilities are normally recorded initially at the transaction cost. There is a subsequent recognition stage which is referred to in chapter 4 as remeasurement. Remeasurement involves changing the monetary amount at which an asset or liability is recorded when the recognition criteria for a change are met. Such a change will normally be attributable to events rather than transactions, for example, the effluxion of time giving rise to the need for depreciation, the diminution in value of an amount owed by a debtor to allow for the possibility of a

bad debt, or a change in value of a marketable security from that used in the initial transaction.

VALUATION OF ASSETS

Measuring assets at monetary amounts is a process of valuation. Historical cost is the method arising from traditional, transactions-based accounting and is used on initial recognition. For remeasurement the method used is usually a form of current value, based upon observations of current market values or the assessment of the current value of the benefits to be derived from using an asset. Current value will usually be the same as historical cost at the initial recognition stage, subsequent events causing the two to diverge at the remeasurement stage. 10

Historical cost

Historical cost is the actual cost of acquiring an asset and thus emerges naturally from the recording of assets. However, there are variants of the historical cost method that arise from the exercise of judgement. These include: 11

(a) transaction costs – the costs of acquisition may include a range of fees and charges incurred in buying the asset;
(b) barter transactions – sometimes assets may be exchanged for other assets and, since the price does not necessarily emerge from the transaction, it will be necessary to impute a historical cost by reference to prices prevailing at the time of the deal; and
(c) allocation across assets – assets may be bought in groups and it may be necessary to allocate the total consideration to the individual assets. An example is the imputation of 'fair value' to assets acquired on the purchase of a business.

Historical cost has the advantage of being widely practised over a long period of time. It is, therefore, familiar to users and preparers of financial statements and it is probably the cheapest valuation method from the point of view of preparers, who have standard methods in place for calculating historical costs (including depreciation and other time allocations), and users, who are used to receiving and interpreting historical cost information. From the point of view of the preparer, the relative cheapness of historical cost is not merely due to its advantage as the incumbent method, but also arises from its transactions base, which avoids regular revaluations. Modifications to the historical cost system are dealt with further in paragraphs 15–17 below. 12

Apart from relative cheapness, historical cost is usually considered to be a relatively objective and therefore reliable method of accounting. This again derives from its transaction base, which provides a dependable and verifiable historical foundation for the valuations that are used. However, this claim has to be moderated to the extent that the time allocations and other accruals in historical cost accounting are based upon a degree of subjective judgement. This is most obvious in such areas as depreciation and the evaluation of work completed under long-term contracts but the difficulty exists potentially on many other occasions when accruals have to be made. The only method of historical cost accounting that could, in principle, be made entirely free of subjective 13 judgement is a cash flow statement, which can avoid the use of any form of accrual information. Thus, any claim for the objectivity and reliability of the historical cost system must be based upon its relative freedom from subjective judgement when compared to alternative systems rather than on its absolute freedom from these problems.

14 The main disadvantages of the historical cost system stem from the fact that it records values at the date of acquisition of the specific assets and, accordingly, historical costs are typically established at dates earlier than that of the financial statements. The dates at which historical costs are recorded will typically be different for different assets and it can thus be argued that, in periods of changing price levels, historical cost lacks the property of comparability, both between different assets owned by the same entity and between different entities at any given time. Moreover, only in the most unusual circumstances will historical cost once recorded continue to represent assets at current prices. Thus, historical costs in financial statements are not expressed in homogeneous units of measurement; the cash received from sales made today is compared with the cost of stock purchased at a previous date; holding gains and trading gains are presented in an aggregate figure the significance of which is not clear.

15 If the effect of changing prices is perceived as important, for example, because there has been rapid inflation, the historical cost measures can be restated in units of current purchasing power by using a general purchasing power index. This is discussed in paragraphs 48–51 below. Such a conversion is essentially a translation exercise and not a revaluation exercise. That is to say it restates historical cost figures which are £'s of different purchasing power into a common unit, usually the current £, rather than attempting to deal with the specific price change of a particular asset. However, the retranslation of the cost of each asset at a common date does avoid the problem of heterogeneous measurement units.

16 Current prices are more relevant than historical costs for measuring the current financial position of a business and the current costs of generating its profits (e.g. in terms of depreciation charges or costs of stock consumed). It has also been suggested that historical cost is poorly understood, particularly by non-accountants; empirical studies confirm that balance sheets are typically interpreted by non-accountants as conveying the current values of assets.

17 It is notable that traditional historical cost accounting has been modified in practice to include revaluations in certain cases. This is evidence of demand for current values and of their relative reliability. On the other hand, revaluations are confined to specific circumstances (as in the use of lower of cost or net realisable value), types of asset (such as investment properties) and industries (such as dealers in marketable securities for the application of the 'marking to market' rule). Thus, current practice is a pragmatic compromise between the tendency to stay with historical cost because of its simplicity and perceived objectivity and the pressure to adopt current values in cases where they are perceived to be particularly relevant and accessible, and significantly different from historical cost. It is not necessarily indicative of a demand for a comprehensive system of current value for all assets in all circumstances, although the trend of practice in recent years has been towards a greater use of current values.

Current values

Current value can be perceived from two points of view, that of the purchaser of the asset (entry value) and that of the seller (exit value). If a market exists for a particular asset, the value that the market puts upon that asset is one means of arriving at its entry and exit values. A further method of arriving at current value is to be found in the value in use (present value) approach. These three methods of arriving at current value are more fully described below: **18**

(a) *Entry values* – these are based upon the cost of acquiring an asset in current market conditions. An important distinction is that between 'reproduction cost' and 'replacement cost'. Reproduction cost is the cost of acquiring an identical asset, whereas replacement cost is concerned with acquiring identical services at the lowest cost, given changes in costs and productive techniques that may have occurred since the original asset was acquired.

    Unless the entity is constrained in the way it is able to replace its assets; replacement cost will always be less than or equal to reproduction cost, reflecting the current least cost burden of replacing the benefits to be derived from an asset, is likely to be of greater relevance to current economic decisions.

(b) *Exit values* – these are based upon selling prices. However, it may not be realistic to assume that an entity has a real opportunity to benefit from current selling prices; there may be costs of sale and the sale process may take time. In such cases, the net realisable value of the asset will be different from its selling price (typically, lower, because selling costs and the delay in receiving the sale proceeds need to be taken into account). Net realisable value rather than selling price is the more relevant concept for decision-making purposes, as this represents the economic opportunity that might be realised if the asset were sold.

(c) *Value in use* – this is the present value of the net future cash flows (including any cash flows resulting from the ultimate disposal of the asset) that can be obtained by retaining the asset in the business and using it in the most 'profitable' manner possible. Instead of being realised by sale in the market the asset is realised by use in the business. Value in use is calculated by discounting the estimated future cash flows associated with the asset at a suitable discount rate.* For example, the method may be used in the evaluation of leasing transactions.

    The higher of value in use and net realisable value is therefore the maximum value that an entity can recover from an asset that it already holds. This is called the asset's recoverable amount.

The various current values share some areas of ambiguity with historical cost and also have some special difficulties of their own. The most obvious difficulty with the current **19**

A wider discussion on discounting, including examples of its application within an historical cost system, can be found in the Discussion Paper TR773 – 'The use of discounting in financial statements' issued in December 1989 by the Institute of Chartered Accountants in England and Wales. (Editor's note: See Part Nine of this volume.**)*

value rules is that they deal with current opportunities that, by definition, have not yet been realised, whereas historical cost has a grounding in actual events (past transactions). Thus, current values are regarded as particularly subjective items of information. The subjectivity increases as the opportunity moves further into the future; value in use (requiring estimates of discount rates and the amount and timing of future cash flows) is usually considered to be the most subjective of all current value measures.

20 There is a further difficulty which is peculiar to current values, being that of aggregation, i.e. at what level is the value of the asset to be assessed: the reporting entity as a whole, the division, the branch or factory, the building or machine, or even the components of the building or machine? The sums of values measured at a more detailed level will not necessarily equal aggregate values measured at a higher level (e.g. the value of a machine is not necessarily the sum of the values of its components) but financial statements record aggregate values. It is thus necessary to take a decision as to the level of aggregation at which the valuation should be made. Historical cost avoids this difficulty by measuring the assets piecemeal as they are acquired.

21 Current values are probably perceived to be less reliable than historical costs. Certainly the historical cost of an asset can usually be established with greater objectivity than its current value except where the asset is traded in active and efficient markets. The estimation of the written down value of a depreciating asset poses difficulties under either historical cost or current value methods unless there is an active second-hand market in the assets, in which case a current value method might be more reliable than a historical cost method as the latter method involves estimates of accumulated depreciation. Thus, the relative reliability of historical cost and current value depends to a great extent on whether a ready market is available in a particular type of asset. For example, there is more reliability in the current values of marketable securities, which are traded in highly efficient and active markets, than in those of highly specific fixed industrial plant, which is not.

22 It should also be noted that current values avoid some of the difficulties of historical cost. Notably, as stated in paragraph 14 above, the dates at which historical costs are recorded are usually different for different assets. Using current values for all assets avoids this problem as all assets are measured on a uniform basis. Also, the allocation problem can be avoided if suitable market values are available, for example, written down values can be based on market prices of part used assets rather than on depreciation, which is an allocation of historical costs.

23 Current values have the advantage of relevance to the current state of the business. They are also likely to be comparable insofar as they reflect economic conditions at a common time and they will be understandable to non-accountants who expect financial statements to be measured in current prices.

Value to the business

24 Each method of valuation (entry values, exit values and value in use) has some potential contribution to make to the economic evaluation of an entity. However it would be expensive and possibly confusing to provide information on several alternative bases. There is a concept of current valuation that makes use of all of the alternatives: the value to the business rule. This is an eclectic concept of valuation drawing on the individual valuation methods. The value to the business rule has been advocated by economists, who see merit in its relevance to the economic opportunities facing the reporting entity; it reflects the potential benefits to an entity from owning an asset (or the potential loss from being deprived of it) by measuring the minimum amount that the proprietor would lose if deprived of the asset. The resulting value has variously been called opportunity value, deprival value and value to the owner, as well as value to the business.

As a practical solution to the problem of deciding which of the current values to use in **25**
the remeasurement process, the application of the value to the business rule provides a means of selecting a valuation method which is appropriate to the circumstances. In situations where there is no economic justification for replacing the services of an asset it would be inappropriate to use replacement cost. Hence, as explained in paragraph 26, the basic value to the business rule is to use replacement cost or recoverable amount, whichever is the lower. The value to the business method focuses on the basic concept of the value of a particular asset to the particular entity. If deprived of an asset, an entity would normally replace that asset if replacement would be worthwhile but, if it is not worth its replacement cost, then the sum its future services are worth is its value to the business.

The value to the business rule values the assets at replacement cost if the recoverable **26**
amount is higher i.e. if the asset is one which the entity would replace. If replacement is not justified the asset is valued at its value in the most profitable use i.e. recoverable amount. Recoverable amount is the higher of value in use and net realisable value. Thus the value to the business of an asset will equal or fall between replacement cost and its net realisable value.

This principle can be stated as follows:

If the asset is worth replacing then use *replacement cost.*

If the asset is not worth replacing, but;
(a) is worth keeping, then use *value in use.*
(b) is not worth keeping, the use ***net realisable value.***

This principle can be illustrated as follows:

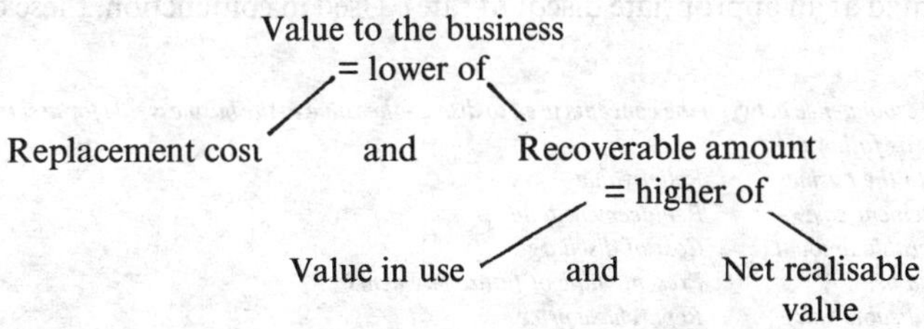

27 The choice between current values is an important issue. In some cases, particularly where there are efficient and inexpensive markets in the asset, the choice between replacement cost and net realisable value will not result in materially different amounts but in other cases the difference may be material. Value in use is a highly subjective method of valuation that would often not pass the test of reliability as a basis for financial reporting and, because of the problem of allocating future cash flows to individual assets, is often more suited to valuing the business as a whole rather than its constituent assets. In those cases where value in use is not a sufficiently reliable measure to result in the recognition of a change in the value of an asset the asset should be valued for financial reporting purposes at replacement cost or net realisable value as appropriate. Despite their subjectivity, estimates of value in use may be of use in making the choice between replacement cost and net realisable value: when the value in use is greater than replacement cost, replacement cost would be used, and when it is lower than both net realisable value and replacement cost, net realisable value would be used. The value is use may also, in certain limited cases, be suitable for valuing assets. Indeed, value in use is a method used for actuarial applications and may also be used in circumstances where there is no market (i.e. no frequent transactions) for the asset concerned.

28 The value to the business rule was the fundamental valuation basis used in the current cost accounting standards issued in the UK by the Accounting Standards Committee (Statement of Standard Accounting Practice No. 16, 1980) and in the USA by the Financial Accounting Standards Board (Financial Accounting Standard 33, 1979), although it was modified for practical purposes (e.g. the explicit use of value in use was not required by SSAP 16).

VALUATION OF LIABILITIES

29 In theory, liabilities can be regarded as negative assets; liabilities are obligations to transfer benefits, whereas assets are rights to receive benefits. If this view is accepted, then the same range of choice of valuation method is available for liabilities as is available for assets.* We thus have a choice between historical cost (the amount originally received for the liability, plus any accrued charges such as 'rolled-up' interest), and current value, namely: replacement loan (the highest loan that could be raised now by incurring the same obligations to pay future interest and repayments of principal as attach to the present loan); repurchase price (the amount at which the loan could be disposed of by repurchase in the market place); and the present value of the future payments required by the loan (including both interest and principal and discounted at an appropriate discount rate). Used in conjunction, these current values

**The correspondence between the concepts used to discuss the value to the business rule for assets and liabilities can be set out as follows:*

Value to the business	*Relief value*
Replacement cost	*Replacement loan*
Recoverable amount	*Cost of discharge*
Value in use	*Present value of future payments*
Net realisable value	*Repurchase price*

provide an equivalent to the value to the business concept which can be applied to liabilities. This is known as relief value.

Relief value

The relief value is the maximum benefit that the entity could obtain if it were relieved of 30
the liability. Relief value is defined as the higher of replacement loan and the cost of discharge. The cost of discharge is the lower of repurchase price and the present value of future payments.

This principle can be illustrated as follows:

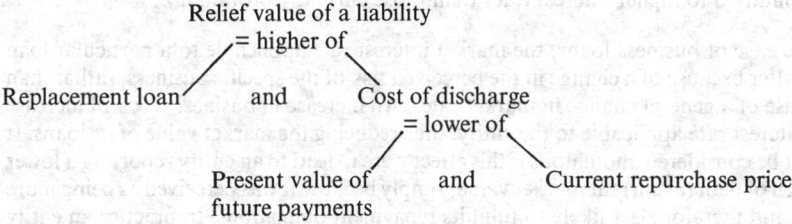

Relief value of a liability
= higher of

Replacement loan — and — Cost of discharge
= lower of

Present value of future payments — and — Current repurchase price

Consideration of the relief value rule suggests that, in practice, the choice between the 31
different current values for loans is probably not a very important issue. If competitive capital markets are available, we would not expect to find a large difference between the repurchase price of a loan and the amount of loan that could be raised in the market for identical terms; any differences being a result of transaction costs (such as arrangement fees or brokerage charges). Equally, we would expect a close correspondence between both of these amounts and the present value of the future outlays necessary to satisfy the loans to maturity. The market value of a traded security is the market's view of the present value of the future cash flows. Apart from transactions costs there would normally be no material differences between the three elements of the relief value model. However, where loan markets are imperfect or incomplete to a serious extent, it may not be possible to determine the value of a replacement loan or the current repurchase cost of the existing loan. In these circumstances the present value of the future payments would need to be used as the valuation basis.

Divergences between the historical amount and current value of liabilities

A more important choice in practice is likely to be whether current value (on any basis) 32
should be used in preference to the historical amount raised. This choice is not likely to be important in all cases. For example, in the case of a bank loan redeemable without penalty at nominal value and subject to a variable market rate of interest, the difference between the historical amount raised and the current value is unlikely to be significant. Divergences between the amount raised historically and the current value are, however, likely to arise where liabilities carry fixed interest rates or where they can only be redeemed other than at their nominal amount. These divergences result from two sources: *(i)* changes in market interest rates; and *(ii)* premiums or discounts on redemption.

(i) Changes in market interest rates

33 Changes in market interest rates are the principal source of the variations in the market prices of fixed interest securities, such as the 'gilt-edged' securities issued by the Government; similar principles apply to business loans. A rise in the market rate of interest will reduce the present market value of a fixed interest loan (because a similar loan would now carry a higher rate of interest) and a fall in interest rates will increase its market value. In such cases there is a change in the effective burden of the loan (as measured by its current market value); an increase in interest rates gives rise to a fall in the burden (the entity gains because it borrowed at lower rates than those currently prevailing) and a decrease in interest rates raises the burden (the entity loses because it is committed to higher interest rates than those currently prevailing).

34 In the case of business loans, the market interest rate applicable to a particular loan may alter because of a change in the perceived risk of the specific business, rather than because of a general change in market rates. An increase in business risk will increase the interest rate applicable to the entity, thus reducing the market value of its loans. It might be considered anomalous if this effect were to lead to an entity reporting a lower burden of debt (at current market value) simply because it was perceived as being more risky and therefore less likely to fulfil its repayment obligations. In practice an entity whose debt reduces in value as a result of increased business risk is unlikely to be able to benefit; any repurchase of the debt (at a discount) would have to be financed by further borrowing which would carry the same interest payments (because at a higher rate) as the bought in debt. The notional capital gain would not, therefore, be recognised until the need for refinancing ceases.

(ii) Premiums or discounts on redemption

35 Premiums or discounts on redemption of a liability can lead to the current value of the loan reflecting 'rolled-up' interest as in the case of a deep discount bond. Even within the historical cost system of measurement, it has been argued that the implicit interest charge in such arrangements should be accrued in such a way that the issue discount or redemption premium is charged over the life of the bond rather than being charged at the time of redemption. The current method of dealing with this under historical cost accounting uses a methodology based on discounting using the same techniques as current valuation. This is not, however, a method of arriving at a current value: it uses a fixed rate of interest (the settlement rate) rather than reflecting changes in interest rates during the life of the loan. Relative to current valuation, this imparts a degree of certainty into the measurement method and a degree of stability into the annual profit and loss charge for the loan, but it does so at the cost of relevance to current economic conditions. Such a method of accruing interest charges will not reflect the current market value of the bond except in the rare circumstances when it is based on the same rates of interest as the market has applied in its valuation of the bond.

Valuation issues

36 One issue which is unlikely to be important in the measurement of liabilities is the unit of measurement. It is inappropriate in the historical cost system to restate liabilities by the application of a general purchasing power index because they are usually denominated in money units. If, as is usual, they are denominated in money units and repayable in those units without adjustment for price changes, restatement would be misleading, as it would imply that the debt was a constant real rather than nominal (money) burden.* The so-called 'gain on borrowing' which arises under current purchasing power accounting systems (under inflationary conditions) is due to the fact that, for income measurement purposes, such systems restate loans along with all other items represented by opening capital but do not restate loans in the closing balance sheet. Such capital maintenance issues are discussed in the next section of this chapter. If, as an alternative to historical cost, liabilities are valued at current market values, these will be expressed in current money units. Provided that current money units are regarded as the appropriate unit of account for financial reporting purposes there would be no need to restate the liabilities.

Liabilities of short duration do not pose a valuation problem (their redemption being imminent). Equally, when the liability is a longer term loan subject to variable interest rates at market rates, divergences between historical costs and current values are unlikely to be material. Liabilities of long duration not subject to variable interest rates at market rates will often have a value that is ascertainable, by a process of discounting, as the amount and timing of the future cash flows required to service and eventually extinguish the liability are usually known with reasonable certainty. **37**

Historical cost will not reflect changes in market interest rates where liabilities carry fixed interest, nor will it necessarily reflect a liability's redemption terms; its use may, therefore, give a misleading view of the entity's current financial position from the point of view of the equity investor and from the point of view of those users of financial statements who attempt to use the balance sheet gearing ratio (debt/equity) as a measure of the burden of indebtedness.† Current values may give more relevant information and should be used where to do otherwise would give a misleading impression of the burden of the reporting entity's indebtedness. **38**

THE INFLUENCE OF CAPITAL MAINTENANCE ON THE MEASUREMENT OF GAINS AND LOSSES

As described in the Introduction to this chapter the measurement of 'gains and losses' involves a calculation of profit and the determination of other gains or losses forming part of total recognised gains and losses. Profit or loss, a major component of total recognised gains and losses, is assessed by comparing the value of the assets consumed in producing the output sold with the revenue from that output. The value of the assets consumed in the production of the output is usually the benchmark to measure profit. It is only after the entity has recovered that value that profit results. Similarly, the **39**

**The same argument applies to assets, such as cash, which are denominated in money units. They give rise to 'losses on holding monetary assets' in a CPP system, under inflationary conditions.*

†This is not to say that the use of the current value of debt will solve entirely the difficulties of using this ratio; the value of the equity interest also has to be assessed on a relevant basis, and this implies an appropriate measure for assets.

opening value of assets and liabilities is used as a benchmark in the assessment of other gains and losses. Accordingly, when calculating total recognised gains and losses in aggregate the value of opening net assets is used as the benchmark against which closing net assets are compared (after allowing for capital withdrawn or introduced) to assess whether an entity has made overall gains or losses during the accounting period.*

40 In the case of both the measurement of total gains and losses and of 'profit or loss' it is necessary to determine the manner in which the benchmark is to be valued. The central problem is one of measuring opening net assets in terms which are suitable for comparing them with closing net assets (for the assessment of total gains and losses) or one of measuring assets consumed for comparison with revenues (for the assessment of 'profit or loss'). The capital maintenance concept adopted, therefore, determines the amount and significance of both the 'total gains and losses' and the 'profit or loss' that are recognised.

41 In a pure historical cost system 'profit' emerges by comparing the selling price of the sold assets (revenue) with their original purchase price (expenses). Where the historical cost system has been modified and certain assets have been revalued to a form of current value, 'profit' reflects the difference between the selling price of the assets and their revalued amounts. The revaluation gain or loss on the assets is part of total recognised gains and losses but is not included in 'profit'.

42 The transactions-based approach and the comparison of opening and closing capital approach will result in the same overall measure of total gains and losses. The transactions-based approach is, however, critical to the measurement of profit or loss and will be appropriate for the purposes of measuring the trading component.

43 Two features of the capital maintenance process should be noted:

(a) the process consists of ensuring that capital at the end of a period is measured on the same basis as that at the beginning. The differences between the various capital maintenance concepts lie in their differing interpretations of what is meant by measuring opening capital and closing capital 'on a common basis';

(b) more than one method of capital maintenance can be used at different levels in a single set of financial statements.

44 There are three alternative basic capital maintenance concepts: nominal money capital; constant money capital; and physical capital. These are discussed below.

Nominal money capital maintenance

45 The nominal monetary unit is the simplest and perhaps the most intuitively appealing of the capital maintenance concepts. It is also the one used traditionally by accountants. To determine total recognised gains and losses the method is simply (after

**Gains and losses other than profit (which together with profit comprise total recognised gains and losses) are calculated in a manner similar to total gains and losses and, to avoid repetition, are not discussed further in the following paragraphs.*

allowing for capital withdrawn or introduced) to deduct the opening nominal money capital (appearing in the opening balance sheet) from the closing nominal money capital (appearing in the closing balance sheet). To measure 'Profit or loss' the original nominal money value (historical cost) of the assets consumed in generating sales is deduced from the revenues produced from those sales.

However, pure historical cost accounting is not always implemented in practice as **46** certain assets are revalued. In addition, certain types of gains or losses are excluded from the profit and loss account and credited (or debited) direct to reserves. For example, unrealised gains arising on the revaluation of fixed assets to current value are carried directly to reserves. Consequently, the profit and loss account (which reflects current law and practice regarding profit recognition) does not on its own measure the increase in nominal money capital in the period. However, the statement of total recognised gains and losses adds the various reserve movements to calculate total gains after maintaining nominal money capital.

As a benchmark to measure total recognised gains and losses the nominal money **47** capital maintenance concept can be used in conjunction with a system of current value or current cost accounting. If in the first period of an entity's operations opening capital were to be shown at its nominal money values and closing capital were to be valued at current values or current cost, total gains and losses would show the change in net assets of the company attributable, not only to its trading, but to the changing values of its portfolio of assets. In later periods the change in net assets would only be reflected on this basis if assets were regularly revalued to current values and opening capital was not restated from closing capital of the prior period.

Current purchasing power (constant money) capital maintenance

Current purchasing power (CPP) or constant money capital maintenance requires that **48** the opening value of net assets (to measure total recognised gains and losses) or assets consumed in the generation of sales (to measure 'profit or loss') be restated by applying a general price level index so that each is measured in the same purchasing power units as closing net assets or sales respectively.

Simply taking the historical cost of the opening assets and restating them by a single **49** general index to reflect the change in purchasing power from the beginning of a period to the date of disposal (or, if retained, the end of the period) would fail to reflect the true change. Instead, opening net assets have to be adjusted initially to ensure that their components are stated in terms of the purchasing power applying at the beginning of the period. Only then can net assets be restated to account for the change in purchasing power during the period.

In a full current purchasing power system the only elements of the closing balance sheet **50** that will not be restated are those denominated in money units (monetary assets and liabilities) since the amount of the claim on or by third parties remains the same in money terms. The CPP system brings out the useful additional information that in real terms there has been a loss on holding money or a gain on borrowing in a period of inflation, when the restated opening balance sheet is compared with the closing CPP balance sheet. However, the CPP system does not reflect any change in the specific value of non-monetary assets (principally fixed assets and stocks) relative to the general price level. The implicit assumption that such asset values follow the general price level may be invalid and, therefore, misleading. This weakness is addressed in the combination of CPP and current value, or current cost, systems considered in the next paragraph.

51 Opening net assets within a current value or current cost system can be restated in terms of current purchasing power to indicate how much the closing amount of the entity's net assets has increased over the period relative to a general purchasing power index. This relative change is what is called a real terms* measure of total recognised gains and losses. This combined system has the advantage that it shows both the total gain or loss for the period in terms of nominal changes in current values (as described in paragraph 47) and that part of the gain or loss which goes beyond a mere reflection of changes in general purchasing power.

Physical capital maintenance

52 Physical capital maintenance concepts underlie the calculation of operating profit in systems of replacement cost or current cost accounting. They are, in essence, based on the specific price changes of the assets (and liabilities) held by the reporting entity rather than the general price level changes used by the current purchasing power or real term methods.

53 Physical capital maintenance implies that opening net assets are measured at current prices at the beginning of the period and are then adjusted to reflect specific price changes during the period. This statement of opening net assets revalued at closing values is then deducted from closing net assets in order to calculate total recognised gains and losses. Current cost operating profit is measured after restating the assets consumed in generating revenues to their current cost or value at the time of their consumption.

54 Physical capital maintenance requires that specific non-monetary attributes of the reporting entity are maintained before gains or losses are recognised. These attributes may consist of the specific assets and liabilities of the entity at the start of the period, or they may embrace a broader concept, such as operating capability.† The latter concept requires maintenance of the entity's capacity to produce goods and services, but allows for the fact that the mix of assets necessary to do this may change as technology and input prices change.

**The term 'real' is interpreted in the sense favoured by economists, indicating, in general, command over goods or services rather than a nominal amount of money.*

†The notion of maintaining the specific assets and liabilities of a business is similar to the 'reproduction cost' of obtaining identical assets whereas operating capability maintenance is similar to the replacement cost notion of valuing assets, i.e. the replacement of the benefits (e.g. output) to be derived from the assets.

Combining capital maintenance concepts

The three basic capital maintenance concepts have been described in the context of particular asset (and liability) valuation systems since the initial capital measure, to which any maintenance adjustment is applied, depends upon the measurement of the assets and liabilities included in that capital. **55**

The simplest and traditional concept of capital maintenance is based on nominal money capital. It has undoubted intuitive appeal (as a simple money amount) and it is consistent with the existing asset and liability valuations currently incorporated in financial statements. It thus seems likely that it will remain an important feature in the profit and loss account and statement of total recognised gains and losses. Its potentially serious weakness is that it does not capture the effect of price changes, but fortunately it does not exclude the use of other methods of capital maintenance since it is possible to combine it with measures reflecting price changes. **56**

Within an accounting system that measures assets and liabilities at current prices, it is possible to combine physical capital maintenance with other methods of capital maintenance. Physical capital maintenance (specific price adjustment of capital) is associated with current cost operating profit. It provides an indication of the current trading margin of the business by charging costs of the assets consumed in the production of output at the prices applying when the revenue was earned. This provides users with an insight into the ability of the business to generate profits from its current operations. **57**

In a period of rising prices an entity may have paid less than current cost for the items consumed in its operations. This applies particularly to stocks and depreciation of equipment. These differences are realised holding gains and there may be further gains (unrealised holding gains) arising on assets (such as stock or equipment) held at the end of the period. Even when the profit and loss account is prepared on a pure current cost (specific price adjustment) basis, these gains can be recorded by adding them to current cost operating profit in a statement of total recognised gains and losses. This would record total gains and losses on a nominal money capital maintenance basis. However, it is also possible to restate opening net assets by applying to them the change in purchasing power over the period (as discussed in paragraph 51). This would enable a measure of total 'real' gains or losses to be shown. This would show by how much the net assets of the entity, measured in current prices, had grown in excess of the amount necessary to compensate for what is commonly termed 'inflation'. A system of this type is illustrated (as the 'real terms' system) in the Accounting Standards Committee's Handbook on 'Accounting for the Effects of Changing Prices'. A similar system was proposed by the Byatt Report on accounting for state-controlled enterprises.* An example is given in the Appendix. **58**

**Accounting for Economic Costs and Changing Prices: A Report to HM Treasury by an Advisory Group. 2 vols. HMSO, 1986.*

CRITERIA FOR CHOOSING METHODS OF MEASUREMENT

59 The qualitative characteristics of financial information and the possible trade-offs between them are discussed in chapter 2 – 'Qualitative characteristics of financial information'. That chapter defined relevance and reliability as the primary qualities to be sought in financial information, with comparability and understandability as secondary, but necessary, qualities. Different methods of measurement are likely to have different degrees of relevance and reliability so that there will often be a trade-off between the two primary characteristics. Equally, the secondary characteristics, comparability and understandability, will not necessarily favour one system of measurement. Moreover, the trade-offs may differ according to the type of asset or liability concerned, so that a decision may have to be made as to whether users gain particular benefit from financial statements being prepared on a single measurement principle, or whether it is acceptable to measure different items in the financial statements using different methods. Finally, preparation costs may vary between alternative measurement methods and these must be taken into account when addressing the balance of benefit and cost. These criteria have been referred to earlier in this chapter when discussing the relative merits of each of the measurement methods.

60 The criteria for choosing methods of measurement used earlier in this chapter have relied heavily on the Board's principles set out in chapter 1 – 'The objectives of financial statements'. Essentially this central objective is to provide information about the financial position, performance and financial adaptability of the reporting entity that is useful to a wide range of users in making economic decisions about the entity as a whole The fundamental choice is between the use of historical cost and some form of current value. The evolution, in a number of respects, of practice, law and accounting standards towards current value suggests that in certain areas at least the disclosure of current value information is meeting a widely felt need.

61 This chapter has argued that no single valuation method can cater for every need or would be sufficiently reliable for financial reporting in all circumstances. Hence, it is desirable to apply a system that chooses the valuation method appropriate to the circumstances. The 'cost or net realisable value whichever is the lower' rule is an example of such a method which has a well established tradition in accounting practice. The current value concept which is equivalent to this is the value to the business concept. This can be interpreted loosely as current cost or market value whichever is the lower. For the reasons given in paragraphs 24 to 28, value to the business is the soundest method of valuing assets at the second (remeasurement) stage of recognition; similar arguments apply to the valuation of liabilities. This conclusion at the level of general principles is consistent with an evolutionary development of eclectic valuation methods in response to developing user needs.

62 All three capital maintenance measures have potential user relevance, provided that they are combined with appropriate valuation systems. Moreover, none of the capital maintenance measures has greater reliability than the valuation measures with which they are associated. Nominal money capital maintenance can be used in association with a current value or historical cost valuation system. A current purchasing power (constant money) method has relevance only in conjunction with current valuation or with adjusted historical cost. A specific index method has relevance only in conjunction with a current valuation system. However, it is possible to combine a number of capital maintenance concepts within a single financial statement so that a current valuation system can measure gains relative to three different capital maintenance benchmarks. The 'real terms' system explained in paragraph 58 demonstrates how this can be achieved. This system provides a comprehensive analysis of the changes in an entity's net assets during a period by breaking them down into the components of trading margins and nominal and real holding gains. Users of financial statements are then able to focus on the particular information they require, by contrast with the more limited choice imposed by other systems or combination of systems.

Appendix – Examples of capital maintenance

A company begins the year with share capital and £100 worth of newly purchased stock. Inflation during the year is 5%. The company sells the stock at the end of the year for £200. Replacement cost of the stock is £150.

Opening balance sheet

Share capital	100	Newly purchased stock	100

Profit and loss account

(i) *Nominal money capital maintenance*
(Opening capital £100 – no adjustment)

Sales	200
Less: cost of sales	100
Nominal money profit	100

(ii) *Current purchasing power (constant money) capital*
(Opening capital £100 × 1.05)

Sales	200
Less: cost of sales	105
Current purchasing power profit	95

or

Nominal money profit	100
Less: capital maintenance measure	5
Current purchasing power profit	95

(iii) *Physical capital maintenance*
(Opening capital £100 + 50 (increase in specific prices))

Sales	200
Less: cost of sales	150
Current cost operating profit	50

(iv) *Real terms capital maintenance*

Profit and loss account

Sales	200
Less: current cost of sales	150
Current cost operating profit	50

Statement of total recognised gains and losses

Current cost operating profit	50
Plus gain from holding stock	50
Nominal money profit	100
Less: capital maintenance measure	5
Current purchasing power profit	95

Statement of Principles Chapter 6
Presentation of financial information

(Issued December 1991)

Contents

Presentation of financial information

INTRODUCTION

... It is a very fundamental principle indeed that knowledge is always gained by the orderly loss of information, that is, by condensing and abstracting and indexing the great buzzing confusion of information that comes from the world around us into a form which we can appreciate and comprehend...

Kenneth E. Boulding*

The objective of financial statements is discussed in Chapter 1 of this Statement of Principles. In summary the objective is to provide information about the financial performance, financial position and financial adaptability of an enterprise that is useful to a wide range of users in making economic decisions. 1

This Chapter of the Statement of Principles analyses the way in which information should be presented in financial statements in order to meet this objective. Accounting information is presented in the form of a structured set of financial statements comprising primary statements and supporting notes. The form of presentation to be adopted in a particular case involves consideration of the appropriate prominence and detail of disclosure of information in the primary statements themselves, in the notes and, in some cases, in supplementary information. 2

The primary statements, which must be read in conjunction with their related notes, are: 3

(a) the profit and loss account;
(b) the statement of total recognised gains and losses;
(c) the balance sheet; and
(d) the cash flow statement.

FEATURES OF FINANCIAL STATEMENTS

Paragraphs 5 to 12 discuss the considerations that guide decisions about the arrangement of information in financial reporting. 4

Aggregation

Financial statements result from processing large quantities of data and involve the need to simplify, to condense and to structure. Transactions and other events that affect a dynamic and complex business enterprise are represented by words and numbers in financial statements, which are necessarily highly simplified. Voluminous transactions and other events are interpreted, condensed, combined, and structured by being aggregated into amounts and totals that appear in financial statements. The 5

**Kenneth E. Boulding, Economics as a Science* (New York: McGraw-Hill Book Company, 1970), p. 2.

decision as to the degree of aggregation will depend on the extent to which the benefit of disclosing more detailed information in helping to meet the objective of financial reporting, is offset by the cost not only of preparing and disclosing but also of using that more detailed information. The resulting financial statements convey information that would be obscured from most users if only great detail, such as descriptions of each transaction or event, were provided.

Classification

6 Classification in financial statements facilitates analysis by grouping items firstly by their nature or function. For example, sales are distinguished from any accompanying sales tax and expenses are analysed by broad categories representing either the nature of the cost, such as purchases or employment costs, or their function in relation to the enterprise, such as production, selling and administrative costs. There is, however, a further rationale underlying the classification imposed on items in financial statements: analysis also requires financial information to be segregated into reasonably homogeneous groups. For example, components of financial statements that consist of items with similar characteristics in one or more respects, such as continuity or recurrence, stability, risk, and reliability, are likely to have more value for analysis purposes than components including items with dissimilar characteristics.

Structure

7 The final stage of the process of aggregation and classification is the presentation of components in individual statements of financial performance, financial position and cash flows along with related notes.

8 The prominence to be given to disclosure should be appropriate to the overall significance of the item to an assessment of the financial performance, financial position or financial adaptability of the reporting enterprise.

Articulation

9 Financial statements articulate (interrelate) because they reflect different aspects of the same transactions or events affecting an enterprise. Articulation is more than just double entry bookkeeping. The different primary statements are in general founded on the same judgements and methods of calculation for the differing aspects of related items. Accordingly, ratio analysis of such items as debtors to sales can be used to obtain further insights into the enterprise's financial position, financial performance and financial adaptability. Primary statements contribute, both individually and collectively, to meeting the objective of financial reporting.

Accounting policies

10 The assessment of the results of a period depends on an understanding of the underlying policies, including the assumptions used in the application of those policies, in recording the effects of the activities and events of the period. Disclosure of the accounting policies and significant assumptions adopted by an enterprise, any changes

in them and the effect of such changes, assists users in identifying differences between the accounting policies for like transactions and other events used by the same enterprise from period to period and by different enterprises.

Notes to financial statements

The notes to financial statements should amplify or explain the items in the primary statements and in certain instances could provide either an alternative view of a particular transaction or event to that included in those primary statements, or information on items not included. For instance, a balance sheet might include a particular asset, such as a debt in dispute, at its expected value whereas the related note could disclose the full range of possible outcomes. Where information is disclosed by way of note the wording should present a balanced view and be clear and unambiguous. If information in the primary statements gives an incomplete picture of the financial performance and position of the enterprise, additional information that is essential for an understanding of the financial performance, financial position and cash flows should be included in the notes. The notes and primary statements form an integrated whole. However, a true and fair view is not given by reliance on the notes to correct a misrepresentation in the primary statements. **11**

Supplementary information

Supplementary information is information that is positioned outside the primary statements and notes. Supplementary information may include information that has a different perspective from that adopted in the financial statements, including information that is highly relevant but low in reliability, or information that is helpful to some users but not essential for all. The basis on which it has been prepared should be disclosed and applied consistently, or any change adequately explained. Supplementary information may also include management's explanation of the information given in financial reporting and their discussion of the significance of that information. Although supplementary information is not required to be audited due care should always be taken in its preparation, and such information may be reviewed by the auditors. A true and fair view is not given by reliance on supplementary information to correct a misrepresentation in the primary statements or notes. **12**

INDIVIDUAL PRIMARY STATEMENTS

The material in paragraphs 14 to 30 builds on the general considerations that guide decisions about the arrangement of information in financial reporting contained in paragraphs 5 to 12 and summarises the information that individual primary statements provide. **13**

Statements of financial performance

Statements of financial performance are the profit and loss account, including a note of historical cost profits and losses, and the statement of total recognised gains and losses (in each case together with related notes). They disclose the major components of an **14** enterprise's gains and losses in the broad sense in which these terms are defined in Chapter 3 of this Statement of Principles. Gains and losses, of which income and expenses are a part, are defined as being elements of financial statements.

15 Statements of financial performance contribute to the purposes of financial reporting by:

(a) giving an account of the results of the stewardship of management to enable users to assess the past performance of management and to form a basis for developing future expectations about financial performance; and
(b) providing feedback to users so that they can check the accuracy of their previous assessments of the financial performance for past periods and, if necessary, modify their assessments for future periods.

16 In assessing the overall financial performance of an enterprise during a period, all changes in equity of the enterprise from activities or events need to be considered. The total of such changes, excluding those deriving from capital contributed by or payments to shareholders, is referred to as total recognised gains and losses.

17 Profit or loss of a period is a component of total recognised gains and losses and focuses on revenues for its output (income) that the enterprise has earned and recognised and what it has sacrificed to obtain that output (expenses). It should be noted that gains that are realised in a period but recognised in previous periods are not components of total recognised gains and losses of the period under review.

18 Although the components of total recognised gains and losses will be common to all enterprises, among different enterprises they will exhibit differing characteristics in terms of continuity or recurrence, stability, risk and reliability. The relative importance of the different components of total recognised gains and losses will, therefore, vary among enterprises.

19 A particular item should be reported separately if its disclosure is likely to be significant for appraising the stewardship of management, or as a factor in assessing or reassessing future performance and cash flows. The optimum number of items to be reported separately depends on the considerations regarding the appropriate level of aggregation discussed in paragraph 5.

20 Information about performance is useful in assessing the capacity of the enterprise to generate cash flows from its existing resource base. It is also useful in forming judgements about the effectiveness with which the enterprise has employed its resources and might employ additional resources. Good presentation involves:

(a) reporting separately items that have been unusual in amount or incidence judged by the experience of previous periods;
(b) distinguishing amounts that are affected in different ways by changes in economic conditions or business activity;
(c) giving enough detail, subject to cost considerations, to enable users to understand the composition of gains and losses and their relationship to receipts and payments. For example, it may be relevant to report separately:

(i) expenses that vary with volume of activity or with various components of income;
(ii) expenses whose amount can be varied within a relatively wide range without significantly affecting current revenues and which have been incurred in a period wholly or partly in order to enhance future profitability;
(iii) income and expenses that are unusual in nature; and
(iv) expenses that have special characteristics such as interest and taxation;

(d) distinguishing between the performance of different business segments;
(e) restricting the set-off of positive and negative items within total recognised gains and losses to those instances where knowledge of the gross amounts is not likely to be useful for the assessment of either future results or the effects of past transactions and events; and
(f) distinguishing between different categories of gains and losses the measurement of which is subject to different levels of reliability.

A good starting point for the assessment of future results is the income generated in those operations which are to continue into the future. Hence, presentation of income from continuing and discontinued operations as separate components of profit or loss will be helpful to users. 21

The assessment of total recognised gains and losses by the users of financial statements may depend partly on their ability to associate results of the enterprise with particular time periods so that they can assess the impact of changes in economic conditions on those results. Moreover the usefulness of financial reporting is increased by consistency from period to period and from enterprise to enterprise. However revisions of judgements made in earlier periods are a normal feature of reporting under conditions of uncertainty. The effects of adjustments to estimates made in the ordinary course of preparing financial statements in previous periods are therefore normally included in the financial performance of the current period. For this reason it will normally only be useful to restate past results by way of a prior year adjustment following the correction of a material fundamental error in the recognition of gains and losses or a change in an accounting policy that would have affected the disclosure of past results. 22

Balance sheet

The balance sheet (together with related notes) provides information about an enterprise's equity, those assets and liabilities which have met the recognition criteria and their relationships to each other at a point of time. The balance sheet delineates the enterprise's resource structure (major classes and amounts of assets) and its financial structure (major classes and amounts of liabilities and equity). 23

The financial position of an enterprise is determined by the economic resources it controls, its financial structure, its liquidity and financial viability, and its capacity to adapt to changes in the environment in which it operates. Information about the economic resources controlled by the enterprise, and the extent to which in the past it has been able to adjust the balance of the components comprising those resources, is useful in assessing the stewardship of management and the ability of the enterprise to generate cash in the future. Information about financial structure is a useful input in 24 assessing future borrowing needs and how future profits and cash flows will be distributed among those with an interest in the enterprise; it is also useful in assessing how successful the enterprise has been in managing its resources and how successful it is likely to be in raising further finance. Information about liquidity and financial viability is useful in predicting the ability of the enterprise to meet is financial commitments as they fall due. Liquidity refers to the availability of cash in the near future after taking account of financial commitments over this period. Financial viability refers to the availability of cash over the longer term to meet financial commitments as they fall due.

25 The elements included in balance sheets are assets, liabilities, and equity, each of which is defined in Chapter 3 of this Statement of Principles. As explained in paragraphs 5 and 6 of this chapter it is helpful to the users of financial statements if those items are reported in classes. The main basis for deciding the number of classes and the content of each is that the result should help users to assess the nature, amounts, and liquidity of available resources, their function in use, and the amounts and timing of obligations that require or may require liquid resources for settlement.

26 Information in the balance sheet can contribute directly to users' estimates of the amounts, timing, and probability of future cash flows. Reporting that distinguishes assets by function is useful for this purpose; for example, assets held for sale should be reported separately from assets held on a continuing basis for use in the enterprise's activities, because the difference is important to prospects for future cash flows.

27 A balance sheet does not purport to show the value of a business enterprise. As a result of limitations stemming from reliability of measurement and cost-benefit considerations, not all assets and not all liabilities are included in a balance sheet (eg some contingent liabilities are not included), and some assets and liabilities that are included may be affected by events, such as price changes or other increases or decreases in value through time, that are not recognised or are only partly recognised. Even if all recognised assets and liabilities were to be included at up-to-date values, the total of assets less the total of liabilities would not, except by coincidence, equal the value of the business. However, together with other financial statements and other information, balance sheets should provide information that is useful to those who wish to make their own assessments of the enterprise's value.

Cash flow statement

28 The objective of financial reporting leads to the conclusion that users need information about cash inflows and outflows to help with assessments of liquidity, financial viability and future cash flows and to provide feedback about previous assessments. A cash flow statement (together with related notes) reflects an enterprise's cash receipts classified by major sources and its cash payments classified by major uses during a period. It provides useful information about an enterprise's activities in generating cash through operations and its expenditure of cash to repay debt, distribute dividends, or reinvest to maintain or expand operating capacity; and about its investing and financing activities, both debt and equity, insofar as they relate to receipts and payments of cash. Important uses of information about an enterprise's current cash receipts and payments include helping to assess factors such as risk, the enterprise's liquidity, financial viability, financial adaptability and the way in which profits are converted into cash.

A cash flow statement provides an incomplete basis for assessing prospects for future cash flows because, for example, of the effect of timing differences. Many current cash receipts, especially from operations, result from activities of earlier periods and many current cash payments are intended or expected to result in future cash receipts. As statements of financial performance are prepared using the accruals concept, they adjust cash flows to measure results for a period. For this reason, statements of financial performance used in conjunction with balance sheets and cash flow statements, together provide a better basis for assessing future cash flow prospects of an enterprise than do cash flow statements alone. **29**

Cash flow statements provide significant information about amounts, causes of differences, and timing differences between: **30**

(a) profits or other aspects of total recognised gains and losses; and
(b) cash receipts and outlays.

Users may consider such information in assessing the amounts, timing and probability of future cash flows.

FINANCIAL ADAPTABILITY

Financial adaptability is the ability of an enterprise to take effective action to alter the amounts and timing of cash flows so that it can respond to unexpected needs or opportunities. Financial adaptability will help an enterprise to survive during a time of low (or possibly negative) cash flows from operations perhaps resulting from an unexpected fall in demand. Financial adaptability may also enable an enterprise to take advantage of profitable and unexpected investment opportunities. **31**

Financial adaptability comes from several sources, for example: the ability to raise new capital, perhaps by issuing debt securities, at short notice; the ability to obtain cash by selling assets without disrupting continuing operations; and the ability to achieve a rapid improvement in the net cash inflows generated by operations. **32**

Financial adaptability generally involves making sacrifices as well as gaining an advantage; for example, holding assets that are readily marketable indicates financial adaptability, but may involve acceptance of a lower rate of return than could be earned from holding less liquid assets. Financial adaptability can affect the risks associated with operations to some extent; for example, financial adaptability reduces the risks of failure in the event of a shortfall in net cash inflows from operations. In general, an enterprise with high financial adaptability will have a lower overall risk than an enterprise with similar operations but with low financial adaptability. However, the risks of a financially adaptable enterprise may still be high if the risk associated with its operations is very high. **33**

The various primary statements all provide information that is useful in assessing **34** financial adaptability; for example, the cash flow statement does so by reporting cash flows from operations. Information about past cash flows may be helpful in predicting future cash flows; and generally, for a given enterprise, the greater the amount of future net cash inflows from operations, the greater the ability of the enterprise to withstand adverse changes in operating conditions. Statements of financial performance can provide information to help assessments of the ability of the enterprise to reduce expenses if income declines. The balance sheet provides information for the assessment of financial adaptability by indicating the nature of available resources and the amounts and timing of claims on those resources.

HIGHLIGHTS AND SUMMARY INDICATORS

35 Highlights and summary indicators are amounts, ratios, and other computations that distil key information about results and financial position.

36 The concepts used in deciding which information should be included in a section of highlights and summary indicators are the same as those used in deciding which information should be included in other parts of financial statements.

37 Although highlights and summary indicators are useful, it is important to avoid focusing attention almost exclusively on 'the bottom line', earnings per share, or other highly simplified condensations. Summary data, such as the amounts of net assets, total recognised gains and losses, profits or earnings per share may be useful as general indicators of the amount of investment or overall past performance and are often used as a basis for comparison of an enterprise with other entities. But, in a complex business enterprise, summary amounts include many heterogeneous transactions and other events and cannot, on their own, adequately describe an enterprise's financial performance, financial position or financial adaptability.

SUPPLEMENTARY INFORMATION

38 Paragraphs 5 to 12 discuss the considerations that guide decisions about the arrangement of information in financial reporting – decisions about whether a particular piece of information should be given in the main body of financial statements, in notes to the financial statements, or elsewhere in financial reporting. The concepts described in paragraphs 5 to 12 to guide decisions on the display of components and of other items apply to information in supplementary financial statements as much as to primary statements. That does not necessarily mean that the same level of detail must be shown in supplementary statements as in primary statements. The amounts of both benefits and costs for a given level of disclosure may be different at the primary and supplementary levels.

39 Paragraphs 40 to 43 give some examples of the kinds of information that may be included in the primary statements and notes, but which on certain occasions may be better presented outside those primary statements and notes, in supplementary information. Four kinds of information are mentioned:

(a) information giving a perspective different from that adopted in the financial statements;
(b) information required for specialised analysis that could be given in the primary statements and notes but is given separately so that different user groups can readily locate the information they require;
(c) statistical information to supplement the information given in the financial statements; and
(d) commentary to supplement the information given elsewhere in the financial statements.

Information giving a different perspective from that adopted in the financial statements, possibly on an experimental basis, can be presented in comprehensive or partial supplementary financial statements or as individual items of information. An example of a different perspective is in the reporting of alternative asset values to those incorporated in the financial statements. **40**

Supplementary information can be used to provide information useful only for specialised analysis of financial statements or specialised industries. In this way, the costs of using financial information can be limited. Users who do not require a great deal of detailed information can avoid the costs involved in reviewing all the information to locate the items that they do require. Positioning of information outside the primary statements and notes also may result in lower costs if that means the information need not be audited, although it may be reviewed by the auditors. **41**

Statistical information may be a useful addition to information in financial statements. For some types of businesses, numbers in the financial statements can be supplemented by other quantitative data to give a more complete picture of the pattern of results of an enterprise. For example, changes in turnover are the joint result of changes in sales volume and changes in selling prices. Information about either or both types of changes can help the assessment of future cash flows by indicating the impact of changes in the environment on past results and by providing a basis for assessment of the relationships between income and expenses. That information can be given by reporting indices of selling prices, indices of sales volume, or actual sales units, depending on the nature and mix of product. Information about changes in the prices of resources used by the enterprise, for example raw materials and labour, may also be useful. **42**

Numerical information cannot provide all the information that is needed for the assessment of future performance. Numerical information typically needs elaboration in a management commentary. An example of this need relates to the reporting of results of unusual activities or particular uncertainties. The reporting of components and other items in the financial statements can help to alert users to the existence of unusual items. However, more information would be needed as a basis for assessing the extent of the impact of the unusual factors and the chances of recurrence. Supplementary discussion can help to provide that information. **43**

Discussion Draft
Statement of Principles Chapter 7
The reporting entity

(Issued July 1994)

Contents

The Reporting Entity – The Principles

A reporting entity is an entity that is the subject of general purpose financial statements which provide information about its financial position, performance and financial adaptability.

An entity should in principle prepare financial statements if there is a demand for that entity's financial statements and if it could supply financial statements that would fulfil that demand.

The demand condition is met if there are those with a legitimate interest in the financial position, performance and financial adaptability of an entity, and in the stewardship of its management, who would rely on its general purpose financial statements as a major source of financial information in making economic decisions about it.

To be able to supply meaningful financial statements an entity must be a cohesive economic unit. An entity is such a unit if it has a unified control structure.

A reporting entity should be required to prepare its financial statements only where the benefits of preparing them outweigh the costs.

Parent entities prepare consolidated financial statements to provide financial information about the economic activities of their groups. Consolidated financial statements reflect a parent's control of the assets and liabilities of its subsidiaries by consolidation, a process that aggregates the assets, liabilities and results of the parent and its subsidiaries using the same accounting bases.

The boundary of the entity that is the subject of a set of financial statements is set by the extent of control, whether it is an individual entity or a group (where the extent of the parent entity's control is the determinant of the group's boundary).

Control is the power to direct. There are two aspects to control:

(i) the ability to deploy the economic resources, whether assets or entities; and
(ii) the ability to benefit (or to suffer) by their deployment.

To have control an entity must have both these abilities.

In most cases, changes in membership of a group do not prevent the group from continuing as the reporting entity as it acquires or disposes of entities in which it has invested. However, in rare circumstances, entities combine not to enlarge one of them but to create a whole new reporting entity in a combination called a merger. In a merger, entities combine on an equal footing, pooling their resources and sharing the risks and benefits, and none of them can be identified as having acquired control over the others.

Acquisition accounting reflects the fact that a purchase has taken place by measuring at fair value the resources applied and the assets and liabilities acquired in exchange, and reports the results of the acquired entity consolidated with those of the acquirer from the date of the acquisition. In contrast, merger accounting reflects the uniting of interests by pooling, normally at book value, the assets and liabilities of the individual merging entities as the basis for the consolidated financial statements of the new reporting entity.

The relationship between an investor and its investee provides the defining features of associates and joint ventures: the investor exercises significant influence over its investee's operating and financial policies and participates as a partner in the business.

The investor should account only for its share of the results and net assets of its associates and joint ventures because, in contrast to its subsidiaries, it does not control its associates and joint ventures, but instead exercises significant influence over their operating and financial policies and participates in their businesses.

1 INTRODUCTION

1.1 **A reporting entity is an entity that is the subject of general purpose financial statements* which provide information about its financial position, performance and financial adaptability**. It is neither practicable nor desirable for every entity to prepare such statements. This chapter considers when it is useful for an entity to prepare them (ie when it should be a reporting entity).

1.2 An entity may prepare financial statements for itself as an individual entity and, if it is a parent, it may also prepare consolidated financial statements for its group. A group is an affiliation of economic interests, some of which may be individual reporting entities in their own right, all within the control of a parent entity. By taking account of relationships between economic interests, consolidated financial statements recognise that business may be conducted through alliances of economic interests rather than by an individual entity acting alone. Consolidated financial statements recognise in particular two close relationships between business interests, first where one controls another (a parent and its subsidiary) and secondly where one has significant influence over another and participates in its business (an investor and its associate or joint venture).

1.3 Although, strictly, consolidated financial statements are prepared by the parent of a group, in this paper, the group itself is sometimes referred to as the reporting entity as shorthand for the parent's reporting role with respect to its group. The group is in fact the *reported* entity – it is the group's assets and liabilities that are reported in the consolidated financial statements. The result is consolidated financial statements that assist users in assessing the financial position, performance and financial adaptability of the group and therefore of its parent.

**The discussion of the reporting entity in this chapter is wholly in the context of general purpose financial statements – which are prepared for those who do not otherwise have access to financial information about that entity. General purpose financial statements contrast with specific purpose financial statements, which are prepared with a particular user or a particular purpose in mind. All references to 'financial statements' in this chapter should be taken as references to 'general financial statements' unless otherwise stated.*

2 IDENTIFYING A REPORTING ENTITY

An entity should in principle prepare financial statements if there is a demand for that entity's financial statements and if it could supply financial statements that would fulfil that demand. 2.1

The demand condition

The demand condition is met if there are those with a legitimate interest in the financial position, performance and financial adaptability of an entity, and in the stewardship of its management, who would rely on its general purpose financial statements as a major source of financial information in making economic decisions about it. This condition is not met if all those with a legitimate interest in an entity have access to alternative sources of financial information about it. For example, owner-managers, the tax authorities, the government and, in some cases, banks may have access to alternative sources of financial information; indeed they may be able to call for information tailored to their own specific purposes. 2.2

The supply condition

To be able to supply meaningful financial statements an entity must be a cohesive economic unit. An entity is a cohesive economic unit if it has a unified control structure. This structure gives the entity determinable boundaries because items are either within its control or outside its control. This structure also enables a reporting entity to have the necessary control of, or obligation for, flows of economic benefit that enables it to have assets and liabilities*. 2.3

Most legal entities fulfil the condition as cohesive economic units and can hold and transfer assets and liabilities. Entities that are not legal entities cannot in law enter into transactions or receive or suffer the relevant inflows and outflows of economic benefits. Although such entities cannot have assets and liabilities in the legal sense, some of them are sufficiently well established as cohesive economic units to be regarded in substance as having assets and liabilities for the purpose of financial reporting. Partnerships (in England and Wales) and groups (made up of a parent and its subsidiaries) are examples of cohesive economic entities with no legal personality that may be reporting entities. 2.4

Determining in practice which entities are reporting entities

Paragraphs 2.1–2.4 set out the conditions that an entity must meet to be a reporting entity. However, **a reporting entity should be required to prepare its financial statements only where the benefits of preparing them outweigh the costs**. If each entity were allowed 2.5

**An entity's assets represent its control of rights or other access to economic benefits and its liabilities represent its obligations to transfer economic benefits (from the definitions of assets and liabilities in paragraphs 7 and 24 of the draft of Chapter 3 of the Statement of Principles 'The elements of financial reporting').*

to decide for itself whether to prepare financial statements by applying its own cost/benefit criteria, the consistency and comparability of financial reporting would be reduced and the availability of financial statements limited. In practice, therefore, reporting requirements are usually set by an arbiter with authority to resolve any conflicting interests arising among those interested in financial statements, particularly between users and preparers of financial statements.*

2.6 In assessing the costs and benefits of an entity preparing financial statements, indirect costs and benefits need to be considered as well as the direct ones. For example, indirect costs to be considered include those relating to loss of competitive advantage through financial reporting requirements and the costs to the user of obtaining the necessary technical competence to use the information in financial statements. The following features are relevant because they affect the benefits that result from an entity preparing financial statements.

The degree of separation of its ownership from its management
As ownership and management diverge, owners lose direct access to financial information about their entity and become increasingly dependent on its financial statements.

Its economic significance
An entity may be economically significant because of its size, or its strategic, economic or political significance, or because the protection of its shareholders is of public interest. The more economically significant an entity is, the more far-reaching become the effects of its activities, and the greater the demand for its financial statements.

Number of users of its financial statements
If only a few users rely on an entity's financial statements as a major source of financial information, the benefits from its presenting financial statements are commensurately limited. This feature, however, has to be evaluated by considering the probable significance of the information for the class of user concerned.

3 CONSOLIDATED FINANCIAL STATEMENTS

3.1 Whether a group is in principle a reporting entity depends on whether it meets the conditions set out in the definition of a reporting entity in Section 2.

The development of consolidated financial statements

3.2 Consolidated financial statements have been developed to reflect the fact that business is often carried on by connected economic interests rather than by individual entities acting alone. **Parent entities prepare consolidated financial statements to provide financial information about the economic activities of their groups. Consolidated financial statements reflect a parent's control of the assets and liabilities of its subsidiaries by consolidation, a process that aggregates the assets, liabilities and results of the parent and its subsidiaries using the same accounting bases.**

**In practice, in the United Kingdom and the Republic of Ireland, legislation sets out which entites are required to prepare financial statements.*

Later developments in business practice have led to consolidated financial statements that reflect the effects of a group carrying on part of its business in partnership with other entities in which it has invested and over which it has significant influence. The equity method of accounting has been developed to show an investing group's share of the net assets and results of its associates. **3.3**

Users of consolidated financial statements

The primary users of consolidated financial statements are investors in the parent because, through their interest in the parent, they have an interest in the group as a whole. However, information about the group as a whole also provides a frame of reference for other users. For example, creditors or lenders whose security is fixed in one member of the group need to refer to the financial statements of the individual entity in which their security is located. However, they may also use the consolidated financial statements to assess the financial strength of the group as a whole and to reach judgements on their effective security as well as the prospects for continuing the trading relationship. The financial strength of the group as a whole is of interest to the creditors of the individual subsidiaries because the parent may guarantee its subsidiary's liabilities; even without formal guarantees, commercial pressures may mean that a parent in effect supports the liabilities of its subsidiaries. **3.4**

Limitations of consolidated financial statements

Consolidated financial statements may overstate the degree of access the parent has to the group's economic resources that are held by its subsidiaries. Consolidated financial statements do not distinguish between the activities and assets of the parent itself and those of its subsidiaries. The parent's access to the resources of its subsidiaries may depend on the way the group is organised, the structure of its subsidiaries, the countries where its subsidiaries are located and the activities they undertake. **3.5**

Where a parent does not wholly own a subsidiary

A parent may control its subsidiary but not own all of the equity. The presence of outside equity interests (minority interests) that may have special statutory or other protection may serve to restrict the parent in some ways in exercising its control, particularly its access to assets. For example, outside equity holders may control sufficient votes to block special resolutions or may be able to invoke legislation against their possible oppression. **3.6**

The presence of outside equity interests in a subsidiary affects the flow of economic benefits from it to its parent because the respective interests held determine the division of distributions. An indication of this effect is useful in assessing the financial position, performance and financial adaptability of the parent. This may be achieved in two ways – full or proportional consolidation. Under full consolidation, the results, assets and liabilities of each subsidiary are consolidated in full and the effect of outside equity interests is indicated by showing their share of the results separately – as a deduction in the performance statements and as a single amount representing their share of net assets in the balance sheet. Proportional consolidation accounts only for the part **3.7** owned, thus including only the parent's proportion of the subsidiary's results, assets and liabilities and excluding the proportion attributable to the outside equity interest.

3.8 Full consolidation presents a more complete picture of a group than proportional consolidation because it includes the full amounts of the assets and liabilities of all subsidiaries, whether or not they are wholly-owned. This reflects the parent's control over its subsidiary, control which is over the whole of that subsidiary regardless of the percentage it owns. As a result of the parent's control, all its subsidiary's economic resources are available to the group for deploying in its business, even though the group's benefit from such deployment is limited to the part it owns. The group's stewardship of its resources should therefore be assessed on the basis of the whole of the resources of its parent and subsidiaries rather than only a proportion. Proportional consolidation does not show in full either the resources available to a parent through its control of other entities or the claims on those resources; it does, however, provide useful information on the components of results and assets and liabilities attributable to the parent through its interest in subsidiaries where there are outside equity interests.

Other restrictions on a parent's access to the resources of its subsidiaries

3.9 The parent's access to the resources of its subsidiaries may also be restricted in the following ways.

(a) Corporate subsidiaries
If they are corporate, the entities that make up the group have separate legal identities. This may restrict the parent's access to its subsidiaries' assets because of the legal duty of care that the directors of the subsidiaries may have to them as individual companies.

(b) Overseas subsidiaries
Some subsidiaries may be established overseas and be subject to restrictions on their activities and the transfer of assets to the parent.

(c) Activities of subsidiaries
Members of the group may operate in different sectors and some may be under special restrictions that do not apply to the group as a whole. For example, some members of the group may operate in regulated industries while others do not.

(d) Financial position of subsidiaries
There may be commercial, financial or economic reasons impeding the parent's ability to deploy funds and resources across the group.

3.10 Paragraphs 3.5–3.9 set out the potential limitations to the information presented in consolidated financial statements because of restrictions on the parent's access to the resources of its subsidiary. However, these limitations do not undermine the case for consolidation as the best way of presenting financial information that recognises the economic effect of a parent's control of its subsidiaries.

3.11 The effect of these limitations is mitigated if users understand the basis of consolidated financial statements and the circumstances causing the limitations. Consolidated financial statements that include segmental information also aid users' understanding of limits on a parent's access to certain group resources. It is inevitable that a process of aggregation such as consolidation may obscure information about individual subsidiaries' financial position, performance and financial adaptability. Any information lost by aggregation can be restored, in part at least, by giving segmental analysis of the group amounts. In particular, showing minority interests by segment provides useful information to assess the effect of these interests on the potential flows of economic benefits within the group.

4 CONTROL DETERMINING THE BOUNDARY OF A REPORTING ENTITY

The boundary of the entity that is the subject of a set of financial statements is set by the extent of control*, whether it is an individual entity or a group (where the extent of the parent entity's control is the determinant of the group's boundary). To include items not within an entity's control in its financial statements would give information of limited use in making assessments of its stewardship or taking economic decisions based on its financial position, performance, and financial adaptability. Determining the boundary of a group can involve difficult distinctions between items where the group's influence amounts to control and those where it does not. 4.1

In general, **control is the power to direct**. In the case of an individual entity control is the power to direct economic resources (as embodied in assets and liabilities). In the case of a group the parent's power to direct applies not just to its own economic resources but also to those of its subsidiaries through its power to direct them. In both cases **there are two aspects to control:** 4.2

(i) the ability to deploy the economic resources, whether assets or entities; and
(ii) the ability to benefit (or to suffer) by their deployment.

To have control an entity must have both these abilities†. In contrast, trusteeship is an example of where the two aspects of control are divided between two parties. The trustee has the power to deploy the trust's assets: the beneficiary benefits from their deployment. In a pure trust neither the trustee nor the beneficiary controls the trust‡.

Determining the extent of control

Individual entities

In most cases the extent of an individual reporting entity's control is clear and it is reasonably simple to identify its assets and liabilities and the performance related to them. Problems may arise, however, in determining the boundary of an individual 4.3

**Control is used to describe a relationship that applies to liabilities and losses as well as to assets and profits. The power to decide on the extent and structure of liabilities is the equivalent of the power to deploy assets, and the obligation to suffer the outflows of benefit related to liabilities and losses is the obverse of the power to benefit from assets and profits.*

†An entity is also regarded as having control of another business interest if it has used its control to set up a continuing arrangement that predetermines the operating and financial policies of that other business.

‡These comments describe how a pure trust works and may not apply to vehicles created in the legal form of a trust where the rights and duties may be divided other than in a pure trust.

entity and it is necessary to identify what aspect of an item constitutes an entity's asset or liability where more than one entity has an interest in a single item, for example where entities share a physical asset such as a pipeline. Problems in determining the extent of an individual entity's assets and liabilities may also arise as a result of complex related transactions, for example those involving options. Financial reporting should report the substance of transactions, which means determining the extent of an entity's control by identifying the items it has the ability both to deploy and to benefit from deploying.

Groups

4.4 In many cases determining the boundary of a group is simple because the extent of the group's control is clear (for example, the group consists of wholly-owned subsidiaries). However, in some cases it may be difficult to determine the extent of the group's control because there is a wide range of possible relationships between business activities making it difficult in some cases to determine whether the group's influence amounts to control. Evidence of control is obtained by examining whether the influence of the group amounts to it enjoying both the deploying and benefiting aspects of control considered above. A group will have both aspects of control with respect to a business activity if it directs the operating and financial policies of the latter with a view to gaining economic benefits from that activity. A group therefore controls activities where this condition is met.

4.5 The extent of a group's control is determined by the actual relationship between business activities, the way they work together in practice. A group's influence over the operating and financial policies of another business in which it has an interest may be anything between absolute and negligible. If its influence is sufficient for it in practice to direct the operating and financial policies of another entity then, providing it exercises its influence with a view to gaining benefits, it controls that entity. Ultimately the question whether a group does or does not have control is a matter of fact*.

4.6 The evidence relevant to determining the extent of a group's control depends on how the group exercises its control, ranging from daily direction, through periodic reviews of overall performance against targets, to predetermining operating and financial policies by contract. Because there are many different ways of exercising control no single piece of evidence can prove in all circumstances that a group has control. The evidence relevant to determining control is obtained by considering:

- the respective rights held;
- the inflows and outflows of benefit; and
- exposure to risk – how and to what extent the group suffers or gains as a result of the outcome of uncertainty as to the amount of benefits generated by the activities under consideration.

These three items of evidence are inter-related because the rights an entity holds in

**As noted earlier, for liabilities these aspects are the power to decide on their extent and structure and the obligation to suffer the relevant economic outflows.*

another usually determine its entitlement to benefits generated by that other and therefore its exposure to risk from variations in the benefits that other generates.

If a group, through either the parent or its subsidiaries, holds a majority of the ordinary shares in another business activity (its 'investee'), it usually has control because its shareholding usually confers a majority of the voting rights too. Holding a majority of the voting rights confers the ability to direct the investee's operating and financial policies and the majority shareholding usually confers proportional rights to any benefits generated by the activities of the investee. However, a parent's control of its subsidiary can be based on any mixture of agreements, formal or informal, and interests held, provided that the overall effect is that it has both of the essential aspects of control. Because a parent's control implies that it has the ability to restrict others from directing the financial and operating policies of its subsidiary, powers of veto and reserve powers may form part of the rights by which the parent exercises control; they are unlikely to form the sole basis of control because they do not provide the basis for deploying the resources of another entity nor do they ensure the necessary flows of benefit. **4.7**

Distinguishing management from control

In some cases it is necessary to determine whether an entity controls or manages another entity. If an entity manages an entity on its own behalf (ie it expects to benefit as a result of the activities of the managed entity other than merely by receiving a management fee*) then it controls the other entity, having both the deploying and benefiting aspects of control. If an entity manages another on behalf of another party, it does not have a parent's exposure to the risks of its subsidiary because the manager's risk in respect of its managed entity is normally limited to its fee. Unlike a parent, a manager operates within guidelines or goals set by another, even if these are very general. If an entity enjoys its powers over another entity for a limited time or by the continuing consent of another party, it is usually the manager of that entity rather than its parent. **4.8**

5 CHANGES IN THE REPORTING ENTITY

Subsidiaries enter and leave a group on the date that they come under or fall out of the control of the parent. **In most cases, changes in membership of a group do not prevent the group from continuing as the reporting entity as it acquires or disposes of entities in which it has invested. However, in rare circumstances, entities combine not to enlarge one of them but to create a whole new reporting entity in a combination called a merger. In a merger, entities combine on an equal footing, pooling their resources and sharing the risks and benefits, and none of them can be identified as having acquired control over the others.** **5.1**

Two methods of accounting reflect the difference between reporting an acquisition and recognising the creation of a new reporting entity. **Acquisition accounting reflects the fact that a purchase has taken place by measuring at fair value the resources applied and** **5.2**

****A management fee may contain a profit-related element as an incentive. However, a fee structure that in substance amounts to an equity interest is to be treated as an equity interest, whatever it is called.***

the assets and liabilities acquired in exchange, and reports the results of the acquired entity consolidated with those of the acquirer from the date of the acquisition. In contrast, merger accounting reflects the uniting of interests by pooling, normally at book value, the assets and liabilities of the individual merging entities as the basis for the consolidated financial statements of the new reporting entity. The results of the merging entities are pooled both for the year of the merger and for the comparative period to give the results of the new entity on a continuous basis. For comparison, the amounts for the previous year are also presented on a merged basis.

6 SIGNIFICANT INFLUENCE AND PARTICIPATION

6.1 This Section considers how an entity's interests in other entities should be treated in its consolidated financial statements where it participates in the other entity's business and exercises significant influence over that entity but does not control it.

6.2 An entity may have interests in businesses that are not its subsidiaries that range from a tiny passively held investment to a near-subsidiary, where the investor's influence falls just short of control. In an entity's individual financial statements this whole range of interests is included as investments. Such an approach is inadequate in consolidated financial statements because their purpose is to assist users to make economic decisions and to assess stewardship by portraying the effect of an entity's interests in other businesses on its financial position, performance and financial adaptability. Consolidated financial statements therefore need to reflect the effect of its having interests in other businesses in which it participates and exercises significant influence. Such investments are used by an investor as media through which to carry on its activities, sometimes as substitutes for developing activities through interests in subsidiaries, and therefore should not be accounted for in the same way as passive investments.

6.3 Investments that are used by the investor as media through which to carry on its activities are traditionally identified as associates and joint ventures. **The relationship between an investor and its investee provides the defining features of associates and joint ventures: the investor exercises significant influence over its investee's operating and financial policies and participates as a partner in the business**. In a joint venture the relationship is based on a joint venture agreement and the sharing of control. The partnership in an associate is between the investor and the management of the associate, representing the other shareholders, while the partnership in a joint venture is between the investor and the other venturers. In practice an investor's participation and significant influence in its associates and joint ventures results in the following conditions being fulfilled:

- the investment is long-term;
- the investor reasonably expects to benefit from the economic benefits accumulated by the activities of its investee;
- in areas of mutual interest the investee generally implements policies that are consistent with the strategy of the investor;
- the investor is able to protect itself against changes in the operating and financial policies of its investee that would change substantially the benefits and risks to which the investor was exposed.

To reflect the effect of an entity's interests in associates and joint ventures in its consolidated financial statements these should include a measure of the results achieved by such investments and their accumulated net assets. Such information is necessary to make assessments of a reporting entity's financial position, performance and financial adaptability and its stewardship of resources. **The investor should account only for its share of the results and net assets of its associates and joint ventures because, in contrast to its subsidiaries, it does not control its associates and joint ventures but instead exercises significant influence over their operating and financial policies and participates in their businesses.** **6.4**

Information on the investor's share of the results and assets of its associates and joint ventures could be included in its consolidated financial statements either by proportional consolidation or by the equity method of accounting. Proportional consolidation brings in the investor's share of results and assets and liabilities of its investment on a line-by-line basis. The equity method brings in the results and net assets of its investment on a net basis although different degrees of detail can be given to show how the net amounts are derived. **6.5**

Proportional consolidation is justified in principle only if the substance of the relationship between investor and investee is that the investor actually controls its proportionate share of the investee's assets and liabilities. This implies that the investor's share should be identifiable and distinct. In most associates and joint ventures the investor shares control or has significant influence over the operating and financial policies of that entity as a whole. In consolidated financial statements based on control, proportional consolidation would therefore misrepresent the extent of the investor's influence over and resulting access to the assets and liabilities of its investee. **6.6**

By contrast, using the equity method for associates and joint ventures is in keeping with the principle that an entity's boundary is set by the extent of its control because the equity method recognises an investor's interest in an associate or joint venture as an investment. In most cases an investor controls its interest in an associate or joint venture but not its share of the individual assets and liabilities of that associate or joint venture. An investor should therefore use the equity method to measure its interest in an associate or joint venture as its asset but, where appropriate, should supplement this in the notes with information on the make-up of the amounts recorded. **6.7**

[FRED 8]
Related party disclosures

(Issued March 1994)

Contents

[Draft] Financial Reporting Standard ● is set out in paragraphs 1–10.

The Statement of Standard Accounting Practice set out in paragraphs 7–10 should be read in the context of the Objective as stated in paragraph 1 and the definitions set out in paragraphs 2–6 and also of the Foreword to Accounting Standards and the Statement of Principles for Financial Reporting currently in issue.

The Explanation set out in paragraphs 11–24 shall be regarded as part of the Statement of Standard Accounting Practice insofar as it assists in interpreting that statement.

Related party disclosures

Preface

This financial reporting exposure draft (FRED) is concerned with the disclosure of information about control relationships and material transactions between the reporting entity and its related parties. It supersedes the proposals of ED 46 'Disclosure of related party transactions' issued by the Accounting Standards Committee in April 1989.

THE NEED FOR DISCLOSURE

The common practice of companies in organising their businesses through the medium of other companies in the same group, associated undertakings and other related entities has caused transactions between related parties to become a routine and necessary part of the operations of many business enterprises. Related parties may nevertheless enter into transactions that unrelated parties either would not undertake, or would undertake only on different terms. Reporting control relationships and related party transactions draws the attention of users of financial statements to the possibility that those statements may have been affected by the relationship.

DISCLOSABLE RELATED PARTY TRANSACTIONS

Paragraph 8 of the FRED requires disclosure of material related party transactions (in aggregated form when appropriate) to make the user aware of their scale and possible commercial importance to the entity. ED 46 proposed the disclosure of 'abnormal' related party transactions, which it defined and illustrated. In the FRED no distinction is made between normal and abnormal transactions since the Board's view is that, when transactions with related parties are material in aggregate, they are of interest whether or not made at arm's length. The FRED's approach of reporting all material related party transactions of the entity and not simply those items deemed to be 'abnormal' by the directors of the reporting entity is the approach of International Accounting Standard 24 'Related Party Disclosures' (1984) and also that of accounting standards on this subject issued in Australia, Canada, New Zealand and the USA.

The FRED incorporates four features that serve to minimise the volume of disclosure.

- Aggregation of similar transactions by type of related party is encouraged unless more detailed disclosure is necessary for an understanding of their impact on the financial statements or is required by law.
- Related party disclosures are not required in the financial statements of a parent when these are presented together with the consolidated financial statements.
- In consolidated financial statements disclosure is not required of transactions eliminated on consolidation.

- In the individual financial statements of wholly-owned subsidiaries* transactions with other entities that are part of the group and associates and joint ventures of the group are not required to be disclosed.

SMALL COMPANIES

Commentators are asked at the end of this Preface whether there are any grounds for exempting small companies from the proposed disclosure requirements of the FRED.

Among possible reasons for exempting small companies are the following:

(a) the external shareholders of all companies already have some protection in the requirements of companies legislation that deal with disclosure of directors' and other officers' transactions; and

(b) other users of small companies' financial statements may have to rely on an abbreviated balance sheet and notes, which are all that need be filed by small companies and which would not include the disclosures required by the FRED.

Against these arguments the case for requiring the related party disclosures for all companies is as follows:

(a) the disclosure of information about related party transactions is no less important to the user of the financial statements of small companies than it is to the user of those of larger entities. Indeed, certain kinds of related party transaction may be more prevalent and of greater significance for the financial statements when the company is small than when it is large (for example those transactions involving individuals); and

(b) the confidential nature of such disclosures need not be a cause for concern, since they would be excluded from the abbreviated accounts available to the public.

No exemption for small companies (however defined) is given in the FRED. At the request of the Board, the Consultative Committee of Accountancy Bodies has set up a working party to recommend general criteria for the Board to use in considering exemptions from standards on the grounds of size or public interest. Pending the working party's report, suggestions from commentators are invited. Small companies, however defined, would be required to state that they had taken advantage of any exemption granted.

PARTICULAR ISSUES ON WHICH COMMENTS ARE INVITED

In addition to general comments on the FRED, respondents' views are especially sought on the matters set out below. It would be helpful if, when giving comments, respondents could state reasons, together with an indication of preferred alternatives.

1. Is the definition of related parties appropriate (paragraph 2)?

**A company is a 'wholly-owned subsidiary' of another company if it has no members except that other and that other's wholly-owned subsidiaries or persons acting on behalf of that other or its wholly-owned subsidiaries (section 736(2) Companies Act 1985). Similar definitions appear in companies legislation in Northern Ireland and the Republic of Ireland.*

2. Are the proposed disclosures for related party transactions satisfactory (paragraph 8)?
3 Is there a risk that the level of aggregation allowed for disclosure of related party transactions will result in disclosures that are too general to be helpful (paragraph 8)?
4. Is the criterion for materiality, namely that which is of significance to users of general purpose financial statements, acceptable (paragraph 20)?
5. Should the reporting entity be required to disclose the name of its controlling party even if there have been no transactions with it in the period (paragraph 9)?
6. Are there any grounds for exempting small companies, as defined by companies legislation (or still smaller companies), from the proposed disclosure requirements?
7. Should wholly-owned subsidiaries be required to disclose transactions with other entities that are part of the group or associates or joint ventures of the group (paragraph 7)?
8. Should the level of shareholding at which parties are presumed to be related be set at 10 per cent (paragraph 2(c)(i))?
9. Should there be a requirement to disclose any material difference between the fair value and the transacted amount in relation to the transfer of assets, liabilities, or services between related parties (paragraph 23)?

Summary

[Draft] Financial Reporting Standard ● 'Related Party Disclosures' requires the disclosure of: **a**

(i) all material related party transactions and
(ii) the name of the party controlling the reporting entity and, if different, that of the ultimate controlling party whether or not any transactions between the reporting entity and those parties have taken place.

Two or more parties are related parties when for all or part of the financial period: **b**

(i) one party has either direct or indirect control of the other party; or
(ii) one party has the ability to influence the financial and operating policies of the other party; or
(iii) the parties are subject to common control from the same source; or
(iv) one of the parties is subject to control and the other to influence (of the kind described in b(ii) above) from the same source.

Examples of related parties are divided into two categories: those where the nature of the relationship is deemed to result in the parties being related and those where the nature of the relationship is presumed to result in the parties being related unless there is evidence to the contrary. **c**

No disclosure is required in consolidated financial statements of intra-group transactions and balances eliminated on consolidation. A parent undertaking is not **d** required to provide related party disclosures in its own accounts when these are presented with consolidated financial statements of its group.

e Disclosure is not required in the financial statements of wholly-owned subsidiaries of transactions with other entities that are part of the group or associates and joint ventures of the group.

[Draft] Financial Reporting Standard ●
Objective

1 The objective of this [draft] FRS is to ensure that financial statements contain the disclosures necessary to draw to the attention of users the possibility that the reported financial position and results may have been affected by the existence of related parties and by material transactions with them.

Definitions

The following definitions shall apply in this [draft] FRS and in particular the Statement of Standard Accounting Practice set out in paragraphs 7–10.

Those of the terms defined below which are also defined in companies legislation have the same meaning as in the legislation notwithstanding that in some cases the definition below is a summary or explanation rather than a repetition of the definition in the legislation.

2 *Related parties:-*

(a) Two or more parties are related parties when for all or part of the financial period:
- (i) one party has either direct or indirect control of the other party; or
- (ii) one party has the ability to influence the financial and operating policies of the other party; or
- (iii) the parties are subject to common control from the same source; or
- (iv) one of the parties is subject to control and the other to influence* from the same source.

In deciding whether parties are related, it is necessary to consider the substance of the relationship.

(b) The following are deemed to be related parties of the reporting entity:
- (i) its ultimate or intermediate parent undertaking or undertakings, subsidiary undertakings, and fellow subsidiary undertakings;
- (ii) associates and joint ventures of itself or any of the undertakings in (b)(i) above;
- (iii) the investor or venturer in respect of which the reporting entity is an associate or a joint venture;

**in terms of paragraph 2(a) (ii)*

(iv) directors of the reporting entity and the directors of its parent undertaking or undertakings and members of the immediate family of such directors;
(v) pension funds for the benefit of employees of the reporting entity or of any entity that is a related party of the reporting entity.

(c) Unless there is evidence to the contrary the following are presumed to be related parties of the reporting entity:
(i) a person owning or able to exercise control over 10 per cent or more of the voting rights of the reporting entity, whether directly, through nominees, or through an entity controlled by that person and members of the immediate family of such a person;
(ii) the key management of the reporting entity and the key management of its parent undertaking and members of the immediate family of a member of such management;
(iii) partnerships, companies, trusts or other entities in which any person in (b)(iv), (c)(i) or (c)(ii) above has a controlling interest;
(iv) each person acting in concert in such a way as to be able to exercise control or influence* over the reporting entity;
(v) an entity managing or managed by the reporting entity under a management contract.

Sub-paragraphs (b) and (c) are not intended to be an exhaustive list of related parties.

(d) For the purposes of the [draft] FRS:
(i) directors include shadow directors;
(ii) key management are those persons having authority or responsibility for directing or controlling the activities and resources of the reporting entity;
(iii) immediate family includes those family members or members of the same household who might influence, or be influenced in relation to, business activities affecting the reporting entity. They would normally include a person's spouse, and parent, child (adult or minor), brother and sister and the spouse of any of these; and
(iv) persons acting in concert comprise persons who, pursuant to an agreement or understanding (whether formal or informal), actively co-operate, through the ownership by any of them of shares in an undertaking, to exercise control or influence over the financial and operating policies of that undertaking.

(e) In the context of the [draft] FRS those parties mentioned at (i) to (iv) below are not deemed to be related parties simply as a result of their role as:
(i) providers of finance in the course of their business in that regard,
(ii) public utilities,
(iii) government departments and agencies, even though they may circumscribe the freedom of action of an eniontity or participate in its decision-making process; and
(iv) a customer, supplier, franchiser, distributor or general agent with whom an entity transacts a significant volume of business.

**in terms of paragraph 2(a) (ii)*

3 *Control:*

The ability of a party to direct the financial and operating policies of an undertaking with a view to gaining economic benefits from its activities.

4 *Related party transaction:*

The transfer of assets or liabilities or the performance of services by, to or for a related party irrespective of whether a price is charged.

5 *Fair value:*

The amount at which an asset or liability could be exchanged in a transaction between informed and willing parties, other than in a forced or liquidation sale.

6 *Companies legislation:*

(a) In Great Britain, the Companies Act 1985;
(b) In Northern Ireland, the Companies (Northern Ireland) Order 1986; and
(c) In the Republic of Ireland, the Companies Acts 1963–90 and the European Communities (Companies: Group Accounts) Regulations 1992.

Statement of standard accounting practice

SCOPE

7 [Draft] Financial Reporting Standard ● applies to all financial statements intended to give a true and fair view of a reporting entity's financial position and profit or loss (or income and expenditure) for a period. The [draft] FRS does not, however, require disclosure:

(a) in consolidated financial statements, of any transactions or balances between group entities that have been eliminated on consolidation;
(b) in a parent's own financial statements when those statements are presented together with its consolidated financial statements;
(c) in the financial statements of wholly-owned subsidiaries, of transactions with entities that are part of the group or associates or joint ventures of the group, provided that the consolidated financial statements in which that subsidiary is included are publicly available;
(d) of pension contributions paid to a pension fund; and
(e) of emoluments in respect of services as an employee of the reporting entity.

Reporting entities taking advantage of any of the exemptions in (b) or (c) above are required to state that fact.

DISCLOSURE OF TRANSACTIONS

8 Financial statements should disclose material transactions undertaken with a related party by the reporting entity. Disclosure should be made irrespective of whether a price is charged. The disclosure should include:

(a) the names of the related parties;
(b) a description of the relationship between the parties;
(c) a description of the transactions;
(d) the amounts involved;
(e) the amounts due to or from related parties at the balance sheet date; and
(f) any other elements of the transactions necessary for an understanding of the financial statements.

Transactions with related parties may be disclosed on an aggregated basis (aggregation of similar transactions by type of related party) unless disclosure of an individual transaction, or connected transactions, is necessary for an understanding of the impact of the transactions on the financial statements of the reporting entity or is required by law.

DISCLOSURE OF CONTROL

When the reporting entity is controlled by another party, there should be disclosure of the name of that party and, if different, that of the ultimate controlling party. If the ultimate controlling party of the reporting entity is not known, that fact should be disclosed. This information should be disclosed irrespective of whether any transactions have taken place between the controlling parties and the reporting entity. **9**

DATE FROM WHICH EFFECTIVE

The accounting practices set out in the [draft] FRS should be regarded as standard in respect of financial statements relating to accounting periods ending on or after (date to be inserted after exposure). Earlier adoption is encouraged but not required. **10**

Explanation

THE EFFECT OF RELATED PARTIES

In the absence of information to the contrary, it is assumed that a reporting entity has independent discretionary power over its resources and transactions and pursues its activities independently of the interests of its individual owners, managers and others. Transactions are presumed to have been undertaken on an arm's length basis – that is, the terms were such as could have obtained in a transaction with an external party, in which each side bargained knowledgeably and freely, unaffected by any relationship between them. **11**

These assumptions may not be justified when related party relationships exist, because the requisite conditions for competitive, free market dealings may not be present. While the parties may endeavour to achieve arm's length bargaining the very nature of the relationship may preclude this occurring. Sometimes the effect of the relationship between the parties may be so pervasive that disclosure of the relationship alone will be sufficient to make users aware of the possible implications of related party trans- **12** actions. For this reason transactions between a wholly-owned subsidiary and other members of the same group are not required to be disclosed in the separate financial statements of the wholly-owned subsidiary.

13 Even when terms are arm's length, the reporting of material related party transactions is useful information, because the terms of future transactions are more susceptible to alteration as a result of the nature of the relationship than they would be in transactions with an unrelated party. Although the existence of a related party relationship sometimes precludes arm's length transactions, non-independent parties can deal with each other at arm's length, as in the situation where a parent undertaking places no restrictions on two subsidiaries, giving them complete freedom in deciding whether to deal with each other and on what terms. However, assertions in financial statements about transactions with related parties should not imply that the related party transactions were effected on terms equivalent to those that prevail in arm's length transactions unless the parties have conducted the transactions in an independent manner.

DISCLOSURE OF CONTROL

14 If the reporting entity is controlled by another party, that fact is relevant information, irrespective of whether transactions have taken place with that party, because the control relationship prevents the reporting entity from being independent in the sense described in paragraph 11. Indeed, the existence and identity of the controlling party may sometimes be at least as relevant in appraising an entity's prospects as are the performance and financial position presented in its financial statements. The controlling party may establish the entity's credit standing, determine the source and price of its raw materials, determine the products it sells, to whom and at what price, and may affect the source, calibre and even the primary concern and allegiance of its management.

APPLYING THE DEFINITION OF 'RELATED PARTY'

15 For the purposes of applying the definition of a related party, a party is: an individual or an entity, such as a company or an unincorporated business; or a group of individuals or entities acting in concert. Groups of individuals or entities are included in this definition because although an independent individual or entity (for example because of small shareholdings) might not be able to divert a particular reporting entity from pursuing its own separate interests, this could be achieved by the individual or entity acting in concert with others.

16 The definition is limited to parties having a relationship with a reporting entity that affects the independence of either the reporting entity or the other party and could have a significant effect on the financial position and operating results of the reporting entity. This does not include relationships between the reporting entity and a major customer or supplier because the reporting entity still retains the freedom to make decisions in its own separate interests.

17 Entities subject to common control are included in the definition of a related party because the controlling entity could cause such entities to transact or not to transact with one another or to transact on particular terms. The relationship could therefore have a material effect on the performance and the financial position of the reporting entity. Common control is deemed to exist when both parties are subject to control from boards having a controlling nucleus of directors in common.

The difference between control and influence is that control brings with it the ability to deploy the resources of the controlled party whilst influence introduces the possibility of such deployment but not the certainty. Hence two entities are not related parties simply because they have a director in common. Furthermore, two related parties of a third entity are not thereby related parties of each other; there must be a related party relationship between themselves. For example, entities are not related parties by being associated companies of the same investor. Since both parties are subject only to influence rather than common control, the relationship between them is too tenuous to justify their being treated as related parties of each other. However, where one of the parties is subject to control and the other to influence over its financial and operating policies from the same source, the relationship between these two parties is deemed to be a related party relationship because the controlled party may be subject to restrictions on its freedom to transact on an arm's length basis with the influenced party. **18**

The fact that certain pension funds are to be regarded as related parties of the reporting entity is not intended to call into question the independence of the trustees with regard to their fiduciary obligations to the members of the pension scheme. Transactions between the reporting entity and the pension fund may be in the interest of members but nevertheless need to be reported in the accounts of the reporting entity. **19**

TRANSACTIONS

Disclosure is required of all material related party transactions. As transactions include donations to or by the entity, related party transactions are required to be disclosed whether or not a price is charged. Transactions are material when their disclosure might reasonably be expected to influence decisions made by the users of general purpose financial statements. **20**

The following are examples of related party transactions that require disclosures by a reporting entity in the period in which they occur: **21**

- purchases or sales of goods (finished or unfinished);
- purchases or sales of property and other assets;
- rendering or receiving of services;
- agency arrangements;
- leasing arrangements;
- transfer of research and development;
- licence agreements;
- provision of finance (including loans and equity contributions in cash or in kind);
- guarantees and the provision of collateral security; and
- management contracts.

AGGREGATION

22 Disclosure of details of particular transactions with individual related parties would frequently be too voluminous to be easily understood. Accordingly, similar transactions may be aggregated by type of related party. In the individual accounts of a group company, for example, purchases or sales with other group companies can be aggregated and described as such. However, this should not be done in such a way as to obscure the importance of significant transactions. For example purchases or sales of goods should not be aggregated with purchases or sales of fixed assets. Nor should a material related party transaction with an individual be concealed in an aggregated disclosure.

OTHER ELEMENTS OF THE TRANSACTION

23 Paragraph 8(f) requires disclosure of 'any other elements of the [related party] transactions necessary for an understanding of the financial statements'. An example falling within this requirement would be a material difference between the fair value and the transacted amount where material transfers of assets, liabilities or services have taken place.

RELATIONSHIP WITH STATUTORY AND LONDON STOCK EXCHANGE REQUIREMENTS

24 There are extensive statutory and London Stock Exchange requirements and reliefs regarding disclosure of related party transactions and relationships. In certain instances, the [draft] FRS will extend existing disclosure requirements; in other instances, the statutory and London Stock Exchange disclosure requirements go beyond those of the [draft] FRS. The location of the principal statutory and London Stock Exchange requirements is given in Appendices I and II respectively.

Appendix I
Note on Legal Requirements

The following table lists only the main parts of the law relating to related party disclosures. 1

GREAT BRITAIN

Companies Act 1985 2

section 231	Disclosure required in notes to the accounts: related undertakings
Schedule 5	Disclosure of information: related undertakings
Part I	*Companies not required to prepare group accounts*
Part II	*Companies required to prepare group accounts*
section 232	Disclosure required in notes to accounts: emoluments and other benefits of directors and others
Schedule 6	Disclosure of information: emoluments and other benefits of directors and others
section 234	Duty to prepare directors' report
Schedule 7	Matters to be dealt with in the directors' report
Schedule 4	Form and content of company accounts
Part I Section B	*The required formats for accounts*
paragraph 50	*Guarantees and other financial commitments*
paragraph 59	*Dealings with or interests in group undertakings*
paragraph 59A	*Guarantees and other financial commitments in favour of group undertakings*
Schedule 4A	Form and content of group accounts
paragraph 1(2)	*General rules – balances attributable to unconsolidated subsidiaries*
paragraph 21	*Amendment to consolidated balance sheet and profit and loss account formats*

NORTHERN IRELAND

The legal requirements in Northern Ireland are identical with those in Great Britain. 3
The following table shows the provisions in the Companies (Northern Ireland) Order 1986 that correspond to the following provisions in the Companies Act 1985 (see paragraph 2 above).

Exposure Drafts in issue

Great Britain	Northern Ireland
section 231	Article 239
Schedule 5 *Parts I and II*	Schedule 5 *Parts I and II*
section 232	Article 240
Schedule 6	Schedule 6
section 234	Article 242
Schedule 7	Schedule 7
Schedule 4 *Part 1 Section B* *paragraphs 50, 59 and 59A*	Schedule 4 *Part I Section B* *paragraphs 50, 59 and 59A*
Schedule 4A *paragraphs 1(2) and 21*	Schedule 4A *paragraphs 1(2) and 21*

REPUBLIC OF IRELAND

4 The following table shows the provisions in the European Communities (Companies: Group Accounts) Regulations 1992, and the Companies Acts 1963 – 90 that correspond to the provisions in the Companies Act 1985 (see paragraph 2 above).

Great Britain	Republic of Ireland
section 231	regulation 36 1992 Regulations
Schedule 5 *Parts I and II*	section 16 Companies (Amendment) Act 1986
	regulation 44 1992 Regulations
	schedule, paragraphs 4, 18–22 1992 Regulations
section 232 Schedule 6	*Disclosure of emoluments and other benefits of directors:* section 191 Companies Act 1963

	schedule, paragraph 16 *1992 Regulations* *Loans, quasi-loans, and other dealings in favour of directors and others:* sections 41–43 Companies Act 1990
	schedule, paragraph 17 1992 Regulations
section 234 Schedule 7	section 158 Companies Act 1963 sections 13, 14 & 16 Companies (Amendment) Act 1986
	regulation 37 1992 Regulations
	section 63 Companies Act 1990
Schedule 4	
Part I Section B	schedule, paragraphs 1–3 Companies (Amendment) Act 1986
paragraph 50	schedule, paragraph 36 Companies (Amendment) Act 1986
paragraph 59	schedule, paragraph 45 Companies (Amendment) Act 1986
paragraph 59A	schedule, paragraph 45A Companies (Amendment) Act 1986
Schedule 4A	
paragraph 1(2)	regulation 15(2) 1992 Regulations
paragraph 21	schedule, paragraph 2 1992 Regulations

Appendix II
Note on London Stock Exchange requirements

'The Listing Rules' published by the London Stock Exchange deal with related party transactions, which are defined somewhat differently from those in the [draft] FRS, albeit with a large degree of overlap. Chapter 11 'Transactions with related parties' defines related party transactions and sets out the requirements and exceptions for such transactions. Further disclosure requirements in respect of related parties are contained in Chapter 12 'Financial information'.

Appendix III
Compliance with International Accounting Standards

Compliance with the [draft] FRS will ensure compliance with International Accounting Standard 24 'Related Party Disclosures' in all material respects.

Part Eight

ASB Discussion Papers in issue

The rôle of valuation in financial reporting

(Issued March 1993)

Contents

The rôle of valuation in financial reporting

PREFACE

This Discussion Paper is being published by the Accounting Standards Board simultaneously with the fifth chapter of the Board's Statement of Principles 'Measurement in Financial Statements'. It describes why the present system of irregular asset valuations is unsatisfactory and sets out the options for reform available to the Board.

In considering these options, the Board has to consider not only the theoretical merits of the various solutions but also the cost of implementation and, in particular, the Board's commitment to a gradual development of existing practice, avoiding disruptive changes. As is explained in the paper, the Board proposes to continue with the present modified historical cost system, but to attempt to remove some of the existing anomalies. The programme would initially involve the development of accounting standards addressing those assets in respect of which supplementary information on current values is already required by law, and which are traded on a ready market.

INTRODUCTION

Chapter 5 of the draft Statements of Principles – 'Measurement in Financial Statements', issued by the Accounting Standards Board (the Board), considers the principles underlying the measurement of an accounting entity's assets, liabilities and proprietors' capital, and describes the two main valuation methods used in accounting – historical cost and some form of current value accounting. British and Irish accounting uses a mixture of both methods with the result that assets and liabilities are measured upon different bases, the residual term, proprietors' capital, being a hybrid measure whose significance is not immediately clear. **1**

The Board's predecessor body, the Accounting Standards Committee (ASC), received representations from both industry and the accounting profession strongly urging the ASC's successor to conduct a review of the fundamental concepts of accounting. For example, responding to the ASC's proposals set out in Exposure Draft ED47 – 'Accounting for goodwill', the CBI commented: **2**

> 'The CBI urges ... the Accounting Standards Board to conduct a review of the fundamental concepts of accounting with a view to developing an approach which places greater emphasis on the value of assets, particularly where present accounting conventions are at variance with business realities.'

This paper discusses one strategy that the Board may follow to remove inconsistencies and options in current accounting practices in order to improve the relevance of information in financial statements while balancing this with the need for reliability, and taking into account the demands for reasonable costs of compliance. The proposals will affect not only the balance sheet but also reported profits. **3**

4 Historical cost accounting has the advantages that it has been widely practised over a long period of time and is, therefore, familiar to users and preparers of financial statements. It is probably the cheapest valuation method from the point of view of the preparers and is deemed to be relatively objective and therefore reliable.

5 The main disadvantage of the historical cost system results from the fact that it records values at the date of acquisition of specific assets. These dates will typically be different for various assets and thus it can be argued that historical cost financial statements lack the property of comparability not only between different companies at any given time but even between different assets owned by the same company. In addition, historical cost accounting allows companies to 'manage income'; that is, to select when to sell assets to realise profits or losses.

6 Current values have the advantage of relevance to the current state of a business – a property that is lacking in historical cost accounting. No banker should ever make a secured loan to a customer based on the historical cost of the security to the customer. Rate of return measures (such as return on capital) and balance sheet measures (such as gearing ratios) are widely employed by users of financial statements. If these crude measures must be used it is more relevant to measure them in terms of current values rather than historical costs. Current values are also more likely to be comparable insofar as they reflect economic conditions at a particular time and will generally be understandable to non-accountants who expect financial statements to be measured in current prices and who may be surprised to find that in traditional accounting this is not the case.

7 Current values, however, may be less reliable than historical costs because their reliability depends largely on whether a ready market is available for a particular type of asset. A current value system, too, is probably more expensive to operate than an historical cost system. Experts would have to be used to determine current values unless a ready market exists and prices are known to the outsider. Additionally, there may be transitional costs in moving to some form of current value accounting given that users are probably attuned to historical cost data and preparers would incur costs in setting up new systems. Despite these costs, however, financial reports in the United Kingdom and Republic of Ireland already contain current value data that presumably have been introduced because of the advantages mentioned above.

8 The question for the Board is whether the present hybrid system, which does not have a clear underlying logic, should be developed into one more clearly founded on principles embracing current values or alternatively whether the system should be pruned back to one rigorously based on the principles of historical cost. The remainder of this paper examines further principles outlined in Chapter 5 of the Statement of Principles in considering present practice in valuing assets in the United Kingdom and Republic of Ireland and the problems associated with the present modified historical cost system.

9 The conclusion, more fully set out in paragraphs 30 to 35 below, states that the present modified historical cost system involving both the retention of historical costs and irregular revaluation is clearly unsatisfactory, but that the Board's approach should be evolutionary rather than revolutionary. Accordingly, the Board believes that the present *modified historical cost system should continue* but an attempt should be made to remove some of the existing anomalies by requiring revaluations of certain assets on a more consistent basis.

The Board proposes that it should issue pronouncements concerned with those assets: **10**

- in respect of which supplementary information on current values is already required by law; and
- which are traded on a ready market.

These pronouncements would require:

(i) the revaluation of properties (excluding fixed assets, such as factories or plant, specific to the business);
(ii) the revaluation of quoted investments; and
(iii) the revaluation of stock of a commodity nature and long-term stock where a market of sufficient depth exists.

For each of these areas the Board will need to consider how gains and losses should be allocated between the profit and loss account and the statement of total recognised gains and losses.

If its strategy is accepted the Board intends to undertake consultation into the scope of **11** any requirements and the forms of valuation to be required and would publish the results of any such consultations in addition to issuing draft proposals in the normal way for accounting standards dealing with the three types of assets mentioned above.

MOVES AWAY FROM PURE HISTORICAL COST

Historical cost accounting systems are rarely found in their pure form. Invariably the **12** 'cost or net realisable value whichever is the lower' formula is adopted when considering the carrying value of assets. In that sense current values are already present in most historical cost systems. Some countries have gone further in introducing current values into systems of financial reporting. The revaluation of fixed assets is common in Australia, New Zealand and South Africa, as well as in the United Kingdom and Republic of Ireland; in the Netherlands a few companies use current value information in their primary financial statements, although many others give such information by way of note disclosure.

Accounting for price level changes

Moves to adopt a system of accounting other than that of traditional historical cost **13** have occurred in recent years. In particular, times of high inflation have inevitably led to pressure to move towards a form of accounting which takes into account the effect of changing prices. Initially these attempts led to the evolution of current purchasing power (CPP) accounting, not only in the United Kingdom and Republic of Ireland but also in Australia, Canada, New Zealand, South Africa and the USA. This was followed by current cost proposals in Australia, Canada, New Zealand, the Netherlands, the

United Kingdom and Republic of Ireland, the USA and (the then) West Germany. Several of these proposals became accounting standards but as inflation diminished the support for these standards also diminished and they were withdrawn.

14 While current cost financial statements are rare today in the United Kingdom and Republic of Ireland, the benefits to be obtained from these financial statements are still perceived to be of sufficient importance to warrant the continuing use of current cost information by former nationalised industries privatised in recent years – in particular the water, electricity and gas industries. Publication of these current cost financial statements is in line with the recommendations of the Byatt Report – Accounting for Economic Costs and Changing Prices – published in 1986. This emphasised the importance of accounting for changing prices – current cost financial statements were deemed to be more useful both to the preparers and users, including regulators, in determining the real return on capital employed and ascertaining realistic measures of costs as a means of ensuring that prices and tariffs were appropriately related thereto. Other companies, however, while not adopting a current cost system, do, within the framework of the law, show certain assets at values other than historical cost as a result of accounting standards, industry practice or individual choice.

Asset valuation – the present position in the United Kingdom and the Republic of Ireland

15 The EC Fourth Directive on Company Law did not attempt to impose a pure historical cost system on the European Community. Within the provisions of the Directive, alternative accounting rules enable a company to use either a current value or an historical cost accounting system for its statutory financial statements. These rules, however, can be applied selectively and as such the law has been used by many UK and Irish companies to enable particular assets to be revalued.

16 Other provisions in the law have indicated that the legislators deem current value information to be of importance when historical cost and current values diverge. Consequently there are requirements for companies to:

(i) give an indication in the directors' report of the difference between the market value of land and buildings held as fixed assets and the amount at which they are included in the balance sheet if the directors think the difference is of such significance that it needs to be drawn to the attention of the members of the company and the debenture holders (CA85 Sch 7 para 1 (2))*;

(ii) give information about the market value of listed investments where it differs from the amount shown in the financial statements (CA85 Sch 4 para 45 (2))†; and

**The Companies (NI) Order 1986 Sch 7 para 1(2) in Northern Ireland; no equivalent requirement in the Republic of Ireland.*

†The Companies (NI) Order 1986 Sch 4 para 45(2) in Northern Ireland; the Companies (Amendment) Act 1986 the Sch para 31(2) in the Republic of Ireland.

(iii) show in a note the replacement cost of stock where it differs materially from the balance sheet amount (CA85 Sch 4 para 27 (3) (b))*.

In addition to legal requirements there has also been pressure to give current value information from the ASC and from industry groups. Further information on these developments and other valuation practice in the United Kingdom and Republic of Ireland is set out in the appendices to this paper. **17**

EXISTING PROBLEMS OF THE MODIFIED HISTORICAL COST SYSTEM

The previous sections of this paper indicated that pure historical cost accounting is not universal practice in the United Kingdom and Republic of Ireland. The scope for revaluations and the move towards marking to market have led many companies' financial statements to be based on what is termed the 'modified historical cost system'. This system also has problems if the valuations are not regularly updated; most of these are shared with the traditional historical cost system. **18**

Difficulties in profit comparisons

There is little consistency in revaluation practice in the United Kingdom and Republic of Ireland as companies are neither obliged to revalue assets nor, if assets are revalued, are companies obliged to keep revaluations updated annually. Consequently, revaluations, if undertaken, can be carried out irregularly. This leads to difficulties in comparing one company with another and has led the Board in Financial Reporting Standard No. 3 – 'Reporting Financial Performance' (FRS 3) to introduce a requirement for a note of historical cost profits, where this differs materially from reported profits. This requirement is intended to enable fair comparisons to be made between companies' profits, since revaluations affect the profit and loss account as well as the balance sheet. **19**

In particular, revaluation of fixed assets has major effects on the comparability of profit among companies for the following reasons: **20**

(i) the law† and SSAP12‡ require that depreciation be based on the carrying value of an asset. Consequently if the value of an asset is increased, depreciation will rise and reported profits will fall;
(ii) under FRS 3 gains in the profit and loss account on disposal are based on carrying values and accordingly when asset values have been revalued upwards such gains

**The Companies (NI) Order 1986 Sch 4 para 27(3)(b) in Northern Ireland; the Companies (Amendment) Act 1986 the Sch para 15(3)(b) in the Republic of Ireland.*

†CA85 Sch 4 para 32(1) in Great Britain; the Companies (NI) Order 1986 Sch 4 para 32(1) in Northern Ireland; and the Companies (Amendment) Act 1986 the Sch para 20(1) in the Republic of Ireland.

‡SSAP 12 para 16.

will be less than those based on historical cost. Gains on revaluations of fixed assets will, however, be recognised as they occur in the statement of total recognised gains and losses and thus will be visible to users.

(iii) when assets are revalued upwards a company's asset base will rise and (as a result of (i) and (ii) above) its profits will fall. The rate of return on investment will therefore be lower than it would have been if the assets had been left at historical cost.

The distinction between holding gains and trading margins

21 In times of rapid movements of relative prices users of financial statements will not easily be able to assess the capacity of a company to generate cash flows from its existing resource base unless profit is analysed between trading margins and holding gains or losses. The key to assisting the user of financial statements to understand the reality of the situation lies in the concepts of capital maintenance adopted.

22 For example, the oil industry was publicly attacked for profiteering during the Gulf War when oil prices rose and petrol prices rose accordingly. Yet an oil company could hardly be expected to continue to sell barrels of oil purchased at (say) $20 for $22 when the replacement cost was $40. If the company were to maintain the same $2 margin, oil sold at $42 would, under the historical cost system, result in a reported profit of $22. If the company were to replace the oil sold only the margin of $2 would remain; the windfall gain of $20 would have been entirely absorbed in the investment necessary to maintain a continuing availability of oil. The distinction between the two types of profit makes an important point about the nature of the company's business and the effect on it of changes in the economic environment.

23 The phenomenon in paragraph 22 above is particularly acute for commodity stocks (such as oil), where prices may fluctuate significantly regardless of the rate of general inflation.

Past gains recorded in present profit

24 At present, under the modified historical cost system where the profit is measured in terms of comparing sales proceeds with the original cost or revalued book amount of the asset sold, gains or losses are recognised at the time of the sale rather than when the change in value took place. There are many examples of this situation (two of which are mentioned below) leading to problems for those who are seeking to obtain a clear idea of a company's economic performance during the reporting period.

(i) Unrecognised holding gains
Companies may hold at historical cost or at outdated revalued amount long-term assets such as land banks bought many years ago and, if land prices have risen appreciably during the period of holding, when the land is eventually used for building the profit recorded in the financial statements will include the holding gains related to many years past not simply the current profit margin. In the past asset-strippers have made substantial profits from such understated values.

(ii) Profit-boosting sales
Companies can sell assets held for many years any time they wish to boost reported profits. Traded investments are particularly prone to 'bed and breakfast' transactions, but companies have even sold major property assets and re-purchased them some months later simply to create profits in the financial statements (circular transactions). Such a profit certainly does not reflect what has happened in that year and does not measure the economic performance of a company during that period – as in (i) above not all the 'profit' arose in the year of sale. Similar problems arise on the realisation of gains on assets contributed to joint ventures or asset gains on 'sale and leaseback' transactions – much of the 'profit' may relate to past periods.

Permanent versus temporary diminutions in value

Sometimes an apparent loss of value of fixed assets (other than investment properties) is not reflected in accounts under present practice because it is considered probable that this loss in value will reverse in the future. In the late 1980s many companies bought or revalued properties at the height of the property market boom. In some cases these asset values have not been written down despite the fact that their value has fallen considerably. It is, of course, extremely difficult in many cases to determine whether a loss in value is temporary or whether it is of a long-term nature. The Companies Act, however, requires that a provision need only be made in respect of diminutions in value of fixed assets if such diminutions are permanent*. The only way this problem could be relieved is if regular revaluations of such assets were required. **25**

The measurement of balance sheet gearing

The gearing ratio is deemed by many to be important, yet historical cost accounting makes it extremely deficient as a measurement device. For example, a loan may be given by a bank for, say, £20m secured on fixed assets which have a value of £30m but are shown in the financial statements at only £5m. Users of the financial statements would have to rely on note information, if given, to obtain a more realistic impression of the company's debt: equity ratio. **26**

Business combinations difficulties

Regular revaluation of certain assets would significantly reduce the difference between acquisition and merger accounting in the treatment of asset valuations and of future profitability. **27**

The two forms of accounting for business combinations, merger accounting and acquisition accounting, result in entirely different balance sheets and profit and loss accounts. There are a number of reasons for this but one factor is that under merger accounting rules the assets of the combining companies need not be revalued whereas under acquisition accounting rules the acquired company's net assets must be restated at their fair values. **28**

****CA85 Sch 4 para 19(2) in Great Britain; the Companies (NI) Order 1986 Sch 4 para 19(2) in Northern Ireland; and the Companies (Amendment) Act 1986 the Sch para 7(2) in the Republic of Ireland.***

29 Following the acquisition of a company, profit is affected by the restatement to fair value of the acquired company's stock and by a depreciation charge based on restated fixed assets. If the market value of stocks diverges markedly from the carrying amount (either because of changes in market prices of commodity stocks or because of the length of time elapsed since purchase or production) the reported profitability of the combined business may be severely reduced for some considerable time. The problem arises because the period by period change in replacement cost of the long-term stocks is ignored in historical cost financial statements until a sale is made, at which time the entire holding gain is shown in profit. An acquirer, however, cannot realise the full profit margin on stocks acquired part way through the maturity period and is unable under the historical cost system to report the increase in value occurring on currently maturing stocks. This may well lead to adverse views being held about the profitability of the new combination.

CONCLUSIONS

30 The present version of the modified historical cost system, a compromise evolved over many years, involving both the retention of historical costs and irregular revaluations is clearly unsatisfactory. Consequently, the Board and other standard setting bodies of the world have been considering ways in which to rationalise present practice. It is the Board's stated policy, set out in its 'Statement of Aims', to introduce accounting changes in an evolutionary manner where that is consistent with its other objectives.

31 In essence, the Board can choose one of three basic options:

(i) a return to historical cost accounting
This would involve excluding all revaluations of assets from financial statements except for the traditional 'cost or net realisable value whichever is the lower' requirement. Current values could obviously be shown by way of note. The advantage of this option is that it would bring practice into line with that of North America and some of the EC countries (but not Australia, New Zealand or South Africa) and would ensure that all companies produced information on a consistent basis. The disadvantages are that it would not solve many of the problems outlined above and it would remove from the primary financial statements values which many companies and users of financial statements clearly believe to be relevant, thereby reversing practices of many years' standing.

(ii) a move to a full current value system
The advantage of this option would be that all costs and assets would be shown at current amounts. The disadvantages would be that there is much work to be done to determine whether or not it is possible to devise a system that would be of economic relevance and acceptable to users and preparers of financial statements in terms of sufficient reliability without prohibitive cost.

(iii) continue with the present modified historical cost system but attempt to remove some of the existing anomalies

This would involve requiring revaluations on a more consistent basis for those assets:

- that represent a store of value (about which current value information has traditionally been given) and for which a ready market is available; and
- that can have potentially major effects on profit measurement (i.e. including assets such as general purpose properties but excluding specialised assets required for the operation of the business).

This course, unlike proposal (ii) above, would be of a hybrid nature but would be evolutionary rather than revolutionary.

The Board believes that a return to historical cost accounting would be inappropriate to the needs of those companies and industry groups that, in the past, have deemed it important to show revaluations in their financial statements. Such a move would be contrary to the trend of accounting development in the United Kingdom and Republic of Ireland towards the provision of more relevant information by the more regular use of current values. Commentators on the ASC's exposure draft ED51 – 'Accounting for fixed assets and revaluations' (May 1990) were asked whether it would be practicable to prohibit the carrying of selected fixed assets at a valuation. Of those who answered the question, 96% believed that it was not practicable. **32**

The Board understands that there are anxieties about the costs and benefits of moving to a full current value system. It believes that there would be a need at least for a considerable period of experimentation and learning before such a major change could be successfully introduced. The Board therefore proposes a strategy that would be based on the existing accounting system and concentrate on those assets whose change in value is an important feature of a company's underlying financial strength. This, the Board believes, would: **33**

- aid comparability and lead to consistency in asset valuation practise;
- be a realistic way of progressing, given that much of the information to be required already has to be provided under companies legislation or is voluntarily provided by many companies;
- remove many of the distortions of profit at present occurring.

The Board proposes that it should issue pronouncements concerned with those assets: **34**

- in respect of which supplementary information on current values is already required by law; and
- which are traded on a ready market.

These pronouncements would require:

(i) the revaluation of properties (excluding fixed assets specific to the business);
(ii) the revaluation of quoted investments; and
(iii) the revaluation of stock of a commodity nature and long-term stock where a market of sufficient depth exists.

If the Board decides to proceed with these proposals following its consideration of the responses to this paper, it would have to consider a number of questions including: **35**

(i) the scope of any requirements
Revaluation will increase costs and the Board must consider whether the benefits of such increased costs apply equally to users of financial statements of all sizes of companies. The Board's present view is that its proposals should apply initially only to the largest companies.

(ii) the form and costs of valuation
Valuations could be undertaken solely by internal valuers, by internal valuers with an external review, or solely by external valuers. Evidence from a survey available to the Board indicates that external valuers undertook approximately half of the property valuations currently shown in financial statements. Costs of compliance depend on the form of valuation required. In considering the form of valuations to be required the Board would hold discussions with the Royal Institution of Chartered Surveyors and other parties to determine the frequency of comprehensive external revaluations needed and the feasibility of updating these for intervening reporting dates by relatively inexpensive reviews, supplemented as necessary by full revaluations of significant blocks of assets that had altered in material respects.

The Board would publish the results of any such consultation in addition to issuing draft proposals in the normal way for accounting standards dealing with the three types of assets mentioned in this paper.

Appendix 1 – The Accounting Standards Committee's approach

SSAP 19 – ACCOUNTING FOR INVESTMENT PROPERTIES (1981)

For investment properties, annual revaluation to open market value has been standard accounting practice for many years. A recent review of the standard undertaken by the Institute of Chartered Accountants of Scotland on behalf of the Board has indicated that there is general satisfaction with its requirements, that there is no desire to return to historical cost and little enthusiasm for the use of discounted cash flows as opposed to open market values.

Concern has been expressed about the potential variability of valuations by different valuers and of the difficulty of reflecting depressed market conditions at a time when there is very little market movement. However, a study by CF Pratten of the Department of Applied Economics at the University of Cambridge following studies* by Drivers Jonas and IPD suggested that 60 per cent of values realised on sales of properties fell within 10 per cent of the surveyors' valuations. He concluded 'Although surveyors' valuations are not ideal they may well be the best estimates of value available for balance sheet purposes. Historical cost data provides a totally unreliable guide to contemporary values of property ... Valuations by surveyors and historical cost data adjusted by changes in indices of property values would provide more accurate assessments of contemporary values than historical cost.'

ED51 – ACCOUNTING FOR FIXED ASSETS AND REVALUATIONS (MAY 1990)

This exposure draft proposed that for each class of fixed asset the directors of an enterprise should determine whether to carry that class of fixed assets at cost or valuation. When a fixed asset was carried at a valuation the exposure draft proposed that:

- The carrying amount should represent the open market value for existing use of the fixed asset except in circumstances in which it was not practical to determine an open market value, in which case the depreciated net replacement cost of the fixed asset concerned should be used.
- No valuation should be more than five years old, although within that restriction a class of fixed assets could be carried at a valuation recognised in previous financial statements less depreciation (and where applicable, provisions for permanent diminutions in value) provided that the directors had reasonable grounds for believing that the value of the class of fixed asset at the balance sheet date was not materially different from that shown in the financial statements previously.
- Normally, external valuers should be used to carry out valuations. If internal valuers were used then a review should be undertaken by an external valuer.

**Covering the period 1988–91.*

ED55 – ACCOUNTING FOR INVESTMENTS (JULY 1990)

This exposure draft proposed that readily marketable investments held as current assets should be included in the balance sheet at their current market value. Where the size and nature of the holding were such that the market was not capable of absorbing the investments without a material effect on their quoted price, the exposure draft proposed that the current market price should be adjusted to reflect the proceeds that the enterprise could realistically expect to raise by disposing of the holding in the ordinary course of business. Where there was no market for the investments the exposure draft proposed that they be included in the balance sheet at the lower of their original cost and net realisable value or at current cost.

ED55 also suggested that a choice be given for on-trading investments shown as fixed assets. They could be carried at their original cost less any provision for permanent diminution or, alternatively, be revalued annually.

Appendix 2 – Specialised industry valuation practice in the United Kingdom and Republic of Ireland

This Appendix summarises some proposals for the use of current values in connection with specialised industries.

BANKS

The Statement of Recommended Practice (SORP) on Securities (September 1990) issued by the British Bankers' Association and the Irish Bankers' Federation and now used in drawing up banks' financial statements recommends that interests in quoted securities should be valued at market price and unquoted securities at the directors' estimate of market value. As in ED55, where a large holding exists a discount should be applied and where hedging is in operation both sides of the hedge should be accounted for by the same accounting method. Investment securities, held for the longer term, are to be carried at cost, less write downs where necessary.

The SORP on Advances (September 1992) states that advances held in a dealing portfolio for the purpose of trading on a secondary market should be carried at their secondary market value. This is to allow the banks maintaining such dealing advances to value them consistently with other dealing assets.

VENTURE CAPITALISTS

The British Venture Capital Association (BVCA) has issued a document entitled 'Principles for the Valuation of Venture Capital Portfolios', Second Edition (March 1991)* which sets out the following treatments:

- Unquoted venture investments (investments in immature companies, including start-up and early stage investments) should be valued at cost (rather than market value) *unless* this basis is untenable, i.e. where later financing transactions, net asset values or significant profits indicate a value other than cost should be used.
- Unquoted development investments (investments in mature companies having a maintainable trend of sustainable profits and where an exit (by way of flotation or trade sale) can be reasonably foreseen (but is not necessarily anticipated)) should after the initial post investment period be revalued with reference to open market value.
- Quoted investments (investments which have achieved an exit by flotation or where regular third party transactions take place) should be valued on the basis of their quoted mid-market value. Any formal restriction or practical limitation on the marketability of the shares should be recognised by applying a discount to the quoted price.

****Editor's note:*** *Superseded by 'Guidelines for the Valuation and Disclosure of Venture Capital Portfolios' issued November 1993.*

LOCAL AUTHORITIES

The Chartered Institute of Public Finance and Accountancy and the Local Authority (Scotland) Accounts Advisory Committee is currently developing a revised Code of Practice for local authority accounting that will be submitted to the Board in due course for issue as a SORP. The draft would require the balance sheet of local authorities to include operational fixed assets at a valuation.*

***Editor's note:** *The final revised Code of Practice published in September 1993 includes this requirement.*

Appendix 3 – Other valuation practice in the United Kingdom and Republic of Ireland

PROPERTY REVALUATIONS

In the United Kingdom property revaluations are probably the most common use of the 'alternative accounting rules' (ie the alternative to the historical cost rules) allowed by law. At the Board's initiative research has been undertaken on the frequency with which companies revalue their assets. A study of 250 companies from 21 industries* has shown that operating properties (that is, properties other than investment properties) were revalued by 64% of the sample overall, and by 70% of listed companies. Only 9% revalued other operating fixed assets. Of the 160 companies which revalued operating properties, 58% had revalued a proportion of them within the previous two years and 83% within the previous five years. The revaluations were equally divided between internal and external revaluations.

COMMODITY TRADING

The practice has developed, principally among commodity dealing companies, of stating stock at market value and also taking into account profits and losses arising on the valuation of forward contracts ('marking to market'). This represents a departure from the SSAP 9 – 'Stocks and long-term contracts' rule that stocks are to be valued at the lower of cost and net realisable value but is normally justified as being necessary in order to show a true and fair view as it results in a better measure of performance and gives less scope for manipulation of results. Marking to market is an international practice. For example, in the USA stocks may be stated at market value even where this is greater than cost in those circumstances where there is an organised and liquid market (eg for precious metals) with little or no selling costs.

**The sample included 184 listed companies and 66 unlisted companies from the following industries:*

Aerospace	*Financial*	*Metals & mining*
Automotive	*Food*	*Office equipment & servicing*
Banking	*Fuel*	*Packaging & containers*
Chemicals	*Health care*	*Publishing & broadcasting*
Conglomerates	*Housing & construction*	*Retail*
Consumer products	*Leisure*	*Service industries*
Electrical & electronics	*Manufacturing*	*Telecommunications*

Goodwill and intangible assets

(Issued December 1993)

Contents

Goodwill and intangible assets

Preface

This Discussion Paper has been prepared so that the issues of accounting for purchased goodwill and for purchased intangible assets can be reconsidered. The Paper looks at four basic methods of accounting for purchased goodwill and examines for each its rationale, related conceptual issues, and practical advantages and disadvantages.

Two possible approaches, derived from the four basic methods that could be adopted, have support amongst Board members; the Board has not yet reached a consensus on a single preferred approach. It is the intention of the Board, after reviewing the responses to this Paper, to issue a Financial Reporting Exposure Draft that will put forward one standard approach to purchased goodwill accounting.

The Paper notes that the nature of purchased intangible assets is closely related to that of purchased goodwill and proposes that most purchased intangible assets should be subsumed within purchased goodwill for reporting purposes.

Internally generated goodwill is touched on briefly in the Paper insofar as it needs to be considered when discussing the treatment of purchased goodwill. It is intended that the current prohibition on the recognition of internally generated goodwill should remain.

Invitation to comment

Comments are invited on the issues set out below as well as on any issues not raised below but which respondents would like to address. Comments will be more helpful if supported by their conceptual or practical justification.

The Board has not reached a consensus supporting any of the methods of purchased 1
goodwill accounting identified in this Paper. However, there is support amongst Board members for each of two approaches:

- a combination of 'capitalisation and predetermined life amortisation' and 'capitalisation and annual review', and
- 'separate write-off reserve'.

These approaches together with their main advantages and disadvantages are summarised in Section 8 of the Paper.

(i) Do you support either of these two approaches and, if so, which one and why?

(ii) If you do not support either of these two approaches:

  (a) which would be your preferred approach to goodwill accounting and why?

  (b) what are your reasons for not supporting either of the approaches described above?

(iii) If your preferred method of goodwill accounting were not to prove acceptable to the Board, which would be your second choice and why?

2 Section 3 of the Paper addresses the proposed treatment of intangible assets, and suggests that they should be subsumed within purchased goodwill for accounting purposes. Do you support this approach? If not, what would be your preferred approach and why?

3 If the Board were to adopt 'capitalisation and predetermined life amortisation' either as a stand-alone method or as part of the combined approach referred to in question 1 above:

(i) do you agree that the maximum allowable amortisation period should be twenty years so as to be consistent with the majority of the international community, or
(ii) do you think that the Canadian and US maximum allowed period of forty years, or some other period, would be more appropriate and why?

4 If the Board were to adopt 'capitalisation and annual review' do you have any specific suggestions as to how the ceiling tests could be improved?

1 INTRODUCTION

1.1 The costs of developing internally generated goodwill are charged to the profit and loss account as incurred and may arise over a period of many years. However, neither these costs nor the value to the business of the goodwill arising are recognised in the balance sheet; instead, the benefits are recognised only at the point when they materialise in the form of profits.

1.2 Purchased goodwill*, however, arises from a distinct transaction that needs to be accounted for. Whichever method is used for dealing with this transaction, there will be inconsistency either with accounting for internally generated goodwill or with accounting for the other assets and liabilities arising from the purchase transaction.

- If the accounting is to recognise as an asset that part of the purchased goodwill considered to represent future benefits to the group, it is inconsistent with the accounting for internally generated goodwill.
- If the accounting is to eliminate purchased goodwill against reserves, which would provide consistency of balance sheet treatment with internally generated goodwill, then it is inconsistent with the accounting for other components of the purchase transaction that are recognised as assets or liabilities.

1.3 Purchased goodwill is thus an accounting anomaly. Every method of accounting for it results in inconsistencies with other aspects of financial reporting. Preferences for one method or another tend to be determined by the conceptual and practical issues deemed to be the most important in the light of each individual's particular experience. This Paper examines these issues in the context of four basic methods of purchased

**In this Paper purchased goodwill is taken as being the difference deduced from performing the fair value exercise after an acquisition, determined arithmetically as: 'purchased goodwill = fair value of consideration for an acquisition less net sum of fair values of recognised assets and liabilities acquired'.*

goodwill accounting, which can be combined or varied to provide six possible approaches.

The methods identified fall into two groups: 1.4

(i) asset-based methods, and
(ii) elimination methods.

These are described in outline in the tables below and are detailed and compared in Sections 4–8 of the Paper.

Asset-based methods

1 Capitalisation and predetermined life amortisation	Purchased goodwill is capitalised, then amortised over a predetermined finite life subject to a maximum of, for instance, 20 years. Its amortised carrying value is assessed each year for recoverability.
2 Capitalisation and annual review	Purchased goodwill is capitalised, then amortised through the application of systematic annual review procedures to estimate the required annual amortisation charges. There may be years when the annual amortisation charge is zero.
Combination of **1** and **2** above	**1** would be the method to use for most acquisitions, but **2** should be used in those special circumstances where the goodwill has an indeterminate life expected to be greater than 20 years.

Elimination methods

3 Immediate write-off	Purchased goodwill is eliminated against reserves immediately on acquisition.
4 Separate write-off reserve	Purchased goodwill is transferred to a separate goodwill write-off reserve immediately on acquisition.
Variant of **4**: Separate write-off reserve with recoverability assessment	Purchased goodwill is transferred to a separate goodwill write-off reserve immediately on acquisition and the balance in this reserve is assessed for recoverability at each year-end. Losses reducing the recoverable amount below the balance in the write-off reserve are charged to the profit and loss account.

1.7 Intangible assets

Accounting for intangible assets is also addressed in the Paper. The proposal is that purchased intangible assets should be subsumed within purchased goodwill and accounted for accordingly. Purchased legal rights attaching to internally created intangible benefits should, however, be capitalised at their historical cost.

1.8 Goodwill acquired on the purchase of an unincorporated business

1.8.1 Where goodwill is acquired as part of the acquisition of an unincorporated business, it must be accounted for within the single entity accounts of the acquiring company. The accounting treatment used should be the same as that adopted by the company for purchased goodwill arising on consolidation.

1.9 Structure of Discussion Paper

1.9.1 Section 2 examines the background and recent developments in respect of goodwill and intangible assets accounting. Section 3 looks at accounting for intangible assets. Sections 4–7 discuss the method, rationale and related conceptual issues for each of the six approaches to goodwill accounting identified, and the practical consequences of applying them. Section 8 concludes the comparative discussion of the different methods of goodwill accounting and indicates the two alternative approaches currently favoured by different members of the Board.

1.9.2 The Appendices address respectively:

A the ceiling tests required for the annual review of the carrying value of purchased goodwill as part of the method of 'capitalisation and annual review',
B current international treatments, and
C consistency of each of the methods discussed with the currently issued draft Statement of Principles.

2 BACKGROUND AND RECENT DEVELOPMENTS

2.1 Existing regulations

2.1.1 The accounting treatment of goodwill in the UK and the Republic of Ireland is currently determined by:

(i) the Companies Act 1985 in Great Britain and the Companies (Northern Ireland) Order 1986 in Northern Ireland,
(ii) the Companies (Amendment) Act 1986, and the European Communities (Companies: Group Accounts) Regulations 1992 in the Republic of Ireland,
(iii) SSAP 22, issued in 1984, with revisions to disclosure requirements in 1989, and
(iv) UITF 3, issued in December 1991.

2.1.2 Companies legislation permits both:

(i) elimination of purchased goodwill against reserves, other than the revaluation reserve or – without the permission of the court – the share premium account, and
(ii) capitalisation of purchased goodwill in the balance sheet, provided that it is depreciated systematically over a period not to exceed its useful economic life.

SSAP 22 allows two different treatments of purchased goodwill: 2.1.3

(i) elimination against reserves, and
(ii) capitalisation and systematic amortisation over its useful economic life, subject to the overriding requirement that purchased goodwill may not be held permanently in the balance sheet.

The alternatives allowed by the SSAP are consistent with companies legislation.

Paragraph 7 of the explanatory note to SSAP 22 explains that purchased goodwill is written off to reserves as a matter of accounting policy and to achieve consistency of treatment with non-purchased goodwill, rather than because it has suffered a permanent diminution in value. 2.1.4

A further requirement was introduced by UITF 3 in December 1991 to the effect that, where a previously acquired business is disposed of or closed, any goodwill relating to it that has not subsequently been charged to the profit and loss account should be removed from reserves and included within the calculation of the profit or loss on disposal or closure. The UITF decided that this treatment was necessary in order to prevent purchased goodwill that has been eliminated against reserves from bypassing the profit and loss account completely. 2.1.5

2.2 Method generally adopted in UK accounts

The significance of accounting for purchased goodwill has increased in recent years; indeed, in a survey of 370 acquisitions, it was found that the amount paid for purchased goodwill as a percentage of the acquirer's net worth pre-acquisition grew from 1 per cent in 1976 to 44 per cent in 1987*. 2.2.1

The method generally adopted for goodwill accounting in the UK is that of elimination against reserves†. Its perceived advantage is that it protects the group profit and loss account from charges for goodwill amortisation. Since the introduction of UITF 3 this protection has lessened because on ultimate disposal or closure of a previously acquired business the related goodwill must be charged to the profit and loss account. 2.2.2

As amounts paid for purchased goodwill have increased, a number of acquisitive groups have found that their reserves have been significantly eroded as a result of the elimination of purchased goodwill. In an attempt to mitigate this effect several such groups have recognised within their accounts, separately from purchased goodwill, 2.2.3

**C Higson, The choice of accounting method in UK mergers and acquisitions, Institute of Chartered Accountants in England and Wales, 1990.*

†Previously unpublished statistics supplied to the Financial Times in November 1993, by Company Reporting, found that in a survey of 500 quoted companies making acquisitions only 4 per cent currently capitalise and amortise goodwill as compared with 96 per cent that write it off direct to reserves.

amounts relating to intangible assets* There has been much variation both in the nature of the intangible assets recognised by different groups and in the procedures used to value them. The accounting treatment adopted has generally been capitalisation, with subsequent write-downs in carrying value being made only to recognise permanent impairment. Automatic annual amortisation charges have generally not been made.

2.3 ED 47 and ED 52

2.3.1 In an attempt to standardise the accounting treatments of purchased goodwill and of purchased intangible assets, the Board's predecessor body, the Accounting Standards Committee, issued two Exposure Drafts in 1990: ED 47 'Accounting for goodwill', and ED 52 'Accounting for intangible fixed assets'.

2.3.2 ED 47 proposed that purchased goodwill should be capitalised and amortised systematically over its estimated useful economic life, which generally should not exceed twenty years and in no circumstances could exceed forty years. It also proposed that the method of elimination against reserves, preferred by SSAP 22 and adopted by the vast majority of UK reporting companies, should no longer be permitted.

2.3.3 These proposals were consistent with those included in the International Accounting Standards Committee's Exposure Draft E 32 'Comparability of Financial Statements', issued in January 1989, which was then the most recent IASC document. Subsequently, in 1992, the IASC issued a further Exposure Draft E 45 'Accounting for Business Combinations', which also proposed that purchased goodwill should not be eliminated against reserves and that it must, instead, be capitalised and amortised over a period that would not usually extend beyond five years and should in no circumstances extend beyond twenty years. These proposals will become effective as part of the revised IAS 22 'Accounting for Business Combinations' for accounting periods beginning on or after 1 January 1995.

2.3.4 ED 52 proposed that intangible fixed assets should be recognised in the balance sheet if, and only if, the historical costs of creating the intangible were known, the characteristics of the intangible could be clearly distinguished from those of goodwill and the cost of the intangible could be measured independently of goodwill. Intangibles satisfying these conditions were to be capitalised at historical cost and amortised over the estimated useful economic life of the intangible, which generally should not exceed twenty years and could in no circumstances exceed forty years. The amortisation proposals for intangible assets were therefore identical to those for goodwill.

2.3.5 The proposals in the two Exposure Drafts met with widespread disapproval†. For both ED 47 and ED 52 there was concern from corporate respondents that mandatory

**P Barwise, C Higson, A Likierman and P Marsh, Accounting for brands, Institute of Chartered Accountants in England and Wales, 1989, page 5 states: 'A survey of company accounts suggests that accounting for tangible assets is common practice in certain industries, and appears to be associated with low book-equity to market capitalisation ratios in many cases'.*

†See tables at paragraphs 2.3.11 and 2.3.12 for analyses of the responses received to ED 47.

annual amortisation charges were inappropriate – 93 per cent of the corporate respondents to ED 47 and 80 per cent of the corporate respondents to ED 52 opposed the fixed-life amortisation proposals. The opposition from the respondents in general was also strong: 73 per cent of all the respondents to ED 47 and 62 per cent of all the respondents to ED 52.

The opposition to the proposals in ED 47 was particularly marked both from the corporate respondents and from the larger firms of accountants. The main reason given was that in many cases management spent heavily to maintain and enhance the value of goodwill and related intangible assets. Managements, therefore, did not believe it appropriate to be forced to make an annual amortisation charge in those cases where the value of the goodwill had not reduced but had been maintained or even increased. Numerous examples were given of goodwill and intangible assets that had already been in existence for significantly longer than the forty-year proposed maximum amortisation period. **2.3.6**

There was clear support from the corporate respondents for a method whereby purchased goodwill would be capitalised, but would not be subjected to automatic annual amortisation charges. Whilst the smaller and medium-sized accounting firms did not in general identify such an approach, the method was identified and supported by half of the six largest accounting firms to respond to the ED. **2.3.7**

Elimination against reserves did not attract such significant disapproval from the corporate respondents as capitalisation and systematic amortisation over a predetermined life, but it was the method least favoured by the accounting firms. **2.3.8**

In response to the evidence that just over half of all the respondents, half of the large accounting firm respondents and over two-thirds of the corporate respondents were in favour of a method whereby purchased goodwill is capitalised and then subjected to an annual review for impairment but not to automatic annual amortisation charges, the Board has researched in some detail how an annual review might be performed. Companies legislation requires that where goodwill is capitalised it should be depreciated systematically over a period not to exceed its useful economic life. The annual review procedures therefore needed to constitute a method of systematic amortisation over the useful economic life of the goodwill. **2.3.9**

Tests known as 'ceiling tests' have been devised to perform the annual review*. The procedures for performing these tests were developed initially following meetings with representatives from thirteen companies, one user of accounts and four firms of accountants. The procedures were then pilot tested by a group of six major companies and subsequently refined to form the tests described in Appendix A. **2.3.10**

****The idea of developing ceiling tests to monitor the carrying value of purchased goodwill was put forward in the report by J Arnold, D Egginton, L Kirkham, R Macve and K Peasnell, Goodwill and other Intangibles: Theoretical Considerations and Policy Issues, Institute of Chartered Accountants in England and Wales, 1992.***

Table analysing companies' and overall responses to ED 47

2.3.11 The following table analyses the responses received to ED 47 from the corporate respondents and from all the respondents. The figures shown are percentages.

	Capitalisation with systematic amortisation over a predetermined life	Capitalisation without automatic annual amortisation charges	Immediate write-off against reserves
Companies support	4	68	20
Companies against	93	26	69
Companies neutral	3	6	11
Companies total	**100**	**100**	**100**
(Total = 70)			
Overall support	14	52	17
Overall against	73	33	66
Overall neutral	13	15	17
Overall total	**100**	**100**	**100**
(Total = 143)			

Table analysing accounting firms' responses to ED 47

2.3.12 The following table analyses the responses received to ED 47 from accounting firms. The figures shown are percentages.

	Capitalisation with systematic amortisation over a predetermined life	Capitalisation without automatic annual amortisation charges	Immediate write-off against reserves
Largest 6 support	17	50	17
Largest 6 against	66	33	66
Largest 6 neutral	17	17	17
Largest 6 total	**100**	**100**	**100**
Other firms support	54	15	8
Other firms against	23	62	69
Other firms neutral	23	23	23
Others total	**100**	**100**	**100**
(Total = 19)			
All firms support	40	20	8
All firms against	32	52	68
All firms neutral	28	28	24
All firms total	**100**	**100**	**100**
(Total = 25)			

3 INTANGIBLE ASSETS

3.1 Internally created intangible assets

Consistent with the treatment of internally generated goodwill, internally created intangible benefits should not be recognised in accounts. Development costs are an exception to this as they are addressed separately in SSAP 13 'Accounting for research and development'. It is not proposed to alter those requirements in any way. **3.1.1**

The benefits related to internally created intangible assets may, however, sometimes be secured through obtaining legal rights. For instance, where a drug has been developed, the right to market it may be secured by a fixed-life patent. In such a case, where the intangible has been developed internally and the legal rights to secure the benefits have been acquired subsequently, there is a clearly defined historical cost for the acquisition of the rights. **3.1.2**

The legal rights will generally, but not always, have a known finite life. Where they have a known finite life, they should be capitalised at historical cost and amortised over a period not to exceed this known life. The amortised carrying value should be assessed each year for impairment. Where they do not have a finite life, they should be capitalised at historical cost and then subjected to an annual assessment for impairment. **3.1.3**

3.2 Intangible assets arising on the acquisition of a company

A clear distinction is not always maintained between what constitutes goodwill and what constitutes intangible assets; in many cases the terms are used interchangeably. For instance, what may be described in one company as a 'brand' held by a particular business may be viewed in another as being part of the 'goodwill' of that business. **3.2.1**

In some cases goodwill may be considered to related to the name of a company without being more specifically identified. For instance an advertising agency with a well-established portfolio of clients may refer more generically to its goodwill than to the intangible benefit of its client list. **3.2.2**

In all these cases goodwill exists, that is, the business as a working whole is worth more than the sum of its component, separable assets and liabilities. The difference in description is one of nomenclature rather than a reflection of inherent differences in the type of intangible benefit described. For accounting purposes it is important that there is consistency of treatment between assets that are essentially the same but to which different people would ascribe different names. **3.2.3**

Companies legislation requirement for separability

Companies legislation defines the identifiable assets and liabilities that should be included in the consolidated balance sheet at fair values at the date of acquisition as 'the **3.2.4** assets or liabilities which are capable of being disposed of or discharged separately without disposing of a business of the undertaking.' Any intangible asset that is to be recognised separately from purchased goodwill, following the post-acquisition fair value exercise, must therefore satisfy this requirement.

3.2.5 Purchased goodwill is in effect defined as being the difference between the amount by which the cost of an acquisition exceeds the net sum of the fair values of the recognised assets and liabilities acquired; any amount of the purchase consideration that cannot be identified with a recognised asset or liability acquired is to be accounted for as purchased goodwill.

3.2.6 Goodwill cannot be disposed of without disposing of a business of the related undertaking, as by its nature it will always attach to a particular business. Where an intangible has the same character as the goodwill of a business it should not be recognised separately but should be included as part of the amount to be accounted for as purchased goodwill and dealt with accordingly. The effect is that, if purchased goodwill is capitalised, such intangibles will be included within the capitalised balance; if purchased goodwill is eliminated against reserves, they will be included within the balance eliminated. Examples of intangible assets that should be treated in this way are brands, publishing titles and newspaper mastheads.

3.2.7 There will sometimes be legal rights securing the benefits of these intangible assets, for instance trade marks or drug patents, such that the intangible asset and the related legal rights are acquired together as part of the acquisition of a company. In these cases it is believed not to be feasible to separate the intangible benefit from the legal right securing it without disposing of a part of the business; hence the appropriate treatment for consistency with companies legislation is to account for both the intangible benefit and the related legal rights within purchased goodwill.

Measurement

3.2.8 Closely related to the issue of separability discussed in paragraphs 3.2.4–3.2.7 above is the question of whether sufficiently reliable methods exist of measuring the benefits represented by intangible assets such as those mentioned in paragraph 3.2.6. This question is particularly pertinent to the accounting treatment of goodwill, as when the required treatment of goodwill is elimination against reserves immediately on acquisition, there is an incentive to preserve the balance sheet net worth by recognising intangible assets. This approach has been followed by a number of companies in the UK and abroad.

3.2.9 Such capitalised intangibles have tended to be recorded initially at cost or allocated value following the post-acquisition fair value exercise and have subsequently been subjected only to an annual assessment for impairment in their carrying value. Automatic annual amortisation charges have generally not been made.

3.2.10 The procedures used to attribute values to these intangibles as part of the post-acquisition fair value exercise and subsequently to assess their carrying values for impairment have varied but include:

- review of incremental earnings streams,
- review of actual earnings streams,
- application of a hypothetical price/earnings ratio, and
- estimation of a notional market value.

The variety of different measurement techniques adopted is recognised in the report 'The Valuation of Intangible Assets' by Arthur Andersen, published by The Economist Intelligence Unit and Business International in January 1992. In its 'Findings' it states (paragraph 4.2): 3.2.11

> 'The valuation of all assets is a subjective process – especially for intangible assets, when there is often no active open market. Given the subjectivities involved in such circumstances, adequate guidelines and standards are required regarding valuation criteria, methods and disclosures, and the qualifications of valuers. Such guidelines and standards will inspire greater public confidence than hitherto in the reliability and consistency of intangible asset valuations for financial reporting purposes.'

The Board does not believe that there is a generally accepted method of measurement for such intangibles. It not only regards these intangible benefits as having the same character as goodwill and therefore requiring to be accounted for accordingly, it has yet to be convinced that sufficiently reliable measurement methods have been developed for separate capitalisation to be acceptable. 3.2.12

Where, however, management believes it can provide a realistic estimate of the value of certain of the intangible benefits included within the goodwill balance, it may, if it wishes, provide a note to the accounts detailing: 3.2.13

- the nature of such intangible benefits,
- an estimate of their value to the business, and
- an explanation of how that estimate was derived.

Management may also wish to include in the Operating and Financial Review commentary of a qualitative nature in respect of the group's intangible assets.

3.3 Intangible assets acquired on the purchase of an unincorporated business

Intangible assets that have been acquired on the purchase of an unincorporated business should be dealt with in the single entity accounts of the acquirer in the same way as those arising on the acquisition of a company are accounted for in the consolidated accounts of a group. They should be subsumed within purchased goodwill and accounted for accordingly. 3.3.1

3.4 Draft Statement of Principles

Consistency of this treatment of intangible assets with the draft Statement of Principles is discussed in Appendix C. 3.4.1

Goodwill – Asset-based methods

4 CAPITALISATION AND PREDETERMINED LIFE AMORTISATION

4.1 Method

4.1.1 Purchased goodwill is capitalised on acquisition, then amortised over its estimated useful economic life. A requirement may be included that there is a fixed maximum period for this estimated life. In this Paper a fixed maximum period of twenty years is assumed.

4.1.2 The amortised carrying value is assessed annually for recoverability, so as to comply with the requirements of companies legislation that the carrying values of fixed assets are written down for any permanent impairment in value. Any write-down identified is charged to the profit and loss account.

4.1.3 The useful economic life is assessed at each year-end and altered if necessary. A requirement is sometimes included that the useful economic life may never be increased following such an assessment.

4.1.4 If an acquired part of the group is disposed of or closed, the amortised carrying value of any related purchased goodwill must be estimated, removed from the balance sheet and charged to the profit and loss account as part of the profit or loss on disposal or closure.

Recoverability assessment

4.1.5 The recoverability assessment of the goodwill balance is applied immediately post-acquisition to ascertain whether any part of the amount paid for goodwill represents a loss and therefore should be charged to the profit and loss account. Recoverability is subsequently assessed at each year-end to identify any losses reducing recoverable amount below the amortised carrying value and to charge such losses to the profit and loss account.

4.1.6 The assessment is performed by considering the recoverable amount of the related investment and, where this has fallen below the carrying amount, deciding whether the shortfall relates to identifiable assets or liabilities or to goodwill. The procedures used in practice for assessing the recoverable amount of the goodwill may be somewhat judgmental but should nevertheless be performed thoroughly. The nature of such an assessment stands in contrast to the more extensive procedures required when applying 'capitalisation and annual review', where the goodwill balance is not subject to other amortisation charges.

4.2 Rationale and related conceptual issues

4.2.1 The rationale of this method is that the amount paid for purchased goodwill represents an asset, provided it satisfies a recoverability assessment, and it should be recognised as such on acquisition. Purchased goodwill is deemed to diminish in value over time even if the related investment retains its value. Retention or enhancement of the value of theinvestment is attributed to the development of internally generated goodwill that replaces the original purchased goodwill. The loss in value of the original purchased goodwill is recorded in the accounts as amortisation and thereby removed from the balance sheet.

The method may not appeal conceptually to those who believe that consistent treatment between purchased goodwill is recognised as an asset, whereas internally generated goodwill is not; this inconsistency could cause difficulties when comparing the accounts of a group that had generated goodwill internally with those of a group possessing goodwill that was of a similar nature but had been purchased. Some view this as a serious deficiency of this method, but others believe that the different ways in which the two types of goodwill have arisen provide sufficient reason for their different accounting treatments. Moreover, users can make adjustments to reported results to remove the effects of recognising purchased goodwill so that different groups can be compared consistently. 4.2.2.

The method does not provide consistency of treatment with accounting for the investment in the accounts of its immediate parent. Automatic annual amortisation charges are made to purchased goodwill but there are no such amortisation charges for the investment, which is written down only to reflect a permanent impairment in value. 4.2.3

Consistency with the draft Statement of Principles is discussed in Appendix C. In general terms, consistency is achieved provided that the procedures for annual assessment of the carrying value of purchased goodwill are deemed to be rigorous. 4.2.4

4.3 Practical advantages and disadvantages

International comparability

The method is required practice in many overseas countries and its adoption here would therefore serve best the goal of international comparability. Detailed requirements differ from country to country in terms of whether or not a fixed maximum period for the useful economic life of goodwill is specified and, if it is, the length of that period. 4.3.1

- The EC Fourth Directive states that the life should generally not exceed five years, but allows a longer period where this can be justified.
- The International Accounting Standards Committee in IAS 22 does not specify a maximum life. However, the revisions to that standard, which are to take effect for accounting periods starting on or after 1 January 1995, include a requirement that the maximum economic life of purchased goodwill should generally be no longer than five years, but may be up to twenty years if such longer period is justified.
- Australia and New Zealand specify a maximum life of twenty years.
- Canada and the USA specify a maximum life of forty years.

A maximum proposed life of twenty years would therefore, to a large extent, provide international consistency.

Accountability

4.3.2 The method provides limited accountability for goodwill. It is difficult to estimate the useful economic life of goodwill accurately and so the annual amortisation charges may not provide effective accountability. The assessment of the amortised carrying value for recoverability should provide some accountability, particularly in the early years after an acquisition when the goodwill balance has not already been significantly reduced by annual amortisation charges, provided the procedures used to perform the assessment are robust.

4.3.3 The Board is concerned that if this method were adopted the assessment procedures to be performed would be similar to those currently required as part of the impairment assessment performed on the carrying value of an investment shown in the single entity accounts of its immediate present. Discussions with representatives from a number of companies indicate that such assessments tend to be of limited scope and to detect only significant losses in value. However, the Board believes that if performed more thoroughly these assessments could in some cases be effective in identifying more promptly and more precisely losses in value of the related investment.

4.3.4 Losses in value, if identified, are recorded in the accounts of the immediate parent company providing accountability for the investment. This accountability is clearer than that provided in the consolidated accounts because it is not confused with the annual amortisation charges made to goodwill. However, not all users of consolidated accounts will obtain copies of the accounts of the various immediate parent companies of the acquired investments.

Views from previous Exposure Drafts

4.3.5 As described in paragraphs 2.3.5 et seq the responses to ED 47 showed that the method was unpopular with commentators from industry, 93 per cent of whom opposed it. They regarded it as inappropriate to impose an automatic annual amortisation charge, arguing that managements who had spent heavily to maintain or enhance the value of their group's goodwill would be penalised unjustifiably through such a charge. They were also concerned that the method results in a double charge being made as both the cost of maintaining the goodwill and the, often inappropriate, amount for amortisation would be charged to the profit and loss account.

Intangible assets

4.3.6 The method can be used to deal simultaneously with accounting for those purchased intangible assets that this Paper proposes should not be capitalised separately from purchased goodwill. Brands, publishing rights and similar purchased intangible benefits would be subsumed within the purchased goodwill balance and amortised over the estimated useful economic life of the complete goodwill balance, subject to the proposed twenty-year maximum life. There may, however, be opposition in some cases to such an approach, as 62 per cent of the respondents to ED 52 stated that they were opposed to mandatory limited-life amortisation for intangible assets.

Simplicity

The method is relatively straightforward to apply. The useful economic life of the goodwill must be estimated but this is subject to a fixed maximum of twenty years. The related investment must be accessed for recoverability each year, but this is a procedure that must in any event be performed for the accounts of the immediate holding company. **4.3.7**

Return on investment

Some believe that the method understates the asset base used for calculating the return on investment earned to the extent of cumulative amortisation charges that do not reflect genuine losses in value. Users of accounts holding this view may find it appropriate to make adjustments to reported results and to the asset base before a return on investment is calculated. Those wishing to calculate a return on tangible assets employed would be able to do so by removing from the asset base the amortised goodwill carrying value. **4.3.8**

5 CAPITALISATION AND ANNUAL REVIEW

5.1 Method

Purchased goodwill is capitalised, then depreciated over its useful economic life through the application of a formal annual recoverability review that determines the appropriate depreciation charges by ascertaining any impairment in the related investment. **5.1.1**

The annual review is performed using tests, known as ceiling tests, which are summarised below and detailed in Appendix A. Application of these tests results in purchased goodwill being depreciated systematically over a period that will not exceed its useful economic life. The tests may in some periods give rise to a nil charge for depreciation but may never reverse depreciation previously charged nor result in an upward revaluation of goodwill. **5.1.2**

If an acquired part of the group is disposed of or closed, the written-down carrying value of any related purchased goodwill must be estimated, removed from the balance sheet and charged to the profit and loss account as part of the profit or loss on disposal or closure. **5.1.3**

Ceiling tests

As there are no automatic amortisation charges, rigorous procedures are required to determine the recoverability of the related investment. Tests known as 'ceiling tests' have been devised to make this determination by estimating the net present value of the investment and comparing it with the sum of the fair values of its individual assets, liabilities and goodwill. Reductions in recoverable amount attributable to the investment's recognised assets and liabilities are adjusted respectively against such assets and liabilities; reductions in recoverable amount not attributable to any recognised **5.1.4** assets or liabilities of the investment must, by default, be attributable to the goodwillpurchased with the investment. A lower recoverable amount for the purchased goodwill is then ascertained and, if necessary, the carrying value of the goodwill is reduced with the reduction being charged to the profit and loss account.

5.1.5 Estimating the net present value of an investment can be a subjective process. To limit this subjectivity the ceiling tests impose certain constraints on the estimation exercise. There are two ceiling tests, known as the 'DCF test' and the 'comparative test'. Each estimates the investment's net present value in a slightly different way from the other.

5.1.6 The 'DCF test' restricts the estimation in three ways.

(i) The cash flow forecasts used must be based on an 'explicit cash flow forecast' (the part of the forecast that makes different assumptions about sales, margins, overhead growth and other relevant parameters from one year to the next) of no more than five years from the start of the forecast period.

(ii) After the explicit cash flow period, the forecast must use a 'continuing value' for the investment based on a steady growth rate of normalised cash flow from one year to the next. This steady growth rate must be appropriate to the business concerned and to the country of operation involved. For UK businesses it may be no higher than 2.5 per cent, which is broadly the average annual growth rate in gross domestic product over the last forty years. Similar restrictions on the growth rate should be placed on business conducted outside the UK.

(iii) The discount rate to be used in the estimation should be the weighted average cost of capital for the part of the business concerned.

5.1.7 In outline, the 'comparative test' bases the cash flows used in the net present value estimation on the level of cash flows actually achieved over the previous five years, or over a shorter period for acquisitions made less than five years earlier. This test is included to ensure that cash flow forecasts are not over-optimistic.

5.1.8 The combination of the two tests is applied every year to each acquisition accounted for using 'capitalisation and annual review'. The tests are described more fully in Appendix A.

5.2 Rationale and related conceptual issues

5.2.1 The rationale is that purchased goodwill is taken to be part of the representation in the consolidated accounts of the related investment recorded in the accounts of the immediate parent. If there were no consolidated accounts, goodwill would not be accounted for separately but would feature as only an implicit part of the related investment. However, consolidated accounts break up the amount of the investment by showing individual categories of assets and liabilities separately and the residual as goodwill. Accountability for the goodwill component can consequently be provided by linking it to the maintenance of value of the investment. Reductions in the recoverable amount of the investment not attributable to any of the other assets or liabilities identified on consolidation are attributed to reductions in the recoverable amount of purchased goodwill, which in turn may require that the carrying value of purchased goodwill is written down. Recoverability reviews are used to determine appropriateannual amortisation charges for purchased goodwill and replace the automatic annual amortisation charges applied under 'capitalisation and predetermined life amortisation'.

The method makes amortisation charges only for genuine losses in value; rather than make a predetermined estimate of the life of goodwill it recognises that such a life may be indeterminate, and that in such cases amortisation over that indeterminate life is appropriate. The method is similar to the non-depreciation in some groups' accounts of assets, such as pipelines or sixteenth-century public houses, that do not have a known finite life since their value is expected to continue without abating for the foreseeable future, as a result of their being effectively maintained. **5.2.2**

The method differs conceptually from that of 'capitalisation and predetermined life amortisation'. Under that method, purchased goodwill is seen as declining over time and possibly being replaced by internally generated goodwill. Supporters of 'capitalisation and annual review' regard it as irrelevant whether there has been a decline in the purchased goodwill and replacement by internally generated goodwill, provided that the goodwill in the related investment is maintained. **5.2.3**

The method does not provide consistency of treatment between purchased goodwill and internally generated goodwill and hence may not appeal to those who consider it important to be able to compare the accounts of a group that has grown by acquisition with the accounts of a similar group that has grown organically. However, if they wish to do so, users can make adjustments to reported results to remove the effects of recognising purchased goodwill so that different groups can be compared consistently. **5.2.4**

Consistency with the draft Statement of Principles is discussed in Appendix C. In general terms consistency is achieved provided that the ceiling tests are viewed as being rigorous. **5.2.5**

5.3 Advantages and disadvantages

Accountability

One of the main advantages of this method is that accountability and predictive information are provided in the consolidated balance sheet and in the consolidated profit and loss account, both for the initial amount spent on goodwill and for the subsequent maintenance of value of that amount. As a result of applying the ceiling tests, this method is more likely than the others to give an early indication of potential problems in respect of the investment. **5.3.1**

The reliability of this accountability depends on the effectiveness of the ceiling tests. When the tests were devised, a trade-off was needed between making them straightforward to apply and making them sufficiently robust to identify promptly losses in value of goodwill. Tests such as the ceiling tests, requiring assumptions about the future, are by their nature always susceptible to over-optimism. If they were to be adopted, managers and auditors would need to consider carefully the assumptions underlying the cash flow forecasts and the degree of realism included when making **5.3.2** them. After extensive consultation, including pilot testing and the introduction of thecomparative test based on past performance, the tests as devised represent a balance between being straightforward to apply and being robust.

Simplicity

5.3.3 The main perceived practical disadvantage of this method is that, as a result of the requirement to perform ceiling tests, it is more onerous to apply than the other methods. However, discussions held on behalf of the Board with representatives from acquisitive groups indicate that many such groups perform similar estimations of the recoverable amount of an investment, both as part of their internal feasibility assessment before making an acquisition, and as a post-acquisition exercise to gauge the continued success of an acquisition. Application of the ceiling tests would essentially be an extension and formalisation of this process.

Legality

5.3.4 The Board believes that this method complies with the requirements of companies legislation that goodwill should be depreciated systematically over a period chosen by the directors that does not exceed its useful economic life. There may, however, be doubt as to whether, on a strict construction, companies legislation read in the context of the EC Fourth Directive, requires that goodwill be 'written off' (ie to zero) over a limited period. Such impediment as that interpretation puts on the adoption of the method can, in the view of the Board, be overcome, if necessary, by resort to the override, which will permit a departure from the legal requirement in regard to the depreciation of goodwill on the grounds of the special circumstances which, as explained in paragraph 5.4.2 below, must obtain to make the adoption of the 'capitalisation and annual review' method appropriate and necessary in order for the accounts to give a true and fair view.

5.3.5 Where there has been resort to the override there must be disclosure of the departure from companies legislation, of the reasons for it and of its effect.

Return on investment

5.3.6 The method provides an appropriate measure of 'return on investment', which can be used to give an effective assessment of management performance. The return is calculated using an asset base that shows goodwill at the lower of its cost and recoverable amount. Those wishing to calculate a return on tangible assets employed can do so by removing capitalised goodwill from the asset base.

International consistency

5.3.7 The method is not adopted overseas. Overseas countries generally capitalise purchased goodwill but then amortise it over a predetermined finite life. Development of the ceiling tests to calculate amortisation charges has been pioneered in the UK. If they were adopted, therefore, UK practice would still not be consistent with international practice. However, interest has been shown by several overseas standard-setters in this method and there is a possibility that some overseas countries could move to it at a later stage.

Views from earlier Exposure Drafts

According to the responses to ED 47 the method appears to be consistent with the way in which most businesses view their investment: 68 per cent of the corporate respondents and 52 per cent of all the respondents supported a method that would not make automatic amortisation charges to the profit and loss account. These respondents believed that it was important to show, where appropriate, the maintenance of value of purchased goodwill. As a result the Board was prompted to undertake research to devise robust tests that would identify genuine losses in value. **5.3.8**

5.4 *Variant: combination of 'capitalisation and predetermined life amortisation' and 'capitalisation and annual review'*

Method

The variant is a combination of the two asset-based methods. **5.4.1**

For most acquisitions the method described in Section 4 of 'capitalisation and predetermined life amortisation' would be used whereby purchased goodwill would be amortised over its estimated useful economic life, subject to a fixed maximum period of twenty years. The method of 'capitalisation and annual review' would be used only in special and limited circumstances, such as where it is impossible to make, with any reasonable degree of precision, a determination of the useful economic life of the goodwill beyond an assessment, on the basis of all relevant factors (including the historical experience of the economic life of goodwill of a similar nature both in the business in question and generally), that the goodwill being assessed has a useful economic life of more than twenty years. **5.4.2**

For any acquisition accounted for using the method of 'capitalisation and annual review' there should be disclosure of the fact that this method has been adopted and of the special circumstances justifying its use. **5.4.3**

Rationale and related conceptual issues

Such a combined approach is likely to appeal to those who see goodwill conceptually as an asset, but do not think that the more accurate reflection of reality provided by the annual review approach to amortisation, as opposed to the predetermined life approach, can always be justified on cost-benefit grounds. In some ways a predetermined life approach to amortisation can be seen as an approximation to the annual review approach to amortisation – indeed even with the predetermined life approach, ceiling tests could be used to replace the informal assessment of the carrying value of the related investment. The combined approach is also likely to appeal to those who believe they have made an investment that will retain its value for more than twenty years, and who believe that economic reality would not therefore be portrayed by predetermined life amortisation over a period not to exceed twenty years. **5.4.4**

5.4.5 The combined approach would bring goodwill accounting in the UK and the Republic of Ireland largely into line with international practice, whilst at the same time satisfying the requirements of companies legislation. It would also meet the concerns of those who objected to the fixed-life amortisation proposals in ED 47 on the grounds that there are cases where goodwill has an indeterminate life and hence that it is inappropriate for such goodwill to be written off over a fixed life.

Advantage and disadvantages

5.4.6 These are the same as those identified in the sections discussing the respective advantages and disadvantages of the two methods.

Goodwill – Elimination methods

6 IMMEDIATE WRITE-OFF

6.1 Method

6.1.1 Purchased goodwill is eliminated immediately against any reserves of the group other than share premium account or the revaluation reserve, which are subject to legal restrictions against their use for the elimination of purchased goodwill.

6.1.2 If an acquired part of the group is disposed of or closed, the amount of any related purchased goodwill must be estimated, removed from the reserve against which it was originally eliminated and charged to the profit and loss account for the period as part of the profit or loss on disposal or closure.

6.1.3 To comply with companies legislation, the cumulative amount spent on purchased goodwill not related to a part of the business that has subsequently been disposed of or closed is shown in a note to the accounts.

6.2 Rationale and related conceptual issues

6.2.1 The rationale is that there should be consistency of treatment between purchased goodwill and internally generated goodwill. As internally generated goodwill may not be recognised in the balance sheet, correspondingly, as a matter of accounting policy and not because it does not have any value, purchased goodwill is eliminated against reserves. In the profit and loss account, however, the treatment of the two kinds of goodwill remains different, as the costs related to the creation of internally generated goodwill are charged, whereas no charge is made for goodwill acquired by purchase.

6.2.2 The method may appeal to those who believe that it is important for there to be consistency of treatment between purchased and internally generated goodwill, so that comparisons can be made, for example, between the accounts of two groups with similar types of intangible benefits comprising goodwill, some of which were acquired by purchase and others built up internally. The method is unlikely to appeal to those who regard purchased goodwill as an asset representing in the consolidated accounts the part of the related investment that cannot be attributed to any of its other recognised assets.

The method does not attempt to link accounting for purchased goodwill with accounting for the related investment in the accounts of its immediate parent. **6.2.3**

As discussed in Appendix C the method is regarded as inconsistent with the draft Statement of Principles. **6.2.4**

6.3 Advantages and disadvantages

Simplicity

The advantage of the method is its simplicity. Once purchased goodwill has been eliminated there is no further accounting required except on disposal or closure of the related part of the business. **6.3.1**

Erosion of reserves and intangible assets accounting

The practical problem with the method is that the reserves of acquisitive groups can, and indeed in many cases have, become significantly and dramatically eroded, so that prosperous acquisitive groups sometimes give the anomalous appearance of being financially weak. In an effort to overcome this appearance many such groups have developed the practice of recognising separately in the balance sheet some of those intangible assets that, in Section 3 above, it is proposed should be subsumed within goodwill for accounting purposes. In the absence of a well-established methodology of recognition and measurement for such assets, inconsistencies have arisen in terms both of the types of intangible assets that have been capitalised and of the methods that have been used for measuring their carrying values. **6.3.2**

This treatment of purchased goodwill, if adopted, will therefore lead either to an acceptance that acquisitive groups, particularly in the service sector, are likely to have a low value for net assets in their consolidated balance sheets or to a need to establish a recognition and measurement methodology for intangible assets. In the latter case, so as to satisfy the companies legislation requirement for fixed assets that 'provisions for diminution in value shall be made in respect of any fixed asset which has diminished in value if the reduction in its value is expected to be permanent...', some system of impairment testing would be needed for capitalised intangible assets. The Board would then be led back either to requiring the amortisation of such intangible assets over a predetermined life, which is known, from the responses to ED 52, to be unpopular, or to the problem of devising tests, possibly similar to the ceiling tests described earlier, to measure the recoverable amounts of intangible assets. Application of the ceiling tests, noted above as being a possible practical difficulty of 'capitalisation and annual review', would, therefore, not necessarily be avoided by applying the method of 'immediate write-off'. **6.3.3**

Accountability

6.3.4 The method does not provide accountability in the consolidated accounts for amounts spent on purchased goodwill. It may appeal to those who consider that the difficulty of providing accountability for purchased goodwill in consolidated accounts is such that it should not be attempted. It is unlikely to appeal to those who believe that accountability can and should be provided in the consolidated accounts for purchased goodwill. Some accountability for the related investment is provided in the accounts of the immediate parent company through the general requirement to write down the carrying value for any permanent impairment in value identified.

6.3.5 Profit and loss account charges for purchased goodwill are recorded in the consolidated accounts only where the related business or part thereof has been disposed of or closed.

International comparability

6.3.6 The method is generally inconsistent with international practice and is even thought by some to result in UK companies overpaying for acquisitions compared with US companies, because there is no requirement to amortise purchased goodwill. Although permitted by some overseas countries, it is far less common than 'capitalisation and predetermined life amortisation'. It is consistent with one of the options within the current IAS 22 'Accounting for Business Combinations' but it is not consistent with the requirements in the revised IAS 22, which are to be effective for accounting periods beginning on or after 1 January 1995. It is permitted by the EC Fourth Directive and is available as an option in some Member States.

Return on investment

6.3.7 The method can lead an uninformed reader to make an incorrect assessment of the return on investment earned. The returns of a group may be increased by the additional income derived from an acquisition whilst the reserve base of the group is reduced by the elimination of the related purchased goodwill. Unless a user makes appropriate adjustments to the asset base, incorrectly high returns on investment may be calculated. Those wishing to calculate a return on tangible assets employed can do so without making any adjustments to the asset base.

Views from earlier Exposure Drafts

6.3.8 The method is much more popular in the UK than the only currently allowable alternative under SSAP 22 of 'capitalisation and predetermined life amortisation', as evidenced by the much higher number of groups that adopt it (see footnote 3 to paragraph 2.2.2). However, as can be seen from the review in Section 2.3, the method was not favoured by respondents to ED 47.

6.3.9 It is possible that this method is sometimes adopted merely because it does not have the perceived disadvantage of 'capitalisation and predetermined life amortisation', namely that the profit and loss account suffers an amortisation charge every year regardless of the continuing value of the purchased goodwill or of the related investment.

7 SEPARATE WRITE-OFF RESERVE

7.1 Method

Purchased goodwill is transferred immediately on acquisition to a separate reserve known as a 'goodwill write-off reserve'. The shareholders' funds of the group are shown in total both before and after inclusion of this write-off reserve. **7.1.1**

If an acquired part of the group is disposed of or closed, the amount of any related purchased goodwill must be estimated, removed from the write-off reserve and charged to the profit and loss account for the period as part of the profit or loss on disposal or closure. **7.1.2**

The method differs from the previous elimination method only in that eliminated goodwill must be held in a separate goodwill write-off reserve, which is shown separately on the face of the balance sheet together with a shareholders' funds subtotal before and after that reserve. **7.1.3**

As noted in paragraph 7.3.3 below, it may be appropriate to present the goodwill write-off reserve in the balance sheet as follows: **7.1.4**

I	Called up share capital	A
II	Share premium account	B
III	Revaluation reserve	C
IV	Other reserves	D
V	Profit and loss account – accumulated results	E
Shareholders' funds before goodwill write-off		*A+B+C+D+E*
	Profit and loss account – cumulative goodwill write-off	(F)
Shareholders' funds after goodwill write-off		*A+B+C+D+E−F*

7.2 Rationale and related conceptual issues

The rationale is that the amount spent on purchased goodwill should be clearly highlighted so that users of accounts can make their own assessment of the success or otherwise of acquisitions. It is assumed to be so difficult to provide reliable information in respect of the continuing value of goodwill in consolidated accounts that this is not attempted. **7.2.1**

It is recognised that the benefits giving rise to the purchased goodwill are similar in **7.2.2** nature to assets, but it is believed that the difficultly involved in measuring such benefits is such that it is inappropriate to show these benefits as assets in the balance sheet.

7.2.3 Consistency with the treatment of internally generated goodwill is largely achieved with this method. Neither is recognised as an asset, but purchased goodwill is shown separately within reserves.

7.2.4 The method does not attempt to link accounting for purchased goodwill with accounting for the related investment in the accounts of its immediate parent.

7.2.5 As discussed in Appendix C the method is regarded as inconsistent with the draft Statement of Principles.

7.3 Advantages and disadvantages

Erosion of reserves and intangible assets accounting

7.3.1 Showing goodwill in a separate write-off reserve eases the problems relating to erosion of reserves that can arise with 'immediate write-off'. As balance sheet totals for reserves are shown separately before and after the goodwill write-off reserve, the anomalous appearance sometimes given by the 'immediate write-off' method of a low balance sheet net worth for a financially healthy group is to a certain extent avoided. Users can clearly see the net worth of the business and management can explain that the separate write-off reserve is simply an accounting adjustment, not related to a loss of value. The clear presentation of net worth before the deduction of cumulative goodwill largely removes the incentive to capitalise intangible assets as a means of preserving net worth.

Accountability

7.3.2 The total spent on purchased goodwill, other than that relating to businesses or parts of them that have subsequently been disposed of or closed, is clearly highlighted. It is left to users to make their own assessments of the success of acquisitions. The method may appeal to those who believe that the difficulty of providing accountability for purchased goodwill in consolidated accounts is so great that it should not be attempted. Some accountability for the investment is provided in the single entity accounts of its immediate parent company through the general requirement to write down for any permanent impairment in value.

Legality

7.3.3 For simplicity this method has been discussed in terms of a separate goodwill write-off reserve. However, some argue that the concept of a negative reserve is self-contradictory. If this view prevails, an equivalent presentation can be achieved by adding a note explaining that the cumulative goodwill write-off reserve should strictly be regarded as part of the aggregate profit and loss account balance, which unlike other reserves may be negative as it is no more than a historical record.

Earlier support

Interest in using a method such as this has already been shown in that several UK publicly quoted companies currently record purchased goodwill in a separate write-off reserve rather than eliminate it against existing reserves. 7.3.4

Simplicity

The method is easy to apply: once goodwill has been transferred to a separate write-off reserve, there is no further accounting required except on disposal or closure of a related part of the business. 7.3.5

Return on investment

The method clearly identifies an amount to be included within the asset-base when calculating the return on investment. However, the amount shown may be overstated because it is not reduced, except on disposal or closure of the related business, for subsequent losses in value of the goodwill. Those wishing to calculate the return on tangible assets employed can do so by using the asset base as reported. 7.3.6

International consistency

The method is not generally adopted overseas. 7.3.7

7.4 Variant: separate write-off reserve with recoverability assessment

Method

Purchased goodwill is transferred immediately on acquisition to a separate goodwill write-off reserve exactly as described in Section 7.1 above. The balance held in this reserve is, however, then either: 7.4.1

(i) assessed informally for recoverability each year by looking at the recoverable amount of the investment in the accounts of its immediate parent, or
(ii) reviewed more formally for recoverability through application of the ceiling tests as required when applying 'capitalisation and annual review'.

In either case any reductions required to the balance held in the goodwill write-off reserve should be charged to the profit and loss account for the period.

If an acquired part of the group is disposed of or closed, the written-down amount of any related purchased goodwill must be estimated, removed from the write-off reserve and charged to the profit and loss account for the period as part of the profit or loss on disposal or closure. 7.4.2

Rationale and related conceptual issues

In a way this variant results in a hybrid treatment between accounting for goodwill similarly to accounting for an asset and providing consistency of treatment with 7.4.3

internally generated goodwill. The accounting is as for an asset in that losses are identified and charged to the profit and loss account, but purchased goodwill is not presented in the balance sheet as an asset. Consistency of balance sheet treatment with internally generated goodwill is achieved in that purchased goodwill is not recognised as an asset; in the profit and loss account, however, the treatment for the two kinds of goodwill remains different.

7.4.4 As for the other elimination methods the variant is regarded as inconsistent with the draft Statement of Principles.

Advantages and disadvantages

7.4.5 Accountability is provided for the amount spent on purchased goodwill in the consolidated balance sheet, and for losses in the value of purchased goodwill in the consolidated profit and loss account. The variant may therefore appeal to those who consider it important that accountability is provided for amounts spent on goodwill, but who, owing to the nebulous nature of goodwill, would prefer to see such amounts as a deduction from reserves rather than as an asset in the balance sheet.

7.4.6 The variant provides an appropriate basis for estimating the return on investment, as the relevant amount of goodwill to be included within the asset base can be identified easily.

7.4.7 It is less straightforward to apply than the basic method, because of the assessment or review required of the recoverable amount of the balance held in the goodwill write-off reserve. The degree of difficulty introduced by applying the variant to the basic method will depend upon whether an informal assessment of the recoverability of the investment is performed or a more formal review is applied using the ceiling tests. If the more formal review is applied, although the method will be more onerous, it will give a more reliable estimate of any losses in recoverable amount.

8 CONCLUSION

8.1 Possible ways forward

8.1.1 The Board has not yet reached a consensus on the appropriate method to use for purchased goodwill accounting. However, when it has considered the responses to this Discussion Paper it intends to identify a single preferred approach. There are two possible approaches that have support amongst Board members:

(i) a combination of 'capitalisation and predetermined life amortisation' and 'capitalisation and annual review'

Most acquisitions would be accounted for using 'capitalisation and predetermined life amortisation'. However, in those special circumstances where purchased goodwill had an indeterminate life believed to be greater than twenty years, it would be accounted for using 'capitalisation and annual review'.

(ii) 'separate write-off reserve'

Purchased goodwill would be eliminated immediately on acquisition by being transferred to a separate goodwill write-off reserve. There would be no further accounting for this balance except on disposal or closure of the related business.

The two approaches reflect different conceptual viewpoints. The first is that accountability can and should be provided for purchased goodwill in both the consolidated profit and loss account and the consolidated balance sheet. The second is that it is not possible to provide accountability for purchased goodwill in the consolidated profit and loss account; instead accountability is provided in the consolidated balance sheet by identifying clearly the total spent on purchased goodwill. Users can then make their own judgement of the success of acquisitions. **8.1.2**

8.2 Asset-based methods

If purchased goodwill is capitalised the treatment that more accurately reflects reality is 'capitalisation and annual review', where the carrying value is reduced only for genuine losses in value; arbitrary annual amortisation charges are not made. However, the disadvantage of this method compared with 'capitalisation and predetermined life amortisation' is that the ceiling test procedures to be applied are more extensive, will take longer and will therefore be more expensive to perform, than the process of calculating an annual amortisation charge and carrying out a less formal and more subjective assessment of the recoverable amount of the related investment. **8.2.1**

Adoption of 'capitalisation and predetermined life amortisation' would result in international comparability, which will not be achieved with any of the other methods, although 'capitalisation and annual review', by recognising purchased goodwill as an asset, would go some way towards achieving this goal. **8.2.2**

Board members supporting an asset-based approach favour a combination of the two methods. 'Capitalisation and annual review' would be used for acquisitions where there were special circumstances such that the related goodwill was believed on the basis of all the relevant factors, including the historical experience of the economic life of goodwill of a similar nature both in the business in question and generally, to have an indeterminate life of more than twenty years. In such cases amortisation over a fixed maximum period not to exceed twenty years would not provide a reasonable approximation to amortisation over the estimated useful economic life of the goodwill. 'Capitalisation and predetermined life amortisation' would be used where the goodwill either had a known life of less than twenty years, or had an indeterminate life but there were no special circumstances for believing that this life was longer than twenty years. **8.2.3**

The fact that consistency of treatment with internally generated goodwill would not be achieved with the asset-based methods is not believed to be critical: through the disclosure provided, the amounts capitalised or charged to the profit and loss account in respect of purchased goodwill in a set of consolidated accounts could be removed by users of the financial statements, and the accounts of a group that had grown by acquisition could then be compared consistently with those of a similar group that had grown organically. Consistency of treatment between purchased goodwill and internally generated goodwill also appears not to be critical to the international **8.2.4** community, the majority of which capitalises purchased goodwill and amortises it over a fixed maximum period but does not recognise internally generated goodwill.

8.3 Elimination methods

8.3.1 If purchased goodwill is eliminated against reserves immediately on acquisition, then the method of presentation of the eliminated balance, and the extent to which it should be accounted for further, need to be considered.

8.3.2 'Immediate write-off' has the disadvantage that the reserves of an acquisitive group can quickly become significantly depleted. This depletion has led many acquisitive groups to capitalise some of their acquired intangible assets. If intangible assets were capitalised, either they would need to be amortised over a fixed maximum period or impairment tests would need to be devised for them, possibly along the lines of the ceiling tests. As discussed earlier, amortisation over a fixed maximum period is known from the responses to ED 52 to be unpopular, whilst application of impairment tests, similar to ceiling tests, for intangible assets would cause the simplicity gained by the 'immediate write-off' method to be lost.

8.3.3 The method of 'separate write-off reserve' seeks to overcome the problem of the erosion of reserves of an acquisitive company by presenting the eliminated goodwill in a separate goodwill write-off reserve. Consequently it is possible that acquisitive groups would not find it necessary to capitalise some of their intangible assets separately from purchased goodwill.

8.3.4 'Separate write-off reserve' also goes some way to overcoming the significant practical disadvantage of the 'immediate write-off' method that it is hard to glean stewardship information in respect of goodwill from the consolidated accounts. 'Separate write-off reserve' without recoverability assessment, although not providing accountability in the profit and loss account for the amount spent on purchased goodwill, highlights this figure in the balance sheet, making it easier for users to draw their own conclusions about the continuing value of such goodwill. Those believing that clear identification in the balance sheet of the amount spent on purchased goodwill is the best accountability that can be provided for purchased goodwill may support this method. Indeed, if the Board were to support this method as the proposed approach to goodwill accounting it might require an analysis of the build-up of the balance in the write-off reserve over the previous five or ten years.

8.3.5 'Immediate write-off' and 'separate write-off reserve' without a recoverability assessment are both simple to adopt. Once eliminated, there is no further accounting for purchased goodwill except on disposal or closure of the related business.

8.3.6 The variant to 'separate write-off reserve', whereby the reserve is subjected to an annual recoverability assessment, results in a hybrid treatment between accounting for goodwill as an asset and providing consistency of treatment with internally generated goodwill. Purchased goodwill is accounted for as an asset in that losses are identified and charged to the profit and loss account for the period, but it is not presented as an asset in the balance sheet. Consistency of balance sheet treatment with internally generated goodwill is then achieved in that goodwill is not recognised as an asset, but the profit and loss account treatment for the two kinds of goodwill is different as a result of the accountability being provided for purchased goodwill.

This variant is not as straightforward to apply as 'separate write-off reserve' without a recoverability assessment, but it provides accountability for the goodwill balance in the consolidated accounts, which is otherwise lacking. It might appeal to those wanting to show accountability for amounts spent on purchased goodwill but who believe that goodwill is such an enigma that to record it as an asset similar to tangible assets would be inappropriate. 8.3.7

Neither of the elimination methods, nor the variant, provides international consistency. 8.3.8

8.4 Profit and loss account effects

From the perspective of their effects on the profit and loss account, the methods discussed offer a spectrum of possible alternatives. At one end of the spectrum are 'immediate write-off' and 'separate write-off reserve' without a recoverability assessment, where no charges are made to the profit and loss account for the period unless the related business or part thereof is disposed of or closed. At the other end is 'capitalisation and predetermined life amortisation', whereby annual profit and loss account amortisation charges arise regardless of whether there is known to have been a loss in value of the goodwill. 8.4.1

Between the two extremes are the other two methods of 'capitalisation and annual review' and 'separate write-off reserve with recoverability assessment'. Each of these charges goodwill to the profit and loss account only where a loss in value has been identified. 8.4.2

8.5 Accountability

Respondents may also wish to consider the extent to which they believe it appropriate to provide accountability for purchases goodwill in consolidated accounts. The strictest accountability is provided when the ceiling tests are used with the method of 'capitalisation and annual review' as actual and expected falls in the value of goodwill are charged to the profit and loss account of the period and adjusted against the reported asset. Similar accountability, again with charges to the profit and loss account for the period, but with adjustments being made against reported reserves rather than against assets, is provided with 'separate write-off reserve with recoverability assessment' in the cases when recoverability is assessed by applying the ceiling tests. Some believe, however, that it is not possible to provide this accountability and that fixed-life amortisation and a judgmental comparison with the value of the related investment is more appropriate. 8.5.1

The elimination methods applied without a recoverability assessment do not provide the same degree of accountability as that achieved by the methods discussed in paragraph 8.5.1 above. 'Separate write-off reserve' without a recoverability 8.5.2

assessment, whilst not providing profit and loss account accountability, does highlight in the consolidated balance sheet the amount spent on purchased goodwill. There is no accountability provided in the consolidated accounts, however, by 'immediate write-off', although limited accountability for the related investment is provided in the single entity accounts of its immediate parent.

8.6 Transitional arrangements

8.6.1 These will be addressed in a subsequent Exposure Draft once the method to be used for purchased goodwill accounting has been decided upon. They will take into account the existing requirements of SSAP 22 and UITF 3.

8.7 Summary

8.7.1 In deciding which method they favour, respondents may wish to start from the conceptual issue of whether they believe:

(i) that purchased goodwill is essentially the representation in the consolidated accounts of the continuing value in an acquired investment, and therefore should be shown as an asset, or
(ii) that because goodwill in effect represents the same type of benefits regardless of whether it has been acquired or developed internally, the accounting treatment of the two types of goodwill should be the same, and hence that purchased goodwill should be removed from a set of accounts by elimination against reserves.

8.7.2 It is suggested that, having determined whether purchased goodwill should be capitalised or eliminated, respondents should decide whether:

(i) if an asset, it should be charged to the profit and loss account:
    (a) by amortisation over a predetermined life, or
    (b) through an annual review of its carrying value; or
(ii) if it is to be eliminated:
    (a) whether the eliminated balance should be presented separately, and
    (b) if it is to be presented separately whether it should be subject to an annual assessment for recoverability.

8.7.3 In making these choices respondents may also wish to take into accounts some of the more detailed accounting effects of each treatment discussed above, and in particular the extent to which they believe that international comparability is desirable.

Appendix A – Ceiling tests

A1 OVERVIEW

This Appendix explains the ceiling tests for monitoring the carrying value of purchased goodwill. **A1.1**

The rationale behind application of these tests is that the net fair value of the related investment, being the sum of the fair values of its recognised assets, liabilities (excluding interest-bearing debt), and goodwill, is monitored with the intention that: **A1.2**

(i) if this value is supported by the recoverable amount of the investment then the amortisation charge for the purchased goodwill will be zero, and
(ii) if this value is not supported by the recoverable amount of the investment, there should be a reduction in the carrying value of the purchased goodwill. This reduction will form the amortisation charge for that year.

For the purpose of applying the ceiling tests, the net fair value of the investment (NFV) is taken to be the net sum of the fair values* of its recognised assets and liabilities, excluding interest-bearing debt, together with the total value of its goodwill. The recoverable amount of the investment is estimated as being the net present value (NPV) of its estimated future cash flows. **A1.3**

To ensure that realistic forecasts of future cash flows are made, some constraints are placed on the procedures used to make these forecasts. There are two parts to the ceiling tests. The first is the discounted cash flow test, 'the DCF test', which includes estimates of the future cash flows subject only to these constraints. The second is 'the comparative test' which links future forecasts with past actual results, as a method of ensuring that management is not over-optimistic about the future bearing in mind the level of actual results achieved in the past. **A1.4**

The DCF test and the comparative test both compare estimates of the NPV of the acquired company with its NFV. The differences in application between the two tests are as follows: **A1.5**

(i) The DCF test uses management's best estimates of the cash flows forecast from the current period onwards after taking into account all relevant factors. The comparative test uses estimates of future cash flows that have been systematically constrained by the level of past actual results achieved.
(ii) Whenever the DCF test indicates that the carrying value of purchased goodwill should be written down, the adjustment must be made immediately. If the comparative test indicates that the carrying value of purchased goodwill should be written down, the adjustment is not mandatory until the third consecutive year for which a reduction in the carrying value of purchased goodwill has been indicated.

****These fair values are computed as being the 'values to the business' of the assets and liabilities concerned as defined in the Measurement chapter of the draft Statement of Principles currently in issue.***

A1.6 It is not always possible to monitor the fair value of the investment directly, as it may have been merged with existing operations of the acquiring group. In such situations the goodwill relating to the acquisition should be monitored by looking at the appropriate units of the combined group: these are the units into which the acquired business has been transferred, and might for instance comprise one or more operating divisions of the combined group. Account will then need to be taken of the internally generated goodwill of such a unit at the time of acquisition to exclude such goodwill from subsequent monitoring of the purchased goodwill.

A1.7 The carrying value of purchased goodwill may be written down following application of the DCF test or of the comparative test, but it may never be written up, even if it is believed that previous losses in value have subsequently been recovered.

A2 DCF TEST

A2.1 The DCF test is applied at each year-end to every acquisition made by the group, or in those cases where the acquired business has been merged with the pre-existing operations of the acquiring company, to each of the units that contain some part of the acquired business.

ACQUISITIONS RUN ON A STAND-ALONE BASIS

A2.2 The NPV of the acquired business should be estimated. This should be done by preparing a five-year explicit cash flow forecast followed by a continuing value based on a steady growth rate. The explicit cash flow forecast should be based on integrated profit and loss account and balance sheet forecasts for each year under review. Components of the profit and loss account and balance sheet should be forecast separately for each year. The cash flow forecast used for the DCF test should be consistent with any internal forecasts prepared for planning and budgeting purposes.

Cash flow forecasts and discount rate

A2.3 The cash flow forecasts and the discount rate used in the NPV calculations should be estimated after tax, with estimations of the tax charge appropriate to a specific part of the business being made if necessary.

A2.4 In dealing with the effects of inflation, either the cash flow forecasts must be estimated at nominal amounts and discounted at a nominal rate, or they must be estimated in real terms and discounted at a real rate.

A2.5 The components of cash flow to be estimated for the explicit forecast period are as follows:

- cash flow = sum of operating free cash flow and non-operating cash flow, where
- operating free cash flow = pre-interest, after-tax operating earnings of acquired company plus non-cash charges (ie depreciation etc.) less investment in working capital, and

- non-operating cash flow = after tax cash flow of non-operating items (ie recurring asset sales, recurring capital expenditure, etc.)

After the explicit forecast period a continuing value should be estimated. This will assume a constant growth rate from that point onwards in perpetuity. The formula to use to estimate the continuing value is: **A2.6**

- Continuing value = C/(W−g),

  where:

  C is the normalised (ie adjusted for cyclical variations) level of cash flow in the first year after the explicit forecast period,

  W is the weighted average cost of capital for the related part of the business, and

  g is the expected growth rate of free cash flow in perpetuity.

The long-term growth rates to be used in the continuing value formula must be reasonable and should take into account the nature of the related industry or industries. For business in the UK the growth rate should be restricted to 2.5 per cent, which is approximately the average annual growth rate in gross domestic product over the last forty years. Similar restrictions should be placed as considered appropriate on growth rates used for overseas businesses. If nominal rates of growth are required the real growth rate should be compounded by the inflation rate used in estimating the weighted average cost of capital (WACC) for the part of the business concerned. **A2.7**

The appropriate discount rate to use is the WACC, for the part of the business concerned. Capital asset pricing model techniques* should be used to estimate the WACC. The WACC may change over time as external economic conditions such as interest rates change, or as the risk profile of the related business changes. The WACC should be made specific to the part of the business concerned by taking the capital structure appropriate to the entire group then adjusting this for the risk attaching to the particular business.† **A2.8**

As the WACC for the part of the business concerned takes into account the cost of debt for the group, it is appropriate that the NFV of the acquired company should be before deduction of its interest-bearing debt. **A2.9**

Application of the DCF test

Once the NPV of the acquired business has been estimated it should be compared with its NFV. **A2.10**

****There are numerous management text-books that explain the principles behind, and the procedures to use in, application of the capital asset pricing model techniques to estimate the WACC. The techniques are addressed by RA Brealy and SC Myers in Principles of Corporate Finance, fourth edition, McGraw-Hill, 1991. The approach to estimating cash flows and discount rates in NPV calculations that has been followed in this Paper is taken from T Copeland, T Koller and J Murrin Valuation – Measuring and Managing the Value of Companies, Wiley, 1991.***

†The risk attaching to a particular part of the business can be taken into account by using the appropriate 'beta' factor when applying capital asset pricing model techniques. Beta factors are published quarterly by 'The Risk Measurement Service' at the London Business School.

A2.11 If the NPV is greater than or equal to the NFV, the DCF test has been passed and no write-down is required, by this test, to the carrying value of the related purchased goodwill.

A2.12 If the NPV is less than the NFV, the DCF test has been failed and the carrying value of the related purchased goodwill should be written down until the NFV has been reduced to the NPV.

A2.13 The NFV of the acquired business must be re-estimated at each year-end for the purposes of applying the ceiling tests.

ACQUISITIONS INTEGRATED AND MERGED WITH THE EXISTING OPERATIONS OF THE ACQUIRING GROUP

A2.14 Where the acquired business is merged with the existing operations of the acquiring group, the procedures described above for applying the DCF test need to be adapted slightly.

A2.15 Any part of the acquired business that is run on a stand-alone basis should have its goodwill monitored as described above. For those parts of the acquired business that have been merged with an existing business of the acquiring company, the goodwill should be monitored separately for each appropriate unit of the combined group. The total amount of the purchased goodwill, calculated as the residual following application of the fair value exercise immediately after the acquisition, as noted in footnote 1 to paragraph 1.2 of the Paper, should be allocated to the different parts of the combined group in the manner that management considers to be the most appropriate. (For example suppose that for a particular unit this amounts to £200,000).

A2.16 Where the acquisition has been merged with the existing operations of the acquiring group it is important that the value of the internally generated goodwill relating to the acquiring business is not confused with the value of the purchased goodwill arising from the acquisition. The value of the internally generated goodwill immediately before the acquisition must therefore be estimated. This can be done by applying the DCF test as described in paragraphs A2.2–A2.13 to the unit as it was immediately before the acquisition. (Suppose that for the unit concerned the internally generated goodwill is found to have a value of £300,000.)

A2.17 The DCF test should then be applied to the combined unit as it is immediately after the acquisition. This will give a value, as opposed to an allocated amount, for the total goodwill of the unit being the sum of the internally generated and the purchased goodwill in the unit. (Suppose that this amounts to £450,000 for the example considered.) The value of the purchased goodwill can then be deduced, and a ratio calculated of the value of the purchased goodwill to that of the internally generated goodwill in the unit. (In the example given, the value of the purchased goodwill will be £150,000, that is £450,000 – £300,000, which is £50,000 less than the amount paid for it. Thus £50,000 should be written off the value of the purchased goodwill and charged immediately to the profit and loss account. This could occur for instance where there had been an initial overpayment for goodwill. The ratio of the purchased goodwill to the internally generated goodwill would then be 1 : 2.)

Thereafter the steps of the DCF test as detailed in paragraphs A2.2–A2.13 should be applied to the combined unit. These will give an upper limit to the value of the total goodwill in the unit. This value should then be apportioned to the purchased goodwill using the ratio calculated at paragraph A2.17. The carrying value of the purchased goodwill should be reduced if necessary. **A2.18**

The ratio calculated at paragraph A2.17 should be assumed to hold until such time as a further acquisition is made resulting in an additional tranche of goodwill being allocated to the unit. At such a stage the ratio should be recalculated. **A2.19**

If purchased goodwill is introduced into a monitoring unit that is found to contain negative internally generated goodwill, any write-down required to the total goodwill of the monitoring unit calculated as a result of applying the DCF test should be applied in its entirety to the purchased goodwill of that unit. **A2.20**

A3 COMPARATIVE TEST

A3.1 Rationale

This test in effect reperforms the DCF test, but it uses cash flow forecasts that are adjusted in the light of the actual level of cash flows achieved in the previous five years. This is done by comparing the last five years' actual cash flows with those forecast in the relevant earlier year's DCF test, as defined in the notes at Section A3.2 below, and, where they fall short of those previously forecast, all of the cash flow estimates from that earlier year's forecast that relate to the future are written down proportionately. The NPV of the appropriate unit is then recalculated using these reduced cash flows and compared with the NFV of the appropriate unit as for the DCF test. **A3.1.1**

The rationale for applying this test is that the actual cash flows achieved over the past five years, as compared with those that were projected to have been achieved, are considered to provide a good indication of the likely level of future cash flows, as compared with those previously forecast. **A3.1.2**

Where it is thought that the cash flow forecast used for comparison purposes has become out of date and no longer provides a realistic pattern of future cash flows, it should be altered but subject to the conditions described in paragraphs A3.2.11 et seq below. **A3.1.3**

The structure of the test, requiring three consecutive years of failure before there is a mandatory write-down to the goodwill carrying value, allows for recessionary periods from which a company could subsequently recover and should ensure that the test does not result in unnecessary write-downs for companies whose business is cyclical. **A3.1.4**

A3.2 APPLICATION OF THE COMPARATIVE TEST

A3.2.1 These notes describe how the test would be applied to one monitoring unit of the consolidated group. It is assumed that an acquisition is made by the acquiring group at its year-end. This date will be known as year 0 in these notes, and subsequent year-ends will be known as years 1,2,3 etc. respectively.

A3.2.2 *At year 0* the comparative test cannot be applied because there is no history available allowing actual cash flows to be compared with those previously forecast.

A3.2.3 *At year 1* the cash flow earned in that year should be compared with that forecast to have been earned in the year 0 DCF test. If the actual cash flow earned is greater than or equal to that forecast to have been earned, the test has been passed and is complete.

A3.2.4 If the actual cash flow earned is less than that forecast to have been earned, the NPV of the unit being monitored should be recomputed using the cash flows that were forecast for year 2 onwards as part of the year 0 DCF forecast, but reduced in the proportion by which the cash flow actually earned in year 1 fell short of that projected to have been earned. This reduced NPV should then be compared with the NFV of the unit.

- If the reduced NPV is greater than or equal to the NFV of the unit the test has been passed and is complete.
- If the reduced NPV is lower than the NFV of the unit the test has been failed. An adjustment should be made to the carrying value of purchased goodwill in exactly the same way as when applying the DCF test unless management believes that when the test is applied in either the following year or the year afterwards it will be passed. In such a case the amount of the indicated write-down to the purchased goodwill should be disclosed together with an explanation of why management does not believe that such a write-down will be indicated in both of the next two year's applications of the test.

A3.2.5 *At year 2* the sum of the first and second years' actual cash flows achieved should be compared with the sum of those projected to have been achieved in those years in the year 0 DCF forecast. If the sum of the actual cash flows earned is greater than or equal to the sum of those forecast to have been earned, the test has been passed and is complete.

A3.2.6 If the sum of the actual cash flows earned is less than the sum of those forecast to have been earned, the NPV of the unit being monitored should be recomputed using the cash flow forecasts that were prepared for the third year-end onwards as part of the year 0 DCF forecast, but reduced in the proportion by which the sum of the cash flows actually earned in the first and second years fell short of the sum of those projected to have been earned. This reduced NPV should then be compared with the NFV of the unit.

- If the reduced NPV is greater than or equal to the NFV of the unit the test has been passed and is complete.

- If the reduced NPV is lower than the NFV of the unit the test has been failed.
  - (a) If the test was also failed in the previous year an adjustment should be made to the carrying value of purchased goodwill, in exactly the same way as when applying the DCF test, unless management believes that when the test is applied in the following year it will be passed.
  - (b) If the test was not failed in the previous year an adjustment should be made to the carrying value of purchased goodwill, in exactly the same way as when applying the DCF test, unless management believes that the test will be passed in either the following year or the year afterwards.

In either case, where the test is failed but no adjustment is made to the goodwill carrying value, the amount of the indicated write-down to the purchased goodwill should be disclosed together with an explanation of why management does not believe that the write-down is required.

At year 3 the sum of the first, second and third years' actual cash flows achieved should be compared with the sum of those projected to have been achieved in the year 0 DCF forecast. If the sum of the actual cash flows earned is greater than or equal to the sum of those forecast to have been earned, the test has been passed and is complete. **A3.2.7**

If the sum of the actual cash flows earned is less than the sum of those forecast to have been earned, the NPV of the unit being monitored should be recomputed using the cash flow forecasts that were prepared for the fourth year-end onwards as part of the year 0 DCF forecast, but reduced in the proportion by which the sum of the cash flows actually earned in the first, second and third years fell short of the sum of those projected to have been earned. This reduced NPV should then be compared with the NFV of the unit. **A3.2.8**

- If the reduced NPV is greater than or equal to the NFV of the unit the test has been passed and is complete.
- If the reduced NPV is lower than the NFV of the unit the test has been failed.
  - (a) If the test was also failed in each of the previous two years the carrying value of the purchased goodwill must be written down in exactly the same way as when applying the DCF test.
  - (b) If the test was failed only in the previous year, an adjustment should be made to the carrying value of purchased goodwill, in exactly the same way as when applying the DCF test, unless management believes that the test will be passed in the following year.
  - (c) If the test was passed in the previous year, an adjustment should be made to the carrying value of purchased goodwill, in exactly the same way as when applying the DCF test, unless management believes that the test will be passed in either the following year or the year after.

In any case, where the test is failed but no adjustment is made to the goodwill carrying value, the amount of the indicated write-down to the purchased goodwill should be disclosed together with an explanation of why management does not believe that the write-down is required.

A3.2.9 *For any years after year 3* the comparative test should be performed in the same way as for year 3 but subject to the following conditions.

(i) The comparison of the sum of actual cash flows with the sum of the projections in the forecast prepared for the year 0 DCF test should be for as many years as are available since the acquisition was made, but subject to a maximum of five years. (Thus for year 6 the comparison will be for years 2–6 inclusive, and for year 7 it will be for years 3–7 inclusive etc.)

(ii) If at any stage the comparative test is failed, then the write-down indicated to the carrying value of purchased goodwill is mandatory if that is the third or subsequent consecutive year for which the comparative test has been failed. If it is only the first or second consecutive year for which the comparative test has been failed the write-down to the carrying value of purchased goodwill need not be made if:

   (a) management believes that the test will be passed before there have been three consecutive years of failing the test, and

   (b) the amount of the indicated write-down is disclosed together with an explanation of why management believes that such a write-down will not be required for three consecutive years.

A3.2.10 In general when a comparison is made of actual cash flows achieved against those forecast, care should be taken that these are compared on a like-for-like basis. It would not be appropriate to determine that the actual cash flows achieved were, in net terms, at the same level as or a higher level than those forecast in a case where operating cash flows achieved were lower than those budgeted, but capital expenditure had been reduced or delayed from that budgeted in order to achieve the required level of net cash flow. Similarly it would be inappropriate to ensure that net cash flows achieved those budgeted by taking unforecast asset sales into the comparison.

Change of forecast used for comparison

A3.2.11 After a while management may consider that the forecast prepared for the first year's DCF test after the acquisition is no longer realistic nor appropriate to use for comparison purposes. In such a case a different forecast may be used for comparison purposes but only provided that:

(i) the revised forecast forms the DCF test forecast for the year in which the alteration is made, and

(ii) comparison is continued with the previous forecast for three years after the forecast has been changed. This comparison will be carried out as described in paragraphs A3.2.2–A3.2.10 above and will run concurrently with, and be additional to, the comparison that is made with the revised forecast that has just been set and is described in paragraph A3.2.12 below.

A3.2.12 Comparisons against the revised forecast will be made in exactly the same way as against the previous forecast. Write-downs to the carrying value of purchased goodwill

will become mandatory if at any stage there have been three consecutive years of failing the test after the forecast was revised. Failure of the test in any year will be deemed to have occurred where it is failed either when comparison is made with the original forecast or when comparison is made with the revised forecast.

Where write-downs are required at any stage by both the application of the comparative test with the old forecast being used for comparison purposes, and by the application of the test with the new forecast being used for comparison purposes, the larger of the two indicated write-downs should be made. **A3.2.13**

A3.3 SUBSEQUENT ADDITIONS TO THE UNIT BEING MONITORED

There may be situations where there is a subsequent addition to the unit being monitored. It will not then be possible in the first year after the subsequent acquisition to apply the comparative test for the new combined unit, for the same reason that it was not possible to apply the comparative test at year 0 for the unit as it existed after the first acquisition was made, namely that no history will be available at that stage. The approach will then be to apportion the cash flows of the combined unit after the subsequent acquisition such that the cash flows of the unit as it stood before the subsequent acquisition can be identified and used for continuing to carry out the comparative test, by comparing against the original forecast, for a period of three years after the subsequent acquisition was made. **A3.3.1**

The apportionment of the cash flows should be performed in the manner considered by management to be the more appropriate, being either in the ratio of the NPV of the unit immediately before the acquisition to that of the unit immediately after the acquisition, or relating more specifically to the respective cash flows expected in each of the three years after the acquisition. **A3.3.2**

A new cash flow forecast will also need to be set, against which the performance of the combined unit will be monitored after the subsequent acquisition. In the first instance this should be the cash flow forecast used for the DCF test at the first year-end after the acquisition. This forecast should be used for the combined unit after the acquisition in exactly the same way as the year 0 forecast was used for the unit before the subsequent acquisition as described in paragraphs A3.2.2 et seq above. Failure of the test in any year will be deemed to have occurred where it is failed either when comparison is made with the original forecast or when comparison is made with the revised forecast. **A3.3.3**

The requirement to monitor the performance of the unit separately, as it was before the acquisition, will cease from three years after the subsequent acquisition. The comparative test to be performed from that point onwards will be that related to the combined unit only and described in paragraph A3.3.3 above. **A3.3.4**

Where write-downs are required at any stage by both the application of the comparative test with the old forecast being used for comparison purposes, and by the application of the test with the new forecast being used for comparison purposes, the larger of the two indicated write-downs should be made. **A3.3.5**

Capital investment

A3.3.6 From time to time further capital investment will be made in the unit being monitored. The procedure to be used for applying the comparative test will then be similar to that described above when there is a subsequent acquisition. The only difference will be that no more purchased goodwill will have been acquired.

A3.3.7 For the first three years after the investment has been made, the cash flows of the unit should be apportioned in a similar way to that described in paragraph A3.3.1 above to the unit as it stood before the subsequent investment and the comparative test then applied, with comparison being made against the original forecast, in the way already described in paragraphs A3.2.2 et seq above.

A3.3.8 In addition the cash flows of the unit must be looked at in aggregate and compared with a new DCF forecast for comparative purposes, being the one prepared for the DCF test immediately after the capital investment. This comparison will then apply and continue in the way described in paragraphs A3.2.2 et seq above.

A3.3.9 Failure of the test in any year will be deemed to have occurred where it is failed either when comparison is made with the original forecast as described in paragraph A3.3.7 above or when comparison is made with the revised forecast as described in paragraph A3.3.8 above.

A3.3.10 The requirement to monitor the performance of the unit separately, as it was before the additional capital investment, will cease three years after such investment. The comparative test to be performed from that point onwards will be that related to the combined unit only and described in paragraph A3.3.8 above.

A3.3.11 Where write-downs are required at any stage by both the application of the comparative test with the old forecast being used for comparison purposes, and by the application of the test with the new forecast being used for comparison purposes, the larger of the two indicated write-downs should be made.

A3.4 COMBINING THE RESULTS OF THE DCF TEST AND THE COMPARATIVE TEST

A3.4.1 If write-downs in the carrying value of purchased goodwill are required by both the DCF test and the comparative test, the larger of the two write-downs should be made.

Appendix B – Summary of international treatments

B1 INTRODUCTION

This section gives a brief summary of the treatments of purchased goodwill and intangible assets adopted internationally. There are no overseas countries that permit capitalisation of internally generated goodwill. **B1.1**

B2 INTERNATIONAL ACCOUNTING STANDARDS

The current relevant standard is IAS 22 'Accounting for Business Combinations', which allows both immediate write-off of goodwill against reserves and recognition as an asset in the consolidated balance sheet. If capitalised, purchased goodwill should be amortised to income on a systematic basis over its useful life. **B2.1**

A revised version of this standard is to be issued shortly* and will become effective for accounting periods commending on or after 1 January 1995. This will require that all purchased goodwill is capitalised, then amortised as an expense over its useful life. This life should not exceed five years unless a longer period can be justified, but such longer period may in no circumstances exceed twenty years. Immediate write-off against reserves is to be prohibited. **B2.2**

The revised standard will not specifically address intangible assets except to state that, as part of the post-acquisition fair value exercise, identifiable intangible assets such as patent rights and licences should initially be included at cost, where cost is determined by allocating purchase price with reference to fair values. The IASC is currently undertaking a project to look at intangible assets and is expected to issue an exposure draft within about a year.† **B2.3**

B3 EUROPEAN COMMUNITY

The EC Fourth Directive (Articles 34 and 37) permits purchased goodwill to be written off immediately against reserves or to be capitalised in the balance sheet. If capitalised, purchased goodwill must be amortised over a maximum period of five years or over a longer but limited period provided that this period does not exceed the useful economic life of the goodwill and that it is disclosed in a note to the accounts together with the supporting reasons for the period chosen. **B3.1**

The Directive includes provisions relating to the treatment of research and develop- **B3.2**

***Editor's note:** Published December 1993.*

*†**Editor's note:** A draft Statement of Principles on Intangible Assets was issued for comment in January 1994 by the IASC Intangible Assets Steering Committee.*

ment expenditure but other intangible assets are not specifically addressed in the Directive beyond the provision of a balance sheet caption for 'concessions, patents, trade marks and similar rights and assets' if they were:

(i) acquired for valuable consideration and need not be shown under goodwill; or
(ii) created by the undertaking itself, insofar as national law permits their being shown as assets.

B4 AUSTRALIA

B4.1 The accounting treatment for purchased goodwill in Australia is regulated by AAS 18, issued in 1984, and by ASRB 1013, issued in 1988. Purchased goodwill is required to be capitalised, then amortised systematically over its estimated useful life, which may not exceed twenty years. The period and method of amortisation must be disclosed.

B4.2 An accounting guidance release 'Accounting for Intangible Assets' was issued in 1985 to clarify the treatment of intangible assets recognised as part of the post-acquisition fair value exercise. This stated that whilst recognition of identifiable intangible assets, separately from purchased goodwill as part of the fair value exercise, had been anticipated, the intention was that such intangibles should be amortised to the profit and loss account over the period of time during which benefits were expected to arise. Incurring costs to maintain the intangible assets would not of itself overcome the need to amortise the assets.

B5 CANADA

B5.1 The accounting treatment for purchased goodwill in Canada is regulated by CICA 1580, issued in 1974. Purchased goodwill is required to be capitalised then amortised using the straight-line method over its useful economic life, which may not exceed forty years. The period of amortisation must be disclosed. Goodwill may not be written off direct to reserves.

B5.2 The requirements for the treatment of intangible assets are included within CICA 3060 dealing with capital assets. Intangible assets are defined as 'capital assets that lack physical substance. Examples of intangible [assets] include brand names, copyrights, franchises, licences, patents, software, subscription lists, and trademarks.' Capital assets are required to be recorded at cost and to be amortised in a systematic manner appropriate to the asset concerned over a period that may not exceed forty years.

B6 NEW ZEALAND

B6.1 The treatment of purchased goodwill is regulated by SSAP 8 issued in 1987 and revised in 1990. Purchased goodwill is required to be capitalised in the balance sheet, then amortised systematically over the period expected to benefit from it. This period is considered unlikely to exceed 10 years and may not in any circumstances exceed twenty years. SSAP 8 is currently under review.

B6.2 As part of the post-acquisition fair value exercise, identifiable intangible assets including contracts, patents, franchises, customer and supplier lists, and favourable leases should be fair valued at estimated or appraised values. The subsequent accounting treatment for intangible assets is that they should be amortised to income on a systematic basis over their expected useful life.

B7 USA

The accounting treatment of purchased goodwill is determined by the requirements of APB Opinion No. 17 issued in 1970, which addresses the accounting treatment of intangible assets in general. Purchased goodwill and identifiable intangible assets are required to be capitalised in the balance sheet, then amortised systemically over their estimated useful lives. In all cases the amortisation period may not exceed forty years. **B7.1**

Appendix C – Draft Statement of Principles

C1 ELEMENTS AND RECOGNITION CHAPTERS

C1.1 The appropriate treatment for goodwill accounting can also be appraised in the light of consistency with the currently issued chapters of the draft Statement of Principles dealing with Elements and Recognition respectively.

C1.2 The draft Elements chapter defines assets as rights or other access to future economic benefits controlled by an entity as a result of past transactions or events.

C1.3 The draft Recognition chapter proposes recognition elements defined as assets where:

(i) there is sufficient evidence that the change in assets or liabilities inherent in the item has occurred, and

(ii) the item can be measured at a monetary amount with sufficient reliability.

C2 APPLICATION OF DRAFT STATEMENT OF PRINCIPLES TO INTANGIBLE ASSETS ACCOUNTING

C2.1 Section 3 of this Paper proposes that purchased intangible assets be subsumed within purchased goodwill for accounting purposes, when they are acquired as part of the acquisition of a company or business. Although they are believed to be assets as defined by the draft Elements chapter of the Statement of Principles, they are not believed to satisfy the draft Recognition requirement of being measurable at a monetary amount with sufficient reliability. It is, therefore, appropriate for consistency with the draft Statement of Principles not to recognise them separately as assets in the balance sheet. When accounted for within purchased goodwill, the accounting treatment will be consistent with the draft Statement of Principles if the method chosen for purchased goodwill accounting is consistent with the draft Statement of Principles, as discussed in Section C3 below.

C2.2 Section 3.1 of the Paper proposes that legal rights, purchased to secure the intangible benefits attaching to an internally created intangible asset, should be capitalised and, if they have a known finite life, amortised over a period not to exceed that known life. Such legal rights satisfy the definition of assets within the draft Elements chapter, as they are rights to the future economic benefit of the related intangible. The transaction of acquiring them ensures that the requirement at C1.3 (i) above of the draft Recognition chapter is satisfied. As the rights have a clearly defined cost, they can be measured reliably and hence satisfy the requirements at C1.3 (ii) above of the draft Recognition chapter. Thus the proposed capitalisation treatment of such legal rights is consistent with the draft Statement of Principles.

C3 APPLICATION OF DRAFT STATEMENT OF PRINCIPLES TO PURCHASED GOODWILL ACCOUNTING

C3.1 Capitalisation and predetermined life amortisation

Any method that recognises goodwill as an asset in the balance sheet must first be robust enough to determine whether the amount paid for purchased goodwill represents 'rights or other access to future economic benefits ... ' or whether there are no such economic benefits to be achieved, for instance in the case of an overpayment on acquisition. The annual assessment of the carrying value of goodwill would have to be performed sufficiently rigorously for amounts representing 'rights or other access to future economic benefits' to be differentiated from losses, which should rightly be charged immediately to the profit and loss account of the period. **C3.1.1**

Secondly, there must be sufficient evidence that the change in assets or liabilities inherent in the item has occurred. The purchase transaction will give sufficient evidence that this has happened. **C3.1.2**

Thirdly, the method of measurement of the item must be sufficiently reliable for different preparers of accounts to arrive at approximately the same carrying value for the goodwill. This in turn would depend not only upon different preparers estimating roughly equal economic lives for the goodwill in question but also upon the annual assessment of the carrying value of the goodwill being performed sufficiently rigorously for different preparers to produce approximately similar carrying values for their goodwill. This would depend upon preparers carefully considering the nature of the benefits they expected to achieve from the acquisitions and in particular being prudent about benefits they did not expect to last for as long as twenty years. **C3.1.3**

Provided that the annual assessment of the carrying value of amortised goodwill is performed thoroughly this method would satisfy the proposals of the draft Elements and Recognition chapters of the Statement of Principles. **C3.1.4**

C3.2 Capitalisation and annual review

Whereas consistency of the method of 'capitalisation and predetermined life amortisation' with the draft Statement of Principles is dependent upon the rigour of the annual assessment procedures for the carrying value of purchased goodwill, the consistency of the method of 'capitalisation and annual review' is dependent upon the rigour of the ceiling tests. **C3.2.1**

The Board believes that the ceiling tests have been devised so that they are sufficiently rigorous for this method to be consistent with the draft Elements and Recognition chapters of the Statement of Principles. **C3.2.2**

C3.3 Elimination methods

None of these methods is consistent with the draft Statement of Principles as currently issued, because immediate write-off against reserves without being charged to the **C3.3.1** profit and loss account or passing through the statement of gains and losses is not a proposed method of recognising any element of the financial statements. However, comments on this Discussion Paper will be taken into account when the draft Statement of Principles is revised.

Associates and joint ventures

(Issued July 1994)

Contents

PREFACE

The Accounting Standards Board has issued this Discussion Paper as its first step in developing an accounting standard on associates and joint ventures.

An important feature of the proposals is that they address the accounting for joint ventures, now a common feature of business, on which there is currently much uncertainty. The Paper proposes resolving the inconsistencies between accounting for associates and joint ventures by identifying both as strategic alliances*, based on the common feature that the investor or venturer is in effect a partner in the business of the entity in which it has invested (its 'investee'). While continuing to define associates by reference to significant influence, the proposals move away from an approach that identifies associates mainly on the basis of an investor's holding in share capital and voting rights, to one that lays more emphasis on the relationship in practice between an investor and its investee.

A difficulty in achieving consistency of treatment for associates and joint ventures is that associates are required by companies legislation and by the EC Seventh Directive to be included by using the equity method, whereas many believe that at least some forms of joint venture are better represented by including the investor's share of their individual assets, liabilities, revenues and expenses (proportional consolidation). The Board believes that the equity method is normally the most appropriate way to represent in the investor's consolidated balance sheet its interest in its associates and joint ventures, because it would be misleading to accumulate with group assets and liabilities the assets and liabilities of associates and joint ventures, which the group does not control. The Paper, however, proposes supplementing the net asset information given in the balance sheet under the equity method by disclosures at a level of detail that depends on the significance of the associates and joint ventures to the investor. For the profit and loss account a fuller exposition is proposed, while distinguishing at each level their turnover, profits and losses from those of the group. The proposals are consistent with companies legislation yet would achieve consistency between the accounting treatment of associates and joint ventures and at the same time provide improved information on the effect of such interests on the financial position, performance and adaptability of an investor.

The accounting standard developed from these proposals would replace the current standard, SSAP 1 'Accounting for associated companies' (which was issued in January 1971 and last revised in April 1982). SSAP 1 has not been fully revised to take account of

The definitions of 'associated undertaking' and 'joint venture' are set out in Section 3 of this Paper. An associate is an associated undertaking that is not a joint venture.

the provisions of the Companies Act*. SSAP 1 has also been criticised for the flexibility with which its definitions are sometimes applied and because it does not deal with joint ventures.

An alternative approach – a limited revision of SSAP 1

The Board notes that certain interests presently qualifying as associated companies under SSAP 1 may cease to qualify as associated undertakings under the definitions proposed in Section 3 of the Paper. Such interests would therefore fall to be reported as fixed asset investments to be carried at one of three possible bases: cost, market value or directors' valuation.

An alternative view has been put to the Board that the present definition of an associated company in SSAP 1, which requires participation by the investor in the financial and operating decisions of that company and is presumed to arise with a holding of 20 per cent or more of the equity voting rights, is basically satisfactory. Given that certain present associated companies will not meet the definition proposed in the Discussion Paper, the alternative view is that the proposals should concentrate on a major criticism of the equity method which concerns the absence of sufficient information on the underlying assets and liabilities, earnings and cash flows of associated companies. On such a view, a revised standard should retain the present definition of an associated company (adjusting the terminology to align with the Companies Act), require the equity method for associated companies as at present, extend the requirement for equity accounting to all joint ventures and concentrate on the expanded disclosures for supplementary analysis set forth in the Paper.

INVITATION TO COMMENT

Comments are invited on the issues set out below as well as on any other aspect you would like to address. Comments will be more helpful if you state reasons for your views and indicate preferred alternatives. Appendix III compares the proposals with the current requirements of the International Accounting Standards Committee (IASC).

1 Do you support a full review of SSAP 1 or would the deficiencies in SSAP 1 be met by requiring the equity method for all joint ventures and expanding the disclosures required, as proposed by the alternative approach (Section 1)?

2 Do you agree that interests in other entities should be divided into three categories: subsidiaries, strategic alliances (including both associates and joint ventures) and investments (Section 2)?

3 Do you agree with the definitions relating to strategic alliances (Section 3):

- 'associated undertaking' (paragraphs 3.3 and 3.4);

**References to the Companies Act are to the Companies Act 1985 in Great Britain. The equivalent reference in Northern Ireland is to the Companies (Northern Ireland) Order 1986 and in the Republic of Ireland is to the Companies Acts 1963–1990 and the European Communities (Companies: Group Accounts) Regulations 1992.*

- 'participating interest' (paragraphs 3.5 and 3.6);
- 'exercise of significant influence' (paragraph 3.7); and
- 'joint venture' (paragraphs 3.9–3.14)?

Do you agree that all strategic alliances, whether associates or joint ventures, should be accounted for by the equity method supplemented by disclosures in the notes (Section 4)? Do you agree that the additional information to be given should depend on whether the associates and joint ventures are substantial or merely material (Section 4)? Should the level at which interests in associates and joint ventures are substantial be measured by whether the amounts for certain items of those interests exceed 15 per cent of the same items for the investor group (paragraph 4.18)? 4

Do you agree that the results of interests in associates and joint ventures should be included in the investor's consolidated profit and loss account as part of operating result with amounts under the subsequent headings relating to such interests shown separately in the consolidated profit and loss account (paragraph 4.15)? 5

Do you agree that the investor's consolidated cash flow statement should include only the dividends received from its associates and joint ventures, including these as cash flows from operating activities (paragraph 4.16)? 6

Do you support the proposed disclosures to supplement the information provided by the equity method (paragraphs 4.17–4.26)? 7

Do you agree with the proposals on other accounting issues set out in Section 5? 8

Section 5 of the Paper makes proposals on several other accounting issues arising in applying the equity method. The issues considered are:

- applying fair values on acquisition, adjusting for transactions between an investor and its associates and joint ventures and using consistent accounting policies, accounting periods and period-ends (paragraphs 5.2–5.6);
- restrictions on disclosure of unpublished information (paragraph 5.7);
- exemptions from equity accounting (paragraph 5.8);
- the treatment of losses and deficiencies in net assets (paragraphs 5.9–5.13);
- non-corporate strategic alliances (paragraph 5.14);
- investing entities that do not prepare consolidated financial statements (paragraph 5.15);
- commencement and cessation of treatment as an associate or joint venture (paragraphs 5.16–5.18);
- permanent impairment in value (paragraph 5.19);
- investments by associates and joint ventures (paragraph 5.20); and
- investments that were formerly associated companies (under the SSAP 1 definition) (paragraphs 5.21–5.23).

1 INTRODUCTION

1.1 One of the features of recent economic development is that entities increasingly carry on some of their economic activities through associates and joint ventures by forming strategic alliances with other entities. Changes in markets and technology mean that for certain activities entities require access to a wide range of resources, some of which may be scarce and best obtained by forming a strategic alliance. Developing business through associates or joint ventures can help by providing access to technology, to local know-how and influence and to finance. Forming strategic alliances can also assist with risk-bearing, for example in the development of new products or in large and risky projects such as large infrastructure schemes.

1.2 Some entities have a policy of expanding through associates and joint ventures rather than through subsidiaries because the former offer access at a lower cost than would be involved in gaining control. Other entities may decide to expand through associates and joint ventures as a matter of necessity rather than choice. For some economic activities it may be impossible for an entity to find a suitable subsidiary or to start a business on its own whereas it may be possible to form a strategic alliance with another entity. Some strategic alliances are formed to carry out a particular project and may have a limited life whereas others are formed as continuing alliances.

1.3 A strategic alliance can be organised in many ways. The investors choose the structure of an alliance according to the particular contribution each party has to make and the benefits each hopes to gain. However, a strategic alliance is always based on one entity's influence over the other resulting either from its holding of equity or from an agreement, formal or informal*. This equity holding and/or the agreement also provides the basis for the investor or venturer to benefit from the activities of its strategic alliance.

The reasons for revising SSAP 1

1.4 Financial reporting has developed to recognise changing business practice. Initially, consolidated financial statements recognised that a parent and its subsidiaries together form an economic entity, a group. SSAP 1 'Accounting for associated companies' was issued in 1971 in response to the growing practice of entities of conducting parts of their business through other entities (frequently consortia and joint ventures) in which they had a substantial but not a controlling interest. The standard was designed to ensure that the investor's financial statements as a whole gave adequate information about the profit streams supporting the investor's own dividend and the scale of the investments in such entities.

1.5 SSAP 1 was last revised in April 1982. The Board believes that it is time to revise the standard again to reflect changes in legislation and business practices, particularly the growing use of strategic alliances as described above. The Board also thinks it appropriate to consider the principles on which accounting for associates should be based, in line with its development of a draft Statement of Principles of Financial Reporting. In developing this Discussion Paper the Board has considered the comments that were received on exposure draft ED 50 'Consolidated accounts' issued by the former

**A strategic alliance is defined in Section 3 using terms from the Companies Act including a requirement to hold a participating interest. To have a participating interest in another entity an entity must have an interest in the shares, which includes an interest convertible into an interest in shares or an option to acquire shares.*

Accounting Standards Committee in the light of the amendments to the Companies Act in 1989.

The Board has identified the following issues that need to be addressed in revising SSAP 1. 1.6

Changes in legislation

Legislation implementing the EC Seventh Company Law Directive has introduced new requirements relating to associated undertakings and joint ventures. The proposals in this Paper are consistent with the new legislation. (The Interim Statement: Consolidated Accounts simply removes by amendment the main inconsistencies between SSAP 1 and the Companies Act; it is not the result of a full-scale review.)

Associated undertakings

The definition of an associated company in SSAP 1 has been criticised as resulting in inconsistent decisions on whether investments should be accounted for as associated companies. The Paper proposes interpreting the terms used in the definition of an 'associated undertaking' in the legislation in a way that narrows the range of investments qualifying as associated undertakings.

Joint ventures

SSAP 1 makes only limited references to joint ventures, yet these forms of business organisation are numerous. The Discussion Paper considers joint ventures from first principles and proposes how they should be defined and treated in consolidated financial statements.

The equity method of accounting

SSAP 1 (and the Companies Act) requires the use of the equity method for associated companies in consolidated financial statements but does not consider why this method of accounting should be used rather than other methods that achieve the same result at the net profit level and include the same amount of net assets. The equity method has also been criticised on the grounds that its net presentation allows scope for off balance sheet financing because it does not show the extent of any borrowings by the associated company. The Paper considers alternative ways of accounting for associates and joint ventures, and evaluates the information provided to assist users in assessing the effect of strategic alliances on the financial performance and position of an entity. It proposes that associates and joint ventures should both be included by the equity method supplemented by information in the notes on a fuller basis than that required by SSAP 1.

2 CLASSIFYING INTERESTS IN OTHER ENTITIES

Section 1 noted that a wide range of different arrangements can be made between entities to further their business interests. If financial reporting is to provide relevant and reliable information, the way that it classifies these arrangements must be based on the way that reporting entities actually conduct their economic activities. 2.1

2.2 Current accounting practice recognises four categories of interests in other entities: subsidiary undertakings, associated undertakings, joint ventures and investments. Joint ventures are sometimes divided into two further categories: corporate and non-corporate joint ventures. In the investor's individual financial statements the treatment of all these interests is the same: they are included as investments, their treatment depending on whether they are fixed or current assets as described in (d) below. However, in consolidated financial statements different treatments are accorded to the different classes of interests as set out below.

(a) Subsidiary undertakings as defined in the Companies Act and FRS 2 (called 'subsidiaries' in the Paper) are in general required to be consolidated.
(b) Associated undertakings as defined in the Companies Act and SSAP 1 (where they are called 'associated companies') are required to be included by the equity method of accounting in consolidated financial statements.
(c) Joint ventures are defined in the Interim Statement: Consolidated Accounts. The Companies Act allows proportional consolidation for non-corporate joint ventures. Corporate joint ventures that qualify as associated undertakings under the Companies Act are required to use the equity method of accounting.
(d) Investments are all other interests in other entities; this category includes any interest that is neither a subsidiary nor an associated undertaking nor a joint venture. The Companies Act requires fixed asset investments to be included at cost (purchase price or production cost), or at market value or directors' valuation, and current asset investments to be included at the lower of cost or net realisable value, or at current cost.

2.3 This Paper proposes changing the classification of interests in other entities to recognise only one intermediate category between subsidiaries and investments. This intermediate category is to include both associates and joint ventures as different forms of strategic alliances. To be consistent with the legal requirements, the proposal is that strategic alliances should be defined by using the definition of associated undertakings in the Companies Act, interpreting this definition to reflect the features of strategic alliances. This Paper proposes that associates and joint ventures, as strategic alliances, should be treated in the same way in consolidated financial statements. The reasons for proposing these changes are given below.

The rationale for identifying any category of interest besides subsidiaries and investments

2.4 A simple division of interests in other entities would be to divide them into interests where the investor controls the investee and those where it does not. The former would be subsidiaries and would be consolidated; the latter would be treated as investments and included in the balance sheet at cost or valuation with accrued dividends included in the profit and loss account.

2.5 The advantage of such a simple division is that there would be a single borderline with a single criterion: does the investor have control? It could be argued that having a single borderline would result in financial statements that were easier to understand and had greater consistency and comparability than financial statements prepared with more than one borderline. Each new borderline introduces new uncertainties, particularly where there are elements of subjectivity in applying the defining criteria.

The disadvantage of having subsidiaries and investments as the only two categories of interests in other entities would be that it leaves a wide range of different interests in other entities to be included as investments. Under such a system investments would include all interests where the investor did not control the investee, even though for some of these the relationship between the investor and investee might be very close. In some cases the relationship is so close that the investor acts as a partner in the business of the investee. It is these cases that the Paper proposes identifying as strategic alliances. **2.6**

Treating strategic alliances as investments because they are not subsidiaries would result in consolidated financial statements that would not fully reflect the effect of an entity's interests in such alliances on its financial position and performance. In order to provide useful information that reflects this effect the investor's share of the results and net assets of its strategic alliances should be brought into its consolidated financial statements. Section 4 considers alternative ways of presenting such information. **2.7**

The rationale for including both associates and joint ventures as strategic alliances

This Paper proposes that for financial reporting purposes both associates and joint ventures form part of a single category of interests in other entities, ie both are forms of strategic alliance. The reasons for this proposal are set out below. **2.8**

(a) *The similarity in role of associates and joint ventures*
An investor may use either an associate or a joint venture to extend its activities. The similarity between the roles that associates and joint ventures play as extensions of an investor's economic activities is more important to their treatment in its consolidated financial statements than any differences in their legal structure or mode of operation. This approach is consistent with the Board's approach to consolidation of subsidiaries. Consolidation recognises the role a subsidiary plays as part of the economic activities of its parent and is based on the investor's control of its investee rather than on the investee's legal structure or mode of operation.

(b) *In both associates and joint ventures the investor is in effect a partner*
The distinguishing feature of a strategic alliance is that the investor acts as a partner in the business of its investee. This distinguishing feature can apply to both associates and joint ventures. In an associate the investor is in effect in partnership with the management of the investee as the representative of the other shareholders; in a joint venture the investor is in partnership with the other venturers.

(c) *Financial reporting benefits from using the minimum of borderlines*
Limiting the categories of interests in other entities to the minimum necessary to describe in full the economic activities of a reporting entity assists in achieving consistency and comparability in financial reporting. Each new category introduces new borderlines and new opportunities for different interpretations resulting in losses in comparability and consistency.

Whether incorporation should affect the way an entity is treated

2.9 The Paper proposes that all strategic alliances, whether or not they are incorporated, should be treated in the same way in an investor's consolidated financial statements. The arguments for and against the different treatment of corporate or non-corporate strategic alliances are set out in the following paragraphs.

Reasons favouring different treatment for corporate and non-corporate strategic alliances

2.10 Those who believe that the treatment of a strategic alliance should depend on whether it is incorporated argue that the investor has a different legal relationship to the assets and liabilities of a non-corporate investee from its relationship to those of a corporate investee. A non-corporate joint venture cannot hold legal title even to the assets and liabilities used in its business; the legal title must be held directly by its venturers. A corporate entity holds its own assets and liabilities and the investor's legal entitlement is to a share in its equity rather than directly to a share of its assets and liabilities.

Reasons favouring the same treatment for corporate and non-corporate strategic alliances

2.11 The Paper rejects the argument that the treatment of interests in other entities should depend on whether they are incorporated.

The reasons are:

(a) An entity's decision on whether to establish a corporate or non-corporate strategic alliance tends to be based on tax, financing and local structural considerations; strategic alliances fulfilling the same purpose may have different structures according to where they are established.
(b) The distinction of incorporation means different things in different jurisdictions: for example, a Scottish partnership has legal personality but a partnership constituted in England or Wales does not.
(c) The comments received on ED 5O were critical of the proposal that a different accounting treatment should be used according to whether a joint venture was incorporated.

Conclusion

2.12 This Section concludes that an entity's interest in other entities can be described in its consolidated financial statements by reference to three categories of interest: subsidiaries, strategic alliances and investments. Keeping the categories to the minimum helps financial reporting to provide information that is comparable and consistent. One effect of this conclusion is that associates and joint ventures, whether or not they are incorporated, are regarded as different forms of a single category of interest called strategic alliances. To reflect the effect of a reporting entity's having strategic alliances, its share of their performance and net assets should be included in its consolidated financial statements.

3 IDENTIFYING ASSOCIATES AND JOINT VENTURES AS ASSOCIATED UNDERTAKINGS

This Section defines associates and joint ventures as strategic alliances in the terms used in the Companies Act to define associated undertakings. It proposes interpreting the terms used in the definition in the Act* to achieve the effect that an 'associated undertaking' becomes synonymous with a 'strategic alliance'. In this way the proposals of the Paper are consistent with the Companies Act and also give effect to the principles set out in Section 2. 3.1

Definition of an associated undertaking

General description of an associated undertaking

An investor uses its interests in an associated undertaking as a strategic alliance to extend its economic activities. The investor does not control its investee but acts as a partner in its business. To act as a partner the investor must have a participating interest and exercise significant influence. The reference to an entity extending its economic activities does not restrict the choice of economic activities that the investor can engage in through strategic alliances. An investor may use strategic alliances to try out new products, markets and processes or to develop an existing business. 3.2

Definition of an associated undertaking

An associated undertaking is an undertaking (other than a subsidiary) in which an undertaking included in the consolidation has a participating interest and over whose operating and financial policies it exercises a significant influence. This definition is consistent with the definition in the Companies Act†. When referring to the Act this Paper uses the term 'undertaking' (defined in section 259) but elsewhere it uses the term 'entity' which means the same as 'undertaking' in the Companies Act. 3.3

The proposed definition identifies two essential parts to the relationship between an investor and its associated undertaking: the investor has a participating interest in its investee and exercises a significant influence over it. An interest in another entity that did not fulfil both of these conditions would not be an interest in an associated undertaking nor therefore a strategic alliance. It is this two-part relationship between the investor and its associated undertaking that gives effect to its role as a partner in the latter's business. The meanings of the two essential terms of the definition are considered below. 3.4

**The reference is to paragraph 20 of Schedule 4A to the Companies Act, to paragraph 20 of Schedule 4A to the 1986 Order in Northern Ireland and to regulation 34 of the 1992 Regulations in the Republic of Ireland.*

*†The references are as in footnote *.*

(1) Participating interest

3.5 The Companies Act defines a participating interest as an interest held in the shares* of another undertaking on a long-term basis for the purpose of securing a contribution to the investor's activities by the exercise of its influence arising from or related to that interest. An interest in the shares of another undertaking includes an interest convertible into an interest in shares or an option to acquire shares. This condition has the following effects when applied to identify strategic alliances.

(a) *The interest must be held on a long-term basis*
Paragraph 10 of FRS 2 'Accounting for Subsidiary Undertakings' defines an interest held on a long-term basis as referring to all interests other than those held exclusively with a view to subsequent resale. The latter are defined as interests where a purchaser has been identified or is being sought and which are reasonably expected to be disposed of within approximately one year of acquisition or those where an interest was acquired as a result of the enforcement of a security, unless the interest has become part of the continuing activities of the group or the holder acts as if it intends the interest to become so. Some take the view that there are 'medium-term' interests that are held neither with the immediate prospect of resale nor for the long-term. However, the Board believes that treating medium-term investments as a separate category from long-term and short-term adds an additional set of borderlines with attendant uncertainties without adding a useful category to the analysis of investments. The Paper, therefore, regards as long-term any interests other than short-term ones, which are those held exclusively with a view to subsequent resale as set out above.

(b) *The interest must be held for the purpose of securing a contribution to the investor's activities by the exercise of its influence arising from or related to that interest*
This condition can be satisfied only if the investor has a beneficial interest and the benefits expected to arise are linked to the exercise of the investor's influence. The latter part of the condition is generally fulfilled if the investor has influence over the investee's operating and financial policies. One effect of this condition is to rule out as interests in an associated undertaking interests limited to those of a trustee or a manager, because these are not beneficial interests. Dividends are not the only way a beneficial interest can be enjoyed; there are other ways of extracting benefit, for example, through a management contract with a fee based on performance (making the receiver of the fee more than just a manager).

3.6 A participating interest describes a continuing relationship between the investor and its investee. Once an investor has a participating interest in another entity, that interest does not cease merely because the investor decides to dispose of its interest. Because a participating interest includes an interest convertible into an interest in shares or an option to acquire shares, strategic alliances include start-up situations where an entity

**The reference to shares is to allotted shares in an entity with a share capital, to rights to share in the profit or liability to contribute to the losses in an entity with capital but no share capital, and to interests either conferring any right to share in the profits or liability to contribute to the losses or giving an obligation to contribute to debts or expenses in a winding up for an entity without capital.*

initially has a close involvement in the strategic operating and financial policies without an equity interest (such as a management contract) but has an option to purchase shares later.

(2) Significant influence

An investor exercises significant influence over the operating and financial policies of another entity if its influence arising from the rights related to the interest it holds in that entity, together with agreements – formal or informal – with other stakeholders or the management of that entity, result in its fulfilling the three conditions set out below. An investor with a substantial, albeit a minority, holding of the voting rights of its investee (for example, 40 per cent when other holdings are widely spread) may fulfil these conditions on the basis of its voting rights alone. In other circumstances to meet these conditions an investor's influence needs additional support from agreements, either formal or informal, between itself and the investee or between the investor and other stakeholders that together have control of the investee. **3.7**

(a) The investor must exercise influence over the operating and financial policies of the investee that is sufficient for it to fulfil its role as a partner in the business of that entity. This means that in the area of their mutual interest the investee will generally implement policies that are consistent with the strategy of the investor.
(b) The investor must reasonably expect to benefit, at least in the long term, from the economic benefits accumulated by the economic activities of its investee. In the long run the value of a business consists of the cash flows it generates. Through its influence over the financial policy of the investee, particularly with respect to dividend policy and investment decisions, the investor must, therefore, have the ability to secure access in the long run to its share of these cash flows if it is to benefit (other than by disposing of its interest) from any increases in the value of its investee. This condition does not imply that the investor must always press for the highest possible dividend: a long-term interest in the future cash flows of the investee may be equally compatible with favouring a policy of re-investment.
(c) The investor's interest must provide it with some protection from changes in the operating and financial policies of the investee that would significantly affect the benefits it expects or the risks to which it is exposed.

The effect of the rebuttable presumptions in the Act

The Companies Act sets out two presumptions that are relevant to determining whether an undertaking is an associated undertaking. **3.8**

(a) A holding of 20 per cent or more of the shares of another undertaking is presumed to be a participating interest. This presumption is based on the percentage of shares held, which is a measure of the level of ownership. It is unlikely that an investor will have the sort of relationship with its investment that makes the latter an associated undertaking unless it has a substantial ownership interest in that undertaking. However, a holding of 20 per cent or more does not ensure that an investor has a participating interest as the presumption is rebutted if the interest held is neither long-term nor beneficial.
(b) Where an undertaking holds 20 per cent or more of the voting rights in another

undertaking it is presumed to exercise significant influence. This presumption is based on the level of voting rights held rather than on the proportion of shares owned, although the two are usually related. This presumption gives effect to the view that it is unlikely that an investor's influence over its investment will amount to the exercise of significant influence unless it has a substantial basis of voting power. However, a 20 per cent holding does not ensure that an investor can exercise significant influence, as the presumption is rebutted if the investor does not exercise influence that meets the definition of the exercise of significant influence and the conditions set out in paragraph 3.7.

Definition of a joint venture

3.9 Strategic alliances formed by an investor sharing control with other investing entities are called joint ventures. The investing entities that share control are called venturers. The Paper proposes that joint ventures, as defined below, are a sub-set of associated undertakings because, if a venturer has joint control of its joint venture, the influence it exercises always amounts to the exercise of significant influence and the interest of a venturer in its joint venture always constitutes a participating interest. If an investor's interest in another entity fulfils the conditions set out below to be a joint venture it also fulfils the conditions as an associated undertaking in paragraphs 3.5–3.7.

General description

3.10 An entity may choose to extend its economic activities through strategic alliances formed as joint ventures. The distinctive feature of a joint venture is that each venturer shares control of the venture with the other venturers. The joint venture agreement that is an essential feature of every joint venture sets out how control is shared as well as determining how the joint venture operates in other ways.

Definitions for joint ventures

3.11 A joint venture is an entity that, as a result of a contractual arrangement, is jointly controlled by the reporting entity and other venturers with a view to benefit. The contractual arrangement may take different forms but will cover matters such as the activities, duration, policies and procedures of the joint venture, the allocation of assets and liabilities, the decision-making process, capital contributions and sharing of output, income, expenses or results of the joint venture.

3.12 An entity jointly controls a venture with other entities if none of the entities alone can control that entity but all together can. Each venturer must, therefore, play an active role in setting the operating and financial policies of the joint venture, at least at a general strategy level. This does not preclude one venturer managing the joint venture provided that the venture's principal operating and financial policies are mutually agreed by the venturers and that the venturers have the power to ensure that these policies are followed. Not all those with interests in a venture need be venturers; those without joint control are merely investors in the venture and treat it as an investment.

3.13 An entity jointly controls another entity only if decisions on operating and financial policy essential to the activities, economic performance and financial position of that other entity require its consent. The requirement for an entity's consent to major strategy decisions does not have to be set out in the joint venture agreement but may describe how the joint venture works in practice.

The Companies Act refers to 'managing jointly' in its description of non-corporate joint ventures*. In the Paper this description is interpreted as requiring joint strategic management rather than day-to-day management. Any entity classed as jointly controlling an entity by applying paragraphs 3.11–3.13 would also therefore be managing that entity jointly for the purposes of the Act. **3.14**

Strategic alliances as long-term relationships

The definitions set out above for associated undertakings and joint ventures describe long-term relationships that should be judged on long-term criteria and not on changes in the relationships that are only short-term. Small or temporary changes in the relationship should not therefore affect the status of an investee once it has qualified as a strategic alliance. In particular, the status of an entity as an associate or joint venture does not change according to whether it is profitable or has net assets or is loss-making or has net liabilities. **3.15**

Shared facilities

The term 'joint venture' is sometimes used to describe any activity undertaken by an entity jointly with other entities. The Paper, however, proposes defining a joint venture as a form of strategic alliance in which the investor acts as a partner in its investee's business. This limits the joint activities that could qualify as joint ventures to those joint activities that constitute a business. The result is that jointly controlled operations or jointly controlled assets† that do not by themselves constitute a business do not amount to a joint venture. **3.16**

Many joint activities stand alone as businesses in their own right. However, some joint activities amount only to a sharing of facilities. A joint activity is a shared facility rather than a business if the joint venturers derive their benefit from product or services taken in kind rather than by receiving a share in the profits of trading. Thus joint activities where the only objective is to share costs are shared facilities. Entities that engage in joint activities to share facilities should account for their share of the costs, assets and liabilities arising from those activities directly in their individual financial statements‡. They should take particular care to disclose any liability contingent on the failure of other entities that are sharing the risks and the costs in a joint activity. **3.17**

**The reference is to paragraph 19 of Schedule 4A to the Companies Act, to paragraph 19 of Schedule 4A to the 1986 Order in Northern Ireland and to regulation 32 of the 1992 Regulations in the Republic of Ireland.*

†Jointly controlled operations and jointly controlled assets are called joint ventures in IAS 31 where the defining feature is the existence of a contractual arrangement rather than the existence of a business that is jointly controlled.

‡This treatment is consistent with the Companies Act because these non-business entities do not qualify as 'undertakings' and therefore are not associated undertakings.

Conclusion

3.18 The substance of the long-term relationship determines whether an investor has a strategic alliance with its investee, either as an associate or as a joint venture. If an investor has a participating interest and exercises significant influence over its investee, it has a strategic alliance with its investee as its associated undertaking. If an investor has a participating interest and exercises significant influence because it jointly controls its investee then its investee is a joint venture. Any associated undertaking that is not a joint venture is an associate. Some joint activities are not joint ventures because they are shared facilities rather than businesses.

4 ACCOUNTING FOR ASSOCIATES AND JOINT VENTURES IN CONSOLIDATED FINANCIAL STATEMENTS

Accounting treatment

4.1 Section 2 of the Paper proposes a system of accounting that recognises the special role of associates and joint ventures, as strategic alliances that extend the economic activities of their investor, by including in its consolidated financial statements its share of their results and assets. This Section considers how such information should be presented to provide useful information about the financial position, performance and financial adaptability of a reporting entity.

4.2 Equity accounting and proportional consolidation are the two main methods of accounting that include in an investor's consolidated financial statements its share of the results and assets of its associates and joint ventures. Consolidation itself also results in the same profit and loss and overall balance sheet totals but reaches these by including line-by-line all the items for its subsidiary, even if not wholly-owned, subtracting the outside equity interest as a single amount called 'minority interest'. This Section considers the advantages and disadvantages of each method. The Paper does not consider in detail how each method is applied, although certain practical issues arising are considered in Section 5.

4.3 The Board proposes to require investing entities to account in their consolidated financial statements for their associated undertakings by the equity method. To supplement the information given under this method, the Board proposes to require additional information that gives a fuller indication of the effect on the investor of its interests in associated undertakings, in particular the potential benefits and risks related to those investments. The disclosures to be proposed are considered in paragraphs 4.17–4.26.

Consolidation

4.4 The justification for requiring consolidation of a parent and its subsidiaries is that the parent controls its subsidiaries and, through them, their results, assets and liabilities. These therefore form part of the economic activities of the group and should be included in full in the parent's consolidated financial statements. Because an investor does not control its associates and joint ventures it would be misleading to consolidate them.

Proportional consolidation

Proportional consolidation is a method of accounting where the investor's share of the results, assets and liabilities of its investee is included in its consolidated financial statements on a line-by-line basis. The same adjustments as those on consolidation should be made to the amounts to be included. **4.5**

The advantages of using proportional consolidation to account for associates and joint ventures as strategic alliances are set out below. **4.6**

(a) Proportional consolidation includes the investor's share of its strategic alliances' assets and liabilities under each format heading, not merely summary or net amounts. This gives an indication of the size of, and liabilities related to, the investor's interests in its associates and joint ventures. Including the investor's share of both the assets and liabilities of its associates and joint ventures also helps users to take account of the structure and financing of the group and its strategic alliances. In total the information provided is useful in assessing the investor's past performance and future prospects.

(b) Some take the view that the best way to present an investor's or venturer's interest in the results and assets of its associate or joint venture is to treat it as having sole control over its proportionate share of these even though, in fact, it shares control over the whole. If this view is held, then proportional consolidation is appropriate and is justified on the same grounds as consolidation for subsidiaries as the investor is bringing in the results and assets it controls.

(c) If the accounting for joint ventures is based on the need for consistency and comparability in accounting for joint activities then proportional consolidation is sometimes justified as being similar to the method used to account for joint activities not involving a separate entity. In the latter case each participant accounts for its part of the results, assets and liabilities of the joint activity directly in its individual financial statements.

The disadvantages of using proportional consolidation to account for associates and joint ventures as strategic alliances are considered below. **4.7**

(a) Unless a clear distinction is maintained between assets and liabilities that are, directly or indirectly, within the control of the investor and those that are not, the performance and resources of the group are obscured. Furthermore, the usefulness of financial statements that aggregate consolidated amounts with proportionally consolidated amounts on a line-by-line basis is questionable. This criticism can be met by using additional lines or a columnar presentation that keeps separate the proportionally consolidated amounts for associated undertakings. However, such a presentation, with the relevant comparatives, would be difficult to fit into the financial statements.

(b) There is a problem in principle in including in financial statements the results, assets and liabilities of entities that are not controlled by their investor. Chapter 3 of the draft Statement of Principles defines assets and liabilities in terms of key relationships, which are (for assets) control of rights or other access to benefits and (for liabilities) present obligations that result in the outflow of benefits. Including the individual assets and liabilities of subsidiaries in the investor's consolidated financial statements is justified by the parent's control of them. However, an investor does not control its associates and joint ventures and so should not, in principle, account directly in its consolidated financial statements for its share of their assets and liabilities but should account instead for what it does control, ie its own asset – the net investment. The issue is then how such an asset should be measured.

(c) The Companies Act allows proportional consolidation only for non-corporate joint ventures. It would therefore be contrary to the Act to include corporate joint ventures or associates by proportional consolidation. The EC Seventh Directive allows proportional consolidation for all joint ventures but not for associates, leaving open the possibility of changing the law but only in respect of joint ventures.

(d) Some consider that including the investor's share of assets and liabilities of associates and joint ventures as strategic alliances by proportional consolidation may lead to fractions of underlying items being recorded in a way that is difficult to understand.

The equity method of accounting

4.8 The equity method of accounting brings in an investment initially at its cost, identifying any goodwill arising. The goodwill element, together with any goodwill in the investee's balance sheet, is accounted for separately according to the relevant requirements. The initial amount for the investment is adjusted in each period by the investor's share of the results of its investee, which the investor recognises in its profit and loss account, and any other changes in the investee's net assets. Dividends received from the investee reduce the carrying amount of the investment.

4.9 The advantages of using the equity method to account for associates and joint ventures as strategic alliances are set out below.

(a) Using the equity method of accounting for strategic alliances is consistent with the Board's principles for consolidated financial statements. It brings into the consolidated financial statements only the assets and liabilities of the parent itself or of entities it controls, ie its subsidiaries. Investments in associates and joint ventures are accounted for as single assets because the investor controls its investment even though it does not control the entity in which the investment is made.

(b) Using the equity method brings into the investor's consolidated financial statements its share of the results and net assets of its associate or joint venture under a few distinct headings, so that the performance and resources of the group itself can be assessed separately from those of its strategic alliances.

(c) Consistent accounting treatment for associates and joint ventures can be achieved within the current legislation only by including joint ventures as associated undertakings and by using equity accounting, as required by the Companies Act, for all associated undertakings. The Board believes that joint ventures and associates should be accounted for in the same way in consolidated financial statements because of their similar roles as different forms of strategic alliances.

(d) The equity method is a method of accounting that is familiar to users and preparers as it has been the method of accounting for associated companies for a number of years.

The disadvantages of using the equity method to account for associates and joint ventures as strategic alliances in the consolidated financial statements of the investor are set out below. 4.10

(a) By bringing in only the net amounts for the results and assets of associates and joint ventures the equity method distorts financial ratios such as gearing and profit margin. Associates and joint ventures extend the economic activities of the investor and the net amounts do not give much information on the operations of such entities and, therefore, the effect on the investor of its interests in them.

(b) The net amounts shown under the equity method do not reveal the level of liabilities held by the associates and joint ventures or the structure of their financing. In general, the potential benefits and risks related to the investor's interests in strategic alliances are obscured by the presentation of net amounts.

Expanded equity method

Most of the criticism of the equity method focuses on the information it traditionally presents, in particular the presentation of only a net amount as 'interests in associated undertakings' in the balance sheet. These criticisms can be met by expanding the information shown in the financial statements for associates and joint ventures. The amount traditionally shown under the equity method in the profit and loss account and balance sheet could be extended, for example, by showing respectively turnover, profit before tax and taxation charge, and gross assets and gross liabilities to give additional information on the benefits and risks associated with investment in associates and joint ventures as strategic alliances and to aid in analysis of performance and financial position. This method is called the expanded equity method*. 4.11

The Board's proposed treatment

The Paper proposes that associates and joint ventures should be included by using a form of the expanded equity method that augments the amounts traditionally shown in the consolidated profit and loss account and the balance sheet under the equity method by giving additional information in the notes to overcome the disadvantages of equity accounting set out above. Paragraphs 4.17–4.26 consider the form that the additional information should take. The Board proposes the use of an expanded equity method as a way of portraying the economic effect of a reporting entity's strategic alliances rather 4.12

****Other forms of the expanded equity method extend the analysis of amounts for associated undertakings into the major headings of the financial statements.***

than as a way of valuing associates and joint ventures. Amounts carried under the equity method will rarely correspond with the current value of an investment, even after they have been adjusted by any related goodwill that has been written off to reserves.

4.13 The Board believes that using the equity method for associates and joint ventures is consistent with the principle that only assets within an entity's control are considered for recognition in its financial statements. The assets the entity controls are its investments in associates or joint ventures. The issue is how to measure these assets in a way that provides useful information about its financial position, performance and adaptability. One possibility would be to use a market value for the investments. However, information on this basis would be inconsistent with the way that consolidated financial statements provide information about a parent and its subsidiaries. For comparability with subsidiaries (for which they may be substitutes) associates and joint ventures should be assessed on the same basis, ie by their profits or losses and changes in their net assets rather than by changes in their market values.

Presentation issues

4.14 Some entities conduct a major part of their business through associates and joint ventures. In these cases it may be helpful to have an indication of the size of the business as whole, including both the group and its interests in associates and joint ventures. In the balance sheet an indication of size can be obtained from the total net assets which include the investor's share of its associates' and joint ventures' net assets. In the profit and loss account turnover is the most common indicator of the size of an entity's operations. Although it is important to show clearly the turnover of the group itself, in some cases it is also useful to give as a memorandum item in the profit and loss account the group's share of the turnover of associates and joint ventures and a total combining this share with group turnover. If this is done, the segmental analysis should be similarly constructed, maintaining the distinction between amounts for the group itself and amounts relating to its associates and joint ventures.

4.15 The operating results of associates and joint ventures should be reported as part of the operating activities of the business, ie in the part of the profit and loss account dealing with operating activities, because the close business alliance between an investor and its associates and joint ventures results in its share of their activities forming part of its operating activities. The effect of this proposal is that all format headings, or those required by FRS 3, occurring after operating profit should include the appropriate share of any similar items appearing in the associate's or joint venture's profit and loss account. If the amounts so included are material, the amount relating to the group and the amount relating to its interests in associates and joint ventures should be shown separately. The statement of recognised gains and losses should also show separately any material amount relating to associates and joint ventures (such as revaluations).

4.16 FRS 1 'Cash Flow Statements' requires dividends from an entity that is equity accounted to be included under 'returns on investments and servicing of finance' in the investor's consolidated cash flow statements. The Board proposes that dividends from associates and joint ventures should be included as part of cash flows from operating activities in the cash flow statement. Comments on this proposal will be taken into account in the current review of FRS 1. The investor's cash flow statement should include only amounts relating to dividends received and other inflows and outflows of cash and cash equivalents in respect of its associates and joint ventures and should not include its share of the cash flows of its associates and joint ventures.

Disclosures

The equity method is sometimes criticised as providing information of only limited use in assessing the effect of strategic alliances on the investor's financial position, performance and adaptability, in particular the potential for benefit and exposure to risk. The Board therefore proposes requiring disclosures to supplement the amounts traditionally shown under the equity accounting method for associates and joint ventures. **4.17**

In order to present information that is relevant but not unduly voluminous, the Paper proposes four levels of disclosure depending on whether interests in strategic alliances are material or substantial, both individually and in aggregate. Associates and joint ventures are material individually or in aggregate if omission or misstatement of information about them might reasonably be expected to influence decisions made by users of financial statements. Associates and joint ventures may be material because of their size or because of the nature of the potential source of risk or benefit they represent. Interests in associates and joint ventures would be deemed to be substantial individually or in aggregate where the investor's share exceeded 15 per cent of any of the following for the investor group (excluding any amount for associates and joint ventures themselves): **4.18**

gross assets;
gross liabilities;
turnover; or
results (ie the profit or loss for the year after tax,
minority interests and extraordinary items).

Aggregate interests

The aggregate interests of the investor in its strategic alliances are material but not substantial

Where aggregate interests in associates and joint ventures are material but not substantial in aggregate, in addition to the information already included for them in the profit and loss account and the balance sheet, the amounts included should be analysed in the notes to show at least the investor's share of the following: **4.19**

turnover;
dividends;
retained result for the year;
other recognised gains and losses; and
total assets and total liabilities.

Unless the interests are material because of their size, the reason why they are considered material should be given. The additional information required in the profit and loss account is limited because paragraph 4.15 already proposes that material amounts relating to associates and joint ventures are shown separately for the profit and loss account headings falling after the determination of operating profit.

The aggregate interests of the investor in its associates and joint ventures are substantial

4.20 Where the investor's interests in associates and joint ventures are substantial in aggregate, the following information should be given:

(a) a set of summarised financial statements in aggregate showing separately the investor's share of each major* balance sheet item, and heading in the profit and loss account and cash flow statements for which there is a material item, together with comparative figures.

(b) an analysis of the investor's share of aggregate borrowings under the statutory format headings and consistent with the requirements of FRS 4 'Capital Instruments', showing how much is with recourse to the investor and how much is without recourse.

(c) a breakdown of the investor's share of the amounts included under the other major headings in (a), if this is necessary to understand the nature of the associates and joint ventures and the effect of investing in them. (For example, it may be necessary to show the breakdown of current assets into stock, debtors and investments and of fixed assets into tangible, intangible and investments.)

(d) the investor's share of any exceptional items in the financial statements of its associates and joint ventures that are in aggregate material in the context of the investing group and any notes to the financial statements of those associates and joint ventures that are material to understanding the effect of investing in them.

Individual interests

The investor's interest in an individual associate or joint venture is material

4.21 For each individually material associate or joint venture, the information required in paragraph 4.19 should be given on an individual basis unless there is a single material associate or joint venture that accounts for nearly all of the amounts that are material in aggregate, in which case only the aggregate information need be given with a note explaining this and identifying the single individually material associate or joint venture.

The investor's interest in an individual associate or joint venture is substantial

4.22 Where the investor's interest in an individual associate or joint venture is substantial, summarised financial statements for that associate or joint venture should be given (including any exceptional items or notes that are material in the context of the

****The major headings are those designated by Roman numerals in Schedule 4 to the Companies Act, Schedule 4 to the 1986 Order in Northern Ireland and the Schedule to the 1986 Act in the Republic of Ireland.***

consolidated financial statements) as described in paragraph 4.20. If there is a single substantial associate or joint venture that accounts for nearly all of the amounts that are substantial in aggregate, only the aggregate information need be given with a note explaining this and identifying the single, individually substantial associate or joint venture.

Retained profits and reserves

The part of the investor's reserves that is attributable to its interests in associates and joint ventures should be shown separately in the notes, indicating the amount relating to its share of retained profits and the amount arising from its share of other accumulated movements in the reserves. **4.23**

Segmental disclosure

SSAP 25 'Segmental reporting' requires the disclosure (unless the information is unobtainable or its publication would be prejudicial to the business of the associate) of segmental information on the results and net assets in relation to an investor's interests in associated undertakings where these account for at least 20 per cent of its total result or 20 per cent of its total net assets. The Board proposes to emphasise this requirement and clarify that the disclosure required is that the activities of associates and joint ventures are analysed across the segments and not that all associates and joint ventures are classified as a single segment, regardless of the nature of their activities or their location. **4.24**

Disclosures on entities becoming or ceasing to be associated undertakings

Where an entity either becomes an associated undertaking or ceases to be an associated undertaking without there being a substantial change in the ownership interest of the investor, the reason for the entity becoming or ceasing to be an associated undertaking should be explained. **4.25**

Disclosures carried forward from SSAP 1

The Board proposes to continue the following disclosure requirements from SSAP 1. **4.26**

(a) *Loans to and from associates and joint ventures*
The total of loans to associates and joint ventures from the investing group and to the investing group from associates and joint ventures should be separately disclosed in the consolidated financial statements (SSAP 1 paragraphs 27 and 28).

(b) *Trading balances*
Balances from unsettled normal trading transactions between the investing group and associates and joint ventures should be included under current assets or liabilities as appropriate and disclosed separately if material (SSAP 1 paragraph 29). In addition the turnover relating to transactions with associates and joint ventures should be disclosed.

(c) *Restrictions on distributions*
If there are significant restrictions on the ability of a associate or joint venture to

distribute its retained profits (other than those shown as non-distributable) because of statutory, contractual or exchange control restrictions, the extent of the restrictions should be indicated (SSAP 1 paragraph 40). However, the existence of significant restrictions may be inconsistent with the investor exercising significant influence because one effect of that influence is that the investor may reasonably expect to benefit, at least in the long term, from the economic benefits accumulated by the economic activities of its investee (paragraph 3.7(b)).

(d) Disclosure of particulars of associates and joint ventures
The names of the principal associates and joint ventures should be disclosed in the financial statements of the investing group showing for each:

(i) the proportion of the number of issued shares in each class held by the investing group; and
(ii) an indication of the nature of its business (SSAP 1 paragraph 49).

5 OTHER ISSUES ARISING FROM THE PROPOSED METHOD OF ACCOUNTING FOR ASSOCIATES AND JOINT VENTURES

5.1 This Section considers various accounting issues arising when applying equity accounting to associates and joint ventures. Any changes from SSAP 1 are noted, as are any departures from the IASC standard dealing with equity accounting, IAS 28 'Accounting for Investments in Associates'.

Adjustments analogous to those on consolidation

5.2 The Board proposes to apply the same adjustments to the amounts included by the equity method for associates and joint ventures as apply in consolidating subsidiaries. This recognises the role of associates and joint ventures as media for extending the economic activities of the investor, even though they are not part of the group itself. Reporting these extended activities needs to be on a basis consistent with that applied to the consolidated activities

When an entity acquires an associate or joint venture

5.3 When an entity acquires an associate or joint venture the proposal is that fair values should be attributed to its underlying assets and liabilities and the consideration paid in acquiring it in the same way as on the acquisition of a subsidiary. The investor's share of these fair values is compared with the consideration paid, in order to calculate any goodwill balance arising on the acquisition. This balance is to be treated in the same way as any other goodwill arising but disclosed separately from the goodwill arising on acquisition of subsidiaries.

Transactions between the investor and its associates and joint ventures

5.4 It is proposed that where profits and losses resulting from transactions between the investor and its associate or joint venture are included in the carrying amount of assets in either entity, the part relating to the investor's or venturer's share should be eliminated. This proposal will also cover any contributions of assets made to an associate or a joint venture in exchange for interests in it. SSAP 1 (paragraph 39) requires adjustment to exclude such items as unrealised profits on stocks transferred to or from associated companies.

Accounting policies

The amounts included for associates and joint ventures are to be based on the same accounting policies as those of the investor. 5.5

Accounting periods and dates

Associates and joint ventures may not have the same accounting period as the investing group. Where the period-ends differ, the associate or joint venture should be included on the basis of interim financial statements prepared to the investor's period-end. If this is not practicable, other financial statements for the associate or joint venture should be used, provided that these relate to a period ending not more than six months before, or shortly after, the period-end of the investor. Any changes that have taken place in the intervening period that materially affect the view given by the investor's financial statements should be taken into account by adjustment. 5.6

Restrictions on disclosure of unpublished information

Regulations on the dissemination of information mean that in general the financial statements of an investor should not contain information about its associates and joint ventures unless such information is available to their other stakeholders at the same time. An investor should plan how to satisfy any regulations on the publishing of information about its associates and joint ventures. 5.7

Exemptions from equity accounting

It is not proposed to carry over into accounting for associates and joint ventures the exemptions that apply in FRS 2 regarding the consolidation of subsidiaries. With one exception, in all cases where those grounds for exemption applied the entity in question would not be a strategic alliance, because the investing group would either not have a participating interest or would not exercise significant influence. The exception is exemption on the grounds of materiality but the Paper does not apply to immaterial items. One ground for exemption that is frequently suggested is where it is impractical to get the necessary information for equity accounting, particularly in respect of any adjustments proposed in paragraphs 5.3–5.6. In certain circumstances it may be reasonable to estimate any necessary adjustments. If the investor is unable to get even the information on which to base reasonable estimates, this suggests that the investor does not exercise the significant influence over its investee that is essential if the investee is its strategic alliance. 5.8

The treatment of losses and deficiencies in net assets

The Board proposes that the investor should take account of any deficiency in net assets of its associates and joint ventures. The only exception is where the investor has 5.9

stated publicly that it is withdrawing from that strategic alliance and has begun the process of withdrawal.

5.10 This proposal is based on the inference that an investor's relationship with its associate or joint venture is for the long term and thus commits it to support its strategic alliance unless there is strong evidence to the contrary. The fact that an entity has been making losses does not affect its status as an associate or joint venture. An analogy is drawn between the treatment of subsidiaries, which are consolidated regardless of any possible deficiency of net assets, and of associates and joint ventures.

5.11 An alternative approach would be to assume no obligation for the losses of an associate or joint venture resulting in an asset deficiency but instead require evidence of any obligation. Those in favour of the alternative approach believe that it is misleading to accumulate losses and record net liabilities for an associate or joint venture that the investor has no obligation to support. They suggest that one anomaly arising from the proposed treatment is that the investor might record a profit (to the extent of the losses previously included) when the investee or joint venture is put into liquidation. They stress that the reason why an investor may choose to operate through the medium of associates and joint ventures is that it may be less committed to support them than it would be to support a subsidiary if the business fails. A record of the losses and profits of an associate or joint venture during a period of asset deficiency could, they say, be set out in a note.

5.12 The Board has rejected the alternative approach because it has the drawback that, where a period of profit succeeded the period of losses for the associate or joint venture, neither the losses nor the ensuing profits would be included in the results of the investor until the accumulated losses were made good. In consequence, potentially useful information for assessing the financial position, performance and financial adaptability of the investor might be missing from the investor's consolidated financial statements. For example, a start-up might incur heavy initial losses. Information about such losses and any return to profitability might be useful in assessing the financial position of the investor but might not be included under the alternative approach.

5.13 Both SSAP 1 and IAS 28 address the treatment of losses of an associate or joint venture that result in a deficiency of net assets. Paragraph 33 of SSAP 1 notes that where an associated company has a deficiency of net assets but is still regarded as a long-term investment it will usually be supported by its shareholders (either by way of loans or by way of an agreement, either formal or informal, to support it). In these circumstances SSAP 1 requires that the investing group should reflect its share of the deficiency of net assets in its consolidated financial statements. IAS 28 requires the investor to discontinue including its share of any losses when the investment is reduced to zero, unless the investor has guaranteed obligations of the associate or is otherwise committed to provide further finance.

Non-corporate associates and joint ventures

5.14 Where an investor has an interest in a non-corporate associate or joint venture, special vigilance is needed to ensure that all liabilities, whether contingent or not, are reported with respect to that non-corporate strategic alliance. Such liabilities might, for example, arise from the joint and several liability of partners in a partnership.

Investing entities that do not prepare consolidated financial statements

The Paper proposes that, where an investor does not prepare consolidated financial statements, supplemental information regarding associates and joint ventures using the equity method should be added to its own balance sheet and profit and loss account or a separate set of financial statements prepared. In requiring a similar treatment SSAP 1 (paragraphs 24 and 35) gives an exemption from this requirement to investing entities that are exempt from preparing consolidated financial statements or would be exempt if they had subsidiaries. The Board proposes to continue this exemption. 5.15

Commencement and cessation of treatment as an associate or joint venture

The Paper proposes that the date on which an associate or joint venture is acquired or disposed of is the date on which the investor respectively commences to fulfil both or ceases to fulfil either of the two key elements of the definition of an associated undertaking: the holding of a participating interest and the exercise of significant influence. SSAP 1 defines the effective date for both acquisition and disposal of any interest, or any portion of an interest, in an associated undertaking as the earlier of: 5.16

(a) the date on which the consideration passes; or
(b) the date on which an offer becomes unconditional.

The changes are proposed to bring the date for acquiring and disposing of an associate or joint venture into line with the date of acquisition and disposal of a subsidiary, which is now determined by when control passes (paragraph 45 of FRS 2).

Where an associate or joint venture is acquired or disposed of in stages, processes similar to those set out in FRS 2 for subsidiaries should be followed. The profit or loss arising when part or all of an interest in a strategic alliance is disposed of is calculated in the same way as for a subsidiary (paragraph 47 of FRS 2). The gain or loss directly arising is therefore calculated by comparing the carrying amount of the net assets of the strategic alliance attributable to the investor before the disposal with the proceeds received together with any remaining carrying amount attributable to the investor after the disposal. The net assets compared should include any related goodwill not previously written off through the profit and loss account. 5.17

An entity ceases to be an associate or joint venture when a transaction or event results in its ceasing to meet the proposed definition of an associated undertaking. The investor may continue to hold at least some interest in the entity, which is now to be treated as an investment. The initial carrying amount of the investor's remaining interest is the proportion it retains of the amount under the equity method for that investment on the date it ceased to be a strategic alliance. This is a surrogate cost because the interest retained has not been directly acquired. The initial carrying amount should be reviewed and written down, if necessary, to its recoverable amount. This treatment is similar to that applied in calculating the initial carrying amount of any remaining interest in an entity that has ceased to be a subsidiary. 5.18

Permanent impairment in value

5.19 SSAP 1 (paragraph 32) requires that where there has been permanent impairment in the value of any goodwill attributable to an investment in a strategic alliance, it should be written down and the amount written off in the accounting period separately disclosed. The paragraph continues, 'because an impairment in the value of the underlying net assets would normally be reflected in the books of the associated company, further provision against the investing group's share of these net assets should not usually be necessary'. The Paper proposes to retain this requirement.

Investments by associates and joint ventures

5.20 SSAP 1 (paragraph 42) requires that where an associated company itself has subsidiary or associated companies, the results and net assets to be dealt with in the investor's consolidated financial statements are its attributable proportion of the results and net assets of the group (including the appropriate proportion of the results and net assets of its associated companies) of which the associated undertaking is the holding company. The Board proposes retaining this requirement in respect of strategic alliances.

Investments in former associated companies

5.21 The Board expects that one effect of implementing the definitions proposed in Section 3 would be that certain interests qualifying as associated companies under SSAP 1 would not qualify as associates or joint ventures. Such former associated companies should therefore be treated as investments and prior years should be adjusted to reflect this. Companies legislation requires that investments that are fixed assets should be carried at purchase price or, under the alternative accounting rules, at market value or at a value determined on any basis that appears to the directors to be appropriate in the circumstances of the company. Investments that are current assets should be included at the lower of purchase price or net realisable value, or at current cost. Former associated companies are likely to be fixed asset investments and would therefore be included at purchase price, market value or directors' valuation.

5.22 An entity's consolidated reserves should reflect only the accumulated retained results of itself and its subsidiaries, together with any other changes in net assets, and its share of these amounts for its associates and joint ventures. Any reserves relating to a former associated company that is not an associate or joint venture under the proposed definitions should be eliminated on implementation of the proposed new standard thus reducing reserves and at the same time reducing the carrying amount for such former associated companies to their original purchase price by this elimination and by bringing back any goodwill relating to that acquisition previously written off to reserves. This amount should be adjusted to take account of any permanent diminution in value. The Board believes that little useful information would be given if former associated companies were carried at their original purchase price. It therefore recommends that they should be carried at either market value or directors' valuation.

5.23 As noted in paragraph 4.12, the equity method is not a valuation method. However, the amount at which a former associated company is carried under the equity method may provide a useful starting point for the valuation process because it shows the initial carrying amount of the investor's share of net assets. For former associated companies that are carried at a market value or directors' valuation, the difference between this amount and the original purchase price should be included in a revaluation reserve.

Appendix I
Example of proposals for disclosures for associates and joint ventures

This example illustrates the disclosures in the notes of XYZ Group's consolidated financial statements for its interests in associates and joint ventures on the basis of the proposals on disclosure in the Paper. The example does not cover how to include amounts for associates and joint ventures in the primary financial statements of an investor.

NOTES TO THE ACCOUNTS OF XYZ GROUP – 31 DECEMBER 1994

Associated Undertakings

XYZ Group has the following interests in associated undertakings.

Oscar's Packaging Limited (Registered in Scotland)	40% of ordinary shares
Alligator Park Inc. (Incorporated in USA)	30% of ordinary shares 45% of redeemable preference ordinary shares
Addresses Partnership (Address – I–4 Round Road Leeds XL2 9PG.)	30% partnership interest

XYZ's interest in Addresses Partnership was sold in February 1995. Because of the joint and several liability of partners, at 31 December 1994 XYZ Group was liable for the liabilities of Addresses Partnership to the extent that these were not met by the joint venture or the other partners. This contingent liability ceased on the sale of XYZ's partnership interest.

XYZ's **aggregate interests** in associate undertakings are **substantial** and the proposed disclosures of paragraph 4.20 are given below.

Aggregate interests in associated undertakings	£million
At 31 December 1992	129
Currency translation adjustment	(5)
Share of revaluing of properties	6
Profit for the year	20
Dividend received	(10)
At 31 December 1993	140

Summarised financial statements showing the aggregate of XYZ Group's share of its individual associated undertakings

Profit and loss account	**Aggregate of XYZ Group's share**
	£ million
Turnover	210
Profit before tax	25
Taxation	5
Profit for the year	20

Exceptional item – Oscar's Packaging

Oscar's Packaging showed an exceptional write-down in the value of its stock because of water penetration of £20,000,000 of which XYZ Group's share is £8,000,000.

Statement of total recognised gains and losses

	Aggregate of XYZ Group's share
	£million
Profit for the financial year	20
Unrealised surplus on revaluation of properties	6
Currency translation differences on foreign currency net investments	(5)
Total gains and losses recognised in the year	21

Balance sheet	**Aggregate of XYZ Group's share**	
	£million	£million
Fixed assets		140
Current assets	120	
Creditors falling due within one year	(60)	
Net current assets		60
Total assets less current liabilities		200
Creditors falling due after more than one year		(45)
Provisions for liabilities and charges		(15)
		140
Capital		
Equity interests	20	
Non-equity interests	25	
		45
Reserves		95
Shareholders' funds		140

Creditors falling due within one year include overdrafts of £5,000,000 and current instalments on bank loans of £2,000,000. Creditors falling due after one year include bank loans of £15,000,000 which are without recourse to XYZ Group. None of the liabilities are convertible.

Cash flow statement

	Aggregate of XYZ Group's share £ million
Net cash inflow from operating activities	41
Net cash outflow from returns of investment and servicing of finance	(3)
Tax paid	(9)
Net cash inflow from financing	1
Increase in cash and cash equivalents	30

XYZ Group's reserves that relate to associated undertakings

	£million
Share of retained profits	47
Accumulated movements in other reserves	15
	62

Additional information – Oscar's Packaging

Oscar's Packaging is a substantial associated undertaking and the disclosures proposed are set out in paragraph 4.22.

Oscar's Packaging – Profit and loss account

	XYZ Group's share £million
Turnover	120
Profit before tax	39
Taxation	(10)
Profit for the year	29

Exceptional item – Oscar's Packaging
See note above on exceptional stock write-down.

Oscar's Packaging – Statement of total recognised gains and losses.

	XYZ Group's share £million
Profit for the financial year	29
Unrealised surplus on revaluation of properties	6
Currency translation differences on foreign currency net investments	2
Total gains and losses recognised in the year	37

Oscar's Packaging – Balance sheet

	£million	XYZ Group's share £million
Fixed assets		80
Current assets	50	
Creditors falling due within one year	(15)	
		35
Total assets less current liabilities		115
Creditors falling due after more than one year		(20)
Provisions for liabilities and charges		(5)
		90
Equity interests		30
Reserves		60
		90

Oscar's Packaging – Cash flow statement

	XYZ Group's share £million
Net cash inflow from operating activities	38
Net cash inflow from returns on investment and servicing of finance	3
Tax paid	(15)
Net cash outflow from financing	(3)
Net increase in cash and cash equivalents	23

Additional information – Alligator Parks

Alligator Parks is a material but not substantial associated undertaking and the disclosures proposed are set out in paragraph 4.21.

XYZ Group's share

	£million		£million
Profit and loss account items		Statement of gains and losses	
Turnover	60	Currency translation differences on foreign currency net investments	(7)
Loss before tax	(6)		
Taxation	2	Balance sheet	
Loss after tax	(4)	Gross assets	55
Dividend paid to XYZ	(1)	Gross liabilities	(35)
Loss retained for the year	(5)	Total net assets	20

Additional information – Addresses Partnership

The same additional information should also be given for Addresses Partnership which is also material but not substantial.

XYZ Group's share

	£million		£million
Profit and loss account items			
Turnover	30		
Loss before tax	(8)		
Taxation	3	Balance sheet	
Loss after tax	(5)	Gross assets	75
		Gross liabilities	(45)
Loss retained for the year	(5)	Total net assets	30

SEGMENTAL ANALYSIS – INCLUDING ASSOCIATED UNDERTAKINGS

Analysis for the group without associated undertakings

	Turnover	Profit before tax	Net assets
	£million	£million	£million
Paper and packaging	200	53	130
Leisure equipment	150	27	101
	350	80	231
Discontinued	72	(16)	52
	422	64	283

Analysis for associated undertakings

	Profit before tax	Net assets
	£million	£million
XYZ Group's share of associated undertakings		
Paper and packaging	36	90
Theme parks	(6)	20
	30	110
Discontinued	(5)	30
	25	140

The example does not show the geographical segments note but it would be prepared on the same basis as the above.

Appendix II

Principal changes from SSAP 1, the interim statement: consolidated accounts and ED 50

PRINCIPAL PROPOSED CHANGES FROM SSAP 1 AND THE INTERIM STATEMENT

A2.1 The FRS developed in the light of the comments received on the Discussion Paper and subsequent exposure draft will supersede SSAP 1 'Accounting for associated companies'. SSAP 1 was initially issued in January 1971 and last revised in April 1982 although some parts were amended to remove inconsistencies with the Companies Act by the Interim Statement: Consolidated Accounts issued in December 1990.

A2.2 The principal changes to the requirements of SSAP 1 (as amended) proposed by the Discussion Paper are set out below.

Definition of strategic alliances as associated undertakings

A2.3 The proposed definitions are similar to those of SSAP 1 in principle but they are supported by more stringent conditions to determine when an entity is an associated undertaking. The purpose of introducing more stringent definitions is to clarify the distinction between associated undertakings and other fixed asset investments on one hand and subsidiaries on the other. One effect will be that fewer investments will qualify as associated undertakings. Paragraphs 5.21–5.23 set out the treatment of associated companies (under SSAP 1) that will not qualify as associated undertakings if the proposals are implemented.

A2.4 SSAP 1 defines an associated company as one where the interest of the investor is for the long term and the investor is in a position to exercise a significant influence over the company in which the investment is made. The Discussion Paper proposes defining a strategic alliance by using the terms and definitions of the Companies Act. On this basis any entity that is an associated undertaking is a strategic alliance. An associated undertaking has two features: the investor holds a participating interest and it exercises significant influence. The Paper proposes how these terms should be interpreted. The Paper also considers the rebuttable presumptions that a holding of 20 per cent or more of the shares amounts to a participating interest and that a holding of 20 per cent or more of the voting rights amounts to the exercise of significant influence. It is proposed that these presumptions should not override the need to meet the conditions set out in paragraph 3.5 for a participating interest and paragraph 3.7 for significant influence.

Definition of a joint venture

A2.5 The major change proposed by the Paper with respect to joint ventures is that these should be part of the class of interests in other entities called strategic alliances and defined by the Companies Act term 'associated undertaking'. The conditions that are proposed to identify associated undertakings therefore also apply to joint ventures.

A2.6 The Interim Statement introduced a definition of a joint venture that is similar to the one proposed in the Paper as the key element is the contractually agreed sharing of control between venturers. The Interim Statement uses the phrase 'expectation to achieve some common purpose or benefit'. The Paper proposes using 'with a view to benefit' because different venturers may have different aims and get different benefits from their participation in a joint venture; defining these in terms of a common purpose or expectation may be too limiting.

Treatment of associated undertakings, including joint ventures

SSAP 1 requires the use of equity accounting for associated undertakings. In the Explanatory Note it states that in some cases partnerships or non-corporate joint ventures can have features that justify using proportional consolidation. The Interim Statement defines joint ventures but does not consider how to account for them. There is therefore currently no accounting standard on joint ventures. The Companies Act allows proportional consolidation for non-corporate joint ventures and requires the equity method for associated undertakings which it defines not to include proportionally consolidated joint ventures. The Paper proposes that joint ventures, whether corporate or non-corporate, should be accounted for as associated undertakings, ie by the equity method supplemented by additional information. The proposals expand the disclosures required in SSAP 1 by attempting to identify the different circumstances when different levels of disclosure would be useful. **A2.7**

Principal proposed changes from ED 50

ED 50 'Consolidated accounts' was issued in June 1990 by the Board's predecessor body, the Accounting Standards Committee. ED 50 proposed that the accounting and definitions for associated undertakings should remain substantially the same as those in SSAP 1 changed only to be consistent with the requirements introduced by the 1989 amendments to the Companies Act 1985. On these matters the changes from ED 50 proposed by the Paper are the same as those from SSAP 1. **A2.8**

ED 50 proposed that corporate joint ventures should be included in the consolidated financial statements by the equity method of accounting, and that non-corporate joint ventures should be included by proportional consolidation. These proposals attracted the most adverse comment in the responses to ED 50: of the twenty-five comments received only seven supported all the proposals. The proposals were criticised because a distinction in accounting treatment was to be based solely on the structure of the investment concerned, ie whether the joint venture was corporate. The Board now proposes that both associates and joint ventures, whether corporate or non-corporate, should be classed as associated undertakings and included, by equity accounting, in the consolidated financial statements of the investing undertaking. **A2.9**

Appendix III
Comparison with international accounting practice

A3.1 The International Accounting Standards Committee (IASC) has two standards that cover the topics considered in this Paper – IAS 28 'Accounting for Investments in Associates' and IAS 31 'Financial Reporting of Interests in Joint Ventures'.

A3.2 The main difference between the proposals in the Paper and the IASC's standards is that the IASC identifies associates and joint ventures as two separate categories of interests in other entities whereas the Paper regards them both as part of a single category, strategic alliances. IAS 28 requires associates to be included in the investor's consolidated financial statements by the equity method and IAS 31 requires joint ventures to be included by proportional consolidation, although the equity method is an allowed alternative treatment. The Paper proposes that associates and joint ventures should both be included in their investor's consolidated financial statements by the equity method. Section 2 sets out the principles on which the Board's proposals are based.

A3.3 IAS 31 defines a joint venture as a contractual arrangement whereby two or more parties undertake an economic activity that is subject to joint control. This definition seems similar to the one proposed by the Paper, but the IASC's definition includes all joint activities as joint ventures, whereas the definition of a joint venture in the Interim Statement and proposed here identifies joint activities as joint ventures only when the joint activities constitute a business (paragraphs 3.16–3.17). The effect of this difference is that jointly controlled assets and jointly controlled operations that are shared facilities are joint ventures under the IASC's definition but not under the one proposed here. The scope of the IASC's definition plays an important role in its justification of proportional consolidation for joint ventures.

A3.4 IAS 31 considers that the venturer's joint control over its joint venture gives it in substance control over its share of the future economic benefits generated by the joint venture. To reflect this substance it argues that the joint venture's results and assets and liabilities should be proportionally consolidated. The Board does not believe it is useful to represent shared control of a whole set of assets and liabilities as in substance equivalent to an investor's sole control of its share of each asset and liability.

A3.5 Another argument used by IAS 31 to support proportional consolidation for joint venture entities is that it results in the activities of the investor being reflected in the same way in its consolidated financial statements, whether its joint activities are carried on through jointly controlled assets, jointly controlled operations or jointly controlled entities. The Board perceives an essential difference between joint activities carried on directly by the reporting entity itself, where the risks and benefits relate only to the entity's share of the assets and liabilities, and joint activities carried on as an undertaking, where there is a sharing of the benefits and risks of the undertaking and its assets and liabilities. The Board believes that useful information results from reflecting, by different accounting treatments, these different ways of carrying on joint activities.

A3.6 The definition of an associate in IAS 28 and an associated undertaking in the Paper are similar in the terms they use. IAS 28 defines an associate as an enterprise in which the investor has significant influence and which is neither a subsidiary nor a joint venture of the investor. If an investor holds 20 per cent or more of the voting power of the investee entity it is presumed to have significant influence unless it can clearly be demonstrated otherwise. However, the Paper proposes defining terms such as 'exercise of significant influence' by setting out further conditions that must be met with the effect that the proposed definition will be more stringent than the one in IAS 28.

IAS 28 requires that an investment in an associate should be accounted for in the consolidated financial statements by the equity method except if acquired and held exclusively with a view to its disposal in the near future, or if the associate operates under severe long-term restrictions that significantly impair its ability to transfer funds to the investor. The Paper does not propose exceptions to the requirement to equity account for associated undertakings. If circumstances were such that the investment was being held for resale, or severe long-term restrictions were in place, the effect in practice would be that the interest failed to meet either or both of the two conditions defining an associated undertaking, ie the holding of a participating interest and the exercise of significant influence. **A3.7**

Accounting for tax

(Issued March 1995)

Contents

Accounting for Tax

Summary of issues and the Board's proposals

This Section summarises the whole Discussion Paper. Those who intend to read the full text may prefer to start at the Preface and invitation to comment on page 1136. Those reading this summary who want further background to any of the issues raised should consult the Chapter indicated in each main heading. 1

The Accounting Standards Board recognises that accounting for tax is a complex subject, affected by many different, often conflicting, considerations. This Discussion Paper has been designed to set out the various issues in sufficient depth to enable readers to form their conclusions on the basis of a rounded view of the subject. 2

To assist in this process, at a number of points the Board's current preferences are stated. In many cases, however, these are no more than tentative first views. The Board looks forward to receiving comments from a wide range of interested parties to assist it in developing firm proposals in a subsequent exposure draft. 3

Reasons for the Board's review of accounting for tax (Chapter 1 and Appendix 2)

The Board has issued this Discussion Paper as the first stage in a project to review accounting for tax in the UK. The current requirements are contained in SSAP 8 (dealing mainly with advance corporation tax (ACT)) and SSAP 15 (dealing with deferred tax). The Board has previously indicated that SSAP 15 was high on its list of existing standards to be reviewed. 4

SSAP 15 requires deferred tax to be provided for under the partial provision method (as described below). It was originally issued in response to the tax system in the UK in the 1970s and early 1980s, under which many companies paid tax at well below the then enacted tax rate of 52 per cent due to the combined effects of first-year allowances, stock relief and high inflation. 5

Subsequently, however, there have been substantial changes both in the tax system and in general economic conditions. SSAP 15 has also been criticised for its inconsistency with international practice and other UK standards, the fact that it takes account of future transactions and its subjectivity. 6

The inconsistency of SSAP 15 with other standards has been particularly highlighted by the issue of pronouncements dealing with accounting for pensions (SSAP 24) and other post-employment benefits (UITF Abstract 6). In order to deal with the inconsistency between SSAP 15 on the one hand and SSAP 24 and UITF 6 on the other, the Board issued the 'Amendment to SSAP 15'. Without the amendment many companies would not be able to recognise the tax relief for pension and other post-employment costs until they are actually paid. In the case of unapproved 7 (unfunded) pension schemes or medical benefits, this may be many years after the costs are first recognised in the financial statements.

8 In view of the wide-ranging criticisms of SSAP 15, the Board believes that SSAP 15 is not capable of further amendment and should be replaced in due course by a new FRS. Accordingly, the Paper explores accounting for tax from first principles.

Main issues in accounting for tax (Chapter 2)

9 In most jurisdictions, including the UK, the starting point for computing corporation tax is the profit as reported in the financial statements. In practice, however, most governments introduce incentives and disincentives into their tax systems in order to implement economic and social policies. As a result, the taxable profit for a particular period may differ significantly from the profit shown in the accounts. Differences between taxable and accounting profit can be analysed into 'permanent' and 'timing' differences.

Permanent differences

10 Permanent differences arise where gains or losses are recognised in financial statements but not in tax computations or vice versa. An example in the UK is most entertainment expenditure, which is disallowed for tax purposes.

Timing differences

11 Timing differences arise where gains or losses are recognised in the financial statements and the tax computation in different periods. An example in the UK is pension costs, which are recognised in the accounts on an accruals basis in accordance with SSAP 24 and in the tax computation on the basis of cash paid to an approved pension scheme (or, in the case of an unfunded scheme, direct to the pensioner).

12 It follows from the above definitions of timing and permanent differences that, over time, cumulative taxable and accounting profits and gains are the same, except for permanent differences. The issue in accounting for tax is whether, and to what extent, the financial statements should seek to bridge the gap between the accounting and taxable profit, by recognising the tax effects of the difference between them. These tax effects are referred to as 'deferred tax'.

13 Some believe that tax is a single net assessment levied on the reporting entity in respect of a particular period, and accordingly that financial statements should record only the immediate liability to the tax authorities (flow-through). Others believe that a wider view should be taken of the reporting entity's tax position than the legal liability to tax, by considering the likely eventual tax consequences of all assets and liabilities, and gains and losses, that have been recognised in the financial statements.

14 Of those who take this wider view, some believe that the tax effects of individual gains and losses should be recognised in full (full provision). Others believe that they

should be recognised only to the extent that tax payments are likely to arise, once the effect of likely future transactions is taken into account (partial provision). An intermediate position would recognise tax effects in full but measure them on a discounted basis.

The Discussion Paper explores these three methods of accounting for tax—flow-through, full provision and partial provision—and, on balance, suggests adoption of the full provision method. The possibility of discounting is considered in paragraphs 32–34 below. **15**

The flow-through method (Chapter 3)

Under the flow-through method, provision is made only for the expected liability to tax in respect of the taxable profit arising in the period. No provision is made for deferred tax. The main advantages of the method are that it is straightforward to apply and the tax liability recognised is closer to many people's idea of a 'real' liability than that recognised under either full or partial provision. **16**

Some also believe that the flow-through method provides the most objective measure of management's ability to control tax expense. By contrast, they see the full provision method as making insufficient distinction between different entities and the partial provision method as too subjective. **17**

The main disadvantage of the flow-through method is that it can lead to large fluctuations in the tax charge shown in the accounts. Some believe that this indicates that the liability recognised may not in some cases be the full liability to tax. The difficulty in extending the items that would be recognised as tax assets and liabilities is knowing where to draw the line. The criteria so far suggested to deal with this problem can produce results that many would find anomalous. **18**

Another difficulty would be that the flow-through method does not allow tax relief relating to long-term liabilities such as pension costs to be recognised in the same period that the costs themselves are recognised. Finally, the method is not used anywhere in the world in countries with significant differences between the fiscal and financial accounts. It is prohibited by the current international standard and a recently published international exposure draft. **19**

For the reasons set out in paragraphs 18 and 19, the Board does not favour adoption of the flow-through method in the UK. **20**

The full provision method (Chapter 4)

Under the full provision method, provision is made for the tax consequences of all gains and losses that have been recognised at the balance sheet date and are expected to enter into the determination of taxable profit at some stage, but have not done so. The full provision method has the advantage that it is consistent with general international practice and is straightforward to apply in most circumstances. **21**

The main disadvantage of the full provision method is that, under certain **22** conditions, it can lead to the establishment of large liabilities that have little apparent significance, because they are seen as falling due only far into the future, if at all, once the effect of likely future transactions is taken into account. In principle, this can be mitigated by discounting deferred tax (see paragraphs 32–34).

23 The Board generally favours adoption of the full provision method in the UK, although there are two distinct views among Board members as to why this is the appropriate option.

24 One view is that deferred tax should be provided for since it is known at the balance sheet date that, as a result of timing differences at that date, the tax assessments of future periods will be greater or less than they would have been if the transactions or events giving rise to those timing differences had not occurred. Accordingly, these known increments and decrements of future tax assets and liabilities should be recognised, irrespective of whether future transactions are expected to occur that will reduce the liability to tax in those future periods.

25 The other view is that deferred tax is more in the nature of a 'valuation adjustment', reflecting the enhancement or impairment of the reporting entity's other assets and liabilities arising from its tax position. For example, a deferred tax asset is recognised in respect of a liability for pension costs because that liability is a smaller burden than one whose settlement attracts no tax relief. A deferred tax liability is recognised in respect of a fixed asset for which accelerated capital allowances have been claimed, because that fixed asset is worth less than an otherwise equivalent asset that is still fully tax-deductible. Such enhancement or impairment results from past transactions and is not affected by future transactions; it should therefore be recognised.

The partial provision method (Chapter 5)

26 Under the partial provision method, provision is made for the tax consequences of all gains and losses that have been recognised at the balance sheet date, but only to the extent that they are expected to result in a payment of tax once the tax effects of expected future transactions are taken into account.

27 The partial provision method is required only in the UK and the Republic of Ireland. It is permitted in the Netherlands, New Zealand and South Africa and by the current International Accounting Standard IAS 12. However, an exposure draft (E49), recently published by the International Accounting Standards Committee seeks to require the full provision method with no allowed alternative.

28 To its supporters, the partial provision method is seen as the best method of accounting for tax, since its objective is to provide only for the amount of tax that is actually expected to be paid. As such the method was widely seen as a pragmatic response to the tax system in place in the UK in the 1970s and early 1980s referred to in paragraph 5 above.

29 However, as noted above, the Board broadly concurs with the criticisms of the methodology of the partial provision method in SSAP 15, as set out in paragraph 6. The Paper examines whether an acceptable alternative methodology for partial provision might be developed, but concludes that it cannot. The Board therefore does not favour retention of the partial provision method in the UK.

The main reason for the Board's rejection of the partial provision method is that it takes account of the tax consequences of future transactions (but not the transactions themselves). This has the effect (for example) that credit is taken in the current period for the tax relief expected to be available in respect of fixed assets that have not yet been recognised in the financial statements. **30**

Moreover the future transactions whose tax effects are taken into account are not, typically, transactions to which the reporting entity is committed. However, in other areas of accounting, the Board believes that items should be recognised only where they arise from past transactions or commitments. **31**

Discounting (Chapter 6)

There is a view that making full provision for deferred tax without taking account of when it will be paid overstates the liability to tax and that discounting is the appropriate method of rectifying this overstatement. However, discounting deferred tax is a complex issue and a number of very different methods have been proposed by commentators and researchers over the years. The Paper discusses the main difficulties, which are to determine on a satisfactory basis (a) the amount and timing of future payments of tax and (b) the appropriate discount rate. **32**

The Paper sets out for comment a methodology of discounting deferred tax whereby deferred tax would be deemed to be paid as the timing differences that gave rise to it reverse. The discount rate used would be the effective rate of a government bond in the particular tax jurisdiction(s) concerned. **33**

Whilst the Board believes that, in principle, deferred tax should be discounted, it would introduce this change only if there were widespread support for, or at least acceptance of, it. However, the Board takes the view that, in the interests of consistency between reporting entities, discounting deferred tax should be either required or prohibited, but not merely permitted. **34**

Disclosures (Chapter 7)

The Board believes that tax accounting must give the reader some insight into the tax 'profile' of the particular reporting entity. For a UK multinational group, this would include such matters as the impact of the mix of tax rates applicable to its profits, the extent to which capital investment postpones payment of deferred tax, the availability of loss relief and double tax relief and the ACT position. No method of accounting for tax can provide this information unless it is reinforced by disclosure. **35**

Some new disclosures are proposed, in particular a simple reconciliation of the **36** actual to the 'expected' tax charge (ie the profit before tax multiplied by the UK corporation tax rate). In developing a new standard, the Board will carefully consider whether any existing disclosures can be abolished.

Fair value adjustments (Chapter 8)

37 The Paper discusses whether deferred tax should be provided for on fair value adjustments made in acquisition accounting. On this issue there are currently two points of view among Board members, which reflect the two views held as to the nature of deferred tax (ie whether it is an increment or decrement of a future tax liability or a 'valuation adjustment' to other assets and liabilities) set out in paragraphs 24 and 25.

38 Those who regard deferred tax as a valuation adjustment to other assets and liabilities believe that deferred tax should generally be provided for on fair value adjustments. For example, they would argue that, if a company attributes a fair value of £600,000 to the stock of an acquired company whose cost to the acquired company (and therefore for tax purposes) was £500,000, that stock cannot be worth as much to the company as stock acquired separately for £600,000 (which would be fully tax-deductible).

39 Those who regard deferred tax as an increment or decrement of a future tax liability believe that deferred tax should not be provided for in respect of fair value adjustments, on the grounds that the new reporting entity's actual tax liability is not altered as a result of the acquisition. In the example above, the cost of the stock for tax purposes will always be £500,000 and the actual amount of tax that will be paid by the combined entity on sale of the stock is not altered as a result of the acquisition.

Revaluations (Chapter 9)

40 The Paper discusses whether deferred tax should be provided for on revaluations. On this issue, too, there are currently two points of view among Board members, which reflect the two views held as to the nature of deferred tax (ie whether it is an increment or decrement of a future tax liability or a 'valuation adjustment' to other assets and liabilities) set out in paragraphs 24 and 25.

41 Those who regard deferred tax as a valuation adjustment to other assets and liabilities believe that deferred tax should be provided for. For example, they would argue that, if a company revalues to £1.5 million land whose historical (and therefore tax) cost was £1 million, that land cannot be worth as much to the company as land acquired separately for £1.5 million (which would be fully tax-deductible). Those who take this view might, however, take into account in measuring such deferred tax the remoteness of its crystallisation, by applying a discounting approach.

42 Those who regard deferred tax as an increment or decrement of a future tax liability believe that deferred tax should not be provided for on the grounds that the new reporting entity's overall tax liability is not altered as a result of the revaluation. In their view no liability to tax arises until there is a commitment to dispose of the revalued asset.

Losses and surplus ACT (Chapter 10)

The Paper discusses the treatment of tax losses and surplus advance corporation tax (ACT) carry-forwards. No change is proposed to current practice (broadly, that they are recognised only where their recovery against future tax liabilities is virtually certain, whether such future tax liabilities are represented by deferred tax at the balance sheet date or are expected to be generated from future trading). **43**

Allocation of the tax charge (Chapter 11)

The Paper discusses an issue arising out of the implementation of FRS 3 'Reporting Financial Performance', on which there is limited guidance in current standards—the allocation of tax expense between the profit and loss account and the statement of total recognised gains and losses. The Board proposes that the tax effect of a gain or loss should be recognised in the same statement as that in which the gain or loss is itself recognised. For example, where a building is revalued with the gain being taken to the statement of total recognised gains and losses, any tax relating to the gain (whether recognised in the same period as the revaluation or in a later period) would also be charged in that statement. **44**

Accounting for ACT (Chapter 12)

The Board has also taken the opportunity in this Discussion Paper to seek comments on the treatment of ACT under SSAP 8 'Taxation under the imputation system'. SSAP 8 requires that ACT should be treated as a payment of tax rather than as a distribution. The Board does not favour changing this requirement, but it will take note of any comments received on the issue. **45**

The Board's proposals

The Board's main initial proposals may be summarised as follows: **46**

(a) SSAP 15 should be withdrawn and replaced with a new FRS requiring that tax should be accounted for using the full provision method. The Board has not yet reached a consensus as to whether tax effects should be recognised in respect of fair value adjustments in acquisition accounting or revaluations.

(b) In principle, deferred tax should be discounted. The Board sets out for comment a methodology that it has developed for discounting deferred tax whereby the reversal of timing differences is treated as a surrogate for future cash flows and discounted using a government bond rate. Any future FRS will either require or prohibit discounting, but not simply permit it.

(c) Disclosures relating to tax should aim to give the reader more insight into the reporting entity's tax affairs than is the case at present. In particular, there should be a reconciliation between the actual and the expected tax charge.

Preface and invitation to comment

PREFACE

The Accounting Standards Board has issued this Discussion Paper as the first stage in its project to review accounting for tax in the UK. The Board has previously indicated that SSAP 15 'Accounting for deferred tax' was high on its list of existing standards to be reviewed.

SSAP 15 was issued in response to the tax system in the UK in the 1970s and early 1980s, under which many companies paid tax at well below the enacted tax rate of 52 per cent due to the combined effects of first-year allowances, stock relief and high inflation. Subsequently, however, there have been substantial changes both in the tax system and in general economic conditions. SSAP 15 has been criticised for its inconsistency with international practice, its conceptual inconsistency with other standards, the fact that it takes account of future transactions and its subjectivity.

The Board believes that SSAP 15 should be replaced by a new FRS. Accordingly, this Discussion Paper explores from first principles three methods of accounting for tax—flow-through, full provision and partial provision—and on balance recommends adoption of the full provision method.

The Board acknowledges that there are attractions in the flow-through method (under which no provision is made for deferred tax), but does not recommend its adoption. Flow-through can lead to large fluctuations in the tax charge shown in the accounts, which suggests to some commentators that the method understates or overstates the liability to tax in individual periods. Attempts to remedy this (eg by providing for deferred tax only on short-term timing differences) can produce anomalous results. To adopt the flow-through method would also move the UK even further away from international practice in accounting for tax than is currently the case.

The full provision method has the advantage that it is consistent with general international practice. However, experience in the UK has shown that, under certain types of corporation tax system, it can lead to the establishment of large liabilities that have little apparent significance, because they are seen as falling due only far into the future, if at all.

The partial provision method seeks to remedy this by providing for deferred tax only to the extent that it is expected to be paid in the foreseeable future. However, the Board takes the view that the methodology of the partial provision method in SSAP 15 is unduly subjective and often leads to counter-intuitive results. The Paper examines whether an acceptable alternative methodology for partial provision might be developed, but concludes that it cannot.

There is a view that the appropriate method of rectifying the apparent overstatement of liabilities under the full provision method is to discount the liability. The Board acknowledges that there is a case for some discounting. However, discounting deferred tax is a complex issue and a number of very different methods have been proposed by commentators and researchers over the years. In order to elicit views on the general acceptability of discounting, the Board proposes a single methodology, which in its view strikes an appropriate balance between theoretical robustness and practical feasibility.

The Board believes that no method of accounting for tax is satisfactory unless it is reinforced by disclosure. Some new disclosures are proposed, in particular a reconciliation of the actual to the 'expected' tax charge (ie the profit before tax multiplied by the UK corporation tax rate). In developing a new FRS, the Board will consider whether certain existing disclosure requirements can be abolished.

The Paper discusses the treatment of tax losses and advance corporation tax (ACT) carry-forwards. No change is proposed to current practice (broadly, that they are recognised only where their recovery against future tax liabilities is virtually assured, whether such future tax liabilities are represented by deferred tax at the balance sheet date or are expected to be generated from future trading).

The Paper contains proposals for dealing with issues where there is limited guidance in the current standards – in particular the allocation of tax expense between the profit and loss account and the statement of total recognised gains and losses, and the deferred tax implications of acquisition accounting and revaluations.

On the question of the allocation of tax expense between the profit and loss account and the statement of total recognised gains and losses, the Board takes the view that, as far as possible, the tax effect of a transaction should be dealt with in the same primary statement as the transaction itself.

On the question of whether deferred tax should be recognised in respect of fair value adjustments and revaluations, there is currently a difference of view among Board members. Some believe that deferred tax should never be recognised in respect of fair value adjustments or revaluations; others believe that it should be provided for in some cases. Essentially, this difference of opinion arises from two different views of the nature of deferred tax. Some Board members see deferred tax as an asset or liability; others see it as an adjustment to the carrying amount of other assets and liabilities. This is discussed in Chapter 2 and more fully in Chapter 4.

The Board has also taken the opportunity in this Discussion Paper to seek comments on the treatment of ACT under SSAP 8 'Taxation under the imputation system'. Whilst the Board does not propose any change to the current requirement that ACT should be treated as a payment of tax rather than a distribution, it will take note of any comments received on this issue.

INVITATION TO COMMENT

The Board seeks comments on any issue raised in this Discussion Paper. However, it would particularly welcome comments on the following matters.

Do you agree that SSAP 15 should be fundamentally reviewed and replaced with a new FRS? (Chapters 1 and 5 and Appendix 2) 1

2 **If you do not, do you agree that the 'Amendment to SSAP 15' made in 1992 should be withdrawn so that all deferred tax (including that relating to pensions and other post-employment benefits) is accounted for on a consistent (partial provision) basis?** (Chapters 1 and 5)

3 **Do you agree that the pure flow-through method is not an appropriate option? Do you consider that the problems of the flow-through method could be remedied by providing for deferred tax in respect of short-term timing differences only?** (Chapter 3)

4 **Do you agree that, taking into account the balance of factors (in particular the changes in the UK tax system since SSAP 15 was issued and the international position), the UK should move onto the full provision method?** (Chapter 4)

The Board is particularly interested to hear of any practical problems that adoption of the full provision method could cause in addition to those acknowledged in the Discussion Paper.

5 **If the full provision method is adopted, do you support discounting on the 'full reversal' basis? Do you agree that the discount rate used should be a universal rate (eg a government bond rate) rather than an entity-specific rate?** (Chapter 6)

6 **Do you consider that the proposed new disclosures, in particular the reconciliation of the tax charge, are a useful improvement on those currently required? Are there any existing disclosure requirements that you believe should be withdrawn?** (Chapter 7)

7 **Do you favour accounting for the tax effects of fair value adjustments made in acquisition accounting either:**

(a) on one of the bases set out in Section 8.4:
- **(i) that deferred tax is not provided for on fair value adjustments; or**
- **(ii) that deferred tax is provided for on items that are expected to be realised through sale or depreciation, or**

(b) on some other basis? (Chapter 8)

8 **Do you favour accounting for the tax effects of revaluations made in acquisition accounting either:**

(a) on one of the bases set out in Section 9.2:
- **(i) that deferred tax is not provided for except in respect of items that the reporting entity is committed to dispose of; or**
- **(ii) that deferred tax is provided for on items that are expected to be realised through sale or depreciation; or**

(b) on some other basis? (Chapter 9)

9 **Do you agree that the tax effects of fair value adjustments and revaluations should be recognised on a consistent basis, or do you believe that there is a basis for treating them differently?** (Chapters 8 and 9)

10 **Do you support the proposal that tax assets arising from losses and ACT carry-**

forwards should be recognised only where they can be offset against deferred tax liabilities or where their recovery is virtually assured? (Chapter 10)

Do you support the proposal that tax relating to items dealt with in the statement of total recognised gains and losses should also be dealt with in that statement? (Chapter 11) **11**

Do you consider that any change should be made to the requirement of SSAP 8 that ACT should be treated as tax rather than as a distribution to shareholders? (Chapter 12) **12**

Chapter 1. Reasons for the Board's review

Existing accounting standards **1.1**

The Accounting Standards Board has issued this Discussion Paper as the first stage in its project to review accounting for tax in the UK, which is currently dealt with by SSAPS 8 and 15. **1.1.1**

SSAP 8 'The treatment of taxation under the imputation system in the accounts of companies' was issued in 1974. It deals with the treatment of advance corporation tax (ACT) and also contains some disclosure requirements of a more general nature. It is discussed briefly in Section 1.5 below and more fully in Chapter 12. **1.1.2**

SSAP 15 'Accounting for deferred tax' was issued in 1978, revised in 1985 and amended in 1992. It requires deferred tax to be provided for under the partial provision method.* **1.1.3**

Reasons for issue of SSAP 15 **1.2**

SSAP 15 was issued in response to the corporation tax system in place in the UK in the 1970s and early 1980s. This is discussed in more detail in Chapter 5, but its key feature was that any company with significant plant and stocks that was a going concern paid tax at well below the nominal tax rate (then 52 per cent of profits). Indeed, during this period some companies paid only ACT and no mainstream corporation tax. **1.2.1**

It was against this background that the Accounting Standards Committee (ASC) issued its first standard on deferred tax, SSAP 11, in 1975. SSAP 11 required full provision for deferred tax, and its timing was particularly unfortunate. Its effect in the tax environment just described was to record large deferred tax liabilities that seemed unlikely to be paid and to show an effective tax rate of 52 per cent in the profit and loss account, although hardly any companies were paying tax at anything approaching this rate. **1.2.2**

Accordingly, the ASC withdrew SSAP 11 before its effective date and in its place issued SSAP 15, which can be seen as a pragmatic attempt to deal with a real economic problem. The objective of SSAP 15 is that deferred tax should be provided for only to the extent that it can be foreseen that it will crystallise. **1.2.3**

**Described in Chapter 5.*

1.2.4 However, experience has shown that the methodology by which this objective is achieved (see paragraph 1.3.2 below) can give rise to problems. This methodology coped fairly well with the long-term deferred tax liabilities that were the main problem of the 1970s, but has proved less adept at handling the long-term deferred tax assets arising from the implementation of standards* on post-retirement employment costs in the 1980s and 1990s.

1.3 *Criticisms of SSAP* 15

1.3.1 Some commentators consider that, whilst SSAP 15 may have been an appropriate pragmatic response to the tax system in place in the UK in the 1970s, it can be criticised for a number of reasons. The main grounds for criticism, which are discussed in more detail below, are that:

- the recognition rule of SSAP 15 is different from that of other standards
- the balances recognised under SSAP 15 are measured by reference to future events and the intentions of management
- there are variations in the application of SSAP 15 in practice
- the partial provision method is not widely used internationally.

Recognition rule different from that of other standards

1.3.2 The core recognition rule of SSAP 15, that deferred tax assets and liabilities should be recognised only when they will not be replaced by equivalent assets and liabilities, is inconsistent with that of any other standard or generally accepted accounting practice. In many companies, the overall level of stocks, debtors and creditors remains relatively static. If the recognition rule in SSAP 15 were applied to these items, a large part of them (including much of the current tax liability) would not be recognised in the financial statements.

1.3.3 The recognition rule in SSAP 15 often gives rise to counter-intuitive results in practice, some examples of which are set out in Appendix 2 to this Paper. Most notably, it was because of the inconsistency between, on the one hand, SSAP 15 and, on the other, SSAP 24 'Accounting for pension costs' and UITF Abstract 6 'Accounting for post-retirement benefits other than pensions' that the Board issued the 'Amendment to SSAP 15' in December 1992.

1.3.4 The Amendment allows companies to recognise tax relief in respect of pensions and other post-employment benefits (OPEBs) as these costs are charged to the profit and loss account. Without the Amendment, this would not be possible, because it would involve recognising a deferred tax asset that would often be replaced by an equivalent asset, contrary to the recognition rule set out in paragraph 1.3.2 above. This problem is intrinsic to SSAP 15 and is not confined to the tax effects of pensions and OPEBs. These highlight the problem merely because of their materiality.

1.3.5 However, some commentators take the view that it is too simplistic to dismiss SSAP 15

**SSAP 24 and UITF Abstract 6.*

on the basis of its recognition rule. They believe that the special nature of deferred tax (some part of which may never be paid) requires a recognition rule different from that applicable to, say, trade creditors (all the individual components of which are paid).

Reliance on future events and intentions of management

SSAP 15 requires account to be taken of the tax effects of future transactions, in particular purchases of fixed assets, by reference to the intentions of management.* Some commentators believe that this is contrary to the Board's draft Statement of Principles, which defines assets and liabilities as benefits or obligations arising from past events and states that the intentions of management alone do not give rise to changes in assets and liabilities. **1.3.6**

However, others believe that criticism of SSAP 15 on these grounds is misplaced. In their view, to assume that fixed assets will be replaced as they wear out is not to anticipate future transactions per se. It is simply an application of the general going concern basis on which the accounts are prepared. Those that take this view agree that management's intention to undertake a course of action does not, in the absence of a commitment, give rise to a liability. They maintain, however, that under SSAP 15 management's intentions are simply used in order to measure a liability that already exists. This is discussed more fully in Chapter 5. **1.3.7**

Inconsistent interpretation of SSAP 15

SSAP 15 has led to some variations in practice. For example, fair value adjustments made in acquisition accounting are not 'timing differences' as defined in SSAP 15† and, therefore, deferred tax should not be provided for in respect of them. However, some companies do provide for deferred tax on at least some categories of fair value adjustments. More generally, there is anecdotal evidence that many (particularly smaller) companies provide for deferred tax in full for simplicity's sake‡ rather than because their circumstances require it. This breaches SSAP 15, which specifically prohibits over-provision for deferred tax.§ **1.3.8**

Partial provision method not used internationally

The partial provision method is required only in the UK and the Republic of Ireland, although it is permitted in some countries (the Netherlands, New Zealand and South Africa) and under the current International Accounting Standard IAS 12. The global trend is towards full provision, particularly in those countries that have adopted, or are developing, a conceptual framework similar to the Board's own draft Statement of Principles. **1.3.9**

**SSAP 15, paragraph 28.*

†This is discussed further in Chapter 8.

‡ie in order to avoid the scheduling of future investment etc required for partial provision.

§SSAP 15, paragraph 26.

1.3.10 Additionally, the International Accounting Standards Committee proposes abolition of the partial provision method in the recently published exposure draft E49. In retaining the partial provision method, the UK will become increasingly isolated internationally.

1.4 *Criticism of SSAP 15 – the Board's views*

1.4.1 The Board accepts that, in view of the criticisms set out in Section 1.3, it is appropriate that SSAP 15 should be reviewed.

1.4.2 Whilst the Board broadly concurs with all the points made by critics of SSAP 15, some Board members believe that some of the criticisms are overstated. These Board members view SSAP 15 as more consistent with the Board's draft Statement of Principles than is implied by the analysis in Section 1.3 above. They believe that the balances recorded under the SSAP are assets and liabilities as defined in the draft Statement of Principles in that they represent a best estimate of the tax that will actually be paid or recovered as a result of the transactions that have been undertaken up to the balance sheet date.

1.4.3 Notwithstanding this difference of emphasis, however, the Board is concerned that retention of the partial provision method leaves accounting for tax in the UK and the Republic of Ireland out of line with the trend of international practice. It is not now possible to argue as it was fifteen years ago that the UK tax system is so different from that of other countries as to require a different accounting treatment. There is also the question of the extent to which accounting for tax, which for many entities includes significant amounts of overseas tax, should be unduly influenced by particular characteristics of a former UK tax system.

1.5 *SSAP 8 – Accounting for ACT**

1.5.1 SSAP 8 requires that ACT (the tax payable by UK companies following a distribution to shareholders) should be treated as a payment of tax. Some believe that this treatment does not reflect what they regard as the economic reality that ACT is a distribution to shareholders rather than a payment of tax. A third view is that recoverable ACT should be treated as tax, but irrecoverable ACT as a distribution. The arguments for each of these views are set out in Chapter 12.

1.5.2 The Board believes that ACT should continue to be treated as a payment of tax, although some Board members see merit in treating irrecoverable ACT as a distribution. The Board will consider whether to include SSAP 8 in its review of accounting for tax in the light of comments received.

**For more detailed discussion, see Chapter 12.*

Chapter 2. The main issues

Introduction **2.1**

In view of the wide-ranging criticisms of SSAP 15, the Board believes that further amendment of SSAP 15 is not a viable option and that it should be replaced with a new FRS. Accordingly, this Discussion Paper considers accounting for tax from first principles. **2.1.1**

The accounting treatment of tax in financial statements depends first on whether tax is regarded as an expense of the business or a distribution of profit. Accounting for tax both in the UK and elsewhere has for many years been developed on the basis that tax is an expense incurred as the result of doing business in a particular tax jurisdiction. The Board shares this view. If tax is an expense, the question arises as to how it should be allocated to different accounting periods. **2.1.2**

Allocation of tax expense to periods **2.2**

In most jurisdictions, including the UK, the starting point for computing corporation tax is the profit* as reported in the financial statements. In practice, however, most governments introduce incentives and disincentives into their tax systems in order to implement economic and social policies. **2.2.1**

In addition, tax systems, both in the UK and elsewhere, typically establish parity of treatment between taxpayers by requiring uniformity of treatment for some items that could be recorded at a range of values in the financial statements. In the UK, for example, tax relief is given for depreciation of fixed assets according to prescribed formulae, irrespective of the treatment in the accounts. **2.2.2**

The result of these modifications of the accounting profit for tax purposes is that in a particular period the taxable profit may differ significantly from the profit shown in the accounts. Differences between taxable and accounting profit can be analysed into 'permanent' and 'timing' differences. **2.2.3**

Permanent differences

Permanent differences arise where gains or losses are recognised in financial statements but not in tax computations or vice versa. An example in the UK is most entertainment expenditure, which is disallowed for tax purposes. **2.2.4**

****Throughout references to 'profits' and 'tax payable' should where applicable be understood to include 'losses' and 'tax recoverable'.***

Timing differences

2.2.5 Timing differences arise where gains or losses are recognised in the financial statements and the tax computation in different periods. An example in the UK is pension costs, which are recognised in the accounts on an accruals basis in accordance with SSAP 24 and in the tax computation on the basis of cash paid to an approved pension scheme (or, in the case of an unfunded scheme, direct to the pensioner).

2.3 *Deferred tax*

2.3.1 It follows from the above definitions of timing and permanent differences that, over time, cumulative taxable and accounting profits are the same, except for permanent differences. The issue in accounting for tax is whether, and to what extent, the financial statements should seek to bridge the gap between the accounting and taxable profit, by recognising the tax effects of the difference between them. These tax effects are referred to as 'deferred tax'.*

2.3.2 Some believe that, although accounting profit is an input to taxable profit, in substance accounting and taxable profit are so different that there is no purpose in trying to bridge the gap between them by recognising deferred tax. Others believe that deferred tax should be recognised. However, there are differing views as to what deferred tax represents and, therefore, the basis on which it should be measured.

2.3.3 Some see deferred tax as an asset or liability. In their view, for example, a deferred tax asset relating to a liability for pension costs represents tax relief that is expected to be received when the liability is settled. A deferred tax liability relating to a fixed asset represents an obligation to refund a temporary cash flow advantage obtained by claiming capital allowances on that asset.

2.3.4 Others focus on the assets and liabilities of the reporting entity and consider whether the entity's tax position affects their recoverable amount. They see deferred tax more as a 'valuation adjustment', reflecting an enhancement or impairment of the entity's other assets and liabilities arising from its tax position. In their view, for example, a deferred tax asset is recognised in respect of a liability for pension costs because that liability is a lower burden than one whose settlement attracts no tax relief. A deferred tax liability is recognised in respect of a fixed asset for which accelerated capital allowances have been claimed, because that fixed asset is worth less than an otherwise equivalent asset that is still fully tax-deductible.

2.3.5 These differing perspectives are discussed in more detail in Chapters 4, 8 and 9. The distinction between them may seem fine, even esoteric, particularly as they produce the same arithmetical result in the great majority of cases. However, their underlying philosophy is radically different, and they produce very different results in some instances—most notably accounting for fair values on an acquisition and revaluations.

**As explained in paragraphs 2.3.3–2.3.5 there are differing views as to whether deferred tax should be recognised only in respect of timing differences between taxable and accounting profit, or whether it should be recognised in respect of some other differences as well.*

Methods of accounting for tax **2.4**

This Section describes the main generally accepted methods of accounting for tax, which are discussed in more detail in Chapters 3–5. After more than half a century of debate, there is still no clear consensus as to which method is most appropriate, for the simple reason that there are a number of possible objectives in accounting for tax, each of which requires a different accounting approach. **2.4.1**

Some believe that tax is a single net assessment levied on the reporting entity in respect of a particular period, and accordingly that financial statements should record only the immediate liability to the tax authorities (flow-through). Others believe that a wider view should be taken of the reporting entity's tax position than the immediate legal liability to tax, by considering the likely eventual tax consequences of all assets and liabilities, and gains and losses, that have been recognised in the financial statements. **2.4.2**

Of those who take this wider view, some believe that the tax effects of individual gains and losses should be recognised in full (full provision). Others believe that they should be recognised only to the extent that tax payments are likely to arise (partial provision). Essentially, full provision focuses more on the individual components of the tax computation, and partial provision emphasises the interaction of those components in a single net assessment. In that sense, the partial provision method is similar to the flow-through method, even though it is more often thought of, and computed, as a modification of the full provision method. **2.4.3**

The flow-through method

Under the flow-through method (discussed in Chapter 3), provision is made in each period for the tax that is expected to be payable on the taxable profit arising in that period. **2.4.4**

*The full provision method**

Under the full provision method (discussed in Chapter 4), the amount provided for consists of two components: current tax, which is the expected present legal liability to tax as recognised under the flow-through method, and deferred tax. Depending on the view taken of the nature of deferred tax as set out in paragraphs 2.3.3 and 2.3.4, deferred tax is recognised to reflect either: **2.4.5**

(a) the extent to which the reporting entity's future tax liabilities will be increased or decreased as a result of cumulative timing differences at the balance sheet date; or

****The variant of full provision long established in the UK and discussed in this Paper is the 'liability' method. Other variants of the full provision method are the 'hybrid' method (discussed in Section 6.7) and the 'deferral' method, the 'net-of-tax' method and the 'temporary difference' approach in FAS 109 (all discussed in Appendix 1).***

(b) the extent to which the recoverable amount of the reporting entity's assets and liabilities is enhanced or impaired as a result of its tax position.

The partial provision method

2.4.6 Under the partial provision method (discussed in Chapter 5), the amount provided for consists of two components: current tax, which is the expected legal liability to tax as recognised under the flow-through method, and deferred tax. Deferred tax is provided for in respect of timing differences arising in the period, but only to the extent that tax is expected actually to be paid, after taking into account the tax effect of likely future transactions.

2.5 *Objectives of accounting for tax and related disclosures*

2.5.1 Tax accounting and the related disclosures must first and foremost give the reader some insight into the tax 'profile' of the particular reporting entity. For a UK multinational group, this would include such matters as the mix of tax rates applicable to its profits, the extent to which capital investment postpones payment of deferred tax, the availability of loss relief and double tax relief and the ACT position.

2.5.2 It is desirable that the method of accounting chosen should indicate the reporting entity's ability to manage its tax affairs. Investors and potential investors regard control of the overall level and timing of tax payments as an important management function. The accounting treatment adopted must also have regard to the tax system itself.

2.5.3 These objectives are, to some extent, mutually exclusive, so that no one method of accounting for tax can achieve all of them on its own. Ultimately, the weight attached to each will vary according to the tax environment that is being portrayed. For example, the partial provision method is more likely to win support in a tax system, such as that in place in the UK for much of the 1970s and the early 1980s, that enables companies to pay tax at well below the enacted tax rate. In other tax systems, the relative complexity and subjectivity of the partial provision method may render it less attractive.

2.5.4 Whichever method is adopted must be reinforced by disclosure. This is discussed further in Chapter 7.

Chapter 3. The flow-through method

3.1 *Method*

3.1.1 Under the flow-through method provision is made in each period for the tax that is expected to be payable on the taxable profit arising in that period. This corresponds to the amount reported as 'current tax' under existing practice in the UK. No provision is made for deferred taxation.

Rationale 3.2

There are broadly three rationales for the flow-through method, as set out below. 3.2.1

Liability only as calculated by tax authorities

Some supporters of the flow-through method argue that tax is assessed annually on profit as determined for tax purposes, not on accounting profits. Although over time these may be substantially the same, in an individual accounting period they are different and it is an 'accounting fiction' to pretend otherwise. On this view, the tax charge in the financial statements should be the amount assessed in respect of the accounting period. 3.2.2

Objective indicator of tax management

It is also argued that the flow-through method provides the most objective measure of the management's control of tax charges. By contrast, the full provision method is seen as making no distinction between the tax management of different reporting entities and the partial provision method as unduly subjective. 3.2.3

Deferred tax not reliably measurable

Other supporters of the flow-through method believe that in principle deferred tax should be recognised in financial statements, but that in practice the estimates and assumptions required are such that deferred tax cannot be measured with sufficient reliability. 3.2.4

Practical considerations 3.3

The main advantage of the flow-through method is its simplicity. It is the easiest of the three methods to apply in practice. The tax charge recorded in each period is simply the tax that will be assessed by the tax authorities in respect of that period. In the UK at least, the basis of assessment of the tax for an accounting period will almost always be fully known at the end of that period; there is no need to make assumptions about the future, such as are required for the full provision and partial provision methods. 3.3.1

A further advantage is that the balance sheet amount recorded under the flow-through method can be seen as a real liability to the tax authorities in the sense that a trade creditor represents a real amount due to a supplier.* As such it may be more readily understood by many users and preparers of financial statements than deferred tax, which is often not seen as a 'real' liability. 3.3.2

The two main practical disadvantages of the flow-through method are that: 3.3.3

**A more accurate analogy would be with an accrual since, at least in the UK, current tax (unlike a trade creditor) does not constitute a legal liability at the balance sheet date since it has not yet been formally assessed by the tax authorities.*

(a) it precludes recognition of deferred tax assets in respect of long-term liabilities such as pensions and other post-employment benefits. This was perceived as a significant failure of SSAP 15, necessitating its amendment in 1992;* and
(b) it can lead to what many would regard as unacceptable variations in the tax charge shown in the profit and loss account. This would necessitate additional disclosures of the contingent liabilities arising from the deferred tax effects of events of the current period.

3.3.4 Point (b) can be illustrated as follows. Two companies (A-Co and B-Co) with a year-end of 31 December both make an annual profit of £1 million comprising loan interest receivable, which is taxed on a receipts rather than an accruals basis. Normally both companies receive all the interest due in respect of a period before the end of that period, so that the taxable profit is the same as the accounting profit. However, A-Co does not receive the loan interest due for 1994 until early 1995, so that it falls to be taxed in the year ending 31 December 1995.

3.3.5 If A-Co and B-Co were to account for tax under the flow-through method, their profit and loss accounts for the years 1993 to 1996 would show the following, assuming a tax rate of 33 per cent:

A-Co

Year ending 31 December	Profit before tax (£000)	Tax charge (£000)	Effective tax rate (%)
1993	1,000	330	33
1994	1,000	NIL	0
1995	1,000	660	66
1996	1,000	330	33

B-Co

Year ending 31 December	Profit before tax (£000)	Tax charge (£000)	Effective tax rate (%)
1993	1,000	330	33
1994	1,000	330	33
1995	1,000	330	33
1996	1,000	330	33

3.3.6 The variations in tax expense both within A-Co and between A-Co and B-Co would probably concern most preparers and users, even if the reasons were explained by supplementary disclosures. A further consideration is that A-Co could, on the basis of the 1994 figures, distribute as dividend assets that will be needed to pay the additional tax falling due in 1995.

**See also paragraphs 1.3.2–1.3.4 and 5.3.3–5.3.7.*

One response to these concerns would be that the accounting reflects the economic reality that accounting profits and taxable profits are different with the result that annual tax bills can fluctuate. As to the risk of over-distribution, it is not difficult to envisage instances where it would be legal, but imprudent, to distribute profits, but this does not influence the accounting treatment. 3.3.7

A less radical view would be that such concerns are valid, but can be dealt with either by a modification of the accounting (discussed below) or by further disclosure (discussed in Chapter 7). 3.3.8

On the face of it, it would appear that the flow-through method could easily be modified to deal with such obviously 'one-off' transactions as that affecting A-Co's 1994 and 1995 accounts in the example in paragraph 3.3.5 above. In practice, however, it is difficult to find a modification that is not arbitrary. 3.3.9

One approach was suggested in the study of SSAP 15 undertaken for the Board by the Institute of Chartered Accountants of Scotland* before the Board's own review of the standard. This study advocates the adoption of the flow-through method modified by the provision of deferred tax in respect of short-term timing differences only. However, this immediately begs the question of what constitutes a 'short-term' timing difference for this purpose. 3.3.10

If a 'short-term' timing difference is taken to mean any difference that reverses within a given time period (such as one year), or is confined to certain transactions (such as those that have a tax effect on a cash basis but are recorded in the financial statements on an accruals basis) there will inevitably be arbitrary distinctions that will lead to apparent anomalies. 3.3.11

An alternative approach is suggested by the distinction made by some authorities (including the ASC in SSAP 15 before its revision in 1985) between timing differences arising from the operation of the capital allowances rules and others. It could be argued that timing differences arising from capital allowances are not true timing differences, but investment incentives that are so deliberately designed to reduce the real burden of tax for companies that their economic effect is best represented by accounting for them on a flow-through basis. However, deferred tax would be provided for in respect of other timing differences, which typically arise because of the use of an accruals basis in the financial statements but a cash basis in the tax computation. 3.3.12

Again, however, the difficulty with this distinction is that it will lead to arbitrary distinctions that are not readily accepted by users and preparers. For example, a company might be required to provide for a deferred tax liability in respect of interest 3.3.13

**SSAP 15 Accounting for deferred taxation, Prof Pauline Weetman (ed), ICAS 1992.*

receivable at the balance sheet date, even though the liability will be offset by capital allowances receivable on plant held at the balance sheet date.

3.4 *Relationship with the Board's draft Statement of Principles*

3.4.1 In examining the compatibility of the flow-through method with the Board's draft Statement of Principles the key issues are:

- Does the balance sheet figure represent an asset or liability (see paragraphs 3.4.2–3.4.4)?
- If so, can it be measured with sufficient reliability to allow its recognition in the financial statements (see paragraphs 3.4.5 and 3.4.6)?
- Is the financial information provided useful (see paragraphs 3.4.7–3.4.9)?

Is the balance sheet amount recorded a 'liability'?

3.4.2 'Assets' and 'liabilities' are defined in Chapter 3 of the draft Statement of Principles ('The elements of financial statements') as follows:

> 'Assets are rights or other access to future economic benefits controlled by an entity as a result of past transactions or events.'*
>
> 'Liabilities are an entity's obligations to transfer economic benefits as a result of past transactions or events.'†

3.4.3 Under the flow-through method, the amount included in the balance sheet in respect of tax represents the amount due to the tax authorities in respect of the taxable profit for the period ending on that date. This is the amount shown as the current tax liability under existing accounting practice in the UK.

3.4.4 As explained in footnote * to paragraph 3.3.2, this amount does not necessarily represent a legal liability at the balance sheet date. Nevertheless, the existence of a taxable profit is sufficient evidence of the existence of a liability under the draft Statement of Principles. There is an obligation to transfer economic benefits (ie to pay tax) as a result of a past event (ie the earning of taxable profit). However, supporters of the full and partial provision methods would take the view that the amount recognised under the flow-through method, although clearly a liability, is not the full liability (see paragraphs 3.4.8 and 3.4.9).

Is it measurable?

3.4.5 Chapter 4 of the draft Statement of Principles ('The recognition of items in financial statements') states that an item should be recognised in financial statements if it:

(a) meets the definition of an 'element' (in this case an asset or liability) in Chapter 3; and

******Draft Statement of Principles, Chapter 3, paragraph 7.*

†*Draft Statement of Principles, Chapter 3, paragraph 24.*

(b) can be measured with sufficient reliability in accordance with the principles set out in Chapter 5 ('Measurement in financial statements').*

The tax liability recorded under the flow-through method is readily measurable. In the UK at least, tax legislation is generally prospective, so that at any balance sheet date the basis of taxation and the relevant tax rate for the period ending on that date will be known.† **3.4.6**

Is the information provided useful?

The information presented by any accounting treatment should seek to achieve the highest possible level of the characteristics of financial information set out in Chapter 2 of the draft Statement of Principles ('The qualitative characteristics of financial information')—relevance and reliability (the primary characteristics), and comparability and understandability (the secondary characteristics). **3.4.7**

The information provided by the flow-through method is reliable and understandable, in the sense that it represents a real (or shortly to be real) liability to the tax authorities that can be measured reliably. However, there must be considerable doubt as to whether the flow-through method recognises the full liability to tax for the period. **3.4.8**

Taking the example in paragraph 3.3.5 by way of illustration, many would regard it as unsatisfactory that a company with identical pre-tax profits in consecutive periods should report no tax charge in one period followed by a double tax charge in the next. This result suggests that the tax liability of A-Co at 31 December 1994 under the pure flow-through method is understated. **3.4.9**

Legal considerations **3.5**

If it is the case, as suggested in paragraph 3.4.9 above, that the pure flow-through method can lead to the tax liability for a particular period being understated, the method may not be permitted by the Companies Act 1985, which requires that: **3.5.1**

> 'all liabilities and losses which have arisen or are likely to arise in respect of the financial year to which the accounts relate.....shall be taken into account'; and
>
> 'All income and charges relating to the financial year to which the accounts relate shall be taken into account, without regard to the date of receipt or payment'.‡

This might necessitate the introduction of the concept of a 'short-term timing difference', as described in paragraphs 3.3.10–3.3.12.

It might also be argued that the existence of the item 'Taxation including deferred **3.5.2**

**Draft Statement of Principles, Chapter 4, paragraph 4.*

†In the UK there may be cases where a company's accounting period ends early in a financial year for which the Finance Bill has not been enacted when the accounts are finalised.

‡Companies Act 1985: Schedule 4 paragraphs 12(b) and 13, Schedule 9 paragraphs 19(b) and 20, Schedule 9A paragraphs 16(b) and 17.

taxation' in the balance sheet formats in the Companies Act 1985 indicates a presumption by the legislators that deferred tax should be provided for. However, it could equally, if not more realistically, be argued that the formats merely indicate where deferred tax should be shown, without prejudice to the issue of whether or not it should be accounted for.

3.6 *International practice*

3.6.1 The flow-through method as described above is not used anywhere in the world and is not permitted under either the current International Accounting Standard IAS 12 or the recently published international exposure draft E49. However, this must be seen in the context that in many countries there are no significant differences between accounting and fiscal profits. In such countries accounting for tax, although nominally using the full provision method, could equally well be described as using the flow-through method.

3.7 *The Board's views*

3.7.1 The Board has initially concluded that it would not favour adoption of the flow-through method in the UK. The main issues considered by the Board in arriving at this conclusion are summarised below.

Accounting versus taxable profit as basis for tax charge

3.7.2 Those who support the flow-through method believe that tax is essentially a net assessment for an accounting period, which can therefore be measured only by reference to a known taxable profit. In their view, it is incorrect to report a liability to tax that is contingent on certain future events (eg earning a taxable profit), as is the case when deferred tax is provided for.

3.7.3 However, the Board is more persuaded by the view that taxable profit is, in form and substance, an adjusted accounting profit. It is possible, and appropriate, to attribute tax effects to individual transactions, even though tax is not legally assessed on this basis.

Stability of tax systems and reliability of measurement of deferred tax

3.7.4 Supporters of the flow-through method also believe that tax can be measured only by reference to a known tax system. In their view, there is no justification for the presumption, implicit in deferred tax accounting, that the tax system will continue in its present form. In the UK the basis of taxation is, as a matter of law, set for only one year at a time. The taxation of companies has undergone some radical changes in the past thirty years. Income tax was replaced by corporation tax in 1965; in the early 1970s ACT on dividends was introduced; 100 per cent first-year allowances and successively amended versions of stock relief were introduced in the same decade, then removed in the 1980s.

3.7.5 However, the Board believes that these changes, significant though they were, were concerned with the detail rather than the continuity of the tax system. In the Board's view, tax systems are generally sufficiently stable for a reasonable estimate to be made of the deferred tax consequences of events reported up to the balance sheet date. It is better to make an uncertain estimate based on the current tax rules than to make no estimate at all.

Consistency with draft Statement of Principles

The Board believes that the amounts recorded under the flow-through method are liabilities as defined in its draft Statement of Principles. However, it is concerned that the information supplied by the method is incomplete, so that in some cases the liability to tax is understated or overstated. **3.7.6**

Inconsistency with international practice

The flow-through method is not used in other countries where the taxation system gives rise to differences between accounting and taxable profit. To change from SSAP 15 to the flow-through method would thus represent a step away from, rather than towards, international harmonisation. **3.7.7**

Chapter 4. The full provision method

Method **4.1**

Provision is made in each period for the potential tax consequences of all gains and losses recognised up to the balance sheet date, irrespective of when those gains and losses will be recognised for tax purposes. The tax effects of possible future transactions are ignored. **4.1.1**

There are a number of variants of the full provision method. The variant discussed in this Chapter is the 'liability' method.* Under this method, the liability† is calculated at the tax rate that will, or is considered likely to, apply when the liability is settled. **4.1.2**

Rationale **4.2**

Historically, deferred tax accounting was adopted in order to match tax expense with the profits giving rise to it, on the basis that, over time, accounting and taxable profit are the same, barring permanent differences. This required that the tax effect of all taxable and tax-deductible gains and losses should be recognised in the accounting period in which the gains and losses themselves are recognised. **4.2.1**

Notwithstanding its origins as a means of matching income and expenditure with their **4.2.2**

****Other variants of the full provision method are the 'hybrid' method (discussed in Section 6.7) and the 'deferral' method, the 'net-of-tax' method and the 'temporary difference' approach in the US standard FAS 109 (discussed in Appendix 1).***

† References to 'liabilities' should be generally understood to include assets.

tax effects, deferred tax is equally valid conceptually (provided that the liability method is used) under models of accounting, such as that in the Board's draft Statement of Principles, that start by identifying assets and liabilities. The relationship of the liability method with the draft Statement of Principles is discussed in Section 4.4.

4.3 *Practical considerations*

4.3.1 The full provision method is relatively straightforward. For a reporting entity with a simple tax position in a stable tax system, deferred tax is the product of timing differences* at the balance sheet date and the expected future tax rate. However, the calculations are more difficult for an entity with a complex tax position. For example:

- Where the enacted future tax rates vary (as was the case in the UK following the Finance Act 1984), it is necessary to schedule timing differences by year of reversal in order to establish the appropriate tax rate to be applied to them.
- Profit forecasts may be required in order to assess the recoverability of deferred tax assets (particularly those arising from losses or surplus ACT).

4.3.2 As regards the financial information provided, the principal advantage of the full provision method, in the view of its supporters, is that the profit and loss account reflects the tax effects of all taxable transactions included in it and the balance sheet reflects the full tax effect of cumulative timing differences. By contrast, under both the flow-through and partial provision methods the full tax effect of a transaction may not become apparent until some time after the transaction is first recorded.

4.3.3 To its critics, however, this aspect of full provision is its great disadvantage. They see it as establishing an ultimate position that takes no account of when (or, some would argue, whether) deferred tax will be paid. Full provision tends, particularly in times of high inflation or under a tax system that gives 'front-loaded' investment incentives, to result in the build-up of material balances that, taken as a whole, are seen as unlikely to be settled or recovered. However, although this conclusion gives a valid description of probable future cash flows, it is valid only if the tax effect of future transactions is taken into account.

4.3.4 Whilst this difficulty has been mitigated to some extent in the UK with the changes to capital allowances initiated in the Finance Act 1984, some problems remain for entities operating in overseas tax jurisdictions. For example, a UK company may have a US subsidiary that accounts for stock under the 'last in, first out' (LIFO) method in its individual financial statements and is taxed on that basis.

4.3.5 If the financial statements of that US subsidiary are adjusted on to a 'first in, first out' (FIFO) basis on consolidation, the effect is to create a timing difference on which a deferred tax liability would, under the full provision method, be provided for. This liability will never reduce unless a reduction in stock levels causes layers of stock carried at old, low prices to pass into cost of sales, generating stock drawdown profits. In many circumstances realisation of such profits on a significant scale appears unlikely and some would therefore question whether the deferred tax liability has any real meaning.

**As explained elsewhere (paragraphs 2.3.3–2.3.5, Section 4.4 and Chapters 8 and 9) there is a view that deferred tax should be applied to some differences other than timing differences.*

So far as the profit and loss account is concerned, the full provision method is open to the criticism that it makes no distinction between a reporting entity that manages its tax affairs well and one that does not. Most users of financial statements attach great importance to management's ability to minimise its effective tax rate. **4.3.6**

The full provision method does not provide this information directly. However, the cash flow statement (and the separate disclosure of current tax in the balance sheet and profit and loss account) indicates actual tax payments and thus enables comparison to be made between different reporting entities. Some users of accounts consulted by the Board have argued that the benefits of careful tax management are also reflected in a lower effective interest rate* for those entities that are able to postpone payment of a large part of their deferred tax liabilities over a long period. **4.3.7**

Some may see the criticism of the full provision method in paragraph 4.3.3 as essentially that it fails to take account of the time value of money. Some of the effects of the time value of money could be dealt with either by the partial provision method (discussed in Chapter 5) or by discounting (discussed in Chapter 6) or by disclosure of the maturity of the deferred tax balance (discussed in Chapter 7). **4.3.8**

Whether discounting or disclosure is chosen as a solution, there is the difficulty of establishing when the deferred tax balance will actually be paid or should be deemed to be paid. Do reversing timing differences represent cash flows? Or must the possible tax effects of future transactions be taken into account, as is done under the partial provision method, which is discussed in Chapter 5? **4.3.9**

Even if the basic premise of partial provision (ie that future transactions will affect the overall level of tax paid in future years) is accepted, it can still be argued that a reversal of a timing difference can be treated as a future cash flow, irrespective of the effect of future transactions. Each reversing timing difference affects the tax assessment in the year in which it reverses, with the result that the amount of tax paid will be higher or lower than it otherwise would have been. On this basis, some argue that reversing timing differences can be treated as future cash flows for the purposes of discounting or disclosure. **4.3.10**

Another consideration is that, once a timing difference is established, the reporting entity is committed either to a higher or lower payment of tax or to some other course of action. For example, suppose that at December 1994 a company forecasts the reversal during 1995 of timing differences of £100,000 relating to accelerated capital allowances. This means that the company must either pay tax or must incur sufficient (eg capital) expenditure during 1995 to generate originating timing differences of at least £100,000. **4.3.11**

There is clearly an important distinction between a tax payment, which is a once and for all loss, and capital investment, which is expected to be recovered by future cash **4.3.12**

**ie interest charge as a percentage of total liabilities (including deferred tax).*

inflows. Nevertheless, as a result of the company's tax position at 31 December 1994 there is a requirement for a cash outflow either to the tax authorities or to a supplier of equipment.

4.3.13 It would still be open to the directors to indicate, either in the notes to the accounts or in the Operating and Financial Review, what steps they intend to take in order to postpone payment of the full liability. Under SSAP 15, these intentions underlie the reported liability for deferred tax but are not explicitly disclosed.

4.4 *Relationship with the Board's draft Statement of Principles*

4.4.1 The key issues to be considered are as set out in paragraph 3.4.1 in the analysis of the flow-through method:

- Is the balance sheet amount an asset or liability?
- If so, is it measurable?
- Is the information provided useful?

4.4.2 Two fundamental assumptions underlying the full provision method are that the tax system in place at the balance sheet date will continue to operate for the foreseeable future and the tax effects of possible future transactions are ignored. The following discussion is predicated on acceptance of these assumptions.

Is the balance sheet amount an asset or liability?

4.4.3 Unlike the flow-through method, which would normally be expected to lead to only credit balances being shown in the balance sheet in respect of tax, the full provision method can lead to either debit or credit balances being shown.

4.4.4 For most UK companies, the major components of the deferred tax balance will be the tax effects of timing differences relating to capital allowances and to the cost of pensions and other post-retirement benefits. The following discussion is based on these two categories of timing difference. They are useful examples for analysis, since each can give rise to deferred tax debits and credits.

CAPITAL ALLOWANCES

4.4.5 Capital allowances are available in the UK for most plant and machinery and many types of building. The discussion in this Section focuses on those given for plant and machinery.* Plant is depreciated in the financial statements over its expected useful life, in most cases on a straight-line basis. Accounting depreciation is disallowed for tax purposes.

4.4.6 Instead, the cost of the plant is allowed as a charge against taxable profits according to a fixed formula, currently 25 per cent of the tax written-down value at the beginning of the period. Tax allowances continue to be given until the tax written-down value

**The summary of the capital allowance provisions that follows is of necessity greatly simplified.*

approaches zero, which may of course be some time after the asset has been fully depreciated in the financial statements.

Suppose that an asset is purchased during 1994 for £1.2 million. It will be depreciated over six years and then scrapped. Deferred tax (on a full provision basis) relating to this asset would be calculated as follows at each year-end, assuming a 33 per cent tax rate. **4.4.7**

Year-end	**Book value (£000) A**	**Tax value (£000) B**	**Difference (£000) (A−B)=C**	**Deferred tax (£000) C×33%**
Purchase date	1200	1200	NIL	NIL
1994	1000	900	100	33.0
1995	800	675	125	41.2
1996	600	506	94	31.0
1997	400	380	20	6.6
1998	200	285	(85)	(28.1)
1999	NIL	214	(214)	(70.6)

There are various views as to the significance of the balance sheet amounts for deferred tax set out above. Some see them as assets and liabilities; others see them as 'valuation adjustments' to the carrying value of the fixed asset.* **4.4.8**

It is worth emphasising that in this example, and in the case of deferred tax relating to pensions described in paragraphs 4.4.15–4.4.21, it makes no difference to the amounts shown in the financial statements whether deferred tax is regarded as an asset or liability or as a 'valuation adjustment'. However, as mentioned earlier, this is not always the case. The two views lead to very different results in the context of acquisition accounting (discussed in Chapter 8) and revaluations (discussed in Chapter 9). **4.4.9**

Those who see the deferred tax in the table in paragraph 4.4.7 as an asset or liability do so on the grounds that, at any point in the life of the asset, the reporting entity's tax assessments for future periods will, as a result of the capital allowances claimed in the current and previous periods, be higher or lower than they would have been if there had been a different pattern of capital allowances claimed. Accordingly, where there is a difference between depreciation and capital allowances claimed, the future cash flows relating to tax assessments will be different from those that would have arisen if capital allowances claimed had equalled depreciation charged. **4.4.10**

**A third view, held by supporters of the 'hybrid' method, regards deferred tax arising from a timing difference that originates in the financial statements as an asset or liability and deferred tax arising from a timing difference that originates in the tax computation as a 'valuation adjustment'. The basis of this view is set out in Section 6.7 in Chapter 6.*

4.4.11 The point can be demonstrated by means of the following table.

Year	Depreciation (£000)	Capital allowances (£000)	Difference (£000)	Tax effect (£000)	Cumulative tax effect (£000)
1994	200	300	100	33.0	33.0
1995	200	225	25	8.2	41.2
1996	200	169	(31)	(10.2)	31.0
1997	200	126	(74)	(24.4)	6.6
1998	200	95	(105)	(34.7)	(28.1)
1999	200	71	(129)	(42.5)	(70.6)
2000–	NIL	214	214	70.6	NIL

The 'cumulative tax effect' column (which is the same as the 'deferred tax' column in the table in paragraph 4.4.7 above) represents the amount by which future tax liabilities will be increased/(reduced) as a result of the interaction between depreciation and capital allowances to date. Any cumulative decrease in the tax burden is eventually paid to the tax authorities in a higher future tax assessment (ie it represents a liability), and any cumulative increase is eventually recovered in a lower future tax assessment (ie it represents an asset).

4.4.12 Those who take this view acknowledge that the actual tax assessments of a future period are not liabilities at the balance sheet date. However, as a result of the cumulative timing differences at the balance sheet date, future tax assessments (whatever their amount in absolute terms) will be higher or lower than they would have been if those timing differences had not arisen. This is the case whether or not future transactions occur that reduce the tax assessments in those periods. It is therefore argued that the known increment or decrement of future liabilities should be recognised immediately.

4.4.13 An alternative approach is to consider the deferred tax as a 'valuation adjustment' to the carrying value of the fixed asset. According to the table in paragraph 4.4.7 above, at 31 December 1994 the book value of the asset is £1 million and its tax written-down value £900,000. The asset must be worth less to the company by an amount of £33,000 (ie the deferred tax at 31 December 1994), compared with an otherwise identical asset whose book value and tax written-down value are both £1 million. This is the case, irrespective of the impact of any future transactions.

4.4.14 In principle, this discrepancy might best be reflected by adjusting the carrying value of the plant. This would be the treatment adopted under the net-of-tax method of full provision as outlined in Appendix 1. However, as explained in Appendix 1, the Board has rejected net-of-tax accounting on a number of grounds, in particular its complexity and the fact that it obscures the overall tax burden of the reporting entity. Those who consider deferred tax as a 'valuation adjustment' believe that it is preferable to pool the tax-related 'valuation adjustments' to all assets and liabilities in the balance sheet under the single heading 'deferred tax'.

PENSIONS AND OTHER POST-RETIREMENT BENEFIT COSTS

The cost of pensions is accounted for in the financial statements on an accruals basis, in accordance with SSAP 24. For tax purposes, however, such costs are allowed only when actually paid by the company (either direct to the beneficiaries or to an approved pension scheme as the case may be). Thus, any balance sheet amount recorded under SSAP 24 is a timing difference on which deferred tax would be provided for under the full provision method. **4.4.15**

Where the balance sheet amount recorded under SSAP 24 is a liability, the implication is that a payment (that will attract tax relief) must eventually be made to a pension scheme or (in the case of an unfunded scheme) direct to a pensioner. Under the full provision method a deferred tax debit balance would be recognised in respect of this tax relief. As in the case of accelerated capital allowances discussed above, some would regard this balance as an asset and others as a 'valuation adjustment' to the pension liability. **4.4.16**

Those who see the deferred tax as an asset would argue that settlement of the liability for pensions will attract tax relief and therefore result in a lower tax assessment for the year in which settlement occurs, irrespective of the effect of future transactions. This known reduction in a future tax liability is itself an asset that should be recognised immediately, even though that future liability is not itself recognised at the balance sheet date. **4.4.17**

Those who view the deferred tax balance as a 'valuation adjustment' to the pension liability do so on the basis that a liability that attracts tax relief when settled must be a lower burden to the reporting entity than an otherwise equivalent liability that does not (eg a trade creditor*). This is the case, irrespective of the impact of any future transactions. **4.4.18**

Where the balance sheet amount recorded under SSAP 24 is an asset, the implication is that a payment (that will have attracted tax relief) has been made to the pension scheme in advance of the pension cost being recognised in the financial statements. Under the full provision method, a deferred tax credit balance would be recognised. Again, some would regard this balance as a liability and others as a 'valuation adjustment' to the pension asset. **4.4.19**

Those who see the deferred tax as a liability would argue that, as a result of the company's decision to pay, and claim tax relief for, pension costs in previous periods, its tax assessments for future periods will be higher than they would have been otherwise, irrespective of the impact of any future transactions. This known increase in a future liability should be recognised immediately, even though that future liability is not itself recognised at the balance sheet date. **4.4.20**

**Tax relief will have been given when the expense represented by the creditor was recognised in the profit and loss account. No tax relief arises on settlement of the liability.*

4.4.21 Those who see the deferred tax balance as a 'valuation adjustment' to the pension asset do so on the basis that the pension asset must be worth less to the business than an asset whose cost will be fully deductible for tax purposes (eg a new machine). This is the case, irrespective of the impact of any future transactions.

Is it measurable?

4.4.22 If it is accepted that, on balance, the tax system is stable rather than unpredictable, a full provision for deferred tax is easily measurable, subject to the potential difficulties highlighted in paragraph 4.3.1.

Is the information provided useful?

4.4.23 To the supporters of the full provision method, the information provided by it is useful since it represents the reporting entity's total liability arising from its tax position at the balance sheet date. The only discretion available to the company is whether it chooses to discharge it when current timing differences reverse or to postpone it by incurring another liability (eg by investing in plant).

4.4.24 However, some users and preparers of accounts, particularly in the UK, believe that the most important information with regard to an entity's tax affairs is its liability actually to pay tax on an ongoing basis. From this point of view, the full provision method does not provide useful information since it takes no account of when tax will become payable, particularly once the tax effect of future transactions is taken into account. If deferred tax were discounted, this difficulty would be mitigated, although not entirely overcome.

4.5 ***Legal considerations***

4.5.1 There are no legal restrictions on the use of the full provision method in the UK. There is currently a minor difficulty, discussed in Chapter 9, concerning the treatment of deferred tax recognised in respect of revaluation gains. The DTI has indicated that it will consider amending the legislation to overcome this.

4.6 ***International practice***

4.6.1 The full provision method is required in most countries where the tax system gives rise to timing differences.* It is also the preferred method in those other countries (the Netherlands, New Zealand and South Africa) that permit the partial provision method. The relevant international standard (IAS 12) permits either full or partial provision. The exposure draft E49 recently published by the IASC proposes that only the full provision method should be permitted.

**In most cases the 'liability' method is prescribed except in Canada, where the deferral method is prescribed, and in New Zealand, where the deferral method is permitted, so long as differences from using the liability method are disclosed.*

The Board's views 4.7

Having considered the various advantages and disadvantages of the possible methods of accounting for tax, the Board has provisionally concluded that the UK should adopt the full provision method. The main issues that influenced the Board in arriving at this conclusion are set out below. 4.7.1

Rejection of the alternatives

In many respects, the Board's reasons for supporting full provision are essentially the counterpart of its reasons for rejecting the flow-through and partial provision methods, which are set out in Chapters 3 and 5 respectively. 4.7.2

Changing circumstances since issue of SSAP 15

Past attempts to adopt the full provision approach (eg in SSAP 11) in the UK have been vigorously resisted, mainly because it seemed inappropriate in the context of the tax system and general economic conditions at the time. However, the Board believes that since the issue of SSAP 15, a number of important changes have taken place that significantly weaken the case for the UK's continued international isolation in accounting for tax: 4.7.3

(a) the withdrawal of first-year allowances and stock relief;
(b) a significant reduction in inflation; and
(c) the development of arrangements for pensions and other post- retirement benefits that are not deductible for tax purposes for a significant period after the costs have been recognised in the financial statements.

The combined effect of these changes is that, whereas in the 1970s the main problem in accounting for tax was how to deal with very long-term tax liabilities, for many companies there is now an equal, if not greater, problem of how to deal with very long-term tax assets. 4.7.4

International harmonisation

As noted in Section 4.6 above, the full provision method is increasingly the method adopted internationally. Its adoption in the UK would therefore represent a step towards international harmonisation, to which the Board is committed where possible. 4.7.5

A broader issue is that, for many companies, the UK will be only one of the many tax jurisdictions in which they operate. It is therefore open to question how far accounting for tax should be unduly influenced by particular aspects of the UK tax system. It is worth recording that, although SSAP 15 was issued just over sixteen years ago, the rules for first-year allowances and stock relief that gave rise to the perceived need for SSAP 15 remained in place for only a relatively short period after its issue. 4.7.6

Consistency with the Board's draft Statement of Principles

The Board believes that the full provision method is consistent with its draft Statement of Principles. The balances recognised arise from past transactions or events and do not 4.7.7

recognise (and are not, in any case, affected by) future transactions or events. However, there are various views among Board members as to what deferred tax represents.

4.7.8 Some take the view, as set out in Section 4.4, that deferred tax represents a known increment or decrement of a future tax liability. Others take the view, as also set out in Section 4.4, that it represents a 'valuation adjustment' to other assets and liabilities at the balance sheet date.

Build-up of long-term assets and liabilities

4.7.9 The Board recognises that a disadvantage of the full provision method is that it may lead to the accumulation of large assets and liabilities that some may see as having little meaning since their date of receipt or payment is so long postponed. This postponement occurs for two distinct reasons:

(a) timing differences at the balance sheet date reverse in later periods; and
(b) new timing differences originating in later periods may cancel the effect of the reversal in those periods of timing differences at the balance sheet date.

4.7.10 The Board currently favours a solution whereby the amount of deferred tax reported in the financial statements would be discounted to take account of reversing current timing differences only (ie (a) in paragraph 4.4.9 above), but the notes to the financial statements would disclose the directors' broad estimate of the effect on tax payments of both reversing current timing differences and originating future timing differences (ie (a) and (b) in paragraph 4.4.9 above).

4.7.11 The Board came to this view on the grounds that disclosure on its own would not deal adequately with the problem. As indicated in paragraph 4.3.9, the two broad options for disclosure would be either:

(a) a maturity analysis of the deferred tax balance by reference to the year of reversal of timing differences at the balance sheet date (see paragraphs 4.7.12 and 4.7.13); or
(b) an estimate of deferred tax payments after taking account of likely future investment (see paragraphs 4.7.14 and 4.7.15).

4.7.12 The Board concluded that simply to disclose the year-by-year reversal of timing differences at the balance sheet date could be misleading. Users could regard a schedule of the reversal of deferred tax as indicating future tax payments, in the same way, for example, as the analysis of future lease commitments indicates future lease payments.

4.7.13 However, this would be a false analogy. The amount of future lease payments is a known, and absolute, liability at the balance sheet date. As explained in Section 4.4, deferred tax at the balance sheet date does not represent the absolute amount of a future tax assessment but the amount by which it is known that a future (as yet unknown) tax assessment will be increased or decreased as the result of events up to the balance sheet date.

4.7.14 The Board accepted that, for the purposes of disclosure, more meaningful information could possibly be given by requiring management's broad estimate of future tax payments in the short term, after taking account of future investment. However, the Board does not believe that it would be appropriate to include such an estimate in the financial statements.

The amount that would be recorded would suffer from the same problems as the estimates of the tax liability currently made using the partial provision method under SSAP 15. For example, it would effectively recognise the tax effects of future transactions to which the reporting entity is not committed, and could be unduly subjective. The Board has provisionally rejected SSAP 15, and the partial provision method in general, for these and other reasons, which are discussed in more detail in Chapter 5. **4.7.15**

These inadequacies in the possible disclosures, if taken in isolation, led the Board to conclude that, in principle, the amount at which the deferred tax is recognised in the financial statements should be discounted. The Board researched whether discounting could deal with postponements of payment of tax arising both from the reversal of current timing differences and from the origination of future timing differences. **4.7.16**

However, as explained more fully in Chapter 6, the Board concluded that discounting on this basis would be both impractical and inconsistent with the full provision method. The Board takes the view that where the full provision method is adopted, discounting should take account of postponements of receipt or payment arising from current timing differences reversing in future periods, but not future timing differences originating in those periods. A proposed methodology for discounting on this basis (the 'full reversal' method) is set out in Chapter 6. **4.7.17**

The Board believes that, in the interests of consistency between reporting entities, discounting deferred tax should be either required or prohibited, rather than merely permitted. However, the Board is concerned that discounting, even under the relatively simple method proposed in Chapter 6, could be difficult, particularly for smaller companies. It will therefore consider comments received on discounting before deciding whether or not it should be required. **4.7.18**

Chapter 5. The partial provision method

Method **5.1**

Provision is made in each period for all the potential tax consequences of all gains and losses recognised in the period, but only to the extent that tax is likely to be actually paid or tax relief received, after taking account of the tax effect of likely future transactions. In practical terms, this is achieved by not providing for the so-called 'hard core' of timing differences. **5.1.1**

Where there is a reasonably constant interval between the recognition of certain transactions in the financial statements and in the tax computation, any company that does not significantly reduce its operations will have a 'hard core' of timing differences, **5.1.2** which never, if considered in aggregate, reverses. In other words, although the individual timing differences making up the 'hard core' at any time reverse, they are simultaneously replaced by new originating timing differences, with the result that the deferred tax balance (considered as a whole) is not reduced.

5.1.3 This 'hard core' represents an effectively permanent, and moreover interest-free, deferral of payment of tax (or receipt of tax relief). Under the partial provision method, the existence of this 'hard core' is acknowledged by not providing for the deferred tax effect of it.

5.2 *Rationale*

5.2.1 Like full provision, partial provision is based on the view that, over time, accounting profit and taxable profit are, except for permanent differences, the same. Profit and tax can (and therefore should) be matched in accordance with the fundamental accruals concept.

5.2.2 The essential difference between the methods lies in the overall amount of tax that each seeks to allocate. The partial provision method seeks to allocate only the amount of deferred tax that, on the evidence available at the balance sheet date, will actually be paid. In that sense, partial provision is comparable to the flow-through method, since the overall amount allocated by both methods should be the amount paid.

5.2.3 The perceived need for the partial provision approach in the UK arose from the tax system in the 1970s and early 1980s. This allowed companies to deduct for tax purposes 100 per cent of the cost of plant and equipment in the year of purchase, together with inflationary increases in the carrying amount of stock. The effect of these deductions was that companies could postpone payment of some or all of their deferred tax indefinitely and actually paid tax at well below the enacted rate of 52 per cent, in some cases paying no tax apart from ACT on dividends.

5.2.4 So long as a company continued to replace its plant and stocks on a regular basis and provided that the tax system did not change, the deferred tax balance would never reduce. Indeed it would increase as a result of inflation, since the cost of plant and stocks (and therefore the tax allowances claimed on them) continually rose. It was thought unrealistic to record a deferred tax liability that would never be paid and to show an effective tax charge in the profit and loss account of the full statutory tax rate when tax paid was well below that rate.*

5.3 *Practical considerations*

5.3.1 The advantage of the partial provision method is that it aims to recognise as an expense and liability only the tax that is expected actually to be paid. It is therefore seen by its supporters as showing a more realistic tax liability and effective tax rate than either the

**Once the level of 'hard core' timing differences reaches a steady 'plateau', the effective tax rate under partial provision becomes the statutory tax rate, and it is only the balance sheet liability that differs from that arising under full provision.*

flow-through or the full provision methods. However, it has a number of disadvantages, which are discussed in paragraphs 5.3.2–5.3.13 below.

Recognition rule

A major disadvantage of the partial provision method, at least as given effect in SSAP 15, is its basic recognition rule—namely that deferred tax assets or liabilities are recognised only to the extent that they are not expected to be replaced by similar items. The conceptual objections to this approach are discussed in Section 5.4. The practical objection to it is that it 'works' only where timing differences are relatively stable. Where the level and/or reversal pattern of timing differences fluctuates (particularly where a new category of timing difference suddenly appears in the financial statements), SSAP 15 produces results that are counter-intuitive. This is discussed in more detail in Appendix 2. **5.3.2**

It was essentially this problem that was highlighted by the issue of SSAP 24 'Accounting for pension costs' and UITF Abstract 6 'Accounting for post-retirement benefits other than pensions'. These required companies to establish for the first time liabilities in respect of pensions and other post-employment benefits (OPEBs), which would be expected to increase over a number of years before resulting in significant payments. **5.3.3**

However, SSAP 15 would not permit any recognition to be given to the tax relief that would be expected to be available when the pensions and OPEBs were paid* until the actual year of payment, because to do so would require a permanent deferred tax asset to be set up, contrary to the recognition criterion described in paragraph 5.3.2 above. **5.3.4**

The treatment required by SSAP 15, considered in terms of the underlying rationale of the standard, is entirely justifiable. In the years when the liability for pensions or OPEBs is first set up, profit before tax will include a charge for pensions or OPEBs that is not tax-deductible. In these periods the company will pay tax at more than the standard rate, in the sense that its current tax liability will be greater than the profit before tax multiplied by the tax rate. **5.3.5**

In the tax computations for the years in which the pensions or OPEBs are paid, tax relief for amounts paid will be offset by add-backs for amounts charged in the profit and loss account.† In other words, tax in those periods will, other things being equal, be paid at the standard rate and the effective 'overpayment' of tax in the earlier years will never be recovered. The accounting treatment required by SSAP 15 before the Amendment reflected this. **5.3.6**

However, at the time of the issue of UITF Abstract 6 the majority of commentators **5.3.7**

In the case of funded pension schemes, tax relief is given in respect of payments to the scheme. In the case of unfunded schemes and OPEBs, tax relief is given in respect of payments to, or on behalf of, the beneficiaries.

† This is the case only when, as is the norm, the company continues to offer such benefits as part of the remuneration package, so that the balance sheet liability for them never reduces. If the company withdraws such benefits for new employees (as some have now done, particularly in respect of medical benefits), the balance sheet liability (and therefore the deferred tax asset) reverses. In such cases, deferred tax assets could have been recognised under SSAP 15 before the amendment (subject to assurance as to their recoverability).

held an alternative view—that the financial statements should reflect the fact that such benefits would attract tax relief when they were paid. Others believed that such long-term, and inevitably not very precise, liabilities as pensions and OPEBs should ideally be provided for on a net-of-tax basis. Accordingly, the Board amended SSAP 15 (pending the current review) to allow full provision in respect of deferred tax on pensions and OPEBs. An inevitable result of this amendment, however, whatever its intrinsic merit, was to create an inconsistency within SSAP 15 that is clearly unsustainable in the longer term.

Complexity

5.3.8 The partial provision method is the most complex of the methods to operate in practice. It requires detailed forecasts of (for example) capital expenditure and the funding policy for the pension scheme, in addition to the scheduling of expected future profits and tax rates that may be required under the full provision method (see paragraph 4.3.1). However, the need for such forecasts is greatly reduced under the sort of tax system, discussed in paragraph 5.2.3 above, that gave rise to the perceived need for the partial provision method in the UK. Under that system it was often obvious, without the need for forecasting, that payment of much or all of the deferred tax liability could be postponed indefinitely.

Subjectivity

5.3.9 Another criticism of the partial provision method is that, because of its reliance on management projections (in order to estimate likely future transactions whose tax effects may be relevant), it is subjective and manipulable. For example, it is possible to reduce the current year's tax charge simply by assuming an increase in future capital expenditure. Some users of financial statements have indicated to the Board that, for this reason, they sometimes find it difficult to accept the tax charges and liabilities of UK companies at face value.

5.3.10 SSAP 15 partly addresses this concern by requiring disclosure of the amount of deferred tax not provided for analysed into its main components,* although this does not give any indication of the basis on which the partial provision has been made (for example the level and timing of future capital investment that has been assumed). However, preparers of accounts could, with some justification, object to such disclosure on the basis that it would reveal information that is commercially sensitive but of only marginal benefit in interpreting the tax charge, and then only in the hands of a highly sophisticated user.

Tax charge may not reflect events of the period

5.3.11 A further, related, drawback of the partial provision method is that it can produce fluctuations in the tax charge for a period that are related neither to transactions nor to changes in the tax law in that period. For example, a decision by management to reduce future capital expenditure will accelerate the net reversal of timing differences and,

**SSAP 15, paragraph 35.*

hence, increase the deferred tax liability recognised and the tax charge for the period. This is particularly the case under the present tax system, where the level of 'hard core' timing differences is much more sensitive to the detailed assumptions made than was the case in the 1970s.

This aspect of the partial provision method can also aggravate the losses of companies that are already experiencing trading difficulties. Such companies will not generate sufficient free cash flow to support a normal capital investment programme. This will lead to an acceleration of the net reversal of timing differences and thus increase tax expense as described in paragraph 5.3.11 above. 5.3.12

Inconsistency with FRS 7

Use of the partial provision method is inconsistent with FRS 7 'Fair Values in Acquisition Accounting'. The basic principle of FRS 7 is that "the assets and liabilities recognised in the allocation of fair values should be those of the acquired entity that existed at the date of acquisition".* In other words, no changes can be made to those fair values to reflect the intentions of the new owner. However, under the partial provision method the deferred tax of a group can be assessed only for the group as a whole and by using the plans of the new owner, rather than those of the acquired entity at the date of acquisition. 5.3.13

Relationship with the Board's draft Statement of Principles 5.4

The key issues to be considered are as set out in paragraph 3.4.1 in the analysis of the flow-through method: 5.4.1

- Is the balance sheet amount an asset or liability?
- If so, is it measurable?
- Is the information provided useful?

Is the balance sheet amount an asset or liability?

The arguments as to whether the balances recorded under the partial provision method represent assets or liabilities are essentially the same as those in respect of the full provision method set out in Section 4.4 of Chapter 4. The additional question that must be considered in connection with the partial provision method is whether it is consistent with the draft Statement of Principles to measure deferred tax by taking account of the tax effects of projected future transactions. 5.4.2

Some believe that the balances resulting from the application of the partial provision method are assets or liabilities, since they purport to represent the actual likely right to receive tax relief or obligation to pay tax, whereas the amount of deferred tax not provided for is at most a contingent liability. However, others take the view that the partial provision method, at least as given effect in SSAP 15, is difficult to reconcile to the draft Statement of Principles in a number of respects: 5.4.3

- the recognition rule (see paragraphs 5.4.4–5.4.9)

***FRS 7, Summary, paragraph (b).*

- the anticipation of future transactions (see paragraphs 5.4.10 and 5.4.11)
- the failure to identify other liabilities that must be incurred in order to defer tax payments (see paragraphs 5.4.12–5.4.14)
- reliance on the intentions of management (see paragraphs 5.4.15- 5.4.18).

RECOGNITION RULE

5.4.4 SSAP 15 states that:

> "... deferred tax should be accounted for in respect of the net amount by which it is probable that any payment of tax will be temporarily deferred or accelerated by the operation of timing differences which will reverse in the foreseeable future without being replaced. Partial provision recognises that ... an enterprise ... will often have what amounts to a hard core of timing differences so that the payment of some tax will be permanently deferred."*

5.4.5 The basic concept—that items that are continually replaced by similar items should not be recognised—does not feature in the draft Statement of Principles and is not used elsewhere; it would lead to strange results if it were. For example, most enterprises have a 'hard core' of trade debtors or creditors that, it could be argued, would not be recognised if the recognition criteria in SSAP 15 were applied to them. Moreover, the so-called 'hard core' of timing differences referred to in SSAP 15 is illusory. Each individual timing difference reverses and increases or decreases the tax assessment in the year of reversal.†

5.4.6 However, some believe that to compare trade creditors with the 'hard core' of non-reversing timing differences is invalid, since trade creditors are regularly (and individually) settled in cash whereas the 'hard core' is not.

5.4.7 A further difficulty in the extract from SSAP 15 quoted in paragraph 5.4.4 above is the reference to payment of tax being "permanently deferred". The UK tax system when SSAP 15 was issued gave some support to the concept of permanent deferral, since some companies then paid no mainstream corporation tax.

5.4.8 Under the current tax system, however, the level of 'hard core' timing differences is more liable to fluctuate in consecutive periods. As a result, the amount of deferred tax provided for today under the partial provision method is much more sensitive to the underlying assumptions than was the case in the 1970s, when a substantial level of 'hard core' differences was thought to be almost certain to remain in place in any company that was a going concern.

5.4.9 It could be argued that the recognition rule in SSAP 15 is in substance a surrogate for discounting the full provision liability, although the ASC probably did not think of it as such. It is not so much that there is no liability, but that there is a liability whose crystallisation is so far in the future that its present value is zero, or at any rate substantially less than the face amount.

SSAP 15, paragraph 12.

†See also paragraphs, 4.3.10–4.3.12.

ANTICIPATION OF FUTURE TRANSACTIONS

The partial provision method can also be criticised on the grounds that it takes account of future transactions, particularly purchases of plant. The case could be made that, in taking account of future transactions, SSAP 15 is incompatible with the draft Statement of Principles, which defines 'assets' and 'liabilities' as, respectively, benefits and obligations arising from past events. **5.4.10**

However, others disagree with this analysis. In their view, the partial provision method is simply a natural reflection of the going concern concept under which financial statements are normally prepared, since any entity that is a going concern must replace its plant regularly. They also point out that the measurement of many other items in financial statements could equally be argued to anticipate future transactions. For example, the classification of an item as a fixed asset effectively presumes that there will be future profits out of which it will be recovered, but this practice is not, as a result, regarded as unacceptable. **5.4.11**

FAILURE TO IDENTIFY ALTERNATIVE LIABILITIES

Strictly speaking, the partial provision method takes account of only the tax effects of future transactions, not the transactions themselves. The partial provision method can thus be argued to reduce the reported liability to tax, but not to identify the other liabilities to which the reporting entity is effectively committed if it is to pay only this reduced amount of tax. **5.4.12**

For example, a company's deferred tax balance on a full provision basis might be £1 million. Under the partial provision method, only £200,000 is recognised because the company plans to invest £3 million in plant over the next five years.* In other words, the accounts have recognised a benefit of £800,000 arising from the deferral of tax, but do not include (or in most cases even disclose) the liability of £3 million that will have to be discharged in order to achieve this benefit. **5.4.13**

However, some believe that this criticism of the partial provision method is misplaced. In their view, it is invalid to compare a payment of tax (which represents a loss to the company) with a payment for plant (which would normally be expected to be recovered out of future earnings). **5.4.14**

MANAGEMENT INTENTION

SSAP 15 requires that: **5.4.15**

> "... deferred tax liabilities or assets ... should be based on reasonable assumptions. The assumptions should take account of all relevant information available

**These are illustrative numbers only.*

up to the date on which the financial statements are approved by the board of directors and also the intentions of management."*

However, the Board's draft Statement of Principles states:

"A mere decision to enter into a transaction in a future period does not of itself provide sufficient evidence for recognition. There will not be sufficient evidence of a change in the entity's assets or liabilities unless and until such time as the entity either enters into a transaction or the circumstances are such that it has a firm commitment."†

5.4.16 Some believe that this principle, which has been embodied in various standards already issued by the Board (FRSS 3, 4, 5 and 7), is incompatible with the explicit reliance on management intent in SSAP 15.

5.4.17 However, others take the view that the Board's draft Statement of Principles is simply meant to indicate that management intention does not, in the absence of a commitment, give rise to an asset or liability. In the present case, however, if the arguments set out in Section 4.4 of Chapter 4 are accepted, deferred tax assets and liabilities are generated not by the intentions of management but by the interaction of the tax system and the financial statements.

5.4.18 Those who take this view argue that the role of management intention under SSAP 15 is not to create a deferred tax asset or liability, but to measure it, in much the same way that the carrying amounts of fixed assets and stocks might be re-appraised in the light of management's future plans. They therefore see no conflict between SSAP 15 and the Board's draft Statement of Principles.

Is the balance sheet amount measurable?

5.4.19 Provided that it is accepted both that the tax system is stable rather than unpredictable, and that the tax effect of likely future transactions can be estimated reliably, a partial provision for deferred tax is measurable with sufficient reliability to be included in financial statements.

Is the information useful?

5.4.20 The partial provision method is seen by its supporters as providing the relevance and comparability lacking in the full provision method. It was generally agreed in the UK that during the era of high first-year allowances and stock relief, full provision did not provide realistic or helpful information. The review of SSAP 15 undertaken for the Board by the Institute of Chartered Accountants of Scotland‡ indicates that, among preparers and some users, there remains a strong preference for retention of the partial provision method on these grounds.

**SSAP 15, paragraphs 27–28.*

†Draft Statement of Principles, Chapter 4 (Recognition), paragraph 39.

‡SSAP 15 Accounting for deferred taxation, Prof Pauline Weetman (ed), ICAS 1992.

By contrast, those users whom the Board has consulted in the course of this project have indicated a preference for the 'harder' numbers provided by the flow-through and full provision methods to be included in the financial statements, amplified if necessary by note disclosure or commentary in the Operating and Financial Review. Those users believed that, even if the partial provision method would give the best answer in an ideal world, its inherent subjectivity renders it unreliable. 5.4.21

Is there an alternative to SSAP 15? 5.5

It could be argued that, even if the criticisms of SSAP 15 in Sections 5.3 and 5.4 above are well made, they do not necessarily mean that the partial provision method is in itself invalid. The Board has therefore considered whether it might be possible to develop an alternative methodology to that of SSAP 15 so as to overcome the difficulties noted above. 5.5.1

The first main criticism of SSAP 15 is its recognition rule. Since this can be argued to be a surrogate for discounting a long-term, non-interest bearing liability, a discounting approach is the obvious alternative. This is discussed in Chapter 6. The other main criticism is that the standard relies on future events and management intentions. 5.5.2

This might be addressed by mandating, or at least constraining, the future transactions to be taken into account. This would remove the subjectivity of management intention altogether and could be argued to be closer to a general extension of the going concern concept. For example, it could be assumed that: 5.5.3

- future investment in fixed assets would be limited to replacement of the current level of plant with an allowance for inflation
- pension costs and funding policy would remain at current levels with an allowance for inflation
- future profits would not be greater than the average of the previous five years' profits with an allowance for inflation (for assessing the recoverability of losses and ACT carried forward).

The Board does not believe that this approach is practicable. In many ways it represents the worst of all possible worlds. It would involve the same level of computation as is currently required for SSAP 15, while being open to the same criticism as the full provision method, ie that it fails to take account of the particular circumstances of individual companies. 5.5.4

Legal considerations 5.6

There are no legal restrictions on the use of the partial provision method in the UK. There is currently a minor difficulty, discussed in Chapter 9, concerning the treatment of deferred tax arising on revaluations. The DTI has indicated that it will consider amending the legislation to overcome this. 5.6.1

International practice 5.7

The UK and the Republic of Ireland are currently the only countries to require the partial provision method. It is permitted in the Netherlands, New Zealand and South 5.7.1

Africa and by the current International Accounting Standard IAS 12. An exposure draft (E49) recently published by the International Accounting Standards Committee proposes abolition of partial provision.

5.8 ***The Board's views***

5.8.1 The Board accepts that the partial provision method has been well accepted practice in the UK for nearly twenty years. However, it has provisionally concluded that the partial provision method should be replaced with full provision, and that deferred tax should be discounted. The issues that have particularly influenced the Board in coming to this preliminary view are set out below.

Inconsistency of SSAP 15 with other standards and the Board's draft Statement of Principles

5.8.2 As explained in Chapter 1 and Section 5.4 above, the Board, whilst believing that some of the criticisms of SSAP 15 are overstated, is concerned that many details of it are difficult to reconcile to other standards and the Board's own draft Statement of Principles. In particular, SSAP 15 recognises the tax effects of future transactions before they have occurred and, in many cases, before the reporting entity is even committed to undertaking them. At a practical level, as shown in Appendix 2, the recognition rule in SSAP 15 produces counter-intuitive answers when the level of 'hard core' timing differences alters significantly.

Internal inconsistency of SSAP 15

5.8.3 The Board believes that, as a short-term measure pending the current review, it was appropriate to issue the 'Amendment to SSAP 15'. Again, however, in the longer term it sits very uneasily with the rest of SSAP 15, since its practical effect is that what for most entities is their biggest deferred tax asset is recognised in full while deferred tax liabilities are only partially recognised. To a jaundiced observer this could well appear a somewhat cynical approach, since, if the arguments in Section 4.4 are accepted, deferred tax credits are just as much liabilities under the Board's draft Statement of Principles as deferred tax debits are assets.

Difficulty of developing an alternative methodology

5.8.4 As explained in Section 5.5, the Board's research so far indicates that it will not be possible to develop a practical and readily acceptable methodology for partial provision in place of that in SSAP 15.

Inconsistency with international practice

5.8.5 The Board is concerned that in retaining the partial provision method, the UK is likely to become isolated internationally while no longer being able to plead with the same justification as in the 1970s that the UK's tax system requires a different approach from that in other countries.

Discounting as the appropriate solution

All deferred tax will (assuming the continuation of the current tax system) eventually become payable. The Board believes that SSAP 15 is flawed in that it deals with this question as an issue of recognition rather than of measurement. In other words, its approach is to ask 'Is this amount a liability?' rather than 'At what amount should this liability be measured?' In principle, this problem should be dealt with by discounting, which is discussed in the following Chapter. **5.8.6**

Chapter 6. Discounting deferred tax

Issues **6.1**

Paragraph 2.5.2 above notes that the accounting treatment adopted for tax should have regard to the tax system itself. A key feature of the UK tax system is that there can be a significant delay between the recognition of certain items in the accounts and the tax computation and vice versa. In particular: **6.1.1**

- the cost of pensions and other post-retirement benefits may be charged to the profit and loss account many years before the cost is allowed for tax purposes
- the provisions relating to capital allowances for plant and machinery may in certain circumstances enable companies to postpone payment of part of their deferred tax balance.

It has been noted in earlier Chapters that the main disadvantage of the full provision method is that, in certain types of tax system, it can lead to the accumulation of large liabilities that are never significantly reduced. The method can therefore be criticised for giving no indication of when (or, some would argue, whether) the deferred tax liability will actually be paid. It thus fails to provide information on what for many users of accounts is an important management function—control of the amount and timing of tax payments. **6.1.2**

It was suggested in Chapter 4 above that this defect could be remedied, or at least mitigated, by discounting. Such an approach has obvious intuitive appeal. Indeed, some parts of the deferred tax balances currently shown by UK companies are in effect discounted. For example, the amounts recognised in respect of pension costs, finance leases and certain capital instruments are discounted and, therefore, any deferred tax effects of such balances are also presented on a discounted basis. **6.1.3**

It should be noted that, whilst discounting will always reduce the balance sheet liability for deferred tax, it will not necessarily always reduce the tax charge in the profit and loss account. For example, if in a particular period interest on the brought forward deferred tax balance is greater than the discount on new items arising during the period, the effect of discounting will be to increase the tax charge for that period. This result is easily explicable, although some may find it surprising. **6.1.4**

Three basic aspects of discounting deferred tax cause some difficulty and are accordingly explored in this Chapter: **6.1.5**

- the validity of discounting deferred tax (see Section 6.2 below)
- choice of a discount rate (see Section 6.3 below)
- determination of the payment schedule (see Section 6.4 below).

6.2 ***The validity of discounting deferred tax***

6.2.1 Deferred tax can be discounted only if it represents a future cash flow, since discounting can be applied only to future cash flows. This Section examines whether deferred tax, as explained in Section 4.4 above, represents a future cash flow.

6.2.2 Section 4.4 sets out two views of the nature of deferred tax. One view is that deferred tax represents the amount by which future tax assessments will be increased or decreased as a result of cumulative timing differences at the balance sheet date. The second view is that deferred tax is a 'valuation adjustment' to the carrying amount of other assets and liabilities recognised at the balance sheet date.

Deferred tax as a reduction or increase in future tax assessments

6.2.3 If deferred tax is an increase or decrease in future tax assessments (which will result in future cash flows), it represents an increase or decrease in future cash flows that can be discounted.

Deferred tax as a valuation adjustment

6.2.4 Some take the view that there is no basis for discounting deferred tax, if it is taken to represent a valuation adjustment to another non-monetary asset or liability that is not itself presented on a discounted basis (eg a fixed asset).*

6.2.5 The opposite view is taken by those Board members who regard deferred tax as a valuation adjustment. They hold that, regardless of whether the asset or liability that is adjusted is a monetary item, the adjustment is made to reflect the effect on future tax assessments of that asset or liability. To the extent that this effect can be predicted, it represents an increase or decrease in a monetary item, which can be discounted.

6.2.6 Essentially the 'valuation adjustment' approach is based on the premise that an asset that is not fully tax-deductible must be worth less than an asset that is tax-deductible. If this is accepted, it must equally be the case that a partially tax-deductible asset that will give rise to higher† tax payments in one year's time must be worth less than an otherwise identical asset that will give rise to higher tax payments in five years' time. Discounting the valuation adjustment reflects this difference.

6.3 ***Determining the discount rate***

6.3.1 Currently in the UK, assets and liabilities that are included in the balance sheet at a discounted amount are discounted at the rate specific to that asset or liability.

**This view is held by those who support the 'hybrid' method of accounting for tax discussed in Section 6.7.*

†ie higher relative to a fully tax-deductible asset.

Examples include finance leases accounted for under SSAP 21, pension and other post-employment benefits (OPEBs) accounted for under SSAP 24 and UITF Abstract 6 and certain capital instruments accounted for under FRS 4.

The difficulty in extending this principle to deferred tax is that the discount rate applicable to deferred tax is not intuitively obvious. Indeed, it has been the subject of lengthy and inconclusive academic debate. The issue is essentially whether a discount rate specific to the reporting entity, or a more general rate, should be used. 6.3.2

Entity-specific rate

The advantage of using an entity-specific discount rate is that this would more closely reflect the circumstances of the reporting company. The main disadvantage is that it is very difficult to determine what rate should be used. For example, a rate such as the marginal cost of borrowing is arguably not appropriate, because borrowings bear interest in any event, whereas deferred tax is payable only in the event of future profits. 6.3.3

A real practical disadvantage of using an entity-specific rate is that, if a company gets into financial difficulty, the rate would increase to reflect the company's deteriorating creditworthiness. This would lead to a reduction in the reported deferred tax liability at the very time when the immediate liability will probably increase because the company is unable to undertake sufficient capital expenditure to maintain the 'hard core' of timing differences.* 6.3.4

General rate

The advantage of using a general rate (eg the effective rate of a government bond) is that it is much simpler than attempting to calculate an entity-specific rate. However, there are difficulties. 6.3.5

For example, the rate used should reflect the estimated maturity profile of the deferred tax balance. Thus, deferred tax expected to be paid in 2005 should be discounted at the rate applicable to a 10-year, rather than a 5-year, bond. There is also the question of whether foreign deferred tax should be discounted at the rate applicable to government bonds in the relevant overseas countries. 6.3.6

The Board believes that, in the absence of any consensus as to the appropriate rate, the only practical solution would be to require deferred tax to be discounted at the effective rate of a government bond appropriate to the tax jurisdiction concerned. The effect of discounting deferred tax would be disclosed. 6.3.7

Determining the payment schedule 6.4

In order to discount a liability it is necessary to know when it is to be settled and the amount of any payment(s) made on the settlement date(s). In the case of most liabilities that are included in financial statements on a discounted basis (eg finance leases, 6.4.1

**This is explained more fully in paragraphs 5.3.11 and 5.3.12.*

deep-discounted bonds), the date and amount of repayments are known in advance, so that calculation of a discounted figure for those liabilities at each balance sheet date presents little or no difficulty.

6.4.2 Where deferred tax is concerned, however, there is no equivalent pre-determined payment schedule. This is not itself a unique difficulty. The balances recorded in respect of pension costs under SSAP 24 essentially represent discounted future cash flows whose precise amount and date are highly uncertain. The problem that is unique to deferred tax is to determine what in principle are the future cash flows to which discounting should be applied.

6.4.3 There are broadly two approaches that can be adopted, the 'full reversal' approach and the 'net reversal' approach, defined for the purposes of this Chapter as follows:*

- *Full reversal*
  The tax effects of individual timing differences constituting the deferred tax balance at the balance sheet date are discounted, based on their expected year of reversal (see Section 6.5 below).
- *Net reversal*
  Estimated payments of deferred tax (after taking account of the tax effects of likely future transactions) are discounted based on their expected year of payment (see Section 6.6 below).

6.4.4 The 'full reversal' approach is applicable to deferred tax calculated on a full provision basis, and the 'net reversal' approach to deferred tax calculated on a partial provision basis.

6.4.5 There is a third view that, for the purposes of discounting, deferred tax cannot be treated as homogeneous. Under this view (the 'hybrid method') deferred tax arising from timing differences that originate in the tax computation ('tax before book' differences) must be treated differently from deferred tax arising from timing differences that originate in the financial statements ('book before tax' differences). The hybrid method is discussed in Section 6.7.

6.5 *The 'full reversal' approach*

Method

6.5.1 The reversals of all timing differences at the balance sheet date are scheduled on a year-by-year basis. The tax effects of those reversals are calculated and discounted.

Rationale

6.5.2 The rationale of the 'full reversal' approach is the same as that for the full provision method. Every individual timing difference reverses and has an incremental or decre-

The names used are not generally recognised terms, but provide a useful shorthand for the purposes of the present discussion.

mental effect on the tax cash flow in the year of reversal. The amount of tax paid (or the amount of any tax loss available for relief) is higher or lower than it would otherwise have been. It is therefore appropriate to discount timing differences based on their year of reversal.

Some argue that it is wrong to equate the reversal of timing differences with cash flows, since originating timing differences in the year of reversal may result in no deferred tax being paid as a result of the reversal. Whilst this may be the case, however, the full provision method is founded on the premise that future transactions should not be recognised until they occur. **6.5.3**

Practical considerations

The 'full reversal' approach is fairly straightforward to apply in practice. By contrast with the 'net reversal' method discussed in Section 6.6 below, it does not require any assumptions as to management's future intentions. For most companies, the major timing differences are likely to consist of three broad types, which can be treated as set out below: **6.5.4**

(a) those relating to pensions and OPEBs. As noted in paragraph 6.1.3 above, these are already effectively discounted, and no further calculation is necessary;
(b) those relating to short-term timing differences, such as interest accounted for in the current period but taxed in the next. Unless these amounts are material, they can be presented on an undiscounted basis, since the effect of discounting them by one year is unlikely to be significant; and
(c) those relating to capital allowances for plant and machinery. Under the 'full reversal' approach, the book and tax depreciation of assets held at the balance sheet date would be projected into future periods. The timing difference reversing in each future period could then be calculated and discounted at the relevant mandated rate.

If this approach is adopted, the only calculation required by preparers is the scheduling and discounting of reversing timing differences relating to plant and machinery. This is a relatively easy exercise. The necessary scheduling is less than that required in order to comply with SSAP 15. **6.5.5**

One consequence of this treatment is that the items falling under (a), (b) and (c) in paragraph 6.5.4 above will not, other than coincidentally, be discounted at the same rate. Whilst this may not be a pure solution, it is probably the only practical one. The alternative would be to restate the deferred tax relating to pensions and OPEBs on an undiscounted basis, and then to re-discount it at the same rate used for other timing differences (eg those relating to plant and machinery). **6.5.6**

In order to restate the deferred tax relating to pensions and OPEBs in this way, it would be necessary to ascertain the asset or liability relating to pensions and OPEBs on an undiscounted basis. This would involve 'unravelling' the actuarial calculations, the cost of which would almost certainly outweigh the benefit. **6.5.7**

One difficult area is the treatment of unrealised gains on (for example) revaluation of **6.5.8** properties and marking to market of investments. The question of whether deferred tax should be recognised on such gains and, if so, how it should be measured is discussed in Chapter 9.

6.6 *The 'net reversal' approach*

Method

6.6.1 Under the 'net reversal' approach, as under the partial provision method, the deferred tax balance is treated as a homogeneous whole. Estimated net reversals of the balance (ie after taking account of the tax effects of likely future transactions) are scheduled on a year-by-year basis and discounted.

Rationale

6.6.2 The rationale for this approach is the same as that for the partial provision method. In other words, it is virtually certain that future timing differences will originate in the periods in which the timing differences at the balance sheet date reverse (eg as the result of investment in new plant), with the result that the deferred tax balance taken as a whole will not be paid in accordance with the reversal pattern of timing differences in existence at the balance sheet date.

Practical considerations

6.6.3 The mechanics of the 'net reversal' approach are much the same as those of SSAP 15 and it therefore has many of the same problems—in particular complexity and subjectivity. The forecasting required for the 'net reversal' method must typically cover a longer timescale than that of projections currently undertaken for SSAP 15, which tend to look no more than three, or at most five, years ahead.

6.6.4 It might be possible to eliminate, or at least reduce, the subjectivity and difficulty of the 'net reversal' approach by mandating, or at least restricting, the assumptions to be used along the lines set out in paragraph 5.5.3 (investment in plant not to exceed current levels with an allowance for inflation etc).

6.6.5 The reported amount of deferred tax under the method suggested in paragraph 6.6.4 would not be a 'best estimate' of future cash flows in the particular circumstances of the individual reporting entity. Rather, it would represent a broad estimate, based on standardised assumptions, of the economic effects of the entity's present tax position. It is likely that neither preparers nor users would readily accept accounts produced on this basis, and it is not discussed further.

6.6.6 The deferred tax effects of pensions and OPEBs present a particular difficulty in 'net reversal' discounting. Under SSAP 15, as currently amended, no forecasting is required in respect of pensions and OPEBs, since the deferred tax relating to them can be recognised in full. By contrast, 'net reversal' discounting requires forecasting and will often have the effect that no deferred tax asset can be recognised. This is because recovery of the asset (in overall net terms) may, depending on the reporting entity's circumstances, be postponed indefinitely (because each reversing difference will be offset by a new originating difference*) and therefore discount to zero.

Another difficulty is that, as pointed out above, timing differences relating to pensions and OPEBs are discounted, whereas most other timing differences are not. The 'net reversal' method focuses on the interaction of timing differences, which can be meaningfully considered only if all timing differences are first stated on a comparable basis. This would require the deferred tax effects of pensions and OPEBs to be restated on an undiscounted basis, which would in turn involve 'unravelling' the actuarial calculations underlying the liability for pensions and OPEBs. 6.6.7

The 'net reversal' method presents some additional technical problems. For example, does the first £1 of tax paid in a year represent current tax of that year or deferred tax of a previous year? Suppose that a company has an (undiscounted) deferred tax balance of £1 million at 31 December 1994. The projected (legal) tax charge for 1995 is £600,000. Does this represent: 6.6.8

(a) entirely current tax for 1995 (in which case the deferred tax balance would be discounted by at least one year);
(b) entirely deferred tax (in which case £600,000 of the balance would be discounted by one year and the remainder by at least one year); or
(c) some combination?

Since the 'net reversal' method focuses on net cash payments rather than individual timing differences, each of these assumptions is equally valid. Whilst it would be quite easy to mandate the basis to be used, the result is to add a further complication to the process. 6.6.9

The 'hybrid' method 6.7

The 'hybrid' method is based on the view that deferred tax is not homogeneous and that 'tax before book' timing differences must be distinguished from 'book before tax' timing differences. 6.7.1

'Tax before book' differences

'Tax before book' differences arise, as their name implies, when items are recognised in the tax computation before they are recognised in the financial statements. The most common example in the UK is the claiming of capital allowances for plant and machinery in advance of depreciation. 6.7.2

Under the hybrid method, it is argued that any deferred tax recognised in respect of a 'tax before book' difference represents a past tax cash flow that becomes absolute once the tax deduction is obtained. There is no future cash flow. 6.7.3

*See paragraphs 5.3.5 and 5.3.6.

6.7.4 It follows from this view that deferred tax arising from a 'tax before book' difference:

(a) is not a monetary asset or liability, but represents a 'valuation adjustment' to the asset or liability to which it relates. For example, deferred tax arising from accelerated capital allowances represents the partial tax-exhaustion of the assets on which allowances have been claimed; and
(b) cannot be discounted.

'Book before tax' differences

6.7.5 'Book before tax' differences arise, as their name implies, when items are recognised in the financial statements before they are recognised in the tax computation. An example in the UK is interest receivable (generally accrued in the accounts before it is received and taxed).

6.7.6 Under the hybrid method, it is argued that any deferred tax recognised in respect of a 'book before tax' difference represents a future tax cash flow. In the case of interest, tax relating to it will be paid when the interest is received. It follows from this view that deferred tax arising from a 'book before tax' difference is a monetary asset or liability that can be discounted.

6.7.7 To its supporters, the hybrid method provides the only valid basis for discounting deferred tax. However, application of the method poses some real practical difficulties, because of the need to analyse timing differences into 'tax before book' and 'book before tax'. In some cases it is straightforward; for example, interest accrued but not received will always be a 'book before tax' difference. However, the position with regard to other timing differences is not so clear-cut.

6.7.8 For example, credit balances recorded under SSAP 24 will generally be 'book before tax' differences (representing pension costs charged to the accounts but not yet paid). However, debit balances will generally be 'tax before book' differences (representing amounts paid to the scheme, and therefore attracting tax relief, but not yet charged in the accounts). The hybrid method would therefore require deferred tax relating to pensions to be treated differently – possibly in consecutive accounting periods.

6.7.9 The position with fixed assets is also complicated. Under a system of fully accelerated capital allowances, any timing difference relating to depreciation must clearly be a 'tax before book' difference. Under the current UK tax system, however, the cumulative timing differences relating to an asset switch round from 'tax before book' to 'book before tax' over the life of the asset.

6.7.10 A simple example will illustrate this. A company buys an item of plant for £100,000, which qualifies for 25 per cent writing-down allowances and is depreciated over five years. The depreciation and capital allowances relating to that asset will be as follows:

	Depreciation	Tax allowances	Difference	Cumulative difference
	£000	£000	£000	£000
Year 1	20	25	(5)	(5)
Year 2	20	19	1	(4)
Year 3	20	14	6	2
Year 4	20	11	9	11
Year 5	20	8	12	23
Years 6–∞		23	(23)	NIL

A negative number in the 'cumulative difference' column indicates a 'tax before book' difference and a positive number a 'book before tax' difference. It is clearly not a practical proposition to keep separate records for each fixed asset and it would be necessary to compare total book and tax values of fixed assets. In making such a comparison, 'tax before book' and 'book before tax' differences on individual assets become mingled, at which point the conceptual rigour of the hybrid method is contaminated. **6.7.11**

Some also believe that the hybrid method focuses on the wrong tax cash flow in relation to 'tax before book' differences. In their view, whilst a 'tax before book' difference clearly arises from a past cash flow as it originates, it also gives rise to a future cash flow as it reverses. Deferred tax represents that second, future, cash flow. **6.7.12**

A simple example will clarify this. A company that pays tax at 33 per cent buys an item of plant for £100,000, which is depreciated over four years. A 100 per cent first-year allowance is available in respect of the plant. Its tax assessments for the four years that it owns the asset will be (decreased)/increased as a result of owning the plant as follows: **6.7.13**

Depreciation		Capital allowances	Difference	Tax effect
	£000	£000	£000	£000
Year 1	25	100	(75)	(24.75)
Year 2	25		25	8.25
Year 3	25		25	8.25
Year 4	25		25	8.25

At the end of Year 1, deferred tax of £24,750 would be recognised on a full provision basis. Supporters of the hybrid method would argue that this represents the cash inflow (or reduction in outflow) that has already occurred by claiming the capital allowance. To others, however, it represents the effective 'refund' of this benefit that will occur in Years 2–4. **6.7.14**

A final concern is that the greater part of many deferred tax liabilities in the UK is composed of 'tax before book' differences in the form of capital allowances claimed in **6.7.15** advance of depreciation. Under the hybrid method, this deferred tax would not be discounted on the grounds that it is a 'valuation adjustment' rather than a liability. However, as set out in paragraphs 6.2.5 and 6.2.6, those Board members who take the view that deferred tax is a 'valuation adjustment' to other assets and liabilities* believe that it is valid to discount it.

6.8 *The Board's views*

Full provision with 'full reversal' discounting

6.8.1 The 'full reversal' approach has the advantage that the calculations involved are fairly simple. If the methodology proposed in paragraph 6.5.4 is adopted, all that is required in most cases is to schedule, in respect of fixed assets held at the balance sheet date, the difference between their book and tax depreciation in future years, and discount these differences. This scheduling is already required in order to calculate the partial provision required by SSAP 15.

6.8.2 Some may criticise the approach for failing to take account of the impact of likely future transactions on the timing and amount of tax payments. However, it is a key feature of the full provision method that no account should be taken of future transactions until they occur.

6.8.3 The Board believes that 'full reversal' discounting strikes the appropriate balance between conceptual robustness and practical feasibility. In recommending adoption of the full provision approach, therefore, the Board proposes that 'full reversal' discounting should be applied to it.

Partial provision with 'net reversal' discounting

6.8.4 It could be argued that, given the benefit of perfect foresight, the 'net reversal' approach would provide the most accurate net present value of future tax cash flows, since it attempts to reflect the true economic effect of the tax system. However, the Board believes that it would add a complexity to the preparation of a deferred tax computation that many would find unacceptable, if not impossible. The Board believes that to rectify this by mandating the assumptions to be used is inappropriate.

6.8.5 Accordingly, the Board does not propose that the 'net reversal' approach should be adopted in practice.

The hybrid method

6.8.6 The Board does not support adoption of the hybrid method for a number of reasons, not least that its practical effect would be that the great majority of deferred tax liabilities (ie those arising from accelerated capital allowances) would not be discounted at all. The Board is concerned that the analysis of timing differences into 'tax before book' and 'book before tax' required by the method renders it unduly complicated.

**See Chapters 2, 4, 8 and 9.*

The Board also disagrees with the main premise on which the method is based, namely that deferred tax arising from a 'tax before book' timing difference does not give rise to a future cash flow that can be discounted. The Board shares the view, set out in paragraphs 6.7.12–6.7.14, that, although 'tax before book' differences arise from a past cash flow, their reversal gives rise to a subsequent future cash flow that can be treated as a liability and discounted. **6.8.7**

Chapter 7. Disclosures

Issues **7.1**

It has been noted in previous Chapters that no one method of accounting for tax can supply all the information regarding the reporting entity's tax affairs that is required by users of financial statements. Whichever method of accounting is adopted in practice must be reinforced by disclosure. **7.1.1**

This Chapter sets out examples of the principal disclosures that would, in the Board's view, be required under the flow-through method, the full provision method (with discounting) and the partial provision method. Disclosures already required by existing standards are printed in italics. The main disclosures in each case are: **7.1.2**

(a) a reconciliation of the 'expected' tax charge (ie the pre-tax profit multiplied by the UK corporation tax rate) to the actual tax charge reported in the accounts. This is discussed further in paragraphs 7.1.4–7.1.7 below; and
(b) a brief outline of the reporting entity's tax 'profile'.

The pro-forma disclosures are based on an imaginary group consisting of the following companies: **7.1.3**

Company	Incorporated in	Tax rate (%)
HoldCo	UK	33
SubCo 1	UK	33
SubCo 2	X-Land	40 (1994), 45 (1993)
SubCo 3	Y-Land	25

Reconciliation of tax charge

The proposed reconciliation of the tax charge is already a disclosure requirement in some overseas countries. UK companies listed in the USA are already required to prepare such a reconciliation for US reporting purposes. The Board believes that this reconciliation gives more useful information than many existing disclosures, a view strongly supported by users of accounts consulted by the Board in the course of the project. **7.1.4**

Such a reconciliation could broadly be expressed in two ways: **7.1.5**

(a) the expected tax charge (ie the profit before tax multiplied by the UK tax rate) to the actual tax charge; or

(b) the UK statutory tax rate to the actual effective tax rate (ie the tax charge divided by the profit before tax).

7.1.6 The pro-forma disclosures adopt a modification of format (a), under which the profit before tax is first adjusted for permanent differences, the UK tax rate is applied to this adjusted profit and the resulting 'expected' charge is reconciled to the actual charge in the accounts. The basis of this format is that permanent differences (by definition) do not have a tax effect and therefore should be shown gross. However, timing differences and losses do have a tax effect. For example, an accelerated capital allowance has a more significant impact on cash flows in a jurisdiction where the tax rate is 50 per cent than in one where the rate is 20 per cent. It is therefore more appropriate to show the tax effect of such items than their gross amount.

General tax information

7.1.7 It is also proposed that companies should disclose, in the broadest terms, the most important influences on their tax charge (tax rates, availability of losses etc). The Board is sensitive to the need to weigh the needs of users for such information against the commercial confidentiality of preparers. It believes that the brief specimen disclosure given in this Chapter strikes an appropriate balance.

Pages 1184–1190 show pro-forma disclosures that the Board believes should be given for each of the three methods of accounting for tax discussed in Chapters 3–5.

Disclosures required by existing standards are shown in italics.

7.2 Pro-forma disclosures – the flow-through method

RECONCILIATION OF TAX CHARGE

	1994 £000	**1993 £000**
Pre-tax profit per the accounts	31,800	28,600
Permanent differences		
Amortisation of goodwill not deductible for tax purposes	1,200	900
Tax free investment grant in Y-Land	(800)	—
Taxable profit	32,200	29,500
UK corporation tax at 33 per cent	10,626	9,735
Overseas tax rate differences	399	880
	11,025	10,615
Timing differences		
Sale of land accounted for in 1993, but taxed in 1994	495	(495)
Capitalised interest deducted for tax purposes	(300)	—
Accelerated capital allowances	(33)	(16)
Interest taxed on receipts basis	50	(50)
Pension costs charged, but not deducted for tax	20	1
	11,257	10,055
Utilisation of losses brought forward	—	(528)
Irrecoverable ACT written off	*100*	*65*
Tax charge per accounts	11,357	9,592
Comprising		
UK tax (including ACT written off)	*6,407*	*4,917*
Overseas tax	*4,950*	*4,675*
	11,357	*9,592*

DEFERRED TAX INFORMATION

The amount of deferred taxation not provided for was as follows:

1994	1993
£000	**£000**
4,031	4,263

The directors consider that of this amount, only £2.5 million (1993: £2.3 million) will become payable in the foreseeable future.*

GENERAL TAX INFORMATION

The group operates in a number of tax jurisdictions, with tax rates ranging from 25 to 40 per cent and expects a reduction in future effective tax rates following a recent fall in the tax rate in X-Land from 45 to 40 per cent. The group has now utilised all brought forward tax losses, which significantly reduced tax payments in the previous two years. The directors do not foresee any scope for reducing the annual cost of irrecoverable ACT significantly below current levels.

**Alternatively, an estimate of the expected effective tax rate (ie the tax charge as a percentage of pre-tax profit) for the next two years could be given.*

'.3 *Pro-forma disclosures – the full provision method*

RECONCILIATION OF TAX CHARGE

	1994	1993
	£000	**£000**
Pre-tax profit per the accounts	31,800	28,600
Permanent differences		
Amortisation of goodwill not deductible for tax purposes	1,200	900
Tax free investment grant in Y-Land	(800)	—
Taxable profit	32,200	29,500
UK corporation tax at 33 per cent	10,626	9,735
Overseas tax rate differences	399	880
	11,025	10,615
Discount	437	(515)
	11,462	10,100
Utilisation of losses brought forward	—	(528)
Irrecoverable ACT written off	*100*	*65*
Tax charge per accounts	11,562	9,637
Comprising		
UK tax		
Current (including ACT written off)	*6,407*	*4,917*
Deferred	*(95)*	*45*
	6,312	*4,962*
Overseas tax		
Current	*4,950*	*4,675*
Deferred	*300*	*—*
	5,250	*4,675*
Total	*11,562*	*9,637*

DEFERRED TAX INFORMATION

The amount provided for deferred taxation has been reduced as result of discounting as follows:

	1994	1993
	£000	**£000**
Undiscounted deferred tax	4,031	4,263
Discount	(1,281)	(1,718)
Amount provided for	*2,750*	*2,545*

Deferred tax relating to pension costs is discounted at the same rate as that used in calculating those costs. Deferred tax relating to accelerated capital allowances is discounted at the effective rates of applicable government bonds ranging from 6.25 to 8.50 per cent a year. The reduction in the amount discounted is primarily due to an decrease in the discount rates used.

In the opinion of the directors, currently projected capital expenditure is sufficient to ensure that the deferred tax paid within the following five years will not exceed £2.5 million (1994: £2.3 million).

GENERAL TAX INFORMATION

The group operates in a number of tax jurisdictions, with tax rates ranging from 25 to 40 per cent and expects a reduction in future tax payments following a recent fall in the tax rate in X-Land from 45 to 40 per cent. The group has now utilised all brought forward tax losses, which significantly reduced tax payments in the previous two years. The directors do not foresee any scope for reducing the annual cost of irrecoverable ACT significantly below current levels.

.4 *Pro-forma disclosures – the partial provision method*

	1994	1993
	£000	**£000**
Pre-tax profit per the accounts	31,800	28,600
Permanent differences		
Amortisation of goodwill not deductible for tax purposes	1,200	900
Tax free investment grant in Y-Land	(800)	—
Taxable profit	32,200	29,500
UK corporation tax at 33 per cent	10,626	9,735
Overseas tax rate differences	399	880
	11,025	10,615
Decrease/(increase) in deferred tax not provided for	*387*	*(215)*
	11,412	10,400
Utilisation of losses brought forward	—	(528)
Irrecoverable ACT written off	*100*	*65*
Tax charge per accounts	11,512	9,937
Comprising		
UK tax		
Current (including ACT written off)	*6,407*	*4,917*
Deferred	*(145)*	*345*
	6,262	*5,262*
Overseas tax		
Current	*4,950*	*4,675*
Deferred	*300*	—
	5,250	*4,675*
Total	*11,512*	*9,937*

DEFERRED TAX INFORMATION

The amount provided for deferred taxation has been reduced as result of application of the partial provision method as follows:

	1994	1993
	£000	**£000**
Total deferred tax	4,031	4,263
Amount not provided for	*(1,531)*	*(1,918)*
Amount provided for	*2,500*	*2,345*

The directors expect that the amount provided for will be paid within the next five years. The amount not provided for relates principally to accelerated capital allowances, and has reduced this year due to the group's decision, discussed in the Operating and Financial Review, to reduce capital expenditure in the medium term. However, in the opinion of the directors, projected capital expenditure is still sufficient to ensure that the effective rate of tax will not be greater than current levels for the foreseeable future.

GENERAL TAX INFORMATION

The group operates in a number of tax jurisdictions, with tax rates ranging from 25 to 40 per cent and expects a reduction in future effective tax rates following a recent fall in the tax rate in X-Land from 45 to 40 per cent. The group has now utilised all brought forward tax losses, which significantly reduced tax payments in the previous two years. The directors do not foresee any scope for reducing the annual cost of irrecoverable ACT significantly below current levels.

Chapter 8. Acquisition accounting

Issues **8.1**

The acquisition of a subsidiary undertaking does not normally give rise to any direct tax consequences, and therefore no legal liability to tax arises in either of the combining entities as a result of the acquisition. **8.1.1**

Where tax is accounted for under the flow-through method, the current tax of the acquired entity would be recognised as an additional liability of the combined group. Where tax is accounted for under the full provision method, any current or deferred tax of the acquired entity also becomes an asset or liability of the new group. **8.1.2**

Where deferred tax is accounted for under the partial provision method, any current tax of the acquired entity becomes a liability of the combined group. In calculating the deferred tax liability, the tax affairs of the combining entities are re-appraised, taking into account the plans of the new group. This may mean that deferred tax of either the acquirer or the acquiree that was not recognised before the acquisition may become recognised (and vice versa) after the acquisition.* **8.1.3**

The issue considered in this Chapter is whether fair value adjustments themselves give rise to deferred tax, if the full provision method is adopted, as proposed in Chapter 4. The current position is that, as explained in paragraph 8.1.5, fair value adjustments are not timing differences, as defined in SSAP 15, but permanent differences. Accordingly deferred tax should not be set up in respect of fair value adjustments, although it is common—but by no means universal—practice in the UK to do so. **8.1.4**

Fair value adjustments are permanent differences as currently defined in SSAP 15 because they have the effect that gains and losses that are charged or deducted in post-acquisition tax computations are never recognised as gains or losses in the financial statements of the combined entity. **8.1.5**

For example, suppose that a company acquires a subsidiary with stock carried at £550,000 to which a fair value of £600,000 is assigned. When the stock is sold, the accounting profit will be based on a cost of £600,000, but the taxable profit on a cost of £550,000 (ie the cost to the acquired entity). The £50,000 difference is therefore a permanent difference. **8.1.6**

It would probably be common ground that, in the example above, the stock is worth less to the acquirer than otherwise identical stock (by reference to which the acquired stock may well have been valued) whose cost is fully tax-deductible. However, views as **8.1.7**

**As explained in paragraph 5.3.13, this is inconsistent with the overall principle of FRS 7 'Fair Values in Acquisition Accounting' and recognised as such in that FRS.*

to how this is best reflected will vary, depending on whether deferred tax is considered as an increment or decrement of future tax liabilities or as a 'valuation adjustment' to other assets and liabilities (see Section 4.4 of Chapter 4).

8.1.8 Those who take the view that deferred tax represents an increment or decrement of a future tax liability believe that no deferred tax arises in this case, since acquisition of the stock does not affect any future tax liability. This is explained in Section 8.3. Those who take the view that deferred tax is a 'valuation adjustment' believe that the effect of acquiring stock that is not fully tax-deductible should be recognised by providing for deferred tax. This is explained in Section 8.4.

8.2 *Practical effect of the two approaches*

8.2.1 The practical effect of the two approaches is that a different tax charge and effective tax rate is shown in the post-acquisition profit and loss account. When the stock is sold, the acquired subsidiary will be assessed to tax of £148,500, calculated as follows:

	£000
Sales proceeds (say)	1,000.0
Cost as recorded in books of subsidiary	550.0
Profit	450.0
Tax at 33 per cent	148.5

8.2.2 The consolidated profit and loss account will show the following:

	No deferred tax (Case A) £000	Deferred tax (Case B) £000
Sales	1,000.0	1,000.0
Cost of sales	600.0	600.0
Profit	400.0	400.0
Current tax (as above)	148.5	148.5
Deferred tax*	—	(16.5)
Tax	148.5	132.0
Profit after tax	251.5	268.0
Effective tax rate (%)	37.1	33.0

***£(600,000–550,000) @ 33%.*

The effect of providing for deferred tax is that the post-acquisition effective tax rate is the statutory rate.* 8.2.3

Arguments against providing for deferred tax 8.3

Those who believe that deferred tax should not be provided for on fair value adjustments do so because such adjustments are made as a consolidation entry only. They are not taxable or tax-deductible transactions in any taxable entity, and therefore do not give rise to an increase or reduction in the reporting entity's tax burden (Case A above). 8.3.1

Those who take this view believe that the objective of deferred tax accounting, like all accrual-based accounting, is to allocate tax paid between periods. In Case B above, however, providing for deferred tax will have the effect that £16,500 of tax paid by the reporting entity in respect of a transaction undertaken by it in the post-acquisition period never appears in a profit and loss account. It is argued that to provide for deferred tax in this case is not an allocation of expense, but a smoothing device. 8.3.2

A further argument might be that the difference between the value of the stocks and that of equivalent stocks bought separately is goodwill, since it represents a difference between acquiring a business as a whole and acquiring the separable net assets of that business individually. 8.3.3

Arguments in favour of providing for deferred tax 8.4

Those who believe that deferred tax should be recognised do so for the reason just mentioned, ie that if the stock had been bought directly for £600,000 its cost would have been fully tax-deductible. It must therefore actually be worth less to the acquirer than £600,000 and this should be reflected by recognising deferred tax as a 'valuation adjustment' to the carrying value of the stock. 8.4.1

Another argument is that acquisition accounting is a construct, and to provide for deferred tax is more consistent with that construct. What actually happens in an acquisition is that the acquirer buys the shares of the acquiree. However, it is agreed to be more useful to portray this transaction in the consolidated accounts as if the acquirer had bought the net assets of the acquiree, in order to reflect the financial position of the group as a whole and to establish a benchmark from which to measure future earnings. 8.4.2

The result of doing so in the example above is to exclude from the post-acquisition earnings of the group income of £50,000 that results from a transaction in the post-acquisition period. It therefore seems necessary, for the sake of consistency, to exclude the tax on that £50,000 from the post-acquisition earnings as well. Put another way, if the acquiree had in fact made this £50,000 profit in the pre-acquisition period (as 8.4.3

**This would not always be the case if the deferred tax were discounted, because of the effect of interest on the discounted amount.*

represented in the consolidated accounts), it would have incurred a tax liability of £16,500, which would have been assumed by the acquirer at the time of the acquisition.

8.4.4 Another argument in favour of providing for deferred tax is the fact that, since an acquisition gives rise to no tax effect, the effective tax rate reported in the profit and loss account should not be distorted as a result of the acquisition. Providing for deferred tax on the fair value adjustments ensures that such distortion does not occur.

8.4.5 If adopted consistently, the 'valuation adjustment' approach to deferred tax would apply to all assets and liabilities. For example, the argument in 8.4.1 above would apply equally well to freehold land acquired in the same acquisition. To the extent that fair value adjustments are made to it, it cannot be worth as much as land bought separately, whose full cost would be deductible in calculating the chargeable gain on disposal. Accordingly, the fair value of the land, just like that of the stocks, should be subject to a 'valuation adjustment' and deferred tax should be provided for.

8.4.6 The effect of such a treatment would be greatly to increase the amount of deferred tax provided for by most UK companies. However, it could be argued that, in the case of a non-depreciable asset where there is no likelihood of disposal, such 'valuation adjustments' are unnecessary. The difference between the tax position of the acquired asset and that of an equivalent asset bought separately will manifest itself only in circumstances so remote that no useful information is given by recognising the deferred tax. This is discussed further in Section 9.2 in the context of revaluations.

8.5 *The Board's views*

8.5.1 The Board takes the view that the current variation in practice in this area is unsatisfactory and is not based on well-defined principles. Accordingly, any new FRS on tax developed following this review will specifically address acquisition accounting and prescribe a single treatment.

8.5.2 At present there are two views among Board members as to the appropriate treatment, which correspond to the differing views, set out in Section 4.4, as to the nature of deferred tax under the Board's draft Statement of Principles.

8.5.3 Those Board members who regard deferred tax as an increment or decrement of future tax liabilities resulting from past timing differences believe that deferred tax should not be provided for on fair value adjustments, because they are permanent, not timing, differences and the future tax liabilities of the combining entities are not altered as a result of them.

8.5.4 Those Board members who regard deferred tax as a 'valuation adjustment' to other assets and liabilities believe that deferred tax should be provided for on fair value adjustments, because an asset acquired as part of an acquisition whose fair value is not fully tax-deductible must be worth less than one acquired separately whose cost would be fully tax-deductible. For the reasons set out in paragraph 8.4.6, they believe that deferred tax should be provided for on fair value adjustments only where these relate to assets and liabilities that are expected to be realised (whether by disposal or depreciation) or settled, rather than retained in the business for the longer term.

Chapter 9. Revaluations

Issues **9.1**

In the UK,* the revaluation of an asset does not give rise to a tax liability.† If, however, a revalued asset is subsequently sold at its revalued amount, a tax liability may arise. The precise nature of the liability arising on disposal of an asset will vary according to the tax status of the asset concerned. **9.1.1**

Where any asset is disposed of at an amount greater than its original cost a chargeable gain may arise. Where the asset disposed of was eligible for capital allowances, a further tax liability may arise by way of a balancing charge, designed to claw back any capital allowances previously claimed in respect of the asset. **9.1.2**

The chargeable gain is computed as the difference between the sale proceeds and the original cost uplifted by an amount ('indexation allowance') intended to exempt purely inflationary gains from taxation. It may be possible to defer immediate payment of the tax on the chargeable gain by taking advantage of 'rollover relief'. **9.1.3**

Rollover relief provides that where the chargeable gain arising on a qualifying asset‡ is reinvested in another qualifying asset, the payment of tax on the gain is deferred (rolled over) until the second asset is disposed of. Rollover relief is again available on the gain on disposal of the second asset, with the result that payment of tax on some chargeable gains can in effect be postponed in perpetuity.§ **9.1.4**

It will be apparent from the summary in paragraphs 9.1.1–9.1.3 above that it is extremely unlikely that the accounting gain recorded on the revaluation of an asset will correspond to the gain that would be assessed for tax if the asset were disposed of at its revalued amount. **9.1.5**

If the flow-through method of accounting for tax were adopted, no tax liability would be recorded on a revaluation, since a revaluation is not a taxable event. However, if the full or partial provision method of accounting for tax is adopted, the question arises whether deferred tax should be provided for at the date of revaluation or at some later date. **9.1.6**

**The discussion in this Chapter concentrates on the UK tax system and is of necessity greatly simplified, but the general principles apply under any tax system where revaluation itself is not a taxable event.*

† Except in the financial sector, where investment gains and losses are commonly taken to the profit and loss account (and taxed) on a 'mark to market' basis.

‡ All the types of asset commonly revalued in the UK are eligible for rollover relief.

§ In the case of gains relating to wasting assets, any amount rolled over becomes payable after 10 years or, if earlier, on disposal of the second asset or its ceasing to be used in the trade.

9.1.7 The current position under SSAP 15 is, in effect, that deferred tax is provided for on a revalued asset only when:

(a) disposal of the asset is likely (whether this is judged to be the case at the time of revaluation or later); and

(b) disposal will result in a taxable gain, after taking account of any expected rollover relief.*

9.1.8 This Chapter explores whether deferred tax should be provided for in respect of a revaluation of an asset at the time of revaluation or at some later date, assuming that the full provision method is adopted, as proposed in Chapter 4. This is discussed in Section 9.2.

9.1.9 A further issue is an apparent legal difficulty in recording deferred tax balances arising on revaluations due to the legal restriction on use of the revaluation reserve. This is discussed in Section 9.4.

9.2 ***Revaluation in absence of a commitment to disposal***

9.2.1 In Section 4.4 of Chapter 4 it was noted that there are two views on the nature of deferred tax. Some regard deferred tax as an increment or decrement of future tax liabilities, and would therefore broadly take the view that deferred tax should be provided for on a revaluation gain only where there is a commitment to dispose of the revalued asset (as explained in paragraphs 9.2.2 and 9.2.3). Others regard deferred tax as a 'valuation adjustment' to other assets and liabilities, and would broadly take the view that deferred tax should be provided for at the time of revaluation (as explained in paragraphs 9.2.5–9.2.16).

Change in liability approach – no deferred tax

9.2.2 Those who regard deferred tax as an increment or decrement of a future tax liability believe that deferred tax should not be provided for on a revaluation gain, unless there is a commitment to dispose of the revalued asset. In the absence of such a commitment, the revaluation gain is a permanent difference, since it will never enter into the determination of taxable profit. Put another way, no additional future tax payments will occur as a result of a revaluation (unless there is a commitment to dispose of the revalued asset) and accordingly no additional deferred tax liability should be recognised.

9.2.3 The advantage of this approach is that it is straightforward and recognises a liability to tax only when the company is committed to a taxable transaction involving the revalued asset. The disadvantage of this approach is that it may have the effect that a tax charge is recognised in neither the year of revaluation nor the year of sale (eg if a commitment to dispose of an asset arises in one period, but disposal does not actually occur until the next).

***SSAP 15, paragraphs 20, 25 and 27.*

This treatment could represent a slight change from current practice, in that the broad effect of SSAP 15, as noted in paragraph 9.1.7 above, is that deferred tax is provided for on revaluation gains that are likely to crystallise. This may mean that in some circumstances deferred tax is currently provided for on the basis of something less than a commitment to disposal. **9.2.4**

'Valuation adjustment' approach – provide for deferred tax

Those who regard deferred tax as a 'valuation adjustment' to other assets and liabilities believe that, whilst a revaluation does not give rise to a direct tax liability, the carrying amount of the revalued asset must be adjusted in order to reflect its tax status compared with that of an equivalent asset. Typically, the revalued asset will be valued by reference to market values for equivalent assets that reflect the amounts at which such assets are traded if purchased separately. **9.2.5**

If an equivalent asset were bought separately its cost would be tax-deductible. However, the carrying amount of the revalued asset will not be fully tax-deductible. Those who regard deferred tax as a 'valuation adjustment' therefore believe that deferred tax should be provided for on the revaluation gain to reflect this difference. **9.2.6**

A further consideration with respect to depreciable assets is that, although the primary purpose of a revaluation is to enable a more up-to-date valuation to be shown in the balance sheet, a consequence is that a more up-to-date depreciation cost is charged in the profit and loss account. Where the asset concerned is of a type eligible for capital allowances, supporters of the 'valuation adjustment' approach would argue that it is necessary to provide for deferred tax in order to reflect the true after-tax cost of the revalued asset. **9.2.7**

A simple example will illustrate the point. A company has a building, eligible for capital allowances, that originally cost £1 million and has an expected remaining useful life of 20 years. Its current book value (and tax written-down value) is £0.8 million and its current market value £1.2 million. The company revalues the building to £1.2 million. **9.2.8**

Henceforth, the annual depreciation charge will be £60,000—ie the amount that would have been charged if the company had actually bought a new equivalent building for £1.2 million. If the company had bought a new building, its cost would have been fully tax-deductible. It could be argued that if the accounts reflect the full depreciation charge for an equivalent asset, they should, for consistency, show the tax relief that such an asset would attract. **9.2.9**

Mechanically, this would be achieved by setting up deferred tax on the revaluation of the asset and releasing this provision as the asset is depreciated. The effect of doing so is that the effective tax charge shown in the profit and loss account as the asset is depreciated is the same as the statutory tax rate, as shown in the example below.* Not recognising deferred tax results in a distortion of the post-revaluation effective tax rate. **9.2.10**

******This would not be the case if deferred tax were discounted, because of the effect of interest on the discounted amount.*

	No deferred tax Case A £000	Deferred tax Case B £000
Profit before depreciation (say)	1,000.0	1,000.0
Depreciation	60.0	60.0
Profit before tax	940.0	940.0
Current tax*	316.8	316.8
Deferred tax†	—	(6.6)
Tax	316.8	310.2
Profit after tax	623.2	629.8
Effective tax rate (%)	33.7	33.0

9.2.11 Those who believe that deferred tax should not be provided for take the view that this is simply a smoothing device and not an allocation of real tax charges. As a result of applying the accounting treatment in Case B above, the amount of tax reported in the profit and loss accounts over the remaining life of the asset will be less than the tax actually paid in that period.‡

9.2.12 The counter-argument to this criticism is that it wrongly focuses on the profit and loss account only. The amount of tax charged to comprehensive income (ie including amounts charged in the statement of total recognised gains and losses) will be the same as that paid. When the liability for deferred tax is set up, the cost is charged to the statement of total recognised gains and losses. As the liability reduces, the credit is taken to the tax charge in the profit and loss account.

9.2.13 The practical effect of this approach is that it would require deferred tax to be provided for in full in respect of all revaluations, irrespective of whether disposal is likely to occur. This would represent a major change to current UK practice.

9.2.14 However, some who broadly support the 'valuation adjustment' approach in principle believe that it is relevant to make such an adjustment only where the revalued asset is both:

****Assuming that historical cost depreciation and industrial buildings allowances are the same and there are no other timing differences, £(1m–0.8m)/20 = £0.96m @ 33% = £316,800.***

†£(1.2m–0.8m)/20 = £20,000 @ 33% = £6,600.

‡Because deferred tax on the original revluation would be charged to the statement of total recognised gains and losses (see Chapter 11).

(a) of a type that is deductible for tax purposes; and
(b) expected to deliver its value through sale or consumption in the business.

In such a case, the difference in value arising from the difference between the tax status of the revalued asset and that of an equivalent separately purchased asset, used as the basis of revaluation, will manifest itself immediately the revalued asset is sold or depreciated.

If, however, the revalued asset is of a type that is never deductible for tax purposes, either on amortisation or ultimate disposal, there is clearly no difference between the tax status of the revalued asset and any equivalent asset used as the basis of revaluation. There is therefore no need to make a 'valuation adjustment'. **9.2.15**

If the revalued asset is expected to give value without being consumed (eg land), the only circumstance in which any difference between its tax status and that of an equivalent asset used as the basis of revaluation will appear is if the revalued asset is sold. Some would argue that the normal expectation is that an asset such as land will be retained in the business rather than sold. It would therefore be inconsistent to recognise a 'valuation adjustment' predicated on an expectation of sale, until such an expectation actually arose. **9.2.16**

The practical effect of this modification of the 'valuation adjustment' approach is that it would require deferred tax to be provided for in full in respect of revaluations of assets that: **9.2.17**

(a) were expected to be sold (in which case the amount provided for would be the estimated chargeable gain and/or balancing charge arising on disposal); or
(b) were expected to be consumed in the business (in which case the amount provided for would be the tax effect of the difference between (i) the amount of the revalued asset deductible for tax purposes and (ii) the amount that would be deductible in respect of an equivalent asset purchased separately for the carrying amount of the revalued asset).

The treatment of items falling under (a) broadly conforms to current UK practice, but that of items falling under (b) would represent a change from current practice.

Rollover relief **9.3**

This Section discusses the extent, if any, to which measurement of a deferred tax liability should take account of the rollover relief provisions as set out in paragraph 9.1.4. **9.3.1**

Rollover relief is relevant: **9.3.2**

(a) in calculating the liability to tax on an asset that the reporting entity is committed to dispose of or in assessing the latent gain in a replacement asset bought with the proceeds of an asset, the gain on the disposal of which was eligible for rollover relief (see paragraph 9.1.4); and
(b) in disclosing the liability to tax on disposal of an asset at its revalued amount.

9.3.3 One view would be that rollover relief must be presumed to be available on any disposal, on the basis that the asset disposed of would have to be replaced in order for the business to remain a going concern in substantially its current form. Supporters of this view would also argue that companies tend to manage major asset disposals very carefully in order to take the maximum advantage of any tax reliefs. It would be wholly exceptional for a company to pass up the opportunity to take advantage of a tax benefit as significant as rollover relief.

9.3.4 The alternative view is that it is inappropriate to take account of the impact of rollover relief until the relief is actually claimed. A decision to take advantage of the relief is a future event, whose effect should be reflected in the period in which the relief is claimed and not be anticipated in the current financial statements.

9.3.5 Another more general objection to the assumption that rollover relief would be taken is that in most businesses the fixed asset profile, and indeed the general focus of operations, shifts over time—especially over the sort of timescale under consideration here. Moreover, a presumption of reinvestment clearly holds less true the more assets qualifying for rollover relief a business owns. A business with a large portfolio of qualifying assets may very well take occasional opportunities to realise particular assets without the need for reinvestment in an equivalent.

9.4 ***Legal considerations***

9.4.1 This Section deals solely with the statutory presentation of any deferred tax expense arising on revaluation. The presentation of the expense under FRS 3 'Reporting Financial Performance' is discussed in Chapter 11.

9.4.2 In statutory terms, revaluation gains are credited to the revaluation reserve. Intuitively, therefore, it would seem appropriate that, for the sake of consistency, any deferred tax provided for on revaluation gains should also be charged to the revaluation reserve.

9.4.3 However, this is currently prohibited by paragraph 34 of Schedule 4* to the Companies Act 1985, which states that the revaluation reserve shall not be reduced except in ways specifically permitted by that paragraph, which do not include a charge for deferred tax. It is not possible to circumvent this difficulty by arguing that deferred tax is not being charged to the revaluation reserve, but rather that the revaluation reserve is being credited only with a net-of-tax revaluation, because this would fall foul of the Alternative Accounting Rules in the Act.

9.4.4 However, although the Act prohibits deferred tax from being charged to the revaluation reserve, there is no such prohibition in the EC Fourth Company Law Directive, from which the relevant provisions of the Act are derived. The Department of Trade and Industry has indicated to the Board that it will consider making an appropriate change to the Act.

**There are equivalent provisions in Schedules 9 and 9A and ion Northern Ireland legislation.*

The Board's views 9.5

At present there are two views among Board members as to whether deferred tax should be provided for on revaluations, which correspond to the differing views, set out in Section 4.4, as to the nature of deferred tax under the Board's draft Statement of Principles. 9.5.1

Those Board members who regard deferred tax as an increment or decrement of future tax liabilities resulting from past timing differences believe, for the reasons set out in paragraphs 9.2.2–9.2.4, that deferred tax should be provided for on revaluations of assets only where there is a commitment to disposal. 9.5.2

However, they take the view that the notes to the accounts should disclose as a contingent liability the amount of tax that would be payable if the revalued assets were sold at their revalued amount. In order to avoid the potentially complex calculations that this could involve (eg establishing a 31 March 1982 value for the asset), the disclosure could be made on an approximate basis (ie the gross gain multiplied by the tax rate), together with an indication of the basis used. 9.5.3

Those Board members who regard deferred tax as a 'valuation adjustment' to other assets and liabilities believe that deferred tax should be provided for on revaluation of assets of a type normally deductible for tax purposes, because a revalued asset whose carrying amount is not fully tax-deductible must be worth less than one acquired separately whose cost would be fully tax-deductible. 9.5.4

However, they believe that, for the reasons set out in paragraphs 9.2.14–9.2.16, deferred tax should be provided for only on revaluation of an asset that is deductible for tax purposes. For non-tax depreciable assets where only capital gains tax would be relevant, the absence of a tax base has a less direct effect on valuation when combined with indexation. In these circumstances, deferred tax would be provided for only once there is a commitment to sell. Any deferred tax not provided for would be disclosed. 9.5.5

On the issue of rollover relief, the Board takes the view that the relief is a future event that merely postpones rather than extinguishes any tax liability. Accordingly, if the full provision method were applied on an undiscounted basis, tax deferred as a result of rollover relief should be recognised (or, where appropriate, disclosed) in full. 9.5.6

Chapter 10. Tax losses and surplus act carry-forwards

Issues 10.1

Tax legislation in the UK provides for the relief of tax losses and surplus advance corporation tax (ACT)* (ie ACT that cannot be relieved against the mainstream 10.1.1

***The treatment of ACT in accounts is discussed in more detail in Chapter 12.*

corporation tax liability of the period in which it is paid). Losses and ACT may be relieved first against the tax liability of previous periods,* with any amounts not so relieved being carried forward for relief against the tax liability of future periods, without time limit (but subject to various restrictions that are beyond the scope of this Chapter).

10.1.2 Where a reporting entity has tax losses or surplus ACT that can be relieved against a tax liability for a previous year, it is clearly appropriate to recognise those losses or surplus ACT as an asset.† Where a deferred tax liability is recognised that represents an increment of a future tax liability against which the losses or surplus ACT may be relieved, it is appropriate to recognise the losses or surplus ACT as an asset, either shown separately or offset against the deferred tax balance.

10.1.3 It is, however, less clear whether it is appropriate to recognise as an asset tax losses or surplus ACT that can be relieved only by carry-forward against future tax liabilities. This raises two issues:

- whether tax loss and surplus ACT carry-forwards are assets (see Section 10.2)
- if so, whether they can be recognised in the financial statements (see Section 10.3).

10.1.4 A further issue concerns the manner in which ACT, if recognised, should be presented in financial statements (see Section 10.4).

10.2 *Are tax loss and surplus ACT carry-forwards assets?*

10.2.1 The central issue, in terms of the Board's draft Statement of Principles, is whether there has been a past event giving rise to an asset. Some would argue that the fact that a company has incurred a tax loss‡ eligible for carry-forward (ie a past event) is sufficient evidence of the existence of an asset. Those who take this view would argue that a company that has incurred a tax loss eligible for carry-forward must be better off than one that has not, but is in other respects identical. This suggests that the tax loss is an asset immediately it is incurred.

10.2.2 Others would argue that, until the profits necessary to recover the loss have been earned (ie a future event), there is no asset, or at best a contingent asset. It might be thought that this point of view is consistent only with the flow-through method of accounting for tax, since both the full provision and partial provision methods assume a future event— ie that the reporting entity will at least break even before tax, thus crystallising the deferred tax liability.

10.2.3 However, some supporters of the full provision method would argue that the future profits needed in order for deferred tax to crystallise are already implicit in the carrying

**The detailed rules for carry-back of losses and ACT are not relevant for the purposes of this Chapter.*

†If the flow-through method of accounting were adopted, such losses and ACT could be recognised as assets only in these circumstances.

‡References to tax losses incurred should be read as including surplus ACT paid.

amounts of assets and liabilities at the balance sheet. By contrast, the additional future profits to absorb tax losses are not implicit in assets and liabilities at the balance sheet date. On this basis, no recognition can be given to tax losses that can be relieved only against future tax not represented by deferred tax at the balance sheet date.*

Recognition of tax loss and surplus ACT carry-forwards 10.3

The argument in favour of recognising a tax loss or surplus ACT carry-forward as an asset in the financial statements as soon as the loss is incurred or ACT paid is that this most closely matches the tax benefit with the event giving rise to it. 10.3.1

The argument against such recognition is that the very event that gives rise to the asset may in many cases cast doubt on its recoverability. For example, if a company incurs a tax loss, it may well have also incurred a trading loss.† This may indicate a decline in the fortunes of the business that calls into question its ability to generate sufficient future taxable profits to enable the loss to be relieved. Again, if the group structure and dividend policy of the reporting entity are such that surplus ACT regularly arises, an opportunity for its recovery is unlikely to occur. 10.3.2

The fact that, in the UK (unlike some overseas tax jurisdictions), tax losses and surplus ACT may be carried forward indefinitely must enhance the prospects of their recovery in the longer term. Against this, however, it could be argued that the tax legislation could change so as to restrict the company's ability to relieve the tax loss. 10.3.3

Presentation of ACT carry-forwards in financial statements 10.4

A recent survey of UK accounting practice‡ has noted the following treatments of ACT among UK companies: 10.4.1

(a) all ACT recoverable is shown separately as an asset;
(b) ACT is set off against that portion of the deferred tax balance that relates to UK corporation tax, to the extent that it could be offset if the deferred tax were a mainstream corporation tax liability (currently 20/33 of the deferred tax balance—see paragraph 12.4.2). Any remaining balance is shown separately as an asset, or in some cases written off as a matter of accounting policy; and
(c) all ACT is set off against the deferred tax liability.

Each of these approaches has a valid conceptual basis.

Those who adopt treatment (a) presumably believe that recoverable ACT and deferred 10.4.2

**The US FASB's first standard on tax (FAS 96) prohibited recognition of loss carry-forwards falling into this category. This was one of the most contentious features of that standard. The current standard (FAS 109) requires tax loss assets to be recognised in the first instance, but then provided against if they are not 'more likely than not' to be recovered.*

† This is not always the case. For example, a 'front-loaded' capital allowance system may generate tax losses even when the underlying trading performance is sound.

‡ 'UK GAAP', fourth edition, Ernst & Young.

tax should not be offset, on the basis that ACT is recoverable only against a future mainstream corporation tax liability and no such liability exists at the balance sheet date.

10.4.3 Those who adopt treatment (b) take the view that, since the deferred tax liability at the balance sheet date is expected to form part of a future mainstream corporation tax liability, ACT can validly be offset against it, subject to the rules regarding the offset of ACT against mainstream corporation tax. Those companies that write off any additional ACT as a matter of policy would also argue that, since the ACT is recognised as an asset solely because of the existence of the deferred tax balance, offset is valid.

10.4.4 Those who adopt treatment (c) presumably take the view that since deferred tax represents an addition to, and recoverable ACT a reduction in, future tax liabilities they may as well be presented as a single figure.

10.5 *The Board's views*

Recognition of tax losses and ACT

10.5.1 The Board takes the view that, for the reasons set out in paragraph 10.2.1, incurring a tax loss or paying surplus ACT gives rise to an asset, and the issue is not whether there is an asset at that stage, but whether it is appropriate to recognise it in the financial statements.

10.5.2 The Board believes, for the reasons set out in paragraph 10.3.2, that it is appropriate to recognise a tax loss or surplus ACT as an asset only where there is strong positive evidence as to its recoverability. Such evidence could take the form of deferred tax at the balance sheet date against which the losses or ACT will be recoverable. Otherwise, it would be necessary to be virtually certain that sufficient future trading profits will be generated. This is essentially the approach currently required by SSAPs 8 and 15.

10.5.3 However, the detailed criteria for recognition of such assets are contained only in the (strictly non-mandatory) appendices to those standards. The Board proposes that in any new FRS on accounting for tax these criteria should be moved to the main body of the standard.

Presentation of recoverable ACT in financial statements

10.5.4 The Board believes that the present variation in practice in this area is unsatisfactory and that it would be preferable if a consistent approach were adopted. The Board is currently inclined to favour treatment (b) as set out in paragraph 10.4.1 above (ie to set off ACT against deferred tax up to the maximum limit for offset of ACT against mainstream corporation tax, and to show any balance as an asset, provided that it meets the recoverability tests).

Chapter 11. Reporting the tax charge in financial statements

Issues 11.1

In October 1992 the Board issued FRS 3 'Reporting Financial Performance'. FRS 3 introduced a new requirement for reporting entities to present a statement of total recognised gains and losses. A key feature of the statement is that once an item has been recognised in it, that item should not subsequently be recognised in the profit and loss account.* 11.1.1

Since the issue of FRS 3 a number of commentators have requested guidance as to how, or indeed whether, tax should be allocated between the profit and loss account and the statement of total recognised gains and losses. The proposals in this Chapter are a response to this request for guidance, and would, subject to comments received, be incorporated in a new standard. 11.1.2

The most common cases where the need for guidance has been identified are: 11.1.3

(a) where a taxable exchange gain or loss is not included in the profit and loss account;
(b) where a gain (or loss) included in the profit and loss account is offset for tax purposes by a loss (or gain) included in the statement of total recognised gains and losses; and
(c) where a previously revalued asset is sold, crystallising a tax liability based on the total gain over historical cost (less any indexation allowance).

The Board's views on how these cases should be treated are set out below. In all cases, the principle is that as far as possible the tax charge or credit should be recorded in the same statement as the gain or loss to which it relates. 11.1.4

Exchange gains and losses 11.2

SSAP 20 'Foreign currency translation' permits exchange gains or losses on a loan that qualifies as a hedge under the standard to be taken direct to reserves. Under FRS 3, such exchange movements are thus included in the statement of total recognised gains and losses. However, those exchange movements may be subject to tax, for example where they arise on a loan held by a parent undertaking that, on consolidation, is treated as hedging the net assets of its foreign investments. 11.2.1

The Board believes that the tax effects of exchange gains and losses dealt with in the statement of total recognised gains and losses should also be dealt with in that statement. 11.2.2

Offsetting gains and losses in different primary statements 11.3

It may happen that a gain (or loss) included in the profit and loss account is offset for tax purposes by a loss (or gain) included in the statement of total recognised gains and losses. For example, suppose that the translated profit and loss account of OverseaCo, an intermediate holding company in a UK group, shows the following: 11.3.1

FRS 3, paragraph 56.

	£000
Trading profit	2,000
Exchange loss on loan	(500)
Profit before tax	1,500
Tax at 40 per cent	600
Profit after tax	900

11.3.2 On consolidation, the loan is treated as a hedge against the net assets of OverseaCo's subsidiary undertakings, so that the exchange loss on it is taken to the statement of total recognised gains and losses. This begs the question of how the subsidiary's total tax charge of £600,000 should be treated. If it is simply taken to the profit and loss account, the effective tax rate shown will be only 30 per cent.* It could be argued that this is misleading, given that the real tax rate is 40 per cent.

11.3.3 One method of dealing with this discrepancy would be to highlight it in the reconciliation of the tax charge proposed in Chapter 7 above. An alternative approach would be to allocate the total tax charge of £600,000 as follows:

	£000
Tax on trading profit (£2m @ 40%)	800
Tax relief on exchange loss (£0.5m @ 40%)	(200)
Total tax charge	600

The profit and loss account would bear a tax charge of £800,000, with £200,000 tax relief being credited to the statement of total recognised gains and losses.

11.3.4 Where the full provision method of accounting for tax is adopted, as is proposed by the Board, the focus is on the tax effects of individual transactions. Accordingly, the Board believes that the treatment set out in paragraph 11.3.3 should be adopted.

11.4 *Tax on gains on disposal of revalued assets*

11.4.1 As noted in Chapter 9, gains arising on revaluation of an asset are taxed only when crystallised by disposal of the asset. When a revalued asset is disposed of, the question

**£600,000/£2,000,000.*

therefore arises as to how the tax charge arising should be allocated between the profit and loss account and the statement of total recognised gains and losses.

A further complication is that deferred tax on the revaluation gain may have been provided for before the date of disposal for some assets but not for others, depending on the circumstances.* 11.4.2

To take the simplest situation, suppose that in 1995 a company sells for £4.5 million a plot of land that cost £2 million in 1980, is carried in the books at £4 million (following a revaluation in 1992), and has a tax value (including indexation allowance) of £3 million. No deferred tax was provided for on the earlier revaluation on the grounds that there was no commitment to sell the land at that time. Assuming that rollover relief is not available, the tax arising on the disposal will be £495,000.† 11.4.3

The Board proposes that, pending any review of FRS 3, this amount should be allocated as shown in the following tables. The figures in the upper table are simply a working to show how the overall tax charge has been allocated. 11.4.4

Working

	Profit and loss account	Statement of total recognised gains and losses	Total
	1995	1992	
	£000	£000	£000
Accounting gain	500	2,000*	2,500
Indexation allowance	—	(1,000)	(1,000)
Taxable gain	500	1,000	1,500

*This amount will already have been recognised in the statement of total recognised gains and losses in the year of revaluation, not the current year.

**The Board's views in this regard are set out in Chapter 9.*

†Sale proceeds (£4.5m) less tax cost (£3m) = £1.5m @ 33% = £495,000.

Financial statements

	Profit and loss account	Statement of total recognised gains and losses	Total
	1995	1992	
	£000	£000	£000
Tax (@ 33%)	165	330	495

11.4.5 The effect of the indexation allowance has been reflected in the amount allocated to the statement of total recognised gains and losses, on the basis that the purpose of the indexation allowance is to exclude from taxation purely inflationary gains. In principle, such gains form part of the holding gains dealt with in the statement of total recognised gains and losses. If the indexation allowance were sufficient to cover all the gain dealt with in the statement of total recognised gains and losses, any balance would be attributed to the profit and loss account. Again, if the gain dealt with in the profit and loss account contained a significant holding gain, it might be appropriate to allocate part of the effect of the indexation allowance to the profit and loss account on an appropriate basis.

11.4.6 If in the above example deferred tax had been provided for before disposal, such deferred tax would have been charged to the statement of total recognised gains and losses. Accordingly on disposal, the amount of the tax on disposal allocated to the statement of total recognised gains and losses in the year of disposal would be reduced by any deferred tax previously provided for.

11.5 *Legal considerations*

11.5.1 The Board has been advised by the Department of Trade and Industry that there is no objection in law to the tax effects of items that have been dealt with in the statement of total recognised gains and losses also being dealt with in that statement. However, as noted in Section 9.4 in Chapter 9, there is a difficulty, when allocating the amounts charged in the statement of total recognised gains and losses to particular statutory reserves, in charging deferred tax to the revaluation reserve.

11.6 *The Board's views*

11.6.1 As set out above, the Board believes that the tax effects of items that are dealt with in the statement of total recognised gains and losses should also be reflected in that statement. Where items that are treated as a single transaction for tax purposes are dealt with for accounting purposes partly in the profit and loss account and partly in the statement of total recognised gains and losses, the Board believes that the tax should be allocated between the two primary statements on a pro-rata basis.

Chapter 12. Accounting for ACT

Issues 12.1

There are, broadly speaking, two methods of taxing the profits of companies – a 'classical' system and an 'imputation' system. 12.1.1

Classical system

Under a classical system, a company's profits are taxed and any dividends paid out of them are treated as taxable income in the hands of shareholders. This means that, in effect, the same profits are taxed twice. A classical system operates in a number of overseas jurisdictions, including the USA. 12.1.2

Imputation system

Under an imputation system, such as operates in the UK, a company's profits and any corporation tax paid on them are 'imputed' to the shareholder. In other words, the shareholder is liable to pay income tax on any distributed profits at the applicable personal tax rate, but such income tax is reduced by any corporation tax already paid on those profits. The economic effect of such a system is that profits are taxed only once in the hands of a shareholder. 12.1.3

ACT

In the UK, the imputation system is applied by means of advance corporation tax (ACT). When a UK company pays a dividend, it must pay ACT equal to one-quarter of the net, or one-fifth of the gross, dividend.* In the hands of the company, ACT is, as its name implies, treated as a payment in advance of corporation tax for the year in which the dividend is paid.† In the hands of the shareholder, ACT is treated as a payment in advance of income tax‡ due on the gross dividend. If the shareholder is not a tax-payer (such as a pension fund), it can reclaim the ACT paid by the company. A simple example of how the system affects a higher-rate UK tax-payer is given in Section 12.2. 12.1.4

The issue in accounting for ACT is whether ACT paid by a company should be shown as tax or as part of the cost of the dividend. The standard currently in force in the UK, SSAP 8 'Taxation under the imputation system', requires ACT to be treated as tax. 12.1.5

****In this context the 'net' dividend is the amount paid to the shareholder and the 'gross' dividend the amount paid to the shareholder plus the associated ACT.***

†The full rules regarding the offset of ACT are complex and beyond the scope of this Chapter.

‡Separate provisions apply where the shareholder is itself a UK company.

12.1.6 Some UK companies believe that this treatment is misleading since it understates the real return to shareholders in comparison with that of similar overseas companies. The arguments in favour of this view are set out in Section 12.2. Those in favour of the approach in SSAP 8 are set out in Section 12.3. There is also a third possible view that, whilst ACT should normally be treated as tax, irrecoverable surplus ACT should be treated as part of the cost of the dividend. This is discussed in Section 12.4.

12.2 *ACT as dividend*

12.2.1 The case for treating ACT as part of the cost of the dividend is best illustrated with a simple example. OverseaCo operates in a country where the corporation tax rate is 20 per cent. The higher personal tax rate, like that in the UK, is 40 per cent, but a classical tax system operates. BritCo is a comparable UK company. Both companies operate a full distribution policy. In the year ended 31 December 1994 both companies make a pre-tax profit, expressed in sterling, of £1 million, so that their reported profit and loss accounts, assuming that BritCo follows SSAP 8, will be as follows:

	BritCo	OverseaCo
	£000	£000
Profit before tax	1,000	1,000
Corporation tax at 33%/20%	330	200
Profit after tax (dividend)	670	800

12.2.2 At first sight, OverseaCo offers the better return to shareholders. However, this is not the case once the effect of the UK ACT system is taken into account. The ultimate cash flow to shareholders (ignoring any withholding tax and double tax relief) can be summarised as follows:

	BritCo		OverseaCo	
	Tax-exempt shareholder	Tax-paying shareholder	Tax-exempt shareholder	Tax-paying shareholder
	£000	£000	£000	£000
Dividend received	670.0	670.0	800.0	800.0
ACT credit	167.5	167.5	N/A	N/A
Gross dividend	837.5	837.5	800.0	800.0
Income tax (at 40%)	N/A	335.0	N/A	320.0
Final cash benefit	837.5	502.5	800.0	480.0

The above table demonstrates that, in economic terms, ACT is a distribution to shareholders, so that the real UK corporation tax rate is not 33 per cent, as reported in the accounts but, assuming a full distribution of profits, 16.25 per cent.* For this reason, some argue that the accounting treatment required by SSAP 8 encourages potential investors to divert funds from UK companies to the disadvantage of both the UK companies and the investors themselves. **12.2.3**

The view that ACT is a distribution to shareholders is supported by SSAP 8 itself, which requires that a company that receives a dividend from another UK company should treat the ACT credit as part of its investment income. Some institutional investors clearly regard ACT as a distribution. For example, many UK pension funds pointed out that the recent reduction in the rate of ACT represented a significant reduction in their income from UK equities. **12.2.4**

ACT as tax **12.3**

The main argument for treating ACT as a payment of tax is set out in SSAP 8, paragraph 4. From the company's perspective, the dividend is the amount declared and paid to the shareholders. ACT paid on that amount is no more than a payment on account of corporation tax.† The fact that the ACT is treated, in assessing the shareholder's liability to tax, as if it had been paid by the shareholder is a matter for the shareholder rather than the company. **12.3.1**

A further argument for treating ACT as part of the tax charge rather than as part of the dividend cost is that the tax charge of otherwise comparable companies would vary depending on whether or not profits were distributed. This can be illustrated using the example of BritCo set out in paragraph 12.2.1 above. The following table shows the different results that would be shown assuming nil and full distribution under both methods of accounting for ACT. **12.3.2**

******£(1,000,000–837,500)/£1,000,000 = 16.25%.*

†The special case of irrecoverable ACT is discussed in Section 12.4.

	ACT as tax charge (SSAP 8)		ACT as distribution	
	A	**B**	**C**	**D**
	Full distribution	**Nil distribution**	**Full distribution**	**Nil distribution**
	£000	**£000**	**£000**	**£000**
Profit before tax	1,000.0	1,000.0	1,000.0	1,000.0
Tax	330.0	330.0	162.5	330.0
Profit after tax	670.0	670.0	837.5	670.0
Dividend	670.0	NIL	837.5	NIL
Retained profit	NIL	670.0	NIL	670.0
Effective tax rate	33%	33%	16.25%*	33%

12.3.3 If BritCo earns a taxable profit of £1 million, it will pay £330,000 to the tax authorities, irrespective of whether or not a dividend is paid. It is simply the allocation of that £330,000 between ACT and mainstream corporation tax that will vary. On this basis the treatment in column C above is misleading because it implies that the company's tax liability is lower as a result of paying a dividend, which is not the case.

12.4 *Irrecoverable ACT as dividend*

12.4.1 A third view would be that, whilst ACT should normally be included in the tax charge, irrecoverable ACT should be treated as a cost of the dividend.

12.4.2 The basic rule is that ACT is treated as a payment in advance of corporation tax payable in respect of the year in which the dividend to which it relates is paid. However, the amount of ACT that can be treated in this way is limited (currently to 20/33 of the total corporation tax liability for the year†). Any ACT that cannot be utilised in this way is called 'surplus ACT' and may be set off against either the corporation tax liability of the previous six years or the corporation tax liability of any future year (in both cases subject to the relevant limit). Any surplus ACT whose recovery in this way cannot be foreseen is written off for accounting purposes and termed 'irrecoverable ACT'.‡

******The effective tax rate could be anywhere between 16.25% and 33%, depending on the amount of dividend paid.*

†*The fraction applicable to any period reflects the rates of ACT and corporation tax for that period.*

‡*SSAP 8, paragraph 22 requires disclosure of the amount ofany irrecoverable ACT included within the tax charge.*

The argument for treating irrecoverable ACT as part of the dividend rather than as part of the tax charge is that it represents an incremental payment that arises directly as a result of paying a dividend and would not have arisen otherwise. 12.4.3

The main argument against this approach is that a company with irrecoverable ACT would appear to pay a higher dividend than one whose ACT was fully recoverable, although the return to shareholders was in both cases the same. A second objection would be that the write-off of irrecoverable ACT and any subsequent recovery would be inconsistently treated. The write-off would be treated as a distribution whereas any recovery would be credited to distributable profits as part of the tax charge. 12.4.4

The Board's views 12.5

The Board appreciates the concerns of those who believe that the current accounting treatment of ACT does not portray economic reality from the perspective of shareholders. However, the Board does not believe that these concerns should be met by changing the basic requirement of SSAP 8 that ACT should be treated as tax. 12.5.1

To treat ACT as a distribution in all circumstances is to confuse the reporting entity with its owners. Moreover, as set out in paragraphs 12.3.2 and 12.3.3, such a treatment would create inconsistencies between UK companies that are more objectionable than any inconsistency between UK and overseas companies under current accounting practice. 12.5.2

Some Board members, however, would support treating irrecoverable ACT as a distribution, on the grounds that it is a cost that arises only as a result of paying a dividend, unlike recoverable ACT, the amount of which must be paid either as ACT or as mainstream corporation tax. 12.5.3

However, the Board would propose a change to current practice only if there were a clear consensus that it should do so. Accordingly, it will take particular note of comments received on this issue. 12.5.4

Appendix 1
Other variants of the full provision method

A1.1 This Appendix briefly discusses variants of the full provision method other than the liability method (discussed elsewhere in the Paper) and the Board's reasons for rejecting them. These variants are:

- the deferral method
- the net-of-tax method
- the 'temporary difference' approach in the US standard FAS 109 and the IASC exposure draft E49.

The deferral method

A1.2 Under the deferral method, deferred tax is provided for at the rate of tax prevailing when the timing difference originates; no adjustments are made to the balance sheet provision for subsequent changes in tax rate. The balance sheet figure for deferred tax under this method, although classified with liabilities, does not seek to measure a future transfer of economic benefits to or from the reporting entity, but is a means of re-allocating tax charges and reliefs between periods.

A1.3 Deferred tax balances established under the deferral method thus represent deferred income or expenditure rather than a liability or asset as defined in the Board's draft Statement of Principles. Accordingly, the Board does not consider that the deferral method is appropriate.

The net-of-tax method

A1.4 Under the net-of-tax method assets, liabilities, gains and losses are reported net of their tax effects. For example, a fixed asset costing £1 million with associated tax allowances of £300,000 would be recorded at £700,000, which would be depreciated over the life of the asset. The balance of £300,000 would be treated as a receivable account, and reduced in line with capital allowances claimed.

A1.5 The Board does not believe that net-of-tax accounting is appropriate because:

(a) it obscures the reporting entity's overall tax position, which would have to be given by way of note disclosure;

(b) in practice, many timing differences cannot be directly related to individual items in the financial statements. For example, under the current rules for capital allowances in the UK, most plant is treated for tax purposes as a fungible 'pool' that cannot, except in the simplest cases, be matched with the fixed assets recorded in the financial statements; and

(c) the method is effectively prohibited by the Companies Act 1985, which:

  (i) requires the tax on profit for the period to be shown on the face of the profit and loss account;

  (ii) forbids the netting of assets and liabilities or income and expenditure; and

(iii) requires assets to be recorded at cost or, in some cases, valuation. It is doubtful whether a net-of-tax carrying amount strictly complies with this.

The 'temporary difference' approach

The temporary difference approach is used in the US standard FAS 109 and is proposed in the recently published IASC exposure draft E49. Under this approach deferred tax is provided for on 'temporary' differences, which are defined in FAS 109 as follows: **A1.6**

> "A difference between the tax basis of an asset or liability and its reported amount in the financial statements that will result in taxable or deductible amounts in future years when the reported amount of the asset or liability is recovered or settled, respectively."*

At first sight, this definition seems little different from that of a timing difference. Indeed, any timing difference would also fall within the definition of temporary difference. However, the scope of the temporary difference approach is wider, because it focuses on the tax payable or recoverable that will arise on the recovery or settlement of all assets and liabilities. **A1.7**

In simple terms the rationalisation of the need for deferred tax is as follows. If an asset† is carried in the balance sheet at, say, £1,000 there is an implicit assumption in the accounts that the asset will ultimately be recovered or realised by a cash inflow of £1,000. That inflow will enter into the determination of taxable income; accordingly, the tax (if any) on that income should be provided for. **A1.8**

The 'basis for conclusions' section in FAS 109‡ puts it thus: **A1.9**

> "A government levies taxes on net taxable income. Temporary differences will become taxable amounts in future years, thereby increasing taxable income and taxes payable, upon recovery or settlement of the recognised and reported amounts of an enterprise's assets or liabilities . . .
>
> A contention that those temporary differences will never result in taxable amounts . . . would contradict the accounting assumption inherent in the statement of financial position that the reported amounts of assets and liabilities will be recovered and settled, respectively; thereby making that statement internally inconsistent."

Suppose that an item of plant with a tax written-down value of £800,000 is carried in the accounts at £1 million. The temporary difference approach argues that this implies future taxable income of £200,000, on which deferred tax should be provided for, calculated as follows: **A1.10**

**FAS 109, paragraph 289.*

†The same broad argument also applies in respect of the settlement of liabilities.

‡FAS 109, paragraphs 77 and 78.

	£000
Carrying amount (ie implicit future taxable cash inflow)	1,000
Tax base (ie tax deductions available in respect of asset)	800
'Temporary' difference	200

This is no different from the timing difference that would be calculated under the 'traditional' approach.

A1.11 Suppose, however, that this asset was not deductible for tax purposes, either on consumption or on disposal. Under the traditional full provision approach, depreciation of such an asset would constitute a permanent difference and would be ignored in calculating deferred tax. Under the temporary difference approach, however, deferred tax would be provided for on a temporary difference of £1 million, calculated as follows:

	£000
Carrying amount (ie implicit future taxable cash inflow)	1,000
Tax base (ie tax deductions available in respect of asset)	NIL
'Temporary' difference	1,000

A1.12 This represents the main practical difference between the traditional approach and the temporary difference approach. Under the traditional approach, the non-deductibility of the asset is reflected by increased tax charges* as the asset is depreciated. Under the temporary difference approach, these increased tax charges are recognised in full in advance by providing for deferred tax on purchase of the asset; the provision is released over the life the asset, so that later tax rates are 'normalised' to the statutory rate.

A1.13 The Board has a number of reservations about the temporary difference approach, even though the concept on which it is based is in many ways the same as that underlying the view of some Board members that deferred tax is a valuation adjustment to other assets and liabilities.

A1.14 In particular the approach can, in the Board's view, be criticised because:

- it is based on an implied premise that the carrying amount of an item represents its recoverable amount
- it provides for only one of many liabilities implicit in the future recovery of an asset.

****Tax charges greater than the 'expected' charge of accounting profit multiplied by the tax rate.***

Carrying amount as recoverable amount

Tax can be meaningfully provided for only on pre-tax cash flows. However, the calculation in paragraph A1.11 effectively takes a post-tax cash flow as its starting point, as explained below. **A1.15**

If the carrying amount of a non-deductible asset does indeed imply a future cash inflow, it must represent a post-tax cash inflow—otherwise it would have to be written down to its (lower) recoverable amount. Thus in the example above, a non-deductible asset with a carrying value of £1 million implies a recoverable amount after tax of £1 million. This is equivalent (assuming the current 33 per cent rate of UK corporation tax) to £1.5 million* before tax. **A1.16**

If the temporary difference approach were applied logically, the asset should be grossed up to £1.5 million (the future pre-tax cash flows implicit in its original carrying value) and deferred tax of £0.5 million provided for on this amount. This seems a meaningless result, in that £1.5 million represents neither cost nor any generally recognised method of valuation. **A1.17**

In the Board's view this result arises because the temporary difference approach is implicitly founded on an invalid interpretation of the measurement base for an asset. The fact that an asset should never be carried at above its recoverable amount does not mean that it is always, or even usually, measured on that basis. Normally cost (whether the historical cost of acquisition or replacement cost) is the basis and is sufficiently below recoverable amount to allow for the recovery of future costs and the earning of profits after tax. **A1.18**

Provision for only one liability arising on realisation of assets

A further concern with regard to the temporary difference approach is that it recognises as a liability one, but only one, of the many future costs associated with the recovery of an asset. In the example above, the temporary difference approach argues that, since the £1 million carrying value implies £1 million of future profit on which tax will be payable, that tax is a liability at the outset. **A1.19**

However, there are many other expenses that must be incurred in order to recover the carrying value of the asset, such as rent, rates, power and wages. If carried to its logical conclusion, the rationale of the temporary difference approach would arguably require these other costs to be recognised as liabilities as well. These other costs are just as certain to arise as the tax, if not (given the potential for changes to the tax system) more so, but they are clearly not liabilities at the balance sheet date. This suggests that deferred tax, as rationalised under the temporary difference approach, is also not a liability. **A1.20**

***£1 million/(100–33)%.*

Appendix 2
SSAP 15 – some practical problems

A2.1 This Appendix explains how SSAP 15 can in certain circumstances produce results that are counter-intuitive. The basic recognition rule of the standard is that deferred tax assets or liabilities should be recognised only to the extent that they are not expected to be replaced by equivalent assets or liabilities.

A2.2 In practice, this rule 'works' only where the level of hard core timing differences is stable. However, SSAP 15 can produce results that are difficult to accept when the level and/or reversal pattern of timing differences changes. The effect is most marked where a new category of timing difference suddenly arises (for example when an asset or liability is recognised for the first time as the result of a new accounting policy).

A2.3 A simple example will illustrate the point. Suppose that a company with a year-end of 31 March has as its sole income intra-group interest receivable of £1 million that is taxed on a receipts basis. In all years up to the year ended 31 March 1994, the interest has been received on 15 March. It therefore forms the taxable profit for the period and no deferred tax arises.

A2.4 During the year ended 31 March 1995 it is decided that, for tax reasons, the interest for that year and all subsequent years will be received on 15 April of the following period. The interest will then form the taxable profit for the year after it is reported as income in the financial statements, so that a timing difference of £1 million arises at each balance sheet date.

A2.5 Under the full provision method, a deferred tax liability of £330,000* would be recognised at 31 March 1995 and each subsequent year. Under SSAP 15, however, no liability is recognised, on the grounds that it is expected to be replaced by an equivalent liability at each successive balance sheet date.

A2.6 During the year ended 31 March 1997, it is decided that with effect from the year ended 31 March 1998, the interest will be received on 15 March as before. This means that the deferred tax of £330,000 arising at 31 March 1997 will not be replaced by an equivalent balance in 1998. Accordingly, under SSAP 15, deferred tax must be provided for at 31 March 1997.

A2.7 The effect on the profit and loss account and balance sheet of accounting for the situation outlined above in accordance with SSAP 15 is as follows:

**£1 million @ 33%.*

Year ended 31 March	**1994**	**1995**	**1996**	**1997**	**1998**
	£000	**£000**	**£000**	**£000**	**£000**
Profit and loss account					
Interest	1,000	1,000	1,000	1,000	1,000
Current tax	(330)	NIL	(330)	(330)	(660)
Deferred tax	NIL	NIL	NIL	(330)	330
Profit after tax	670	1,000	670	340	670
Balance sheet					
Current tax	330	NIL	330	330	660
Deferred tax	NIL	NIL	NIL	330	NIL

The effect of applying the recognition rule in SSAP 15 has been, in simple terms, that no tax is charged in 1995 whereas 1997 suffers a double tax charge. Any attempt to remedy this by overriding the detailed requirements of the standard would simply shunt the problem into another year. If deferred tax had not been provided for in 1997, 1998 would have suffered the double tax charge instead. Alternatively, if deferred tax had been provided for in 1995, and the company had not taken the decision in 1997 to change the payment date of interest, either: **A2.8**

(a) the balance sheet would have shown a deferred tax liability in perpetuity (ie the true and fair override would have had to be invoked every year); or
(b) the deferred tax liability would have had to be written back at some stage, creating a nil tax charge in the year of write-back.

This is a simple, even a trivial, example, but the principle that it illustrates always holds good. When the level of hard core timing differences changes significantly for any reason, the tax charge reported under SSAP 15 will be distorted in the year(s) of change.* **A2.9**

It was exactly this problem that was highlighted by the issue of UITF Abstract 6 'Accounting for post-retirement benefits other than pensions'. This is discussed in more detail in paragraphs 1.3.3 and 1.3.4 and 5.3.2–5.3.7. **A2.10**

Implementation of FRS 4 has highlighted the same problem for some companies. FRS 4 broadly requires that the cost of a financial instrument should be allocated over the life of the instrument on a systematic (usually actuarial) basis. However, tax relief for such costs is generally given on a cash basis. Thus any liability recorded under FRS 4 that represents interest charged to the profit and loss account but not yet paid is a timing difference. **A2.11**

Under a full provision system, a deferred tax asset would be set up in respect of this **A2.12**

**It is only changes in the hard core timing differences that have this effect. The tax effects of changes in other timing differences will, under SSAP 15, be fully provided for.*

timing difference. Under SSAP 15, however, a company cannot record the related deferred tax asset where it is likely to remain a permanent feature of the balance sheet (eg where a company has a 'rolling' debt issue programme and there are no deferred tax liabilities against which the asset can be offset). Such a company is thus required by FRS 4 to record a liability for interest which, when paid, will attract tax relief, but is prevented by SSAP 15 from recording a deferred tax balance in respect of that tax relief.

A2.13 The inability of SSAP 15 to deal with changing circumstances was also shown after the issue of the Finance Act 1984. This abolished first-year allowances over a three-year period, which had the effect of reducing the level of timing differences relating to depreciation. For some companies, this had the effect of increasing tax payments significantly. For many companies, however, the overall level of tax payments did not change, because the tax rate was lowered.

A2.14 However, since the effect of the legislation was to accelerate the reversal of hard core timing differences, and therefore to increase the amount of tax provided for on a partial provision basis, application of SSAP 15 required nearly all companies to provide for an additional tax charge, irrespective of whether or not they expected to pay more tax on an ongoing basis under the new rules. This seemed an odd result from a standard whose objective is to indicate likely expected tax payments.*

**In practice, the problem was mitigated to some extent because SSAP 6 permitted a change in the basis of taxation to be treated as an extraordinary item. If FRS 3 had been in force, however, the full additional charge would have been treated as part of the tax charge for the year.*

Part Nine

Relevant Technical Releases issued by ASC and ICAEW

[TR707]
Statement by the Accounting Standards Committee on the withdrawal of SSAP 16 'Current Cost Accounting'

(Issued July 1988)

On 22 April 1988, The Chartered Association of Certified Accountants joined the other members of the Consultative Committee of Accountancy Bodies in agreeing to withdraw SSAP 16 'Current Cost Accounting'. SSAP 16 was therefore formally withdrawn on 22 April 1988, having been suspended since June 1985. **1**

The Accounting Standards Committee reaffirms its view that where historical cost accounts are materially affected by changing prices, information about the effects of changing prices is necessary for an appreciation of a company's results and financial position. Companies are encouraged to give information about these effects, where material, in their financial statements. The ASC is continuing to explore effective means of developing a standard on accounting for the effects of changing prices. **2**

The ASC also reaffirms its belief in current cost accounting as an acceptable method of accounting for the effects of changing prices. ASC's Handbook 'Accounting for the effects of changing prices', issued in 1986, is an authoritative reference work based on the experience gained in developing SSAP 16 and represents the ASC's latest thinking on the subject. Entities that present current cost information in their financial statements may where appropriate state in the accounting policy note that the current cost accounts are drawn up in accordance with the principles set out in the Accounting Standards Committee publication 'Accounting for the effects of changing prices: a Handbook', specifying which capital maintenance concept has been adopted. **3**

[TR805]
Legal and taxation anomalies in statements of standard accounting practice

*(Issued July 1990)**

1 INTRODUCTION

In February and March 1990 the Accounting Standards Committee received two reports which recommended that a number of existing statements of standard accounting practice should be updated to take account of changes in statute. The ASC does not make piecemeal changes to SSAPs, because the consultative and approval processes required are appropriate only in the case of a full review. However, apart from identifying more far-reaching anomalies, the two reports also noted simple references that were no longer correct. As such updating is a matter of fact, the ASC has extracted these uncontentious matters from the reports and presents them here for the convenience of readers. They do not represent changes of practice or substantive changes to the standards, nor have they been formally approved by the Councils of the governing bodies, and are listed as a matter of record only. The full reports on which the proposed changes are based have been published and are available separately from their issuing bodies.† **1.1**

The following standards were under review by the ASC at the time the reports were compiled, and are not, therefore, covered by the updating review. **1.2**

SSAP1	(Revised) Accounting for associated companies;
SSAP2	Disclosure of accounting policies;
SSAP4	The accounting treatment of government grants;
SSAP10	Statements of source and application of funds;
SSAP14	Group accounts;
SSAP22	Accounting for goodwill; and
SSAP23	Accounting for acquisitions and mergers.

2 TAXATION

SSAP3 Earnings per share

Delete paragraph 4 and insert: **2.1**

'One of the features of the imputation system of corporation tax is that earnings

***Editor's note:** This TR does not deal with changes subsequent to July 1990.*

†*Technical Release 791* Memorandum to the ASC on the review of extant SSAPs *is available from the Publications Department, The Institute of Chartered Accountants in England and Wales, Gloucester House, 399 Silbury Boulevard, Witan Gate East, Central Milton Keynes, MK9 2HL.* Review of tax references in SSAPs *is available from the Chartered Institute of Management Accountants, 63 Portland Place, London W1N 4AB.*

after corporation tax are available to cover the actual cash dividends payable to the shareholders.'

2.2 The following amendments are necessary:

Paragraph 3, line 3: Delete 'after the transitional period'
Paragraph 5, line 1: Delete 'not the former gross dividend but'
Paragraph 6, line 1: Delete 'under the new system'
Paragraph 3, line 5: Change 'will' to 'are'.

SSAP5 Accounting for VAT

2.3 In paragraph 1, line 1, insert the words 'by way of business' after 'goods and services' to reflect the fact that VAT only applies to transactions done in furtherance of business.

2.4 In paragraph 4, line 2, delete the word 'certain' following the removal of overseas and customer entertainment relief.

SSAP8 The treatment of taxation under the imputation system in the accounts of companies

2.5 In the fourth sentence of paragraph 1, the words '(but not on its chargeable gains)' should be deleted. Delete the word 'income' in lines 2 and 8 and replace by 'taxable profits'. In line 4, delete 'on a date which may be a year or more' and insert 'nine months' to bring it into line with the Companies Act.

2.6 Delete paragraph 2 and insert:

'The ACT set off against the final corporation tax bill, assuming a basic rate of income tax of 25%, is effectively restricted to one quarter of the company's taxable profits. Any ACT thereby unrelieved, that is ACT on that part of a distribution that is in excess of the company's taxable profits, can be carried back to accounting periods beginning in the six years preceding the accounting period in which the surplus ACT arose. The unrelieved ACT can also be carried forward without time limit.'

2.7 Delete paragraph 5 and insert:

'5. ACT is primarily recovered by being set off against the corporation tax on the taxable profits of the year in which the related distribution is made. In the case of dividends paid during the year under review, the taxable profits of that year and of the six previous years will normally be available to absorb the relief. Where a proposed dividend is to be paid in the following year, then the related ACT falls to be set off against the corporation tax on the taxable profits of the year of payment of the proposed dividend and in default of that, against the taxable profits of the year under review or of the five years previous to that. In both cases, ACT can be carried forward indefinitely if necessary. In each year there is an overriding restriction on the use of ACT for set off by reference to the taxable profits of that year.'

The following amendments are necessary: **2.8**

Paragraph 6, line 3: delete 'income', insert 'profits';
line 5: delete 'income is', insert 'profits are';
Paragraph 7, line 9: delete '30', insert '25';
Paragraph 7, last sentence: delete;
Paragraph 16, line 4: delete 'at least';
Paragraph 22(a) (i) line 2: delete 'income', insert 'taxable profits';
Appendix 1, line 3: delete '1967', insert '1985';
Appendix 2: delete paragraphs 3 to 7.

Delete paragraph 1, Appendix 2 and insert: **2.9**

'Prior to 31 March 1984, where a company had UK and overseas income, it was necessary to allocate such items as charges on income and ACT among the different sources so as to calculate the amount of UK corporation tax attributable to that foreign income. For accounting periods ending on or before that date, the Inland Revenue view was that foreign tax could only be deducted after any available ACT. In cases where the corporation tax (net of ACT) was less than foreign tax, the excess was lost since unused double taxation relief cannot be carried forward.

'For accounting periods ending after 31 March 1984, the foreign credit is deductable before the ACT. Accordingly, it is no longer necessary to set ACT against UK source income as opposed to foreign source income.

'For accounting periods ending after 2 June 1986, the amount of ACT which may be set against the company's corporation tax liability in respect of foreign income from which double taxation relief has been deducted is limited to the lesser of:
(a) the ACT limit calculated as if that foreign income were the company's only income for the relevant accounting period; and
(b) the amount of corporation tax, which, after deducting the foreign tax credit, the company is liable to pay in respect of that income.'

SSAP15 Accounting for deferred tax

In paragraph 17 of the Appendix, delete the words 'excluding chargeable gains' to accommodate the ACT set off changes. Change three references to 'income' in paragraph 16 to 'profits'. **2.10**

Delete paragraphs 63–72 and insert paragraphs 63–80 in the attached annex which outlines the tax position in Northern Ireland and the Republic of Ireland. Paragraph 73 should be renumbered as paragraph 81. **2.11**

In the Appendix, delete the sentence 'stock relief in the Republic of Ireland is effectively a permanent difference' from paragraph 3. **2.12**

3 LEGAL MATTERS

SSAP3 Earnings per share

3.1 In paragraph 13, last sentence, delete 'other than companies claiming exemption from the disclosure requirements under Part III of Schedule 2 of the Companies Act 1967' and insert 'other than banking and insurance companies, as defined in section 744 of the Companies Act 1985, preparing accounts in accordance with section 255 of and paragraphs 27 and 28 of Part I of Schedule 9 to the Companies Act 1985.'

3.2 On page 1, Appendix 1, footnote: insert 'and revised August 1986' after 1974.

SSAP5 Accounting for value added tax

3.3 Delete paragraph 7 relating to purchase tax.

3.4 Insert 'Part 3 – legal requirements

11. Section 262(1) of the Companies Act 1985 states that 'turnover, in relation to a company, means the amounts derived from the provision of goods and services falling within the company's ordinary activities, after deduction of (i) trade discounts, (ii) value added tax, and (iii) any other taxes based on the amounts so derived.'

SSAP6 (Revised) Extraordinary items and prior year adjustments

3.5 In paragraph 41, delete 'companies preparing accounts in compliance with sections 228 and 230 of the Companies Act 1985' and insert 'companies preparing accounts in accordance with sections 226 and 227 of the Companies Act 1985.'

3.6 References to sections 258 and 259 of the Companies Act 1985 should be deleted and replaced by references to sections 255 and 255A of the Companies Act 1985.

SSAP12 (Revised) Accounting for depreciation

3.7 Change references to section 228 and 230 of the Companies Act 1985 in paragraph 29 to sections 226 and 227 respectively.

3.8 In paragraph 32, delete the word 'cost' and insert 'purchase price or production cost.'

SSAP13 (Revised) Accounting for research and development

3.9 Delete references to special category companies in paragraphs 20 and 22 and insert 'banking and insurance companies as defined in section 744 of the Companies Act 1985, preparing accounts in accordance with sections 255 and 255A of and Schedule 9 to the Companies Act 1985.'

SSAP15 (Revised) Accounting for deferred tax

3.10 The following revisions are necessary to Part 4 'Note on legal requirements in Great Britain'

- In the heading above paragraph 46: delete sections 228 and 230 and insert sections 226 and 227 respectively.
- In the heading above paragraph 58: delete sections 258 and 259 and insert sections 255 and 255A respectively.
- In paragraph 58 delete reference to shipping companies.

In paragraph 47, delete the first two sentences and insert 'paragraph 47 requires deferred tax balances to be disclosed separately from other provisions for taxation.' **3.11**

SSAP19 Accounting for investment properties

In paragraph 13, delete reference to 'paragraph 10 of SSAP6' and insert 'Paragraph 24 of SSAP6 (Revised).' **3.12**

SSAP20 Foreign currency translation

In paragraphs 35 and 62, delete references to sections 149 and 152 of the Companies Act 1948 and insert sections 226 and 227 of the Companies Act 1985. In paragraph 62, delete 'Schedule 8 to the Companies Act 1948' and insert 'Schedule 4 to the Companies Act 1985.' **3.13**

SSAP24 Accounting for pension costs

In paragraph 98, delete 'paragraphs 61 and 68 of Schedule 4' and insert 'paragraph 1 of Schedule 4A to the Companies Act 1985.' **3.14**

In paragraph 99, delete 'Banking, Insurance and Shipping companies' and insert 'Banking and Insurance companies as defined in section 744 of the Companies Act 1985, preparing accounts in accordance with sections 255 and 255A of and Schedule 9 to the Companies Act 1985.' **3.15**

Annex SSAP15: Accounting for deferred tax – proposed Part 5

NORTHERN IRELAND

63 The legal references in Part 4 to Schedule 4 (before amendment by the Companies Act 1989) of the Companies Act 1985, apply equally in Northern Ireland by virtue of Schedule 4 to the Companies (Northern Ireland) Order 1986. The Schedule references are the same except for paragraph 89 for which the equivalent reference in Northern Ireland is paragraph 88.

64 The legal references in Part 4 to Schedule 9 (before amendment by the Companies Act 1989) apply equally in Northern Ireland by virtue of Schedule 9 to the Companies (Northern Ireland) Order 1986. The Schedule references are the same in both enactments.

REPUBLIC OF IRELAND

65 This section applies to companies subject to Section 3 of the Companies (Amendment) Act 1986.

66 The references below to "the Act" and to "the Schedule" are to the Companies (Amendment) Act 1986 and the Schedule to that Act.

67 Deferred tax provisions should be included in the balance sheet under the heading 'Provisions for liabilities and charges' as part of the provision for 'Taxation, including deferred taxation' (balance sheet format 1.6, format 2 – liabilities B, 2). Paragraph 70 of the Schedule describes provision for liabilities or charges as 'any amount retained as reasonably necessary for the purpose of providing for any liability or loss which is either likely to be incurred, or certain to be incurred but uncertain as to the amount or as to the date on which it will arise.'

68 The amount of any provisions for taxation other than deferred taxation has to be stated (paragraph 33 of the Schedule). Taking this requirement together with that referred to in paragraph 4 above, the balance of deferred tax will be ascertainable as the remaining figure. Tax provisions are distinguished from tax liabilities falling due within, or after more than, one year, which are shown separately under creditors in the balance sheet (balance sheet format 1-C, 8 and F8, format 2 – liabilities C, 8 and note 7 on the balance sheet formats).

69 Paragraph 32(1) of the Schedule requires the information set out in paragraph 32(2) of the Schedule to be given where any amount is transferred to any provision for liabilities and charges or from any provision for liabilities and charges, except where the transfer is for the purpose for which the provision was established. The information required in paragraph 32(2) of the Schedule is:

(a) the amount of the reserve or provisions as at the date of the beginning of the financial year and as at the balance sheet date respectively;

(b) any amounts transferred to or from the reserves or provisions during that year; and

(c) the source and application respectively of any amounts so transferred.

Any deferred tax carried forward as an asset should be included under the heading of 'Prepayments and accrued income' within 'current Assets/Debtors'. Any amount falling due after more than one year should be shown separately (note 4 on the balance sheet formats). 70

In determining the aggregate amount of deferred tax, this statement requires deferred tax debit balances to be matched with deferred tax liabilities against which they will be able to be offset. This is in accordance with Section 5(e) of the Act as individual deferred tax debit balances and liabilities which can be offset for tax purposes are not separate items, which under section 4(11) of the Act cannot be offset but are elements of an aggregate deferred tax asset or liability. 71

The amount of any item has to be determined on a prudent basis. In particular, all liabilities and losses which have arisen or are likely to arise in respect of the financial year to which the accounts relate or a previous financial year have to be taken into account (Section 5(c) of the Act). 72

Paragraph 36(2) of the Schedule requires information to be given with respect to the amount or estimated amount of any contingent liability not provided for, its legal nature and any valuable security provided. The ASC has obtained legal advice to the effect that unprovided deferred tax is a contingent liability, except where the prospect of it becoming payable is so remote that it does not amount to a contingent liability at all. 73

Where a company is a member of a group, any contingent deferred tax liability on behalf of other members of the group has to be shown separately in the financial statements of any company which has undertaken the commitment, analysed between amounts in respect of any subsidiary and amounts in respect of any holding company or fellow subsidiary (paragraph 36(6) of the Schedule). 74

The tax treatment of amounts credited or debited to the revaluation reserve has to be disclosed (paragraph 22(5) of the Schedule). 75

The basis on which the charge for taxation is computed has to be stated (paragraph 40(1) of the Schedule). Particulars are required of any special circumstances affecting the tax liability for the financial year or succeeding financial years (paragraph 40(2) of the Schedule). 76

Paragraph 40(3) of the Schedule requires the amounts shown under the items 'tax on profit or loss on ordinary activities' and 'tax on extraordinary profit or loss', to be analysed between: 77

(a) corporation tax;
(b) income tax; and
(c) other taxation on profits or capital gains including taxation payable outside the State (distinguishing where practicable between corporation tax and other taxation).

Deferred tax is not specifically referred to in the profit and loss account formats. However, this statement requires any deferred tax to be separately shown as part of the tax on profit or loss on ordinary activities or of the tax on extraordinary profit or loss, as appropriate, either on the face of the profit and loss account or in a note.

78 Differences exist between United Kingdom law and Republic of Ireland law on advance corporation tax. Deferred tax is affected by advance corporation tax in the following respects:

(a) the off-set of advance corporation tax against a deferred tax liability; and

(b) the carry forward of a net debit balance on the deferred tax account represented by advance corporation tax. The general provisions of the statement in regard to these two matters will be applicable to Republic of Ireland companies with one exception. Because advance corporation tax is payable six months from the end of the accounting period in which the dividend is paid, it will be necessary to consider the possibility of offsetting an advance corporation tax liability against the asset representing advance corporation tax recoverable. If such an offset were probable the advance corporation tax recoverable would not be deducted from a deferred tax credit balance under paragraph 29 – or recognised as a deferred tax debit balance under paragraphs 31 and 32. The treatment of advance corporation tax in the Republic of Ireland is dealt with more fully in Appendix 3 to SSAP8.

79 Certain Irish companies and branches of foreign companies have been totally relieved of corporation tax or have been subject to tax at reduced rates on profits arising from the export of manufactured goods and services (Export Sale Relief and 'Shannon' relief). Where such companies have timing differences originating during the period of total relief or of reduced relief and it is probable that these differences will reverse after expiry of the relief period – or when the reduced rates no longer apply – and that a tax liability will crystallise, then provision should be made for taxation deferred. The amount of tax to be deferred in respect of such timing differences should be calculated by reference to the effective rate estimated to be applicable in the years of reversal. It should be noted that Export Sales Relief and "Shannon" relief expired on 5 April 1990.

80 A reduced rate of corporation tax applies to companies in regard to income arising from the sale of goods manufactured in the Republic of Ireland. Under present legislation the relief is for sales made in periods up to 31 December 2000. In calculating deferred tax provisions where a reduced rate applies, similar considerations to those given in the preceding paragraphs should be taken into account.

APPENDIX

The reference to Republic of Ireland stock relief in paragraph 3 should be deleted.

[TR773]
A discussion paper – The use of discounting in financial statements

(Issued December 1989)

This discussion paper, Technical Release (TR) 773, is issued by the Technical Committee of The Institute of Chartered Accountants in England and Wales.

Contents

A discussion paper – The use of discounting in financial statements

INTRODUCTION

It is well accepted that a sum of money receivable at a future date is worth less to the recipient than the same sum receivable immediately, even after allowing for changes in the purchasing power of that money. Similarly an obligation to make a payment in the future is less onerous for the payer than one to make an immediate payment of the same amount. The difference between present value and future value results from a feature of the nature of money as an asset: that, if invested, it has the capacity to earn interest and grow into a larger sum. Putting it simply, money has a time value. 1

Discounting is a technique that gives recognition to the time value of money. The technique is not currently used extensively in the preparation of financial statements although it is accepted practice to discount long term assets and liabilities in certain specialised cases. Accounting for pensions in accordance with SSAP 24 'Accounting for pension costs' and for deep discount bonds in accordance with TR677 'Accounting for complex capital issues'* are examples of uses of discounting. The principle of discounting is specifically referred to in SSAP 21 'Accounting for leases and hire purchase contracts', in SSAP 24, in the ED Auditing Guideline 'General Business Insurers'† and in the ASC's discussion paper 'Fair value in the context of acquisition accounting'.‡ 2

It is not always clear when preparers of financial statements have used discounting. A recent research project, 'Discounting in corporate financial reporting', sponsored by the Institute's Research Board, indicated that the use of discounting to determine the amount of assets and liabilities is increasing in practice, but that there is a lack of adequate disclosure of accounting policies in this area. The research project reviewed UK and US literature on discounting and studied the current use of discounting in published accounts in the UK. The project showed that the uses of discounting do not appear to have a clear, generally accepted, conceptual basis; that interest rates are defined in a variety of ways in official pronouncements; that these definitions are not always consistent with one another; and that, in some instances, the choice of the interest rate used for discounting is left to the discretion of other professional experts. 3

The Technical Committee has considered the possible applications of discounted cash flow techniques, how these can be used in preparing financial statements and the factors that need to be considered, including the interest rate to be used. The Technical Committee believes that the recognition of the time value of money is required in certain instances in order that financial statements should give a true and fair view. 4

**See now FRS 4 'Capital Instruments'.*

†See Auditing Guideline 'General business insurers in the United Kingdom'.

‡See now FRS 7 'Fair values in acquisition accounting'.

PURPOSE

5 The purpose of this TR is to publicise the Technical Committee's views on this topic and to promote discussion.

6 The TR sets out the concepts involved. An appendix is attached giving two examples of how the concepts could be applied in practice.

7 The paper does not attempt to say how other professionals that use discounting techniques, such as valuers and actuaries, should apply those techniques.

8 In order to promote discussion the Technical Committee has specifically set out, in paragraph 44, a number of issues on which it would welcome views. Comments on the discussion paper should be addressed to Mrs E A Buckley, Secretary to the Technical Committee, The Institute of Chartered Accountants in England and Wales, Chartered Accountants' Hall, Moorgate Place, London, EC2P 2BJ and are requested by 31 March 1990. All comments will be regarded as being on public record unless confidentiality is requested by the commentator.

POSSIBLE APPLICATIONS OF DISCOUNTED CASH FLOW TECHNIQUES

9 There are three potential applications of discounted cash flow techniques. These are:

(a) Allocation of cash inflows and outflows as revenues or expenses over accounting periods in a manner that is consistent with the time value of money;
(b) Valuation where there is no ready external market for the item and where no cash alternative is available. A valuation can be calculated as the present value of 'known' (see paragraph 10 below) cash flows arising; and
(c) Projection to estimate future cash flows from knowledge of present values and yields.

10 There are three principal variables involved in applying discounting techniques and it is possible to calculate a value for one of them only if a value is known, or can be estimated with reasonable certainty, (referred to below as 'known') for the other two variables. The three applications are summarised in the table below which shows the different informational needs for each of them.

	Cash flow	Cost or Present value	Interest rate
Allocation	known	known	calculate
Cost/Valuation	known	calculate	known
Projection	calculate	known	known

Taking the issue of a deep discount bond on normal commercial terms as an example: the present value is the initial cash inflow; the future cash outflows will be stipulated in the contract. Consequently the issuer of the bond can calculate the rate that, when used to discount the future cash outflows, will equal the present value. This rate can then be used to allocate the interest and discount to the profit and loss accounts over the life of the bond.

Discounting as a method of allocation can be used in relation to items of revenue or expense in financial statements. The use of discounting as a valuation technique can be used to determine disaggregated amounts for groups of assets or liabilities, as well as a more generalised valuation tool in specific applications (such as pension obligations). The use of discounted techniques to assist with projections is found mainly in a decision making context. It is the first two applications that are relevant to financial reporting and that are considered in this paper. **11**

USES OF DISCOUNTING IN FINANCIAL STATEMENTS

The uses of discounting as a technique for allocation and for ascertaining cost or present value are considered in turn below. **12**

Allocation

The common theme to the examples already mentioned is that they all involve transactions which have effect over a long period of time and, hence, where the effect of discounting is likely to be material. The materiality of discounting will be a function of length of time and rate of interest: the longer the period of time and the higher the rate of interest the more likely it is that there will be a material effect. Except in hyper-inflationary conditions, this is unlikely to be the case for current assets and liabilities. **13**

In accordance with the fundamental concept of matching, costs should be allocated to accounting periods so as to match expected benefits. Some of the methods of allocation currently used are essentially arbitrary or for arithmetical convenience rather than being based on any economic analysis. Where costs and benefits extend over a long period of time their economic incidence will be affected by the time value of money. The method of matching should reflect this by the use of discounting as a method of allocation over a succession of accounting periods. **14**

Taking an expense as an example, most transactions are such that the expense is incurred and payable with almost immediate effect. There are no discounting implications in such instances. However, when an expense is incurred immediately and payable over an extended period then, depending on the length of the credit period relative to rates of interest, there may be a benefit to the business. If so, only the present value of the future amount should be allocated in the accounts (either charged against profits or capitalised) in the first accounting period. Additional amounts will be allocated in the accounts in each of the subsequent periods benefiting from the extended credit period. **15**

Cost or Present Value

Discounting may be used as a technique to calculate the present value at a point in time of a single or a series of cash flows in the future. Such a calculation may be used to **16** derive the cost of certain items at the point of acquisition. For instance, when an asset is acquired using deferred consideration the credit period may be a material benefit that should be recognised in stating the asset at a cost less than the aggregate of the gross cash outflow.

17 In other circumstances, the calculation of present value may represent a valuation. The preparation of financial statements often requires such valuations, particularly if a current cost convention is adopted. Discounting can assist in the valuation of an asset or liability for which there is neither a ready external market nor an immediate cash alternative.

18 Under a current cost convention, Appendix 1 of the ASC's Handbook 'Accounting for the effects of changing prices' recommends that the current cost of an asset is the lesser of:

(a) the net current replacement cost; and
(b) the greater of:
  (i) the net realisable amount on sale; and
  (ii) the economic value.

19 The net current replacement cost and the net realisable amount are values which should, ordinarily, be capable of being established by reference to external sources; but the economic value is calculated as the discounted present value, at the date of valuation, of the future cash flows associated with ownership of the asset.

PRINCIPLES OF DISCOUNTING

20 Three factors need to be considered when applying discounting: the amount of the future cash flows; the timing of those future cash flows; and the interest rate to be used to discount the cash flows.

AMOUNT OF FUTURE CASH FLOWS

21 Determining the absolute amount of future cash flows is not a matter particular to discounting. It includes the problems of uncertainty inherent in all cases of accounting estimates. The following matters relating to the amount of cash flows in applying discounting techniques deserve particular attention:

(a) Some cash flows may vary in amount depending upon their timing. Estimates of future cash flows may be subject to variation due to general inflation. It is not uncommon for commercial agreements to make provision for cash flows to be indexed either by reference to a general inflation rate or to the prices of some more specific commodities. Allowance must be made for any such indexation or other similar variation in the discounting calculation. If the cash flows have been increased by the expected inflation rate then the interest rate applied to those cash flows should be a money rate, whereas a real rate should be applied to cash flows that have not been increased to take account of inflation.
(b) It is not unknown for preparers of financial statements to apply some form of

implicit discounting in arriving at estimates of assets and liabilities that will be realised or will crystallise in the future. The extent of such implicit discounting can be difficult to ascertain particularly in cases where the estimation process involves a significant degree of judgement. Discounting calculations, either as a method of allocation or of valuation, should be applied only to gross cash flows. Where the degree of implicit discounting in the estimates is uncertain, it may not be appropriate to apply further discounting calculations.

TIMING OF CASH FLOWS

As explained above (paragraph 13), when all the cash flows are within a future period sufficiently close to the present that the time value of money is not material to them, discounting is not relevant. 22

In many circumstances the pattern of cash flows over an extended period is such that in estimating the cash flows, the effect of uncertainty in the timing of one of them would not give rise to a material error, for instance where there is a large number of discrete events. However, where the pattern of cash flows is such that uncertainty in estimating the timing of one of them would give rise to a material error (e.g., where there is a small number of individually large cash flows) then the concept of prudence would imply that discounting be applied on the basis that: 23

(a) the timings used for cash outflows should tend towards the earlier of the estimates; and
(b) the timings used for cash inflows should tend towards the later of the estimates.

For any pattern of cash flows there will be a point beyond which the weight of the discount factor being applied becomes so large that it produces a present value approaching nil. There will therefore be no material error if the cash flows subsequent to that point are ignored. At the other end of the spectrum, that is, in the short-term, the effect of discounting may be so small that its effect is immaterial. The present value will approximate to the cash flows as the discount factor becomes close to unity. Pragmatically, the area where a discounting calculation is at its most sensitive is in the medium term, far enough in the future that discounting has an effect, but not so far in the future that its effect is overwhelming. It is in that area that the greatest care is needed in determining how the calculation is made. 24

CHANGES IN THE ESTIMATION OF THE TIMING OF CASH FLOWS

Estimating future events and their effects requires the exercise of judgement and will require reappraisal as new events occur. The effect of changes in the estimated timing of future cash flows in the allocation process is an adjustment arising as a natural result of estimates inherent in accounting. As indicated in SSAP 6 (Revised) 'Extraordinary items and prior year adjustments'* the adjustment should not be given retrospective effect by restatement of prior years, the adjustment should be prospective. In accord- 25

**SSAP 6 has been superseded by FRS 3 'Reporting Financial Performance'.*

ance with SSAP 6* the adjustment will usually be dealt with in arriving at the profit on ordinary activities. It will be treated as an extraordinary item only if it is derived from an extraordinary event.

26 When using discounting to produce an asset value relating either to the date of acquisition or to a subsequent revaluation, a change in the estimated timing of future cash flows would produce a different value if the discounted value were recalculated using the revised estimates. The same would equally apply where liabilities have been valued using discounting techniques. However, the Technical Committee envisages that the basis and assumptions underlying the value, once determined, will not change unless:

(a) the change in the estimates of the timing of future cash flows arises from the correction of a fundamental error;
(b) it is the entity's policy to reappraise its valuations regularly; or
(c) there is a permanent impairment in the value of an asset due to other reasons.

Any such revisions to a valuation should take into account any corresponding changes in interest rates.

INTEREST RATE

27 The determination of the interest rate to be used in a discounting calculation depends upon the purposes of the discounting: whether it is to provide a means of allocation or to calculate a cost or present value.

28 For a problem of allocation when cash flows and present value are both known the internal rate of return (IRR) should be used. The IRR is the rate which equates the initial outlay (proceeds) on an asset (liability) with the present value of the future inflows (outflows) discounted at that rate. Were another rate to be used in the allocation process, a windfall gain or loss would arise.

29 Use of the IRR is consistent with current accounting practice, for example, SSAP 21 'Accounting for leases and hire purchase contracts' and TR677 'Accounting for complex capital issues'. The main advantage of the IRR is its objectivity: if the cash flows are fixed or determinable, the IRR is uniquely defined except in relatively rare circumstances.

30 To use the IRR both the initial cost and the cash flows must be known. This will not be the case when discounting is being used to calculate a present value as an estimate of cost or as a valuation. This situation is recognised in the guidance notes to SSAP 21 in the case of a leased asset for which no market value is known. The guidance notes suggest that a rate of interest should be estimated.

31 In the circumstances where discounting is being used to derive a present value (either as a cost or a valuation) the Technical Committee believes that the rate to be used should normally be a current rate that takes account of the riskiness of the asset and the costs of available finance.

****Editor's note:*** *SSAP 6 has been superseded by FRS 3 'Reporting Financial Performance'.*

The only circumstances where it may not be appropriate to use a current market rate of interest are those where a company is limited in the amount of funds it is able to invest. If the amount available for investment is fixed and cannot be increased even by raising new funds externally (commonly known as 'capital rationing') market rates are less relevant. In such circumstances a more meaningful rate of interest would be the rate of return that could be earned on the best alternative capital purchase by the company. **32**

CHANGES IN THE RATE OF INTEREST

When discounting is used to allocate costs and revenues over time there is no need to revise the calculation as market rates change since market rates are not used in the calculations. If the change in market rates results in a change to the terms of the transaction the effect of which is material the adjustment, being a natural result of estimates inherent in accounting, should be recognised in the accounts in accordance with SSAP 6 (Revised) 'Extraordinary items and prior year adjustments'* (see paragraph 25 above). An example might be when there is a change resulting in a permanent impairment in the benefits to be allocated to future periods. **33**

When using discounting to value an asset or liability, the present value calculation uses a current rate. Accordingly, as this changes over time, the valuation, if recalculated periodically, will change. The Technical Committee envisages that the value of the asset or liability, once determined, will not be changed in the accounts unless there is a subsequent fundamental change in the rate used, or it is the entity's policy to revalue regularly. **34**

CHANGES IN VALUE ARISING FROM DISCOUNTING

Changes in value arising from using discounting as part of the allocation process, (other than changes arising from correction of fundamental errors), should be taken directly to the profit and loss account. There are potentially two places within the detailed profit and loss account that the discounting increment could appear: within the caption appropriate to the relevant benefit or expense subject to allocation or within financing charges. The Technical Committee believes that the presentation should reflect the substance of the item and that discounting increments should be included with other finance items separately disclosed if material. **35**

The treatment of changes in value arising from the valuation basis should be accounted for in accordance with generally accepted accounting principles. The Accounting Standards Committee is currently developing a proposed Statement of Standard Accounting Practice on the topic of Accounting for Fixed Assets including revaluations thereof which will address, *inter alia*, accounting for adjustments to valuations.† **36**

****Superseded by FRS 3.***

*†**Editor's note** See ED 51 'Accounting for fixed assets and valuations'.*

TAXATION

37 Pre-tax cash flows should be used in an allocation calculation. For a valuation calculation the cash flows and interest rate should both be either gross or net of taxation.

38 The calculation of a partial provision for deferred tax in accordance with SSAP 15 could involve the use of discounting. The use in practice of a fixed time horizon is a pragmatic application of the point discussed above in paragraph 24. The Technical Committee advocates the application of discounting to the foreseeable future cash tax liabilities to calculate the deferred tax provision.

PURCHASE PRICE

39 For companies subject to Schedule 4 of the Companies Act 1985 assets are to be carried at purchase price or production cost. Purchase price is defined as the actual price paid plus any expenses incidental to its acquisition. It can be argued therefore that it is not acceptable to show an asset at a discounted amount. However, as indicated in paragraph 16 above this paper adopts the approach that a deferred consideration represents the purchase of two separate assets; the item acquired and the right to pay over an extended period. Accordingly the discounted amount does represent the purchase price of the asset.

LIABILITIES

40 Where discounting is applied to liabilities it may be necessary in certain instances to record in the balance sheet the ultimate liability under creditors and to record the discount as an asset. The Companies Act 1985 does not contain any valuation rules (either historical cost accounting rules or alternative accounting rules) for liabilities. Paragraph 24, Schedule 4, Companies Act 1985 states:

> '(1) Where the amount repayable on any debt owed by a company is greater than the value of the consideration received in the transaction giving rise to the debt, the amount of the difference may be treated as an asset.
>
> (2) Where any such amount is so treated –
>
> (a) it shall be written off by reasonable amounts each year and must be completely written off before repayment of the debt; and
>
> (b) if the current amount is not shown as a separate item in the company's balance sheet it must be disclosed in a note to the accounts.'

41 Taking as an example a company that issues a three year bond, receiving £6,000 at the date of issue and having to pay £10,000 to the bondholders at the end of year three. If the terms of the contract are such that if the contract is terminated early the company still has to pay the full £10,000 then the balance sheet should record the liability over the life of the bond as £10,000 together with a corresponding debit balance equal to the deferred charge. However, if the liability gradually increases from £6,000 to £10,000 over the three year period then the balance sheet

liability should not be recorded as the full £10,000 at each intervening balance sheet date but should start at £6,000 and gradually build up to £10,000 by the end of year three.

DISCLOSURE

The accounting policy followed in respect of discounting should be explained in the notes to the accounts. **42**

In order to assist the user of financial statements the following disclosures are necessary for each class of similar items to which discounting has been applied except in the cases of expert valuations such as pension costs and property where specific disclosures are already prescribed: **43**

(1) Rate used
(2) Timescale involved
(3) The balance sheet value of the items that have been subject to the discounting process
(4) The undiscounted amount.

QUESTIONS FOR COMMENTATORS

The Technical Committee would welcome comments on any part of this discussion paper and, in particular, on the following: **44**

- is the recognition of the time value of money required in certain instances in order that financial statements can give a true and fair view (paragraph 4)?
- do commentators agree that discounting can be used in both allocating costs and calculating a revaluation (paragraphs 13 to 19)?
- do commentators agree that the internal rate of return is the most appropriate rate for allocation within the historical cost accounting framework (paragraph 28)?
- do commentators agree with the views regarding changes in the estimation of the timing of cash flows (paragraphs 25 and 26) and of the interest rate (paragraphs 33 and 34)?
- do commentators agree with the approach suggested to setting an interest rate in circumstances where discounting is used to arrive at a present value and, if so, can commentators suggest specific rates that should be used in specific circumstances (paragraphs 31 and 32)?
- do commentators agree with the suggested disclosures, in particular do commentators believe that additionally an indication of the sensitivity of the discounting calculation would be appropriate (for example the disclosure of the effect of a one-tenth change in interest rate or timing of cash flows)?
- can commentators identify particular items, e.g. deferred tax, for which they may feel discounting is particularly appropriate or inappropriate?
- do commentators consider that either or both of (a) netting (see paragraphs 40 and 41) and (b) allocating the total cash outflows into, say, the cost of a fixed asset and interest payable (see paragraph 39) are contrary to statutory requirements?

Appendix

EXAMPLES

Tax has been ignored in the following examples

1 A company issues a deep discount bond on 1.1.X1 for £157,763. Interest of 4% is payable annually on 31 December. The bond will be redeemed on 31.12.X5 for £200,000.

The company wishes to charge the cost of borrowing (that is, actual interest payable plus an appropriate part of the rolled-up interest) through its profit and loss account each year and has decided that it will use discounting techniques to allocate an equal charge to the profit and loss account in each of the five years.

The total cost of borrowing thus to be charged through the profit and loss account over the five year period is made up as follows:

Annual interest payments (5 x £8,000)	£40,000
Deep discount (£200,000 – £157,763)	£42,237
	£82,237

The internal rate of return, which is the average rate of interest that equates the payments (both interest and principal) on the bond over time to the bond's original issue value, is 9.5%.

Accordingly, the total interest cost charged through the profit and loss account each year will in the circumstances described be equal to 9.5% of the present value at the beginning of each year:

The book-keeping entries each year are:

DR Interest expense CR Cash – for payments
DR Interest expense CR Bond – for rolled up portion

Year	*Profit & Loss a/c charge*	*Interest payable*	*Rolled-up interest charged to P&L a/c*	*Liability* in closing balance sheet*
	(a)	(b)	(a) – (b)	
	£	£	£	£
19X1	14,988 (W1)	8,000	6,988	164,751
19X2	15,651 (W2)	8,000	7,651	172,402
19X3	16,378 (W3)	8,000	8,378	180,780
19X4	17,174 (W4)	8,000	9,174	189,954
19X5	18,046 (W5)	8,000	10,046	200,000
	82,237	40,000	42,237	

*[The liability shown here is the net effect and it may be necessary to show the gross liability of £200,000 and a corresponding debit balance.]

W1 14,988 = 0.095 × £157,763
W2 15,651 = 0.095 × £(157,763 + 6,988) = 0.095 × 164,751
W3 16,378 = 0.095 × £(164,751 + 7,651) = 0.095 × 172,402
W4 17,174 = 0.095 × £(172,402 + 8,378) = 0.095 × 180,780
W5 18,046 = 0.095 × £(180,780 + 9,174) = 0.095 × 189,954

A company sells, on 31.12.X1, an asset for £10,000 receivable on 31.12.X3. The net 2
book value of the asset at the date of sale is £7,500.

The company has adopted an accounting policy of discounting. Accordingly the sale proceeds, at the date of sale, will be recorded as the present value of the future receivable.

The company has agreed that the appropriate rate of interest is 10%.

The company will reflect the following transactions in its financial statements:

Year	*Balance sheet*	*Profit and loss a/c*
	£	£
19X1	8,265 debtor (W1)	765 credit (W2) – profit on sale
19X2	9,091 debtor (W3)	826 credit (W4) – interest receivable
19X3	{ 10,000 cash nil debtor	909 credit (W5) – interest receivable

W1 At 31.12.X1 – Present value of proceeds receivable $= \dfrac{£10,000}{(1.1)^2} = £8,265$

W2 Profit on sale = £8,265 (W1) – £7,500 = £765

W3 At 31.12.X2 – Present value of proceeds receivable $= \dfrac{£10,000}{(1.1)} = £9,091$

W4 Credit to P&L a/c representing the notional interest on the debtor, being £9,091 – £8,265 which is equal to 10% of £8,265

W5 Credit to P&L a/c representing the notional interest on the debtor, being £10,000 – £9,091 which is equal to 10% of £9,091

[FRAG 3/93]
Provisions for claims in the financial statements of non-life insurers

Guidance issued in February 1993 on behalf of the Council of the Institute of Chartered Accountants in England and Wales on information to be given in financial statements of non-life insurers in respect of claims provisions in cases of material inherent uncertainty.

Contents

Provisions for claims in the financial statements of non-life insurers

INTRODUCTION

This Technical Release addresses the accounting treatment of provisions for claims for non-life business in the financial statements of insurers in cases where there is material inherent uncertainty. 1

The purpose of this Technical Release is to provide guidance on the information to be disclosed in financial statements in relation to: 2

- the bases of accounting adopted;
- material inherent uncertainty in establishing the appropriate level of claims provisions; and
- adjustments to claims provisions made in previous accounting periods.

A distinction needs to be drawn between normal accounting estimates of the level of provisions required for the purposes of financial statements and estimates where there is a wide range of potential outcomes and there is a particular difficulty in determining where a reasonable level of provisions should lie. The former situation may be adequately dealt with by adjustments to financial statements in following years and, consequently, no detailed disclosure may be necessary. However, in the latter situation, the position may, depending on the extent of the uncertainty and its materiality in relation to the financial statements as a whole, need to be explained. 3

Insurance is, by its nature, concerned with risk and uncertainty and the position as explained in paragraph 3 for the generality of companies is therefore of particular importance to users of financial statements of insurers. Whilst there will be many types of insurance business where it will not be necessary to explain the position in the notes of financial statements, there will be situations, such as London Market business, where, subject to materiality in relation to the financial statements as a whole, it may be appropriate to do so. Examples of situations where there is likely to be material inherent uncertainty in relation to a reasonable level of claims provisions would include significant exposure to 'long-tail' business such as latent diseases and environmental pollution. 4

This guidance takes into account the work on inherent uncertainties contained in the Exposure Draft 'Auditors' Reports on Financial Statements' issued by the Auditing Practices Board in May 1992.* It may be necessary to revise this guidance on the publication of the full Statement of Auditing Standards. Until that time, the guidance should be regarded as indicative of best practice. 5

***Editor's note:** *The wording on inherent uncertainties in the final Statement of Auditing Standards differs from that in the expsoure draft – see paragraph 54 of SAS 600, issued May 1993.*

BACKGROUND

6 In July 1991, the Accounting Standards Board issued a draft Statement of Principles entitled 'The Objective of Financial Statements and the Qualitative Characteristics of Financial Information' which stated (*inter alia*):

> 'To be useful, information must be reliable. Information has the quality of reliability when it is free from material error and bias and can be depended upon by users to represent faithfully in terms of valid description that which it either purports to represent or could reasonably be expected to represent.'

7 The ASB's statement went on to address the primary characteristics of reliable information and stated (*inter alia*):

> 'Most financial information is subject to some risk of being less than a faithful representation of that which it purports to portray. This is not due to bias, but rather to inherent difficulties either in identifying the transactions and other events to be measured or in devising and applying measurement and presentation techniques that can convey messages that correspond with those transactions and events. In certain cases, the measurement of the financial effect of items could be so uncertain that enterprises generally would not recognise them in financial statements. In other cases, however, it may be relevant to recognise items and to disclose the risk of error surrounding their recognition and measurement.'

8 In May 1992, the Auditing Practices Board issued an Exposure Draft of a Statement of Auditing Standards entitled 'Auditors' Reports on Financial Statements'; Standard 6 is as follows:

> 'Auditors should draw attention in their report to inherent uncertainties in order to ensure that the reader appreciates fully the context in which the auditors' opinion was formed, when those uncertainties:
> - affect the validity of the going concern assumption; or
> - involve possible outcomes falling within a range which is unusually or exceptionally wide in relation to the financial statements; or
> - involve possible outcomes which are so material and pervasive in their possible effects that resolution of the matter could significantly alter the view given by the financial statements;
>
> notwithstanding that in the auditors' opinion the inherent uncertainties have been properly accounted for and adequate disclosure made such that there is no cause for qualification of their opinion in this respect.
>
> When the disclosures of such uncertainties contained in the financial statements are, in the auditors' opinion, inadequate they should issue a qualified opinion.'

INHERENT UNCERTAINTY

9 In an insurance transaction, there is typically uncertainty as to:

- whether a claim will occur;

- when it will occur;
- what the cost will be; and
- when it will be paid.

The degree of uncertainty inherent in the estimation of claims provisions depends not only on the nature of the business written but also on: 10

- the basis of underwriting.
  An insurer can underwrite a risk either directly or through reinsuring the risk from another insurer. In the case of reinsurance, the reinsurer can agree, in return for a proportion of the original premium, to accept liability for the same proportion of each related claim (proportional reinsurance) or can accept liability for claims above a certain agreed level which is normally subject to an upper limit (non-proportional reinsurance).
- the structure of the reinsurance programme.
  The insurer may choose to seek to reinsure much of the business accepted or may prefer to reinsure only higher than anticipated claims. Additionally, it is possible to cover fully certain layers of insurance or alternatively to cover such layers only partially.
- the claims' settlement pattern.
  For some claims, such as property damage, the settlement of claims is finalised within a short time of the expiry of the period covered ('short-tail' business). In other instances, such as latent diseases, the loss may only become apparent many years after the period in which the event giving rise to the loss occurred. It may then take a further significant period to determine the nature and extent of the insurer's liability before the claim can be settled ('long-tail' business).

Thus, an insurer with a 'short-tail' book of business with a comprehensive reinsurance programme may be able to establish the net amount likely to be required for claims with reasonable certainty, notwithstanding that there may be uncertainties regarding the appropriate level of gross provisions. However, for a company with a 'long-tail' book of business, there may be considerable uncertainty as to the appropriate level of the provision for claims, irrespective of the nature of the reinsurance programme. 11

BASES OF ACCOUNTING

The majority of insurance business is accounted for on an annual basis. However, it is not always possible to determine a result with the required degree of certainty using the annual accounting basis because of the extent of the inherent uncertainty attaching to certain classes of business; accordingly: 12

- where this is the case but a result can be determined with the required degree of certainty after a further twelve months, the 'deferred annual basis' of accounting is used; and
- where a result cannot be determined with reasonable certainty on a deferred annual basis, the 'fund basis' is used, the fund not being 'closed' until there is sufficient information available to provide the requisite degree of certainty (usually after three years but sometimes longer); whilst profits are not recognised on funded

business until the account is closed, any anticipated deficiencies in the fund are made good as soon as they are identified.

13 Details of these three methods are set out in the Statement of Recommended Practice 'Accounting for insurance business' issued by the Association of British Insurers in May 1990.

ADJUSTMENTS TO ACCOUNTING ESTIMATES

14 Because of the difficulty in estimating claims costs, provisions need to be adjusted in the light of subsequent information or events, such adjustments being reflected in the accounting period in which they are made. For accounting periods commencing on or after 1 January 1995, UK insurers will be required to disclose information in the notes to financial statements relating to material adjustments made to claims provisions established in previous accounting periods (in accordance with the requirements of Article 38(2) of the EC Insurance Accounts Directive*).

RECOMMENDATIONS

15 Financial statements of non-life insurers should indicate the basis on which they have been prepared, the policies adopted and should disclose any material inherent uncertainties; accordingly, it is recommended that:

- the basis of accounting should be stated and, where a basis of accounting other than the annual basis is used, the basis should be explained and the reasons for adopting it indicated; an example of appropriate disclosure for an insurer drawing up its financial statements on an annual basis is given in the Appendix.
- where there is material inherent uncertainty in relation to the potential cost of claims, which are material in relation to the accounts as a whole, appropriate disclosure should be made in the financial statements which explains the type of business and the factors which give rise to the uncertainty. An example of appropriate disclosure for an insurer drawing up its financial statements on an annual basis is given in the Appendix.
- where the adjustment made to claims provisions in respect of previous years is material, the fact and the amount should be disclosed in the financial statements.

16 Where there is material inherent uncertainty in relation to the potential cost of claims, which are material in relation to the accounts as a whole, the auditor will need to consider carefully the content of the audit report in the light of the particular circumstances and the extent of the disclosures and explanations by the directors in the financial statements.

***Editor's note:** *Implemented in the UK by the Companies Act 1985 (Insurance Companies Accounts) Regulations 1993 (SI 1993 No 3246).*

Appendix

Example of disclosure in financial statements

Accounting policy

Provision is made on the basis of available information for the estimated ultimate cost of claims notified but not settled at the date of the balance sheet and for claims incurred but not notified at that date; the provision reflects claims' settlement expenses and anticipated reinsurance and other recoveries.

Note

The claims provision includes amounts in respect of potential claims relating to environmental pollution. Legislative and judicial actions to date have failed to determine the basis of liability to indemnify losses. These claims are not expected to be settled for many years and there is considerable uncertainty as to the amounts at which they will be settled.

The level of the provision has been set on the basis of the information which is currently available, including potential outstanding loss advice, experience of development of similar claims and case law. Whilst the directors consider that the gross provision for claims and the related reinsurance recoveries are fairly stated on the basis of the information currently available to them, the ultimate liability will vary as a result of subsequent information and events and may result in significant adjustments to the amount provided. Adjustments to the amounts of provisions are reflected in the financial statements for the period in which the adjustments are made. The methods used, and the estimates made, are reviewed regularly.

Interim financial reporting – a consultative paper

(Issued September 1993)

Contents

Interim financial reporting – a consultative paper

I – Preface

INTRODUCTION

Listed companies have published interim financial reports ('interim reports') for many years. Interim reports are generally seen as a very important aspect of financial reporting, particularly as far as the stock market is concerned. Despite this there have been no accounting standards or similar guidance issued on the subject in the UK, except that for listed companies the Stock Exchange has laid down a number of specific requirements. These have recently been updated and are summarised in the Appendix. **1.1**

The increasing importance of interim financial reporting has been underlined by the 'Report of the Committee on the Financial Aspects of Corporate Governance' (the Cadbury Report). The Cadbury Committee recommended the disclosure of balance sheet *information*, and for consideration to be given to the inclusion of cash flow *information*. The Cadbury Committee called on the Accounting Standards Board (ASB), in conjunction with the Stock Exchange, to clarify the rules on interim financial reporting. The ASB has asked the Financial Reporting Committee of the Institute of Chartered Accountants in England and Wales (the Committee) to assist it in this regard. The project is being carried out by a working party which includes representatives from the profession, the business sector, financial analysts and some of the other CCAB bodies. **1.2**

The present document is in the form of a draft set of proposals prepared by the Committee for the ASB. The ASB is likely in due course to publish a formal exposure draft prior to finalising a statement on the subject. Although these proposals are written in the style of a proposed accounting standard, their ultimate form is at this stage not clear. **1.3**

Accounting standards generally apply to annual financial statements which are intended to give a true and fair view. Interim reports are much briefer than annual financial statements and, even if their content is improved as a result of this present exercise, they will still be substantially briefer than full financial statements. In general, the same measurement principles should be used for interim reporting as those set out in accounting standards and UITF abstracts which are used in preparing annual financial statements, except where this paper specifies a different treatment. **1.4**

Another important issue which is at present unclear is that of enforcement. In the context of annual financial statements, not only do accounting standards apply to them but also they are policed (in the case of public companies) by the Financial Reporting Review Panel. The ASB consider that the enforcement of an accounting standard that applies to interim reporting would be outside the terms of reference of the Review Panel. Quite apart from the position of the Review Panel, compliance with the Stock Exchange requirements is supervised by the Stock Exchange. However, in so far as this current project increases the disclosure and measurement requirements relating to **1.5** interim reports, it is at this stage unclear whether the Stock Exchange would adopt those enhanced requirements and incorporate them within a future version of its Yellow Book.

GENERAL APPROACH

1.6 Against this background, the proposals in this paper deal with:

- the disclosure requirements relating to interim reports;
- the measurement basis to be adopted;
- the meaning of 'balance sheet information'; and
- the meaning of 'cash flow information'

The proposals for balance sheet and cash flow information are put forward in response to the Cadbury Report, rather than being based on detailed research analysing the cost/benefit considerations.

1.7 The proposals do not deal with:

- the frequency of interim reports (for example, whether they should be half-yearly or quarterly); or
- the timeliness of interim reporting (that is, how soon after the end of the interim period an interim report should be published).

These two matters are seen as the province of the Stock Exchange and not of the accounting standard setters.

1.8 Furthermore, the proposals do not deal with the audit or review of interim financial statements, although the Auditing Practices Board is developing guidance on such matters in parallel with this project.*

BALANCE SHEET INFORMATION

1.9 In using the term 'balance sheet information', the Cadbury Committee evidently had in mind that companies might be asked to give some information about the balance sheet, but less than a full balance sheet. The Financial Reporting Committee has considered what form or extent of disclosure would be useful to users of accounts but, at the same time, would not be unduly burdensome on preparers. It has considered the possibility of requiring companies to publish selected figures from the balance sheet (such as fixed assets, net current assets, total debt etc.); but has rejected this on the grounds that individual figures of that nature would be very difficult to interpret without the context of the other figures in the balance sheet. On the other hand, the Committee takes the view that it is not necessary to give a balance sheet in the full detail that is required at the year end. It appears that the most useful approach would be to require companies to give a summarised balance sheet, with all the main headings but dropping some of the detail found at the year end. For this purpose, the degree of summarisation used in Summary Financial Statements seems appropriate.

***Editor's note:** *Bulletin 1993/1 'Review of interim financial information' was issued in November 1993.*

CASH FLOW INFORMATION

In a similar way, the Committee has considered what the phrase 'cash flow information' should be taken to mean. It is also mindful of the fact that the Cadbury recommendation relating to cash flow statements was weaker than that relating to interim balance sheets. Despite this, the Committee believes that cash flow information is very important and, at the interim date, at least as important as the balance sheet. **1.10**

It, therefore, believes that companies should give summarised cash flow statements at the interim date, at about the same level of detail as the summarised balance sheet. Cash flow statements do not form part of Summary Financial Statements and, therefore, that model cannot be used. However, it seems that a similar level of detail would be given by requiring a total for each of the five main categories of cash flows specified by FRS 1 (that is: operating activities; returns on investment and servicing of finance; taxation; investing activities; and financing; with a sub-total after investing activities, and with the total being the movement in cash and cash equivalents).

As with all the proposed requirements, this would be the minimum disclosure. Companies might, for example, wish to provide in addition a reconciliation from operating profit to operating cash flow. Companies may find it useful or necessary to give further analysis of other categories. An example would be where the 'investing' heading is distorted by major inflows or outflows relating to non-cash equivalent short-term investments. **1.11**

PROFIT AND LOSS ACCOUNT – DEGREE OF DETAIL

The present requirements relating to the profit and loss account are those laid down by the Stock Exchange. The Committee consider it is appropriate to increase these requirements slightly, in two respects: **1.12**

- to add the lines that are required by the regulations for Summary Financial Statements, that is: income from interests in associated undertakings; interest receivable and similar income; and interest payable and similar charges.
- to add a requirement for disclosure of those exceptional items that are required by FRS 3 to be shown after trading profit and before the interest line. Although not exactly the same as former extraordinary items under SSAP 6, they are similar and in that sense the requirement is not really additional to SSAP 6.

Directors' emoluments are required to be disclosed in Summary Financial Statements but the Committee does not propose that item should be included in the interim report. **1.13**

STATEMENT OF TOTAL RECOGNISED GAINS AND LOSSES/INTERIM VALUATIONS

If a balance sheet as well as the profit and loss account is to be published at the interim stage, then it seems appropriate for companies also to publish a statement of total recognised gains and losses, as being both an important part of the reporting of **1.14** performance in its own right, and also a link between the profit and loss account and the balance sheet. The Committee proposes that this statement should be included to show, as at the year end, all gains and losses that have been recognised in the financial statements for the interim period. However, this is not to say that all value changes and other gains and losses should be recognised at the end of the interim period; merely that the statement should include them if they are recognised. For instance, foreign currency translation differences arising in the period would normally be included. By contrast, the Committee does not believe it is appropriate to require companies to reflect, at the interim stage, changes in the value of fixed assets. The Committee takes the view that revaluations adopted in annual financial statements are adequate. On the other hand, if revaluations are made (for example an investment company that continuously revalues its fixed asset investments), then such gains and losses should be included in the statement.

MEASUREMENT OF INTERIM RESULTS

1.15 One of the major issues is whether interim reporting should involve the same accounting principles as are used at the year end or whether different principles should be applied. There are two fundamentally different theoretical approaches: the 'discrete period' approach and the 'integral' approach. The discrete period approach treats each interim period as an accounting period in isolation, whereas the integral approach treats the interim period as a part of the annual period and attempts to relate the interim results to the expected results for the year. The essential difference between the two approaches is that, under the integral approach, items are allocated to interim periods based on estimates of the total annual revenue and expenses. Consequently, profits fluctuate less under the integral approach than under the discrete period approach. However, the resulting assets and liabilities would not fit the definitions in the ASB's proposed Statement of Principles.

1.16 On the other hand, the discrete period approach has the important advantage that the elements of financial statements – assets, liabilities, revenues and expenses – are defined in the same way as for annual financial statements. Volatility, previously regarded as a disadvantage of the discrete approach, will often be a feature of financial statements following the introduction of FRS 3.

1.17 Neither the discrete period nor the integral approaches in their pure, or extreme, form produces entirely sensible results. As a result, a 'combined' approach is often applied in practice. Interim reports are prepared under the discrete period approach, in the same manner as annual financial statements, but 'integral' adjustments are made so as the ensure that the interim reports are not misleading. The combined approach has no theoretical basis but reflects a pragmatic view that interim reports need to be interpreted in conjunction with the annual financial statements.

1.18 There can be difficulties associated with defining the terms 'discrete period method' and 'integral method' and with prescribing one or the other method for us in practice. The Committee proposes that the general principle of measurement should be that the same accounting principles should be adopted at the interim reporting date as are used at the year end. This approach should ensure consistency of treatment without the need to define new bases of accounting. However, if different accounting policies are used, the interim report should contain an explanation of the reasons for, and quantification of the effect of, the departure.

II – Proposed statement

SCOPE

Principles adopted for interim financial reporting should apply to all entities that are required to issue interim financial reports ('interim reports'). Other entities, including non-profit organisations, that voluntarily issue such reports are encouraged to comply with the principles set out in this statement. 2.1

This statement is primarily concerned with clarification of the accounting procedures – measurement and disclosure – to be followed in preparing interim reports, rather than the frequency and timeliness of interim reports which, in the case of listed companies, is regulated by the Stock Exchange. However, timeliness is important and the value of interim reports to users is that more frequent and timely information is available than that provided by the annual financial statements. 2.2

This statement does not address the need for interim reports to be audited although it is likely that, in most cases, they will have been reviewed by an auditor. 2.3

PRESENTATION OF FINANCIAL INFORMATION

Interim reports should be presented on a consolidated basis by entities that present their annual financial statements on a consolidated basis. In addition to the primary statements, interim reports should include an explanation of the main factors underlying the performance during the interim period and the financial position at the end of the period. 2.4

An interim report should include a summarised profit and loss account. As a minimum, the summarised profit and loss account should comprise the following information: 2.5

- Turnover;
- Income from interests in associated undertakings;
- Operating profit;
- Interest receivable and similar income;
- Interest payable and similar charges;
- Profit or loss on ordinary activities before tax;
- Tax on profit or loss on ordinary activities;
- Profit or loss on ordinary activities after tax;
- Minority interests;
- [Extraordinary items] (included only to show positioning);
- Profit or loss for the period; and
- Dividends paid and proposed.

The following items should be shown separately in the summarised profit and loss account after operating profit and before interest:

- Profits and losses on the sale or termination of an operation;
- Costs of a fundamental reorganisation or restructuring having a material effect on the nature and focus of the reporting entity's operations; and
- Profits or losses on the disposal of fixed assets.

2.6 Earnings per share, based on the profit for the period and calculated in accordance with SSAP3 'Earnings per share' (as amended), should be disclosed.

2.7 Turnover and results relating to discontinued operations should be separately disclosed and included in the determination of profit or loss for the interim period in which they occur, in accordance with FRS3 'Reporting financial performance'.

2.8 Exceptional items and extraordinary items should be shown separately in the summarised profit and loss account. Exceptional items should not be aggregated under one heading. An adequate description of each exceptional item and each extraordinary item should be given to enable the nature of the item to be understood.

2.9 An interim report should include a summarised balance sheet. As a minimum, the summarised balance sheet should comprise the following information:

- Fixed assets;
- Current assets;
- *Prepayments and accrued income;
- Creditors: amounts falling due within one year;
- Net current assets (liabilities);
- Total assets less current liabilities;
- Creditors: amounts falling due after more than one year;
- Provisions for liabilities and charges;
- *Accruals and deferred income;
- Capital and reserves; and
- Minority interests.

* Only relevant for separate disclosure if the 'alternative format' is normally used for the balance sheet in the annual accounts.

2.10 A statement of total recognised gains and losses should be included in the interim report where gains or losses are recognised in the interim period. However, where an entity has no recognised gains or losses other than the profit or loss for the period, a statement of total recognised gains and losses need not be provided. A note explaining the reason for excluding the statement should be included immediately below the summarised profit and loss account. Where it is an entity's policy to revalue assets only at the year-end, or on a less frequent basis, and no valuation has been carried out in the interim period, this should be stated.

2.11 An interim report should include a summarised cash flow statement. The summarised cash flow statement should include the totals of each of the principal categories of cash flows, together with the movement in cash and cash equivalents. Supporting notes may also be provided.

As a minimum, the summarised cash flow statement should comprise the following cash flows: 2.12

- Net cash flow from operating activities;
- Returns on investment and servicing of finance;
- Taxation;
- Investing activities;
- Net cash flow before financing; and
- Financing.

The following items should be disclosed in notes to the interim report of in a statement forming part of the interim report, together with an explanation where applicable: 2.13

- changes in capital structure and financing since the previous year-end;
- any major fixed asset or investment acquisitions and disposals during the period;
- significant changes in contingencies and commitments since the previous year-end;
- Significant events arising after the end of the period; and
- any other matters of significance to users.

CORRESPONDING AMOUNTS

Corresponding amounts should be shown for the previous corresponding interim period and for the whole of the previous year. 2.14

SEASONALITY

Where an entity's business is seasonal, the interim report should include a description of the seasonal nature of the activities and should provide adequate information to enable the performance of the business during the interim period and its financial position at the end of the period to be understood, in the context of the whole year. 2.15

CHANGES IN ACCOUNTING POLICY AND PRIOR PERIOD ADJUSTMENTS

Changes in accounting policy and other prior period adjustments should be applied retrospectively, with restatement of prior periods, in accordance with FRS3 'Reporting financial performance'. An adequate description of each item should be given to enable the nature of the change or adjustment to be understood. 2.16

ACCOUNTING TREATMENT AND RELATED DISCLOSURE

The preparation of financial information presented in interim reports should be based on accounting principles and practices consistent with those used in the preparation of annual financial statements except as regards taxation (see paragraph 2.19 below). A statement to this effect should be included in the interim report. 2.17

2.18 The interim report should also state:

- the period to which the interim report relates;
- the date on which the interim report is approved by the board of directors;
- that the interim report should be read in conjunction with the most recent annual financial statements; and
- if an accounting policy used for preparing the interim report is not consistent with the accounting policy used in preparing the most recent annual financial statements, the interim accounting policy used and the effect of adopting a different policy.

TAXATION

2.19 Taxation for an interim period should be recognised on the following basis:

- current and deferred taxation should be included at the end of the interim period using an estimate of the likely effective tax rate for the whole year and should be disclosed separately in the interim report.
- tax effects relating to exceptional and extraordinary items should be shown separately in the profit and loss account.
- deferred tax assets should not be carried forward, except to the extent that they are expected to be recoverable without replacement by equivalent debit balances.

SEGMENTED INFORMATION

2.20 Financial information segmented by industry and geographical area should be disclosed in the interim report, using the same segment classification as that adopted in the annual financial statements. The information presented should comprise:

- segment turnover, distinguishing between external sales and inter-segment sales if inter-segment sales are significant; and
- segment operating profit or loss before taxation, minority interests and extraordinary items; and
- segment net assets, where there has been a significant change since the previous year-end.

III – Explanation

GENERAL

3.1 Interim financial reports provide a useful source of information about an entity's activities between the release of the previous year's annual report and the current year's preliminary profit announcement. However, the information contained in interim reports is less extensive than that in annual reports. Particular attention therefore needs to be given to its relevance and reliability, characteristics that may often conflict. It must also be timely and understandable.

FREQUENCY

The Stock Exchange currently requires only half-yearly reports, although some companies, particularly those subject to US filing regulations, issue quarterly reports. Whilst there may be a gradual trend towards more frequent reporting, it is considered more important to improve the relevance and reliability of information contained in interim reports than to increase their frequency. The proposed statement is therefore framed on the basis that interim reports should be prepared regularly and should present information for a period comprising the first part of the financial year, normally the first six months. Where a change in year-end is proposed, a listed company is required to consult the Stock Exchange as to the period to be covered by the interim report. 3.2

CONTENT OF INTERIM REPORTS

In the past, the content of interim reports has varied widely but most UK companies have provided little more than the minimum information required by the Stock Exchange (see Appendix). However, there are indications that an increasing proportion of large listed companies are including balance sheets and, to a lesser extent, cash flow statements, in their interim reports. This trend is consistent with practices in a number of other countries, such as the US and Canada, Australia and New Zealand. 3.3

In addition, the Cadbury Report has recommended the inclusion of balance sheet information and has proposed that consideration be given to producing cash flow information. 3.4

There are some advantages of including full interim balance sheets and cash flow statements, for example: 3.5

(a) if an item is required to be disclosed in order to show a true and fair view in the annual financial statements, there is a view that it also needs to be disclosed in the interim report;
(b) when making investment or credit decisions based on interim reports, users need a balance sheet to evaluate a company's capital structure, solvency and operational efficiency;
(c) presentation of full financial statements assists the user of interim reports in understanding, interpreting and analysing the information presented.

However: 3.6

(a) interim reports are subordinate to, and should be read in conjunction with, annual financial statements;
(b) information needs of users are different at the interim stage to those at the year-end and can be adequately met by providing summarised information;
(c) presentation of selected financial information rather than a full interim balance sheet and cash flow statement may better serve the interests of users and shareholders in providing timely information at an acceptable cost.

Avoiding unnecessary detail will normally increase the cost-effectiveness of an interim 3.7

report, bearing in mind that such statements are not often read in isolation but are used to update information contained in previously issued annual financial statements. A requirement for *summarised information* is therefore consistent with the role of interim reports in a continuing reporting process.

MANAGEMENT COMMENTARY

3.8 As part of the continuing reporting process, the issue of an interim report provides an opportunity to discuss and explain the main factors underlying the entity's performance and financial position. Many interim reports already include a detailed commentary of this nature so as to meet, as a minimum, the Stock Exchange requirement for 'an explanatory statement on group activities that ... includes any significant information enabling investors to make an informed assessment of the trend of the group's activities and profit and loss.'

3.9 In July 1993, the ASB issued a statement setting out the recommended content of an Operating and Financial Review (OFR) to supplement the annual accounts of large companies. The statement provides a voluntary framework for presenting information in two broad sections. The *operating* section would normally include a discussion of the result and business trends, the main influences that may have an impact on the business, and the ways in which the business is investing to meet future needs. The *financial* review would cover such aspects as the capital structure, treasury policies, cash flow and current liquidity, borrowing requirements and any restrictions on the transfer of funds held overseas.

3.10 To enable the users of interim reports to gain a better understanding of the financial circumstances of the business, companies should consider which of the OFR items should be included in order to meet the requirements of the Stock Exchange and of this statement. For instance, amongst the areas identified in the ASB statement, the following may include several issues that require comment:

(a) the operating results (including a discussion of the main factors and influences that may affect future results, reference to the main risks and uncertainties, any new or discontinued activities, acquisitions or disposals, and any significant external factors, such as changes in exchange rates or interest rates); and

(b) the company's financial needs and resources (including a discussion of treasury policy, current liquidity and the reasons for any changes in capital structure since the year-end).

3.11 In addition, the commentary may need to refer to such matters as dividend policy, in that many financial analysts regard the interim dividend as an indicator of the expected dividend for the year; where business is seasonal, management often discuss the extent to which the interim results reflect the level to be expected, bearing in mind the company's previous trading pattern and its probable performance for the year.

ACCOUNTING TREATMENT

The proposed statement is based on the view that, for the reporting entity, an interim period, like a financial year, is a distinct financial period. Interim reports should therefore be prepared on the same basis as annual financial statements. With certain exceptions, identified below, similar problems of allocation will arise in the measurement of income and expenditure for an interim period as for a full year. The same accounting treatment should therefore be followed, based on the fundamental accounting concepts set out in SSAP2. **3.12**

The issues that need to be considered separately are: **3.13**

(a) Taxation, which is normally assessed on an annual basis and therefore requires the use of an estimated effective tax rate for the year (paragraph 3.25);
(b) Expenses (and income) determined on an annual basis (paragraph 3.15); and
(c) Seasonal businesses, for which expenses and income are not spread evenly throughout the year (paragraph 3.16).

Expenses that are directly associated with, or allocated to, products sold or services rendered should be recognised in the same interim period as the income. All other cost and expenses should be recognised in interim periods on the basis of time expired, benefit received, or activity associated with the period. As in the case of annual financial statements, if the actual amounts are not known, appropriate estimates and assumptions should be made to recognise costs and revenues in the period to which they relate. Where, either due to the nature of the item or the short period involved, an estimate may be subject to substantial adjustment at the year-end, this fact should be disclosed. **3.14**

ANNUALLY DETERMINED EXPENDITURE AND INCOME

Certain items of expenditure and income are only formally determined once each year. Examples are management bonuses, staff profit sharing, volume discount (on both purchases and sales), sales commissions and rent based on income or sales. An estimate of the effective rate at which each item will accrue during the year should be made so as to determine the element relating to the interim period. The same approach should be taken as would be the case in annual financial statements if the bonus, discount etc related to a date which differed from the accounting year end. **3.15**

SEASONALITY

Where the seasonal nature of a business follows an annual cycle, disclosure of figures for the comparative period in the prior year will not show the effect of seasonality. Where seasonality is a factor, additional information should therefore be provided so that users of interim reports may understand the seasonal nature of the business and assess the impact of seasonality on the interim results. One or more of the following methods are normally used: **3.16**

- to provide results for both interim periods of the prior year;
- to present a historical summary covering a number of previous years; or

- to include a table showing results in the interim period and the previous interim period as percentages of those for the respective year.

  As the type of seasonality varies from one business to another, it may not be possible to identify a single most appropriate method of presenting its impact. However, notwithstanding the method adopted, it will be necessary to provide a narrative explanation of the seasonality of the business.

CORRESPONDING AMOUNTS

3.17 The selection of comparative figures is not generally an issue in preparing annual financial statements because the format is well established. However, in an interim report, comparative figures are a potential area of divergence in that different 'comparative periods' could be used:

(a) the corresponding period in the previous year, thus enabling year-on-year comparison to be made; or
(b) the previous year's annual result, assisting a user to evaluate trends and to forecast annual results.

3.18 Current reporting practice favours a three-column approach comprising the current period, the prior year's corresponding period and the most recent annual figures. As a minimum, it is envisaged that interim reports should provide comparative figures that include those for the previous corresponding interim period and those for the most recent financial year. The presentation adopted should indicate the extent to which information for each of these periods has been audited.

DISCONTINUED OPERATIONS

3.20 Turnover and results relating to discontinued operations should be separately disclosed and included in the determination of profit or loss for the interim period in which the discontinuation occurs, in accordance with FRS3. For this purpose, operations are classified as discontinued when the sale or termination is completed *either* in the interim period *or* before the earlier of three months after the end of the interim period and the date on which the interim report is approved. It may be appropriate to disclose separately in the interim report the results of operations which, although not discontinued, are in the process of being discontinued or it has been announced will be discontinued before the year-end.

EXCEPTIONAL ITEMS AND EXTRAORDINARY ITEMS

3.21 In general, exceptional and extraordinary items do not extend over more than a year nor is it normally logical to allocate them over the different parts of a year. By definition, exceptional and extraordinary items are both unusual in nature and significant in amount and it is important that they are separately disclosed in the profit and loss account for the interim period. Exceptional and extraordinary items should therefore be recognised in the interim period in which they occur, with appropriate explanation in the notes to the interim report. In assessing the significance of an exceptional item or extraordinary item arising in the interim period, its materiality should be judged in the context of the interim period rather than in relation to the expected results or total assets for the year.

EARNINGS PER SHARE

Interim earnings per share should be based on the results of the interim period. FRS3 requires that, where a reporting entity wishes to present an additional earnings per share figure, calculated on another level of earnings, the reason for doing so should be stated; the additional figure should be presented on a consistent basis and with no greater prominence than that calculated in accordance with FRS3. If an entity presents an additional earnings per share figure in its annual financial statements, it may also wish to provide this information in its interim report. In this case, it should be calculated in the same way as at the year-end and reconciled to the earnings per share figure calculated in accordance with FRS3, which should be presented with no less prominence than the alternative earnings per share figure. 3.22

CHANGES IN ACCOUNTING POLICIES AND FUNDAMENTAL ERRORS

When a change in accounting policy or the correction of a fundamental error occurs during an interim period, the question arises as to whether it should be dealt with in the interim report or whether its presentation should await the annual financial statements. 3.23

- The Stock Exchange's basic requirement is that the accounting policies and presentation of figures in interim reports should be consistent with those in the annual financial statements. Decisions to change an accounting policy are normally made at the year-end. However, in the event of such a decision being taken during an interim period, the change should be applied retroactively. In their interim reports, entities are encouraged to use accounting policies that will be used at the year-end and therefore to apply any changes in accounting policy retroactively to the figures for the interim period. Figures for the comparative interim period should be restated or, where they are not restated, the effect of the change should be disclosed.
- When a fundamental error is discovered during an interim period, the prior period adjustment should be applied in full as soon as it is recognised.

All prior period adjustments required by FRS3 should therefore be applied in interim periods in the same way as they are in annual financial statements. 3.24

TAXATION

Unlike most items, the tax charge for an interim period cannot be absolutely determined until the end of the financial year. Many UK companies adopt an approach which recognises that taxation is an annual charge. The effective tax rate for the year is therefore calculated, based on a prudent estimate of the taxation charge (or credit) for 3.25

the year expressed as a percentage of the expected accounting profit (or loss). This rate is then applied to the interim profit (or loss). Use of the effective rate for the year consequently results in taxation, including permanent and timing tax differences, being recognised ratably over the year as a whole.

3.26 The general approach of making a prudent estimate of the effective tax rate for the year should be employed even where, for example, a company's result in the first half of the year is expected to be wholly or completely offset by its result in the second half year. Even if the overall result is a break-even, there will still be an effective tax rate (say 30%). The full year's tax of nil is, conceptually, 30% of no profit, rather than 0%. Thus that tax rate should be applied to both profits and losses. However, if tax relief is booked against a loss in the interim period, the deferred tax asset should be carried forward at the interim date only when it is expected to be recoverable without replacement by an equivalent debit balance.

STOCK

3.27 Stock at the end of an interim period should normally be recognised on the same basis as that used in preparing annual financial statements. If the basis used at the end of the interim period differs from that used at the year-end, the method used, the reason for adopting a different method and the effect should be disclosed.

3.28 Stock diminutions resulting from a decline in market prices should not be deferred beyond the interim period in which the decline occurs unless the diminution is temporary and no loss in value is expected at the year-end. In certain circumstances, the application of year-end stock valuation policies at an interim date can be misleading. This may occur, for example, if diminutions in the value of stock during an interim period are written off to the profit and loss account even though, due to seasonality, such diminutions would be expected to reverse by the year-end. Whilst it may be appropriate to require that stock diminutions resulting from a decline in market prices are not deferred beyond the interim period in which the decline occurs, temporary diminutions need not be recognised in interim results if no loss is expected at the year-end.

FOREIGN EXCHANGE

3.29 In the past, some companies have translated interim figures on the basis of exchange rates relating to the previous year. This approach is inconsistent with the accounting treatment proposed. Foreign exchange translation should be based on the exchange rate relating to the interim period; this could be the average rate or the closing rate, according to the accounting policy adopted at the year-end.

Appendix – Summary of the Stock Exchange Yellow Book requirements for interim reports

An explanatory statement on group activities that '... *includes any significant information enabling investors to make an informed assessment of the trend of the group's activities and profit and loss*'

There should also be:

- an explanation of any special factor which has influenced the activities and the profit or loss for the period;
- information to enable a comparison to be made with the corresponding previous period; and
- so far as possible, a reference to the group's prospects in the current financial year.

The accounting policies and presentation of figures must be consistent with those applied to the annual statements.

A profit and loss account that includes:

- net turnover;
- profit or loss before taxation and extraordinary items;
- taxation on profits;
- minority interests;
- profit or loss attributable to shareholders, before extraordinary items;
- extraordinary items (net of taxation);
- profit or loss attributable to shareholders;
- rates of dividends paid and proposed and amount absorbed thereby;
- earnings per share expressed as pence per share; and
- comparative figures for all of the above for the corresponding period in the preceding financial year.

If figures are not audited, a statement to that effect; where figures are audited, the report of the auditors, including any qualification, to be reproduced in full.

[FRAG 35/94]
The application of FRS 5 to general insurance transactions

Guidance issued in December 1994 by the Institute of Chartered Accountants in England and Wales in relation to the treatment in annual financial statements of general (non-life) insurance transactions under the requirements of FRS 5. This guidance finalises the draft guidance issued in October 1994 as FRAG 27/94 and supersedes TR 862 'Accounting for non-life financial reinsurance: a discussion paper' issued in December 1991.

Contents

INTRODUCTION

Purpose and scope of the Technical Release

Financial Reporting Standard 5 'Reporting the substance of transactions' ('FRS5') applies to all financial statements which are intended to show a true and fair view. In determining the substance of a transaction, all its aspects and implications should be identified and greater weight given to those more likely to have a commercial effect in practice. Transactions are required to be analysed in terms of the assets and liabilities which result from the transaction so that these can be reflected in the financial statements. 1

This Technical Release provides guidance on the application of the requirements of FRS5 to general (ie non-life) insurance transactions (including reinsurance transactions), by both the insured and the insurer; for this purpose insurers include overseas captive insurance subsidiaries of UK groups, Lloyd's syndicates and any other UK entity undertaking such transactions in addition to authorised insurers. 2

This Technical Release uses the terms 'insured' and 'insurer' in relation to insurance transactions; accordingly, where the transaction includes reinsurance, the cedent will be described as the 'insured' and the reinsurer as the 'insurer'. 3

Certain of the principal areas covered by FRS5, in particular linked presentation for certain non-recourse finance arrangements, offset, and identification, accounting for and disclosure of quasi subsidiaries, may be applicable to companies or other reporting entities which undertake insurance transactions. This Technical Release does not, however, expand on the requirements of FRS5 in respect of these areas. 4

FRS5 emphasises the fact that a reporting entity's financial statements should report the substance of the transactions into which it has entered. Contracts which are described as insurance may be structured in a wide range of different ways. It is important that the transaction is fully understood and analysed in order that its substance and the appropriate accounting treatment can be correctly identified. 5

The provisions of this Technical Release should be applied in respect of both prospective and retrospective contracts of insurance. Prospective insurance is where an insurer agrees to indemnify an insured for losses that may be incurred as a result of future insurable events. Retrospective insurance is where an insurer agrees to indemnify an insured for losses that may be incurred as a result of past insurable events. 6

DETERMINATION OF THE SUBSTANCE OF AN INSURANCE TRANSACTION

Insurance is an arrangement whereby one party ('the insurer'), in return for a premium, indemnifies another party ('the insured') against loss, liability or other consequence of an adverse event, in circumstances where, when the indemnity arrangement is entered into, it is uncertain whether such loss event will occur, when it will occur, or what cost it will have. 7

8 A key characteristic of insurance is therefore the transfer and assumption of risk. The risk assumed by the insurer may be underwriting risk (ie the uncertainty as to whether or not the loss event will occur and/or the ultimate amount of any claim payments in respect of the loss event). The insurer may also assume timing risk (ie the uncertainty as to when claim payments will be made). 'Insurance risk', which is transferred under a contract of insurance, may comprise either or both of underwriting risk and timing risk.

9 In considering whether or not a significant transfer of insurance risk has taken place under a contract of insurance, the entity should consider first whether it is reasonably possible that the insurer may realise a significant loss from the contract, and secondly whether there is reasonable possibility of a significant range of outcomes under the contract. Insurance risk will not have been transferred unless both of these conditions exist. 'Significant' should be assessed in the context of the commercial substance of the contract or contracts being evaluated as a whole, and should be judged with reference to the range of outcomes that would reasonably be expected to occur in practice.

10 The assessment in paragraph 9 above should be made having regard to the net present value of all cash flows anticipated under the contract and any related contract. The assessment should also include the risk being insured, where this is necessary to obtain an understanding of the overall commercial effect of the contract.

11 The assessment as to whether insurance risk is transferred should be made prospectively, at the time the contract is entered into. The method of accounting should be followed consistently over the whole period of the contract. If there has been a material change in contract terms during the period of the contract, the entity should perform a new assessment of whether or not a significant transfer of insurance risk has occurred.

12 If there is a significant degree of uncertainty in respect of the timing of claim payments then, depending on the effect of the contract as a whole, timing risk alone may be sufficient to constitute a transfer of insurance risk. This will only be the case provided there are no other features of the contract of insurance which affect or compensate for the timing of claim payments under the contract and provided the conditions in paragraph 9 are met. Insurance risk will not exist in respect of contracts where the insurer effectively receives no more than a lender's return under all reasonably possible scenarios.

ACCOUNTING BY INSUREDS

Recognition and de-recognition of assets and liabilities

13 Payment of a premium under a contract of insurance involves the transfer of an asset to the insurer. If the insurance risk transferred under the contract is significant, the asset, generally cash, should cease to be recognised by the insured and expensed over the period of the risk.

14 A claim recovery under a contract of insurance gives rise to an asset for the insured. If a

claim event arises under a contract where there is significant transfer of insurance risk, the insured should recognise that asset. The insured should follow the provisions of paragraph 20 of FRS5 in determining whether and when the asset should be recognised in the balance sheet. Recognition of the asset will generate entries in the profit and loss account.

If the insurance risk transferred under the contract is not significant, the premium paid under the contract should continue to be recognised in the balance sheet of the insured under a heading which reflects the terms and commercial substance of the contract, provided that it meets the normal rules for asset recognition. **15**

The profit and loss account should record the payment of premiums and receipt of claims only in circumstances where there is a significant transfer of insurance risk. Where this is not the case, the insured should not account for the premium paid through the profit and loss account but in accordance with paragraph 15. **16**

Where a contract covers more than one accounting period, the insured should remeasure future entitlements and liabilities under the contract at each balance sheet date. This remeasurement should have regard to experience under the contract up to the balance sheet date and the amount and timing of expected future cash flows. The insured should follow the provisions of paragraph 20 of FRS5 in determining whether an asset or liability should be recognised in the balance sheet. The remeasurement should not include a reassessment of whether or not the contract transfers significant insurance risk unless, as noted in paragraph 11, there has been a material change in contract terms. **17**

Analysis by an insured of a contract of insurance may, in certain circumstances, result in the contract being divided into two parts, one accounted for in accordance with paragraph 13 and the other in accordance with paragraph 15 . This will be appropriate in circumstances where the contract involves clearly distinct and separable elements, only certain of which result in significant insurance risk being transferred. **18**

ACCOUNTING BY INSURERS

Recognition and de-recognition of assets and liabilities

Where an insurer has entered into a contract of insurance under which there is a significant transfer of insurance risk, an asset should be recognised when the premium under the contract is receivable. Until a claim event arises under the policy, no liability to the insured should be recognised other than in respect of unearned premium or contractual arrangements such as profit sharing. Premiums receivable, and claims payable, will generate corresponding entries in the profit and loss account. **19**

The conditions set out in paragraph 20 of FRS5 are relevant to the recognition of liabilities by insurers under circumstances where there is significant transfer of insurance risk. **20**

Where a premium is received by an insurer under a contract which does not involve a **21** significant transfer of insurance risk, an asset, usually the cash it has received under the contract, should be recognised. The insurer should also recognise the liability to the insured under the contract. The recording of these assets and liabilities will not generate corresponding entries in the profit and loss account. The insurer should record profit and loss account entries only to the extent that the contract gives rise to income and expenditure, being the net return attributable to the insurer under the contract.

OTHER MATTERS

Disclosure

22 Disclosures in the financial statements of entities undertaking insurance transactions should be sufficient to enable the users of the financial statements to understand the commercial effect of individually material contracts, or groups of contracts. Particularly where there is no significant transfer of insurance risk, such contracts may result in the recognition of assets or liabilities whose nature differs from that of items usually included under the relevant balance sheet headings. Where this is the case, the differences should be explained. Entities should note the guidance given in paragraphs 92–94 of FRS5 relating to appropriate disclosure.

Applicability

23 FRS5 applies to accounting periods ending on or after 22 September 1994. Accordingly, all existing contracts of insurance entered into during that accounting period or in prior accounting periods will need to be reviewed in the light of this Technical Release and restated where appropriate. There are special transitional arrangements for Lloyd's syndicates, set out in an amendment to FRS5 issued in December 1994, which do not require restatement for such transactions in the financial statements of syndicates drawing up accounts to 31 December 1993 or earlier.

[FRAG 1/95] Materiality in financial reporting – a discussion paper

(Issued January 1995)

Contents

Materiality in Financial Reporting

PREFACE

This discussion paper is issued for comment by the Financial Reporting Committee of the Institute of Chartered Accountants in England and Wales. The paper is intended to form the basis of a revision of the current Members' Handbook statement *The interpretation of 'material' in relation to accounts.* Before putting forward a revised statement, the Committee considered that it should acknowledge the importance of the subject of materiality to all those involved in financial reporting by seeking the views of members, standard setters, regulators, users and preparers of accounts and other interested parties.

Views are invited on any aspects of the paper and particularly in relation to the questions set out below. It will be helpful if supporting reasons are given and preferred alternatives suggested.

Do you agree with how the discussion paper: **1**

(a) summarises the ways in which the concept of materiality is applied and the demands these place on reporting systems? (paragraphs 2, 3)
(b) identifies and classifies references to materiality in Accounting Standards and the Companies Act 1985? (4–7)
(c) excludes from its scope the application of materiality in relation to the requirements of Schedules 6 and 7 to the Companies Act 1985 and the subject of rounding? (8, 9)

Do you think that the paper is right to argue that users' expectations of accuracy are not relevant to materiality judgements? If not, is this because you reject the central role the ASB gives to the economic decisions of users or do you have some other reason? (10–15) **2**

Do you believe that the three essential determinants of materiality are the nature of an item or error, its size and the circumstances of its occurrence or presentation? (16–22) **3**

Do you agree with the paper's view that accountants should only hold themselves out as being expert in making judgements about materiality in relation to items or errors that are quantifiable in monetary terms and capable of being assessed in the context of other accounting information? (23–25) **4**

Do you share the paper's view that the materiality of an item or error cannot be judged without reference to: comparative figures and trends; users' expectations including, where relevant, projections and forecasts; and the financial statements of comparable entities? (30) **5**

Is the paper right to reject reliance on materiality rules but to encourage their use in identifying matters requiring particular consideration? (31–39) **6**

7 Do you think that the paper adequately addresses practical issues concerning materiality faced by preparers of accounts, including:

(a) relevant aspects of the nature of an item or error? (26, 27)
(b) the context in which an item or error should be judged? (28, 29)
(c) the dangers of 'playing safe'? (40)
(d) identifying users whose needs are relevant to making materiality judgements? (41, 42)
(e) ascertaining users' needs? (41, 43–44)
(f) responding to users' needs at critical points, for example in relation to violation of debt covenants? (41, 45)

Responses should be addressed to:

Robert E Langford
Head of Financial Reporting
The Institute of Chartered Accountants in England and Wales
PO Box 433
Moorgate Place
London EC2P 2BJ

The period for comment will end on 31 March 1995. Comments will only be treated as confidential if this is specifically requested.

Materiality in Financial Reporting

INTRODUCTION

The Financial Reporting Committee of the Institute of Chartered Accountants in England and Wales (ICAEW) is issuing this discussion paper for comment. The paper is intended to form the basis of a revised ICAEW Members Handbook statement *The interpretation of 'material' in relation to accounts* for the guidance of members with responsibility for preparing financial information. It deals with the application of the concept of materiality presented in the draft *Statement of Principles* issued by the Accounting Standards Board (ASB). Chapter 2 of the draft Statement of Principles states that financial information must have the primary qualitative characteristics of relevance and reliability if it is to be useful. However, the draft Statement of Principles also recognises that no information can be useful if it is not also material. Paragraph 39 explains the 'threshold quality' of materiality as follows: 1

> 'Information is material if its omission or misstatement could influence the economic decisions of users taken on the basis of the financial statements. Materiality depends on the size of the item or error judged in the particular circumstances of its omission or misstatement. Thus, materiality provides a threshold or cut-off point rather than being a primary qualitative characteristic that information must have if it is to be useful.'

APPLICATIONS OF MATERIALITY

In presenting any accounting information, the concept of materiality is applied in three ways: 2

(a) If it is material, an item of accounting information is reported in a way that makes it relevant and reliable.
(b) Material errors arising from the omission of a material item of accounting information or the material misstatement of accounting information are corrected.
(c) An immaterial item of accounting information is not reported and an immaterial error is not corrected unless there is a legal requirement or a professional duty to do so.

Applying the concept of materiality requires that reporting systems are established: 3

(a) to gather all accounting information which might be material in aggregate in such a way that it will be relevant and reliable; and
(b) to prevent and detect material misstatement of that information.

Accounting information that is to be regarded as relevant, reliable and properly stated is specified in a variety of requirements: Accounting Standards in the form of FRSs, SSAPs and UITF Abstracts, legislation such as the Companies Act applicable to specific entities and regulations covering certain types of organisation. Many of these reporting requirements acknowledge the concept of materiality for external financial reporting purposes. Consequently, those with responsibility for external reporting need to be able to apply the concept if they are to meet their legal and regulatory 4 obligations. This point is illustrated by paragraph 20 of the *Foreword to Accounting Standards* which notes that the Financial Reporting Review Panel is concerned with material departures from those standards and apparent departures from the accounting provisions of the Companies Act. In the event of such departure, the Panel is empowered to require company directors to prepare revised accounts. The Department of Trade and Industry has similar powers.

5 There are numerous references to materiality in the reporting requirements of Accounting Standards and the Companies Act 1985. These are summarised in the appendix to this discussion paper under the following headings:

(a) items to be disclosed when they are material;
(b) accounting methods to be applied to material items;
(c) items to be disclosed when a material difference exists;
(d) accounting methods to be used when a material difference exists;
(e) items to be disclosed when there are material events or conditions; and
(f) accounting methods required when there are material events or conditions.

6 Only requirements under the first heading involve applying the concept of materiality directly and simply to an item of accounting information to determine whether it should be reported. The most pervasive example is Section 86 of Schedule 4 to the Companies Act 1985 *Form and Content of Company Accounts*. This states that amounts which in the particular context of any provision of Schedule 4 are not material may be disregarded. Schedules 4A and 5 contain similar references in relation to group accounts and disclosures about related undertakings.

7 Other important references to materiality arise under the second heading identifying accounting methods to be applied to material items. Paragraph 13 of the *Foreword to Accounting Standards* states that Standards need not be applied to immaterial items. Paragraph 9 of the *Foreword to UITF Abstracts* and the preamble to each Statement of Standard Accounting Practice contain similar provisions. Paragraph 27 of the *Foreword to Accounting Standards* asserts the corollary that Standards should be applied to all material transactions.

8 Unlike the provisions of Schedule 4 to the Companies Act 1985, the requirements of Schedule 6 *Disclosure of Information: Emoluments and other benefits of Directors and others* and Schedule 7 *Matters to be dealt with in Directors' Report* apply regardless of the materiality of the amounts involved. As a consequence, in the areas covered by these requirements, there is no scope for exercising judgement in deciding what constitutes useful and relevant information for public reporting purposes.

9 The convention of rounding items to the nearest pound or some other reporting unit substantially below any possible materiality threshold means that precise monetary amounts are generally not reported in financial statements. Such rounding is adopted as a matter of practical convenience and does not constitute an application of the concept of materiality.

RELEVANCE TO DECISION-MAKING

An item is material if it could influence the economic decisions of users of accounting information. This principle applies to an item of accounting information, an error, a difference, an event or a condition and is reflected in paragraph 39 of Chapter 2 of the ASB's draft Statement of Principles, quoted in paragraph 1 above. It also follows paragraph 30 of the *Framework for the Preparation and Presentation of Financial Statements* of the International Accounting Standards Committee (IASC). **10**

Both the ASB and the IASC state that 'information is material if its omission or misstatement could influence the economic decisions of users'. In a situation where only amounts over £900,000 are considered material, this statement rightly implies that a debtor balance of £1 million is material. Less convincingly, the statement implies that, in the same situation, a debtor balance of £1 is also material because its misstatement at £1 million could influence the economic decisions of users. On the assumption that the latter implication is not intended, this discussion paper supports the more precisely stated view that information is material if its omission could influence the economic decisions of users and that a misstatement other than an omission is also material if it could influence the economic decisions of users. **11**

The emphasis that the ASB and the IASC place on influencing decisions has important practical consequences. For example, the concept of materiality can be invoked to justify not reporting items if they are immaterial. The reporting of immaterial and therefore irrelevant information imposes unnecessary costs on preparers; it also impedes decision-making by users by obscuring material information amid excessive detail. **12**

Furthermore, when making materiality judgements, those engaged in financial reporting should be concerned with users' needs and decisions but they should not be specifically concerned with users' expectations of accuracy. For example, a user who regards the reporting of turnover in a particular business as straightforward might expect it to be misstated by at most 0.5%. However, pursuing the same illustration, if turnover has to be misstated by at least 5% to cause a user to make a different decision from the one he or she would make on the basis of accurate information, then only a misstatement of 5% or more is material. It is the degree of accuracy the user requires for decision-making rather than the degree of accuracy the user expects which affects materiality judgements. **13**

Problems sometimes arise when the accuracy that a user requires is greater than the accuracy that can reasonably be expected. In these circumstances, material information might contain material undetected errors and so lack the ASB's primary qualitative characteristic of reliability. Such information should only be reported with disclosure of the circumstances that limit its reliability. **14**

The primacy of users' decision-making needs is also important in considering the application of the materiality concept to legal and regulatory reporting requirements. Users of financial statements might reasonably expect a high degree of accuracy in disclosures about directors' emoluments made under Schedule 6 to the Companies Act **15**

1985. Nonetheless, if the concept of materiality were applied to such disclosures, it would be wrong to assert that materiality should be set very low as a consequence of users' high expectations.

DETERMINANTS OF MATERIALITY

16 Three aspects of an item or error are important in determining whether an item or error could influence the economic decisions of users:

(a) size,
(b) nature, and
(c) circumstances.

Thus, it is impossible to say whether a balance of a given size, such as £1 million, is material without knowing both the nature of the balance and the circumstances of its occurrence or presentation.

17 The three determinants of materiality mean that it is similar to 'tallness'. As the size of an item increases it becomes taller and at some point it becomes tall. However, it is impossible to say whether something is tall simply upon being told that it is 500 feet high. The point at which an item becomes tall is determined not just by its size but also by the nature of the item involved and the circumstances in which it appears. It matters whether a building or a hill top is being described and whether it is in New York State or Nepal.

18 Paragraph 29 of the IASC Framework also stresses the importance of nature, size and circumstances. It states that the relevance of information, and therefore the need to report it, depends upon its nature and materiality, where materiality is seen as depending upon size and circumstances. This generally means that the nature of an item helps determine whether it is material and in need of reporting.

19 The ASB takes the view that the IASC's discussion of the nature of an item is incomplete and so omits all reference to it from Chapter 2 of its draft Statement of Principles. This discussion paper proposes introducing the nature of an item as a determinant of materiality on the grounds that it is impractical to consider the materiality of an item or error purely on the basis of its size and circumstances without knowing what sort of item or error it is.

20 The guidance proposed in this paper would not however endorse the IASC's view that some accounting information might be relevant to users solely on the basis of its nature, regardless of size and circumstances. Where the nature of an item or error is of overriding importance, the IASC believes that its concept of materiality does not apply. This view that the size and circumstances of an item may be irrelevant in deciding whether it should be reported is inconsistent with the ASB's characterisation of materiality as a threshold concept. According to the ASB's draft Statement of Principles, information must be material to be useful.

21 The IASC's example of a situation where the nature of an item is of overriding importance is where a new segment needs to be reported simply because of its relevance in assessing the risks and opportunities facing an enterprise. The example is unhelpful in a UK context because the segmental disclosure requirements of the relevant standard, SSAP 25, need not be applied to immaterial items. More generally, it seems implausible to suggest that the size of the numbers involved need not matter in deciding whether to disclose a new segment.

The IASC's contention that relevance and the consequential need to report might be **22** established purely by reference to the nature of an item is also not supported by considering other examples of information that might be treated as material on this basis:

(a) As regards the statutory requirement to disclose details of directors' transactions, it is true that size and circumstances have no role to play in deciding what disclosures should be made, but relevance has no role to play either.
(b) In the case of illegal or fraudulent acts and related party transactions, this discussion paper does not consider it relevant to users' decision-making needs that such items be reported simply because of their nature without having regard to size and circumstances. For example, even disclosure of theft by a related party would generally not seem as relevant if it involves a paper clip that is bought by a major company before being taken for private use by an employee.

THE QUANTIFICATION OF MATERIALITY

The view that size is an essential determinant of materiality means that, for financial **23** reporting purposes, materiality can only be judged in relation to items or errors which are quantifiable in monetary terms. As illustrated in paragraph 5 above, certain accounting methods and disclosures are required when specified material events occur or conditions exist. Although the nature and circumstances of such events and conditions are relevant to determining their materiality, a final judgement as to whether they are material depends on their ultimate monetary impact in the context of other financial information.

In relation to financial reporting matters, accountants restrict their exercise of judge- **24** ments about materiality to specific types of situation. For example, they generally judge whether a material event or change has occurred only if they can assess its monetary impact in the context of other accounting information available to someone who might rely on their judgement for decision-making purposes. It is particularly important for members to recognise the proper extent of their expertise when the word 'material' is encountered outside accounting legislation, standards and other regulation.

For example, when drafting agreements or terms of engagement that will be binding on **25** themselves or others as accountants, it is proposed that members should seek to ensure that the word 'material' is only applied in relation to financial information specified elsewhere in the relevant agreement or terms of engagement. The purpose of this guidance would be to establish clear and realistic expectations amongst all the parties concerned.

THE NATURE OF AN ITEM OR ERROR

26 Reviewing the nature of an item or error as a basis for determining its materiality should have regard to matters which could have an impact on users' decisions. By considering what might alter a user's view of the materiality of an item of a given size in a given set of circumstances, relevant matters can be identified.

27 In making judgements about materiality, the following aspects of the nature of an item or error should be considered:

(a) the events or transactions giving rise to it;
(b) the legality, sensitivity, normality and potential consequences of the event or transaction;
(c) the identity of any other parties involved; and
(d) the account captions and disclosure notes affected.

The expected degree of accuracy associated with an item and the existence or absence of any statutory requirement to disclose it regardless of size should not be regarded as relevant.

CIRCUMSTANCES AFFECTING MATERIALITY JUDGEMENTS

28 The ASB's draft Statement of Principles recognises that the materiality of an item or error depends upon the circumstances of its occurrence. This discussion paper proposes further guidance regarding the circumstances which are relevant and the way in which they affect the materiality of an item or error of a given nature and size. Two types of relevant circumstances can be distinguished:

(a) the *context* of the accounting information in which an item or error occurs; and
(b) the economic *decision-making processes* employed by the users of the accounting information in which an item or error occurs.

29 The content of an item or error is in part defined by its effect on the entity's financial statements, in particular:

(a) primary financial statement captions and subtotals;
(b) the relevant primary financial statement as a whole;
(c) any individual disclosure note; and
(d) the financial statements as a whole.

30 However, the context of an item or error cannot be defined purely in terms of the entity's financial statements for the period to which the item or error relates. In isolation, the financial statements of a single period for a single entity are generally of limited value for decision-making purposes and users will normally refer to such information in the context of:

(a) comparative figures and trends;
(b) users' expectations including, where relevant, projections and forecasts; and
(c) the financial statements of comparable entities.

31 The relative importance of the different aspects of the nature and context of an item or error identified in the preceding paragraphs will depend largely on preparers' views about users' decision-making processes. There are two basic ways of determining whether an item or error of a given size and nature in a given context could affect users' decision-making and consequently be material:

(a) to devise rules or formulae which seek to reflect users' decision-making processes and thus replace the individual judgement of the preparer; or
(b) to develop principles and guidelines to assist individual judgements about what is likely to affect users' decisions.

For the reasons discussed in the following section, this discussion paper rejects reliance on rules or formulae in making judgements about materiality. Nevertheless, it does endorse their use insofar as they assist in the identification of items requiring particularly careful judgement. The paper also supports adherence to a deliberate policy as regards the factors to consider in making such judgements. **32**

MATERIALITY RULES AND THEIR LIMITATIONS

Devising and publishing rules to decide what is material relieves preparers of the need to make judgements about the circumstances of an item or error. For example, in assessing whether an omitted sales transaction is material, a rule might state that: **33**

(a) the relevant context of such an omission is its relationship to current year profit before taxation; and
(b) users' decision-making processes are deemed to be such that their decisions are affected by items exceeding a specified percentage of current year profit before taxation.

Advantages of published materiality rules are that: **34**

(a) users do not have false expectations about the accounting information on which they base their economic decisions; and
(b) preparers save the time they would otherwise spend on identifying users' needs and decision-making processes in specific cases and deliberating over individual judgements.

Despite the advantages, there are two overwhelming arguments against relying solely on materiality rules: **35**

(a) any rules that are adequately drafted to reflect real decision-making processes relating to different types of items in different contexts are likely to be extremely complex and costly to apply; and
(b) if simpler and less costly rules are devised, they are likely to be seen as rules of 'technical' materiality and, because technically immaterial items might still be judged to be material and in need of special treatment and disclosure, the rules would neither satisfy users' needs nor make judgement redundant.

In rejecting reliance on rules, this discussion paper is encouraging those with financial reporting responsibilities to respond in an efficient and professional way to the needs of users of financial information and to be responsible for their own judgements. **36**

37 Where rules are devised to assist in judging materiality, such rules should only be used as part of a system of control over the process of preparing financial statements. Rules should not be cited as the sole authoritative basis for making a judgement but should be used to identify matters requiring careful consideration, especially in view of the fact that others might quote rules if a preparer's judgement is subsequently called into question. For these reasons, a preparer might consult with others on all decisions not to adjust for an error or disclose an item over an amount indicated by a particular rule. Such consultation would seek to ensure that the member's judgement is supported by a proper consideration of how the item might affect users' decisions, with particular reference to its nature and circumstances.

38 The following guidance should be borne in mind by preparers when drawing up procedures for highlighting potentially material matters requiring specific consideration or consultation:

(a) the one explicit materiality rule in UK Accounting Standards is contained in paragraph 16.ii of SSAP 3 which requires fully diluted earnings per share to be disclosed when such earnings are at least 5% less than basic earnings per share;
(b) paragraph 76 of FRS 6 refers to a material minority and indicates that this is defined as 10%;
(c) a 'substantial acquisition' is seen as being larger than a material acquisition and arises under paragraph 37 of FRS 6 when the net assets or operating profits of the acquired entity exceed 15% of those of the acquiring entity or the fair value of the consideration given exceeds 15% of the net assets of the acquiring entity; and
(d) the staff of the US Securities and Exchange Commission has an informal rule of thumb that items and errors of more than 10% are material, those between 5% and 10% may be material and those under 5% are usually not material. These percentages are normally applied to gross profit, net income, equity and any specific line item in the financial statements that is potentially misstated.

39 Preparers might also wish to bear in mind that Accounting Standards and related guidance provide the following indications of the context in which the materiality of items should be considered, albeit without discussing users' decision-making processes in further detail:

(a) in assessing the materiality of convertible debt for disclosure purposes, consideration should be given to the implications of conversion (FRS 4.100);
(b) an investing group's share of an associate's extraordinary items should be disclosed by the investing group where that share is material in the context of the group's result (SSAP 1.21);
(c) details of balances within an associate's accounts should be disclosed where results and balance sheet items are material in the context of the financial statements of the investing group having regard not merely to the net carrying value of the investment in the associate but also to the scale of the associate's operations compared to those of the group (SSAP 1.23 and SSAP 1.30);

(d) trading balances with associates within debtors and creditors should be disclosed where they are material in the context of the financial statements of the investing group (SSAP 1.29);
(e) non-adjusting events of sufficient materiality to require disclosure should be determined having regard to all matters which are necessary to enable users of financial statements to assess, and reach a proper understanding of, financial position (SSAP 17.13 and SSAP 17.23);
(f) to interpret the provision that SSAP 21 need not be applied to immaterial items, the relevant criterion is the size of the lease or leases in the context of the size of the lessee or lessor (SSAP 21 Guidance Notes 7); and
(g) in deciding whether a lease is material, regard should be had to the effect on the financial statements as a whole, so that a lessee need not capitalise a lease if it would have no material effect on total fixed assets, total borrowings and obligations, the gearing ratio and profit or loss for the year (SSAP 21 Guidance Notes 8).

RESPONDING TO USERS' NEEDS

In making materiality judgements, it is generally inadvisable to 'play safe'. Where accounting methods have to be applied and disclosures made in relation to material items, differences, events or conditions, these requirements apply regardless of cost. Similarly, there is no justification for not correcting a material misstatement on grounds of cost. Consequently, if materiality levels are set too low, unnecessary costs are incurred that cannot be justified in terms of the related benefit to users. A level of materiality that is too low leads not only to extra cost but also to the reporting of financial information which is too detailed and complex. As a result, the benefit users derive from such information might be diminished. **40**

In responding to users' needs, those with responsibility for preparing financial information should be encouraged to use materiality rules to challenge their judgements about materiality whilst recognising that rules cannot replace their own views about: **41**

(a) which users' needs should be reflected in materiality judgements;
(b) what is important to users in making decisions; and
(c) how to handle users' needs around critical points.

These matters are dealt with in the remainder of this discussion paper.

The wide range of users of financial statements envisaged by the ASB in the introduction to its draft Statement of Principles includes actual and potential investors, employees, lenders, suppliers and other trade creditors, customers, governments and their agencies, and members of the public with access to financial statements. A potentially serious challenge for preparers is that virtually any item or error could tip the balance in some users' decisions and so become material. To meet this challenge, it is proposed that preparers should consider the needs of users who are: **42**

(a) average members of a class whose use of financial statements could reasonably be foreseen;

(b) reasonable in their use of and reliance on historical information as part of a broader range of financial information that is relevant to making decisions;
(c) aware that the needs of different users have to be balanced and accommodated within financial statements that give a true and fair view and are not cluttered by excessive disclosure likely to be of interest only to a few potential users; and
(d) aware that the ASB sees investors as the primary users of financial statements who are mainly interested in accounting information that is relevant for predicting future cash flows.

43 Preparers should judge users' needs based on the preparers' experience of:

(a) general discussions with users;
(b) observing users' responses to information, eg. comments by the press or by analysts on particular disclosures, numbers, ratios or trends and their effects on decisions to buy, hold or sell an investment or to reappoint or replace management;
(c) the impact on market prices of specific items of news; and
(d) their own reactions and attitudes as users of financial information in similar situations.

44 On the basis of experience, a preparer might reasonably decide to attach particular importance to the materiality of items or errors in a company's financial statements in the context of the trend of earnings and the margins of other companies in the same sector. Such considerations might be particularly appropriate in situations of marginal or break-even profitability. Consequently, items or errors that could appear to be material or even substantial if judged purely in the context of a company's earnings for one year might nonetheless be properly regarded as immaterial.

45 Notwithstanding the preceding paragraph, at certain critical points, a proper assessment of users' needs will sometimes indicate a requirement for very low levels of materiality and potentially unrealistic demands for accuracy, eg. where trends reverse, profits become losses, technical insolvency occurs or compliance with debt covenants is in doubt. In responding to such circumstances, preparers should:

(a) question whether users will actually make different decisions depending upon which side of a thin dividing line an answer falls;
(b) adopt a neutral approach in areas where the required degree of accuracy is difficult to achieve so that there is perceived to be an equal chance of mistakenly falling on either side of a critical divide;
(c) be sensitive to the potentially misleading cumulative effect of individually immaterial items or errors; and
(d) consider whether the information concerned is so unreliable in relation to its potential use that it should only be reported in conjunction with disclosure of the circumstances of its preparation and its inherent limitations.

Appendix
References to Materiality in Accounting Standards and the Companies Act 1985

Items to be disclosed when they are material **(a)**

- Departures from Accounting Standards (Foreword to Accounting Standards 7 and 19)
- Cash flows under five standard headings (FRS 1.13)
- Effects on five standard cash flow headings of acquisitions and disposals in period (FRS 1.42 and FRS 6.34)
- Non-cash transactions (FRS 1.43)
- As exceptional, items which derive from ordinary activities (FRS 3.5)
- As extraordinary, highly abnormal items which do not derive from ordinary activities (FRS 3.6)
- Material gross gains or losses on the sale of fixed assets or the sale or termination of an operation should be disclosed in the notes even when the immateriality of the net amount would normally preclude disclosure on the face of the profit and loss account (FRS 3.20)
- Transfers between amounts attributable to different classes of shareholders (FRS 3.58)
- Non-equity interests in shareholders' funds and minority interests, and convertible debt on the face of the balance sheet (FRS 4.100)
- Effect of any uncertainty regarding the gain or loss arising from a 'special case' transaction which does not result in an entire asset either ceasing or continuing to be recognised (FRS 5.24)
- Main headings of a quasi-subsidiary's financial statements (FRS 5.38)
- Subsequent adjustments to provisional fair values on acquisition with corresponding adjustments to goodwill (FRS 6.27)
- Impact of an acquisition on a major business segment (FRS 6.28)
- Associates' extraordinary items (SSAP 1.21)
- Unsettled trading balances between associates and the investing company (SSAP 1.29)
- Accounting policies (SSAP 2.11, 2.12 and 2.18)
- Departures from fundamental accounting concepts (SSAP 2.17)
- Differences in results arising from government grants (SSAP 4.18)
- Irrecoverable ACT (SSAP 8.9)
- Separate elements of taxation charge including adjustments in respect of previous periods (SSAP 8.22)
- Difference between replacement cost and book amount of stocks (SSAP 9.40 and CA 85 Sch 4.27(3))
- Effects on depreciation charge of a change in method (SSAP 12.26)
- Effects on depreciation charge of a revaluation (SSAP 12.27)
- Non-adjusting post-balance sheet events (SSAP 17.13 and 23)
- Contingent losses which are neither probable nor remote (SSAP 18.16)
- Probable contingent gains (SSAP 18.17)
- Separable intangible fixed assets acquired in an acquisition (SSAP 22.37)

- Goodwill recognised as a result of any acquisition (SSAP 22.44)
- Effects on future pension costs of changes in the law (SSAP 24.50)
- Debtors due after one year on the face of the balance sheet (UITF 4.3)
- Balance sheet provisions for post-retirement benefits other than pensions (UITF 6.9)
- Statutory format captions with Arabic numbers (CA 85 Sch 4.3(4))
- Departures from applicable Accounting Standards (CA 85 Sch 4.36A)
- Each provision within 'other provisions' (CA 85 Sch 4.46(3))
- Apply statutory disclosure requirements to material amounts (CA 85 Sch 4.86)
- Financial information on subsidiaries (CA 85 Sch 5.3(4))
- Details of significant holdings in undertakings which are not subsidiaries (CA 85 Sch 5.9(4))
- Financial information about non-consolidated subsidiaries (CA 85 Sch 5.17(3))
- Details of other significant holdings (CA 85 Sch 5.25(3) and 28(3))

(b) Accounting methods to be applied to material items

- Applying Accounting Standards to all material items and transactions no matter when they are entered into (Foreword to Accounting Standards 13 and 27)
- Make material adjustments to prior periods when they result from policy changes or fundamental errors (FRS 3.7)
- Eliminate material effects of intercompany transactions and differences in accounting policies when accounting for associates in group accounts (SSAP 1.39)
- Include irrecoverable VAT in items when it is material (SSAP 5.9)
- Adjust for material adjusting post balance sheet events (SSAP 17.22.a)
- Accrue material probable contingent losses (SSAP 18.15)
- Consider applying 'rule of 78' or actuarial methods of interest allocation to finance leases and hire purchase contracts where total finance charges are material (SSAP 21 Guidance Notes 36)
- Accelerate recognition of a pension fund deficit when, inter alia, it is material (SSAP 24.82)
- Apply UITF Abstracts to material items and transactions no matter when they are entered into (Foreword to UITF Abstracts 9 and 17)
- Include material goodwill not previously charged to profit and loss in profit or loss on disposal (UITF 3.7)
- Apply statutory accounting requirements to material amounts (CA 85 Sch 4.86)
- Apply statutory consolidation accounting requirements to material amounts (CA 85 4A.5)
- Eliminate material group transactions (CA 85 4A.6(4))
- Apply equity method of accounting to associates in consolidated accounts when amounts are material (CA 85 Sch 4A.22(3))

(c) Items to be disclosed when a material difference exists

- Historic cost profit when there is a material difference from reported profit (FRS 3.26)
- Use of non-coterminous financial statements for associates when differences from using conterminous statements would be material (SSAP 1.37)

- Nil basis EPS when it is materially different from the net basis (SSAP 3.9)
- Fully diluted EPS when materially different from basic EPS (SSAP 3.16.ii)
- Turnover by destination when materially different from turnover by origin (SSAP 25.18)

(d) Accounting methods to be used when a material difference exists

- Adjust on consolidation for use of non-coterminous financial statements when differences are material (FRS 2.43)
- Perform fair valuation exercise to calculate goodwill on increase to stake in subsidiary where a material difference arises by comparison to existing carrying values (FRS 2.51)
- Account for finance costs at a constant rate on the carrying amount of debt except where this is not materially different from the nominal yield (FRS 4.75)
- Account for the effect on accumulated depreciation of a revision of the useful economic life of a fixed asset as an exceptional item when future results or financial position would be materially distorted by writing off the effect over the remaining revised life (SSAP 12.18)
- Apply actuarial method of interest allocation where there is a material difference from straight-line or 'rule of 78' approximations (SSAP 21 Guidance Notes 35)
- Make consolidation adjustments for the application of consistent accounting policies where differences are material (CA 85 Sch 4A.3(3))

(e) Items to be disclosed when there are material events or conditions

- Disclosures of material undertakings ceasing to be subsidiary undertakings (FRS 2.48)
- Significant restrictions on distributions by a subsidiary undertaking when the restrictions materially limit the parent's access to distributable profits (FRS 2.53)
- Disclosures of acquisitions, sales or terminations having a material impact on a major business segment (FRS 3.15)
- Fair value and other disclosures for individual material acquisitions as required by FRS 6.24–35 (FRS 6.23.a)
- Current year pre-acquisition profits and prior year profits of the acquired entity for each material acquisition (FRS 6.35)
- If the result of one or more associated companies are material, their turnover, depreciation charges, profits less losses before taxation and profits less losses attributable to the investing group should be disclosed (SSAP 1.23)
- If the interests in associated companies are material, their tangible and intangible assets and liabilities should be disclosed (SSAP 1.30)
- Disclosures for material disposals of previously acquired businesses or segments (SSAP 22.52)
- Comments where a material actuarial surplus or deficiency exists in an employer's pension scheme (SSAP 24.88.h.iv)
- Post-retirement benefits where their cost is expected to be material (UITF 6.10)

(f) Accounting methods required when there are material events or conditions

- Consolidate subsidiaries which are individually or collectively material (FRS 2.24 and CA 85 s 229 (2))
- Account for discontinued operations when a sale or termination has a material effect on the nature and focus of operations and represents a material reduction in operating facilities whether caused by withdrawal from a market or a material reduction of turnover in a continuing market (FRS 3.4.c and FRS 3.43)
- Record related costs as exceptional items below operating profit when a reorganisation or restructuring has a material effect on nature and focus of operations (FRS 3.20.b)
- Consolidate material quasi-subsidiaries in group accounts or, for a company not preparing group accounts, present the accounts of the quasi-subsidiary with the same prominence as the company accounts (FRS 5.101.a)
- Merger account for a business combination where, as well as satisfying four other criteria, it satisfies the criterion that any non-equity consideration represents an immaterial proportion of the fair value of the consideration and 'consideration' excludes an interest in a peripheral business that can be disposed of without having a material effect on the nature and focus of operations (FRS 6.9 and 10)
- Merger account for a business combination when no equity shareholders of any of the combining entities retain any material interest in the performance of only part of the combined entity and four other criteria are satisfied (FRS 6.11)
- Use carrying value based on historical cost as a proxy for fair value where prices have not changed materially (FRS 7.51)
- Do not fair value a subsidiary held for resale at its net proceeds where the acquirer makes material changes to it or events occur during the holding period which materially change its fair value (FRS 7.69)
- Include approved variations in the sales value of a contract if, inter alia, they are likely to be a material factor in outcome (SSAP 9 Appendix I.26)
- Adjust for post balance sheet events which indicate that the going concern concept is inappropriate for a material part of a company (SSAP 17.22.b)
- Apply investment property accounting when the sale of a property would not materially affect trading or manufacturing (SSAP 19.2)
- Adjust for hyper inflation where operations in hyperinflationary economies are material (UITF 9.5)
- Do not account for certain assets at fixed amounts when their quantity, value and composition are subject to material change (CA 85 Sch 4.25(2))

[FRAG 12/95]
Financial reporting of environmental liabilities – a discussion paper

(Issued April 1995)

INTRODUCTION

This discussion paper sets out a number of issues relating to the financial reporting of environmental costs, liabilities and impaired assets that may arise in the preparation or use of financial statements and has been prepared by a working party set up by the ICAEW Environment Steering Group. At this stage, the primary audience for the paper is the accounting profession and those who are directly involved with financial reporting. For convenience, the issues are stated in the form of questions and fall within four main areas: 1

I Definition and treatment of environmental costs.
II Recognition of environmental liabilities.
III Impairment of assets.
IV Disclosure.

The paper has possible implications for all entities for which environmental considerations are significant and is not directed solely at large companies.

In its statement on the operating and financial review, the Accounting Standards Board (ASB) lists environmental protection costs and potential environmental liabilities as examples of matters that may be relevant, depending on the nature of a company's business, for inclusion in a discussion of the risks and uncertainties relating to the business. 2

The aim of the working party was to identify the issues involved and to consider whether, in each case, the existing accounting principles are adequate to ensure that the treatment adopted is appropriate. To the extent the ambiguity exists, the paper puts forward ideas on possible treatment. These ideas are not intended to preempt any guidance the ASB may develop but may add a further dimension to the debate which will follow the publication of the ASB's forthcoming discussion paper on provisions. 3

Whilst questions relating to the recognition and disclosure of environmental liabilities and impairment of assets are almost invariably the more important issues to be considered, it is logical to deal first with definition and treatment of environmental costs, in viewe of the different approaches that are possible and the consequent difficulties in making comparisons or drawing conclusions. 4

The working party has deliberately avoided widening the scope of the paper to include environmental matters that do not have any direct implications for financial reporting. For example, the paper is not concerned with the more extensive environmental reports in which some companies describe the steps being taken to conserve the environment, 5 nor does it deal with the related management systems or the subject of environmental verification. Separate environmental reports often include information on emissions, performance targets and achievements, as well as remedial action to eliminate or reduce unsatisfactory environmental performance. Much of this information is often of a non-financial nature, such as input–oputput reconciliations showing volumes of materials and gases involved in the process.

6 Amongst matters associated with financial reporting, it should be noted that the paper does not cover:

(a) the treatment of environmental costs that arise after a site has been cleaned up and vacated ('post exit costs');
(b) environmental costs that relate to specific industries, such as decommissioning and abandonment costs; or
(c) the discounting of future environmental liabilities, which are not regarded as unique in this respect.

7 In addition to existing financial reporting standards, exposure drafts and statements issued by the ASB (or its predecessor), the paper draws on a research report issued by the Canadian Institute of Chartered Accountants (the 'CICA'), the report on accounting for future events prepared by a joint working group of five standard-setting bodies and a working document being prepared for the EC Accounting Advisory Forum ('the Forum'). The paper also mentions US guidance issued by the SEC. Reference to these documents is included only to the extent that this may assist in interpreting UK requirements.

8 No account has been taken at this stage of two initiatives expected to give rise to guidance for auditors on environmental issues. We understand, for instance, that the American Institute of Certified Public Accountants has a task force considering the matter. There is also a proposed discussion paper 'The audit profession and the environment' being developed by a sub-committee of IFAC. Whilst there will no doubt be a view that some of the proposed auditing guidance is pre-empting the corresponding accounting and reporting requirements, such initiatives will almost certainly lead to a demand for any gaps in the financial reporting requirements to be filled.

9 In broad terms, the working party believes that the financial reporting of environmental costs, liabilities and impaired assets is covered by existing UK accounting requirements and that most of the issues involved are not particular contentious. However, the application of certain principles may be difficult, due to the more extended timeframes that need to be considered and the degree of judgement required, which may be greater than that in reporting other liabilities. There is also a general perception that existing accounting principles are not adequate to deal with environmental factors. The likelihood of more onerous environmental legislation may therefore put a strain on the existing accounting rules.

10 The working party considers that additional guidance may be needed on some issues, particularly the treatment of impaired assets, and is pleased to note that the ASB's current project on provisions will also deal with impairment generally. Whilst many responsible companies are already addressing the issues covered in the paper, the need for a 'level playing field' should be recognised. The paper therefore supports the development of more uniform disclosure. In particular, it may be appropriate for some of the existing rules to be strengthened by specific disclosures.

The paper is issued as a basis for discussion and comments are invited on any of the issues raised or on any related matters. Responses will be treated as being on public record unless the commentator specifically requests confidentiality and should be addressed to: **11**

Robert E Langford
Head of Financial Reporting
Chartered Accountants' Hall
Moorgate Place
London EC2P 2BJ

so as to arrive not later than 30 June 1995.

I DEFINITION AND TREATMENT OF ENVIRONMENTAL COSTS

Q1 What constitutes environmental costs and how are such costs to be distinguished from the costs of increasing efficiency or capability? Should environmental costs include:

(a) costs of environmental measures, ie steps taken to prevent, reduce or repair damage to the environment;
(b) expenditure on health and safety;
(c) losses through the impairment of assets;
(d) commitments involving future expenditure; and/or
(e) the payment of fines, penalties and damages?

1.1 Increasing public concern about the environment is accompanies by a common perception that little guidance exists on accounting for or disclosing environmental costs. There is also a likelihood that different users of financial information will place a variety of interpretations on what environment costs represent. It is therefore logical to begin by discussing possible definitions.

1.2 The definitions set out below are based on those in the CICA* research report. 'Environmental costs' include:

(i) the costs of environmental measures; and
(ii) environmental losses

'Environmental measures' are steps taken by an entity or, on its behalf, by others, to prevent, reduce or repair damage to the environment or to deal with the conservation of resources.

'Environmental losses' are costs incurred by an entity in relation to the environment for which there is not return or benefits, for example:

(i) assets whose costs are irrecoverable due to environmental concerns;
(ii) damages paid to others for environmental damages; or
(iii) fines or penalties for non-compliance with environmental regulations.

1.3 Environmental costs do not include expenditure on health or safety to the extent that such measures relate to produce and process safety. Product safety involves measures to ensure the safe use of products. Process safety involves measures to reduce risks to employees engaged in the process.

1.4 The working party concurs with the definitions and principles set out above.

1.5 Costs of environmental measures are sometimes difficult to distinguish. There is an argument that such costs should be confined to those which relate 'wholly and exclusively' to preventing, reducing or repairing damage to the environment and

*'Environmental costs and liabilities: Accounting and financial reporting issues', *a research report published by the Canadian Institute of Chartered Accountants, February 1993.*

should exclude, for example, costs incurred so as to conserve energy, and closure costs, even if the closure takes place for environment reasons. On the other hand, it is important that any information about future costs should be as complete as possible, subject to the technical constraints in quantifying such costs. On balance, the working party therefore take the view that, provided disclosure is accompanied by adequate explanation, a 'wholly and exclusively' condition would be unduly restrictive. To avoid misleading a user of the accounts due to the possible overlap with other costs and benefits, disclosure of what environmental costs include or, in some cases, exclude is therefore important.

In the case of capital expenditure, the renewal of a plant, incorporating the latest technology, will often result in other efficiencies, such as improved production levels, as well as better environmental performance. Isolating the element of cost relating to environmental benefits is therefore difficult. A judgemental allocation, based on the best information available and including, where appropriate, an engineering assessment, may need to be made if a separate figure is required. For instance, in the operating and financial review, discussion of capital expenditure in a particular segment may require information about the amount spent on environmental protection. **1.6**

There is also a problem of different perceptions in the minds of users of financial statements as to whether a high or increasing environmental spend is a favourable or an unfavourable factor. Whereas users from the 'green lobby' might welcome a large figure, investors may take this as a sign that future profits will be significantly reduced and that the expenditure involved does not represent productive investment. Where manufacturing processes are re-engineered so that emissions are diminished and environmental costs are reduced, then a lower level of spend would reflect an improved environmental performance. Nor is there any suggestion that a particular level of environmental spend is 'appropriate' for the business concerned. **1.7**

Similar problems arise in the case of research and development expenditure, where there is no agreement on the levels of investment necessary to sustain technological growth. Some industries may spend large sums on research and development, yet innovate little, whereas small but well-targeted investments can achieve major benefits. To reduce the risk of misinterpretation, it may therefore be necessary not only to describe what is included in for environmental costs and related capital expenditure but also to include a commentary and corresponding figures for previous years. **1.8**

With regard to fines or penalties, it should be noted that a draft working document* prepared for the Forum states that ... 'costs incurred as a result of fines or penalties for non-compliance with environmental regulations, compensation to third parties as a result of loss or injury caused by past environmental pollution and similar environmentally related costs are *excluded* from ... the definition of environmental expenditure'. **1.9**

A supplementary question concerns the definition of environmental costs within a **1.10**

**Working document for the EC Accounting Advisory Forum* 'Environmental Issues in Financial Reporting' *(Draft)*.

group where the main activity of one of the subsidiaries comprises environmental measures and it might be argued that all the costs arising in that subsidiary constitute environmental costs for the group. The working document for the Forum specifically excludes from the definition all expenditure in a company engaged in the environmental business, such as the treatment of waste.

1.11 The working party's view is that, if such costs incurred by a subsidiary relate to environmental work done for other entities within the group, those costs and associated overheads would be classified as environmental costs of the group. However, where the costs are incurred in connection with environmental work done for third parties, they would not be treated as environmental costs of the subsidiary concerned or the group.

Q2 Should environmental costs be charged directly to the profit and loss account, capitalised or deferred? If different treatment is appropriate in different circumstances, what are the relevant criteria? Are there any circumstances in which treatment as a prior period adjustment would be appropriate?

2.1 Environmental costs are often embedded in other operating expenditure and sometimes similar in nature, with the result that, in principle, their treatment is similar. However, their potential order of magnitude and the political and social implications which may be involved suggest that separate disclosure may be appropriate if the amounts are material.

2.2 In the view of the working party, the appropriate treatment of environmental costs may be summarised as follows:

- The costs of environmental measures should be charged directly to the profit and loss account unless the costs can be directly associated with the future economic benefits of identifiable assets. Environmental losses, for which there is no return or benefit, should always be charged directly to the profit and loss account.
- Material environmental costs, including those that relate to continuing activities or to discontinued activities, should be charged in arriving at the profit or loss on ordinary activies. If additional disclosure is necessary to show a true and fair view, the costs should be reported separately as an exceptional item under FRS 3 'Reporting financial performance'. Costs that are not material should not be separately disclosed.
- Where costs are incurred during the construction or development of a related capital asset to alleviate future damage to the environment arising from the asset, or to conserve natural resources, such costs should be capitalised as part of the cost of the asset.
- The cost of assets used for the clean up of past environmental damage should be treated the same way as other costs related to the clean up.
- A fine or penalty that relates to past operating activities should be treated as a current period item.

2.3 Prior period adjustments are defined in FRS 3 as 'material adjustments applicable to prior periods arising from changes in accounting policies or from the correction of fundamental errors. They do not include normal recurring adjustments or corrections of accounting estimates made in prior periods'.

The definition in FRS 3 would generally prevent environmental costs being treated as a prior period adjustment. The only exceptions to this principle would be where there is a change in accounting policy or where there was a fundamental error in estimating environmental costs recognised in a prior period. When an estimate that has been made in a prior period is subsequently adjusted, the adjustment would be treated as a current period item. Since estimation of environmental liabilities often involves inherent uncertainty, improvements in technology that enable a more reliable figure to be presented than was available previously do not lead to a prior year adjustment. **2.4**

The revised international accounting standard IAS 8 'Net profit or loss for the period, fundamental errors and changes in accounting policies' restricts the adjustment of information relating to prior periods to: **2.5**

(a) the correction of a fundamental error that relates to prior periods; and
(b) a change in accounting policy, where the amount of the adjustment is reasonably determinable.

In all other cases, items of expense recognised in a period are included in determining the net result for the period.

Where environmental costs relate to previous acitivities that have been discontinued, the costs would be included within discontinued operations under FRS 3 and the information relating to such activities would normally be shown in a separate segment for the purpose of segmented reports. In cases where such costs are material, it would be appropriate to treat them as an exceptional item. **2.6**

The working document for the Forum takes the position that environmental expenditures are normally expense in the current period and that, where such expenditures are incurred to clean up past environmental damages, they should be regarded as maintenance or repair costs. However, where environmental expenditures are incurred to prevent or reduce future environmental damage or conserve resources, they may qualify for recognition as an asset if they are intended for use on a continuing basis for the purpose of the undertaking's activities and if, in addition, one of the following criteria is met: **2.7**

(a) the costs relate to anticipated environmental benefits and extend the life, increase the capacity, or improve the safety or efficiency of assets owned by the company; or
(b) the costs reduce or prevent environmental contamination that is likely to occur as a result of future operations.

It would appear that the working document for the Forum would permit the costs of staff training to be recognised as an asset if one of the above criteria are satisfied. It seems more likely to be the intention that this paragraph is only applicable to the acquisition of physical assets. Subject to this proviso, the working party concurs with the principles set out above. **2.8**

Q3 In the case of environmental costs that are incurred subsequent to the acquisition of a capital asset, should capitalisation be dependent on an increase in the future economic benefits expected from the asset? Where environmental cost are capitalised, how should the depreciation period be determined?

3.1 The revised international accounting standard IAS 16 'Accounting for property, plant and equipment' states that expenditure which is made for safety or environmental reasons, while not directly increasing the future economic benefit of any particular item of property, plant and equipment, may be necessary to obtain future economic benefits from an enterprise's other assets. Such expenditure qualifies for recognition as an asset but only to the extent that the amounts capitalised do not exceed the recoverable amount of that asset and related assets.

3.2 This treatment needs to be distinguished from that proposed in a subsequent paragraph of IAS 16 regarding the costs of cleaning the environment and the payment of fines for breaches of environmental regulations resulting from the operation of plant and equipment – costs for which there is no future economic benefit – which are recognised as expended when incurred and are not capitalised.

3.3 In the case of environmental costs that are incurred after the related capital asset is acquired, constructed or developed, the CICA Study Group did not reach a conclusion but identified two possible approaches as to whether such costs can be associated with future benefits and therefore capitalised:

(a) Under the 'increased future benefits' approach, such environmental costs must result in an increase in expected future *economic* benefits from the asset.

(b) Under the 'additional cost of future benefits' approach, such costs are capitalised if they are considered to be a cost of expected future benefits from the asset – *irrespective* of whether there are any *increased economic* benefits.

However, a key consideration is whether the term 'economic benefits' is interpreted in the narrow sense, for example, cash flow, profits, asset life or output, or whether it is interpreted in a wider sense, such as the ability to operate an asset in conformity with new or existing laws, regulations and reasonable public expectations. It is also necessary in any event to consider whether the expenditure results from an impairment of the asset or whether, following capitalisation of the expenditure, the asset is stated at a figure above its recoverable amount.

3.4 Additional expenditure may avoid an impairment that would otherwise arise. Provided the expected future benefits, after incurring such expenditure, exceed the increased total cost, it would be possible to justify capitalisation. Clearly it will often be difficult to distinguish the benefits expected to result from particular costs. On balance, the working party therefore takes the view that the first of the approaches described in paragraph 3.3, with a reasonably wide interpretation of the term 'economic benefits', should be the principle adopted.

3.5 Where environmental expenditure relating to a specific plant is capitalised, the depreciation period may be shorter than that of the plant itself, if the period expected to benefit is itself shorter than the life of the plant. For example, new legislation may necessitate an alteration to an existing item of plant but the additional part fitted to the plant may need to be replaced over a shorter timescale than the remaining life of the plant itself.

II RECOGNITION OF ENVIRONMENTAL LIABILITIES

4 **When should future environmental expenditure be recognised as a liability? Does this depend on whether the related environmental damage has already occurred? Or on when the obligation for clean up was incurred?**

Under SSAP 2 'Disclosure of accounting policies', provision is made for all known 4.1
liabilities (expenses and losses) whether the amount of these is known with certainty or is a best estimate in the light of the information available'. To qualify as liabilities under the ASB's proposed Statement of Principles, environmental liabilities would need to represent 'an entity's obligations to transfer economic benefits arising from past transactions or events'. Consequently, the cost of future environmental measures would only represent a liability if the entity has an obligation to incur such costs.

When an entity has a legal obligation, or is otherwise committed, to incur future 4.2
expenditure to prevent, reduce or repair environmental damage, the costs involved represent an environmental liability.

As regards the timing of recognition, a liability may crystallise if laws are introduced 4.3
that require environmental measures to be taken or if, as the result of a public statement or declared policy, management is otherwise *irrevocably* committed to take such measures. A liability may also be expected to crystallise as a result of a decision to close, or dispose of, a site. Until such time as the liability crystallises, it should be regarded as contingent if it meets the criteria in SSAP 18. Whereas the application of the prudence concept might require that provisions be made for the liability as soon as such a decision is taken, the ASB's proposed statement of principles emphasises that decisions do not, in themselves, give rise to liabilities.

In a different scenario, new laws may simply raise the level of acceptable standards so 4.4
that the environmental measures previously adopted are no longer sufficient to satisfy the new requirements. Even though such legislation may operate retrospectively, in that the requirements affect existing plant used in continuing operations, the working party believes that the effects should be dealt with in the period in which the legislation is introduced. Where the legislation affects discontinued operations but there is still a liability, for example if a disused site has been retained awaiting disposal, a similar treatment should be adopted but with appropriate disclosure.

New laws sometimes impose an obligation for progressive reductions in environmental 4.5
contamination. Subsequent environmental measures that would be necessary in such cases do not represent an obligation until the new law becomes effective. At that future date, there is also a possibility that clean up costs will be affected by improvements in technology. The working party therefore considers that, where there is an element of

uncertainty, the future obligation should be disclosed as an impending obligation for which the entity expects to be liable. However, there may be circumstances in which it would be imprudent to await the effective date of the new legislation before recognising that a liability exists.

4.6 The working party considers that the effects of future legislation should not be anticipated and that fugture environmental expenditure should therefore be recognised when the entity has an obligation to incur future sacrifices as a result of past events and the expenditure involved is reasonably determinable. This is often triggered by new legislation which requires an entity to close, or dispose of, the business.

4.7 Factors to consider in deciding what information to disclose would therefore normally include:

(a) the legal position;
(b) the extent of public commitment by management;
(c) whether any change of use is planned, such as a decision to dispose of the business or to close the site and vacate; and
(d) the nature of contamination and the standard of cleanliness required.

4.8 In a recent* report on accounting for future events, the consensus was that, although liabilities are generally measured in terms of future sacrifices, they represent an *existing obligation* to incur these sacrifices. The prospect of future sacrifices, although necessary, was not regarded as a sufficient condition for recognition. Thus, in assessing whether provisions should be made for future expenditures, 'the mere fact that a future loss is probable does not justify recognition of a liability... Losses may be recognised in circumstances which the entity is *irrevocably committed* to incur losses in the future...'. Various examples are given, including liabilities arising from an obligation imposed by law. As regards the role of future legal requirements, such as the possibility of new laws that would introduce or increase environmental liabilities, the joint working group's consensus was that, 'regardless of likelihood, only changes in future legal requirements that have already been enacted, or substantially enacted, into law should be assumed in accounting for (assets and) liabilities'.

Q5 How should the liability be recognised if the amount involved is difficult or impossible to estimate? Should a liability be recognised net of expected recoveries through counter-claims or from sale of the related asset?

5.1 Where an entity has an environmental liability, provision should be made in the balance sheet if the related expenditure is probable and the amount can be estimated with a reasonable degree of accuracy. Where the amount cannot be estimated, the nature of the liability and expected timing of the expenditure should be disclosed, commensurate with the nature of the liability.

5.2 If the entity has a joint and several liability for environmental costs, a characteristic

*'Future events', *a research report issued in August 1994 by a joint working group comprising five standard-setting bodies, including the ASB. The report was based on a study designed to develop a common conceptual basis that individual standard-setting bodies can use for establishing their own accounting standards.*

that is largely peculiar to the US, this will also make the measurement of the liability more difficult, in that, if any of the other parties do not meet their share of the liability, if may fall on the reporting entity. To the extent that there is doubt, the working party's view is that the liability should be recognised in accordance with the principles in SSAP 18.

The working document for the Forum notes that the Fourth Directive prohibits the offsetting of assets and liabilities, except where a legal right of set off exists. The Companies Act, Schedule 4, paragraph 5 includes a similar prohibition of set off. On the basis that the liability for environmental damage and the expected recovery comprise two separate transactions, each with its own associated risks and uncertainties, the document for the Forum is expected to recommend that the gross liability and the expected net recovery are evaluated and presented separately in the balance sheet, unless a legal right of set off exists. The working party believes that this is an acceptable approach although inclusion of the recovery in the balance sheet must depend on the degree of certainty involved. **5.3**

It is often argued that, as a result of the Companies Act, Schedule 4 paragraph 12, the amount accrued as a liability may take account of the probable outcome of related counterclaims against third parties. Nevertheless, the working party believes that expected recoveries should not be taken into account in recognising liabilities for future environmental expenditure, for a number of reasons, in particular: **5.4**

(a) the uncertainty involved and the different degrees of responsibility attaching to the liability and the recovery;
(b) the more stringent criteria for recognising contingent gains compared with contingent losses; and
(c) the general principle whereby assets and liabilities are not offset except in very limited circumstances, such as where the third party in each case is the same entity.

As suggested in paragraph 5.3 above, however, separate disclosure may be necessary to provide a balanced view.

Q6 In the case of contingent environmental liabilities, do existing accounting standards and company law provide sufficient guidance?

SSAP 18 defines a contingency as 'a condition which exists at the balance sheet date, where the outcome will be confirmed only on the occurrence or non-occurrence of one or more uncertain future events'. It requires that provision should be made for a material contingent loss where: **6.1**

(a) it is *probable* that a future event will confirm the loss; and
(b) the loss can be estimated with reasonable accuracy at the date when the accounts are formally approved by the directors.

This requirement is reflected in the Companies Act, Schedule 4 para 12(b).

Where no provision is made, the contingent loss should be disclosed unless the *possibility* of loss is remote. Such disclosure includes the nature of the contingency, a **6.2** summary of the uncertainty involved and, where possible, an estimate of the financial effects. Where it is not possible to quantify the effects, this should be disclosed.

6.3 The same principles apply in the case of contingencies involving environmental expenditure.

6.4 The conclusions reached by the CICA Study Group were that disclosure should include:

(a) 'reasonable possible' future environmental expenditure related to past events or transactions; and
(b) 'reasonably possible' environmental losses that could have a significant effect on future cash flows.

If the possibility of an environmental loss relating to past events or transactions is remote, but the impact could have a significant impact on future cash flows, the CICA research report concludes that it is desirable to disclose this possibility.

6.5 Such disclosure would go further than the current UK requirement under SSAP 18 and the working party believes that there would be a risk that users may draw unreliable conclusions from this information.

6.6 Under the US approach, a company might typically make a broad statement to the effect that the company is subject to environmental regulations that may result in a liability to meet the costs of environmental measures. Such disclosure might include further information as to the number of sites involved and an indication of the environmental policy adopted by management.

6.7 The working document for the Forum states simply that contingent liabilities should be disclosed in accordance with the Fourth and Seventh Directives, with sufficient narrative information to enable the nature of the contingency to be understood.

6.8 The working party takes the view that SSAP 18 provides an adequate basis on which to deal with disclosure of contingent environmental liabilities, although the uncertainty involved and the period to which it relates will often present particular difficulties as regards recognition and measurement. Therefore, there is often greater uncertainty in measuring the liability than for other contingencies.

III IMPAIRMENT OF ASSETS

Q7 Are existing accounting principles sufficiently clear as regards the recognition of impairment of the value of assets resulting from environmental concerns? Is there adequate distinction between an asset write-down and an accrual for a probable future loss due to impairment?

7.1 The issue of impairment is not unique to assets that are affected by environmental factors and the general principles of reviewing asset values for possible impairment apply equally to environmental impairment. Nevertheless, the working party took the view that existing principles in this area are not sufficiently clear for assessing any type of impairment. However, as the uncertainties as to timescale and amount are often likely to be greater in the case of environmental impairment, there is a more urgent need for guidance.

The ASB's proposed Statement of Principles (Chapter 4) deals with the recognition of assets and liabilities, including subsequent remeasurement, stating that, following initial recognition, events may occur that affect the recognised item and it is therefore necessary to test at intervals thereafter to see if the recorded amount needs to be changed. However, the ASB has not issued any specific guidance that relates to impaired assets, either generally or in connection with impairment of an asset as a result of environmental considerations. 7.2

In Chapter 5 of the ASB's proposed Statement of Principles, the asset measurement basis considered to be the most appropriate is that of *value to the business*. Applying this to the case of an asset that is impaired as a result of environmental concerns, an entity would be expected to measure the asset at its *recoverable amount*, which would usually be its *value in use*, as the net realisable value would in most cases be lower than the value is use as a result of the impairment. However, where legislation prohibits the use of an asset which has a material scrap value, the recoverable amount would be its net realisable value. 7.3

In ED 51 'Accounting for fixed assets and revaluations', the ASC proposed that a *permanent diminution* in the value of a fixed asset to below its carrying amount should be recognised in the profit and loss account for the period in which it occurs or is first perceived. 7.4

In November 1993, the FASB issued an exposure draft on the impairment of assets 'Accounting for the impairment of long-lived assets'. This proposed that the *recognition* of impairment should be based on a consideration of the undiscounted cash flows from the asset concerned bu that the impairment should be *measured* on the basis of discounted cash flows. 7.5

The CICA research report concluded that, if the impairment of assets as a result of environmental concerns is recognised through a loss accrual, the accrued loss should be shown as a separate liability. However, the report also stated that there is a need to clarify the distinction between an asset write-down and a contingent loss accrual for the impairment of an asset. 7.6

When legislation is introduced which requires reductions in the level of environmental contamination, it may be necessary to consider whether existing assets are impaired. In certain circumstances, such as the announcement of forthcoming legislation, it may be imprudent to await the actual date on which the new regulations become effective. 7.7

As regards the measurement of impairment, the net recoverable amount of an asset would normally be determined by reference to the estimated future net cash flow from its use, based on a projection using management's best estimates. As in other cases involving the consideration of future cash flows, the use of discounting may be appropriate. 7.8

7.9 The working party do not share the concern expressed in the CICA report, on the basis that in the case of an asset write-down, the entity has already incurred the loss, whereas in the case of a future loss accrual, the loss has not yet been incurred but its future occurrence is known with a reasonable degree of certainty. The impairment of an asset should be recognised by reducing the carrying amount of the asset rather than by introducing a liability. Such an item would not, in any case, meet the definition of a liability in the ASB's proposed Statement of Principles.

IV DISCLOSURE

Q8 **Are any additional disclosures appropriate, eg as regards accounting policies, environmental costs, liabilities and commitments, or possible future expenditure?**

8.1 Under SSAP 2 'Disclosure of accounting policies', the accounting policies followed for dealing with items which are judged material or critical in determining profit or loss for the year and in stating the financial position should be disclosed by way of note to the accounts.

8.2 In addition, the working document for the Forum states that 'the valuation methods applied on environmental issues' should be disclosed. It is not clear what information would be provided under this heading or whether it would differ from other valuation methods.

8.3 The CICA research study concludes that disclosure should comprise:

(a) a description of what is included in the definition of 'environmental costs';
(b) the basis on which environmental costs are expenses or capitalised;
(c) if environmental costs are capitalised the basis on which such costs are amortised to income; and
(d) the basis on which environmental liabilities are recognised.

8.4 The working party supports the broad principles set out above as being consistent and applicable to all entities for which environmental considerations are significant. A specific accounting policy for recognition and measurement of environmental costs and liabilities should be provided when such items are material to the financial statements. In addition, specific disclosures will follow from the principles set out in the preceding sections of this paper.

8.5 The working document for the Forum states that disclosure of costs incurred as a result of fines and penalties and similar environmentally-related costs, if not separately disclosed as extraordinary items, would be *useful*. The view of FEE is that separate disclosure should be *required*. Where fines or penalties incurred represent a significant proportion of total environmental costs, the working party believes that separate disclosure is important so as not to distort the view presented as regards spending on beneficial environmental work, i.e. costs for which there is a return or benefit.

8.6 The unique nature of environmental costs and liabilities is not a sufficient criterion for separate disclosure; this should depend on the likelihood of information, or its omission, influencing the economic decisions of users. Consequently, in deciding what information to disclose, it is essential to have regard to the purpose of disclosure and the materiality of the amounts involved. The difficulty of making comparisons and the danger of drawing unreliable conclusions need to be borne closely in mind.

The measurement of liabilities may be difficult and is particularly vulnerable to the effect of changes in the current state of environmental technology. For example, to be useful, disclosure needs to strike a balance between a broad unquantified statement and a very detailed description of specific valuation methods that may tend to confuse the reader. **8.7**

Disclosure of environmental liabilities is an example of the trade off between relevance and reliability, identified as qualitative characteristics of financial statements in the ASB's proposed Statement of Principles. In particular, such 'information may be relevant although so unreliable in nature or representation that its recognition in the financial statements may be potentially misleading'. **8.8**

Part Ten

ICAEW Accounting Recommendations

Trust accounts

*(Issued October 1986)**

Contents

****Editor's note:*** *No attempt has been made to footnote any changes in taxation or other legislation referred to in these recommendations.*

Trust Accounts

The Council of The Institute of Chartered Accountants in England and Wales makes the following recommendations to members regarding the accounts of deceased persons' estates and the more general types of trusts in England and Wales (excluding special trusts such as pension funds, unit trusts and public charitable foundations). Generally the recommendations in this statement will be most appropriate to private trusts formed in connection with estate planning and other personal purposes. Whilst it is recognised that, subject to the observance of any relevant legal considerations, the form in which accounts are prepared is a matter within the discretion of the trustees, it is hoped that these recommendations as to what is regarded as best practice will be helpful to members who either act as trustees themselves or whose advice or assistance is sought by trustees.

Introduction

The main object of trust accounts is to demonstrate that the trust funds, including the **1** income thereof, have been applied in accordance with the provisions of the trust instrument. They should also convey to beneficiaries and other interested parties, as well as to the trustees, information about the transactions and the current state of affairs of the trust. Trust accounts may also be useful for taxation and other purposes. To this extent trust accounts are special purpose accounts and SSAPs will not generally be applicable. However, where a trust account includes trading activities, SSAPs should be applied so far as they are relevant to these activities.

Special considerations, which are not necessarily dealt with in the following para- **2** graphs, obtain in the case of trusts under the Settled Land Act 1925 and those for which prescribed forms of account exist (e.g., certain charities).

Trust accounts differ from ordinary commercial accounts in a number of ways because **3** of different underlying circumstances. For instance there are many trusts where income is separately accounted for, thus lessening the need for production of annual accounts, and, in the case of established trusts, where changes of investments are infrequent and the income is mandated to a single life tenant, the interval between accounting dates may be several years and the accounts may deal only with capital transactions. Accounts dealing with all or selected aspects of the trust will be required in the following circumstances:

(a) where there is a distribution or other significant changes in the trust fund or in the rights in it;
(b) in the case of the estate of a deceased person which is settled for any period, when the initial administration of the estate has been completed (i.e., when the final inheritance tax figures have been settled, testamentary expenses paid, and the investments assembled into a fairly permanent portfolio); and
(c) at selected intervals, to show changes in capital accounts, even when there are no other matters to be dealt with.

If accounts are prepared less frequently than annually, particular care will be necessary to ensure that the underlying records are kept up to date and that the investments come under regular review by the trustees.

4 The following taxes and duties have been repealed, or were operative for one year only:

special charge, imposed by the Finance Act 1968, by reference to investment income for the year to 5 April 1968

special contribution, imposed by the Finance Act 1948, by reference to investment income for the year to 5 April 1948

legacy and succession duties, repealed by the Finance Act 1949 as respects deaths occurring on or after 30 July 1949

Inasmuch as the aforementioned taxes were chargeable to capital and, where separate funds are involved, perhaps disproportionately to those funds, their incidence may still be relevant in trust accounts. In paragraph 59 guidance is offered as to the treatment of special charge; the same general principles would have applied to special contribution and legacy and succession duties, but these are not dealt with in detail.

betterment levy, imposed by Part III of the Land Commission Act 1967 on the increase in the value of land as a result of a change in its use and repealed with effect from 22 July 1970

development gains tax, imposed by the Finance Act 1974 on land subject to development and disposals of such land and interests in settled property, at least three quarters of whose assets were represented by land, and repealed on the introduction of development land tax on 1 August 1976

development land tax, imposed by the Development Land Tax Act 1976 on gains arising on land made available for development, or when the proceeds of sale of land reflected the prospects of development, and repealed by the Finance Act 1985

In so far as these taxes have been paid as a result of land being developed and that land is retained by a trust, guidance is offered in paragraph 39 of the treatment in the accounts and in paragraph 44 on the enhanced base cost of that land for the purposes of other taxes.

estate duty, first imposed by the Finance Act 1894 on property passing before and on death and finally repealed on 13 November 1974 following the introduction of capital transfer tax

Where exemption from estate duty was granted on a death occurring before 13 November 1974 on works of art, historic buildings, or land of historic, scenic or scientific interest, this duty may still be payable in certain circumstances, and guidance is offered in paragraph 57 which deals with the incidence of inheritance tax in similar circumstances.

capital transfer tax, first imposed by the Finance Act 1975, repealed for certain lifetime gifts with effect from 18 March 1986 and renamed as inheritance tax as from 25 July 1986 for property passing 7 years prior to or on death.

In addition to be accountable for money and other assets actually coming into their hands trustees are responsible for the administration of the trust. The extent of their responsibility and the way it has been discharged will, therefore, not be apparent unless the periodical accounts deal with both these aspects. This will involve the recording of all the assets and liabilities of the trust, real or contingent, including for example, interests in expectancy and foreign estate. Where assets and liabilities cannot be quantified, or are subject to contingencies (e.g., foreign assets subject to exchange control regulations, contingent liabilities to inheritance tax, capital transfer tax and estate duty as a result of conditional exemptions and deductions allowed from possible future tax liabilities), attention should be drawn to their existence in notes to the balance sheet. The balance sheet will then show the position of the trust as a whole and not merely those assets which have come into the hands of the trustees. **5**

There is a fundamental distinction in trust accounts between income and capital. Often there are interests in income and interests in capital which conflict and the drawing of this distinction is essential to show the relative positions of those concerned. **6**

Various special aspects of the administration of trusts make it necessary to consider how to deal with: **7**

(a) the three ranges of investments ('narrower', wider' and 'special') if the Trustee Investments Act 1961 is applied (see also **Members' Handbook Statement 2.204** on the Trustee Investments Act 1961);
(b) investments acquired by the trustees from a testator or settlor which, but for special powers to postpone sale or to retain, would be unauthorised;
(c) assets which have not yet come into the trustees' hands;
(d) accumulations of income and investments made therefrom;
(e) special legal considerations such as statutory and equitable apportionments, deeds of family arrangement, court orders; and
(f) the linking of taxes (e.g., inheritance tax, capital gains tax, income tax) with the particular funds out of which they are payable.

Some trustees, and many beneficiaries, may know little about accounting. Trust accounts should, therefore, be as simple and clear as is consistent with the showing of sufficient detail for a proper understanding of the transactions. These requirements can be fulfilled by using schedules and subsidiary accounts for many matters of detail, cross-referencing them to the main accounts. It is desirable that trustees should sign the accounts and that beneficiaries should formally signify agreement with their personal accounts; clarity and simplicity of presentation, by making the accounts more easily understood, will help adoption of this procedure. **8**

The accounts and their underlying records may have to be examined to establish what deductions are available for capital gains tax purposes on the disposal of chargeable assets, or because of a dispute (e.g., between trustees and beneficiaries) or, in the case of **9** a discretionary settlement, to calculate inheritance tax on a ten-year periodic charge, or on a beneficiary becoming entitled to call for income and/or the settled property. In addition to emphasising the need for clarity and adequate detail, these possibilities indicate that accounts, vouchers and records generally should be kept for a longer period than if they were commercial documents. Where members discover that such records are inadequate, they should draw to the attention of the trustees, preferably in writing, the need to maintain and retain appropriate records.

10 Trust accounts are the responsibility of the trustees. An accountant preparing accounts for trustees should submit them with a report reciting any instructions given to him and stating the principles adopted in presentation and any special factors, problems or outstanding matters. These recommendations do not deal with the form of either such reports or audit reports. However, the accountant should make it clear whether or not he has audited the accounts.

11 It will usually facilitate a clear understanding of the accounts if a short history is attached showing the incidents which led up to the position displayed by the accounts, the names of the trustees and a brief explanation of the devolution of the funds. If the trust instrument(s) is complex, such explanation may be restricted to present interests in income and such indication of succeeding interests as is feasible within the compass of a short note.

12 For listed investments, a valuation of the portfolio as at the balance sheet date may accompany the accounts and this valuation, together with the accounts, should ideally give sufficient information to enable the capital gains tax implications of investment policy to that date to be considered.

13 The recommendations below may not apply fully throughout the entire field of trust accounts but it is considered that the fundamental principles should not differ in substance from those now recommended. It must, however, be emphasised that trusts are so varied in their nature that there should be flexibility in the manner of presenting accounts and that a standard form is neither practicable nor desirable.

14 The following paragraphs contain references to statutory and equitable apportionments, and to the operation of the Trustee Investments Act 1961. Nowadays, many wills and settlements specifically exclude the former and, by incorporating their own wide investment powers, override those in the Act.

Recommendations

15 It is recommended that the following principles should normally be applied in connection with records and the preparation of accounts of trusts.

GENERAL PRINCIPLES

Trustees should maintain records from which, in the light of the trust instrument(s) and legal considerations, periodical statements of account and tax returns can be prepared. The records and/or trust accounts should preserve all the information that may be required at future dates (possibly long deferred) for any review of the trustees' transactions and for capital gains tax and inheritance tax purposes. Although traditionally it has been recommended that this should be achieved by keeping books on complete double-entry principles, less formal methods are now acceptable provided that those principles govern the preparation of the trust accounts. Similar considerations apply to the presentation of the accounts. There should be prepared and kept with the trust documents a short history of the trust and a summary of the relevant provisions of the will or other trust instrument(s). However, the original terms should be consulted where necessary. Other information which might be suitably recorded and kept readily available and up to date would include: **16**

(a) the settlor's name and present address, his domicile, residence and ordinary residence status for tax purposes and his deemed domicile status for inheritance tax purposes, the dates he created and transferred any property into the trust and, where relevant, his date of death;
(b) any reference adopted by the Capital Taxes Office for the settlor's and the trustees' affairs;
(c) the trustees' names and addresses;
(d) the names and addresses of present and future beneficiaries, their dates of birth (especially where the attainment of a specified age is relevant to the will or settlement), the dates of their marriages (where this is likewise relevant), and their relationship to the testator or settlor;
(e) the dates on which the trustees lose powers to accumulate income and/or to exercise discretions over the devolution of the settled property;
(f) in the case of discretionary settlements, the dates and amounts of each chargeable occasion for inheritance tax (formerly capital transfer tax) purposes.

It may be appropriate to set out some or all of the above information in a statement attached to the accounts. **17**

The date to which accounts are made up should be decided according to the circumstances and will not necessarily be the anniversary of the creation of the trust. Having regard to the taxation liabilities of the trust and of the beneficiaries, it may frequently be convenient for accounts to be made up to the anniversary of the trust's creation if the rules of law relating to equitable apportionments are applicable or if there are other special circumstances. The nature of the trust assets, the dates on which income is receivable, the due dates of annuities, are all factors that may affect the selection of the most convenient accounting date. **18**

Income and capital transactions should be segregated clearly. This may be assisted by the use of separate columns in accounting records. **19**

Periodic accounts should normally consist of: **20**

(a) balance sheet of the whole of the trust estate;
(b) capital account, summarising capital transactions either from the commencement of the trust or since the last account;
(c) income account, where appropriate; and
(d) schedules and subsidiary accounts explaining in greater detail the major items appearing in the balance sheet, capital account and income account;

showing separately the figures for any special funds.

21 The balance sheet, capital account and income account should be presented as simply as possible, all details being relegated to the schedules and subsidiary accounts.

BALANCE SHEET

22 The various items in the balance sheet should be grouped under appropriate headings, so that significant totals are readily apparent. Presentation becomes ever more important when the Trustee Investments Act 1961 has been applied and the capital account and the assets represented by it have been divided into narrower-, wider-, and special-range parts.

23 Where there are differing interests in the same trust the accounts will consist of two or more self-balancing sections, and can be made more understandable if the balance sheet layout is designed with this in mind. For instance, if there are few liabilities, it will probably be better to deduct them from the assets than to show them on the liabilities side. In this way the liabilities would be confined to the various funds and beneficiaries' current account balances, and the net assets by which they are represented would appear by sections immediately opposite them. This form of presentation is not always possible but, whenever it is, it should be adopted.

Distinction between capital and income

24 In most cases, capital items should be clearly segregated from income balances, either by appropriate grouping, or possibly by the use of separate columns. However, where a balance on income account represents income received and held temporarily on a bank account for distribution to a life tenant(s) and the member is satisfied that the realisable assets on capital account exceed the associated current liabilities, the distinction may be ignored in the balance sheet, although it must be clear from the underlying records.

Comparative figures

25 Comparative figures should be included if they serve a useful purpose. Normally, however, the supporting schedules will be more informative than any comparison of total figures with those on the previous accounting date.

Capital account

26 Generally, the capital account in the balance sheet will show the balance of the capital funds held, so far as they have been ascertained. If the Trustee Investments Act 1961 has been applied, the division of the fund in two or three parts should be shown, but in that case it is important to show the total of the capital accounts and not merely the amounts of its parts. Where distributions of capital have been made to beneficiaries it is permissible, and sometimes necessary (e.g., where advancement has taken place), to show the original capital available for distribution and the amount of the distributions to date.

The capital account should be amplified by way of notes for any contingencies of significance to the trustees and/or the beneficiaries, including notes on both contingent liabilities and assets (see paragraphs 32 and 51). This would also apply where the value of assets is known to differ materially from their balance sheet amount. **27**

Where appropriate, liabilities on capital account (e.g., inheritance tax, capital gains tax, unpaid legacies) should be distinguished from those in income account, which themselves should be analysed so as to segregate balances due to beneficiaries from other liabilities. **28**

Current liabilities and those payable more than one year after the date of the balance sheet should be segregated. Details of the arrangements for the payment of those liabilities due more than one year hence, any interest thereon and the translation of any amounts due in a currency other than sterling (including the exchange rate used) should appear in notes to the balance sheet. **29**

Where liabilities, or rights to advances are payable only out of the proceeds of sale of particular assets and the payments are secured thereon, such liabilities should be shown as a deduction from the values at which those assets are carried in the accounts. **30**

Accruing liabilities on capital account are normally provided for but in special or difficult circumstances may alternatively be recorded by way of note. An example would be where the Trustee Investments Act 1961 has been applied and it is not known from which part of the fund a liability will be paid. (For treatment of accruals on income account see paragraph 70.) **31**

It is normally preferable to deal by way of note with: **32**

(a) known liabilities whose amounts cannot be determined with substantial accuracy;
(b) contingent liabilities including:

guarantees given by a deceased, or the trustees (unless claims may be expected, in which case they should be provided for in full in the accounts)

potential capital gains tax on an unrealised but recorded appreciation of the trust's investments

potential risk of further sterling liabilities when loans or significant other debts are repayable in foreign currencies and not matched by corresponding readily realisable assets in the same currencies

where the value of any assets associated with charges to inheritance tax, capital gains tax, or stamp duty have yet to be agreed for those purposes;

where, following a lifetime gift, a donee and trustees have agreed that any chargeable gains arising as a result of the gift should be held over for capital gains tax purposes

where personal representatives and/or trustees have given undertakings to the Treasury in order to obtain the conditional exemption from estate duty and/or capital transfer tax and/or inheritance tax on gifts of property of national interest

inheritance tax and capital gains tax due on property transferred to the trust to the extent that these taxes have not been paid by the settlor

where, following distributions from the trust, the trustees and the beneficiaries have held over a gain and the trustees remain responsible for paying the associated capital gains tax if the beneficiary ceases to be resident or ordinarily resident in the United Kingdom

where personal representatives and/or trustees have elected to defer the payment of capital transfer tax or inheritance tax on growing timber until disposal of that timber

further inheritance tax on the death of a settlor to the extent that the tax at the death rates at that time exceeds the tax due on the lifetime gift

inheritance tax on the termination of a right to call for income or on the death of a life tenant (subject to the exemption under the surviving spouse rule)

inheritance tax on:

the creation of interests in possession; or accumulation and maintenance settlements for children; or any tenth anniversary of the creation of the settlement; where the settled property is or was held on discretionary trusts

(c) contingent legacies.

Where it is desirable to indicate the financial effect to the beneficiaries, an amount should be set aside to meet the possible liability covered by the note, or should be dealt with in the covering report.

Tax on capital gains and chargeable transfers

33 In normal cases it will be possible to quantify any outstanding liability in respect of tax on capital gains. In these cases it should be treated as a creditor and charged against the surplus which has been added to capital.

34 Where a trust has been appropriated into separate funds to meet differing interests but is still regarded as a single settlement for capital gains tax purposes:

(a) any tax payable by the trustees should be divided amongst and charged to the funds to which chargeable gains have arisen in the accounting period in proportion to those gains; and

(b) no amounts should be transferred to those funds to whom allowable losses have arisen for the capital gains tax that has been saved by those funds with chargeable gains utilizing those losses;

in the absence of a direction to the contrary in the will or other trust instrument.

Where trustees hold shares in a company: 35

which is not resident in the United Kingdom; which would be regarded as a close company if resident here; which disposes of assets not associated with trading activities; and which does not distribute that gain on winding up within two years;

they face liabilities to capital gains tax on a proportion of any gains arising to that company equal to the proportion of its assets they would receive on a winding up (unless that proportion is less than 5 per cent). Unless the tax is paid direct by the company to the Inland Revenue, provision should be made in the capital account for the capital gains tax payable by the trustees and the accounts should include a note drawing attention to the possibility of the tax paid being a deduction from any subsequent chargeable gain arising on the disposal of the shares. If any tax is paid by the company, the payment should be shown in the accounts as a deduction from the capital gains tax payable and not as income arising to the trustees.

Where allowable losses have been established, the cumulative total available to be carried forward should be noted. 36

If the payment of capital gains tax has been postponed under the provisions of Section 8, Capital Gains Tax Act 1979, or capital transfer tax or inheritance tax has been postponed under the provisions of the Inheritance Tax Act 1984, or the trustees have assumed the responsibility for the payment of any taxes due by the settlor, provision should be made for the whole of the tax, and a note added explaining the period over which the instalments are payable. 37

Where chargeable gains have arisen to trustees on the realisation of foreign property, the proceeds of which cannot be remitted due to local exchange control regulations, and the trustees have applied for the payment of the tax to be deferred, provision should be made for the tax payable after deducting any double taxation relief and a note added explaining the circumstances under which the tax is payable. 38

In certain circumstances a deduction may be allowed from any chargeable gains subsequently arising to the trustees on the sale of the relevant assets if they have paid any of the following taxes (or similar taxes which may be introduced) on these assets and then retained them: 39

betterment levy

development gains tax

development land tax

capital transfer tax or inheritance tax (e.g., where either tax has been paid on chargeable assets, but the chargeable gains have been held over for capital gains tax purposes)

inheritance tax (e.g., where a donor dies within 7 years of his gift).

Details of the nature and value of each deduction should appear in notes to the accounts.

Assets

40 In normal circumstances investments will appear in the balance sheet under a few broad classifications with the detail appearing in schedules attached. Where, however, there are few investments, no changes having taken place during the year, it would be permissible to detail them in the balance sheet. The total market value of the listed investments should always appear on the face of the balance sheet as well as in the schedules.

41 Where the trustees have applied the Trustee Investments Act 1961 they should have earmarked specific investments to each part of the fund. It is most important that this allocation should be strictly maintained at all times and that the total of the investments of each part of the fund should appear, either in the balance sheet, or in the investment schedules.

42 Where the trustees of a deceased person's estate have power to postpone the sale of unauthorised investments, such holdings may need to be distinguished in the accounts so that points of equitable apportionment or investment policy can be understood.

43 The circumstances in which an asset is acquired by a trust will determine the value at which it is brought into the trust books. If it devolves on the trustees as part of a deceased person's estate, the probate value (normally the market value at the date of death) will be adopted. If it is a gift from a living settlor and he pays capital gains tax thereon by reference to the market value at the date of the gift, that value will likewise become the book value. Where the settlor and the trustees agree to any chargeable gains arising on the gift being held over, the book value of any assets should be the market value, less any associated held over gain, and a note should appear on the accounts accordingly (see paragraph 32(b)). If the asset is purchased at arm's length by the trustees, cost will be the basis adopted.

44 On the eventual disposal of an asset, its cost or its market value at the date of acquisition, as appropriate, will generally become relevant for the purpose of computing capital gains tax. It will be convenient if the cost or market value appearing in the accounts is made to agree with that which will govern the capital gains tax position on disposal before indexation allowance. Such cost or market values may also take account of any enhancements following charges to other taxes (paragraph 4). However, following the introduction of and the changes to the identification rules, this may no longer be possible, particularly after partial disposals of listed securities. In such circumstances, listed securities should be carried in accounts at their average cost to the trustees, the profits and losses calculated accordingly and the basis adopted explained in a note.

45 Where small realisations of investments (e.g., sales of fractional shares and rights to new shares) have taken place and where the proceeds are less than 5 per cent of the value of the investments, the proceeds would be deducted from the cost or market value. It is not suggested, however, that assets acquired before 6 April 1965, or 31 March 1982, should be restated at their market value at either of those dates, unless there is some circumstance or occurrence such as a part-disposal which renders it obligatory to adopt that value for capital gains tax purposes subsequently.

The other significant departure from the general principle set out in paragraphs 43 and 44 would be where, because of a provision in the trust instrument, the accounts would be difficult to understand or inappropriate if capital gains tax base values were adopted. **46**

The assets of a trust may become subject to inheritance tax, or capital gains tax, or both, while remaining within the ownership of the trustees (e.g., on the cesser of a life interest, or when an interest in possession is created over settled property previously subject to discretionary trusts). On the happening of such an event, the current values agreed for tax purposes should appear in the accounts. However, the current values should be adopted in the accounts only if the trustees discharge the associated capital gains tax; where they elect to hold over the gains the current value of the relevant assets should be written down and the capital account adjusted accordingly. In this way not only will the tax borne be shown to bear a proper relationship to the assets involved, but, at least initially, the base cost for subsequent capital gains tax liabilities will normally be established in the books. **47**

There may be a revaluation of trust assets for reasons unconnected with taxation (e.g., in order to effect a division of the trust funds for the provision of applying the Trustee Investments Act 1961, or of carrying out some provision of the trust instrument). If such a revaluation is adopted in the accounts, consideration should be given to the impact of capital gains tax should the assets be disposed of at their new book amounts. If a material liability to tax would result, the position should be disclosed in a note on the accounts. **48**

Valuations by investment advisers may be attached to trust accounts, and if they are made at the balance sheet date, they may be used as a substitute for the investment schedules. It must, however, be remembered that in many cases they will not agree with the balance sheet total for investments because the book amount will not be included as part of the information. **49**

The composition of cash and bank balances as between capital, income and special funds should be shown. If material, cash and bank balances in currencies other than sterling should be shown separately for each currency. If the grouping adopted for the balance sheet as between capital, income and special funds makes it necessary, the bank balance(s) will have to be divided so that the appropriate amounts appear under their proper headings in the balance sheet, but the aggregate bank balances should also be shown. **50**

A note should be made in respect of: **51**

(a) any known assets, the amount of which cannot be determined with substantial accuracy, for example, reversions and claims for damages;

(b) any known assets of a contingent nature, for example, restrictive covenants over realty or personalty and contingent reversions; and
(c) the rates of exchange used to translate any assets and/or liabilities appearing in the accounts and expressed in currencies other than sterling.

Special Funds

52 Where special funds arise by reason of the existence of separate trusts or settled funds within the main administration, the capital and liabilities of such special funds should be stated under separate headings and the corresponding assets should also be stated separately. The treatment of special charges on different funds will depend on the circumstances of the life tenants or annuitants (see paragraph 59). Where it is desired to show a special relationship between the funds (e.g., they are particular fractions of residue) it will be necessary to show the original capital of each fund inset, with the charge and related professional fees as deductions.

Capital Account

53 The opening entries for any form of trust record will be derived from the cost or acquisition values of the assets concerned (see paragraph 43).

54 For deceased persons' estates, the opening entries should show the assets and liabilities at the figures applicable for inheritance tax purposes, a balance being struck to show the net estate subdivided, if necessary, to show:

(a) property on which tax either has been paid or is currently payable;
(b) property not currently assessable to tax; and
(c) property exempt from tax.

55 The capital account for any period should show, suitably classified and in adequate detail, the extent to which the trust capital account has been affected by matters such as:

(a) surpluses or deficits on realisations;
(b) taxation of capital gains arising directly to the trustees showing separately those taxes payable in the United Kingdom and overseas and any double taxation relief;
(c) taxation of capital gains arising as a result of interest in overseas companies and trusts, showing separately taxes payable in the United Kingdom and overseas, any double taxation relief and tax provided for in previous years and then paid direct by the companies and/or trusts;
(d) adjustments of book figures to capital gains tax base values;
(e) inheritance tax;
(f) special charges, such as that imposed by the Finance Act 1968;
(g) administration expenses;
(h) changes for inheritance tax purposes as shown in corrective affidavits;
(i) surpluses or deficits on revaluations;
(j) legacies, or appropriations to special funds; and

(k) statutory or equitable apportionments.

Separate figures should be presented for each part of a trust which has been split in accordance with the provisions of the Trustee Investments Act 1961; this may be achieved by presenting one account with several columns. 56

Inheritance tax

Where appropriate, the capital account should show the total on which inheritance tax is payable and the amount paid; also the information relating to inheritance tax should include matters such as: 57

business relief available;

agricultural relief claimed;

conditional exemptions for:
growing timber
works of art
historic buildings and land of historic, scenic or scientific interest;

quick succession relief;

surviving spouse exemption;

annual exemptions surrendered by beneficiaries;

any other reliefs and exemptions;

the trustees' assumed cumulative chargeable transfers to the date of charge;

any property aggregable for inheritance tax purposes though not forming part of the estate, or settled property for which the trustees are accountable;

any similar foreign tax charges and double taxation relief;

incidence of inheritance tax and foreign taxes amongst the beneficiaries; and

taxes paid to date and still outstanding.

Any other material matters affecting inheritance tax should also be stated in the capital account. If the detail is considerable, it should be relegated to a supporting schedule.

In some cases the agreement of valuations for inheritance tax purposes may be a protracted matter extended over several years (for example, where the estate includes interests in land, unlisted shares or business goodwill). Where this occurs, the fact of the 58 inheritance tax being provisional should be stated with an indication, where appropriate and practicable, whether the outstanding amount involved may be material.

Special charges

59 Where a tax such as a special charge (see paragraph 4) is paid out of a trust it is charged to capital in the same way as inheritance tax. Where particular funds are directed by a will to be free from tax, special charges may prove to be a charge against the residuary estate, but normally it will be a charge upon the funds whose income gives rise to the tax paid. Where more than one person is interested in the income of one undivided fund then the various payments of the special charges will be charged to the capital of that fund and future shares of income will be adjusted. Professional charges for dealing with special charges will be dealt with in the same way as the tax itself.

Comparative figures

60 Comparative figures for the preceding period will not normally serve a useful purpose in the capital account.

Special funds

61 Special funds, dealt with separately in the balance sheet, should have their separate capital accounts (see also paragraph 23).

INCOME ACCOUNT

62 The purpose of an income account is to inform those interested as to the amount, sources and division of income and, occasionally, to assist in the understanding of the taxation position. The main emphasis, according to circumstances, should be one or more of:

(a) the stewardship of the trustees, when much detail will be shown;
(b) the pattern of income, when the grouping of the figures will be used to produce significant totals, for instance, the income from fixed interest and other types of investment or, possibly, the significant diversification of investments. This will help the appraisal of future requirements and budgeting;
(c) division of income, as in cases where apportionments are made or there are several funds each with a different life tenant;
(d) assistance to beneficiaries and trustees in adjusting or understanding their taxation, where, for example, relief is available against higher rate taxes for inheritance tax on accrued income (Section 430, Taxes Act 1970) or there are assessments on property income.

63 The form of the accounts must be that which is most apt to the trust, comprehensible to trustees and beneficiaries (who may not be business-trained) and useful in managing the trust. Items should be grouped in appropriate classifications (for example, interest on Government Securities, dividends, interest of mortgages, rents, business profits, credit from realised capital on equitable apportionments). All items involving considerable detail, such as investment income, should be included in total only, with supporting schedules showing the details. If appropriate, comparative figures should be given.

Income

In circumstances where other arrangements might be onerous, for convenience trustees are usually allowed to account to beneficiaries for income when it is receivable so that the account need not necessarily include accruing income. However, a life tenant is not entitled to income that is earned and accrues prior to the purchase of securities. Therefore, now that income tax is normally payable on accrued interest included in the proceeds of sale of fixed-interest and certain similar securities (and corresponding relief for income tax purposes is available for such interest on the purchase of such securities), where a life tenant may be interested in such accruals consideration should be given to accounting for such interest and the associated tax on an accruals basis when such securities are purchased or sold. **64**

Income collected by agents, such as rents collected, but not handed over to the trustees, should be regarded for accounting purposes as having been received. Consideration should also be given to the effect of any distortion caused by the exclusion of other accrued income, for example, where a company alters its dividend-paying timetable and, as a result, the accounts include more or less than a normal year's income. Where material distortion occurs, a note to the accounts or a reference in the accompanying report will be necessary in most cases. Income received in advance of the due date should be carried forward as a creditor in the balance sheet. **65**

Where a trade is carried on by trustees, the usual accounting principles applicable to a trading concern should be followed so far as relates to the trading profit and a note on the accounts will be necessary to indicate that this basis has been applied. The trading activity will sometimes have an accounting year which does not coincide with the trust accounting year, and the results should then be incorporated in the trust accounts on the basis of the trading year. Again an explanatory note on the accounts will be necessary. **66**

Where there are relatively few changes on capital account, an income account, not accompanied by a balance sheet, may be acceptable. There will also be cases where no formal account is needed, for example where all income is mandated to one life tenant (in which case a note to that effect should appear in the accounts) or where the disposal of income is so straightforward that a copy of the Inland Revenue Form R59 (Trust Estate: Statement of Income for the year ending 5 April) is an acceptable substitute. **67**

Income may be received: **68**

(a) gross but liable to income tax by direct assessment;
(b) net after deduction of United Kingdom and/or overseas tax at the basic rate;
(c) net after deduction of overseas withholding tax;
(d) with an associated tax credit;
(e) net under special arrangements (e.g., building society and bank deposit interest);

(f) exempt from tax (e.g., National Savings Certificates interest and supplement on tax repayments).

It should be made clear whether the income is shown gross or net and any charge for tax should be related to the income being taxed. The form of presentation will depend largely on the circumstances of the trust, in particular the types and number of sources of income and the period(s) covered by the accounts.

Statutory apportionments

69 In accounting for deceased persons' estates, investments are normally shown cum dividend. Therefore, unless accrued interest on any fixed-interest securities to the date of death has been taxed as income (in which case the interest should be deducted from the book value of the investment), where, in such a case, all or part of the dividend after death is apportioned to capital, it should not be deducted from the book value of the investment, but should be added to the balance of the estate capital account. Thus the investments will continue to be accounted for at capital gains tax values. Where an investment is shown ex-dividend, then the dividend apportioned to capital will usually be credited to the account for those dividends which are separately shown in the Inland Revenue affidavit. Ultimately, any balance on this account will be written off to estate capital account.

Expenditure

70 The income account should include all amounts payable in respect of the accounting period including, where material to a proper view of the distributable income, amounts accrued up to the accounting date but not then due for payment. Annuities payable are not normally accounted for on an accruals basis, although there will be cases where an income account would give an incorrect view of the amount of the surplus income if no accrual were made.

71 Items of expenditure and other deductions from income should be grouped in appropriate classifications; for example, administration expenses, interest on overdraft, income tax, interest on inheritance tax and other taxes, annuities, transfers to capital as a result of apportionments.

Tax on income

72 As indicated in paragraph 68, the treatment of the charge for tax on income will depend upon the form of presentation of the accounts. Where tax has still to be assessed on income shown in the accounts, due provision should be made. Any adjustment to the tax of earlier years should be shown separately.

73 There may be cases where the presentation alone cannot make clear how the tax is related to the income shown in the accounts, for instance where:

(a) tax is assessed under Schedules B or D and the charge does not represent the basic rate on the income for a particular accounting year;

(b) the rule in *re Pettit* applies (i.e., certain annuities paid free of tax);
(c) trust income is assessed to tax directly on the life tenant;
(d) the accrued income rules on the purchase or sale of fixed interest securities reduce or increase, respectively, the taxable income; or
(e) in the case of charitable trusts, income tax may be due by reference to:
  (i) expenditure and donations not regarded as for charitable purposes
  (ii) amounts invested in non-qualifying investments
  (iii) amounts lent on non-qualifying loans.

In all cases an appropriate explanatory note should be made in the accounts.

Balance of Income

The income account should show the balance available after debiting all items chargeable against income. It should show the manner in which the net balance has been applied by the trustees; for example, amounts divided amongst the beneficiaries and transfers to accumulation accounts, indicating the bases of division in cases such as those where adjustment is required for interest on advances of capital to beneficiaries. 74

If the income account is being accumulated or is to be distributed at the trustees' discretion: 75

(a) the amount of the tax credit available to frank such distributions in accordance with Section 17, Finance Act 1973; and
(b) the extent to which there is insufficient credit to do so on the balance available for distribution (e.g., as a result of the trustees claiming allowances or receiving tax-free income);

should be disclosed in a note.

SCHEDULES AND SUBSIDIARY ACCOUNTS

Whenever possible, details should be relegated to schedules and subsidiary accounts, leaving only the significant totals in the main accounts. 76

Appropriate cross-references should be given in both the main and the subsidiary documents. 77

Investments

The investment schedule should be so prepared as to enable totals in the main accounts to be identified readily. The grouping of the items in the schedule should therefore correspond with the grouping adopted in the balance sheet and it may be necessary to present more than one schedule. Where the trustees have applied the Trustee Investments Act 1961 the schedule(s) should show clearly to which part of the fund each investment has been allocated. 78

Special funds dealt with separately in the balance sheet or income account should in any case have their separate investment schedules. 79

80 The following information will normally be relevant in the investment schedule(s) although it may not all be necessary in every case:

(a) description and opening and closing nominal amounts and book amounts of securities; also in the case of listed securities, movements to both nominal and book amounts, including acquisitions, disposals, rights and bonus issues, share uplifts, exchanges, surrenders and revaluations and resulting surpluses and deficits during the period, the values at 6 April 1965 where relevant for capital gains tax purposes and, unless a valuation by an investment adviser is attached, the base cost of each security and the associated indexation allowance to the date of the balance sheet. In the case of unlisted securities a valuation will not normally be available. It may, however, be helpful for the schedule to include the date of the latest valuation and the value placed on them;

(b) in the case of mortgages, details of the opening and closing amounts and movements, security, rate of interest and due dates thereof, with particulars of any arrears of interest;

(c) the gross or net amount of interest and dividends, any associated tax credits and, separately, income tax and overseas withholding taxes deducted at source (see paragraph 68);

(d) opening and closing book values of acquisitions, disposals and revaluations of other investments during the period and resultant surpluses or deficits;

(e) statutory apportionments of dividends between capital and income, shown item by item, and the proportion of the interest received immediately following the acquisition of fixed interest securities with a nominal value greater than £5,000 which is not taxable in the hands of the life tenant. (Equitable apportionments do not usually fall to be dealt with item by item and should therefore be explained in the capital and income accounts by narration, or, if appropriate, by reference to a separate schedule);

(f) in the case of real estate and leasehold estate, the probate value, cost or other book amount, as applicable, with such details as tenure, property expenses suitably analysed, rents receivable and particulars of any arrears; and

(g) in the case of life assurance policies, the aggregate premiums paid to date (plus, in the case of an existing policy acquired, the value at the date of acquisition), brief details of the sums assured and maturity dates of the policies and, if relevant, their surrender values.

Accounts with beneficiaries

81 Accounts with beneficiaries should generally be presented. This is particularly important when the details are complicated; for example, where there are periodical payments on account of income, accumulation accounts on which income tax at the additional rate is payable, maintenance accounts, or special difficulties. It is desirable that beneficiaries should be able to verify easily any amounts shown in the accounts as having been paid to them.

Capital cash summary accounts

A capital cash summary account, containing in summarised form all significant information regarding the receipts and payments on capital account during the period covered by the accounts, may sometimes be helpful in larger estates. The information shown by such a summary account is not normally apparent in the capital account, which includes transactions other than receipts and payments. The summary account therefore provides a link between the capital cash shown in the balance sheet and that shown in the previous balance sheet. **82**

Other schedules

Examples of other matters, for which separate schedules should be prepared where the detail involved makes it desirable, are the following: **83**

(a) debtors;
(b) creditors;
(c) taxation, where the tax position of the trust is complex;
(d) executorship, administration or management expenses on both income and capital accounts;
(e) pecuniary and specific legacies, showing those paid or satisfied;
(f) inheritance tax where the detail is considerable, showing specifically any amounts charged to individual beneficiaries.

The interpretation of 'material' in relation to accounts

(Issued December 1985)

*The Council of the Institute of Chartered Accountants in England and Wales issues the following statement for the guidance of members on the meaning to be attached to the expression 'material' as used in the Companies Act 1985, particularly with reference to provisions relating to accounts and also as used generally in the Council's statements, including Statements of Standard Accounting Practice.**

INTRODUCTION

1 By literal definition the adjective 'material' can vary in meaning from 'significant' to 'essential'. In an accounting sense, however, a matter is material if knowledge of the matter would be likely to influence the user† of the financial or other statements under consideration. The use of the word 'material' in relation to accounting matters is intended to allow scope for different interpretations according to the variety of circumstances which can arise. It is not possible or desirable therefore to give a definition of 'material' in the sense of a formula which can be applied mechanically.

STATUTORY ACCOUNTING REQUIREMENTS AND STATEMENTS OF STANDARD ACCOUNTING PRACTICE

2 Paragraph 86 of the fourth schedule of the Companies Act 1985 provides that: 'Amounts which in the particular context of any provision of this schedule are not material may be disregarded for the purposes of that provision'. This and the other references to 'material' and its derivatives in companies legislation and the Statements of Standard Accounting Practice should be construed in the light of this statement, subject to the responsibility of the Courts to interpret the law in relation to specific cases.

3 In the context of accounts that are required or intended to give a true and fair view, Counsel's opinion obtained by the Accounting Standards Committee draws attention to the fact that the law distinguishes between the meaning of 'a true and fair view', which is constant, and the content of accounts required to give a true and fair view which may change over time. This opinion supports the advice in this statement that

***Editor's note:** A Discussion Paper 'Materiality in Financial Reporting' (FRAG 1/95) was issued in January 1995. It was designed to form the basis of revised guidance for members and is reproduced in Part Nine of this volume.*

†See Statement 1.311 in ICAEW Members Handbook, Professional Liability of Accountants and Auditors, paragraphs 14 to 18 on liability to third parties.

whether an item is material to the true and fair view can only be judged in the particular circumstances of that item and the accounts to which it relates.

GENERAL ACCOUNTING REQUIREMENTS

4 The principle of materiality pervades the whole process of accountancy and is not therefore confined to the statutory requirements referred to in the preceding paragraphs, nor to accounts intended to give a true and fair view. Questions of materiality arise in connection with all accounts, including those legally exempt from giving a true and fair view, specific purpose accounts, simple receipts and payments accounts and detailed profit and loss accounts. The process of preparing accounts, which entails the measurement, aggregation, classification and presentation of all relevant events, gives rise to two classes of question relating to materiality: (a) whether an item needs to be disclosed; (b) what margin of error (if any) is acceptable in the amount attributed to an item.

APPLICATION

5 The interpretation of what is 'material' is a matter for the exercise of professional judgement based on experience and the requirements of the accounts concerned (e.g., to give a true and fair view).

6 Considerations of materiality can arise in connection with various questions relating to the preparation of accounts, including whether or not:

(a) an item should be disclosed:
- (i) by description in an omnibus item
- (ii) separately
- (iii) as an important reservation or a matter of deliberate emphasis in presentation (e.g., profit of the year before deducting an exceptional loss);

(b) an error or oversight needs correction;

(c) a method of computation, basis or formula properly allows for relevant factors.

7 The application of the term 'material' to any item will include consideration of:

(a) the amount itself, in relation to:
- (i) the overall view of the accounts
- (ii) the total of which it forms or should form part
- (iii) associated items (whether in the profit and loss account or in the balance sheet)
- (iv) the corresponding amount in previous years;

(b) the description, including questions of emphasis;

(c) the presentation and context; and

(d) any statutory requirements for disclosure.

8 Materiality can only be considered in relation to context. On the question of disclosure, those responsible for preparing accounts have to decide which, out of the many facts available to them, are the ones which are likely to influence users of these accounts. In a small business, £100 may be material, whereas £1 million may not be material in classifying the expenditure of a very large undertaking, especially as too much elaboration could result in failure to communicate a clear overall picture. On the question of the required degree of accuracy, a difference of 10 per cent or more might be acceptable in some circumstances, but in other circumstances any difference might be unacceptable. While appropriate percentage comparisons can constitute useful broad guides, they should not be applied indiscriminately without regard to the particular circumstances.

Any item may be material in either a general or a particular context. The general context refers to the accounts as a whole. The particular context relates to the total of which an item forms or should form part and any directly associated items. If an item is not material in the general context, the degree of latitude acceptable in the particular context may depend upon its nature. **9**

There is an important distinction between cases where the amount at issue is arrived at on the basis of assumptions and the exercise of judgement and those where it is capable of precise and objective determination. In the former case the acceptable margin of error needs to be judged in the context of the fact that, for the item in question, there may be a range of figures (depending on the assumptions and judgements applied) which would not be regarded as incorrect. This may lead to the acceptable margin of error being greater than for items in the latter category, where in the ordinary course of events no departure from the exact figure would be expected. **10**

In the case of items such as directors' emoluments, audit fees and investment income which are subject to specific disclosure requirements (implying that they are expected to be of particular interest or importance to shareholders); an error which is trivial in the general context, and indeed may not even be large in relation to the item itself, may nevertheless be considered material. **11**

Some specific points are listed below: **12**

(a) *Degree of approximation*
The degree of estimation or approximation which is unavoidably inherent in arriving at the amount of an item may be a factor in deciding on materiality. Examples include contingency provisions, the valuation of stock and work in progress, and taxation provisions.

(b) *Excessive detail*
Excessive detail concerning immaterial items can serve to obscure the true and fair view. Examples are, (i) detailed description of items of little importance to the accounts as a whole; (ii) the use of spuriously exact figures for amounts which are inherently estimates (e.g., some contingencies); and (iii) the statement of amounts in full, where confining disclosure to the first few significant figures materially assists comprehension.

(c) *Critical points*
Inaccuracy which would not otherwise be judged to be material could have the effect of reversing a trend, or turning a profit into a loss, or creating or eliminating

the margin of solvency in a balance sheet. When an item affects such a critical point in accounts, then its materiality has to be viewed in that narrower context.

(d) *Losses or low profits*

The use of the profit figure as a point of comparison tends to be vitiated when the profits are abnormally low or where there is a loss; when judging the materiality of individual items in the profit and loss account in such cases, the more normal results of the business activities have to be considered.

(e) *Disproportionate significance*

An item of small amount may nevertheless be material in the context of a company's particular circumstances, especially if that context would lead the user to expect the item to be of substantial amount.

(f) *Offset and aggregation*

It frequently happens that two items, which would each be material if considered separately, are of opposite effect. Care should be taken before offsetting such items. It may also be necessary, where there are a large number of small items, for them to be aggregated to ascertain if they are material in total.

Accounting for goods sold subject to reservation of title

(Issued July 1976)

The following statement of guidance on the accounting treatment of goods sold subject to reservation of title is issued by the Council of The Institute of Chartered Accountants in England and Wales (in association with The Institute of Chartered Accountants of Scotland, The Institute of Chartered Accountants in Ireland, The Association of Certified Accountants, The Institute of Cost and Management Accountants and The Chartered Institute of Public Finance and Accountancy).

INTRODUCTION

1 The Romalpa case (*Aluminium Industrie Vaassen B.V. v Romalpa Aluminium Limited*), decided in the Court of Appeal on 16th January 1976, and reported in [1976] 1 W.L.R. 676, focused attention on certain terms of sale whereby the seller retains title to the goods sold and, in some cases, the right to other goods produced from them and the ultimate sale proceeds. Such terms of sale, which have in the past been more common in some Continental countries, are now being introduced by an increasing number of companies in the United Kingdom.

2 It should be noted that the Romalpa case was concerned with the construction of a particular contractual relationship which in itself is not of general relevance.

3 Whether an effective reservation of title exists will depend on the construction of the particular contract in each case and this construction may vary, to some extent, according to the law of the country in which the goods are situated. The main effect of trading with reservation of title is that the position of the unpaid seller may be improved if the purchaser becomes insolvent. This is because goods sold by the seller which are still in the purchaser's possession remain the seller's property and the proceeds of on-sales by the purchaser may be regarded in law as being held in trust for the seller. It follows that the position of other creditors, either with the security of a floating charge or no security, may be adversely affected.

ACCOUNTING TREATMENT

4 In drawing up the accounts of undertakings trading on terms whereby goods are supplied subject to a reservation of title, it is necessary to decide at what stage they should be treated as sold by the supplier and purchased by the party to whom they are supplied ('the customer'). In reaching this decision, it is considered that the commercial

substance of the transaction should take precedence over its legal form where they conflict. The substance of transactions of this nature has to be decided from consideration of all the surrounding circumstances.

5 The circumstances surrounding the transaction may indicate that the reservation of title is regarded by the parties as having no practical relevance except in the event of the insolvency of the customer. The goods concerned may be supplied and payment for them may be due in a manner identical with other goods which are not subject to a reservation of title. In such circumstances, where the customer is a going concern, it is considered that the omission of the stock (or, if resold, the debtors) and of the corresponding liabilities from the balance sheet of the customer would prevent it from showing a true and fair view of the state of affairs. Similarly, the accounts of the supplier would also be distorted by the omission of such goods from sales and debtors. Accordingly it is recommended that in such circumstances the goods should be treated as purchases in the accounts of the customer and as sales in the accounts of the supplier.

6 In some instances goods may be supplied on terms such that the intention of the parties is that they are consignment stocks. It will then be appropriate to treat them as continuing to belong to the supplier until some event inconsistent with the supplier's ownership occurs. Indications that stocks should be regarded as consignment stocks might include:

(a) the right of the customer to return them to the supplier;
(b) deferment of the obligation to pay for the goods until they have been sold by the customer;
(c) acceptance by the Customs and Excise authorities that Value Added Tax is not payable by reference to the time of delivery of the goods but to some later event, e.g., the appropriation of the goods by the customer.

7 Precedents for the accounting treatment of goods supplied as sales by reference to the substance rather than to the strict legal form of the transaction already exist in, for example, hire purchase sales and in certain export sales, which are often included in sales on despatch from the supplier's factory even though legal title may not have passed.

DISCLOSURE IN ACCOUNTS

8 Where the accounts are materially affected by the accounting treatment adopted in relation to sales or purchases subject to reservation of title, the treatment should be disclosed.

9 Where such transactions are accounted for by the customer on the basis recommended in paragraph 5 it will also be necessary to disclose the fact that the liability to suppliers may, in effect, be secured. It is not entirely clear whether such a liability is secured 'otherwise than by operation of law' so that its disclosure would be necessary to comply with paragraph 9 of the Second Schedule to the Companies Act 1967* . Nevertheless,

Editor's note: *Superseded by paragraph 48(4) of Schedule 4 to the Companies Act 1985.*

the fact that certain trade creditors might in an insolvency be in a position to obtain payment of the amounts due to them ahead of the holder of a floating charge and of the unsecured creditors would normally need to be disclosed if such amounts were material.

QUANTIFICATION

The extent to which the liability to creditors may be secured should whenever possible be disclosed in the relevant note and the amount due to creditors protected by reservation of title should therefore be shown. There should be little difficulty in doing this if, for example, the reservation of title applies only to the purchase of a particular fixed asset or to goods from a single supplier. **10**

It is recognised that in many businesses there would be major practical difficulties in quantifying the amounts protected by reservation of title. There are considerable variations in the form in which suppliers may seek to reserve title and doubt as to the legal effectiveness of some of them may exist. It would, therefore, be necessary to form a view on the legal construction of each such contract before the amount of liabilities to be treated as secured could be assessed. A further difficulty would arise in the need to establish accounting procedures which not only enabled suppliers' ledger balances to be split according to the terms of sale, but also identified the amounts due to the secured suppliers in respect of unprocessed goods received notes. **11**

If the amount of the liability to suppliers who have reserved title to the goods supplied cannot reasonably be quantified, it is recommended that the situation should be explained in the relevant note in terms that provide as good an indication as possible of the extent to which the creditors are protected in this way. **12**

RELEVANCE OF THE GOING CONCERN CONCEPT

The accounting treatment of goods supplied subject to reservation of title recommended in paragraph 5 would only be appropriate in the context of a going concern. If the financial position of the company or other considerations throw doubt on the going concern concept, the accounting treatment of goods supplied on such terms will need particular consideration. In the rare circumstances in which accounts are drawn up on some basis other than the going concern basis, it would be necessary to have regard to the strict legal position in relation to the liabilities, stock, debtors and cash. **13**

EFFECT ON OTHER SECURITIES

The purchase of goods subject to reservation of title by the supplier may affect the position of the customer in relation to security given to other creditors. Such purchases might, for example, lead to a failure to maintain a required level of asset cover or the borrowing limits being exceeded. The implications on other securities can only be assessed by considering the terms of the relevant trust deeds or other instruments constituting the security. **14**

INLAND REVENUE ATTITUDE TO THE STATEMENT ON 'ACCOUNTING FOR GOODS SOLD SUBJECT TO RESERVATION OF TITLE'

15 The accountancy bodies have received the following reply dated 25th June 1976 from the Board of Inland Revenue in response to their request for clarification of the Revenue's practice on the publication of the Statement V24 (now Statement 2.207) *'Accounting for goods sold subject to reservation of title'*:

> 'You sent me on 7th June your proposed statement on this subject. We regard your approach as entirely reasonable and do not want to make difficulties. At the same time we obviously see a risk that the 'sensible' basis may be used by one party and the strict legal basis by another so that relief would be claimed by both. I must make it clear therefore that while we would accept accounts made up on the basis of your statement so long as it is followed for tax purposes by all the parties to the transaction, we must reserve the right to insist on the legal basis for all those concerned if one party claims it. We see no other taxation implications which would be unacceptable to us.'

16 It follows from the above reply received from the Board of Inland Revenue that where both parties to the transaction follow the recommendations set out in Statement V24 (now Statement 2.207) no taxation difficulties will normally arise.

The determination of realised profits and disclosure of distributable profits in the context of the Companies Act

(Issued September 1982)

***(Editor's note:** For ease of reference the text reproduced below has been amended to refer to the Companies Act 1985 and to FRS 2.)*

The following statement of guidance on the determination of realised profits and disclosure of distributable profits in the context of the Companies Act is issued by the Council of The Institute of Chartered Accountants in England and Wales (in association with the Institute of Chartered Accountants of Scotland, the Institute of Chartered Accountants in Ireland, the Association of Certified Accountants, the Institute of Cost and Management Accountants and the Chartered Institute of Public Finance and Accountancy). The guidance given in this statement may need to be amended as the law is interpreted in particular cases, or as existing accounting standards are revised and new standards are issued.

The statement and its appendix have been considered and approved by Counsel. They are, however, not definitive. Interpretation of the law rests ultimately with the courts.

References to 'the Act' are to the Companies Act 1985.

REALISED PROFITS: THE STATUTORY FRAMEWORK

The term 'realised profits' was introduced into UK company law statutes as a result of the implementation of the 2nd and 4th EEC directives on company law: 1

(a) Part VIII of the Act imposes statutory restrictions on the distribution of profits and assets by companies. These restrictions include a prohibition on the distribution of unrealised profits.*

(b) Paragraph 12 (a) of the 4th schedule requires that 'only profits realised at the balance sheet date shall be included in the profit and loss account'. Paragraph 34 (3) contains a similar requirement applicable to transfers from the revaluation reserve to the profit and loss account. These requirements are extended to consoli-

****There is an exception to this rule where distributions are made in kind (see section 276).***

dated accounts by paragraphs 1 of Schedule 4A. They do not apply to accounts prepared under old Schedule 9A.*

2 Section 262(3) states that 'references to realised profits . . . are references to such profits . . . as fall to be treated as realised profits . . . in accordance with principles generally accepted with respect to the determination for accounting purposes of realised profits at the time when those accounts are prepared'. The term 'principles generally accepted' for the determination of realised profits is not defined in the Act.

3 This statement gives guidance as to the interpretation of 'principles generally accepted' for the determination of realised profits in the context of these statutory requirements. Both the statutory requirements and the following guidance must throughout be viewed in the context of section 226 which states that the requirement for company accounts to give a true and fair view overrides all other provisions of the Companies Act as to the matters to be included in a company's accounts. Section 227 imposes a corresponding requirement for group accounts.

'PRINCIPLES GENERALLY ACCEPTED' FOR REALISED PROFITS

4 'Principles generally accepted' for the determination of realised profits should by considered in conjunction with, *inter alia*, the legal principles laid down in Schedule 4, statements of standard accounting practice (SSAPs), and in particular the fundamental accounting concepts referred to in SSAP 2 'Disclosure of accounting policies.' As stated in the explanatory foreword to accounting standards, SSAPs describe methods of accounting for all accounts intended to give a true and fair view. They must therefore, where applicable, be considered to be highly persuasive in the interpretation of 'principles generally accepted' for the determination of realised profits.†

5 Accounting thought and practice develop over time. This is recognised in the statutory requirement that realised profits should be determined 'in accordance with principles generally accepted . . . at the time when those accounts are prepared'. Because of this, the guidance set out in this statement is itself liable to amendment from time to time.

6 In determining whether a profit is realised, particular regard should be had to the statutory accounting principles at paragraphs 12 and 13 of Schedule 4, and to the parallel fundamental accounting concepts of 'prudence' and 'accruals' as set out in SSAP 2.

7 Paragraph 12 of Schedule 4 requires that 'The amount of any item shall be determined

****Editor's note:*** *Insurance companies may use old Schedule 9A for financial years commencing before 23 December 1994. The new Schedule 9A inserted by The Companies Act 1985 (Insurance Companies Accounts) Regulations 1993 (SI. 1993 No. 3246) includes in paragraph 16(a) a similar requirement to paragraph 12(a) of Schedule 4, but subject to note 9 on the profit and loss account format (unrealised gains and losses on investments).*

†Editor's note: *The ASB Foreword to Accounting Standards discusses the scope and application of accounting standards and the Appendix addresses their status under UK legislation.*

on a prudent basis' and, in particular, as already noted, that 'only profits realised at the balance sheet date shall be included in the profit and loss account'. SSAP 2 amplifies the prudence concept as follows:

> 'revenues and profits are not anticipated, but are recognised by inclusion in the profit and loss account only when realised in the form either of cash or of other assets the ultimate cash realisation of which can be assessed with reasonable certainty'.

In the light of the new statutory requirements, it should be borne in mind that the phrases 'ultimate cash realisation' and 'assessed with reasonable certainty' are intended to clarify the extent to which a profit can be said to be 'realised' under the prudence concept in circumstances other than where the profit has already been realised in the form of cash. 'Reasonable certainty' is the limiting factor.

This approach is consistent with paragraph 13 of Schedule 4 which requires that: **8**

> 'All income and charges relating to the financial year to which the accounts relate shall be taken into account, without regard to the date of receipt or payment.'

The statutory requirement corresponds with the accruals concept as explained at paragraph 14 (b) of SSAP 2. This states that:

> 'revenue and costs are accrued (that is, recognised as they are earned or incurred, not as money is received or paid), matched with one another so far as their relationship can be established or justifiably assumed, and dealt with in the profit and loss account of the period to which they relate'.

In determining realised profits, it is also necessary to comply with paragraph 12 (b) of **9**
Schedule 4, which states that:

> 'all liabilities and losses which have arisen or are likely to arise in respect of the financial year to which the accounts relate or a previous financial year shall be taken into account, including those which only become apparent between the balance sheet date and the date on which it is signed on behalf of the board of directors . . . '.

This statutory requirement corresponds with the prudence concept as explained at paragraph 14 (d) of SSAP 2. This states that:

> 'provision is made for all known liabilities (expenses and losses) whether the amount of these is known with certainty or is a best estimate in the light of the information available'.

Realised profits: summary of guidance

A profit which is required by statements of standard accounting practice to be **10**
recognised in the profit and loss account should normally be treated as a realised profit, unless the SSAP specifically indicates that it should be treated as unrealised.*

**See appendix.*

11 A profit may be recognised in the profit and loss account in accordance with an accounting policy which is not the subject of a SSAP, or, exceptionally, which is contrary to a SSAP. Such a profit will normally be a realised profit if the accounting policy adopted is consistent with paragraphs 12 and 13 of Schedule 4 and with the accruals and prudence concepts as set out in SSAP 2.

12 Where, in special circumstances, a true and fair view could not be given, even if additional information were provided, without including in the profit and loss account an unrealised profit, the effect of section 226 is to require inclusion of that unrealised profit notwithstanding paragraph 12 (a) of Schedule 4. Moreover, paragraph 15 of Schedule 4 allows the directors to include an unrealised profit in the profit and loss account where there are special reasons for doing so. Where unrealised profits are thus recognised in the profit and loss account, particulars of this departure from the statutory accounting principle, the reasons for it and its effect are required to be given in a note to the accounts.

DISTRIBUTABLE PROFITS

13 The definition of realised profits contained in Schedule 4 is extended by section 742(2) to apply to any provision of the Act. It therefore applies to the provisions of Part VIII, dealing with distributions. In that context this guidance should be read in conjunction with the statutory rules as to what constitute distributable profits and losses in particular circumstances for the purposes of that part of the Act.

14 It is essential that all companies should keep sufficient records to enable them to distinguish between those reserves which are distributable and those which are not. While most realised profits will be passed through the profit and loss account, there may be some realised profits which will originally have been brought into the accounts as unrealised profits by way of direct credit to reserves. Similarly, while most unrealised profits will be credited direct to reserves, there may be some unrealised profits passed through the profit and loss account (see paragraph 12 above). Subsequently, when such profits are realised either in whole or in part, a reclassification needs to be made between unrealised and realised profits.

15 There is not legal requirement for a company to distinguish in its balance sheet between distributable and non-distributable reserves as such. However, where material non-distributable profits are included in the profit and loss account or in other reserves which might reasonably be assumed to be distributable, it may be necessary for this to be disclosed and quantified in a note to the accounts in order for them to give a true and fair view.

16 Distributions are made by companies and not by groups. It follows that the profits of a group are only distributable to members of the group's holding company to the extent of the holding company's distributable profits. The concept of distributable profit is not, therefore, strictly applicable to groups. However, it is reasonable to assume that the distributable retained profits of subsidiaries can be distributed to the holding company. Where this is not the case, the requirements of paragraph 53 of FRS 2. 'Accounting for subsidiary undertakings' should be complied with. This states:

'Where significant statutory contractual or exchange control restrictions on distributions by subsidiary undertakings materially limit the parent undertakings access to distributable profits the nature and extent of the restrictions should be disclosed.'

Appendix

ACCOUNTING STANDARDS AND REALISED PROFITS: EXAMPLES

1 As statements of standard accounting practice are revised and as new standards are issued, it is expected that they will deal with any matters relevant to the determination of realised profits.

2 This has already been done in the case of SSAP 1 'Accounting for associated companies', revised in April 1982. This provides an example of the way in which the true and fair view requirements should be satisfied by giving additional information rather than by including unrealised profits in profit and loss account (see paragraph 12 above). As far as an investing company is concerned, the profits of its associated companies are not realised until they are passed on as dividends; the true and fair view, however, requires that they should be reflected in the investing company's financial statements. There is no problem where group accounts are prepared because specific provision is made for this situation in paragraph 22 of Schedule 4A*. Where, however, the investing company does not prepare group accounts, the revised SSAP 1 states that it should show the information required as to its share of the associated company's profit by preparing a separate profit and loss account or by adding the information to its own profit and loss account in supplementary form in such a way that its share of the profits of the associated company is not treated as realised.

3 An example of the principle that profit recognised in accordance with an accounting standard should normally be treated as realised (see paragraph 10 above) is provided by SSAP 9 'Stocks and long-term contracts'. This requires that long-term contract work in progress should be stated in periodic financial statements at cost plus any attributable profit, less any foreseeable losses and progress payments received and receivable. There was initially some concern as to whether profit thus recognised on long-term contract work in progress would be construed as realised profit within the provisions of the Companies Acts. However, the relevant principles of recognising profits in SSAP 9 are based on the concept of 'reasonable certainty' as to the eventual outcome and are not in conflict with the statutory accounting principles. Such profits should be treated as realised profits. The Department of Trade does not dissent from this view.

***Editor's note:** Under paragraph 22 equity accounting is required, whereas when this statement was issued equity accounting was merely permitted.*